SOURCEBOOK ON CRIMINAL LAW

Cavendish
Publishing
Limited

London • Sydney

SOURCEBOOK ON CRIMINAL LAW

Peter Hungerford-Welch, LLB, Barrister
Senior Lecturer in Law
Inns of Court School of Law

Alan Taylor, BA, MPhil, Barrister
Senior Lecturer in Law
Inns of Court School of Law

Cavendish
Publishing
Limited

London • Sydney

First published in Great Britain 1997 by Cavendish Publishing Limited,
The Glass House, Wharton Street, London WC1X 9PX
Telephone: 0171-278 8000 Facsimile: 0171-278 8080

British Library Cataloguing-in-Publication Data A catalogue record for this book is available from the British Library.

Hungerford-Welch, Peter
Sourcebook on Criminal Law – (Sourcebook Series)
I Title II Taylor, Alan III Series
344.205

ISBN 1 85941 100 2

Printed and bound in Great Britain by
Biddles Ltd, Guildford and King's Lynn

PREFACE

This Sourcebook should be a helpful handbook for anyone studying the criminal law. It addresses both general principles and a number of specific offences. The statutory framework is set out, together with extracts from the case law which put flesh (often a great deal of it) on the statutory skeleton. There is also a commentary to guide the reader through the materials.

Our heartfelt thanks goes to Jane Hungerford-Welch, without whose assistance the enormous pile of photocopies and scribbled notes would never have turned into a book. Our thanks also go to Cavendish Publishing, and especially Elaine Tuffery, who edited this book.

Any errors that this book contains are there for the entertainment of those who enjoy hunting for other people's mistakes.

We have endeavoured to state the law as at 30 April 1997.

Alan Taylor
Peter Hungerford-Welch
Inns of Court School of Law

ACKNOWLEDGMENTS

Grateful acknowledgment is made to the Controller of Her Majesty's Stationery Office for permission to reproduce Crown Copyright materials; to the Incorporated Council of Law Reporting for England and Wales for permission to reproduce extracts from the *Law Reports* and *Weekly Law Reports*; to Butterworths for permission to reproduce extracts from the *All England Reports;* to Sweet & Maxwell for permission to reproduce extracts from the *Criminal Appeal Reports;* and the *Criminal Law Review.*

Every effort has been made to trace all the copyright holders but if any have been inadvertently overlooked the publishers will be pleased to make the necessary arrangement at the first opportunity.

CONTENTS

TABLE OF CASES

TABLE OF STATUTES

CHAPTER 1

ACTUS REUS: THE EXTERNAL ELEMENTS OF AN OFFENCE

For a person to be guilty of a criminal offence, he must have carried out the 'external elements' (or '*actus reus*') of the offence. This will usually be an act or a series of acts (for example, hitting the victim or taking the goods).

However, where the accused is under a duty to act, the *actus reus* of the offence may be an omission to act. Similarly, there are cases where the *actus reus* is not an act or omission but instead consists of nothing more than the existence of a state of affairs. The acts must be voluntary (that is, controlled by the mind of the accused), since the law exculpates those who are not properly in control of themselves (defences such as non-insane automatism, insanity, duress and intoxication are considered in separate chapters).

Part of the *actus reus* of an offence may well be the bringing about of a certain consequence. That consequence must be caused by the accused's act(s) or omission(s). The prosecution have to prove that the consequence would not have arisen 'but for' what the accused did or failed to do. The question of causation is dealt with Chapter 4.

Unless the offence is one of strict liability (see Chapter 14), the defendant must also have the necessary state of mind (or '*mens rea*') at the time of the act or omission which constitutes the *actus reus* of the offence. The requirement of *mens rea* is considered in detail in Chapter 2.

A voluntary act

An act which is involuntary does not give rise to criminal liability. This would be the case, for example, where the defendant was conscious at the relevant time but his mind was not controlling his actions.

In later chapters we consider the following defences, all of which relate to the voluntariness of the defendant's acts:

(1) Intoxication (Chapter 7);

(2) Duress (Chapter 9);

(3) Insanity and non-insane automatism (Chapter 6).

A state of affairs amounting to an *actus reus*

R v Larsonneur (1933) 24 Cr App R 74 (CA)

Lord Hewart CJ: ... The fact is, as the evidence shows, that the appellant is an alien. She has a French passport, which bears this statement under the date 14 March 1933, 'Leave to land granted at Folkestone this day on condition that the holder does not enter any employment, paid or unpaid, while in the United Kingdom', but on 22 March that condition was varied and one finds these words: 'The condition attached to the grant of leave to land is hereby varied so as to require departure from the United Kingdom not later than 22 March 1933'. Then follows the signature of an Under-Secretary of State. In fact, the appellant went to the Irish Free State and afterwards, in circumstances which are perfectly immaterial, so far as this appeal is concerned, came back to Holyhead. She was at Holyhead on 21 April 1933, a date after the day limited by the condition on her passport ...

The appellant was, therefore, on 21 April 1933, in the position in which she would have been if she had been prohibited from landing by the Secretary of State and, that being so, there is no reason to interfere with the finding of the jury. She was found here and was, therefore, deemed to be in the class of persons whose landing had been prohibited by the Secretary of State, by reason of the fact that she had violated the condition on her passport. The appeal, therefore, is dismissed and the recommendation for deportation remains.

Winzar v Chief Constable of Kent (1983) Times, 28 March (DC)

The appellant was convicted of being drunk on the highway (contrary to s 12 of the Licensing Act 1872). The appellant had been taken to a hospital. The doctor decided that he was merely drunk and asked him to leave. He remained in the hospital and the police were called. They placed the appellant in a police car parked in the road outside the hospital. The appellant was then charged with being drunk on the highway. It was held that the fact that his presence on the highway was not of his own volition and was momentary did not amount to a defence.

An omission to act as an *actus reus*

A failure to act can only amount to the *actus reus* of an offence if the defendant was under a duty to act.

R v Gibbins and Proctor (1918) 13 Cr App R 134 (CA)

Darling J: The two appellants were indicted and tried together for the wilful murder of Nelly Gibbins, the daughter of Gibbins. The facts were that Gibbins's wife had left him, and he was living in adultery with Proctor. There were several children, one of whom was the child of Proctor, in the house. He earned good wages, which he brought home and gave to Proctor to maintain the house and those in it. There is no evidence that there was not enough to keep them all in health. And all were looked after except one, namely Nelly, who was starved to death. Her organs were healthy, and there was no reason why she should have died if she had been supplied with food. She was kept upstairs apart from the others, and there was evidence that Proctor hated her and cursed her, from which the jury could infer that she had a very strong interest in her death ...

It has been said that there ought not to have been a finding of guilty of murder against Gibbins. The court agrees that the evidence was less against Gibbins than Proctor, Gibbins gave her money, and as far as we can see it was sufficient to provide for the wants of themselves and all the children. But he lived in the house and the child was his own, a little girl of seven, and he grossly neglected the child. He must have known what her condition was if he saw her, for she was little more than a skeleton. He is in this dilemma; if he did not see her the jury might well infer that he did not care if she died; if he did he must have known what was going on. The question is whether there was evidence that he so conducted himself as to show that he desired that grievous bodily injury should be done to the child. He cannot pretend that he showed any solicitude for her. He knew that Proctor hated her, knew that she was ill and that no doctor had been called in, and the jury may have come to the conclusion that he was so infatuated with Proctor, and so afraid of offending her, that he preferred that the child should starve to death rather than that he should be exposed to any injury or unpleasantness from Proctor. It is unnecessary to say more than that there was evidence that Gibbins did desire that grievous bodily harm should be done to the child; he did not interfere in what was being done, and he comes within the definition which I have read, and is therefore guilty of murder.

The case of Proctor is plainer. She had charge of the child. She was under no obligation to do so or to live with Gibbins, but she did so, and receiving money, as it is admitted she did, for the purpose of supplying food, her duty was to see that the child was properly fed and looked after, and to see that she had medical attention if necessary. We agree with what Lord Coleridge CJ said in *R v Instan* [1893] 1 QB 450: 'There is no case directly in point, but it would be a slur upon, and a discredit to the administration of, justice in this country if there were any doubt as to the legal principle, or as to the present case being within it. The prisoner was under a moral obligation to the deceased from which arose a legal duty towards her; that legal duty the prisoner has wilfully and deliberately left unperformed, with the consequence that there has been and acceleration of the death of the deceased owing to the non-performance of that legal duty.' Here Proctor took upon herself the moral obligation of looking after the children; she was *de facto*, though not *de jure*, the wife of Gibbins and had excluded the child's own mother. She neglected the child undoubtedly, and the evidence shows that as a result the child died. So a verdict of manslaughter at least was inevitable.

But it is necessary to go further and see whether it was murder. The evidence is that she had plenty of money; that she kept the child upstairs insufficiently supplied with food; that she hated the child and hit her. There is also evidence that when the child died of starvation both appellants took part in hiding the body and preventing the death from being known. They concocted a story that she had been sent away and was still alive. There is evidence that Proctor told Gibbins to bury the child out of sight, and that he did so in the brickyard where he worked. The jury came to the conclusion that she had done more than wickedly neglect the child; she had deliberately withheld food from it, and therefore we come to the conclusion that there was evidence which justified the jury in returning a verdict against her, not merely of manslaughter, but of murder. The appeals are therefore dismissed.

R v Lowe [1973] QB 702 (CA)

Phillimore LJ: Robert Lowe appeals against his conviction at Nottingham Crown Court on 25 July 1972 ... [H]e was convicted on count 2 of the indictment of cruelty to a child by wilfully neglecting it so as to cause unnecessary suffering or injury to health contrary to the provisions of s 1(1) of the Children and Young Persons Act 1933. He was also convicted on count 1 of manslaughter of the child on the grounds that his cruelty alleged under count 2 caused its death ...

The trial judge ... directed the jury that if they found the appellant guilty of the second count they must, as a matter of law, find him guilty of the first, namely of manslaughter. Having found him guilty of the second count they also found him guilty of the first and made it clear that they did so solely as a result of the direction by the trial judge; in other words, they did *not* find the appellant guilty of reckless conduct resulting in the child's death.

... This court feels that there is something inherently unattractive in a theory of constructive manslaughter. It seems strange that an omission which is wilful solely in the sense that it is not inadvertent, the consequences of which are not in fact foreseen by the person who is neglectful should, if death results, automatically give rise to an indeterminate sentence instead of the maximum of two years which would otherwise be the limit imposed.

We think there is a clear distinction between an act of omission and an act of commission likely to cause harm. Whatever may be the position in regard to the latter it does not follow that the same is true of the former. In other words if I strike a child in a manner likely to cause harm it is right that if the child dies I may by charged with manslaughter. If, however, I omit to do something with the result that it suffers injury to health which results in its death, we think that a charge of manslaughter should not be an inevitable consequence, even if the omission is deliberate.

R v Stone and Dobinson [1977] QB 354 (CA)

Geoffrey Lane LJ: ... In 1972, at 75 Broadwater, Bolton-on-Dearne in Yorkshire, there lived three people. Stone, an ex-miner now aged 67, widowed for 10 years, who is partially deaf, almost totally blind and has no appreciable sense of smell; Gwendoline Dobinson, now aged 43, who had been his housekeeper and mistress for some eight years, and Stone's son called Cyril, aged 34, who is mentally subnormal. Stone is of low average intelligence, Dobinson is described as ineffectual and somewhat inadequate.

There was an addition to that household in 1972. Stone had a younger sister called Fanny, about 61 at the date of her death. She had been living with another sister called Rosy. For some reason, probably because Rosy could not tolerate her any longer, she had decided to leave. She came to live at no 75, where she occupied a small front room. She was in receipt of a pension of £11.60 per week and gave her brother £1.50 towards the rent. She was eccentric in many ways. She was morbidly and unnecessarily anxious about putting on weight and so denied herself proper meals. She would take to her room for days. She would often stay in her room all day until the two appellants went to the public house in the evening, when she would creep down and make herself a meal.

In early spring 1975 the police called at the house. Fanny had been found wandering about in the street by herself without apparently knowing where she was. This caused the appellants to try and find Fanny's doctor. They tried to trace him through Rosy, but having walked a very considerable distance in their search they failed. It transpired that they had walked to the wrong village. Fanny herself refused to tell them the doctor's name. She thought she would be 'put away' if she did. Nothing more was done to enlist outside professional aid.

In the light of what happened subsequently there can be no doubt that Fanny's condition over the succeeding weeks and months must have deteriorated rapidly. By July 1975 she was, it seems, unable or unwilling to leave her bed and, on 19 July, the next-door neighbour, Mrs Wilson, gallantly volunteered to help the female appellant to wash Fanny. She states:

> On the 19 July Mrs Dobinson and I went to Fanny's room in order to clean her up. When I went into the room there was not a strong smell until I moved her. Her nightdress was wet and messed with her own excreta and the dress had to be cut off. I saw her back was sore; I hadn't seen anything like that before. I took the bedclothes off the bed. They were all wet through and messed. And so was the mattress. I was there for about two hours and Mrs Dobinson helped. She was raw, her back, shoulders, bottom and down below between her legs. Mrs Dobinson appeared to me to be upset because Fanny had never let her attend to her before. I advised Mrs Dobinson to go to the Social Services.

Emily West, the licensee of the local public house, the Crossed Daggers, gave evidence to the effect that during the whole of the period, from 19 July onwards, the appellants came to the public house every night at about 7.00 pm. The appellant Dobinson was worried and told Emily West that Fanny would not wash, go to the toilet or eat or drink. As a result Emily West immediately advised Dobinson to get a doctor and when told that Fanny's doctor lived at Doncaster, Emily West suggested getting a local one. It seems that some efforts were made to get a local doctor, but the neighbour who volunteered to do the telephoning (the appellants being incapable of managing the instrument themselves) was unsuccessful.

On 2 August 1975 Fanny was found by Dobinson to be dead in her bed. The police were called. On arrival they found there was no ventilation in the bedroom, the window had to be hammered open and the bed was so sited that it was impossible to get the door fully open.

At one side of the bed on a chair was an empty mineral bottle and on the other chair a cup. Under the bed was an empty polythene bucket. Otherwise there was no food, washing or toilet facilities in the room. There was excrement on the bed and floor. It was a scene of dreadful degradation.

The pathologist, Dr Usher, gave evidence that the deceased was naked, emaciated, weighing five stone and five pounds, her body ingrained with dirt, lying in a pool of excrement. On the bed on which she was lying were various filthy and crumpled bed-clothes, some of which were soaked in urine. There was excrement on the floor and wrapped in newspapers alongside the bed. There was a tidemark of excreta corresponding with the position in which her body was lying.

At the mortuary Dr Usher found the deceased's body to be ulcerated over the right hip joint and on the underside of the left knee; in each case the ulceration went down to the bone. There were maggots in the ulcers. He found pressure sores over the back of her right shoulder, the outside of the left kneecap to the underside of the left knee, over the right hip joint, to the inner aspect of the left shin and on the left instep where the body had been lying. Such ulcers could not have been produced in less than two to three weeks. The ulcers were due to the general poor condition of the skin and the protruding bones which would have had a greater effect on her than a normal person. She was soaked in urine and excreta.

Her stomach contained no food products but a lot of bile-stained fluid. She had not eaten recently. He found no natural disease. The disinclination to eat was a condition of anorexia nervosa which was not a physical condition but a condition of the brain or mind.

She had been requiring urgent medical attention for some days or even weeks. He said:

> If two weeks prior to my seeing the body she had gone into hospital there is a distinct possibility that they may have saved her; and three weeks earlier the chances would have been good. If her condition on 19 July was no worse than that described by Mrs Wilson, then her survival would have been probable.

He said that the cause of death was (1) toxaemia spreading from the infected pressure areas (this could have been alleviated by keeping her clean) and (2) prolonged immobilisation. There was no physical reason for her being immobile. Death was due to immobilisation, which caused the pressure sores, and lack of food. Depression might have caused the lack of mobility. The sores on the left knee he thought did not develop in two weeks. Lack of ventilation would have aggravated the other matters. With regard to the condition of the mattress, he thought it would take weeks to get into that condition.

The Crown alleged that in the circumstances the appellants had undertaken the duty of caring for Fanny who was incapable of looking after herself, that they had, with gross negligence, failed in that duty, that such failure had caused her death and that they were guilty of manslaughter ...

There is no dispute, broadly speaking, as to the matters on which the jury must be satisfied before they can convict of manslaughter in circumstances such as the present. They are: (1) that the defendant undertook the care of a person who by reason of age or infirmity was unable to care for herself; (2) that the defendant was grossly negligent in regard to his duty of care; (3) that by reason of such negligence the person died. It is submitted on behalf of the appellants that the judge's direction to the jury with regard to the first two items was incorrect.

At the close of the Crown's case submissions were made to the judge that there was no, or no sufficient, evidence that the appellants, or either of them, had chosen to undertake the care of Fanny.

That contention was advanced by counsel for the appellant before this court as his first ground of appeal. He amplified the ground somewhat by submitting that the evidence which the judge had suggested to the jury might support the assumption of a duty by the appellants did not, when examined, succeed in doing so. He suggested that the situation here was unlike any reported case. Fanny came to this house as a lodger. Largely, if not entirely due to her own eccentricity and failure to look after herself or feed herself properly, she became increasingly infirm and immobile and eventually unable to look after herself. Is it to be said, asks counsel for the appellants rhetorically, that by the mere fact of becoming infirm and helpless in these circumstances, she casts a duty on her brother and Mrs Dobinson to take steps to have her looked after or taken to hospital? The suggestion is that, heartless though it may seem, this is one of those situations where the appellants were entitled to do nothing; where no duty was cast on them to help, any more than it is cast on a man to rescue a stranger from drowning, however easy such a rescue might be.

This court rejects that proposition. Whether Fanny was a lodger or not she was a blood relation of the appellant Stone; she was occupying a room in his house; Mrs Dobinson had undertaken the duty of trying to wash her, of taking such food to her as she required. There was ample evidence that each appellant was aware of the poor condition she was in by mid-July. It was not disputed that no effort was made to summon an ambulance or the social services or the police despite the entreaties of Mrs Wilson and Mrs West. A social worker used to visit Cyril. No word was spoken to him. All these were matters which the jury were entitled to take into account when considering whether the necessary assumption of a duty to care for Fanny had been proved.

This was *not* a situation analogous to the drowning stranger. They *did* make efforts to care. They tried to get a doctor; they tried to discover the previous doctor. Mrs Dobinson helped with the washing and the provision of food. All these matters were put before the jury in terms which we find it impossible to fault. The jury were entitled to find that the duty had been assumed. They were entitled to conclude that once Fanny became helplessly infirm, as she had by 19 July, the appellants were, in the circumstances, obliged either to summon help or else to care for Fanny themselves.

Counsel for the appellants' second submission presents greater difficulty. It is that the judge's direction on the nature of the negligence or recklessness required was wrongly stated. This is how the matter was left to the jury:

> Have the Crown proved that either or both of these defendants was guilty of gross neglect of Fanny amounting to a reckless disregard for the health and well-being of that woman. Do not place your judgment ... on the question of recklessness as to whether she died or not. What has to be proved is not that, but that there was a reckless disregard for their duty of care. It may well be that that will involve a consideration of what they thought would be the consequences of their reckless disregard, if you found there was one. For example, if I were in charge of a person and I was guilty of some major neglect, but I genuinely did not appreciate that it would lead to any dire results, you would probably say, 'That person is not very bright, but I am not sure he is guilty of recklessness'.

Then at a later stage in the direction:

> ... were either or both of these defendants in grave neglect of that duty, were they reckless, or did they show a reckless disregard for their obligations. Again it depends to a large extent on the extent of their knowledge of her condition; of their individual appreciation of the need to act. It depends to some extent on their appreciation of the consequences of inaction; it depends on the facilities which were available or which they could readily have made available ... Mr Stone says: 'Nothing was done because I was not aware of the gravity of the matter, of the danger to Fanny's life and of the situation. I did not know the actual conditions in which my sister was lying'. If that is true or if it may be true then you will acquit him. If you are sure that he did know then you ask yourselves: what did he do about it, and what could he have done ... you do not judge him on what you would have done yourselves; but you take the man as you find him ... So far as Mrs Dobinson is concerned ... did she do her incompetent best? Certainly if she did that, then you would acquit her.

The appellants' contention is that the Crown in order to succeed must show recklessness on the part of the defendant; that recklessness in this context means foresight of the likelihood or possibility of death or serious injury and a determination nevertheless to persist in the omission to provide care. We were referred to a number of 19th-century decisions which are historically interesting but of small practical assistance. Counsel for the appellants relied principally on the decision of this court in *R v Lowe* [1973] QB 702. In that case there were two counts, one alleging manslaughter of a child on the grounds that the defendants' cruelty alleged under the second count caused its death, and the second count charging cruelty to a child by wilfully neglecting it so as to cause unnecessary suffering or injury to health under s 1(1) of the Children and Young Persons Act 1933. The judge had directed the jury that if they found the appellant guilty on the second count they must find him guilty under the first count of manslaughter, even though they acquitted him of recklessness.

That was held to be a misdirection. Phillimore LJ, delivering the judgment of the court, went on to say this:

> Now in the present case the jury negatived recklessness. How then can mere neglect albeit wilful amount to manslaughter? This court feels that there is something inherently unattractive in a theory of constructive manslaughter. It seems strange that an omission which is wilful solely in the sense that it is not inadvertent, the consequences of which are not in fact foreseen by the person who is neglectful, should if death results, automatically give rise to an indeterminate sentence ...

Counsel for the appellants submits that that passage is support for his argument that there must be an appreciation by the defendant of the risk of death or serious injury before a conviction for manslaughter in these circumstances can result. We disagree. The court is saying simply that there must be proved the necessary high degree of negligence, and a direction which fails to emphasise that requirement will be defective. It is to *Andrews v DPP* [1937] AC 576 that one must turn to discover the definition of the requisite degree of negligence. Lord Atkin cites, with approval, the words of Hewart CJ in *R v Bateman* (1925) 94 LJKB 791, and goes on to say this:

> Simple lack of care such as will constitute civil liability is not enough. For purposes of the criminal law there are degrees of negligence; and a very high degree of negligence is required to be proved before the felony is established. Probably of all the epithets that can be applied 'reckless' most nearly covers the case. It is difficult to visualise a case of death caused by 'reckless' driving, in the connotation of that term in ordinary speech which would not justify a conviction of manslaughter; but it is probably not all-embracing, for 'reckless' suggests an indifference to risk whereas the accused may have appreciated the risk and intended to avoid it, and yet have shown in the means adopted to avoid the risk such a high degree of negligence as would justify a conviction.

It is clear from that passage that indifference to an obvious risk and appreciation of such risk, coupled with a determination nevertheless to run it, are both examples of recklessness.

The duty which a defendant has undertaken is a duty of caring for the health and welfare of the infirm person. What the Crown has to prove is a breach of that duty in such circumstances that the jury feel convinced that the defendant's conduct can properly be described as reckless. That is to say a reckless disregard of danger to the health and welfare of the infirm person. Mere inadvertence is not enough. The defendant must be proved to have been indifferent to an obvious risk of injury to health, or actually to have foreseen the risk but to have determined nevertheless to run it.

The direction given by the judge was wholly in accord with these principles. If any criticism is to be made it would be that the direction was unduly favourable to the defence. The appeals against conviction therefore fail ...

R v Dytham [1979] QB 722 (CA)

Lord Widgery CJ read the following judgment of the court prepared by **Shaw LJ**: The appellant was a police constable in Lancashire. On 17 March 1977 at about one o'clock in the morning he was on duty in uniform and was standing by a hot-dog stall in Duke Street, St Helens. A Mr Wincke was inside the stall and a Mr Sothern was by it. Some 30 yards away was the entrance to Cindy's Club. A man named Stubbs was ejected from the club by a bouncer. A fight ensued in which a number of men joined. There arose cries and screams and other indications of great violence. Mr Stubbs became the object of a murderous assault. He was beaten and kicked to death in the gutter outside the club. All this was audible and visible to the three men at the hot-dog stall. At no stage did the appellant make any move to intervene or any attempt to quell the disturbance or to stop the attack on the victim. When the hubbub had died down he adjusted his helmet and drove away. According to the other two at the hot-dog stall, he said that he was due off and was going off.

His conduct was brought to the notice of the police authority. As a result he appeared on 10 October 1978 in the Crown Court at Liverpool to answer an indictment which was in these terms:

> ... the charge against you is one of misconduct of an officer of justice, in that you ... misconducted yourself whilst acting as an officer of justice in that you being present and a witness to a criminal offence, namely a violent assault upon one ... Stubbs by three others deliberately failed to carry out your duty as a police constable by wilfully omitting to take any steps to preserve the Queen's Peace or to protect the person of the said ... Stubbs or to arrest or otherwise bring to justice [his] assailants.

On arraignment the appellant pleaded not guilty and the trial was adjourned to 7 November. On that day before the jury was empanelled counsel for the appellant took an objection to the indictment by way of demurrer. The burden of that objection was that the indictment as laid disclosed no offence known to the law. Neill J ruled against the objection and the trial proceeded. The defence on the facts was that the appellant had observed nothing more than that a man was turned out of the club. It was common ground that in that situation his duty would not have required him to take any action. The jury were directed that the crucial question for their consideration was whether the appellant had seen the attack on the victim. If he had, they could find him guilty of the offence charged in the indictment. The jury did return a verdict of guilty. Hence this appeal which is confined to the matters of law raised by the demurrer pleaded at the court of trial.

At the outset of his submissions in this court counsel for the appellant conceded two matters. The first was that a police constable is a public officer. The second was that there does exist at common law an offence of misconduct in a public office.

From that point the argument was within narrow limits though it ran deep into constitutional and jurisprudential history. The effect of it was that not every failure to discharge a duty which devolved on a person as the holder of a public office gave rise to the common law offence of misconduct in that office. As counsel for the appellant put it, non-feasance was not enough. There must be a malfeasance or at least a misfeasance involving an element of corruption. In support of this contention a number of cases were cited from 18th and 19th century reports. It is the fact that in nearly all of them the misconduct asserted involved some corrupt taint; but this appears to have been an accident of circumstance and not a necessary incident of the offence. Misconduct in a public office is more vividly exhibited where dishonesty is revealed as part of the dereliction of duty. Indeed in some cases the conduct impugned cannot be shown to have been misconduct unless it was done with a corrupt or oblique motive ...

In the present case it was not suggested that the appellant could not have summoned or sought assistance to help the victim or to arrest his assailants. The charge as framed left this answer open to him. Not surprisingly he did not seek to avail himself of it, for the facts spoke strongly against any such answer. The allegation made was not of mere non-feasance but of deliberate failure and wilful neglect. This involves an element of culpability which is not restricted to corruption or dishonesty but which must be of such a degree that the misconduct impugned is calculated to injure the public interest so as to call for condemnation and punishment. Whether such a situation is revealed by the evidence is a matter that a jury has to decide. It puts no heavier burden on them than when in more familiar contexts they are called on to consider whether driving is dangerous or a publication is obscene or a place of public resort is a disorderly house ...

The judge's ruling was correct. The appeal is dismissed.

R v Miller [1982] QB 532 (CA)

Facts: The appellant lit a cigarette and lay down on a mattress in the room he was using. He fell asleep before he had finished the cigarette, and it dropped onto the mattress, setting it alight. He awoke later when the mattress was smouldering, but did nothing to extinguish it, and merely moved to another room. The house caught fire.

May LJ: The issue in this case is whether the actual omission of the appellant to act to put out the fire in the mattress was in law a sufficient *actus reus* to constitute the offence alleged. This appeal therefore raises the question to what extent, if at all, except as specifically provided by statute, an omission to act can sufficiently found criminal liability ...

Counsel ... drew our attention to *Fagan v Metropolitan Police Commissioner* [1969] 1 QB 439. [His Lordship summarised the facts of that case, which is set out in Chapter 22 below, and went on:] Counsel argued, we think correctly, that the majority in the Divisional Court decided the case on its own particular facts. In their judgment the defendant's act of which complaint could be made had not been completed at the moment when the car wheel came to rest on the constables foot, but had to be regarded as a continuing act operating until the wheel was removed. Looking at the facts in this way, although the original mounting of the foot may have been accidental, there was thereafter a sufficient *actus reus* together with a coincident *mens rea*. It was on this basis they dismissed the appeal.

... [W]e do not dissent from the proposition that unless a statute so provides, or the case is one in which in the criminal context the common law imposes a duty on one person to act in a particular way towards another, such as a parent to his or her child, then a *mere* omission to act, with nothing more, cannot make the person who so fails to do something guilty of a criminal offence. Further, save in exceptional cases and subject to what follows, we think that normally the *actus reus* and the *mens rea* must coincide. Nevertheless, we also think that the answer to the problem which arises in the instant case depends on what is really meant by that last proposition. Some criminal offences are committed and complete in a second, others occupy a much longer period of time. We feel that it may well be artificial to consider merely the parts of what is alleged to be criminal conduct and to conclude that just because they are separate in point of time an *actus reus* cannot be conjoined to either a previous or subsequent *mens rea* to complete the commission of a crime.

Further, in both *Fagan's* case [1969] 1 QB 439 and the present, justice and good sense required that the defendant should not escape liability merely because the last thing that happened in the relevant story was an omission on his part. With respect to the Divisional Court in *Fagan's* case, we agree with Professor Glanville Williams's criticism of the reasoning of the majority of the court. In reality, driving the car wheel on to the policeman's foot was an act, was something which the driver did: the latter's failure thereafter to drive it off, despite the officer's request, was something which the driver did not do, it was an omission, and we think that it is unreal to describe it as any more than that.

On the other hand, in the driver's failure to release the officer's foot in the knowledge that he had just driven on to it, we think that there was clearly a substantial element of adoption by the driver, at the later stage, of what he had done a little earlier. We think that the conduct of the driver in that case can and should have been looked at as a whole and as the whole contained both the *actus reus* and the *mens rea* they were sufficiently coincident to render the driver guilty of an assault, without having to resort to the somewhat artificial reasoning of the majority of the Divisional Court. In our opinion, an unintentional act followed by an intentional omission to rectify that act or its consequences can be regarded *in toto* as an intentional act. We do not seek to define the rule, if rule it be, any more precisely because each case must depend on its own facts and we prefer to leave it to the trial judge to give the jury what he considers to be the appropriate direction in any given case. We would only say that an unintentional act followed by an intentional omission to rectify it or its consequences, or a reckless omission to do so when recklessness is a sufficient *mens rea* for the particular case, should only be regarded *in toto* as an intentional or reckless act when reality and common sense so require; this may well be a matter to be left to the jury. Further, in the relevant analysis we think that whether or not there is on the facts an element of adoption on the part of the alleged offender of what he has done earlier by what he deliberately or recklessly fails to do later, is an important consideration.

In these circumstances, although we doubt whether the recorder was correct in holding that when the appellant in the present case woke up there was any duty on him at criminal law to extinguish the smouldering mattress, nevertheless we do think that the whole of the appellant's conduct in relation to the mattress from the moment he lay on it with a lighted cigarette until the time he left it smouldering and moved to the adjoining room, can and should be regarded as one act. Clearly his failure with knowledge to extinguish the incipient fire had in it a substantial element of adoption on his part of what he had unintentionally done earlier, namely set it on fire. In these circumstances, we think that on the admitted facts the recorder was nevertheless correct in leaving the case to the jury, as he did, on the basis that the question was whether the appellant's failure to act was reckless, as defined by their Lordships' House in *R v Caldwell* [1981] 2 WLR 509.

For these reasons, this appeal is dismissed.

See also the decision of House of Lords dismissing an appeal from the decision of the Court of Appeal:

R v Miller [1983] 2 AC 161

See Chapter 20.

R v Adomako [1995] 1 AC 171 (HL)

See Chapter 21.

CHAPTER 2

MENS REA: THE MENTAL ELEMENT

The term *mens rea* refers to the state of mind of the accused at the time of the commission of the *actus reus* of an offence. The traditional maxim is '*actus non facit reum nisi mens sit rea*': the act is not guilty unless the mind is also guilty. The only offences for which this is not a requirement are offences of 'strict liability' (as to which, see Chapter 14). In this chapter, we look at the general principles of *mens rea*. The *mens rea* required for specific offences is dealt with in later chapters.

Any discussion of *mens rea* requires an examination of concepts such as 'intention' and 'recklessness'.

INTENTION

A person who acts deliberately to bring about a certain consequence may be said to 'intend' the consequence of his acts.

Foresight of consequences

DPP v Smith [1961] AC 290 was taken to have laid down an irrebuttable presumption that a person intends the natural and probable consequences of his actions. The effect of *Smith* was reversed by s 8 of the Criminal Justice Act 1967. The effect of s 8 is this: the fact that something is the natural and probable consequence of the defendant's actions does not mean that the defendant must, as a matter of law, be taken to have intended that consequence. The fact that something is the natural and probable consequence of the defendant's act is, however, evidence from which it may be inferred that the defendant intended that result to occur. The practical effect of this provision has been considered by the courts on numerous occasions, for example in *R v Moloney* [1985] AC 905 and *R v Hancock and Shankland* [1986] AC 455.

Section 8 of the Criminal Justice Act 1967

A court or jury, in determining whether a person has committed an offence:

(a) shall not be bound in law to infer that he intended or foresaw a result of his actions by reason only of its being a natural and probable consequence of those actions; but

(b) shall decide whether he did intend or foresee that result by reference to all the evidence, drawing such inferences from the evidence as appear proper in the circumstances.

R v Moloney [1985] AC 905 (HL)

See Chapter 21.

R v Hancock and Shankland [1986] AC 455 (HL)

See Chapter 21.

R v Nedrick [1986] 1 WLR 1025 (CA)

See Chapter 21.

R v Woolin [1996] 1 Cr App R 97 (CA)

See Chapter 21.

RECKLESSNESS

As a result of the decisions of the House of Lords in *R v Caldwell* [1982] AC 341 and *R v Lawrence* [1982] AC 510 a person may be regarded as having been reckless with regard to something happening if either:

(a) he fails to consider a risk which a reasonable person would have said was an obvious risk; or

(b) he is aware of the risk but decides to carry on nonetheless.

The first of these is sometimes called 'objective recklessness' and the second is sometimes called 'subjective recklessness'. Criminal liability attaches to the first situation because the accused has taken the conscious decision to ignore the risk; in the second situation, criminal liability arises because the accused ought to have appreciated the existence of the risk.

In *R v S* (1983) 78 Cr App R 149 the Court of Appeal held that *Caldwell* does not apply to the offence of rape.

R v Lawrence [1982] AC 510 (HL)

Lord Diplock: My Lords, on Good Friday, 13 April 1979, after night had fallen, the respondent ('the driver') was riding his motor cycle along an urban street in Lowestoft. The street was subject to a 30 mph speed limit and there was a good deal of other traffic using it at the time. The driver ran into and killed a pedestrian who was crossing the road to return from an off-licence shop to her car which was parked on the opposite side of the street. The driver was in due course tried upon indictment for the offence of causing her death by driving a motor vehicle on a road recklessly, contrary to s 1 of the Road Traffic Act 1972.

Apart from the very tragic consequences of this accident the case that the jury had to try was about as simple and straightforward as any case can be in which the charge is one of driving recklessly. The only question of fact that was in issue was the speed at which the driver was travelling immediately before the impact. The prosecution's case was that the motor cycle was being driven at between 60 and 80 mph and probably much nearer the latter. The case for the defence was that the speed of the motor cycle was no more than 30 or, at most, 40 mph and probably near to the former ...

My Lords, this House has very recently had occasion in *R v Caldwell* [1982] AC 341 to give close consideration to the concept of recklessness as constituting *mens rea* in criminal law. The conclusion reached by the majority was that the adjective 'reckless' when used in a criminal statute, ie the Criminal Damage Act 1971, had not acquired a special meaning as a term of legal art, but bore its popular or dictionary meaning of careless, regardless, or heedless of the possible harmful consequences of one's acts. The same must be true of the adverbial derivative 'recklessly'.

The context in which the word 'reckless' appears in s 1 of the Criminal Damage Act 1971 differs in two respects from the context in which word 'recklessly' appears in ss 1 and 2 of the Road Traffic Act 1972, as now amended. In the

Criminal Damage Act 1971 the *actus reus*, the physical act of destroying or damaging property belonging to another, is in itself a tort. It is not something that one does regularly as part of the ordinary routine of daily life, such as driving a car or a motor cycle. So there is something out of the ordinary to call the doer's attention to what he is doing and its possible consequences, which is absent in road traffic offences. The other difference in context is that in s 1 of the Criminal Damage Act 1971 the *mens rea* of the offences is defined as being reckless as to whether particular harmful consequences would occur, whereas in ss 1 and 2 of the Road Traffic Act 1972, as now amended, the possible harmful consequences of which the driver must be shown to have been heedless are left to be implied from the use of the word 'recklessly' itself. In ordinary usage 'recklessly' as descriptive of a physical act such as driving a motor vehicle which can be performed in a variety of different ways, some of them entailing danger and some of them not, refers not only to the state of mind of the doer of the act when he decides to do it but also qualifies the manner in which the act itself is performed. One does not speak of a person acting 'recklessly', even though he has given no thought at all to the consequences of his act, unless the act is one that presents a real risk of harmful consequences which anyone acting with reasonable prudence would recognise and give heed to. So the *actus reus* of the offence under ss 1 and 2 is not simply driving a motor vehicle on a road, but driving it in a manner which in fact creates a real risk of harmful consequences resulting from it. Since driving in such a manner as to do no worse than create a risk of causing inconvenience or annoyance to other road users constitutes the lesser offence under s 3, the manner of driving that constitutes the *actus reus* of an offence under ss 1 and 2 must be worse than that; it must be such as to create a real risk of causing physical injury to someone else who happens to be using the road or damage to property more substantial than the kind of minor damage that may be caused by an error of judgment in the course of parking one's car ...

I turn now to the *mens rea*. My task is greatly simplified by what has already been said about the concept of recklessness in criminal law in *R v Caldwell* [1982] AC 341. Warning was there given against adopting the simplistic approach of treating all problems of criminal liability as soluble by classifying the test of liability as being either 'subjective' or 'objective'. Recklessness on the part of the doer of an act does presuppose that there is something in the circumstances that would have drawn the attention of an ordinary prudent individual to the possibility that his act was capable of causing the kind of serious harmful consequences that the section which creates the offence was intended to prevent, and that the risk of those harmful consequences occurring was not so slight that an ordinary prudent individual would feel justified in treating them as negligible. It is only when this is so that the doer of the act is acting 'recklessly' if before doing the act, he either fails to give any thought to the possibility of there being any such risk or, having recognised that there was such risk, he nevertheless goes on to do it.

In my view, an appropriate instruction to the jury on what is meant by driving recklessly would be that they must be satisfied of two things:

> *first*, that the defendant was in fact driving the vehicle in such a manner as to create an obvious and serious risk of causing physical injury to some other person who might happen to be using the road or of doing substantial damage to property; and
>
> *second*, that in driving in that manner the defendant did so without having given any thought to the possibility of there being any such risk or, having recognised that there was some risk involved, had nonetheless gone on to take it.

It is for the jury to decide whether the risk created by the manner in which the vehicle was being driven was both obvious and serious and, in deciding this, they may apply the standard of the ordinary prudent motorist as represented by themselves.

If satisfied that an obvious and serious risk was created by the manner of the defendant's driving, the jury are entitled to infer that he was in one or other of the states of mind required to constitute the offence and will probably do so; but regard must be given to any explanation he gives as to his state of mind which may displace the inference ...

R v Caldwell [1982] AC 341 (HL)

See Chapter 20.

R v Satnam S and Kewal S (1983) 78 Cr App R 149 (CA)

See Chapter 23.

R v Morrison (1989) 89 Cr App R 17 (CA)

Lord Lane CJ: ... The facts of the case were somewhat unusual. They are these. In the early morning of 10 September 1987, police officers, five of them in all, were detailed to enter a vacated property in Hyde in order to evict people who were squatting in that house and also to make arrests for burglary. Some of the police officers went upstairs and amongst them was a Woman Detective Constable Matthews. She went upstairs and entered a room, where the appellant was hiding behind a door. According to her, and it is plain that the jury accepted her evidence so far as this matter was concerned, she said, 'We are police officers, you are under arrest', whereupon this appellant ran towards the window. The Woman Detective Constable seized hold of him by the clothes, but he dived forward through the glass of the window on to the pavement some 20 feet down below, dragging her as far as the window with him. The result of that was that her face unfortunately came in contact with the broken glass of the window and she sustained very serious and disfiguring injuries, in the shape of a long jagged cut from the hairline over her right eye right down over the eyebrow into her right eyelid, necessitating a number of stitches. Perhaps the most serious matter from her point of view is that the injury is not a proper subject for cosmetic surgery and she will be scarred for life. Those were the facts.

The appellant gave an account to the jury that he had been woken by banging. He had been unable to see that the people involved in the arrest were police. They were in plain clothes. He had not heard the policewoman saying anything about police and he did not know that she was hanging on to him and in any event he had not intended any harm to her ...

Unhappily there are now in the law of this country two types of recklessness according to the nature of the crime which is charged. The first is that defined by Lord Diplock in *R v Caldwell* [1982] AC 341. He examines the history and then, dealing as he is not with the 1861 Act with which we are here concerned, but with the Criminal Damage Act 1971, s 1(1), has this to say: (at 20 and 354):

> In my opinion, a person charged with an offence under s 1(1) of the Criminal Damage Act 1971 is 'reckless as to whether any such property would be destroyed or damaged' if (1) he does an act which in fact creates an obvious risk that property will be destroyed or damaged and (2) when he does the act he either has not given any thought to the possibility of there being any such risk or has recognised that there was some risk involved and has nonetheless

> gone on to do it. That would be a proper direction to the jury; cases in the Court of Appeal which held otherwise should be regarded as overruled.

The way in which Lord Diplock so defined recklessness is sometimes described, although Lord Diplock would not approve of it, as being the objective test, namely not what the defendant himself was thinking but what an observer, an ordinary reasonable and prudent observer, would in those circumstances have thought. That is the sense, thanks to that opinion of Lord Diplock, in which the word 'reckless' must be construed when one is considering the Criminal Damage Act 1971 at least.

The other type of recklessness is that defined by Byrne J in the Court of Criminal Appeal in *Cunningham* (1957) 41 Cr App R 155, [1957] 2 QB 396. Let me say, in parentheses, that Lord Diplock in the opinion from which I have just cited a passage, considered *Cunningham*. He distinguished *Cunningham* in *R v Caldwell*, but did not in fact disapprove of it. So the decision in *Cunningham* still stands and is still binding upon this court.

Byrne J in *Cunningham*, having set out the various cases under the 1861 Act, said at 159 and 399 respectively:

> We have considered those cases, and we have also considered, in the light of those cases, the following principle which was propounded by the late Professor C S Kenny in the first edition of his *Outlines of Criminal Law* published in 1902 and repeated at p 186 of the 16th edition edited by Mr J W Cecil Turner and published in 1952: 'In any statutory definition of a crime, malice must be taken not in the old vague sense of wickedness in general but as requiring either (1) An actual intention to do the particular kind of harm that in fact was done; or (2) [this is the important passage] recklessness as to whether such harm should occur or not (ie the accused has foreseen that the particular kind of harm might be done and yet has gone on to take the risk of it). It is neither limited to nor does it indeed require any ill will towards the person injured.

The same principle is repeated by Mr Turner in his 10th edition of *Russell on Crime* at 1592:

> We think that this is an accurate statement of the law. It derives some support from the judgments of Lord Coleridge and Blackburn J in *Pembliton* (1874) LR 2 CCR 119. In our opinion the word 'maliciously' in a statutory crime postulates foresight of consequences.

In the present case the word 'maliciously' appears in the section with which we are dealing and it appears in the indictment. Consequently it is that definition of 'recklessness' which applies here ...

R v Reid [1992] 1 WLR 793 (HL)

Lord Keith of Kinkel: My Lords, the question principally debated at the hearing of this appeal was whether the formulation by Lord Diplock in *R v Lawrence* [1982] AC 510 at 525-26 of the meaning of 'driving recklessly' in s 1 of the Road Traffic Act 1972 (as amended) was incorrect, so that the decision in that case should be departed from under the 1966 practice statement (see *Note* [1966] 1 WLR 1234). It was argued for the appellant that the formulation was mistaken in respect that Lord Diplock expressed the *mens rea* for the statutory offence as including not only a state of mind where the accused drove as he did recognising that his action created a risk of injury or of substantial damage to property but nevertheless went on to take that risk, but also a state of mind where the accused drove as he did without giving any thought to the possibility of there being any such risk, notwithstanding that the risk was obvious (see [1982] AC 510 at 526–27). In truth, so it was maintained, it was only the former state of mind which constituted the relevant *mens rea*. In common with my noble and learned friends Lord Ackner and Lord Goff of Chieveley I am satisfied that, for the reasons they give, the argument is unsound. Lord Diplock described the *actus reus* of the offence as driving a vehicle in such a manner as to create an obvious and serious risk of causing physical injury to some other person who might happen to be using the road or of doing substantial damage to property. The important thing here is that the risk created must be an obvious and serious one. No criticism has been or could be made of that. The precise state of mind of a person who drives in the manner indicated must in the vast majority of cases be quite incapable of ascertainment. Absence of something from a person's mind is as much part of his state of mind as its presence. Inadvertence to risk is no less a subjective state of mind than is disregard of a recognised risk. If there is nothing to go upon apart from what actually happened, the natural inference is that the driver's state of mind was one or other of those described by Lord Diplock. It would, however, be quite impossible for any juryman to say which it was, and in particular for him to be satisfied beyond reasonable doubt that it was the first state of mind rather than the second. So logically, if only the first state of mind constituted the relevant *mens rea*, it would be impossible ever to get a conviction. There is no room for doubt, in my opinion, that a large proportion of drivers who drive in such a manner as to create the relevant sort of risk do so without giving any thought to the possibility of risk. Indeed, the very attempt to exclude such drivers from the ambit of the statutory offence recognises that this must be so. Driving a motor vehicle is potentially an extremely dangerous activity, requiring a high degree of self-discipline. Those who fail to display the requisite degree of self-discipline through failing to give any thought to the possibility of the serious risks they are creating may reasonably be regarded as no less blameworthy than those who consciously appreciate a risk but nevertheless go on to take it. The word 'reckless' in its ordinary meaning is apt to embrace the former category no less than the latter, and I feel no doubt that Parliament by its use intended to cover both of them.

The substance of Lord Diplock's formulation of a specimen jury direction is accordingly apt, in my opinion, to cover the generality of cases. But I do not rule out that in certain cases there may be special circumstances which require it to be modified or added to, for example where the driver acted under some understandable and excusable mistake or where his capacity to appreciate risks was adversely affected by some condition not involving fault on his part. There may also be cases where the driver acted as he did in a sudden dilemma created by the actions of others. The specific certified question as to whether the jury should always be directed in the *ipsissima verba* of Lords Diplock's formulation I would answer in the negative. In some cases when the only relevant issue is one of disputed fact it may not be necessary to use it at all. In others it may require to be modified or adapted to suit the circumstances of the case ...

Lord Goff of Chieveley: My Lords, the judge's direction to the jury on the meaning in law of the expression 'driving recklessly' in s 1 of the Road Traffic Act 1972 (as amended) followed the specimen direction set out by Lord Diplock in his speech in *R v Lawrence* [1982] AC 510 at 526–27. The appeal to your Lordships' House, concerned as it is with the question whether a jury in such a case as this should be directed in the precise terms of Lord Diplock's specimen direction, has taken the form of a frontal attack upon the validity of that direction. It is, of course, well known that the speeches in *R v Lawrence* were delivered on the same day as (although immediately after) the speeches in *R v Caldwell* [1982] AC 341, a case concerned not with driving recklessly but with the meaning of the word 'reckless' as used in s 1 of the Criminal Damage Act 1971; and that the leading speech in *R v Lawrence* was delivered by Lord Diplock who there drew heavily upon the definition of the mental element in recklessness contained in his own speech (the leading speech of the majority) in *R v Caldwell*. So, although the present appeal is concerned only with driving recklessly, it is inevitable that some reference should be made to *R v Caldwell*. Even so, your Lordships are in the present case concerned with the meaning of the word 'recklessly' as used in ss 1 and 2 of the Road Traffic Act 1972 and are not directly concerned with the meaning of the word 'reckless' as used in s 1 of the Criminal Damage Act 1971 ...

I think it right that I should at this stage set out the passage from Lord Diplock's speech in *R v Lawrence* [1982] AC 510 at 526–27, from which the judge in the present case drew his direction to the jury on the meaning of the words 'driving recklessly'. It reads as follows:

> In my view, an appropriate instruction to the jury on what is meant by driving recklessly would be that they must be satisfied of two things: first, that the defendant was in fact driving the vehicle in such a manner as to create an obvious and serious risk of causing physical injury to some other person who might happen to be using the road or of doing substantial damage to property; and, second, that in driving in that manner the defendant did so without having given any thought to the possibility of there being any such risk or, having recognised that there was some risk involved, had nonetheless gone on to take it. It is for the jury to decide whether the risk created by the manner in which the vehicle was being driven was both obvious and serious and, in deciding this, they may apply the standard of the ordinary prudent motorist as represented by themselves. If satisfied that an obvious and serious risk was created by the manner of the defendant's driving, the jury are entitled to infer that he was in one or other of the states of mind required to constitute the offence and will probably do so; but regard must be given to any explanation he gives as to his state of mind which may displace the inference.

The first limb of this direction is directed towards the *actus reus* of the offence; the second limb is directed towards the *mens rea*, and set out two alternative forms which the *mens rea* may take. This definition of the *mens rea* (which mirrors Lord Diplock's definition in *R v Caldwell* [1982] AC 341 at 354 of the *mens rea* of recklessness in s 1 of the Criminal Damage Act 1971) has proved to be most controversial. It has provoked a very hostile reaction from some of our leading academic lawyers specialising in criminal law. Their view has been that the mental element in crimes involving recklessness should be restricted to the second of the two alternatives referred to by Lord Diplock, *viz* disregarding a recognised risk, which is usually called the subjective test. The first of these two alternative formulations, *viz* acting without giving any thought to the possibility of there being any risk of the relevant kind, they have rejected as contrary to principle and contrary to previous Court of Appeal authority (see, in particular, *R v Stephenson* [1979] QB 695, a decision under the Criminal Damage Act 1971, disapproved in *R v Caldwell*).

The central question in this appeal is whether, in cases concerned with driving recklessly, your Lordships' House should reject Lord Diplock's alternative form of recklessness and restrict that concept to the so-called subjective approach. It came as no surprise that Mr Michael Hill QC, for the appellant Mr Reid, placed this submission at the forefront of his argument, seeking to persuade your Lordships to reconsider *R v Lawrence* and, in so far as the decision extended the mental element in cases of recklessness beyond the category of disregarding a recognised risk, to exercise the power under the 1966 practice statement (see *Note* [1966] 1 WLR 1234) to hold that it was wrongly decided and, on that basis, to allow the appeal.

In order to consider the submission advanced by Mr Hill for the appellant, it is first necessary to ascertain precisely what led to the formulation of Lords Diplock's specimen direction in *R v Lawrence*, and in particular to his introduction of his first alternative form of the mental element in recklessness in that case. I am anxious not to indulge in long quotations from Lord Diplock's speeches in *R v Caldwell* and *R v Lawrence* so I will summarise, as best I can, the steps to his reasoning. Central to his reasoning in *R v Caldwell* [1982] AC 341 at 351–55 was the idea that recklessness, in its ordinary meaning, covers a whole range of states of mind, from failing to give any thought to whether there is any risk of the relevant kind, to recognising the existence of the risk and nevertheless deciding to ignore it. From this it followed that to concentrate on one type of recklessness (disregarding a recognised risk) to the exclusion of others would impose an unnaturally narrow meaning upon the word; and, since disregarding a recognised risk was not necessarily more blameworthy than failing to give any thought to the possibility of risk, to restrict recklessness to the former meaning was undesirable as a matter of policy. Furthermore, to require a jury to convict a defendant of recklessness only if he had in fact foreseen the relevant risk and nevertheless disregarded it was in reality to impose an impossible task upon juries, since in real life disregarding a recognised risk and failing to address one's mind to the possibility of risk are states of mind which shade into each other and in many cases are very difficult, if not impossible, to segregate and so identify in any particular case. To the suggestion that disregarding a recognised risk constituted a test of *mens rea* which was subjective (and therefore acceptable as a criterion of blameworthiness), whereas failing to address one's mind to the possibility of risk was essentially objective and therefore not acceptable, Lord Diplock's response was to disparage the use of the terms 'subjective' and 'objective', and to assert that in any event both criteria were, in their different ways, subjective. Even so he recognised that, before a man could be held to have been reckless, there must have been something which ought to have drawn the attention of an ordinary prudent person to the possibility of the relevant harm occurring; and he laid down the further requirement that the ordinary prudent person would not, on consideration, have treated the risk as negligible.

In *R v Lawrence* [1982] AC 510 at 525–26 Lord Diplock developed this reasoning to render it more appropriate to the rather different case of driving recklessly. He considered that, in ordinary usage, the word 'recklessly' as descriptive of a physical act such as driving a motor vehicle not only refers to the state of mind of the driver, but also qualifies the manner in which his act of driving is performed. In his opinion, the *actus reus* of such an offence must be driving the vehicle in a manner which in fact creates a real risk of harm. Furthermore, since driving recklessly must be intended to be worse than merely careless driving punishable under s 3 of the same Act, it must be such as to create a risk of damage more substantial than the kind of minor damage associated with an error of judgment. It was his reasoning in *R v Caldwell* together with his further reasoning in *R v Lawrence*, which led him to formulate the specimen direction in *R v Lawrence* which I have already quoted.

Now the fundamental reason for the academic hostility to *R v Caldwell* and *R v Lawrence* lies in the perception that the appropriate definition of the mental element in recklessness is to be found in the idea of acting in disregard of a recognised risk. Thus, in cl 5.12 of the draft Criminal Code (Legislating the Criminal Code: Offences Against the Person and General Principles (Law Commission Consultation Paper no 122) (1992)), of which Professor Smith is the leading draftsman, we find the following definition of recklessness:

> a person acts ... 'recklessly' with respect to: (1) a circumstance when he is aware of a risk that it exists or will exist; (2) a result when he is aware of a risk that it will occur; and it is, in the circumstances known to him, unreasonable to take the risk.

Likewise, we find Professor Glanville Williams asserting in para 5.1 of his *Textbook of Criminal Law*, 2nd edn, 1983, p 96, that recklessness 'normally involves conscious and unreasonable risk-taking'. This is generally accepted as constituting a form of recklessness. But the question is whether this is the only form which recklessness is understood to take, and indeed whether recklessness should properly be understood to take only one form. This is the point on which Lord Diplock challenged academic opinion, by embracing within the concept of recklessness his alternative category. It is evident from his reasoning that he would include within this alternative category cases where the defendant's perception is impaired by drink or by blind rage or by some other excitement, with the result that he fails to give any thought to the possibility of such risk. But there may well be other cases. For example, the defendant's state of mind may be such that he does not care whether any such risk exists or not, which has been described as an attitude of indifference, or of not caring less. Such a state of mind does not necessarily involve awareness of risk; despite Professor Smith's assertion that such a state of mind certainly seems to require foresight of the risk (see [1981] Crim LR 395), I myself doubt whether this need be so, where the defendant acts regardless of the consequences (*cf R v Pigg* [1982] 1 WLR 762 and *R v Kimber* [1983] 1 WLR 1118). In other cases, the defendant's state of mind may be one of wilful blindness, where he simply closes his mind to the possibility of risk. In yet other case, perhaps the most common, the defendant simply does not think about the matter at all, perhaps because he is acting impetuously on the spur of the moment without addressing his mind to the possibility of risk.

It is not difficult to give examples of cases of this kind in the context of driving. I can for example see no difficulty in envisaging a driver who drives at high speed in traffic or in a built-up area or both, just not caring whether any risk of personal injury or damage to other vehicles exists or not. It does not matter whether in such a case he is indifferent to the existence of the risk, or whether he has closed his mind to any such thing; the point is that in such circumstances he may not even address his mind to the possibility of risk. Likewise, when driving down the motorway many of us must have seen small groups of motorcyclists weaving in and out of the traffic at enormous speeds, with their eyes apparently glued to their speedometers to see how fast they are going. Again, these young men may very well not even address their minds to the possibility of risk, concentrating only on the speed at which they are travelling. Then there are the young joyriders who take other people's cars, often fast cars such as GTIs, and drive them at high speed around housing estates. They, too, may well give no thought to the possibility of risk to other people or other vehicles in the vicinity. These are everyday examples of cases which we have either seen ourselves on the road or have read about in the newspapers. I cannot help thinking that in ordinary speech all these people would be described as driving recklessly. Certainly, I do not think that ordinary people would regard it as a relevant inquiry to ascertain whether these drivers had in fact addressed their minds to the possibility of risk before they could be said to have acted recklessly. Indeed, I would go further and say that this category of recklessness on the roads may well be as prevalent as the category in which the driver actually foresees the risk and decides to disregard it. This is because on the roads decisions to act, for example to overtake or to go for a gap, are often split-second decisions which may be taken virtually without thought. In retrospect after the event, a driver may say, 'Yes, I did think about it and I did realise that there was a risk'; but he may be just as likely, if not more likely, to say, 'I am afraid that I just did not think but, if I had done, I would have realised that there was a risk'. In circumstances such as these, an enquiry into the existence of actual foresight of the risk would seem to be unrealistic for the purpose of assessing blameworthiness or criminality. Indeed, it can be argued with force that, in many cases of failing to think, the degree of blameworthiness to be attached to the driver can be greater than that to be attached in some cases to the driver who recognised the risk and decided to disregard it. This is because the unspoken premise which seems to me to underlie Lord Diplock's statement of the law in *R v Lawrence* (and perhaps also in *R v Caldwell*) is that the defendant is engaged in an activity which he knows to be potentially dangerous. Every driver knows that driving can be dangerous; and if when a man is in fact driving dangerously in the sense described by Lord Diplock, he does not even address his mind to the possibility of risk, then, in the absence of special circumstances (to which I will refer later) it is right that he should, if the risk was obvious, be held to have been driving recklessly, even though he was not in fact aware of the risk. It cannot be right that in such circumstances he should be able to shelter behind his ignorance, or be given preferred treatment as compared with another person who, having recognised and considered the risk, has wrongly decided to disregard it. If the policy underlying this category of recklessness were to be explained to a jury, I would be surprised if they had difficulty in understanding it ...

It follows that in cases of driving recklessly (with which your Lordships are here concerned), I find myself to be in respectful agreement with the conclusion of Lord Diplock, that recklessness cannot sensibly be restricted to the so-called subjective test, but must be extended to embrace cases where the defendant has failed to give any thought to the possibility of risk. At the very least his view is, in my opinion, perfectly tenable; and in these circumstances it would not be an appropriate exercise of the power under the 1966 practice statement (see *Note* [1966] 1 WLR 1234) to depart from the decision in *R v Lawrence*.

I recognise that it has been suggested that, if this is right, driving recklessly cannot be so sharply differentiated from careless driving, ie driving without due care and attention, as it would be if the purely subjective test were to be adopted as the sole criterion of recklessness, in which case a clear distinction could be drawn between cases where the defendant was aware of the risk and nevertheless disregarded it, and cases where the defendant failed to advert to the relevant risk. But the answer to this criticism is, I believe, as follows. First, as I have already said, we have to recognise that there are cases where, although the defendant is unaware of the risk, his conduct coupled with his state of mind is such that, in ordinary speech, he can properly be described as driving recklessly. Second, these cases can be differentiated from mere careless driving, because they are cases in which the defendant's driving would be described as dangerous in the sense that he was driving in such a manner as to create a serious risk of causing physical injury to other people or substantial damage to other people's property, and yet he did not even address his mind to the possibility of there being any such risk. This is different from a case where, for example, momentary inadvertence happens incidentally to create a risk; for the recklessness arises from the combination of the dangerous character of the driving coupled with failure by the driver even to address his mind to the possibility of risk. I for my part see no real difficulty, in practice, in perceiving a sufficiently clear differentiation between cases of this kind and cases of driving without due care and attention, which we see happening so often on the roads and of which many of us may, I fear, be guilty from time to time. Take the simple case of a man driving his car on the motorway in a group of other cars, all travelling at say 60 mph, and he fails for a moment or so to keep his eye on the car in front – perhaps his attention is caught by a pretty girl in the car alongside – with the result that he does not notice that the car in front has had to brake suddenly and he drives straight into it causing it damage. This is a classic case of careless driving; I do not think that on these simple facts anybody would say that he was driving recklessly. This is not a case of a man driving dangerously (in the sense described by Lord Diplock) and nevertheless failing to address his mind to the possibility of risk; it is a case of a man who failed to drive with due care and attention, and no more.

It has been pointed out that, although Lord Diplock's two categories of recklessness taken together have the effect that, in most cases where the defendant is driving dangerously in the sense I have described, he will in fact be driving recklessly, nevertheless there are cases in which this is not so. This may occur where the defendant considers the possibility of risk but nevertheless concludes that there is none. But we have to remember that, *ex hypothesi*, the defendant is driving dangerously in the sense I have described; and in practice his evidence that in such circumstances he thought that there was no risk is only likely to carry weight if he can point to some specific fact as to which he was mistaken and which, if true, would have excluded the possibility of risk which might occur if, for example, as my noble and learned friend Lord Ackner has pointed out, he misunderstood in good faith some direction or instruction, or if he drove the wrong way down a one-way street at a normal speed in the mistaken belief that it was a two-way street. If that was indeed the case, his driving might well not be described as reckless, though such cases are likely to be rare. It has been suggested that there is therefore a 'loophole' or 'lacuna' in Lord Diplock's definition of recklessness. I feel bound to say that I myself regard these expressions as misleading. The simple fact is that Lord Diplock was concerned to define driving recklessly, not dangerous driving; and it is not in every case where the defendant is in fact driving dangerously that he should be held to be driving recklessly, although in most cases the two will coincide. Another example where they may not coincide would occur where a driver who, while driving, is afflicted by illness or shock which impairs his capacity to address his mind to the possibility of risk; it may well not be right to describe him as driving recklessly in such circumstances. Likewise (as my noble and learned friend has pointed out), if a driver takes evasive action in an emergency, his action may involve the taking of a risk which is regarded as justified in the special circumstances, so that he cannot be described as driving recklessly. Such cases, which again are likely to be rare, can be dealt with if and when they arise. It is however unnecessary to consider any such case on the present appeal.

I turn to consider Lord Diplock's specimen direction to the jury, designed for use in cases concerned with driving recklessly, set out in his speech in *R v Lawrence* [1982] AC 510 at 526–27. This has, I think, to be approached sensibly, and not considered like a statutory provision. It is after all described simply as 'an appropriate instruction'. Like all such specimen directions, it should be regarded as no more than epitomising the relevant law. Specimen directions such as these should be regarded as models to be adapted to fit the facts of the particular case; and they should also be regarded as capable of adaptation, as necessary, where new situations arise, because it is always difficult to foresee every situation which may occur in the future ...

It is against this background that I turn to the first question posed for your Lordships' consideration, which is whether, in a case of reckless driving, the jury should be directed in the terms of the *ipsissima verba* of Lord Diplock's specimen instruction to the jury from *R v Lawrence*, without modifications. I myself would regard such a statement as too sweeping ... Indeed ... there are cases of reckless driving in which it is unnecessary to define recklessness at all; for some turn on simple questions of fact in which an analysis of the elements of recklessness may serve only to complicate the issues. *R v Lawrence* was itself such a case. I have also referred to the possibility that special fact-situations may arise which may call for a specific qualification of Lord Diplock's summary of the law. My own belief is that judges of the Crown Court should take the law as epitomised by Lord Diplock in *R v Lawrence*, and bring that abstract statement to life for the jury by means of relevant examples taken from ordinary life, and then relate it to the case before the jury by drawing their attention to the specific issues to which they have to address their minds ...

Speaking for myself, it has helped me to start with the fact that there are two relevant driving offences which have to be differentiated: careless driving (ie driving without due care and attention) and driving recklessly. Driving recklessly is to be differentiated from careless driving in two ways. First, the driving itself must be of a certain dangerous character – the defendant must in fact have been driving in such a manner as to create a serious risk of harm, and that harm must be more substantial than the kind of minor damage associated with an error of judgment. So the defendant must be driving the vehicle in such a manner as to create a serious risk of causing physical injury to some other person who might happen to be using the road or of doing substantial damage to property ...

But, in addition, to establish that the defendant was driving recklessly, it has to be shown that he possessed a certain state of mind. I find it relatively straightforward to follow Lord Diplock's thinking on this point, provided that the abstract principle is brought down to earth with practical examples. I first bear in mind that recklessness is an ordinary English word, but that, as used in ordinary speech, and likewise as used in our law, it has more than one meaning. I then find it best to take first Lord Diplock's second category of recklessness – recognising that there is some risk of the relevant kind involved, and nevertheless going on to take it – and relate it to simple examples drawn from ordinary life, always based upon dangerous driving in the sense described by Lord Diplock. After that, I find it easier to turn to Lord Diplock's first category, recalling that there are circumstances, which in the context of driving are probably just as common (because drivers do from time to time act impetuously without thinking), in which a driver may, although he is driving dangerously, nevertheless fail to address his mind at all to the possibility of there being any risk of the relevant kind ... I do not think that a jury would be surprised to hear that where a man is driving dangerously (in the sense described) he cannot escape responsibility by simply sheltering behind his own ignorance of the risk, provided that the risk was obvious; for if he drives a motor vehicle in such a manner on the public road without even addressing his mind to the possibility of risk, we would describe him in ordinary speech as driving recklessly, and the law considers him to be blameworthy in the same way as a driver who realises there is a risk and nevertheless goes on to take it is regarded as blameworthy. There are therefore these two states of mind which the law regards as reckless; but in real life they can shade into each other, and may not be easy to distinguish.

On this approach ... it is, I believe, relatively easy to understand Lord Diplock's encapsulation of the law in his specimen direction, which is to the effect that a jury should only convict a defendant of driving recklessly if they are sure of the following:

(1) that he was in fact driving in such a manner as to create a serious risk of causing physical injury to some other person who might happen to be using the road, or doing substantial damage to property; and

(2) either:

    (a) that he recognised that there was some risk of that kind involved, but nevertheless went on to take it; or

    (b) that, despite the fact that he was driving in such a manner, he did not even address his mind to the possibility of there being any such risk, and the risk was in fact obvious ...

Lord Browne Wilkinson: ... My first comment is that, in the absence of a general statutory definition of the work 'reckless', I do not accept that the constituent elements of recklessness must be the same in all statutes. In particular the following factors may lead to the word being given different meanings in different statutes. First, the history of the legislation. Lord Goff has demonstrated the statutory derivation of the phrase 'driving recklessly' in the road traffic legislation. That history is markedly different from that of s 1 of the Criminal Damage Act 1971 which was under consideration in *R v Caldwell*. Second, the statutory provision (as in s 1 of the Criminal Damage Act 1971) may require proof of recklessness as to a specified consequence or, as in the present case, the word may be used on its own simply as a description of the prohibited act. It is not apparent to me that these two different uses of the word necessarily postulate the same ingredients in the *mens rea* of the offence. Third, the single word 'recklessness' may be used as in the Road Traffic Act, to describe both the nature of the *actus reus* – the type of driving – and also the mental state of the defendant in driving in that manner. This is to be contrasted with cases such as those under the Criminal Damage Act 1971, where the word is directed only to the mental state of the accused and not to the act itself. Finally, the word 'reckless' may be used in relation to the doing of one or more isolated acts, as in the Criminal Damage Act 1971, or as in the present case in relation to a continuous course of action (driving) which is part of life for nearly everybody and which, although capable of being done safely, is inherently dangerous. For these reasons, I propose to deal with the decision in *R v Lawrence* alone and, despite the close link between the two cases, express no view on the decision in *R v Caldwell.*

... In the present context, I would have thought that the correct usage of the word 'subjective' is to connote a requirement that the offence is committed only if the mental state of the accused himself, as opposed to the mental state of the reasonable man, were such as to satisfy the requirements of *mens rea* for that offence. An objective test, on the other hand, would be satisfied if it could be shown that the state of mind of a reasonable man in those circumstances would satisfy the requirements of mens rea for that offence.

That being my understanding of the words, I am puzzled by the criticism of the direction in *R v Lawrence* that it lays down an objective test since in my judgment it plainly does not. First, the answer given by this House to the first question posed in *Lawrence* – '*mens rea* is involved in the offence of driving recklessly' – shows that it is not an absolute offence. Lord Diplock in his speech when dealing with *mens rea* refers to the necessary mental state of the accused himself ...

As I understand the criticisms of *R v Lawrence*, they are founded on the proposition that 'recklessness' requires it to be shown that the defendant was aware of the risk and disregarded it, which I shall call 'advertence'. It is said that a 'couldn't care less' attitude in which the defendant does not address his mind at all to whether or not there is a risk (non-advertence) is not sufficient. Non-advertence is characterised by the critics as being not subjective. In my judgment this is to confuse the issue; both advertence and non-advertence to risk are states of mind of the defendant himself. Therefore the test is, on my terminology, subjective in both cases ...

... In its ordinary or dictionary meaning the word 'reckless' includes the concept of heedlessness of risk (non-advertence). I can see no reason for giving the word a more limited meaning in this Act ...

As to the so called 'loophole' or 'lacuna' in Lord Diplock's direction ... [t]here may be cases where, despite the defendant being aware of the risk and deciding to take it, he does so because of a reasonable misunderstanding, sudden disability or emergency which render it inappropriate to characterise his conduct as being reckless. Lord Diplock in *R v Lawrence* was not seeking to lay down a test applicable to all cases and the facts in the present case do not fall within this special category ...

[Note: s 2 of the Road Traffic Act 1988 replaces the offence of reckless driving with that of dangerous driving.]

MENS REA WORDS

Some crimes have, in their definition, a specific requirement of *mens rea*. For example, the accused must have been acting 'wilfully' or 'maliciously' or 'knowingly'.

Wilfully

R v Sheppard [1981] AC 394 (HL)

Lord Diplock: My Lords, the appellants ('the parents') were convicted in the Crown Court at Northampton of an offence under s 1(1) of the Children and Young Persons Act 1933 of wilfully neglecting their infant child, Martin, between 1 July 1978 and 29 January 1979 in a manner likely to cause him unnecessary suffering or injury to health.

The child, who had been a slow developer, died, at the age of 16 months, on 28 January 1979 of hypothermia associated with malnutrition, a condition which increases the susceptibility of infants to hypothermia. If Martin had received timely medical attention his life might well have been saved. For five days or more before his death he had probably suffered from gastro-enteritis which had caused him to vomit up and so fail to ingest the food that had been offered to him; but the details of such symptoms of serious illness as were apparent during the period before his death do not affect the question which falls to be decided by your Lordships in this appeal and is a question of law alone.

The gravamen of the charge against the parents was that they had failed to provide Martin with adequate medical aid on several occasions during the seven months to which the charge related and, in particular, during the week immediately preceding his death. In the light of the trial judge's instructions given to the jury as to the law applicable to the offence charged, it can safely be inferred from the verdicts of guilty that the jury found (1) that injury to Martin's health had in fact been caused by the failure by each of the parents to have him examined by a doctor in the period prior to his death and (2) that any reasonable parents, ie parents endowed with ordinary intelligence and not indifferent to the welfare of their child, would have recognised from the manifest symptoms of serious illness in Martin during that period that a failure to have him examined by a doctor might well result in unnecessary suffering or injury to his health.

The parents, a young couple aged 20 and 22 respectively, occupied poor accommodation, particularly as respects heating, where the family, which included another (older) child, subsisted on a meagre income. They would appear, on the evidence, to have been of low intelligence. Their real defence, if it were capable of amounting to a defence in law, was that they did not realise that the child was ill enough to need a doctor; they had observed his loss of appetite and failure to keep down his food, but had genuinely thought that this was due to some passing minor upset to which babies are prone, from which they recover naturally without medical aid and which medical treatment can do nothing to alleviate or to hasten recovery.

We do not know whether the jury would have thought that this explanation of the parents' failure to have Martin examined by a doctor might be true. In his instructions the judge had told the jury that to constitute the statutory offence with which the parents were charged it was unnecessary for the Crown to prove that at the time when it was alleged the parents should have had the child seen by a doctor either they in fact knew that their failure to do so involved a risk of causing him unnecessary suffering or injury to health or they did not care whether this was so or not. Following a line of authority by appellate courts that was binding on him, the trial judge treated the offence as one of strict liability and told the jury that the test of the parents' guilt was objective only: 'Would a reasonable parent, with knowledge of the facts that were known to the accused, appreciate that failure to have the child examined was likely to cause him unnecessary suffering or injury to health?' That was the question that the jury by their verdict answered Yes, not any question as to the parents' own state of mind.

The Court of Appeal, regarding themselves as bound by the same line of authority, felt compelled to dismiss the parents' appeal, but expressed their opinion that the law on this subject was worthy of review by your Lordships' House and gave the parents leave to appeal. They certified as the point of law of general public importance involved in their decision to dismiss the appeal: 'What is the proper direction to be given to a jury on a charge of wilful neglect of a child under s 1 of the Children and Young Persons Act 1933 as to what constitutes the necessary *mens rea* of the offence?'

The relevant provisions of s 1 are in the following terms:

(1) If any person who has attained the age of 16 years and has the custody, charge, or care of any child or young person under that age, wilfully assaults, ill-treats, neglects, abandons, or exposes him, or causes or procures him to be assaulted, ill-treated, neglected, abandoned, or exposed, in a manner likely to cause him unnecessary suffering or injury to health (including injury to or loss of sight, or hearing, or limb, or organ of the body, and any mental derangement), that person shall be guilty of a misdemeanour, and shall be liable: (a) on conviction on indictment, to a fine, or alternatively, or in addition thereto, to imprisonment for any term not exceeding two years ...

(2) For the purposes of this section: (a) a parent or other person legally liable to maintain a child or young person shall be deemed to have neglected him in a manner likely to cause injury to his health if he has failed to provide

> adequate food, clothing, medical aid or lodging for him, or if, having been unable otherwise to provide such food, clothing, medical aid or lodging, he has failed to take steps to procure it to be provided under enactments applicable in that behalf ...

The presence of the adverb 'wilfully' qualifying all five verbs, 'assaults, ill-treats, neglects, abandons, or exposes', makes it clear that any offence under s 1 requires *mens rea*, a state of mind on the part of the offender directed to the particular act or failure to act that constitutes the *actus reus* and warrants the description 'wilful'. The other four verbs refer to positive acts, 'neglect' refers to failure to act, and the judicial explanation of the state of mind denoted by the statutory expression 'wilfully' in relation to the doing of a positive act is not necessarily wholly apt in relation to a failure to act at all. The instant case is in the latter category, so I will confine myself to considering what is meant by wilfully neglecting a child in a manner likely to cause him unnecessary suffering or injury to health.

In construing the statutory language it is not always appropriate and may often be misleading to dissect a compound phrase and to treat a particular word or words as intended to be descriptive only of the *mens rea* of the offence and the remainder as defining only the *actus reus*. But s 1 of the 1933 Act contains in subsection(2)(a) a clear indication of a dichotomy between 'wilfully' and the compound phrase 'neglected him [sc the child] in a manner likely to cause injury to his health'. When the fact of failure to provide adequate food, clothing, medical aid or lodging has been established, the deeming provision applies only to that compound phrase; it still leaves the prosecution with the burden of proving the required *mens rea*, the mental element of 'wilfulness' on the part of the accused.

The *actus reus* of the offence with which the accused were charged in the instant case does not involve construing the verb 'neglect', for the offence fell within the deeming provision; and the only question as respects the *actus reus* was: did the parents fail to provide for Martin in the period before his death medical aid that was in fact adequate in view of his actual state of health at the relevant time? This, as it seems to me, is a pure question of objective fact to be determined in the light of what has become known *by the date of the trial* to have been the child's actual state of health at the relevant time. It does not depend on whether a reasonably careful parent, with knowledge of those facts only which such a parent might reasonably be expected to observe for himself, would have thought it prudent to have recourse to medical aid. The concept of the reasonable man as providing the standard by which the liability of real persons for their actual conduct is to be determined is a concept of civil law, particularly in relation to the tort of negligence; the obtrusion into criminal law of conformity with the notional conduct of the reasonable man as relevant to criminal liability, though not unknown (eg in relation to provocation sufficient to reduce murder to manslaughter), is exceptional, and should not lightly be extended: see *Andrews v DPP* [1937] AC 576 at 582–83. If failure to use the hypothetical powers of observation, ratiocination and foresight of consequences possessed by this admirable but purely notional exemplar is to constitute an ingredient of a criminal offence it must surely form part not of the *actus reus* but of the *mens rea*.

It does not, however, seem to me that the concept of the reasonable parent, what he would observe, what he would understand from what he had observed and what he would do about it, has any part to play in the mens rea of an offence in which the description of the mens rea is contained in the single adverb 'wilfully'. In the context of doing to a child a positive act (assault, ill-treat, abandon or expose) that is likely to have specified consequences (to cause him unnecessary suffering or injury to health), 'wilfully', which must describe the state of mind of the actual doer of the act, may be capable of bearing the narrow meaning that the wilfulness required extends only to the doing of the physical act itself which in fact results in the consequences described, even though the doer thought that it would not and would not have acted as he did had he foreseen a risk that those consequences might follow. Although this is a possible meaning of 'wilfully', it is not the natural meaning even in relation to positive acts defined by reference to the consequences to which they are likely to give rise; and, in the context of the section, if this is all the adverb 'wilfully' meant it would be otiose. Section 1(1) would have the same effect if it were omitted; for even in absolute offences (unless vicarious liability is involved) the physical act relied on as constituting the offence must be wilful in the limited sense, for which the synonym in the field of criminal liability that has now become the common term of legal art is 'voluntary'.

So much for 'wilfully' in the context of a positive act. To 'neglect' a child is to omit to act, to fail to provide adequately for its needs, and, in the context of s 1 of the 1933 Act, its physical needs rather than its spiritual, educational, moral or emotional needs. These are dealt with by other legislation. For reasons already given the use of the verb 'neglect' cannot, in my view, of itself import into the criminal law the civil law concept of negligence. The *actus reus* in a case of wilful neglect is simply a failure, for whatever reason, to provide the child whenever it in fact needs medical aid with the medical aid it needs. Such a failure as it seems to me could not be properly described as 'wilful' unless the parent *either* (1) had directed his mind to the question whether there was some risk (though it might fall far short of a probability) that the child's health might suffer unless he were examined by a doctor and provided with such curative treatment as the examination might reveal as necessary, and had made a conscious decision, for whatever reason, to refrain from arranging for such medical examination, *or* (2) had so refrained because he did not care whether the child might be in need of medical treatment or not.

As regards the second state of mind, this imports the concept of recklessness which is a common concept in *mens rea* in criminal law. It is not to be confused with negligence in the civil law of tort (see *Andrews v Director of Public Prosecutions* [1937] AC 576 at 582–83). In speaking of the first state of mind I have referred to the parent's knowledge of the existence of some risk of injury to health rather than of a probability. The section speaks of an act or omission that is 'likely' to cause unnecessary suffering or injury to health. This word is imprecise. It is capable of covering a whole range of possibilities from 'it's on the cards' to 'it's more probable than not'; but, having regard to the ordinary parent's lack of skill in diagnosis and to the very serious consequences which may result from failure to provide a child with timely medical attention, it should in my view be understood as excluding only what would fairly be described as highly unlikely ...

To give to s 1(1) of the 1933 Act the meaning which I suggest it bears would not encourage parents to neglect their children nor would it reduce the deterrent to child neglect provided by the section. It would afford no defence to parents who do not bother to observe their children's health or, having done so, do not care whether their children are receiving the medical examination and treatment that they need or not; it would involve the acquittal of those parents only who through ignorance or lack of intelligence are genuinely unaware that their child's health may be at risk if it is not examined by a doctor to see if it needs medical treatment. And, in view of the abhorrence which magistrates and juries feel for cruelty to helpless children, I have every confidence that they would not readily be hoodwinked by false claims by parents that it did not occur to them that an evidently sick child might need medical care.

In the instant case it seems likely that on the evidence the jury, if given the direction which I have suggested as correct, would have convicted one or both of the accused; but I do not think it possible to say with certainty that they would. It follows that in my opinion these appeals must be allowed and that the certified question should be answered: 'The proper direction to be given to a jury on a charge of wilful neglect of a child under s 1 of the Children and Young Persons Act 1933 by failing to provide adequate medical aid is that the jury must be satisfied (1) that the child did in fact need medical aid at the time at which the parent is charged with failing to provide it (the *actus reus*) and (2) either that the parent was aware at that time that the child's health might be at risk if it was not provided with medical aid or that the parent's unawareness of this fact was due to his not caring whether his child's health was at risk or not (the *mens rea*).'

Maliciously

R v Cunningham [1957] 2 QB 396 (CA)

Byrne J: The appellant was convicted at Leeds Assizes upon an indictment framed under s 23 of the Offences Against the Person Act, 1861, which charged that he unlawfully and maliciously caused to be taken by Sarah Wade a certain noxious thing, namely, coal gas, so as thereby to endanger the life of the said Sarah Wade ...

The facts were not really in dispute, and in a statement to a police officer the appellant said: 'All right, I will tell you. I was short of money, I had been off work for three days, I got eight shillings from the gas meter. I tore it off the wall and threw it away.' Although there was a stop tap within two feet of the meter the appellant did not turn off the gas, with the result that a very considerable volume of gas escaped, some of which seeped through the wall of the cellar and partially asphyxiated Mrs Wade, who was asleep in her bedroom next door, with the result that her life was endangered.

... The act of the appellant was clearly unlawful and therefore the real question for the jury was whether it was also malicious within the meaning of s 23 of the Offences Against the Person Act 1861 ...

With the utmost respect to the learned judge, we think it is incorrect to say that the word 'malicious' in a statutory offence merely means wicked. We think the judge was, in effect, telling the jury that if they were satisfied that the appellant acted wickedly – and he had clearly acted wickedly in stealing the gas meter and its contents – they ought to find that he had acted maliciously in causing the gas to be taken by Mrs Wade so as thereby to endanger her life.

In our view it should have been left to the jury to decide whether, even if the appellant did not intend the injury to Mrs Wade, he foresaw that the removal of the gas meter might cause injury to someone but nevertheless removed it. We are unable to say that a reasonable jury, properly directed as to the meaning of the word 'maliciously' in the context of s 23, would without doubt have convicted.

Knowingly

R v Ellis, Street and Smith (1987) 84 Cr App R 235 (CA)

O'Connor LJ: ... All three appellants accepted that they participated in importing large quantities of cannabis into this country concealed in secret compartments in motor cars. They were indicted in the ordinary form for being knowingly concerned in the fraudulent evasion of the prohibition on the importation of a controlled drug contrary to s 170(2) of the Customs and Excise Management Act 1979. The particulars of offence were that on the relevant dates they were in relation to a class B controlled drug, namely in the case of Ellis and Street 29.3 kilogrammes and in the case of Smith 24.85 kilogrammes of cannabis, 'knowingly concerned in the fraudulent evasion of the prohibition on importation imposed by s 3(1) of the Misuse of Drugs Act 1971'.

In both cases the defendants as they then were pleaded not guilty and at once asked for a ruling as to whether they had a defence in law if the facts were that they knew that they were participating in the importation of prohibited goods but believed that the goods were pornographic goods which they knew to be subject to a prohibition and which were in fact subject to a prohibition.

In both cases the trial judges, holding themselves bound by the decision of this court in *Hennessey* (1979) 68 Cr App R 419, ruled that they had no defence in law on those assumed facts. Thereupon they changed their pleas to guilty and were sentenced.

Mr Shaw has appeared for all three appellants in this court. He accepted that these three cases could not be distinguished from *Hennessey*. In a carefully thought-out, concise and lucid argument, for which we express our gratitude, he submitted that *Hennessey* is no longer good law because it cannot stand with subsequent decisions in the House of Lords.

Before we turn to *Hennessey* it is necessary to start the consideration of the law by looking at *Hussain* [1969] 2 QB 567...

In *Hussain* the defendant was a seaman on a ship which came into Liverpool. In his cabin customs officers found a secret compartment in the bulkhead full of cannabis. In due course he said, and this was his defence, that while he was in his cabin the first officer and a carpenter had come there and threatened him. They had opened up the bulkhead to create the secret compartment, had put something in it, he did not know what it was, and had told him that if he said anything about it they would cut him up. So that on analysis his defence was that he did not know what was in the secret compartment. His real defence was duress. He was indicted on two counts, one an offence against what was then s 304 of the Customs and Excise Act 1952, which is the same offence as that indicated here under s 170(2) of the 1979 Act, and the other a count of possessing a controlled drug. He was convicted of both. In the Court of Appeal Widgery LJ, as he then was, gave the judgment of the court. In the summing up the chairman had directed the jury that the phrase they had to consider was 'being knowingly concerned in a fraudulent evasion of the prohibition against importation of cannabis resin'. At 451 and 571 respectively Widgery LJ said:

> Then he proceeded to go through that phrase in some detail; he pointed out there was a prohibition against the importation of cannabis (which was not disputed); and he further pointed out that there was an importation of cannabis in the present case: any difficulties on the law in that regard having disappeared in the course of the trial. He then proceeded: 'The question is: Has it been proved that the defendant was knowingly concerned in that

> operation? ... Knowingly concerned in that operation means that he was co-operating with the smugglers, if I may so put it, and it does not matter if he did not know precisely the nature of the goods the smugglers were dealing with. He would be just as guilty if he had thought they were dealing with brandy, for instance, but what has to be proved is that he was knowingly and to that extent consciously and deliberately concerned in co-operating in what he must have known was an operation of smuggling or getting prohibited goods into this country' ... Two main complaints are made against that passage in the summing up. First of all, it is said that the learned chairman was wrong in saying that the Crown did not have to prove that the accused knew that cannabis was the subject of the importation. It is submitted on behalf of the appellant that proof of knowledge on the part of the accused that the goods being smuggled were cannabis was part of the obligation of the prosecution, and since the learned chairman had directed that it was not necessary for the accused to know precisely the nature of the goods there was a misdirection. The court is not prepared to accept that submission. It seems perfectly clear that the word 'knowingly' in the section in question is concerned with knowing that a fraudulent evasion of a prohibition in respect of goods is taking place. If, therefore, the accused knows that what is afoot is the evasion of a prohibition against importation and he knowingly takes part in that operation, it is sufficient to justify his conviction, even if he does not know precisely what kind of goods are being imported. It is, of course, essential that he should know that the goods which are being imported are goods subject to a prohibition. It is essential he should know that the operation with which he is concerning himself is an operation designed to evade that prohibition and evade it fraudulently. But it is not necessary he should know the precise category of the goods the importation of which has been prohibited. Accordingly, in our judgment, there is nothing in that point taken on behalf of the appellant.

There is a clear statement of the law construing s 304 of the 1952 Act. The 1979 Act was a consolidating statute and, as will appear later in our judgment, there is no difference to be made in construing s 170.

Hussain was in 1969. In 1978 came *Hennessey* (1979) 68 Cr App R 419. In *Hennessey* the defence raised was what in shorthand can be called the 'blue-film' defence, namely that although there was a large quantity of cannabis concealed in the motor car the defendant said he thought he was bringing in obscene material. It was exactly the same as this case. Lawton LJ, who gave the judgment of the court, had this to say about it, at 422:

> Customs officers searched his car and found ... cannabis resin ... Hennessey said, 'I don't know anything about them'. About a month later he made a written statement in which he said that he thought he was bringing back 'blue' films to England and the context in which he said it showed that he knew that what he claimed to be bringing back was a prohibited import. This was the basis of his defence at his trial. It did not succeed.

At the foot of p 422 Lawton LJ said this:

> Mr Godfrey on behalf of Hennessey submitted that Judge Abdela had misdirected the jury. He told the jury what the relevant section of the Customs and Excise Act 1952, namely s 304(b), provided and went on at pp 5–6 of the transcript of the summing up as follows: 'You can see from the terms in which the statement of offence is set out that the crux of the matter is, in fact, being knowingly concerned in the fraudulent evasion of a prohibition. Now this is where I have to correct Mr Godfrey when he was addressing you

> about the question of knowledge and I noticed that one or two of you were taking down what he said and I must correct it. "Knowingly" in this section of this statute is concerned with knowing that a fraudulent evasion of a prohibition in respect of goods is taking place. It is not a question of knowing whether you have got a particular commodity in your pocket or container or car and there is quite a considerable amount of legal authority for that proposition. If, therefore, an accused person knows that what is afoot is the evasion of a prohibition against importation and he knowingly takes part in that operation, it is sufficient to justify his conviction under this section of the Act, even if he does not know precisely what kind of goods are being imported.' By directing the jury in these terms Judge Abdela was following, as he told the jury he was, the judgment of Widgery LJ (as he then was) in Hussain (*above*). In that case the appellant had submitted that the trial judge should have directed the jury that the prosecution had to prove that the accused knew what was the subject of the prohibited importation. Mr Godfrey made the same submission in this case. The Court in Hussain rejected the submission. Mr Godfrey boldly submitted that this court had been wrong to do so and that we should not follow Hussain. We intend to follow it for the best of reasons, it was correctly decided. On his own story Hennessey did know that he was concerned in a fraudulent evasion of a prohibition in relation to goods. In plain English he was smuggling goods. It matters not for the purpose of conviction what the goods were as long as he knew that he was bringing into the United Kingdom goods which he should not have been bringing in. Hennessey's appeal against conviction is dismissed.

In 1983 the case of *Taaffe* (1983) Cr App R 82, came before this court. *Taaffe* had this difference. In that case the defendant, when he was found to have a lot of cannabis stowed in the spare tyre of his motor car and a lot more strapped to his body, said that he thought that what he was bringing into this country was currency, and that he thought that currency was prohibited. In fact, there was no prohibition on bringing currency into this country. It was in those circumstances that *Taaffe* came to this court because once again the trial judge had ruled that those facts afforded no defence, relying on the decisions in *Hussain (above)* and *Hennessey (above)* ...

In the House of Lords *R v Taaffe* [1984] AC 539 is an important case in the present circumstances. It is necessary to look shortly at the argument. First of all, we must point out that the members of the House in *Taaffe* were Lord Fraser of Tullybelton, Lord Scarman, Lord Roskill, Lord Bridge of Harwich and Lord Brightman. It is particularly important to note that Lord Scarman and Lord Bridge were members of the House ...

It is important that Lord Rawlinson of Ewell who appeared for the defendant made the following submissions, at 542:

> (1) The requisite element of *mens rea* that arises in offences against s 170(2) is imparted by the word 'knowingly' and governs all the material elements of the offence. (2) An offence under s 170(2) may be committed in one or more of three ways, as set out in paragraphs (a), (b) and (c). The essence of an offence under s 170(2)(a)(b)(c) is not merely a fraudulent evasion of a regulation; rather, the essence of the offence is being 'knowingly concerned' in any fraudulent evasion of a regulation. (3) It is not sufficient for the commission of an offence to be 'involved in a smuggling operation'. For a person to be convicted of an offence, he must be knowingly concerned in (a) a fraudulent evasion, or attempt thereat, of (b) a prohibition or restriction in

force. (4) There is no issue as to the state of the defendant's mind on any question of reasonableness of belief or recklessness, for, on the agreed facts, he (1) mistakenly believed that the packages, etc contained money and (2) mistakenly believed money to be subject to a prohibition. (5) Had a jury accepted those facts, he could not have been 'knowingly concerned' as to the fraudulent evasion of the prohibition of drugs.

I now come to the important submission made, which is (6):

> It is immaterial that a person charged under this section is mistaken as to the particular prohibition that he breaches or whether the goods that he carried are dutiable. Certainly, where a person knows that the goods hidden are subject to a prohibition and he designs to evade that prohibition fraudulently, it is not necessary that he should know the precise category of goods nor the precise prohibition: see *Hussain*. (7) That does not, however, arise in this case, since the goods that the defendant believed that he was carrying and that he believed to be prohibited were not in fact prohibited.

Lastly, Lord Rawlinson said in his argument at 544 D:

> The House is fixed with the agreed facts. It should not be led into interpreting 'knowingly' lightly. The first part of subsection (2) governs any offence created. People may be involved in smuggling operations innocently. 'Knowingly' is the word most apt to introduce an element of *mens rea*. It is the clearest word that Parliament could have used to indicate that requirement. *Hussain (above)* and *Hennessey (above)* are to be distinguished because there the defendants did have the *mens rea*; they did believe that there was a fraudulent evasion. If the defendant here honestly believed (and it is an agreed fact that he did) that he was bringing money into the country, which is not an offence, how can it be said that he was knowingly concerned in the fraudulent evasion of the prohibition on the importation of a controlled drug? To believe that he was bringing in coffee (prohibited) would not be a defence.

It is in the light of those submissions that Lord Scarman dealt with the appeal quite shortly in his speech. He read the certified question at 546:

> When a defendant is charged with an offence, contrary to s 170(2) of the Customs and Excise Management Act 1979, of being knowingly concerned in the fraudulent evasion of the prohibition on the importation of a controlled drug, does the defendant commit the offence where he: (a) imports prohibited drugs into the United Kingdom: (b) intends fraudulently to evade a prohibition on importation; but (c) mistakenly believes the goods to be money and not drugs; and (d) mistakenly believes that money is the subject of a prohibition against importation?
>
> In effect, the learned recorder answered the question in the affirmative and the Court of Appeal in the negative.
>
> There was no trial: for the respondent changed his plea to guilty after the learned recorder's ruling. On his appeal against conviction, the judgment of the Court of Appeal was delivered by Lord Lane CJ. The judgment recites the history of the case and the assumptions upon which a decision had to be taken. It is unnecessary to burden the House with a repetition of what is there so clearly set forth.
>
> Lord Lane CJ construed the subsection under which the respondent was charged as creating not an offence of absolute liability but an offence of which an essential ingredient is a guilty mind. To be 'knowingly concerned'

> meant, in his judgment, knowledge not only of the existence of a smuggling operation but also that the substance being smuggled into the country was one the importation of which was prohibited by statute. The respondent thought he was concerned in a smuggling operation but believed that the substance was currency. The importation of currency is not subject to any prohibition. Lord Lane concluded: '(The respondent) is to be judged against the facts that he believed them to be. Had this indeed been currency and not cannabis, no offence would have been committed.' Lord Lane went on to ask this question: 'Does it make any difference that the (respondent) thought wrongly that by clandestinely importing currency he was committing an offence?' The Crown submitted that it does. The court rejected the submission: the respondent's mistake of law could not convert the importation of currency into a criminal offence: and importing currency is what it had to be assumed that the respondent believed he was doing. My Lords, I find the reasoning of the Lord Chief Justice compelling. I agree with his construction of s 170(2) of the Act of 1979: and the principle that a man must be judged upon the facts as he believes them to be is an accepted principle of the criminal law when the state of a man's mind and his knowledge are ingredients of the offence with which he is charged ...

How does Mr Shaw seek to escape from the situation? He submitted that the true ratio of *Hussain* is not that the defendant mistakenly thought he was bringing in some other prohibited material, as in *Hennessey* and in *R v Taaffe* and in the present cases, but that in *Hussain* the defendant was simply not concerned at all with what it was, that he did not care what the material was; and that in those circumstances *Hussain* can be distinguished from *Hennessey* and from these cases. The difficulty about that argument is that it seems to us when the history of *Hussain*, through *Hennessey*, through *R v Shivpuri* is examined, it is the passage from Widgery LJ's judgment which we have cited at the beginning of this judgment that remains in full force (ie (1969) 53 Cr App R 448, 451; [1969] 1 QB 567, 571). That shows that "knowingly" in the section in question is concerned with knowing that a fraudulent evasion of a prohibition in respect of goods is taking place'. It seems to us that it cannot make any difference whether a particular defendant says: 'I don't know what the goods were; I only know they were prohibited' or a defendant says: 'I didn't know what the goods in fact were. I thought that they were some other prohibited goods' (*Hennessey*). The House of Lords having had the opportunity in *R v Shivpuri* to take up Lord Scarman's question in *R v Taaffe* as to whether *Hennessey* was correctly decided, did not deal with it. Therefore *Hennessey* as we have already said remains good law ...

TEMPORAL COINCIDENCE OF *ACTUS REUS* AND *MENS REA*

In order to be guilty of an offence, the defendant must have the necessary *mens rea* at the time of the *actus reus*.

Thabo Meli and Others v R [1954] 1 WLR 228 (PC)

Lord Reid: The four appellants in this case were convicted of murder ... The appeal which has been heard by this Board dealt with two matters: first, whether the conclusions of the learned judge on questions of fact were warranted: and, second, whether, on a point of law, the accused are entitled to have the verdict quashed.

On the first matter, there really is no ground for criticising the learned judge's treatment of the facts. It is established by evidence, which was believed and which is apparently credible, that there was a preconceived plot on the part of the four accused to bring the deceased man to a hut and there to kill him, and then fake an accident, so that the accused should escape the penalty for their act. The deceased man was brought to the hut. He was there treated to beer and was at least partially intoxicated; and he was then struck over the head in accordance with the plan of the accused. Witnesses say that while the deceased was seated and bending forward he was struck a heavy blow on the back of the head with a piece of iron like the instrument produced at the trial. But a post mortem examination showed that his skull had not been fractured and medical evidence was to the effect that a blow such as the witnesses described would have produced more severe injuries than those found at the post mortem examination. There is at least doubt whether the weapon which was produced as being like the weapon which was used could have produced the injuries that were found, but it may be that this weapon is not exactly similar to the one which was used, or it may be that the blow was a glancing blow and produced less severe injuries than those which one might expect. In any event, the man was unconscious after receiving the blow, but he was not then dead. There is no evidence that the accused then believed that he was dead, but their Lordships are prepared to assume from their subsequent conduct that they did so believe; and it is only on that assumption that any statable case can be made for this appeal. The accused took out the body, rolled it over a low krantz or cliff, and dressed up the scene to make it look like an accident. Obviously, they believed at that time that the man was dead, but it appears from the medical evidence that the injuries which he received in the hut were not sufficient to cause the death and that the final cause of his death was exposure when he was left unconscious at the foot of the krantz.

The point of law which was raised in this case can be simply stated. It is said that two acts were done: first, the attack in the hut; and, second, the placing of the body outside afterwards; and that they were separate acts. It is said that, while the first act was accompanied by *mens rea*, it was not the cause of death; but that the second act, while it was the cause of death, was not accompanied by *mens rea*; and on that ground, it is said that the accused are not guilty of murder, though they may have been guilty of culpable homicide. It is said that the *mens rea* necessary to establish murder is an intention to kill, and that there could be no intention to kill when the accused thought that the man was already dead, so their original intention to kill had ceased before they did the act which caused the man's death. It appears to their Lordships impossible to divide up what was really one series of acts in this way. There is no doubt that the accused set out to do all these acts in order to achieve their plan, and as parts of their plan; and it is much too refined a ground of judgment to say that, because they were under a misapprehension at one stage and thought that their guilty purpose had been achieved before, in fact, it was achieved, therefore they are to escape the penalties of the law. Their Lordships do not think that this is a matter which is susceptible of elaboration. There appears to be no case, either in South Africa or England, or for that matter elsewhere, which resembles the present. Their Lordships can find no difference relevant to the present case between the law of South Africa and the law of England; and they are of opinion that by both laws there can be no separation such as that for which the accused contend. Their crime is not reduced from murder to a lesser crime merely because the accused were under some misapprehension for a time during the completion of their criminal plot.

Their Lordships must, therefore, humbly advise Her Majesty that this appeal should be dismissed.

Fagan v Metropolitan Police Commissioner [1969] 1 QB 439 (DC)

See Chapter 22.

Attorney General's Reference (No 4 of 1980) [1981] 1 WLR 705 (CA)

Ackner LJ: This is a reference to the court by the Attorney General of a point of law seeking the opinion of the court pursuant to s 36 of the Criminal Justice Act 1972. It raises yet again the problem of the supposed corpse, and the facts, which I take from the terms of the reference itself, are inevitably macabre.

The deceased was the fiancée of the accused and for some months before her death they had lived together in a maisonette consisting of two floors of a house connected by two short flights of carpeted wooden stairs. The deceased was employed locally and was last seen at work on 17 January 1979 at about 5 pm. Thereafter no one, other than the accused, ever saw her alive again.

The deceased met her death on 18 January 1979, although this fact was not known until over three weeks later when the defendant so informed a friend. His account, the first of a number, was that in the course of an argument on the evening of 17 January he had slapped her on the face causing her to fall downstairs and bang her head. He said that he had then put her to bed but discovered next morning that she was dead. He then took her body to his home town and buried her.

On the following day, 14 February, he gave his second account, telling the same friend that after the deceased had 'fallen downstairs' he had dragged her upstairs by a piece of rope tied round her neck. He subsequently cut up her body with a saw before burying it. The next day, on the advice of his friend, the accused went to see a superior and gave an account similar to the one he had given his friend.

We now come to the statements which he made to the police. On 27 February, having consulted solicitors, the accused was interviewed by the police at his solicitors' office. He began by giving the police substantially the same account that he had given to his friend and his superior but added that instead of burying the deceased he had 'dumped' the various parts of her body on a tip. At the police station later that day he amplified his statement by saying that the incident when the deceased 'fell downstairs' occurred at about 7 pm on 17 January and that it was the following day, when he found her motionless, that he pulled her upstairs by a rope around her neck and then cut up her body in the bathroom. On the following day after much questioning by the police he changed his account stating that everything had happened on Thursday, 18 January at about 7 am. This is what he then said happened. (1) He and the deceased had an argument on the landing in the course of which each slapped the other; he seized the deceased and shook her hard; she dug her nails into him and he pushed her away instinctively, causing her to fall backwards over the handrail, down the stairs head first onto the floor. (2) He went downstairs immediately to find her motionless and on a very cursory examination discovered no pulse, and no sign of breath but frothy blood coming from her mouth. (3) Almost immediately thereafter he dragged her upstairs by a rope tied around her neck, placed her in the bath and cut her neck with a penknife to let out her blood, having already decided to cut up her body and dispose of the pieces.

He agreed that his previous account was untrue and he made a detailed voluntary statement along the lines set out in (1), (2) and (3) above describing how subsequently he had cut up and disposed of her body.

In the course of these interviews at the police station, after the defendant had given his revised account, the following conversation took place:

Officer: How long was it from the time that she went backwards over the handrail to when you started pulling her up the stairs with a piece of rope around her neck?

Accused: I went downstairs when she went backwards. I looked at her, tried her pulse. I tried to lift her and she wee'd, so I put her down again. Then two girls went past [the glass fronted door] so I covered the door with the blanket. Then I got the piece of rope and pulled her up the stairs.

Officer: When did you decide you were going to cut the body up and dispose of it?

Accused: Just before I pulled her up the stairs.

Later he was questioned by the officer:

Q: Is it correct that you hauled [her] to the bathroom, and put her into the bath and then cut her neck with a knife to let the blood out and these were all a continuous series of events?

A: Yes, they all happened together.

Subsequently the police discovered evidence which corroborated the accused's account of how, where and when he had cut up the body. They also found the saw he had used and the shopkeeper who sold it to him. However, the body of the deceased was never found, only some minute fragments of bone, which were discovered in the maisonette. There was thus no expert evidence as to the cause of death. The deceased died either as a result of being pushed and thus caused to fall backwards over the handrail and backwards down the stairs head first onto the floor, or by being strangled with the rope, or having her throat cut. The Crown conceded that it was not possible for them to prove whether the deceased died as the result of the 'fall' downstairs or from what the accused did to the deceased thereafter.

The indictment charged the accused with (1) manslaughter, (2) obstructing the coroner in the execution of his duty, and (3) preventing the burial of a corpse.

The accused pleaded guilty to the third count, the Crown offered no evidence on the second and the trial proceeded on the count of manslaughter.

At the close of the Crown's case counsel for the accused stated that he proposed to submit that on the facts proved there was no case of manslaughter capable of going to the jury. It is not easy to follow from the transcript the exact basis of his submissions, but what he appears to have been contending was that (a) it was not possible for the jury to be sure what caused the deceased's death and (b) whether the death was caused as a result of her 'fall' down the stairs or from what the accused subsequently did, believing her to be dead, in neither event was there a *prima facie* case of manslaughter.

The judge, although expressing his reluctance to accept that the accused could be in a better position as a result of his dismembering the body of the deceased, appeared to have been very concerned at what he described as 'an insuperable problem of sentencing', were the accused to be convicted of manslaughter. He expressed the view that the real criminality of the accused's behaviour was in disposing of the body, a view which this court is unable to accept. These views appear to have influenced his decision, which was to withdraw the case from the jury and to direct an acquittal on the ground that the Crown had failed to prove the cause of the death of the deceased.

On the above facts this reference raises a single simple question, *viz* if an accused kills another by one or other of two or more different acts each of which, if it caused the death, is a sufficient act to establish manslaughter, is it necessary in order to found a conviction to prove which act caused the death? The answer to that question is No, it is not necessary to found a conviction to prove which act caused the death. No authority is required to justify this answer, which is clear beyond argument, as was indeed immediately conceded by counsel on behalf of the accused.

What went wrong in this case was that counsel made jury points to the judge and not submissions of law. He was in effect contending that the jury should not convict of manslaughter if the death had resulted from the 'fall', because the push which had projected the deceased over the handrail was a reflex and not a voluntary action, as a result of her digging her nails into him. If, however, the deceased was still alive when he cut her throat, since he then genuinely believed her to be dead, having discovered neither pulse nor sign of breath, but frothy blood coming from her mouth, he could not be guilty of manslaughter because he had not behaved with gross criminal negligence. What counsel and the judge unfortunately overlooked was that there was material available to the jury which would have entitled them to have convicted the accused of manslaughter, whichever of the two sets of acts caused her death. It being common ground that the deceased was killed by an act done to her by the accused and it being conceded that the jury could not be satisfied which was the act which caused the death, they should have been directed in due course in the summing up, to ask themselves the following questions: (1) 'Are we satisfied beyond reasonable doubt that the deceased's 'fall' downstairs was the result of an intentional act by the accused which was unlawful and dangerous?' If the answer was No, then they would acquit. It the answer was Yes, then they would need to ask themselves a second question, namely (2) 'Are we satisfied beyond reasonable doubt that the act of cutting the girl's throat was an act of gross criminal negligence?' If the answer to that question was No, then they would acquit, but if the answer was Yes, then the verdict would be guilty of manslaughter. The jury would thus have been satisfied that, whichever act had killed the deceased, each was a sufficient act to establish the offence of manslaughter.

The fact of this case did not call for a 'series of acts direction' following the principle in *Thabo Meli v R* [1954] 1 All ER 373, [1954] 1 WLR 228 ...

R v Le Brun [1992] 1 QB 61 (CA)

Lord Lane CJ: ... The facts giving rise to the charge were these. In September 1989 the appellant, who was then serving in the Royal Navy, was living at an address in Plymouth with his wife, who was the victim in the present case. They went out for the evening to some friends, the Cartwrights, on 23 September 1989. They left the house of the friends in the early hours at about 2 am. They did not have very far to go to their own home. They had been drinking. They were both described as merry, but neither, it was said, was drunk.

It was only two or three minutes' walk to get to their own home. But during that short journey it is quite plain that a heated argument developed between the two of them. To come to the end of the story, after a short interval, which was really only sufficient for the friends whose house they had visited to have tidied up the house, taken the dog for a walk and prepared for bed, the appellant returned to the Cartwrights, banged on the door and shouted 'It's Joannie ... she's collapsed. There's blood everywhere. Get an ambulance.'

In fact the wife (as I shall call her now) was lying near the top of some steps leading from the pathway to their home. She had sustained two wounds to her head: a fracture to the back of the skull and a severe injury to her chin which had produced what might be described as a star shaped wound. That wound had broken the jaw and caused bleeding into the joints on each side. She had sustained also a bruise on the outer edge of the lip on the left, a fracture to both wings of the hyoid bone at the top of the neck. As can be seen from the photographs, there was a good deal of blood at the scene and – a matter of some importance – some hair, which had plainly been pulled by the roots out of her scalp, was lying at the scene. The cause of death was bruising to the brain which in its turn had been caused by the fracture to the back of the skull.

There was abundant evidence from the neighbours of the argument which had taken place between these two. For example Mrs Luke whose house overlooked the area where the incident took place, heard a man sounding very angry and aggressive, plainly wanting a woman (the wife in this case) to go into the house. Indeed it is plain from her evidence and from the evidence of other eye witnesses or other witnesses who heard what was going on, that one reason for the altercation between these two was the woman's wish not to go into the house and the man's wish that she should.

Mrs Luke saw two people arguing. Eventually she heard a thump and a moan and saw the woman kneeling against the metal railing and the man taking hold of her with a hand on her head. She next saw the woman lying on the ground, the man telling her to get up and then pulling her by the arms or shoulders towards the road. It then seemed to her that he let go of her. So she fell and her head hit the ground and that thump could be heard.

Mr Hislop, whose evidence is referred to by the judge in his summing up, said that the man was shouting 'get on home', and the woman was saying 'get off me'. They were saying that sort of thing repeatedly and there was a lot of swearing, he said, from both of them. He said that he went to the window and saw a man and a woman struggling in the middle of the road, pulling and pushing at each other. He tried to pull her in the direction which it emerged was the direction of the appellant's house and she resisted. Further evidence was given by a Mrs Bradford, whose evidence had certain unsatisfactory features about it.

There was medical evidence from a pathologist and also an expert in dental and facial injuries. The effect of that evidence was that the injury to the back of the skull would have to have been caused by the body falling at least from waist height. The importance of that evidence was that there was one witness who had said that the head had been lifted an inch or two from the ground and let fall. On the pathological evidence it seems that that would not have been sufficient to cause the fracture to the back of the skull which in its turn was responsible for the death ...

When the police arrived at the scene they found the appellant in a hysterical state trying to revive his wife. He was arrested. He continued to struggle on his way to the police station, shouting that he wanted to see his wife. He said that she had slipped on the steps and hit her head. He had not touched her. When interviewed he declined to answer any questions.

He gave evidence at the trial. He said the two of them had been happy when they left the house of the Cartwrights, but an argument which became heated developed as they made their way towards home. He had asked his wife for the house keys which she had. She was standing by the railings at the steps. She would not give him the keys. He tried to persuade her. He took hold of her arm, whereupon she shouted 'get off me', as one of the witnesses had heard. He started walking back to the house away from her, and all of a sudden he heard a scream, a thud behind him, he turned round and saw the deceased on the ground. He told her to get up. She seemed to be unconscious. He described how he had tried to lift her, but she had slipped from his hold and had fallen. Eventually he held her upright against himself, with her legs trailing along the ground, and tried to drag her backwards, but she slipped through his arms so that her back and then her head hit the roadway. He then realised she was seriously hurt and went for help. He never hit her, he said. He did not know how she had sustained her injuries. He had tried to revive her and then all he had wanted to do was to get her home ...

Problems of causation and remoteness of damage are never easy of solution. We have had helpful arguments from both counsel on this point, the point in the present case being, to put it in summary before coming to deal with it in more detail, that the intention of the appellant to harm his wife one way or another may have been separated by a period of time from the act which in fact caused the death, namely the fact of her falling to the ground and fracturing her skull. The second incident may have taken place without any guilty mind of the part of the appellant.

The authors of Smith and Hogan, *Criminal Law*, 6th edn, 1988, p 320, say:

> An intervening act by the original actor will not break the chain of causation so as to excuse him, where the intervening act is part of the same transaction, but it is otherwise if the act which causes the *actus reus* is part of a completely different transaction. For example, D, having wounded P, visits him in hospital and accidentally infects him with smallpox of which he dies.

The problem in the instant case can be expressed in a number of different ways, of which causation is one. Causation on the facts as the jury in this case must have found them – I say at the best from the point of view of the appellant – is in one sense clear. Death was caused by the victim's head hitting the ground as she was being dragged away by the appellant. The only remoteness was that between the initial unlawful blow and the later moment when the skull was fractured causing death.

The question can be perhaps framed in this way. There was here an initial unlawful blow to the chin delivered by the appellant. That, again on what must have been the jury's finding, was not delivered with the intention of doing really serious harm to the wife. The guilty intent accompanying that blow was sufficient to have rendered the appellant guilty of manslaughter, but not murder, had it caused death. But it did not cause death. What caused death was the later impact when the wife's head hit the pavement. At the moment of impact the appellant's intention was to remove her, probably unconscious body to avoid detection. To that extent the impact may have been accidental. May the earlier guilty intent be joined with the later non-guilty blow which caused death to produce in the conglomerate a proper verdict of manslaughter?

It has usually been in the previous decisions in the context of murder that the problem has arisen. We have had our attention directed to a Privy Council case, *Meli v The Queen* [1954] 1 WLR 228 ...

That decision of course is not binding upon us. It is of very persuasive authority and it was adopted by another division of this court in 1975 in *R v Moore* [1975] Crim LR 229.

However, it will be observed that the present case is different from the facts of those two cases in that death here was not the result of a preconceived plan which went wrong, as the case in those two decisions which were have cited. Here the death, again assuming the jury's finding to be such as it must have been, was the result of an initial unlawful blow, not intended to cause serious harm, in its turn causing the appellant to take steps possibly to evade the consequences of his unlawful act. During the taking of those steps he commits the *actus reus* but without the mens rea necessary for murder or manslaughter. Therefore the mens rea is contained in the initial unlawful assault, but the *actus reus* is the eventual dropping of the head on to the ground.

Normally the *actus reus* and *mens rea* coincide in point of time. What is the situation when they do not? Is it permissible, as the prosecution contend here, to combine them to produce a conviction for manslaughter? ...

It seems to us that where the unlawful application of force and the eventual act causing death are parts of the same sequence of events, the same transaction, the fact that there is an appreciable interval of time between the two does not serve to exonerate the defendant from liability. That is certainly so where the appellant's subsequent actions which caused death, after the initial unlawful blow, are designed to conceal his commission of the original assault.

It would be possible to express the problem as one of causation. The original unlawful blow to the chin was a *causa sine qua non* of the later *actus reus*. It was the opening event in a series which was to culminate in death: the first link in the chain of causation, to use another metaphor. It cannot be said that the actions of the appellant in dragging the victim away with the intention of evading liability broke the chain which linked the initial blow with the death.

In short, in circumstances such as the present, which is the only concern of this court, the act which causes death, and the necessary mental state to constitute manslaughter, need not coincide in point of time ...

TRANSFERRED MALICE

Under the doctrine of transferred malice a person may be guilty of an offence if he intends to harm one person but in fact harms another.

R v Pembliton (1874) LR 2 CCR 119

Lord Coleridge CJ: I am of opinion that the conviction should be quashed. The facts of the case are that there was fighting going on in the streets of Wolverhampton near the prosecutor's house, and the prisoner, after fighting for some time, separated himself from the crowd and threw a stone, which missed the person he aimed at, but struck and broke a window, doing damage to the extent of upwards of £5. The question is, whether under an indictment for unlawfully and maliciously injuring the property of the owner of the plate-glass window, these facts will support the indictment when coupled with the other facts found by the jury, that the prisoner threw the stone at the people intending to strike one or more of them, but not intending to break a window. I am of opinion that the evidence does not support the conviction. The indictment is under the 24 and 25 Vict c 97, s 51, which deals with malicious injuries to property, and the section expressly says that the act is to be unlawful and malicious. There is also the 58th section, which makes it immaterial whether the offence has been committed from malice against the owner of the property or otherwise, that is, from malice against someone not the owner of the property. In both these sections it seems to me that what is intended by the statute is a wilful doing of an intentional act. Without saying that if the case had been left to them in a different way the conviction could not have been supported, if, on these facts the jury had come to a conclusion that the prisoner was reckless of the consequence of his act, and might reasonably have expected that it would result in breaking the window, it is sufficient to say that the jury have expressly found the contrary. I do not say anything to throw doubt on the rule under the common law in cases of murder which has been referred to, but the principles laid down in such cases have no application to the statutable offence we have to consider.

R v Latimer (1886) 17 QB 359 (CCR)

Facts: The defendant aimed a blow with his belt at one person, striking him slightly. The belt also struck someone else, causing a severe wound. The court had to decide whether A can be guilty of unlawfully wounding C where A intends to strike B but strikes C instead.

Lord Coleridge CJ: ... It is common knowledge that a man who has an unlawful and malicious intent against another, and, in attempting to carry it out, injures a third person, is guilty of what the law deems malice against the person injured, because the offender is doing an unlawful act, and has that which the judges call general malice, and that is enough ... [His Lordship then referred to *R v Hunt* 1 Moo CC 93 and said:] There a man intended to injure A, and said so, and, in the course of doing it, stabbed the wrong man, and had clearly malice in fact, but no intention of injuring the man who was stabbed. He intended to do an unlawful act, and in the course of doing it the consequence was that somebody was injured ...

Lord Esher MR: I am of the same opinion. The only case which could be cited against the well-known principle of law applicable to this case was *R v Pembliton* (1874) Law Rep 2 CC 119, but, on examination, it is found to have been decided on this ground, *viz* that there was no intention to injure any property at all. It was not a case of attempting to injure one man's property and injuring another's, which would have been wholly different.

Bowen LJ: I am of the same opinion. It is quite clear that the act was done by the prisoner with malice in his mind. I use the word 'malice' in the common law sense of the term, *viz* a person is deemed malicious when he does an act which he knows will injure either the person or property of another. The only case that could be cited for the prisoner is *R v Pembliton* (1874) Law Rep 2 CC 119, which was founded not upon malice in general, but upon a particular form of malice, *viz* malicious injury to property; and the court held that though the prisoner might have been acting maliciously in the common law sense of the term, he was not malicious in the sense of the Act directed against malicious injury to property. That decision does not apply to a case under the Act where the indictment is for injury to the person. *R v Pembliton* might have been ground for an argument of some plausibility if the prisoner meant to strike at a pane of glass and had hit a person. It might have been that the malice in that case was not enough. But when, as here, an intent to injure a person is proved, that is enough.

Manisty J: I will add only a few words, for all has been said that could be said, but the facts of this case, no doubt, raise an exceedingly important question, for the man Chapple, whom the prisoner intended to strike, and who was struck, with the belt, was standing close by the woman, and the belt bounded off and struck the prosecutrix. It seems to me that the first and second findings of the jury are quite sufficient to justify the verdict, for they find that the blow was unlawful and malicious, and that it wounded the prosecutrix. That being so, the third finding does not entitle the prisoner to acquittal. The third finding is that the striking of the prosecutrix was purely an accident, and so it was in one sense. The prisoner did not intend to strike her, but in the unlawful and malicious act of striking Chapple the prisoner did unlawfully and maliciously wound the prosecutrix, and the third finding is quite immaterial.

Attorney General's Reference (No 3 of 1994) [1996] 2 All ER 10 (CA)

See Chapter 21.

CHAPTER 3

PARTIES TO OFFENCES

ACCESSORIES

A crime can be committed by more than one party, even though only one person actually carries out the acts which constitute the commission of the offence. For example, a burglary may be committed by two people: D1 enters the property and steals the goods, while D2 merely stands outside to check that no one is approaching. In this example, D1 is the 'principal offender' and D2 is a 'secondary party' or 'accessory'.

A secondary party is one who 'aids, abets, counsels or procures' the commission of an offence. Section 8 of the Accessories and Abettors Act provides that a secondary party 'shall be liable to be tried, indicted, and punished as a principal offender'. Section 44(1) of the Magistrates' Courts Act 1980 makes similar provision for summary offences (ie offences triable only in a magistrates' court). The result is that secondary parties may be charged as if they were principal offenders. This is only possible where the offenders are acting in concert – in other words, there is a 'joint enterprise'. In such a case, where all the participants are charged as principal offenders, the distinction between primary and secondary participation is relevant only to the question of what sentence is appropriate in the event of conviction.

Nonetheless, it is possible for a person to be charged, not as a principal offender, but with aiding, abetting, counselling or procuring an offence. The words aid, abet and counsel are given their ordinary meaning and connote the giving of assistance, encouragement or advice. The word 'procure' means taking certain steps to bring about a desired consequence.

Attorney General's Reference (No 1 of 1975) [1975] QB 773 (CA)

Lord Widgery CJ: This case comes before the court on a reference from the Attorney General, under s 36 of the Criminal Justice Act 1972, and by his reference he asks the following question:

> Whether an accused, who surreptitiously laced a friend's drinks with double measures of spirits when he knew that his friend would shortly be driving his car home, and in consequence his friend drove with an excess quantity of alcohol in his body and was convicted of the offence under s 6(1) of the Road Traffic Act 1972, is entitled to a ruling of no case to answer on being later charged as an aider and abettor counsellor and procurer, on the ground that there was no shared intention between the two, that the accused did not by accompanying him or otherwise positively encourage the friend to drive, or on any other ground.

... The present question has no doubt arisen because in recent years there have been a number of instances, where men charged with driving their motor cars with an excess quantity of alcohol in the blood have sought to excuse their conduct by saying that their drinks were 'laced', as the jargon has it; that is to say, some strong spirit was put into an otherwise innocuous drink and as a result the driver consumed more alcohol than he had either intended to consume or had the desire to consume. The relevance of all that is not that it entitles the driver to an acquittal because such driving is an absolute offence, but that it can be relied on as a special reason for not disqualifying the driver from driving. Hence no doubt the importance which has been attached in recent months to the possibility of this argument being raised in a normal charge of driving with excess alcohol.

The question requires us to say whether on the facts posed there is a case to answer and, needless to say, in the trial from which this reference is derived the judge was of the opinion that there was no case to answer and so ruled. We have to say in effect whether he is right.

The language in the section which determines whether a 'secondary party', as he is sometimes called, is guilty of a criminal offence committed by another embraces the four words 'aid, abet, counsel or procure'. The origin of those words is to be found in s 8 of the Accessories and Abettors Act 1861, which provides:

> Whosoever shall aid, abet, counsel or procure the commission of any misdemeanour, whether the same be a misdemeanour at common law or by virtue of any Act passed or to be passed, shall be liable to be tried, indicted and punished as a principal offender.

Thus, in the past, when the distinction was still drawn between felony and misdemeanour, it was sufficient to make a person guilty of a misdemeanour if he aided, abetted, counselled or procured the offence of another. When the difference between felonies and misdemeanours was abolished in 1967, s 1 of the Criminal Law Act 1967 in effect provided that the same test should apply to make a secondary party guilty either of treason or felony.

Of course it is the fact that in the great majority of instances where a secondary party is sought to be convicted of an offence there has been a contact between the principal offender and the secondary party. Aiding and abetting almost inevitably involves a situation in which the secondary party and the main offender are together at some stage discussing the plans which they may be making in respect of the alleged offence, and are in contact so that each knows what is passing through the mind of the other.

In the same way it seems to us that a person, who counsels the commission of a crime by another, almost inevitably comes to a moment when he is in contact with that other, when he is discussing the offence with that other and when, to use the words of the statute, he counsels the other to commit the offence.

The fact that so often the relationship between the secondary party and the principal will be such that there is a meeting of minds between them caused the trial judge in the case from which this reference is derived to think that this was really an essential feature of proving or establishing the guilt of the secondary party and, as we understand his judgment, he took the view that in the absence of some sort of meeting of minds, some sort of mental link between the secondary party and the principal, there could be no aiding, abetting or counselling of the offence within the meaning of the section.

So far as aiding, abetting and counselling are concerned we would go a long way with that conclusion. It may very well be, as I said a moment ago, difficult to think of a case of aiding, abetting or counselling when the parties have not met and have not discussed in some respects the terms of the offence which they have in mind. But we do not see why a similar principle should apply to procuring. We approach s 8 of the Act of 1861 on the basis that the words should be given their ordinary meaning, if possible. We approach the section on the basis also that if four words are employed here, 'aid, abet, counsel or procure', the probability is that there is a difference between each of those four words and the other three, because, if there were no such difference, then Parliament would be wasting time in using four words where two or three would do. Thus, in deciding whether that which is assumed to be done under our reference was a criminal offence we approach the section on the footing that each word must be given its ordinary meaning.

To procure means to produce by endeavour. You procure a thing by setting out to see that it happens and taking the appropriate steps to produce that happening. We think that there are plenty of instances in which a person may be said to procure the commission of a crime by another even though there is no sort of conspiracy between the two, even though there is no attempt at agreement or discussion as to the form which the offence should take. In our judgment the offence described in this reference is such a case.

If one looks back at the facts of the reference: the accused surreptitiously laced his friend's drink. This is an important element and, although we are not going to decide today anything other than the problem posed to us, it may well be that, in similar cases where the lacing of the drink or the introduction of the extra alcohol is known to the driver, quite different considerations may apply. We say that because, where the driver has no knowledge of what is happening, in most instances he would have no means of preventing the offence from being committed. If the driver is unaware of what has happened, he will not be taking precautions. He will get into his car seat, switch on the ignition and drive home and, consequently, the conception of another procuring the commission of the offence by the driver is very much stronger where the driver is innocent of all knowledge of what is happening, as in the present case where the lacing of the drink was surreptitious.

The second thing which is important in the facts set out in our reference is that, following and in consequence of the introduction of the extra alcohol, the friend drove with an excess quantity of alcohol in his blood. Causation here is important. You cannot procure an offence unless there is a causal link between what you do and the commission of the offence, and here we are told that in consequence of the addition of this alcohol the driver, when he drove home, drove with an excess quantity of alcohol in his body.

Giving the words their ordinary meaning in English, and asking oneself whether in those circumstances the offence has been procured, we are in no doubt that the answer is that it has. It has been procured because, unknown to the driver and without his collaboration, he has been put in a position in which in fact he has committed an offence which he never would have committed otherwise. We think that there was a case to answer and that the trial judge should have directed the jury that an offence is committed if it is shown beyond reasonable doubt that the defendant knew that his friend was going to drive, and also knew that the ordinary and natural result of the additional alcohol added to the friend's drink would be to bring him above the recognised limit of 80 milligrammes per 100 millilitres of blood.

It was suggested to us that, if we held that there may be a procuring on the facts of the present case, it would be but a short step to a similar finding for the generous host, with somewhat bibulous friends, when at the end of the day his friends leave him to go to their own homes in circumstances in which they are not fit to drive and in circumstances in which an offence ... is committed. The suggestion has been made that the host may in those circumstances be guilty with his guests on the basis that he has either aided, abetted, counselled or procured the offence.

The first point to notice in regard to the generous host is that that is not a case in which the alcohol is being put surreptitiously into the glass of the driver. That is a case in which the driver knows perfectly well how much he has to drink and where to a large extent it is perfectly right and proper to leave him to make his own decision.

Furthermore, we would say that, if such a case arises, the basis on which the case will be put against the host is, we think, bound to be on the footing that he has supplied the tool with which the offence is committed. This, of course is a reference back to such cases as those where oxy-acetylene equipment was bought by a man knowing it was to be used by another for a criminal offence: see *R v Bainbridge* [1960] 1 QB 129. There is ample and clear authority as to the extent to which supplying the tools for the commission of an offence may amount to aiding and abetting for present purposes.

Accordingly, so far as the generous host type of case is concerned we are not concerned at the possibility that difficulties will be created, as long as it is borne in mind that in those circumstances the matter must be approached in accordance with well-known authority governing the provision of the tools for the commission of an offence, and never forgetting that the introduction of the alcohol is not there surreptitious, and that consequently the case for saying that the offence was procured by the supplier of the alcohol is very much more difficult.

Our decision on the reference is that the question posed by the Attorney General should be answered in the negative.

R v Calhaem [1985] 1 QB 808 (CA)

Parker LJ: ... The prosecution case was that the applicant had counselled or procured the commission of the offence by one Zajac, a private detective, on 23 February 1983. On 5 September 1983 Zajac pleaded guilty to the murder and was duly sentenced therefor. The prosecution case against the applicant was that she had hired Zajac to commit the murder in order to get rid of the victim, who had for some time had an affair with the applicant's solicitor, Mr Pigot, with whom she was infatuated; that she had made a down-payment to Zajac of some £5,000 at a meeting on 28 January 1983 and that he had thereafter committed the murder.

The principal witness for the prosecution was Zajac. He testified to the hiring, the receipt of the money, and the murder itself. He said that on the day of the murder he went to Mrs Rendell's house, having first ensured that her husband was out, taking with him a hammer, a knife, and a shotgun loaded with cartridges from which he had removed the shot, the gun being in a gift-wrapped parcel. He had, he said, no intention of killing Mrs Rendell, having decided in the preceding days not to do so. He had on arrival at the house rung the bell, and when Mrs Rendell came to the door he had asked her to sign for the gift-wrapped parcel. She went to get a pen, and when she returned and found him in the hall she screamed. He had intended to do no more than act out a charade, so that both Mrs Rendell and the applicant would think that an attempt had been made to murder her. However, when Mrs Rendell screamed, he said, he had gone berserk, hit her several times with the hammer and killed her. Thereafter, it appears, he had stabbed her in the neck with his knife.

The first point taken by Mr Carman on the applicant's behalf was that the judge had seriously misdirected the jury on the law as to the ingredients of the offence of counselling ... Put in summary form, the submission which was made was that (a) the Crown were bound by Zajac's evidence as to his state of mind before and at the time of the murder; (b) both procuring and counselling require a substantial causal connection between the acts of the secondary offender and the commission of the offence; and (c) on Zajac's evidence there was no causal connection, or at any rate no substantial causal connection.

So far as presently material, at the end of [this] submission ... the judge ruled as follows:

> In my judgment, therefore, the appropriate direction in this case is to this effect. 'To counsel' means to incite, solicit, instruct or authorise. The Crown have to prove that the defendant counselled Zajac in this sense to kill Mrs Rendell and that in fact Mrs Rendell was killed by Zajac in circumstances that amounted to murder, and that such killing was within the scope of that instruction or authorisation.

... The direction given by the judge was, Mr Carman submits, wrong in law. He should have directed the jury that, in the case of counselling as in the case of procuring, the counselling must be a 'substantial cause' ...

Such authority as there is does not, in our view, take the matter much further; although assistance as to the general approach is to be gained from *Attorney General's Reference (No 1 of 1975)* [1975] QB 773 at 778 ...

We must ... approach the question raised on the basis that we should give to the word 'counsel' its ordinary meaning, which is, as the judge said, 'advise', 'solicit', or something of that sort. There is no implication in the word itself that there should by any causal connection between the counselling and the offence. It is true that, unlike the offence of incitement at common law, the actual offence must have been committed, and committed by the person counselled. To this extent there must clearly be, first, contact between the parties, and, second, a connection between the counselling and the murder. Equally, the act done must, we think, be done within the scope of the authority or advice, and not, for example, accidentally when the mind of the final murderer did not go with his actions. For example, if the principal offender happened to be involved in a football riot in the course of which he laid about him with a weapon of some sort and killed someone who, unknown to him, was the person whom he had been counselled to kill, he would not, in our view, have been acting within the scope of his authority; he would have been acting entirely outside it, albeit what he had done was what he had been counselled to do ...

The natural meaning of the word does not imply the commission of the offence. So long as there is counselling – and there was ample evidence in this case of that fact – so long as the principal offence is committed by the one counselled, and so long as the one counselled is acting within the scope of his authority, and not in the accidental way or some such similar way as I have suggested with regard to an incident in a football riot, we are of the view that the offence is made out ...

Attorney General v Able and Others [1984] 1 QB 795 (CA)

Woolf J: In this case, Her Majesty's Attorney General applies by originating summons for declaratory relief that, in the circumstances specified by him, the distribution of a booklet entitled 'A guide to self-deliverance', which is published by the executive committee of the Voluntary Euthanasia Society (which also used to be known as Exit), is unlawful as being either an offence or an attempted offence contrary to the provisions of s 2(1) of the Suicide Act 1961.

That Act, by s 1, abrogated the rule of law whereby it was a crime for a person to commit suicide. Section 2(1) provides:

> A person who aids, abets, counsels or procures the suicide of another, or an attempt by another to commit suicide, shall be liable on conviction on indictment to imprisonment for a term not exceeding 14 years.

The respondents to the summons, whose names were changed at the outset of the proceedings, are members of the executive committee of the society. The society is an unincorporated association of members. Its amended constitution recites the purposes for which the society was established. These are:

> (2) The society shall work for the legalisation of voluntary euthanasia and for the enactment and beneficial working of any other measure seeking to establish the right, within properly defined limits, to avoid suffering and to die peacefully. (3) The society shall publish and distribute a form of declaration enabling members and others to make known their wishes with regard to terminal and emergency treatment. (4) The society may take any other steps intended to promote a general acceptance and understanding of the principles of voluntary euthanasia. (5) The society may consider and evaluate questions relating to the avoidance of suffering and to peaceful death and may provide information and practical and other advice to members of mature years and reasonable length of membership (by, for example, publication and distribution of a pamphlet or booklet) as to how most appropriately a prolonged and painful death can be avoided, and a life can be ended painlessly by someone hopelessly and painfully ill who has decided to embark on self-deliverance. (6) The society may carry our research in relation to all the above purposes and apply funds accordingly.

The respondents dispute the claim for relief on two main grounds. First, it is said that this is not a case in which it would be proper for the court to exercise its jurisdiction to grant declaratory relief, since it is for the criminal courts and not this court to apply the criminal law and if the law is unclear, the proper body to clarify the law is Parliament and not the courts. Second, they submit that the distribution of the booklet is not unlawful. The respondents go on to contend that if it is appropriate to grant declaratory relief, then a declaration should be granted that:

> No offence against s 2 of the Suicide Act is committed by publishing or supplying factual information about methods of committing suicide or arguments about the property of so doing, if its publisher or supplier (a) has no knowledge that the recipient has a present intention of committing suicide, or (b) lacks an intention to persuade a particular recipient to commit suicide, or (c) where the information or argument published is by its nature or by the circumstances attending its publication unlikely to precipitate suicidal attempts ...

... I consider it appropriate to proceed to consider whether, on the evidence which is before me, the Attorney General has established that he is entitled to the declaratory relief which he seeks. A starting point of such consideration must be the terms of s 2(1) itself. The intent of the subsection is clear. Section 1 of the Act having abrogated the criminal responsibility of the suicide, s 2(1) retains the criminal liability of an accessory at or before the fact. The nature of that liability has, however, changed. From being a participant in an offence of another, the accessory becomes the principal offender. This has the result that to attempt to 'aid, abet, counsel or procure the suicide of another, or an attempt by another to commit suicide' can be an offence even if the person concerned does not attempt to commit suicide: see *R v McShane* (1978) 66 Cr App R 97 and s 3 of the Criminal Attempts Act 1981. This is of significance in relation to the present issues because if the distribution of the booklet amounts to an offence under s 2(1) when the person to whom the booklet is distributed commits suicide or attempts to commit suicide, then the distribution to that person, if there is no attempt to commit suicide, could be an attempt to commit an offence under s 2(1) in the appropriate circumstances.

This being the general effect of s 2(1), the issue can be confined to considering whether to distribute the booklet to someone who commits suicide or attempts to commit suicide makes the distributor 'an accessory before the fact' to the suicide or attempted suicide, the position so far as the distributor is concerned being exactly the same as it would be if either suicide or attempted suicide were still a criminal offence.

Of the opening words of s 2(1), the words 'aids, abets' are normally regarded as referring to an accessory at the fact, and the words 'counsels or procures' to an accessory before the fact. However, it is not right to ignore the words 'aids, abets' in considering whether a person is an accessory before the fact.

As is pointed out in *Russell on Crime*, 12th edn, 1964, p 150, the conception of accessories before the fact is one of great antiquity and it cannot properly be understood without consideration of its history. Coke used both the word 'aide' and the word 'abetting' in dealing with accessories before the fact. Hale said in his *Pleas of the Crown*, 1778 edn, p 615: 'An accessory before, is he, that being absent at the time of the felony committed, doth yet procure, counsel, command, or abet another to commit a felony.'

Therefore, in the ordinary case, in deciding whether or not an offence has been committed, it is preferable to consider the phrase 'aids, abets, counsels or procures' as a whole. However, some of the previous decisions of the courts are explained by the fact that in the particular circumstances of that case, the court was considering only one part of the phrase.

The editor of *Russell* also provides assistance as to what is the 'bare minimum' which is necessary to constitute a person an accessory before the fact. At 151, it is stated that:

> the conduct of an alleged accessory should indicate (a) that he knew the particular deed was contemplated, and (b) that he approved of or assented to it, and (c) that his attitude in respect of it in fact encouraged the principal offender to perform – and I would here add 'or attempt to perform' – the deed.

In relation to the first minimum requirement, those responsible for publishing the booklet, because of its terms, would almost certainly know that a significant number of those to whom the booklet was intended to be sent would be contemplating suicide. They would not know precisely when, where or by what means the suicide was to be effected, if it took place, but this does not mean they cannot be shown to be accessories. As Lord Parker CJ said In *R v Bainbridge* [1960] 1 QB 129 at 134:

> If the principal does not totally and substantially vary the advice or the help and does not wilfully and knowingly commit a different form of felony altogether, the man who has advised or helped, aided or abetted, will be guilty as an accessory before the fact.

As the judge had directed the jury in that case: 'It must be proved he knew the type of crime which was in fact committed was intended.'

In relation to the second requirement, if the recipients of the booklet attempted to commit or committed suicide, the contents of the booklet indicate that the publishers approved or assented to their doing so. To conclude otherwise is inconsistent with the whole object of the booklet, which is to assist those who feel it necessary to resort to self-deliverance.

I turn, therefore, to the final minimum requirement. I have no doubt that in the case at least of certain recipients of the booklet, its contents would encourage suicide. Ignorance as to how to commit suicide must by itself be a deterrent. Likewise, the risks inherent in an unsuccessful attempt must be a deterrent. The contents of the booklet provide information as to methods which are less likely to result in an unsuccessful attempt. This assistance must encourage some readers to commit or attempt to commit suicide. This is clearly appreciated by the publishers, thus their care to control the persons to whom the booklet is to be sold and their advice as to the safe-keeping of the booklet.

I, therefore, have come clearly to the conclusion that there could be circumstances in which to supply the booklet could amount to an offence ...

The fact that the supply of the booklet could be an offence does not mean that any particular supply is an offence. It must be remembered that the society is an unincorporated body and there can be no question of the society committing an offence. Before an offence under s 2 can be proved, it must be shown that the individual concerned 'aided, abetted, counselled or procured' an attempt at suicide or a suicide and intended to do so by distributing the booklet. The intention of the individual will normally have to be inferred from facts surrounding the particular supply which he made. If, for example, before sending a copy of the booklet, a member of the society had written a letter, the contents of which were known to the person sending the booklet, which stated that the booklet was required because the member was intending to commit suicide, then, on those facts, I would conclude that an offence had been committed or at least an attempted offence contrary to s 2 of the Act. However, in the majority of cases, a member requesting the booklet will not make clear his intentions and the supply will be made without knowledge of whether the booklet is required for purposes of research, general information, or because suicide is contemplated. Is it, therefore, enough that in any particular case the person responsible for making the supply would appreciate that there is a real likelihood that the booklet is required by one of the substantial number of members of the society who will be contemplating suicide? It is as to this aspect of the case that there is the greatest difficulty and little assistance from the authorities.

[Counsel], on behalf of the society, contends that before a person can be an accessory, there must be a consensus between the accessory and the principal, and there can be no consensus where the alleged accessory does not even know whether the principal is contemplating (in this case) suicide. As, however, is pointed out in Smith and Hogan, *Criminal Law*, 4th edn, 1978, while counselling implies consensus, procuring and aiding do not. The editors say at 116:

> the law probably is that: (1) 'procuring' implies causation but not consensus; (2) 'abetting' and 'counselling' imply consensus but not causation; and (3) 'aiding' requires actual assistance but neither consensus nor causation.

As a matter of principle, it seems to me that as long as there is the necessary intent to assist those who are contemplating suicide to commit suicide if they decide to do so, it does not matter that the supplier does not know the state of mind of the actual recipient. The requirement for the necessary intent explains why in those cases where, in the ordinary course of business, a person is responsible for distributing an article, appreciating that some individuals might use it for committing suicide, he is not guilty of an offence. In the ordinary way, such a distributor would have no intention to assist the act of suicide. An intention to assist need not, however, involve a desire that suicide should be committed or attempted ...

Counsel for the respondents points out, and this I accept, that in some cases the booklet, far from precipitating someone to commit suicide, might have the effect of deterring someone from committing suicide when they might otherwise have done so. In such circumstances, he submits, it would be quite nonsensical to regard the supply of the booklet as being an attempted offence contrary to s 2. I agree, though I recognise that on one approach the result would be different. The reason why I agree with the submission is because, in such a case, the booklet has not provided any assistance with a view to a contemplated suicide. Such assistance is necessary to establish the *actus reus* for even the attempted offence.

There will also be cases where, although the recipient commits or attempts to commit suicide, the booklet has nothing to do with the suicide or the attempted suicide; for example, a long period of time may have elapsed between the sending of the booklet and the attempt. In such a case, again, I would agree with counsel for the respondents that there would not be a sufficient connection between the attempted suicide and the supply of the booklet to make the supplier responsible. This does not mean that it has to be shown that the suicide or attempted suicide would not have occurred but for the booklet. However, if 'procuring' alone is relied upon, this may be the case. As Lord Widgery CJ stated in *Attorney General's Reference (No 1 of 1975)* [1975] QB 773, at 779–80:

> To procure means to produce by endeavour. You procure a thing by setting out to see that it happens and taking the appropriate steps to produce that happening ... You cannot procure an offence unless there is a causal link between what you do and the commission of the offence ...

However, you do not need to procure to be an accessory and the same close causal connection is not required when what is being done is the provision of assistance.

I therefore conclude that to distribute the booklet can be an offence. But, before an offence can be established to have been committed, it must at least be proved: (a) that the alleged offender had the necessary intent, that is, he intended the booklet to be used by someone contemplating suicide and intended that person would be assisted by the booklet's contents, or otherwise encouraged to attempt to take or take his own life; (b) that while he still had that intention he distributed the booklet to such a person who read it; and, (c) in addition, if an offence under s 2 is to be proved, that such a person was assisted or encouraged by so reading the booklet to attempt to take or to take his own life, otherwise the alleged offender cannot be guilty of more than an attempt.

If these facts can be proved, then it does not make any difference that the person would have tried to commit suicide anyway. Nor does it make any difference, as the respondents contend, that the information contained in the booklet is already in the public domain. The distinguishing feature between an innocent and guilty distribution is that in the former case the distributor will not have the necessary intent, while in the latter case he will.

However, in each case it will be for a jury to decide whether the necessary facts are proved. If they are, then normally the offence will be made out. Nevertheless, even if they are proved, I am not prepared to say it is not possible for there to be some exceptional circumstance which means that an offence is not established.

The situations with which I have just sought to deal illustrate the problems in this case of granting any form of declaration to Her Majesty's Attorney General. However, as I am clearly of the view that the supply of this booklet can amount to an offence contrary to s 2, if the recipient commits or attempts to commit suicide, there can be no question of the respondents being granted a declaration ...

R v Gianetto [1997] 1 Cr App R 1 (CA)

Kennedy LJ: [The appellant had been charged with the murder of his wife. There was no scientific evidence to connect him with the crime and the prosecution relied upon a number of items of circumstantial evidence.]

It was the prosecution case that the appellant had either murdered her himself, or got someone else to do so ...

... The appellant complains that the trial judge erred in law when he failed to direct the jury that they must be unanimous as to which of the two competing versions of events put forward by the Crown they accepted. The failure was not accidental. The trial judge deliberately chose to give no such direction. [Counsel] for the appellant contends that the jury should have been told that before they could convict they must all agree either that the appellant was the murderer or that someone else murdered Julia Giannetto on his behalf. If they were unable to choose between those alternatives, or were divided as to which alternative they found to be proved, then, it is submitted, the appellant was entitled to be acquitted, because a jury can only convict if they can all find each essential element in an offence proved ...

In the context of the present case it seems to us that the starting point must be s 8 of the Accessories and Abettors Act 1861, as amended, which reads:

> Whosoever shall aid, abet counsel or procure the commission of any indictable offence ... at common law or by virtue of any Act passed or to be passed, shall be liable to be tried, indicted and punished as a principal offender.

The effect of that section is that even if the appellant did no more than encourage someone else to kill his wife he was liable to be tried, indicted and punished as a principal offender, and where, as here, the prosecution, for good reason, is unable to say whether the defendant did more than encourage, it must be open to the prosecution to invite the jury as a whole to find that at least the defendant encouraged. If the jury does convict it may do so with some jurors satisfied that the defendant was actually the killer, but all will be satisfied that if not himself the killer at least he encouraged and by reason of the statutory provision in the 1861 Act which we have cited no more is necessary to prove the offence. If that approach is correct, then this ground of appeal must fail...

In *Gaughan* [1990] Crim LR 880, the prosecution alleged that the appellant had damaged the complainant's motorcar, or got someone else to do so. On appeal he contended that the two alternatives should have been spelt out in separate counts. That was rejected by this court, Lloyd LJ (as he then was) saying at p 7G of the transcript that 'committing an offence as a principal and committing an offence as an accessory are two different ways of participating in the same offence. They are not separate offences'... Commenting [in the Criminal Law Review] on the case of *Gaughan* Professor Smith said:

> It is fundamental that the defendant should be told as precisely as possible what he is alleged to have done and that he should not be charged with doing one thing and convicted of doing something else. There will be occasions, however, when it is impossible to specify the mode of participation before the trial and where the case may have to be left to the jury on the basis that the defendant was either a principal or an accessory. It has long been established that this is permissible: *Swindall v Osborne* (1846) 2 C & K 230.

> We respectfully agree ...
>
> Having considered the authorities with some care we are satisfied that in the circumstances of this case the trial judge was right not to direct the jury that before they could convict they must all be satisfied either that the appellant killed his wife or that he got someone else to do so. They were entitled to convict if they were all satisfied that if he was not the killer he at least encouraged the killing, and accordingly this ground of appeal fails.
>
> There are two cardinal principles. The first is that the jury must be agreed upon the basis on which they find a defendant guilty. The second is that a defendant must know what case he has to meet. When the Crown allege, fair and square, that on the evidence, the defendant must have committed the offence either as principal or as secondary offender, and make it equally clear that they cannot say which, the *basis* on which the jury must be unanimous is that the defendant, having the necessary *mens rea*, by whatever means caused the result which is criminalised by the law. The Crown is not required to specify the means, because the legal definition of the crime does not require it; and the defendant knows perfectly well what case he has to meet. Of course, if (as will very often be so) the Crown nail their colours to a particular mast, their case will, generally, have to be established in the terms in which it is put. Our judgment should give no encouragement to prosecutors casting around for alternative possibilities where the essential evidence does not show a clear case against the defendant. But the facts of the present appeal are by no means an instance of that ...

MENS REA

To be guilty as a secondary party to an offence, the defendant must know 'the essential matters which constitute that offence' (*Johnson v Youden* [1950] 1 KB 544, 546, *per* Goddard CJ). In addition, there must be an 'intention to aid': see *National Coal Board v Gamble* [1959] 1 QB 11 at 20, *per* Devlin J. In other words, the accessory must intend or know that his conduct will have the effect of aiding, abetting, counselling or procuring the commission of an offence. Recklessness or negligence as to the effect of his conduct will not suffice.

Johnson v Youden and Others [1950] 1 KB 544 (DC)

Facts: One Dolbear, a builder, built a house under the authority of a licence granted under a Defence Regulation subject to a condition limiting the price for which the house might be sold to £1,025. The builder induced a purchaser to agree to pay for the house £250 in excess of the price permitted. That £250 was paid to the builder in advance. He then instructed a firm of solicitors, in which the three defendants were partners, to act for him in the sale. He concealed from the defendants the fact that he had received the additional £250, and the first two defendants did not know of it at any material time. On 6 April 1949, however, the purchaser's solicitors wrote a letter to the third defendant stating that they had not proceeded to completion because the builder was in breach of s 7 of the Building Materials and Housing Act 1945. The third defendant sought an explanation from the builder, who said that he had placed the £250 in question in a separate deposit account, and that it was to be spent on payment for work, as and when he would be able lawfully to execute it in the future, on the house on the purchaser's behalf. The third defendant accepted that explanation, and, having read the Act of 1945, formed the opinion that the payment of £250 was lawful and called on the purchaser to complete.

The builder was charged on information with offering to sell the house for a greater price than that permitted, contrary to s 7(1) of the Building Materials and Housing Act 1945; and informations were preferred against the three defendants charging them with aiding and abetting him in the commission of that offence.

On 5 July 1949, the builder was convicted, but the justices dismissed the three informations against the other defendants as they were of opinion that *mens rea* was a constituent of the offence of aiding and abetting an offence under s 7(1) of the Act of 1945. They found that the third defendant honestly believed the explanation given to him by the builder regarding the £250.

The prosecutor appealed.

Lord Goddard CJ: Before a person can be convicted of aiding and abetting the commission of an offence he must at least know the essential matters which constitute that offence. He need not actually know that an offence has been committed, because he may not know that the facts constitute an offence and ignorance of the law is not a defence. If a person knows all the facts and is assisting another person to do certain things, and it turns out that the doing of those things constitutes an offence, the person who is assisting is guilty of aiding and abetting that offence, because to allow him to say, 'I knew of all those facts but I did not know that an offence was committed', would be allowing him to set up ignorance of the law as a defence.

The reason why, in our opinion, the justices were right in dismissing the informations against the first two defendants is that they found, and found on good grounds, that they did not know of the matters which in fact constituted the offence; and, as they did not know of those matters, it follows that they cannot be guilty of aiding and abetting the commission of the offence.

With regard to their partner, the third defendant, a different state of affairs arises. His client, the builder, told him a story which, even if it were true, was on the face of it obviously a colourable evasion of the Act. The builder told him that he had received another £250, that he had placed the sum in a separate deposit account, 'and that it was to be spent on payment for work as and when he, the builder, would be lawfully able to execute it in the future on the house on behalf of the said purchaser'. It seems impossible to imagine that anyone could believe such a story. Who has ever heard of a purchaser putting money into the hands of the builder when he bought a house from him because he might want some work done thereafter? Surely, if the builder did not think that the purchaser could pay for the work, he would say: 'Will you pay something on account?' A story of that kind, on the face of it, is a mere colourable evasion of the Act.

It is more than likely, I think, that, in reading the Act, the third defendant did not read as carefully as he might have done s 7(5). If he had read that subsection carefully, I cannot believe that he – or indeed any solicitor, or even a layman – would not have understood that the arrangement which the builder said that he had made was just the kind of thing that subsection prohibited.

How could anybody say that the story which the builder told the third defendant was not a story with regard to a transaction with which the sale was associated? If that subsection had been read by the third defendant and appreciated by him, he would have seen at once that the extra £250 which the builder was obtaining was an unlawful payment; but unfortunately he did not realise it, but either misread the Act or did not read it carefully; and the next day he called on the purchaser to complete. Therefore he was clearly aiding and abetting the builder in the offence which the latter was committing.

The result is that, as far as the first two defendants are concerned, the appeal fails and must be dismissed; but as far as the third defendant is concerned, the case must go back to the justices with an intimation that an offence has been committed, and that he must be convicted.

National Coal Board v Gamble [1959] 1 QB 11 (QBD)

Facts: On 3 October 1957, an employee of a firm of hauliers took his lorry to a National Coal Board colliery, where it was filled with coal from a hopper and was then taken to a weighbridge, where the weighbridge operator (an employee of the NCB) weighed the lorry and its load and told the driver that the load was nearly four tons overweight. The driver, saying that he would risk taking the overload, took the weighbridge ticket from the weighbridge operator and left the colliery. He was subsequently stopped by the police. His employers were later convicted of contravening the Motor Vehicles (Construction and Use) Regulations 1955. The hauliers were collecting the coal for carriage to a power station, to whom the NCB were bound by contract to supply a bulk quantity of coal. The NCB were charged with aiding and abetting the hauliers in the commission of an offence.

Lord Goddard CJ: ... In my opinion it is quite clear that neither side could have intended the property in the coal to pass when it was put from the hopper into the lorry. The quantity would have to be ascertained in order to enable the price to be ascertained. The lorry is then taken to the weighbridge to be weighed and in my opinion no sale takes place whereby the property is passed until the weighing is completed and assented to by the buyer, and this is shown by the handing to him and the acceptance by him of a weighbridge ticket. In my opinion, therefore, no property passes until the weighbridge ticket was accepted by Mallender [the lorry driver].

As soon as Haslam [the weighbridge operator] weighed the coal he knew it was overweight and called Mallender's attention to that fact. From Mallender's answer he knew that Mallender intended to drive the overweighted lorry on the highway and with that knowledge he completed the sale and handed the weight ticket to Mallender whose duty then was to give it to the purchasers, namely the Central Electricity Authority. Haslam could, in my opinion, have refused to allow the overweight amount of 3 tons 18 cwts to leave the colliery. No specific amount had been asked for. The board were no doubt bound to deliver coal to the electricity authority under their contract, but were not bound to deliver any particular amount of coal at any particular moment.

The justices drew the inference, and it was not disputed, that the Board were bound by contract to supply a bulk quantity of coal to the authority. It was urged on behalf of the Board that they had no right to require Mallender to unload the coal or rather the excess, but with this I cannot agree. For the reasons I have already given the property had not passed until the delivery was completed, and it could only be completed by the weighing and the delivery and acceptance of the ticket.

Suppose a purchaser took his lorry to the hopper and asked for 10 tons of coal or the Coal Board had offered to supply him with 10 tons of coal. Nobody would know how much the hopper delivered until it had been weighed. If it was found that more than 10 tons had been put into the lorry it seems to me beyond question that the Board could insist upon the excess being taken out. Here no specific amount was asked for, but the Board, by their servant, knew that more had been put into the lorry than could be lawfully carried on the road and with that knowledge completed the sale. In my opinion that amounted to an aiding and abetting of the offence, as Haslam knew Mallender was going there and then to drive the lorry on the highway, in other words, a specific offence was contemplated ...

Devlin J: A person who supplies the instrument for a crime or anything essential to its commission aids in the commission of it; and if he does so knowingly and with intent to aid, he abets it as well and is therefore guilty of aiding and abetting. I use the words 'supplies' to comprehend giving, lending, selling, or any other transfer of the right of property ... In the transfer of property there must be either a physical delivery or a positive act of assent to a taking. But a man who hands over to another his own property on demand, although he may physically be performing a positive act, in law is only refraining from detinue. Thus in law the former act is one of assistance voluntarily given and the latter is only a failure to prevent the commission of the crime by means of a forcible detention, which would not even be justified except in the case of felony. Another way of putting the point is to say that aiding and abetting is a crime that requires proof of *mens rea*, that is to say, of intention to aid as well as of knowledge of the circumstances, and that proof of the intent involves proof of a positive act of assistance voluntarily done ...

It was contended on behalf of the Board that Haslam had no option after weighing but to issue the ticket for the amount then in the lorry. I think that this contention is unsound. In the circumstances of this case the loading must be taken as subject to adjustment; otherwise, if the contact were for a limited amount, the seller might make an over-delivery or an under-delivery which could not thereafter be rectified and the carrier might be contractually compelled to carry away a load in excess of that legally permitted. I think that the delivery of the coal was not completed until after the ascertained weight had been assented to and some act was done signifying assent and passing the property. The property passed when Haslam asked Mallender whether he intended to take the load and Mallender said he would risk it and when the mutual assent was, as it were, sealed by the delivery and acceptance of the weighbridge ticket. Haslam could therefore after he knew of the overload have refused to transfer the property in the coal.

This is the conclusion to which the justices came. Mr Thompson submits on behalf of the Board that it does not justify a verdict of guilty of aiding and abetting. He submits, first, that even if knowledge of the illegal purpose had been acquired before delivery began, it would not be sufficient for the verdict; and second, that if he is wrong about that, the knowledge was acquired too late, and the Board was not guilty of aiding and abetting simply because Haslam failed to stop the process of delivery after it had been initiated.

On his first point Mr Thompson submits that the furnishing of an article essential to the crime with knowledge of the use to which it is to be put does not of itself constitute aiding and abetting; there must be proved in addition a purpose or motive of the defendant to further the crime or encourage the criminal. Otherwise, he submits, there is no *mens rea*.

I have already said that in my judgment there must be proof of intent to aid. I would agree that proof that the article was knowingly supplied is not conclusive evidence of intent to aid ... But *prima facie* ... a man is presumed to intend the natural and probable consequences of his acts, and the consequence of supplying essential material is that assistance is given to the criminal. It is always open to the defendant, as in *R v Steane*, to give evidence of his real intention. But in this case the defence called no evidence. The *prima facie* presumption is therefore enough to justify the verdict, unless it is the law that some other mental element besides intent is necessary to the offence.

This is what Mr Thompson argues, and he describes the additional element as the purpose or motive of encouraging the crime. No doubt evidence of an interest in the crime or of an express purpose to assist it will greatly strengthen the case for the prosecution. But an indifference to the result of the crime does not of itself negative abetting. If one man deliberately sells to another a gun to be used for murdering a third, he may be indifferent about whether the third man lives or dies and interested only in the cash profit to be made out of the sale, but he can be still an aider and abettor. To hold otherwise would be to negative the rule that *mens rea* is a matter of intent only and does not depend on desire or motive ...

The case chiefly relied on by Mr Thompson was *R v Coney* (1882) 8 QBD 534. In that case the defendants were charged with aiding and abetting an illegal prize fight at which they had been present. The judgments all refer to 'encouragement', but it would be wrong to conclude from that that proof of encouragement is necessary to every form of aiding and abetting. Presence on the scene of the crime without encouragement or assistance is no aid to the criminal; the supply of essential material is. Moreover, the decision makes it clear that encouragement can be inferred from mere presence. Cave J, who gave the leading judgment, said of the summing up: 'It may mean either that mere presence unexplained is evidence of encouragement, and so of guilt, or that mere presence unexplained is conclusive proof of encouragement, and so of guilt. If the former is the correct meaning I concur in the law so laid down; if the latter, I am unable to do so'. This *dictum* seems to me to support the view I have expressed. If voluntary presence is *prima facie* evidence of encouragement and therefore of aiding and abetting, it appears to me to be a *fortiori* that the intentional supply of an essential article must be *prima facie* evidence of aiding and abetting.

As to Mr Thompson's alternative point, I have already expressed the view that the facts show an act of assent made by Haslam after knowledge of the proposed illegality and without which the property would not have passed. If some positive act to complete delivery is committed after knowledge of the illegality, the position in law must, I think, be just the same as if the knowledge had been obtained before the delivery had been begun. Of course, it is quite likely that Haslam was confused about the legal position and thought that he was not entitled to withhold the weighbridge ticket. There is no *mens rea* if the defendant is shown to have a genuine belief in the existence of circumstances which, if true, would negative an intention to aid ... But this argument, which might have been the most cogent available to the defence, cannot now be relied upon, because Haslam was not called to give evidence about what he thought or believed.

The fact that no evidence was called for the defence makes this case a peculiar one. We were told that the Board desired to obtain a decision on principle which would enable them to regulate their practice in the future. They therefore accepted responsibility for Haslam's act without going into any questions of vicarious liability; and they called no evidence in order, we were told, that the decision might be given on facts put against them as strongly as might be. What they wished to establish was that responsibility for overloaded lorries rested solely with the carrier and that the sale and delivery of the coal could not, if that was all that could be proved, involve them in a breach of the criminal law. For the reasons I have given I think that the law cannot be so stated and that the appeal should be dismissed.

Gillick v West Norfolk and Wisbech Area Health Authority and Department of Health and Social Security [1986] 1 AC 112 (HL)

Lord Fraser of Tullybelton: My Lords, the main question in this appeal is whether a doctor can lawfully prescribe contraception for a girl under 16 years of age, without the consent of her parents ...

In December 1980, the DHSS issued guidance on family planning services for young people ... which stated, or implied, that, at least in certain cases which were described as 'exceptional', a doctor could lawfully prescribe contraception for a girl under 16 without her parents' consent. Mrs Gillick, who is the mother of five daughters under the age of 16, objected to the guidance and she instituted the proceedings which have led to this appeal, and in which she claims a declaration ... that the advice given in the guidance was unlawful ...

Is a doctor who gives contraceptive advice or treatment to a girl under 16 without her parents' consent likely to incur criminal liability?

The submission was made to Woolf J on behalf of Mrs Gillick that a doctor who provided contraceptive advice and treatment to a girl under 16 without her parents' authority would be committing an offence under s 28 of the Sexual Offences Act 1956 by aiding and abetting the commission of unlawful sexual intercourse. When the case reached the Court of Appeal counsel on both sides conceded that whether a doctor who followed the guidelines would be committing an offence or not would depend on the circumstances. It would depend upon the doctor's intentions; this appeal is concerned with doctors who honestly intend to act in the best interests of the girl, and I think it is unlikely that a doctor who gives contraceptive advice or treatment with that intention would commit an offence under s 28. It must be remembered that a girl under 16 who has sexual intercourse does not thereby commit an offence herself, although her partner does: see the Sexual Offences Act 1956, ss 5 and 6. In any event, even if the doctor would be committing an offence, the fact that he had acted with the parents' consent would not exculpate him as Woolf J pointed out [1984] QB 581, 595 G. Accordingly, I regard this contention as irrelevant to the question that we have to answer in this appeal. Parker LJ in the Court of Appeal at 118a, dealt at some length with the provisions of criminal law intended to protect girls under the age of 16 from being seduced, and perhaps also to protect them from their own weakness. Parker LJ expressed his conclusion on this part of the case as follows at 137f–g:

> It appears to me that it is wholly incongruous, when the act of intercourse is criminal, when permitting it to take place on one's premises is criminal and when, if the girl were under 13, failing to report an act of intercourse to the police would up to 1967 have been criminal, that either the department [or] the area health authority should provide facilities which will enable girls under 16 the more readily to commit such acts. It seems to me equally incongruous to assert that doctors have the right to accept the young, down, apparently, to any age, as patients, and to provide them with contraceptive advice and treatment without reference to their parents and even against their known wishes.

My Lords, the first of those two sentences is directed to the question, which is not in issue in this appeal, of whether contraceptive facilities should be available at all under the National Health Service for girls under 16. I have already explained my reasons for thinking that the legislation does not limit the duty of providing such facilities to women of 16 or more. The second sentence, which does bear directly on the question in the appeal, does not appear to me to follow necessarily from the first and with respect I cannot agree with it. If the doctor complies with the first of the conditions which I have specified, that is to say if he satisfies himself that the girl can understand his advice, there will be no question of his giving contraceptive advice to very young girls ...

Lord Scarman: ... If this case should be made good, the discussion of parental right is, of course, an irrelevance. If it be criminal or contrary to public policy to prescribe contraception for a girl under the age of 16 on the ground that sexual intercourse with her is unlawful and a crime on the part of her male partner, the fact that her parent knew and consented would not make it any less so. I confess that I find the submission based upon criminality or public policy surprising. So far as criminality is concerned, I am happy to rest on the judgment of Woolf J whose approach to the problem I believe to be correct. Clearly a doctor who gives a girl contraceptive advice or treatment not because in his clinical judgment the treatment is medically indicated for the maintenance of restoration of her health but with the intention of facilitating her having unlawful sexual intercourse may well be guilty of a criminal offence. It would depend, as my noble and learned friend, Lord Fraser of Tullybelton, observes, upon the doctor's intention - a conclusion hardly to be wondered at in the field of criminal law. The department's guidance avoids the trap of declaring that the decision to prescribe the treatment is wholly a matter of the doctor's discretion. He may prescribe only if she has the capacity to consent or if exceptional circumstances exist which justify him in exercising his clinical judgment without parental consent. The adjective 'clinical' emphasises that it must be a medical judgment based upon what he honestly believes to be necessary for the physical, mental, and emotional health of his patient. The *bona fide* exercise by a doctor of his clinical judgment must be a complete negation of the guilty mind which is an essential ingredient of the criminal offence of aiding and abetting the commission of unlawful sexual intercourse.

The public policy point fails for the same reason. It cannot be said that there is anything necessarily contrary to public policy in medical contraceptive treatment if it be medically indicated as in the interest of the patient's health: for the provision of such treatment is recognised as legitimate by Parliament: s 5 of the National Health Service Act 1977. If it should be prescribed for a girl under 16 the fact that it may eliminate a health risk in the event of the girl having unlawful sexual intercourse is an irrelevance unless the doctor intends to encourage her to have that intercourse. If the prescription is the *bone fide* exercise of his clinical judgment as to what is best for his patient's health, he has nothing to fear from the criminal law or from any public policy based on the criminality of a man having sexual intercourse with her.

It can be said by way of criticism of this view of the law that it will result in uncertainty and leave the law in the hands of the doctors. The uncertainty is the price which has to be paid to keep the law in line with social experience, which is that many girls are fully able to make sensible decisions about many matters before they reach the age of 16. I accept that great responsibilities will lie on the medical profession. It is, however, a learned and highly trained profession regulated by statute and governed by a strict ethical code which is vigorously enforced. Abuse of the power to prescribe contraceptive treatment for girls under the age of 16 would render a doctor liable to severe professional penalty. The truth may well be that the rights of parents and children in this sensitive area are better protected by the professional standards of the medical profession than by *a priori* legal lines of division between capacity and lack of capacity to consent since any such general dividing line is sure to produce in some cases injustice, hardship, and injury to health ...

Smith v Mellors and Soar (1987) 84 Cr App R 279 (DC)

Croom-Johnson LJ: ... The facts as found by the justices are as follows. At 3.30 am on 7 February 1985, police officers observed a stationary motor vehicle on a building site. It was a building site to which access could only have been obtained by driving on public roads. The doors were open. The two defendants were seen running away from the vehicle. We were told, without objection, that the ignition keys were in the motor vehicle. The justices went on to find that the vehicle had been driven there on public roads and finally abandoned, that Mellors and Soar were or had been the only occupants and that either Mellors or Soar was the driver of the vehicle. Mellors was arrested and taken to the police station where he was tested by an Intoximeter. His blood alcohol was found to be 64 microgrammes per 100 millilitres. Soar was not arrested, it appears, but was brought to the police station at 3.55 am where he, too, was tested. His blood alcohol was shown to have been 79 microgrammes per 100 millilitres.

Thereafter, the case took a somewhat peculiar form. The motor vehicle, we have been told, belonged to Mellors' father. It also appears that he had not had his father's permission to use the car that night.

The two defendants were separately interviewed. I can summarise the effect of the interviews as follows. Mellors said that Soar was the driver. Soar said that Mellors was the driver. Reference has been made to the evidence because one of the grounds of this appeal has been that the justices came to a wholly unreasonable conclusion on the evidence. When Mellors was interviewed and said that Soar was the driver, that was not evidence against Soar. When Soar was interviewed and said that Mellors was the driver, that was not evidence against Mellors. To this day the mystery has never been cleared up. It was not cleared up before the justices.

The solution which was adopted by the prosecution was to charge them both as principals in accordance with s 44 of the Magistrates' Courts Act 1980, on the basis that either Mellors was the driver and in breach of s 6, in which case Soar was aiding and abetting in the commission of that offence, or that Soar was the driver and in breach of s 6, and that Mellors was aiding and abetting. It does not matter, says the prosecution, if that dispute is unresolved. This was one of the grounds upon which the justices, on a submission of no case, ruled that there was no case to answer against each of the defendants, on the basis that it had not been proved which of them was driving.

I can deal with that matter straight away. It is quite clear that either could be charged as a principal, notwithstanding that he might only be a passenger in the motor car, provided it could be proved that as a passenger he was aiding and abetting the other one in the driving of the car ...

So far as whether it is necessary to decide the point whether there was evidence to pin the driving on one person rather than upon the other we have come to the conclusion that upon this part of the case the justices came to a wrong decision. The opinion which they gave upon the submission of no case is this:

> Our view was that the prosecution must prove which defendant drove the vehicle and which defendant was aider and abettor. We accept that we could convict the aider and abettor of the principal offence in accordance with s 44 of the Magistrates' Courts Act 1980 but nonetheless the appellant must still adduce evidence to identify the driver and the aider and abettor. There was no evidence in our opinion from which any court could find who was the driver of this vehicle and accordingly we could find no case to answer against each defendant and accordingly dismissed the informations.

We are not saying that it is enough to leave the matter in the air and give the court a choice as to who is the driver, but the circumstances must be such as to compel the court to come to the conclusion that it really does not matter for the purposes of the case which is being put before it whether A was in the driving seat and B in the passenger seat or whether it was the other way about. If the case really is that they were both equally guilty regardless of who was doing the driving and who was being driven, then, it would be open to the court to convict both driver and passenger as principal in respect of the offence under s 6 of the Road Traffic Act. It does not mean to say that this situation will apply in every case. I emphasise that it must be in circumstances where it does not matter who was doing what at the particular time.

We now come to the much more substantial point in this case. There was a second string to the appellant's bow. The fact that there was no direct evidence as to who was driving the vehicle at the material time only had no significance if the prosecution was able to establish that Mellors and Soar, on this journey in the motor car, were on a joint enterprise which required knowledge by both defendants that the other one had had too much to drink to be fit to be driving a motor car for the purposes of s 6. It would not do, for example, to assume that Mellors was the driver and Soar the passenger unless Soar had knowledge or was reckless that Mellors had had too much to drink. Equally, it would be quite unsafe to make that assumption if the situation were the other way round. Accordingly, the justices had to consider this question on the basis to which I have referred.

The question of recklessness does not appear to have been argued before the justices and accordingly it has not been argued before us. It might be that an aider and abettor would be an aider and abettor if he were simply reckless as to whether or not the driver had the requisite amount of alcohol in his blood. This case has been put fairly and squarely before us on the basis of knowledge.

In those circumstances, the justices came to this conclusion:

> We were satisfied that this motor vehicle had been driven on a public road by one of the defendants and that both defendants had consumed alcohol in excess of the prescribed limit. However, on the evidence as presented, we were of the opinion that it was unreasonable to infer that both respondents were aware the other had consumed alcohol in excess of the prescribed limit.

It is said that without knowing who was the driver it has to be both. We have therefore been urged to say that the justices in making their finding made a finding which no reasonable tribunal could have come to. Accordingly, we have been referred to the evidence ...

... It is always very difficult for an appellate court to assess matters of opinion as they were put before the justices. These are not simply questions of fact. They are the impressions which were made on the police officers. There is no direct evidence in relation to either of the defendants as to what impression the other one made upon him. The justices saw and heard the witnesses. They had to assess what weight was to be given to the evidence of the officers of the opinions which they formed at the times at which they formed them and as they were expressed by them when they came to give evidence in the witness box. That was essentially a matter for the justices. On the basis of the note which has been provided for us, we are quite unable to come to the conclusion that the justices were not entitled to come to the opinion to which they did.

In those circumstances, this case falls short of the degree of proof which is required to show that it really does not matter who was driving and who was the passenger. We are unable to say that the decision was wholly unreasonable and perverse. In those circumstances, this appeal must be dismissed.

R v Lomas (1913) 9 Cr App R 220 (CA)

Facts: A burglary was committed by a man named King, who had used for the purpose a housebreaking implement known as a jemmy, and was convicted as a principal. It appears that on the day on which the burglary was committed the jemmy was in possession of the appellant, who originally received it from King. At King's request he returned it to him, and subsequently, after the burglary had been committed, received it again, together with the sum of 2d. Appellant, who was indicted as an accessory before the fact, was charged with King with housebreaking.

The jury found: 'Lomas guilty: that he had a certain knowledge that the jemmy was wanted for an illegal purpose – that he handed the jemmy to King with the knowledge that it was wanted for a burglary. He did not know that it was wanted for this particular burglary.'

Lord Isaacs CJ: ... The question is, do the facts found by the jury in their verdict show that the appellant was an accessory before the fact to the commission of this burglary? It has been argued by Mr Willes with great clearness that an accessory is one who gives assistance with the knowledge that a crime is to be committed. Here the finding is not enough to bring the case even within that statement of the law. We do not say that we agree with it as a definition of an accessory before the fact, but it is sufficient for us to say that the facts as found by the jury are not enough to constitute the offence.

R v Petters and Parfitt [1995] Crim LR 501 (CA)

Facts: Petters and Parfitt were both acquitted of murder and convicted of manslaughter. The victim died as a result of an incident in a car park, the evidence suggesting that the fatal blow had been caused by a kick. Petters and Parfitt arrived on the scene independently. Both admitted punching the victim. One witness said that Parfitt had kicked the victim, but later retracted that statement. Another witness said that Petters kicked the victim, but later said that the kick missed. The case was put as a joint enterprise. The judge directed the jury that there was a joint enterprise, even if there was no prearranged plan, if both were attacking the victim at the same time with the same type of weapon (ie punching and/or kicking) and there was a common intention or common purpose that the victim should suffer harm (and the fatal blow was part of the common intention). On appeal, complaint was made against that direction.

Held, allowing the appeal, that in such a case, what needed to be said to the jury was that the common purpose or intention had to be more than merely them both separately intending to do some harm to the victim. They had to share a common purpose to harm the victim, and make it clear by their actions to the other that that was their common intention. In the light of that criticism, taken with another relating to the way in which the evidence was put to the jury by the judge, the convictions were unsafe.

Note: In *R v JF Alford Transport Ltd* (1997), *The Times*, March 31, a company, its managing director and its transport manager were charged with aiding and abetting the making of false tachograph entries by drivers employed by the company. It was held by the Court of Appeal:

(1) That the prosecution had to prove that the particular defendant intended to do the acts which he knew to be capable of assisting or encouraging the commission of the crime, but he need not have intended that the crime be committed.

(2) If the management's reason for turning a blind eye was to keep the drivers happy rather than to encourage the production of false tachograph records, that would afford no defence.

(3) Knowledge, together with passive acquiescence to the commission of the offence, was insufficient to amount to aiding and abetting. However, knowledge, together with the ability to control the actions of the principal offender and the taking of a deliberate decision to refrain from preventing the commission of the offence, could amount to aiding and abetting.

SCOPE OF JOINT VENTURE

If D1 enters a house and steals something while D2 stands watch outside, the burglary is clearly within the scope of their joint enterprise.

However, what if D1 is armed with a knife and stabs the occupant of the house. Is D2 liable for the attack on the householder? The answer to this question depends on the extent to which this further crime was within D2's contemplation. The question is whether D1 went beyond the agreed scope of the joint enterprise. If the jury or magistrates decide that D2 contemplated a real risk that a weapon might be used, D2 may be convicted of the further offence.

It follows that a person may be a secondary party to a crime, provided that he knows the basic type of crime to be committed, even if he does not know the precise details of that crime. Where the crime committed goes beyond what was actually agreed between the parties, contemplation or foresight of a real or serious risk of that occurring is enough.

R v Bainbridge [1960] 1 QB 129 (CA)

Facts: On the night of 30 October 1958 the Stoke Newington branch of the Midland Bank was broken into by cutting the bars of a window, the doors of the strong room and of a safe inside the strong room. This was done by a means of oxygen cutting equipment. The cutting equipment was left behind and it was later discovered that it had been bought by the appellant some six weeks earlier. The appellant was convicted of being an accessory before the fact to the burglary.

Lord Parker CJ: The case against him [the appellant] was that he had bought this cutting equipment on behalf of one or more of the thieves with the full knowledge that it was going to be used, if not against the Stoke Newington branch of the Midland Bank, at any rate for the purposes of breaking and entering premises.

The appellant's case, as given in his evidence, was this:

> True, I had bought this equipment from two different firms. I had gone there with a man called Shakeshaft to buy it for him. As a result of a conversation which I had with him I was suspicious that he wanted it for something illegal, I thought it was for breaking up stolen goods which Shakeshaft had received, and as a result in those purchases I gave false names and addresses, but I had no knowledge that the equipment was going to be used for any such purpose as it was used.

The complaint here is that Judge Aarvold, who tried the case, gave the jury a wrong direction in regard to what it was necessary for them to be satisfied of in order to hold the appellant guilty of being an accessory before the fact. The passages in question are these. He said:

> To prove that, the prosecution have to prove these matters: first of all they have to prove the felony itself was committed. Of that there is no doubt. That is not contested. Second, they have to prove the defendant, this man Bainbridge, knew that a felony of that kind was intended and was going to be committed, and with that knowledge he did something to help the felons commit the crime. The knowledge that is required to be proved in the mind of this man Bainbridge is not the knowledge of the precise crime. In other words, it need not be proved he knew the Midland Bank, Stoke Newington branch, was going to be broken and entered and money stolen from that particular bank, but he must know the type of crime that was in fact committed. In this case it is a breaking and entering of premises and the stealing of property from those premises. It must be proved he knew that sort of crime was intended and was going to be committed. It is not enough to show that he either suspected or knew that some crime was going to be committed, some crime which might have been a breaking and entering or might have been disposing of stolen property or anything of that kind. That is not enough. It must be proved he knew the type of crime which was in fact committed was intended ...

Mr Simpson, who has argued this case very well, contends that that direction is wrong. As he puts it, in order that a man should be convicted of being accessory before the fact, it must be shown that at the time he bought the equipment in a case such as this he knew that a particular crime was going to be committed, and by a particular crime Mr Simpson means that the premises in this case which were going to be broken into were known to the appellant and contemplated by him, and not only the premises in question but the date when the breaking was going to occur; in other words, that he must know that on a particular date the Stoke Newington branch of the Midland Bank is intended to be broken into.

The court fully appreciates that it is not enough that it should be shown that a man knows that some illegal venture is intended. To take this case, it would not be enough if he knew – he says he only suspected - that the equipment was going to be used to dispose of stolen property. That would not be enough. Equally, this court is quite satisfied that it is unnecessary that knowledge of the particular crime which was in fact committed should be shown to his knowledge to have been intended, and by 'particular crime' I am using the words in the same way in which Mr Simpson used them, namely on a particular date and particular premises.

It is not altogether easy to lay down a precise form of words which will cover every case that can be contemplated but, having considered the cases and the law this court is quite clear that the direction of Judge Aarvold in this case cannot be criticised ...

Judge Aarvold in this case, in the passage to which I have referred, makes it clear that there must be not merely suspicion but knowledge that a crime of the type in question was intended, and that the equipment was bought with that in view. In his reference to the felony of the type intended it was, as he stated, the felony of breaking and entering premises and the stealing of property from those premises. The court can see nothing wrong in that direction ...

DPP for Northern Ireland v Maxwell [1978] 1 WLR 1350 (HL)

Lord Fraser of Tullybelton: My Lords, the appellant was convicted of, *inter alia*, two offences under s 3 of the Explosive Substances Act 1883. In count 1 he was charged with doing an act with intent to cause an explosion by a pipe bomb and in count 2 with possession of a pipe bomb. In fact, he did not physically do an act of placing the bomb in position, nor did he physically have the bomb in his possession, but he was a member of a gang of four or five men, acting in concert, other members of which conveyed the bomb to the place where they intended to explode it and placed it in position. The appellant's part in the enterprise was to act as guide by leading the way in his own motor car, while other members of the gang followed in another car. He led them to the Crosskeys Inn, where the bomb was placed and the fuse ignited. His part was important because the other members were strangers to the district, and he was familiar with the road.

In these circumstances, the answer to the question whether he was rightly convicted depends on the extent of his knowledge of the common plan when he took part in it. If he had known full details of the plan, the time, place and nature of the crimes intended, he would unquestionably be guilty as a principal because he had aided and abetted their commission. Even if he had not known the intended time and place, but had known the nature of the crimes that were planned, there would be no question of his guilt: see *R v Bainbridge* [1960] 1 QB 129. In the present case it was not proved that the appellant knew that a pipe bomb was to be used, nor that it was being carried in the second car, and the argument was that he was therefore not guilty of the crimes charged. The trial judge held that the appellant knew the men in the second car 'were going to attack the inn', but with great respect I have some doubt whether that finding is justified. It seems to me doubtful whether the proof went further than showing that the inn was the place to which the appellant was to guide the gang for the purpose of the operation, and that the inn might have been merely a convenient rendezvous for an attack on some other place nearby. But whether my doubt is justified or not it does not affect my view that the appellant was rightly convicted ...

In my opinion there is no substance in the argument for the appellant, having regard to the facts in this case. The appellant was a member of the Ulster Volunteer Force ('UVF') and there was evidence from a police officer that the UVF had been responsible for various kinds of violent incidents, including murders and bombings of public houses and other premises owned by Roman Catholics. (The owner of the Crosskeys Inn was a Roman Catholic.) On the occasion in question, the appellant knew that he was being sent on a 'job'. The trial judge found that:

> As used by the accused the word 'job' is synonymous with military action which raises, having regard to the proven activities of the UVF, the irresistible inference [that] the attack would be one of violence in which people would be endangered or premises seriously damaged.

In my opinion it is clear that when the appellant was ordered, as his part in the job, to lead another car to the Crosskeys Inn, he must have contemplated that a violent attack of some kind was to be made either on the inn itself or on some neighbouring place. When he obeyed the order he must therefore have intended to assist in carrying out such an attack. Although he is not proved to have known exactly what form the attack was to take, whether a murder or a bombing of the premises, he must have known that either or both of these (and any form of attack which was practised by the UVF) was to be expected as the plan for that night. Further he must have known that the bombing of premises necessarily involved doing an act with intent to cause an explosion by explosive substances, and also being in possession of explosive substances. If he did not know the particular type of operation planned when he took part in it, he must have intended to assist in any one or more of these types of operations, with all that it necessarily involved, while being content to leave the choice of the actual operation to others, perhaps members of the gang or some higher commander. As Lowry LCJ expressed it in his judgment in the Court of Criminal Appeal: 'He was therefore in just the same situation, so far as guilty knowledge is concerned, as a man who had been given a list of jobs and told that one of them would be carried out.' He was guilty of any or all of the jobs on the list that were in fact carried out.

The possible extent of his guilt was limited to the range of crimes any of which he must have known were to be expected that night. Doing acts with explosives and possessing explosives were within that range and when they turned out to be crimes committed on that night he was therefore guilty of them. If another member of the gang had committed some crime that the appellant had no reason to expect, such as perhaps throwing poison gas into the inn, the appellant would not have been guilty of using poison gas.

The same reasoning applies to count 2, possession of the pipe bomb. The appellant must have known that use of such a bomb was to be expected, and he must have known that whatever weapon or device was to be used would almost certainly be carried in the second car ...

Lord Scarman: My Lords, I also would dismiss this appeal. The question it raises is as to the degree of knowledge required by law for the attachment of criminal responsibility to one who assists another (or others) to commit or attempt crime.

In *Johnson v Youden* [1950] 1 KB 544 the Divisional Court held that before a person can be convicted of aiding and abetting the commission of an offence he must at least know the essential matters which constitute the offence. He does not have to know that the facts constitute an offence: for ignorance of the law is no defence. In *R v Bainbridge* [1960] 1 KB 129 the Court of Criminal Appeal for England and Wales held that it was not necessary that the accused should know the particular crime intended or committed by those whom he assisted, and upheld a direction in which the judge had made it clear that it was enough if the accused knew the type of crime intended ...

I think *R v Bainbridge* was correctly decided. But I agree with counsel for the appellant that in the instant case the Court of Criminal Appeal in Northern Ireland has gone further than the Court of Criminal Appeal for England and Wales found it necessary to go in *R v Bainbridge*. It is not possible in the present case to declare that it is proved, beyond reasonable doubt, that the appellant knew a bomb attack on the inn was intended by those whom he was assisting. It is not established therefore, that he knew the particular type of crime intended. The court, however, refused to limit criminal responsibility by reference to knowledge by the accused of the type or class of crime intended by those whom he assisted. Instead, the court has formulated a principle which avoids the uncertainties and ambiguities of classification. The guilt of an accessory springs, according to the court's formulation, 'from the fact that he contemplates the commission of one (or more) of a number of crimes by the principal and he intentionally lends his assistance in order that such a crime will be committed': *per* Lowry LCJ.

Lowry LCJ continues:

> The relevant crime must be within the contemplation of the accomplice and only exceptionally would evidence be found to support the allegation that the accomplice had given the principal a completely blank cheque.

The principle thus formulated has great merit. It directs attention to the state of mind of the accused: not what he ought to have in contemplation, but what he did have. It avoids definition and classification, while ensuring that a man will not be convicted of aiding an abetting any offence his principal may commit, but only one which is within his contemplation. He may have in contemplation only one offence, or several; and the several which he contemplates he may see as alternatives. An accessory who leaves it to his principal to choose is liable, provided always the choice is made from the range of offences from which the accessory contemplates the choice will be made. Although the court's formulation of the principle goes further than the earlier cases, it is a sound development of the law and in no way inconsistent with them. I accept it as good judge-made law in a field where there is no statute to offer guidance.

On the facts as found by the trial (there was no jury because of the Northern Ireland (Emergency Provisions) Act 1973), the appellant knew he was guiding a party of men to the Crosskeys Inn on a UVF military-style 'job', ie an attack by bomb, incendiary or bullet on persons or property. He did not know the particular type of offence intended, but he must have appreciated that it was very likely that those whom he was assisting intended a bomb attack on the inn.

If the appellant contemplated, as he clearly did, a bomb attack as likely, he must also have contemplated the possibility that the men in the car, which he was leading to the inn, had an explosive substance with them. Though he did not know whether they had it with them or not, he must have believed it very likely that they did. In the particular circumstances of this case, the inference that the two offences of possessing the explosive and using it with intent to cause injury or damage were within the appellant's contemplation is fully justified on the evidence. The appellant was rightly convicted, and I would dismiss his appeal.

Chan Wing-Siu and Others v The Queen [1985] 1 AC 168 (PC)

Sir Robin Cooke: ... The case for the prosecution depended on the evidence of Madam Lam. She was a prostitute carrying on her trade with her husband's consent in a flat in which he was also habitually present. Advertisements were placed regularly in Chinese newspapers indicating that her services were available there. She testified that during the afternoon of 31 May 1980 her doorbell rang and she went to answer it, her husband as usual discreetly withdrawing to the kitchen. At first she saw only the accused Tse. Assuming that he was a client, she opened the door to let him in, but the other two accused then rushed round a corner and the three forced their way into the flat. They all drew knives. She was ordered to kneel down, keep still and not make a sound. Her husband appeared at the kitchen door and Chan and Wong then forced him back into the kitchen, while Tse remained on guard over her. She heard one of the other two say 'Stab him down' and then a scream from her husband. Shortly afterwards one of the other two shouted 'Run'. All three left, but as they did so she heard one say 'Stab her down too'. She was slashed across the head, receiving a wound which bled profusely but in the event proved to be comparatively superficial. She found her husband dying in the kitchen. He had been stabbed several times.

At different times later on the same day, Madam Lam and Chan and Wong each went separately to the casualty department of the same hospital, where she happened to see and recognised Chan. The two men both had wounds and injuries sufficiently serious for them to be kept in hospital for two days. In particular, Wong had a 2½-inch wound on his face involving the nose and penetrating the nasal cavity; there was a compound fracture of his hard palate. Tse had not been hurt and was not arrested until some three months later.

The men left behind them in the flat three knives, two of which were heavily stained with blood of the same group as that of the deceased. The third knife had only some spots of blood, too small for grouping. A ring worn by the deceased, and said by his wife to fit firmly round his finger, was found lying in the living room. The possibility that it had been wrenched from the deceased's finger and then dropped by one of the accused in flight was relevant to the Crown's theory at the trial that the motive for the attack on the deceased was robbery.

Each accused made several statements to the police. These were put in evidence by the prosecution. None of the accused, however, gave evidence at the trial, nor was any evidence called for them. In their respective statements all the accused admitted, at least ultimately, having gone to the flat that day. (Chan and Wong had initially given quite different accounts of how they came by their wounds.) They claimed that their purpose had been to collect a debt owing by the deceased to Tse. Chan and Wong each admitted taking a knife, allegedly for self-protection, and knowing that the others also had knives. Tse made no admission of having himself taken a knife, and he denied knowing that his friends were armed with knives. The general tenor of the statements of all three was that, as soon as they entered, the deceased attacked them savagely with a chopper or knives – this despite the fact that, as the judge underlined in his summing up, a client was expected, rather than a party of invaders. Only Wong admitted to using violence himself. He maintained that, immediately they entered, the woman called out 'Robbery' and proceeded to lock the door; whereupon the man attacked him with a chopper. He said that after having been chopped three times and warding off a fourth blow, he stabbed his assailant many times and ran. He claimed to have acted in self-defence. It should be mentioned that the judge gave the necessary direction that the statements of each accused were admissible only against the maker ...

... [O]ne way in which the Crown case at the trial was put against all three accused, and on both counts, was that crimes of the type charged must have been contemplated by the accused as possible occurrences in the course of their joint venture. Both in the summing up and later in answer to questions from the jury regarding the necessary intent, Macdougall J directed them to the effect that an accused was guilty on both counts if proved to have had in contemplation that a knife might be used on the occasion by one of his co-adventurers with the intention of inflicting serious bodily injury. The judge's words varied slightly, but the following is a sufficient example of what he said:

> The Crown does not have to prove which accused inflicted the fatal blow. You may convict any accused of murder if you come to the conclusion that he either personally inflicted the fatal wound on the deceased with the intention of causing at least serious bodily injury or that one of his companions inflicted that wound and that the accused contemplated that either of his companions might use a knife to cause serious bodily injury on any one or more to the occupants of that flat.

... The present appeal involves solely an attack on the summing up, albeit in relation to both counts. As in the Court of Appeal, it is submitted for the appellants that it was not enough if an appellant foresaw death or grievous bodily harm as a *possible* consequence of the joint enterprise: that the jury ought to have been directed that it must be proved that he foresaw that one of those consequences would *probably* result. Refining the argument somewhat, counsel for the appellants conceded before their Lordships that a person who is charged with murder on the basis of having been a party to an unlawful enterprise, and who was aware that weapons were being carried, need not have foreseen as more probable than not a contingency in which a weapon might be used by one of his companions (for example, resistance by the victim of an intended robbery). The main proposition submitted for the appellants remained, however, that such an accused does at least have to be proved to have foreseen that, if such a contingency eventuated, it was more probable than not that one of his companions would use a weapon with intent to kill or cause grievous bodily harm.

In considering that argument it should first be recalled that a person acting in concert with the primary offender may become a party to the crime, whether or not present at the time of its commission, by activities variously described as aiding, abetting, counselling, inciting or procuring it. In the typical case in that class, the same or the same type of offence is actually intended by all the parties acting in concert. In view of the terms of the directions to the jury here, the Crown does not seek to support the present convictions on that ground. The case must depend rather on the wider principle whereby a secondary party is criminally liable for acts by the primary offender of a type which the former foresees but does not necessarily intend.

That there is such a principle is not in doubt. It turns on contemplation or, putting the same idea in other words, authorisation, which may be express but is more usually implied. It meets the case of a crime foreseen as a possible incident of the common unlawful enterprise. The criminal culpability lies in participating in the venture with that foresight ...

In agreement with the courts in Hong Kong, Australia and New Zealand, their Lordships regard as wholly unacceptable any argument that would propose, as any part of the criteria of the guilt of an accomplice, whether on considering in advance the possibility of a crime of the kind in the event actually committed by his co-adventurers he thought that it was more than an even risk. The concession that the contingency in which the crime is committed need not itself be foreseen as more probable than not, while virtually inevitable in the light of the reasoning in *Johns v The Queen* (1980) 143 CLR 108 and the other cases, complicates the argument without improving it. What public policy requires was rightly identified in the submissions for the Crown. Where a man lends himself to a criminal enterprise knowing that potentially murderous weapons are to be carried, and in the event they are in fact used by his partner with an intent sufficient for murder, he should not escape the consequences by reliance upon a nuance of prior assessment, only too likely to have been optimistic.

On the other hand, if it was not even contemplated by the particular accused that serious bodily harm would be intentionally inflicted, he is not a party to murder. This is reflected in a passage in the speech of Lord Simonds LC in *Davies v DPP* [1954] AC 378, 401:

> ... I can see no reason why, if half a dozen boys fight another crowd, and one of them produces a knife and stabs one of the opponents to death, all the rest of his group should be treated as accomplices in the use of a knife and the infliction of mortal injury by that means, unless there is evidence that the rest intended or concerted or at least contemplated an attack with a knife by one of their number, as opposed to a common assault. If all that was designed or envisaged was in fact a common assault, and there was no evidence that Lawson, a party to that common assault, knew that any of his companions had a knife, then Lawson was not an accomplice in the crime consisting in its felonious use.

The test of *mens rea* here is subjective. It is what the individual accused in fact contemplated that matters. As in other cases where the state of a person's mind has to be ascertained, this may be inferred from his conduct and any other evidence throwing light on what he foresaw at the material time, including of course any explanation that he gives in evidence or in a statement put in evidence by the prosecution. It is no less elementary that all questions of weight are for the jury. The prosecution must prove the necessary contemplation beyond reasonable doubt, although that may be done by inference as just mentioned. If, at the end of the day and whether as a result of hearing evidence from the accused or for some other reason, the jury conclude that there is a reasonable possibility that the accused did not even contemplate the risk, he is in this type of case not guilty of murder or wounding with intent to cause serious bodily harm.

In some cases in this field it is enough to direct the jury by adapting to the circumstances the simple formula common in a number of jurisdictions. For instance, did the particular accused contemplate that in carrying out a common unlawful purpose one of his partners in the enterprise might use a knife or a loaded gun with the intention of causing really serious bodily harm?

The present was such a case. It is not necessary for the trial judge to say more on the subject than he did. He drew the jury's attention fully to the unsworn statements of each accused. He emphasised that if the jury were to conclude that it was reasonably possible that an accused had an intention less than the infliction of serious bodily injury on any occupant of the flat, or that he did not foresee that one of his colleagues was going to inflict injury of a serious bodily nature, then that accused did not have the necessary intent or foresight of consequences for murder. He told them that if Tse thought that the knives would be used to do no more than frighten the occupants, then he would be guilty not of murder but of manslaughter.

On the second count the judge went as far as to give as his opinion on the facts that it was very difficult to convict any of the accused, saying:

> you may well think it is unlikely that the thought ever occurred to any of the accused that one of their number would suddenly out of the blue gratuitously suggest that someone should slash down a woman who happened to be kneeling on the floor and who was offering no resistance.

The jury were entitled to and did take a different view of the facts. They were entitled to remember that disastrous violent action on the impulse of a moment of emergency is very apt to occur when intruders have weapons.

Further, the judge made it plain that it was for the jury to decide whether they accepted Madam Lam's evidence. And, as he said, if they did so then 'debt or no debt, the accused had no right to be in the deceased's premises displaying knives'. Evidently Tse did not claim in anything that he said to the police that he knew that knives were being taken but never thought that they would be used except to threaten. On the contrary, he denied all advance knowledge of the knives and being a party to any plan to take them. Once the jury accepted Madam Lam's evidence that all three accused drew knives as soon as they forced their way in, there was no evidential foundation for an argument that, if Tse foresaw the use of knives by the other two, it was only as a risk so remote that he disregarded it. No more elaborate direction was called for on the evidence in this case.

Where there is an evidential foundation for a remoteness issue, it may be necessary for the judge to give the jury more help. Although a risk of a killing or serious bodily harm has crossed the mind of a party to an unlawful enterprise, it is right to allow for a class of case in which the risk was so remote as not to make that party guilty of a murder or intentional causing of grievous bodily harm committed by a co-adventurer in the circumstances that in the event confronted the latter. But if the party accused knew that lethal weapons, such as a knife or a loaded gun, were to be carried on a criminal expedition, the defence should succeed only very rarely.

In cases where an issue of remoteness does arise it is for the jury (or other tribunal of fact) to decide whether the risk *as recognised by the accused* was sufficient to make him a party to the crime committed by the principal. Various formulae have been suggested – including a substantial risk, a real risk, a risk that something might well happen. No one formula is exclusively preferable; indeed it may be advantageous in a summing up to use more than one. For the question is not one of semantics. What has to be brought home to the jury is that occasionally a risk may have occurred to an accused's mind – fleetingly or even causing him some deliberation – but may genuinely have been dismissed by him as altogether negligible. If they think there is a reasonable possibility that the case is in that class, taking the risk should not make that accused a party to such a crime of intention as murder or wounding with intent to cause grievous bodily harm. The judge is entitled to warn the jury to be cautious before reaching that conclusion; but the law can do no more by way of definition; it can only be for the jury to determine any issue of that kind on the facts of the particular case ...

R v Slack [1989] QB 775 (CA)

Lord Lane CJ: ... The facts were as follows. In the early afternoon of 5 June 1987 the appellant and one Buick went to the home of a 78-year-old widow, Mrs Crowder, in Lincoln. She was tiny, 4 feet 9 inches in height, and frail. She wore a hearing aid. They believed she kept money in the flat, of which they intended to rob her.

The prosecution, so far as direct evidence was concerned, were largely dependent on what the appellant told the police. He did not go into the witness box. The appellant had said in interview that Buick told him to go and get the money while he, Buick, held Mrs Crowder, or that he was to stand outside until Buick shouted that the coast was clear when the appellant could come in and get the money.

The appellant heard a scuffle and heard Buick shout, 'Come on, she's down'. In went the appellant, and as he did so he saw Buick with his arm round Mrs Crowder's neck. He searched unsuccessfully, so he said, for the money, inquired about Mrs Crowder, to be told that she had passed out. Then, continued the appellant, 'she was beginning to come to ... He says to me to pass us a knife, I says what for, he says to threaten her with in case she comes round and starts screaming.'

He told the police how he then got a knife from the kitchen and gave it to Buick, who at this time was in the hallway with his arm round Mrs Crowder's neck as she lay on her back on the floor. He said that he didn't know Buick was going to use the knife on Mrs Crowder. He just 'thought he was going to use it in case she came to ... He just said he was going to threaten her.'

He told the police that after he had passed the knife, Buick had been sick and Buick's sweatshirt and hand were bloodstained. Eventually he had said to Buick that he was getting out of the flat. At that stage, according to the appellant, Buick said, 'hang on a minute'. So he, the appellant, left through the front door to be followed by Buick straight away. He said that he heard the woman moan and groan but when he got outside he said to Buick to phone the police up to check to see if she is all right, which he said he was going to do.

In fact all that was done was that they telephoned to the Fire Brigade to say that there was a gas leak at the address. They did this 'just for a laugh'. According to him he was later told that the police were looking for him 'in connection with a murder involving the cutting of someone's throat', although this fact had not been revealed by the police.

The circumstantial evidence painted a somewhat different picture. Mrs Crowder was found lying where she had been assaulted. Her throat had been cut as she lay there. There were blood splashes elsewhere. Buick had plainly been into the bedroom with the knife. The flat had been ransacked. Mrs Crowder's pension money, £39.50, which she had collected that morning, was missing, so were some partly consumed bottles of spirits. The men or one of them had taken the keys to the flat and had locked the door after them.

The pathologist was able to cast light on the cause of death. Mrs Crowder's assailant must have been behind her with his arm around her neck. Pressure from the arm had obstructed her air-passage and had broken the cartilage of her voice box. As she was dying, or probably just after she was dead, her throat was cut at least five times, the cuts extending from the angle of the jaw to the ear. Three ribs on the right-hand side and four on the left had been fractured, whilst she was still alive. At some stage whilst he was in the flat, as had been described by the appellant, Buick had vomited.

The prosecution submitted, *inter alia*, to the jury that the appellant could not fail to have seen these terrible injuries at least as he left the flat, and the fact that the two men remained together until Buick was arrested hours later was hard to explain except on the basis that the appellant had been party to the murder.

The appellant's case put forward by counsel was simply that although he was undoubtedly jointly guilty of robbery, he was in no way party to the murder.

[Counsel] submits on behalf of the appellant that the judge misdirected the jury as to the mental element which the prosecution must prove before the secondary participant in a joint enterprise can be convicted of murder, the actual killing having been done by the primary party ...

Some confusion has arisen as to the proper direction to be given to a jury in these circumstances. That seems to be partly due to some of the observations of the Judicial Committee of the Privy Council in *Chan Wing-Siu v The Queen* [1985] AC 168 ...

The Judicial Committee seems primarily to have been concerned with the problem posed by a conditional agreement, eg 'We do not want to kill or seriously injure, but if necessary we will.'

... A must be proved to have intended to kill or do serious harm at the time he killed. B may not be present at the killing: he may be a distance away, for example, waiting in the getaway car; he may be in another part of the house; he may not know that A has killed; he may have hoped, and probably did hope, that A would not kill or do serious injury. If however as part of their joint plan it was understood between them expressly or tacitly that if necessary one of them would kill or do serious harm as part of their common enterprise, then B is guilty of murder.

As appears from the cases we have cited, the direction may be in a variety of different forms. Provided that it is made clear to the jury that B, to be guilty, must be proved to have lent himself to a criminal enterprise involving the infliction, if necessary, of serious harm or death or to have had an express or tacit understanding with A that such harm or death should, if necessary, be inflicted, the precise form of words in which the jury are directed is not important. As Sir Robin Cooke observed in *Chan Wing-Siu v The Queen* [1985] AC 168 at 179C–D: 'No one formula is exclusively preferable; indeed it may be advantageous in a summing up to use more than one. For the question is not one of semantics.'

The principle was expressed authoritatively by the House of Lords in *R v Maxwell* [1978] 1 WLR 1350, to which reference has already been made. Maxwell was a subordinate member of a terrorist organisation in Northern Ireland. He was ordered to drive a vehicle to an inn. He knew that others who were following his lead car were armed and that they would make some terrorist attack, whether by guns, bombs or incendiary devices he did not know. In fact the others planted a bomb. He was held to have been rightly convicted of doing an act with intent to cause an explosion likely to endanger life, contrary to s 3(a) of the Explosive Substances Act 1883, and of an offence of being in possession of a bomb with like intent under s 3(b).

Sir Robert Lowry CJ, whose judgment in the Northern Ireland Court of Criminal Appeal was upheld by the House of Lords, said at 1374–75:

> The situation has something in common with that of two persons who agree to rob a bank on the understanding, either express or implied from conduct (such as the carrying of a loaded gun by one person with the knowledge of the other), that violence *may* be resorted to. The accomplice knows, not that the principal *will* shoot the cashier, but that he may do so; and, if the principal does shoot him, the accomplice will be guilty of murder. A different case is where the accomplice has only one offence, A, in contemplation and the principal commits offence B. Here the accomplice, although morally culpable (and perhaps guilty of conspiring to commit offence A), is not guilty of aiding and abetting offence B. The principle with which we are dealing does not seem to us to provide a warrant, on the basis of combating lawlessness generally, for convicting an alleged accomplice ... and only exceptionally would evidence be found to support the allegation that the accomplice had given the principal a completely blank cheque.

Lord Scarman having cited with approval that final sentence, went on, at 1362–63:

> The principle thus formulated has great merit. It directs attention to the state of mind of the accused – not what he ought to have in contemplation, but what he did have; it avoids definition and classification, while ensuring that a man will not be convicted of aiding and abetting any offence his principal may commit, but only one which is within his contemplation. He may have in contemplation only one offence, or several: and the several which he contemplates he may see as alternatives. An accessory who leaves it to his principal to choose is liable, provided always the choice is made from the range of offences from which the accessory contemplates the choice will be made.

In our judgment the second question posed by the judge in the instant case in his written directions to the jury was in accordance with the principles we have endeavoured to express. The question made it clear to the jury that the appellant must have at least tacitly agreed that, if necessary, serious harm should be done to Mrs Crowder, or that he lent himself to the infliction of such harm. There was ample evidence before the jury upon which they could come to the conclusion that the prosecution had satisfied them so as to feel sure upon these matters so far as the appellant was concerned ...

R v Hyde, Sussex and Collins [1991] 1 QB 134 (CA)

Lord Lane CJ: ... The incident resulting in the death of Gallagher took place outside the Merlin public house, Andover, at about 10.25 pm on 3 June 1988. There was no dispute that Gallagher sustained a violent blow to the forehead, consistent with a heavy kick from a shod foot, which crushed the front of his skull. He died

73 days later, having never regained consciousness. The prosecution case was that the three appellants carried out a joint attack on the victim and were all equally responsible for his death, even though it was not possible to say who had actually struck the fatal blow or blows; furthermore, that their situation had been to cause serious injury, or that each knew that such was the intention of the others when he took part.

By 10 pm that evening all three, who were regular customers at the Merlin public house, had probably had too much to drink. Sussex and Collins were both overheard making unspecific threatening remarks. When Gallagher left he was closely followed by Hyde and Sussex, and then Collins. Other customers, in the belief that serious trouble was about to break out, gathered on the balcony to watch events unfold.

Gallagher was accompanied by a man called Burkwood, who related how Hyde had said to Gallagher, 'Hey, feller, you've got a problem.' When Gallagher asked 'Why?' he was felled by a blow. Collins told Burkwood, 'Get out if you know what's good for you.' Burkwood was then knocked against a car, and when he recovered his breath he saw all three appellants round Gallagher (who was already on the ground) kicking him. Other witnesses saw Hyde kicking Gallagher's legs from under; Sussex punching Gallagher's head; Hyde kicking him between the legs, saying 'This is for Norma (or Nora),' and Collins running back for five yards as they left and kicking Gallagher on the head. Witnesses spoke of Hyde and Sussex going back into the public house with blood on their hands and clothes. It was said that they looked pleased with themselves, and later that evening Hyde told someone, 'It was a favour for a friend.' Collins told a friend of his the following day that he had kicked Gallagher twice ...

All three gave evidence before the jury denying that there was any joint enterprise or any intent to do serious harm to Gallagher. Hyde and Sussex said each had acted on his own with no intention beyond a simple assault. Collins, according to them, was responsible for the fatal blow. His actions and intention were nothing to do with them, nor did they foresee what he might intend to do. Collins for his part maintained that there was no joint attack or, if there was, it involved only Hyde and Sussex. The jury, it was submitted, could not be sure whose act caused the death, and that therefore no one should be convicted as the killer ...

Before us the primary ground advanced by counsel was the contention that the judge misdirected the jury on the law of joint enterprise. The passages in the summing up of which complaint is made are these:

> As I say, ordinarily speaking, if he does something which is beyond the scope of the agreement, that is as you might say the end of the agreement. But, what if the others anticipated that he might do some such thing – and here we have to apply common sense. Fights do get out of hand and escalate. A man who starts by punching may get excited and decide to kick. If there was a tacit agreement to punch and kick, a man who is kicking may decide to give a kick like that which was allegedly given by Collins and which has been described as a place kick or a penalty kick, a description which if the basic facts are right is not a bad description of the kick. If either of the other two, and you have to consider the case of each of them separately, foresaw and contemplated a real possibility that one of his fellows might in the excitement of the moment go beyond the actual plan and intend to do and do grievous bodily harm, then you have to consider whether that man, the one who had the foresight, did not in truth intend that result himself.

The judge then went on to explain to the jury the distinction which may, in some cases, exist between what a man desires should happen and what a man intends should happen. He explained to the jury that foresight that something will happen is not necessarily the same as an intention that it should happen, though it may be powerful evidence of such intention. The judge concluded this part of his summing up with the following words:

> We may summarise it shortly by saying that if all three intended to do grievous bodily harm, then that is that, they are all guilty of murder. If they did not, but one of them decided to do it, then if either of the others can be shown to have had the same intention, in as much as he foresaw the real possibility that that might be the result of the fight which he was putting in train, then he too shares in the responsibility as in common sense he must.

The judgment of this court in *R v Slack* [1989] QB 775 was not delivered until some four months after the conclusion of the hearing of the instant case. Consequently the judge here did not have before him the distinction which we endeavoured to draw in *Slack's* case between the mental element required to be proved *vis-à-vis* the secondary party (hereinafter called 'B') and that required in the case of the principal party, the actual killer (hereinafter called 'A'). In the passages we have cited from the summing up of which complaint is made, the judge was endeavouring to apply the principles which were, prior to *Slack's* case, thought to apply to cases of joint enterprise. The question is whether the directions in the present case were sufficient to comply with the law as it now stands.

There are, broadly speaking, two main types of joint enterprise cases where death results to the victim. The first is where the primary object of the participants is to do some kind of physical injury to the victim. The second is where the primary object is not to cause physical injury to any victim but, for example, to commit burglary. The victim is assaulted and killed as a possibly unwelcome incident of the burglary. The latter type of case may pose more complicated questions than the former, but the principle in each is the same. A must be proved to have intended to kill or to do serious bodily harm at the time he killed. As was pointed out in *R v Slack* [1989] QB 775 at 781, B, to be guilty, must be proved to have lent himself to a criminal enterprise involving the infliction of serious harm or death, or to have had an express or tacit understanding with A that such harm or death should, if necessary, be inflicted.

We were there endeavouring, respectfully, to follow the principles enunciated by Sir Robin Cooke in *Chan Wing-Siu v The Queen* [1985] AC 168 at 175:

> The case must depend rather on the wider principle whereby a secondary party is criminally liable for acts by the primary offender of a type which the former foresees but does not necessarily intend. That there is such a principle is not in doubt. It turns on contemplation or, putting the same idea in other words, authorisation, which may be express but is more usually implied. It meets the case of a crime foreseen as a possible incident of the common unlawful enterprise. The criminal culpability lies in participating in the venture with that foresight.

It has been pointed out by Professor J C Smith, in his commentary on *R v Wakely* [1990] Crim LR 119 at 120–21, that in the judgments in *R v Slack* [1989] QB 775 and also in *R v Wakely* [1990] Crim LR 119 itself, to both of which I was a party, insufficient attention was paid by the court to the distinction between on the one hand tacit agreement by B that A should use violence, and on the other hand a realisation by B that A, the principal party, may use violence despite B's refusal to authorise or agree to its use. Indeed in *R v Wakely* we went so far as to say:

> The suggestion that a mere foresight of the real or definite possibility of violence being used is sufficient to constitute the mental element of murder is *prima facie*, academically speaking at least, not sufficient.

On reconsideration, that passage is not in accordance with the principles set out by Sir Robin Cooke which we were endeavouring to follow and was wrong, or at least misleading. If B realises (without agreeing to such conduct being used) that A may kill or intentionally inflict serious injury, but nevertheless continues to participate with A in the venture, that will amount to a sufficient mental element for B to be guilty of murder if A, with the requisite intent, kills in the course of the venture. As Professor Smith points out, B has in those circumstances lent himself to the enterprise and by so doing he has given assistance and encouragement to A in carrying out an enterprise which B realises may involve murder.

That being the case it seems to us that the judge was correct when he directed the jury in the terms of those passages of the summing up which we have already quoted ...

R v O'Brien [1995] 2 Cr App R 649 (CA)

Glidewell LJ: ... On the night of Saturday/Sunday 6/7 June 1992 PC Alexander Kelly and SC Glenn Goodman were on patrol duty in the Tadcaster area of North Yorkshire in a police car. At about 3 am they saw a red Ford Sierra car which moved off quickly when the police car appeared. They followed the Sierra car to the slip road leading from the Tadcaster road onto the A64 Leeds-York road. At that point PC Kelly signalled for the Sierra to stop, which it did. PC Kelly went to the side of the car. The appellant was driving the Sierra, and Magee was sitting in the front passenger seat. Neither gave any sensible explanation of what they were doing in the area. In particular they said that they had been to a public house which the police officers soon established did not exist. The appellant gave a false name and address.

Throughout those enquiries, which lasted some 25 minutes, Magee remained seated in the Sierra car. At the end of that time Magee got out of the Sierra, walked towards SC Goodman who was standing beside the police car and shot him twice in the chest with a 0.45 pistol. SC Goodman later died from his wounds. Magee then turned and pointed the gun at PC Kelly who was sitting in the police car, and fired two shots at him through the windscreen of the car. PC Kelly fell sideways onto the passenger seat, and Magee then came to the driver's side and fired four or five further shots at PC Kelly, two or three from the 0.45 and two others from a second revolver, a 0.38. Despite being hit by four bullets PC Kelly survived. He identified Magee as the man who had fired at him. He was unable to identify the appellant, but there was a fingerprint of the appellant on a police form in the car, and in any case the appellant admitted being the driver of the Sierra. PC Kelly did not see the appellant do anything to assist or to encourage Magee to murder Goodman or to attempt to murder himself.

Magee and the appellant then got back into the Sierra and drove off, the appellant again driving the car. Despite his injuries PC Kelly had managed to send an SOS message to his control room. Two different police cars took up the pursuit of the Sierra, which turned onto the A1. In one of them, a Peugeot, the driver was PC Whitehouse accompanied by WPC Larkin. About 4 am, which was about 10 minutes after the Sierra had driven away from PC Kelly's car, PCs Whitehouse and Larkin saw a red Ford Orion car approaching them on the road from the village of Burton Salmon. They stopped this car and started to question the five occupants. Hardly had they started doing so when they saw the red Sierra approaching.

The Sierra passed very close to the police car, but avoided collision. The police officers, realising that this was the car that they should be investigating, immediately followed it. A short distance further away, the Sierra stopped at another road junction and the police car pulled up 15–20 feet behind it. Magee got out of the passenger side of the Sierra holding a Kalashnikov rifle. Magee took slow, deliberate aim at the Peugeot and fired a single shot which hit the front of the vehicle. PC Whitehouse immediately put the police car into reverse and pushed WPC Larkin down into the footwell. He saw Magee starting to run towards the Peugeot and that the Sierra was also reversing. He then heard a continuous burst of further shots from the rifle, some of which struck the road surface and some the front of the car on the driver's side. A single shot hit the windscreen of the Peugeot which reversed into a fence and came to a halt. Whitehouse then clambered out of the car and went to assist WPC Larkin. During this time, although Whitehouse was a target, Magee did not fire any further shots from the rifle but instead returned to the Sierra which again drove away. At this point the red Ford Orion came on the scene, despite the fact that the police officers had told the occupants that the men in the Sierra were armed. The occupants of the Orion assisted the two police officers.

The Sierra was driven to a nearby wood where it was set on fire and burned out.

The appellants and Magee abandoned the car and went into hiding, living rough for four days. On 11 June 1992 they were both arrested within a few hours of each other in Pontefract. At that time neither of them was armed. Save that O'Brien admitted being the driver of the Sierra, neither he nor Magee said anything at interview.

... At the trial neither Magee nor the appellant gave evidence, nor was any other evidence called on their behalf ...

We now consider the first ground of appeal. Throughout the trial, the place at which the offences in counts 1 and 2 took place was described as scene 1, and the scene of counts 3 and 4 as scene 2. In his summing up, Laws J directed the jury that before they could convict the appellant on either counts 3 or 4, they had to be sure, first, that Magee intended to kill when he fired the Kalashnikov; second, that the appellant knew when he stopped the Sierra car at scene 2 that Magee might shoot to kill; and third, that with such knowledge, he assisted Magee by stopping to allow him to get out of the Sierra and thereafter reversing the car towards the police car. As to count 5, the judge said:

> ... if you are sure that the driver knew that his companion had the rifle and intended if the occasion arose to use it in a manner which would endanger the life of another or others, and with that knowledge assisted him in the way I have described for the purposes of counts 3 and 4 he would be as guilty as his passenger on count 5.

There was a major issue at the trial, based on the evidence of the firearms expert called by the prosecution and on the fact that when PC Whitehouse had got out of his car and was an open target Magee made no further attempt to shoot at him, whether the jury could be sure that at scene 2 Magee did shoot with the intention of killing. By their verdicts in relation to Magee, the jury must have been sure that he did intend to kill both the officers at scene 2. There was clear evidence which entitled the jury to find as a fact that this appellant stopped the Sierra to allow Magee to get out, and then reversed the car. Thus if the third part of the judge's direction to the jury on this part of the case, that is that before they could convict O'Brien they had to be sure that he knew when he stopped the car that Magee might shoot to kill, was a correct direction in law, the judge was in our view correct in rejecting the submission of no case to answer. The correctness of the judge's direction on that third point is the subject of the second ground of appeal, to which Mr Mansfield directed his main argument. We now therefore turn to consider this ground ...

The second ground of appeal is that, if O'Brien were to be found guilty of attempted murder, whether as a participant in a joint enterprise with Magee or as aider and abettor of Magee, the jury had to find that he knew before the firing of the shots by Magee at scene 2 that Magee did intend to kill. In other words, O'Brien was only guilty if he knew that Magee *would* shoot to kill, not that he *might* do so.

We have been referred to a number of recent authorities concerning the state of mind which a secondary party, who does not himself commit the fatal act, must have if he is to be found guilty of murder.

These authorities were all appeals in cases of joint enterprise, but Mr Mansfield QC agrees that the same principle applies equally to an aider and abettor.

The first of these decisions was *Chan Wing-Siu v R* [1985] AC 168, a decision of the Privy Council. A passage from the judgment of the Board in that case, delivered by Sir Robin Cooke at p 121 and p 175 respectively, was approved and adopted in the judgments of this court in *Ward* (1987) 85 Cr App R 71, and *Slack* [1989] 775 QB 775, and quoted and approved in *Hyde* [1991] 1 QB 134 ...

The passage from the judgment of Sir Robin Cooke in *Chan Wing-Siu* and its adoption in *Hyde* were referred to with approval in the most recent decision, that of the Privy Council in *Hui Chi-Ming v R* [1992] 1 AC 34.

Mr Mansfield QC submits that, though this is the test to establish guilt of a person who aids and abets, or is party to a joint enterprise which results in a murder, the same test does not suffice for attempted murder. He argues that since the intention of the principal in attempted murder must be to kill, so a secondary party is only guilty if he knows that the principal does intend to kill – in the judge's phrase in this case, that he 'will shoot to kill'.

We do not follow the logic of this argument. The jury clearly found that O'Brien knowing that Magee had the rifle assisted him by stopping the car at scene 2 and thereafter reversing it. If, following the judge's direction, they concluded that O'Brien knew that Magee might shoot to kill and if he had actually killed PC Whitehouse or WPC Larkin, on the authorities to which we have referred O'Brien would have been guilty of murder. There is in our judgment no logical reason why the same knowledge should not make him guilty of an attempt to commit that offence. We therefore reject Mr Mansfield's argument on the second and principal ground of appeal.

R v Powell and Daniels [1996] 1 Cr App R 14 (CA)

Lord Taylor CJ: ... It was the Crown's case that the appellants, together with another man, called at the deceased's home in South London. Seconds after he had answered his doorbell, one of the group shot the deceased at point-blank range and he died a short while later. It was alleged this was a joint enterprise.

Rachel Hickey gave evidence that on Saturday 29 May 1993, she was asked on the telephone by the appellant, Daniels to give him a lift. She agreed and went in a van provided by her employer. She collected the two appellants and the third man known as 'Mikey' who was not brought to justice. She was instructed to drive to Daniels' home where the three men got out. They returned a few minutes later, Daniels carrying a plastic bag. She was then asked to drive back to Upper Norwood where again the three men got out of the van. Hickey said she did not see where they went. They in fact went to some stairs leading to the first floor of a block of flats where the deceased, David Edwards, lived alone. He was apparently a small-time dealer in drugs frequently supplying cannabis. On this night, four of his friends were at his home when the appellants and 'Mikey' arrived there at about 11.20 pm. One or more of the group of three knocked at the door. Seconds after the deceased opened it, he was shot in the chest. There was evidence from his friends in the flat and from neighbours that they heard the bang just after the door was opened. Lisa Steel, who lived nearby, also heard the bang from the gun. Looking out of her window she saw three black men running along the pathway towards Hickey's van. They ran one after the other, the middle man being the tallest and the other two of similar height. She said the tallest was carrying in one hand, horizontally, what she thought was an iron bar. She helped in the creation of a photofit of the tallest of the three. Later she attended an identification parade at which both appellants appeared but she did not pick out either of them.

Shortly after dropping the three men off, Hickey also heard the bang. All three of the men returned to the van and shouted at her to get out of the area. Daniels got into the front passenger seat, Powell and 'Mikey' in the back. According to Hickey, Daniels shouted at Powell: 'You should not have gone up there and done that.' He was, she said, 'going mad at Powell'. The latter responded merely by complaining about the blood on his clothes and at no time ventured any denial. At the end of the journey Hickey found a gun in the passenger footwell where Daniels had been sitting. The plastic bag, now empty, was also on the floor. She was told to dispose of the gun and took it into her flat. Next day, she cleaned out the van and found blood on the carpet in the back. In cross-examination she agreed that she was devoted to Daniels and disliked Powell. She pleaded guilty to doing an act in relation to the gun intended to pervert the course of justice.

In interview, both appellants exercised their right to remain silent. Daniels did not give evidence or call any evidence at the trial. Powell did testify. He said he had been introduced to 'Mikey' for the first time that evening. The three men had arranged to go to Norwood to buy some cannabis from a man known to the other two but not to him. They drove first to the home of Daniels who went inside and returned with something in a plastic bag. Although when they got to a block of flats all three got out of the van, he, Powell, did not go to the deceased's front door. He was present at the scene purely to purchase cannabis. He never saw a gun or knew anything about it until after it was fired. He claimed that as the three ran away Daniels was in the lead, 'Mikey' was in the middle and he was at the back. He denied that there was any blood on this clothing and in that he was supported by evidence from his father's girlfriend who did his laundry and said there was no blood on any garment of his which she handled.

... [B]efore the recorder summed up, there was legal argument as to the appropriate direction on *mens rea* in relation to a secondary party on a charge of murder. After conflicting submissions inviting him to sum up in accordance with two different lines of authority, the learned recorder directed the jury as follows:

> If you are satisfied on the evidence as to the identity of that person – the one who fired – you may consider that he has no defence to the charge of murder. Whoever he was he was not alone. Two other men were with him the whole or part of the relevant time. About them the law says this: where two or more persons embark on a joint criminal enterprise, each is liable for the acts done in pursuance of that joint enterprise, and that includes liability for unusual consequences if they arise from the execution of the joint enterprise, but if one of the adventurers goes beyond what has been tacitly agreed as part of the common enterprise, his co-adventurer is not liable for

> the consequences of the unauthorised act. It is for you to decide whether what was done was part of the joint enterprise or went beyond it and was, in fact, an act unauthorised by the joint enterprise.
>
> I referred to a tacit agreement because you may consider that is the commonest situation, and may be it is the one here. There is no evidence about an express agreement other than one to purchase cannabis.
>
> The law goes further and adds this: if B or C realised, without agreeing to such conduct being used, that A may kill or intentionally inflict serious injury and they nevertheless continue to participate with A in the venture, that will amount to a sufficient mental element for B or C to be guilty of murder if A with the requisite intent kills in the course of the venture. In those circumstances B and C have lent themselves to the enterprise and by so doing have given assistance and encouragement to A in carrying out an enterprise which they realised may involve murder.

That direction is in accordance with the line of authority starting with *Chan Wing-Siu v R* [1985] AC 168, and, as one would expect from the recorder, is expressed with total clarity. Mr Feinberg QC accepts that the preponderance of authorities and in particular the more recent cases, have followed that line. He also conceded that he could not in principle distinguish the present case from *Chan Wing-Siu*. Nevertheless, supported by Mr Wolkind for Daniels, he submits that the recorder was wrong and should have followed the other line of authority to which we will later refer ...

Hyde [1991] 1 QB 134 was another case in which three appellants had attacked the deceased and it was impossible to determine who struck the fatal blow. Lord Lane CJ was at pains to follow the principles stated in *Chan Wing-Siu*. At 139 he corrected what he had said in *Slack* [1988] 1 QB 775, and went on as follows:

> On reconsideration, that passage is not in accordance with the principles set out by Sir Robin Cooke which were endeavouring to follow and was wrong, or at least misleading. If B realises (without agreeing to such conduct being used) that A may kill or intentionally inflict serious injury, but nevertheless continues to participate with A in the venture, that will amount to a sufficient mental element for B to be guilty of murder if A with the requisite intent, kills in the course of the venture. As Professor Smith points out, B has in those circumstances lent himself to the enterprise and by so doing he has given assistance and encouragement to A in carrying out an enterprise which B realises may involve murder.

The learned recorder's direction in the present case followed that formulation almost verbatim. It is sufficient, without lengthening this judgment unnecessarily, to say that Lord Lane's formulation was approved and followed in *Hui Chi-Ming v R* [1992] 1 AC 34, 51C, in *Roberts* (1993) 96 Cr App R 291, 297, in *Rook* (1993) 97 Cr App R 327, 331, in *Day* (December 1994) at p 6 of the transcript, and most recently in *O'Brien* [1995] 2 Cr App R 649.

Mr Feinberg contends that these cases are all wrong in that they equate foresight with intent. He submits that to prove a charge of murder, whether against the principal actor or a secondary party, the prosecution must establish an intent to kill or to cause grievous bodily harm. He relies principally upon *R v Maloney* [1985] AC 905; *R v Hancock and Shankland* [1986] AC 455, and *Nedrick* (1986) 83 Cr App R 267. The first two of those cases were House of Lords' decisions. However, it must be stressed that in all three cases the appellants had been the principal actors who had committed in each case the *actus reus*. They were not secondary parties in a joint enterprise.

Mr Feinberg relies especially on a passage in the speech of Lord Scarman in *Hancock and Shankland* at 471 where, referring to *Maloney* he said:

> Second, the House made it absolutely clear that foresight of consequences is no more than evidence of the existence of the intent; it must be considered, and its weight assessed, together with all the evidence in the case. Foresight does not necessarily imply the existence of intention, though it may be a fact from which, when considered with all the other evidence, a jury may think it right to infer the necessary intent.

The decisions in those cases were considered by this court in *Ward* (1987) 85 Cr App R 71 which, by contrast, was a case of joint enterprise. Lord Lane CJ at 76 said:

> The second ground of appeal reads as follows: 'The learned judge misdirected the jury in relation to the joint enterprise, wrongly directing that one is responsible for the acts of another if the one contemplates and foresees the acts of the other as a possible part or result of a planned joint enterprise.'
>
> It is submitted by Mr Steer in regard to that ground of appeal that the decisions of the House of Lords in *R v Maloney* and *R v Hancock* have had the effect of completely altering the law relating to joint enterprise ... No man, he submits, can be convicted of murder unless it is specifically decided against him that he had a murderous intent and that could only be decided against him if the judge directed the jury that that was what they had to find.
>
> Each member of this court is bound to confess that he was unable to understand the submission. It is enough to say that we do not consider that the cases of *R v Maloney* and *R v Hancock* have had any effect at all upon the well-known and well-established principles of joint enterprise: in short, the principles set out in *Anderson and Morris* [1966] 2 QB 110, still hold good.

The first paragraph of the learned recorder's summing up in the present case, quoted above, accurately stated the principle set out in *Anderson and Morris*. After referring to *Chan Wing-Siu*, Lord Lane went on in *Ward* at 77 as follows:

> It was suggested by Mr Steer that the decision in that case, which came from Hong Kong, is not in accordance with the decisions of the House of Lords in *R v Maloney* and *R v Hancock*. We disagree. We think that what appears in that case, if we may say so respectfully, is good law ...

Reliance is also placed upon half a sentence in the judgment of Lawton LJ in *Reid* (1976) 62 Cr App R 109. In that case the appellant had accompanied two others who were convicted of murdering a colonel at his home by shooting him. The appellant was convicted only of manslaughter. His defence was that he was a mere spectator who had gone to see if the other two would actually carry out what they said they intended, namely to kill the colonel. At 112, after referring to *Anderson and Morris (above)*, Lawton LJ said:

> When two or more men go out together in joint possession of offensive weapons such as revolvers and knives and the circumstances are such as to justify an inference that the very least they intend to do with them is to use them to cause fear in another, there is, in our judgment, always a likelihood that, in the excitement and tensions of the occasion, one of them will use his weapon in some way which will cause death or serious injury. <u>If such injury was not intended by the others, they must be acquitted of murder</u>; but having started out on an enterprise which envisaged some degree of violence, albeit nothing more than causing fright, they will be guilty of manslaughter.

It is the underlined passage 'If such injury was not intended by the others, they must be acquitted of murder' which is relied upon. In so far as it should be construed as in conflict with the preponderant line of authority reviewed above, we do not think it can prevail. It was, in any event, *obiter* since no question arose of whether *Reid* was guilty of murder. Furthermore, the formulation in *Hyde* involved, as Professor Smith points out, an intention or agreement by the secondary party to participate in a joint enterprise which he realises may involve murder by another participant. There is a distinction between the manslaughter situation identified by Lawton LJ and murder of the basis of the *Hyde* formulation. The former does not involve a realisation by the accused that his co-participant may commit murder. It depends upon an objective likelihood that 'in the excitement and tensions of the occasion' death may result. The *Hyde* formulation requires subjective realisation by the accused that his co-participant may commit murder and, notwithstanding that, his agreement to participate himself.

The strongest support for Mr Feinberg's proposition is to be found in the judgment of Russell LJ in *Smith* [1988] Crim LR 616. Unlike *Maloney*, *Hancock* and *Nedrick* this was a case of joint enterprise. The appellant had been convicted of causing grievous bodily harm with intent, arising from a fight in which he and two others were alleged to have kicked the victim on the ground. The trial judge summed up in accordance with *Chan Wing-Siu*. In allowing the appeal, Russell LJ referred to *R v Maloney* and *R v Hancock*. It does not seem, however, that *Ward* was drawn to the court's attention and although there was passing reference to *Chan Wing-Siu*, *Hyde* and the other cases cited above had not yet been decided. Russell LJ said at 13 of the transcript:

> We have to observe that it is a thousand pities in the instant case that at no stage in the summing up did the learned judge make it plain to the jury that the foresight, to which he repeatedly drew the jury's attention, was not of itself to be regarded as an intent, though it could properly be regarded as evidence and powerful evidence, supporting the existence of the intent necessary to establish the offence with which this appellant was charged.

As a matter of principle, it has been strongly argued that there is an anomaly in requiring proof against a secondary party only of a lesser *mens rea* than needs to be provided against the principal who commits the *actus reus*. This was taken up by the Law Commission in their Consultation Paper No 131 entitled 'Assisting and Encouraging Crime'. The paper states at 63:

> First, it is one thing to think that a person should be guilty of murder if he engages in an unlawful enterprise and foresees that his co-adventurer may intentionally kill, but rather different to convict such a person of murder when he merely foresees that his co-adventurer may intentionally inflict serious injury. Second, it is anomalous that in such a case the law now requires a less blameworthy mental standard for the non-acting co-adventurer than for the person who actually commits the murderous act.

Despite those observations, we feel bound to follow and apply the *Hyde* formulation having regard to the approval which it has received in a number of decisions in this court and to the fact that it is in accordance with the House of Lords' decision in *Maxwell*. If the result is an unacceptable anomaly, it must now be for the House of Lords or the legislature to say so. Accordingly, the first ground of appeal fails.

By way of subsidiary argument, it is contended that the recorder failed (to use Mr Feinberg's phrase) 'to quantify the risk' of his co-adventurer committing murder. The defendant would have to realise the risk and not just have a fleeting thought which he dismisses. This point was mentioned by Sir Robin Cooke in *Chan Wing-Siu*. Again, how grave a risk would the appellant have to foresee? A real risk, a substantial risk? This was a matter also raised by Sir Robin Cooke. However, we are satisfied that, following *dicta* in *Roberts* (1993) 96 Cr App R 291, 298, in a passage based upon Lord Lane's judgment in *Hyde* and approved by this court in *Day*, the recorder's direction – 'realised, without agreeing to such conduct being used, that A may kill or intentionally inflict serious injury' – was correct and sufficient for the purposes of this case ...

R v Dunbar and Others [1988] Crim LR 693 (CA)

Facts: The appellant was convicted of manslaughter. Her co-defendants were convicted of murder. It was the prosecution case that the appellant had incited her co-defendants to murder her former lover. The victim died after being hit on the head with a metal bar; the cause of death was asphyxiation when the metal bar used to garotte her with such force that her voice box was shattered. The appellant denied inciting murder; she admitted that she may have expressed a wish to see the victim dead but claimed that was rambling associated with drink and drugs. She had suspected that the co-defendants planned to burgle the victim's flat and that in the course of the burglary some violence might be done to her former lover. The appellant appealed against conviction on the ground that the verdict of manslaughter was not open to the jury.

Held, allowing the appeal and quashing the conviction, the jury's verdict must have been reached upon the basis that while the appellant contemplated the use of some unlawful violence, short of the infliction of grievous bodily harm, one or other or both of her co-defendants must have gone beyond the scope of that design and used the extreme violence which was intended to cause grievous bodily harm or death. The judge's direction in the appellant's case did not deal with that situation [or with] the appropriate verdict of not guilty should the jury find the second and/or third defendant went beyond what was contemplated by the appellant. On the facts of the case there were only two verdicts open to the jury, guilty or not guilty of murder. If, as the Crown contended, she was a party to an agreement to kill, she was guilty of murder. If she was a party to an agreement to inflict some harm, short of grievous bodily harm, then she was guilty of neither murder nor manslaughter. The victim's killing and the manner of the killing could not be within the ambit of the agreement to which the appellant was a party, if the ambit was confined on her part to an intention that only some harm should befall the deceased albeit not death or really serious injury. The issues involved could not be distinguished from those adumbrated by Widgery LJ in *Lovesey and Peterson* (1969) 53 Cr App R 461. The judge failed to remind the jury of the law as laid down in *Anderson and Morris* (1966) 50 Cr App R 216 and followed in *Lovesey and Peterson* (1969) 53 Cr App R 461. The result of that non-direction was that the jury returned a verdict which was not open to them.

R v Roberts [1993] 1 All ER 583 (CA)

Lord Taylor of Gosforth CJ: ... On 4 August 1990 John Davies, a 69-year-old recluse, was robbed and beaten to death at his home near Merthyr Tydfil. The case for the Crown was that the appellant and Gray were jointly responsible for his murder. For their part the appellant and Gray blamed one another.

John Davies lived mainly on his pension, but he had some £300 left from a Criminal Injuries Compensation Board award, which he kept in a building society. As a result of the attack upon him which gave rise to that award, he kept an axe by his chair for self-protection.

The appellant was 5 ft 2 ins, weighed only 8 stone 5 lb and was 39 at the time of the killing. The co-accused, Gray, was 49 and a much bigger man. The accused knew one another, but were not friends. Gray knew the victim slightly, but the appellant did not.

Gray spent the day of the murder drinking. The appellant, who lived in Swansea, had left his wife the day before the killing and had hitchhiked to Merthyr Tydfil. He had lost all his money in a betting shop and bumped into Gray by chance in the street on 4 August. They went for a drink at a rugby club and from there set off for the victim's home. Each suggested in evidence that it was the other's idea. The appellant admitted he knew they were going to rob an old man.

Gray's account was that the appellant went into the victim's house first to collect some money which the victim gave to him. Gray thought this was consensual but, as the two men were walking out, the victim made a grab for Gray, who fell to the ground. As he was trying to fend the victim off, he claimed to have seen the appellant hit the victim on the back of the head with a shovel. The appellant then, according to Gray, struck the victim again with the shovel on the front of the head knocking him to the ground. By the time Gray got up the appellant had gone.

The police interviewed the appellant three times and he gave evidence at the trial. By contrast to Gray's account, in his first interview the appellant initially said that he had followed Gray into the house. Gray had demanded money in a menacing way. The victim had picked up an axe, there was a struggle between Gray and the victim and the appellant ran away. Eventually he admitted that he had returned and there had been a struggle between the victim and Gray in the yard during which he, the appellant, had pulled the victim off Gray and had seen Gray hit the victim repeatedly with an axe. The appellant denied that he had ever struck the victim.

In his second interview the appellant admitted taking the victim's wallet, which had fallen to the floor in the course of the struggle with Gray. This formed the basis of the appellant's plea of guilty to robbery. He also admitted that he was prepared to contemplate the use of violence when he and Gray went to the house although not to the extent of killing the victim. In both the second and third interviews the appellant reiterated that only Gray had used violence and his own role had been confined to pulling the victim off Gray.

In evidence the appellant gave substantially the same account, repeating that only Gray had struck the victim. He admitted that he had contemplated there might be some violence when they went to the victim's house. He gave inconsistent answers as to the degree of violence he foresaw, but twice said that he foresaw the risk of really serious injury ...

[Counsel for the appellant] submits that, in the circumstances of the present case, the learned judge's directions were incorrect, or at least insufficient. This was not a case in which the object of the joint venture was to assault the victim; not was it a case in which lethal weapons or indeed any weapons were being carried. In those circumstances [counsel] argues that it was wrong or insufficient for the judge to identify the degree of foresight required to be proved against the appellant as merely that Gray 'may' or 'might' intentionally kill or inflict really serious injury. She submits he should have emphasised that the requisite foresight to be proved against the appellant must be that such an intentional killing or infliction of really serious injury by Gray was a 'real' or 'substantial' or 'serious' possibility ...

In our judgment the principle stated by Lord Lane CJ in *R v Hyde* is of general application, whether weapons are carried or not and (as Lord Lane CJ expressly said) whether the object of the enterprise be to cause physical injury or to do some other unlawful act, eg burglary or robbery. True, it will be easier for the Crown to prove that B participated in the venture realising that A might wound with murderous intent if weapons are carried or if the object is to attack the victim or both. But that is purely an evidential difference, not a difference in principle.

With regard to the passage relied upon in *Chan Wing-Siu v R* we are doubtful whether the defendant B, who fleetingly thinks of the risk of A using violence with murderous intent in the course of a joint enterprise only to dismiss it from his mind and go on to lend himself to the venture, can truly be said, at the time when he so lends himself, to 'foresee' or 'realise' that A might commit murder. In such a case B can hardly have such foresight or realisation at the time he lends himself to the venture because he has banished the risk from his mind. The words 'realise' and 'realisation' used by Lord Lane CJ and by the trial judge here aptly described the test, because to realise something may happen is surely to contemplate it as a real, not fanciful, possibility. Accordingly, we are inclined to the view that seeking to distinguish between a fleeting but rejected consideration of a risk and a continuing realisation of a real risk will, in most cases, be unnecessary. It would also overcomplicate directions to juries and possibly lead to confusion.

However, even accepting that it may be necessary or desirable in some cases, due to possible remoteness of the risk, for the judge to give the jury more help, we do not think the present case fell into that category. This was not, to take an extreme example, a case of burglars entering in the erroneous belief that the householder was on holiday and one of them encountering and killing the householder. Here, the appellant knew the plan was to rob an old man in his cottage. He consistently conceded in evidence that he knew the victim was unlikely to yield up his money or goods without resistance. The nub of the case was therefore not whether the appellant realised force might be used but whether he realised only that some physical harm might be done or that really serious injury might be inflicted. As to that, the learned judge gave the clearest possible directions of law to the jury both at the beginning of his summing up and after their question ...

R v Wan and Chan [1995] Crim LR 296 (CA)

Facts: The appellants were convicted of aiding and abetting, counselling or procuring, persons unknown unlawfully and maliciously to inflict grievous bodily harm (count 2). They were acquitted of aiding and abetting, counselling or procuring the causing of grievous bodily harm with intent to do grievous bodily harm (count 1). The prosecution case was that the appellants believed that the victim had stolen Chan's Rolex watch and arranged for her to be beaten up. The appellants denied having anything to do with the beating. The appellants appealed against conviction, submitting, *inter alia*, that either the appellants had the intention that grievous bodily harm be caused to the victim, and should have been convicted of count 1, or they did not and should not have been convicted on count 2. If the prosecution had wanted an alternative to count 1 to cover a situation where the jury were not satisfied that the appellants intended that more than superficial injuries should be caused to the victim, the proper alternative charge would have been one of inciting an assault.

Held, allowing the appeal and quashing the convictions, applying *Dunbar* [1988] Crim LR 693 the court concluded that on the prosecution evidence there was no doubt but that the assailants intended to cause grievous bodily harm and to acquit on count 1 the jury must have decided that the attackers may have gone beyond the scope of what the appellants had asked them to do. The judge did not direct the jury on the basis that the appellants need only have foreseen that the infliction of grievous bodily harm by the attackers was a substantial risk and the court could not assume that the jury could convict on count 2 on that basis.

R v Perman [1996] 1 Cr App R 24 (CA)

Roch LJ: ... The jury were concerned with events which occurred on 22 February 1993 at a newsagent's shop in Hammersmith. Both the appellant and his co-defendant lived in that part of London. The evidence indicated that on that evening the co-defendant had taken drugs and alcohol. He was carrying a loaded single-barrelled 12-bore shotgun, the barrel of which had been cut down to just under 11 inches and the stock of which had been shortened to resemble a pistol grip. The appellant had taken two Valium tablets that evening which had been given him by his co-defendant. The appellant knew the co-defendant had a gun when he and the co-defendant left the appellant's home some time after 5 pm. They went to a public house at which it would seem the co-defendant took heroin and where they both drank alcohol. From there they went into a shop in King Street owned by a Mr Kumar so that the co-defendant could buy cigarettes. In that shop the appellant had taken a Cadbury's cream egg without paying for it. Mr Kumar saw him do that and became angry, and the co-defendant told the appellant to put the egg back as Mr Kumar's shop was the place where his family shopped. The co-defendant apologised to Mr Kumar for the appellant's behaviour.

From Mr Kumar's shop they walked some distance, deciding to go to an off-licence in Goldhawk Road to buy some beer. That off-licence was chosen because the appellant knew that he would be served although he was under age. Before reaching there, the co-defendant and the appellant entered the newsagent's shop of a Cyril Fernando in which the co-defendant produced his gun and threatened people in the shop with it. The co-defendant took the money from the till, both notes and coins. Cigarettes were handed over. At some point Mr Cyril Fernando, his wife and his brother, Luigi, and Luigi's wife were able to leave the shop through a rear storeroom, leaving in the shop a man called Nath Banda, who was there waiting for the Fernando family to close their shop because he, Nath Banda, was to have supper with the Fernandoes that evening. It is clear that the co-defendant turned his attention to Nath Banda and that the shotgun was fired with the muzzle at a distance of approximately 18 inches from Mr Banda's stomach, inflicting a fatal wound.

The appellant gave evidence to the jury. He told the jury that as they were going to the off-licence, his co-defendant suddenly said that he wanted cigarettes and went across the road into Mr Fernando's shop. He, the appellant, thought it odd that his co-defendant, who had just bought cigarettes in Mr Kumar's shop should want more cigarettes, and consequently he followed his co-defendant into the shop. They did not enter the shop together. The appellant's face was not covered in any way. He could see that his co-defendant was robbing the shop with the gun out. It was the co-defendant who took the money and who asked for the cigarettes and took them. His co-defendant had thrown some cigarettes at him which may have hit him. He, the appellant, might have bent down, but he did not bend down to pick the coins up off the floor that had spilled from the drawer of the till. He might have picked up some cigarettes. He turned and left the shop, walked round the corner into West Croft Square and some 10 yards or so further. Then he decided to go back to see what was going on. As he reached the shop window on the corner, the gun went off. The appellant denied in his evidence that he was acting as a look out. Although he knew that the co-defendant had a gun, he did not know the gun was loaded. Indeed, he did not know that his co-defendant had ammunition for the gun. He had never seen ammunition or heard of the co-defendant having ammunition. We observe that the Crown called evidence which contradicted this part of the appellant's evidence to the jury, namely the witnesses Cotton and Flemming.

The co-defendant had come flying out of the shop saying that it was an accident and had run past him. Momentarily he, the appellant, had considered whether to go back into the shop or whether to run away, and he had run away because he did not want to be blamed for anything. They had both run back to the appellant's home by a back way. Once at the appellant's home the co-defendant had told him that it was an accident; the gun just went off. They had persuaded the appellant's mother to take them to the flat of the co-defendant's girlfriend in North London, where both of them had spent the night and stayed until the early afternoon of the next day.

He had not had any of the proceeds of the robbery. He told the jury that he had had no idea that his co-defendant was going into the shop in order to commit a robbery. He knew that his co-defendant had the gun, but not that it was loaded. He believed it to be unloaded. He did not participate in the robbery at all ...

The Crown's case against the appellant was that there was a joint enterprise between the appellant and his co-defendant to rob this newsagent's, that the appellant had known that his co-defendant had a gun and would use it to threaten and intimidate those in the shop and that in the shop the appellant had played an active, albeit minor, part in the robbery. The unlawful use of the gun had been part of and within the scope of the joint enterprise. Consequently the appellant was guilty of manslaughter, although in the circumstances of the case the Crown did not seek conviction of the appellant on the charge of murder. The appellant's case, as we have already observed, was simply that there was no such joint enterprise and that he had not taken any part at all in the robbery ...

Because of the conclusion we have reached on the third ground of appeal, it is unnecessary for us to reach a concluded view on Mr Robertson's second ground. We would simply raise the question whether once the criminal activity contemplated in a joint enterprise has commenced, it is possible for a party to the joint enterprise to withdraw, and whether it is ever open to a party to a joint enterprise to say that he is not criminally responsible for all that is done in that criminal activity which is within the scope of the joint enterprise. In this case, saying that the appellant withdrew may be no more than another way of saying that the robbery of Mr Banda was outside the scope of the original joint enterprise. Certainly most of the instances given in Smith and Hogan, 7th edn p 153, of withdrawal, are cases of withdrawal from a joint enterprise before the start of the contemplated criminal activity.

The case of the *Becerra and Cooper* (1976) 62 Cr App R 212 is an instance of an alleged withdrawal after the criminal activity had commenced. However, in that case the submission that the defendant had withdrawn from the joint enterprise failed. If the conduct of the defendant in that case did not amount to a withdrawal from the joint enterprise, we doubt whether the appellant's act of leaving the shop in the present case could amount to a withdrawal from a joint enterprise ...

In the present case, if the appellant did not know that the gun was loaded, and believed that it was unloaded, the scope of the joint enterprise in which he joined was the robbery of those in the shop by the putting of such persons as were in the shop in fear by the use of an unloaded and therefore innocuous gun. The appellant's knowledge that the gun was loaded was crucial to the Crown's case, because if it were proved that he knew the gun was loaded then he was party to a joint enterprise in which those in the shop were to be threatened with a lethal weapon, that is to say were to be subjected to the obvious risk of that weapon being fired in the excitement and tensions of the occasion. That would make him guilty of manslaughter, as is demonstrated by the case of *Reid*.

A joint enterprise to cause fright or hysteria through threats being made with an unloaded and innocuous gun was not sufficient to found a conviction of manslaughter in the circumstances of this case. It was, of course, sufficient to found convictions in respect of the counts of robbery and possession of an offensive weapon with intent. Nevertheless, the judge directed that the defence to the manslaughter count was the same as the defence to the counts of robbery and possession of the offensive weapon with intent. Here again the implication was that even if the appellant did not know the gun was loaded, and believed it to be unloaded, he would be not guilty of murder but he would be guilty of all the other charges he faced, including manslaughter. The true distinction between the appellant being guilty of murder and the appellant being guilty of manslaughter in the circumstances of this case was not the appellant's knowledge that the gun was loaded but the appellant's knowledge that the co-defendant was likely to use the loaded gun to kill or cause grievous bodily harm on the one hand, or was simply going to use the loaded gun to frighten on the other. We conclude that there was here a material misdirection in respect of count 4 ...

R v Mahmood [1995] RTR 48 (CA)

Lord Taylor of Gosforth CJ: ... The circumstances of the case were disturbing in the extreme. Unhappily, they seem to be symptomatic of a spate of such offences which were being committed about the time of this one, especially in the north east of England where this occurred. At about 6.00 pm on 14 November 1990, an Austin Montego motor car was stolen by three youths. They abandoned the car a couple of hours later, having had their enjoyment. They told a group of friends, including the appellant and his co-defendant, what they had done. Later, at about 10.20 pm, a witness met the co-defendant driving the car alone. The co-defendant asked the witness to join him, which the witness declined.

At 11.17 pm two police officers, who incidentally were investigating a car crash which had been caused by the bad driving of other youths, saw the Montego being driven by the co-defendant. The appellant was a passenger. The vehicle passed them in a built-up area at a speed of between 60 to 70 mph, swerving about the road. The officers abandoned what they were doing, got into their car and pursued the appellant and his co-defendant. They had their beacons flashing, but that did not stop the Montego. They temporarily lost sight of it, but came upon it a little later. It was standing in the entrance to a cul-de-sac pointing towards the main road. At the appearance of the police car, it sprang into action and crossed the path of the police car, quickly achieving a speed of about 60 mph, and causing another motorist in its path to brake sharply. That motorist said that the car thereafter slowed to a fairly slow speed before accelerating away. He was shocked by the incident. The Montego then turned the corner and slowed to a 'fast walking pace'. As they came around the corner, the officers saw both front doors of the car open and the occupants rolling in the road. A civilian witness saw the driver jump out at the corner, but not the passenger. Another witness did not see the driver jump out until a very late stage of the vehicle's progress. The vehicle, still in gear, went up on to the pavement and, as one witness thought, accelerated. It struck a pram, or buggy, in which there was a 10-month-old child, before colliding with a fence. The child was thrown out into a garden and was found to be grievously injured. On arrival at hospital the child was dead ...

At the end of the prosecution case there was a submission to the judge that he ought to withdraw the case from the jury because there was no evidence that the appellant gave any encouragement to the driver to drive the way he did, or abandon the car in the way he did; that there was insufficient evidence to enable the jury, properly directed, to conclude that what had happened was merely an unforeseen consequence of a joint enterprise which the appellant and his co-defendant had agreed should be carried out.

In ruling on the submission, the judge posed three questions of which the jury would have to be satisfied before they could convict. The first was:

> Was the co-defendant Ali guilty of manslaughter by driving recklessly?

He came to the conclusion that there was clear evidence on which the jury could answer that question, 'Yes'. The second was:

> Did the appellant whilst a passenger in the vehicle driven by Ali, contemplate that Ali might drive recklessly?

The third was:

> Did the appellant, in addition to being present in the vehicle, wilfully and intentionally encourage Ali to drive recklessly?

In relation to the second and third questions and the evidence to go to the jury, the judge said:

> As to the second question the prosecution evidence taken at its highest will establish, if accepted, that this 15-year-old [appellant] accepted from his 14-year-old friend the offer of a joyride late at night in a car which he must have known was stolen, and thereby embarked on a journey which was likely to involve, in addition to the ordinary hazards of the motor car with a juvenile at the wheel, the high possibility of a police pursuit. That evidence would be amply sufficient, in my judgment, to found a finding by any reasonable jury that [the appellant] contemplated that Ali would drive the car recklessly.
>
> As to the third question, there is no direct evidence before the jury as to what these two boys said to each other as they continued their journey. The circumstances already mentioned, however, taken together with the evidence in this particular case of deliberate baiting of the police, as well as common knowledge on which any reasonable jury would be entitled to draw, of the exhibitionist courting of danger which [taking without authority] invariably involves would, in my judgment, provide sufficient basis for a jury to be sure that [the appellant] by his words and conduct wilfully and intentionally encouraged Ali to drive recklessly.

Accordingly, the judge rejected the submission and allowed the case to go to the jury.

It is of significance that when he came to direct the jury on the questions to which they would need to address themselves, he added two which he had not posed to himself in considering his ruling. The first was:

> Did the obvious and serious risk of causing physical injury to another road user include a possibility that the car might, when still in motion, be abandoned by its driver and that a person might be injured by the empty vehicle thereafter?

The second was:

> Did [the appellant] now a passenger in the vehicle driven by Ali, contemplate that Ali might drive in that sense recklessly? ...

In our judgment, had the fatality occurred by reason of the car driven by the co-defendant colliding with a pedestrian, or colliding with some other car and killing the driver or passenger therein, it might well have been possible to leave it to the jury to take the view that what had occurred had resulted from a common unlawful enterprise which had culminated in unforeseen consequences. However, in our view the present case falls into a different category. Whilst it is true that the phrase 'reckless driving' can be applied both to that part of the co-defendant's driving during which he was at the wheel, swerving about, driving with excessive speed and putting other car users in a state of shock, and to the abandonment of the vehicle at the end, leaving it to career on its own, the two elements in this history were very different in character. One can well understand that someone in the appellant's position might be inferred by the jury to have contemplated the former kind of driving, but we do not consider that the evidence sufficiently supported a contention that he contemplated the second type of reckless driving, namely the abandonment of the vehicle. It is of interest to compare what the judge asked himself when considering his ruling on the submission with what he asked the jury to consider when he came to review the evidence. The two supplementary questions, which have already been quoted in this judgment, raised the point which we have just addressed. Had the judge asked himself those two supplementary questions at the time he considered his ruling, he may well have concluded that his decision ought to have been to the contrary effect. That is the view we take. We consider that the evidence here did not support sufficiently a case from which a jury could infer that the appellant had entered a joint enterprise in which he contemplated the abandonment of the vehicle, leaving it in gear to drive itself in a manner which caused the death. Nor do we consider that there was any evidence to show, even in the absence of an original plan which would have contemplated such conduct, any encouragement by the appellant of the co-defendant to adopt the course he did. In those circumstances, we take the view that the judge ought to have withdrawn the case from the jury.

[Counsel for the Crown] submits that since the judge did leave the supplementary questions to the jury, and since they convicted, it must follow that they found there was here a contemplation by the appellant of the abandonment of the car as a foreseeable consequence of embarking on this piece of driving. However, we are very conscious of the fact that this case was conducted at a time when, in the area where it was tried, this type of offending was causing great anguish and anxiety to the public. The jury's concern about this type of offending may very well have played a part in their deliberations. Therefore, it was extremely important that unless there was evidence which could properly be relied upon by the jury to support an inference of guilt, the case ought to have been withdrawn.

We bear in mind that the passenger in the vehicle was a young boy of only 15 who, it is true, had no business to be taking this car away without consent, but had never had any part in the actual direction of the vehicle or its abandonment so far as the driving was concerned. We consider that leaving the case to the jury in the circumstances exposed him to a risk of conviction to which he should never have been exposed. Accordingly, we allow this appeal against conviction ...

R v Stewart and Schofield [1995] 3 All ER 159 (CA)

Hobhouse LJ: In *R v Reid* (1975) 62 Cr App R 109 at 112 Lawton LJ, delivering the judgment of the court, said:

> When two or more men go out together in joint possession of offensive weapons such as revolvers and knives and the circumstances are such as to justify an inference that the very least they intend to do with them is to use them to cause fear in another, there is, in our judgment, always a likelihood that, in the excitement and tensions of the occasion, one of them will use his weapon in some way which will cause death or serious injury. If such injury was not intended by the others, they must be acquitted of murder; but having started out on an enterprise which envisaged some degree of violence, albeit nothing more than causing fright, they will be guilty of manslaughter.

It has been argued on behalf of the appellants in this case, with the support of the authors of Smith and Hogan, *Criminal Law*, 7th edn, 1992, p 146, that this statement of the law cannot stand with other decisions of the Court of Appeal and should not be regarded as good law ...

On the evening of Thursday 23 January 1992 Mr Dada, a 60-year-old Pakistani, was in his shop, the Popular Delicatessen in Wilmslow Road, Withington. During the early evening two young women, Dawn Rothwell and Heather Stewart, went into the shop. They bought some cigarettes. Whilst there, Stewart noticed Mr Dada removing some money from the till and putting it into his pocket. After they had left the shop and were walking along the road they met Lambert, who was known to Stewart. He was driving a car and Schofield was with him. Stewart told them about what she had seen in the shop and suggested that they should rob Mr Dada of the cash which they had seen him put in his pocket. They agreed. The four of them then drove back to near the shop, where Lambert, Schofield and Stewart got out. Rothwell stayed in the car and did not take any further part. There was evidence that the trio took out of the car a scaffolding bar and a knife. Lambert put on a balaclava and a long coat. Whilst Schofield kept watch outside, the other two went into the shop. On the evidence that the jury must have accepted, Lambert had the bar and Stewart had the knife. The upshot was that Mr Dada was viciously beaten with the bar, seriously injured, and a relatively small amount of cash was stolen from him. He died a few days later in hospital as a result of the injuries he had received; these included four skull fractures. The money taken from Mr Dada was less than £100 cash. After the incident the three ran off to the car where the money was divided up.

Both Stewart and Schofield had answered questions at interview but only Stewart gave evidence at the trial. Schofield had admitted knowledge of the weapons with which Lambert and Stewart were armed. Stewart said she did not know but the jury must have disbelieved her. They both said that they had not contemplated that Mr Dada would be more than threatened. They did not know at that time that Lambert was a person who was deeply motivated by racial hatred or would be liable to use such excessive violence ...

They said it went far beyond anything that they contemplated or that they had any reasons to contemplate. His attack on Mr Dada was motivated not by the needs of the robbery but by vicious racial hatred and was so excessive that it did not form part of any joint enterprise upon which the three of them engaged. They said that the jury should not be satisfied that they were parties to the unlawful killing of Mr Dada ...

The primary ground of appeal of the appellants is:

> Having regard to the decision of the Court of Criminal Appeal in *R v Anderson and Morris* [1966] 2 QB 110 and notwithstanding the subsequent authority of *R v Reid (Barry)* (1975) 62 Cr App R 109, it is not open to a jury which acquits a secondary party of murder to convict him of manslaughter in the alternative, where the principal is guilty of murder ...

Joint enterprise

The allegation that a defendant took part in the execution of a crime as a joint enterprise is not the same as an allegation that he aided, abetted, counselled or procured the commission of that crime. A person who is a mere aider or abettor etc is truly a secondary party to the commission of whatever crime it is that the principal has committed although he may be charged as a principal. If the principal has committed the crime of murder, the liability of the secondary party can only be a liability for aiding and abetting murder. In contrast, where the allegation is joint enterprise, the allegation is that one defendant participated in the criminal act of another. This is a different principle. It renders each of the parties to a joint enterprise criminally liable for the acts done in the course of carrying out that joint enterprise. Where the criminal liability of any given defendant depends upon the further proof that he had a certain state of mind, that state of mind must be proved against that defendant. Even though several defendants may, as a result of having engaged in a joint enterprise, be each criminally responsible for the criminal act of one of those defendants done in the course of carrying out the joint enterprise, their individual criminal responsibility will, in such a case, depend upon what individual state of mind or intention has been proved against them. Thus, each may be a party to the unlawful act which caused the victim's death. But one may have had the intent either to kill him or to cause him serious harm and be guilty of murder, whereas another may not have had that intent and may be guilty only of manslaughter.

Mens rea

An allegation that a defendant was part of a criminal joint enterprise with others includes an allegation that he was aware of the character of the joint enterprise in which he was joining and foresaw that the relevant criminal acts were liable to be involved. Thus, the allegation of joint enterprise involves an allegation concerning the state of the defendant's mind at the time of his participation in the joint enterprise. Normally the fact that the defendant had the state of mind sufficient to prove his guilt of the offence charged is proved by proof that he was a party to the joint enterprise in the course of which the criminal acts were committed. But joint enterprises vary. They may have a purpose, say the infliction of grievous bodily harm, which corresponds to the specific intent for a particular crime, say murder or an offence contrary to s 18 of the Offences Against the Person Act 1861, in which case participation in the joint enterprise will prove the relevant *mens rea*. But in other cases the purpose of the joint enterprise may have been more limited and the relevant criminal liability may only have arisen from some undesired consequence. Provided that the joint enterprise is proved in relation to the relevant acts, then it is not an answer that consequences of those acts were unusual or unexpected. Even if unusual or unexpected consequences arose from the execution of the plan, each participant is responsible for those consequences. In such cases the liability of an individual defendant may depend upon whether his intention at the time the act was done included an intention that the consequences should follow. A defendant who had that intention may have a more serious criminal liability than one who did not. This is because the *mens rea* for the more serious offence can by proved against the one but not against the other.

Archbold

The analysis which we have shortly summarised is that followed by the editors of Archbold and by way of summary we are content to adopt what they say:

> A person who is a party to a joint enterprise, the pursuance of which results in the causing of another's death may be criminally liable for that death either on the basis that he is guilty of murder or on the basis that he is guilty of manslaughter. It is fundamental to a conviction of either offence that the accused must have been a party to the act which caused death. The application of the law concerning joint enterprise in cases of homicide in practice raises two problems, (1) whether in the circumstances the accused was party to the act which caused death; (2) if he was, whether his state of mind was such as to make him guilty of murder or of manslaughter.

The editors go on to refer to *R v Richards, R v Stober* (1992) 96 Cr App R 258 in which it was recognised that difference pleas might be accepted from defendants involved in a joint enterprise on this basis. The editors also treat *R v Reid* (1975) 62 Cr App R 109 and *R v Betty* (1963) 48 Cr App R 6, as exemplifying and confirming their analysis.

The authorities

The main case upon which [counsel for Schofield] founded his submission was *R v Anderson and Morris*, [1966] 2 QB 110. But like him we will start with *R v Betty*. Betty and another man were charged with manslaughter and both were convicted. The killing arose out of a fight in which they were both involved. Their defences at trial were self-defence. But Betty also argued that in truth his co-defendant had murdered the victim and that this meant that he, Betty, should not have been convicted of manslaughter. The Court of Criminal Appeal rejected that argument, saying that the point was covered by an earlier decision of a five-judge court, *R v Smith* [1963] 1 WLR 1200 at 1205–06, in which the court had expressly approved the direction:

> Anybody who is a party to an attack which results in an unlawful killing which results in death is a party to the killing ... Only he who intended that unlawful and grievous bodily harm should be done is guilty of murder. He who intended only that the victim should be unlawfully hit and hurt will be guilty of manslaughter if death results.

The court dismissed Betty's appeal. They applied *R v Smith* and held that the point raised was no defence unless the unlawful act which resulted in death was not done in the court of the joint enterprise.

In *R v Anderson and Morris* the court was again a five-judge court. Two men had been involved in an attack on a man. One of the men, Anderson, stabbed him with a knife and killed him. The other man, Morris, said that he had not known that Anderson was going to use a knife. Anderson was convicted of murder and Morris of manslaughter. Morris's appeal was allowed because the trial judge had directed the jury that neither the fact that Morris had not known about the knife nor the fact that Anderson did an act outside the common design to which Morris was a party could provide Morris with a defence to manslaughter. This was a clear misdirection. The court approved and adopted the submission of Mr Lane QC, counsel for Morris, that whilst a party to a joint enterprise would be liable for the acts done in pursuance of the joint enterprise, including:

> liability for unusual consequences if they arise from the execution of the agreed joint enterprise but ... if one of the adventurers goes beyond what has been tacitly agreed as part of the common enterprise, his co-adventurer is not

> liable for the consequences of that unauthorised act. (See [1966] 2 QB 110 at 221.)

The court did not question in *R v Smith* and *R v Betty* (by which they were anyway bound). What they did was to confirm and stress the need for the Crown, if it seeks to rely upon joint enterprise, to prove that the criminal act was done as part of the joint enterprise ...

In *R v Lovesey, R v Peterson* [1970] 1 QB 352, following *R v Anderson and Morris* and applying the 'Lane' formulation, the court refused to substitute a verdict of manslaughter for an unsatisfactory conviction for murder because they considered that the degree of violence used led to the conclusion that if the acts were within the common design it had to be murder and, if they were not, there was no other basis for any finding of guilt.

R v Reid 62 Cr App R 109 was decided in 1975. The court included Lane LJ, who had been involved in both the previously cited cases and must have had them fully in mind. Three men, alleged by the Crown to be supporters of the IRA, armed with weapons, went to the house of an army officer at night. When he opened the door one of them shot him. Two were convicted of murder; the third, Reid, was acquitted of murder but convicted of manslaughter. His defence had been that he was not part of the joint venture but had gone along with them in order to see whether the other two were really IRA terrorists, which he did not believe they were. The judge had given the jury direction on manslaughter based upon *R v Church* [1966] 1 QB 59. The appeal of Reid was based upon the factual submission that on the evidence it must have been murder or nothing. The court rejected that submission. They stressed the common possession of the weapons. Lawton LJ said (62 Cr App R 109 at 112):

> If men carrying offensive weapons – indeed deadly – weapons go to a man's house in the early hours of the morning for no discernible lawful purpose, they must, in our judgment, intend to do him harm of some kind, and the very least kind of harm is causing fright by threats to use them.

Having cited *R v Anderson and Morris*, they asked (at 112):

> Was O'Connaill's deliberate firing of the revolver 'a mere unforeseen consequence' of the unlawful possession of offensive weapons? We adjudge it was.

There then followed the passage quoted at the outset of this judgment. They dismissed Reid's appeal.

It is not possible to suggest that this decision was in any way *per incuriam*. Unless it is inconsistent with other binding authority, it is binding upon us.

R v Penfold (1979) 71 Cr App R 4 did not involve the use of weapons, but the court held that the fact that one defendant used excessive violence during a robbery, killing the victim, did not preclude a conviction for manslaughter on the basis of joint enterprise. The court strongly commented upon the need to proceed on the basis of realistic inferences as to what was to be contemplated by those involved in crimes of violence and not to be drawn into unrealistic theoretical distinctions. This echoed the language in *R v Reid* ...

A case upon which [counsel for Schofield] has particularly relied, and which he says is inconsistent with *R v Reid* is *R v Dunbar* [1988] Crim LR 693 (for which we also have a transcript). The victim was a prostitute. She was found dead in the bath in her flat. She had been garrotted with a metal bar. She had also received other injuries. The evidence was that she had been killed by two burglars; they were convicted of murder. The case of the Crown was that they had been recruited by Dunbar, another prostitute. The allegation against her was, therefore, not that she had participated in a joint enterprise, but that she was an accessory before the fact and had counselled or procured the commission of the crime. She denied any incitement to murder. She knew that a burglary was being planned and appreciated that some minor violence might be done to the victim in the course of the burglary; she knew nothing about the intention to use an iron bar and did not contemplate any serious violence. She was acquitted of murder but convicted of manslaughter. The Court of Appeal, applying *R v Anderson and Morris* and *R v Lovesey, R v Peterson*, considered that the verdict of the jury was only consistent with the conclusion by the jury that:

> one or both of her co-defendants must have gone beyond the scope of that design and used the extreme violence which was intended to cause grievous bodily harm or death.

The court stressed that it was 'on the facts of this case' that they had concluded that there were only two verdicts open to the jury, guilty or not guilty of murder. The court also considered the summing up in her case to be defective because it did not sufficiently cover the law incorporated in the Lane formulation.

The transcript of the judgment of the Court of Appeal does not justify the conclusion that the law was being stated or applied in any different way from the earlier case. Leaving on one side defective directions of law by the trial judges, the distinction between the outcome of *R v Smith, R v Betty* and *R v Reid* on the one hand and *R v Anderson and Morris, R v Lovesey, R v Peterson* and *R v Dunbar* on the other is that a different view was taken of the facts of the cases and whether the act in question was, or was to be treated as being, within or without the scope of the joint enterprise. *R v Dunbar* is not authority for the proposition that the cases falling on the other side of the line were wrongly decided, nor for the proposition that, in a suitable case, a jury cannot properly find one participant in a joint enterprise guilty of murder and another of manslaughter. We do not agree with the views to the contrary expressed in the notes in the *Criminal Law Review* (see [1988] Crim LR 693 at 694–95) and in Smith and Hogan p 145; that discussion also does not seem to take account of the fact that *R v Dunbar* probably should not be categorised as a case of joint enterprise at all. *R v Hyde* [1991] 1 QB 134, a case of joint enterprise, however, illustrates and confirms that a joint enterprise to commit a non-violent crime, burglary, may become more serious if one participant continues appreciating that another may kill or intentionally inflict serious injury; a conviction for murder on that basis was upheld.

Finally, we should refer to the advice of the Judicial Committee delivered by Lord Lowry in *Hui Chi-Ming v R* [1992] 1 AC 34 which involved a group attack on a man in the course of which one of the attackers used a piece of piping and the man was killed. The fatal blow was struck by a man who had been acquitted of murder at an earlier trial but convicted of manslaughter. At the appellant's trial the Crown's case was that it had, nevertheless, been a case of a joint enterprise to inflict serious harm or kill. The appellant was convicted of murder. The main discussion related to what common enterprise was necessary to prove the *mens rea* for murder; *R v Hyde* was followed. But for present purposes the interest in the case is that the trial judge had directed the jury ([1992] 1 AC 34 at 46):

> If on the other hand, you are satisfied that the accused was present and that he shared an intention with his companions that the victim should be assaulted and caused some injury, but some injury less than some really serious bodily injury, then he would not be guilty of murder but he would be guilty of manslaughter. If you conclude that it was a reasonable possibility

> that the accused though present did not share any intention with the others that the victim should in any way be assaulted, then he would be entitled to an acquittal.

These directions recognised that, although the victim may have been murdered by another participant in the joint venture, the appellant, although a participant in a joint venture with others, may have lacked the *mens rea* for murder but could still be guilty of manslaughter. They were implicitly approved by Lord Lowry ([1992] 1 AC 34 at 47).

The authorities do not support the appellants' submission. There is no suggestion that *R v Reid* was wrongly decided nor that there is an inconsistency between what Lawton LJ there said and what was said in *R v Anderson and Morris* by Lord Parker CJ. The distinction between the various cases is that, as one would expect, in different factual situations there may be different verdicts open to a jury. The latest case, *Hui Chi-Ming v R*, confirms again that it is possible that a person may be a party to a joint enterprise which leads to death and be guilty of manslaughter although the actual killer may be guilty of murder.

Conclusion

The directions given by Morland J in the present case disclose no error of law. The verdicts of manslaughter were properly open to the jury and were correctly left to them. It is possible to identify a number of confusions in the appellants' arguments and, it appears, in the academic comment. Cases of joint enterprise, properly so termed, should not be confused with cases of counselling or procuring. It may often be the case that the proof of a defendant's *mens rea* is sufficiently proved by proof of this participation in the joint enterprise; the cases cited emphasise this. But it does not follow that this will, or must, always be the case. It is possible that a defendant, whilst being a participant in a joint enterprise and responsible for the unintended consequences of acts done in the course of carrying out that joint enterprise, may lack a specific intent possessed by another participant. In any given case the issue may arise what was the scope of the joint enterprise; depending upon what answer is given to that question, a further question may arise where a crime of specific intent is charged, what was the state of mind of the defendant. The *mens rea* of the defendant may be proved by either method, by proof of participation in a joint enterprise having the requisite character, or, where the joint enterprise proved does not have that character, by proof of a specific intent. Where proof of participation in the joint enterprise during the course of which the relevant act was done is considered to prove only the *mens rea* appropriate to a lesser offence, only the lesser crime will have been proved against that defendant, although the act in question may have involved the commission of a more serious crime by another against whom a specific intent can be proved.

The question whether the relevant act was committed in the course of carrying out the joint enterprise in which the defendant was a participant is a question of fact not law. If the act was not so committed then the joint enterprise ceases to provide a basis for a finding of guilt against such a defendant. He ceases to be responsible for the act. This is the fundamental point illustrated by *R v Anderson and Morris* and *R v Lovesey, R v Peterson*. But it does not follow that a variation in the intent of some of the participants at the time the critical act is done precludes the act from having been done in the course of carrying out the joint enterprise, as is illustrated by *R v Betty* and *R v Reid*.

The appeals against conviction must accordingly be dismissed.

18 May 1995: the Appeal Committee of the House of Lords (**Lord Keith of Kinkel, Lord Lloyd of Berwick** and **Lord Hoffmann**) refused leave to appeal.

R v Bamborough [1996] Crim LR 744 (CA)

Facts: The appellant and his co-accused burst into their victim's flat, apparently intent on carrying out a robbery. The co-accused had a gun. The victim was badly beaten about the face, and suffered a broken nose which was consistent with his having been hit with the gun. He was then shot in the thigh at very close range by the co-accused, and bled to death within minutes. The appellant and the co-accused were both convicted of murder. The appellant's case at trial was that, although he knew that a gun was being carried, he had no idea until it was fired that it was loaded. His ground of appeal was that the trial judge should have directed the jury that if they found that the appellant might have been a party to the use of the gun only to cause grievous bodily harm in the form of pistol-whipping – which was not the cause of death – then he should be convicted only of manslaughter. It was argued that the summing up failed to distinguish, as was necessary in this context, between fatal and non-fatal grievous bodily harm.

Held: that it made no difference what form of really serious harm was contemplated. It was most unlikely that the jury accepted that the appellant might have thought that the gun was unloaded; but in any event, if the appellant knew that really serious harm, of whatever type, was going to be inflicted with the gun then he was properly convicted of murder.

LIABILITY OF ACCESSORY WHERE THERE IS NO PRINCIPAL OFFENDER

A person can be liable as an accessory even though no principal offender has been identified, or a person alleged to have been a principal offender has been acquitted, so long as it is proved that the *actus reus* of the offence was committed: *Hui Chi-Ming* [1992] 1 AC 34. This is true even if the offence is one which the accessory could not have committed as a principal offender (as where a woman aids and abets a rape). Similarly, it is possible for an accessory to be convicted of a more serious offence than the principal.

Hui Chi-Ming v The Queen [1992] 1 AC 34 (PC)

Lord Lowry: ... Miss Lo Kwai-Ying ('Mui Mui') had a boyfriend, Ah Po, of whom her parents and her brother strongly disapproved. He asked his friend, Ah Hung, to speak to his sister. He attempted to frighten her by describing Ah Hung as the 'Southern Boxing Champion': this was quite untrue. Ah Hung tried to intimidate her into giving up Ah Po. She was upset. After he left, she telephoned Ah Po at a park at Lei Yue Mun pier, told him what had happened and gave him a description of Ah Hung, in particular, that he was tall, wearing glasses and had a red stain on his chest. Ah Po told his friends, including the defendant, that Mui Mui had been bullied. He wanted his friends to go to the Yau Tong Estate to look for Ah Hung and 'to look for someone to hit'.

Ah Po left with two other youths in a taxi: he was carrying a length of water pipe. The defendant went with two others in a following taxi. At the estate, they stood together in the vicinity of a bus stop, waiting for a man answering to the description of Ah Hung. A number of people were approached by some of the youths and asked if they were the 'Southern Boxing Champion'. A bus arrived and a number of passengers climbed on board. As the bus moved off, a tall man wearing glasses ran after it to catch it. He was seized by four, five or six of the group: the evidence conflicted as to the number. He was struck by the metal pipe, wielded, as the Crown alleged, by Ah Po. The man, who was not Ah Hung and was a perfectly innocent victim, received numerous bruises, three wounds to the head and fractures in two places to his skull. He later died from his injuries. Some time after this Ah Po called out 'Let's go' and the group of six left. When they got back to the pier, a number of them remonstrated with Ah Po who agreed that he had gone over the top. The group then went by ferry to Ah Po's house, where they spent the night. No witness saw the defendant speak to anyone or strike a blow, or play any particular part in the assault on the victim. Ah Po was arrested on 30 June 1986.

On 6 January 1987, Ah Po and three of the group who had accompanied him, were indicted for murder before the High Court of Hong Kong. All four pleaded not guilty. Ah Po was tried by a jury before Hooper J. The second defendant changed his plea to guilty of manslaughter on the 14th day of the trial and was remanded in custody for a new trial, at which he renewed his plea of guilty to manslaughter and was sentenced to three years' imprisonment. The third defendant pleaded guilty to manslaughter at the outset and his plea was accepted by the Crown: he was sentenced to five years' imprisonment; this sentence was reduced to four years on appeal. The fourth defendant was acquitted and discharged on the fourth day of the trial by direction of the judge, the Crown offering no further evidence against him. The trial lasted until 6 February 1987.

The defence of Ah Po at his trial was that he had nothing to do with the incident. He did not suggest provocation or diminished responsibility. By unanimous decision of the jury, Ah Po was acquitted of murder and convicted of manslaughter. He was sentenced to six years' imprisonment.

The defendant, who had no previous convictions, was arrested on 19 October 1987. He was initially charged with manslaughter by the police, on advice from the Legal Department of the Attorney General's Chambers. But on the advice of another Crown counsel, Mr Gerber, who received the brief to prosecute, the defendant was indicted for murder. The same procedure was followed with another friend of Ah Po, Sze Hoi-Tai, who was arrested on 3 November 1987, charged with manslaughter but subsequently jointly indicted with the defendant for murder.

On the first day of the trial, Sze pleaded not guilty to murder but guilty to manslaughter, and the Crown accepted the plea: he was subsequently sentenced to three years' imprisonment. Crown counsel offered to accept a plea of guilty to manslaughter from the defendant, but the offer was refused ...

At the trial of the defendant the judge, when charging the jury, gave directions with regard to the doctrine of acting unlawfully in concert which their Lordships think it convenient to set out in full, adding numbers to the paragraphs for ease of reference:

1 The Crown does not suggest that it was the [defendant] who held the water pipe at any stage nor does the Crown suggest that it was the [defendant] who inflicted the fatal blow or blows. But the Crown does not have to prove to you that the [defendant] even laid a finger on the deceased. It is not necessary for the Crown to prove which particular individual caused the fatal blow or blows which resulted in the death of the deceased. The Crown says that, in the circumstances of this case, to constitute murder, it is not necessary for the Crown to prove who precisely struck the fatal blow or blows.

2 The Crown in this case relies on the well-known doctrine of acting in concert, and the law on that is this: where two or more persons embark

upon a joint unlawful enterprise and going to assault someone – even punching someone on the nose is an unlawful enterprise – each is liable for the consequences of such acts of the others as are done in the pursuance of that joint enterprise and also for the unusual consequences of such acts if these arise from the execution of the agreed joint enterprise.

3 But if one of the adventurers goes beyond what has been expressly, or tacitly, agreed as part of the common enterprise, his co-adventurers are not liable for the consequences of that unauthorised act. It is for you, as a jury, to decide whether what was done was part of the joint enterprise, or went beyond it and was an act unauthorised by the joint enterprise.

4 Let me give you an example of that – that last portion. Let's say three men decide to go and burgle a house and, whilst two of them are going round looking for things to steal, the third man comes across a woman and he there and then rapes her. Now all three men would be guilty of burglary but the other two would not be guilty of rape because that was never in their contemplation. The intention was to steal and it was not within their contemplation that anyone should be raped.

5 It is important that you thoroughly understand the doctrine or the concept of common intent, so I will rephrase what I have just said to you a moment ago.

6 It was not only the person who inflicts the fatal blow or blows who is criminally responsible. The law says that if two or more persons reach an understanding or arrangement that they will commit a crime, and, as I have said, assaulting someone is a crime, and whilst that arrangement is still in being, they are both present and one or other of them does, or they do between them, in accordance with their arrangement all the things necessary to constitute the crime, then they are all equally guilty of it provided the crime does not go beyond their understanding or arrangement.

7 It is not necessary that the understanding or arrangement be express. It can be tacit. It can be arrived at by means of actions or words. People who go and do something wrong do not go to a solicitor's office and have a contract drawn up and signed, sealed and delivered. They do not want to advertise what they are going to do.

8 The Crown may establish the count of murder against the [defendant] by proving the [defendant] was present and that the deceased was killed in accordance with an understanding or arrangement to which the [defendant] was a party and that that understanding or arrangement included the intent charged, that is either to kill or to cause grievous bodily harm.

9 The Crown may establish the offence charged against the [defendant] by proving that the [defendant] was present when the victim was attacked in accordance with an understanding or arrangement to which the [defendant] was a party, and that understanding or arrangement included the intent either to kill or to cause grievous bodily harm.

10 The [defendant] would also be guilty if he lent himself to a criminal enterprise knowing that a potentially lethal weapon was being carried by one of his companions, and in the event it is in fact used by one of his partners with an intent sufficient for murder. Then he too will be guilty of that offence if you are sure beyond reasonable doubt that the

> [defendant] contemplated that in the carrying out of the common unlawful purpose, one of his partners in the enterprise might use a lethal weapon with the intention of at least causing really serious bodily harm. It is what the [defendant] in fact contemplated that matters.
>
> 11 You may remember, members of the jury, that the [defendant] was asked by Mr Gerber this question ... 'You realised very well that there was a very real danger that somebody was going to get a terrible beating, didn't you?' And the [defendant's] answer was 'That was just what I thought.' And you may interpret that to mean, it is a matter for you, that the [defendant] foresaw the very real possibility that somebody was going to receive a terrible beating.
>
> 12 You may also remember the evidence of the [defendant] that Ah Po whom he had known for a number of years, several years, and I think he had been at school together with him although in different classes. He told you that Ah Po was comparatively hot-tempered.
>
> 13 Members of the jury, if you are satisfied that the [defendant] was present and that he shared an intention with his companions that the victim should be assaulted, you might ask yourselves 'Did the [defendant] contemplate that in the carrying out of the common unlawful purpose, that is the assault of the victim, that one of his partners in the enterprise *might*,' I did not say 'would', '*might* use that water pipe with the intention of causing at least really serious bodily injury?' If the answer is 'Yes', then you would find the [defendant] guilty.
>
> 14 If the other hand, you are satisfied that the [defendant] was present and that he shared an intention with his companions that the victim should be assaulted and caused some injury, but some injury less than some really serious bodily injury, then he would not be guilty of murder but he would be guilty of manslaughter.
>
> 15 If you conclude that it was a reasonable possibility that the [defendant] though present did not share any intention with the others that the victim should in any way be assaulted, then he would be entitled to an acquittal.

The defendant's case at the trial was put by his counsel, Mr Percy, in the following terms:

> He went along not to join with the others in any common purpose that they believed amongst themselves but to prevent his friends or friend getting into trouble. He was there in the opposite capacity, not to assist them attack someone, but to dissuade them from getting into trouble.

In the alternative he argued that the common intention of the group of six was not the intention to kill or to cause grievous bodily harm and that if, as the Crown contended, Ah Po had any such intention the whole group did not share it. Mr Percy put it thus:

> I would suggest that if there was indeed a common purpose shared by all of them, then you would expect all of them to equip themselves even with a water pipe either to use in defence or attack, but that wasn't done. No other person except for Ah Po armed himself with any weapon, that is the evidence. And the simple reason for that is that Ah Po was the only one who wanted revenge. No one had any interest in protecting Ah Po's girlfriend from anything. What interest did the others have? Misguided loyalty, is that going to be suggested as the reason for assisting Ah Po? I would suggest, members of the jury, that that dissolves this so-called common purpose?

The directions in paragraph 15 above were clearly designed to cover the defendant's primary case, but the only inference which can be drawn is that the jury did not accept the reasonable possibility that either paragraph 14 or paragraph 15 accorded with the facts. On the contrary, the jury must have been satisfied that what happened accorded with the situation described in paragraphs 8 and 9 or else in paragraphs 10 and 13 of the directions. This of course also necessarily involves the jury's acceptance that Ah Po was guilty of murder.

The defendant's basic proposition in his written case was:

> On the trial of a secondary party for murder on the basis of a 'common intent', the Crown must prove: (a) that the act was in the contemplation of both the principal and secondary party as an act which might be done in the course of carrying out the primary criminal intention; and (b) that the principal party intended to kill or to do serious bodily injury at the time he killed.

No question arises on this appeal in relation to proposition (b), because the judge (in paragraph 10) gave the appropriate direction to the jury. It is with the defendant's basic proposition (a) that their Lordships are here concerned. The case then noted that the trial judge left the issue of intent to the jury on two bases. Having explained that a party is liable for the consequences of such acts of the others as are done pursuant to a common criminal enterprise, and emphasising that a party is not liable for the consequences of an act which goes beyond that which has been expressly or tacitly agreed, he said:

> (1) The Crown may establish the count of murder against the [defendant] by proving the [defendant] was present and that the deceased was killed in accordance with an understanding or arrangement to which the [defendant] was as party and that that understanding and arrangement included the intent charged, that is either to kill or to cause grievous bodily harm.

The judge's alternative direction on intent was recited in the [defendant's] case as follows:

> (2) Then [the defendant] too will be guilty of [murder], if you are sure beyond reasonable doubt that the [defendant] contemplated that in the carrying out of the common unlawful purpose, one of his partners in the enterprise might use a lethal weapon with the intention of at least causing really serious harm. It is what the [defendant] in fact contemplated that matters ... if you are satisfied that the [defendant] was present and that he shared an intention with his companions that the victim should be assaulted, you might ask yourselves, 'Did the [defendant] contemplate that in the carrying out of the common unlawful purpose, that is the assault of the victim, that one of his partners might' ... I did not say 'would' ... 'might use the water pipe with the intention of causing at least really serious bodily injury?' If the answer is 'Yes', then you would find the [defendant] guilty.

Their Lordships would here observe that direction (1) noted above (which corresponds to paragraphs 8 and 9 of the directions) contemplates the straightforward case where a crime is agreed upon and carried out according to plan: the principal and the accomplices will all be guilty. Direction (2) (which corresponds to paragraphs 10 and 13) contemplates that one partner (the principal) may *in carrying out the common unlawful purpose* commit an act which, although *not mutually arranged in advance*, is within the contemplation of an accessory, who will in this case also be guilty of murder in the circumstances described. The typical example is of a group of men who set out on a bank robbery as the planned crime. One, who to the knowledge of his companions has a loaded revolver, shoots a bank clerk or a watchman dead and generally all will be guilty of murder. What the judge said adapts that concept to the possible circumstances of the present case.

The printed case, when adverting to contemplation of the consequences, cites the observation of Sir Robin Cooke in *Chan Wing-Siu v The Queen* [1985] AC 168, 175:

> It turns on contemplation or, putting the same idea in other words, authorisation, which may be express but is more usually implied. It meets the case of a crime foreseen as a possible incident of the common unlawful enterprise. The criminal culpability lies in participating in the venture with that foresight.

The defendant's basic proposition was then repeated:

> The correct principle is expressed in *Johns v The Queen* (1980) 143 CLR 108 where the High Court of Australia approved the statement by Street CJ in the Supreme Court of New South Wales: 'an accessory before the fact bears, as does a principle in the second degree, a criminal liability for an act which was *within the contemplation of both himself and the principal* in the first degree as an act which might be done in the course of carrying out the primary criminal intention – an act contemplated as a possible incident of the originally planned particular venture.' The crux of that *dictum* is that the act must be *within the contemplation of both parties.* For the Crown to establish murder against a secondary party on the basis that he contemplated, or authorised, an attack with murderous intent, it is necessary to prove that the primary party himself so contemplated. (Emphasis supplied.)

The written submissions on this part of the appeal concluded with this proposition:

> If reliance is to be placed simply on the foresight of the secondary party, then the judge ought in any event to direct the jury to consider whether the risk *as recognised by the accused* was sufficient to make him a party to the crime committed by the principal.

As to this last submission, which was based on a passage in *Chan Wing-Siu v The Queen* [1985] AC 168, 179, their Lordships consider that on the facts of the present case the judge put the case to the jury both adequately and correctly in paragraphs 10 – 13 of his directions.

Mr Thomas, who appeared for the defendant before the Board, made two further points. The first, which stemmed from the defendant's basic proposition, was that the judge should have told the jury that, for the defendant to be guilty of murder, it was necessary that Ah Po contemplated the possibility of at least grievous bodily harm being caused when the unlawful agreement to assault Ah Hung was made; otherwise his severe attack on the victim, though intended when it was made, would have gone beyond what was authorised by the agreement. The second point was that Sir Robin Cooke's equation in *Chan Wing-Siu v The Queen* [1985] AC 168 of contemplation with authorisation meant that an accomplice who merely foresees the further and additional act of the principal is not thereby rendered liable for that act. Neither point poses any problem on the assumed basis that the jury found the unlawful joint enterprise to be one of the first type, which was covered by paragraphs 8 and 9 of the judge's directions ('type 1'). Both points were directed to the question of guilty intent on the part of the accomplice in relation to an unlawful joint enterprise of the second type (as their Lordships for the purposes of argument will assume the crime to have been), which was dealt with in paragraphs 10 and 13 of the directions ('type 2'). Paragraph 10 clearly recalls Sir Robin Cooke's reference in *Chan Wing-Siu v The Queen* at 175, to the accomplice's 'contemplation' of 'a crime foreseen as a possible incident of the common unlawful enterprise', which tends to indicate, not surprisingly, that the judge's directions were based on *Chan Wing-Siu v The Queen.*

The principle enunciated in *Chan Wing-Siu v The Queen* has since been clearly stated by Lord Lane CJ in the Court of Appeal (Criminal Division in *R v Ward* (1986) 85 Cr App R 71 and *R v Slack* [1989] QB 775, in both of which *Chan Wing-Siu v The Queen* [1985] AC 168 was expressly approved and applied, and most recently in *R v Hyde* [1991] 1 QB 134 which also applied *Chan Wing-Siu v The Queen.*

... [T]he judgment in *R v Hyde* correctly states, in their Lordships' opinion, the law applicable to a joint enterprise of the kind described, which results in the commission of murder by the principal as an incident of the joint enterprise.

Against that background their Lordships consider the two arguments set out above. The first can be readily disposed of on the facts by pointing out that Ah Po's arming himself with the water pipe before setting out showed unequivocally what he *did* contemplate at that stage. The connection between the argument and the facts to which it was directed was tenuous, to say the least.

Counsel's submission, however, was based on the passage already cited from *Johns v The Queen* (1980) 143 CLR 108 at 130–31. The issue in that case was whether an accessory before the fact is, like a principal in the second degree, responsible for an act constituting the offence charged if such act was contemplated as a *possible* incident of the common purpose, or whether it has to be established as a *likely or probable* consequence of the way in which the crime was to be committed. The court unanimously accepted the former alternative. But, in the course of their judgment, Mason, Murphy and Wilson JJ stated the law in the manner already quoted, requiring the act to have been within the contemplation of *both the principal and the accessory* as an act which might be done in the course of carrying out the primary criminal intention. It is on the basis of that passage that the defendant contends that the secondary party cannot be liable unless the relevant act was within the contemplation of both the principal and the secondary party.

Johns v The Queen is a leading case on the law relating to accessories. It was specifically relied on by Sir Robin Cooke in *Chan Wing-Siu v The Queen* [1985] AC 168, in which the same central issue fell to be considered. It is, however, plain that, in the passage upon which the defendant relies, attention was being concentrated on those cases in which the question is whether the act of the principal falls within the common purpose of the parties. This appears from the immediately succeeding sentence in the judgment of Mason, Murphy and Wilson JJ at 131 (not quoted in the written case for the defendant), which reads:

> Such an act is one which falls within the parties' own purpose and design precisely because it is within their contemplation and is foreseen as a possible incident of the execution of their planned enterprise.

In such a case the contemplation of both parties will be relevant. But, as appears from Sir Robin Cooke's judgment in *Chan Wing-Siu v The Queen* (and as was recognised by Lord Lane CJ in *R v Hyde* [1991] 1 QB 134, departing in this respect from some of the observations contained in the earlier judgments in *R v Slack* [1989] QB 775 and *R v Wakely* [1990] Crim LR 119), the secondary party may be liable simply by reason of his participating in the joint enterprise with foresight that the principal may commit the relevant act as part of the joint enterprise. We therefore find Sir Robin Cooke focusing upon the contemplation of the secondary party alone, as in the following passage at 178:

> In some cases in this field it is enough to direct the jury by adapting to the circumstances the simple formula common in a number of jurisdictions. For instance, did the particular accused contemplate that in carrying out a common unlawful purpose one of his partners in the enterprise might use a knife or a loaded gun with the intention of causing really serious bodily harm?

In practice, of course, in most cases the contemplation of both the primary and the secondary party is likely to be the same; if there is an alleged difference, it will arise where the secondary party asserts in his defence that he did not have in contemplation the act which was in the contemplation of the principal. But their Lordships are unable to accept that in every case the relevant act must be shown to have been in the contemplation of *both* parties before the secondary party can be proved guilty.

Let it be supposed that two men embark on a robbery. One (the principal) to the knowledge of the other (the accessory) is carrying a gun. The accessory contemplates that the principal may use the gun to wound or kill if resistance is met with or the pair are detected at their work but, although the gun is loaded, the only use initially contemplated by the principal is for the purpose of causing fear, by pointing the gun or even by discharging it, with a view to overcoming resistance or evading capture. Then at the scene the principal changes his mind, perhaps through panic or because to fire for effect offers the only chance of escape, and shoots the victim dead. His act is clearly an incident of the unlawful enterprise and the possibility of its occurrence as such was contemplated by the accomplice. According to what was said in *Chan Wing-Siu v The Queen* [1985] AC 168 the accomplice, as well as the principal, would be guilty of murder. Their Lordships have to say that, having regard to what is said in *Chan Wing-Siu v The Queen* and the cases which applied it, they do not consider the prior contemplation of the principal to be a necessary additional ingredient. In their opinion the judge had no duty to direct the jury to that effect in paragraphs 10 and 13 of the relevant passage in his summing up.

In none of the cases reviewed, including the case under appeal, was the prior contemplation of the principal a live issue. But it must be recognised that to hold the accomplice to be guilty in the example their Lordships have posed is consistent with *Chan Wing-Siu v The Queen* and *R v Hyde* [1991] 1 QB 134.

Their Lordships appreciate that the hypothetical example they have given is largely theoretical. Rarely, if ever, will a case arise in which the accessory, but not the principal, contemplates the possibility of a further relevant offence and, if the facts appeared to support such a hypothesis, the defence would no doubt seize the opportunity to contend that the accomplice himself had not been proved to have contemplated something which was not in the mind of the principal. Alternatively, he might contend that the principal's further act had gone beyond the contemplated area of guilty conduct, with the result that the accessory to the planned offence was not criminally liable for the new offence. In truth, the point taken by the defendant was academic; but, for the reasons they have given, their Lordships reject it as unsound.

The defendant's second point relies on Sir Robin Cooke's use of the word 'authorisation' as a synonym for contemplation in the passage already cited from his judgment in *Chan Wing-Siu v The Queen* [1985] AC 168, 175. Their Lordships consider that Sir Robin used this word – and in that regard they do not differ from counsel – to emphasise the fact that mere foresight is not enough: the accessory, in order to be guilty, must have foreseen the relevant offence which the principal may commit *as a possible incident of the common unlawful enterprise* and must, with such foresight, still have participated in the enterprise. The word 'authorisation' explains what is meant by contemplation, but does not add a new ingredient. That this is so is manifest from Sir Robin's pithy conclusion to the passage cited: 'The criminal culpability lies in participating in the venture with that foresight.'

Their Lordships are satisfied that the trial judge accurately conveyed that idea to the jury by paragraph 10 of his directions.

This was a strong case of at least tacit agreement that Ah Hung should be attacked accompanied by foresight, as admitted by the defendant, that a very serious assault might occur, even if that very serious assault had not been planned from the beginning. It is, moreover, easier to prove against an accomplice that he contemplated and by his participation accepted the use of extra force in the execution of the planned assault than it normally would be to show contemplation and acceptance of a new offence, such as murder added to burglary.

Their Lordships therefore reject all the criticisms of the judge's directions to the jury on joint enterprise ...

R v Bourne [1939] 1 KB 687 (CA)

Lord Goddard CJ: The appellant was indicted before Hallett J at the last assizes for Worcestershire and convicted of aiding and abetting his wife to commit the offence commonly called bestiality. The circumstances were such that nobody can approach this case without feeling the utmost repulsion, and indeed the learned judge thought it right, and I think he was quite right, to have a special report on the sanity of the appellant before he tried him. Without going into more of the revolting facts of this case than one can help, the appellant, who is only 28 years of age, his wife being a year or two younger, compelled her on two occasions to submit to the insertion of the male organ of a dog which he had excited into her vagina. That such a man should be allowed to be at large is almost intolerable and dreadful. Though he denied the offence when he went into the witness box, he had admitted it to the police. He had gone to the police to inquire where his wife and children were. The police meantime had been informed of what had been going on, I suppose on complaint by the wife, and they told him what had been suggested and he made a full confession to them, saying he admitted he had been a brute to his wife ...

The case against the appellant was that he was a principal in the second degree to the crime of buggery which was committed by his wife, because if a woman has connection with a dog, or allows a dog to have connection with her, that is the full offence of buggery. She may be able to show that she was forced to commit the offence. I will assume that the plea of duress could have been set up by her on the evidence, and in fact we have allowed Mr Green to argue this case on the footing that the wife would have been entitled to be acquitted on the ground of duress. The learned judge left no question to the jury on duress, but the jury have found that she did not consent ... I am willing to assume for the purpose of this case, and I think my brethren are too, that if this woman had been charged herself with committing the offence, she could have set up the plea of duress, not as showing that no offence had been committed, but as showing that she had no *mens rea* because her will was overborne by threats of imprisonment or violence so that she would be excused from punishment. But the offence of buggery whether with man or beast does not depend upon consent; it depends on the act, and if an act of buggery is committed, the felony is committed.

A point is raised here that the appellant was charged with being not merely an accessory before the fact but with being an aider and abettor. So he was, because the charge is: 'you being present aided and abetted, counselled and procured ...'

In the opinion of the court, there is no doubt that the appellant was properly indicted for being a principal in the second degree to the commission of the crime of buggery. That is all that it is necessary to show. The evidence was, and the jury by their verdict have shown they accepted it, that he caused his wife to have connection with a dog, and if he caused his wife to have connection with a dog he is guilty, whether you call him an aider and abettor or an accessory, as a principal in the second degree. For that reason, this appeal fails and is dismissed.

R v Cogan and Leak [1976] 1 QB 217 (CA)

Lawton LJ: ... The indictment in the statement of offence charged Cogan with rape and Leak as 'being aider and abettor to the same offence'. The particulars of offence against Cogan were in common form. As against Leak they were as follows: 'at the same time and place did aid and abet counsel and procure John Rodney Cogan to commit the said offence'.

The victim of the conduct which the prosecution submitted was rape by both defendants was Leak's wife, a slightly built young woman in her early 20s. They had been married in 1969. There had been many quarrels and some violence. On 9 July 1974, Leak came home in the evening under the influence of alcohol. He asked his wife for money. She refused to give him any. Shortly afterwards he attacked her. He knocked her down and while she was on the floor he kicked her many times. She sustained numerous bruises on her back and hip. At his trial he pleaded guilty to this assault.

The next day Leak came home at about 6 pm with Cogan. Both had been drinking. Leak told his wife that Cogan wanted to have sexual intercourse with her and that he, Leak, was going to see she did. She was frightened of him and what he might do, as well she might have been. He made her go upstairs where he took her clothes off and lowered her on to a bed. Cogan then came into the room. Leak asked him twice whether he wanted sexual intercourse with her. On both occasions he said that he did not. Leak then had sexual intercourse with her in the presence of Cogan. When he had finished, Leak again asked Cogan if he wanted sexual intercourse with his wife. This time Cogan said he did. He asked Leak to leave the room but he refused to do so. Cogan then had sexual intercourse with Mrs Leak. Her husband watched. While all this was going on for most of the time, if not all, Mrs Leak was sobbing. She did not struggle when Cogan was on top of her but she did try to turn away from him. When he had finished, he left the room. Leak then had intercourse with her again and behaved in a revolting fashion to her. When he had finished he joined Cogan and the pair of them left the house to renew their drinking. Mrs Leak dressed. She went to a neighbour's house and then to the police. The two defendants were arrested about three-quarters of an hour later. Both made oral and written statements. Leak did not give evidence.

Leak's statement amounted to a confession that he had procured Cogan to have sexual intercourse with his wife. He admitted that while Cogan was having sexual intercourse with her she was 'sobbing on and off not all the time'. There was ample evidence from the terms of his statement that she had not consented to Cogan having intercourse with her. The whole tenor of this statement was that he had procured Cogan to do what he did in order to punish her for past misconduct. He intended that she should be raped and that Cogan's body should provide the physical means to an end.

Cogan, in his written statement, admitted that he had had sexual intercourse with Mrs Leak at Leak's suggestion and that while he was on top of her she had been upset and had cried. At the trial Cogan gave evidence that he thought Mrs Leak had consented. The basis of his belief was what he had heard from her husband about her. The drink he had had seems to have been a reason, if not the only one, for mistaking her sobs and distress for consent ...

Cogan's appeal against conviction was based on the ground that the decision of the House of Lords in *R v Morgan* [1976] AC 182 applied. It did. There is nothing more to be said. It was for this reason that we allowed the appeal and quashed his conviction.

Leak's appeal against conviction was based on the proposition that he could not be found guilty of aiding and abetting Cogan to rape his wife if Cogan was acquitted of that offence as he was deemed in law to have been when his conviction was quashed: see s 2(3) of the Criminal Appeal Act 1968 ...

... [H]ere one fact is clear – the wife had been raped. Cogan had had sexual intercourse with her without her consent. The fact that Cogan was innocent of rape because he believed that she was consenting does not affect the position that she was raped.

Her ravishment had come about because Leak had wanted it to happen and had taken action to see that it did by persuading Cogan to use his body as the instrument for the necessary physical act. In the language of the law the act of sexual intercourse without the wife's consent was the *actus reus*: it had been procured by Leak who had the appropriate *mens rea*, namely his intention that Cogan should have sexual intercourse with her without her consent. In our judgment it is irrelevant that the man whom Leak had procured to do the physical act himself did not intend to have sexual intercourse with the wife without her consent. Leak was using him as a means to procure a criminal purpose.

Before 1861 a case such as this, pleaded as it was in the indictment, might have presented a court with problems arising from the old distinctions between principals and accessories in felony. Most of the old law was swept away by s 8 of the Accessories and Abettors Act 1861 and what remained by s 1 of the Criminal Law Act 1967. The modern law allowed Leak to be tried and punished as a principal offender. In our judgment he could have been indicted as a principal offender ...

Had Leak been indicted as a principal offender, the case against him would have been clear beyond argument. Should he be allowed to go free because he was charged with 'being aider and abettor to the same offence'? If we are right in our opinion that the wife had been raped (and no one outside a court of law would say that she had not been), then the particulars of offence accurately stated what Leak had done, namely he had procured Cogan to commit the offence. This would suffice to uphold the conviction. We would prefer, however, to uphold it on a wider basis. In our judgment convictions should not be upset because of mere technicalities of pleading in an indictment. Leak knew what the case against him was and the facts in support of that case were proved. But for the fact that the jury thought that Cogan in his intoxicated condition might have mistaken the wife's sobs and distress for expressions of her consent, no question of any kind would have arisen about the form of pleading. By his written statement Leak virtually admitted what he had done. As Judge Chapman said in *R v Humphreys* [1965] 3 All ER 689, 692:

> It would be anomalous if a person who admitted to a substantial part in the perpetration of a misdemeanour as aider and abettor could not be convicted

> on his own admission merely because the person alleged to have been aided and abetted was not or could not be convicted.

In the circumstances of this case it would be more than anomalous: it would be an affront to justice and to the common sense of ordinary folk ...

ACQUITTAL OF ALLEGED PRINCIPAL OFFENDER

Thornton v Mitchell [1940] 1 All ER 339 (KBD)

Lord Hewart LCJ: In my opinion, it is quite clear that this appeal must be allowed. Informations were preferred by the respondent, a superintendent of police, against a certain motor driver, one Hollinrake, for driving a motor vehicle – that is to say, an omnibus – without due care and attention, contrary to s 12(1) of the Road Traffic Act 1930, and also against the same driver for driving a motor vehicle – that is to say, a motor omnibus - without reasonable consideration for other persons using the road. At the same time, the bus conductor was charged as an aider and abettor. The information alleged that Hollinrake did unlawfully drive the motor vehicle without due care and attention, and that the present appellant, who was a bus conductor, unlawfully did aid, abet counsel and procure Hollinrake to do and commit that offence. There was a further charge against the bus conductor under the second information, whereby the driver was charged with driving 'without reasonable consideration for other persons using the road'. In the result, the justices dismissed the two charges against the driver, but convicted the appellant of unlawfully aiding, abetting counselling and procuring the driver to do and commit the offence of driving without due care and attention, contrary to s 12(1). They say in para 8:

> We, being of opinion that the conductor [had been very negligent], held that he was guilty of aiding and abetting, counselling and procuring the said Hollinrake to drive without due care and attention, and accordingly we inflicted a fine.

In my opinion, this case is a *fortiori* upon *Morris v Tolman* [1923] 1 KB 166, to which our attention has been directed. I will read one sentence from the judgment of Avory J at 171:

> ... in order to convict, it would be necessary to show that the respondent was aiding the principal, but a person cannot aid another in doing something which that other has not done.

That, I think is the very thing which these justices have decided that this bus conductor did. In one breath they say that the principal did nothing which he should not have done, and in the next breath they hold that the bus conductor aided and abetted the driver in doing something which had not been done or in not doing something which he ought to have done. I really think that, with all respect to the ingenuity of counsel for the respondent, the case is too plain for argument, and this appeal must be allowed and the conviction quashed.

R v Howe and Others [1987] 1 AC 417 (HL)

Lord Mackay of Clashfern: ... The material facts in Burke's case are, that on 9 July 1983 Burke shot dead one Henry Botton at point blank range with a sawn off shotgun. The victim was due to give evidence at Inner London Crown Court on 18 July 1983 in a trial in which Burke's co-defendant, William Clarkson, was accused with others of conspiracy to handle stolen goods. The victim was to have given evidence in support of the defence of duress by Clarkson, which was raised by one of Clarkson's co-defendants. Burke's defence at his trial was that he had agreed to shoot the victim only because of his fear that Clarkson would kill him if he did not, but when it came to the event, the gun actually went off accidentally and the killing was therefore unintentional and amounted to no more than manslaughter. At the trial it was submitted on behalf of Burke that he was entitled to be acquitted completely of murder and manslaughter by reason of duress and that if this submission failed he was entitled to be acquitted of murder and found guilty of manslaughter by reason of accident in an unlawful act. The judge who presided at the trial, the then Common Sergeant, Judge Tudor Price, directed the jury that Burke, as the actual killer, was not entitled to rely upon the defence of duress to the charge of murder but since he considered there was evidence in support of the defence of duress he left it to the jury in respect of manslaughter. He further directed the jury that they could not convict Clarkson of murder unless the convicted Burke of murder and that if Burke was guilty of manslaughter then Clarkson could be convicted, at most, only of manslaughter and that if the appellant was acquitted on the grounds of duress then Clarkson, the author of the duress, must be convicted of manslaughter ...

... In dismissing the appeals the court certified three points of law of general public importance were involved in the decisions to dismiss the appeals, namely:

> ... (2) Can the one who incites or procures by duress another to kill or to be a party to a killing be convicted of murder if that other is acquitted by reason of duress?...

... Clarkson's appeal is concerned with the second question in respect of which he contends that if Burke was acquitted by reason of duress he could not be convicted of murder as one who had incited or procured by duress Burke to kill or to be a party to a killing ...

Question 2

I turn now to the second certified question. In the view that I take on question one the second does not properly arise. However, I am of opinion that the Court of Appeal reached the correct conclusion upon it as a matter of principle.

Giving the judgment of the Court of Appeal Lord Lane CJ said [1986] QB 626 at 641–42:

> The judge based himself on a decision of this court in *R v Richards* [1974] QB 776. The facts in that case were that Mrs Richards paid two men to inflict injuries on her husband which she intended should 'put him in hospital for a month'. The two men wounded the husband but not seriously. They were acquitted of wounding with intent but convicted of unlawful wounding. Mrs Richards herself was convicted of wounding with intent, the jury plainly, and not surprisingly, believing that she had the necessary intent, though the two men had not. She appealed against her conviction on the ground that she could not properly be convicted as accessory before the fact to a crime more serious than that committed by the principals in the first degree. The appeal was allowed and the conviction for unlawful wounding was substituted. The court followed a passage from *Hawkins' Pleas of the Crown*, Vol 2 c 29, para 15: 'I take it to be an uncontroverted rule that [the offence of the accessory can never rise higher than that of the principal]; it seeming incongruous and absurd that he who is punished only as a partaker of the guilt of another, should be adjudged guilty of a higher crime than the other.'
>
> James LJ delivering the judgment in *R v Richards* [1974] QB 776 said at 780: 'If there is only one offence committed, and that is the offence of unlawful wounding, then the person who has requested that offence to be committed,

> or advised that that offence be committed, cannot be guilty of a graver offence than that in fact which was committed.' The decision in *R v Richards* has been the subject of some criticism. Counsel before us posed the situation where A hands a gun to D informing him that it is loaded with blank ammunition only and telling him to go and scare X by discharging it. The ammunition is in fact live, as A knows, and X is killed. D is convicted only of manslaughter, as he might be on those facts. It would seem absurd that A should thereby escape conviction for murder. We take the view that *R v Richards* was incorrectly decided, but it seems to us that it cannot properly be distinguished from the instant case.

I consider that the reasoning of Lord Lane CJ is entirely correct and I would affirm his view that where a person has been killed and that result is the result intended by another participant, the mere fact that the actual killer may be convicted only of the reduced charge of manslaughter for some reason special to himself does not, in my opinion in any way, result in a compulsory reduction for the other participant ...

R v Millward [1994] Crim LR 527 (CA)

Facts: The appellant was convicted of aiding, abetting, counselling or procuring another person to cause death by reckless driving. The prosecution case was that the appellant had given one of his employees instructions which involved him using a tractor belonging to the appellant to tow a trailer on a main road. The tractor's hitch was poorly maintained and during the journey the trailer became detached and hit a car, causing the death of a passenger. The recklessness alleged was confined to the state of the hitch mechanism, and the appellant was said to have procured the offence by his instructions to his employee. It was argued on appeal that there was no reported case of a procurer being convicted following the acquittal of a principal offender. Further, in the instant case, the word 'reckless' imported a mental element into the *actus reus* of the offence. The acquittal thus implied that the *actus reus* had not been committed.

Held, dismissing the appeal,

(1) a passage in Blackstone's *Criminal Practice* was approved, to the effect that an accessory can be liable provided that there is the *actus reus* of the principal offence even if the principal offender is entitled to be acquitted because of some defence personal to him. Procuring does not require a joint intention between accessory and principal. The procurer may, therefore, be convicted where the principal lacks the necessary *mens rea*.

(2) In the instant case, the *actus reus* was taking of the vehicle in its defective condition on to the road so as to cause the death. It was procured by the appellant.

(3) The ratio of *Thornton and Mitchell* [1940] 1 All ER 339 was that the driver did not commit the *actus reus* of careless driving, the offence in that case. He relied on the conductor's signals.

(4) *Cogan and Leak* [1976] QB 217 was, contrary to the submissions of the defence, essentially a case of procuring rather than aiding and abetting, and could not be distinguished from the present case.

R v Loukes [1996] 1 Cr App R 444 (CA)

Auld LJ: ... Mr Loukes and his brother, Ian Loukes, were partners in a haulage contractors. Mr Loukes's role in the business was to oversee the maintenance and servicing by the firm's mechanics of its fleet of vehicles. Ian Loukes drove some of the vehicles and had other responsibilities, but none of them included the servicing of vehicles. Ronnie Kennedy was one of the firm's drivers.

On 10 July 1993 Mr Kennedy was driving an ERF tipper truck of the firm along the northbound carriageway of the M1. Part of the prop shaft broke free and flew across the crash barrier into the path of a vehicle travelling in the southbound carriageway, killing its driver. The police examined the vehicle, and as a result Mr Kennedy was charged with causing death by dangerous driving, and Mr Loukes and his brother were charged with aiding, abetting, counselling or procuring that offence.

At the trial the prosecution case against Mr Loukes was that he caused the truck to be driven by Mr Kennedy when he, Mr Loukes, knew or ought to have known that it was in a dangerous state. PC Logan, an accident investigation officer, gave evidence about the truck's transmission system of which the prop shaft was a part. He said that the system had several pre-accident defects which, together, had caused lateral movements in the sliding joints of the system, which in turn had caused the prop shaft to become loose and fly off ...

As to the mechanics of the prop shaft breaking free, PC Logan's opinion was that the nut had become loose and had eventually become detached from the flange, allowing the flange to move partly away from the shaft, hence the worn splines and grooves on the shaft. He said that he would have expected that last damage to have occurred about four hours before the castellated nut worked its way completely free of the flange, allowing the prop shaft to break away. He added that during that period of loosening of the nut there would have been additional noise and vibration detectable to the driver. His conclusion in summary was that an examination of the underside of the vehicle before the accident would have revealed the defects in the flange, and that it would have been obvious there was a danger of that part of the prop shaft breaking free and causing an accident ...

At the close of the prosecution case the judge upheld submissions of no case to answer on behalf of Ian Loukes and Ronnie Kennedy, but rejected a similar submission on behalf of Mr Loukes.

Mr Loukes did not give evidence or call any witnesses. His defence, as presented by his counsel to the jury, was that, although the truck had been in a dangerous state, there was no evidence that the defects alleged to have been dangerous and to have caused the accident, did cause it, and, in any event, no evidence that he had known of its dangerous state.

The first ground of appeal is that the judge, having directed the jury to acquit Mr Kennedy of the principal offence, misdirected the jury by directing them that Mr Loukes could be found guilty of the secondary offence. His case, in reliance on the well-known authority of *Thornton v Mitchell* [1940] 1 All ER 339, is that the judge directed the acquittal of Mr Kennedy because there was no evidence that he had committed the *actus reus* of the offence, and that, therefore, he, Mr Loukes, could not be convicted of procuring it. He accepts, in reliance on *Millward* [1994] Crim LR 527, that if the judge properly directed the acquittal of Mr Kennedy only for want of evidence of *mens rea*, he, Mr Loukes, could be convicted of the secondary offence.

The principle upon which the court proceeded in *Millward* was that the procurer of another to commit the *actus reus* of an offence may be convicted of procuring it even if that other is not guilty of it for want of *mens rea*. The critical question here is 'What is the *actus reus* of the new offence of causing death by dangerous driving?'

Mr Loukes was charged with aiding, abetting, counselling or procuring Mr Kennedy to cause death by dangerous driving, contrary to ss 1 and 2A(2) of the

Road Traffic Act 1988, as amended on 1 July 1992 by the Road Traffic Act 1991. The effect of that amendment was to substitute the offence of causing death by dangerous driving for that of causing death by reckless driving. The material provisions of ss 1 and 2A of the 1988 Act read:

1 A person who causes the death of another by driving a mechanically propelled vehicle dangerously on a road or other public place is guilty of an offence.

2A(1) For the purposes of s 1 ... above a person is to be regarded as driving dangerously if (and, subject to subsection (2) below, only if):

(a) the way he drives falls far below what would be expected of a competent and careful driver, and

(b) it would be obvious to a competent and careful driver that driving in that way would be dangerous.

(2) A person is also to be regarded as driving dangerously for the purposes of s 1 ... if it would be obvious to a competent and careful driver that driving the vehicle in its current state would be dangerous.

(3) ... in determining ... what would be ... obvious to ... a competent and careful driver in a particular case, regard shall be had not only to the circumstances of which he could be expected to be aware but also to any circumstances shown to have been within the knowledge of the accused.

By reference to ss 1 and 2A(2), the principal offence charged, giving rise to the secondary charge against Mr Loukes, was that Mr Kennedy caused death by driving the vehicle when it would have been obvious to a competent and careful driver that to do so in its then state would be dangerous ...

It is implicit in the judge's ruling on the submission on behalf of Mr Loukes that he did not regard the *actus reus* as including any element of constructive knowledge of a notional competent and careful driver. In his definition of the *actus* he was clearly influenced by the decision of this court in *Millward*, a case concerning the procuring of the former offence of causing death by reckless driving, the recklessness relating to a defect in the vehicle and not to the manner of driving. The court there held that the *actus reus* of the principal offence lay in the taking of the vehicle on the road in a defective condition so as to cause death. It held that a procurer could be found guilty even though the driver was not, and that the *mens rea* of the procurer lay in the causing of that *actus reus* knowing of the vehicle's defective condition, whether or not it was or should have been known to the driver. The decision has been expressly approved by another division of this court in *Wheelhouse* [1994] Crim LR 756. As Professor Sir John Smith observed in a commentary in [1994] Crim LR 528–30, it:

> ... breaks new ground, being the first case to decide that procuring the *actus reus* of an offence is itself that offence ...

The drafting of the new provisions is tortuous, but their intent is plain, namely that a driver is guilty of an offence if, measured by an objective standard, his driving is dangerous. The standard might be said to be one of constructive blameworthiness, namely a constructive knowledge of danger – what should have been obvious to him because it would have been obvious to a competent and careful driver who also knew what he did. This is close to the first, alternative part of the *Lawrence* test of recklessness applicable to the former offence of reckless driving, namely driving in a way so as to create an obvious risk of danger without having given any thought to it. See *R v Lawrence* [1982] AC 510 HL, *per* Lord Diplock at p 526e. We say 'close to' because of the logical uncertainty that that formula left as to the relevance of what was or what should have been in the mind of a person accused of reckless driving and the tangled jurisprudence to which the formula gave rise ...

The purpose of the 1991 amendment was to resolve that uncertainty by introducing a wholly objective test and thus an absolute offence. In our view, it has achieved that. *Mens rea* plays no part in the principal offence. Proof of guilt depends on an objective standard of driving, namely what would have been obvious to a competent and careful driver. The accused driver's state of mind is relevant only if and to the extent that it attributes additional knowledge to the notional competent and careful driver. See the commentary to *Woodward* [1995] Crim LR 487; and the commentary to *Skelton* [1995] Crim LR 635. It should be noted too that the threshold of proof is high. It must be shown that the defect was 'obvious' to a 'competent and careful driver'. It is not enough to show in the case of such a driver that, say, if he had examined the vehicle by going underneath it, he would have seen the defect. See *Strong* [1995] Crim LR 428.

The effect of the judge's ruling in withdrawing from the jury the case against Mr Kennedy was that there was no dangerous driving here because, not only was there no evidence that he knew of the dangerous condition, but also – the critical test – no evidence that it would have been obvious to a competent and careful driver. It follows that the effect, though not the form, of the judge's ruling was that there was no evidence of the commission of the *actus reus* of the offence.

Where does that conclusion leave the conviction of Mr Loukes as an alleged procurer of a non-existent offence? We do not consider *Millward* to be of help in the new statutory context. It was essential to the decision in that case that there was evidence of the commission of the *actus reus*. Scott Baker J, giving the judgment of the court, said:

> ... the *actus reus* ... was the taking of the vehicle in the defective condition on the road so as to cause the death.

For reasons we have given, the *actus reus* of the new offence of dangerous driving is broader, its criterion being the objective one of obviousness to a competent and careful driver, whether or not supplemented by any particular knowledge of the accused driver. In the offence of reckless driving, there was scope for consideration of *mens rea*, however faint on the first alternative in the *Lawrence* test, and it was certainly an element of the second alternative. Here there is no room for it.

Accordingly, we are of the view that the *Millward* principle does not enable conviction of an alleged procurer of causing death by dangerous driving where the dangerous driving as defined in s 2A(2) has not been established. In our view, this case is governed by *Thornton v Mitchell*. A man cannot be convicted of procuring an offence where the *actus reus* is not established. That is enough to dispose of the appeal in Mr Loukes's favour ...

... [F]or the reasons that we have given, we allow the appeal on the first ground, that Mr Loukes could not procure an offence, the *actus reus* of which all of the offence in this case – has not been committed. The case of *Millward* [1994] Crim LR 527 was decided after the change in the law, and the problem that the court had to consider there does not appear to have been considered in the Road Traffic Review Report ('the North Report'), Department of Transport and Home Office 1988, the Government White Paper, 'The Road User and the Law', February 1989 (Cmd CM576) or in the passage of the bill which became the 1991 Act through Parliament. If we are correct in our interpretation of the new provisions, a person who, knowing of the dangerous state of a vehicle, procures another, innocent of that dangerous state, to drive it, and where there is no evidence that that state would have been obvious to a competent and careful driver, will escape conviction. In our view, that injustice can only be cured by legislation ...

PRESENCE AT THE SCENE OF THE CRIME

To be guilty as a secondary party, a person who has encouraged the commission of an offence need not be present when the offence is actually committed. On the other hand, mere presence at the scene of a crime or failure to prevent someone else from committing an offence, is insufficient to give rise to liability as an accessory. There are, however, some instances where presence at the scene of a crime will be regarded as encouragement (eg *Wilcox v Jeffery* [1951] 1 All ER 464; *R v Allan* [1965] 1 QB 130; *R v Jefferson* [1994] 1 All ER 270)

R v Coney and Others (1882) 8 QBD 534

Cave J: ... The evidence was that on the 16 June last, at the close of Ascot races, Burke and Mitchell had engaged in a fight near the road from Ascot to Maidenhead; that a ring was formed with posts and ropes; that a large number of persons were present looking on, some of whom were undoubtedly encouraging the fight; that the men fought for some time; and that the three prisoners were seen in the crowd, but were not seen to do anything, and there was no evidence how they got there or how long they stayed there.

The chairman of quarter sessions directed the jury in the words of *Russell on Crimes*, Vol 1, p 818: 'There is no doubt that prize-fights are illegal, indeed just as much so as that persons should go out to fight with deadly weapons, and it is not at all material which party strikes the first blow, and all persons who go to a prize-fight to see the combatants strike each other, and who are present when they do so are, in point of law, guilty of an assault.' And the chairman added, in the words of Littledale J, in *R v Murphy* 6 C and P 103: 'If they were not casually passing by, but stayed at the place, they encouraged it by their presence, although they did not say or do anything.'

... Now it is a general rule in the case of principals in the second degree that there must be participation in the act, and that, although a man is present whilst a felony is being committed, if he takes no part in it, and does not act in concert with those who commit it, he will not be a principal in the second degree merely because he does not endeavour to prevent the felony, or apprehend the felon ...

... Where presence may be entirely accidental, it is not even evidence of aiding and abetting. Where presence is *prima facie* not accidental it is evidence, but no more than evidence, for the jury ...

This summing up unfortunately appears to me capable of being understood in two different ways. It may mean either that mere presence unexplained is evidence of encouragement, and so of guilt, or that mere presence unexplained is conclusive proof of encouragement, and so of guilt. If the former is the correct meaning, I concur in the law so laid down, if the latter, I am unable to do so. It appears to me that the passage tending to convey the latter view is that which was read by the chairman in this case to the jury, and I cannot help thinking that the chairman believed himself, and meant to direct the jury, and at any rate I feel satisfied that the jury understood him to mean, that mere presence unexplained was conclusive proof of encouragement, and so of guilt; and it is on this ground I hold that this conviction ought not to stand.

Lopes J: ... I understand the ruling of the chairman to amount to this, that mere presence at a prize-fight, unexplained, is conclusive proof of aiding and abetting, even if there be no evidence that the person or persons so present encouraged, or intended to encourage the fight by his or their presence. I cannot hold, as a proposition of law, that the mere looking on is *ipso facto* a participation in or encouragement of a prize-fight. I think there must be more than that to justify a conviction for an assault. If, for instance, it was proved that a person went to a prize-fight, knowing it was to take place, and remained there for some time looking on, I think that would be evidence from which a jury might infer that such person encouraged, and intended to encourage, the fight by his presence. In the present case, the three prisoners were merely seen in the crowd, were not seen to do anything, and there was no evidence why or how they came there, or how long they stayed.

Applying the direction of the chairman to this state of facts, I think it was wrong.

Hawkins J: ... In summing up the case the chairman directed the jury that all persons who went to a prize-fight to see the combatants strike each other, and who were present when they did so, were, in point of law, guilty of an assault, for 'if they were not casually passing by, but stayed at the place, they encouraged it by their presence, although they did not do or say anything'. The jury, on that direction, found the defendants guilty, but they also found expressly that they were not aiding or abetting. The whole question, therefore, for us to determine, as a matter of law, is not whether voluntary presence at a prize-fight is evidence of an aiding and abetting, but whether inactive presence at a prize-fight as a voluntary spectator thereof, amounts of itself to such encouragement of it as to render a man amenable to the criminal law as an aider and abettor in that breach of the peace ...

In my opinion, to constitute an aider and abettor some active steps must be taken by word, or action, with the intent to instigate the principal, or principals. Encouragement does not of necessity amount to aiding and abetting, it may be intentional or unintentional, a man may unwittingly encourage another in fact by his presence, by misinterpreted words, or gestures, or by his silence, on non-interference, or he may encourage intentionally by expressions, gestures, or actions intended to signify approval. In the latter case he aids and abets, in the former he does not. It is no criminal offence to stand by, a mere passive spectator of a crime, even of a murder. Non-interference to prevent a crime is not itself a crime. But the fact that a person was voluntarily and purposely present witnessing the commission of a crime, and offered no opposition to it, though he might reasonably be expected to prevent and had the power so to do, or at least to express his dissent, might under some circumstances, afford cogent evidence upon which a jury would be justified in finding that he wilfully encouraged and so aided and abetted. But it would be purely a question for the jury whether he did so or not. So if any number of persons arrange that a criminal offence shall take place, and it takes place accordingly, the mere presence of any of those who so arranged it would afford abundant evidence for the consideration of a jury of an aiding and abetting ...

Huddleston B: ... The mere staying at the place where a fight is going on is not necessarily encouragement; the detective sent to report what is taking place and to bring the offenders to justice cannot be said to be encouraging what is going on; a person casually passing, but who stays to see what happens and interferes to prevent, or retires in disgust, or is hemmed in so that he cannot retire, cannot be said to be encouraging ... The finding of the jury was in fact one of not guilty. They bow with respect to the chairman's direction in point of law, but by adding that the prisoners were not aiding and abetting, I conclude that they intend to convey that by no act of theirs were they countenancing or encouraging the fight, a conclusion fully supported by the evidence in the case.

Manisty J: ... It is said that if the ruling of the chairman is not upheld a great impetus will be given to prize fighting. I do not share in that apprehension. It is well-settled law that every person who by his presence or otherwise encourages a fight, be it a prize or an ordinary fight, is guilty of a criminal offence, that is to say, of an assault or manslaughter, as the case may be, but it is for the jury in each particular case to say as a matter of fact whether the accused did by his presence or otherwise encourage the combatants to fight. To hold the contrary would, in my opinion, be erroneous in point of law, and very injurious in its consequences.

Suppose that the fight in question had resulted in the death of one of the combatants, then, if the direction given to the jury was right, every person who was in the crowd was in point of law guilty of manslaughter, though he neither spoke nor did anything, and notwithstanding that in the opinion of the jury he neither aided nor abetted the combatants. I cannot believe such is the law of England ...

Wilcox v Jeffery [1951] 1 All ER 464 (KBD)

Lord Goddard CJ: This is a case stated by the metropolitan magistrate at Bow Street Magistrates' Court before whom the appellant, Herbert William Wilcox, the proprietor of a periodical called 'Jazz Illustrated', was charged on an information that 'on 11 December 1949, he did unlawfully aid and abet one Coleman Hawkins in contravening Art 1(4) of the Aliens Order, 1920, by failing to comply with a condition attached to a grant of leave to land, to wit, that the said Coleman Hawkins should take no employment paid or unpaid while in the United Kingdom, contrary to Art 18(2) of the Aliens Order, 1920'. Under the Aliens Order, Art 1(1), it is provided that:

> ... an alien coming ... by sea to a place in the United Kingdom: (a) shall not land in the United Kingdom without the leave of an immigration officer ...

It is provided by Art 1(4) that:

> An immigration officer, in accordance with general or special directions of the Secretary of State, may, by general order or notice or otherwise, attach such conditions as he may think fit to the grant of leave to land, and the Secretary of State may at any time vary such conditions in such manner as he thinks fit, and the alien shall comply with the conditions so attached or varied ...

If the alien fails to comply, he is to be in the same position as if he has landed without permission, ie he commits an offence.

The case is concerned with the visit of a celebrated professor of the saxophone, a gentleman by the name of Hawkins who was a citizen of the United States. He came here at the invitation of two gentlemen of the name of Curtis and Hughes, connected with a jazz club which enlivens the neighbourhood of Willesden. They, apparently, had applied for permission for Mr Hawkins to land and it was refused, but, nevertheless, this professor of the saxophone arrived with four French musicians. When they came to the airport, among the people who were there to greet them was the appellant. He had not arranged their visit, but he knew they were coming and he was there to report the arrival of these important musicians for his magazine. So, evidently, he was regarding the visit of Mr Hawkins as a matter which would be of interest to himself and the magazine which he was editing and selling for profit. Messrs Curtis and Hughes arranged a concert at the Princes Theatre, London. The appellant attended that concert as a spectator. He paid for his ticket. Mr Hawkins went on the stage and delighted the audience by playing the saxophone. The appellant did not get up and protest in the name of the musicians of England that Mr Hawkins ought not to be here competing with them and taking the bread out of their mouths or the wind out of their instruments. It is not found that he actually applauded, but he was there having paid to go in, and, no doubt, enjoying the performance, and then lo and behold, out comes his magazine with a most laudatory description, fully illustrated, of this concert. On those facts the magistrate has found that he aided and abetted.

Reliance is placed by the prosecution on *R v Coney* (1882) 8 QBD 534 which dealt with a prize-fight. This case relates to a jazz band concert, but the particular nature of the entertainment provided, whether by fighting with bare fists or playing on saxophones, does not seem to me to make any difference to the question which we have to decide. The fact is that a man is charged with aiding and abetting an illegal act, and I can find no authority for saying that it matters what that illegal act is, provided that the aider and abettor knows the facts sufficiently well to know that they would constitute an offence in the principal. In *R v Coney* the prize-fight took place in the neighbourhood of Ascot, and four or five men were convicted of aiding and abetting the fight. The conviction was quashed on the ground that the chairman had not given a correct direction to the jury when he told them that, as the prisoners were physically present at the fight, they must be held to have aided and abetted. That direction, the court held, was wrong, it being too wide. The matter was very concisely put by Cave J, whose judgment was fully concurred in by that great master of the criminal law, Stephen J. Cave J said (8 QBD 534 at 540):

> Where presence may be entirely accidental, it is not even evidence of aiding and abetting. Where presence is *prima facie* not accidental it is evidence, but no more than evidence, for the jury.

There was not accidental presence in this case. The appellant paid to go to the concert and he went there because he wanted to report it. He must, therefore, be held to have been present, taking part, concurring, or encouraging, whichever word you like to use for expressing this conception. It was an illegal act on the part of Hawkins to play the saxophone or any other instrument at this concert. The appellant clearly knew that it was an unlawful act for him to play. He had gone there to hear him, and his presence and his payment to go there was an encouragement. He went there to make use of the performance, because he went there, as the magistrate finds and was justified in finding, to get 'copy' for his newspaper. It might have been entirely different, as I say, if he had gone there and protested, saying: 'The musicians' union do not like you foreigners coming here and playing and you ought to get off the stage.' If he had booed, it might have been some evidence that he was not aiding and abetting. If he had gone as a member of a claque to try to drown the noise of the saxophone, he might very likely be found not guilty of aiding and abetting. In this case it seems clear that he was there, not only to approve and encourage what was done, but to take advantage of it by getting 'copy' for his paper. In those circumstances there was evidence on which the magistrates could find that the appellant aided and abetted, and for these reasons I am of opinion that the appeal fails.

R v Allan and Others [1965] 1 QB 130 (CA)

Facts: On 8 September 1962, a fight with knives took place between a number of Somalis and white men in streets in the vicinity of the Oswald Hotel in

Scunthorpe. During the evening a Somali named Yusef was stabbed to death in Allanby Street. The fight appeared to have lasted 15 minutes; a large number of people had collected in Frances Street, West Street and Allanby Street, where the principal fighting occurred, and during its course Allan, Ballantyne and Mooney received knife wounds.

Edmund Davies J: ... [T]he judge ... directed the jury that they were duty bound to convict an accused who was proved to have been present and witnessing an affray if it was also proved that he nursed an intention to join in if help were needed by the side he favoured and this notwithstanding that he did nothing by words or deeds to evince his intention and outwardly played the role of a purely passive spectator. It was said that, if that direction be right, where A and B behave themselves to all outward appearances in an exactly similar manner, but it be proved that A had the intention to participate if needs be, whereas B had no such intention, then A must be convicted of being a principal in the second degree to the affray, whereas B should be acquitted. To do that, it is objected, would be to convict A on his thoughts, even though they found no reflection in his actions. For the Crown, on the other hand, it is contended that the direction was unimpeachable, and that in the given circumstances a jury doing its duty would be bound to convict A of aiding and abetting in an affray even though he uttered no word of encouragement and acted throughout in exactly the same manner as all the other spectators of what was happening.

The *locus classicus* on this branch of the law is the majority decision of the Court of Crown Cases Reserved in *R v Coney* (1882) 8 QBD 534, whereby the conviction of mere spectators of a prize-fight as being aiders and abettors in the fight was quashed ...

... [W]e have come to the conclusion that, in effect the trial judge here dealt with facts which, at most might provide some evidence of encouragement as amounting to conclusive proof of guilt. The jury were in terms told that a man who chooses to remain at a fight, nursing the secret intention to help if the need arose, but doing nothing to evince that intention, *must* in law be held to be a principal in the second degree and that, on these facts being proved, the jury would have no alternative but to convict him. In our judgment that was a misdirection. As Cave J said in *R v Coney*: 'Where presence is *prima facie* not accidental it is evidence, but no more than evidence, for the jury', and it remains no more than evidence for the jury even when one adds to presence at an affray a secret intention to help ...

... In our judgment, before a jury can properly convict an accused person of being a principal in the second degree to an affray, they must be convinced by the evidence that, at the very least, he by some means or other encouraged the participants. To hold otherwise would be, in effect, as the appellants' counsel rightly expressed it, to convict a man on his thoughts, unaccompanied by any physical act other than the fact of his mere presence.

Indeed, in our judgment, encouragement in one form or another is a minimal requirement before an accused person may properly be regarded as a principal in the second degree to any crime. It is true that in *National Coal Board v Gamble* [1959] 1 QB 11, 24 Devlin J, referring to *R v Coney* (1882) 8 QBD 584, said: 'It would be wrong to conclude ... that proof of encouragement is necessary to every form of aiding and abetting.' But when the facts of that case are examined, it does not, in our judgment, affect the validity of the proposition we have stated, for there the accused had intentionally supplied an article essential to the perpetration of the crime charged, and this Devlin J described as an *a fortiori* case to that of voluntary presence. In that case there was what was judicially described as 'proof of intent to aid', which may properly be regarded as but one of the numerous possible manifestations of encouragement ...

R v Clarkson and Others [1971] 1 WLR 1402 (Courts-Martial Appeal Court)

Megaw LJ: ... It is unnecessary to go into much detail as to the disgraceful and shameful events which took place on the night of 9/10 May 1970 in which beyond all the appellants, as well as others, were concerned. On no view can the conduct of any of them be regarded as other than deplorable. The question, however, is whether their respective convictions for criminal offences can be sustained.

The relevant facts will be recited as briefly as possible. The victim of the offences was an 18-year-old girl named Elke von Groen. On 9 May 1970 she, having recently come out of hospital where she had undergone an operation to her womb, went to a party at the barracks at Menden. At about midnight she left the party to go to see a soldier with whom she had in the past been familiar. She went to his room. He was not there but other soldiers were there. Eventually she went to another room, room 64, where the rapes occurred. There she was raped at least by Newton, by Holloway and by Marshall at one time or another between midnight and about 3.15 am. She was physically injured and her clothes were torn to shreds. To say that those who attacked her behaved like animals would be unjust to animals. At some time after the raping began and when she had been screaming and moaning, there were clustered outside the door of room 64 a number of men, including the three appellants, no doubt listening to what was going on inside. The only thing to be said in their favour is that they may have been in a drunken condition when their moral sense and sense of the requirements of human decency had left them. The door of room 64 opened and they, including the three appellants, in the words of a witness 'piled in' to the room. There is no doubt that they remained there for a considerable time and there is no doubt that during that time the unfortunate girl was raped. There is no doubt that some of those present actively assisted by helping to hold down the unfortunate girl. However, so far as the appellants Clarkson and Carroll are concerned, there was no evidence – no admissible evidence and therefore no evidence – of their having done any positive act to assist. There was no evidence – no admissible evidence – that either of them helped to hold down the girl ...

As has been said, there was no evidence on which the prosecution sought to rely that either the appellant Clarkson or the appellant Carroll had done any physical act or uttered any words which involved direct physical participation or verbal encouragement. There was no evidence that they had touched the girl, helped to hold her down, done anything to her, done anything to prevent others from assisting her or to prevent her from escaping, or from trying to ward off her attackers, or that they had said anything which gave encouragement to the others to commit crime or to participate in committing crime. Therefore, if there was here aiding and abetting by the appellants Clarkson or Carroll it could only have been on the basis of inferences to be drawn that by their very presence they, each of them separately as concerns himself, encouraged those who were committing rape. Let it be accepted, and there was evidence to justify this assumption, that the presence of those two appellants in the room where the offence was taking place was not accidental in any sense and that it was not by chance, unconnected with the crime, that they were there. Let it be accepted that they entered the room when the crime was committed because of what they had heard, which indicated that a woman was being raped, and they remained there.

R v Coney (1882) 8 QBD 534 decided that non-accidental presence at the scene of the crime is not conclusive of aiding and abetting. The jury has to be told by the judge, or as in this case the court-martial has to be told by the judge-advocate, in clear terms what it is that has to be proved before they can convict of aiding and abetting; what it is of which the jury or the court-martial, as the case may be, must be sure as matters of inference before they can convict of aiding and abetting in such a case where the evidence adduced by the prosecution is limited to non-accidental presence. What has to be proved is stated by Hawkins J in a well-known passage in his judgment in *R v Coney* (1882) 8 QBD at 557, 558 where he said:

> In my opinion, to constitute an aider and abettor some active steps must be taken by words, or action with the intent to instigate the principal, or principals. Encouragement does not of necessity amount to aiding and abetting, it may be intentional or unintentional, a man may unwittingly encourage another in fact by his presence, by misinterpreted words, or gestures, or by his silence, or non-interference, or he may encourage intentionally by expressions, gestures, or actions intended to signify approval. In the latter case he aids and abets, in the former he does not. It is no criminal offence to stand by, a mere passive spectator of a crime, even of a murder. Non-interference to prevent a crime is not itself a crime. But the fact that a person was voluntarily and purposely present witnessing the commission of a crime, and offered no opposition to it, though he might reasonably be expected to prevent and had the power so to do, or at least to express his dissent, might under some circumstances, afford cogent evidence upon which a jury would be justified in finding that he wilfully encouraged and so aided and abetted. But it would be purely a question for the jury whether he did so or not.

It is not enough, then, that the presence of the accused has, in fact, given encouragement. It must be proved that the accused intended to give encouragement; that he *wilfully* encouraged. In a case such as the present, more than in many other cases where aiding and abetting is alleged, it was essential that that element should be stressed; for there was here at least the possibility that a drunken man with his self-discipline loosened by drink, being aware that a woman was being raped, might be attracted to the scene and might stay on the scene in the capacity of what is known as a voyeur; and, while his presence and the presence of others might in fact encourage the rapers or discourage the victim, he himself, enjoying the scene or at least standing by assenting, might not intend that his presence should offer encouragement to rapers and would-be rapers or discouragement to the victim; he might not realise that he was giving encouragement; so that, while encouragement there might be, it would not be a case in which, to use the words of Hawkins J, the accused person 'wilfully encouraged'.

A further point is emphasised in passages in the judgment of the Court of Criminal Appeal in *R v Allan* [1965] 1 QB 130 at 135, 138. That was a case concerned with participation in an affray. Edmund Davies J, giving the judgment of the court, said:

> In effect, it amounts to this: that the learned judge thereby directed the jury that they were duty bound to convict an accused who was proved to have been present and witnessing an affray if it was also proved that he nursed an intention to join in if help were needed by the side which he favoured, and this notwithstanding that he did nothing by words or deeds to evince his intention and outwardly played the role of purely passive spectator. It was said that, if that direction be right, where A and B behave themselves to all

> outward appearances in an exactly similar manner, but it be proved that A had the intention to participate if needs be, whereas B had no such intention, then A must be convicted of being a principal in the second degree to the affray, whereas B should be acquitted. To do that, it is objected, would be to convict A on his thoughts, even though they found no reflection in his actions.

The other passage in the judgment is this:

> In our judgment, before a jury can properly convict an accused person of being a principal in the second degree to an affray, they must be convinced by the evidence that, at the very least, he by some means or other encouraged the participants. To hold otherwise would be, in effect, as counsel for the appellants rightly expressed it, to convict a man on his thoughts, unaccompanied by any physical act other than the fact of his mere presence.

From that it follows that mere intention is not in itself enough. There must be an intention to encourage; and there must also be encouragement in fact, in cases such as the present case.

So we come to what was said by the judge-advocate ...

The judge-advocate draws the analogy which is commonly drawn where direction is given of two persons jointly indicted, for example, of committing burglary. One actually enters the house and the other stands outside to keep watch. That analogy, in the view of this court, is misleading in relation to what was involved in the present case, for it presupposes a prior meeting of minds between the persons concerned as to the crime to be committed. The man who stands outside and does not go in is guilty of burglary; but it cannot in such a case properly be said that he has taken no active step in the commission of the offence. He has gone to the place where he is, and he has conducted himself as he does, as a part of the joint plan which, in its totality, is intended to procure commission of the crime.

In the view of this court the echo of that false analogy unfortunately continued throughout when the judge-advocate came to sum up the matter to the court-martial ...

R v Tait [1993] Crim LR 538 (CA)

Facts: The appellant was charged, along with a co-defendant, with assault occasioning actual bodily harm. The Crown alleged that the appellant, who was the licensee of a public house, assaulted a customer; the latter had brought with him a person banned from the public house and when the appellant refused to serve them he swept glasses off the bar and knocked over a table before leaving. It was said that the appellant and his co-defendant decided to teach the customer a lesson and, upon the customer leaving the building, the co-defendant jumped on his back, knocking him to the ground, and the appellant kicked him while he was on the ground (one Crown witness said that the appellant did not kick the customer at all and the customer gave evidence only of being kicked by someone). After the incident the appellant said words to the effect of 'no one messes with me'. There was no medical evidence that the customer was injured as a result of any kicks. The defence was that the customer fell over and the injuries (to his face) were accidental. In his summing up the judge directed the jury that a tacit agreement was sufficient; that the Crown's case was that both defendants took an active part in the assault but at the least if there were no physical act on the part of either they could find them guilty on the basis of a joint enterprise if the (non-active) person was physically present and ready and willing to assist in the assault. Both defendants were convicted.

The basis of the appellant's appeal was that the judge misdirected the jury on the question of joint enterprise.

Held, allowing the appeal, where the Crown relied on joint enterprise, it must prove an intention to encourage and wilful or actual encouragement. The judge's direction to the jury was therefore incomplete because it omitted any reference to actual encouragement. The Crown had submitted that evidence of a tacit agreement would have been sufficient and the court agreed; however the last words of the summing up did not refer to the alternative method of finding joint enterprise established by a tacit agreement. The jury could have been misled into thinking that they could convict the appellant without either a tacit agreement or actual encouragement on his part; his being present and ready and willing to assist was of itself insufficient. The conviction would be quashed.

R v Jefferson and Others [1994] 1 All ER 270 (CA)

Auld J: On the evening of 21 June 1990 there was serious and widespread public disorder in Bedford. It immediately followed and was occasioned by the victory by England over Egypt in a World Cup football match played that evening. The match, which had been televised, had been watched by many football fans in a number of public houses in the centre of Bedford. They spilled out onto the streets in what began as a celebration of victory but ended in widespread and sustained public disorder involving much violence and damage to property. The disorder, which eventually involved a crowd of about 300 youths, moved around the central area of Bedford. As the crowd moved about there were various individual incidents of violence and of criminal damage, and certain participants in the disorder were observed in various permutations at a number of such incidents. In the result, 30 youths were arrested and variously charged with offences under the Public Order Act 1986, and the Offences Against the Person Act 1861.

These four appeals against conviction arise from separate trials of two groups of the 30 arrested, which took place in April and May 1991 before Judge May and a jury sitting in the Crown Court in Bedford. The appellants Jefferson, Skerritt and Readman were among the defendants in the first trial, and the appellant Keogh was one of the defendants in the second trial. All four appellants were charged with riot contrary to s 1(1) of the 1986 Act and in the alternative with violent disorder contrary to s 2(1) of the 1986 Act. Skerritt and Readman were convicted of riot and Jefferson and Keogh were convicted of violent disorder. Skerritt and Readman, who also faced alternative counts of causing grievous bodily harm with intent and assault occasioning actual bodily harm in relation to a particular incident, were acquitted of both charges. A number of the other defendants in both trials, who were jointly charged with the appellants, were convicted of riot or violent disorder and a number were acquitted of those charges. Skerrit and Readman now appeal against their respective convictions for riot and Jefferson and Keogh against their respective convictions for violent disorder.

The prosecution case against all the appellants on the counts of riot and violent disorder was that their presence at various of the specific incidents of disturbance and violence demonstrated a willing and persistent involvement in the disorder. The prosecution maintained that, although there might be no evidence of specific violence by any one of them, their presence at what took place was, and was intended by them to be, an encouragement to others to use violence. In short the prosecution case was that each of them aided and abetted the violence of the night.

The defence of each appellant was that his presence, to the extent that it had been proved, at various of the incidents of violence was merely that of an onlooker, not a participant ...

Jefferson and Keogh – violent disorder – aiding and abetting

Counsel for Jefferson and Keogh submitted that the prosecution case against them was that they were aiders and abettors to, and not principles in, the use of violence, and that s 2 of the 1986 Act, which defines the offence of violent disorder, creates an offence for principals only. Whilst he was only concerned with s 2, under which the appellants Jefferson and Keogh were convicted, he made the same submissions about s 1, riot, s 3, affray, s 4, fear or provocation of violence, and s 5, harassment, alarm or distress. Section 2(1) of the 1986 Act provides:

> Where three or more persons who are present together use or threaten unlawful violence and the conduct of them (taken together) is such as would cause a person of reasonable firmness present at the scene to fear for his personal safety, each of the persons using or threatening unlawful violence is guilty of violent disorder.

Counsel submitted that the offence of violent disorder, in common with the other offences created by ss 1, 3, 4 and 5, is confined to the person who actually commits the *actus reus* by virtue of s 6 of the Act. Section 6, in a series of subsections, deals with the mental element respectively required for each of the offences in ss 1–5. The formula in each subsection is the same, namely that a person is guilty of the specified offence 'only if he intends' a particular consequence appropriate to that offence. In the case of violent disorder sub-s (2) provides that a person is guilty of it 'only if he intends to use or threaten violence or is aware that his conduct may be violent or threaten violence'. Counsel submitted that the scheme of s 6, in particular the use of the term in the case of each offence 'only if he intends', is to exclude the operation of s 8 of the Accessories and Abettors Act 1861. That section provides:

> Whosoever shall aid, abet, counsel, or procure the commission of any indictable offence, whether the same be an offence at common law or by virtue of any Act passed or to be passed, shall be liable to be tried, indicted, and punished as a principal offender.

Thus, counsel submitted that aiding and abetting by encouragement – the essence of the prosecution case against all these appellants – of an offence under the 1986 Act is not itself an offence under the Act. He also relied in support of that submission on the scheme of s 6 in its reflection of the grading in ss 1–5 of the seriousness of public order offences. We should, therefore, set out the material provisions of the section in full:

> 6(1) A person is guilty of riot only if he intends to use violence or is aware that his conduct may be violent.
>
> (2) A person is guilty of violent disorder or affray only if he intends to use or threaten violence or is aware that his conduct may be violent or threaten violence.
>
> (3) A person is guilty of an offence under s 4 only if he intends his words or behaviour, or the writing, sign or any other visible representation, to be threatening, abusive or insulting, or is aware that it may be threatening, abusive or insulting.
>
> (4) A person is guilty of an offence under s 5 only if he intends his words or behaviour, or the writing, sign or other visible representation, to be

> threatening, abusive or insulting, or is aware that it may be threatening, abusive or insulting or (as the case may be) he intends his behaviour to be or is aware that it may be disorderly ...

In our judgment, the offences created by the 1986 Act may be committed by aiders and abettors as well as by principals. As counsel for the Crown pointed out, the question is not whether s 6 of the 1986 Act excludes s 8 of the 1861 Act, and it is only in part one of construction. An aider and abettor of an offence is a common law notion, not a creation of statute. It is of general application to all offences, whether at common law or of statutory creation, unless expressly excluded by statute. Section 8 of the 1861 Act is merely a deeming provision as to how aiders and abettors are to be dealt with at trial. The proper approach is to consider whether there is anything in the 1986 Act which excludes, in relation to the public order offences created by it, the general common law principles of aiding and abetting.

In our view, s 6 is concerned only with identifying, in statutory form, the requisite *mens rea* for each of the offences provided for in ss 1 – 5. It does not exclude or cut down in relation to any of those offences the liability of an aider and abettor who is aware of and party to the requisite intent of the principal offender.

As to the reliance of counsel for Jefferson and Keogh on the scheme of grading in ss 1–5, as reflected in s 6(1)–(4), we do not see that it is harmed by the application to it of the ordinary common law principles of aiding and abetting of offences. There is already some overlap between the different provisions, and that will not be significantly increased by applying those principles to them.

In the case of violent disorder, of which Jefferson and Keogh were convicted, the application of those principles made them guilty under s 6(2) if they aided and abetted, by encouraging and intending to encourage, others as described in s 2 intentionally to use or threaten violence or, where appropriate, to use conduct that they were aware might be violent or threaten violence. That is just how the judge put it to the jury. For convenience, we repeat just one of the passages in the summing up in which he put the point accurately, clearly and shortly:

> ... in order to prove that the defendant participated in this offence by encouraging others it is not enough to prove merely that he was present. It must be proved that he gave encouragement, and did so intending to encourage others to use unlawful violence ...

Rubie v Faulkner [1940] 1 KB 571

Facts: The appellant, while in a motor vehicle driven by the holder of a provisional licence (a 'learner-driver') who was driving under his supervision in accordance with reg 16(3)(a) of the Motor Vehicles (Driving Licences) Regulations 1937, was in a position to see that the driver was about to overtake another vehicle by pulling considerably to the offside at a pronounced bend of the road, but he neither said nor did anything to prevent it. An accident occurred and the driver was convicted of driving without due care and attention.

Lord Hewart CJ: ... The regulation contemplates a duty and the presence of a person, properly to be called a supervisor, who is to perform that duty, and the duty is obviously comprised in the task of supervision ...

In this court it appeared to be argued that, partly because the time occupied by the events leading to the accident had been short, the appellant was not called on to do or to say anything, but was justified in what the justices described as his 'passive conduct'. That argument gives the go-by to the obvious intention of the regulation. The condition on which the holder of a provisional licence is allowed to drive a motor vehicle on a highway is that he is under the supervision of an experienced driver. The very essence of the matter is that there should be a supervisor competent to supervise. The duty being clear on the face of the regulation, it was a pure question of fact for the justices to decide whether that duty had been performed.

It seems to me that it was open to the justices to find that the appellant, by his passive conduct in circumstances which required him to be active, if only by exclaiming 'Keep in!', failed to discharge the duty which he had undertaken, and thus was guilty of the offence with which he was charged. In my opinion, therefore, this appeal should be dismissed.

Hilbery J: I agree. The regulation is framed to make some provision for the protection of the public against the dangers to which they are exposed through a car being driven on the road by a driver who is still a learner and therefore assumed to be not fully competent. It is, I can only suppose, because a learner-driver is assumed to be not fully competent that the regulation provides that a supervisor shall accompany him. This being so, the supervisor must be intended by the regulation to have the duty, by supervision, of making up as far as possible for the driver's incompetence. In other words, it is the supervisor's duty, when necessary, to do whatever can reasonably be expected to be done by a person supervising the acts of another to prevent that other from acting unskilfully or carelessly or in a manner likely to cause danger to others, and to this extent to participate in the driving.

In this case it was found that the supervisor could see the driver was about to do the unlawful act of which he was convicted and the magistrates found that the supervisor remained passive. There is no hint in the case that the supervisor in evidence ever asserted that he did anything. For him to refrain from doing anything when he could see that an unlawful act was about to be done, and his duty was to prevent an unlawful act if he could, was for him to aid and abet.

Tuck v Robson [1970] 1 WLR 741 (QBD)

Lord Parker CJ: This is an appeal by way of case stated from a decision of one of the magistrates of the magistrates' courts of the metropolis sitting at Lambeth, who convicted the appellant of an offence contrary to the licensing laws. The informations, three in number, alleged that on a certain day he being the licensee of certain premises aided and betted three customers to consume intoxicating liquor out of hours.

The relevant statutory provision is to be found in s 59(1) of the Licensing Act 1964, which, so far as it is material, provides:

> subject to the provisions of this Act, no person shall, except during the permitted hours: (a) himself or by his servant or agent sell or supply to any person in licensed premises ... any intoxicating liquor, whether to be consumed on or off the premises; or (b) consume in or take from such premises any intoxicating liquor.

Accordingly, if liquor is bought during permitted hours and is being consumed after the permitted hours, the consumer commits an offence and the licensee could only be guilty if anything of aiding and abetting.

What happened in the present case was that at 11.23 pm on 11 April 1969 police officers went into the Canterbury Arms public house in Maddocks Way, London,

SE17, of which the appellant was a joint licensee. At the time the police entered the main lights in the saloon bar had been extinguished, leaving those on behind the bar, and there was a barmaid standing behind the bar. In the saloon bar the police found 20 customers, 12 of whom were consuming intoxicating liquor, including the three involved in these three informations. They were drinking alcoholic drinks, some of them standing and others sitting at tables.

No consumption of intoxicating liquor is permitted on the premises after 11.10 pm and the justices found that at 11.00 pm the appellant had called 'time' and had switched off some of the main lights, and at 11.05 pm had called 'glasses please'.

Having done that, he went into the public bar to clear away glasses and assist customers from that part of the premises. He knew, so the finding is, that during that period from 11.10 pm until the time the police arrived at 11.23 pm, ie 13 minutes, that customers were consuming liquor in the saloon bar, and took no steps to stop them. Evidence was given of a conversation between the appellant and the police, during which the appellant said:

> I thought that if I called out 'time' and asked customers to leave, that is all I am required to do ...

As it seems to me, two things must be proved before an accused can be held to be guilty of aiding and abetting the commission of the offence: first, he must have full knowledge of the facts which constitute the offence. I interpose, there is no question of that here; there is a finding that the appellant knew full well that after 11.10 pm drink was being consumed. Second, there must be some form of voluntary assistance in the commission of the offence. Sometimes the word used is 'encouragement', and the real question here is how far inaction, passive tolerance, can amount to assistance so as to make the accused guilty of aiding and abetting ...

... Here is a licensee who is in control of his premises; he has full knowledge that liquor is being consumed after hours; he takes no steps in the matter other than to call 'time' and ask customers to leave, which he did at 11.00 pm, and as he himself puts it 'I thought that if I called out "time" and asked customers to leave, that is all I am required to do'.

The question as it seems to me is whether the magistrate, as a reasonable tribunal, was entitled in all the circumstances to draw the inference that here there was passive assistance in the sense of presence with no steps being taken to enforce his right either to eject the customers or at any rate to revoke their licence to be on the premises. In my judgment the magistrate was entitled to draw that inference, and accordingly I would dismiss this appeal.

WITHDRAWAL

A party who has a change of mind and wishes to withdraw from a joint enterprise must communicate to the other parties his intention to withdraw from the enterprise and must do in sufficient time before the commission of the offence: *R v Becerra* (1975) 62 Cr App R 212; *R v Whitefield* (1983) 79 Cr App R 36; *R v Rook* [1993] 1 WLR 1005.

R v Becerra and Cooper (1975) 62 Cr App R 212 (CA)

Roskill LJ: ... The facts were horrifying for they reveal acts of brutality almost unequalled even in this day and age. On 13 June 1974, in the early hours of the morning, these appellants and the third man entered this old lady's house at 8 Gore Terrace, Swansea, intending to steal some money that they had been told, as a result of a conversation in a public house, she kept in a drawer in her kitchen. It was said – whether truthfully or not does not matter – she might have as much as £4,000 there.

When they entered this house through the old lady's bedroom window, the applicant Becerra was carrying a clasp knife which had according to undisputed evidence, a handle 4½ and a blade 3½ inches long; and once that knife blade was opened, it remained rigid until a lever on the handle was released. The evidence was beyond question that Cooper knew that Becerra had that knife, and indeed Cooper borrowed it to cut the telephone wires leading to the house.

It is not necessary to go through the details, but some of the story must be related. Cooper climbed in through the window. The old lady began to switch her bedside light on and off. Cooper went over to her. He punched her, knelt and jumped on her, and covered her head with a pillow. Becerra and the third man followed Cooper. On Cooper's instructions the third man, somewhat reluctantly, took over the holding of the pillow over the old lady's face and Becerra cut the wires of the telephone by the side of the bed with the knife I have already mentioned.

Cooper then took Becerra's knife in his left hand and went out into the hall, going towards the kitchen. Why he took that knife and why he was given that knife was matter of acute controversy at the trial. Mr Lewis, who was the occupier of a first floor flat in the house came downstairs, obviously having been aroused by what he heard was going on. Becerra and the third man heard him, climbed out of the window and ran away. Cooper tried the back door, but it was locked and so he turned back and was confronted by Lewis. There was a struggle in which beyond question Lewis was stabbed four times on the left-hand side of his body and one of the stab wounds was 3½ inches deep and penetrated the right ventricle of his heart and he died. Cooper then made his escape through the window leaving the knife behind.

Only by the mercy of providence was the old lady not killed by the brutal treatment which she received. But she was greatly shocked and an innocent tenant of this house lost his life. Mrs Francis herself was in such a state of shock that she was unable to speak and the medical evidence showed she had bruising on her chest and face. Mercifully there was no damage to her central nervous system.

The basic prosecution case against Becerra and Cooper was that they had entered into a common agreement to use such force as was necessary against anyone in the house to get the money or to avoid identification or arrest. It was urged that this common agreement included the use, if necessary, of the knife to inflict serious bodily injury, if not death, and it was alleged that Cooper, in furtherance of that common agreement, murdered Lewis with the knife in his left hand while he pinioned Lewis from behind with his right arm around Lewis's shoulder ...

... It was argued in the alternative on behalf of Becerra, that ... Becerra had open to him a second line of defence, namely that – I hope I do Mr Owen's argument on the second ground no injustice if I put it this way – whatever Cooper did immediately before and at the time of the killing of Lewis, Becerra had by then withdrawn from that common design and so should not be convicted of the murder of Lewis, even though the common design had previously been that which I have stated ...

It is necessary, before dealing with that argument in more detail, to say a word or two about the relevant law. It is a curious fact, considering the number of times in which this point arises where two or more people are charged with criminal offences, particularly murder or manslaughter, how relatively little authority there is in this country upon the point. But the principle is undoubtedly of long standing.

Perhaps it is best first stated in *Saunders and Archer* (1577) 2 Plowd, 473 (in the 18th year of the first Queen Elizabeth) at 476, in a note by *Plowden*, thus: '... for if I command one to Kill J S and before the Fact done I go to him and tell him that I have repented, and expressly charge him not to kill J S and he afterwards kills him, there I shall not be Accessory to this Murder, because I have countermanded my first Command, which in all Reason shall discharge me, for the malicious Mind of the Accessory ought to continue to do ill until the Time of the Act done, or else he shall not be charged; but if he had killed J S before the Time of my Discharge or Countermand given, I should have been Accessory to the Death, notwithstanding my private Repentance.'

The next case to which I may usefully refer is some 250 years later, but over 150 years ago: *Edmeads and Others* (1828) 3 C and P 390, where there is a ruling of Vaughan B at a trial at Berkshire Assizes, upon an indictment charging Edmeads and others with unlawfully shooting at gamekeepers. At the end of his ruling the learned Baron said on the question of common intent at 392, 'that is rather a question for the jury; but still, on this evidence, it is quite clear what the common purpose was. They all draw up in lines, and point their guns at the gamekeepers, and they are all giving their countenance and assistance to the one of them who actually fires the gun. If it could be shown that either of them separated himself from the rest, and showed distinctly that he would have no hand in what they were doing, the objection would have much weight in it.'

I can go forward over 100 years. Mr Owen (to whose juniors we are indebted for their research into the relevant Canadian and United States cases) referred us to several Canadian cases, to only one of which is it necessary to refer in detail, a decision of the Court of Appeal of British Columbia in *Whitehouse (alias Savage)* (1941) 1 WWR 112. I need not read the headnote. The Court of Appeal held that the trial judge concerned in that case, which was one of murder, had been guilty of misdirection in his direction to the jury on this question of 'withdrawal'. The matter is, if I may most respectfully say so, so well put in the leading judgment of Sloan JA, that I read the whole of the passage at pp 115 and 116: 'Can it be said on the facts of this case that a mere change of mental intention and a quitting of the scene of the crime just immediately prior to the striking of the fatal blow will absolve those who participate in the commission of the crime by overt acts up to that moment from all the consequences of its accomplishment by the one who strikes in ignorance of his companions' change of heart? I think not. After a crime has been committed and before a prior abandonment of the common enterprise may be found by a jury there must be, in my view, in the absence of exceptional circumstances, something more than a mere mental change of intention and physical change of place by those associates who wish to dissociate themselves from the consequences attendant upon their willing assistance up to the moment of the actual commission of that crime. I would not attempt to define too closely what must be done in criminal matters involving participation in a common unlawful purpose to break the chain of causation and responsibility. That must depend upon the circumstances of each case but it seems to me that one essential element ought to be established in a case of this kind: Where practicable and reasonable there must be timely communication of the intention to abandon the common purpose from those who wish to dissociate themselves from the contemplated crime to those who desire to continue in it. What is 'timely communication' must be determined by the facts of each case but where practicable and reasonable it ought to be such communication, verbal or otherwise, that will serve unequivocal notice upon the other party to the common unlawful cause that if he proceeds upon it he does so without the further aid and assistance of those who withdraw. The unlawful purpose of him who continues alone is then his own and not one in common with those who are no longer parties to it nor liable to its full and final consequences.' The learned judge then went on to cite a passage from *Hales's Pleas of the Crown* 618 and the passage from *Saunders and Archer* (*above*) to which I have already referred.

In the view of each member of this court, that passage, if we may respectfully say so, could not be improved upon and we venture to adopt it in its entirety as a correct statement of the law which is to be applied in this case.

The last case, an English one, is *Croft* [1944] 1 KB 295, a well-known case of a suicide pact where, under the old law, the survivor of a suicide pact was charged with and convicted of murder. It was sought to argue that he had withdrawn from the pact in time to avoid liability (as the law then was) for conviction for murder.

The Court of Criminal Appeal, comprising Lawrence J (as he then was), Lewis and Wrottesley JJ dismissed the appeal and upheld the direction given by Humphreys J to the jury at the trial. Towards the end of the judgment Lawrence J said at pp 297 and 298 '... counsel for the appellant complains – although I do not understand that the point had ever been taken in the court below – that the summing up does not contain any reference to the possibility of the agreement to commit suicide having been determined or countermanded. It is true that the learned judge does not deal expressly with that matter except in a passage where he says: "Even if you accept his statement in the witness box that the vital and second shot was fired when he had gone through that window, he would still be guilty of murder if she was then committing suicide as the result of an agreement which they had mutually arrived at that that should be the fate of both of them, and it is no answer for him that he altered his mind after she was dead and did not commit suicide himself." ... The authorities, such as they are, show in our opinion, that where a person has acted as an accessory before the fact, in order that he should not be held guilty as an accessory before the fact, he must give express and actual countermand or revocation of the advising, counselling, procuring, or abetting which he had given before.'

It seems to us that those authorities make plain what he law is which has to be applied in the present case.

We therefore turn back to consider the direction which the learned judge gave in the present case to the jury and what was the suggested evidence that Becerra had withdrawn from the common agreement. The suggested evidence is the use by Becerra of the words 'Come on, let's go', coupled, as I said a few moments ago, with his act in going out through the window. The evidence, as the judge pointed out, was that Cooper never heard that nor did the third man. But let it be supposed that that was said and the jury took the view that it was said.

On the facts of this case, in the circumstances then prevailing, the knife having already been used and being contemplated for further use when it was handed over by Becerra to Cooper for the purpose of avoiding (if necessary) by violent means the hazards of identification, if Becerra wanted to withdraw at that stage, he would have to 'countermand', to use the word that is used is some of the cases or 'repent' to use another word so used, in some manner vastly different and vastly more effective than merely to say 'Come on, let's go' and go out through the window.

It is not necessary, on this application, to decide whether the point of time had arrived at which the only way in which he could effectively withdraw, so as to free himself from joint responsibility for any act Cooper thereafter did in furtherance of the common design, would be physically to intervene so as to stop Cooper attacking Lewis, as the judge suggested, by interposing his own body between them or somehow getting in between them or whether some other action might suffice. That does not arise for decision here. Nor is it necessary to decide whether or not the learned judge was right or wrong, on the facts of this case, in that passage which appears at the bottom of p 206, which Mr Owen criticised: 'and at least take all reasonable steps to prevent the commission of the crime which he had agreed the others should commit.' It is enough for the purposes of deciding this application to say that under the law of this country as it stands, and on the facts (taking them at their highest in favour of Becerra), that which was urged as amounting to withdrawal from the common design was not capable of amounting to such withdrawal. Accordingly Becerra remains responsible, in the eyes of the law, for everything that Cooper did and continued to do after Becerra's disappearance through the window as much as if he had done them himself.

Cooper being unquestionably guilty of murder, Becerra is equally guilty of murder. Mr Owen's careful argument must therefore be rejected and the application by Becerra for leave to appeal against conviction fails ...

R v Whitefield (1983) 79 Cr App R 36 (CA)

Dunn LJ: ... The facts of the burglary were as follows. Between 4 pm on 3 November and 11 pm on 5 November 1982, a quantity of goods were taken from a flat in London SE16 when the occupier was away. On his return the latter reported the matter to the police. On 23 November the police interviewed the appellant after two other persons (Anthony Gallagher and Helen Coffey) had been arrested and charged with the burglary. Contemporaneous notes of the interviews were made and signed by the appellant. The appellant stated at the interview that he never took part in the burglary, but admitted telling Gallagher one evening that the flat that was next to his own was unoccupied. He also admitted that he had agreed to break into the flat with Gallagher by way of his own flat and balcony. They discussed how the property should be disposed of and the proceeds divided. Subsequently the appellant decided that he would not take part, and so informed Gallagher before the burglary took place. However he knew that the burglary was to take place on a particular night. He heard it being committed, but did nothing to prevent it. He denied having spoken to Gallagher since the burglary. He had received none of the property or proceeds from its disposal ...

The law upon withdrawal is stated in *Becerra and Cooper* (1976) 62 Cr App R 212 and *Grundy* [1977] Crim LR 543. So far as material to the facts of this case, the law may be shortly stated as follows. If a person has counselled another to commit a crime, he may escape liability by withdrawal before the crime is committed, but it is not sufficient that he should merely repent or change his mind. If his participation is confined to advice or encouragement, he must at least communicate his change of mind to the other, and the communication must be such as 'will serve unequivocal notice upon the other party to the common unlawful cause that if he proceeds upon it he does so without the aid and assistance of those who withdraw'. (See the Canadian case of *Whitehouse* [1941] 1 WWR 112, 116 *per* Sloan JA, approved in *Becerra and Cooper* and *Grundy*.)

In this case there was, if the jury accepted it, evidence in the answers given by the appellant to the police that he had served unequivocal notice on Gallagher that if he proceeded with the burglary he would do so without the aid or assistance of the appellant. In his ruling the judge stated that such notice was not enough, and that in failing to communicate with the police or take any other steps to prevent the burglary he remained 'liable in law for what happened, for everything that was done that night'. In the judgment of this court, in making that statement the judge fell into an error of law. The direct result of it was that the appellant changed his plea to one of guilty. A change of plea founded upon an error of law by the judge cannot stand, and the conviction must be quashed and the appeal allowed ...

R v Rook [1993] 1 WLR 1005 (CA)

Lloyd LJ: ... The case concerns a so-called contract killing. Afsar was a taxi driver in Nottingham. He wished to be rid of his wife, Shaheen. On Tuesday 19 December 1989 he met the appellant, Armstrong, and a man called Barker, when they hired his taxi. During the journey there was some conversation. Afsar asked whether the appellant wanted to earn some money. A friend of his, said Afsar, wanted to have a woman beaten up. As the conversation continued, it became clear that the 'friend' wanted the woman murdered. There was some discussion between the appellant, Afsar and Armstrong about money. The appellant named a price of £20,000. The price agreed was £15,000 cash, and £5,000 worth of jewellery which the woman would be wearing. Afsar said it was to be a murder on credit. In the event he paid no more than £50.

Barker said he wanted nothing to do with it; so the following day, Wednesday 20 December 1989, the appellant recruited Leivers. He said to Leivers: 'Look Mark, it's murder.' Leivers replied: 'Yea, it's all right. I'll be there.' It was arranged that Afsar would pick up the other three at about 4.30 pm. They drove to Colwick Park, by the side of the lake. There was some discussion between all four as to how the murder should be committed. Afsar said that when they were ready he would bring the woman in his car. It was agreed that the murder would take place the following day.

On the evening of Wednesday 20 December there was a further discussion between the appellant, Armstrong and Leivers about the method of killing. They decided to use a knife and a piece of wood. Armstrong said that he wanted some money 'up front'. The appellant said that they would need money in order to buy new clothes after the murder.

On Thursday 21 December 1989 Afsar drove Armstrong and Leivers to Colwick Park, and dropped them as arranged. The appellant could not be found. Afsar went back to collect Shaheen. When he returned, Armstrong and Leivers dragged her from the car and killed her most brutally. Her body was found in the lake the next day.

The appellant was interviewed and made certain admissions. He also gave evidence at the trial. His defence was that he never intended the woman to be killed. He hoped to get some money from Afsar 'up front', and then disappear. At first he 'tagged along' to see how serious the others were. He was not sure whether they would go through with it or not. Then he tried to stall them, because he never intended to go through with it himself. Finally, on the Thursday, he deliberately absented himself. He said he thought that, if he were not there, Armstrong and Leivers would not go ahead without him ...

... It is now well established that in a case of joint enterprise, where the parties are both present at the scene of the crime, it is not necessary for the prosecution to show that the secondary party intended the victim to be killed, or to suffer serious injury. It is enough that he should have foreseen the event, as a real or substantial risk: see *Chan Wing-Siu v R* [1985] AC 168, *R v Hyde* [1991] 1 QB 134 and *Hui Chi-Ming v R* [1992] 1 AC 34. Thus, a secondary party may be liable for the unintended consequences of the principal's acts, provided the principal does not go outside the scope of the joint enterprise.

We see no reason why the same reasoning should not apply in the case of a secondary party who lends assistance or encouragement before the commission of the crime. Indeed Lowry LCJ in the Court of Appeal in Northern Ireland drew this very analogy in *DPP for Northern Ireland v Maxwell* [1978] 1 WLR 1350 at 1363. That was a case where the defendant was charged, in effect, with aiding and abetting.

> His guilt springs from the fact that he contemplates the commission of one (or more) of a number of crimes by the principal and he intentionally lends his assistance in order that such a crime will be committed. (See [1978] 1 WLR 1350 at 1374 Lowry LCJ.)

Lord Scarman, in the House of Lords, approved Lowry LCJ's formulation ([1978] 1 WLR 1350 at 1362–63):

> The principle thus formulated has great merit. It directs attention to the state of mind of the accused: not what he ought to have in contemplation, but what he did have. It avoids definition and classification, while ensuring that a man will not be convicted of aiding and abetting any offence his principal may commit, but only one which is within his contemplation.

It follows that it is no defence to a secondary party to say that he did not intend the victim to be killed, or to suffer serious harm, if he contemplated or foresaw the event as a real or serious risk. In *Lynch v DPP for Northern Ireland* [1975] AC 653, overruled on another point in *R v Howe* [1987] AC 417, the accomplice drove the principal to a place where he knew the principal intended to kill a policeman. Lord Morris said that the intentional driving of the car was enough to render the accomplice liable for aiding and abetting the murder, even though he regretted the plan, and indeed was horrified by it (see [1975] AC 653 at 678). In *Smith and Hogan* p 133 the *mens rea* for a secondary party is stated as follows:

> It must be proved that D intended to do the acts which he knew to be capable of assisting or encouraging the commission of the crime ...

We now come to the second part of the case, which raises, potentially at least, more difficult questions. Mr Maxwell QC submits that where a person has given assistance, for example by providing a gun, in circumstances which would render him liable as a secondary party if he does not withdraw, then in order to escape liability he must 'neutralise' his assistance. He must, so it was said, break the chain of causation between his act of assistance, and the subsequent crime, by recovering the gun, or by warning the victim to stay away, or by going to the police. Mr Hockman submits, on the other hand, that the Crown must prove that the defendant continued ready to help until the moment the crime is committed; and if there is doubt as to the defendant's state of mind on the day in question, or his willingness to provide further help if required, then the jury must acquit.

As between these two extreme views, we have no hesitation in rejecting the latter. In *R v Croft* [1944] KB 295 the surviving party of a suicide pact was held to be guilty of murder. Lawrence J, giving the judgment of the court, said ([1944] KB 295 at 298):

> The authorities, however, such as they are, show, in our opinion, that the appellant, to escape being held guilty as an accessory before the fact must

> establish that he expressly countermanded or revoked the advising, counselling, procuring or abetting which he had previously given.

In *R v Whitehouse* [1941] 1 WWR 112 at 114 Sloan JA said:

> Can it be said on the facts of this case that a mere change of mental intention and a quitting of the scene of the crime just immediately prior to the striking of the fatal blow will absolve those who participate in the commission of the crime by overt acts up to that moment from all the consequences of its accomplishment by the one who strikes in ignorance of his companions' change of heart? I think not. After a crime has been committed and before a prior abandonment of the common enterprise may be found by a jury there must be, in my view, in the absence of exceptional circumstances, something more than a mere mental change of intention and physical change of place by those associates who wish to dissociate themselves from the consequences attendant upon their willing assistance up to the moment of the actual commission of that crime. I would not attempt to define too closely what must be done in criminal matters involving participation in a common unlawful purpose to break the chain of causation and responsibility. That must depend upon the circumstances of each case but it seems to me that one essential element ought to be established in a case of this kind: Where practicable and reasonable there must be timely communication of the intention to abandon the common purpose from those who wish to dissociate themselves from the contemplated crime to those who desire to continue in it. What is 'timely communication' must be determined by the facts of each case but where practicable and reasonable it ought to be such communication, verbal or otherwise, that will serve unequivocal notice upon the other party to the common unlawful cause that if he proceeds upon it he does so without the further aid and assistance of those who withdraw. The unlawful purpose of him who continues alone is then his own and not one in common with those who are no longer parties to it nor liable to its full and final consequences.

In *R v Becerra* (1975) 62 Cr App R 212 this court approved that passage as a correct statement of the law. The facts of *R v Becerra* were that the victim was killed in the course of a burglary. The appellant had provided the knife shortly before the murder. The court held that the appellant's sudden departure from the scene of the crime with the words 'Come on, let's go' was an insufficient communication of withdrawal. So the appellant's conviction as a secondary party to the murder was upheld. In *R v Whitefield* (1983) 79 Cr App R 36 at 39–40 Dunn LJ stated the law as follows:

> If a person has counselled another to commit a crime, he may escape liability by withdrawal before the crime is committed, but it is not sufficient that he should merely repent or change his mind. If his participation is confined to advice or encouragement, he must at least communicate his change of mind to the other, and the communication must be such as 'will serve unequivocal notice upon the other party to the common unlawful cause that if he proceeds upon it he does so without the aid and assistance of those who withdraw'.

In the present case the appellant never told the others that he was not going ahead with the crime. His absence on the day could not possibly amount to 'unequivocal communication' of his withdrawal. In his evidence-in-chief, in a passage already quoted, he said that he made it quite clear to *himself* that he did not want to be there on the day. But he did not make it clear to the others. So the minimum necessary for withdrawal from the crime was not established on the facts. In these circumstances, as in *R v Becerra*, it is unnecessary for us to consider whether communication of his withdrawal would have been enough, or whether he would have had to take steps to 'neutralise' the assistance he had already given.

Mr Maxwell rightly drew our attention to a sentence in the judgment of Sloan JA, already quoted, where he refers to the service of notice on the other party that if he proceeds he does so without *further* aid from those who withdraw. This may suggest that aid *already* afforded need not be neutralised. We agree with Mr Maxwell that this attaches too much importance to a single word. But that is as far as we are prepared to go in this case. We are not prepared, as at present advised, to give our approval to his proposition in its extreme form. In *Criminal Law: The General Part*, 2nd edn, 1961, para 127, Glanville Williams quotes a graphic phrase from an American authority (*Eldredge v US* (1932) 62 F 2d 449 *per* McDermott J): 'A declared intent to withdraw from a conspiracy to dynamite a building is not enough, if the fuse has been set; he must step on the fuse.' It may be that this goes too far. It may be that it is enough that he should have done his best to step on the fuse. Since this is as much a question of policy as a question of law, and since it does not arise on the facts of the present case, we say no more about it ...

R v Baker [1994] Crim LR 444 (CA)

Facts: A man with the same name as the deceased had earlier been robbed in his own home and there was evidence that the deceased had paid the robbers to commit the offence. He was called out one night and killed with two knives belonging to the appellant. Witnesses said that the appellant had said that he had done the killing. At trial, a co-defendant gave evidence in his own defence which implicated the appellant. He said that on the night of the killing, the appellant said he wanted to see Sam, which was the nickname of the deceased, because, he said, the appellant had been a party to the robbery. They went to waste ground where he expected the appellant to have a word with Sam but instead he attacked him and went mad, stabbing him repeatedly. Death was caused by 48 stab wounds, each of which was fatal. The appellant's evidence was that he knew that his co-defendant was a violent man who had kicked and punched him previously and threatened to finish him off. He and others had told him that Sam was going to the police about the robbery and wanted him to go with them to see Sam. He went out of fear, and they took his knives. Once on the open ground, the co-defendant handed the appellant a knife and told him to kill Sam. He then went berserk and was waving the other knife at the appellant, who was petrified. The appellant swung the knife which penetrated Sam somewhere near the shoulder or the throat, Sam staggered back and the co-defendant went on screaming for the appellant to kill Sam and so he swung the knife twice more. He did not know where it went in. The appellant then passed the knife back to the co-defendant and said 'I'm not doing it'. He did not touch Sam again but moved a short distance away and turned his back. He then heard more thuds caused by the others continuing to stab Sam. He then saw him on the ground.

The defence was that insofar as he was involved in any joint enterprise, it was a joint enterprise to do serious harm to Sam but not to kill him, and he did it under duress. It could not be proven that any of the three stab wounds he had inflicted would have killed Sam or that they did kill him. That he passed over the knife and thereafter disassociated himself from what the others did meant that the joint enterprise had come to an end. The witnesses were tainted by their close relationship with the co-defendant.

Held: It would be considered how far in practice a direction to the jury to consider a s 18 count would have benefited or might have benefited the appellant. The defence would have relied on duress by the co-defendant but if that had succeeded there would have been a complete acquittal. The risk that the jury might be unwilling to acquit him completely and should therefore have been allowed to consider convicting on a lesser charge presupposed that they would convict him after satisfying themselves that he did not act under duress. In that situation, according to his story, the appellant was told by the co-defendant to kill Sam and stabbed him three times before turning away and saying that he wasn't doing it. He then stayed there until Sam was on the ground dead or dying, whereupon he left with the other two. If that account were accepted by the jury the court was far from confident that the appellant, by his words and actions, had effectively put an end to the joint enterprise so that he had no criminal responsibility for what happened after the three stab wounds which he inflicted. The words 'I'm not doing it' and the turning around and moving a few feet away were far from unequivocal notice that the appellant was wholly disassociating himself from the entire enterprise. The words were quite capable of meaning no more than 'I will not myself strike any more blows'. They were not an unequivocal indication that he did not intend to take any further part in any further assault on Sam and indeed he did no more than withdraw by a few feet (see *Becerra* (1976) 62 Cr App R 212; *Rook* [1993] 1 WLR 1005).

VICTIMS AS ACCESSORIES

Where a statute creates an offence aimed at protecting a class of people, a member of that class cannot be an accessory to such an offence, even if the offence is committed with his or her assistance, encouragement or consent.

R v Whitehouse [1977] 1 QB 868 (CA)

See Chapter 13.

R v Tyrell [1894] 1 QB 710 (CCR)

See Chapter 13.

CHAPTER 4

CAUSATION

A causal link has to be established between the *actus reus* (the act, omission, or state of affairs) and the consequence which has to occur for an offence to have been committed. For example, in a murder case, it has to be proved that the defendant's actions caused the death of the victim. In other words, it has to be proved that the particular consequence would not have occurred 'but for' the accused's action.

R v Bracewell (1979) 68 Cr App R 44 (CA)

Ormrod LJ: ... [The trial judge (Boreham J), in the course of directing the jury had said:] ... You must remember this, that a doctor, and you may have thought that Dr Green was a splendid example of fairness, is speaking from a scientific point of view. He was saying, 'I cannot as a scientific certainty rule out that which you postulate, namely partial asphyxia, recovery and then a heart attack', but, he said, 'I incline strongly against that view'. You will remember, ladies and gentlemen, that your duty is not to judge scientifically or with scientific certainty. You judge so that as sensible people you feel sure and even say that what might not satisfy Dr Green as a scientific certainty, might, with propriety, satisfy you so that you felt sure. Do not be misled. There is no such thing as certainty in this life, absolute certainty. You ask yourselves the simple question upon the whole of the evidence do I feel sure? Take account of course of the doctor's evidence. It is the most important evidence on this aspect. He is really the only one qualified to speak here. Take account of his reservation fully.

That direction, in our judgment, correctly draws the distinction between what might be described as scientific proof on the one hand and legal proof on the other. It is, with respect, an admirably lucid and succinct way of dealing with a problem which often arises in connection with scientific evidence. It is, of course, part of cross-examining counsel's duty to invite expert witnesses to consider alternative hypotheses and, after examining them in detail, to conclude by asking 'Can you exclude the possibility?' The available data may be inadequate to *prove* scientifically that the alternative hypothesis is false, so the scientific witness will answer 'No, I cannot exclude it', though the effect of his evidence as a whole can be expressed in terms such as 'But for all practical purposes (including the jury's), it is so unlikely that it can safely be ignored'. That is in substance what Dr Green said ...

R v Dawson, Nolan and Walmsley (1985) 81 Cr App R 150 (CA)

Facts: The three appellants attempted to rob a petrol filling station but fled when the attendant pressed an alarm button. The attendant, who suffered from a heart condition, collapsed and died shortly afterwards. The appellants were convicted of manslaughter. At their trial, medical experts were of the opinion that the attempted robbery was responsible for the attendant's death; but they could not rule out the possibility of a heart attack having occurred before the attempted robbery.

Watkins LJ: ... [Following a submission of no case to answer, the trial judge (Glidewell J) had declined to withdraw the case from the jury and in doing so] had based himself in part upon what was said by Ormrod LJ in giving the judgment of this court in *R v Bracewell* (1979) 68 Cr App R 44 at 49 [*quoted in the preceding extract – ed*] ...

In dealing with the burden of proof with particular regard to the medical evidence the judge based himself upon the direction given by Boreham J to the jury in *Bracewell* as set out above. He put the matter thus:

> How then should you approach the doctor's evidence? Your task, using your experience and your common sense, is to ask yourselves whether you are sure of guilt beyond a reasonable doubt. You are not asked to say you are absolutely certain. Indeed there are few things in this trial which are absolutely certain. The doctors gave their evidence to you as experts. Their standard is the standard of medical science. So when they say in effect, in my opinion it is highly probable that Mr Black's death was caused by the shock of the attempted robbery but I cannot rule out the possibility that it was caused by an episode of heart disease unconnected with the attempted robbery, you may think that it is in the context of medical science that they are using the phrases 'highly probable' and 'cannot rule out the possibility'. The doctors' opinions do not necessarily oblige you to say that you cannot be sure. If they did then of course there would have been no point in inviting you to judge this matter. Of course, the doctors' opinions are of the utmost importance in this case and you will take full account of them. But when you have done so make up your own minds on the whole of the evidence.

His intention so to direct the jury must, in our view, have been a strong influence upon his decision to refuse to withdraw the case from the jury in that he thought, justifiably we think, that upon the whole of the evidence it was open to the jury to decide that the possibility of heart failure having been caused by something unconnected with attempted robbery could safely be excluded.

Can the judge be properly criticised for allowing the jury to reach their own conclusions? The facts in *Bracewell* (*above*) were very dissimilar to those in the present case, but the considerations arising from the medical evidence in both cases bore such a similarity as, in our view, to entitle the judge to take the *Bracewell* direction, suitably altered to accord with the evidence he had to bear in mind, as a guide in his endeavour to direct the jury into a permissible way of regarding the medical evidence alongside the overall requirement to be, if minded to convict, sure of guilt.

When account is also taken of all the other evidence, the judge, whilst obviously conscious of the difficult task, as he put it, confronting the jury, cannot be said, we think, to have offended in principle in allowing the trial to run its course. His, too, was a difficult decision in that respect. Whilst it could possibly and understandably have gone either way, as it was, we can see no reason to hold that it was wrong. We reach the same conclusion about the judge's version of the *Bracewell* direction ...

R v Watson [1989] 1 WLR 684 (CA)

Lord Lane CJ: ... The facts of the case, insofar as they are relevant, were as follows. Late at night on 11 December 1986 two men, one of whom was the appellant, broke into the home of a man called Harold Moyler. Mr Moyler was 87 years old and suffered from a serious condition of the heart. He lived alone. The two men first threw a brick through the window and, having made entry to the house, confronted Mr Moyler as he woke up, abused him verbally and then made off without stealing anything.

Mr Moyler died an hour and a half later as the result of a heart attack. The case for the Crown was that the heart attack was a direct consequence of the unlawful actions of the appellant and his colleague.

The defence put forward by the appellant was that he was not responsible for the death. Mr Moyler's heart condition could have caused his death at any time, quite apart from any question of excitement or shock. Furthermore, there were two events subsequent to the burglary, either of which might have precipitated the heart attack: first, the arrival of the police and, second, the arrival of council workmen to board up the broken window. Any adverse effect of the burglary, it was suggested, would have ceased long before the death occurred.

There was a sharp of evidence conflict on the medical issue. Dr West, who was called on behalf of the prosecution, had performed the autopsy. He was sure that the burglary was the cause of death. He described for the benefit of the jury how excitement causes the production of adrenalin, making the heart beat faster. The heart therefore needs more blood and oxygen but is unable to obtain it if there is a chronic heart disease, as there was here, with the result that the arteries leading to the heart are substantially narrowed. The heart then begins to beat irregularly, it eventually stops beating and thus death ensues.

He said that his opinion was that this chain of events began with burglary and continued up to the time of death. The initial shock caused by the burglary could last for a considerable period of time, and certainly for the one and a half hours which was the length of time involved in the present case ...

The appellant himself did not give evidence, but Dr Matterson was called to give evidence on his behalf. His opinion was that the excitement and stress caused by the burglary could not have been a subsisting and operating cause of death one had a half hours later. If any extraneous incident was responsible for the heart attack, it must have been the arrival of the police or that of the council workmen. However, the victim's condition was such that a heart attack could have occurred at any time without the necessity of any excitement or shock ...

The second ground of appeal arises in the following way. The prosecution, as already indicated, based their case on the proposition advanced by Dr West that the burglary had caused the heart attack to occur one and a half hours later. The judge had correctly directed the jury on these lines, setting out Dr West's opinion and the conflicted opinion of Dr Matterson, to the effect that the stress caused by the burglary would have subsided in 20 minutes and that the fatal heart attack was therefore either spontaneous or the result of the arrival of the police or the council workmen.

Finally on this point, the judge said:

> So, what do you do? You must consider all these opinions very carefully. You must say to yourselves, where you have someone as skilled and experienced as Dr Matterson expressing the views as he did, it might be very difficult for you to reject his opinion out of hand. If you do say to yourselves: 'Well, Dr Matterson is right', or 'He may be right', that is all you need to say to yourself. If he may be right it would be proper for you to return a verdict of not guilty in this case.

That, like the rest of his directions to the jury prior to their retirement, was simple, concise and clear.

However, after the jury had been in retirement for some time, they returned with two questions. The second of the two questions was not easy to understand, but the effect was to ask what should be the verdict if the victim's heartbeat had returned to normal after the burglary but the arrival either of the police or of the council workmen had caused a second crisis which resulted in death 'as a direct result of the emotional stress which was continuing in the victim'.

A discussion took place in the absence of the jury as to how the judge should deal with this difficult matter. The judge was clearly minded at first to direct the jury to acquit if that was the conclusion at which they had arrived.

Counsel for the prosecution, however, by a submission, which he tells us he now regrets, persuaded the judge to change his mind in the upshot of the following further direction which was given:

> Now, if you were to say to yourself: 'Well, I am sure that the heart rate had returned to normal some 20 minutes afterwards, but the two succeeding incidents did cause a further increase in the heart rate, and it was one or other, or both, of those incidents which caused death', the burglary would still be responsible for the death, provided that you are satisfied that the two subsequent incidents were natural consequences of the burglary. That would be a matter for your determination.

That was introducing a fresh dimension into the jury's task, namely a consideration of whether it could be said that as a matter of logic the burglary was the cause of the police arriving and of the necessity to board up the window and so for the arrival of the council workmen and so for the heart attack, whichever of the three matters may have been the precipitating event. It may be that counsel for the appellant would have been able to say little of assistance to his client had he had the opportunity to address the jury on this fresh topic. Nevertheless, the fact that he was deprived of that opportunity, coupled with the fact that the jury were not, it seems, wholly convinced that Dr West's opinion was correct, lead us, not without some hesitation, to say that this verdict of guilty of manslaughter is unsatisfactory. The conviction is accordingly quashed.

R v Armstrong [1989] Crim LR 149 (Owen J at St Albans Crown Court)

The defendant, a drug addict, supplied to the victim, who had already consumed a potentially lethal quantity of alcohol, heroin and the means by which to mix and inject the heroin. There was no evidence that the defendant had injected the heroin into the victim. The case proceeded upon the assumption that the victim had injected himself. Shortly after injecting himself, the victim died.

The defendant was charged, *inter alia*, with manslaughter. At the trial the Crown called a pathologist and a toxicologist: the former opined that death was caused primarily by the deceased's alcohol intake and said that it was 'possible' that heroin had been a contributory cause; the latter initially expressed a different view but deferred to the pathologist's opinion.

It was submitted at the close of the Crown's case (1) that there was no or insufficient evidence that heroin had been a substantial cause of death, alternatively (2) that if heroin did cause death, the deceased injecting himself was a *novus actus interveniens* breaking the chain of causation flowing from the defendant's acts.

Held, upholding the submissions: (1) that if the expert could not be sure that heroin caused the deceased's death, the jury could not be and (2) that the alternative submission was well-founded. Regard was had to *Cato* 62 Cr App R 41 and *Dalby* 74 Cr App R 348: the facts proved were closest to *Dalby*.

OPERATING AND SUBSTANTIAL CAUSES

In many instances, the accused's actions will not be the only cause of a particular consequence. A consequence may be caused by several different actions or sets of circumstances. For the accused to be criminally liable, it has to be shown that his acts were an 'operating and substantial cause'. This means that the accused's acts must have had a more than minimal effect.

R v Hennigan [1971] 3 All ER 133 (CA)

Lord Parker CJ: ... In view of the point that is made, it is really unnecessary to go into the facts in full in this case. Quite shortly what happened was that a Mrs Lowe driving a Vauxhall car with two passengers was emerging from a road called Old Road in order to cross the Wigan to Ashton Road and go into Nicol Road opposite. Old Road and Nicol Road were minor roads and indeed there was a 'Give way' sign where Mrs Lowe was approaching. The evidence was that she stopped at the entrance and then moved forward, and her evidence was that she had looked to her left towards Wigan and that the only traffic that she saw was a long way down by a railway bridge. However, she had only just got astride the middle of the road when a Ford Cortina driven by the appellant from Wigan towards Ashton crashed into her broadside and unfortunately as a result Mrs Lowe's two passengers were killed.

There was a considerable body of evidence that the appellant was driving at a fast speed; the estimates went up to 80 miles an hour, and almost immediately before the accident he appears to have overtaken a Jaguar, regaining his side of the road and then crashing into Mrs Lowe's car. It at once occurs to one that if this was a civil action, Mrs Lowe might be held substantially to blame, emerging from a minor road, because she clearly was at fault; on the other hand the appellant in a restricted area at night – it was 11.00 pm – was clearly going too fast, and dangerously too fast.

The trouble that has arisen in this case is in regard to a direction that the judge gave when the jury, after retirement, came back and asked a question. In the course of the summing up he told the jury that it must be shown that the appellant's manner of driving caused the collision and that the collision caused the death. He said this:

> It is admitted by the defence here very properly that the death of both Mr Twiss and Miss Twiss was the result of the collision, so the only issue you have to try is whether it is established, first of all, that the manner of his driving his car was dangerous, and, second, if it was, that that dangerous driving on his part was a substantial cause of the collision which is admitted resulted in the death of those two people.

A little later he said addressing the jury:

> You then say: 'If I think it was dangerous was it a substantial cause – not necessarily the whole cause – was it a substantial cause of the collision which caused the death?'

Then as I said the jury returned for a further direction, and they had probably been considering this from the point of view of blameworthiness as in a civil action. They asked: 'We would like further guidance on what you mean by "substantial", my Lord.' The judge then said:

> 'Substantial' means that it is not a remote cause of the death, but it is an appreciable cause of the death. It is rather like this: in a collision between two

> motor cars there may be both drivers each 50% to blame, and each would be a substantial cause of the collision. If on the other hand you get a situation where you can say that one of the drivers was four-fifths to blame and the other was one-fifth, you can say: 'I don't regard one-fifth as being a substantial cause of the accident; if it is as low as that then the fellow who really caused the accident was the one who is four-fifths to blame'. It is hard to define, but it means the real cause as opposed to being a minimal cause. Do you follow me? Would you like to retire again?

Then the foreman, clearly indicating what was in his mind, said: 'There is some doubt as to whether we can apportion blame'. The trial judge quite rightly said:

> You have only one man before you, and you are not concerned in any civil claim or with compensation. All you have to find is whether [the appellant] in your charge, was guilty of dangerous driving which was a substantial cause of the death of these two people, and I hope I have explained 'substantial' to you effectively.

What is said, as the court understands it, is that that conveyed the impression to the jury that they could find the appellant guilty if he was only little more than one-fifth to blame. The court would like to emphasise this, that there is of course nothing in s 1 of the Road Traffic Act 1960 which requires the manner of the driving to be a substantial cause, or a major cause, or any other description of cause, of the accident. So long as the dangerous driving is a cause and something more than *de minimis*, the statute operates. What has happened in the past is that judges have found it convenient to direct the jury in the form that it must be, as in one case it was put, the substantial cause ...

Although the word does not appear in the statute, it is clearly a convenient word to use to indicate to the jury that it must be something more than *de minimis*, and also to avoid possibly having to go into details of legal causation, remoteness and the like. That appears from the further direction of the trial judge, who in terms said that it must not be remote, and that it must be a real cause as opposed to being a minimal cause. It is perhaps unfortunate that he dealt with the matter in the illustration he gave on the basis of apportioning blame, but when one analyses it, it is quite clear that the direction, if anything, was much too favourable to the appellant in that the court is quite satisfied that even if he was in this case only one-fifth to blame, he was a cause of the death of these two people. In these circumstances the appeal is dismissed.

R v Cato and Others [1976] 1 WLR 110 (CA)

Lord Widgery CJ: ... The victim, as I have said, was a young man called Anthony Farmer. The events leading up to his death occurred on 25 July 1974. On that day Cato and Farmer had been in each other's company for most of the day. The evidence suggests certain intervals when they were apart, but by and large they seem to have been together all that day, and they spent much of the day with Morris and Dudley as well. All four of them at that time were living at a house called 34 Russell Street, and on 25 July their activities brought them to the Crown public house where they were until closing time, and after closing time they went back to 34 Russell Street.

There were others living in the house. They went to bed, and the four (that is to say, Cato, Morris, Dudley and the deceased Farmer) remained downstairs for a time. The moment came when Farmer produced a bag of white powder and some syringes and invited the others to have a 'fix' with him; and so they did. The white powder was put in its bag on the mantelpiece, the syringes were distributed amongst the four who were to participate, and the procedure which they adopted (which may or may not be a common one) was to pair off so that each could do the actual act of injection into the other half of his pair. Following this procedure Morris and Dudley paired off together and so did Cato and Farmer (the deceased). All four had a number of injections following this procedure, but the time came when Dudley and Morris went to bed, leaving Cato and Farmer downstairs in the sitting room. Cato and Farmer continued to give each other these injections from time to time right through the night.

The actual method, which I have probably described sufficiently already, may deserve a moment's repetition because so much hinges on it. The method, as I have already indicated, was that each would take his own syringe. He would fill it to his own taste with whatever mixture of powder and water he thought proper. He would then give his syringe to the other half of his pair – in this case Farmer would give his syringe to Cato – and the other half of the pair would conduct the actual act of injection. It is important to notice that the strength of the mixture to be used was entirely dictated by the person who was to receive it because he prepared his own syringe; but it is also to be noticed that the actual act of injection was done by the other half of the pair, which of course has a very important influence on this case when one comes to causation.

When the following morning came Farmer and Cato were still downstairs. They were apparently fast asleep, although everybody thought they were well enough at 8 am when they were seen. But as the next hour or two passed it became apparent that they were both in difficulties. Cato indeed was having difficulty in breathing, and probably his life was saved only because somebody gave him some rudimentary first aid. No one was able to do the same for Farmer, and by 11 am Farmer was dead. The cause of death was that his respiratory system ceased to function consequent on intoxication from drugs ...

We can now turn to look more precisely at counsel's submissions in supporting Cato's appeal against conviction. We have had a long and very helpful argument from counsel for Cato in which all the features of this difficult, and in some respects intriguing, case have been considered. It seems to us that the first and most important single factor to which he directed our attention was concerned with causation, that is to say with the link alleged to exist between the injection of heroin and the death of Farmer.

First of all, he invited us to look at the evidence of causation, and he pointed out that the medical evidence did not at any point say 'This morphine killed Farmer'; the actual link of that kind was not present. The witnesses were hesitant to express such a view and often recoiled from it, saying it was not for them to state the cause of death.

It is perfectly true, as counsel for Cato says, that the expert evidence did not in positive terms provide a link, but it was never intended to. The expert witnesses here spoke to factual situations, and the conclusions and deductions therefrom were for the jury. The first question was: was there sufficient evidence on which the jury could conclude, as they must have concluded, that adequate causation was present?

When one looks at the evidence it is important to realise that no other cause of Farmer's death was supplied. Dr Robinson thought that there might have been another drug, and she said at one stage it might have been cocaine, but there was never any cocaine found in the body. The only cause of death actually supplied by the evidence was morphine. No natural disease was present and no other drug was identified. Furthermore, the symptoms of the external appearance of the body, and the nature of the final terminal cause, were consistent with poison by the administration of heroin in the way which was described.

Further, when the people who lived in the house were giving their evidence about the death of Farmer, it was, as the judge pointed out, quite clear that they thought there was no doubt about what the cause had been. It may be of course that young people living in those circumstances know a great deal about the symptoms of heroin poisoning: I know not.

The judge said:

> Members of the jury, it seems to me that that evidence about the condition of Cato when he was senseless on the floor and was put to bed, what he looked like and so forth is quite material in regard to the cause of Tony Farmer's death because Cato and he had both been dosing themselves with the same sort of thing, in the same sort of way, in the same sort of number of times, and that is clear evidence in this particular case. The opinion of the people in the house is of course not medical opinion but everybody there seemed to draw the conclusion that probably the heroin injections had caused both of them to be in the condition they were in.

That is an important and proper conclusion, if the jury thought fit to adopt it, because the fact that Cato very nearly suffered the same fate as Farmer, and showed the same kind of symptoms following the same kind of injections, is a pointer to indicate that the cause of Farmer's condition was the heroin which he had taken; and, furthermore, the jury were entitled, if they thought fit, to be influenced by the fact that the non-medical evidence from the residents was of the kind which the judge related.

Of course behind the whole question of the sufficiency of evidence of causation is the fact that it was not necessary for the prosecution to prove that the heroin was the only cause. As a matter of law, it was sufficient if the prosecution could establish that it was a cause, provided it was a cause outside the *de minimis* range, and effectively bearing on the acceleration of the moment of the victim's death.

When one has that in mind it is, we think, really possible to say if the jury had been directed to look for heroin as a cause, not *de minimis* but a cause of substance, and they came back with a verdict of not guilty, the verdict could really be described as a perverse one. The whole background of the evidence was the other way and there certainly was ample evidence, given a proper direction, on which a charge of manslaughter could be supported.

But what about the proper direction? It will be noted that in none of the versions which I have quoted of the judge's direction on this point, nor in any of those which I have not quoted which appear in the summing up, is there any reference to it being necessary for the cause to be a substantial one. It is said in clear terms in one of the six questions that the jury can consider whether the administration of the heroin was a cause or contributed to or accelerated the death, and in precise terms the word 'contributed' is not qualified to show that a substantial contribution is required.

Counsel for Cato, whose eagle eye misses nothing, sees here, and seeks to exploit here, what is a misdirection on the part of the trial judge. In other words, taking the judge's words literally, it would be possible for the jury to bring in a verdict of guilty of manslaughter even though the contribution was not of substance.

Before pursuing that, it is worth reminding oneself that some of the more recent *dicta* in the textbooks about this point do not support as strongly as was once the case the theory that the contribution must be substantial.

In Smith and Hogan, *Criminal Law*, 3rd edn, 1973, p 217 there is this rather interesting extract:

> It is commonly said by judges and writers that, while the accused's act need not be the sole cause of the death, it must be a substantial cause. This appears to mean only that a minute contribution to the cause of death will not entail responsibility. It may therefore be misleading to direct a jury that D is not liable unless his conduct was a 'substantial' cause. Killing is merely an acceleration of death and factors which produce a very trivial acceleration will be ignored.

Whether that be so or not, and we do not propose to give that passage the court's blessing today at all events, if one looks at the circumstances of the present case with any real sense of reality, we think there can be no doubt that when the judge was talking about contribution the jury knew perfectly well that he was talking about something more than the mere *de minimis* contribution. We have given this point particular care in our consideration of the case because it worried us to some extent originally, but we do feel in the end, having looked at all the circumstances, that there could not have been any question in this case of the jury making the mistake of thinking that the contribution would suffice if it were *de minimis*. Therefore in our judgment there is no substance in the attack of counsel for Cato on the basis of causation, whether it be an attack on the available evidence or on the trial judge's treatment of that evidence ...

R v Notman [1994] Crim LR 518 (CA)

Facts: The defendant was acquitted of affray and convicted of assault occasioning actual bodily harm. The defendant and others entered a shop from which he had been banned and created a disturbance. A police officer arrived and the defendant charged at him. The officer moved out of the way and put out his leg to stop the defendant, thereby sustaining an injury to his ankle. The recorder directed the jury that the conduct of the defendant must have been a substantial cause of the officer's injury for them to convict. It was argued on appeal that the recorder should not have used the expression 'a substantial cause', but should have directed the jury in accordance with the test in *Roberts* (1972) 56 Cr App R 95.

Held: (1) The case was on all fours with *Hennigan* (1971) 55 Cr App R 262 (causing death by dangerous driving). In that case it was said that the expression 'a substantial cause' was convenient to indicate to the jury that the cause must have been more than just *de minimis*, which was the only necessary qualification. It also avoided the necessity to go into the details of legal causation and remoteness.

(2) The test set out in *Roberts* (was the injury the natural result of what the assailant said and did, in the sense that it was something that could reasonably have been foreseen as the consequence of what he was saying and doing) did not invalidate the simple direction given by the trial judge in that case (was the harm 'as a result' of the assailant's act). The test in *Roberts* is not one always to be applied and about which there should always be a direction.

R v Kimsey [1996] Crim LR 35 (CA)

Facts: The appellant was convicted of causing death by dangerous driving. A close friend of the appellant overtook him and the two engaged in a high-speed chase with the appellant driving a few feet from the rear of his friend's car. Both cars had just overtaken another car at 75 mph, when the friend's car swerved on to the verge. The prosecution evidence was that the appellant overtook his friend at that point and struck her car, either because she swerved back to the right, or because he pulled to the left as he overtook. The friend, not in control of her car, struck an oncoming car, and was killed. One of her tyres was underinflated, which could have led to the car being difficult to control. The appellant's case was that the friend had lost control before his car hit hers and the first collision did not have any effect on her loss of control, which in turn led to the second, fatal collision. The prosecution case was that the appellant's driving had caused the friend's loss of control and the first collision, which in turn led to the fatal collision, or alternatively that his driving encouraged her to drive too fast and lose control; or that by driving so closely behind, when she did lose control, the first collision occurred, occasioning further loss of control. The recorder told the jury that they did not have to be sure that the appellant's driving 'was the principal, or a substantial, cause of the death, as long as you are sure that it was a cause and that there was something more than a slight or a trifling link'.

On appeal, it was argued that it was wrong to say that the cause did not have to be a substantial cause.

Held, dismissing the appeal, that the test in *Hennigan* (1971) 55 Cr App R 262 was whether the contribution of the dangerous driving to the death was more than minute. To use the expression 'a substantial cause' is no doubt a convenient way of putting the test to the jury, as was suggested in that case. But the jury may well give the word 'substantial' a larger meaning. The recorder's reference to a 'slight or trifling link' was a permissible and useful way to avoid the term *de minimis*. His direction was faithful to the logic of *Hennigan*.

NOVUS ACTUS INTERVENIENS

It cannot be said that the accused's act caused a consequence if there is a new (intervening) act which breaks the chain of causation between the accused's act and the consequence. There are three types of intervening causes which need to be considered: third-party intervention, act of God, and act of the victim.

Third party intervention

An act of a third party can only amount to a *novus actus interveniens* if that act was a voluntary act (see *R v Pagett* (1983) 76 Cr App R 279).

It is clear from cases such as *R v Smith* [1959] 2 QB 35 and *R v Cheshire* [1991] 1 WLR 844 that medical treatment will only be regarded as a *novus actus interveniens* in exceptional cases.

R v Pagett (1983) 76 Cr App R 279 (CA)

Facts: In the early hours of one morning on the first floor of a block of flats where he lived, the appellant, who was armed with a shotgun and cartridges, shot at police officers who were attempting to arrest him for various serious offences. The appellant had with him a 16-year-old girl who was pregnant by him, and against her will used her body to shield him from any retaliation by the officers. The officers in fact returned the appellant's fire and as a result the girl was killed. The appellant was charged, *inter alia*, with her murder.

Robert Goff LJ: ... [I]t was pressed upon us by Lord Gifford [counsel for the appellant] that there either was, or should be, a comparable rule of English law, whereby, as a matter of policy, no man should be convicted of homicide (or, we imagine, any crime of violence to another person) unless he himself, or another person acting in concert with him, fired the shot (or, we imagine, struck the blow) which was the immediate cause of the victim's death (or injury).

No English authority was cited to us in support of any such proposition, and we know of none. So far as we are aware, there is no such rule in English law; and, in the absence of any doctrine of constructive malice, we can see no basis in principle for any such rule in English law. Lord Gifford urged upon us that, in a case where the accused did not, for example, fire the shot which was the immediate cause of the victim's death, he will inevitably have committed some lesser crime, and that it would be sufficient that he should be convicted of that lesser crime. So, on the facts of the present case, it would be enough that the appellant was convicted of the crime of attempted murder of the two police officers, DS Sartain and DC Richards. We see no force in this submission. In point of fact, it is not difficult to imagine circumstances in which it would manifestly be inadequate for the accused merely to be convicted of a lesser offence; for example, a man besieged by armed terrorists in a house might attempt to make his escape by forcing some other person to act as a shield, knowing full well that that person would in all probability be shot, and possibly killed, in consequence. For that man merely to be convicted of an assault would, if the person he used as a shield were to be shot and killed, surely be inadequate in all the circumstances; we can see no reason why he should not be convicted at least of manslaughter. But in any event there is, so far as we can discern, no basis of legal principle for Lord Gifford's submission. We are therefore unable to accept it.

In our judgment, the question whether an accused person can be held guilty of homicide, either murder or manslaughter, of a victim the immediate cause of whose death is the act of another person must be determined on the ordinary principles of causation, uninhibited by any such rule of policy as that for which Lord Gifford has contended. We therefore reject the second ground of appeal.

We turn to the first ground of appeal, which is that the learned judge erred in directing the jury that it was for him to decide *as a matter of law* whether by his unlawful and deliberate acts the appellant caused or was a cause of Gail Kinchen's death ...

We have no intention of embarking in this judgment on a dissertation of the nature of causation, or indeed of considering any matters other than those which are germane to the decision of the issues now before us. Problems of causation have troubled philosophers and lawyers throughout the ages; and it would be rash in the extreme for us to trespass beyond the boundaries of our immediate problem. Our comments should therefore be understood to be confined not merely to the criminal law, but to cases of homicide (and possibly also other crimes of violence to the person); and it must be emphasised that the problem of causation in the present case is specifically concerned with the intervention of another person (here one of the police officers) whose act was the immediate cause of the death of the victim, Gail Kinchen.

In cases of homicide, it is rarely necessary to give the jury any direction on causation as such. Of course, a necessary ingredient of the crimes of murder and manslaughter is that the accused has by his act caused the victim's death. But how the victim came by his death is usually not in dispute. What is in dispute is more likely to be some other matter: for example, the identity of the person who committed the act which indisputably caused the victim's death; or whether the accused had the necessary intent; or whether the accused acted in self-defence, or was provoked. Even where it is necessary to direct the jury's minds to the question of causation, it is usually enough to direct them simply that in law the accused's act need not be the sole cause, or even the main cause, of the victim's death, it being enough that his act contributed significantly to that result. It is right to observe in passing, however, that even this simple direction is a direction of law relating to causation, on the basis of which the jury are bound to act in concluding whether the prosecution has established, as a matter of fact, that the accused's act did in this sense cause the victim's death. Occasionally, however, a specific issue of causation may arise. One such case is where, although an act of the accused constitutes a *causa sine qua non* of (or necessary condition for) the death of the victim, nevertheless the intervention of a third person may be regarded as the sole cause of the victim's death, thereby relieving the accused of criminal responsibility. Such intervention, if it has such an effect, has often been described by lawyers as a *novus actus interveniens*. We are aware that this time-honoured Latin term has been the subject of criticism. We are also aware that attempts have been made to translate it into English; though no simple translation has proved satisfactory, really because the Latin term has become a term of art which conveys to lawyers the crucial feature that there has not merely been an intervening act of another person, but that act was so independent of the act of the accused that it should be regarded in law as the cause of the victim's death, to the exclusion of the act of the accused. At the risk of scholarly criticism, we shall for the purposes of this judgment continue to use the Latin term.

Now the whole subject of causation in the law has been the subject of a well-known and most distinguished treatise by Professors Hart and Honore, *Causation in the Law*. Passages from this book were cited to the learned judge, and were plainly relied upon by him; we, too, wish to express our indebtedness to it. It would be quite wrong for us to consider in this judgment the wider issues discussed in that work. But, for present purposes, the passage which is of most immediate relevance is to be found in Chapter 12, in which the learned authors consider the circumstances in which the intervention of a third person, not acting in concert with the accused, may have the effect of relieving the accused of criminal responsibility. The criterion which they suggest should be applied in such circumstances is whether the intervention is voluntary, ie whether it is 'free, deliberate and informed'. We resist the temptation of expressing the judicial opinion whether we find ourselves in complete agreement with that definition; though we certainly consider it to be broadly correct and supported by authority. Among the examples which the authors give of non-voluntary conduct, which is not effective to relieve the accused of responsibility, are two which are germane to the present case, *viz* a reasonable act performed for the purpose of self-preservation, and an act done in performance of a legal duty.

There can, we consider, be no doubt that a reasonable act performed for the purpose of self-preservation, being of course itself an act caused by the accused's own act, does not operate as a *novus actus interveniens*. If authority is needed for this almost self-evident proposition, it is to be found in such cases as *Pitts* (1842) C & M 284, and *Curley* (1909) 2 Cr App R 96. In both these cases, the act performed for the purpose of self-preservation consisted of an act by the victim in attempting to escape from the violence of the accused, which in fact resulted in the victim's death. In each case it was held as a matter of law that, if the victim acted in a reasonable attempt to escape the violence of the accused, the death of the victim was caused by the act of the accused. Now one form of self-preservation is self-defence; for present purposes, we can see no distinction in principle between an attempt to escape the consequences of the accused's act, and a response which takes the form of self-defence. Furthermore, in our judgment, if a reasonable act of self-defence against the act of the accused causes the death of a third party, we can see no reason in principle why the act of self-defence, being an involuntary act caused by the act of the accused, should relieve the accused from final responsibility for the death of the third party. Of course, it does not necessarily follow that the accused will be guilty of the murder, or even of the manslaughter, of the third party; though in the majority of cases he is likely to be guilty at least of manslaughter. Whether he is guilty of murder or manslaughter will depend upon the question whether all the ingredients of the relevant offence have been proved; in particular, on a charge of murder, it will be necessary that the accused had the necessary intent ...

No English authority was cited to us, nor we think to the learned judge, in support of the proposition that an act done in the execution of a legal duty, again of course being an act itself caused by the act of the accused, does not operate as a *novus actus interveniens* ... Even so, we agree with the learned judge that the proposition is sound law, because as a matter of principle such an act cannot be regarded as a voluntary act independent of the wrongful act of the accused. A parallel may be drawn with the so-called 'rescue' cases in the law of negligence, where a wrongdoer may be held liable in negligence to a third party who suffers injury in going to the rescue of a person who has been put in danger by the defendant's negligent act. Where, for example, a police officer in the execution of his duty acts to prevent a crime, or to apprehend a person suspected of a crime, the case is surely a *fortiori*. Of course, it is inherent in the requirement that the police officer, or other person, must be acting in the execution of his duty that his act should be reasonable in all the circumstances: see s 3 of the Criminal Law Act 1967. Furthermore, once again we are only considering the issue of causation. If intervention by a third party in the execution of a legal duty, caused by the act of the accused, results in the death of the victim, the question whether the accused is guilty of the murder or manslaughter of the victim must depend on whether the necessary ingredients of the relevant offence have been proved against the accused, including in particular, in the case of murder, whether the accused had the necessary intent.

The principles which we have stated are principles of law. This is plain from, for example, the case of *Pitts* (1842) C & M 284, to which we have already referred. It follows that where, in any particular case, there is an issue concerned with what we have for convenience called *novus actus interveniens*, it will be appropriate for the judge to direct the jury in accordance with these principles. It does not however follow that it is accurate to state broadly that causation is a question of law. On the contrary, generally speaking causation is a question of fact for the jury. Thus in, for example, *Towers* (1874) 12 Cox C C 530, the accused struck a woman; she screamed loudly, and a child whom she was then nursing turned black in the face, and from that day until it died suffered from convulsions. The question whether the death of the child was caused by the act of the accused was left by the judge to the jury to decide as a question of fact. But that does not mean that there are no principles of law relating to causation, so that no directions on law are ever to be given to a jury on the question of causation. On the contrary, we have already pointed out one familiar direction which is given on causation, which is that the accused's act need not be the sole, or even the main, cause of the victim's death for his act to be held to have caused the death. Similarly, it was held by this court in the case of *Blaue* [1975] 1 WLR 1411 that:

> [I]t has long been the policy of the law that those who use violence on other people must take their victims as they find them. This in our judgment means the whole man, not just the physical man. It does not lie in the mouth of the assailant to say that his victim's religious belief which inhibited her from accepting certain kinds of treatment was unreasonable. The question for decision is what caused her death. The answer is the stab wound. The fact

> that the victim refused to stop this end coming about did not break the causal connection between the act and death. (See at pp 274 and 1415, *per* Lawton LJ delivering the judgment of the court).

This was plainly a statement of a principle of law. Likewise, in cases where there is an issue whether the act of the victim or of a third party constituted a *novus actus interveniens*, breaking the causal connection between the act of the accused and the death of the victim, it would be appropriate for the judge to direct the jury, of course in the most simple terms, in accordance with the legal principles which they have to apply. It would then fall to the jury to decide the relevant factual issues which, identified with reference to those legal principles, will lead to the conclusion whether or not the prosecution have established the guilt of the accused of the crime of which he is charged ...

There is however one further aspect of the present case to which we must advert. On the evidence, Gail Kinchen was not just an innocent bystander killed by a shot fired from the gun of a police officer who, acting in reasonable self-defence, fired his gun in response to a lethal attack by the appellant: though on those facts alone it would, in our opinion, have been open to the jury to convict the appellant of murder or manslaughter. But if, as the jury must have found to have occurred in the present case, the appellant used Gail Kinchen by force and against her will as a shield to protect him from shots fired by the police, the effect is that he committed not one but two unlawful acts, both of which were dangerous – the act of firing at the police, and the act of holding Gail Kinchen as a shield in front of him when the police might well fire shots in his direction in self-defence. Either act could in our judgment, if on the principles we have stated it was held to cause the death of Gail Kinchen, constitute the *actus reus* of the manslaughter or, if the necessary intent were established, murder of Gail Kinchen by the appellant, even though the shot which killed her was fired not by the appellant but by the police officer.

In the light of these principles, we do not consider that any legitimate criticism can be made, on behalf of the appellant, of the direction given by the learned judge to the jury on the issue of causation in the present case ...

R v Jordan (1956) 40 Cr App R 152 (CA)

Hallett J: ... The facts of the case, so far as I need refer to them, are as follows. The appellant, together with three other men, all serving airmen of the United States Forces, were charged with the murder of a man named Beaumont as the result of a disturbance which arose in a cafe at Hull. Beaumont was stabbed with a knife. There was no evidence that any one of the other three men used a knife on Beaumont or was acting in concert with the man who did use the knife, and accordingly Byrne J, who tried the case, directed the acquittal of those three men. With regard to the appellant it was ultimately conceded by Mr Veale, who appeared for him in the court below and in this court, that he did use the knife and stab Beaumont. Beaumont was admitted to hospital very promptly and the wound was stitched up, but nonetheless he died not many days after. In those circumstances the appellant was tried for murder. Various defences were raised, accident, self-defence, provocation and stabbing in the course of a quarrel. On all of those defences the direction of the learned judge is not in any way challenged and the jury rejected them.

Mr Veale told us, with his usual frankness, that the original intention of the defence was not to lodge an appeal, but certain information reached the United States authorities and the defence became in a position to put forward further evidence, and in particular the evidence of two doctors, Dr Keith Simpson and Mr Blackburn, whose standing is beyond question ...

The further evidence is said to show that death was not, to use words of Byrne J, 'consequent upon the wound inflicted'. On the contrary, both the doctors called are of opinion that, from the medical point of view, it cannot be described as caused by the wound at all. Whether from the legal point of view it could be described as caused by the wound is a more doubtful question ...

... There were two things other than the wound which were stated by these two medical witnesses to have brought about death. The stab wound had penetrated the intestine in two places, but it was mainly healed at the time of death. With a view to preventing infection it was thought to administer an antibiotic, terramycin.

It was agreed by the two additional witnesses that that was the proper course to take, and a proper dose was administered. Some people, however, are intolerant to terramycin, and Beaumont was one of those people. After the initial doses he developed diarrhoea, which was only properly attributable, in the opinion of those doctors, to the fact that the patient was intolerant to terramycin. Thereupon the administration of terramycin was stopped, but unfortunately the very next day the resumption of such administration was ordered by another doctor and it was recommenced the following day. The two doctors both take the same view about it. Dr Simpson said that to introduce a poisonous substance after the intolerance of the patient was shown was palpably wrong. Mr Blackburn agreed.

Other steps were taken which were also regarded by the doctors as wrong – namely the intravenous introduction of wholly abnormal quantities of liquid far exceeding the output. As a result the lungs became waterlogged and pulmonary oedema was discovered. Mr Blackburn said that he was not surprised to see that condition after the introduction of so much liquid, and that pulmonary oedema leads to bronchopneumonia as an inevitable sequel, and it was from bronchopneumonia that Beaumont died.

We are disposed to accept it as the law that death resulting from any normal treatment employed to deal with a felonious injury may be regarded as caused by the felonious injury, but we do not think it necessary to examine the cases in detail or to formulate for the assistance of those who have to deal with such matters in the future the correct test which ought to be laid down with regard to what is necessary to be proved in order to establish causal connection between the death and the felonious injury. It is sufficient to point out here that this was not normal treatment. Not only one feature, but two separate and independent features, of treatment were, in the opinion of the doctors, palpably wrong and these produced the symptoms discovered at the post mortem examination which were the direct and immediate cause of death, namely the pneumonia resulting from the condition of oedema which was found.

The question then is whether it can be said that, if that evidence had been before the jury, it ought not to have, and in all probability would not have, affected their decision. We recognise that the learned judge, if this matter had been before him, would have had to direct the jury correctly on how far such supervening matters could be regarded as interrupting the chain of causation; but we felt that in the end it would have been a question of fact for the jury depending on what evidence they accepted as correct and the view they took on that evidence. We feel no uncertainty at all that, whatever direction had been given to the jury and however correct it had been, the jury would have felt precluded from saying that they were satisfied that death was caused by the stab wound.

For these reasons we come to the conclusion that the appeal must be allowed and the conviction set aside.

R v Smith [1959] 2 QB 35 (CA)

Facts: The appellant, Thomas Joseph Smith, a private soldier in the King's Regiment, took part in a fight between a company of his regiment and a company of the Gloucestershire Regiment, who were sharing barracks in Germany, on the night of 13 April 1958. Three men of the Gloucesters received stab wounds. One of them subsequently died.

Lord Parker CJ: ... The second ground concerns a question of causation. The deceased man in fact received two bayonet wounds, one in the arm and one in the back. The one in the back, unknown to anybody, had pierced the lung and caused haemorrhage. There followed a series of unfortunate occurrences. A fellow member of his company tried to carry him to the medical reception station. On the way he tripped over a wire and dropped the deceased man. He picked him up again, went a little farther, and fell apparently a second time, causing the deceased man to be dropped onto the ground. Thereafter he did not try a third time but went for help, and ultimately the deceased man was brought into the reception station. There, the medical officer, Captain Millward, and his orderly were trying to cope with a number of other cases, two serious stabbings and some minor injuries, and it is clear that they did not appreciate the seriousness of the deceased man's condition or exactly what had happened. A transfusion of saline solution was attempted and failed. When his breathing seemed impaired he was given oxygen and artificial respiration was applied, and in fact he died after he had been in the station about an hour, which was about two hours after the original stabbing. It is now known that having regard to the injuries which the man had in fact suffered, his lung being pierced, the treatment that he was given was thoroughly bad and might well have affected his chances of recovery. There was evidence that there is a tendency for a wound of this sort to heal and for the haemorrhage to stop. No doubt his being dropped on the ground and having artificial respiration applied would halt or at any rate impede the chances of healing. Further, there were no facilities whatsoever for blood transfusion, which would have been the best possible treatment. There was evidence that if he had received immediate and different treatment, he might not have died. Indeed, had facilities for blood transfusion been available and been administered, Dr Camps, who gave evidence for the defence, said that his chances of recovery were as high as 75%.

In these circumstances Mr Bowen urges that not only was a careful summing up required but that a correct direction to the court would have been that they must be satisfied that the death of Private Creed was a natural consequence and the sole consequence of the wound sustained by him and flowed directly from it. If there was, says Mr Bowen, any other cause, whether resulting from negligence or not, if, as he contends here, something happened which impeded the chance of the deceased recovering, then the death did not result from the wound. The court is quite unable to accept that contention. It seems to the court that if at the time of death the original wound is still an operating cause and a substantial cause, then the death can properly be said to be the result of the wound, albeit, that some other cause of death is also operating. Only if it can be said that the original wounding is merely the setting in which another cause operates can it be said that the death does not result from the wound. Putting it in another way, only if the second cause is so overwhelming as to make the original wound merely part of the history can it be said that the death does not flow from the wound ...

Mr Bowen placed great reliance on a case decided in this court of *R v Jordan* (1956) 40 Cr App R 152 and in particular on a passage in the headnote which says: '... that death resulting from any normal treatment employed to deal with a felonious injury may be regarded as caused by the felonious injury, but that the same principle does not apply where the treatment employed is abnormal.' Reading those words into the present case, Mr Bowen says that the treatment that this unfortunate man received from the moment that he was struck to the time of his death was abnormal. The court is satisfied that *Jordan's* case was a very particular case depending upon its exact facts. It incidentally arose in this court on the grant of an application to call further evidence, and leave having been obtained, two well-known medical experts gave evidence that in their opinion death had not been caused by the stabbing but by the introduction of terramycin after the deceased had shown that he was intolerant to it, and by the intravenous introduction of abnormal quantities of liquid. It also appears that at the time when that was done the stab wound which had penetrated the intestine in two places had mainly healed. In those circumstances the court felt bound to quash the conviction because they could not say that a reasonable jury properly directed would not have been able on that to say that there had been a break in the chain of causation; the court could only uphold the conviction in that case if they were satisfied that no reasonable jury could have come to that conclusion.

In the present case it is true that the judge-advocate did not in his summing up go into the refinements of causation. Indeed, in the opinion of this court he was probably wise to refrain from doing so. He did leave the broad question to the court whether they were satisfied that the wound had caused the death in the sense that the death flowed from the wound, albeit that the treatment he received was in the light of after-knowledge a bad thing. In the opinion of this court that was on the facts of the case a perfectly adequate summing up on causation; I say 'on the facts of the case' because, in the opinion of the court, they can only lead to one conclusion: a man is stabbed in the back, his lung is pierced and haemorrhage results; two hours later he dies of haemorrhage from that wound; in the interval there is no time for a careful examination, and the treatment given turns out in the light of subsequent knowledge to have been appropriate and, indeed, harmful. In those circumstances no reasonable jury or court could, properly directed, in our view possibly come to any other conclusion than that the death resulted from the original wound. Accordingly, the court dismisses this appeal.

R v Malcherek; R v Steel [1981] 1 WLR 690 (CA)

Lord Lane CJ: ... The facts of the two cases are as follows. I start with the applicant Steel. This man, on 13 December 1979, in the Crown Court at Leeds before Boreham J and a jury, was convicted of murder, and he now applies to this court for leave to appeal against conviction and also to call certain witnesses, two medical men.

The victim of the attack was a girl called Carol Wilkinson. She was 20 years of age at the time. She lived in the Ravenscliffe area of Bradford with her fiancé and worked at a bakery which was situated about half a mile away from her home. Steel was then aged 21. He lived not far away in another house of the same Ravenscliffe estate. He was sharing accommodation with a girl named Pamela Ward, but at the same time he was carrying on an association with another girl whom he eventually married. Steel was employed by the local council as a gardener.

It was on 10 October 1977, at about 9 am, that Carol Wilkinson was walking to work from her home to the bakery. At some time on that morning, between about 9.00 and 9.30, she was savagely attacked by someone who stripped off the greater part of her clothing and then battered her about the head with a 50 lb stone which was found nearby. She was found shortly afterwards, in a field by the road, unconscious. She was taken as rapidly as could be to hospital. She had multiple fractures of the skull and severe brain damage as well as a broken arm and other superficial injuries which need not concern us. She was put almost immediately on a life support machine in the shape of a ventilator.

On 12 October the medical team in whose charge she was, after a number of tests, came to the conclusion that her brain had ceased to function and that, accordingly, the ventilator was in effect operating on a lifeless body. The life support machine was switched off and all bodily functions ceased shortly afterwards.

The judge withdrew the issue of causation from the jury on the fifth day of that trial, and the jury were accordingly left to decide the issue, hotly contested, of whether they were sure that it was Steel who had been the girl's assailant ...

So far as that issue is concerned, namely the issue of causation, the following facts are material. On admission to the casualty department of the Bradford Royal Infirmary at about 10.15 am on Monday 10 October, Carol was seen by a Dr Nevelos, who found her to be deeply unconscious with no motor activity, her eyes open and the pupils fixed. She was breathing only with the aid of the ventilator. An hour later she was admitted to the intensive care unit of the Royal Infirmary and during the whole of that day she remained deeply unconscious and unresponsive. At 10.00 pm the consultant neuro-surgeon, a Mr Price, examined her. He found her to be in a deep coma, unresponding to any stimulus. He carried out a test for electrical activity in the brain which proved negative. The total absence of any motor activity since the girl had been admitted to hospital and the early fixation of the pupils, which I have already mentioned, led him to the conclusion that there had been a devastating impact injury to the brain.

The cerebral function monitor showed no activity. Her eyes were too occluded, so it is said, to allow any caloric testing. The suggestion was made by Mr Price that her temperature should be raised and that if by the morning her cerebral function remained as it had been up to date, namely zero, they should declare her brain to be dead. In fact, shortly after 10.00 am the next day, a cerebral blood flow test was carried out which indicated that there was no blood circulating in the brain. Several electroencephalogram tests were made during that day. None of them had any positive result.

On Wednesday 12 October, two days after the injuries had been inflicted, another electroencephalogram test was made in the morning and another one at 6.00 pm but none of these tests showed any signs of electrical activity at all. After that there was a consultation between the doctors who were in charge of the patient, and it was agreed amongst them that the continued use of the ventilator was without any purpose. At 6.15 pm the patient was withdrawn from the ventilator, and at 6.40 pm she was declared to be dead. There is an indication, though we are told it was not part of the evidence at the trial, that on post mortem 50 minutes later it was found that her brain was already in the process of decomposition. Much of the cross-examination of the medical men was taken up with suggestions that they had failed to conform to certain criteria which have been laid down by the Royal Medical Colleges on the subject of the ascertainment of brain death.

The matter which counsel for Steel invites this court to take into consideration as possibly differentiating the case of *Steel* from that of *Malcherek* is that he says that two of the suggested tests were not carried out properly, namely the corneal reflex test and the vestibulo-ocular reflex test. The corneal reflex test consists of touching the cornea of the eye with a piece of cotton wool to see if that creates any reaction in the patient and, as we understand it, the vestibulo-ocular reflex test consists of putting ice cold water into the aperture of the ear, again to see if that produces any reflex in the patient. Reasons were given for neither of those tests having been carried out.

We now turn to the facts in the case of Malcherek. On 12 November 1979, this time in the Crown Court at Winchester before Willis J and a jury, Malcherek was convicted of murder. He appeals against the conviction by leave of the single judge. The victim was Christian Malcherek, his wife, who was then aged 32. It seems that in November 1978 she left Malcherek in order to go and live with her daughters at Poole. There was a non-molestation order in force, directed at Malcherek, but on the evening of 26 March 1979 he went to her flat where she was living. There was a quarrel and, to cut a long story short, he stabbed his wife nine times with a kitchen knife. One of the stabs resulted in a deep penetrating wound to Mrs Malcherek's abdomen.

She was taken to Poole General Hospital and there was preliminary treatment in order to try to rectify her very low blood pressure, which was ascertained on admission. The surgical registrar then performed a laparotomy and removed rather more than one and half litres of blood from the abdomen. There was a section of the intestine which was damaged, and he excised that and joined up the two ends. For several days it seemed as though Mrs Malcherek was making an uneventful recovery. Indeed, she was clearly confidently expected to survive. However, on 1 April she collapsed and the preliminary diagnosis was that she had suffered a massive pulmonary embolism. She was resuscitated and arrangements were made for her admission to the Western Hospital at Southampton, which was equipped to deal with this type of emergency. She arrived there shortly before midnight. A couple of hours later her condition suddenly deteriorated and her heart stopped. She was taken straight away to the operating theatre and given cardiac massage. The surgeon then opened her chest. He found that her heart was distended and not beating. He made an incision into the pulmonary artery and extracted from the pulmonary artery a large clot of blood some 12 inches long, which had plainly formed in one of the veins of the leg (which, we are told, is a common complication of major abdominal surgery), and had then moved on from the leg to the pulmonary artery with the results already described.

When the clot was removed the heart started again spontaneously. It will be appreciated that since the heart was not beating for a period of something like 30 minutes there was a grave danger of anoxic damage to the brain. She was returned to the ward and connected to a ventilator. Throughout the Monday she remained on that machine receiving intensive care, but in the afternoon an electroencephalogram showed that there were indeed symptoms of severe anoxic damage to the brain. The prognosis was poor.

The consultant neurologist saw her at 7.00 pm. She was unresponsive to any stimulus save that her pupils did react to light. He suggested a further electroencephalogram because at that stage it was not clear how much brain damage had been suffered. On the morning of Tuesday, Dr Manners decided to dispense with the ventilator if that could possibly be done. When that was done she was able, first of all, to breathe adequately by herself, but towards midday she suffered a sharp and marked deterioration and the diagnosis was that she had suffered a cerebral vascular accident, possibly a ruptured blood vessel, possibly a clot, causing further brain damage. In any event, by quarter to two in the afternoon her attempts to breathe were inadequate and she was put back onto the ventilator. There was a continued deterioration and by the following day she was deeply unconscious and seemed to have irreversible brain damage. There was less electrical activity than before when a further electroencephalogram was carried out.

On 5 April the situation had deteriorated still more, and it was quite obvious at 1.15 pm on that day, when Dr Lawton made an examination, that her brain was irretrievably damaged. He carried out five of the six Royal Medical College's confirmatory tests. The one he omitted was the 'gag reflex' test, again for reasons which he explained. The patient's relations were consulted and a decision was made to disconnect the ventilator, which was done at half past four. A supply of oxygen was fed to her lungs in case she should make spontaneous efforts to breathe but she did not, and shortly after 5.00 pm she was certified to be dead.

In these circumstances, as in the earlier case, the judge decided that the question of causation should not be left for the jury's consideration. Consequently, the only issue they had to decide was the one of intent, there being no argument but that Malcherek had in fact inflicted the knife wound or wounds on Mrs Malcherek.

In this case the principal and, in effect, the only ground of appeal, as counsel for Malcherek has told us, is that the judge should have left the issue of causation to the jury.

This is not the occasion for any decision as to what constitutes death. Modern techniques have undoubtedly resulted in the blurring of many of the conventional and traditional concepts of death. A person's heart can now be removed altogether without death supervening; machines can keep the blood circulating through the vessels of the body until a new heart can be implanted in the patient, and even though a person is no longer able to breathe spontaneously a ventilating machine can, so to speak, do his breathing for him, as is demonstrated in the two cases before us. There is, it seems, a body of opinion in the medical profession that there is only one true test of death and that is the irreversible death of the brain stem, which controls the basic functions of the body such as breathing. When that occurs it is said the body has died, even though by mechanical means the lungs are being caused to operate and some circulation of blood is taking place.

We have had placed before us, and have been asked to admit, evidence that in each of these two cases the medical men concerned did not comply with all the suggested criteria for establishing such brain death. Indeed, further evidence has been suggested and placed before us that those criteria or tests are not in themselves stringent enough. However, in each of these two cases there is no doubt that whatever test is applied the victim died; that is to say, applying the traditional test, all body functions, breathing and heartbeat and brain function came to an end, at the latest, soon after the ventilator was disconnected.

The question posed for answer to this court is simply whether the judge in each case was right in withdrawing from the jury the question of causation. Was he right to rule that there was no evidence on which the jury could come to the conclusion that the assailant did not cause the death of the victim?

The way in which the submissions are put by counsel for Malcherek on the one hand and by counsel for Steel on the other is as follows: the doctors, by switching off the ventilator and the life support machine, were the cause of death or, to put it more accurately, there was evidence which the jury should have been allowed to consider that the doctors, and not the assailant, in each case may have been the cause of death.

In each case it is clear that the initial assault was the cause of the grave head injuries in the one case and of the massive abdominal haemorrhage in the other. In each case the initial assault was the reason for the medical treatment being necessary. In each case the medical treatment given was normal and conventional. At some stage the doctors must decide if and when treatment has become otiose. This decision was reached, in each of the two cases here, in circumstances which have already been set out in some detail. It is no part of the task of this court to inquire whether the criteria, the Royal Medical College confirmatory tests, are a satisfactory code of practice. It is no part of the task of this court to decide whether the doctors were, in either of these two cases, justified in omitting one or more of the so called 'confirmatory tests'. The doctors are not on trial; Steel and Malcherek respectively were.

There are two comparatively recent cases which are relevant to the consideration of this problem. The first is *R v Jordan* (1956) 40 Cr App R 152 ...

In the view of this court, if a choice has to be made between the decision in *R v Jordan* and that in *R v Smith*, which we do not believe it does (*R v Jordan* being a very exceptional case), then the decision in *R v Smith* is to be preferred.

The only other case to which reference has been made, it having been drawn to our attention by counsel for Steel, is *R v Blaue* [1975] 1 WLR 1411. That was the case where the victim of a stabbing incident was a Jehovah's Witness who refused to accept a blood transfusion although she had been told that to refuse would mean death for her, a prophecy which was fulfilled. The passage that has been drawn to our attention in that case is the last paragraph of the judgment of Lawton LJ ([1975] 1 WLR 1411 at 1416):

> The issue of the cause of death in a trial for either murder or manslaughter is one of fact for the jury to decide. But if, as in this case, there is no conflict of evidence and all the jury has to do is apply the law to the admitted facts, the judge is entitled to tell the jury what the result of that application will be. In this case the judge would have been entitled to have told the jury that the appellant's stab wound was an operative cause of death. The appeal fails.

There is no evidence in the present case here that at the time of conventional death, after the life support machinery was disconnected, the original wound or injury was other than a continuing, operating and indeed substantial cause of the death of the victim, although it need hardly be added that it need not be substantial to render the assailant guilty. There may be occasions, although they will be rare, when the original injury has ceased to operate as a cause at all, but in the ordinary case if the treatment is given *bona fide* by competent and careful medical practitioners, then evidence will not be admissible to show that the treatment would not have been administered in the same way by other medical practitioners. In other words, the fact that the victim has died, despite or because of medical treatment for the initial injury given by careful and skilled medical practitioners, will not exonerate the original assailant from responsibility for the death. It follows that so far as the ground of appeal in each of these cases relates to the direction given on causation, that ground fails. It also follows that the evidence which it is sought to adduce now, although we are prepared to assume that it is both credible and was not available properly at the trial (and a reasonable explanation for not calling it at the trial has been given), if received could, under no circumstances, afford any ground for allowing the appeal.

The reason is this. Nothing which any of the two or three medical men whose statements are before us could say would alter the fact that in each case the assailant's actions continued to be an operating cause of the death. Nothing the doctors could say would provide any ground for a jury coming to the conclusion that the assailant in either case might not have caused the death. The furthest to which their proposed evidence goes, as already stated, is to suggest, first, that the criteria or the confirmatory tests are not sufficiently stringent and, second, that in the present case they were in certain respects inadequately fulfilled or carried out. It is no part of this court's function in the present circumstances to pronounce on this matter, nor was it a function of either of the juries at these trials. Where a medical practitioner adopting methods which are generally accepted comes bona fide and conscientiously to the conclusion that the patient is for practical purposes dead, and that such vital functions as exist (for example, circulation) are being maintained solely by mechanical means, and therefore discontinues treatment, that does not prevent the person who inflicted the initial injury from being responsible for the victim's death. Putting it in another way, the discontinuance of treatment in those circumstances does not break the chain of causation between the initial injury and the death.

Although it is unnecessary to go further than that for the purpose of deciding the present point, we wish to add this thought. Whatever the strict logic of the matter may be, it is perhaps somewhat bizarre to suggest, as counsel have impliedly done, that where a doctor tries his conscientious best to save the life of a patient brought to hospital *in extremis*, skilfully using sophisticated methods, drugs and machinery to do so, but fails in his attempt and therefore discontinues treatment, he can be said to have caused the death of the patient.

For these reasons we do not deem it either necessary under s 23(2) of the Criminal Appeal Act 1968 nor desirable or expedient under s 23(1) to receive the proposed evidence of the doctors which, in statement form, has been placed before us. Likewise, there is no ground for saying that the judge in either case was wrong in withdrawing the issue of causation from the jury. It follows that the appeal of Malcherek is dismissed. It now remains to consider the application in the case of Steel in so far as it relates to the matters other than causation ...

R v Cheshire [1991] 1 WLR 844 (CA)

Beldam LJ: ... At about midnight on 9/10 December 1987 the appellant was in the 'Ozone' fish and chip shop in Greenwich when he became involved in an argument with Trevor Jeffrey, the deceased. The appellant produced a handgun and fired it at the ceiling. The deceased grappled with him but the appellant fired two more shots. They were fired at the deceased at close range. One bullet entered the top of the thigh and shattered the thigh bone. The other entered the deceased's stomach. The appellant fled from the shop, and an ambulance and the police were summoned. The deceased was taken to the accident and emergency department of the Greenwich District Hospital. There, in the early hours of the morning, he underwent surgery. Both bullets had caused extensive damage. The thigh injury was cleaned, the bone joined and his leg placed in traction. There was substantial damage in the abdominal cavity, which was contaminated. A fairly extensive bowel resection and wound toilet was carried out and he was given blood transfusions. In due course he was transferred to the intensive care unit. He there developed respiratory problems and his breathing had to be maintained by a ventilator using a tube placed in the windpipe. A week later this tube was replaced by a tracheotomy tube, which remained in place for the next four weeks. His condition did not improve and after a marked deterioration on Christmas Day a further operation to explore his abdomen was carried out.

From time to time he suffered from chest infections, from vomiting and from discharges from the abdominal wound and it was not until 2 February 1988 that he began to show improvement. During his time in intensive care the deceased's lungs had become congested and filled with fluid and he suffered considerable difficulty with breathing. On 8 February he again complained of difficulty in breathing and it was at first thought that this was a recurrence of the problem with his lungs. An X-ray was taken but it showed no recurrence of lung trouble. Whilst in intensive care the deceased had on several occasions shown signs of anxiety and a tentative diagnosis was made that the intermittent problem with his breathing of which he complained after 8 February was due to attacks of anxiety. He was seen by several doctors of differing experience during the ensuing week. He was probably seen by Mr Harrison, the consultant general surgeon at Greenwich District Hospital, on one occasion. He was also seen by the surgical registrar, Mr Saunders, and the orthopaedic registrar. Later, on the evening of 14 February, he complained of further difficulty with breathing and was attended by a house surgeon, Dr Clare Jones. Dr Jones had qualified in the summer of 1987 and had been a medical houseman for six months before becoming house surgeon on 1 February. She was worried about the deceased's condition and sat with him for three-quarters of an hour recording in the notes that he was making a noise through his respiratory passages which she described as 'stridor'. The deceased's condition deteriorated and the medical registrar was called. Urgent resuscitation, including cardiac massage, was given but the deceased died shortly after midnight.

At post mortem it was found that the deceased's windpipe had become obstructed due to narrowing near the site of the tracheotomy scar. Such a condition is a rare but not unknown complication of intubation of the windpipe. The deceased's windpipe had become so narrowed that even a small amount of mucus could block it and cause asphyxiation.

The experienced pathologist who conducted the post mortem gave evidence that the immediate cause of death was cardio-respiratory arrest:

> due to a condition which was produced as a result of treatment to provide an artificial airway in the treatment of gunshot wounds of the abdomen and leg.

And he said:

> in other words, I give as the cause of death cardio-respiratory arrest due to gunshot wounds of the abdomen and leg.

For the appellant it was conceded that the sequence of events which had led to the deceased's death was that described by the pathologist but a consultant surgeon, Mr Eadie, gave it as his opinion that by 8 February 1988 the wounds of the thigh and the abdomen no longer threatened the life of the deceased and his chances of survival were good. In his view:

> The cause of his death was the failure to recognise the reason for his sudden onset and continued breathlessness after the 18 February [and the] severe respiratory obstruction, including the presence of stridor [on 14 February] ...

The doctors who examined and treated the deceased in the week before his death ought to have diagnosed the serious clinical condition from which he was suffering. Mr Eadie was particularly critical of the failure to appreciate the serious implications of 'stridor' on the evening of 14 February. The deceased would not have died if his condition had been diagnosed and properly treated. The doctors had been negligent and this was the cause of his death ...

One question for the jury at trial therefore was whether the Crown had proved, so that they were sure, that the shots fired by the appellant had caused the deceased's death ...

A case in which the facts bear a close similarity to the case with which we are concerned is *R v Evans and Gardiner (No 2)* [1976] VR 523. In that case the deceased was stabbed in the stomach by the two applicants in April 1974. After operation the victim resumed an apparently healthy life but nearly a year later, after suffering abdominal pain and vomiting and undergoing further medical treatment, he died. The cause of death was a stricture of the small bowel, a not uncommon sequel to the operation carried out to deal with the stab wound inflicted by the applicants. It was contended that the doctors treating the victim for the later symptoms ought to have diagnosed the presence of the stricture, that they had been negligent not to do so and that timely operative treatment would have saved the victim's life.

The Supreme Court of Victoria held that the test to be applied in determining whether a felonious act has caused a death which follows, in spite of an intervening act, is whether the felonious act is still an operating and substantial cause of the death.

The summing up to the jury had been based on the passage already quoted from Lord Parker CJ's judgment in *R v Smith* and the Supreme Court indorsed a direction in those terms. It commented upon the limitations of *R v Jordan* and made observations of the difference between the failure to diagnose the consequence of the original injury and cases in which medical treatment has been given which has a positive adverse effect on the victim. It concluded (at 528):

> But in the long run the difference between a positive act of commission and an omission to do some particular act is for these purposes ultimately a question of degree. As an event intervening between an act alleged to be felonious and to have resulted in death, and the actual death, a positive act of commission or an act of omission will serve to break the chain of causation only if it can be shown that the act or omission accelerated the death, so that it can be said to have caused the death and thus to have prevented the felonious act which would have caused death from actually doing so.

Later in the judgment the court said (at 534):

> In these circumstances we agree with the view of the learned trial judge expressed in his report to this court that there was a case to go to the jury. The failure of the medical practitioners to diagnose correctly the victim's condition, however, inept or unskilful, was not the cause of death. It was the blockage of the bowel which caused death and the real question for the jury was whether that blockage was due to the stabbing. There was plenty of medical evidence to support such a finding, if the jury chose to accept it.

It seems to us that these two passages demonstrate the difficulties in formulating and explaining a general concept of causation but what we think does emerge from this and the other cases is that when the victim of a criminal attack is treated for wounds or injuries by doctors or other medical staff attempting to repair the harm done, it will only be in the most extraordinary and unusual case that such treatment can be said to be so independent of the acts of the accused that it could be regarded in law as the cause of the victim's death to the exclusion of the accused's acts.

Where the law requires proof of the relationship between an act and its consequences as an element of responsibility, a simple and sufficient explanation of the basis of such relationship has proved notoriously elusive.

In a case in which the jury have to consider whether negligence in the treatment of injuries inflicted by the accused was the cause of death we think it is sufficient for the judge to tell the jury that they must be satisfied that the Crown have proved that the acts of the accused caused the death of the deceased, adding that the accused's act need not be the sole cause or even the main cause of death, it being sufficient that his acts contributed significantly to that result. Even though negligence in the treatment of the victim was the immediate cause of his death, the jury should not regard it as excluding the responsibility of the accused unless the negligent treatment was so independent of his acts, and in itself so potent in causing death, that they regard the contribution made by his acts as insignificant.

It is not the function of the jury to evaluate competing causes or to choose which is dominant provided they are satisfied that the accused's acts can fairly be said to have made a significant contribution to the victim's death. We think the word 'significant' conveys the necessary substance of a contribution made to the death which is more than negligible ...

R v Mellor [1996] 2 Cr App R 245 (CA)

Schiemann LJ: ... The deceased was 71 years old and was attacked by some hooligans at 11.15 pm on 15 January 1994. He was taken to hospital suffering from bruising to the eyes, a damaged nose, and complaining of chest pain and a pain in his right shoulder. He died in hospital two days later. The defence of Mr Mellor who gave evidence was twofold:

1 He was not the man who attacked Mr Sims.

2 The substantial cause of Mr Sims's death was not the beating which he had received from the hooligan who attacked him but rather the actions and inactions of the hospital ...

The immediate cause of death was broncho-pneumonia which, upon the evidence, was brought on directly by the injuries inflicted by the appellant. Those injuries were certainly the cause of death. Probably if the appellant had been administered sufficient oxygen in time, the broncho-pneumonia would not have been fatal, and therefore the failure to administer sufficient oxygen could be regarded as a cause of death. It was asserted on behalf of the appellant, and supported by expert evidence, that the failure to administer sufficient oxygen in time amounted to negligence or incompetence in the care of Mr Sims in hospital.

The question for the trial judge was how he should frame his direction to the jury in these circumstances. The question was debated with counsel before leading counsels' final speeches and the case of *Cheshire* [1992] 1 WLR 844, was considered.

In homicide cases, where the victim of the alleged crime does not die immediately, supervening events will occur which are likely to have some causative effect leading to the victim's death; for example, a delay in the arrival of the ambulance, a delay in resuscitation, the victim's individual response to medical or surgical treatment, and the quality of medical, surgical and nursing care. Sometimes such an event may be the result of negligence or mistake or bad luck. It is a question of fact and degree in each case for the jury to decide, having regard to the gravity of the supervening event, however caused, whether the injuries inflicted by the defendant were a significant cause of death.

The onus on the Crown is to make the jury sure that the injuries inflicted by the defendant were a significant cause of death. However, the Crown has no onus of establishing that any supervening event was not a significant cause of death or that there was no medical negligence in the deceased's treatment.

If the issue of medical negligence is raised, the jury must have regard to the evidence adduced on the issue. If they conclude that there was or may have been medical negligence, they must have regard to that conclusion when answering the all-important question: 'Has the Crown proved that the injuries inflicted by the defendant were *a* significant cause of death?' In appropriate cases the jury can be told that there may be a number of significant causes leading to a victim's death. So as long as the Crown proves that the injuries inflicted by the defendant were at least a significant, if not the only, cause of death that will be sufficient to prove the nexus between injury and death ...

In *Cheshire* Beldam LJ said [1992] 1 WLR 884 at p 847:

> In the criminal law, and in particular in the law of homicide, whether the death of a deceased was the result of the accused's criminal act is a question of fact for the jury, but it is a question of fact to be decided in accordance with legal principles explained to the jury by the judge. We think the matter cannot be better put than it was by Goff LJ, as he then was, in the case of *Pagett* (1983) 76 Cr App R 279, 288.

With that opinion this court respectfully entirely agrees. Goff LJ said at p 288:

> ... where it is necessary to direct the jury's mind to the question of causation, it is usually enough to direct them simply that in law the accused's act need not be the sole cause, or even the main cause, of the victim's death, it being enough that his act contributed significantly to that result. It is right to observe in passing, however, that even this simple direction of law relating to causation, on the basis of which the jury are bound to act in concluding whether the prosecution has established, as a matter of fact, that the accused's act did in this sense cause the victim's death.

In *Cheshire* the facts were that the appellant had fired two shots at a man who died about two months later in hospital. The cause of death was given as 'cardio-respiratory arrest due to gunshot wounds of the abdomen and leg'; but the appellant, who was charged with murder, called expert evidence at his trial to the effect that the victim had suffered a rare but not unknown complication due to the treatment he had received and that medical negligence had caused his death.

In the latter part of the judgment Beldam LJ considered the impact of medical negligence on causation of death. He said at p 851:

> In a case in which the jury have to consider whether negligence in the treatment of injuries inflicted by the accused was the cause of death we think it is sufficient for the judge to tell the jury that they must be satisfied that the Crown have proved that the acts of the accused caused the death of the deceased adding that the accused's acts need not be the sole cause or even the main cause of death, it being sufficient that his acts contributed significantly to that result. Even though negligence in the treatment of the victim was the immediate cause of his death, the jury should not regard it as excluding the responsibility of the accused unless the negligent treatment was so independent of his acts, and in itself so potent in causing death, that they regard the contribution made by his acts as insignificant.
>
> It is not the function of the jury to evaluate competing causes or to choose which is dominant provided they are satisfied that the accused's act can fairly be said to have made a significant contribution to the victim's death. We think the word 'significant' conveys the necessary substance of a contribution made to the death which is more than negligible.

In our judgment, Beldam LJ was not intending to put any gloss on Goff LJ's suggested direction in *Pagett*, which was not a medical negligence case, but relating it to a medical negligence case. He made it clear at the end of the passage which we have cited that the question for the jury was whether they were satisfied that the accused's acts significantly contributed to the victim's death. That was the question for the jury in the present case.

What the Crown had to prove in the present case were the injuries inflicted by the appellant significantly contributed to Mr Sims's death. There was no onus whatever on the Crown to negative medical negligence. Equally, there was no onus on the appellant to establish medical negligence. However, if negligence was established it was a factor to be taken into account by the jury in deciding whether the Crown had established that, notwithstanding this negligence, the injures inflicted by the appellant had significantly contributed to Mr Sims's death. In the event of a jury being sure that medical negligence has been negatived by the Crown as a significant contributory cause of death, the medical negligence factor would be out of the equation.

In our judgment, it is undesirable in most cases for juries to be asked to embark upon the question of whether medical negligence as a significant contributory cause of death has been negatived because it diverts the jury from the relevant question, namely has the accused's act contributed significantly to the victim's death?...

An appropriate, but we do not suggest the only appropriate, form of words on the particular facts of this case would have been:

> You must acquit the defendant of murder unless the Crown has made you sure that the injuries that he inflicted contributed significantly to Mr Sims's death. Provided you are sure of that, it matters not whether incompetence or mistake in treatment at the hospital may have also contributed significantly to the death.

In our judgment, if the medical/causation issue had been put in this way there could only have been one answer. The evidence was overwhelming that having regard to the extent and nature of the injuries inflicted upon the 71-year-old Mr Sims those injuries significantly contributed to his death less than two days later ...

Act of God

This is an event which is entirely unforeseen and entirely unconnected with the accused's act. If it would have been sufficient on its own to bring about the consequence in question, it breaks the chain of causation.

Southern Water Authority v Pegrum and Pegrum [1989] Crim LR 442 (DC)

Facts: The respondents were charged with an offence contrary to s 31(1) of the Control of Pollution Act 1974, causing polluting matter (pig effluent) to enter a stream. The respondents reared pigs; effluent produced by the pigs was held initially in tanks and then transferred by gravity into a lagoon constructed for the purpose. The lagoon itself was emptied of liquid content for use as manure several times a year and of sediment annually. In the winter of 1987, after heavy rain, a blocked drain resulted in rain water flowing into the lagoon. A fissure developed at the top of one side of the lagoon and polluting liquid escaped, finding its way into a stream and eventually into a river. The magistrates found that the overflow from the lagoon was caused by an act of God – the ingress of rainwater - and that it was unnecessary to consider whether the respondents were negligent either in not inspecting the drain or discovering the overflow promptly enough or in not providing an adequate drain. They further found that the blocked drain causing the ingress of rainwater was an intervening event 'breaking the chain of causation'. They dismissed the information and the prosecutor appealed by way of case stated.

Held, allowing the appeal and remitting the case with a direction to convict, the following principles applied: (1) where the defendant conducts some active operation involving the storage, use or creation of material capable of polluting a river should it escape, then if it does escape and pollute, the defendant is liable if he 'caused' that escape; (2) the question of causation is to be decided in a common sense way; (3) a defendant may be found to have caused that escape even though he did not intend that escape and even though the escape happened without his negligence; (4) it is a defence to show that the cause of the escape was the intervening act of a third party or act of God or *vis major* which are the *novus actus interveniens* defences to strict civil liability referred to in *Rylands v Fletcher* (1868) LR 3 HL 330; (5) in deciding whether the intervening cause affords a defence the test is whether it was of so powerful nature that the conduct of the defendant was not a cause at all, but was merely part of the surrounding circumstances. On the facts of the present case, the active operations or positive acts of the respondents were the storage and re-use of the effluent which resulted in the formation of the toxic sediment which polluted the stream. The magistrates erred in finding that the ingress of rainwater was an act of God; an act of God is an operation of natural forces so unpredictable as to excuse a defendant all liability for its consequences. The quantity of rain could not properly be regarded in itself as an act of God and in any event the ingress of rainwater into the lagoon was the result of the overflow from the blocked drain. Although unpredictable and unforeseeable operation of animate forces can amount to an act of God (see *Carstairs v Taylor* (1870) LR 6 Exch 217), there was no factual basis for such finding in the present case. The respondents submitted that the blocked drain was an effective intervening cause relegating the respondent's effluent operation to a mere surrounding circumstance; it was sought to distinguish *Alphacell Ltd v Woodward* [1972] AC 824 on the basis that in that case the blockage and breakdown was within the system of the 'active operations' which led to the creation and storage of the pollutant, while in the present case the drainage system was nothing to do with the system for storing and using the effluent. That factual difference made no difference in law. The submission must fail on a proper understanding of the strict liability established by s 31. It would defeat the object of the legislation if a landowner who chooses to keep on his land matter capable of polluting should it escape is liable for the non-negligent breakdown of the system for dealing with the matter but is not liable for the non-negligent breakdown of another system (in the present case drainage) within his control and utilised for his purpose.

Act of the victim

There are some instances where the victim's own actions can be said to break the chain of causation. According to *R v Williams* [1992] 1 WLR 380, the victim's actions will only break the chain of causation if they are not within the range of reasonable responses which might be anticipated from a victim in the situation in which the present victim found himself (although the decision in *R v Dalby* [1982] 1 WLR 425 – see Chapter 21 – is inconsistent with this principle).

R v Roberts (1971) 56 Cr App R 95 (CA)

See Chapter 22.

R v Williams and Another [1992] 1 WLR 380 (CA)

Stuart-Smith LJ: ... The facts were these. On 15 June 1989 the deceased, John Shephard, was hitch-hiking to a free festival at Glastonbury. He was picked up in a car driven by Williams; Davis and the co-accused Bobat were passengers. After some five miles, while the car was travelling at bout 30 mph, the deceased jumped from the car, and died from head injuries caused by falling onto the road.

The key issue in the case was whether anything had happened in the car, and, if so, what, to cause him to jump.

The prosecution case was that this was a planned robbery of the hitch-hiker, conceived before the deceased got into the car and involving all three occupants, and that the deceased met his death trying to escape.

The deceased, John Shephard, was 28. He smoked cannabis quite often. At the post mortem cannabinoids were found in his blood, consistent with his having smoked one or two joints. The psychiatric evidence was that the cannabis would not have caused him to act in an irrational manner.

A Mr Brickell was driving behind the car (a Toyota) in which the deceased had been given a lift. He noticed that the car was drifting across the road and narrowly missed an oncoming lorry but he saw nothing untoward going on inside the car. Suddenly the rear nearside door opened, someone looked out and then jumped from the car into the path of Mr Brickell's car. At the same time an object went up in the air, almost certainly the deceased's wallet. The door closed and the car sped away ...

Davis's appeal

In the forefront of Mr Perry's submission on behalf of Davis is the contention that the judge misdirected the jury on the law relating to manslaughter where death follows a threat of violence in that he failed to give them any guidance on the question of causation.

... [I]n some cases, and in our judgment this is one of them, it is necessary to give the jury a direction on causation, and explain the test by which the voluntary act of the deceased may be said to be caused by the accused's act and not a *novus actus interveniens*, breaking the chain of causation between the threat of violence and the death. There must be some proportionality between the gravity of the threat and the action of the deceased in seeking to escape from it ...

The necessary causal link can be traced through the old cases and also the judgments of Stephenson LJ in *R v Roberts* (1971) 56 Cr App R 95 and *R v Mackie* (1973) 57 Cr App R 453 ...

In *R v Roberts* (1971) 56 Cr App R 95 the complainant had jumped from a moving car because she said the appellant had assaulted and threatened her. The appellant was convicted of assault occasioning actual bodily harm. The issue was one of causation. In giving the judgment of the court Stephenson LJ said (at 102):

> The test is: Was it the natural result of what the alleged assailant said and did, in the sense that it was something that could reasonably have been foreseen as the consequence of what he was saying or doing? As it was put in one of the old cases, it had got to be shown to be his act, and if of course the victim does something so 'daft', in the words of the appellant in this case, or so unexpected, not that this particular assailant did not actually foresee it but that no reasonable man could be expected to foresee it, then it is only in a very remote and unreal sense a consequence of his assault, it is really occasioned by a voluntary act on the part of the victim which could not

> reasonably be foreseen and which breaks the chain of causation between the assault and the harm or injury.

In *R v Mackie* 57 Cr App R 453 the Crown's case was that the victim, a child of three, was fleeing from fear of his father's violence and fell downstairs and was killed. Stephenson LJ, after citing the case to which we have just referred, said (at 459):

> Where the injuries are not fatal, the attempt to escape must be the natural consequence of the assault charged, not something which could not be expected, but something which any reasonable and responsible man in the assailant's shoes would have foreseen. Where the injuries are fatal, the attempt must be the natural consequence of an unlawful act and that unlawful act 'must be such as all sober and reasonable people would inevitably recognise must subject the other person to, at least, the risk of some harm resulting therefrom, albeit not serious harm' ...

It is plain that in fatal cases there are two requirements. The first, as in non-fatal cases, relates to the deceased's conduct, which would be something that a reasonable and responsible man in the assailant's shoes would have foreseen. The second, which applies only in fatal cases, relates to the quality of the unlawful act, which must be such that all sober and reasonable people would inevitably recognise must subject the other person to some harm resulting therefrom albeit not serious harm. It should be noted that the headnote is inaccurate and tends to confuse these two limbs.

The harm must be physical harm. Where the unlawful act is a battery, there is no difficulty with the second ingredient. Where however the unlawful act is merely a threat unaccompanied and not preceded by any actual violence, the position may be more difficult. In the case of a life-threatening assault, such as pointing a gun or knife at the victim, all sober and reasonable people may well anticipate some physical injury through shock to the victim, as for example in *R v Dawson* (1985) 81 Cr App R 150, where the victim died of a heart attack following a robbery in which two of the appellants had been masked, armed with a replica gun and pickaxe handles. But the nature of the threat is of importance in considering both the foreseeability of harm to the victim from the threat and the question whether the deceased's conduct was proportionate to the threat, that is to say that it was within the ambit of reasonableness and not so daft as to make it his one voluntary act which amounted to a *novus actus interveniens* and consequently broke the chain of causation. It should of course be borne in mind that a victim may in the agony of the moment do the wrong thing.

In this case there was an almost total lack of evidence as to the nature of the threat. The prosecution invited the jury to infer the gravity of the threat from the action of the deceased. The judge put it this way:

> ... what he was frightened of was robbery, that this was going to be taken from him by force, and the measure of the force can be taken from his reaction to it. The prosecution suggest that if he is prepared to get out of a moving car, then it was a very serious threat involving him in the risk of, as he saw it, serious injury.

In our judgment that was a wholly impermissible argument and was simply a case of the prosecution pulling itself up by its own bootstraps.

Moreover in a case of robbery the threat of force is made to persuade the victim to hand over money: if the money is handed over actual violence may not eventuate. The jury should consider two questions: first, whether it was reasonably foreseeable that some harm, albeit not serious harm, was likely to result from the threat itself; and, second, whether the deceased's reaction in jumping from the moving car was within the range of responses which might be expected from a victim placed in the situation which he was. The jury should bear in mind any particular characteristic of the victim and the fact that in the agony of the moment he may act without thought and deliberation ...

R v Corbett [1996] Crim LR 594 (CA)

Facts: The appellant was convicted of manslaughter. The victim was a mentally handicapped man of 26 who suffered from time to time with mental illness and had problems with high alcohol consumption. The appellant and the victim had been drinking all day. At about 9.30 pm the appellant had an argument with the victim and started to hit and head-butt him. The victim ran away and fell into the gutter where he was struck by a passing car and killed. In the course of his summing up the judge gave a direction on manslaughter and told the jury that they had to consider whether what the victim had done was within the foreseeable range. The judge referred to the fact that the victim had been immensely drunk and asked the jury to decide whether what the victim had done was something that might be expected as a reaction of somebody in that state. On appeal counsel for the appellant contended that the judge should have told the jury that the Crown had to prove the death occurred as *the* natural consequence of what the defendant had done and that if there had been scope for any other consequence the Crown would not have discharged the burden of proof on them.

Held, dismissing the appeal, the judgment in *Roberts* (1971) 56 Cr App R 95 at 102 undermined the submission made by counsel for the appellant because it clearly envisaged a foreseeable range of consequences and held that it would only be a daft reaction on the part of a victim which would be beyond that range and which would thus break the chain of causation. Here the judge had emphasised to the jury that the victim's reaction had to be in the foreseeable range.

R v Dear [1996] Crim LR 595 (CA)

Facts: The appellant appealed against his conviction of murder. The prosecution case was that, following allegations by the appellant's 12-year-old daughter that the deceased had sexually interfered with her, the appellant had slashed the deceased repeatedly with a Stanley knife, and that he had died two days later as a result of the wounds inflicted. The appellant's case was that he had been provoked, but that in any event the chain of causation had been broken between his actions and the death because the deceased had committed suicide either by reopening his wounds or, the wounds having reopened themselves, by failing to take steps to staunch the consequent blood flow. It was argued on the appeal that the suicide of the deceased would have been a *novus actus interveniens* and that the judge had misdirected the jury on the issue of causation.

Held, dismissing the appeal, that the real question in the case was, as the judge had correctly directed the jury, whether the injuries inflicted by the appellant were an operating and significant cause of the death. That had been enunciated as the correct approach in *Smith* [1959] 2 QB 35; *Blaue* [1975] 1 WLR 1411; *Malcherek* [1981] 1 WLR 690; *Cheshire* (1991) 93 Cr App R 251, and Smith and Hogan, *Criminal Law*, 7th edn. It would not be helpful to juries if the law required them to decide causation in a case such as the present by embarking on an analysis of whether a victim had treated himself with mere negligence or gross neglect, the latter breaking but former not breaking the chain of causation between the defendant's wrongful act and the victim's death. It would be a retrograde step if the niceties of apportionment of fault and causation in the civil law, and the roles which the concepts of *novus actus interveniens* and foreseeability did or should play in causation, were to invade the criminal law. In the present case the cause of the deceased's death was bleeding from the artery which the defendant had severed. Whether or not the resumption or continuation of that bleeding was deliberately caused by the deceased, the jury were entitled to find that the appellant's conduct made an operative and significant contribution to the death.

THE 'EGGSHELL SKULL' RULE

The rule in criminal law is the same as that in tort: the accused takes his victim as he finds him.

R v Blaue [1975] 1 WLR 1411 (CA)

Lawton LJ: ... The victim was a young girl aged 18. She was a Jehovah's Witness. She professed the tenets of that sect and lived her life by them. During the late afternoon of 3 May 1974 the appellant came into her house and asked her for sexual intercourse. She refused. He then attacked her with a knife inflicting four serious wounds. One pierced her lung. The appellant ran away. The girl staggered out into the road. She collapsed outside a neighbour's house. An ambulance took her to hospital, where she arrived at about 7.30 pm. Soon afterwards she was admitted to the intensive care ward. At about 8.30 pm she was examined by the surgical registrar who quickly decided that serious injury had been caused which would require surgery. As she had lost a lot of blood, before there could be an operation there would have to be a blood transfusion. As soon as the girl appreciated that the surgeon was thinking of organising a blood transfusion for her, she said that she should not be given one and that she would not have one. To have one, she said, would be contrary to her religious beliefs as a Jehovah's Witness. She was told that if she did not have a blood transfusion she would die. She said that she did not care if she did die. She was asked to acknowledge in writing that she had refused to have a blood transfusion under any circumstances. She did so. The Crown admitted at the trial that had she had a blood transfusion when advised to have one she would not have died. She did so at 12.45 am the next day. The evidence called by the Crown proved that at all relevant times she was conscious and decided as she did deliberately, and knowing what the consequences of her decision would be. In his final speech to the jury, counsel for the Crown accepted that the girl's refusal to have a blood transfusion was a cause of her death. The prosecution did not challenge the defence evidence that the appellant was suffering from diminished responsibility.

Towards the end of the trial and before the summing up started counsel on both sides made submissions as to how the case should be put to the jury. Counsel then appearing for the appellant invited the judge to direct the jury to acquit the appellant generally on the count of murder. His argument was that the girl's refusal to have a blood transfusion had broken the chain of causation between the stabbing and her death. As an alternative he submitted that the jury should be left to decide whether the chain of causation had been broken. Counsel for the Crown submitted that the judge should direct the jury to convict, because no facts were in issue and when the law was applied to the facts there was only one possible verdict, ie manslaughter by reason of diminished responsibility ...

There have been two cases in recent years which have some bearing on this topic: *R v Jordan* (1956) 40 Cr App R 152 and *R v Smith* [1959] 2 QB 35 ... We share Lord Parker CJ's opinion in *Smith* that *Jordan* should be regarded as a case decided on its own special facts and not as an authority relaxing the common law approach to causation ...

The physical cause of death in this case was bleeding into the pleural cavity arising from the penetration of the lung. This had not been brought about by any decision made by the deceased girl but by the stab wound.

Counsel for the appellant tried to overcome this line of reasoning by submitting that the jury should have been directed that if they thought the girl's decision not to have a blood transfusion was an unreasonable one, then the chain of causation would have been broken. At once the question arises – reasonable by whose standards? Those of Jehovah's Witnesses? Humanists? Roman Catholics? Protestants of Anglo-Saxon descent? The man on the Clapham omnibus? But he might well be an admirer of Eleazar who suffered death rather than eat the flesh of swine (see 2 *Maccabees*, Chapter 6 vv 18-31) or of Sir Thomas Moore who, unlike nearly all his contemporaries, was unwilling to accept Henry VIII as Head of the Church of England. Those brought up in the Hebraic and Christian traditions would probably be reluctant to accept that these martyrs caused their own deaths.

As was pointed out to counsel for the appellant in the course of argument, two cases, each raising the same issue of reasonableness because of religious beliefs, could produce different verdicts depending on where the cases were tried. A jury drawn from Preston, sometimes said to the most Catholic town in England, might have different views about martyrdom to one drawn from the inner suburbs of London ... It has been the policy of the law that those who use violence on other people must take their victims as they find them. This in our judgment means the whole man, not just the physical man. It does not lie in the mouth of the assailant to say that his victim's religious beliefs which inhibited her from accepting certain kinds of treatment were unreasonable. The question for decision is what caused her death. The answer is the stab wound. The fact that the victim refused to stop this end coming about did not break the causal connection between the act and death.

If a victim's personal representatives claim compensation for his death the concept of foreseeability can operate in favour of the wrongdoer in the assessment of such compensation; the wrongdoer is entitled to expect his victim to mitigate his damage by accepting treatment of a normal kind: see *Steele v George & Co Ltd* [1942] AC 497. As counsel for the Crown pointed out, the criminal law is concerned with the maintenance of law and order and the protection of the public generally. A policy of the common law is applicable to the settlement or tortious liability between subjects may not be, and in our judgment is not, appropriate for the criminal law.

The issue of the cause of death in a trial for either murder or manslaughter is one of fact for the jury to decide. But if, as in this case, there is no conflict of evidence and all the jury has to do is to apply the law to the admitted facts, the judge is entitled to tell the jury what the result of that application will be. In this case the judge would have been entitled to have told the jury that the appellant's stab wound was an operative cause of the death. The appeal fails.

CHAPTER 5

GENERAL DEFENCES

INTRODUCTION

Where an accused puts forward a defence, he bears what is known as an 'evidential' burden of proof in relation to it. This does *not* mean that he has to prove his defence to the satisfaction of the jury. All it means is that the accused has to adduce sufficient evidence of the defence for the judge or magistrates to decide that it is worthy of consideration. Thus, the 'legal' burden of proof is borne by the prosecution: it is for the prosecution to prove beyond reasonable doubt that the defence is negated. These rules apply whether the case is being tried in a magistrates' court or in the Crown Court.

In practice, the evidential burden is not an onerous one for the accused to discharge. If, for example, the defence is one of self-defence, the accused may:

(1) give evidence himself that he was acting in self-defence; and/or

(2) call witnesses to testify that he was acting in self-defence; and/or

(3) cross-examine prosecution witnesses on the basis that he was acting in self-defence.

All that is required is that the judge or magistrates take the view that there is sufficient basis for holding that self-defence is a 'live' issue. As long as this is so, it is for the prosecution to disprove self-defence beyond reasonable doubt. Unless the jury or magistrates are satisfied so that they are sure that the accused was not acting in self-defence, they must acquit the accused. The one exception as regards the burden of proof is in the context of the defence of insanity, as to which see Chapter 6.

We now turn to consider the various defences which can be raised, starting with mistake.

MISTAKE

The defence of mistake is a denial that the accused had the appropriate *mens rea*. The nature of this defence therefore depends on the *mens rea* required for the particular offence which the accused is alleged to have committed.

If an offence requires what may be called 'subjective fault' (eg crimes requiring intention or malice), a person is not guilty of that offence if he mistakenly believed that the facts were such that he would not be committing an offence. For example, someone who shoots a person, believing that person to be an inanimate object, cannot be guilty of murder. In such a case, there is no requirement that the mistake is one which a reasonable person could have made (although the more unreasonable the mistake, the less likely it is that a jury or bench of magistrates will believe that the accused was indeed mistaken). See *W (A Minor) v Dolbey* (1983) 88 Cr App R 1 and *DPP v Morgan* [1976] AC 182.

On the other hand, if an offence can be committed with what may be called 'objective recklessness' (ie failure to appreciate an obvious risk – see *Caldwell*

[1982] AC 341, dealt with in Chapter 2) a mistake can only amount to a defence if a reasonable person could have made the same mistake as the accused. See *R v S* (1983) 78 Cr App R 149 (rape); *R v Kimber* [1983] 1 WLR 1118 (indecent assault); *Chief Constable of Avon* and *Somerset v Shimmen* (1986) 84 Cr App R 7 and *R v Merrick* [1995] Crim LR 802 (criminal damage).

A mistake of law will only amount to a defence if it is a mistake as to civil law, not criminal law. For example, it is a defence to say 'I thought that I was – as a matter of civil law – the legal owner of the property I damaged' (as in *R v Smith* [1974] QB 354) but it is not a defence to say 'I thought that a wild creature could not be "property" for the purposes of theft' [*cp* s 4(4) of the Theft Act 1968]. See also *Secretary of State for Trade and Industry v Hart* [1982] 1 WLR 481.

R v Tolson (1889) 23 QBD 168 (CCR)

Wills J: In this case the prisoner was convicted of bigamy. She married a second time within seven years of the time when she last knew of her husband being alive, but upon information of his death, which the jury found that she upon reasonable grounds believed to be true. A few months after the second marriage he reappeared.

The statute upon which the indictment was framed is the 24 and 25 Vict c 100, s 57, which is in these words: 'Whoever, being married, shall marry any other person during the life of the former husband or wife shall be guilty of felony, punishable with penal servitude for not more than seven years, or imprisonment with or without hard labour for not more than two years', with a proviso that 'nothing in this Act shall extend to any person marrying a second time whose husband or wife shall have been continually absent from such person for the space of seven years last past, and shall not have been known by such person to be living within that time'.

There is no doubt that under the circumstances the prisoner falls within the very words of the statute. She, being married, married another person during the life of her former husband, and, when she did so, he had not been continually absent from her for the space of seven years last past.

It is, however, undoubtedly a principle of English criminal law, that ordinarily speaking a crime is not committed if the mind of the person doing the act in question be innocent. 'It is a principle of natural justice and of our law', says Lord Kenyon CJ, 'that *actus non facit reum, nisi mens sit rea*. The intent and act must both concur to constitute the crime': *Fowler v Padget* 7 TR 509, 514. The guilty intent is not necessarily that of intending the very act or thing done and prohibited by common or statute law, but it must at least be the intention to do something wrong. That intention may belong to one or other of two classes. It may be to do a thing wrong in itself and apart from positive law, or it may be to do a thing merely prohibited by statute or by common law, or both elements of intention may co-exist with respect to the same deed. There are many things prohibited by no statute - fornication or seduction, for instance - which nevertheless no one would hesitate to call wrong; and the intention to do an act wrong in this sense at the least must as a general rule exist before the act done can be considered a crime. Knowingly and intentionally to break a statute must, I think, from the judicial point of view, always be morally wrong in the absence of special circumstances applicable to the particular instance and excusing the breach of the law, as, for instance, if a municipal regulation be broken to save life or to put out a fire. But to make it morally right some special matter of excuse must exist, inasmuch as the administration of justice and, indeed, the foundations of civil society rest upon the principle that obedience to the law, whether it be a law approved of or disapproved of by the individual, is the first duty of a citizen ...

Now in the present instance one consequence of holding that the offence is complete if the husband or wife is *de facto* alive at the time of the second marriage, although the defendant had at the time of the second marriage every reason to believe the contrary, would be that though the evidence of death should be sufficient to induce the Court of Probate to grant probate of the will or administration of the goods of the man supposed to be dead, or to prevail with the jury upon an action by the heir to recover possession of his real property, the wife of the person supposed to be dead who had married six years and eleven months after the last time that she had known him to be alive would be guilty of felony in case he should turn up 20 years afterwards. It would be scarcely less unreasonable to enact that those who had in the meantime distributed his personal estate should be guilty of larceny. It seems to me to be a case to which it would not be improper to apply the language of Lord Kenyon when dealing with a statute which literally interpreted led to what he considered an equally preposterous result, 'I would adopt any construction of the statute that the words will bear in order to avoid such monstrous consequences'. *Fowler v Padget* 7 TR 509 at 514.

Again, the nature and extent of the penalty attached to the offence may reasonably be considered. There is nothing that need shock any mind in the payment of a small pecuniary penalty by a person who has unwittingly done something detrimental to the public interest. To subject him, when what he has done has been nothing but what any well-disposed man would have been very likely to do under the circumstances, to the forfeiture of all his goods and chattels, which would have been one consequence of a conviction at the date of the Act of 24 and 25 Vict, to the loss of civil rights, to imprisonment with hard labour, or even to penal servitude, is a very different matter; and such a fate seems properly reserved for those who have transgressed morally as well as unintentionally done something prohibited by law. I am well aware that the mischiefs which may result from bigamous marriages, however innocently contracted, are great: but I cannot think that the appropriate way of preventing them is to expose to the danger of a cruel injustice persons whose only error may be that of acting upon the same evidence as has appeared perfectly satisfactory to a Court of Probate, a tribunal emphatically difficult to satisfy in such matters, and certain only to act upon what appears to be the most cogent evidence of death. It is, as it seems to me, undesirable in the highest degree without necessity to multiply instances in which people shall be liable to conviction upon very grave charges when the circumstances are such that no judge in the kingdom would think of pronouncing more than a nominal sentence.

It is said, however, in respect of the offence now under discussion, that the proviso in 24 and 25 Vict c 100, s 57, that 'nothing in the section shall extend to any person marrying a second time whose husband or wife shall have been continually absent from such person for seven years last past, and shall not have been known by such person to be living within that time', points out the sole excuse of which the Act allows. I cannot see what necessity there is for drawing any such inference. It seems to me that it merely specifies one particular case, and indicates what in that case shall be sufficient to exempt the party without any further inquiry from criminal liability ...

Stephen J: ... My view of the subject is based upon a particular application of the doctrine usually, though I think not happily, described by the phrase *non est reus, nisi mens sit rea*. Though this phrase is in common use, I think it most unfortunate, and not only likely to mislead, but actually misleading, on the following grounds. It naturally suggests that, apart from all particular definitions of crimes, such a thing exists as a *mens rea*, or 'guilty mind', which is always expressly or by implication involved in every definition. This is obviously not the case, for the mental elements of different crimes differ widely. *Mens rea* means in the case of murder, malice aforethought; in the case of theft, an intention to steal; in the case of rape, an intention to have forcible connection with a woman without her consent; and in the case of receiving stolen goods, knowledge that the goods were stolen. In some case it denotes mere inattention. For instance, in the case of manslaughter by negligence it may mean forgetting to notice a signal. It appears confusing to call so many dissimilar states of mind by one name. It seems contradictory indeed to describe a mere absence of mind as a *mens rea*, or guilty mind. The expression again is likely to and often does mislead. To an unlegal mind it suggests that by the law of England no act is a crime which is done from laudable motives, in other words, that immorality is essential to crime ...

The principle involved appears to me, when fully considered, to amount to no more than this. The full definition of every crime contains expressly or by implication a proposition as to a state of mind. Therefore, if the mental element of any conduct alleged to be a crime is proved to have been absent in any given case, the crime so defined is not committed; or, again, if a crime is fully defined, nothing amounts to that crime which does not satisfy that definition. Crimes are in the present day much more accurately defined by statute or otherwise than they formerly were. The mental element of most crimes is marked by one of the words 'maliciously', 'fraudulently', 'negligently', or 'knowingly', but it is the general – I might, I think, say, the invariable – practice of the legislature to leave unexpressed some of the mental elements of crime. In all cases whatever, competent age, sanity, and some degree of freedom from some kinds of coercion are assumed to be essential to criminality, but I do not believe they are ever introduced into any statute by which any particular crime is defined.

The meanings of the words 'malice', 'negligence', and 'fraud' in relation to particular crimes has been ascertained by numerous cases. Malice means one thing in relation to murder, another in relation to the Malicious Mischief Act, and a third in relation to libel, and so of fraud and negligence ...

... It could not be the object of Parliament to treat the marriage of widows as an act to be if possible prevented as presumably immoral. The conduct of the women convicted was not in the smallest degree immoral, it was perfectly natural and legitimate. Assuming the facts to be as they supposed, the infliction of more than a nominal punishment on them would have been a scandal. Why, then, should the legislature be held to have wished to subject them to punishment at all?

If such a punishment is legal, the following amongst many other cases might occur. A number of men in a mine are killed, and their bodies disfigured and mutilated, by an explosion; one of the survivors secretly absconds, and it is supposed that one of the disfigured bodies is his. His wife sees his supposed remains buried; she marries again. I cannot believe that it can have been the intention of the legislature to make such a woman a criminal; the contracting of an invalid marriage is quite misfortune enough. It appears to me that every argument which showed in the opinion of the judges in *R v Prince* LR 2 CCR 154 that the legislature meant seducers and abductors to act at their peril, shows that the legislature did not mean to hamper what is not only intended, but naturally and reasonably supposed by the parties, to be a valid and honourable marriage, with a liability to seven years' penal servitude. It is argued that the proviso that a remarriage after seven years' separation shall not be punishable, operates as a tacit exclusion of all other exceptions to the penal part of the section. It appears to me that it only supplies a rule of evidence which is useful in many cases, in the absence of explicit proof of death. But it seems to me to show not that belief in the death of one married person excuses the marriage of the other only after seven years' separation, but that mere separation for that period has the effect which reasonable belief of death caused by other evidence would have at any time. It would to my mind be monstrous to say that seven years' separation should have a greater effect in excusing a bigamous marriage than positive evidence of death, sufficient for the purpose of recovering a policy of assurance or obtaining probate of a will, would have, as in the case I have put, or in others which might be even stronger ...

R v Lamb [1967] 2 QB 981 (CA)

See Chapter 21.

R v Smith (David) [1974] 1 QB 354 (CA)

See Chapter 20.

DPP v Morgan [1976] AC 182 (HL)

Lord Hailsham of St Marylebone: ... Although each appellant was originally separately represented, their appeals raise the same point, and they were accorded single representation before this House. The question certified as being of general public importance by the Court of Appeal, and the only point of principle raised on their behalf is:

> Whether, in rape, the defendant can properly be convicted notwithstanding that he in fact believed that the woman consented if such belief was not based on reasonable grounds.

The question arises in the following way. The appellant Morgan and his three co-appellants, who were all members of the RAF, spent the evening of 15 August 1973 in one another's company. The appellant Morgan was significantly older than the other three, and considerably senior to them in rank. He was, as I have said, married to the alleged victim, but not, it seems, at the time habitually sleeping in the same bed. At this time, Mrs Morgan occupied a single bed in the same room as her younger son aged about 11 years, and by the time the appellants arrived at Morgan's house, Mrs Morgan was already in bed and asleep, until she was awoken by their presence.

According to the version of the facts which she gave in evidence, and which was evidently accepted by the jury, she was aroused from her sleep, frog-marched into another room where there was a double bed, held by each of her limbs, arms and legs apart, by the four appellants, while each of the three young appellants in turn had intercourse with her in the presence of the others during which time the other two committed various lewd acts on various parts of her body. When each had finished and had left the room, the appellant Morgan completed the series of incidents by having intercourse with her himself.

According to Mrs Morgan she consented to none of this and made her opposition to what was being done very plain indeed. In her evidence to the court, she said that her husband was the first to seize her and pull her out of bed. She then 'yelled' to the little boy who was sleeping with her to call the police, and later, when the elder boy came out on the landing, she called to him also to get the police, and 'screamed'. Her assailants, however, covered her face and pinched her nose, until she begged them to let her breathe. She was held, wrists and feet, 'dragged' to the neighbouring room, put on the bed where the various incidents occurred. At this stage she was overcome by fear of 'being hit'. There was never a time when her body was free from being held. When it was all over she grabbed her coat, ran out of the house, drove straight to the hospital and immediately complained to the staff of having been raped. This last fact was fully borne out by evidence from the hospital.

In their evidence in court, the appellants made various damaging admissions which certainly amounted to some corroboration of all this. They admitted that some degree of struggle took place in the bedroom, that Mrs Morgan made some noise which was forcibly suppressed, and that she was carried out forcibly into the other bedroom, and that her arms and legs were separately held. In addition to this, Mrs Morgan's evidence was far more fully corroborated by a number of statements (each, of course, admissible only against the maker) which virtually repeated Mrs Morgan's own story but in far greater and more lurid detail. Of course, the appellants repudiated their statements in the witness box, saying that the words were put into their mouths by the police, even though at least one was written out in the hand of the maker of the statement. I think it likely to the extent of moral certainty that the jury accepted that these statements were made as alleged and contained the truth. But I need not rest my opinion on this, since the undeniable fact is that the jury accepted, after an impeccable summing up and adequate corroboration, that Mrs Morgan was telling the truth in her evidence. I mention all these details simply to show, that if, as I think plain, the jury accepted Mrs Morgan's statement *in substance* there was no possibility whatever of any of the appellants holding any belief whatever, reasonable or otherwise, in their victim's consent to what was being done.

The primary 'defence' was consent. I use the word 'defence' in inverted commas, because, of course, in establishing the crime of rape, the prosecution must exclude consent in order to establish the essential ingredients of the crime. There is no burden at the outset on the accused to raise the issue. Nevertheless, at the close of the prosecution case the appellants had a formidable case to answer, and they answered by going into the witness box and swearing to facts which, if accepted, would have meant, not merely that they reasonably believed that Mrs Morgan had consented, but that, after she entered the bedroom where the acts of intercourse took place, she not merely consented but took an active and enthusiastic part in a sexual orgy which might have excited unfavourable comment in the court of Caligula or Nero.

All four appellants explained in the witness box that they had spent the evening together in Wolverhampton, and by the time of the alleged offence had had a good deal to drink. Their original intention had been to find some women in the town but, when this failed, Morgan made the surprising suggestion to the others that they should all return to his home and have sexual intercourse with his wife. According to the three younger appellants (but not according to Morgan who described this part of their story as 'lying') Morgan told them that they must not be surprised if his wife struggled a bit, since she was 'kinky' and this was the only way in which she could get 'turned on'. However this may be, it is clear that Morgan did invite his three companions home in order that they might have sexual intercourse with his wife and, no doubt, he may well have led them in one way or another to believe that she would consent to their doing so. This, however, would only be a matter predisposing them to believe that Mrs Morgan consented, and would not in any way establish that, at the time, they believed she did consent whilst they were having intercourse.

I need not enter into the details of what the appellants said happened after they arrived at the house. As I have said they admitted that some degree of struggle took place in the wife's bedroom. But all asserted that after she got into the double bedroom she not merely consented to but actively co-operated with and enjoyed what was being done. She caressed and masturbated their private parts, she licked their private parts, she made noises and 'moans' of pleasure. When it was all over she said, 'Have you all had a go?', but not in a sarcastic sense. In other words, she was actively participating in a sexual orgy, and was anxious to see that each of the participants had enjoyed himself as much as she.

The choice before the jury was thus between two stories each wholly incompatible with the other, and in my opinion it would have been quite sufficient for the judge, after suitable warnings about the burden of proof, corroboration, separate verdicts and the admissibility of the statements only against the makers, to tell the jury that they must really choose between the two versions, the one of a violent and unmistakable rape of a singularly unpleasant kind, and the other of active co-operation in a sexual orgy, always remembering that if in reasonable doubt as to which was true they must give the appellants the benefit of it. In spite of the valiant attempts of counsel to suggest some way in which the stories could be taken apart in sections and give rise in some way to a situation which might conceivably have been acceptable to a reasonable jury in which, while the victim was found not to have consented, the appellants, or any of them could conceivably either reasonably or unreasonably have thought she did consent, I am utterly unable to see any conceivable half-way house. The very material which could have introduced doubt into matter of consent goes equally to belief and *vice versa*. As the judge's summing up, so far as relevant to this point, was wholly impeccable, and as the jury obviously accepted the victim's story in its substance there is in my view no conceivable way in which a miscarriage of justice can have taken place and therefore no possibility of quashing these convictions, even though, as I shall show, the substantial question of principle should be answered in favour of the appellants' contention.

The certified question arises because counsel for the appellants raised the question whether, even if the victim consented, the appellants may not have honestly believed that she did. As I have pointed out, the question was wholly unreal, because if there was reasonable doubt about belief, the same material must have given rise to reasonable doubt about consent, and *vice versa*. But, presumably because, at that stage, the jury's view of the matter had not been sought, the matter was left to them, as the appellants complain, in a form which implied that they could only acquit if the mistaken belief in consent was reasonable, and it was not enough that it should be honest. This ruling was originally made at the close of the case for the prosecution, but, as it was subsequently embodied in the summing up, it is sufficient to refer to this. I will quote the principal passage *in extenso* from the record.

[His Lordship then quoted from the summing up, in the course of which the trial judge directed the jury that where a defendant says that he believed that the woman was consenting to sexual intercourse, 'his belief must be a reasonable belief; such a belief as a reasonable man would entertain if he applied his mind and thought about the matter ...']

... [It was submitted on behalf of the appellants that an] honest belief in consent ... is enough. It matters not whether it be also reasonable ... [T]he appellants contend [that] ... the fact to be refuted by the prosecution is honesty and not honesty plus reasonableness ...

... If ... it is necessary for any belief in the woman's consent to be 'a reasonable belief' before the defendant is entitled to an acquittal, it must either be because the mental ingredient in rape is not 'to have intercourse and to have it without her consent' but simply 'to have intercourse' subject to a special defence of 'honest and reasonable belief', or alternatively to have intercourse without a reasonable belief in her consent ... [I]n my view each [of these alternatives] is open to insuperable objections of principle. No doubt it would be possible, by statute, to devise a law by which intercourse, voluntarily entered into, was an absolute offence, subject to a 'defence' of belief whether honest or honest and reasonable, of which the 'evidential' burden is primarily on the defence and the 'probative' burden on the prosecution. But in my opinion such is not the crime of rape as it has hitherto been understood. The prohibited act in rape is to have intercourse without the victim's consent. The minimum *mens rea* or guilty mind in most common law offences, including rape, is the intention to do the prohibited act ...

[His Lordship held that the trial judge had correctly stated the law when he said:]

> ... Further, the prosecution has to prove that each defendant intended to have sexual intercourse with this woman without her consent. Not merely that he intended to have intercourse with her but that he intended to have intercourse without her consent. Therefore, if the defendant believed or may have believed that Mrs Morgan consented to him having sexual intercourse with her, then there would be no such intent in his mind and he would not be guilty of the offence of rape, but such a belief must be honestly held by the defendant in the first place ...

The only qualification I would make to [this part of the] direction of the learned [judge] ... is the refinement ... that if the intention of the accused is to have intercourse *nolens volens*, that is recklessly and not caring whether the victim be a consenting party or not, that is equivalent on ordinary principles to an intent to do the prohibited act without the consent of the victim ...

Once one has accepted, what seems to me abundantly clear, that the prohibited act in rape is non-consensual sexual intercourse, and that the guilty state of mind is an intention to commit it, it seems to me to follow as a matter of inexorable logic that there is no room either for a 'defence' of honest belief or mistake, or of a defence of honest and reasonable belief and mistake. Either the prosecution proves that the accused had the requisite intent, or it does not. In the former case it succeeds, and in the latter it fails. Since honest belief clearly negatives intent, the reasonableness or otherwise of that belief can only be evidence for or against the view that the belief and therefore the intent was actually held, and it matters not whether, to quote Bridge J [giving the judgment of the Court of Appeal in the present case], 'the definition of a crime includes no specific element beyond the prohibited act' ...

... I am content to rest my view of the instant case on the crime of rape by saying that it is my opinion that the prohibited act is and always has been intercourse without consent of the victim and the mental element is and always has been the intention to commit that act, or the equivalent intention of having intercourse willy-nilly not caring whether the victim consents or no. A failure to prove this involves an acquittal because the intent, an essential ingredient, is lacking. It matters not why it is lacking if only it is not there, and in particular it matters not that the intention is lacking only because of a belief not based on reasonable grounds ...

For the above reasons I would answer the question certified in the negative, but would apply the proviso to s 2(1) of the Criminal Appeal Act 1968 on the ground that no miscarriage of justice has or conceivably could have occurred. In my view, therefore these appeals should be dismissed.

Lord Cross of Chelsea and **Lord Fraser of Tullybelton** delivered concurring speeches.

Lord Simon of Glaisdale and **Lord Edmund-Davies** dissented.

[Note that s 1 of the Sexual Offences (Amendment) Act 1976 provides that the presence or absence of reasonable grounds for a belief that the victim was consenting to sexual intercourse is a matter to which the jury shall have regard in considering whether the accused did in fact hold that belief – *ed*]

Secretary of State for Trade v Hart [1982] 1 WLR 481 (DC)

Woolf J: This is a case stated by a metropolitan stipendiary magistrate in respect of his adjudication whilst sitting at Wells Street, on 7 April 1981, when he dismissed two informations which had been preferred against the defendant by the prosecutor, the Secretary of State for Trade and Industry. The first of those two offences related to the fact that the defendant in the case of a company (AMF Ashby Metal Fabrications Ltd) of which he was a director and secretary, acted as an auditor when he knew he was disqualified for such appointment. The second offence was similar in nature in that he had acted as auditor of a company called Auger Safety Equipment Ltd, knowing that he was disqualified for appointment as auditor of a company in that he was also a director of that company. The offences were alleged to be contrary to s 161(2) of the Companies Act 1948 and s 13 of the Companies Act 1976.

The fact that the defendant, during the relevant period, had acted as auditor of those companies, at a time when he was disqualified as alleged in the information, was not in dispute before the magistrate. The only matter that was in issue was whether or not the defendant had the necessary *mens rea* to constitute the offences which were alleged ...

The defendant had contended, before the magistrate, that he was not guilty because he was ignorant of the statutory provisions which made him disqualified as a matter of law from holding the office of auditor of the respective companies. The Secretary of State is concerned that such ignorance is treated as amounting to a defence in law, and I can well understand that concern because of the important part the auditor plays in company law. He is relied upon to act as a watch-dog in relation to the affairs of companies and clearly it is very much in the public interest that persons should not act as auditors at a time when they are as a matter of fact disqualified from so acting. However, it has to be remembered that the defendant was charged with a criminal offence and therefore it is, in my view, necessary to answer the question which is raised by the case stated, by reference to the relevant statutory provisions ...

[The] position has now been radically changed by the provisions of s 13 of the Companies Act 1976. Subsection (1) of that Act deals with persons who are qualified for appointment as auditors. Subsection (5) provides:

> No person shall act as auditor of a company at a time when he knows that he is disqualified for appointment to that office; and if an auditor of a company to his knowledge becomes so disqualified during his term of office he shall thereupon vacate his office and give notice in writing to the company that he has vacated it by reason of such disqualification.

Subsection (5) therefore creates the disqualification which arises as a result of persons holding particular offices. It is significant that the provisions of subsection (5) are very different in terms to those of s 161(2) of the Act of 1948. Section 161 of the Act of 1948 contained an absolute prohibition certain persons holding the office of appointment as an auditor of a company. Subsection (5) puts it in a different way: 'No person shall act as auditor of a company at a time when he knows that he is disqualified for appointment ...' and requires a person who becomes aware that he is so disqualified to vacate the office and give notice of that matter. Section 13(6) of the Act of 1976 widens the categories of persons who could be guilty of a criminal offence in relation to this matter. It provides:

> Any person who acts as auditor in contravention of subsection (5) above or fails without reasonable excuse to give notice of vacating his office as required by that subsection shall be guilty of an offence and liable on conviction on indictment to a fine and on summary conviction to a fine not exceeding £40 for every day during which the contravention continues.

It is subsections (5) and (6) that this court is primarily concerned with in answering the question posed by this appeal. Mr Moses, on behalf of the Secretary of State, argues that when subsection (5) and subsection (6) are read together the position is one where a person is guilty of an offence under those provisions if he knows the facts of circumstances which cause him to be disqualified but nonetheless acts as an auditor. He contends that it is not necessary for a person charged with an offence under those subsections also to know that as a matter of law he is disqualified. He submits that it is sufficient if he knows the facts and circumstances, because like anyone else a person acting as an auditor should be aware of the provisions of law which deal with the disqualification for an appointment to the office of auditor.

This is, however, as I have already pointed out, a criminal offence which is created by s 13(5) and (6). In my view it is at least equally consistent with the ordinary meaning of the words which are used in those subsections, that their effect is that a person is not guilty of an offence and is not disqualified from acting as an auditor unless he in fact knows not only the relevant facts but also that in consequence of the facts he is disqualified by the law for appointment to the office. The words in their ordinary interpretation are wholly consistent with a view of the subsections which means that a person in the position of the defendant must be aware of the statutory restrictions which exist against his holding the appointment ...

Ormrod LJ: ... We have to begin by construing the relevant section which, as Woolf J has pointed out, is the combined effect of subsections (5) and (6) of s 13 of the Companies Act 1976. We have to construe those words in the context of the Act itself and to a limited extent in relation to the legislative history, which in this case strikes me as quite important.

Up until 1976, it was not a criminal offence for an officer (or a company director or secretary) to act as auditor of the company if he were otherwise qualified to do so. The fact that he was disqualified had possibly various effects from a civil point of view, but it was not a criminal offence. It was, however, a criminal offence from 1948 onwards (and perhaps earlier) for a body corporate to act as an auditor to a company, and subsection (5) of s 161 of the Act of 1948 imposed a fine of £100 on a body corporate which so acted.

In 1976 it was presumably considered necessary to insert, in the process of 'topping up' the qualifications for auditors, a provision which made it a criminal offence to act in contravention of the section dealing with the qualifications. The language which Parliament has chosen to use seems to me to be explicit, straightforward and quite simple. [His Lordship read s 13(5) and continued:]

Subsection (6) makes it an offence to act in contravention of subsection (5). In other words, the offence, as was correctly set out in the information, is that the defendant acted as an auditor of a company at a time when he knew that he was disqualified for that appointment. And interpreting the language quite simply, it seems to me to indicate that the defendant is not guilty of a criminal offence unless he knew that he was disqualified.

If that means that he is entitled to rely on ignorance of the law as a defence, in contrast to the usual practice and the usual rule, the answer is that the section gives him that right. Whether it does so intentionally or not is another matter. Whether it is easy for anyone to prove or establish that, in the defendant's position, he did not know he was disqualified, will be problematical.

But in this case the facts are unusual. The magistrate who heard the facts, and who saw the defendant give his evidence, accepted him as a person who gave a true and honest account of his position, however improbable it may seem, and accordingly he acquitted the defendant. In my judgment he was fully entitled to do so ...

R v Kimber [1983] 1 WLR 1118 (CA)

See Chapter 23.

Chief Constable of Avon and Somerset v Shimmen (1987) 84 Cr App R 7 (DC)

See Chapter 20.

W (A Minor) v Dolbey (1989) 88 Cr App R 1 (DC)

Robert Goff LJ: ... The facts found by the justices fall into a very short compass and are as follows. The defendant was a young man born on 12 June 1966, which makes him just under 16 at the time of the incident. It appears that on 11 June 1982, he took from home an air rifle which belonged to his elder brother. He had not been given proper instruction in the use of the gun, but had seen his brother use it. It seems he had a number of pellets with him. With the gun he shot at a number of bottles.

Later on he walked towards a farm. When he got there, Philip Rimmer was standing at the barn door. The defendant lay down on the ground and pointed the gun at Rimmer. Rimmer told the defendant to put the gun down. The defendant then stood up and walked towards Rimmer and when he was about 25 feet away from him he stood there, put the rifle to his shoulder and aimed at Rimmer. Rimmer forcefully told the defendant to desist and the defendant then said: 'There is nothing in the gun, I have got no pellets'. He then pulled the trigger. There was a pellet in the gun. He fired at Rimmer and struck him on the forehead between the eyes. By striking Rimmer on the forehead, the pellet caused a wound which required hospital treatment.

The justices found that the defendant did indeed believe the gun to be unloaded at the time when he aimed at Rimmer, because he believed that he had used his last pellet shooting at the bottles. They further found as a fact that the defendant honestly had this belief at the time of the offence. The justices also found that the defendant did not open the gun to ascertain that it was unloaded before aiming it at the victim, but believed at that time that the weapon was not loaded. It appears from a later passage in the case that they formed the view that the defendant ignored the risk that the gun might be loaded before pulling the trigger.

The justices were referred to certain case, including *R v Caldwell* and *R v Lawrence*, and they stated the following conclusion in paragraph 6 of the case:

> We were of opinion following the cases of *Lawrence* (1981) and *Metropolitan Police Commissioner v Caldwell* (1981) that on the facts proved the defendant acted recklessly. We particularly took into account the fact that the defendant ignored the risk that the gun might be loaded before pulling the trigger. We found that this was enough to constitute the malicious intent required by the statute and accordingly we found the defendant guilty and made an order of conditional discharge.

The question stated for the opinion of the court is whether the justices were correct in law in finding the defendant guilty of malicious wounding on the basis of their finding of recklessness.

On behalf of the defendant, Mr Clegg has drawn our attention in particular to two authorities. The first is *Cunningham* [1957] 2 QB 396. That was a case concerned with an offence under s 23 of the Offences Against the Person Act 1861 of unlawfully and maliciously causing a certain person to take a noxious thing, namely coal gas, so as thereby to endanger her life. A question arose as to the meaning of the word 'maliciously' in that section. The trial judge had directed the jury that the word 'maliciously' imported the requirement of wickedness. The Court of Criminal Appeal allowed an appeal on conviction on the ground of a misdirection. Byrne J gave the judgment of the Court. At p 159 and p 399 of the respective reports, after referring to certain cases, he said:

> We have considered those cases, and we have also considered, in the light of those cases, the following principle which was propounded by the late Professor C S Kenny in the first edition of his *Outlines of Criminal Law*, published in 1902, and repeated at 186 of the 16th edition edited by Mr J W Cecil Turner and published in 1952: 'In any statutory definition of a crime, malice must be taken not in the old vague sense of wickedness in general but as requiring either (1) an actual intention to do the particular kind of harm that in fact was done; or (2) recklessness as to whether such harm should occur or not (ie the accused has foreseen that the particular kind of harm might be done and yet has gone on to take the risk of it). It is neither limited to nor does it indeed require any ill will towards the person injured.' The same principle is repeated by Mr Turner in his 10th edition of *Russell on Crime* at 1592.
>
> We think that this is an accurate statement of the law. It derives some support from the judgments of Lords Coleridge C J and Blackburn J in *Pembliton's* case. In our opinion the word 'maliciously' in a statutory crime postulated foresight of consequence.

That decision was considered by Lord Diplock in *Caldwell* [1982] AC 341. The decision of the House of Lords in *Caldwell* was concerned with the interpretation to be placed on the word 'reckless' in s 1 of the Criminal Damage Act 1971 and was not therefore concerned with the interpretation of the word 'maliciously' in the Offences Against the Person Act 1861. In *Caldwell* the *ratio decidendi* of the case is to be found in the speech of Lord Diplock, who gave the leading judgment. In his judgment he gave a definition of the meaning of the word 'reckless' as used in the Act of 1971 in terms which are different from those adopted by the Court of Criminal Appeal in *Cunningham*. But Lord Diplock was careful to distinguish his definition of recklessness from any definition of the word 'maliciously' in a case such as Cunningham, to which he expressly referred. At p 351 he referred to Professor Kenny's definition of malice which had been quoted in *Cunningham*, and he then said:

> My Lords, in this passage Professor Kenny was engaged in defining for the benefit of students the meaning of 'malice' as a term of art in criminal law. To do so he used ordinary English words in their popular meaning. Among the words he used was 'recklessness', the noun derived from the adjective 'reckless', of which the popular or dictionary meaning is: careless, regardless, or heedless, of the possible harmful consequences of one's acts. It presupposes that if thought were given to the matter by the doer before the act was done, it would have been apparent to him that there was a real risk of its having the relevant harmful consequences; but, granted this, recklessness covers a whole range of states of mind from failing to give any thought at all to whether or not there is any risk of those harmful consequences, to recognising the existence of the risk and nevertheless deciding to ignore it. Conscious of this imprecision in the popular meaning of recklessness as descriptive of a state of mind, Professor Kenny, in the passage quoted, was, as it seems to me, at pains to indicate by the words in brackets the particular species within the genus reckless states of mind that constituted 'malice' in criminal law. This parenthetical restriction on the natural meaning of recklessness was necessary to an explanation of the meaning of the adverb 'maliciously' when used as a term of art in the description of an offence under the Malicious Damage Act 1861 (which was the matter in point in *Cunningham* [1957] 2 QB 396); but it was not directed to and consequently has no bearing on the meaning of the adjective 'reckless' in s 1 of the Criminal Damage Act 1971. To use it for that purpose can, in my view, only be misleading.

From that it follows, in my judgment, that Lord Diplock was concerned to distinguish the meaning of the word 'maliciously' as used in the Offences Against the Person Act 1861 from the meaning of the word 'reckless' as used in s 1 of the Criminal Damage Act 1971. No guidance can be derived from the definition of the latter word in Lord Diplock's speech in the consideration of the problem in the present case. It also follows that it was the view of Lord Diplock that *Cunningham* was still good law so far as the subject-matter of that case was concerned, and that what he was saying in *Caldwell* was not considered by him to have any impact on either the decision or the reasoning in that case. So we can put on one side the definition of 'reckless' in *Caldwell* and it follows from what Lord Diplock said that we are simply concerned with the meaning of the word 'maliciously' used as a term of art, as he put it, in criminal law.

That being so, referring again to the case of *Cunningham*, it appears from the passage which I have quoted from the judgment of Byrne J that the word 'maliciously' postulates foresight of consequences. That means, in the ordinary sense of the words, that the accused person must have actually foreseen, as it was put by Professor Kenny, that a particular kind of harm might be done.

Here, Mr Clegg submitted, on the facts as known to the accused, the gun was not loaded, because he honestly believed that the gun was not loaded. Therefore, says Mr Clegg, this young man, the defendant, did not foresee the risk of any harm happening at all to Rimmer if he pointed the gun at him and pulled the trigger, however foolhardy the ordinary man might think that act to have been.

For the prosecutor, Mr Collins made the following submission. He said:

> Let us stand back and look at what the defendant did. He picked up a gun, pointed it at Rimmer and pulled the trigger in the belief, honestly held, that the gun was not loaded. But if we look further into the matter and ask ourselves the question: 'Why did he form the view that the gun was not loaded', the answer must be: 'Because he did not bother to check the gun and

> see if there was a pellet in the gun'. He simply assumed, on the basis of his recollection, that the gun was not loaded without checking it.

Mr Collins submitted that, if the facts are looked at in that way, it can be seen that this young man recklessly disregarded the risk of the gun being loaded and therefore was reckless as to the possible consequence that if the gun was loaded, Rimmer might be injured. In my judgment, however, this submission is contrary to authority; because, as I read the decision of the Court of Criminal Appeal in *Cunningham*, what is required is actual foresight, on the facts known to the accused person, that the particular kind of harm might be done. If there was not such foresight, then it is not permissible to ask the question: 'Why did the accused not appreciate that there was such a risk?' and then on an investigation of the circumstances form an opinion as to whether his action could be described as reckless. It is not to be forgotten that the relevant authority is one which has been described by Lord Diplock as authority on the meaning of 'malice' as a term of art, not on the meaning of the word 'reckless'.

In my judgment, on the findings of fact in this case the defendant did not foresee that any physical harm might come to Rimmer at all, however foolhardy he was in pointing the gun at Rimmer and pulling the trigger without checking to see if the gun was loaded.

I, for my part, would answer the question of law posed by the justices in the negative. It was not correct in law to find the defendant guilty of malicious wounding on the basis of the justices' finding of recklessness on the facts stated in the case.

Attorney General's Reference (No 1 of 1995) [1996] 1 WLR 970 (CA)

Lord Taylor of Gosforth CJ: ... This is a reference by the Attorney General (No 1 of 1995) under s 36 of the Criminal Justice Act 1972.

On 22 November 1994 the respondents were convicted in the Crown Court at Teesside of a number of offences under s 35 of the Banking Act 1987. They were sentenced to a term of imprisonment. The offences involved fraudulent inducements to make deposits.

They were, however, acquitted on the trial judge's directions of two counts charged under s 3(1) of the Banking Act 1987. The judge withdrew those counts from the jury's considerations following submissions at the conclusion of the case for the Crown. Her Majesty's Attorney General now seeks the option of this court on points of law, namely:

> (1) Whether on a charge against a company director of consenting to the acceptance of a deposit contrary to ss 3 and 96 of the Banking Act 1987, ignorance of the law as to the requirement of the authorisation of the Bank of England is a defence; and (2) what *mens rea* is required to be proved to show 'consent'.

The terms of the two relevant sections of the Banking Act 1987 are as follows, so far as is relevant. Section 3(1):

> No person shall ... accept a deposit in the course of carrying on ... a business which for the purposes of this Act is a deposit-taking business unless that person is an institution for the time being authorised by the Bank [of England] under ... this Act.

Section 96(1):

> Where an offence under this Act committed by a body corporate is proved to have been committed with the consent or connivance of, or to be attributable

> to any neglect on the part of any director, manager, secretary or other similar officer of the body corporate, or any person who was purporting to act in any such capacity, he, as well as the body corporate, shall be guilty of that offence ...

It is convenient for completeness to refer also to s 96(4), which provides:

> In any proceedings for an offence under this Act it shall be a defence for the person charged to prove that he took all reasonable precautions and exercised all due diligence to avoid the commission of such an offence by himself or any person under his control.

The facts of the present case can be shortly stated. The respondents were directors of a company trading in the north of England. It was a small company dealing in insurance and investment brokerage. The first respondent, F was the chairman. He ran the business. He and his wife were the only directors. The second respondent, B was his right-hand man and acted as a *de facto* director.

There was evidence that from 1987 onwards the company was accepting deposits in the course of carrying on a deposit-taking business and that both were men who were directly concerned in that activity. Large sums of money were deposited, amounting to some £750,000 in total. In order to induce such deposits the respondents told a number of the depositors that the money would be lent on as bridging loans for which the company would hold charges as security. In fact the money thus raised was being diverted into a night club venture. When that venture failed in 1989, most of the money was lost. It was in respect of the representations made by respondents to the depositors that the charges which were proved against the respondents were based.

The company was not authorised by the bank to accept deposits. In February 1992 the respondents were arrested and in October 1992 they were charged. Following their arrest interviews were sought with the two respondents. They declined to answer questions. However, in September 1992 the second respondent volunteered an interview. Towards the end of it the detective sergeant asked the second respondent what explanation he could give for the unlicensed deposit-taking of the company. In the course of questioning it emerged from the second respondent that he had no idea that in order to take people's money on deposit or to take people's money on investment you have to be licensed by the Bank of England.

The two counts in question were specimen offences. Count 1 related to Mrs B. She had originally invested a total of about £20,000 through the company. She said that at some point after her initial investment the second respondent offered her 17% on her money and the respondents had *carte blanche* from her to invest the money where it would get 17%. The money was then deposited in the company's 'bridging fund'. The deposit was evidenced by a document called a 'property bridging bond' which was signed by the second respondent. It referred to an 'investment', which the prosecution said was truly a deposit, of £19,210 on 25 November 1988 at a flat rate interest of 17%. The first respondent later acknowledged in a letter dated 27 December 1989 that Mrs B had been offered participation in the bridging fund scheme with fixed interest.

Count 2 concerned Mr and Mrs G who placed £54,511 in the company's bridging fund via an intermediary. That transaction was evidenced by an agreement with the company signed by the second respondent, which was found at the first respondent's house.

At the end of the prosecution case the defence submitted that there was no case to answer on these two counts. It was argued on their behalf that in order to be guilty of consenting to the offence by the company a defendant director must be aware of the relevant facts. If the director was not aware that the business is as a matter of fact deemed to be a deposit-taking business for the purposes of the Act, he cannot give informed consent and therefore cannot consent to the acceptance of the deposit in contravention of s 3 ...

On behalf of the Attorney General, Mr Worsley submits that the judge's rulings and observations to the jury were incorrect. He relies on the well-known principle that ignorance of the law is no excuse. That proposition is not, and indeed could not be, in dispute. The issue on this reference is as to what state of mind has to be established against the accused to make him guilty of 'consenting' under s 96(1).

Mr Worsley submits that if a person mentioned in that subsection knows the facts which constitute the offence under s 3(1) committed by the body corporate and consents to that body's affairs being carried on in accordance with those facts, he is guilty of the offence under s 96(1), subject to any defence he may have under s 96(4). It is no defence to say 'I had no idea it was an offence to carry on that business without authorisation from the bank'.

Mr Worsley relies upon *dicta* in two cases. *Johnson v Youden* [1950] 1 KB 544, was a case in the Divisional Court concerned with aiding and abetting. Lord Goddard CJ said, at p 546:

> If a person knows all the facts and is assisting another person to do certain things, and it turns out that the doing of those things constitutes an offence, the person who is assisting is guilty of aiding and abetting that offence, because to allow him to say, 'I knew all those facts but I did not know that an offence was committed', would be allowing him to set up ignorance of the law as a defence.

That passage was expressly approved in the decision of the House of Lords in *R v Churchill (No 2)* [1967] 2 AC 224, a conspiracy case. Viscount Dilhorne, with whom all the other members of the Appellate Committee agreed, said at 237:

> The question is, 'What did they agree to do?' If what they agreed to do was, on the facts known to them, an unlawful act, they are guilty of conspiracy and cannot excuse themselves by saying that, owing to their ignorance of the law, they did not realise that such an act was a crime.

Mr Collier's submission reflected in the judge's rulings was that unless the accused directors were shown to have addressed their minds specifically to the absence of authorisation or, as it has been called throughout these proceedings, a licence from the Bank of England, they could not be guilty of consenting under s 96(1) ...

... Mr Collier referred the court to *Secretary of State for Trade and Industry v Hart* [1982] 1 WLR 481 upon which the judge relied. There, a defendant audited the annual accounts of companies of which he was a director, although the Companies Act disqualified him from doing so. He was charged with an offence under s 13(5) of the Companies Act 1976, which provided: 'No person shall act as auditor of a company at a time when he knows that he is disqualified for appointment to that office'. The metropolitan stipendiary magistrate acquitted the defendant since the prosecution had not, in his judgment, established that the defendant had the requisite knowledge. The decision was challenged on appeal on the grounds that ignorance of the law is no defence. However, the Divisional Court upheld the decision because of the specific wording of the subsection which made it an ingredient of the offence that the defendant must know he is disqualified. In our judgment that case was crucially different from the present one. There, knowledge of the unlawfulness of his acting as an auditor was an ingredient of the offence which had to be proved against the defendant.

Here, we are satisfied that the correct approach is that suggested on behalf of the Attorney General. A director who knows that acts which can only be performed by the company if it is licensed by the bank, are being performed when in fact no licence exists and who consents to that performance is guilty of the offence charged. The fact that he does not know it is an offence to perform them without a licence, ie ignorance of the law, is no defence.

Mr Collier's suggestion that the director must actively have addressed his mind to the question of licences is wholly unreal. If the two directors, who were wholly responsible for the company's business activity, were ignorant of the need for a licence it can readily be inferred that they knew they did not have one. The concept of a director who is ignorant of the law requiring a licence, focusing his mind on the question of whether he has or has not obtained one is wholly academic. Had anyone approached the defendant directors and asked: 'Have you a licence or authorisation from the Bank of England?' the ready answer would have been 'No', probably supplemented by 'I did not know I needed one'. There would have been no need for a search, an inquiry or a focusing of the mind. Since the question had not occurred to them they would know that the company did not have one.

The ignorance of the law on the point necessarily must in the context of this case point to the knowledge that the company is operating unlicensed. That is not to say that s 96(1) creates an absolute offence in respect of directors. There could, for example, in a company with a number of directors responsible for different limbs of the company's business, be a director who believed the licence had been obtained and was not therefore consenting to the offences committed by the company. That was not the situation here. In our view the judge was wrong to withdraw counts 1 and 2 from the jury.

Our answers to the two questions posed are as follows: (1) No. (2) A defendant has to be proved to know the material facts which constitute the offence by the body corporate and to have agreed to its conduct of its business on the basis of those facts.

R v Merrick [1995] Crim LR 802 (CA)

See Chapter 20.

CHAPTER 6

INSANITY AND AUTOMATISM

INSANITY

The defence of insanity is governed by the rules laid down in *M'Naghten's* case (1843) 10 Cl & F 200.

M'Naghten's case (1843) 10 Cl & F 200

Tindal CJ: ... The jurors ought to be told in all cases that every man is to be presumed to be sane, and to possess a sufficient degree of reason to be responsible for his crimes, until the contrary be proved to their satisfaction; and that to establish a defence on the ground of insanity, it must be clearly proved that, at the time of the committing of the act, the party accused was labouring under such a defect of reason, from disease of the mind, as not to know the nature and quality of the act he was doing; or, if he did know it, that he did not know he was doing what was wrong.

The following elements may be derived from the M'Naghten Rules:

(1) The accused is presumed to be sane unless he proves (and the burden is on him to show), on the balance of probabilities, that he was insane at the time of the alleged offence. It follows that the jury do not have be satisfied beyond reasonable doubt that the defendant was insane; it is sufficient that they are satisfied that it is more likely than not that he was insane at the relevant time: see *Sodeman v The King* [1936] 2 All ER.

(2) The insanity must amount to a 'defect of reason': see *R v Clarke* [1972] 1 All ER 219.

(3) The defect of reason must result from a 'disease of the mind': see *R v Sullivan* [1984] AC 156.

(4) Either:

   (a) the accused did not know the 'nature and quality of the act he was doing' (ie he did not know what he was doing); or

   (b) he did not know that what he was doing was wrong: see *R v Codère* (1916) 12 Cr App R 21; see *R v Sullivan* [1984] AC 156.

Sodeman v The King [1936] 2 All ER 1138 (PC)

Facts: The petitioner (appellant) was convicted of the murder of a young girl. His defence was that he was insane at the time of the killing. At the trial three doctors gave evidence to support the defence of insanity. No expert evidence on the issue of insanity was tendered by the prosecution.

Viscount Hailsham LC: ... First, it is suggested by the petitioner that the rules in *M'Naghten* are no longer to be treated as an exhaustive statement of the law with regard to insanity, and that there is to be engrafted upon those rules another rule that where a man knows that he is doing what is wrong, nonetheless he may be held to be insane if he is caused to do the act by an irresistible impulse produced by disease ... Their Lordships do not think that the argument is a sound one ... The other point [concerned the burden and standard of proof] ... [I]t is certainly plain that the burden in cases in which an accused has to prove insanity may fairly be stated as not being higher than the burden which rests upon a plaintiff or defendant in civil proceedings. [*ie the balance of probabilities; more likely than not – ed.*]

Bratty v Attorney General for Northern Ireland [1963] AC 386 (HL)

Viscount Kilmuir LC: ... To establish the defence of insanity within the M'Naghten Rules the accused must prove on the preponderance of probabilities, first a defect of reason from a disease of the mind, and, second, as a consequence of such a defect, ignorance of the nature and quality (or the wrongfulness) of the acts. We have to consider a case in which it is sought to do so by medical evidence to the effect that the conduct of the accused might be compatible with psychomotor epilepsy, which is a disease of the mind affecting the reason, and that psychomotor epilepsy could cause ignorance of the nature and quality of the acts done, but in which the medical witness can assign no other cause for that ignorance. Where the possibility of an unconscious act depends on, and only on, the existence of a defect of reason from disease of the mind within the M'Naghten Rules, a rejection by the jury of this defence of insanity necessarily implies that they reject the possibility.

The Court of Criminal Appeal also took the view that where the alleged automatism is based solely on a disease of the mind within the M'Naghten Rules, the same burden of proof rests on the defence whether the 'plea' is given the name of insanity or automatism. I do not think that statement goes further than saying that when you rely on insanity as defined by the Rules you cannot by a difference of nomenclature avoid the road so often and authoritatively laid down by the courts.

What I have said does not mean that, if a defence of insanity is raised unsuccessfully, there can never, in any conceivable circumstances, be room for an alternative defence based on automatism. For example, it may be alleged that the accused had a blow on the head, after which he acted without being conscious of what he was doing or was a sleep-walker. There might be a divergence of view as to whether there was a defect of reason from disease of the mind (compare the curious position which arose in *R v Kemp* [1957] 1 QB 399). The jury might not accept the evidence of a defect of reason from disease of the mind, but at the same time accept the evidence that the prisoner did not know what he was doing. If the jury should take that view of the facts they would find him not guilty. But it should be noted that the defence would only have succeeded because the necessary foundation had been laid by positive evidence which, properly considered, was evidence of something other than a defect of reason from disease of the mind. In my opinion, this analysis of the two defences (insanity and automatism) shows that where the only cause alleged for the unconsciousness is a defect of reason from disease of the mind, and that cause is rejected by the jury, there can be no room for the alternative defence of automatism. Like the Court of Criminal Appeal, I cannot therefore accept the submission that the whole of the evidence directed to the issue of insanity should have been left to the jury to consider whether there was automatism due to another cause. It was conceded before this House, and this is stated in the judgment of the Court of Criminal Appeal, that there was nothing to show or suggest that there was any other pathological cause for automatism.

I next consider the submission that, even so, the question of automatism ought to have been left to the jury ...

Where the defence succeeds in surmounting the initial hurdle (see *Mancini v DPP* [1942] AC 1), and satisfies the judge that there is evidence fit for the jury to consider, the question remains whether the proper direction is: (a) that the jury will acquit if, and only if, they are satisfied on the balance of probabilities that the accused acted in a state of automatism, or (b) that they should acquit if they are left in reasonable doubt on this point. In favour of the former direction it might be argued that, since a defence of automatism is (as Lord Goddard said in *Hill v Baxter* [1958] 1 QB 277, 282) very near a defence of insanity, it would be anomalous if there were any distinction between the onus in the one case and in the other. If this argument were to prevail it would follow that the defence would fail unless they established on a balance of probabilities that the prisoner's act was unconscious and involuntary in the same way as, under the M'Naghten Rules, they must establish on a balance of probabilities that the necessary requirements are satisfied.

Nevertheless, one must not lose sight of the overriding principle, laid down by this House in *Woolmington's* case [1935] AC 462, that it is for the prosecution to prove every element of the offence charged. One of these elements is the accused's state of mind; normally the presumption of mental capacity is sufficient to prove that he acted consciously and voluntarily, and the prosecution need go no further. But if, after considering evidence properly left to them by the judge, the jury are left in real doubt whether or not the accused acted in a state of automatism, it seems to me that on principle they should acquit because the necessary *mens rea* – if indeed the *actus reus* – has not been proved beyond reasonable doubt.

I find support for this view in the direction given by Barry J to the jury in *R v Charlson* [1955] 1 WLR 317. In that case the prisoner was charged on three counts, namely causing grievous bodily harm with intent to murder, causing grievous bodily harm with intent to cause grievous bodily harm, and unlawful wounding. The defence raised the issue of automatism and called medical evidence in support of it. The learned judge, on the basis – which has aroused some discussion – that insanity did not come into the case, after directing the jury that on each of the first two charges the prosecution must prove the specific intent, went on to deal with the third charge, that is, unlawful wounding, in these words: 'Therefore, in considering this third charge you will have to ask yourselves whether the accused knowingly struck his son, or whether he was acting as an automaton without any knowledge of or control over his acts ... If you are left in doubt about the matter, and you think that he may well have been acting as an automaton without any real knowledge of what he was doing, then the proper verdict would be "not guilty" ...'

My conclusion is, therefore, that once the defence has surmounted the initial hurdle to which I have referred and has satisfied the judge that there is evidence fit for the jury's consideration, the proper direction is that, if that evidence leaves them in a real state of doubt, the jury should acquit ...

Lord Denning: My Lords, in the case of *Woolmington v DPP* [1935] AC 462, 482 Viscount Sankey LC said that 'when dealing with a murder case the Crown must prove (a) death as the result of a voluntary act of the accused and (b) malice of the accused'. The requirement that it should be a voluntary act is essential, not only in a murder case, but also in every criminal case. No act is punishable if it is done involuntarily; and an involuntary act in this context – some people nowadays prefer to speak of it as 'automatism' – means an act which is done by the muscles without any control by the mind, such as a spasm, a reflex action or a convulsion; or an act done by a person who is not conscious of what he is doing, such as an act done whilst suffering from concussion or whilst sleep-walking. The point was well put by Stephen J in 1889: 'Can anyone doubt that a man who, though he might be perfectly sane, committed what would otherwise be a crime in a state of somnambulism, would be entitled to be acquitted? And why is this? Simply because he would not know what he was doing'; see *R v Tolson* (1889) 23 QBD 168, 187. The term 'involuntary act' is, however, capable of wider connotations: and to prevent confusion it is to be observed that in the criminal law an act is not to be regarded as an involuntary act simply because the doer does not remember it. When a man is charged with dangerous driving, it is no defence for him to say 'I don't know what happened. I cannot remember a thing'; see *Hill v Baxter* [1958] 1 QB 277. Loss of memory afterwards is never a defence in itself, so long as he was conscious at the time; see *Russell v H M Advocate* [1946] SC(J) 37; *R v Podola* [1960] 1 QB 325. Nor is an act to be regarded as an involuntary act simply because the doer could not control his impulse to do it. When a man is charged with murder and it appears that he knew what he was doing, but he could not resist it, then his assertion 'I couldn't help myself' is no defence in itself; see *Attorney General for South Australia v Brown* [1960] AC 432: though it may go towards a defence of diminished responsibility, in places where that defence is available; see *R v Byrne* [1960] 2 QB 396: but it does not render his act involuntary so as to entitle him to an unqualified acquittal. Nor is an act to be regarded as an involuntary act simply because it is unintentional or its consequences are unforeseen. When a man is charged with dangerous driving, it is no defence for him to say, however truly, 'I did not mean to drive dangerously'. There is said to be an absolute prohibition against that offence, whether he had a guilty mind of not; see *Hill v Baxter* [1958] 1 QB 277 at 282 by Lord Goddard CJ. But even though it is absolutely prohibited, nevertheless he has a defence if he can show that it was an involuntary act in the sense that he was unconscious at the time and did not know what he was doing, see *H M Advocate v Ritchie* 1926 S C (J) 45, *R v Minor* (1955) 15 W W R (N S) 433 and *Cooper v McKenna, Ex parte Cooper* [1960] Qd L R 406.

Another thing to be observed is that it is not every involuntary act which leads to a complete acquittal. Take first an involuntary act which proceeds from a state of drunkenness. If the drunken man is so drunk that he does not know what he is doing, he has a defence to any charge, such as murder or wounding with intent, in which a specific intent is essential, but he is still liable to be convicted of manslaughter or unlawful wounding for which no specific intent is necessary, see *Beard's* case [1920] AC 479 at 494, 498, 504.

Again, if the involuntary act proceeds from a disease of the mind, it gives rise to a defence of insanity, but not to a defence of automatism. Suppose a crime is committed by a man in a state of automatism or clouded consciousness due to a recurrent disease of the mind. Such an act is no doubt involuntary, but it does not give rise to an unqualified acquittal, for that would mean that he would be let at large to do it again. The only proper verdict is one which ensures that the person who suffers from the disease is kept secure in a hospital so as not to be a danger to himself or others. That is, a verdict of guilty but insane.

Once you exclude all the cases I have mentioned, it is apparent that the category of involuntary acts is very limited. So limited, indeed, that until recently there was hardly any reference in the English books to this so-called defence of automatism ... In striking contrast to *Charlson's* case, *ibid* 317, is *R v Kemp* [1957] 1 QB 399. A devoted husband of excellent character made an entirely motiveless and irrational attack upon his wife. He struck her violently with a hammer. He was charged with causing her grievous bodily harm. It was found that he suffered from hardening of the arteries which might lead to a congestion of blood in the brain. As a result of such congestion, he suffered a temporary lack of consciousness, so that he was not conscious that he picked up the hammer or that he was striking his wife with it. It was therefore an involuntary act. Note again the important point – no plea of insanity was raised but only the defence of automatism. Nevertheless, Devlin J put insanity to the jury. He held that hardening of the arteries was a 'disease of the mind' within the M'Naghten Rules and he directed the jury they ought so to find. They accordingly found Kemp guilty but insane.

My Lords, I think that Devlin J was quite right in *Kemp's* case in putting the question of insanity to the jury, even though it had not been raised by the defence. When it is asserted that the accused did an involuntary act in a state of automatism, the defence necessarily puts in issue the state of mind of the accused man: and thereupon it is open to the prosecution to show what his true state of mind was. The old notion that only the defence can raise a defence of insanity is now gone. The prosecution are entitled to raise it and it is their duty to do so rather than allow a dangerous person to be at large ...

Upon the other point discussed by Devlin J, namely what is a 'disease of the mind' within the M'Naghten Rules, I would agree with him that this is a question for the judge. The major mental diseases, which the doctors call psychoses, such as schizophrenia, are clearly diseases of the mind. But in *Charlson's* case, Barry J seems to have assumed that other diseases such as epilepsy or cerebral tumour are not diseases of the mind, even when they are such as to manifest themselves in violence. I do not agree with this. It seems to me that any mental disorder which has manifested itself in violence and is prone to recur is a disease of the mind. At any rate it is the sort of disease for which a person should be detained in hospital rather than be given an unqualified acquittal.

It is to be noticed that in *Charlson's* case and *Kemp's* the defence raised only automatism, not insanity. In the present case the defence raised both automatism and insanity. And herein lies the difficulty because of the burden of proof. If the accused says he did not know what he was doing, then, so far as the defence of automatism is concerned, the Crown must prove that the act was a voluntary act, see *Woolmington's* case. But so far as the defence of insanity is concerned, the defence must prove that the act was an involuntary act due to disease of the mind, see *M'Naghten's* case (1843) 10 Cl and F 200, 210 HL ...

My Lords, I think that the difficulty is to be resolved by remembering that, whilst the *ultimate* burden rests on the Crown of proving every element essential in the crime, nevertheless in order to prove that the act was a voluntary act, the Crown is entitled to rely on the *presumption* that every man has sufficient mental capacity to be responsible for his crimes: and that if the defence wish to displace that presumption they must give some evidence from which the contrary may reasonably be inferred. Thus a drunken man is presumed to have the capacity to form the specific intent necessary to constitute the crime, unless evidence is given from which it can reasonably be inferred that he was incapable of forming it; see the valuable judgment of the Court of Justiciary in *Kennedy v H M Advocate* 1944 S C (J) 171, 177 which was delivered by Lord Normand. So also it seems to me that a man's act is presumed to be a voluntary act unless there is evidence from which it can reasonably be inferred that it was involuntary. To use the words of Devlin J, the defence of automatism 'ought not to be considered at all until the defence has produced at least *prima facie* evidence'; see *Hill v Baxter* [1958] 1 QB 277, 285; and the words of North J in New Zealand 'unless a proper foundation is laid'; see *R v Cottle* [1958] N Z L R 999 at 1025. The necessity of laying the proper foundation is on the defence: and if it is not so laid, the defence of automatism need not be left to the jury, any more than the defence of drunkenness (*Kennedy v H M Advocate* 1944 S C (J) 171), provocation (*R v Gauthier* (1943) 29 Cr App R 113, C C A) or self-defence (*R v Lobell* [1957] 1 QB 547) need be.

What, then, is a proper foundation? The presumption of mental capacity of which I have spoken is a provisional presumption only. It does not put the legal burden on the defence in the same way as the presumption of sanity does. It leaves the legal burden on the prosecution, but nevertheless, until it is displaced, it enables the prosecution to discharge the ultimate burden of proving that the act was voluntary. Not because the presumption is evidence itself, but because it takes the place of evidence. In order to displace the presumption of mental capacity, the defence must give sufficient evidence from which it may reasonably be inferred that the act was involuntary. The evidence of the man himself will rarely be sufficient unless it is supported by medical evidence which points to the cause of the mental incapacity. It is not sufficient for a man to say 'I had a black-out': for 'black-out' as Stable J said in *Cooper v Mc Kenna, Ex parte Cooper* 'is one of the first refuges of a guilty conscience and a popular excuse'. The words of Devlin J in *Hill v Baxter* should be remembered: 'I do not doubt that there are genuine cases of automatism and the like, but I do not see how the layman can safely attempt without the help of some medical or scientific evidence to distinguish the genuine from the fraudulent'. When the only cause that is assigned for an involuntary act is drunkenness, then it is only necessary to leave drunkenness to the jury, with the consequential directions, and not to leave automatism at all. When the only cause that is assigned for it is a disease of the mind, then it is only necessary to leave insanity to the jury and not automatism. When the cause assigned is concussion or sleep-walking, there should be some evidence from which it can reasonably be inferred before it should be left to the jury. If it is said to be due to concussion, there should be evidence of a severe blow shortly beforehand. If it is said to be sleep-walking, there should be some credible support for it. His mere assertion that he was asleep will not suffice.

Once a proper foundation is thus laid for automatism, the matter becomes at large and must be left to the jury. As the case proceeds, the evidence may weigh first to one side and then to the other: and so the burden may appear to shift to and fro. But at the end of the day the legal burden comes into play and requires that the jury should be satisfied beyond reasonable doubt that the act was a voluntary act.

This brings me to the root question in the present case: Was a proper foundation laid here for the defence of automatism, apart from the plea of insanity? There was the evidence of George Bratty himself that he could not remember anything because 'this blackness was over me'. He said 'I did not realise exactly what I was doing', and added afterwards 'I didn't know what I was doing. I didn't realise anything.' He said he had four or five times previously had 'feelings of blackness' and frequently headaches. There was evidence, too, of his odd behaviour at times, his mental backwardness and his religious leanings. Added to this there was the medical evidence. Dr Sax, who was called on his behalf, said that there was a possibility that he was suffering from psychomotor epilepsy. It was, he said, practically the only possibility that occurred to him. Dr Walker, his general practitioner, said you could not leave the possibility out of account. Dr Robinson, a specialist, who gave evidence on behalf of the Crown, said he thought it was extremely unlikely that it was an epileptic attack, but could not rule it out. All the doctors agreed that psychomotor epilepsy, if it exists, is a defect of reason due to disease of the mind: and the judge accepted this view. No other cause was canvassed.

In those circumstances, I am clearly of opinion that, if the act of George Bratty was an involuntary act, as the defence suggested, the evidence attributed it solely to a disease of the mind and only defence open was the defence of insanity.

There was no evidence of automatism apart from insanity. There was, therefore, no need for the judge to put [non-insane automatism] to the jury. And when the jury rejected the defence of insanity, they rejected the only defence disclosed by the evidence ...

Lord Morris of Borth-y-Gest delivered a concurring speech; **Lord Tucker** and **Lord Hodson** agreed.

Defect of reason

R v Clarke [1972] 1 All ER 219 (CA)

Ackner J: ... The facts are simple. It was common ground that on 2 March 1971 the appellant went to the International Stores supermarket at Leicester. She there shopped with the aid of a wire basket provided by the store to enable her, not only to carry the goods of her choice, but also to keep them separate and apart from any other goods and thus enable the cashier readily to calculate the cost of the goods she had purchased from the store. While she was in the store the appellant selected various items, three of which consisted of a pound of butter, a jar of coffee and a jar of mincemeat. At some stage before she went to the check-out point the appellant transferred those goods out of the wire basket and into her own bag so that when she presented her basket those three items were no longer in the wire basket and were not therefore paid for. Understandably enough it was alleged that these goods were secreted into the appellant's own shopping bag with the object of stealing them and taking them out of the store without paying for them.

The appellant's defence was that she had no intention of stealing these goods. She had not been feeling well on the morning in question nor for quite some time. She suffers from sugar diabetes. In the previous year she had gone down with 'flu and on the Friday previous to that occurrence her husband had broken his collarbone. He had to look after her and was in fact, because of his own condition, off work for several months. What with one thing and another she had become very depressed. On a number of occasions she had been very forgetful; for example, she had put sugar in the refrigerator instead of in the cupboard and the sweeping brush in the dustbin and then put the dirt where the brush should have been put. In her own words 'everything seemed to get on top of me'.

On the morning in question she woke up with a very bad head which persisted despite her taking her pills. Her husband rang up at about 11.00 am to say that he would be home for lunch late. She put their meal in the oven on a low flame and went out to fetch the groceries. She had no recollection of putting these three items into her shopping bag and as for the jar of mincemeat neither she nor her husband ever ate this. In short her defence was that she had no intention to steal these articles, but in a moment of absent-mindedness had put them in her own shopping bag.

Had the matter rested there, there would have been no complications and the assistant recorder would no doubt have directed the jury to consider her explanation and ask themselves whether they were satisfied beyond reasonable doubt that she had the necessary intent to sustain the charge. However, to support the validity of her explanation medical evidence was called. These witnesses were her general practitioner and a consultant psychiatrist. These two gentlemen both spoke to the fact that she was suffering from depression, which one of them accepted to be a minor mental illness. The general practitioner described the symptoms. The patient feels a lack of energy – he finds it difficult to concentrate – he may be short-tempered or absent-minded. The psychiatrist stated that it can produce states of absent-mindedness in which the patient would do things he would not normally do in periods of 'confusion and memory lapses'. All this evidence was entirely consistent with the appellant's story.

Unfortunately the medical witnesses were pressed to, what it seems to us, an unreasonable degree to explain the workings of this particular illness. The psychiatrist stated that what happens in these cases is 'that there is a patchy state of affairs, that the consciousness, if you like goes off at times and comes on again, changing every few minutes and not in proper control of the patient'.

The effect of this evidence on the assistant recorder was to convince him that the defence was in truth a defence of 'not guilty by reason of insanity' under the M'Naghten Rules (see *M'Naghten's* case (1843) 10 Cl and Fin 200, [1843–60] All ER Rep 229). He was undoubtedly influenced to this decision by the evidence that the depression was an illness which he translated as meaning also a disease and by the fact that on the medical evidence, as he understood it, a possible explanation was that there had been a total lack of consciousness at the moment when the offence was committed. In order to sustain a defence under the M'Naghten Rules it is necessary to show that the party accused was labouring under *such a defect of reason from the disease of the mind as not to know the nature and quality of the act he was doing* or if he did know, that he did not know that what he was doing was wrong.

It may be that on the evidence in this case the assistant recorder was entitled to the view that the appellant suffered from a disease of the mind but we express no concluded view on that. However, in our judgment the evidence fell very short either of showing that she suffered from a defect of reason or that the consequences of that defect in reason, if any, were that she was unable to know the nature and quality of the act she was doing. The M'Naghten Rules relate to accused persons who by reason of a disease of the mind are deprived of the power of reasoning. They do not apply and never have applied to those who retain the power of reasoning but who in moments of confusion or absent-mindedness fail to use their powers to the full. The picture painted by the evidence was wholly inconsistent with this being a woman who retained her ordinary powers of reason but who was momentarily absent-minded or confused and acted as she did by failing to concentrate properly on what she was doing and by failing adequately to use her mental powers ...

Disease of the mind

R v Kemp [1957] 1 QB 399 (Devlin J, Bristol Assizes)

Devlin J: ... The facts of the case in relation to which this point has to be considered are that the accused, who is charged with causing grievous bodily harm to his wife, struck her during the night with a hammer with such violence as to inflict a grievous wound. The accused is an elderly man of excellent character and he and his wife have always been thought to be a devoted couple, and it seems that there is strong evidence to show that the act was entirely motiveless and irrational. I say strong evidence to show, though that is a matter which the jury will have in due course to decide: for the purpose of my ruling I assume that in accordance with the evidence to which I have referred, the act was committed, as the doctors on all sides think it was, while the accused was in a mental condition which made him not responsible for his actions. Their view upon this – and all three are agreed – is that he did the act, as he says he did, not knowing anything about it and that he has not any real memory of it. It is not merely a question of his striking his wife when in some mental derangement, nor appreciating that what he was doing was wrong; it is a case in the view of all three doctors in which he was not conscious at the time that he did the act, that he picked up the hammer or that he was striking his wife with it ...

It is common ground on the evidence that the accused was suffering from a physical disease, namely arteriosclerosis, or hardening of the arteries. It had not reached – and this, I think, is clear from the evidence, at any rate I assume so for this purpose – the stage at which the accused was showing any general sign of mental trouble. Apart from a depression, not an irrational depression, produced by his poor state of health, there were no signs of mental trouble ...

I shall say by way of commencement that there is, according to the evidence, no general medical opinion upon what category of diseases are properly to be called diseases of the mind. Both doctors have expressed their views, but they have expressed their views as personal views and not ones for which they can call in aid any general body of medical opinion. Doctors' personal views, of course, are not binding upon me. I have to interpret the rules according to the ordinary principles of interpretation, but I derive help from their interpretations in as much as they illustrate the nature of the disease and the matters which from the medical point of view have to be considered in determining whether or not it is a disease of the mind.

The broad submission that was made to me on behalf of the accused was that this is a physical disease and not a mental disease; arteriosclerosis is a physical condition primarily and not a mental condition. But that argument does not go so far as to suggest that for the purpose of the law diseases that affect the mind can be divided into those that are physical in origin and those that are mental in origin. There is such a distinction medically. I think it is recognised by medical men that there are mental diseases which have an organic cause, there are disturbances of the mind which can be traced to some hardening of the arteries, to some degeneration of the brain cells or to some physical condition which accounts for mental derangement. It is also recognised that there are diseases functional in origin where it is not possible to point to any physical cause but simply to say that there has been a derangement of the functioning of the mind, such as melancholia, schizophrenia and many other of those diseases which are usually handled by psychiatrists. This medical distinction is not pressed as part of the argument for the accused in this case, and I think rightly. The distinction between the two categories is quite irrelevant for the purposes of the law, which is not concerned with the origin of the disease or the cause of it but simply with the mental condition which has brought about the act. It does not matter, for the purposes of the law, whether the defect of reason is due to a degeneration of the brain or to some other form of mental derangement. That may be a matter of importance medically, but it is of no importance to the law, which merely has to consider the state of mind in which the accused is, not how he got there.

The distinction that emerges from the evidence of Dr Gibson and which has been argued by [counsel for the accused] is a different one. It is that this is something which is capable of becoming a mental disease but has not yet become one. It has not created any degeneration of the brain and the argument is that it is merely interfering temporarily with the working of the brain by cutting off the supply of blood in the same way as concussion might, or something of that sort. I am invited to say that this disease at this stage is purely physical; when it interferes with the brain cells so that they degenerate, it then becomes a disease of the mind. This would be a very difficult test to apply for the purposes of the law. I should think it would be a matter of great difficulty medically to determine precisely at what point degeneration of the brain sets in, and it would mean that the verdict depended upon a doubtful medical borderline.

The law is not concerned with the brain but with the mind, in the sense that 'mind' is ordinarily used, the mental faculties of reason, memory and understanding. If one read for 'disease of the mind' 'disease of the brain', it would follow that in many cases pleas of insanity would not be established because it could not be proved that the brain had been affected in any way, either by degeneration of the cells or in any other way. In my judgment the condition of the brain is irrelevant and so is the question of whether the condition of the mind is curable or incurable, transitory or permanent. There is no warranty for introducing those considerations into the definition in the M'Naghten Rules. Temporary insanity is sufficient to satisfy them. It does not matter whether it is incurable and permanent or not.

I think that the approach of [counsel for the Crown] to the definition in the rules is the right one. He points out the order of the words 'a defect of reason, from disease of the mind'. The primary thing that has to be looked for is the defect of reason. 'Disease of the mind' is there for some purpose, obviously, but the prime thing is to determine what is admitted here, namely whether or not there is a defect of reason. In my judgment, the words 'from disease of the mind' are not to be construed as if they were put in for the purpose of distinguishing between diseases which have a mental origin and diseases which have a physical origin, a distinction which in 1843 was probably little considered. They were put in for the purpose of limiting the effect of the words 'defect of reason'. A defect of reason is by itself enough to make the act irrational and therefore normally to exclude responsibility in law. But the rule was not intended to apply to defects of reason caused simply by brutish stupidity without rational power. It was not intended that the defence should plead: 'Although with a healthy mind he nevertheless had been brought up in such a way that he had never learned to exercise his reason, and therefore he is suffering from a defect of reason'. The words ensure that unless the defect is due to a diseased mind and not simply to an untrained one there is insanity within the meaning of the rule.

Hardening of the arteries is a disease which is shown on the evidence to be capable of affecting the mind in such a way as to cause a defect, temporarily or permanently, of its reasoning, understanding and so on, and so is in my judgment a disease of the mind which comes within the meaning of the rules ...

R v Quick and Paddison [1973] 1 QB 910 (CA)

Lawton LJ: ... In their broadest aspects these appeals raise the question as to what is meant by the phrase 'a defect of reason from disease of the mind' within the meaning of the M'Naghten Rules. More particularly the question is whether a person who commits a criminal act while under the effect of hypoglycaemia can raise a defence of automatism, as the defendants submitted was possible, or whether such a person must rely on a defence of insanity if he wishes to relieve himself of responsibility for his acts, as Bridge J ruled.

The defendants were both employed at Farleigh Mental Hospital, Flax Bourton, Somerset. Quick was a charge nurse, Paddison a state enrolled nurse. At the trial it was not disputed that at about 4 pm on 27 December 1971, one Green, a paraplegic spastic patient, unable to walk, was sitting in Rosemount Ward at the hospital, watching television. Quick was on duty; Paddison had gone off duty at 2 pm but was still present in the ward. Half an hour later, Green had sustained two black eyes, a fractured nose, a split lip which required three stitches and bruising of his arm and shoulders. There was undisputed medical evidence that these injuries could not have been self-inflicted.

The prosecution's case was that Quick had inflicted the injuries on Green and that Paddison had been present aiding and abetting him, not by actual physical participation, but by encouragement. On arraignment Quick pleaded not guilty. At the close of the evidence, following a ruling by the judge as to the effect in law of the evidence relied upon by Quick to support a defence of automatism, he pleaded guilty to count 2 of the indictment. The judge's ruling was to the effect that that evidence could only be relied upon to support a defence of insanity.

The evidence upon which the judge ruled came partly from witnesses for the prosecution and partly from Quick's own evidence and that of a consultant physician, Dr Cates, who was called on his behalf ... In the course of his own evidence Quick said that he could not remember assaulting Green. He admitted that he had been drinking and that his drinks had included whisky and a quarter of a bottle of rum. He also said that he was, and had been since the age of seven, a diabetic and that that morning he had taken insulin as prescribed by his doctor. After taking insulin he had had a very small breakfast and no lunch. Dr Cates said that on 12 or more occasions Quick had been admitted to hospital either unconscious or semi-conscious due to hypoglycaemia, which is a condition brought about when there is more insulin in the bloodstream than the amount of sugar there can cope with. When this imbalance occurs, the insulin has much the same effect as an excess of alcohol in the human body. At the onset of the imbalance the higher functions of the mind are affected. As the effects of the imbalance become more marked, more and more mental functions are upset; and unless an antidote is given (and a lump of sugar is an effective one) the sufferer can relapse into coma. In the later stages of mental impairment a sufferer may become aggressive and violent without being able to control himself or without knowing at the time what he was doing or having any recollection afterwards of what he had done. The following answer by Dr Cates sums up his evidence about hypoglycaemia and his opinion as to whether Quick could have been doing what he was proved to have been doing in the course of a suggested hypoglycaemic reaction:

> If a patient is going unconscious with a falling blood sugar, for a while he will be aggressive, for a while he will be more than aggressive, for a while he may start being physically violent and then he will be in a semi-conscious state when he could be struggling and resisting people's efforts to give him sugar. Then he may have a fit, then he may stay deeply unconscious for quite a while. It would sound from the evidence that this man developed an increasing effect of a falling blood sugar from some time in the afternoon till when he collapsed after the episode of attack. At least the events fit with that.

Dr Cates said that on three or four occasions while in hospital under treatment for diabetes Quick had behaved violently when his blood sugar had got too low.

As is well-known, insulin is prescribed by doctors in order to ensure that only the requisite amount of sugar is in the patient's bloodstream; but from time to time the sugar level may get too low. Dr Cates said that there were a number of causes for that. The doctor may have prescribed too much insulin; the patient may have eaten too little or have been overactive. He accepted that on the occasion when Green was attacked, Quick's own conduct that day might well have caused a severe fall in blood sugar.

At the trial and before this court it was accepted by the prosecution that the evidence to which we have referred was enough to justify an issue being left to the jury whether Quick could be held responsible for what he had done to Green. If the jury were to accept the evidence relied on by Quick, what should their verdict be? Quick's counsel submitted, 'not guilty'; Sir Joseph Moloney on behalf of the Crown submitted that it should be 'not guilty by reason of insanity'. The judge ruled in favour of the Crown. As Quick did not want to put forward a defence of insanity, after consulting with his counsel, he pleaded guilty to count 2. As that plea had been made as a result of the judge's ruling, it was accepted by the prosecution before this court that if that ruling was adjudged to be wrong it would not be a bar to an appeal by Quick against his conviction ...

Our examination of such authorities as there are must start with *Bratty v Attorney General for Northern Ireland* [1963] AC 386, because the judge ruled as he did in reliance on that case. Bratty had been accused of the murder of a young girl. He put forward three defences; first, that at the material time he was in a state of automatism by reason of suffering from an attack of psychomotor epilepsy; second, that he was guilty only of manslaughter since he was incapable of forming an intent on the ground that his mental condition was so impaired and confused and he was so deficient in reason that he was not capable of forming such intent; and third, that he was insane. The trial judge left the issue of insanity to the jury (which they rejected) but refused to leave the other two issues. The House of Lords adjudged on the evidence in *Bratty's* case that he had been right to rule as he did, but accepted that automatism as distinct from insanity could be a defence if there was a proper foundation in the evidence for it. In this case, if Quick's alleged condition could have been caused by hypoglycaemia and that condition, like psychomotor epilepsy, was a disease of the mind, then Bridge J's ruling was right. The question remains, however, whether a mental condition arising from hypoglycaemia does amount to a disease of the mind. In *Bratty v Attorney General for Northern Ireland* [1963] AC 386, all their Lordships based their speeches on the basis that such medical evidence as there was pointed to Bratty suffering from a 'defect of reason from disease of the mind' and nothing else. Lord Denning discussed in general terms what constituted a disease of the mind. [His Lordship then quoted from the speech of Lord Denning at 412].

If [Lord Denning's] opinion is right and there are no restricting qualifications which ought to be applied to it, Quick was setting up a defence of insanity. He may have been at the material time in a condition of mental disorder manifesting itself in violence. Such manifestations had occurred before and might recur. The difficulty arises as soon as the question is asked whether he should be detained in a mental hospital. No mental hospital would admit a diabetic merely because he had a low blood sugar reaction; and common sense is affronted by the prospect of a diabetic being sent to such a hospital, when in most cases the disordered mental condition can be rectified quickly by pushing a lump of sugar or a teaspoonful of glucose into the patient's mouth.

The 'affront to common sense' argument, however, has its own inherent weakness, as Sir Joseph Moloney pointed out. If an accused is shown to have done a criminal act while suffering from a 'defect of reason from disease of the mind', it matters not whether the condition of the mind is curable or incurable, transitory or permanent: see *per* Devlin J in *R v Kemp* [1957] 1 QB 399, 407. If the condition is transitory, the Secretary of State may have a difficult problem of disposal; but what happens to those found not guilty by reason of insanity is not a matter for the courts.

In *R v Kemp* [1957] 1 QB 399, where the violent act was alleged to have been done during a period of unconsciousness arising from arteriosclerosis, counsel for the accused submitted that his client had done what he had during a period of mental confusion arising from a physical, not a mental, disease. Devlin J rejected that argument, saying at 407:

> It does not matter, for the purposes of the law, whether the defect of reason is due to a degeneration of the brain or to some other form of mental derangement. That may be a matter of importance medically, but it is of no importance to the law, which merely has to consider the state of mind in which the accused is, not how he got there.

Applied without qualification of any kind, Devlin J's statement of the law would have some surprising consequences. Take the not uncommon case of the rugby player who gets a kick on the head early in the game and plays on to the end in a state of automatism. If, while he was in that state, he assaulted the referee, it is difficult to envisage any court adjudging that he was not guilty by reason of insanity. Another type of case which could occur is that of the dental patient who kicks out while coming round from an anaesthetic. The law would be in a defective state if a patient accused of assaulting a dental nurse by kicking her while regaining consciousness could only excuse himself by raising the defence of insanity.

In *Hill v Baxter* [1958] 1 QB 277, the problem before the Divisional Court was whether the accused had put forward sufficient evidence on a charge of dangerous driving to justify the justices adjudging that he should be acquitted, there having been no dispute that at the time when his car collided with another one he was at the driving wheel. At the trial the accused had contended that he became unconscious as a result of being overcome by an unidentified illness. The court (Lord Goddard CJ Devlin and Pearson JJ) allowed an appeal by the prosecution against the verdict of acquittal. In the course of examining the evidence which had been put forward by the accused the judges made some comments of a general nature. Lord Goddard CJ at 282, referred to some observations of Humphreys J in *Kay v Butterworth* (1945) 61 TLR 452 which seemed to indicate that a man who became unconscious while driving due to the onset of a sudden illness should not be made liable at criminal law and then said at 283:

> I agree that there may be cases where the circumstances are such that the accused could not really be said to be driving at all. Suppose he had a stroke or an epileptic fit, both instances of what may properly be called acts of God; he might well be in the driver's seat even with his hands on the wheel, but in such a state of unconsciousness that he could not be said to be driving ... In this case, however, I am content to say that the evidence falls far short of what would justify a court holding that this man was in some automatous state.

Lord Goddard CJ did not equate unconsciousness due to a sudden illness, which must entail the malfunctioning of the mental processes of the sufferer, with disease of the mind, and in our judgment no one outside a court of law would. In *Hill v Baxter* [1958] 1 QB 277, 285, Devlin J accepted that some temporary loss of consciousness arising *accidentally* (the italics are ours) did not call for a verdict based on insanity. It is not clear what he meant by 'accidentally'. The context suggests that he may have meant 'unexpectedly' as can happen with some kinds of virus infections. He then said at 285:

> But if disease is present, the same thing may happen again, and therefore, since 1800, the law has provided that persons acquitted on this ground should be subject to restraint.

If that be right anyone suffering from a tooth abscess, who knows from past experience that he reacts violently to anaesthetics because of some constitutional bodily disorder which can be attributed to disease, might have to go on suffering or take the risk of being found insane unless he could find a dentist who would be prepared to take the risk of being kicked by a recovering patient. It seems to us that the law should not give the words 'defect of reason from disease of the mind' a meaning which would be regarded with incredulity outside a court ...

In this quagmire of law seldom entered nowadays save by those in desperate need of some kind of a defence, *Bratty v Attorney General for Northern Ireland* [1963] AC 386, 403, 412, 414 provides the only firm ground. Is there any discernible path? We think there is. Judges should follow in a common sense way their sense of fairness. This seems to have been the approach of the New Zealand Court of Appeal in *R v Cottle* [1958] NZLR 999, 1011 and of Sholl J in *R v Carter* [1959] VR 105, 110. In our judgment no help can be obtained by speculating (because that is what we would have to do) as to what the judges who answered the House of Lords' questions in 1843 meant by disease of the mind, still less what Sir Matthew Hale meant in the second half of the 17th century. A quick backward look at the state of medicine in 1843 will suffice to show how unreal it would be to apply the concepts of that age to the present time. Dr Simpson had not yet started his experiments with chloroform, the future Lord Lister was only 16 and laudanum was used and prescribed like aspirins are today. Our task has been to decide what the law means now by the words 'disease of the mind'. In our judgment the fundamental concept is of a malfunctioning of the mind caused by disease. A malfunctioning of mind of transitory effect caused by the application to the body of some external factor such as violence, drugs, including anaesthetics, alcohol and hypnotic influences cannot fairly be said to be due to disease. Such malfunctioning unlike that caused by a defect of reason from disease of the mind, will not always relieve an accused from criminal responsibility. A self-induced incapacity will not excuse (see *R v Lipman* [1970] 1 QB 152), nor will one which could have been reasonably foreseen as a result of either doing, or omitting to do something, as, for example, taking alcohol against medical advice after using certain prescribed drugs, or failing to have regular meals while taking insulin. From time to time difficult borderline cases are likely to arise. When they do, the test suggested by the New Zealand Court of Appeal in *R v Cottle* is likely to give the correct result, *viz*, can this mental condition be fairly regarded as amounting to or producing a defect of reason from disease of the mind?

In this case Quick's alleged mental condition, if it ever existed, was not caused by his diabetes but by his use of the insulin prescribed by his doctor. Such malfunctioning of his mind as there was, was caused by an external factor and not by a bodily disorder in the nature of a disease which disturbed the working of his mind. It follows in our judgment that Quick was entitled to have his defence of automatism left to the jury and that Bridge J's ruling as to the effect of the medical evidence called by him was wrong. Had the defence of automatism been left to the jury, a number of questions of fact would have had to be answered. If he was in a confused mental condition, was it due to a hypoglycaemic episode or to too much alcohol? If the former, to what extent had he brought about his condition by not following his doctor's instructions about taking regular meals? Did he know that he was getting into a hypoglycaemic episode? If yes, did he not use the antidote of eating a lump of sugar as he had been advised to do? On the evidence which was before the jury Quick might have had difficulty in answering these questions in a manner which would have relieved him of responsibility for his acts. We cannot say, however, with the requisite degree of confidence, that the jury would have convicted him. It follows that his conviction must be quashed on the ground that the verdict was unsatisfactory.

If Quick's conviction is quashed, what happens to Paddison's having regard to the fact that he was said to have aided an abetted Quick? The quashing of

Quick's conviction amounts in law to an acquittal. Can Paddison be deemed to have aided and abetted someone who has been adjudged 'not guilty'? As a general proposition of law, the answer to this question is a qualified 'yes'. The facts of each case, however, have to be considered and in particular what is alleged to have been done by way of aiding and abetting. In this case the allegation against Paddison was encouraged by conduct. The case against him was that he knew what Quick was going to do and encouraged him to do it by getting the other patients out of the way. If Quick acted without conscious volition, it is most unlikely that Paddison would have known what he intended to do. The quashing of Quick's conviction in our judgment introduced an element of unreality into the verdict against Paddison. It follows that that verdict too must be quashed as being unsatisfactory.

R v Sullivan [1984] 1 AC 156 (HL)

Lord Diplock: My Lords, the appellant, Mr Sullivan, a man of blameless reputation, has the misfortune to have been a lifelong sufferer from epilepsy. There was a period when he was subject to major seizures known as *grand mal*; but, as a result of treatment which he was receiving as an out-patient of the Maudsley Hospital from 1976 onwards, these major seizures had, by the use of drugs, been reduced by 1979 to seizures of less severity known as *petit mal*; or psychomotor epilepsy, though they continued to occur at a frequency of one or two per week.

One such seizure occurred on 8 May 1981, when Mr Sullivan, then aged 51, was visiting a neighbour, Mrs Killick, an old lady aged 86 for whom he was accustomed to perform regular acts of kindness. He was chatting there to a fellow visitor and friend of his, a Mr Payne aged 80, when the epileptic fit came on. It appears likely from the expert medical evidence about the way in which epileptics behave at the various stages of a *petit mal* seizure that Mr Payne got up from the chair to help Mr Sullivan. The only evidence of an eyewitness was that of Mrs Killick, who did not see what had happened before she saw Mr Payne lying on the floor and Mr Sullivan kicking him about the head and body, in consequence of which Mr Payne suffered injuries severe enough to require hospital treatment.

As a result of this occurrence Mr Sullivan was indicted upon two counts: the first was of causing grievous bodily harm with intent contrary to s 18 of the Offences Against the Person Act 1861; the second of causing grievous bodily harm contrary to s 20 of that Act. At his trial, which took place at the Central Criminal Court before Judge Lymbery and a jury, Mr Sullivan pleaded not guilty to both counts. Mrs Killick's evidence that he had kicked Mr Payne violently about the head and body was undisputed and Mr Sullivan himself gave evidence of his history of epilepsy and his absence of all recollection of what had occurred at Mrs Killick's flat between the time that he was chatting peacefully to Mr Payne there and his return to the flat somewhere else to find that Mr Payne was injured and that an ambulance had been sent for. The prosecution accepted his evidence as true. There was no cross-examination.

Counsel for Mr Sullivan wanted to rely upon the defence of automatism or, as Viscount Kilmuir LC had put it in *Bratty v Attorney General for Northern Ireland* [1963] AC 386, 405, 'non-insane' automatism; that is to say, that he had acted unconsciously and involuntarily in kicking Mr Payne, but that when doing so he was not 'insane' in the sense in which that expression is used as a term of art in English law, and in particular in s 2 of the Trial of Lunatics Act 1883, as amended by s 1 of the Criminal Procedure (Insanity) Act 1964. As was decided unanimously by this House in Bratty, before a defence of non-insane automatism may properly be left to the jury, some evidential foundation for it must be laid.

The evidential foundation that counsel laid before the jury in the instant case consisted of the testimony of two distinguished specialists from the neuropsychiatry epilepsy unit at the Maudsley Hospital, Dr Fenwick and Dr Taylor, as to the pathology of the various stages of a seizure due to psychomotor epilepsy. Their expert evidence, which was not disputed by the prosecution, was that Mr Sullivan's acts in kicking Mr Payne had all the characteristics of epileptic automatism at the third or post-ictal stage of petit mal; and that in view of his history of psychomotor epilepsy and hospital records of his behaviour during previous seizures, the strong probability was that Mr Sullivan's acts of violence towards Mr Payne took place while he was going through that stage.

The evidence as to the pathology of a seizure due to psychomotor epilepsy can be sufficiently stated for the purposes of this appeal by saying that after the first stage, the prodram, which precedes the fit itself, there is a second stage, the ictus, lasting a few seconds, during which there are electrical discharges into the temporal lobes of the brain of the sufferer. The effect of these discharges is to cause him in the post-ictus stage to make movements which he is not conscious that he is making, including, and this was a characteristic of previous seizures which Mr Sullivan had suffered, automatic movements of resistance to anyone trying to come to his aid. These movements of resistance might, though in practice they very rarely would, involve violence ...

The M'Naghten Rules have been used as a comprehensive definition for this purpose by the courts for the last 140 years. Most importantly, they were so used by this House in *Bratty v Attorney General for Northern Ireland* [1963] AC 386. That case was in some respects the converse of the instant case. Bratty was charged with murdering a girl by strangulation. He claimed to have been unconscious of what he was doing at the time he strangled the girl and he sought to run as alternative defences non-insane automatism and insanity. The only evidential foundation that he laid for either of these pleas was medical evidence that he might have been suffering from psychomotor epilepsy which, if he were, would account for his having been unconscious of what he was doing. No other pathological explanation of his actions having been carried out in a state of automatism was supported by evidence. The trial judge first put the defence of insanity to the jury. The jury rejected it; they declined to bring in the special verdict. Thereupon, the judge refused to put to the jury the alternative defence of automatism. His refusal was upheld by the Court of Criminal Appeal of Northern Ireland and subsequently by this House ...

In the instant case, as in *Bratty*, the only evidential foundation that was laid for any finding by the jury that Mr Sullivan was acting unconsciously and involuntarily when he was kicking Mr Payne, was that when he did so he was in the post-ictal stage of seizure of psychomotor epilepsy. The evidential foundation in the case of Bratty, that he was suffering from psychomotor epilepsy at the time he did the act with which he was charged, was very weak and was rejected by the jury; the evidence in Mr Sullivan's case, that he was so suffering when he was kicking Mr Payne, was very strong and would almost inevitably be accepted by a properly directed jury. It would be the duty of the judge to direct the jury that if they did accept that evidence the law required them to bring in a special verdict and none other. The governing statutory provision is to be found in s 2 of the Trial of Lunatics Act 1883. This says 'the jury *shall* return a special verdict ...'

My Lords, I can deal briefly with the various grounds on which it has been submitted that the instant case can be distinguished from what constituted the *ratio decidendi* in *Bratty v Attorney General for Northern Ireland* [1963] AC 386, and that it falls outside the ambit of the M'Naghten Rules.

First, it is submitted that the medical evidence in the instant case shows that psychomotor epilepsy is not a disease of the mind, whereas in *Bratty* it was accepted by all the doctors that it was. The only evidential basis for this submission is that Dr Fenwick said that in medical terms to constitute a 'disease of the mind' or 'mental illness', which he appeared to regard as interchangeable descriptions, a disorder of brain functions (which undoubtedly occurs during a seizure in psychomotor epilepsy) must be prolonged for a period of time usually more than a day; while Dr Taylor would have it that the disorder must continue for a minimum of a month to qualify for the description 'a disease of the mind'.

The nomenclature adopted by the medical profession may change from time to time; *Bratty* was tried in 1961. But the meaning of the expression 'disease of the mind' as the cause of 'a defect of reason' remains unchanged for the purposes of the application of the M'Naghten Rules. I agree with what was said by Devlin J in *R v Kemp* [1957] 1 QB 399, 407, that 'mind' in the M'Naghten Rules is used in the ordinary sense of the mental faculties of reason, memory and understanding. If the effect of a disease is to impair these faculties so severely as to have either of the consequences referred to in the latter part of the rules, it matters not whether the aetiology of the impairment is organic, as in epilepsy, or functional, or whether the impairment itself is permanent or is transient and intermittent, provided that it subsisted at the time of commission of the act. The purpose of the legislation relating to the defence of insanity, ever since its origin in 1800, has been to protect society against recurrence of the dangerous conduct. The duration of a temporary suspension of the mental faculties of reason, memory and understanding, particularly if, as in Mr Sullivan's case, it is recurrent, cannot on any rational ground be relevant to the application by the courts of the M'Naghten Rules, though it may be relevant to the course adopted by the Secretary of State, to whom the responsibility for how the defendant is to be dealt with passes after the return of the special verdict of 'not guilty by reason of insanity'.

To avoid misunderstanding I ought perhaps to add that in expressing my agreement with what was said by Devlin J in *Kemp*, where the disease that caused the temporary and intermittent impairment of the mental faculties was arteriosclerosis, I do not regard that learned judge as excluding the possibility of non-insane automatism (for which the proper verdict would be a verdict of 'not guilty') in cases where temporary impairment (not being self-induced by consuming drink or drugs) resulted from some external physical factor such as a blow on the head causing concussion or the administration of an anaesthetic for therapeutic purposes. I mention this because *R v Quick* [1973] QB 910, Lawton LJ appears to have regarded the ruling in *Kemp* as going as far as this. If it had done, it would have been inconsistent with the speeches in this House in *Bratty* [1963] AC 386, where *Kemp* was alluded to without disapproval by Viscount Kilmuir LC at 403, and received the express approval of Lord Denning at 411. The instant case, however, does not in my view afford an appropriate occasion for exploring possible causes of non-insane automatism.

The only other submission in support of Mr Sullivan's appeal which I think it necessary to mention is that, because the expert evidence was to the effect that Mr Sullivan's acts in kicking Mr Payne were unconscious and thus 'involuntary' in the legal sense of that term, his state of mind was not dealt with by the M'Naghten Rules at all, since it was not covered by the phrase 'as not to know the nature and quality of the act he was doing'. Quite apart from being contrary to all three speeches in this House in *Bratty v Attorney General for Northern Ireland* [1963] AC 386, this submission appears to me, with all respect to counsel, to be quite unarguable. Dr Fenwick himself accepted it as an accurate description of Mr Sullivan's mental state in the post-ictal stage of a seizure. The audience to whom the phrase in the M'Naghten Rules was addressed consisted of peers of the realm in the 1840s when a certain orotundity of diction had not yet fallen out of fashion. Addressed to an audience of jurors in the 1980s it might more aptly be expressed as 'He did not know what he was doing'.

My Lords, it is natural to feel reluctant to attach the label of insanity to a sufferer from psychomotor epilepsy of the kind to which Mr Sullivan was subject, even though the expression in the context of a special verdict of 'not guilty by reason of insanity' is a technical one which includes a purely temporary and intermittent suspension of the mental faculties of reason, memory and understanding resulting from the occurrence of an epileptic fit. But the label is contained in the current statute, it has appeared in this statute's predecessors ever since 1800. It does not lie within the power of the courts to alter it. Only Parliament can do that. It has done so twice; it could do so once again ...

R v Hennessy [1989] 1 WLR 287 (CA)

Lord Lane: ... The facts which gave rise to the charges, is so far as material, were these. On Thursday 28 May 1987, two police constables, Barnes and Grace, were on duty in St Leonards-on-Sea on the Sussex coast, among other things looking for a Ford Granada car which had been stolen. They found the car. It was unattended. They kept it under watch. As they watched they saw the appellant get into the car, switch on the headlights and ignition, start the car and drive off. The appellant at the wheel of the car correctly stopped the car at a set of traffic lights which were showing red against him. PC Grace then went over to the car as it was stationary, removed the ignition keys from the ignition lock, but not before the appellant had tried to drive the motor car away and escape from the attention of the policeman. The appellant was put in the police car. On the way to the police station an informal conversation about motor vehicles took place between the appellant and the police officers, in particular about the respective merits of the new Rover motor car and the Ford Sierra. Indeed, the appellant appeared to PC Barnes not only to be fully in possession of his faculties but to be quite cheerful and intelligent. Indeed he went so far as to say to the police officer that if he had only got the car, which he was in the process of removing, into the open road, he would have given the policemen a real run for their money.

However after having been at the police station for a time, the appellant was at a later stage escorted by PC Barnes to hospital. He seemed to be normal when he left the cell block at the police station, but when he arrived at the hospital he appeared to be dazed and confused. He complained to the sister in the casualty ward that he had failed to take his insulin and indeed had had no insulin since the previous Monday when he should have had regular self-injection doses. He was given insulin, with which he injected himself, and the hospital discharged him and he was taken back to the police station.

The appellant gave evidence to the effect that he had been a diabetic for about 10 years. He needed, in order to stabilise his metabolism, two insulin injections on a daily basis, morning and afternoon. The amount required would depend on factors such as stress and eating habits. He was on a strict carbohydrate diet. At the time of the offence he said he had been having marital and employment problems. His wife had submitted a divorce petition some time shortly before, and he was very upset. He had not been eating and he had not been taking his insulin. He remembered very few details of the day. He could recall being handcuffed and taken to the charge room at the police station. He remembered being given insulin at the hospital and injecting himself and he remembers feeling better when he got back to the police station afterwards. He said he did not recall taking the car ...

The defence to these charges accordingly was that the appellant had failed to take his proper twice-a-day dose of insulin for two or three days and at the time the events in question took place he was in a state of automatism and did not know what he was doing. Therefore it is submitted that the guilty mind, which is necessary to be proved by the prosecution, was not proved, and accordingly that he was entitled to be acquitted.

The judge took the view, rightly in our view, that the appellant, having put his state of mind in issue, the preliminary question which he had to decide was whether this was truly a case of automatism or whether it was a case of legal 'insanity' within the M'Naghten Rules (see *M'Naghten's* case (1843) 10 Cl and Fin 200, [1843–60] All ER Rep 229). He concluded that it was the latter, and he so ruled, whereupon the appellant changed his plea to guilty and was sentenced to the terms of imprisonment suspended which we have already mentioned. The judge then certified the case fit for appeal in the terms which I have already described.

The M'Naghten Rules in the earlier part of the last century have in many ways lost their importance; they certainly have lost the importance they once had, but they are still relevant in so far as they may affect the defence of automatism. Although the rules deal with what they describe as insanity, it is insanity in the legal sense and not in the medical or psychological sense ...

The importance of the rules in the present context, namely the context of automatism, is this. If the defendant did not know the nature and quality of his act because of something which *did not* amount to defect of reason from disease of the mind then he will probably be entitled to be acquitted on the basis that the necessary criminal intent which the prosecution has to prove is not proved. But, if, on the other hand, his failure to realise the nature and quality of his act was due to a defect of reason from disease of the mind, then in the eyes of the law he is suffering from insanity, albeit M'Naghten insanity ...

The question in many cases, and this is one such case, is whether the function of the mind was disturbed on the one hand by disease or on the other hand by some external factor. The matter was discussed, as counsel for the appellant has helpfully pointed out to us, by the House of Lords in *R v Sullivan* [1984] AC 156 at 172 in the speech of Lord Diplock, which reads as follows:

> I agree with what was said by Devlin J in *R v Kemp* [1957] 1 QB 399 at 407 that 'mind' in the M'Naghten Rules is used in the ordinary sense of the mental faculties of reason, memory and understanding. If the effect of a disease is to impair these faculties so severely as to have either of the consequences referred to in the latter part of the rules, it matters not whether the aetiology of the impairment is organic, as in epilepsy, or functional, or whether the impairment itself is permanent or is transient and intermittent, provided that it subsisted at the time of commission of the act. The purpose of the legislation relating to the defence of insanity, ever since its origin in 1880, has been to protect society against recurrence of the dangerous conduct. The duration of a temporary suspension of the mental faculties of reason, memory and understanding, particularly if, as in the appellant's case, it is recurrent, cannot on any rational ground be relevant to the application by the courts of the M'Naghten Rules, though it may be relevant to the course adopted by the Secretary of State, to whom the responsibility for how the defendant is to be dealt with passes after the return of the special verdict of not guilty by reason of insanity.

The point was neatly raised in *R v Quick, R v Paddison* [1973] QB 910, also referred to us by counsel for the appellant, in which Lawton LJ reviewed the authorities.

It might perhaps help if I read a short passage from the headnote ([1973] QB 910):

> The defendants, Q and P, nurses at a mental hospital, were jointly and severally charged with assaulting a patient occasioning actual bodily harm. Both pleaded not guilty. Q, a diabetic, relied on the defence of automatism. He gave evidence that he had taken insulin as prescribed on the morning of the assault, had drunk a quantity of spirits and eaten little food thereafter and had no recollection of the assault. He called medical evidence to the effect that his condition at the material time was consistent with that of hypoglycaemia. The judge ruled that that evidence could only support a defence of insanity, not automatism. Q then pleaded guilty and P was convicted of aiding and abetting Q by encouragement. The defendants appealed against conviction.

I turn to the passage in the judgment where Lawton LJ said ([1973] QB 910 at 922–23):

> A malfunctioning of the mind of transitory effect caused by the application to the body of some external factor such as violence, drugs, including anaesthetics, alcohol and hypnotic influences cannot fairly be said to be due to disease. Such malfunctioning, unlike that caused by a defect of reason from disease of the mind, will not always relieve an accused from criminal responsibility ... In this case Quick's alleged mental condition, if it ever existed, was not caused by his diabetes but by his use of the insulin prescribed by his doctor. Such malfunctioning of his mind as there was, was caused by an external factor and not by bodily disorder in the nature of a disease which disturbed the working of his mind. It follows in our judgment that Quick was entitled to have his defence of automatism left to the jury and that Bridge J's ruling as to the effect of the medical evidence called by him was wrong.

Thus in *R v Quick* the fact that his condition was, or may have been, due to the injections of insulin meant that the malfunction was due to an external factor and not to the disease. The drug it was that caused the hypoglycaemia, the low blood sugar. As suggested in another passage of the judgment of Lawton LJ, hyperglycaemia, high blood sugar, caused by an inherent defect and not corrected by insulin is a disease, and if, as the defendant was asserting here, it does cause a malfunction of the mind, then the case may fall within the M'Naghten Rules.

The burden of the argument of counsel for the appellant to us is this. It is that the appellant's depression and marital troubles were a sufficiently potent external factor in his condition to override, so to speak, the effect of the diabetic shortage of insulin on him. He refers us not only to the passage which I have already cited in *R v Quick*, but also to a further passage in *Hill v Baxter* [1958] 1 QB 277 at 285 which is part of the judgment of Devlin J, sitting with Lord Goddard CJ and Pearson J, in the Divisional Court of Queen's Bench Division. It reads as follows:

> I have drawn attention to the fact that the accused did not set up a defence of insanity. For the purposes of the criminal law there are two categories of mental irresponsibility, one where the disorder is due to disease and the other where it is not. The distinction is not an arbitrary one. If disease is not the cause, if there is some temporary loss of consciousness arising accidentally, it is reasonable to hope that it will not be repeated and that it is safe to let an acquitted man go entirely free. If, however, disease is present, the same thing may happen again and therefore since 1800 the law has provided that persons acquitted on this ground should be subject to restraint.

That is the submission made by counsel as a basis for saying the judge's decision was wrong and that this was a matter which should have been decided by the jury.

In our judgment, stress, anxiety and depression can no doubt be the result of the operation of external factors, but they are not, it seems to us, in themselves separately or together external factors of the kind capable in law of causing or contributing to a state of automatism. They constitute a state of mind which is prone to recur. They lack the feature of novelty or accident, which is the basis of the distinction drawn by Lord Diplock in *R v Sullivan*. It is contrary to the observations of Devlin J, to which we have just referred in *Hill v Baxter*. It does not, in our judgment, come within the scope of the exception 'some external physical factor such as a blow on the head ... or the administration of an anaesthetic ...' (see *R v Sullivan* [1984] AC 156 at 172) ...

R v Bingham [1991] Crim LR 433 (CA)

Facts: Following arrest for shoplifting, the defendant, a diabetic, was charged with theft of a can of 'Coke' and sandwiches, worth £1.16, at a time when he had £90 in his pocket. He had paid for one can of Coke, and was stopped on leaving the store, following which he replied to questions with 'no comment'. His defence was automatism based on the claim that, at the time, he was suffering from hypoglycaemia and was unaware of his actions. The judge refused to leave that defence to the jury.

Held, allowing the appeal, the arguments put to the judge failed to distinguish between hyperglycaemia and hypoglycaemia, the former being too much sugar in the blood, and the latter too little. Hyperglycaemia might raise difficult problems about the M'Naghten Rules and verdicts of not guilty by reason of insanity. Hypoglycaemia was not caused by the initial disease of diabetes, but by the treatment in the form of too much insulin, or by insufficient quality or quantity of food to counterbalance the insulin. Generally speaking, that would not give rise to a verdict of not guilty by reason of insanity but would, if it were established and showed that the necessary intent was or might be lacking, provide a satisfactory defence to an alleged crime such as theft, due to lack of *mens rea*. Those simple facts would be plain to anyone who troubled to read *Quick* (1973) 57 Cr App R and *Hennessy* [1989] 1 WLR 287. In the present case, the problem was hypoglycaemia and the judge had to decide whether, on the evidence, there was a *prima facie* case for the jury to decide whether the defendant was suffering from its effects and, if so, whether the Crown had shown that he had the necessary intent under the Theft Act. It was not doubted that the defendant was a diabetic and there was evidence that he might have been suffering from the effects of a low blood sugar level at the relevant time. That evidence should have been left to the jury.

R v Burgess [1991] 1 QB 92 (CA)

Lord Lane CJ: On 20 July 1989 in the Crown Court at Bristol before Judge Sir Ian Lewis and a jury the appellant was found not guilty by reason of insanity on a charge of wounding with intent. He was ordered to be admitted and detained in such hospital as the Secretary of State should direct.

He now appeals against that verdict by certificate of the trial judge under s 12 of the Criminal Appeal Act 1968.

The appellant did not dispute the fact that in the early hours of 2 June 1988 he had attacked Katrina Curtis hitting her on the head first with a bottle when she was asleep, then with a video recorder and finally grasping her round the throat. She suffered a gaping 3 cm laceration to her scalp requiring sutures.

His case was that he lacked the *mens rea* necessary to make him guilty of the offence, because he was 'sleep-walking' when he attacked Miss Curtis. He was, it was alleged, suffering from 'non-insane' automatism and he called medical evidence, in particular from Dr d'Orban and Dr Eames, to support that contention.

The prosecution on the other hand contended that this was not a case of automatism at all, but that the appellant was conscious of what he was doing. If, contrary to that contention, he was not conscious of what he was doing, then the case fell within the M'Naghten Rules, and accordingly the verdict should be not guilty by reason of insanity. The prosecution called an equally eminent expert in the shape of Dr Fenwick.

Where the defence of automatism is raised by a defendant two questions fall to be decided by the judge before the defence can be left to the jury. The first is whether a proper evidential foundation for the defence of automatism has been laid. The second is whether the evidence shows the case to be one of insane automatism, that is to say a case which falls within the M'Naghten Rules, or one of non-insane automatism.

The judge in the present case undertook that task and on the second question came to the conclusion that (assuming the appellant was not conscious at the time of what he was doing), on any view of the medical evidence so far as automatism was concerned, it amounted to evidence of insanity within the M'Naghten Rules and not merely to evidence of non-insane automatism.

The sole ground of appeal is that the ruling was wrong.

The jury then had to decide on the basis of the judge's direction, which of course followed his ruling, whether the appellant was conscious when he struck Miss Curtis, in which case the verdict would be guilty, or whether he was not guilty by reason of insanity. As already indicated, they came to the latter conclusion.

The facts required setting out in a little more detail.

Miss Curtis occupied the flat immediately above that of the appellant. The two were on friendly terms. They were in the habit of watching video tapes together in her flat. She realised that the appellant was probably in love with her. She did not wish to allow their relationship to develop beyond mere friendship. The appellant was then 32 years of age. He was sexually inexperienced and of a somewhat solitary disposition. He had always behaved impeccably towards her and had made no physical advances. He had hopes that her friendship towards him might develop into something deeper.

On the evening in question the appellant came up to her flat with the video tapes. They had one glass of Martini each. There is no suggestion of any intoxication. Having watched one video tape, she fell asleep on the sofa. The next thing she knew was that something hard had hit her on the head. This must have been about one to one and a half hours later, so it seems. She woke up, dazed, to find herself surrounded by broken glass and confronted by the appellant with the video recorder held up high, clearly intending to bring it down on her head, which he did. He was speaking loudly. He seemed vicious and angry – quite out of character. She fell to the floor, whereupon he put a hand round her throat. With great presence of mind, she managed to say, 'I love you Bar', whereupon he appeared to come to his senses and to show great anxiety for what he had done. He later telephoned for an ambulance. It seems that he must have unplugged the video recorder detaching the various leads and then carried it round to where Miss Curtis lay ...

[His Lordship quoted the material part of the M'Naghten Rules (set out at the start of this chapter) and went on:]

The reason for the finding of not guilty in these circumstances is of course the absence of the intent which must be proved to accompany the defendant's actions before guilt can be established.

What the law regards as insanity for the purposes of these enactments may be far removed from what would be regarded as insanity by a psychiatrist.

There can be no doubt but that the appellant, on the basis of the jury's verdict, was labouring under such a defect of reason as not to know what he was doing when he wounded Miss Curtis. The question is whether that was from 'disease of the mind'.

The first point that has to be understood is that the phrase is 'disease of the mind' and not 'disease of the brain' ...

The appellant plainly suffered from a defect of reason from some sort of failure (for lack of a better term) of the mind causing him to act as he did without conscious motivation. His mind was to some extent controlling his actions, which were purposive rather than the result simply of muscular spasm, but without his being consciously aware of what he was doing. Can it be said that that 'failure' was a *disease* of the mind rather than a defect or failure of the mind not due to disease? That is the distinction, by no means always easy to draw, upon which this case depends, as others have depended in the past.

One can perhaps narrow the field of enquiry still further by eliminating what are sometimes called the 'external factors' such as concussion caused by a blow on the head. There were no such factors here. Whatever the cause may have been, it was an 'internal' cause. The possible disappointment or frustration caused by unrequited love is not to be equated with something such as concussion. On this aspect of the case, we respectfully adopt what was said by Martin JA giving the judgment of the court in the Ontario Court of Appeal in *R v Rabey* (1977) 17 OR (2d) 1 at 17, 22, which was approved by a majority in the Supreme Court of Canada (see [1980] 2 SCR 513 at 519 where the facts bore a similarity to those in the instant case although the diagnosis was different):

> Any malfunctioning of the mind, or mental disorder having its source primarily in some subjective condition or weakness internal to the accused (whether fully understood or not), may be a 'disease of the mind' if it prevents the accused from knowing what he is doing, but transient disturbances of consciousness due to certain specific external factors do not fall within the concept of disease of the mind ... In my view, the ordinary stresses and disappointments of life which are the common lot of mankind do not constitute an external cause constituting an explanation for a malfunctioning of the mind which takes it out of the category of a 'disease of the mind'. To hold otherwise would deprive the concept of an external factor of any real meaning.

This distinction between 'internal' and 'external' factors appears in the speech of Lord Diplock in *R v Sullivan* [1984] AC 156 at 172 [from which his Lordship then quoted].

What help does one derive from the authorities as to the meaning of 'disease' in this context? Lord Denning in *Bratty v Attorney General for Northern Ireland* [1963] AC 386 at 412 said:

> On the other hand discussed by Devlin J, namely what is a 'disease of the mind' within the M'Naghten Rules, I would agree with him that this is a

> question for the judge. The major mental diseases, which the doctors call psychoses, such as schizophrenia, are clearly diseases of the mind. But in *R v Charlson* [1955] 1 WLR 317, Barry J seems to have assumed that the other diseases such as epilepsy or cerebral tumour are not diseases of the mind, even when they are such as to manifest themselves in violence. I do not agree with this. It seems to me that any mental disorder which has manifested itself in violence and is prone to recur is a disease of the mind. At any rate it is the sort of disease for which a person should be detained in hospital rather than be given an unqualified acquittal.

It seems to us that if there is a danger of recurrence that may be an added reason for categorising the condition as a disease of the mind. On the other hand, the absence of the danger of recurrence is not a reason for saying that it cannot be a disease of the mind. Subject to that possible qualification, we respectfully adopt Lord Denning's suggested definition.

There have been several occasions when during the course of judgments in the Court of Appeal and the House of Lords observations have been made, *obiter*, about the criminal responsibility of sleep-walkers, where sleep-walking had been used as a self-evident illustration of non-insane automatism. For example, in the speech of Lord Denning, from which we have already cited an extract, appears this passage at ([1963] AC 386 at 409):

> No act is punishable if it is done involuntarily: and an involuntary act in this context – some people nowadays prefer to speak of it as 'automatism' – means an act which is done by the muscles without any control by the mind such as a spasm, a reflex action or a convulsion; or an act done by a person who is not conscious of what he is doing such as an act done whilst suffering from concussion or whilst sleep-walking. The point was well put by Stephen J in 1889: '... can anyone doubt that a man who, though he might be perfectly sane, committed what would otherwise be a crime in a state of somnambulism, would be entitled to be acquitted? And why is this? Simply because he would not know what he was doing'; see *R v Tolson* ((1889) 23 QBD 168 at 187, [1886–90] All ER Rep 26 at 37) ...

One turns then to examine the evidence upon which the judge had to base his decision and for this purpose the two medical experts called by the defence are the obvious principal sources. Dr d'Orban in examination-in-chief said:

> On the evidence available to me, and subject to the results of the tests when they became available, I came to the same conclusion as Dr Nicholas and Dr Eames, whose reports I had read, and that was that [the appellant's] actions had occurred during the course of a sleep disorder.

He was asked, 'Assuming this is a sleep-associated automatism, is it an internal or external factor?' He answered: 'In this particular case, I think that one would have to see it as an internal factor.'

Then in cross-examination:

> *Q*: Would you go so far as to say that it was liable to recur?
>
> *A*: It is possible for it to recur, yes.
>
> *Judge Lewis:* Is this a case of automatism associated with a pathological condition or not?
>
> *A*: I think the answer would have to be Yes, because it is an abnormality of the brain function, so it would be regarded as a pathological condition.

Dr Eames in cross-examination agreed with Dr d'Orban as to the internal rather than the external factor. He accepted that there is a liability to recurrence of sleepwalking. He could not go so far as to say that there is no liability of recurrence of serious violence but he agreed with the other medical witnesses that there is no recorded case of violence of this sort recurring.

The prosecution, as already indicated, called Dr Fenwick, whose opinion was that his was not a sleep-walking episode at all. If it was a case where the appellant was unconscious of what he was doing, the most likely explanation was that he was in what is described as a hysterical dissociative state. That is a state in which, for psychological reasons, such as being overwhelmed by his emotions, the person's brain works in a different way. He carries out acts of which he has no knowledge and for which he has no memory. It is quite different from sleep-walking.

He then went on to describe features of sleep-walking. This is what he said:

> First, violent acts in sleep-walking are very common. In just an exposure of one day to a sleep-walking clinic, you will hear of how people are kicked in bed, hit in bed, partially strangled – it is usually just arms round the neck, in bed, which is very common. Serious violence fortunately is rare. Serious violence does recur, or certainly the propensity for it to recur is there, although there are very few cases in the literature – in fact I know of none – in which somebody has come to court twice for a sleep-walking offence. This does not mean that sleep-walking violence does not recur; what it does mean is that those who are associated with the sleeper take the necessary precautions. Finally, should a person be detained in hospital? The answer to that is: Yes, because sleep-walking is treatable. Violent night terrors are treatable. There is a lot which can be done for the sleep-walker, so sending them to hospital after a violent act to have their sleep-walking sorted out makes good sense.

Dr Fenwick was also of the view that in certain circumstances hysterical dissociative states are also subject to treatment.

It seems to us that on th[e] evidence the judge was right to conclude that this was an abnormality or disorder albeit transitory, due to an internal factor, whether functional or organic, which had manifested itself in violence. It was a disorder or abnormality which might recur, though the possibility of it recurring in the form of serious violence was unlikely. Therefore, since this was a legal problem to be decided on legal principles, it seems to us that on those principles the answer was as the judge found it to be. It does however go further than that. Dr d'Orban, as already described, stated it as his view that the condition would be regarded as pathological. Pathology is the science of diseases. It seems therefore that in this respect at least there is some similarity between the law and medicine.

The judge was alive to the apparent incongruity of labelling this sort of disability as insanity. He drew attention, as we would also wish to do, to the passage of the speech of Lord Diplock in *R v Sullivan* [1984] AC 156 at 173 where he said:

> ...it is natural to feel reluctant to attach the label of insanity to a sufferer from psychomotor epilepsy of the kind to which the appellant was subject, even though the expression in the context of a special verdict of not guilty by reason of insanity is a technical one which includes a purely temporary and intermittent suspension of the mental faculties of reason, memory and understanding resulting from the occurrence of an epileptic fit. But the label is contained in the current statute, it has appeared in this statute's predecessors ever since 1800. It does not lie within the power of the courts to

> alter it. Only Parliament can do that. It has done so twice; it could do so once again.

This appeal must accordingly be dismissed.

R v Thomas [1995] Crim LR 314 (CA)

The appellant was convicted of burglary and acquitted of an alternative count of robbery. The prosecution case was that the appellant and another broke into a private house and stole four candlesticks and two statues. At the time of her arrest, the appellant was very drunk. She did not give evidence. Medical evidence from the appellant's doctor was called to the effect that the appellant had a mental condition, hypomania, which was aggravated by drink or drugs, and which, if aggravated, rendered her so confused that she would be unable to form the specific intents for the offences of burglary and robbery. A doctor called by the prosecution gave evidence that hypomania meant slight or mania of little degree. His view was that the appellant would have been able to form the specific intents for the offences. At the end of the cross-examination of the appellant's doctor, the judge put certain questions to him, the answers to which were to the effect that hypomania was a disease of the mind and that the appellant would have been unaware of the nature or quality of her acts. In the absence of the jury, the judge raised the question of leaving the defence of insanity to the jury. Counsel for the appellant indicated that the defence did not wish to raise the issue, and submitted that this was not an appropriate case for the judge to raise it. The judge ruled that the question of insanity should be left to the jury and he so directed them.

On appeal against conviction, counsel for the appellant submitted, *inter alia*, that: (1) where medical evidence was called to the effect that the appellant could not have formed the specific intent for the offences, the judge erred in leaving to the jury, against the wishes of the appellant's counsel, the defence of insanity and in ruling that he was obliged to do so; (2) to leave such a defence overcomplicated the case: it failed to differentiate between the ability to form a specific intent and the ability to appreciate the nature and quality of her acts; and (3) the judge's direction was not sufficiently clear.

Held, allowing the appeal, the judge's decision to raise the issue of insanity and his direction to the jury on the matter were material irregularities. Insanity was not a defence raised by the appellant or her counsel. Her defence was simply that by reason of her hypomania, and the drink that she had taken, the jury could not be sure that she had been capable of forming the specific intents required by the indictment. It was then for the Crown to rebut that. The judge thought that he had a duty to raise the issue of insanity. As a practical matter, the issue did not provide an additional defence for the appellant. A judge might well have a duty in an appropriate case to raise defences open to a defendant where the burden of disproving that defence rested on the prosecution. However, the situation was not the same where the defence placed a burden of proof upon a defendant. The principle was correctly stated in *Archbold*, at paragraph 17.111, and was consistent with the views expressed in *Dickie* (1984) 79 Cr App R 213 at 218, *per* Watkins LJ, namely that in certain exceptional circumstances a judge can of his own volition raise an issue of insanity and leave it to the jury, providing there is evidence embracing all the relevant considerations in the M'Naghten Rules. There might be cases, for example, of homicide, where an accused had raised a defence of diminished responsibility, where a judge would be entitled of his own volition to raise the issue. However, it would have to be a rare and exceptional case. It was to be regretted that the judge asked the questions of the appellant's doctor, a consequence of which was that the jury might well have supposed that the appellant would only have been incapable of forming the necessary specific intentions if she had been legally insane. The judge's direction might well have misled the jury as to the burden of proof on one issue left to them, namely had the appellant the necessary intent to support a charge of robbery or, alternatively, a charge of burglary. The issue of insanity was a complication which the judge should have avoided and from which the jury should have been spared.

Either: not knowing nature of act or not knowing act wrong

R v Codère (1916) 12 Cr App R 21 (CA)

Lord Reading CJ: ... The appellant was a lieutenant in the Canadian militia for 18 months or two years before the war. After the war broke out he came to this country with the Canadian contingent as lieutenant, and in December last his regiment was quartered at Bramshot camp; the appellant was living in a house with the colonel and major of the regiment. On 3 December he seems to have induced the bank to cash two cheques for £60 and £90 on the promise that he would bring Canadian currency there to be changed into English money. About that time, at what precise moment is not clear, it appears that Ozanne was in possession of Canadian notes of the value of about $1,500, and discussed the question of changing them at mess, when the appellant was present. Having got the two cheques cashed without having money sufficient to meet them, the appellant was bound to find money to put his account in funds. Ozanne appears to have been taken by him to Arundel House, and there beyond all question to have been put to death by him.

It is said that the evidence shows that the appellant was not a person who ought to be convicted of murder, but that the right verdict should have been that he was guilty of the act charged, but was insane so as not to be responsible according to law for his actions at the time. Mr Foote [for the appellant] has addressed an argument to us based on *M'Naghten's* case, which is the classic authority on the subject, which in substance resolved itself into this, that we must assume that when the law says that the question is whether the accused was labouring under such a defect of reason, from disease of the mind, as not to know the nature and quality of the act he was doing, we must read 'nature' to have reference to the physical act, and 'quality' to refer to the morality of the act, and that therefore the jury should be asked if he knew he was doing wrong. The argument advanced is that the judge ought to tell the jury that 'quality' means, 'Did the accused person know that the act was immoral?' and when one stops and asks the meaning of 'immoral' we get to the first of the difficulties which faced Mr Foote.

It is said that 'quality' is to be regarded as characterising the moral, as contrasted with the physical, aspect of the deed. The court cannot agree with that view of the meaning of the words 'nature and quality'. The court is of opinion that in using the language 'nature and quality' the judges were only dealing with the physical character of the act, and were not intending to distinguish between the physical and moral aspects of the act. That is the law as it has been laid down by judges in many directions to juries, and as the court understands it to be at the present time.

We then come to the second branch of the test, namely if he knew the physical nature of the act did he know that he was doing wrong? Mr Foote has argued that it is not enough that he knew the act was contrary to law and punishable by law, and that, even if he did know that when killing Ozanne, yet the jury ought to have been told that they must find a special verdict under s 2(1) of the Trial of Lunatics Act, 1883, unless they came to the conclusion that he knew that the act was morally wrong. The question of the distinction between morally and legally wrong opens wide doors. In a case of this kind, namely killing, it does not seem debatable that the appellant could have thought that the act was not morally wrong, judged by the ordinary standards, when the act is punishable by law, and is known by him to be punishable by law. It was suggested at one time in the course of the argument that the question should be judged by the standard of the accused, but it is obvious that this proposition is wholly untenable, and would tend to excuse crimes without number, and to weaken the law to an alarming degree. It is conceded now that the standard to be applied is whether according to the ordinary standard adopted by reasonable men the act was right or wrong. There may be cases where it is difficult to decide that question, but that is not the case here. The judges in *M'Naghten's* case, in answering the second and third questions put to them, said, 'If the accused was conscious that the act was one which he ought not to do, and if that act was at the same time contrary to the law of the land, he is punishable; and the usual course, therefore, has been to leave the question to the jury, whether the party accused had a sufficient degree of reason to know that he was doing an act that was wrong'. That is the accepted test, and applying it in this case there can be no room for doubt; once it is clear that the appellant knew that the act was wrong in law, then he was doing an act which he was conscious he ought not to do, and as it was against the law, it was punishable by law; assuming, therefore, that he knew the nature and quality of the act, he was guilty of murder, and was properly convicted.

The difficulty no doubt arises over the words 'conscious that the act was one which he ought not to do', but, looking at all the answers in *M'Naghten's* case, it seems that if it is punishable by law it is an act which he ought not to do, and that is the meaning in which the phrase is used in that case. There may be minor cases before a court of summary jurisdiction where that view may be open to doubt, but in cases such as these the true view is what we have just said.

In approaching the facts it is right to say undoubtedly on the evidence the appellant is possessed of a mind of very inferior quality. He was always known as being abnormal mentally; he was called in Quebec and in the regiment *'Le fou Codère'*. Instances were given and statements made in evidence that show, both from his own want of mental capacity and from his family history, that he cannot be regarded as an ordinary person. On the other hand, evidence was given to show that he knew quite enough to know the nature and quality of the act, namely that he was killing a man in order to retain money which it was his duty to hand over to the deceased and which he was not in a position to hand over, at any rate without putting himself in a very serious position. If Ozanne were out of the way, it might appear that he had run away with the money, and unless the crime could be brought home to the appellant it might never have been proved that he had the money. Then he takes Ozanne to the house and kills him, tries to conceal the fact that he is killed, and actually gets the two men to help him to conceal the body. It is true he had spoken to other men in a way which showed that he viewed very lightly the purpose which he had formed. All of these facts show that there was evidence which it was proper to leave to the jury that he was conscious of the act he was doing within the rules in *M'Naghten's* case. It was open to the jury to find that he did know, although he was a person of this peculiar type of mind ...

R v Windle [1952] 2 QB 526 (CA)

Facts: The appellant was convicted of the murder of his wife. He was a man, 40 years of age, of little resolution and weak character, and was married to a woman 18 years his senior. His married life was very unhappy; his wife was always speaking of committing suicide and the doctors who gave evidence at the trial were of opinion, from the history of the case, that she was certifiably insane. The appellant frequently discussed his home life with his workmates, until, as one of them said, they were sick and tired of hearing about it. Eventually a workmate said to the appellant, 'Give her a dozen aspirins', and on the following day the appellant gave his wife 100 tablets. He sent for a doctor and told him that he had given his wife so many aspirins. She was taken to hospital, where she died. The appellant informed the police that he had given his wife 100 aspirins, and added: 'I suppose they will hang me for this?' At his trial a defence of insanity was put forward. A doctor was called for him who said that the appellant was suffering from a form of communicated insanity known as *folie à deux*. It was said that if a person was in constant attendance on another of unsound mind, in some way the insanity might be communicated to the attendant, so that, for a time at any rate, the attendant might develop a defect of reason or of mind. Rebutting medical evidence was allowed to be called for the prosecution, and the doctors called on either side expressed the opinion that the appellant, when administering the fatal dose of aspirin to his wife, knew that he was doing an act which the law forbade.

The trial judge, Devlin J, having heard the evidence, ruled that there was no evidence of insanity, as defined in the rules in *M'Naghten's* case (1843) 10 Cl and F 200, to be left to the jury. He accordingly withdrew that issue from them, and they found the appellant guilty of murder.

Lord Goddard CJ: ... In this particular case, the only evidence given on the issue of insanity was that of the doctor called by the appellant and of the prison doctor who was allowed to be called by the prosecution to rebut, if indeed it were necessary, any evidence which had been given. It was probably right that the prison doctor should be called as he had had the appellant under constant observation. Both the doctors gave their evidence in a way that commended itself to the judge, and both, without hesitation, expressed the view that the appellant knew, when administering this poison, for such as it was, to his wife, that he was doing an act which the law forbade. I need not put it higher than that.

It may well be that, in the misery in which he had been living, with this nagging and tiresome wife who constantly expressed the desire to commit suicide, he thought that she would be better out of this world than in it. He may have thought that it would be a kindly act to release her from what she was suffering from – or thought she was suffering from – but that the law does not permit. In the present case there was some exceedingly vague evidence that the appellant was suffering from a defect of reason. In the opinion of his own doctor, there was a defect of reason which he attributed to communicated insanity. In my opinion, if the only question in this case has been whether the appellant was suffering from a disease of the mind, I should say that that was a question which must have been left to the jury. That, however, is not the question.

... A man may be suffering from a defect of reason, but if he knows that what he is doing is 'wrong', and by 'wrong' is meant contrary to law, he is responsible. Mr Shawcross, in the course of his very careful argument, suggested that the word 'wrong', as it was used in the M'Naghten Rules, did not mean contrary to law but had some kind of qualified meaning, such as morally wrong, and that if a person was in such a state of mind through a defect of reason that, although he knew that what he was doing was wrong in law, he thought that it was beneficial or kind or praiseworthy, that would excuse him ...

... Counsel for the appellant argued that the M'Naghten Rules only applied to cases in which delusions were present. The court cannot agree with that. It is true that when the judges who formulated the rules were summoned by the House of Lords the occasion had special reference to *M'Naghten's* case, but ever since that date the rules have been generally applied in all cases of insanity, whatever the nature of the insanity or disease of the mind from which the person accused is suffering.

In the opinion of the court there is no doubt that in the M'Naghten Rules 'wrong' means contrary to law and not 'wrong' according to the opinion of one man or of a number of people on the question whether a particular act might or might not be justified. In the present case, it could not be challenged that the appellant knew that what he was doing was contrary to law, and that he realised what punishment the law provided for murder. That was the opinion of both the doctors who gave evidence ...

R v Sullivan [1984] 1 AC 156 (HL)

See *above*.

AUTOMATISM

To distinguish 'automatism' from insanity, it is convenient to use the label 'non-insane automatism'.

The basis for the defence of non-insane automatism is that the accused's acts were not 'voluntary'. The classic case is the sleepwalker, who is not in control of his actions. There must have been a total loss of voluntary control: impaired or reduced control is not enough: *Attorney General's Reference (No 2 of 1992)* [1994] QB 91.

Automatism is difficult to establish where the accused was conscious at the time of the offence, but reflex actions (as in *Hill v Baxter* [1958] 1 QB 277) may give rise to a plea of automatism.

The automatism must not be self-induced: this includes the situation where the defendant is at fault, in that (for example) he has failed to follow medical advice (eg *R v Quick* [1973] QB 910; *R v Bailey* [1983] 1 WLR 760).

Involuntary act

Hill v Baxter [1958] 1 QB 277 (DC)

Lord Goddard CJ: This special case stated by justices for the County Borough of Brighton concerns two informations preferred against the respondent, the first for the dangerous driving of a motor vehicle contrary to s 11(1) of the Road Traffic Act, 1930, and the second for failing to conform to a Halt sign contrary to s 49(b) of the Act. The facts found by the justices are that at 10.45 pm on the evening of 12 April this year the respondent drove a motor van along Springfield Road, Brighton, in a westerly direction and where that road crosses Beaconsfield Road he ignored an illuminated Halt sign, drove across the road junction at a fast speed and came into collision with a car which was being driven northwards in Beaconsfield Road. The respondent's van then carried on for a short distance and overturned. A police constable arrived and found the respondent in a dazed condition and at the hospital to which he was taken he said:

> I remember being in Preston Circus going to Withdean. I don't remember anything else until I was searching for my glasses. I don't know what happened.

The justices found that to be in Springfield Road on the way to Withdean from Preston Circus involved a substantial and unnecessary detour but that the respondent must have exercised skill in driving in order to reach Springfield Road by whatever route he took. The justices apparently accepted the respondent's evidence and found that he remembered nothing from the time when he was at Preston Circus till the accident had happened. They were of opinion that the respondent was not conscious of what he was doing after leaving Preston Circus and to this finding they add the words 'with the implication that he was not capable of forming any intention as to his manner of driving'. They dismissed the informations, accepting a submission that loss of memory could only be attributed to the respondent being overcome by illness without warning ...

The first thing to be remembered is that the statute contains an absolute prohibition against driving dangerously or ignoring Halt signs. No question of *mens rea* enters into the offence; it is no answer to a charge under those sections to say 'I did not mean to drive dangerously' or 'I did not notice the Halt sign'. The justices' finding, that the respondent was not capable of forming any intention as to the manner of driving, is really immaterial. What they evidently meant was that the respondent was in a state of automatism ...

I agree that there may be cases where the circumstances are such that the accused could not really be said to be driving at all. Suppose he had a stroke or an epileptic fit, both instances of what may properly be called Acts of God; he might well be in the driver's seat even with his hands on the wheel but in such a state of unconsciousness that he could not be said to be driving. A blow from a stone or a swarm of bees I think introduces some conception akin to *novus actus interveniens*. In this case, however, I am content to say that the evidence falls far short of what would justify a court holding that this man was in some automatous state. There was no evidence that he was suffering from anything to account for what is so often called a 'black-out' and which probably, if genuine, is epileptic in origin ...

Attorney General's Reference (No 2 of 1992) [1994] QB 91 (CA)

Lord Taylor of Gosforth CJ: ... The point is defined in the reference as follows: 'Whether the state described as "driving without awareness" should, as a matter of law, be capable of founding a defence of automatism.' This formulation relates to expert evidence given in the particular case. However, we take the point more generally to raise the question: 'What are the requirements and limits of the defence of automatism?'

On 6 September 1991 in the Crown Court at Worcester, the respondent was acquitted after a five-day trial of two offences of causing death by reckless driving.

On 16 April 1991 the respondent, who was a professional heavy-goods-lorry driver, drove his lorry from Lincolnshire to Liverpool between the hours of 10 am and 4 pm. At about 6 pm he set off again, driving south on the M6 and then on the M5. Throughout the day he had taken appropriate breaks to comply with regulations. He ate a full meal at a service station between 10 and 10.30 pm. He stopped at another service station later and put on an extra coat. He then drove a further 22 miles before the accident occurred. After junction 6 on the M5, the motorway narrowed from three to two lanes. On passing junction 7, the respondent steered, apparently deliberately, on to the hard shoulder. He drove some 700 metres along that shoulder with only inches to spare on either side before crashing into a stationary white van. The van had its hazard lights flashing and in front of it was a recovery vehicle with rotating yellow lights. Standing between the two vehicles were the two victims who received fatal injuries as the van was pushed into the recovery vehicle. Marks on the road showed that braking had occurred only at the very last moment. The respondent had been driving for over six hours out of the preceding 12 and had covered 343 miles.

It was the prosecution case that the respondent had been overcome by sleep at the wheel. In the course of a lengthy interview with the police, he ultimately acknowledged that he was tired but had decided to push on to the next service station and must have fallen asleep.

Both the prosecution and the defence had obtained expert evidence. For the defence, there was a report from Professor Brown, a chartered psychologist and assistant director of the Medical Research Council's Applied Psychology Unit in Cambridge. The Crown had obtained a report from Professor Horne, director of the Sleep Research Laboratory at Loughborough University. It was agreed by counsel that the evidence of each of these experts should be adduced and the judge admitted it. Professor Horne was called as part of the prosecution case. The respondent did not give evidence but relied upon Professor Brown's expert testimony which is central to this reference.

Professor Brown described to the court a condition known as 'driving without awareness' and on the basis of his evidence it was contended for the defence that the respondent was in a state of automatism at the time of the accident and was therefore not to be regarded as driving at all. Professor Horne did not accept Professor Brown's analysis. However, the judge in summing up to the jury left the defence of automatism based upon Professor Brown's evidence as an issue properly open for the jury's consideration.

It is common ground that, for the purposes of this reference, the court should proceed on the basis of Professor Brown's evidence at its highest. He said that 'driving without awareness' is not a scientific term but a provisional, or interim, descriptive phrase coined at a conference he had attended. He said that there are two essential components to the act of driving: collision avoidance and steering within highway lanes. In a state of 'driving without awareness', the driver's capacity to avoid a collision ceases to exist. This is because repetitive visual stimuli experienced on long journeys on straight, flat, featureless motorways can induce a trance-like state in which the focal point of forward vision gradually comes nearer and nearer until the driver is focusing just ahead of his windscreen. He therefore fails to see further ahead in the central field of vision. However, peripheral vision continues to send signals which are dealt with subconsciously and enable the driver to steer within highway lanes.

Professor Brown said this condition can occur insidiously without the driver being aware it is happening. However, he also said that usually a driver would 'snap out' of the condition in response to major stimuli appearing in front of him. Thus flashing lights would usually cause him to regain full awareness. Professor Brown was unable to explain why that had not happened in the present case. In fact, the respondent told the police when interviewed that he had seen the flashing lights some quarter of a mile before reaching them. Professor Brown was also unable to explain why the respondent should have steered, apparently deliberately, onto the hard shoulder.

Despite his phrase 'driving without awareness', Professor Brown agreed that the driver's body would still be controlling the vehicle, that there would be subconscious motivation to his steering and that although 'largely unaware of what was happening ahead' and 'largely unaware of steering either' the unawareness was not total. Asked if nothing intrudes into the driver's consciousness when he is in this state, the professor said: 'I would not go so far as to say nothing, but very little'. There must, as a matter of common sense, be some awareness if, as Professor Brown accepted, the driver will usually be caused to 'snap out' of the condition by strong stimuli noticed by his eyes.

Against this evidential background, the recorder directed the jury as follows:

> Professor Brown ... has told you that in his opinion [the respondent] was driving in a state which he describes as 'driving without awareness' in which he moved onto the hard shoulder, mistaking it for the nearside lane, and then continued steering subconsciously until a fraction of a second before the collision. Indeed, Professor Brown's view was that that state of driving without awareness had persisted for quite a long time and had included not only that last half mile, but had included the manoeuvre at junction 6 illustrated in the photograph some miles before. As a matter of law I direct you that if, because of this state of driving without awareness, [the respondent's] consciousness was, or may have been, so impaired that his mind did not control his action, he is not guilty of the offence and it is for the prosecution to make you sure that that was not his condition.

The contention on behalf of the Attorney General is that on the evidence given by Professor Brown, even taken at its highest, there was no basis for leaving the defence of automatism to the jury.

[Counsel for the Attorney General] submits that automatism as a defence in a driving case arises only where there is such total destruction of voluntary control that the defendant cannot be said to be driving at all. He cited *Hill v Baxter* [1958] 1 QB in which Lord Goddard CJ said at 283:

> I agree that there may be cases where the circumstances are such that the accused could not really be said to be driving at all. Supposed he had a stroke or an epileptic fit, both instances of what may properly be called acts of God; he might well be in the driver's seat even with his hands on the wheel, but in such a state of unconsciousness that he could not be said to be driving.

Pearson J at 286, gave as examples an epileptic fit, a coma, a blow on the head from a stone thrown up from the roadway and an attack by a swarm of bees so that the driver is:

> prevented from exercising any directional control over the vehicle, and any movement of his arms and legs are solely caused by the action of the bees. In each of these cases it can be said that at the material time he is not driving and, therefore, not driving dangerously. Then suppose that the man in the driving seat falls asleep. After he has fallen asleep he is no longer driving, but there was an earlier time at which he was falling asleep and therefore

> failing to perform the driver's elementary and essential duty of keeping himself awake and therefore he was driving dangerously.

In *Bratty v Attorney General for Northern Ireland* [1963] AC 386, a defence of automatism due to an attack of psychomotor epilepsy was raised. Lord Denning said of the *actus reus*, at 409:

> No act is punishable if it is done involuntarily: and an involuntary act in this context – some people nowadays prefer to speak of it as 'automatism' – means an act which is done by the muscles without any control by the mind, such as a spasm, a reflex action or a convulsion; or an act done by a person who is not conscious of what he is doing, such as an act whilst suffering from concussion or whilst sleep-walking.

The extent of the loss of control is crucial in the present case. [Counsel for the Attorney General] referred to three other authorities in support of his proposition that automatism requires there to be total destruction of voluntary control and that impairment or reduction of voluntary control is insufficient.

Watmore v Jenkins [1962] 2 QB 572 was a decision by a court of five judges in a case where the defendant was a diabetic and sought to raise automatism due to hypoglycaemia as a defence to driving charges. Giving the judgment of the court, Winn J said, at 586:

> It is ... a question of law what constitutes a state of automatism. It is salutary to recall that this expression is no more than a modern catch-phrase which the courts have not accepted as connoting any wider or looser concept than involuntary movement of the body or limbs of a person.

Later, at p 587, he referred to the need for 'such a complete destruction of voluntary control as could constitute in law automatism'.

Second, [counsel for the Attorney General] relies on *Roberts v Ramsbottom* [1980] 1 WLR 823, a civil case in which the defendant driver sought to rely on automatism due to a stroke. Neill LJ said, at p 831G: '... I am not concerned with the total loss of consciousness but with a clouding or impairment of consciousness'. He then referred, *inter alia*, to *Watmore v Jenkins* [1962] 2 QB 572 and *Hill v Baxter* [1958] 1 QB 277 and concluded [1962] 2 QB 572, 832:

> I am satisfied that in a civil action a similar approach should be adopted. The driver will be able to escape liability if his actions at the relevant time were wholly beyond his control. The most obvious case is sudden unconsciousness. But if he retained some control, albeit imperfect control, and his driving, judged objectively, was below the required standard, he remains liable. His position is the same as a driver who is old or infirm. In my judgment unless the facts establish what the law recognises as automatism the driver cannot avoid liability on the basis that owing to some malfunction of the brain his consciousness was impaired. [Counsel] put the matter accurately, as I see it, when he said: 'One cannot accept as exculpation anything less than total loss of consciousness'.

The third case relied upon by [counsel for the Attorney General] is *Broome v Perkins* [1987] RTR 321, where again a driver charged with careless driving relied on an attack of hypoglycaemia as creating automatism. Glidewell LJ referred to *Bratty's* case [1963] AC 386 and to *Watmore v Jenkins* [1962] 2 QB 572. He said [1987] RTR 321 at 330:

> The question which is posed in the case can be rephrased to ask: 'On the evidence, could the justices properly conclude that the defendant was not conscious of what he was doing and that his actions were involuntary and

> automatic throughout the whole of the five-mile journey over which the erratic driving was observed?' If, during a part or parts of that journey, they were satisfied his actions were voluntary and not automatic, at those times he was driving ... When driving a motor vehicle, the driver's conscious mind receives signals from eyes and ears, decides on the appropriate course of action as a result of those signals, and gives directions to the limbs to control the vehicle. When a person's actions are involuntary and automatic his mind is not controlling or directing his limbs.

[Counsel for the respondent] concedes that he can find no authority which runs counter to the principle illustrated by those three cases. Moreover, he conceded that despite Professor Brown's phrase 'driving without awareness', the professor's description of the condition showed that it amounts only to reduced or imperfect awareness. There remains the ability to steer the vehicle straight. There is also usually a capacity to react to stimuli appearing in the road ahead. In the present case the respondent admitted he had actually seen the flashing lights a quarter of a mile from the scene ...

We were referred to a number of decisions drawing a distinction between insane automatism and non-insane automatism: see *R v Quick* [1973] QB 910; *R v Sullivan* [1984] AC 156; *R v Hennessy* [1989] 1 WLR 287 and *R v Burgess* [1991] 2 QB 92.

The effect of those decisions is that if the defence of automatism is said to arise from internal causes so as to bring the defendant within the *M'Naghten Rules* (see *M'Naghten's* case), then if it succeeds the verdict should be one of not guilty by reason of insanity. An epileptic seizure, in *R v Sullivan*, a stress disorder, prone to recur and lacking the features of novelty or accident, in *R v Hennessy*, and sleep-walking, in *R v Burgess*, were all regarded as internal causes. If, however, automatism is said to arise from an external cause, for example a stone hitting the driver on the head, then a successful defendant is entitled to be acquitted.

Here, [counsel for the respondent] argues that the precipitating cause of the condition described by Professor Brown was the external factor of motorway conditions. However that may be, the proper approach is that prescribed by Lord Lane CJ in *R v Burgess* [1991] 2 QB 92 at 96:

> Where the defence of automatism is raised by a defendant, two questions fall to be decided by the judge before the defence can be left to the jury. The first is whether a proper evidential foundation for the defence of automatism has been laid. The second is whether the evidence shows the case to be one of insane automatism, that is to say, a case which falls within the M'Naghten Rules, or one of non-insane automatism.

The first of those questions is the one raised by this reference. In our judgment, the 'proper evidential foundation' was not laid in this case by Professor Brown's evidence of 'driving without awareness'. As the authorities cited above show, the defence of automatism requires that there was a total destruction of voluntary control of the defendant's part. Impaired, reduced or partial control is not enough. Professor Brown accepted that someone 'driving without awareness' within his description, retains some control. He should be able to steer the vehicle and usually to react and return to full awareness when confronted by significant stimuli.

Accordingly, in our judgment the recorder ought not to have left the issue of automatism to the jury in this case and the answer to the point of law as formulated is, 'No'.

Self-induced automatism

R v Quick [1973] QB 910 (CA)

See *above*.

R v Bailey [1983] 1 WLR 760 (CA)

Griffiths LJ: ... The appellant is a diabetic and has been so for some 30 years. He requires to take insulin to control his condition. His defence at the trial was that he was acting in a state of automatism caused by hypoglycaemia.

In early January 1982, the woman with whom the appellant had been living for the previous two years left him and formed an association with the victim, Mr Harrison. At about 7 pm on 20 January 1982, the appellant, seeming upset, visited Mr Harrison at his home. They had a cup of tea and discussed the matter. After 10 or 15 minutes the appellant said that he felt unwell and asked Mr Harrison to make him some sugar and water, which the appellant drank. About 10 minutes later the appellant started to leave. He then said that he had lost his glove and that it might be down the side of the chair on which he had been sitting. Mr Harrison bent down to look and the appellant struck him on the back of the head with an iron bar, which was a case opener about 18 inches long. The appellant remained there holding the iron bar. Mr Harrison ran from the house. His wound required 10 stitches.

The Crown's case was that although it was theoretically possible, from a medical point of view, for there to have been a temporary loss of awareness due to hypoglycaemia, as the appellant claimed, this was not what had happened. On the contrary, it was contended that the appellant, upset and jealous about Mr Harrison's relationship with his girlfriend, had armed himself with the iron bar and gone to Mr Harrison's house with the intention of injuring him ...

Automatism resulting from intoxication as a result of a voluntary ingestion of alcohol or dangerous drugs does not negative the *mens rea* necessary for crimes of basic intent, because the conduct of the accused is reckless and recklessness is enough to constitute the necessary *mens rea* in assault cases where no specific intent forms part of the charge: see *R v Majewski* [1977] AC 443, 476 in speech of Lord Elwyn Jones LC and in the speech of Lord Edmund-Davies where he said, at p496, quoting from Stroud, *Mens Rea*, 1914, p 115:

> The law therefore establishes a conclusive presumption against the admission of proof of intoxication for the purpose of disproving *mens rea* in ordinary crimes. Where this presumption applies, it does not make 'drunkenness itself' a crime, but the drunkenness is itself an integral part of the crime, as forming together with the other unlawful conduct charged against the defendant, a complex act of criminal recklessness.

The same considerations apply where the state of automatism is induced by the voluntary taking of dangerous drugs: see *R v Lipman* [1970] 1 QB 152 where a conviction for manslaughter was upheld, the appellant having taken LSD and killed his mistress in the course of an hallucinatory trip. It was submitted on behalf of the Crown that a similar rule should be applied as a matter of public policy to all cases of self-induced automatism. But it seems to us that there may be material distinctions between a man who consumes alcohol or takes dangerous drugs and one who fails to take sufficient food after insulin to avert hypoglycaemia.

It is common knowledge that those who take alcohol to excess or certain sorts of drugs may become aggressive or do dangerous or unpredictable things, they may be able to foresee the risks of causing harm to others but nevertheless persist in their conduct. But the same cannot be said without more of a man who fails to take food after an insulin injection. If he does appreciate the risk that such a failure may lead to aggressive, unpredictable and uncontrollable conduct and he nevertheless deliberately runs the risk or otherwise disregards it, this will amount to recklessness. But we certainly do not think that it is common knowledge, even among diabetics, that such is a consequence of a failure to take food and there is no evidence that it was known to this appellant. Doubtless he knew that if he failed to take his insulin or proper food after it, he might lose consciousness, but as such he would only be a danger to himself unless he put himself in charge of some machine such as a motor car, which required his continued conscious control.

In our judgment, self-induced automatism, other than that due to intoxication from alcohol or drugs, may provide a defence to crimes of basic intent. The question in each case will be whether the prosecution have proved the necessary element of recklessness. In cases of assault, if the accused knows that his actions or inaction are likely to make him aggressive, unpredictable or uncontrolled with the result that he may cause some injury to others and he persists in the action or takes no remedial action when he knows it is required, it will be open to the jury to find that he was reckless ...

In the present case the recorder never invited the jury to consider what the appellant's knowledge or appreciation was of what would happen if he failed to take food after his insulin or whether he realised that he might become aggressive. Nor were they asked to consider why the appellant had omitted to take food in time. They were given no direction on the elements of recklessness. Accordingly, in our judgment there was also a misdirection in relation to the second count in the indictment of unlawful wounding.

But we have to consider whether, notwithstanding these misdirections, there has been any miscarriage of justice and whether the jury properly directed could have failed to come to the same conclusion. As Lawton LJ said in *Quick's* case at 922 [*R v Quick* (1973) QB 910], referring to the defence of automatism, it is a 'quagmire of law seldom entered nowadays save by those in desperate need of some kind of a defence ...' This case is no exception. We think it very doubtful whether the appellant laid a sufficient basis for the defence to be considered by the jury at all. But even if he did we are in no doubt that the jury properly directed must have rejected it. Although an episode of sudden transient loss of consciousness or awareness was theoretically possible it was quite inconsistent with the graphic description that the appellant gave to the police both orally and in his written statement. There was abundant evidence that he had armed himself with the iron bar and gone to Mr Harrison's house for the purpose of attacking him because he wanted to teach him a lesson and because he was in the way ...

CHAPTER 7

GENERAL DEFENCES – INTOXICATION

VOLUNTARY AND INVOLUNTARY INTOXICATION

Involuntary intoxication (where, for example, the accused did not realise that he was drinking alcohol) is only a defence if it prevents the accused from forming the *mens rea* which is a necessary ingredient of the offence with which the accused is charged: *R v Kingston* [1994] 3 WLR 519.

Intoxication is regarded as voluntary if the accused knowingly took alcohol or other intoxicating drugs. It is irrelevant that the accused misjudged the extent to which he would become intoxicated: *R v Allen* [1988] Crim LR 698.

What counts as an intoxicating drug was considered in *R v Bailey* [1983] 1 WLR 760 and *R v Hardie* [1985] 1 WLR 64.

R v Kingston [1995] 2 AC 355 (HL)

Lord Mustill: My Lords, this appeal concerns the effect on criminal liability of involuntary intoxication ...

The relevant facts are simple. The respondent was in dispute over business matters with a couple named Foreman, who employed Penn to obtain damaging information which they could use against the respondent, who is a homosexual with paedophiliac predilections. As part of this plan Penn invited the youth to his room. According to the evidence given by the youth at the trial he remembered nothing between a time when he was sitting on the bed and when he woke up, still in Penn's room, the following morning. It was the case for the prosecution, which the jury by their verdict on the second count must have accepted, that the boy fell asleep because Penn had secretly given him a soporific drug in a drink. On the same evening the respondent went to the room where the youth lay unconscious. He and Penn indulged in gross sexual acts with him. As part of the plan Penn made a recording of what was going on, and also took some photographs ...

At the outset of the trial counsel for the respondent foreshadowed a defence on the lines that as part of the plan Penn had secretly administered drugs not only to the boy but also to the respondent. It was not said, and in the light of the recordings and photographs could not have been said, that the consequence was to make the respondent, like the boy, insensible; nevertheless his case was he had suffered effects which annulled the criminal liability which his acts would otherwise have involved ...

... [T]here are three grounds on which the respondent might be held free from criminal responsibility. First, that his immunity flows from general principles of the criminal law. Second, that this immunity is already established by a solid line of authority. Finally, that the court should, when faced with a new problem, acknowledge the justice of the case and boldly create a new common law defence.

It is clear from the passage already quoted that the Court of Appeal [which allowed Kingston's appeal] adopted the first approach. The decision was explicitly founded on general principle. There can be no doubt what principle the court relied upon, for at the outset the court [1994] QB 81, 87, recorded the submission of counsel for the respondent:

> The law recognises that, exceptionally, an accused person may be entitled to be acquitted if there is a possibility that although his act was intentional, the intent itself arose out of circumstances for which he bears no blame.

The same proposition is implicit in the assumption by the court that if blame is absent the necessary *mens rea* must also be absent.

My Lords, with every respect I must suggest that no such principle exists or, until the present case, had ever in modern times been thought to exist. Each offence consists of a prohibited act or omission coupled with whatever state of mind is called for by the statute or rule of the common law which create the offence. In those offences which are not absolute the state of mind which the prosecution must prove to have underlain the act or omission – the 'mental element' – will in the majority of cases be such as to attract disapproval. The mental element will then be the mark of what may properly be called a 'guilty mind'. The professional burglar is guilty in a moral as well as a legal sense; he intends to break into the house to steal, and most would confidently assert that this is wrong. But this will not always be so. In respect of some offences the mind of the defendant and still less his moral judgment, may not be engaged at all. In others, although a mental activity must be the motive power for the prohibited act or omission the activity may be of such a kind or degree that society at large would not criticise the defendant's conduct severely or even criticise it at all. Such cases are not uncommon. Yet to assume that contemporary moral judgments affect the criminality of the act, as distinct from the punishment appropriate to the crime one proved, is to be misled by the expression *mens rea*, the ambiguity of which has been the subject of complaint for more than a century. Certainly, the *mens* of the defendant must usually be involved in the offence; but the epithet *rea* refers to the criminality of the act in which the mind is engaged, not to its moral character ...

I would therefore reject that part of the respondent's argument which treats the absence of moral fault on the part of the appellants as sufficient in itself to negative the necessary mental element of the offence ...

... His second ground is more narrow, namely that involuntary intoxication is already recognised as a defence by authority which the House ought to follow ...

[His Lordship discussed the older authorities, and then went on:] There is, however, another line of authority to be considered, for it is impossible to consider the exceptional case of involuntary intoxication without placing it in the context of intoxication as a whole. The area of the law is controversial, as regards the content of the rules, their intellectual foundations, and their capacity to furnish a practical and just solution. Since the law was not explored in depth during the arguments and since it is relevant only as part of the background it is better not to say any more about it than is strictly necessary. Some consideration of the law laid down in *R v Majewski* [1977] AC 443 is however inevitable. As I understand the position it is still the law that in the exceptional case where intoxication causes insanity the M'Naghten Rules (*M'Naghten's* case (1843) 10 Cl & F 200) apply: see *DPP v Beard* [1920] AC 479, 501 and *Attorney General for Northern Ireland v Gallagher* [1963] AC 349. Short of this, it is no answer for the defendant to say that he would not have done what he did had he been sober, provided always that whatever element of intent is required by the offence is proved to have been present. As was said in *R v Sheehan* [1975] 1 WLR 739, 744c, 'a drunken intent is nevertheless an intent'. As to proof of intent, it appears that at least in some instances self-induced intoxication can be taken into account as part of the evidence from which the jury draws its conclusions; but that in others it cannot. I express the matter in this guarded way because it has not yet been decisively established whether for his purpose there is a line to be drawn between offences of 'specific' and of 'basic' intent. That in at least some cases a defendant cannot say that he was so drunk that he could not form the required intent is however clear enough. Why is this so? The answer must I believe be the same as that given in other common law jurisdictions: namely that such evidence is excluded as a matter of policy ...

There remains the question by what reasoning the House put this policy into effect. As I understand it two different rationalisations were adopted. First that the absence of the necessary consent is cured by treating the intentional drunkenness (or more accurately, since it is only in the minority of cases that the drinker sets out to make himself drunk, the intentional taking of drink without regard to its possible effects) as a substitute for the mental element ordinarily required by the offence. The intent is transferred from the taking of drink to the commission of the prohibited act. The second rationalisation is that the defendant cannot be heard to rely on the absence of the mental element when it is absent because of his own voluntary acts. Borrowing an expression from a far distant field it may be said that the defendant is estopped from relying on his self-induced incapacity.

Your Lordships are not required to decide how these two explanations stand up to attack, for they are not attacked here. The task is only to place them in the context of an intoxication which is not voluntary. Taking first the concept of transferred intent, if the intoxication was not the result of an act done with an informed will there is no intent which can be transferred to the prohibited act, so as to fill the gap in the offence. As regards the 'estoppel' there is no reason why the law should preclude the defendant from relying on a mental condition which he had not deliberately brought about. Thus, once the involuntary nature of the intoxication is added the two theories of *Majewski* fall away, and the position reverts to what it would have been if *Majewski* [1977] AC 443 had not been decided, namely that the offence is not made out if the defendant was so intoxicated that he could not form an intent. Thus, where the intoxication is involuntary *Majewski* does not *subtract* the defence of absence of intent; but there is nothing in *Majewski* to suggest that where intent is proved involuntary intoxication *adds* a further defence ...

To recognise a new defence of this type would be a bold step. The common law defences of duress and necessity (if it exists) and the limited common law defence of provocation are all very old. Since counsel for the appellant was not disposed to emphasise this aspect of the appeal the subject was not explored in argument, but I suspect that the recognition of a new general defence at common law has not happened in modern times. Nevertheless, the criminal law must not stand still, and if it is both practical and just to take this step, and if judicial decision rather than legislation is the proper medium, then the courts should not be deterred simply by the novelty of it. So one must turn to consider just what defence is now to be created. The judgment under appeal implies five characteristics:

1 The defence applies to all offences, except perhaps to absolute offences. It therefore differs from defences such as provocation and diminished responsibility.

2 The defence is a complete answer to a criminal charge. If not rebutted it leads to an outright acquittal, and unlike provocation and diminished responsibility leaves no room for conviction and punishment for a lesser offence. The underlying assumption must be that the defendant is entirely free from culpability.

3 It may be that the defence applies only where the intoxication is due to the wrongful act of another and therefore affords no excuse when, in circumstances of no greater culpability, the defendant has intoxicated himself by mistake (such as by shortsightedly taking the wrong drug). I say that this may be so, because it is not clear whether, since the doctrine was founded in part on the *dictum* of Park J in *Pearson's* case, 2 Lew 144, the 'fraud or stratagem of another' is an essential element, or whether this was taken as an example of a wider principle.

4 The burden of disproving the defence is on the prosecution.

5 The defence is subjective in nature. Whereas provocation and self-defence are judged by the reactions of the reasonable person in the situation of the defendant, here the only question is whether this particular defendant's inhibitions were overcome by the effect of the drug. The more susceptible the defendant to the kind of temptation presented, the easier the defence is to establish.

My Lords, since the existence or otherwise of the defence has been treated in argument at all stages as a matter of existing law the Court of Appeal had no occasion to consider the practical and theoretical implications of recognising this new defence at common law, and we do not have the benefit of its views. In their absence, I can only say that the defence appears to run into difficulties at every turn. In point of theory, it would be necessary to reconcile a defence of irresistible impulse derived from a combination of innate drives and external disinhibition with the rule that irresistible impulse of a solely internal origin (not necessarily any more the fault of the offender) does not in itself excuse although it may be a symptom of a disease of the mind: *Attorney General for South Australia v Brown* [1960] AC 432. Equally, the state of mind which founds the defence superficially resembles a state of diminished responsibility, whereas the effect in law is quite different. It may well be that the resemblance is misleading, but these and similar problems must be solved before the bounds of a new defence can be set.

On the practical side there are serious problems. Before the jury could form an opinion on whether the drug might have turned the scale witnesses would have to give a picture of the defendant's personality and susceptibilities, for without it the crucial effect of the drug could not be assessed; pharmacologists would be required to describe the potentially disinhibiting effect of a range of drugs whose identity would, if the present case is anything to go by, be unknown; psychologists and psychiatrists would express opinions, not on the matters of psychopathology familiar to those working within the framework of the Mental Health Acts but on altogether more elusive concepts. No doubt as time passed those concerned could work out techniques to deal with these questions. Much more significant would be the opportunities for a spurious defence. Even in the field of road traffic the 'spiked' drink as a special reason for not disqualifying from driving is a regular feature. Transferring this to the entire range of criminal offences is a disturbing prospect. The defendant would only have to assert, and support by the evidence of well-wishers, that he was not the sort of person to have done this kind of thing, and to suggest an occasion when by some means a drug might have been administered to him for the jury to be sent straight to the question of a possible disinhibition. The judge would direct the jurors that if they felt any legitimate doubt on the matter – and by its nature the defence would be one which the prosecution would often have no means to rebut – they must acquit outright, all questions of intent, mental capacity and the like being at this stage irrelevant.

My Lords, the fact that a new doctrine may require adjustment of existing principles to accommodate it, and may require those involved in criminal trials to learn new techniques, is not of course a ground for refusing to adopt it, if that is what the interests of justice require. Here, however, justice makes no such demands for the interplay between the wrong done to the victim, the individual characteristics and frailties of the defendant, and the pharmacological effects of whatever drug may be potentially involved can be far better recognised by a tailored choice from the continuum of sentences available to the judge than by the application of a single yea-or-nay jury decision. To this, there is one exception. The mandatory life sentence for murder, at least as present administered, leaves no room for the trial judge to put into practice an informed and sympathetic assessment of the kind just described. It is for this reason alone that I have felt any hesitation about rejecting the argument for the respondent. In the end however I have concluded that this is not a sufficient reason to force on the theory and practice of the criminal law an exception which would otherwise be unjustified. For many years mandatory sentences have impelled juries to return merciful but false verdicts, and have stimulated the creation of partial defences such as provocation and diminished responsibility whose lack of a proper foundation has made them hard to apply in practice. I do not think it right that the law should be further distorted simply because of this anomalous relic of the history of the criminal law.

All this being said, I suggest to your Lordships that the existing work of the Law Commission in the fields of intoxication could usefully be enlarged to comprise questions of the type raised by this appeal, and to see whether by statute a merciful, realistic and intellectually sustainable solution could be newly created. For the present, however, I consider that no such regime now exists, and that the common law is not a suitable vehicle for creating one ...

R v Allen [1988] Crim LR 698 (CA)

Facts: The appellant was convicted of buggery and indecent assault. It was the appellant's alternative line of defence that if, contrary to his basic assertion that he was not the attacker, he was so drunk at the time that he was not responsible for his actions and was in effect acting in a state of automatism; and that that drunken condition was due to his involuntarily having imbibed a quantity of alcohol which he was not responsible for consuming. The appellant gave evidence that he had consumed some drink in a public house and had later been given wine by a friend. He had not realised that the wine had a high alcohol content. The second line of defence was not left to the jury by the judge. The appellant appealed against conviction on the ground that the judge erred in ruling that involuntary drunkenness could not be a defence to a crime of non-specific intent.

Held, dismissing the appeal, the judge was correct in ruling that there was no evidence before him that the drinking was other than voluntary. Further, where an accused knows that he is drinking alcohol, such drinking does not become involuntary for the reason alone that he may not know the precise nature or strength of the alcohol that he is consuming.

R v Hardie [1985] 1 WLR 64 (CA)

Parker LJ: ...Shortly after 9.15 pm on 2 January 1982, fire broke out in a wardrobe in the bedroom of the ground floor flat at 55, Bassingham Road, London SW10. At that time there were in the flat the appellant, Mrs Jeanette Hardie, with whom the appellant had been living at the premises since May 1974, and who had changed her name to Hardie by deed poll in 1976, and her daughter Tonia. The upstairs flat was occupied by a Mrs Young. Shortly before 2 January, the appellant's relationship with Mrs Hardie had broken down and she had insisted that he must leave. He did not wish to do so, but on the morning of 2 January he packed a suitcase. At about lunchtime the appellant found two bottles of tablets in a cabinet. One contained Valium which Mrs Hardie had had in 1974 and the other tablets to assist urination.

The appellant's evidence in regard to this was that he had never taken Valium before, that he took one about 12 pm to calm him down for he was in a distressed state, that it did not have much effect, that he and Mrs Hardie had then gone shopping, that he had taken two more in front of her and she had said, 'take as many as you like, they are old stock and will do you no harm', that he taken two more shortly afterwards, that he may have taken two of the other tablets also, and that shortly thereafter on return to the house he had fallen into a deep sleep and could thereafter remember only periods. He was in fact collected from the flat by his mother and remained with her until returning to the flat again at 9.15 pm. It was not disputed that he must have started the fire for he was alone in the bedroom when it started. Having started it, he emerged, returned to the sitting room where were Mrs Hardie and Tonia and stayed there. Shortly afterwards Mrs Hardie heard sounds from the bedroom, went there and found smoke and flames coming from the wardrobe. There was evidence that before, at the time of and after the fire the appellant was exhibiting signs of intoxication and that such signs might have resulted from the taking of Valium some hours earlier.

The defence was that the appellant was so affected by the Valium that he could remember nothing about the fire and had not the necessary *mens rea* to constitute either of the offences charged. On the basis no doubt of *R v Majewski* [1977] AC 443 and *R v Caldwell* [1982] AC 341, the judge directed the jury in effect that, as the Valium was voluntarily self-administered, it was irrelevant as a defence and its effect could not negative *mens rea* ...

... It is clear from *R v Caldwell* [1982] AC 341 that self-induced intoxication can be a defence where the charge is only one specific intention. It is equally clear that it cannot be a defence where, as here, the charge included recklessness. Hence, if there was self-intoxication in this case the judge's direction was correct. The problem is whether, assuming that the effect of the Valium was to deprive the appellant of any appreciation of what he was doing it should properly be regarded as self-induced intoxication and thus no answer ...

R v Majewski was a case of drunkenness resulting from alcoholic consumption by the accused whilst under the influence of non-medically prescribed drugs. *R v Caldwell* [1982] AC 341 was a case of plain drunkenness. There can be no doubt that the same rule applies both to self-intoxication by alcohol and intoxication by hallucinatory drugs, but this is because the effects of both are well-known and there is therefore an element of recklessness in the self-administration of the drug. *R v Lipman* [1970] 1 QB 152 is an example of such a case.

'Intoxication' or similar symptoms may, however, arise in other circumstances. In *R v Bailey (John)* [1983] 1 WLR 760 this court had to consider a case where a diabetic had failed to take sufficient food after taking a normal dose of insulin and struck the victim over the head with an iron bar. The judge directed the jury that the defence of automatism, ie that the mind did not go with the act, was not available because the incapacity was self-induced. It was held that his was wrong on two grounds (a) because on the basis of *R v Majewski* [1977] AC 443 it was clearly available to the offence embodying specific intent and (b) because although self-induced by the omission to take food it was also available to negative the other offence which was of basic intent only ...

In the present instance the defence was that the Valium was taken for the purpose of calming the nerves only, that it was old stock and that the appellant was told it would do him no harm. There was no evidence that it was known to the appellant or even generally known that the taking of Valium in the quantity taken would be liable to render a person aggressive or incapable of appreciating risks to others or have other side effects such that its self-administration would itself have an element of recklessness. It is true that Valium is a drug and it is true that it was taken deliberately and not taken on medical prescription, but the drug is, in our view wholly different in kind from drugs which are liable to cause unpredictability or aggressiveness. It may well be that the taking of a sedative or soporific drug will, in certain circumstances, be no answer, for example, in a case of reckless driving, but if the effect of a drug is merely soporific or sedative the taking of it, even in some excessive quantity, cannot in the ordinary way raise a *conclusive* presumption against the admission of proof of intoxication for the purpose of disproving *mens rea* in ordinary crimes, such as would be the case with alcoholic intoxication or incapacity or automatism resulting from the self-administration of dangerous drugs.

In the present case the jury should not, in our judgment, have been directed to disregard any incapacity which resulted or might have resulted from the taking of Valium. They should have been directed that if they came to the conclusion that, as a result of the Valium, the appellant was, at the time, unable to appreciate the risks to property and persons from his actions they should then consider whether the taking of the Valium was itself reckless. We are unable to say what would have been the appropriate direction with regard to the elements of recklessness in this case for we have not seen all the relevant evidence, nor are we able to suggest a model direction, for circumstances will vary infinitely and model directions can sometimes lead to more rather than less confusion. It is sufficient to say that the direction that the effects of Valium were necessarily irrelevant was wrong.

In *R v Bailey (John)* [1983] 1 WLR 760 the court upheld the conviction notwithstanding the misdirection, being satisfied that there had been no miscarriage of justice and that the jury properly directed could not have failed to come to the same conclusion. That is not so in the present case. Properly directed the jury might well have come to the same conclusion. There was, for example evidence that the Valium really did not materially affect the appellant at all at the relevant time, but we are quite unable to say that they must have come to the same conclusion ...

VOLUNTARY INTOXICATION

Voluntary intoxication is only a defence to offences of 'specific intent' (as opposed to 'basic intent').

Unfortunately, the definition of these terms is not as clear as it could be. In *DPP v Morgan* [1976] AC 182 Lord Simon said that a crime of basic intent was a crime in which the *mens rea* does not go beyond the *actus reus*. Assault would be one example. A crime of specific intent is therefore one where the *mens rea* goes beyond the *actus reus*. An example would be wounding with intent to cause grievous bodily harm (s 18 of the Offences Against the Person Act 1861) where the *actus reus* is the wounding but the *mens rea* goes further.

Another way of looking at it is to say (as Blackstone's *Criminal Practice*, section A3.10) that 'any offence for which only intention will suffice as the mental element can be regarded as an offence of specific intent'.

Where there is a statutory defence of 'honest mistake' (eg s 5(2) of the Criminal Damage Act 1971), a mistake brought about by intoxication still amounts to a defence (see *Jaggard v Dickinson* [1981] QB 527). However, in relation to common law defences, such as self-defence, a mistake induced by intoxication falls outside the scope of the defence (see *R v O'Grady* [1987] QB 995).

DPP v Majewski [1977] AC 443 (HL)

Lord Elwyn-Jones LC: My Lords, Robert Stefan Majewski appeals against his conviction on 7 November 1973, at Chelmsford Crown Court on three counts of assault occasioning actual bodily harm and three counts of assault on a police constable in the execution of his duty ...

The appellant's case was that when the assaults were committed he was acting under the influence of a combination of drugs (not medically prescribed) and alcohol, to such an extent that he did not know what he was doing and that he remembered nothing of the incidents that had occurred ...

The appeal raises issues of considerable public importance. In giving the judgment of the Court of Appeal Lawton LJ rightly observed at 404, that

> The facts are commonplace – indeed so commonplace that their very nature reveals how serious from a social and public standpoint the consequences would be if men could behave as the [appellant] did and then claim that they were not guilty of any offence.

Self-induced alcoholic intoxication has been a factor in crimes of violence, like assault, throughout the history of crime in this country. But voluntary drug taking with the potential and actual dangers to others it may cause has added a new dimension to the old problem with which the courts have had to deal in their endeavour to maintain order and to keep public and private violence under control. To achieve this is the prime purpose of the criminal law. I have said 'the courts', for most of the relevant law has been made by the judges. A good deal of the argument in the hearing of this appeal turned on that judicial history, for the crux of the case for the Crown was that, illogical as the outcome may be said to be, the judges have evolved for the purpose of protecting the community a substantive rule of law that, in crimes of basic intent as distinct from crimes of specific intent, self-induced intoxication provides no defence and is irrelevant to offences of basic intent, such as assault ...

What then is the mental element required in our law to be established in assault? This question has been most helpfully answered in the speech of Lord Simon of Glaisdale in *R v Morgan* [1976] AC 182, 216:

> By 'crimes of basic intent' I mean those crimes whose definition expresses (or, more often, implies) a *mens rea* which does not go beyond the *actus reus*. The *actus reus* generally consists of an act and some consequence. The consequence may be very closely connected with the act or more remotely connected with it: but with a crime of basic intent the *mens rea* does not extend beyond the act and its consequence, however remote, as defined in the *actus reus*. I take assault as an example of a crime of basic intent where the consequence is very closely connected with the act. The *actus reus* of assault is an act which causes another person to apprehend immediate and unlawful

> violence. The *mens rea* corresponds exactly. The prosecution must prove that the accused foresaw that his act would probably cause another person to have apprehension of immediate and unlawful violence, or would possibly have that consequence, such being the purpose of the act, or that he was reckless as to whether or not his act caused such apprehension. This foresight (the term of art is 'intention') or recklessness is the *mens rea* in assault. For example of a crime of basic intent where the consequence of the act involved in the *actus reus* as defined in the crime is less immediate, I take the crime of unlawful wounding. The act is, say, the squeezing of a trigger. A number of consequences (mechanical, chemical, ballistic and physiological) intervene before the final consequence involved in the defined *actus reus* – namely, the wounding of another person in circumstances unjustified by law. But again here the *mens rea* corresponds closely to the *actus reus*. The prosecution must prove that the accused foresaw that some physical harm would ensue to another person in circumstances unjustified by law as a probable (or possible and desired) consequence of his act, or that he was reckless as to whether or not such consequence ensued.

How does the fact of self-induced intoxication fit into that analysis? If a man consciously and deliberately takes alcohol and drugs not on medical prescription, but in order to escape from reality, to go 'on a trip', to become hallucinated, whatever the description may be and thereby disables himself from taking the care he might otherwise take and as a result by his subsequent actions causes injury to another – does our criminal law enable him to say that because he did not know what he was doing he lacked both intention and recklessness and accordingly is entitled to an acquittal?

Originally the common law would not and did not recognise self-induced intoxication as an excuse. Lawton LJ spoke of the 'merciful relaxation' to that rule which was introduced by the judges during the 19th century, and he added, at 411:

> Although there was much reforming zeal and activity in the 19th century, Parliament never once considered whether self-induced intoxication should be a defence generally to a criminal charge. It would have been a strange result if the merciful relaxation of a strict rule of law had ended, without any Parliamentary intervention, by whittling it away to such an extent that the more drunk a man became, provided he stopped short of making himself insane, the better chance he had of an acquittal ... The common law rule still applied but there were exceptions to it which Lord Birkenhead LC tried to define by reference to specific intent.

There are, however, decisions of eminent judges in a number of Commonwealth cases in Australia and New Zealand, (but generally not in Canada nor in the United States) as well as impressive academic comment in this country, to which we have been referred, supporting the view that it is illogical and inconsistent with legal principle to treat a person who of his own choice and volition has taken drugs and drink, even though he thereby creates a state in which he is not conscious of what he is doing, any differently from a person suffering from various medical conditions like epilepsy or diabetic coma and who is regarded by the law as free from fault. However our courts have for a very long time regarded in quite another light the state of self-induced intoxication. The authority which for the last half century has been relied upon in this context has been the speech of the Earl of Birkenhead LC in *DPP v Beard* [1920] AC 479, who stated at 494:

> Under the law of England as it prevailed until early in the 19th century voluntary drunkenness was never an excuse for criminal misconduct; and indeed the classic authorities broadly assert that voluntary drunkenness must be considered rather an aggravation than a defence. This view was in terms based upon the principle that a man who by his own voluntary act debauches and destroys his will power shall be no better situated in regard to criminal acts than a sober man.

Lord Birkenhead LC made a historical survey of the way the common law, from the 16th century on, dealt with the effect of self-induced intoxication upon criminal responsibility. This indicates how, from 1819 on, the judges began to mitigate the severity of the attitude of the common law in such cases as murder and serious violent crime when the penalties of death or transportation applied or where there was likely to be sympathy for the accused, as in attempted suicide. Lord Birkenhead LC concluded at 499, that (except in cases where insanity is pleaded) the decisions he cited:

> establish that where a specific intent is an essential element in the offence, evidence of a state of drunkenness rendering the accused incapable of forming such an intent should be taken into consideration in order to determine whether he had in fact formed the intent necessary to constitute the particular crime. If he was so drunk that he was incapable of forming the intent required he could not be convicted of a crime which was committed only if the intent was proved ... In a charge of murder based upon intention to kill or to do grievous bodily harm, if the jury are satisfied that the accused was, by reason of his drunken condition, incapable of forming the intent to kill or to do grievous bodily harm ... he cannot be convicted of murder. But nevertheless unlawful homicide has been committed by the accused, and consequently he is guilty of unlawful homicide without malice aforethought, and that is manslaughter: *per* Stephen J in *R v Doherty* (1887) 16 Cox CC 306, 307.

He concludes the passage:

> the law is plain beyond all question that in cases falling short of insanity a condition of drunkenness at the time of committing an offence causing death can only, when it is available at all, have the effect of reducing the crime from murder to manslaughter.

From this it seemed clear – and this is the interpretation which the judges have placed upon the decision during the ensuing half century – that it is only in the limited class of cases requiring proof of specific intent that drunkenness can exculpate. Otherwise in no case can it exempt completely from criminal liability ...

I do not for my part regard that general principle as either unethical or contrary to the principles of natural justice. If a man of his own volition takes a substance which causes him to cast off the restraints of reason and conscience, no wrong is done to him by holding him answerable criminally for any injury he may do while in that condition. His course of conduct in reducing himself by drugs and drink to that condition in my view supplies the evidence of *mens rea*, of guilty mind certainly sufficient for crimes of basic intent. It is a reckless course of conduct and recklessness is enough to constitute the necessary *mens rea* in assault cases: see *R v Venna* [1976] QB 421, *per* James LJ at 429. The drunkenness is itself an intrinsic, an integral part of the crime, the other part being the evidence of the unlawful use of force against the victim. Together they add up to criminal recklessness ...

My noble and learned friends and I think it may be helpful if we give the following indication of the general lines on which in our view the jury should be directed as to the effect upon the criminal responsibility of the accused of drink or drugs or both, whenever death or physical injury to another person results from something done by the accused for which there is no legal justification and the offence with which the accused is charged is manslaughter or assault at common law or the statutory offence of unlawful wounding under s 20, or of assault occasioning actual bodily harm under s 47 of the Offences Against the Person Act 1861.

In the case of these offences it is no excuse in law that, because of drink or drugs which the accused himself had taken knowingly and willingly, he had deprived himself of the ability to exercise self-control, to realise the possible consequences of what he was doing, or even to be conscious that he was doing it. As in the instant case, the jury may be properly instructed that they 'can ignore the subject of drink or drugs as being in any way a defence' to charges of this character ...

Lord Salmon: ... I accept that there is a degree of illogicality in the rule that intoxication may excuse or expunge one type of intention and not another. This illogicality is, however, acceptable to me because the benevolent part of the rule removes undue harshness without imperilling safety and the stricter part of the rule works without imperilling justice. It would be just as ridiculous to remove the benevolent part of the rule (which no one suggests) as it would be to adopt the alternative of removing the stricter part of the rule for the sake of preserving absolute logic. Absolute logic in human affairs is an uncertain guide and a very dangerous master. The law is primarily concerned with human affairs. I believe that the main object of our legal system is to preserve individual liberty. One important aspect of individual liberty is protection against physical violence.

If there were to be no penal sanction for any injury unlawfully inflicted under the complete mastery of drink or drugs, voluntarily taken, the social consequence could be appalling. That is why I do not consider that there is any justification for the criticisms which have been made of the Court of Appeal's decision in *R v Lipman* [1970] 1 QB 152. Lipman was convicted of manslaughter because he had killed his companion by stuffing bedclothes down her throat under the illusion, induced by the hallucinatory drugs he had taken, that he was fighting for his life against snakes. Had she survived his attack he could have been properly convicted of causing grievous bodily harm or of assault occasioning actual bodily harm under ss 20 and 47 respectively of the Act of 1861. These, like manslaughter, are all offences of basic intent and do not require the proof of any specific intent in order to establish guilt. According to our law as it has stood for about 150 years, in such cases evidence that the injuries were inflicted by a man not knowing what he was doing because he was intoxicated by drinks or drugs which he has voluntarily taken is wholly irrelevant. Certainly this rule seems, in practice, to have worked well without causing any injustice. The judge always carefully takes into account all the circumstances (which vary infinitely from case to case) before deciding which of the many courses open should be adopted in dealing with the convicted man.

If, as I think, this long-standing rule was salutary years ago when it related almost exclusively to drunkenness and hallucinatory drugs were comparatively unknown how much more salutary is it today when such drugs are increasingly becoming a public menace? My Lords, I am satisfied that this rule accords with justice, ethics and common sense, and I would leave it alone even if it does not comply with strict logic. It would, in my view, be disastrous if the law were changed to allow men who did what Lipman did to go free. It would shock the public, it would rightly bring the law into contempt and it would certainly increase one of the really serious menaces facing society today. This is too great a price to pay for bringing solace to those who believe that, come what may, strict logic should always prevail ...

Lord Russell of Killowen: ... There are those who consider that the pendulum should swing the whole way from the old attitude of the criminal law that self-induced intoxication was if anything an aggravation of the crime committed while under its influence, to an attitude whereunder if the intoxication deprives a man of the ability to appreciate what he was doing he cannot be held guilty of any crime at all, save one of absolute liability or in which drunkenness is itself a constituent element of the crime. A man who has no knowledge of what he does cannot, it is said, be a guilty man, whatever may have deprived him of that knowledge. There is, at least superficially, logic in that approach: but logic in criminal law must not be allowed to run away with common sense, particularly when the preservation of the Queen's Peace is in question. The ordinary citizen who is badly beaten up would rightly think little of the criminal law as an effective protection if, because his attacker had deprived himself of ability to know what he was doing by getting himself drunk or going on a trip with drugs, the attacker is to be held innocent of any crime in the assault. *Mens rea* has many aspects. If asked to define it in such a case as the present I would say that the element of guilt or moral turpitude is supplied by the act of self-intoxication reckless of possible consequences. (In the early history of the criminal law it was always recognised that intoxication *not* self-induced – the surreptitiously laced drink – gave rise to quite different considerations: and this was because it was not the man's 'fault'. And so nowadays.) If, however, the crime charged was, as described in *DPP v Beard* [1920] AC 479, one which required a 'specific intent' to constitute the crime, and the self-induced intoxication was such that he had not the required specific intent, the accused is not to be found guilty of that particular crime: though commonly there will be a lesser crime to which the intoxication – however mind-stealing – will be no defence: murder and manslaughter are such: assault causing grievous bodily harm with intent to cause grievous bodily harm, and assault causing grievous bodily harm or actual bodily harm is another example ...

R v Lipman [1970] 1 QB 152 (CA)

See Chapter 21.

R v Woods (1982) 74 Cr App R 312 (CA)

Griffiths LJ: ... [The appellant's conviction of rape] arose out of a disgraceful incident on Saturday 29 September 1979. The victim, who was aged only 19, had been drinking at a club in Blackburn. I can summarise the facts by saying that after she left the club it was alleged that these young men had raped her one after the other.

The appellant made admissions of his part in it to the police. He said he had felt sick ever since it happened and he was disgusted with himself and asked if the girl was all right. When charged with rape he said that he was glad that he had been caught and he admitted that he had been attempting to have intercourse with the girl. He said, and no doubt this is true, it would never have happened if he had not been drunk. Forensic evidence showed that he had seminal staining on his underpants and there were fragments of grass on the outside of his jacket and a small amount of soil, all consistent with taking part in this rape in the car park.

At his trial he went back on those admissions and said in effect that he had so much to drink that he was not sure what had happened. He did not know whether he had raped her or not and did not realise that she was not consenting to anything that went on. The sole ground of this appeal is that the learned judge wrongly directed the jury that the appellant's self-induced intoxication afforded him no defence to the allegation that he was reckless as to whether the complainant consented to sexual intercourse.

[Counsel for the appellant] founded his submission upon the wording of s 1 of the Sexual Offences (Amendment) Act 1976. Subsection (1) provides:

> For the purposes of section 1 of the Sexual Offences Act 1956 (which relates to rape) a man commits rape if: (a) he has unlawful sexual intercourse with a woman who at the time of the intercourse does not consent to it; and (b) at the time he knows that she does not consent to the intercourse or he is reckless as to whether she consents to it; and references to rape in other enactments (including the following provisions of this Act) shall be construed accordingly.

[Counsel for the appellant] concedes that if the section ended there he could not pursue this appeal in the face of the decision of the House of Lords in *DPP v Majewski* [1977] AC 443, and in the very recent case of *Caldwell* [1981] 1 All ER 961. To show that he is correct to make his concession at that stage it is only necessary to read a short passage from the speech of Lord Diplock in *Caldwell*. [His Lordship then quoted the words of Lord Diplock at 967G].

[Counsel for the appellant], however, relies upon the wording of subsection (2) which [then provided:]

> It is hereby declared that if at a trial for a rape offence the jury has to consider whether a man believed that a woman was consenting to sexual intercourse, the presence or absence of reasonable grounds for such a belief is a matter to which the jury is to have regard, in conjunction with any other relevant matters, in considering whether he so believed.

He submits that the language of this subsection is directing the jury to take into account a defendant's drunken state as a possible reasonable ground for his belief that a woman is consenting to intercourse.

As the law stood immediately before the passing of this Act self-induced intoxication was no defence to a crime of rape (see *DPP v Majewski*). If Parliament had intended to provide in future that a man whose lust was so inflamed by drink that he ravished a woman, should nevertheless be able to pray in aid his drunken state to avoid the consequences we would have expected them to have used the clearest words to express such a surprising result which we believe would be utterly repugnant to the great majority of people. We are satisfied that Parliament had no such intention and that this is clear from the use of the word 'relevant' in the subsection. Relevant means, in this context, legally relevant. The law, as a matter of social policy, has declared that self-induced intoxication is not a legally relevant matter to be taken into account in deciding as to whether or not a woman consents to intercourse.

Accordingly, the appellant's drunkenness was not a matter that the jury were entitled to take into consideration in deciding whether or not reasonable grounds existed for the appellant's belief that the woman consented to intercourse. The learned judge rightly directed the jury on this issue. In fact we believe that the object of subsection (2) is the very reverse of that contended by the appellant. It was not intended to make it easier for a man who rapes a woman to escape punishment by saying, in spite of the other evidence, that he thought she consented. The subsection directs the jury to look carefully at all the other relevant evidence before making up their minds on this issue ...

R v Fotheringham (1989) 88 Cr App R 206 (CA)

See Chapter 23.

R v Bennett [1995] Crim LR 877 (CA)

Facts: The appellant appealed against her conviction of arson, intending to endanger life. A fire was started in the kitchen of the flat which she shared with her friend. She denied being responsible for the fire, both in interview with the police and in evidence. The interviewing officer and the appellant's friend gave evidence that the appellant was drunk on the night of the fire. The appellant denied being drunk, saying she was 'merry'.

She appealed against conviction on the ground that the jury should have been directed that there was evidence of drunkenness which they ought to take into account when deciding whether or not the prosecution had proved that she intended to destroy or damage property and by the damage to endanger life.

Held, allowing the appeal and substituting a conviction for arson being reckless as to whether life was endangered, a judge must direct the jury, not only on those issues specifically raised by a defendant, but also on issues which, though not pursued by the defendant, are on the evidence capable of serving as a defence or bearing on facts which the prosecution must prove to bring home the offence to the accused. Unlike a case in which the judge has to decide whether or not to direct on an alternative defence inconsistent with a defence advanced by the defendant, the judge in the appellant's case had to give a direction on an essential element of the offence which the Crown had to prove. In that context evidence of voluntary intoxication had to be treated like any other evidence which tended to show that the defendant may have lacked the state of mind necessary to support the offence. The judge ought to have drawn the jury's attention to the significance of the evidence of intoxication and to have given the direction suggested in *Sheehan and Moore* (1974) 60 Cr App R 308.

Jaggard v Dickinson [1981] QB 527 (DC)

See Chapter 20.

R v O'Grady [1987] 1 QB 995 (CA)

Lord Lane CJ: ... The appellant was addicted to drinking large quantities of alcohol, as were the friends and acquaintances with whom he consorted, one of whom was McCloskey, the deceased man. On Thursday 26 September 1985, the appellant, McCloskey and another man called Brennan spent the day drinking. The appellant had drunk huge quantities of cider (some eight flagons), and he and Brennan and McCloskey repaired to the appellant's flat.

Early on Friday morning Brennan woke up to see that the appellant was covered in blood. 'We' – meaning McCloskey and himself – 'had a fight', said the appellant, 'and I felt him and he was cold.' The appellant went to the police station saying he wished to report a murder. He was medically examined. He had a number of cuts and bruises to the head, hands and legs which were consistent with (a) fighting and (b) grasping broken glass ...

... He said, 'I did not want to kill him. I wanted him alive, not dead. I had no enmity to him. If I had not hit him I would be dead myself.'

... How should the jury be invited to approach the problem? One starts with the decision of this court in *R v Williams (Gladstone)* (1983) 78 Cr App R 276, namely that where the defendant might have been labouring under a mistake as to the facts he must be judged according to that mistaken view, whether the mistake was reasonable or not. It is then for the jury to decide whether the defendant's reaction to the threat, real or imaginary, was a reasonable one. The court was not in that case considering what the situation might be where the mistake was due to voluntary intoxication by alcohol or some other drug.

We have come to the conclusion that where the jury are satisfied that the defendant was mistaken in his belief that any force or the force which he in fact used was necessary to defend himself and are further satisfied that the mistake was caused by voluntary induced intoxication, the defence must fail. We do not consider that any distinction should be drawn on this aspect of the matter between offences involving what is called specific intent, such as murder, and offences of so called basic intent, such as manslaughter. Quite apart from the problem of directing a jury in a case such as the present where manslaughter is an alternative verdict to murder, the question of mistake can and ought to be considered separately from the question of intent. A sober man who mistakenly believes he is in danger of immediate death at the hands of an attacker is entitled to be acquitted of both murder and manslaughter if his reaction in killing his supposed assailant was a reasonable one. What his intent may have been seems to us to be irrelevant to the problem of self-defence or no ...

This brings us to the question of public order. There are two competing interests. On the one hand the interest of the defendant who has only acted according to what he believed to be necessary to protect himself, and on the other hand that of the public in general and the victim in particular who, probably through no fault of his own, has been injured or perhaps killed because of the defendant's drunken mistake. Reason recoils from the conclusion that in such circumstances a defendant is entitled to leave the court without a stain on his character.

We find support for that view in the decision of the House of Lords in *R v Majewski* [1977] AC 443, and in particular in the speeches of Lord Simon of Glaisdale and Lord Edmund-Davies. [His Lordship quoted from the speech of Lord Simon at 476 and the speech of Lord Edmund-Davies at 492].

[His Lordship then referred to *R v Lipman* [1970] 1 QB 152 and went on to say that if the arguments put forward by the appellant in the present case were correct] Lipman could successfully have escaped conviction altogether by raising the issue that he believed he was defending himself legitimately from an attack by serpents. It is significant that no one seems to have considered that possibility ...

THE 'DUTCH COURAGE' RULE

A person who deliberately becomes intoxicated in order to give himself the courage to commit a crime cannot use his intoxication as a defence even if the crime is one of specific intent.

Attorney General for Northern Ireland v Gallagher [1963] AC 349 (HL)

Lord Denning: My Lords, every direction which a judge gives to a jury in point of law must be considered against the background of facts which have been proved or admitted in the case. In this case the accused man did not give evidence himself. And the facts proved against him were:

> He had a grievance against his wife. She had obtained a maintenance order against him and had been instrumental in getting him detained in a mental hospital.

> He had made up his mind to kill his wife. He bought a knife for the purpose and a bottle of whiskey – either to give himself Dutch courage to do the deed or to drown his conscience after it.
>
> He did in fact carry out his intention. He killed his wife with the knife and drank much of the whiskey before or after he killed her.

There were only two defences raised on his behalf: (1) Insanity; (2) Drunkenness.

The Lord Chief Justice directed the jury that the *time* when they had to consider whether he was insane or not (within the M'Naghten Rules) was before he started on the bottle of whiskey. 'You should direct your attention', he said to them, 'to the state of his mind before he opened the bottle of whisky.' If he was sane at that time, he could not make good the defence of insanity 'with the aid of that bottle of whiskey'. Immediately after the jury retired, Mr Kelly took up this point of *time*. He suggested that it was inaccurate and inconsistent with the M'Naghten Rules. But the Lord Chief Justice adhered to his view. He declined to modify his charge to the jury on the matter. 'If I'm wrong', he said, 'I can be put right.' It was on this very point of *time* that the Court of Criminal Appeal reversed him. His direction was, they said, 'inconsistent with the M'Naghten Rules', which fix the crucial time as 'the time of the committing of the act', that is, the time of the killing and not at an earlier time.

The question is whether the direction of the Lord Chief Justice as to the *time* was correct. At least that is how I read the question posed by the Court of Criminal Appeal. It is complicated by the fact that, according to the medical evidence, the accused man was a psychopath. That does not mean that he was insane. But it sharpens the point of the question. He had a disease of the mind. It was quiescent before he started on the whiskey. So he was sane then. But the drink may have brought on an explosive outburst in the course of which he killed her. Can he rely on this self-induced defect of reason and put it forward as a defence of insanity?

My Lords, this case differs from all the others in the books in that the accused man, whilst sane and sober, before he took to the drink, had already made up his mind to kill his wife. This seems to me to be far worse – and far more deserving of condemnation – than the case of a man who, before getting drunk, has no intention to kill, but afterwards in his cups, whilst drunk, kills another by an act which he would not dream of doing when sober. Yet by the law of England in this latter case his drunkenness is no defence even though it has distorted his reason and his will power. So why should it be a defence in the present case? And is it made any better by saying that the man is a psychopath?

The answer to the question is, I think, that the case falls to be decided by the general principle of English law that, subject to very limited exceptions, drunkenness is no defence to a criminal charge, nor is a defect of reason produced by drunkenness. This principle was stated by Sir Matthew Hale in his Pleas of the Crown, 1, p 32, in words which I would repeat here: 'This vice' (drunkenness) 'both deprive men of the use of reason, and puts many men into a perfect, but temporary frenzy ... By the laws of England such a person shall have no privilege by this voluntary contracted madness, but shall have the same judgment as if he were in his right senses.'

This general principle can be illustrated by looking at the various ways in which drunkenness may produce a defect of reason:

(a) It may impair a man's powers of perception so that he may not be able to foresee or measure the consequences of his actions as he would if he were sober. Nevertheless he is not allowed to set up his self-induced want of perception as a defence. Even if he did not himself appreciate that what he was doing was dangerous, nevertheless if a reasonable man in his place, who was not befuddled with drink, would have appreciated it, he is guilty: see *R v Meade* [1909] 1 KB 895, as explained in *DPP v Beard* [1920] AC 479, 502–04.

(b) It may impair a man's power to judge between right or wrong, so that he may do a thing when drunk which he would not dream of doing while sober. He does not realise he is doing wrong. Nevertheless he is not allowed to set up his self-induced want of moral sense as a defence. In *Beard's* case Lord Birkenhead LC distinctly ruled that it was not a defence for a drunken man to say he did not know he was doing wrong.

(c) It may impair a man's power of self-control so that he may more readily give way to provocation than if he were sober. Nevertheless he is not allowed to set up his self-induced want of control as a defence. The acts of provocation are to be assessed, not according to their effect on him personally, but according to the effect they would have on a reasonable man in his place. The law on this point was previously in doubt (see the cases considered in *Beard's* case), but it has since been resolved by *R v McCarthy* [1954] 2 QB 105, *Bedder v DPP* [1954] 1 WLR 1119 and s 3 of the Homicide Act 1957.

The general principle which I have enunciated is subject to two exceptions:

1 If a man is charged with an offence in which a specific intention is essential (as in murder, though not in manslaughter), then evidence of drunkenness, which renders him incapable of forming that intention, is an answer: see *Beard's* case. This degree of drunkenness is reached when the man is rendered so stupid by drink that he does not know what he is doing (see *R v Moore* (1852) 3 Car & Kir 319), as where, at a christening, a drunken nurse put the baby behind a large fire, taking it for a log of wood (*Gentleman's Magazine*, 1748, p 570); and where a drunken man thought his friend (lying in his bed) was a theatrical dummy placed there and stabbed him to death (1951) *Times*, 13 January. In each of those cases it would not be murder. But it would be manslaughter.

2 If a man by drinking brings on a distinct disease of the mind such as *delirium tremens*, so that he is temporarily insane within the M'Naghten Rules, that is to say, he does not at the time know what he is doing or that it is wrong, then he has a defence on the ground of insanity: see *R v Davis* (1881) 14 Cox CC 563 and *Beard's* case.

Does the present case come within the general principle or the exceptions to it? It certainly does not come within the first exception. This man was not incapable of forming an intent to kill. Quite the contrary. He knew full well what he was doing. He formed an intent to kill, he carried out his intention and he remembered afterwards what he had done. And the jury, properly directed on the point, have found as much, for they found him guilty of murder. Then does the case come within the second exception? It does not, to my mind, for the simple reason that he was not suffering from a disease of the mind brought on by drink. He was suffering from a different disease altogether. As the Lord Chief Justice observed in his summing up: 'If this man was suffering from a disease of the mind, it wasn't of a kind that is produced by drink.'

So we have here a case of the first impression. The man is a psychopath. That is, he has a disease of the mind which is not produced by drink. But it is quiescent. And whilst it is quiescent he forms an intention to kill his wife. He knows it is wrong but still he means to kill her. Then he gets himself so drunk that he has an explosive outburst and kills his wife. At that moment he knows what he is doing but he does not know it is wrong. So in that respect – in not knowing it is wrong – he has a defect of reason at the moment of killing. If that defect of reason is due to the drink, it is no defence in law. But if it is due to the disease of the mind, it gives rise to a defence of insanity. No one can say, however, whether it is due to the drink or to the disease. It may well be due to both in combination. What guidance does the law give in this difficulty? That is, as I see it, the question of general public importance which is involved in this case.

My Lords, I think the law on this point should take a clear stand. If a man, whilst sane and sober, forms an intention to kill and makes preparation for it, knowing it is a wrong thing to do, and then gets himself drunk so as to give himself Dutch courage to do the killing, and whilst drunk carries out his intention, he cannot rely on this self-induced drunkenness as a defence to a charge of murder, nor even as reducing it to manslaughter. He cannot say that he got himself into such a stupid state that he was incapable of an intent to kill. So also when he is a psychopath, he cannot by drinking rely on his self-induced defect of reason as a defence of insanity. The wickedness of his mind before he got drunk is enough to condemn him, coupled with the act which he intended to do and did so. A psychopath who goes out intending to kill, knowing it is wrong, and does kill, cannot escape the consequences by making himself drunk before doing it. That is, I believe, the direction which the Lord Chief Justice gave to the jury and which the Court of Criminal Appeal found to be wrong. I think it was right and for this reason I would allow the appeal.

I would agree, of course, that if before the killing he had discarded his intention to kill or reversed it – and then got drunk – it would be a different matter. But when he forms the intention to kill and without interruption proceeds to get drunk and carry out his intention, then his drunkenness is no defence and nonetheless so because it is dressed up as a defence of insanity. There was no evidence in this case of any interruption and there was no need for the Lord Chief Justice to mention it to the jury.

I need hardly say, of course, that I have here only considered the law of Northern Ireland. In England a psychopath such as this man might now be in a position to raise a defence of diminished responsibility under s 2 of the Homicide Act 1957 ...

Lord Morris of Borth-y-Gest: ... On the part of the case dealing with insanity the issue before the jury was whether the accused at the time of the killing was suffering from a disease of the mind, which disease had the effect of producing a defect of reason so that either he did not know the nature and quality of the act he was doing or that he did not know that it was wrong. If he had any disease of the mind, he had it prior to and in the morning of 7 September; it was immaterial how it was caused, though if the accused had any disease of the mind it was not of a kind that was caused by drink. If he had a disease of the mind in the morning, I do not read the medical evidence as suggesting that some later consumption of alcohol altered the nature of the disease. Nor do I read the medical evidence as suggesting that any disease of the mind originated during the day. It was said that the accused had a disease of the mind which was 'episodic' in that it made him liable to have outbursts. If there was some explosive outburst resulting either in his not knowing what he was doing or not knowing that it was wrong, there would only be applicability of the M'Naghten Rules if such explosive outburst was a manifestation of, or a result of, some disease of the mind which existed in the morning. If there was some explosive outburst which resulted from drink and not from disease of the mind, then the M'Naghten Rules would not be applicable. It was for the accused at the trial to show that his actions at the time of the killing were manifestations of a disease of the mind and not manifestations of being under the influence of alcohol.

Since in the present case it was not suggested that if the accused had some disease of the mind it had not existed at the start of the day and throughout the day, a consideration as to whether such disease existed in the morning was equally a consideration as to whether it existed 'at the time of the committing of the act'. When the learned Lord Chief Justice told the jury in his summing up that they should come to their conclusion without reference to the drink that the accused took on 7 September, and should direct their attention to the state of his mind in the morning before he opened the bottle of whiskey, he was helpfully reminding them that, for the M'Naghten Rules to apply, the defect of reason producing a condition of either not knowing the nature and quality of the act being done or of not knowing that it was wrong must be the result of a disease of the mind and not the result of being under the influence of drink. The learned Lord Chief Justice was pointing the differences between the possible case where a psychopath does something because he is drunk and the possible case where a psychopath does something because he is a psychopath.

The many references in the summing up to the tests in regard to the knowledge of the accused (ie his knowledge as to the nature and quality of the act he was doing or as to whether it was wrong) must in the nature of things have had reference to the moment of time of the act (ie the killing) which was in question. The Learned Lord Chief Justice summarised all the medical evidence very carefully. The most that Dr Dawson could say in regard to the accused's knowledge was that assuming that the accused 'may have been under the influence of alcohol' he (Dr Dawson) expressed a 'very real doubt' as to the accused's knowledge in the material respects: if it were assumed that the accused had not had alcohol Dr Dawson expressed 'a doubt' as to the accused's knowledge.

If the jury thought that the accused did have a disease of the mind, then such disease of the mind existed on the morning of 7 September, and before the defence of insanity could succeed the jury would have had to have been of the opinion that that disease of the mind was of such a kind that it could produce, and that it did produce, a defect of reason which had the result that the accused either did not know what he was doing or did not know it was wrong.

Having these considerations in mind, it seems to me that, read as a whole, the summing up did not wrongly direct the jury in their consideration of the issue of insanity.

I would allow the appeal.

CHAPTER 8

GENERAL DEFENCES – SELF-DEFENCE

A person may use such force as is reasonable in the circumstances for the purposes of:

(1) self-defence

(2) defence of another person

(3) defence of property

(4) the prevention of crime (see s 3(1) of the Criminal Law Act 1967)

(5) making a lawful arrest (see s 3(1) of the Criminal Law Act 1967).

See, for example, *Beckford v The Queen* [1988] AC 130 and *R v Clegg* [1995] 1 AC 482.

This defence applies only to crimes which involve the use of force (*R v Renouf* [1986] 1 WLR 522).

A person can use reasonable force to ward off an anticipated attack, so long as he believes the attack to be imminent. Where the threat of force is likely to be sufficient, it may well be unreasonable to use actual force. See *R v Cousins* [1982] 1 QB 526.

Where the defence relied upon is defence of another person, there has to be a link between the accused and that other person. How close that link must be is unclear. In most cases, the defence of another person will in any event also be action to prevent a crime. See, for example, *R v Duffy* [1967] 1 QB 63.

It is clear that one can defend one's own property, but it is not so clear to what extent one can defend the property of other people. However, action to defend another person's property will usually be action to prevent a crime and so will be a defence on that basis.

Beckford v The Queen [1988] AC 130 (PC)

Lord Griffiths: ... The defendant was a police officer who on 8 March 1983 was issued with a shotgun and ammunition and sent with a number of other armed police officers to a house at Greenvale Park in Manchester. The prosecution called no evidence to explain the circumstances in which this armed posse was sent out that morning but according to the defendant, in a statement he made from the dock, he and other police officers, including a Police Constable Reckord, were told by Deputy Superintendent Wilson that a report had been received from Heather Barnes that her brother Chester Barnes was terrorising her mother with a gun and that the police must come immediately to save her life. The defendant said that they were warned that the man appeared to be a dangerous gunman and that they must take special care. Heather Barnes, however, who was the first witness called by the prosecution, denied in cross-examination that she had made a telephone call to the police or that her brother Chester Barnes was armed ...

The prosecution case, based primarily on the evidence of Heather Barnes and a witness named Peart, was that the defendant armed with a shotgun and Police Constable Reckord, armed with a revolver, had aggressively entered the house whereupon the unarmed Chester Barnes had fled from the house, run across the yard, jumped over a wall and tried to hide by a pigsty on the adjoining common.

Heather Barnes said the defendant had fired at her brother in the yard and then he and Police Constable Reckord had pursued him over the wall on to the common from whence she heard more shots. Peart said he saw Chester Barnes jump the wall pursued by the police. Later he saw Barnes hiding by a pigsty, he put his hands in the air and both police officers fired at him. He heard Barnes say 'do officer, don't shoot me, because me a cook' [*sic*]. He said Barnes had nothing in his hands, and when he fell after the first shots the defendant shot the deceased in the belly ...

At the conclusion of the defence case the only live issue for the jury was whether the prosecution had proved that the defendant had not killed in self-defence. The first ground of appeal before the Court of Appeal in Jamaica, and the only ground with which their Lordships are concerned, was that the trial judge had misdirected the jury on the issue of self-defence ...

It is accepted by the prosecution that there is no difference on the law of self-defence between the law of Jamaica and the English common law and it therefore falls to be decided whether it was correctly decided by the Court of Appeal in *R v Williams (Gladstone)* (1983) 78 Cr App R 276 that the defence of self-defence depends upon what the accused 'honestly' believed the circumstances to be and not upon the reasonableness of that belief ...

The common law recognises that there are many circumstances in which one person may inflict violence upon another without committing a crime, as for instance, in sporting contests, surgical operations or, in the most extreme example, judicial execution. The common law has always recognised as one of these circumstances the right of a person to protect himself from attack and to act in the defence of others and if necessary to inflict violence on another in so doing. If no more force is used than is reasonable to repel the attack such force is not unlawful and no crime is committed. Furthermore a man about to be attacked does not have to wait for his assailant to strike the first blow or fire the first shot; circumstances may justify a pre-emptive strike.

It is because it is an essential element of all crimes of violence that the violence or the threat of violence should be unlawful that self-defence, if raised as an issue in a criminal trial, must be disproved by the prosecution. If the prosecution fail to do so the accused is entitled to be acquitted because the prosecution will have failed to prove an essential element of the crime, namely that the violence used by the accused was unlawful.

If, then, a genuine belief, albeit without reasonable grounds, is a defence to rape because it negatives the necessary intention, so also must a genuine belief in facts which, if true, would justify self-defence, be a defence to a crime of personal violence because the belief negatives the intent to act unlawfully. Their Lordships therefore approve the following passage from the judgment of Lord Lane CJ in *R v Williams (Gladstone)* 78 Cr App R 276, 281, as correctly stating the law of self-defence:

> The reasonableness or unreasonableness of the defendant's belief is material to the question of whether the belief was held by the defendant at all. If the belief was in fact held, its unreasonableness, so far as guilt or innocence is concerned, is neither here nor there. It is irrelevant. Were it otherwise, the defendant would be convicted because he was negligent in failing to recognise that the victim was not consenting or that a crime was not being committed and so on. In other words the jury should be directed first of all that the prosecution have the burden or duty of proving the unlawfulness of the defendant's actions; second, if the defendant may have been labouring under a mistake as to the facts, he must be judged according to his mistaken

> view of the facts; third, that is so whether the mistake was, on an objective view, a reasonable mistake or not.
>
> In a case of self-defence, where self-defence or the prevention of crime is concerned, if the jury came to the conclusion that the defendant believed, or may have believed, that he was being attacked or that a crime was being committed, and that force was necessary to protect himself or to prevent the crime, then the prosecution have not proved their case. If, however, the defendant's alleged belief was mistaken and if the mistake was an unreasonable one, that may be a powerful reason for coming to the conclusion that the belief was not honestly held and should be rejected. Even if the jury come to the conclusion that the mistake was an unreasonable one, if the defendant may genuinely have been labouring under it, he is entitled to rely upon it.

... There may be a fear that the abandonment of the objective standard demanded by the existence of reasonable grounds for belief will result in the success of too many spurious claims of self-defence. The English experience has not shown this to be the case. The Judicial Studies Board with the approval of the Lord Chief Justice has produced a model direction on self-defence which is now widely used by judges when summing up to juries. The direction contains the following guidance:

> Whether the plea is self-defence or defence of another, if the defendant may have been labouring under a mistake as to the facts, he must be judged according to his mistaken belief of the facts: that is so whether the mistake was, on an objective view, a reasonable mistake or not.

Their Lordships have heard no suggestion that this form of summing up has resulted in a disquieting number of acquittals. This is hardly surprising, for no jury is going to accept a man's assertion that he believed that he was about to be attacked without testing it against all the surrounding circumstances. In assisting the jury to determine whether or not the accused had a genuine belief, the judge will of course direct their attention to those features of the evidence that make such a belief more or less probable. Where there are no reasonable grounds to hold a belief it will surely only be in exceptional circumstances that a jury will conclude that such a belief was or might have been held ...

R v Clegg [1995] 1 AC 482 (HL)

Lord Lloyd of Berwick: My Lords, on the night of 30 September 1990 the appellant, Lee William Clegg, a soldier serving with the Parachute Regiment, was on patrol in Glen Road, West Belfast, when the driver of a stolen car and one of his passengers were shot and killed. Private Clegg was charged with murder of the passenger, and attempted murder of the driver. His defence was that he fired in self-defence. He was convicted on 4 June 1993, after a trial before Campbell J without a jury. His appeal to the Court of Appeal was dismissed. The Court of Appeal held that the firing of the shot which killed the passenger was, on the facts found by the judge, a grossly excessive and disproportionate use of force, and that any tribunal of fact properly directed would so have found. The certified question of law for your Lordships is whether a soldier on duty, who kills a person with the requisite intention for murder, but who would be entitled to rely on self-defence but for the use of excessive force, is guilty of murder or manslaughter.

The patrol consisted of 15 men under the command of Lieutenant Oliver. It was accompanied by a police constable from the Royal Ulster Constabulary. The purpose of the patrol was to catch joyriders. But this was not explained to Private Clegg. The patrol was divided into four teams or 'bricks'. Brick 11 formed a vehicle checkpoint at a bridge on the Glen Road about six miles west of Belfast. Brick 10A, consisting of Lieutenant Oliver, Private Clegg, Private Aindow and another, were moving down the road towards Belfast. Private Aindow was on the right-hand side of the road. The others were all on the left-hand side. Bricks 12 and 14 were still further down the road, around a corner. As the stolen car approached the bridge from the west, it was stopped by a member of Brick 11. The car then accelerated away in the centre of the road towards Brick 10A with its headlights full on. Someone in Brick 11 shouted to stop it. All four members of Brick 10A fired at the approaching car. Private Clegg's evidence was that he fired three shots at the windscreen, and a fourth shot into the side of the car as it was passing. He then replaced his safety-catch. According to Private Clegg he fired all four shots because he thought Private Aindow's life was in danger. However, scientific evidence showed, and the trial judge found as a fact, that Private Clegg's fourth shot was fired *after* the car had passed, and was already over 50 feet along the road to Belfast. It struck a rear-seat passenger, Karen Reilly, in the back. It was later found lodged beneath her liver. The judge found that Private Clegg's fourth shot was an aimed shot fired with the intention of causing death or serious bodily harm. Although another bullet passed through Karen Reilly's body, Private Clegg's fourth shot was a significant cause of the death.

In relation of the first three shots, the judge accepted Private Clegg's defence that he fired in self-defence or in defence of Private Aindow. But with regard to the fourth shot he found that Private Clegg could not have been firing in defence of himself or Private Aindow, since, once the car had passed, they were no longer in any danger.

Having rejected Private Clegg's defence in relation to the fourth shot, the judge went on to consider, as was his duty, whether there was any other defence open on the evidence, even though Private Clegg had not raised the defence himself. One possible defence was that Private Clegg fired the fourth shot in order to arrest the driver. Section 3(1) of the Criminal Law Act (Northern Ireland) 1967 provides:

> A person may use such force as is reasonable in the circumstances in the prevention of crime, or in effecting or assisting in the lawful arrest of offenders or suspected offenders or of persons unlawfully at large.

The judge held that there was insufficient evidence to raise such a defence. Accordingly he convicted Private Clegg of murder.

When the case reached the Court of Appeal, the court reviewed the whole of Private Clegg's evidence. In a number of his answers he had said that he fired to stop the driver of the car after it had, as he thought, struck Private Aindow. Accordingly there was, in the court's view, evidence on which the judge should have considered the defence under s 3 of the Act of 1967.

It should be noted in passing that the car did not, in fact, strike Private Aindow. The judge held that bruising found of Private Aindow's left leg was caused, not by the car, but by another soldier stamping on him in order to create the appearance that he had been struck by the car. In those circumstances, Private Aindow was charged with perverting the course of justice as well as attempted murder. He was convicted on the former count and sentenced to two years' imprisonment. His appeal on that count was dismissed.

Having held that there was evidence to raise the defence under s 3, the Court of Appeal went on to consider whether any miscarriage of justice had actually occurred by reason of the failure of the judge to consider that defence. Section 3 of the Act of 1967 allows a person to use 'such force as is reasonable in the circumstances'. So the question for the Court of Appeal was whether Private Clegg, in firing the fourth shot, used only such force as was reasonable in the circumstances, or whether the force which he used was excessive.

In the course of his cross-examination Private Clegg was asked whether he was aware of any circumstances which would have justified him in firing after the car had passed. He replied that he had no reason to fire at that stage.

> *Q 29*: And if you had fired any more you know of no justification for that action?
>
> *A 29*: That's correct. That's why I applied my safety-catch as the car went past me.

There was no suggestion in Private Clegg's evidence, as the Court of Appeal pointed out, that he thought that the driver was a terrorist, or that if the driver escaped he would carry out terrorist offences in the future. In those circumstances the use of lethal force to arrest the driver of the car was, in the court's view, so 'grossly disproportionate to the mischief to be averted' that any tribunal of fact would have been bound to find that the force used was unreasonable. It follows that if the defence under s 3 had been raised, which it was not, it would have failed. Accordingly, Private Clegg's appeal was dismissed ...

The point raised in the present case might have arisen for decision by your Lordships in *Attorney General for Northern Ireland's Reference (No 1 of 1975)* [1977] AC 105. That case also concerned a soldier on patrol in Northern Ireland. He shot and killed an unarmed man, who ran away when challenged. The trial judge found that, unlike the present case, the prosecution had failed to prove that the soldier intended to kill or cause serious bodily harm, and further found that the homicide was justifiable under s 3 of the Act of 1967 on the ground that the use of force was reasonable in the circumstances. The questions for the opinion of the House were first whether, on the facts set out in the reference, the soldier had committed a crime at all and second whether, if so, the crime was murder or manslaughter. The House held that the first question was not a question of law at all, but a pure question of fact, which, on the facts proved at the trial, had been answered in favour of the soldier; and that the second question, though a question of law, did not arise on the facts. But it is to be observed that Viscount Dilhorne said in relation to the second question at 148:

> I now turn to the second point of law referred, whether if a crime was committed in the circumstances stated in the reference it was murder or manslaughter. The Attorney General indicated that he would like it to be held that it was manslaughter and, while I appreciated his reasons for doing so, I can find no escape from the conclusion that if a crime was committed, it was murder if the shot was fired with intent to kill or seriously wound. To hold that it could be manslaughter would be to make entirely new law. If a plea of self-defence is put forward in answer to a charge of murder and fails because excessive force was used though some force was justifiable, as the law now stands the accused cannot be convicted of manslaughter. It may be that a strong case can be made for an alteration of the law to enable a verdict of manslaughter to be returned where the use of some force was justifiable but that is a matter for legislation and not for judicial decision.

... I do not find it necessary to go through the earlier English authorities relied on by counsel, since they were all reviewed at length by Lord Morris of Borth-y-Gest in *Palmer v The Queen* [1971] AC 814. I respectfully agree with his analysis. Counsel did not advance any fresh arguments. In my opinion the law of England must now be taken to be settled in accordance with the decision of the Privy Council in that case. Thus, the consequence of the use of excessive force in self-defence will be the same in the law of England, Scotland, Australia, Canada and the West Indies. I consider later whether, despite this uniformity, some change in the law may, nevertheless, be desirable.

The second question is whether there is any distinction to be made between excessive force in self-defence and excessive force in the prevention of crime or in arresting offenders. In *Attorney General for Northern Ireland's Reference (No 1 of 1975)* [1977] AC 105 Lord Diplock said at 139, that the two cases were quite different. But I do not think it possible to say that a person who uses excessive force in preventing crime is always, or even generally, less culpable than a person who uses excessive force in self-defence; and even if excessive force in preventing crime were in general less culpable, it would not be practicable to draw a distinction between the two defences, since they so often overlap. Take, for example, the facts of the present case. The trial judge held that Private Clegg's first three shots might have been fired in defence of Private Aindow. But he could equally well have held that they were fired in the prevention of crime, namely to prevent Private Aindow's death being caused by dangerous driving. As is pointed out in Smith and Hogan, *Criminal Law*, 6th edn, 1988, p 244; 7th edn, 1992, p 255, the degree of permissible force should be the same in both cases. So also should the consequences of excessive force.

The third question is whether it makes any difference that Private Clegg was a member of the security forces, acting in the course of his duty ...

... In most cases of a person acting in self-defence, or a police officer arresting an offender, there is a choice as to the degree of force to be used, even if it is a choice which has to be exercised on the spur of the moment, without time for measured reflection. But in the case of a soldier in Northern Ireland, in the circumstances in which Private Clegg found himself, there is no scope for graduated force. The only choice lay between firing a high-velocity rifle which, if aimed accurately, was almost certain to kill or injure, and doing nothing at all.

It should be noticed that the point at issue here is not whether Private Clegg was entitled to be acquitted altogether, on the ground that he was acting in obedience to superior orders. There is no such general defence known to English law, nor was any such defence raised at the trial ... The point is rather whether the offence in such a case should, because of the strong mitigating circumstances, be regarded as manslaughter rather than murder. But so to hold would, as Viscount Dilhorne said in *Attorney General for Northern Ireland's Reference (No 1 of 1975)* [1977] AC 105, 148, be to make entirely new law. I regret that under existing law, on the facts found by the trial judge, he had no alternative but to convict of murder ...

DPP (Jamaica) v Bailey [1995] 1 Cr App R 257 (PC)

Lord Slynn: The respondent, who was a Special Constable in Jamaica, was indicted for the murder of Granville Angus on 20 February 1988. The jury on 9 October 1989 returned a unanimous verdict of not guilty of murder but guilty of manslaughter ...

The respondent came upon the deceased and his brother Patrick with other young men on 19 February 1988 in the street. There was an altercation. The respondent's account in his unsworn statement at the trial was that Patrick

Angus used indecent language and threatened to shoot him. Patrick Angus, on the other hand, said that the respondent warned him that he would arrest him. The respondent said that he had no intention of doing so. Whatever was said the respondent told the policeman on duty at the Harbour View Police Station of what had happened.

It is common ground that on the next day the respondent saw Patrick Angus again. The prosecution evidence was to the effect that whilst the respondent was speaking to Patrick the deceased came out of the house and sat on a pipe. The respondent pushed the deceased and pointed a gun in his face threatening to shoot him. When the deceased dared the respondent to shoot he did so causing the death ...

On the respondent's case there was ... a struggle with the two men who were antagonistic to him trying to get his gun which he sought to protect from them. At the trial the principal defence was that what happened was an accident, the alternative defence being that the respondent was provoked. The learned judge summed up on these two defences in a way which has not been criticised. He added however:

> So also, Mr Foreman and members of the jury, such killing that is a deliberate, intentional killing done in lawful self-defence is no offence at all, but let me tell you this here and now that self-defence does not arise in this case so you will not hear more from me about self-defence. It does not arise in this case. I am only telling you for your own edification that killing done in lawful self-defence is no offence at all ...

It was this withdrawal of the issue of self-defence from the jury's consideration which provided the ground of appeal. The Court of Appeal took the view that 'it is too clear for words that self-defence arose on the appellant's unsworn statement'. They thought that the jury should have been told that the respondent was obliged and entitled to protect his firearm (he was a police officer) and to protect himself from any intended or actual attack on him by the two brothers. 'Self-defence as a concept embraces not only aggressive action such as a pre-emptive strike or aggressive reaction but applies equally to a wholly defensive posture.' The Court of Appeal added:

> It seems to us absolutely illogical that the judge left to the jury the issue of provocation which has all the ingredients of self-defence in a murder case, but omitted to mention self-defence. The actus remains the same in both situations ...

It is clear that perfectly hopeless defences which have no factual basis of support do not have to be left to the jury. But it is no less clear, in their Lordship's view, that if the accused's account of what happened includes matters which, if accepted, could raise a *prima facie* case of self-defence this should be left to the jury even if the accused has not formally relied upon self-defence.

Where, as here, there was a struggle between three men, two of them wanting to get the gun held by the other, then it is possible that the killing was murder, or that it was provoked and so was manslaughter, or that it was an accident, or that it happened deliberately but in self-defence. Self-defence in this context could well include stopping antagonistic men from trying to get a gun which they might have used to injure the accused.

Whether self-defence can fairly be said to arise depends in any case on an analysis of the facts relied on by the accused. Even if the appellant is right in saying that the evidence here, from which self-defence could be deduced once accident is rejected, was not strong, it seems to their Lordships that the Court of Appeal was entitled to conclude on the facts that self-defence should have been explained to and left to the jury. As the appellant accepts, if accident is rejected, then the shooting here was deliberate. It is at that stage necessary to consider whether in the struggle the shooting took place by way of self-defence ...

R v Renouf [1986] 1 WLR 522 (CA)

Lawton LJ: ... On the evening of 2 September 1984 the appellant was working in the forecourt of his garage near Salisbury when a Volvo motor car drew up. Its occupants threw various articles at him. The windscreen of his own motor car was damaged and he was struck on his arm, causing an injury which amounted to 'actual bodily harm' within the meaning of s 47 of the Offences Against the Person Act 1861. Whoever threw that which caused his injury had committed an arrestable offence since it was punishable with imprisonment for not more than five years (see s 2 of the Criminal Law Act 1967). The appellant, in these circumstances, was entitled lawfully to arrest the person throwing the object and those who were aiding and abetting him; and any policeman who, on the appellant's information, tried to arrest the alleged offenders could lawfully do so without a warrant (see s 2 of the Criminal Law Act 1967).

The offenders drove off in the Volvo. The appellant, after telling his wife to telephone the police, followed them in his own motor car. They drove along the A30 road in the direction of Salisbury. This road is straight. The appellant followed them with the object, so he said, of keeping them in view so that they could be identified and arrested by the police. He followed them at a speed of about 60 mph. It was not suggested that the appellant's driving in pursuit of the offenders was reckless.

The prosecution's case was that when later he was near the Pheasant Inn on the A30 road the appellant carried out a manoeuvre which made the Volvo go onto the grass verge and stop. The appellant in evidence said that he had acted as he did in order to make sure that it, and its occupants, were still there when the police arrived, as he expected them to do. The prosecution challenged his evidence as to why he had acted as he did; but if it was relevant evidence, it was for the jury to decide whether to accept it. The evidence relating to edging the Volvo off the road was what the prosecution alleged amounted to the reckless driving as charged. It did create an obvious and serious risk of causing physical harm to the occupants of the Volvo and of damage to it. On the evidence this was the only risk on which the allegation of recklessness could be based. There was no risk to oncoming traffic; and nothing more than a tenuous suggestion that there might have been a risk to any traffic there may have been (and there was none) on a side road nearby. Counsel for the appellant accepted that he had created this risk. His submission, however, was that in creating it he was using 'such force as [was] reasonable in the circumstances ... in ... assisting in the lawful arrest of offenders' (see s 3(1) of the Criminal Law Act 1967). This being so, he was putting forward a defence which the trial judge should have left to the jury.

Counsel for the Crown submitted that no such defence was available to the appellant or, indeed, to anyone charged with reckless driving. Once the prosecution has proved that the accused, having the appropriate *mens rea*, has driven a vehicle in a manner which creates a risk of injury or damage, he has to be convicted, no matter how worthy his reasons were for creating that risk. In the course of argument he submitted, in answer to a question from the bench, that a police officer who forced a criminal off the road in the same kind of way and for the same reason as the appellant said he had done, there being a child in the criminal's car reasonably suspected of having been kidnapped, would in law be guilty of reckless driving. Whether he would be prosecuted would be a matter for the exercise of discretion by the prosecuting authority. This seemed to be a startling proposition; but so would a proposition that motorists could excuse themselves from the consequences of reckless driving merely by alleging that when doing so they were trying to assist in the lawful arrest of offenders.

This case has to be considered in the light of the evidence which was said to have amounted to reckless driving. This evidence had two facts: one was what the prosecution alleged to be the acts of recklessness; and the other was that these same acts amounted to the use of reasonable force for the purpose of assisting in the lawful arrest of offenders. In our judgment it is only when the evidence has these two facets that s 3(1) of the 1967 Act can apply. This being so, the occasions for relying on that section will be rare, certainly not when the reckless acts were antecedent to the use of force. In our judgment the alleged presence of these two facets in the appellant's evidence concerning why he did the acts which the prosecution said were reckless was capable of providing him with a defence. It is no answer for the prosecution to submit, as counsel for the Crown did, that the wording of ss 1 and 2 of the Road Traffic Act 1972 shuts out any possibility of such a defence because they contained no words such as 'lawful excuse'. Nor does s 20 of the Offences Against the Person Act 1861; but s 3(1) has been used to provide a defence to charges under that section.

The only other point which calls for consideration is whether what the appellant said he did amounted to the use of 'force'. That word is one of ordinary usage in English and does not require judicial interpretation. In that usage a jury might consider that the appellant had forced the Volvo off the road onto the grass verge. The trial judge used the word 'force' in this sense in the course of his summing up.

In our judgment, on the unusual evidence in this case, the judge should have left to the jury the appellant's defence based on s 3(1) of the 1967 Act ...

R v Cousins [1982] 1 QB 526 (CA)

Milmo J: ... On 23 April 1981 William Reed, a notoriously violent man, was attacked and beaten up when leaving a public house where the appellant had been. There was no evidence that the appellant had anything to do with this assault, as a result of which William Reed was detained in hospital for a few days.

On the afternoon of 29 April 1981, the appellant, carrying a double-barrelled shotgun, came to the Reeds' home where he enquired as to the whereabouts of Kelly Reed, the son of Mr and Mrs Reed. Mr Reed asked the appellant what he was going to do with the gun and, according to him, the reply was, 'I am coming after Kelly with a gun. When I see him I'm going to kill him. I'm going to blow his brains out, when I see him.' Mrs Reed confirmed this evidence. She said that the appellant had pointed the gun at her husband's head and said: 'I am after your Kelly. I want to see Kelly because he is after me and I'm going to blow his head off.' Both Mr and Mrs Reed said that they believed the appellant intended to carry out the threat he had made and the appellant in cross-examination conceded that he meant them to do so ...

The appellant gave evidence denying that he had anything to do with the beating up of William Reed. He said that three days after the incident, three men whom he knew told him in a public house that he ought to watch out, because they had heard that there was a contract out to shoot him. These men said that Kelly Reed and a cousin of his had put out a contract because they had heard that the appellant was the man who had beaten up William Reed. The appellant said that he had panicked. He had borrowed the gun from a nephew and had gone to the

Reeds' house to give them warning of what he would do if he was attacked or his wife or children endangered. He admitted that at a later stage he had converted the weapon into a sawn-off shotgun which he intended to use if attacked by Kelly Reed ...

It was argued on behalf of the appellant that he in making the threat to William Reed was both seeking to forestall an attack which he reasonably believed that Kelly Reed was planning to make upon him, and also to prevent the commission of the crime which such an attack would have involved. Section 3 of the Criminal Law Act 1967 was relied upon, the relevant parts of which read:

> 3 (1) A person may use such force as is reasonable in the circumstances in the prevention of crime ... (2) Subsection (1) above shall replace the rules of the common law on the question when force used for a purpose mentioned in the subsection is justified by that purpose.

It is, of course, true that the charge against the appellant was not that he used force but that he threatened to use force. However, if force is permissible, something less, for example a threat, must also be permissible if it is reasonable in the circumstances. Moreover, in criminal proceedings the common law recognises that it is lawful for a person to use reasonable means for self-defence. Consequently it can amount to a lawful excuse for a threat to kill if the threat is made of the prevention of crime or for self-defence, provided it is reasonable in the circumstances to make such a threat. What is reasonable in the circumstances is always a question for the jury, never a 'point of law' for the judge: see *Attorney General for Northern Ireland's Reference (No 1 of 1975)* [1977] AC 105, 137, *per* Lord Diplock. As is pointed out in Smith and Hogan, *Criminal Law*, 4th edn, 1978:

> A threat to kill may, however, be excusable where actual killing would not. To cause fear of death might be reasonable to prevent crime or arrest an offender whereas actually to kill would be quite unreasonable.

It will be desirable in many cases to tell the jury this.

In order to obtain the conviction of the appellant under count 1, the onus lay upon the prosecution to establish (a) the making by the appellant to William Reed of a threat to kill Kelly Reed; (b) that the appellant made the threat intending that William Reed would fear that the threat would be carried out; and (c) that there was no lawful excuse for making the threat. Of these elements, (a) and (b) were pure questions of fact for the jury. As to (c), if there was evidence of facts which could give rise to lawful excuse, it was the duty of the judge to direct the jury to these facts and having reminded them that the onus lay with the prosecution to prove the absence of lawful excuse, to have left it to the jury to decide whether the existence of lawful excuse had been disposed of. On the other hand if there was no evidence of any facts which would give rise to a lawful excuse, it was the duty of the judge to direct the jury accordingly.

One ground only is given for the appeal against conviction. It reads as follows:

> The judge erred in directing the jury that there could be no question of lawful excuse for the issue of the said warning threat because 'the life of the defendant was not in immediate jeopardy' and that, accordingly, the defendant was not entitled to use the threat of force in self-defence or in prevention of crime. The judge thereby wrongly withdrew from the jury the question which should have been for them to decide: 'Did the defendant act in reasonable self-defence/prevention of crime in issuing a deterrent threat?'

In the judgment of this court this criticism of the summing up is well founded. What the judge in fact did was to withdraw from the jury the issue whether the appellant had any lawful excuse for making to William Reed the threat alleged.

Throughout the summing up one finds that the judge is directing the jury that lawful excuse does not come into the matter at all ...

R v Duffy [1967] 1 QB 63 (CA)

Edmund Davies J: ...The facts were these. The victim of the affair was a Pakistani named Mohammed Akbar who said that on the night of 1 May he visited the Barracks Tavern in Bradford, where the two accused women were. Kathleen Duffy abused him and then hit him in the face with a glass. He said he did not see the appellant do anything and did not know whether she hit him or not. The licensee said that he saw Kathleen Duffy break a glass, and when he next looked he saw Akbar bleeding profusely, and he sent for the police. He testified that he had not seen the appellant at the start of the trouble, but she appeared from the toilet at a time when her sister was fighting with Akbar on the floor, and it is not unimportant to note that at that time there was blood on both Akbar and on her sister, and the appellant then went to help her sister.

A witness named Hant said he heard a commotion and he saw a Pakistani holding on to Kathleen Duffy and the appellant hitting him with a glass until it broke.

A police officer who was called to the scene said he saw Kathleen on the floor fighting with Akbar. The appellant was in the midst of the battle with a bottle in her hand, and as he and another constable approached, he saw the appellant fight her way towards the Pakistani, raise her right arm and strike him a severe blow on the back of the head with a bottle which smashed, and blood gushed from the back of his head. Both women pummelled the Pakistani with their fists ...

It appears to this court that the trial unfortunately developed along the wrong lines. The inception of the errors was that defending counsel throughout relied upon the plea that the appellant was acting in self-defence, a plea which he submitted extended to the action of the appellant in seeking to rescue her sister. It is established that such a defence is not restricted to the person attacked. It has been said to extend to 'the principal civil and natural relations'. Hale's *Pleas of the Crown*, Vol 1, p 484, gives as instances master and servant, parent and child, and husband and wife who, if they even kill an assailant in the necessary defence of each other, are excused, the act of the relative assisting being considered the same as the act of the party himself ...

The source of the error in this case, as it appears to this court is as we have said, that everyone, including counsel at the trial and again before us, seems to have overlooked that in reality and in law the case of Lilian Duffy was not trammelled by any technical limitations on the application of the plea of self-defence, and this court is not here concerned to consider what those limitations are. Quite apart from any special relations between the person attacked and his rescuer, there is a general liberty even as between strangers to prevent a felony. That is not to say, of course, that a newcomer may lawfully join in a fight just for the sake of fighting. Such conduct is wholly different in law from that of a person who in circumstances of necessity intervenes with the sole object of restoring the peace by rescuing a person being attacked. That, credible or otherwise, was the basic defence advanced by the appellant ...

Section 3(1) of the Criminal Law Act 1967

A person may use such force as is reasonable in the circumstances in the prevention of crime, or in effecting or assisting in the lawful arrest of offenders or suspected offenders or of persons unlawfully at large.

DUTY TO RETREAT?

Where the accused had an opportunity of retreating, rather than using force, the key question is whether the accused acted reasonably in using force rather than retreating: see *R v McInnes* [1971] 1 WLR 1600.

R v Julien [1969] 1 WLR 839 (CA)

Widgery LJ: ... The third point taken by counsel for the appellant is that the learned deputy chairman was wrong in directing the jury that before the appellant could use force in self-defence he was required to retreat. The submission here is that the obligation to retreat before using force in self-defence is an obligation which only arises in homicide cases. As the court understands it, it is submitted that if the injury results in death then the accused cannot set up self-defence except on the basis that he had retreated before he resorted to violence. On the other hand, it is said that where the injury does not result in death (as in the present case) the obligation to retreat does not arise. The sturdy submission is made that an Englishman is not bound to run away when threatened, but can stand his ground and defend himself where he is. In support of this submission no authority is quoted, save that counsel for the appellant has been at considerable length and diligence to look at the textbooks on the subject, and has demonstrated to us that the textbooks in the main do not say that a preliminary retreat is a necessary prerequisite to the use of force in self-defence. Equally, it must be said that the textbooks do not state the contrary either; and it is, of course, well-known to us all that for very many years it has been common form for judges directing juries where the issue of self-defence is raised in any case (be it a homicide case or not) that the duty to retreat arises. It is not, as we understand it, the law that a person threatened must take to his heels and run in the dramatic way suggested by counsel for the appellant; but what is necessary is that he should demonstrate by his actions that he does not want to fight. He must demonstrate that he is prepared to temporise and disengage and perhaps to make some physical withdrawal; and to the extent that that is necessary as a feature of the justification of self-defence, it is true, in our opinion, whether the charge is a homicide charge or something less serious. Accordingly, we reject counsel for the appellant's third submission ...

R v Bird [1985] 1 WLR 816 (CA)

Lord Lane CJ: ... The facts of the case are these. On 10 March 1984 the appellant was celebrating her 17th birthday. There was a party at a house in Harlow. Unhappily it was at that party that the events occurred which ended with her being sent to youth custody.

There was a guest at the party called Darren Marder, who was to be the victim of the events which occurred thereafter. He and the appellant had been friendly and had been going out together between about January and the middle of 1983. That close friendship had come to an end, but Marder arrived at the party with his new girlfriend and, for reasons which it is not necessary to explore, an argument broke out. After a great deal of bad language and shouting, the appellant told Marder to leave, and leave he did.

A little later he unwisely came back and a second argument took place together with a second exchange of obscenities between the two of them. What happened thereafter was the subject of dispute between the parties, though not so much dispute as often arises in these sudden events. The appellant poured a glassful of

Pernod over Marder, and he retaliated by slapping her around the face. Further incidents of physical force took place between them. The appellant said that the time came when she was being held and held up against a wall, at which point she lunged at Marder with her hand, which was the hand, unhappily, which held the Pernod glass. The glass hit him in the face, broke, and his eye as a result was lost. It was a horrible event in the upshot, but of course she would not realise the extent to which she was going to cause injury to this young man.

The prosecution case was this, that Marder only slapped the appellant once and that was in order to calm her down, the commonly believed remedy for hysterics. The jury were accordingly invited to infer from that that she could not possibly have been acting in reasonable self-defence when she retaliated against that slap with a weapon as grave as a glass. Second, there was evidence of Marder, and also a Miss Bryant, who was his new girlfriend, that so far from showing remorse after the event the appellant said that she would do it again if the same situation arose. Third, there was the evidence of Mrs Sharpe, the owner of the house where the party was taking place, who said that after the incident the appellant had admitted to her, Mrs Sharpe, that she had slashed Marder in the face with a glass after he had punched her.

The appellant herself was interviewed by the police. She said that it was only afterwards that she realised that a glass was in her hand, the hand with which she struck the appellant.

The appellant gave evidence. She insisted that she had been acting in self-defence. She was being pushed. Marder had said to her that he would hit her if she did not shut up. He slapped her in the face, she was being held by him and thought the only thing for her to do was to strike back to defend herself. In the agony of the moment, so to speak, she did not realise that she was holding the glass. Those are the comparatively simple facts of the case.

The grounds of appeal are these. First of all, the judge was in error in directing the jury that before the appellant could rely on a plea of self-defence, it was necessary that she should have demonstrated by her action that she did not want to fight. That really is the essence of the appellant's case put forward by her counsel to this court ...

The court in *R v Julien* was anxious to make it clear that there was no duty, despite earlier authorities to the contrary, actually to turn round or walk away from the scene. But, reading the words which were used in that judgment, it now seems to us that they placed too great an obligation on a defendant in circumstances such as those in the instant case, an obligation which is not reflected in the speeches in *Palmer v R*.

The matter is dealt with accurately and helpfully in Smith and Hogan, *Criminal Law*, 5th edn, 1983, p 327 as follows;

> There were formerly technical rules about the duty to retreat before using force, or at least fatal force. This is now simply a factor to be taken into account in deciding whether it was necessary to use force, and whether the force was reasonable. If the only reasonable course is to retreat, then it would appear that to stand and fight must be to use unreasonable force. There is, however, no rule of law that a person attacked is bound to run away if he can; but it has been said that: '... what is necessary is that he should demonstrate by his actions that he does not want to fight. He must demonstrate that he is prepared to temporise and disengage and perhaps to make some physical withdrawal'. It is submitted that it goes too far to say

> that action of this kind is *necessary*. It is scarcely consistent with the rule that it is permissible to use force, not merely to counter an actual attack, but to ward off an attack honestly and reasonably believed to be imminent. A demonstration by D [the defendant] at the time that he did not want to fight is, no doubt, the best evidence that he was acting reasonably and in good faith in self-defence; but it is no more than that. A person may in some circumstances so act without temporising, disengaging or withdrawing; and he should have a good defence.

We respectfully agree with that passage. If the defendant is proved to have been attacking or retaliating or revenging himself, then he was not truly acting in self-defence. Evidence that the defendant tried to retreat or tried to call off the fight may be a cast-iron method of casting doubt on the suggestion that he was the attacker or retaliator or the person trying to revenge himself. But it is not by any means the only method of doing that ...

R v McInnes [1971] 1 WLR 1600 (CA)

Edmund Davies LJ: ... The incident which led to the murder charge was of a kind only too frequently occurring in these days, namely a fracas between two perfect strangers which resulted in the violent death of one of them as the result of a knife wound. The appellant belonged to a group of youths commonly called 'greasers', who adopted a particular form of dress which includes leather jackets. Hostility generally exists between them and 'skinheads', who are youths differently dressed and having close-cropped heads. The deceased belonged to neither of these groups. The deceased was killed at about 9.30 pm on Saturday 22 August 1970, at a fair being held at Platt Fields in Manchester, and his death was caused by a knife wound in the left side of the body. The knife used had penetrated the heart. The wound was about 2 inches deep and about 3 feet 11 inches from the deceased's left heel ...

Self-defence

We turn to the two criticisms advanced in relation to the manner in which the learned judge treated the topic of self-defence. Before doing this, however, it should again be observed that, while both prosecuting and defence counsel (very understandably in all the circumstances) dealt at length with this plea, it was one never advanced by the appellant himself in evidence. On the contrary, he insisted throughout that he never thrust the knife forward, and that the wounding and killing of the deceased were due to no aggressive action on his part.

The first criticism of the learned judge's treatment of self-defence is that he misdirected the jury in relation to the question of whether an attacked person must do all he reasonably can to retreat before he turns on his attacker. The direction given was in these terms:

> In our law if two men fight and one of them after a while endeavours to avoid any further struggle and retreats as far as he can, and then when he can go no further turns and kills his assailant to avoid being killed himself, that homicide is excusable, but notice that to show that homicide arising from a fight was committed in self-defence it must be shown that the party killing had retreated as far as he could, or as far as the fierceness of the assault would permit him.

... In our judgment, the direction was expressed in too inflexible terms and might, in certain circumstances, be regarded as significantly misleading. We prefer the view expressed by the High Court of Australia (in *R v Howe* (1958) 100 CLR 448 at 462, 464, 469) that a failure to retreat is only an element in the considerations on which the reasonableness of an accused's conduct is to be judged (see *Palmer v R* [1971] 2 WLR 831 at 840), or, as it is put in Smith and Hogan's *Criminal Law*, 1969, 2nd edn, p 231:

> ... simply a factor to be taken into account in deciding whether it was necessary to use force, and whether the force used was reasonable.

The modern law on the topic was, in our respectful view, accurately set out in *R v Julien* ([1969] 1 WLR 839 at 843) by Widgery LJ in the following terms:

> It is not, as we understand it, the law that a person threatened must take to his heels and run in the dramatic way suggested by counsel for the appellant; but what is necessary is that he should demonstrate by his actions that he does not want to fight. He must demonstrate that he is prepared to temporise and disengage and perhaps to make some physical withdrawal; and to the extent that that is necessary as a feature of the justification of self-defence, it is true, in our opinion, whether the charge is a homicide charge or something less serious.

In the light of the foregoing, how stands the direction given in the present case? Viewed in isolation, that is to say, without regard to the evidence adduced, it was expressed in too rigid terms. But the opportunity to retreat remains, as the trial judge said, 'an important consideration', and, when regard is had to the evidence as to the circumstances which prevailed, in our view it emerges with clarity that the appellant could have avoided this fatal incident with ease by simply walking or running away – as, indeed, he promptly did as soon as the deceased had been stabbed ...

Excessive force in self-defence

The final criticism levelled against the summing up is that the learned judge wrongly failed to direct the jury that, if death resulted from the use of excessive force by the appellant in defending himself against the aggressiveness of the deceased, the proper verdict was one of not guilty of murder but guilty of manslaughter. Certainly no such direction was given, and the question that arises is whether its omission constitutes a defect in the summing up.

The Privy Council decision in *Palmer v R* provides high persuasive authority which we, for our part, unhesitatingly accept, that there is certainly *no* rule that, in every case where self-defence is left to the jury, such a direction is called for. But where self-defence fails on the ground that the force used went clearly beyond that which was reasonable in the light of the circumstances as they reasonably appeared to the accused, is it the law that the inevitable result must be that he can be convicted of manslaughter only, and not of murder? It seems that in Australia that question is answered in the affirmative (see Professor Colin Howard's article, 'Two Problems in Excessive Defence' (1968) 84 LQR 343), but not, we think, in this country. On the contrary, if self-defence fails for the reason stated, it affords the accused no protection at all. But it is important to stress that the facts on which the plea of self-defence is unsuccessfully sought to be based may nevertheless serve the accused in good stead. They may, for example, go to show that he may have acted under provocation or that, although acting unlawfully, he may have lacked the intent to kill or cause serious bodily harm, and in that way render the proper verdict one of manslaughter ...

Section 3(1) of the Criminal Law Act 1967 provides: 'A person may use such force as is reasonable in the circumstances in the prevention of crime ...' and in our judgment the degree of force permissible in self-defence is similarly limited. Deliberate stabbing was so totally unreasonable in the circumstances of this case, even on the appellant's version, that self-defence justifying a complete acquittal was not relied on before us, and rightly so. Despite the high esteem in which we hold our Australian brethren, we respectfully reject as far as this country is concerned the refinement sought to be introduced that, if the accused, in defending himself during a fisticuffs encounter, drew out against his opponent (who he had no reason to think was armed) the deadly weapon which he had earlier unsheathed and then 'let him have it', the jury should have been directed that, even on those facts, it was open to them to convict of manslaughter. They are, in our view, the facts of this case. It follows that in our judgment no such direction was called for ...

Priestnall v Cornish [1979] Crim LR 310 (DC)

Facts: The defendant, driving his Ford Cortina car with a girlfriend as his only passenger, was involved in an incident with a Hillman Imp car carrying three men. The Hillman then pursued the Cortina, overtook it twice, and slowed down on each occasion. After a further chase, the Cortina stopped, and the Hillman stopped behind it. Both drivers got out; the defendant was holding a metal steering-wheel lock ('Krooklock') at the sight of which the other retreated into his car but was hit several times and his windscreen was broken by the defendant with the Krooklock. The defendant was charged, *inter alia*, with assault occasioning actual bodily harm; and damaging property, contrary to s 1(1) of the Criminal Damage Act 1971. The justices upheld his contention that he acted in self-defence and, accordingly, they dismissed the informations. The prosecutor appealed by case stated to the Queen's Bench Divisional Court.

Held, allowing the appeal that, since the victim, by retreating into his car, had ceased to be a threat, so that the defendant had had every means of retreat open to him, the defendant could not rely on self-defence. The case would go back to the justices for a conclusion to be reached on the basis that the defence was not available.

DEGREE OF FORCE

For this defence to be available, the accused must have used such force as was reasonable in the circumstances, as the accused honestly believed them to be. In essence, the accused must have believed that the degree of force which he used was reasonable.

Palmer v The Queen [1971] AC 814 (PC)

Lord Morris of Borth-y-Gest: ... The only question that is raised for determination is whether in cases where on a charge of murder an issue of self-defence is left to the jury it will in all cases be obligatory to direct the jury that if they found that the accused while intending to defend himself had used more force than was necessary in the circumstances they should return a verdict of guilty of manslaughter ...

... Their Lordships conclude that there is no room for criticism of the summing up or of the conduct of the trial unless there is a rule that in every case where the issue of self-defence is left to the jury they must be directed that if they consider that excessive force was used in defence then they should return a verdict of guilty of manslaughter. For the reasons which they will set out, their Lordships consider that there is no such rule ...

On behalf of the appellant it was contended that if, where self-defence is an issue in a case of homicide, a jury came to the conclusion that an accused person was intending to defend himself, then an intention to kill or to cause grievous bodily harm would be negatived: so it was contended that if in such a case the jury came to the conclusion that excessive force had been used the correct verdict would be one of manslaughter: hence it was argued that in every case where self-defence is left to a jury they must be directed that there are the three possible verdicts, *viz* guilty of murder, guilty of manslaughter, and not guilty. But in many cases where someone is intending to defend himself he will have had an intention to cause serious bodily injury or even to kill, and if the prosecution satisfy the jury that he had one of these intentions in circumstances in which or at a time when there was no justification or excuse for having it, then the prosecution will have shown that the question of self-defence is eliminated. All other issues which on the facts may arise will be unaffected.

An issue of self-defence may of course arise in a range and variety of cases and circumstances where no death has resulted. The test as to its rejection or its validity will be just the same as in a case where death has resulted. In its simplest form the question that arises is the question: Was the defendant acting in necessary self-defence? If the prosecution satisfy the jury that he was not then all other possible issues remain ...

In their Lordships' view the defence of self-defence is one which can be and will be readily understood by any jury. It is a straightforward conception. It involves no abstruse legal thought. It required no set words by way of explanation. No formula need be employed in reference to it. Only common sense is needed for its understanding. It is both good law and good sense that a man who is attacked may defend himself. It is both good law and good sense that he may do, but may only do, what is reasonably necessary. But everything will depend upon the particular facts and circumstances. Of these a jury can decide. It may in some cases be only sensible and clearly possible to take some simple avoiding action. Some attacks may be serious and dangerous. Others may not be. If there is some relatively minor attack it would not be common sense to permit some action of retaliation which was wholly out of proportion to the necessities of the situation. If an attack is serious so that it puts someone in immediate peril then immediate defensive action may be necessary. If the moment is one of crisis for someone in imminent danger he may have to avert the danger by some instant reaction. If the attack is all over and no sort of peril remains then the employment of force may be by way of revenge or punishment or by way of paying off an old score or may be pure aggression. There may no longer be any link with a necessity of defence. Of all these matters the good sense of a jury will be the arbiter. There are no prescribed words which must be employed in or adopted in a summing up. All that is needed is a clear exposition, in relation to the particular facts of the case, of the conception of necessary self-defence. If there has been no attack then clearly there will have been no need for defence. If there has been attack so that defence is reasonably necessary it will be recognised that a person defending himself cannot weigh to a nicety the exact measure of his necessary defensive action. If a jury thought that in a moment of unexpected anguish a person attacked had only done what he honestly and instinctively thought was necessary that would be most potent evidence that only reasonable defensive action had been taken. A jury will be told that the defence of self-defence, where the evidence makes its raising possible, will only fail if the prosecution show beyond doubt that what the accused did was not by way of self-defence. But their Lordships consider, in agreement with the approach in the *De Freitas* case (1960) 2 WLR 523, that if the prosecution have shown that what was done was not done in self-defence then that issue is eliminated from the case. If the jury consider that an accused acted in self-defence or if the jury are in doubt as to this then they will acquit. The defence of self-defence either succeeds so as to result in an acquittal or it is disproved in which case as a defence it is rejected. In a homicide case the circumstances may be such that it will become an issue as to whether there was provocation so that the verdict might be one of manslaughter. Any other possible issues will remain. If in any case the view is possible that the intent necessary to constitute the crime of murder was lacking then that matter would be left to the jury ...

R v Shannon (1980) 71 Cr App R 192 (CA)

Ormrod LJ: ... [Counsel] for the appellant has criticised the learned judge's summing up on the basis of the well-known passage in the speech of Lord Morris of Borth-y-Gest giving the advice of the Privy Council in *Palmer v R* [1971] AC 814, 831 and 832. He submits that the learned judge overlooked one important sentence in that advice which reads thus: 'If a jury thought that in a moment of unexpected anguish a person attacked had only done what he honestly and instinctively thought was necessary, that would be most potent evidence that only reasonable defensive action had been taken.'

This proposition is, as it were, a bridge between what is sometimes referred to as 'the objective test', that is what is reasonable judged from the viewpoint of an outsider looking at a situation quite dispassionately, and 'the subjective test', that is the viewpoint of the accused himself with the intellectual capabilities of which he may in fact be possessed and with all the emotional strains and stresses to which at the moment he may be subjected.

The learned judge dealt fully with the relevant evidence and the law, and finally left this question to the jury: 'Has the prosecution satisfied you that Mr Shannon used more force than was reasonable in the circumstances; because that goes solely to the question: Did he lawfully kill Mr Meredith?' This summarises the burden of his direction to the jury. [Counsel for the appellant] argues that the judge ought to have invited the jury to consider whether the appellant, at the moment of stabbing, 'honestly and instinctively thought that this action was necessary' to his defence and to have told them that if they thought that that was right and provided an adequate reason for the stabbing, it would be strong evidence that only reasonable defensive action had been taken.

[Counsel for the appellant] in effect urged that the learned judge had concentrated so much on the state of the appellant's mind in relation to the intent necessary to establish the charge of murder that he had, unwittingly, obscured this subjective element in self-defence.

Taken in isolation it is not an easy concept to explain to a jury, or for a jury to understand and apply, although Lord Morris regarded the defence of self-defence as 'one which can and will be readily understood by any jury'. It is however easier to understand in its context and, if full justice is to be done to [counsel's] submission in this case, it is necessary to read what Lord Morris said *in extenso* at [1971] AC 814, 831, 832. [See the passage in *Palmer* beginning 'In their Lordships' view ...' quoted *above – ed*].

... The whole tenor of this statement of the law [ie what Lord Morris said] is directed to the distinction which has to be drawn between acts which are essentially defensive in character and acts which are essentially offensive, punitive, or retaliatory in character. Attack may be the best form of defence, but not necessarily in law. Counter-attack within limits is permissible; but going over to the offensive when the real danger is over is another thing. This, we think, is the distinction which Lord Morris was endeavouring to explain, and which he thought a jury would readily understand.

Various indicators are used by the judges to enable juries to make this crucial distinction. If the act or acts go beyond what the jury think reasonably necessary for defensive purposes, that points to the offensive rather than the defensive character of the act; if the attack is finished, the subsequent employment of force may be, in Lord Morris's words, 'by way of revenge or punishment or by way of paying off an old score or may be pure aggression'; if other people have come to the assistance of the person attacked before some act of violence is done to the assailant, this too may indicate that the victim has gone over to the offensive. But these are only indicators to be used by the jury in making their common sense assessment on the facts as they find them; they are not conclusive tests in themselves of self-defence on the one hand or of aggression on the other. This is where Lord Morris's references come in to 'a person defending himself cannot weigh to a nicety the exact measure of his necessary defensive action' and to such a person's 'honest and instinctive' belief that his act was necessary. These considerations, depending on the facts of the particular case, may have to be weighed by the jury before coming to their conclusion 'self-defence' or 'no self-defence'.

The learned judge, in the course of his summing up, used verbatim several extracts from Lord Morris's statement of the law in *Palmer v R* (*above*), but throughout the summing up, and at the end he left the jury with the bald question, 'Are you satisfied that the appellant used more force than was necessary in the circumstances?' without Lord Morris's qualification that if they came to the conclusion that the appellant honestly thought, without having to weigh things to a nicety, that what he did was necessary to defend himself, they should regard that as 'most potent evidence' that it was actually reasonably necessary. In other words, if the jury came to the conclusion that the stabbing was the act of a desperate man in extreme difficulties, with his assailant dragging him down by the hair, they should consider very carefully before concluding that the stabbing was an offensive and not a defensive act, albeit it went beyond what an onlooker would regard as reasonably necessary ...

In the judgment of this court the evidence of the appellant, if accepted by the jury, raised the questions (a) whether the stabbing was in fact the act of a desperate man trying to defend himself and to force his assailant to let go of his hair and (b) whether, although not reasonably necessary by an objective standard, nonetheless, to use Lord Morris's words, the appellant honestly and instinctively thought that it was; in which case his honest belief would be 'most potent evidence' that he had only taken defensive action; in other words, in the circumstances the stabbing was essentially defensive in character. The case for the prosecution, on the other hand, if accepted by the jury, was a perfect illustration of a man going over to the offensive and stabbing by way of revenge, punishment, retaliation or pure aggression.

The learned judge touched on this aspect of the matter when he was directing the jury on the issue of intent in relation to the charge of murder. At the end of the summing up he said this:

> If you think that he lashed out because he lost his temper, having been treated in this painful, humiliating, frightening way, then you may think – it is a matter for you – that because he lost his temper in those circumstances he gave little or no thought to what might be the consequences of lashing out and in those circumstances he did not form the intent suggested. That is the matter which you must consider, clearly. The more a man loses his temper,

> the less likely he may be to consider what are likely to be the consequences of his acts even though when he is in a balanced state of mind he realises that if you lash out with scissors and it lands and you do it with force then it is going to do a lot of personal injury.

But on the issue of self-defence he, effectively excluded the state of the accused's mind. In other words, by leaving that issue to the jury on the bald basis of 'Did the appellant use more force than was necessary in the circumstances?' the learned judge may have precluded the jury from considering the real issue, which, to paraphrase Lord Morris in *Palmer v R* (*above*) was: 'Was this stabbing within the conception of necessary self-defence judged by the standards of common sense, bearing in mind the position of the appellant at the moment of the stabbing, or was it a case of angry retaliation or pure aggression on his part?'

It is, we think, significant that in relation to intent, that is applying the test of what was in the accused's mind, the jury concluded that it was not murder but only manslaughter on the basis of no intent to cause really serious bodily harm, but seem to have excluded the appellant's state of mind in considering self-defence ...

R v Whyte [1987] 3 All ER 416 (CA)

Lord Lane CJ: ... The facts of the case were these. The appellant and his brother lived in an upstairs flat in a road called Pyrland Road, London N5. Their neighbours were a Mr and Mrs Holmes. Mr and Mrs Holmes owned a dog, which apparently was not fully house-trained. Mr and Mrs Holmes lived in the downstairs flat, but the appellant's flat and the Holmes's flat shared a common landing and it seems that the door leading to the upstairs flat was close to the door which led into the Holmes's flat. What happened was this. On the evening of 30 March Mr and Mrs Holmes were in a public house, and they met a man called Michael Khan, who had been an acquaintance of theirs for many years but whom they had not seen for some time. After they finished drinking in the public house they returned to the Holmes's flat.

Thereafter there is a sharp divergence in the account of what happened, because according to Mr Khan, who was the eventual victim of the incident, the appellant's voice was heard outside the flat. Mr Khan went to the door to see what was required. When he opened the door, according to Mr Khan, the appellant punched him and said: 'the dog's pissed against my door'. Mr Khan, according to him, tried to calm the appellant down because he was very agitated, but the appellant reached round into the door which led into his, the appellant's, premises, produced a lock-knife, the blade of which was already open, and tried to stab Mr Khan in the stomach. Mr Khan put his arm across his stomach to protect himself, and as a result the arm received the effect of the knife. It was very severely cut. Mr Khan, having blocked the blow in that way, punched the appellant and slammed the door, and that, according to Mr Khan, was the end of the incident.

The appellant was interviewed by the police. To the police he was uncommunicative. He declined to answer any of the questions which they posed to him. The account of the events which he gave at the trial was this. He said first of all that he had not deliberately stabbed Mr Khan at all. It remained to some degree a mystery in those circumstances how Mr Khan received the wound that he did. But his defence was that he was acting in self-defence of himself and also of his brother. He said that what happened was this. He said that there was a knock at his door. He opened the door, but before he did so, he placed his lock-knife, the six-inch blade of which he had already opened, in his back pocket. This was before the door was open at all. He opened the door and there was Mrs Holmes, who asked him to join her for a drink. At that moment, he said, Mr Khan stepped in front of him, though it is not quite clear why. The appellant, according to himself, said: 'The dog's pissed on the floor'. Mr Khan told him to calm down, but then Mr Khan made a gesture towards him which he endeavoured to avoid, but he did not avoid. In other words Mr Khan struck him on the face. The appellant then took out the knife, according to him, but dropped it on the floor. There was then a struggle. He managed to pick up the knife. He tried to push away Mr Khan, and in some way, which he could not explain, the knife had penetrated Mr Khan's arm. The appellant then threw away the knife and ran away from the flat. Eventually, having seen his solicitor some two days later, he went to see the police seven or eight days later.

Those were the two conflicting versions.

... What the judge said to the jury on the question of self-defence, having given them an impeccable direction on the general effect of that defence, was this:

> ... If a man does use violence and claims he was only violent in self-defence, he may only use such force to defend himself as was reasonable in all the circumstances. It is for you, the jury, to decide as a matter of common sense whether a blow with a knife was in self-defence, and if it was, if the use of a knife against a man who is not alleged to have been armed was reasonable ... So before you can convict Mr Whyte of either count 1 or count 2, you must be satisfied so that you are sure that Mr Whyte struck Mr Khan a blow with a knife as an assailant, and that the blow was not a blow in self-defence, or if it was, it was an unreasonable amount of force, having regard to the danger Mr Whyte himself was in at the hands of Mr Khan.

In most cases, where the issue is one of self-defence, it is necessary and desirable that the jury should be reminded that the defendant's state of mind, that is his view of the danger threatening him at the time of the incident, is material. The test of reasonableness is not, to put it at its lowest, a purely objective test.

We have been referred to two authorities. The first is an opinion of the Privy Council in *Palmer v R* [1971] AC 814 and the second is *R v Shannon* (1980) 71 Cr App R 192, a decision of this court which of course is binding on us. The effect of those two decisions seems to be this. A man who is attacked may defend himself, but may only do what is reasonably necessary to effect such a defence. Simple avoiding action may be enough if circumstances permit. What is reasonable will depend on the nature of the attack. If there is relatively a minor attack, it is not reasonable to use a degree of force which is wholly out of proportion to the demands of the situation. But if the moment is one of crisis for someone who is in imminent danger, it may be necessary to take instant action to avert that danger.

Although the test is what is sometimes called an objective one, yet nevertheless, to quote the words of Lord Morris in *Palmer v R* [1971] AC 814 at 832:

> If a jury thought that in a moment of unexpected anguish a person attacked had only done what he honestly and instinctively thought was necessary, that would be most potent evidence that only reasonable defensive action had been taken.

In *R v Shannon*, to which we have already referred, the trial judge had directed the jury to consider the question, 'Are you satisfied that the defendant used more force than necessary in the circumstances?' without going on to consider the qualification what the defendant may have done in a 'moment of unexpected anguish'. On the facts of *R v Shannon*, that was clearly a fatal flaw which led to the conviction being quashed.

The judge in the present case likewise omitted to mention the qualification which Lord Morris had suggested should be made and which *R v Shannon* says should be made in appropriate circumstances.

It is a trite observation, but nevertheless true, that the requirements of a summing up will depend on the particular facts of the case. Whereas on the facts of *R v Shannon* the court correctly held that the qualifying effect mentioned by Lords Morris should have been given, one has to look at this case to see whether it was similarly necessary here. The jury in convicting him of the s 18 offence must have come to the conclusion that he had deliberately stabbed Mr Khan with the knife, despite what he himself said. They were directed correctly on the question of accident. The appeal on that point has been abandoned. So the jury must have decided that the knife was deliberately used by the appellant on Mr Khan. At the very best, from the appellant's point of view, the jury must have come to the conclusion that he stabbed Mr Khan because Mr Khan had hit him in the face with his hand. Now I am assuming in favour of the appellant that the facts were, with that small amendment about accident, as the appellant himself stated them to be. It is highly likely that the jury entirely disbelieved the appellant.

Was it necessary in those circumstances that the judge should mention the qualifying factor as mentioned by Lord Morris? In our judgment it was not. There was no question raised by the appellant that he, acting in the agony of the moment, went too far, that he failed to weigh accurately the precise degree of the attack which he was suffering. It is perfectly plain that on any view the use of an already prepared knife, the blade having been extended, in circumstances such as this, could not possibly be reasonable under any circumstances, whether the direction in *Palmer v R* was given or not.

For those reasons we think that in this particular case it was not necessary for the judge to give the *Palmer* direction, although as a matter of abundance of caution he might perhaps have given it ...

R v Scarlett [1993] 4 All ER 629 (CA)

See Chapter 21.

R v Owino [1996] 2 Cr App R 128 (CA)

Collins J: ... The appellant and his wife had both been married before but were divorced when they first met in 1992 when they were working at a hospital in Kent, he as a doctor and she as a nurse. They were attracted and decided that they would get married.

The appellant was to move to a new post in London in 1993, and obtained a flat in Southgate. On 3 September 1993 they were married and went to live together at that flat. Very shortly after the marriage things began to go wrong. She said that he was extraordinarily jealous, and this led to arguments in which he treated her with physical violence. He said that she had a very violent temper and would blow up and go for him in a physical way, and that any violence that he did to her was purely in order to restrain her.

It is necessary to give a short account of the circumstances of each of the alleged assaults in order fully to follow the points made by Mr Mendelle on this appellant's behalf.

The first occurred on 2 October 1993 and resulted in the appellant's wife's wrist being fractured. Mrs Owino (she was referred to at trial by her maiden name of

Miss Coulson) said that a row developed following a visit to the flat of the appellant's daughter by his previous marriage and, in the course of that argument, he grabbed her by the wrists, twisted her left wrist outwards, causing the ulna to break. She said that he refused to take her to hospital for some time, an allegation which was not supported by his daughter, who was called to give evidence.

There was evidence from the surgeon who treated her that the fracture was more likely to have been caused by a twist than a fall.

That was relevant because the appellant said that his wife had fallen off a chair when standing on it to reach for something in a cupboard in the kitchen when he was not even in the room, and it was that that caused her to break her wrist. That is indeed the story that she told various people, including the casualty officer when she went to hospital. Although some considerable time later in December, and of course when she gave her evidence, she said that the story was incorrect and that her husband had caused the fracture by twisting her wrist.

Count 2 related to an incident on 15 November. Miss Coulson alleged that the appellant had, in the course of an argument, punched her in the face a number of times, causing her to suffer a black eye. She undoubtedly did receive a black eye and she did attend hospital as a result. The hospital notes record that she could not recall what had happened because she was drunk. The appellant said that he saw the black eye the next morning. It had appeared overnight, and his wife told him that it had been caused when she had gone into the kitchen to get a glass of water and had unfortunately walked into the kitchen door.

Count 3 was an incident on 30 November 1993. There was an argument about sleeping arrangements. She said that this developed into him hitting her repeatedly about the head, causing her, among other things, to fear that she had damaged her eardrum. She telephoned the police.

Again she went to the hospital. She saw a Dr Shakani, who had photographs taken. There was a fresh bruise to the back of her head and old bruising to her left eye, her jaw and her arms, but the doctor said the bruising had 'several different ages' and was unlikely to have been caused, he thought, in merely restraining her.

The appellant's account was that they did have a quarrel in which they both pushed each other. She was screaming that she did not want him to sleep with her. She then calmed down. She woke him again at 3 am, wanting to talk to him. He refused to talk. She called him a 'selfish bastard' and began pushing and shoving him, and so he picked her up to take her from the room. She broke away and things calmed down. Any injuries she sustained were thus, if he was right, caused when he was using force to restrain her from attacking him.

After this incident she left him. She returned of her own volition in mid-December, about a fortnight or so later. There was no improvement in her temper, according to him, but they did spend Christmas together. She had been staying with her sister and had completed a list of matters which had aggravated the relationship. This did not include violence by him. Her explanation for that was that she was listing things which might create violence; she was not listing violent episodes themselves.

Finally, we come to count 4, which occurred on 3 January 1994. He was decorating the bathroom. There was a quarrel about her using the lavatory. This developed into a tussle of some sort. She said he hit her and threw her out of the flat, injuring her right thumb. Again, Dr Shakani was seen. He was not able to observe any new bruising, save for some reddening to the top of her back, but there were other bruises of variable age.

The appellant's case was that there had indeed been a quarrel. She made some very offensive remarks, and so he had lifted her up and put her out of the house.

Generally in the course of this interview with the police he denied any violence, with the exception of slaps, which were admitted towards the end of the interview, when he said:

> I don't deny she has bruises, but usually when Marie starts lunging, I usually hold her and that's where there is some pushing and falling. I don't deliberately hit her. I have never punched or kicked her or shoved her head against a wall or the floor. I've slapped her, yes; most I've done.

He denied that he had ever deliberately used violence to her except in those circumstances.

It is clear that in relation to counts 3 and 4, self-defence was being raised, the appellant's case being that any bruising suffered by his wife for which he was responsible was caused only by reasonable force used in restraining her and in preventing her from assaulting him. In those circumstances it was obviously incumbent upon the learned judge to give a full and proper direction as to the elements of self-defence and also to draw the jury's attention to the distinction between provocation by words or by conduct, which would not, and threats or actual attack which could raise an issue of self-defence. If there is material which raises this issue, the burden is of course on the prosecution to prove that the violence used was excessive and was not used in self-defence.

Unfortunately, the learned judge did not refer to self-defence at all in his summing up, and the jury retired shortly after 1 pm without any such direction being given to them. It was perfectly plain that such a direction ought to have been given ...

With the greatest of respect to the learned judge, if, as indeed was clear, the issue of self-defence had been raised on the evidence, he had a duty to put it to the jury and to direct the jury upon it. The fact, if it be a fact, that counsel had not specifically referred to self-defence in the course of their speeches was no reason for the learned judge not to deal with it in his summing up.

We are told by Mr Mendelle that he did not specifically use the word self-defence in the course of his submissions to the jury, nor, as we understand it, did counsel for the prosecution, Miss Kamill. But it was a matter, he says, that the jury were well aware of because the interview which the appellant had had with the police made it perfectly plain, in the passage to which we have already referred, that any violence that he had used to his wife was used only when he was restraining her when she was attacking or, perhaps, threatening to attack him. So, as we have said, in those circumstances, it was clearly necessary for the learned judge, whatever counsel may or may not have said, to have dealt with the matter in the course of his summing up. But the jury having sent the note, he then proceeded to deal with it.

Complaint is made by Mr Mendelle that he did not deal with it even then as adequately as he ought to have done. Mr Mendelle essentially submits that he failed to direct the jury, as he ought to have done, that any force used must be unlawful, in the sense that it must have been excessive – more than was reasonable for self-defence; and further, that the test of what was reasonable was subjective, in the sense that the defendant could not be convicted unless he intended to use force which was more than was necessary for lawful self-defence. He relies on the authority of *Scarlett* [1993] 4 All ER 629 to support that proposition.

Before I come to the case of *Scarlett* specifically, it is our view that the law does not go as far as Mr Mendelle submits that it does. The essential elements of self-defence are clear enough. The jury have to decide whether a defendant honestly believed that the circumstances were such as required him to use force to defend himself from an attack or a threatened attack. In this respect a defendant must be judged in accordance with his honest belief, even though that belief may have been mistaken. But the jury must then decide whether the force used was reasonable in the circumstances as he believed them to be.

Scarlett was a case where a landlord of a public house had been ejecting and perfectly lawfully and properly ejecting, a drunken customer from his public house. The allegation was that he had used excessive force in the course of ejecting him so that the customer fell down the steps of the entrance to the pub and unfortunately hit his head and was killed. What Mr Mendelle relies upon in the case of *Scarlett* is a passage at pp 295, 296 and p 636 of the respective reports, where Beldam LJ, giving the judgment of the court, said this:

> Where, as in the present case, an accused is justified in using some force and can only be guilty of an assault if the force used is excessive, the jury ought to be directed that he cannot be guilty of an assault unless the prosecution prove that he acted with the mental element necessary to constitute his action an assault, that is 'that the defendant intentionally or recklessly applied force to the person of another'. Further, they should be directed that the accused is not to be found guilty merely because he intentionally or recklessly used force which they consider to have been excessive. They ought not to convict him unless they are satisfied that the degree of force used was plainly more than was called for by the circumstances as he believed them to be and, provided he believed the circumstances called for the degree of force used, he is not to be convicted even if his belief was unreasonable.
>
> In this case the learned judge gave no direction to the jury that the prosecution, to establish an assault, had to prove that the appellant intentionally or recklessly applied excessive force in seeking to evict the deceased.

The passage which we have cited could, if taken out of context, give rise to a suggestion that the submission by Mr Mendelle is well-founded. But what, in the context, the learned Lord Justice was really saying was, in our view, this: he was indicating that the elements of an assault involved the unlawful application of force. In the context of an issue of self-defence or reasonable restraint, which was what *Scarlett* was essentially about, then clearly a person would not be guilty of an assault unless the force used was excessive; and in judging whether the force used was excessive, the jury had to take account of the circumstances as he believed them to be. That is what is made clear in the first part of the sentence, which we will isolate and read again:

> They ought not to convict him unless they are satisfied that the degree of force used was plainly more than was called for by the circumstances as he believed them to be and, provided be believed the circumstances called for the degree of force used, he is not to be convicted even if his belief was unreasonable.

So far as the second half of the sentence is concerned, what we understand the learned Lord Justice to have been saying was that, in judging what he believed the circumstances to be, the jury are not to decide on the basis of what was objectively reasonable; and that even if he, the defendant, was unreasonable in his belief, if it was an honest belief and honestly held, that he is not to be judged by reference to the true circumstances. It is in that context that the learned Lord

Justice talks about '[belief] that the circumstances called for the degree of force used', because clearly you cannot divorce completely the concept of degree of force and the concept of the circumstances as you believe them to be. In our judgment, that is effectively all that the learned Lord Justice was saying.

What he was not saying, in our view (and indeed if he had said it, it would be contrary to authority) was that the belief, however ill-founded, of the defendant that the degree of force he was using was reasonable, will enable him to do what he did. As Kay J indicated in argument, if that argument was correct, then it would justify, for example, the shooting of someone who was merely threatening to throw a punch, on the basis that the defendant honestly believed, although unreasonably and mistakenly, that it was justifiable for him to use that degree of force. That clearly is not, and cannot be, the law.

In truth, in the view of this court, the law was properly and adequately set out in the case of *Williams* (1983) 3 All ER 411, which was cited and referred to in *Scarlett* and the court in *Scarlett* was not going beyond what is set out in *Williams* ...

In the light of all that, we have to decide whether the direction given by the learned judge after the question was asked was adequate.

He told the jury that an assault was a deliberate, unlawful, hostile act committed against the person of another; he went on:

> If that occurs, you are entitled to defend yourself if attacked or if threatened with attack.

He then gave the classic direction in relation to self-defence. Unfortunately, he did not indicate that the burden was on the Crown to disprove self-defence. That was raised by Mr Mendelle, and the learned judge, that having been raised, said:

> You are absolutely right; I am grateful, members of the jury, self-defence is, of course, a plea of not guilty. In other words, 'I did not assault. I did not do what the Crown allege.' The burden is always on the Crown to prove their case and to establish that the force used or the restraint used was not reasonable in the circumstances. The burden shifts to the Crown to negative and destroy the defence of self-defence if it is put forward by a defendant. That was your point, was it not, Mr Mendelle?
>
> *Mr Mendelle*: 'Yes.'

Mr Mendelle rightly criticises that because it indicates that there is a defence of self-defence and the burden shifts to the Crown. In one sense, of course, technically it does, because there is an evidential burden on the defence to raise the issue of self-defence in the first place. But it is not a helpful way of putting it.

Nonetheless, we have to ask ourselves whether, in the context of the direction as a whole, that really can have muddled the jury or led them to believe that there was any burden on the defence. In the light of the direction as a whole, we do not think that can reasonably have been the impression gained by the jury.

But it did not stop there, because the foreman of the jury then himself asked a question; he said:

> The question is about lifting people out of the room against their will while struggling.

That, clearly, was highly material on count 4 and may have been material too on count 3. The learned judge then said this:

> That must be a question of fact for you. You must look at all the circumstances of the case and you may say, 'In those circumstances, was that

> reasonable force?' Indeed, you must go further than that because it is not only whether it is reasonable force objectively looked at, it is whether or not the person so acting genuinely and instinctively believed it was other than reasonable force – genuinely believed that it was reasonable force, but it is upon the prosecution to establish that there was not such genuine belief. It is important to remember that.
>
> That direction was, on the face of it, as favourable, in our view, as the defence could have hoped. Indeed it went further in favour of the defence than the law made necessary ...

MISTAKES OF FACT

The defence of self-defence is still available to a person who mistakenly believes that he is being attacked or is mistaken as to the nature of the attack. The belief does not have to be a reasonable one, but the reasonableness or otherwise of the accused's belief will be relevant to the question of whether he actually held that belief.

R v Williams [1987] 3 All ER 411 (CA)

See Chapter 22.

R v Oatridge (1992) 94 Cr App R 367 (CA)

Mustill LJ: ... The appellant and the deceased began to associate during 1988, and started to live together in July 1990. Their relationship seems always to have been stormy. The deceased was a diabetic. He is said to have been reasonable when sober, but he drank too much and on occasions failed to keep his blood sugar under control. He then became abusive and violent. There was ample evidence from other witnesses besides the appellant that there had been several instances when he had struck her. She herself spoke of occasions when he got hold of her by the neck. On the evening in question, 14 October 1990, the appellant had gone out for the evening with friends. She had a fair amount to drink. The deceased had also been drinking, much more heavily. He returned to their flat in the evening, very drunk. The appellant arrived soon afterwards by taxi. After an initial hesitation she went inside. A quarrel then broke out, in the course of which she stabbed him once with a knife, just below the sternum, severing a main pulmonary artery. A pathologist was to say at the trial that a moderate degree of force was required, and that it was unlikely that the deceased had fallen forward on to the knife. Soon after the incident the appellant called the emergency services. Ambulance workers, and later police officers, found the appellant in the flat with the deceased on the floor, either dying or dead. The knife was lying on a work surface. The police asked how he was stabbed. She said 'I stabbed him, he was at me, what else could I do ... He came in drunk, we had a fight. What could I do, I had to defend myself' ...

It is convenient to pause at this point to summarise the material law on self-defence, drawn from *Williams (Gladstone)* (1984) 78 Cr App R 276 and *Beckford v R* [1988] AC 130. In many cases of self-defence the following questions must be asked: (1) Was the defendant under actual or threatened attack by the victim? (2) If yes, did the defendant act to defend himself against this attack? (3) If yes, was his response commensurate with the degree of danger created by the attack? In answering this question allowance must of course be made for the fact that the defendant has to act in the heat of the moment and cannot be expected to measure his response exactly to the danger. (These questions are of course a considerable oversimplification, particularly since they omit reference to burden of proof. But they will suffice to illustrate the point at issue in the present appeal). There are however occasions where a further question must be asked: (1a) Even if the defendant was not in fact under actual or threatened attack, did he nevertheless honestly believe that he was? (The relevance of the reasonableness of the supposed belief is explained by Lord Lane CJ in *Williams, above*, at pp 280, 281.) If this question is answered in the affirmative (or, more correctly, the prosecution does not establish that it should be answered in the negative), then the third question must be modified, so as to read: (3a) Was the response commensurate with the degree of risk which the defendant believed to be created by the attack under which he believed himself to be?

We return to the present case ...

In our opinion two questions arise on the appeal against the verdict of guilty. First, did the judge in fact give direction on mistaken belief? Second, if he did not should he have done so, in the light of the issues arising on the evidence? The first question does not bear elaborate analysis. Although there was a reference to honest belief, this was in the context of the 'agony of the moment' aspect of reasonable response, which is only indirectly linked with mistake as to the nature of the attack. The thrust of the summing up was, as the quoted passages will demonstrate, to point up the radical issue as to whether the deceased really was setting out to strangle the appellant, and the question whether she might honestly have believed that he was even if in fact he was not, was explored at all. We are fortified in the view that when [counsel for the defendant] raised the question of subjective belief, [counsel] for the Crown submitted that any direction on the topic would have to include a reference to the effect of drink on the appellant's belief, the judge did not say anything further to the jury. As we understand the matter it was not disputed before us, or at any rate not disputed with any great vigour, that the summing up did not deal with honest mistake, and as the argument developed it emerged that the real question for decision was whether in the circumstances any such direction was required.

To this we now turn. In doing so we wish to make it quite plain from the outset that nothing we are about to say detracts from the principle, constantly emphasised by this court, that directions to a jury should be tailored to the occasion, and that the jury should not be burdened with propositions of law which have no practical bearing on the case. This will be so in many trials where self-defence is in issue. Often, the central question will be whether the acts relied upon as justifying the counter-attack took place as the defendant described them, and whether the circumstances rule out any possibility of mistake. If the defendant gives evidence that the victim attacked him with an axe in broad daylight and that after one blow had narrowly missed was preparing to deliver another, and where the witnesses for the prosecution deny that any such attack took place, it is pointless to confuse the jury with talk of subjective belief. Either there was an attack or there was not, and questions of mistake cannot come into it. So also if the fact and character of the attack are undisputed, and the defence turns on matters such as the proportionality of the response, or the possibility of escape. In all such cases it would be wrong for the judge to give such direction as the appellant contends for here, and the more so if (as frequently happens) the case is already complicated by the fact that defences of provocation, lack of intent and self-defence are all in play at once.

We therefore have to consider whether the possibility that the appellant mistook the victim's intentions towards her was sufficiently realistic for it to merit an express and distinct direction to the jury. This is not an easy task, since counsel appearing on the appeal differ as to their recollection of the way in which the case was conducted. Since of course no record exists of their closing submissions to the jury we thought it proper to postpone the delivery of judgment (the appellant being no longer in custody) whilst a transcript of the exchange with the judge after the jury retired was obtained, to see whether it cast any light on the problem. After a regrettably long delay this transcript is now available, but advances the matter very little further. All one can glean from it is that counsel for the defendant thought that honest mistake was a feasible middle ground between a rejection of the appellant's case that the victim was making as if to kill her, and an acceptance that this might be true.

We are therefore obliged to fall back on the evidence itself. Two points stand out: (1) Although the medical evidence suggests that the attack actually made was in pure physical terms not of great severity, it took place against the background of quite serious violence and threats of worse. (2) In one of the passages quoted the choice was not between a potentially lethal attack and a trifling assault. Even on the prosecution's case the victim tried unsuccessfully to get the appellant out of the front door by force, and then (being unsuccessful) grasped her by the throat.

It seems to us on these facts that the possibility of the appellant honestly believing that on this particular occasion the victim was really going to do what he had previously threatened – even if in fact this was not what he was going to do – was not so fanciful as to require its exclusion from the case as a piece of unnecessary clutter. This being so, although we respectfully endorse the learned judge's desire to keep the case as simple as possible, we consider that on this occasion he went too far. What the jury would have made of it if the point had been developed we cannot tell, but each of us considers that the jury might have felt that the possibility of mistake could not be excluded, in which case the question on proportionate response would have been crucially different. Thus, although conscious of differing from a judge of great experience who was present at the trial and had a chance to take the measure of it which we have not, we are constrained to hold that there was a misdirection. Since there can be no question of applying the proviso the appeal must be allowed.

CHAPTER 9

DURESS AND NECESSITY

These defences amount to a plea that special circumstances justify or excuse the actions of the accused.

DURESS

Unless the defendant is charged with murder or attempted murder, he may seek to exculpate himself by saying that he acted under duress. The key elements of duress are:

(1) that the accused was subject to coercion through threats;

(2) that the accused must have acted as any sober person of reasonable firmness would have done (in other words, his participation in the commission of an offence must have been a not unreasonable response to the duress to which he was subjected).

The threat

The threat must be one of death or serious physical harm: see *R v Graham* [1982] 1 WLR 294. Threats to third parties are capable of constituting duress: see *R v Ortiz* (1986) 83 Cr App R 173.

The threat is insufficient to give rise to the defence of duress if a person of reasonable firmness, sharing the characteristics of the defendant, would not have given way to the threats: see *R v Graham* [1982] 1 WLR 294; *R v Howe* [1987] AC 417.

Some of the characteristics of the defendant are ignored: for example, that the accused is unusually vulnerable to pressure (*R v Horne* [1994] Crim LR 584; *R v Hegarty* [1994] Crim LR 353) or the fact that the accused was voluntarily intoxicated (*R v Graham, above*). See also *R v Bowen* [1997] 1 WLR 372.

The effect of the possibility of the accused seeking protection from the police, rather than giving in to the duress, was considered in *R v Hudson* [1971] 2 QB 202.

The ambit of the defence

Duress is not a defence to murder, and this is so whether the accused is a principal offender or an accessory: see *R v Howe* [1987] AC 417 (where the House of Lords declined to follow its earlier decision in *DPP for Northern Ireland v Lynch* [1975] AC 653). Similarly, duress is not available on a charge of attempted murder: see *R v Gotts* [1992] 2 AC 412.

A person cannot rely on duress if he voluntarily exposed himself to risk by joining a criminal organisation or gang: see *DPP for Northern Ireland v Lynch* [1975] AC 653; *R v Sharp* [1987] QB 853.

R v Steane [1947] 1 KB 997 (CA)

Facts: The appellant, a British subject, entered the service of the German broadcasting system, and on several occasions broadcast through that system. The evidence called by the prosecution was that of one witness who proved that the appellant did, in fact, so broadcast and said that he had seen a telegram, in the appellant's possession, signed Emmie Goering, which stated that he could expect to be released and be home very shortly. The principal evidence against him was a statement taken from him by an officer of the British Intelligence Service in October 1945, purporting to give an account of his activities in the German broadcasting service, concluding with the words: 'I have read this statement over and to the best of my knowledge and belief it is all true, and must request it to be used in conjunction with my written report dated 5 July 1945 to the American C-I-C in Augsburg'. This earlier report was not produced in evidence. Before the war, the appellant was employed in Germany as a film actor and was so engaged when the war broke out. His wife and two sons were living in Germany. On the outbreak of war the appellant was at once arrested, but his wife and two sons remained in Oberammergau.

The only other evidence was that of the appellant. He said that on his arrest he was questioned and that the interview ended with the order: 'Say *Heil Hitler*, you dirty swine'. He refused and was thereupon knocked down losing several teeth, and he was interned on 11 September 1939. Just before Christmas of that year he was sent for by Goebbels, who asked him to broadcast. He refused. He was thereupon warned that he was in an enemy country and that they had methods of making people do things. A week later an official named von Bockman saw him and dropped hints as to German methods of persuasion. A professor named Kossuth also warned him that these people could be dangerous to those who gave trouble. In consequence he submitted to a voice test, trying to perform as badly as he could. The next day he was ordered to read news three times a day, and did so until April 1940. In that month he refused to do any more broadcasting. Two Gestapo men called on him. They said: 'If you don't obey, your wife and children will be put in a concentration camp'. In May three Gestapo men saw him and he was badly beaten up, one ear being partly torn off. He agreed to work for his old employers, helping to produce films. There was no evidence that the films he helped to produce were or could be of any assistance to the Germans or at all harmful to this country. He swore that he was in continual fear for his wife and children. He asserted, and said he had asserted, in his report of 5 July 1945, that he never had the slightest idea or intention of assisting the enemy, and that what he did was done to save his wife and children and that what he did could not have assisted the enemy except in a very technical sense. There was no record of the actual broadcasts made by the appellant ...

Lord Goddard CJ: ... That a record of the appellant's broadcasts in Germany was not given in evidence again was, no doubt, inevitable, but unfortunate, as the actual tone of the broadcast might have thrown some light upon the motives and intentions of the appellant, but, in the opinion of the court, there was undoubtedly evidence from which a jury could infer that the acts done by the appellant were acts likely to assist the enemy.

The far more difficult question that arises, however, is in connection with the direction to the jury with regard to whether these acts were done with the intention of assisting the enemy...

In this case the court cannot feel that some confusion arose with regard to the question of intent by so much being said in the case with regard to the subject of duress. Duress is a matter of defence where a prisoner is forced by fear of violence or imprisonment to do an act which in itself is criminal. If the act is a criminal act, the prisoner may be able to show that he was forced into doing it by violence, actual or threatened, and to save himself from the consequences of that violence. There is very little learning to be found in any of the books or cases on the subject of duress and it is by no means certain how far the doctrine extends, though we have the authority both of Hale and of Fitzjames Stephen, that while it does not apply to treason, murder and some other felonies, it does apply to misdemeanours; and offences against these regulations are misdemeanours. But here again, before any question of duress arises, a jury must be satisfied that the prisoner had the intention which is laid in the indictment. Duress is a matter of defence and the onus of proving it is on the accused. As we have already said, where an intent is charged on the indictment, it is for the prosecution to prove it, so the onus is the other way.

Now, another matter which is of considerable importance in this case, but does not seem to have been brought directly to the attention of the jury, is that very different considerations may apply where the accused at the time he did the acts is in subjection to an enemy power and where he is not. British soldiers who were set to work on the Burma road or, if invasion had unhappily taken place, British subjects who might have been set to work by the enemy digging trenches would undoubtedly be doing acts likely to assist the enemy. It would be unnecessary surely in their cases to consider any of the niceties of the law relating to duress, because no jury would find that merely by doing this work they were intending to assist the enemy. In our opinion it is impossible to say that where an act was done by a person in subjection to the power of others, especially if that other be a brutal enemy, an inference that he intended the natural consequences of his act must be drawn merely from the fact that he did it. The guilty intent cannot be presumed and must be proved. The proper direction to the jury in this case would have been that it was for the prosecution to prove the criminal intent, and that while the jury would be entitled to presume that intent if they thought that the act was done as the result of the free uncontrolled action of the accused, they would not be entitled to presume it, if the circumstances showed that the act was done in subjection to the power of the enemy, or was as consistent with an innocent intent as with a criminal intent, for example, the innocent intent of a desire to save his wife and children from a concentration camp. They should only convict if satisfied by the evidence that the act complained of was in fact done to assist the enemy, and if there was doubt about the matter, the prisoner was entitled to be acquitted.

It is to be observed also in this case that in summing up the learned judge did not remind that jury of the various threats to which the prisoner swore he had been exposed. The jury might, of course, have disbelieved his evidence. The matters of these threats depended upon his evidence alone, and while it is fair to say that he does not appear to have been in any way shaken in cross-examination on these matters, the jury were not necessarily bound to believe it. But we do not think that the summing up contained anything like a full enough direction as to the prisoner's defence. The defence must be fully put to the jury and we think they ought to have been reminded of various matters upon which the accused relied as negativing the intent ...

R v Graham [1982] 1 WLR 294 (CA)

Lord Lane CJ: ... The facts of the case were as follows. The appellant was the victim's husband. He is a practising homosexual. His wife was aware of this and indeed at the material time they were living in a bizarre ménage à trois with another homosexual called King. They were living in the flat above two other homosexuals, named Gillis and Minter, with whom the appellant occasionally had sexual relations. The appellant and King were jointly charged with the murder. King pleaded guilty. The appellant admitted playing an active part in the events leading to the killing and admitted seeking to conceal the killing after it had happened.

His defence was twofold: first, that he lacked the necessary intent, and he drew attention particularly to the drink and drugs he had taken; and, second, that whatever his intentional actions may have been, they were performed under duress because of his fear of King.

We are satisfied that the directions given to the jury by the trial judge, on the issues of murder and manslaughter, on joint enterprise and on the relevance of drink and drugs to those issues, were impeccable. Other minor complaints made in the notice of appeal are also without foundation. The only live issue is, as counsel for the appellant concedes, whether the direction to the jury on the question of duress was correct.

The evidence relevant to this issue was this. The appellant had suffered for some time from an anxiety state. He was taking Valium tablets on prescription. There was medical evidence to the effect that Valium, if taken in excess, would make him more susceptible to bullying, but that by mid-1980 he would have developed some tolerance to the drug. King was said to be a man of violence. There was evidence of altercations. In 1978 King had tipped the appellant and his wife off a settee because they were embracing and he was jealous. The appellant, it seems, knew of another incident in 1978 when some other woman had been assaulted by King and had had her ribs broken. In June 1980, said the appellant, King had 'swiped him over the head'.

On Friday 27 June 1980, the day before the killing, King attacked the wife with a knife. The appellant intervened and, for his trouble, cut his finger when he tried to grab the knife. As a result of this incident, the wife on the following day left and went to the appellant's mother's home. The appellant and King stayed behind and, together with the man Gillis, occupied their time in the flat drinking, talking and indulging in homosexual activities. The appellant said that he had a lot to drink during this time and had taken Valium tablets in excess of the quantity which had been prescribed for him. He also said that during the time that the three were together, he thought that King was going to attack him with a knife, but the incident came to nothing. Gillis left soon after midnight.

King then suggested getting rid of the wife once and for all. The two of them hatched a plan. The appellant telephoned his wife in the small hours, told her falsely that he had cut his wrists and asked her to come home at once. Meanwhile, King bandaged both of the appellant's wrists and he, the appellant, lay face down on the floor pretending to be seriously hurt. When the wife arrived, she knelt down beside the appellant to see how he was. King had the flex from a coffee percolator in his hands. He attempted unsuccessfully to put it round the wife's neck while she was kneeling. The appellant and his wife then both got up and King said: 'What's it feel like to know that you are going to die, Betty?' That remark was repeated. King then put the flex round the wife's neck and pulled it tight, hauling her off her feet onto his back as if she were a sack of coals. She put her hands up to the flex at her neck, whereupon King told the appellant to cut her fingers away. The appellant said in evidence that he picked up a knife but could not bring himself to use it. King thereupon put the wife on the floor, still holding the flex. He told the appellant to take hold of one end of it. The appellant said in evidence that he did so. He added that it was only in fear of King that he complied with the order. He said that, in any event, the plug at the end of the flex which he was holding came off as he exerted pressure on it. If that were the case, it would remain in doubt whether the appellant's act made any contribution to the death. It should, however, be noted that in the voluntary statement, which he made to the police, he had admitted pulling on the flex for about a minute. Whatever the precise sequence of events, it was beyond doubt that the ligature around the wife's neck was responsible for her death.

Thereafter, the appellant helped King to dispose of her body by wrapping it up, carrying her out of the flat and dumping it over an embankment. Each of the two men then took one of her earrings; the appellant rifled her handbag for anything he could find of use, and spread the rest of the contents near her body to make it look as though she had been robbed. He then made telephone calls suggesting that she had gone missing.

The Crown at the trial conceded that, on those facts, it was open to the defence to raise the issue of duress. In other words, they were not prepared to take the point that the defence of duress is not available to a principal in the first degree to murder. Consequently, the interesting question raised by the decisions in *Lynch v DPP for Northern Ireland* [1975] AC 653, and *Abbott v R* [1977] AC 755 was not argued before us. We do not have to decide it. We pause only to observe that the jury would no doubt have been puzzled to learn that whether the appellant was to be convicted of murder or acquitted altogether might depend on whether the plug came off the end of the percolator flex when he began to pull it ...

The direction which the judge gave to the jury required them to ask themselves two questions. First, a subjective question which the judge formulated thus: 'Was this man at the time of the killing taking part because he feared for his own life or personal safety as a result of the words or the conduct on the part of King, either personally experienced by him, or genuinely believed in by him?' Neither side in the present appeal has taken issue with the judge on this question. We feel, however, that for purposes of completeness, we should say that the direction appropriate in this particular case should have been in these words: 'Was this man at the time of the killing taking part because he held a well-grounded fear of death (or serious physical injury) as a result of the words or conduct on the part of King?' The bracketed words may be too favourable to the defendant. The point was not argued before us.

The judge then went on to direct the jury that if the answer to that first question was 'Yes', or 'He may have been', the jury should then go on to consider a second question importing an objective test of reasonableness. This is the issue which arises in this appeal. Counsel for the appellant contends that no second question arises at all; the test is purely subjective. He argues that if the appellant's will was in fact overborne by threats of the requisite cogency, he is entitled to be acquitted and no question arises as to whether a reasonable man, with or without his characteristics, would have reacted similarly.

Counsel for the Crown, on the other hand, submits that such *dicta* as can be found on the point are in favour of a second test; this time an objective test. He argues that public policy requires this and draws an analogy with provocation. He submits that while the judge was right to pose a second question, he formulated it too favourably to the appellant. The question was put to the jury in the following terms:

> Taking into account all the circumstances of the case, including the age, sex, sexual propensities and other characteristics personal to the defendant, including his state of mind and the amount of drink or drugs he had taken, was it reasonable for the defendant to behave in the way he did, that is to take part in the murder of his wife as a result of the fear present at the time in his mind? The test of reasonableness in this context is: would the defendant's behaviour in all the particular circumstances to which I have just referred reflect the degree of self-control and firmness of purpose which everyone is entitled to expect that his fellow citizens would exercise in society as it is today? ...

There is no direct binding authority on the questions whether the test is solely subjective or, if objective, how it is to be formulated ...

As a matter of public policy, it seems to us essential to limit the defence of duress by means of an objective criterion formulated in terms of reasonableness. Consistency of approach in defences to criminal liability is obviously desirable. Provocation and duress are analogous. In provocation the words or actions of one person break the self-control of another. In duress the words or actions of one person break the will of another. The law requires a defendant to have the self-control reasonably to be expected of the ordinary citizen in his situation. It should likewise require him to have the steadfastness reasonably to be expected of the ordinary citizen in his situation. So too with self-defence, in which the law permits the use of no more force than is reasonable in the circumstances. And, in general, if a mistake is to excuse what would otherwise be criminal, the mistake must be a reasonable one.

It follows that we accept counsel for the Crown's submission that the direction in this case was too favourable to the appellant. The Crown having conceded that the issue of duress was open to the appellant and was raised on the evidence, the correct approach on the facts of this case would have been as follows: (1) was the defendant, or may he have been, impelled to act as he did because, as a result of what he reasonably believed King had said or done, he had good cause to fear that if he did not so act King would kill him or (if this is to be added) cause him serious physical injury? (2) if so, have the prosecution made the jury sure that a sober person of reasonable firmness, sharing the characteristics of the defendant, would not have responded to whatever he reasonably believed King said or did by taking part in the killing? The fact that a defendant's will to resist has been eroded by the voluntary consumption of drink or drugs is not relevant to this test.

We doubt whether the Crown was right to concede that the question of duress ever arose on the facts of this case. The words and deeds of King relied on by the defence were far short of those needed to raise a threat of the requisite gravity. However, the Crown having made the concession, the judge was right to pose the second objective question to the jury. His only error lay in putting it too favourably to the appellant.

R v Ortiz (1986) 83 Cr App R 173 (CA)

Farquharson J: ... The appellant is a citizen of Columbia. It appears that during and before 1983 he had developed a fashion business in his own country. This involved him travelling abroad to buy materials for his shops and for his connections. During the course of his business activities, he met a man named

Ronch and, as a result of the influence of Ronch, his area of purchasing extended to Europe. It appears that Ronch introduced him to suppliers in Italy. In the autumn of 1983, Ronch invited him to make a further trip to Europe for the purpose of purchasing materials and to spend some time in London. He made available to the appellant a flat in Chelsea. Ronch further suggested that, as part of the exercise, the appellant should have a holiday with his wife and child and that they too should accompany him. So it was that during the month of November 1983 the appellant arrived here with his wife and family.

On the evening of November 12 that same year Ronch took the appellant to another flat and introduced him to a man called Carrera. Without more ado, Carrera informed the appellant that he was involved in a substantial drugs operation and required the assistance of a courier. He then went on to inform the appellant that if he failed to assist him, as he was now in possession of knowledge of Carrera's plans, his wife and child would suffer harm. By way of substantiating those threats, Carrera told him that if the appellant did not comply with Carrera's wishes, the appellant's family could 'disappear'. The threats, according to the appellant, were real ones; he himself gave evidence of the circumstances obtaining in his country at the time and indeed called the evidence of a further witness to the effect that such was the state of drug-running in that country that a very large number were killed if they cut across the interests of the drug barons. It was not a threat, in the view of the appellant, that could be lightly dismissed.

Therefore, according to the evidence the appellant gave to the jury, on some three occasions he was driven to Victoria Station by Ronch and collected from various other couriers bags of cocaine ...

When the appellant was arrested, he gave a totally untrue account of the circumstances in which he had come into possession of the drugs and also failed to identify or misidentified the persons with whom he was concerned in the running of the drug racket.

The defence which he presented to the jury when the case came on for trial was one of duress. It was his case that, because of the threats issued by Carrera and his own observation of a gun in Carrera's possession, he had been compelled to act as he did.

The complaint made before us by Mr Corrigan, counsel for the appellant, is that on more than one occasion when defining the meaning of duress, the learned judge told the jury that, for that defence to succeed, the defendant should have committed the crime charged solely by reason of the threats made to him. The emphasis was on the word 'solely'. The relevant passages of the summing up disclose these directions: 'So what, members of the jury, is duress? Duress is a defence if a man acts solely as a result of threats of death or serious injury to himself or another. The threats can be immediate or they can be in the future.' The learned judge then went on to give illustrations of the kind of duress that would come within the meaning of that definition ...

Before us counsel has submitted that the learned judge was in error by reason of her emphasis of the word 'solely'. He submits that there is no direct authority which supports this proposition. Counsel goes on to canvass the possibility that a man may commit a crime, partly because of the threats of death or serious bodily injury to himself or to another and partly because of greed, or some other motive. In such a situation, he claims that the defence of duress would still be open to the defendant.

Whatever may be the theoretical justification for such an argument, it is difficult to conceive of a situation where a man could reasonably say that he committed a criminal act because his will was overborne by the threats made to him and also because he wanted to make money. Inevitably, one would suppose that the jury, in those circumstances, would reject the claim that he acted under duress. The essence of that defence is that the will of the subject of the threats is no longer entirely under his own control because of the fear engendered by those threats. There is no room in his mind for other motives for his acts.

In the judgment of this court the question is essentially one of proof, the burden of which, as the judge correctly pointed out, lies on the prosecution. While we would not dissent from the use of the word 'solely' in this context, we are of the opinion that it is best omitted in a summing up as it may raise unnecessary complications in the minds of a jury. The question posed to them should simply be: 'Has the prosecution made you sure that the defendant was not acting under duress, in the sense that he did not commit the crime charged because of threats being made, either of death or serious injury to himself or to another?'

In the present case the issue never really arose of whether the defendant acted as he did as a result of influences other than the threats made. Mr Corrigan has pointed out to us, however, that there was a considerable body of evidence which disclosed substantial material benefits to the appellant. He points, first, to the trade facilities which had been made available to the appellant by his association with the man, Ronch. He points to the fact that evidence was given during the course of the trial that he had come into possession of substantial sums of money because of his participation in the drug smuggling. He also referred to the accommodation that the appellant was enjoying with his wife and child in London. It should, therefore, have been open to the jury, argues Mr Corrigan, to take into account those factors; in other words, that the appellant may have been influenced in acting as he did by these material benefits and, therefore, by the judge's use of the word 'solely' she ruled out that possibility from the minds of the jury; and, accordingly, the appellant did not have the opportunity of a defence which was clearly open to him being considered. In short, he is saying that the definition of 'duress' as put forward by the learned judge was too restrictive.

We have been referred to another passage, during the course of argument, by Mr Austin-Smith on behalf of the Crown, in the summing up which immediately follows the part I last cited. The learned judge went on to say this: 'In duress, a man is forced to do what he does not wish to do; he would not do it save for the threats; the sole reason, the only reason, he does what he does is the fear of the threats being carried out. I have told you that the burden of proof is upon the prosecution. Consequently, it is for the prosecution to make you sure that there was not that duress which excuses a man from guilt.' Mr Austin-Smith points to that passage as elucidating in the minds of the jury precisely the realm and extent of the defence as it was open to this appellant.

Our view of the matter is that notwithstanding the evidence of these benefits which were laid before the jury, the case was never run on the basis that the appellant was influenced partly by the threats and partly from the attraction of the material benefits which were made available to him. The whole thrust of the defence case before the jury was that he had been forced to do what he did simply by reason of the threats to which I have already adverted. In those circumstances, in our judgment, it would have been unreal, especially in a summing up involving as much factual material as this, for the learned judge to have had to canvass that matter before the jury. It was not the way the defence put the case ...

R v Howe [1987] AC 417 (HL)

Lord Hailsham of St Marylebone LC: ... I take the facts of these truly horrible cases almost verbatim from the judgment of Lord Lane CJ [1986] QB 626 in the instant appeal. First, as to the case of Howe and Bannister, Murray and Bailey, the facts were as follows. At the time of the offences Howe and Bailey were 19, Bannister was 20 and Murray was 35. Howe had one minor conviction for motoring offences. Bannister had convictions for theft and burglary but none for violence. He was on probation. Bailey had convictions for burglary and theft. Murray had 25 previous court appearances, including two convictions for assault occasioning actual bodily harm, and in 1974 he had been convicted of assault with intent to rob and robbery in respect of which he had been sentenced to eight years' imprisonment.

Bannister met Murray in Risley Remand Centre. Howe and Bailey met in Stockport when Bailey was living in a hostel and Howe happened to be living next door with his grandmother. Murray came to visit Bailey when he was on six days' home leave from a sentence of two and a half years' imprisonment. Bailey introduced Howe to Murray. Lord Lane CJ continued, at pp 635–36:

> *Count 1: murder of Elgar*. The first victim was a 17-year-old youth called Elgar. He was offered a job as a driver by Murray. On the evening of 10 October 1983 all five men were driven by Murray up into the hills between Stockport and Buxton, eventually stopping at some public lavatories at a remote spot called Goytsclough. Murray at some stage told both appellants in effect that Elgar was a 'grass', and that they were going to kill him. Bannister was threatened with violence if he did not give Elgar 'a bit of a battering'. From thenceforward Elgar, who was naked, sobbing and begging for mercy, was tortured, compelled to undergo appalling sexual perversions and indignities, he was kicked and punched. Bannister and Howe were doing the kicking and punching. The *coup de grâce* was executed by Bailey who strangled Elgar with a headlock. It is unnecessary to go into further details of the attack on Elgar which are positively nauseating. In brief the two appellants asserted that they had only acted as they did through fear of Murray, believing that they would be treated in the same way as Elgar had been treated if they did not comply with Murray's directions. The prosecution were content to assent to the proposition that death had been caused by Bailey strangling the victim, although the kicks and punches would have resulted in death moments later even in the absence of the strangulation. The body was hidden by the appellants and the other two men. On this basis the appellants were in the position of what would have earlier been principals in the second degree and duress was left to the jury as an issue on this count.
>
> *Count 2: murder of Pollitt*. Very much the same course of conduct took place as with Elgar. On 11 October 1983 the men picked up Pollitt, a 19-year-old labourer, and took him to the same place where all four men kicked and punched the youth. Murray told Howe and Bannister to kill Pollitt, which they did by strangling him with Bannister's shoe lace. As the appellants were in the position of principals in the first degree, the judge did not leave duress to the jury on this count.
>
> *Count 3: conspiracy to murder Redfern*. The third intended victim was a 21-year-old man. The same procedure was followed, but Redfern suspected that something was afoot and managed with some skill to escape on his motorcycle from what would otherwise have inevitably been another horrible murder. The judge left the defence of duress to the jury on this charge of conspiracy to murder.

The grounds of appeal, which are the same in respect of each of these appellants, are as follows. That the judge erred in directing the jury (1) in respect of count 2, that the defence of duress was not available to a principal in the first degree to the actual killing; (2) in respect of counts 1 and 3, that the test as to whether the appellants were acting under duress contains an 'objective' element; that is to say, if the prosecution prove that a reasonable man in the position of the defendant would not have felt himself forced to comply with the threats, the defence fails ...

Lord Griffiths: ... For centuries it was accepted that English criminal law did not allow duress as a defence to murder. It was so stated in Hale's *Pleas of the Crown* (1736), Vol 1, p 51, repeated by Blackstone in his *Commentaries on the Laws of England*, 1857 edn, Vol 4, p 28, and so taught by all the authoritative writers on criminal law. It was accepted by those responsible for drafting the criminal codes for many parts of the British Empire and they provided, in those codes, that duress should not be a defence to murder. In *R v Tyler and Price* (1838) 8 C & P 616, Denman CJ told the jury in emphatic language that they should not accept a plea of duress that was put up in defence to a charge of murder against those who were not the actual killers. Fifty years later, in *R v Dudley and Stephens* (1884) 14 QBD 273, the defence of necessity was defined to the men who had killed the cabin boy and eaten him in order that they might survive albeit only Stephens was the actual killer. The reasoning that underlies that decision is the same as that which denies duress as a defence to murder. It is based upon the special sanctity that the law attaches to human life and which denies to a man the right to take an innocent life even at the price of his own or another's life.

There are surprisingly few reported decisions on duress but it cannot be gainsaid that the defence has been extended, particularly since the second war, to a number of crimes. I think myself it would have been better had this development not taken place and that duress had been regarded as a factor to be taken into account in mitigation as Stephen suggested in his *History of the Criminal Law of England* (1883) Vol 2, p 108. However, as Lord Morris of Borth-y-Gest said in *DPP for Northern Ireland v Lynch* [1975] AC 653, 670, it is too late to adopt that view. And the question now is whether that development should be carried a step further and applied to a murderer who is the actual killer, and if the answer to this question is no, whether there is any basis upon which it can be right to draw a distinction between a murderer who did the actual killing and a murderer who played a different part in the design to bring about the death of the victim ...

In *Abbot v The Queen* [1977] AC 755, the majority in the Privy Council applied the law of duress in accordance with English authority and denied it as a defence to a murderer who took part in the actual killing. The minority would have extended the defence even to the actual killer, pointing out the illogicality of allowing it to the principal in the second degree or the aider and abettor and denying it to the principal in the first degree.

Since that time the whole question of duress has been studied by the Law Commission: see Law Commission Report, 'Criminal Law, Report on Defences of General Application' (Law Com No 83), dated 27 July 1977. The report sets out the arguments for and against the defence and deals in particular with whether it should apply to murder. They balanced the argument based upon the sanctity of human life that denies the defence to a murderer against the argument urged by the majority in *DPP for Northern Ireland v Lynch* [1975] AC 653, that the law should not demand more than human frailty can sustain. They preferred the latter argument and accordingly recommended that a defence of duress should be available to all crimes including murder ...

Against this background are there any present circumstances that should impel your Lordships to alter the law that has stood for so long and to extend the defence of duress to the actual killer? My Lords, I can think of none. It appears to me that all present indications point in the opposite direction. We face a rising tide of violence and terrorism against which the law must stand firm recognising that its highest duty is to protect the freedom and lives of those that live under it. The sanctity of human life lies at the root of this ideal and I would do nothing to undermine it, be it ever so slight.

On this question your Lordships should, I believe, accord great weight to the opinion of the Lord Chief Justice who by virtue of his office and duties is in far closer touch with the practical application of the criminal law and better able to evaluate the consequence of a change in the law than those of us who sit in this House. This is what Lord Lane CJ had to say in his judgment in this case [1986] QB 626, 641:

> It is true that to allow the defence to the aider and abettor but not to the killer may lead to illogicality, as was pointed out by this court in *R v Graham (Paul)* [1982] 1 WLR 294, where the question in issue in the instant case was not argued, but that is not to say that any illogicality should be cured by making duress available to the actual killer rather by removing it from the aider and abettor. Assuming that a change in the law is desirable or necessary, we may perhaps be permitted to express a view. The whole matter was dealt with *in extenso* by Lord Salmon in his speech in *Abbott v The Queen* [1977] AC 755 to which reference has already been made. He dealt there with the authorities. It is unnecessary for us in the circumstances to repeat the citations which he there makes. It would, moreover, be impertinent for us to try to restate in different terms the contents of that speech with which we respectfully agree. Either the law should be left as it is or the defence of duress should be denied to anyone charged with murder, whether as a principal in the first degree or otherwise. It seems to us that it would be a highly dangerous relaxation in the law to allow a person who has deliberately killed maybe a number of innocent people, to escape conviction and punishment altogether because of a fear that his own life or those of his family might be in danger if he did not; particularly so when the defence of duress is so easy to raise and may be so difficult for the prosecution to disprove beyond reasonable doubt, the facts of necessity being as a rule known only to the defendant himself. That is not to say that duress may not be taken into account in other ways, for example, by the parole board. Even if, contrary to our views, it were otherwise desirable to extend the defence of duress to the actual killer, this is surely not the moment to make any such change, when acts of terrorism are commonplace and opportunities for mass murder have never been more readily to hand.

My Lords, in my view we should accept the advice of Lord Lane CJ and the judges who sat with him, and decline to extend the defence to the actual killer. If the defence is not available to the killer what justification can there be for extending it to others who have played their part in the murder. I can, of course, see that as a matter of common sense one participant in a murder may be considered less morally at fault than another. The youth who hero-worships the gangleader and acts as lookout man whilst the gang enter a jeweller's shop and kill the owner in order to steal is an obvious example. In the eyes of the law they are all guilty of murder, but justice will be served by requiring those who did the killing to serve a longer period in prison before being released on licence than the youth who acted as lookout. However, it is not difficult to give examples where more moral fault may be thought to attach to a participant in murder who was not the actual killer; I have already mentioned the example of a contract killing, when the murder would never have taken place if a contract had not been placed to take the life of the victim. Another example would be an intelligent man goading a weak-minded individual into a killing he would not otherwise commit.

It is therefore neither rational nor fair to make the defence dependent upon whether the accused is the actual killer or took some other part in the murder. I have toyed with the idea that it might be possible to leave it to the discretion of the trial judge to decide whether the defence should be available to one who was not the killer, but I have rejected this as introducing too great a degree of uncertainty into the availability of the defence. I am not troubled by some of the extreme examples cited in favour of allowing the defence to those who are not the killer such as a woman motorist being hijacked and forced to act as getaway driver, or a pedestrian being forced to give misleading information to the police to protect robbery and murder in a shop. The short, practical answer is that it is inconceivable that such persons would be prosecuted; they would be called as the principal witnesses for the prosecution.

As I can find no fair and certain basis upon which to differentiate between participants to a murder and as I am firmly convinced that the law should not be extended to the killer, I would depart from the decision of this House in *DPP for Northern Ireland v Lynch* [1975] AC 653 and declare the law to be that duress is not available as a defence to a charge of murder, or to attempted murder. I add attempted murder because it is to be remembered that the prosecution have to prove an even more evil intent to convict of attempted murder than in actual murder. Attempted murder requires proof of an intent to kill, whereas in murder it is sufficient to prove an intent to cause really serious injury.

It cannot be right to allow the defence to one who may be more intent upon taking a life than the murderer. This leaves, of course, the anomaly that duress is available for the offence of wounding with intent but not to murder if the victim dies subsequently. But this flows from the special regard that the law has for human life, it may not be logical but it is real and has to be accepted.

I do not think that your Lordships should adopt the compromise solution of declaring that duress reduces murder to manslaughter. Where the defence of duress is available it is a complete excuse. This solution would put the law back to lines upon which Stephen suggested it should develop by regarding duress as a form of mitigation. English law has rejected this solution and it would be yet another anomaly to introduce it for the crime of murder alone. I would have been more tempted to go down this road if the death penalty had remained for murder. But the sentence for murder, although mandatory and expressed as imprisonment for life, is in fact an indefinite sentence, which is kept constantly under review by the parole board and the Home Secretary with the assistance of the Lord Chief Justice and the trial judge. I have confidence that through this machinery the respective culpability of those involved in a murder case can be fairly weighed and reflected in the time they are required to serve in custody ...

R v Horne [1994] Crim LR 584 (CA)

Facts: The appellant, an employee of the DSS, conspired with others to make fraudulent claims for income support, totalling £17,741.22. He admitted creating the fictitious claims, saying he had been induced to do so by one of his co-conspirators, who offered him money, and said he would be looked after when the job had been done. He had been pressurised by telephone calls and visits to his home, had never been threatened directly with violence, but this person had implied that his brother, a drug dealer, knew a lot of people who could 'sort people out'. The issue at trial was whether the defence of duress had been negatived by the Crown. Following conviction, one of the grounds of appeal related to the judge's direction on duress and to his ruling that psychiatric evidence was inadmissible.

Held, dismissing the appeal, the judge directed the jury that the threats must have been such as would have driven a person of reasonable firmness to have behaved in the same way. A person of reasonable firmness was an average member of the public; not a hero necessarily, not a coward, just an average person. It was submitted for the appellant that the test was too narrowly stated. The classic statement of the law was laid down in *Graham* (1982) 74 Cr App R 235, which provided a two-limbed test. The first being subjective: was the defendant threatened with such violence that he acted as he did or might have been? The second, being objective, required the jury to consider whether a person of reasonable fairness, sharing the characteristics of the defendant and in his circumstances would have responded to the threat as he had done? That test was approved by the House of Lords in *Howe* [1987] AC 417, where one question was whether the defence of duress failed if the Crown proved that a person of reasonable firmness, sharing the characteristics of the defendant, would not have given way to the threats as he did? Lord Mackay cited with approval a passage from Lord Lane's judgment in *Howe* in the Court of Appeal [1986] 1 QB 626, and the relevant passage from *Graham*.

Counsel for the appellant submitted that the judge was wrong to construe the word 'characteristics' narrowly; it should be construed much more widely and should include such matters as the defendant's psychological characteristics.

During the trial, he had applied for leave to call a psychiatrist whose evidence was designed to show the jury that the appellant was a man who was unusually pliable and vulnerable to pressure. His report covered such matters as past history of giving way to bullying at school, and also expressed the view that his vulnerability was greater at the time of the offence due to the death of his father the previous year. However, it made clear that he had no history of psychiatric illness. In refusing to admit the evidence the judge considered *Graham* and *Howe* and said that if the word 'characteristics' was given the natural wide meaning it would include personal mental characteristics and if these were included the objective test would be undermined completely. Therefore, there must be a limited meaning in this context and it seemed to the judge it would include such things as age, sex, and serious physical disability, but he did not consider it included mental characteristics such as inherent weakness, vulnerability and susceptibility to threats. The history was inadmissible as hearsay and the doctor could not say whether the appellant was in fact threatened nor could he say whether he was affected by any threats which might have been made. The psychiatrist's opinion that the appellant was by nature pliable or vulnerable could not concern the jury because that would circumvent the objective test. The death of his father a year or more before the offences was something within the ordinary scope of human experience (see *Turner* (1974) 60 Cr App R 80).

In support of his argument that the judge was wrong, counsel relied on a passage from the Law Commission report (No 83, para 228), which said that the personal characteristics of a defendant were most important. Threats directed against a weak, immature or disabled person might well be much more compelling than against a normal healthy person. However, that recommendation was not enacted by Parliament and did not represent the law. The court was bound by *Graham* and *Howe*, and Lord Lane's judgment in *Graham* did not comply with the suggestion of the Law Commission. The second limb of the test, which passed an objective test, required the jury to ask themselves whether a person of reasonable firmness, otherwise sharing the characteristics of the defendant, would or might have responded as he did to the threats to which he was subjected. If the standard for comparison was a person of reasonable firmness it must be irrelevant for the jury to consider any characteristics of the defendant which showed that he was not such a person, but was pliant or vulnerable to pressure. It would be a contradiction in terms to ask the jury this question, and then to ask them to take into account, as one of his characteristics, that he was pliant or vulnerable.

For the purposes of this appeal, evidence of personal vulnerability or pliancy falling short of psychiatric illness was not relevant.

R v Hegarty [1994] Crim LR 353 (CA)

Facts: At the appellant's trial for robbery, and possession of an imitation weapon, his defence was duress. He claimed that some Asian men who accommodated him when he was on the run later attacked him and threatened violence against his family unless he carried out the robberies. The Crown challenged the existence of the Asians or the threats. In support of the plea of duress the appellant sought to put before the court the evidence of two medical witnesses who would testify to his mental instability. He had a conviction for manslaughter of his wife on grounds of diminished responsibility, and the reports described him as 'emotionally unstable' and in a 'grossly elevated neurotic state'. The judge refused to admit the evidence, and on appeal following conviction it was contended that he was wrong. The primary contention was that the appellant's pre-existing mental condition made him vulnerable to threats.

Held, dismissing the appeal, the duress relied upon was duress by threats, but in some cases a defendant might be able to rely on 'duress by circumstances' (see *Conway* [1989] QB 290; *Martin* [1989] 1 All ER 652), and although not argued in this way it was proposed to consider whether the medical evidence could have been introduced on the basis that Hegarty might have been able to set up such a defence.

Duress by threats provided a defence to a charge of any offence other than murder (see *Howe* [1987] AC 417), attempted murder (see *Gotts* [1982] 2 AC 412) and some forms of treason. It was founded on public policy considerations (see *Attorney General v Whelan* [1934] IR 518). The fact that the defendant's mind had been 'overborne' by the threats did not mean that he lacked the requisite intent to commit the crime (see *DPP for Northern Ireland v Lynch* [1975] AC 653, 703B). It followed that the law might have developed on the lines that, when considering duress, a purely subjective test should be applied, and it might well develop in this way in the future (see Law Com No 218, para 29.14, November 1993, Cmnd 2370 and draft Criminal Law Bill, cl 25(2)).

As the law stood however the test was not purely subjective but required an objective test to be satisfied (*Howe*). The jury had to consider the response of a sober person of reasonable firmness 'sharing the characteristics of the defendant'. They could take account of age, sex and physical health, but it was open to consideration whether the shared characteristics could include a personality disorder of the kind suffered by the appellant. His counsel argued that the expert evidence was relevant to explain the reaction of a man like him to threats of violence to himself and his family, and admissible because the pathological aspects of his personality and the effect of his disorder on his behaviour were matters which lay outside the knowledge and experience of a judge and jury. Counsel referred to a passage in *Emery* (1993) 14 Cr App R (S) 394, 398 where

Lord Taylor CJ said that: '... The question for the doctors was whether a woman of reasonable firmness with the characteristics of [the appellant], if abused in the manner which she said, would have had her will crushed so that she could not have protected her child'.

It was accepted that for the purposes of the subjective test medical evidence was admissible if the mental condition or abnormality was relevant and its effects lay outside the knowledge and experience of laymen. In the present case, the reports before the judge did not go that far, and the judge had to decide on the material before him.

There were no grounds for disturbing his decision. As the evidence was not admissible to explain the reaction of the appellant himself, it was clearly not admissible on the objective test. The passage cited could not be read in isolation, and it was not considered that Lord Taylor CJ intended to throw any doubt on the general rule which presently applied to cases of provocation and duress that the application of the objective test was a matter for the jury (see speech of Lord Simon in *Camplin* [1978] AC 705). The medical evidence was not admissible as the law stood on the objective test in a case of duress. Further, as that test predicated a 'sober person of reasonable firmness' there was no scope for attributing to that hypothetical person as one of the characteristics of the defendant a pre-existing mental condition of being 'emotionally unstable' or in a 'grossly elevated neurotic state'.

That left consideration of whether the position would have been different had 'duress by circumstances' been asserted. It was plain from *Martin* that an objective test applied, and one of the questions to be addressed was whether a sober person of reasonable firmness, sharing the accused's characteristics, would have responded to the situation confronting him by acting as he did. The medical evidence in this case did not address that question. The judge was right to exclude it as inadmissible.

R v Flatt [1996] Crim LR 576 (CA)

Facts: The appellant was convicted on four counts of possession of drugs with intent. His defence was duress. He was addicted to crack cocaine and owed his supplier £1,500. Some 17 hours before the police searched his flat, the drug dealer told him to look after the drugs found, saying that if he did not, he would shoot the appellant's mother, grandmother and girlfriend.

On appeal, it was argued that the judge should have told the jury that, in assessing the response of the hypothetical person of reasonable firmness to the threats, they should have invested that person with the characteristic of being a drug addict.

Held, dismissing the appeal, that drug addiction was a self-induced condition, not a characteristic. There was no evidence that the appellant's addiction (or indeed that of anyone else) would have had an effect on a person's ability to withstand a threat from a drugs dealer. It was not sought to adduce psychiatric or other evidence to say that the appellant's ability to withstand threats was in any way weakened. It may well be that he felt under some obligation to look after the supplier's drugs.

R v Bowen [1997] 1 WLR 372 (CA)

Stuart-Smith LJ: On 2 August 1995 in the Crown Court at Luton the appellant was convicted of five counts of obtaining services by deception. He was subsequently sentenced to 18 months' imprisonment, concurrent on each count. He now appeals against his convictions with leave of the single judge.

The five counts were specimen counts reflecting a large number of incidents during the period January 1992 to June 1994. On some 40 occasions the appellant had visited shops selling electrical goods and obtained a large number of them by applying for 'instant credit'. On all occasions he had paid a proportion of the cost by way of deposit. He had not completed payment for any of the goods concerned. Payments were to be made in some cases by payment book and in others by direct debit. There was evidence that some of the direct debits had been cancelled by the appellant.

On all occasions he had given his correct name and bank details. On some occasions he had given his correct address; on others not. The total amount of credit obtained was about £20,000.

The appellant was arrested on 14 June 1994 as he attempted to buy a camcorder using the same method. He was interviewed at some length without a solicitor being present, though he had received some advice over the telephone. After some initial prevarication he told the officers that he had obtained a large number of goods that he subsequently sold and that, although he had made some payments for them, he stopped paying the finance company.

He was interviewed against on 10 August 1994 when details of the various agreements were put to him and he accepted that he had obtained the goods in question. He said that he had stopped paying for the credit because he could see little point in doing so when it was so easy and he had sold the goods as a way of making a 'quick buck'. He said that he had not realised that what he was doing was a criminal offence; he thought he was just getting himself into debt ...

Apart from an oblique reference to threats in these last two interviews there was no mention of the events which were to form the basis of his defence of duress. The Crown's case was that the appellant had no intention of paying the amounts of the credit outstanding in respect of any of the goods in question.

The appellant gave evidence; he accepted that he had obtained the goods on credit and had made few payments. He asserted that throughout the period he had acted under duress. He had been approached first by an acquaintance when buying a television for himself, and asked what was needed to obtain credit. Thereafter two men had accosted him in a public house, and he had been threatened by them that he and his family would be petrol-bombed if he did not obtain goods for them. On each occasion he was told what goods the men required. He was told that if he went to the police his family would be attacked. He said that he had not told the police this in interview because he was worried about the possible repercussions ...

The appeal is based on what [counsel for the appellant] submits was a misdirection in law in relation to the defence of duress ...

At the conclusion of the summing up [counsel for the appellant] submitted that the judge should have included in his direction that the sober person of reasonable firmness was someone who shared the defendant's characteristics. The judge accepted that he had not used this expression; he considered that he did not have to do so ...

[Counsel for the appellant] submits to this court that the judge was in error in omitting these words.

The classic statement of the law is to be found in the judgment of the Court of Appeal in *Graham* [1982] 1 WLR 294 at 299 ...

But the question remains, what are the relevant characteristics of the accused to which the jury should have regard in considering the second objective test? This question had given rise to considerable difficulty in recent cases. It seems clear that age and sex are, and physical health or disability may be, relevant characteristics. But beyond that it is not altogether easy to determine from the authorities what others may be relevant ...

What principles are to be derived from [the] authorities? We think they are as follows:

(1) The mere fact that the accused is more pliable, vulnerable, timid or susceptible to threats than a normal person are not characteristics with which it is legitimate to invest the reasonable/ordinary person for the purpose of considering the objective test.

(2) The defendant may be in a category of persons who the jury may think less able to resist pressure than people not within that category. Obvious examples are age, where a young person may well not be so robust as a mature one; possibly sex, though many women would doubtless consider they had as much moral courage to resist pressure as men; pregnancy, where there is added fear for the unborn child; serious physical disability, which may inhibit self-protection; recognised mental illness or psychiatric condition, such as post-traumatic stress disorder leading to learned helplessness.

(3) Characteristics which may be relevant in considering provocation, because they relate to the nature of the provocation itself, will not necessarily be relevant in cases of duress. Thus homosexuality may be relevant to provocation if the provocative words or conduct are related to this characteristic; it cannot be relevant in duress, since there is no reason to think that homosexuals are less robust in resisting threats of the kind that are relevant in duress cases.

(4) Characteristics due to self-induced abuse, such as alcohol, drugs or glue sniffing, cannot be relevant.

(5) Psychiatric evidence may be admissible to show that the accused is suffering from mental illness, mental impairment or recognised psychiatric condition provided persons generally suffering from such condition may be more susceptible to pressure and threats and thus to assist the jury in deciding whether a reasonable person suffering from such a condition might have been impelled to act as the defendant did. It is not admissible simply to show that in the doctor's opinion an accused, who is not suffering from such illness or condition, is especially timid, suggestible or vulnerable to pressure and threats. Nor is medical opinion admissible to bolster or support the credibility of the accused.

(6) Where counsel wishes to submit that the accused has some characteristic which falls within (2) above, this must be made plain to the judge. The question may arise in relation to the admissibility of medical evidence of the nature set out in (5). If so, the judge will have to rule at that stage. There may, however, be no medical evidence, or, as in this case, medical evidence may have been introduced for some other purpose, eg to challenge the admissibility or weight of a confession. In such a case counsel must raise the question before speeches in the absence of the jury, so that the judge can rule whether the alleged characteristic is capable of being relevant. If he rules that it is, then he must leave it to the jury.

(7) In the absence of some direction from the judge as to what characteristics are capable of being regarded as relevant, we think that the direction approved in *R v Graham* without more will not be as helpful as it might be, since the

jury may be tempted, especially if there is evidence, as there was in this case, relating to suggestibility and vulnerability, to think that these are relevant. In most cases it is probably only the age and sex of the accused that is capable of being relevant. If so, the judge should, as he did in this case, confine the characteristics in question to these.

How are these principles to be applied in this case? [Counsel for the appellant] accepts, rightly in our opinion, that the evidence that the appellant was abnormally suggestible and a vulnerable individual is irrelevant. But she submits that the fact that he had, or may have had, a low IQ of 68 is relevant since it might inhibit his ability to seek the protection of the police. We do not agree. We do not see how low IQ, short of mental impairment or mental defectiveness, can be said to be a characteristic that makes those who have it less courageous and less able to withstand threats and pressure. Moreover, we do not think that any such submission as is now made, based solely on the appellant's low IQ, was ever advanced at the trial. Furthermore, it is to be noted that in two places the judge told the jury that if they thought the appellant passed the subjective test they should acquit him. We are quite satisfied that in the circumstances of this case the judge's direction was sufficient. He directed the jury to consider the only two relevant characteristics, namely age and sex. It would not have assisted them, and might well have confused them, if he had added, without qualification, that the person of reasonable firmness was one who shared the characteristics of the appellant. For these reasons, the appeal will be dismissed.

R v Hudson and Taylor [1971] 2 QB 202 (CA)

Lord Parker CJ: ... On 6 April 1969, a fight took place in a Salford public house between one Wright and one Mulligan with the result that Wright was charged with wounding Mulligan. Each of the present appellants gave statements to the police and they were the principal prosecution witnesses at Wright's trial. Elaine Taylor is 19, and Linda Hudson is 17.

Wright's trial took place on 4 August 1969, but when called to give evidence the appellants failed to identify Wright as Mulligan's assailant. Taylor said that she knew no one called Jimmy Wright, and Hudson said that the only Wright she knew was not the man in the dock. Wright was accordingly acquitted and, in due course, the appellants were charged with perjury. At their trial they admitted that the evidence which they had given was false but set up the defence of duress. The basis of the defence was that, shortly after the fight between Wright and Mulligan, Hudson had been approached by a group of men including one Farrell who had a reputation for violence and was warned that if she 'told on Wright in court' they would get her and cut her up. Hudson passed this warning to Taylor who said that she had also been warned by other girls to be careful or she would be hurt. The appellants said in evidence that, in consequence of these threats, they were frightened and decided to tell lies in court in order to avoid the consequences which might follow if they testified against Wright. This resolve was strengthened when they arrived at court for Wright's trial and saw that Farrell was in the gallery.

The recorder directed the jury as a matter of law that the defence of duress was not open to the appellants in these circumstances ...

... Despite the concern expressed in Stephen's *History of the Criminal Law of England*, Vol 2, 1883, p 107 that it would be 'a much greater misfortune for society at large if criminals could confer [immunity] upon their agents by threatening them with death or violence if they refuse to execute their commands' it is clearly established that duress provides a defence in all offences including perjury (except possibly treason or murder as a principal) if the will of the accused had been overborne by threats of death or serious personal injury so that the commission of the alleged offence was no longer the voluntary act of the accused.

This appeal raises two main questions; first, as to the nature of the necessary threat and, in particular, whether it must be 'present and immediate'; second, as to the extent to which a right to plead duress may be lost if the accused has failed to take steps to remove the threat as, for example, by seeking police protection.

It is essential to the defence of duress that the threat shall be effective at the moment when the crime is committed. The threat must be a 'present' threat in the sense that it is effective to neutralise the will of the accused at that time. Hence an accused who joins a rebellion under the compulsion of threats cannot plead duress if he remains with the rebels after the threats have lost their effect and his own will has had a chance to re-assert itself: *R v M'Growther* (1746) Fost 13; *Attorney General v Whelan* [1934] IR 518. Similarly a threat of future violence may be so remote as to be insufficient to overpower the will at that moment when the offence was committed, or the accused may have elected to commit the offence in order to rid himself of a threat hanging over him and not because he was driven to act by immediate and unavoidable pressure. In none of these cases is the defence of duress available because a person cannot justify the commission of a crime merely to secure his own peace of mind.

When, however, there is no opportunity for delaying tactics, and the person threatened must make up his mind whether he is to commit the criminal act or not, the existence at that moment of threats sufficient to destroy his will ought to provide him with a defence even though the threatened injury may not follow instantly, but after an interval. This principle is illustrated by *Subramaniam v Public Prosecutor* [1956] 1 WLR 965, when the appellant was charged in Malaya with unlawful possession of ammunition and was held by the Privy Council to have a defence of duress, fit to go to the jury, on his plea that he had been compelled by terrorists to accept the ammunition and feared for his safety if the terrorists returned.

In the present case the threats of Farrell were likely to be no less compelling, because their execution could not be effected in the courtroom, if they could be carried out in the streets of Salford the same night. In so far, therefore, as the recorder ruled as a matter of law that the threats were not sufficiently present and immediate to support the defence of duress we think that he was in error. He should have left the jury to decide whether the threats had overborne the will of the appellants at the time when they gave the false evidence.

[Counsel for the Crown], however, contends that the recorder's ruling can be supported on another ground, namely that the appellants should have taken steps to neutralise the threats by seeking police protection either when they came to court to give evidence, or beforehand. He submits on grounds of public policy that an accused should not be able to plead duress if he had the opportunity to ask for protection from the police before committing the offence and failed to do so. The argument does not distinguish cases in which the police would be able to provide effective protection, from those when they would not, and it would, in effect, restrict the defence of duress to cases where the person threatened had been kept in custody by the maker of the threats, or where the time interval between the making of the threats and the commission of the offence had made recourse to the police impossible. We recognise the need to keep the defence of duress within reasonable bounds but cannot accept so severe a restriction upon it. The duty, of the person threatened, to take steps to remove the threat does not seem to have arisen in an English case but, in a full review of the defence of duress in the Supreme Court of Victoria (*R v Harley and Murray* [1967] VR 526), a condition of raising the defence was said to be that the accused 'had no means, with safety to himself, of preventing the execution of the threat'.

In the opinion of this court it is always open to the Crown to prove that the accused failed to avail himself of some opportunity which was reasonably open to him to render the threat ineffective, and that upon this being established the threat in question can no longer be relied upon by the defence. In deciding whether such an opportunity was reasonably open to the accused the jury should have regard to his age and circumstances, and to any risks to him which may be involved in the course of action relied upon.

In our judgment the defence of duress should have been left to the jury in the present case, as should any issue raised by the Crown and arising out of the appellants' failure to seek protection ...

R v Sharp [1987] 1 QB 853 (CA)

Lord Lane CJ: ... The circumstances which gave rise to the charge of murder were the culmination of what was in effect a series of armed robberies committed upon sub-post offices. They culminated in the Wraysbury offence which resulted in the death of the subpostmaster at that place.

Count 2, the Hounslow robbery, to which the appellant pleaded guilty, concerned the following facts, and they are of relevance to the main issue. At about midday on 23 August Alderson and Hussey, both of whom were armed with sawn-off shotguns in the company of the appellant held up a sub-post office in Hounslow. They wore wigs. Hussey threatened the wife of the postmaster, whereupon the postmaster himself pressed the alarm. All three then ran off to the getaway car empty handed, because they had not time, after the sounding of the alarm, to take any of the money which they had coveted. Hussey tried to fire his gun in the air in order to discourage anyone who was minded to pursue them. His first attempt to fire the gun failed, but his second attempt succeeded, and a pellet from that gun in fact hit Alderson, one of the other miscreants, in the ear.

The importance of that incident is this, that both Alderson and Sharp as a result of that knew the sort of man with whom they were associating in the commission of these offences and the predilection which Hussey had for loaded weapons. They must have known also that any attempt in the future by an unlucky postmaster to press the alarm button would be viewed by Hussey with disfavour to say the least.

On 14 September 1984 the sub-post office at Wraysbury, near Staines, was subject of a reconnaissance by the appellant and the two other men. Then they determined to attack the office. Alderson and Hussey once again carried loaded sawn-off shotguns. A further weapon, a pump action shotgun, was left in the getaway car. Hussey's gun was loaded with a particularly venomous sort of shot, namely buckshot. Sharp was responsible for locking the post office door after the three of them had entered.

Alderson moved towards the wife of the subpostmaster and Hussey went to the post office area of this little shop. Hussey then shot the subpostmaster in the head at close range: the ballistics expert thought about two or three feet. The unfortunate postmaster died instantly. As he fell, so money was scattered. Alderson took the opportunity to hit the subpostmaster's wife on the head with his gun three times. That was in order to try to stop her screaming, which, not surprisingly, she had started to do. Once outside, Alderson shot at the tyre of a parked vehicle which belonged to the subpostmaster in order plainly to impede anyone who might be minded to pursue them.

Hussey, as already stated, was convicted of murder. The jury, not unnaturally, rejected his contention that the gun may have been discharged by accident. Alderson at first denied that he had taken part in the matter at all, but eventually went on to admit his part in the affair and he was in due course convicted of manslaughter.

Sharp put forward the contention that he had been invited indeed to take part in these robberies and had willingly acceded to the invitation. He was the 'bagman', as he put it, the man carrying the bag in which the loot, if any would be contained. He regarded Hussey in the vernacular as a 'nutcase'. He, Sharp, did not wish any weapons to be used, so he said. He said that he panicked when he saw the guns being loaded into the car. He thought they were blanks, so he said. He wanted to pull out, but he lost his nerve and he carried on despite his wish to withdraw from the conspiracy, because Hussey pointed a gun at him and threatened to blow his head off if he did not carry on with the plan to rob the post office. He, Sharp, did not carry a gun. He said he had thought of sabotaging either the gun or the ammunition by using some salt, but he did not get the opportunity ...

...[Counsel for the appellant] now agrees that everything in this appeal depends upon whether the judge was correct or not in ruling that a defendant who has voluntarily joined a gang such as this cannot subsequently rely upon the defence of duress.

So we turn to examine the situation which lies behind [counsel's] submission to the judge, and again the submissions to this court, namely that the common law knows no such exception to the defence of duress. [Counsel for the appellant] realistically is the first to concede that pragmatically, to use his own word, and realistically, the judge's interpretation of the law was desirable, if not essential, if justice is to be done in circumstances such as existed in the present case. But he submits that it is not for this court, or indeed any other court, to usurp the function of Parliament and to introduce into the common law a rule which, in his submission, has never previously been held to form part of it.

No one could question that if a person can avoid the effects of duress by escaping from the threats, without damage to himself, he must do so. In other words if there is a moment at which he is able to escape, so to speak, from the gun being held at his head by Hussey, or the equivalent of Hussey, he must do so. It seems to us to be part of the same argument, or at least to be so close to the same argument as to be practically indistinguishable from it, to say that a man must not voluntarily put himself in a position where he is likely to be subjected to such compulsion.

... [W]e are fortified in the view which I indicate, which, to jump ahead, is that this is part of the common law and always has been, by certain matters which appear in the speeches of their Lordships in *DPP for Northern Ireland v Lynch* [1975] AC 653. Although *Lynch's* case has been the subject of certain adverse comment since the date of those speeches, nevertheless the passages to which we wish to refer have not, as far as we know, been the subject of criticism.

First of all in the speech of Lord Morris of Borth-y-Gest appears this passage, at 668:

> Where duress is in issue many questions may arise such as whether threats are serious and compelling or whether (as on the facts of the present case may specially call for consideration) a person the subject of duress could reasonably have extricated himself or could have sought protection or had

> what has been called a 'safe avenue of escape'. Other questions may arise such as whether a person is only under duress as a result of being in voluntary association with those whom he knew would require some course of action. In the present case, as duress was not left to the jury, we naturally do not know what they thought of it all.

A little later Lord Morris of Borth-y-Gest again said, at p 670:

> In posing the case where someone is 'really' threatened I use the word 'really' in order to emphasise that duress must never be allowed to be the easy answer of those who can devise no other explanation of their conduct nor of those who readily could have avoided the dominance of threats nor of those who allow themselves to be at the disposal and under the sway of some gangster-tyrant. Where duress becomes an issue courts and juries will surely consider the facts with care and discernment.

Here of course, I interpolate, Hussey was the archetypal gangster-tyrant.

I turn form Lord Morris of Borth-y-Gest to the speech of Lord Wilberforce, at 679:

> It is clear that a possible case of duress, on the facts, could have been made. I say 'a possible case' because there were a number of matters which the jury would have had to consider if this defence had been left to them. Among these would have been whether Meehan, though uttering no express threats of death or serious injury, impliedly did so in such a way as to put the appellant in fear of death or serious injury; whether, if so, the threats continued to operate throughout the enterprise; whether the appellant had voluntarily exposed himself to a situation in which threats might be used against him if he did not participate in a criminal enterprise (the appellant denied that he had done so); whether the appellant had taken every opportunity open to him to escape from the situation of duress. In order to test the validity of the judge's decision to exclude this defence, we must assume on this appeal that these matters would have been decided in favour of the appellant.

Finally, so far as the passages in favour of the contention which we are supporting are concerned, in the speech of Lord Simon of Glaisdale appears this passage, at p 687:

> I spoke of the social evils which might be attendant on the recognition of a general defence of duress. Would it not enable a gang leader of notorious violence to confer on his organisation by terrorism immunity from the criminal law? Every member of his gang might well be able to say with truth, 'It was as much as my life was worth to disobey'. Was this not in essence the plea of the appellant? We do not, in general, allow a superior officer to confer such immunity on his subordinates by any defence of obedience to orders: why should we allow it to terrorists? Nor would it seem to be sufficient to stipulate that no one can plead duress as a defence who has put himself into a position in which duress could be exercised on himself ...

In other words, in our judgment, where a person has voluntarily, and with knowledge of its nature, joined a criminal organisation or gang which he knew might bring pressure on him to commit an offence and was an active member when he was put under such pressure, he cannot avail himself of the defence of duress ...

R v Shepherd (1988) 86 Cr App R 47 (CA)

Mustill LJ: ... The offences were all of a similar character. The appellant, in the company of a varying number of other men, would enter retail premises. Some would distract the shopkeeper, whilst others would carry away boxes of goods, usually cigarettes. In this simple way the thieves were able to make off with goods of very considerable value. Ultimately some of them, including the appellant, were caught. In the last of a series of interviews the appellant admitted what he had done, and pointed out to the police the premises concerned.

There was reason to believe that another man, whom we shall call P, was also involved in some of the offences, but he was not charged with any of them. P is a man with many convictions for offences of dishonesty and violence.

On these facts it would seem that the appellant had no choice but to plead guilty to all the charges. In the event however he sought to raise a defence on the following lines. He had originally been recruited to the joint enterprise by P. The very first of the offences took place during April 1986, and the appellant played a willing part. It was a stroke of great good fortune for the appellant that this offence was on the list of those taken into consideration, and was not the subject of a plea of guilty. But he was unnerved by the experience and wanted to give it up. He was however threatened by P with violence to himself and his family, and was compelled to carry on with the thefts and did so until he was caught some weeks later.

The story, which was not mentioned in the police records of his interviews, receives some colour from the undoubted fact that P was subsequently sent to prison for an assault on the appellant committed within the precincts of the court whilst the case was awaiting trial, and there was evidence of another assault on him at much the same time.

On the appellant's pleas of not guilty the matter came for trial in the Crown Court on 5 January 1987. We mention this date because it was some three months before another division of this court gave judgment in *Sharp* [1987] 3 WLR 1. If the order of events had been different, and the guidance given in that judgment had been available to counsel and the learned assistant recorder, it may well be that a different course would have been adopted.

At all events what happened was this. Counsel for the appellant very properly informed the prosecution that the defence of duress was to be raised, and of the basis for it. Counsel for the prosecution intimated that he would contend that on the authorities the defence was unsound, even if the appellant's story were true, since his original participation in the joint venture had been voluntary. Since the validity of this argument would affect the scope of the evidence and cross-examination, it was thought proper to raise the question of the law at the outset in order to save a possible waste of time and cost. The learned assistant recorder agreed to this proposal, and after argument he ruled in favour of the prosecution.

In spite of this the appellant maintained his pleas, and gave evidence on his own behalf. For reasons which we do not follow, he was permitted to give his story of duress, even though the assistant recorder had already ruled that it was immaterial – as indeed he was to direct the jury when he reminded them of what the appellant had said. The story was not however tested in any way.

The jury retired for only 10 minutes before returning verdicts of guilty, having really been left no choice in the matter.

The appellant now appeals, contending that the issue of duress should not have been withdrawn from the jury.

The basis for this contention, as it was developed in the course of the appeal, was substantially different from the argument presented at the trial. It was (and still is) accepted on behalf of the prosecution that duress may in appropriate circumstances be available as a defence to a person charged with offences such as the present. It was (and still is) accepted on behalf of the appellant that this defence is not available when the defendant has, to put the matter neutrally, voluntarily brought himself into the situation from which the duress has arisen. The problem concerns the breadth of this exception.

At the trial no recourse was had to authority beyond a very compressed account in Archbold, *Criminal Pleading, Evidence and Practice*, 42nd edn, para 17.58, of the judgment delivered by the Lord Chief Justice of Northern Ireland in *Fitzpatrick* [1977] NILR 20. This was relied on by counsel for the appellant in support of a submission that the accused forfeits the right to rely on duress only where he has joined an 'organisation' possessing some kind of formal, although illicit, structure such as has existed in Northern Ireland and elsewhere. The judge rejected this contention. Any doubts about whether he was right to do so have been laid to rest by *Sharp* (*above*), and we need say no more about this point. The exclusion from the defence of duress is undoubtedly capable of operating where the persons with whom the defendant involves himself are simply co-conspirators banded together for a single offence or a group of offences.

This was not however the only question of principle which arose on the facts which we have summarised. Does a voluntary participation in any joint criminal act entail that any act of duress thereafter committed by another participant is to be excluded from consideration when the defence is raised? Or is the exception to be more narrowly understood? ...

At the conclusion of the argument we had arrived at the following opinion:

(1) Although it is not easy to rationalise the existence of duress as a defence rather than a ground of mitigation, it must in some way be founded on a concession to human frailty in cases where the defendant has been faced with a choice between two evils.

(2) The exception which exists where the defendant has voluntarily allied himself with the person who exercises the duress must be founded on the assumption that, just as he cannot complain if he had the opportunity to escape the duress and failed to take it, equally no concession to frailty is required if the risk of duress is freely undertaken.

(3) Thus, in some instances it will follow inevitably that the defendant has no excuse: for example, if he has joined a group of people dedicated to violence as a political end, or one which is overtly ready to use violence for other criminal ends. Members of so-called paramilitary illegal groups, or gangs of armed robbers, must be taken to anticipate what may happen to them if their nerve fails, and cannot be heard to complain if violence is indeed threatened.

(4) Other cases will be difficult. There is no need for recourse to extravagant examples. Common sense must recognise that there are certain kinds of criminal enterprises the joining of which, in the absence of any knowledge of propensity to violence on the part of one member, would not lead another to suspect that a decision to think better of the whole affair might lead him into serious trouble. The logic which appears to underlie the law of duress would suggest that if trouble did unexpectedly materialise, and if it put the defendant into a dilemma in which a reasonable man might have chosen to act as he did, the concession to human frailty should not be denied to him.

Having arrived at these conclusions on the argument addressed to us, it appeared to us plain there had been a question which should properly have been put to the jury and that the appeal must accordingly be allowed. We intimated that this would be so, whilst taking the opportunity to put our reasons in writing.

Naturally a proper scepticism would have been in order when the defence came to be examined at the trial, for there were many aspects on which the appellant could have been pressed. In particular, his prior knowledge of P would require investigation. At the same time the trial would not have been a foregone conclusion, since the concerted shoplifting enterprise did not involve violence to the victim either in anticipation or in the way it was actually put into effect. The members of the jury have had to ask themselves whether the appellant could be said to have taken the risk of P's violence simply by joining a shoplifting gang of which he was a member. Of course even if they were prepared to give the appellant the benefit of the doubt in this respect, an acquittal would be far from inevitable. The jury would have then to consider the nature and timing of the threats, and the nature and persistence of the offences, in order to decide whether the defendant was entitled to be exonerated. It may well be that, in the light of the evidence as it emerged, convictions would have followed. But the question was never put to the test. The issues were never investigated. The jury were left with no choice but to convict.

In these circumstances we saw no alternative but to hold that the convictions could not stand. The sentences necessarily fell away, leaving the fortunate appellant with no penalty attached to the first offence of which he was undeniably guilty, but which was not the subject of any charge.

That was the position at the conclusion of the argument. Since then we have been able to study a transcript of the ruling of the trial judge in *Sharp* (Kenneth Jones J), a ruling which was approved on appeal (see *above*) ...

This ruling, if we may say so, corresponds exactly with the view which we had independently formed. In the interests of accuracy it must be acknowledged that it was the ruling itself, rather than the whole of the passage in which it was expressed, which was the subject of the approval on appeal. Nevertheless the terms of the judgment delivered by the Lord Chief Justice were such as to make it clear, to our mind, that the approach of the trial judge was correct. In the context of that case, given the facts, such a conclusion was fatal to the appeal. Here, by contrast, it demonstrates that the issue ought to have been left to the jury ...

R v Ali [1995] Crim LR 303 (CA)

Facts: The appellant was convicted of robbery, having an imitation firearm with intent and possessing an imitation firearm when committing an offence. The appellant robbed a building society of £1,175, in the course of which he threatened cashiers with a gun. At trial he gave evidence that he had gone to Pakistan in 1987 and had become a heroin addict. One of the suppliers to whom he resorted was X, whom he refused to name but whom he knew to be a very violent person. He said the arrangement was that he would sell on the heroin he received from X and hand on the proceeds to him, as well as taking a certain amount for his own use. One day instead of selling on the bulk of the heroin, he used it all for his own purposes. That put him in debt to X, who threatened him and told him on several occasions that he would be shot. The appellant moved house, but X caught up with him, gave him a gun and told him he wanted the money the following day. The appellant was to get it from a bank or building society, otherwise he would be killed. The appellant was scared that X would return for him if he went to the police and so he committed the robbery. X took the money from him. On appeal, it was argued that the judge had not directed the jury correctly on the defence of duress, which was the burden of the appellant's case. The judge had posed four questions for the jury, the last of which was whether the appellant, in obtaining heroin from X and supplying it to others for gain, after he knew of X's reputation for violence, voluntarily put himself in a position where he knew that he was likely to be forced by X to commit a crime. It was submitted that it was not sufficient for the appellant knowing of X's reputation for violence, voluntarily to put himself in a position where he knew he was likely to be forced by X to commit a crime; the judge should have said 'forced by X to commit armed robbery'.

Held, dismissing the appeal, the jury could not have read the words 'a crime' as referring back to the drug dealing, as opposed to some crime other than that which was the common currency of the relationship between the appellant and X. The crux of the matter was knowledge in the defendant of either a violent nature to the gang or the enterprise which he had joined, or a violent disposition in the person or persons involved with him in the criminal activity he voluntarily joined. If a defendant voluntarily participated in criminal offences with a man 'X', whom he knows to be of a violent disposition and likely to require him to perform other criminal acts, he could not rely on duress if 'X' does so. The judge's summing up had expressed that proposition accurately. He had made it clear that, if there was no reason for a defendant to anticipate violence, then he would be entitled to rely on duress. But if he knew of a propensity for violence in those with whom he was working, then he could hardly rely on duress if they had threatened him with violence to make him do their bidding.

NECESSITY AND DURESS OF CIRCUMSTANCES

A distinction must be drawn between 'necessity' and 'duress of circumstances'.

Necessity is where criminal conduct may be regarded as the lesser of two evils and is not accepted as a defence to a criminal charge. See *R v Dudley and Stephens* [1884] 14 QBD 273. However, where an offence is defined as doing a particular act 'unlawfully', the act may be regarded as lawful if it was necessary (eg *R v Bourne* [1939] 1 KB 687).

Duress of circumstances is where force of circumstance causes or compels the accused to act in the way he does. Provided that the accused acts in a way that is reasonable, duress of circumstances is a defence to any charge except murder or attempted murder. See *R v Pommell* [1995] 2 Cr App R 607.

Necessity

R v Dudley and Stephens [1884] 14 QBD 273

Lord Coleridge CJ: ... [T]his is clear, that the prisoners put to death a weak and unoffending boy upon the chance of preserving their own lives by feeding upon his flesh and blood after he was killed, and with the certainty of depriving him of any possible chance of survival. The verdict finds in terms that 'if the men had not fed upon the body of the boy they would probably not have survived', and that 'the boy being in a much weaker condition was likely to have died before them'. They might possibly have been picked up next day by a passing ship; they might possibly not have been picked up at all; in either case it is obvious that the killing of the boy would have been an unnecessary and profitless act. It is found by the verdict that the boy was incapable of resistance, and, in fact, made none; and it is not even suggested that his death was due to any violence on his part attempted against, or even so much as feared by, those who killed him ...

There remains to be considered the real question in the case – whether killing under the circumstances set forth in the verdict be or be not murder. The contention that it could be anything else was, to the minds of us all, both new and strange, and we stopped the Attorney General in his negative argument in order that we might hear what could be said in support of a proposition which appeared to us to be once dangerous, immoral, and opposed to all legal principle and analogy. All, no doubt, that can be said has been urged before us, and we are now to consider and determine what it amounts to. First it is said that it follows from various definitions of murder in books of authority, which definitions imply, if they do not state, the doctrine, that in order to save your own life you may lawfully take away the life of another, when that other is neither attempting nor threatening yours, nor is guilty of any illegal act whatever towards you or any one else. But if these definitions be looked at they will not be found to sustain this contention ...

... Now it is admitted that the deliberate killing of this unoffending and unresisting boy was clearly murder, unless the killing can be justified by some well-organised excuse admitted by the law. It is further admitted that there was in this case no such excuse, unless the killing was justified by what has been called 'necessity'. But the temptation to the act which existed here was not what the law has ever called necessity. Nor is this to be regretted. Though law and morality are not the same, and many things may be immoral which are not necessarily illegal, yet the absolute divorce of law from morality would be of fatal consequence; and such divorce would follow if the temptation to murder in this case were to be held by law an absolute defence of it. It is not so. To preserve one's life is generally speaking a duty, but it may be the plainest and the highest duty to sacrifice it. War is full of instances in which it is a man's duty not to live, but to die. The duty, in case of shipwreck, of a captain to his crew, to the crew to the passengers, of soldiers to women and children, as in the noble case of the *Birkenhead*; these duties impose on men the moral necessity, not the preservation, but of the sacrifice of their lives for others, from which in no country, least of all, it is to be hoped, in England, will men ever shrink, as indeed, they have not shrunk. It is not correct, therefore, to say that there is any absolute or unqualified necessity to preserve one's life ... It is not needful to point out the awful danger of admitting the principle which has been contended for. Who is to be the judge of this sort of necessity? By what measure is the comparative value of lives to be measured? Is it to be strength, or intellect, or what? It is plain that the principle leaves to him who is to profit by it to determine the necessity which will justify him in deliberately taking another's life to save his own. In this case the weakest, the youngest, the most unresisting, was chosen. Was it more necessary to kill him than one of the grown men? The answer must be 'No':

> So spake the Fiend, and with necessity,
>
> The tyrant's plea, excused his devilish deeds.

It is not suggested that in this particular case the deeds were 'devilish', but it is quite plain that such a principle once admitted might be made the legal cloak for unbridled passion and atrocious crime. There is no safe path for judges to tread but to ascertain the law to the best of their ability and to declare it according to their judgment; and if in any case the law appears to be too severe on individuals, to leave it to the sovereign to exercise that prerogative of mercy which the constitution has intrusted to the hands fittest to dispense it.

It must not be supposed that in refusing to admit temptation to be an excuse for crime it is forgotten how terrible the temptation was; how awful the suffering; how hard in such trials to keep the judgment straight and the conduct pure. We are often compelled to set up standards we cannot reach ourselves, and to lay down rules which we could not ourselves satisfy. But a man has no right to declare temptation to be an excuse, though he might himself have yielded to it, nor allow compassion for the criminal to change or weaken in any manner the legal definition of the crime. It is therefore our duty to declare that the prisoners' act in this case was wilful murder, that the facts as stated in the verdict are no legal justification of the homicide; and to say that in our unanimous opinion the prisoners are upon this special verdict guilty of murder.

R v Bourne [1939] 1 KB 687 (Central Criminal Court)

Facts: On 14 June 1938, the defendant performed an operation on the girl in question at St Mary's Hospital, and thereby procured her miscarriage. The following facts were also proved. On 27 April 1938, the girl, who was then under the age of 15, had been raped with great violence in circumstances which would have been most terrifying to any woman, let alone a child of 14, by a man who was in due course convicted of the crime. In consequence of the rape the girl became pregnant. Her case was brought to the attention of the defendant, who, after examination of the girl, performed the operation with the consent of her parents.

The defence put forward was that, in the circumstances of the case, the operation was not unlawful. The defendant was called as witness on his own behalf and stated that, after he had made careful examination of the girl and had informed himself of all the relevant facts of the case, he had come to the conclusion that it was his duty to perform the operation ... In his opinion the continuance of the pregnancy would probably cause serious injury to the girl, injury so serious as to justify the removal of the pregnancy at a time when the operation could be performed without any risk to the girl and under favourable conditions.

Macnaghten J: ... The charge against Mr Bourne is made under s 58 of the Offences Against the Person Act 1861, that he unlawfully procured the miscarriage of the girl who was the first witness in the case ...

... That section is a re-enactment of earlier statutes, the first of which was passed at the beginning of the last century in the reign of George III. (43 Geo 3, c 58, s 1). But long before then, before even Parliament came into existence, the killing of an unborn child was by the common law of England a grave crime: see Bracton, Book 3 (*De Corona*), fol 121. The protection which the common law afforded to human life extended to the unborn child in the womb of its mother. But, as in the case of homicide, so also in the case where an unborn child is killed, there may be justification for the act.

Nine years ago Parliament passed an Act called the Infant Life (Preservation) Act, 1929. Section 1(1) of the Act provides that 'any person who, with intent to destroy the life of a child capable of being born alive, by any wilful act causes a child to die before it has an existence independent of its mother, shall be guilty of felony, to wit, of child destruction, and shall be liable on conviction thereof on indictment to penal servitude for life: provided that no person shall be found guilty of an offence under this section unless it is proved that the act which caused the death of the child was not done in good faith for the purpose only of preserving the life of the mother'. It is true, as Mr Oliver has said, that this enactment provides for the case where a child is killed by wilful act at the time when it is being delivered in the ordinary course of nature; but in my view the proviso that it is necessary for the Crown to prove that the act was not done in good faith for the purpose only of preserving the life of the mother is in accordance with what has always been the common law of England with regard to the killing of an unborn child. No such proviso is in fact set out in s 58 of the Offences Against the Person Act 1861; but the words of that section are that any person who 'unlawfully' uses an instrument with intent to procure miscarriage shall be guilty of felony. In my opinion the word 'unlawfully' is not, in that section, a meaningless word. I think it imports the meaning expressed by the proviso in s 1(1) of the Infant Life (Preservation) Act 1929, and that s 58 of the Offences Against the Person Act 1861, must be read as if the words making it an offence to use an instrument with intent to procure a miscarriage were qualified by a similar proviso.

In this case, therefore, my direction to you in law is this: that the burden rests on the Crown to satisfy you beyond reasonable doubt that the defendant did not procure the miscarriage of the girl in good faith for the purpose only of preserving her life. If the Crown fails to satisfy you of that, the defendant is entitled by the law of this land to a verdict of acquittal. If, on the other hand, you are satisfied that what the defendant did was not done by him in good faith for the purpose only of preserving the life of the girl, it is your duty to find him guilty. It is said, and I think said rightly, that this is a case of great importance to the public and, more especially, to the medical profession; but you will observe that it has nothing to do with the ordinary case of procuring abortion to which I have already referred. In those cases the operation is performed by a person of no skill, with no medical qualifications, and there is no pretence that it is done for the preservation of the mother's life. Cases of that sort are in no way affected by the consideration of the question which is put before you today.

What then is the meaning to be given to the words 'for the purpose of preserving the life of the mother'? ...

... I think those words ought to be construed in a reasonable sense, and, if the doctor is of opinion, on reasonable grounds and with adequate knowledge, that the probable consequence of the continuance of the pregnancy will be to make the woman a physical or mental wreck, the jury are quite entitled to take the view that the doctor who, under those circumstances and in that honest belief, operates, is operating for the purpose of preserving the life of the mother ...

Duress of circumstances

R v Willer (1986) 83 Cr App R 225 (CA)

Watkins LJ: ... Mark Edward Willer is 19 years of age. He is of excellent character. He appeals against his conviction for reckless driving.

What happened to bring him to conviction was that at about half past nine in the evening of 24 April 1984 he and two school friends, Martin and Richard Jordan, were driving around the town of Hemel Hempstead in the appellant's Vauxhall Cavalier car. They heard a broadcast on the car's, what is known as, Citizen's Band radio. From what they heard, the appellant was persuaded to drive to a shopping precinct at Leverstock Green. There they expected to meet another enthusiast of Citizen's Band radio. At one stage of the journey the appellant had to drive up a very narrow turning off a road called Green Lane in order to keep his assignment with the other enthusiast mentioned. As he made his way up what is called Leaside, which is, as we see from the photographs, an alleyway, he was suddenly confronted with a gang of shouting and bawling youths, 20 – 30 strong. He heard one of them shouting: 'I'll kill you Willer' and 'I'll kill you Jordan'. He stopped and tried to turn the car round. These youths surrounded him. They banged on the car. A youth called Smallpiece opened the rear door of the car and dived upon Richard Jordan who was sitting in the back of it. Martin Jordan, his brother, got out of the front seat to help. The appellant realised that the only conceivable way he could somehow escape from this formidable gang of youths, who were obviously bent upon doing further violence, was to mount the pavement on the right-hand side of Leaside and on the pavement to drive through a small gap into the front of the shopping precinct. That he did quite slowly, it was accepted, at about 10 mph.

Having gained the security, if that was what it could be called, of the front of the shopping precinct and moved somewhere in the vicinity of a car park which was there, he realised that he had lost one of his companions. So he turned the car round and drove very slowly, at 5 mph, back towards the gap and through it. He had to make a couple of turns in his search for his missing companion. All this time Smallpiece was in the back of the car fighting with Richard Jordan. With that going on the appellant drove to the local police station and reported the matter. For his pains he was prosecuted, a very surprising turn of events indeed.

He was charged with reckless driving. Very properly, so it seems to us, he chose trial by jury. He appeared at the Crown Court at St Albans on 16 April 1985. The trial was presided over by Mr Curwen, an assistant recorder. During the course of the trial an argument developed between the assistant recorder and counsel over the question as to whether or not the defence of necessity was available to the appellant. The assistant recorder ruled that it was not. The submissions were made very carefully, and authorities, some from America and Australia were referred to. We do not see the need to refer to them in this judgment. I say that because we doubt that the defence of necessity was in point here. There was however a very different defence available to the appellant to which I shall later return ...

Returning to how the appellant came to change his plea, one begins with the reasons advanced by the assistant recorder for declaring that the defence of necessity was not available to the appellant. He seems to have based himself upon the proposition, though saying that necessity was a defence known to English law, that it was not, albeit available to the appellant in respect of the journey through the gap into the car park in front of the shopping precinct, available to him upon the return journey because he was not at that stage being besieged by the gang of youths. We feel bound to say that it would have been for the jury to decide, if necessity could have been a defence at all in those circumstances, whether the whole incident should be regarded as one, or could properly be regarded as two separate incidents so as to enable them to say that necessity applied in one instance but not in the other. For that reason alone the course adopted by the assistant recorder was we think seriously at fault. Beyond that upon the issue of necessity we see no need to go further, for what we deem to have been appropriate in these circumstances to raise as a defence by the appellant was duress. The appellant in effect said: 'I could do no other in the face of this hostility than to take the right turn as I did, to mount the pavement and to drive through the gap out of further harm's way, harm to person and harm to my property'. Thus the offence of duress, it seems to us, arose but was not pursued. What ought to have happened therefore was that the assistant recorder upon those facts should have directed that he would leave to the jury the question as to whether or not upon the outward or the return journey, or both, the appellant was wholly driven by force of circumstance into doing what he did and did not drive the car otherwise than under that form of compulsion, ie under duress ...

R v Conway [1989] 1 QB 290 (CA)

Woolf LJ: ... The prosecution evidence was that on the day in question, 6 July 1987, two police officers were on duty in an unmarked police vehicle when they saw the appellant's motor car parked. The appellant was in the driving seat, there was a passenger in the front seat, and another passenger, named Giulio Tonna, in the rear seat. Tonna was known to the police officers as being the subject of a bench warrant and, having seen him in the appellant's car, they pulled their vehicle up alongside his car, blocking the vehicle, and one of the police officers leaned over towards the appellant, showed him his warrant card, and said to him: 'Police; wait there. I want to have a word with your passenger'. He then walked to the rear passenger door of the Rover to speak to Tonna, when he heard Tonna shout: 'Go, I am wanted', and, subsequently, 'It's the Old Bill, go, I am wanted', at which the appellant drove off at speed. The police officers followed and saw the appellant's car being driven in a way which would undoubtedly normally be regarded as reckless. The appellant's car performed a four-wheel skid around a corner, and drove down a very narrow road, in which there were cars parked on both sides, at speeds in excess of 40 mph. At one stage a car had to move on to the footway to avoid a collision. The appellant approached a junction on the wrong side of the road, forcing another car to swerve on to the pavement to avoid a collision. He also turned sharp left at a junction without stopping, cutting directly in front of a car on the near side, causing that car to perform an emergency stop, and drove through a 'No Entry' sign round a blind corner and along a one-way street until forced to stop by traffic coming in the opposite direction. He was then apprehended by the officers, but Tonna was no longer in the car, and when asked what he was doing he indicated that he wanted to avoid the police catching Tonna.

The appellant's evidence, which was supported by his witnesses, who included his passengers, differed substantially as to detail from that of the prosecution witnesses. The effect of the defence evidence is accurately summarised in the grounds of appeal, as follows:

> A few weeks before 6 July Tonna had been in a vehicle when another man was shot by a 12-bore shotgun and severely injured and on that occasion Tonna was chased and narrowly escaped. That this event had occurred was not disputed by the prosecution. The appellant understood that Tonna was the main target and intended victim of that incident. Immediately before the alleged reckless driving, two young men in civilian clothes came running towards the vehicle and Tonna then screamed hysterically 'drive off'. The men never identified themselves as police officers, and the appellant drove off because he feared a fatal attack on Tonna. When he drove off the two persons whom he assumed to be intended attackers gave chase in a motor vehicle. It was only after he had dropped off Tonna and ceased driving that he realised the persons were police officers. At all times during the chase he had believed the two men were potential assassins. He did, however, deny many of the details of the alleged reckless driving, maintaining that although

> he drove at excessive speeds he did not carry out many of the dangerous manoeuvres alleged by the police. He accepted that nevertheless, were it not for the believed emergency, his manner of driving might well have been reckless. He was however petrified and when he saw the 'No Entry' sign he took no notice because he was in a panic ...

... [Counsel for the appellant] submits that the jury should have been given an additional direction. He says:

> The jury should be directed to consider whether the prosecution had proved beyond reasonable doubt that the appellant did not believe that he was acting in an emergency to save Tonna from serious bodily injury. If the jury found that the appellant so believed or may have so believed the jury should be directed to consider whether the manner of the appellant's driving was justified or excused having regard to the circumstances in which he drove.

Although [counsel] in his careful and helpful submissions was anxious not to put forward any proposition which was wider than was absolutely necessary for the purposes of this appeal, it appears from this suggested direction that what he is contending for is a defence of necessity based upon subjective belief which would justify what would otherwise amount to reckless driving. In doing this he is departing from the approach which was adopted by counsel who appeared for the appellant in the Crown Court. In submissions made at the end of the evidence and prior to the summing up counsel accepted that it would be 'impossible to run the defence of necessity in this particular case', and that the judge was not required to leave it to the jury. However, he contended that the jury nonetheless could consider whether the appellant's explanation was reasonable and, if it was, find him not guilty ...

We conclude that necessity can only be a defence to a charge of reckless driving where the facts establish 'duress of circumstances', as in *R v Willer* 83 Cr App R 225, ie where the defendant was constrained by circumstances to drive as he did to avoid death or serious bodily harm to himself or some other person.

As the editors point out in Smith and Hogan, *Criminal Law*, 6th edn, 1988, p 225, to admit a defence of 'duress of circumstances' is a logical consequence of the existence of the defence of duress as that term is ordinarily understood, ie 'do this or else'. This approach does no more than recognise that duress is an example of necessity. Whether 'duress of circumstances' is called 'duress' or 'necessity' does not matter. What is important is that, whatever it is called, it is subject to the same limitations as 'do this or else' species of duress. As Lord Hailsham of St Marylebone LC said in his speech in *R v Howe* [1987] AC 417 at 429:

> There is, of course, an obvious distinction between duress and necessity as potential defences; duress arises from the wrongful threats or violence of another human being and necessity arises from any other objective dangers threatening the accused. This, however, is ... a distinction without a relevant difference, since on this view of duress it is only that species of the genus of necessity which is caused by wrongful threats. I cannot see that there is any way in which a person of ordinary fortitude can be excused from the one type of pressure on his will rather than the other ...

It follows that a defence of 'duress of circumstances' is available only if *from an objective standpoint* the defendant can be said to be acting in order to avoid a threat of death or serious injury. The approach must be that indicated by Lord Lane CJ in *R v Graham (Paul)* [1982] 1 WLR 294 at 300 ...

Adopting the approach indicated by Lord Lane CJ, and not that argued by [counsel for the appellant], which involved a subjective element, we ask ourselves whether the judge in the Crown Court should have left the defence of 'duress of circumstances' to the jury, notwithstanding the submission made by his counsel that it was 'impossible to run the defence of necessity ... or indeed (to) leave it to the jury'.

On the facts alleged by the appellant we are constrained to hold that the judge was obliged to do so, notwithstanding his counsel's submission at the hearing... [H]is client's defence was that he drove as he did because he was in fear for his life and that of Tonna. Although it is unlikely that the outcome of the jury's deliberations would have been any different, they should have been directed as to the possibility that they could find the appellant not guilty because of duress of circumstances, although they were otherwise satisfied that he had driven recklessly ...

R v Martin [1989] 1 All ER 652 (CA)

Simon Brown J: ... The appellant now appeals against his conviction as of right on a pure point of law. The point is whether the defence of necessity is available to a charge of driving whilst disqualified when that driving occurs in circumstances such as the appellant was contending arose in his case. To those circumstances I shall come in a moment. In a private-room hearing before the appellant was arraigned, the judge held not. He concluded that, once it was established that the defendant was driving and that he was disqualified at the time, the offence was established. It was, in short, in those circumstances an absolute offence ...

The circumstances which the appellant desired to advance by way of defence of necessity were essentially these. His wife has suicidal tendencies. On a number of occasions before the day in question she had attempted to take her own life. On the day in question her son, the appellant's stepson, had overslept. He had done so to the extent that he was bound to be late for work and at risk of losing his job unless, so it was asserted, the appellant drove him to work. The appellant's wife was distraught. She was shouting, screaming, banging her head against a wall. More particularly, it is said she was threatening suicide unless the appellant drove the boy to work ...

The appellant's case on the facts was that he genuinely, and he would suggest reasonably, believed that his wife would carry out that threat unless he did as she demanded. Despite his disqualification he therefore drove the boy. He was in fact apprehended by the police within about a quarter of a mile of the house.

Sceptically though one may regard that defence on the facts (and there were, we would observe, striking difficulties about the detailed evidence when it came finally to be given before the judge in mitigation), the sole question before this court is whether those facts, had the jury accepted they were or might be true, amounted in law to a defence. If they did, then the appellant was entitled to a trial of the issue before the jury. The jury would of course have had to be directed properly on the precise scope and nature of the defence, but the decision on the facts would have been for them. As it was, such a defence was pre-empted by the ruling. Should it have been?

In our judgment the answer is plainly not. The authorities are now clear. Their effect is perhaps most conveniently to be found in the judgment of this court in *R v Conway* [1988] 3 WLR 1238. The decision reviews earlier relevant authorities.

The principles may be summarised thus: first, English law does in extreme circumstances recognise a defence of necessity. Most commonly this defence arises as duress, that is pressure on the accused's will from the wrongful threats or violence of another. Equally however it can arise from other objective dangers threatening the accused or others. Arising thus it is conveniently called 'duress of circumstances'.

Second, the defence is available only if, from an objective standpoint, the accused can be said to be acting reasonably and proportionately in order to avoid a threat of death or serious injury.

Third, assuming the defence to be open to the accused on his account of the facts, the issue should be left to the jury, who should be directed to determine these two questions: first, was the accused, or may he have been, impelled to act as he did because as a result of what he reasonably believed to be the situation he had good cause to fear that otherwise death or serious physical injury would result; second, if so, would a sober person of reasonable firmness, sharing the characteristics of the accused, have responded to that situation by acting as the accused acted? If the answer to both those questions was Yes, then the jury would acquit; the defence of necessity would have been established.

That the defence is available in cases of reckless driving is established by *R v Conway* itself and indeed by an earlier decision of the court in *R v Willer* (1986) 83 Cr App R 225. *R v Conway* is authority also for the proposition that the scope of the defence is no wider for reckless driving than for other serious offences. As was pointed out in the judgment, 'reckless driving can kill' (see [1988] 3 WLR 1238 at 1244).

We see no material distinction between offences of reckless driving and driving whilst disqualified so far as the application and scope of this defence is concerned. Equally we can see no distinction in principle between various threats of death; it matters not whether the risk of death is by murder or by suicide or indeed by accident. One can illustrate the latter by considering a disqualified driver being driven by his wife, she suffering a heart attack in remote countryside and he needing instantly to get her to hospital.

It follows from this that the judge quite clearly did come to a wrong decision on the question of law, and the appellant should have been permitted to raise this defence for what it was worth before the jury ...

DPP v Bell [1992] Crim LR 176 (DC)

Facts: The appellant was driving a car with an alcohol reading of 74 microgrammes/100 ml breath. He had been drinking with friends. Some trouble occurred which caused the appellant to run back to his car pursued by others. Finding himself outnumbered and in fear of serious personal injury he got into the car, reversed away and drove off for some distance down the road. In reversing he accidentally drove over one of his own passengers who had failed to get into the car in time. The magistrates' court convicted him of driving with excess alcohol but the Crown Court allowed his appeal against conviction on the basis of duress. The prosecutor appealed against the Crown Court decision by way of case stated.

Held, dismissing the appeal, it was clear that the defence of duress was made out where fear engendered by threats caused a person to lose complete control of his will (see *Willer* (1986) 83 Cr App R 225; *Ortiz* (1986) 83 Cr App R 173, 176 *per* Farquharson J). On the facts found by the Crown Court the appellant was in terror when he drove off and it was a hypothetical question whether he might have driven in the same way if he had not been in fear from the threats. A further important finding of fact was that he drove off only 'some distance' down the road and not, for example, all the way home so that the defence of duress/necessity continued to avail him. (*DPP v Jones* [1990] RTR 33 distinguished.) The prosecution had failed to negative the defence of duress.

R v Cole [1994] Crim LR 582 (CA)

Facts: The appellant's defence to robbing two building societies was his inability to repay money lenders, who had threatened him, hit him with a baseball bat, and threatened his girlfriend and child. At trial, the judge ruled that duress was only available where the threats were directed to the commission of the particular offence charged. Here, the threat related to the debt, and it was not contended that he was threatened with the unpleasant consequences if he did not commit the robbery. In *Willer* (1986) 83 Cr App R 225, *Conway* [1989] QB 290 and *Martin* [1989] 1 All ER there was a direct link between the threats and the offence. The appellant changed his plea and appealed.

Held, dismissing the appeal, two distinct defences had developed: duress by threats and duress of circumstances (necessity). The first applied when the threatener nominated the crime (*Hudson*) (1972) 56 Cr App R 1; *DPP for Northern Ireland v Lynch* (1975) 61 Cr App R 6. The appellant could not rely on duress by threats since the money lenders had not stipulated that he commit robbery to meet their demands. Whilst not suggesting that *Martin* was incorrectly decided, it was questioned whether it properly reflected the distinction between the two types of duress. The *Martin* principles, even supposing they correctly laid down the approach to both defences, were not regarded as determinative of the main appeal. On the contrary, they begged the root question, namely what nexus must exist between the threatened peril and the, otherwise, criminal course of action for the defence of duress properly to arise for the jury's consideration on the facts?

In the present case the imminent peril, which was a necessary precondition to the defence properly arising, was lacking. True, the appellant had said that he had no choice, and had to have the money by a particular time, but that fell short of the degree of directness and immediacy required of the link between the suggested peril and the offence charged. The connection between the threat and the criminal act was not as close and immediate as in *Willer*, *Conway* and *Martin*, where the offence was virtually a spontaneous reaction to the physical risk arising.

Separating the two types of duress might on occasion appear to involve an imperfect logic, but the dichotomy was proposed to be continued in the draft Criminal Law Bill (Law Com No 218). The court echoed the urgent call for legislation in *Hurst*, (1994) Times, 2 February, albeit provoked by rather different concerns than arose here. Meanwhile, this was not the time to give duress any wider ambit than had hitherto been recognised. Until all aspects of the defence had been put on a statutory footing, including as presently envisaged, shifting the burden of proof from the Crown to the accused, duress should be rigidly confined to its established present limits.

DPP v Davis; DPP v Pittaway [1994] Crim LR 600 (DC)

Facts: The respondents were charged separately with driving with excess alcohol, contrary to s 5(1)(a) of the Road Traffic Act 1988. Magistrates dismissed the charges finding that, in each case, the defence of duress had been proved. The DPP appealed by way of case stated.

Davis: Magistrates found Davis had been suffering stress and anxiety when he had accepted an invitation to go for a meal with a male acquaintance. After the meal he returned to the other man's flat where he became the subject of an unwelcome homosexual advance. Magistrates found he feared for his life and had run from the flat. After breaking free from the other man's clutches, he had driven away. Magistrates applied a subjective test in deciding it was more likely than not that events had caused Davis to lose complete control of his will.

Pittaway: Pittaway had recently divorced her husband who had been violent towards her. Magistrates found that, as a result of the violence she was frightened of men. She formed a new relationship with the appellant. At a party, she and the appellant had a row, leading to an angry exchange of words outside the party and unspecified threats being made by the appellant. Magistrates found the respondent believed she would suffer immediate violence from the appellant and, although she ran to her house which was about 200 yards from the party, she decided instead to hide in her car. After five minutes or so, she drove 200 yards before being stopped. The appellant was not in the vicinity at the time.

Held, allowing both appeals and remitting the cases to the magistrates with a direction to convict, there was not evidence raising the defence of duress.

Davis: Although the defence of duress was subjective, it also had objective elements to it, namely whether there was good cause to fear death or serious injury would occur unless the respondent acted as he had done, and whether a sober person of reasonable firmness, sharing the respondent's characteristics, would have responded in the same way (*Graham* and *Howe.*) The magistrates had focused on loss of will at the invitation of the prosecution, and this may have led them to overlook the objective elements. There was no finding that the respondent had been in fear of his life or serious injury at the moment he drove off, or that he continued to be frightened during the two miles he drove before being stopped. The only finding was that the respondent feared for his life when still in the flat. The magistrates did not consider whether there was good cause for the fear. Had they done so, it would have been impossible to conclude that the other man drawing near and undoing the respondent's shirt buttons could provide cause for such fear. Neither did the other man's attempts to pull the respondent from his car, which were accompanied by unspecified abuse but no actual blows.

The magistrates had also erred in deciding that it was not unreasonable for the respondent to drive two miles as it would have been difficult for him to stop. They should have considered whether it was necessary for him to continue driving.

Pittaway: The magistrates had again applied a subjective test, concerning themselves with the effect on the respondent of a man behaving violently towards her. They had not found that the threats amounted to threats of death or serious injury. They were wrong to apply a subjective test, and also wrong in considering whether the distance driven was reasonable, rather then necessary. Neither did they consider the significance of the respondent sitting in her car for five minutes, unpursued by the appellant, before driving off. They should have considered whether there was good cause for her to fear, which there was not.

R v Pommell [1995] 2 Cr App R 607 (CA)

Kennedy LJ: ... [T]he prosecution case was that at about 8 am on 4 June 1993 police officers entered the appellant's home to execute a search warrant. He was found lying in bed with a loaded gun in his right hand. He was asked if the gun was his and he replied, 'I took it off a geezer who was going to do some people some damage with it'. In the same bedroom police officers found a brown holdall containing ammunition. The appellant was arrested and interviewed. When interviewed he was asked to explain his possession of the gun, and he said:

> Last night someone come round to see me, this guy by the name of Erroll, and he had it with him with the intention to go and shoot some people

> because they had killed his friend and he wanted to kill their girlfriends and relatives and kids, and I persuade him, I took it off him and told him that it's not right to do that.

The appellant went on to say that Erroll had called between 12.30 am and 1 am and, after he left, the appellant took the gun upstairs and kept it from his girlfriend and took the bullets out of it. He appears to have achieved this by removing a loaded magazine containing 23 rounds. He then decided to wait until morning and decided to put the bullets back into it. To do this he must have inserted the loaded magazine back into the gun. He agreed that at the time of his arrest he was lying in bed with the gun against his leg because, he said, he did not want his girlfriend to see it. He said that he was going to hand the gun to his brother so that he could hand it to the police because his brother gets on with the police and had handed in guns in the past ...

We now turn to the events of 27 October 1993. In the course of an *ex parte* application as to discovery, prosecuting counsel advised the judge that the defence was going to be that the defendant had the weapon in his possession, holding it for another, so that the defence might be described as a defence of necessity. The judge said that he could not see that giving rise to an issue which it would be proper for a jury to consider, so the matter was explored further in open court. After arraignment, prosecuting counsel drew the attention of the judge to what the defendant had said in interview, and said that he understood that to be the basis of the defence. The judge said that he did not see any defence, and would need persuasion that a jury needed to be sworn. Defence counsel appears to have accepted that the judge should proceed on the basis that the contents of the interview were true. He drew the attention of the judge to the decision of this court in the case of *Martin* (1989) 88 Cr App R 343. There the court acknowledged that in extreme circumstances there can be a defence of necessity. Most commonly it arises when wrongful acts put pressure upon the accused, but it can arise from other objective dangers threatening the accused or others, then it is conveniently referred to as 'duress of circumstance'. Simon Brown J, as he then was, giving the judgment of the court, said:

> ... the defence is available only if, from an objective standpoint, the accused can be said to be acting reasonably and proportionately in order to avoid a threat of death or serious injury.

He went on to say that:

> ... assuming the defence to be open to the accused on his account of the facts, the *issue should be left to the jury*, who should be directed to determine these two questions: first, was the accused, or may he have been, impelled to act as he did because as a result of what he reasonably believed to be the situation he had good cause to fear that otherwise death or serious physical injury would result? Second, if so, may a sober person of reasonable firmness, sharing thc characteristics of the accused, have responded to that situation by acting as the accused acted? If the answer to both questions was yes, then the jury would acquit: the defence of necessity would have been established.

[The italics are ours.]

Martin had been charged with driving whilst disqualified, and asserted that he drove when he did because his wife, who was suicidal, threatened to kill herself. Obviously the circumstances of the present case are different and having had his attention drawn to the case of *Martin*, the trial judge said that in his view necessity could not be an issue here:

> ... because assuming that he was originally driven by necessity to take possession of it [the gun] ... his failure to go immediately to the police robs him of a defence ...

Before us there is substantially one ground of appeal. It is that the judge should not have ruled as he did and when he did in relation to the defence of necessity. [Counsel] for the appellant contends that the defence which he was seeking to advance should not have been so summarily dismissed. Evidence should have been called in the normal way, and then, if the evidence emerged as was anticipated, the judge should have left to the jury the issue of whether or not the defence of necessity was made out ...

... [W]e turn to consider the defence of necessity. There is an obvious attraction in the argument that if A finds B in possession of a gun which he is about to use to commit a crime, and if A is then able to persuade B to hand over the gun so that A may hand it to the police, A should not immediately upon taking possession of the gun become guilty of a criminal offence. However, if that is right, then in 1974, at least in the result, the case of *Woodage v Moss* was wrongly decided.

The strength of the argument that a person ought to be permitted to breach the letter of the criminal law in order to prevent a greater evil befalling himself or others has long been recognised (see, for example, Stephen's *Digest of Criminal Law*), but it has, in English law, not given rise to a recognised general defence of necessity, and in relation to the charge of murder, the defence has been specifically held not to exist (see *Dudley and Stephens* (1884) 14 QBD 273). Even in relation to other offences, there are powerful arguments against recognising the general defence. As Dickson J said in the Supreme Court of Canada in *Perka et al v R* (1985) 13 DLR (4th) 1 at 14:

> '... no system of positive law can recognise any principle which would entitle a person to violate the law because in his view the law conflicted with some higher social value.' The Criminal Code has specified a number of identifiable situations in which an actor is justified in committing what would otherwise be a criminal offence. To go beyond that and hold that ostensibly illegal acts can be validated on the basis of their expediency, would import an undue subjectivity into the criminal law. It would invite the courts to second-guess the legislature and to assess the relative merits of social policies underlying criminal prohibitions.

However, that does not really deal with the situation where someone commendably infringes a regulation in order to prevent another person from committing what everyone would accept as being a greater evil with a gun. In that situation it cannot be satisfactory to leave it to the prosecuting authority not to prosecute, or to individual courts to grant an absolute discharge. The authority may, as in the present case, prosecute because it is not satisfied that the defendant is telling the truth, and then, even if he is vindicated and given an absolute discharge, he is left with a criminal conviction which, for some purposes, would be recognised as such.

It was, as it seems to us, to meet this difficulty that the limited defence of duress of circumstances has been developed in English law in relation to road traffic offences. It was first recognised in *Willer* (1986) 83 Cr App R 225, where the accused drove onto a pavement and in and out of a shopping centre in order to escape a gang of youths seeking to attack him and his passenger. *Willer* was followed and applied in *Conway* (1989) 88 Cr App R 159, in which the Court of Appeal quashed a conviction on a charge of reckless driving. Having considered existing authorities, textbooks and the proposals of the Law Commission, the court in that case said at 164:

> ... it is still not clear whether there is a general defence of necessity or, if there is, what are the circumstances in which it is available.

In our judgment, that is still the position, but the court in *Conway* went on to say that necessity can be a defence to a charge of reckless driving where the facts establish duress of circumstances, that is to say when the defendant is constrained to drive as he did to avoid death or serious bodily harm to himself or some other person.

Then came *Martin*, a decision to which we referred earlier in this judgment, and *DPP v Bell* [1992] RTR 335, where the defendant, whose alcohol level was over the prescribed limit, was pursued to his car and, fearing serious injury, drove some distance down the road. The Crown Court allowed his appeal on the basis of duress of circumstances, and an appeal by way of case stated was dismissed. The Divisional Court particularly noted the finding of fact that the appellant drove only some distance down the road and not, for example, all the way home, so that the defence of duress of circumstances continued to avail him. In *DPP v Jones* [1990] RTR 33, it was held that any defence of necessity available to a driver would cease to be available if he drove for a longer period than necessary. Commenting on the case of *Bell*, Professor Sir John Smith has written:

> All the cases so far have concerned road traffic offences but there are no grounds for supposing that the defence is limited to that kind of case. On the contrary, the defence, being closely related to the defence of duress by threats, appears to be general, applying to all crimes except murder, attempted murder and some forms of treason ... (see [1992] Crim LR 176)

We agree.

That leads us to the conclusion that in the present case the defence was open to the appellant in respect of his acquisition of the gun. The jury would have to be directed to determine the two questions identified in the passage which we have cited from the judgment in *Martin*. That leaves the question as to his continued possession of the gun thereafter. In our judgment, the test laid down in *Martin* is not necessarily the appropriate test for determining whether a person continues to have a defence available to him. For example, a person takes a gun off another in the circumstances in which this appellant says he did and then locks it away in a safe with a view to safeguarding it while the police are informed. When the gun is in the safe, the test laid down in *Martin* may not be satisfied: there would then be no immediate fear of death or serious injury. In our judgment, a person who has taken possession of a gun in circumstances where he has the defence of duress by circumstances must 'desist from committing the crime as soon as he reasonably can' (Smith and Hogan, *Criminal Law*, 7th edn, p 239). This test is similar to the test in *Jones*, to which we have already referred. In deciding whether a defendant acted reasonably, regard would be had to the circumstances in which he finds himself. Can it be said, in this case, that there was no evidence upon which a jury could have reached the conclusion that the appellant did desist, or may have desisted, as soon as he reasonably could? In answering this question, the jury would have to have regard to the delay that had occurred between, on the appellant's account, his acquisition of the gun and ammunition at 12.30 to 1 am, and the arrival of the police some hours later. The appellant has offered an explanation for that delay but, as it seems to us, the defence of duress of circumstances could not avail him once a reasonable person in his position would have known that the duress, in this case the need to obtain and retain the firearm, had ceased. In the present case the judge said that the failure of the appellant to go immediately to the police 'robs him of a defence'. We accept that in some cases a delay, especially if unexplained, may be such as to make it clear that any duress must have ceased to operate, in which case the judge would be entitled to conclude that even on the defendant's own account of the facts, the defence was not open to him. There would then be no reason to leave the issue to the jury. However, the situation does not seem to us to have been sufficiently clear cut to make that an appropriate step in the present case. In the first place, the delay of a few hours overnight might not be regarded as being unduly long and, second, the defendant did offer an explanation for it, therefore, in our judgment, the proposed defence should have been left to the jury.

We have considered whether the reloading of the gun and the fact that the appellant had the gun in his bed deprived him of the defence. Must a person who has acquired a gun in circumstances in which he has the defence of duress of circumstances not only desist from committing the offence as soon as he reasonably can but, in the meanwhile, act in a reasonable manner with the gun? The answer is that if he does not do so, it will be difficult for the court to accept that he desisted from committing the offence as soon as he reasonably could. Therefore, in our judgment, the acts of reloading and putting the gun in the bed do not of themselves deprive him of the defence, but are matters which may be taken into account by the jury in deciding the issues to which we have already made reference ...

CHAPTER 10

INFANCY

There is an irrebuttable presumption that a child who has not attained the age of 10 is incapable of forming criminal intent.

In the case of a child who has attained the age of 10 but is under 14, that presumption becomes a rebuttable one; in such a case, the prosecution must prove that the child knew that his or her actions were seriously wrong (*C v DPP* [1994] 3 WLR 888). In a number of subsequent cases the Divisional Court had given guidance on the evidence required to rebut the presumption.

Section 50 of the Children and Young Persons Act 1933

It shall be conclusively presumed that no child under the age of 10 can be guilty of an offence.

The Presumption: 10–13 year olds

C v DPP [1996] AC 1 (HL)

Lord Jauncey of Tullichettle: ... It is, no doubt, undesirable that a young person who commits an offence and who genuinely does not know that he is doing something seriously wrong should suffer the rigours of the criminal law. But is a blanket presumption such as exists in England and Wales at the moment the best way to achieve protection for such a person? There must be many youthful offenders under the age of 14 who are very well aware that what they are doing is seriously wrong. Indeed it is almost an affront to common sense to presume that a boy of 12 or 13 who steals a high-powered motor car, damages other cars while driving it, knocks down a uniformed police officer and then runs away when stopped is unaware that he is doing wrong.

The presumption has been subject to weighty criticism over many years by committees, by academic writers and by the courts as explained in detail in the speech of my noble and learned friend. I add my voice to those critics and express the hope that Parliament may once again look at the presumption, perhaps as part of a larger review of the appropriate methods in a modern society of dealing with youthful offenders.

No such presumption operates in Scotland, where normal criminal responsibility attaches to a child over eight, and I do not understand that injustice is considered to have resulted from this situation. In this connection it is worth mentioning that the system of children's hearings constituted by the Social Work (Scotland) Act 1968, which enables many offending children between eight and 16 years of age to be effectively dealt with outside the criminal courts, works extremely well.

Lord Lowry: My Lords, the point of this appeal is:

> Whether there continues to be a presumption that a child between the ages of 10 and 14 is *doli incapax* and, if so, whether that presumption can only be rebutted by clear positive evidence that he knew that his act was seriously wrong, such evidence not consisting merely in the evidence of the acts amounting to the offence itself.

That was the question certified as a point of law of general public importance by the Divisional Court when granting leave to appeal to this House after dismissing the appellant's appeal by case stated from the decision of a youth court convicting the appellant of interfering with a motor cycle with the intent that an offence of theft or of taking and driving away without consent should be committed contrary to s 9(1) of the Criminal Attempts Act 1981. The question arose in this way.

About 3 pm on 8 June 1992 two policemen on mobile patrol saw a Honda 125 cc motor cycle parked in the private driveway of a house in Liverpool. Two boys were tampering with the motor cycle. The appellant was holding the handlebars while the other boy tried with a crowbar to force open the chain and padlock securing the motor cycle. The police approached on foot and both boys ran off. One policeman chased the appellant, who then climbed over a wall at the rear of the property and was arrested by another policeman. The damage to the motor cycle included the detaching of the leads to the coil and battery and the dislodging of the mounting. There was, as your Lordships have been told, no evidence of any admission or statement by the appellant. At the conclusion of the prosecution's case the appellant's solicitor called no evidence but submitted that the prosecution had not adduced sufficient evidence to prove that the appellant, who was born on 29 June 1979 and was therefore just under 13 years old at the time of the alleged offence, had guilty knowledge and knew that what he was doing was seriously wrong as opposed to merely naughty or mischievous.

As the case stated reveals, the justices found that the appellant knew that what he had done was seriously wrong, observing that the damage done to the motor cycle was substantial and that the appellant and his accomplice ran from the police, leaving the crowbar behind. They drew from these facts the inference that the appellant 'knew he was in serious trouble because he had done something seriously wrong'. They therefore convicted the appellant and fined him 15 units at £4, payable by his mother, who was also bound over to ensure his future good behaviour. The question in the case stated for the opinion of the High Court was:

> whether or not there was any, or any sufficient, evidence to justify the finding of fact made by us, that this particular defendant knew that what he was doing was seriously wrong.

On the hearing of the appeal the Divisional Court ([1994] 3 WLR 888), constituted by Mann LJ and Laws J, of its own motion took a point which had not been raised either in that court or in the youth court by either party, namely that it was a matter for consideration whether the presumption of *doli incapax* (which I shall refer to as 'the presumption') had outlived its usefulness and should no longer be regarded as part of the common law ...

My Lords, [counsel] for the appellant has argued cogently that the Divisional Court was not justified in holding that the presumption is 'no longer part of the law of England'. He referred to 1 Hale's *Pleas of the Crown* (6th edn, Leach 1788) and *Blackstone* (already noted) and to up-to-date editions of *Russell on Crime* (12th edn, Vol 1, 1964, Kenny's *Outlines of Criminal Law*, 19th edn, 1966; Smith and Hogan, *Criminal Law*, 7th edn, 1992; 11(1) Halsbury's *Law of England,* 4th edn reissue and Cross and Ashworth, *The English Sentencing System* (3rd edn, 1981). The doctrine is summarised in Archbold's *Criminal Pleading Evidence and Practice,* Vol 1, 1993, para 1.96:

> At common law a child under 14 years is presumed not to have reached the age of discretion and to be *doli incapax;* but this presumption may be rebutted by strong and pregnant evidence of a mischievous [disposition] ... Between 10 and 14 years a child is presumed not to know the difference between right and wrong and therefore to be incapable of committing a crime because of

> lack of *mens rea* ... Wrong means gravely wrong, seriously wrong ... evil or morally wrong ...

In the 17th century the 'age of discretion' was fixed by Coke at 14. It was accepted as such by Hale.

Counsel pointed to the long line of cases, most of which were noted in the judgment of Laws J (and the latest of which was *A v DPP* [1992] Crim LR 34 in the Divisional Court), in which the presumption has without exception been recognised and applied. He also traced the doctrine in the cases, legislation and textbooks of other jurisdictions in the Commonwealth ...

My Lords, I think it is time that I took a look at the reasons given by Laws J for his conclusions, not for the purpose of refuting them, but to show that they do not conclude the matter.

(1) It is true that there is (and has been for a considerable time) compulsory education and, as the judge said, perhaps children now grow up more quickly. But better formal education and earlier sophistication do not guarantee that the child will more readily distinguish right from wrong.

(2) The presumption is 'out of step with the general law'. True enough, but the *general* law was not meant to apply without qualification to children under 14.

(3) I agree that the phrase 'seriously wrong' is conceptually obscure, and that view is confirmed by the rather loose treatment accorded to the *doli incapax* doctrine by the textbooks, but, when the phrase is contrasted with 'merely naughty or mischievous', I think its meaning is reasonably clear.

(4) The rule is said to be illogical because the presumption can be rebutted by proof that the child was of normal capacity *for his age*; this leads to the conclusion that every child is initially presumed not to be of normal mental capacity *for his age*, which is absurd. This argument involves a point which I must deal with when considering the second part of the certified question (how to prove that the child is *doli capax*), but at this stage I will focus on the illogicality. We start with a benevolent presumption of *doli incapax*, the purpose of which was to protect children between 7 (now by statute 10) and 14 years from the full rigour of the criminal law. The fact that the presumption was rebuttable has led the courts to recognise that the older the child (*B v R* (1958) 44 Cr App R 1 at 3) and the more obviously heinous the offence, the easier it is to rebut the presumption. Proof of mental normality has in practice (understandably but perhaps not always logically) been largely accepted as proof that the child can distinguish right from wrong and form a criminal intent. The presumption itself is not, and never has been, completely logical; it provides a benevolent safeguard which evidence can remove. Very little evidence is needed but it must be adduced as part of the prosecution's case, or else there will be no case to answer.

(5) The need for the prosecutor to rebut the presumption may give rise to injustice where the rebuttal involves proving previous convictions. I remind your Lordships of the relevant passage in the judgment ([1994] 3 WLR 88 at 895):

> ... the presumption's application may also give rise to the risk of injustice. In *R v B, R v A* [1979] 1 WLR 1185, to which I have already referred, the Court of Appeal held that a child's previous convictions may in principle be admitted in evidence to rebut the presumption. If that were to happen before a jury, in a case where the child defendant disputed the primary facts, the prejudicial consequences can only too readily be imagined. It is no answer to say that the

> judge would possess a discretion to exclude such evidence. So he would; but the case might be one where there was no other evidence available to counter the presumption's application, and the judge would then be faced with an impossible choice between doing rank injustice to the defendant and doing rank injustice to the prosecution. No doubt that would be an extreme case. But it illustrates the needlessly distortive effect which this rule produces in the execution of criminal justice.

The last sentence above makes the point: there must be something badly wrong with a doctrine which can involve such unjust results. This proposition needs to be scrutinised.

One would, of course, have to know the nature of the earlier convictions before accepting that they might properly prove a guilty mind in relation to the offence charged. Second, can the *opinion* of an earlier court of jury prove the guilty mind *vis-à-vis* the later charge? I can see the argument that the child, if convicted and, a *fortiori*, if punished for the offence, could be said to know thenceforward right from wrong. But I think there is a simpler answer to the problem. If the primary facts are disputed, my own opinion is that, despite *R v B, R v A* [1979] 1 WLR 1185, a child defendant ought not to be put in a worse position than an adult by having evidence of his previous convictions admitted unless they can be admitted under a generally applicable principle, for example, if he has put his character in issue or attacked the character of prosecution witnesses or if the earlier convictions come within the 'similar facts' rule (see on this point *Kenny* p 80, note 2). In *R v B, R v A* the offence charged was blackmail and the report does not disclose what the earlier convictions were for. The only clue is to be found in the trial judge's observation that:

> it seems to be blindingly obvious that if a person charged with an offence of dishonesty has been before the juvenile court and there has been recorded a finding of guilt in respect of such a case, that must be relevant whether or not he knows the difference between right or [*sic*] wrong. (See [1979] 1 WLR 1185 at 1187.)

Later, referring to what evidence may be admitted to prove knowledge of right and wrong, the judge said:

> And it must, in my view, include evidence of convictions, provided those are relevant. [I assume that this means relevant to prove knowledge of the difference between right and wrong.] It does seem to me that a situation could arise where the prosecution might be seeking to prove findings of guilt which could really have no bearing on this issue, and if that were the situation then one would without hesitation say that the prejudicial effect of such evidence would outweigh any possible beneficial value and that such evidence should be excluded. But that is not the situation which arises in this case.

Unfortunately, as I have said, the report of the case does not show what the previous convictions were for. The judge's observations would exclude evidence of a conviction of assault or riding a bicycle on the footpath but not necessarily a conviction for stealing, which would not be admitted under the similar facts rule. Such a conviction could well be relevant to prove 'knowledge', but it would be inadmissible (though very prejudicial) to prove the primary facts. What the report does reveal is that the defence abandoned the presumption once the judge had ruled against them. Therefore I would infer that there was a working defence on the primary facts. Assuming that the previous convictions were allowed to be put in evidence but were not admissible under the similar facts rule, it would clearly have been in vain for the judge to tell the jury to disregard them when considering the primary issue but then to take account of them if they had to decide the 'knowledge' issue.

[Lord Widgery CJ] delivering the judgment of the Court of Appeal in *R v B, R v A*, said ([1979] 1 WLR 1185 at 1187):

> The judge in clear terms was taking the view that where the presumption applies the prosecution can seek to remove the effect of the presumption and to call evidence to that effect. A moment's thought will make it clear that that is so. If the presumption is allowed to stand and the prosecution did not call evidence to rebut it, then, at the close of the prosecution case, there would be a ruling that there was no case to answer. It seems to us, as it seemed to the judge below, that to guard against that ridiculous result one must accept the fact that the prosecution can call relevant evidence which is relevant on the issue of the young man's capacity to know good from evil.

The cases cited in *R v B, R v A* were concerned with the evidence of the defendant's general background and, so far as the above passage deals with that kind of evidence, I freely concur in what was said. But I do not think it right (assuming that to be the position) to admit non-similar fact evidence which would be inadmissible on issue 1 for the purpose of proving the prosecution's case on issue 2. If the prosecution's case must sometimes fail because some or all of the probative evidence cannot be given, that is not a unique situation and it must be borne with fortitude in the interests of fairness to the accused. To hold a split trial, dividing issues 1 and 2, would not be practicable and such a procedure would soon conduce to the inference at an early stage of the trial that evidence of previous convictions will be tendered if issue 1 is decided against the accused. I hope your Lordships will forgive me for devoting some time to the previous convictions argument, which appears to me to involve a general principle and to be something which will concern trial judges for so long as they have to cope with the *doli incapax* doctrine.

(6) It has also been said that the rule is divisive because it bears hardly on perhaps isolated acts of wrongdoing done by children from 'good homes', and also perverse because it absolves children from 'bad homes', who are most likely to commit 'criminal' acts. One answer to this observation (not entirely satisfying, I agree) is that the presumption contemplated the conviction and punishment of children who, possibly by virtue of their superior upbringing, bore moral responsibility for their actions, and the exoneration of those who did not. The Divisional Court's argument provides support for the modern outlook in favour of prescribing suitable treatment (which may or may not be punitive) for the many children who commit antisocial acts, instead of searching for moral culpability, which should then be visited with retribution.

(7) It is then said (with considerable force, I would admit) that the presumption is an outmoded survival from an age in which criminal guilt was inevitably followed by ferocious retribution. But, while times have greatly changed since the days when children of eight and 10 years were hanged for offences much less heinous than murder, it should be observed that the purpose and effect of the presumption is still to protect children between 10 and 14 from the full force of the criminal law ...

A long and uncontradicted line of authority makes two propositions clear. The first is that the prosecution must prove that the child defendant did the act charged and that when doing that act he knew that it was a wrong act as distinct from an act of mere naughtiness or childish mischief. The criminal standard of proof applies. What is required has been variously expressed as, in *Blackstone*, 'strong and clear beyond all doubt or contradiction', or in *R v Gorrie* (1919) 83 JP 136, 'very clear and complete evidence', or in *B v R* (1958) 44 Cr App R 1 at 3 *per* Lord Parker CJ, 'It has often been put in this way, that ... "guilty knowledge must be proved and the evidence to that effect must be clear and beyond all possibility of doubt"'. No doubt the emphatic tone of some of the directions was due to the court's anxiety to prevent merely naughty children from being convicted of crimes and in a sterner age to protect them from the draconian consequences of conviction.

The second clearly established proposition is that evidence to prove the defendant's guilty knowledge, as defined above, must not be the mere proof of the doing of the act charged, however horrifying or obviously wrong that act may be. As Erle J said in *R v Smith* (1845) 1 Cox CC 260:

> ... a guilty knowledge that he was doing wrong ... must be proved by the evidence, and cannot be presumed from the mere commission of the act. You are to determine from a review of the evidence whether it is satisfactorily proved that at the time he fired the rick (if you should be of opinion he did fire it) he had guilty knowledge that he was committing a crime.

... The cases seem to show, logically enough, that the older the defendant is and the more obviously wrong the act, the easier it will generally be to prove guilty knowledge. The surrounding circumstances are of course relevant and what the defendant said or did before or after the act may go to prove his guilty mind. Running away is usually equivocal, as Laws J rightly said it was in the present case, because flight from the scene can easily follow a naughty action as a wicked one. There must, however, be a few cases where running away would indicate guilty knowledge, where an act is either wrong or innocent and there is no room for mere naughtiness. An example might be selling drugs at a street corner and fleeing at the sight of a policeman.

The Divisional Court here, assuming that the presumption applied, would have reversed the youth court, rightly, in my opinion, because there was no evidence, outside the commission of the 'offence', upon which one could find that the presumption had been rebutted.

In order to obtain that kind of evidence, apart from anything the defendant may have said or done, the prosecution has to rely on interviewing the suspect of having him psychiatrically examined (two methods which depend on receiving co-operation) or on evidence from someone who knows the defendant well, such as a teacher, the involvement of whom adversely to the child is unattractive ...

My Lords, I have reached without difficulty the conclusion that both parts of the certified question should be answered Yes. I would therefore allow the appeal and remit the case to the High Court in order that it may be sent back to the youth court with a direction to dismiss the charge against the appellant. But the judges in the court below have achieved their object, at least in part, by drawing renewed attention to serious shortcomings in an important area of our criminal law ...

I believe that the time has come to examine further a doctrine which appears to have been inconsistently applied and which is certainly capable of producing inconsistent results, according to the way in which courts treat the presumption and depending on the evidence to rebut it which is available in each case ...

The distinction between the treatment and the punishment of child 'offenders' has popular and political overtones, a fact which shows that we have been discussing not so much legal as a social problem, with a dash of politics thrown in, and emphasises that it should be within the exclusive remit of Parliament. There is need to study other systems, including that which holds sway in Scotland, a task for which the courts are not equipped. Whatever change is made, it should come only after collating and considering the evidence and after taking account of the effect which a change would have on the whole law relating to children's antisocial behaviour. This is a classic case for Parliamentary investigation, deliberation and legislation ...

Rebutting the presumption

J M (A Minor) v Runeckles (1984) 79 Cr App R 255 (DC)

Mann J: ... On 2 July 1982 the defendant was aged 13. The circumstances of the offence alleged were as follows. The defendant and another girl had a discussion with the victim in a public open space. After that discussion the victim went home, to which house the defendant and her companion then went. On their arrival at the home, the front door was opened. The victim was hit by the defendant with a milk bottle and was then stabbed by the defendant with the now broken bottle. The defendant and her companion ran off.

The defendant and her companion shortly afterwards were seen in a street by a police officer, whereupon appreciating the sighting, they fled and sought to hide in a garden. They were apprehended.

In those circumstances the justices convicted this defendant and her companion. It is argued before this court that the defendant's conviction must be quashed because of the operation of the presumption which applies in regard to the acts of children between 10 and 14. That presumption is this: at common law a child under 14 is presumed not to have reached the age of discretion and is to be deemed *doli incapax*. The presumption is a rebuttable presumption, and the burden of rebutting it is upon the prosecution. I do not doubt that the prosecution has to discharge that burden by reference to the standard of proof which the prosecution has ordinarily to establish in a criminal case.

[Counsel] for the appellant argued that the prosecution could rebut this presumption only by showing that the child appreciated that that which he or she had done was morally wrong; and that this could not have been done on the facts of this case.

... The question which the justices posed for the decision of this court is whether or not there was evidence on which they could come to the conclusion that the defendant had (what in the old language is called) a mischievous discretion.

The court has been referred to the direction of Salter J in *Gorrie* (1919) 83 JP 136, where he said:

> The boy was under 14, and the law presumed that he was not responsible criminally; and if the prosecution sought to show that he was responsible although under 14, they must give them (that is, the jury) very clear and complete evidence of what was called mischievous discretion: that meant that they must satisfy the jury that when the boy did this he knew that he was doing what was wrong – not merely what was wrong, but what was gravely wrong, seriously wrong.

I would respectfully adopt the learned judge's use of the phrase 'seriously wrong'. I regard an act which a child knew to be morally wrong as being but one type of those acts which a child can appreciate to be seriously wrong. I think it is unnecessary to show that the child appreciated that his or her action was morally wrong. It is sufficient that the child appreciated the action was seriously wrong. A court has to look for something beyond mere naughtiness or childish mischief.

In this case the justices had before them the actions of the defendant; that is, a blow with a milk bottle and a stab with a remnant part of that bottle. They had before them her immediate running away. They had before them her hiding when the police were observed. They also had the defendant's statement under caution, a statement which was coherent in content and which contained the caption written in the defendant's handwriting.

In my judgment, taking the matter together, the justices were justified in finding that they were satisfied so as to be sure that the presumption had been rebutted, and that this 13-year-old girl (who from her statement seemed of normal intelligence) appreciated that what she did to her victim was a seriously wrong thing to do. For those reasons, I would answer the question in the case by saying there was evidence on which the justices could conclude that the defendant had mischievous discretion ...

L v DPP; T v DPP; W, GH and CH v DPP (1996) 160 JP 528 (DC)

Otton LJ: [His Lordship referred to *C v DPP* [1994] 3 WLR 888 and continued:] Thus five principles relevant to these appeals emerge which are not contentious:

(1) The presumption of *doli incapax* can only be rebutted by clear positive evidence that a child knew that his act was seriously wrong.

(2) Evidence of the commission of the acts amounting to the offence itself is not sufficient to rebut the presumption.

(3) Interviews with the child are capable of providing the necessary insight into the mental functions of the child from which inferences may be drawn to rebut the presumption.

(4) The conduct of the child before or after the act may go to prove his guilty mind.

(5) The older the child is and the more obviously wrong the act, the easier it will generally be to prove guilty knowledge.

In the case of each of the appellants the defence was that there was no, or insufficient evidence 'outside the offence' upon which the court could find the presumption rebutted.

A second line of argument was advanced, based upon the passage of the speech of Lord Lowry:

> In order to obtain that kind of evidence, apart from anything the defendant may have said or done, the prosecution has to rely on interviewing the suspect or having him psychiatrically examined (two methods which depend on receiving co-operation) or on evidence from someone who knows the defendant well, such as a teacher, the involvement of whom adversely to the child is unattractive.

Counsel for each of the appellants submitted that in order to rebut the presumption the prosecution was required to call evidence specifically relating to the child's perception of the seriousness of what he did. That is, evidence independent of the facts of the events and from an independent source such as a teacher or psychiatrist or one who knew the suspect well. Such evidence should have included an interview with the suspect and questions should have been put to him specifically to elicit responses which would have indicated his state of mind at the time of the offence, and his appreciation of the seriousness of what he had done.

I am unable to accept that interpretation of the passage. Lord Lowry was not laying down the principle that in every case brought before the youth court the prosecution is required to adduce such evidence. In practice, the prosecuting authority would find it frequently impossible to obtain such evidence. Teachers would be placed in an invidious position even if they knew of the child's disposition to naughtiness or mischief. In simple, straightforward cases an interview by a psychiatrist would introduce an undesirable and unnecessary element into the prosecution process. It is for the court to decide as a fact whether what the suspect did or said before or after the incident indicates his state of mind at the time of the offence and his appreciation of the seriousness of what he has done. This essential function must not be usurped by or delegated to psychiatrists, teachers, or other persons who know the suspect well.

In summary, in seeking to establish that a child knows that his actions were seriously wrong as distinct from merely naughty it is not usually necessary to lead direct evidence on this point. In *IPH v Chief Constable of South Wales* [1987] Crim LR 42, Woolf LJ suggested that a police officer, when interviewing the suspect, should incorporate some questions designed to probe the issue of whether he knew his acts were seriously wrong. He proffered a direct question such as, 'Did you appreciate that what you were doing was seriously wrong?' I consider this to be helpful guidance and not inconsistent with Lord Lowry's *dicta*. I would further suggest that police officers who are engaged in dealing with child suspects should be trained and encouraged to ask such direct questions. The questions should not suggest the answer that the child may perceive the person in authority wishes to hear. The language should be suited to the age and literacy of the suspect. The answers may well give the court (which is constituted of persons specially selected for the task) a useful insight, one way or the other, into the child's state of mind at the time of the offence and his appreciation of the seriousness of what he has done. If this were adopted as the usual practice it would only be in exceptional cases that the necessity to call independent evidence would arise.

With these principles and observations in mind I approach each of the appeals in turn.

L v DPP

... On 29 August 1995, the applicant was convicted of possession, without the authority of the Secretary of State, of a weapon, namely a KO 5001 CS gas canister which was designed or adapted for the discharge of a noxious liquid contrary to s 5(1)(b) of the Firearms Act 1968.

The appellant was born on 1 May 1981 and thus on the date of the offence was aged 13 years and 10 months.

The justices found that two police constables from their marked police car saw the appellant together with another youth in Erconwald Street on 23 February 1995 at about 4.05 pm. The appellant looked towards the police car and stepped into an entrance to his right so that he was partly concealed by a low wall. The police car stopped and PC Davison ran from it, saw the appellant pull out his right hand from his trouser pocket and drop a small red object. PC Croome picked up the object and said to the appellant, 'It's a CS gas canister which is illegal' and asked him why he had got it, to which the appellant replied, 'I didn't have it on me'. The object was a CS gas canister. He was arrested and cautioned to which he made no comment ...

The justices were of the opinion that as the appellant was nine weeks away from his 14th birthday, the presumption that he was *doli incapax* was almost negated.

They further considered that as the case concerned the possession of a CS gas canister, which is an illegal item in itself, the appellant must have known that to possess it was seriously wrong rather than naughty or mischievous because such an item was not readily available to the public. It was in a different category from a knife or a pair of scissors which could become an offensive weapon if possessed with requisite intention. They considered the appellant's conduct in disposing of the canister on seeing the police car was sufficient evidence to demonstrate that he knew that it was seriously wrong to possess it. Accordingly, they found the case proved.

The question for the opinion of this court was whether they were correct to find that there was sufficient evidence before them for the presumption that the appellant was *doli incapax* to be rebutted ...

Conclusion

The approach of the justices cannot be faulted. They directed themselves correctly on the law, as propounded in *C v DPP*. This was a statutory offence of possession and did not require proof of *mens rea*. Moreover, the act of possessing a weapon was either wrong or innocent. There was no room for mere naughtiness when he was in possession of a CS gas canister which could not be legitimately (or innocently) in his possession. The justices did not confine themselves to the evidence of the acts amounting to the offence itself. They were entitled to and did consider the actions immediately after the appellant saw the police arrive. He dropped the can in order to dispossess himself of it. It would also have been open to them to take account of the fact that, when confronted at the scene, he told a deliberate and blatant lie. In fact the justices did not do so. The facts upon which they did rely might not have been sufficient in a much younger person but the justices were entitled to take into consideration the fact that the appellant was only nine weeks short of his 14th birthday.

... [T]he youth court was correct to find that there was sufficient evidence of the presumption that the appellant was *doli incapax* to be rebutted ...

T v Crown Prosecution Service

...[It was alleged that T] stole two packs of sandwiches, belonging to Boots Company plc, contrary to s 1 of the Theft Act 1968. At the material time the appellant was aged 11 years and nine months.

The justices found as fact that at approximately 10 am on the day in question, T was in the Boots store together with two other youths, one older and one younger. They were seen by a store detective in the food area of the store. The youths were observed looking at the sandwiches and then seemed to select and replace sandwiches from the chiller. T was seen to select two packs of sandwiches but did not replace them. The smallest boy was seen to place a plastic bottle of orange juice in his hand. All three boys left the food area together with the items they had selected and walked across the shop floor in the direction of the chemist's counter. The applicant and the smallest boy carried the sandwiches openly in their hands at all times as they walked across the store. The three boys passed by the tills and made no attempt to pay for the items they had selected. As they approached the exit doors (on the far side of the store from the area where they had selected the sandwiches and the orange juice) the appellant passed one of the two packs of sandwiches he was holding to the oldest boy. All three boys left the store without paying or making any attempt to pay for the items selected.

They crossed the road followed by the store detective and a uniformed security guard. They realised they were being followed, whereupon all three youths began to run pursued by the store detective and the guard. In the course of the pursuit the older boy threw the sandwiches to the ground and the smallest boy threw down the orange juice. The three boys were conveyed back to the security office in the Boots store. They were subsequently arrested and taken to the police station. During an interview under caution at which his mother and his solicitor were present the appellant made mixed admissions and denials. He acknowledged that he had no money and knew when he walked out of the store that the sandwiches were stolen. Initially he said that another boy took them from Marks and Spencer. He subsequently admitted they had been taken from Boots. He was asked if he realised 'that taking stuff from a store is stealing?' (but the answer was not adduced) ...

On the basis that the acts constituting theft were completed when they made their exit from the store without payment being made, the justices were satisfied that the only reason why the boys chose to run outside the store was because they knew they had stolen the sandwiches (and orange juice) and on realising they were being followed by a uniformed security guard (and store detective) they wished to get away and avoid being caught. In the opinion of the justices this finding was supported by the additional evidence of each of the boys throwing away stolen items in the course of the pursuit, which they believed was a clear attempt by the boys to rid themselves of the evidence. Furthermore, the fact that the appellant made both admissions and denials in the course of interview was clear evidence that he understood the concept of stealing. In particular, he alleged that one of the other boys had 'nicked' the sandwiches from another store. This demonstrated that he was trying to evade liability for his own actions and in so doing attempted to pass the responsibility on to another boy. All of this convinced the justices that the appellant must have known that what he did was seriously wrong.

The question posed in the case is 'whether or not the prosecution called sufficient evidence to justify the findings of fact made by us, ie that this particular defendant (appellant) knew what he did was seriously wrong' ...

Conclusion

... There were facts as found by the court, based on evidence, from which they could safely find that the presumption had been rebutted. They were entitled to find that, from their conduct inside the store before the theft was committed and from their running away and throwing away the sandwiches when being pursued they wished to avoid being caught because they knew they had stolen the sandwiches. The magistrates were not wrong to treat the interview as amounting to admissions and denials, or to interpret the expression 'nicked' in the way they did. There was no need for a psychiatric assessment or the evidence of those able to assess the child. The police officer asked a pertinent question but the answer was not adduced.

Accordingly, I would answer the question posed in the affirmative. The prosecution did call sufficient evidence to justify the findings of fact made by the court that this appellant knew what he did was seriously wrong ...

W, GH and CH v DPP

... [T]he appellants [were charged as follows:]

1 On 13 August 1994 they together assaulted N thereby occasioning him actual bodily harm, contrary to s 47 of the Offences Against the Person Act 1861.

2 On the same day they together falsely imprisoned N and detained him against his will, contrary to common law.

The justices heard evidence over two days and made detailed findings of fact. On 13 August 1994 at about 12.30 pm N (the victim) then aged seven years was playing with his friend O, (aged eight years), on the Tarzan swing in The Meadows near Catcote Road, Hartlepool. Shortly after, the appellants and a fourth boy arrived at the scene and began to bully N. The appellants and the fourth boy had three dogs and a dog chain with them. The appellant GH and the fourth boy pushed N whilst the appellants CH and W wrapped the chain around N's neck causing him considerable pain and distress because he was being choked. The victim was pushed down the hill and sustained a cut to his knee but the justices were unable to make a finding as to who was responsible for inflicting this injury. CH and the fourth boy pushed the victim into the stream and later the appellants W and CH and the fourth boy took N into a field where they forced him to eat horse faeces. W pushed N as a result of which N sustained an injury to his elbow causing soreness.

CH on several occasions whipped the victim with the chain across his back. He admitted to the police in interview that he had punched N in the face and back. As a result the victim suffered pain and distress. He was pushed into some nettles but the justices were unable to make a finding as to who was responsible for that act.

GH put the child into an old bath used as a horse trough containing water and insects. The three appellants and the fourth boy then urinated on N whilst he was in the horse trough. (This incident was the subject-matter of the false imprisonment allegation). CH put a bucket over the child's head and then kicked the bucket causing him pain and distress. The victim was subjected to a sustained and vicious attack by the three appellants which lasted approximately an hour.

The victim was later seen at the accident and emergency department, Hartlepool General Hospital. There were multiple bruises all over the victim's body; contusions, abrasions, scratches over both arms, the front of his chest and the back of both legs. Such injuries were consistent with the evidence given by the boy as to the conduct of the three appellants at the scene of the incident.

When the appellants saw PC Elliott leaving O's house (who had been with N at the scene), and suspecting that PC Elliott was investigating the incident, they ran away. This demonstrated to the justices that the appellants knew they had been involved in a wrongdoing and that their conduct amounted to more than mere mischievousness. The appellants and the fourth boy were arrested and interviewed under caution. All accepted being at the scene of the incident but denied being responsible for assaulting N. The justices formed the view from all the surrounding circumstances of the case that all three appellants appreciated that what they did was seriously wrong.

At the date of the offence W was aged 11 years and 10 months, GH was 13 years and three months and CH was 11 years and three days ...

The justices found that the prosecution had discharged the burden of adducing sufficient evidence to rebut the presumption of *doli incapax* by showing that the appellants had the requisite criminal intent and capacity to commit acts constituting the offences charged. They believed that W and CH by their admissions at interview assaulted N and knew what they had done was seriously wrong. The attack was a joint enterprise. GH was responsible on his own for keeping N in the horse trough against his will. The appellants clearly understood questions put to them in interview by the police. The appellants demonstrated in answer to those questions that they knew that what they had done was seriously wrong as opposed to mere naughtiness. The motivation of the appellants for the attack was to avenge N's conduct towards the younger sister of two of the appellants. The appellants intended to carry out the attack and made use of the opportunity which presented itself to them. GH interviewed for the benefit of N when the dog chain was wrapped round his neck so as to prevent further harm. He told the other appellants not to pull the chain any tighter. This demonstrated an understanding of the potential serious consequences and wrongfulness of such an act. Each appellant had lied to the police about his involvement and had implicated the other appellants. The justices were satisfied that all the appellants had been involved in a vicious attack on N, a younger child, and had the requisite capacity to understand the seriousness of their actions.

Accordingly they convicted CH and W of assault occasioning actual bodily harm and dismissed the charge of false imprisonment against both appellants. They convicted GH of false imprisonment and dismissed the charge of assault occasioning actual bodily harm against him. The question posed for the consideration of this court is:

> In convicting the appellants as we did were we right in concluding that the evidence was sufficiently clear to rebut the presumption of *doli incapax* ...

Conclusion

This was an incident of bullying of the grossest kind. It lasted for an hour. The actual incident of the assault occasioning actual bodily harm took a very short time to commit. The period of the false imprisonment in the horse trough was also quite short. There was abundant evidence of the conduct of each of the appellants before and after the offences themselves to rebut the presumption.

The motive was revenge and the incident took place at a time and place where there was little hope of assistance. There was evidence of distress to the victim which the appellants admitted they were aware of at the time, yet they persisted. Each sought to dissociate himself from the attack, to minimise the part played and blatantly to blame the others. The justices were accordingly fully entitled to conclude that there was an awareness on the part of each appellant that what they were doing was seriously wrong and not mere naughtiness, that each was a party to a joint enterprise, though to a different extent. Following such conduct, the act of running away was unlikely to be considered merely equivocal.

There was certainly no necessity for evidence from an independent source such as a teacher or psychiatrist or from someone who knew each appellant well to indicate his state of mind. Questions were put by the investigating police officers to each appellant, in the presence of his mother, designed to probe the issue of whether he knew that his (and their joint) conduct was seriously wrong. Their answers went some way (according to how the justices evaluated them) to indicate that they did appreciate that what they were doing was seriously wrong.

Accordingly, I would answer the question posed in the affirmative. In convicting each of the appellants the justices were right in concluding that the evidence was sufficiently clear to rebut the presumption of *doli incapax* ...

Director of Public Prosecutions v K & B [1997] 1 Cr App R 36 (DC)

Russell LJ: In September 1994, two girls whom I shall refer to as K and B were respectively 14 years and 11 years of age. On September 9 they encountered another girl W who was 14 years of age.

During the ensuing two-and-a-half hours or so, they subjected W to what must have been an appalling ordeal. W was threatened, falsely imprisoned and robbed. Eventually, a boy became involved. W was told by K and B to remove some of her clothing and to have sexual intercourse with the boy.

All four youngsters were by now in a block of flats. In the privacy of a room there the boy had sexual intercourse with W. There was partial penetration. It was followed by further sexual intimacy. W was distressed. There was no suggestion that she consented to any of the sexual activity. The boy left the scene and has never been traced. He was or may well have been under the age of 14 years but certainly over 10 years.

... There were a number of informations laid against K and B, but the material one, for the purposes of this case, alleged that they with two others, later acquitted, aided, abetted, counselled and procured the commission of the offence of rape upon W by an unknown person.

The magistrate [in the Youth Court] found that the Crown had negatived *doli incapax* in relation to B and she was convicted as was K of false imprisonment and robbery. However, as to the charge of rape, the magistrate made a number of findings which lead to his dismissing the information charging rape against both K and B. The Director of Public Prosecution appeals against that dismissal of the charge of rape and of indecent assault where precisely the same questions arise by way of case stated. In addition to the case we have also had the advantage of perusing written reasons prepared by the magistrate to support his findings ...

[The magistrate] considered the position of the respondents K and B in the light of his finding *vis-a-vis* the boy. He concluded and I cite from the case stated:

> [4](i)[W], the alleged victim, was born on April 25, 1980. She was aged 14 at the time of the events giving rise to the charges, and 15 at the date when she gave her evidence.
>
> (ii) On September 9, 1994 [W] was on her way to visit her grandmother when she was approached by [K] and [B] in the car park of a block of flats.
>
> (iii) W remained in the company of [K] and [B] and other young persons during the next two and a half hours or so, during which time she was subjected to threats and violence and was (as I found) robbed of articles and falsely imprisoned. I do not go into the detail of my findings this far since I respectfully believe such detail to be immaterial to the point raised in the Case which I herein stated.
>
> (iv) There came a time during the incident when [W], operating under threats of [K] and [B], went with an unknown male and acts of sexual intimacy took place which, as I respectfully believe them to be material to this case, I state in detail in the following paragraphs (v) to (xiii).
>
> (v) [K] and [B] were acting in concert. By threat and violence they made [W] remove her cardigan and bra and made clear they expected her to have sexual intercourse with the boy.
>
> (vi) [W] and the unknown boy went into a room apart from [K] and [B].
>
> (vii) The boy said 'Do you want me to do this?' and [W] replied 'I don't exactly want you to do it but I haven't got a choice'. In saying this she was affected by threats uttered to her by [K] and [B].
>
> (viii)The boy touched the breasts of [W], told [W] to lie on the floor, [W] took down her tights and knickers to a position below the knees and the boy unzipped his trousers and lay on top of [W].
>
> (ix) The boy inserted his erect or partially erect penis in the vagina of [W] sufficient to amount to penetration, but no ejaculation took place.

(x) [W], in purporting to consent to the act of sexual penetration, was moved by fear of violence induced by threats to her by [K] and [B] who remained in close proximity throughout the act. It was not established whether at the time of the act of penetration the boy knew whether [W] was or was not consenting.

(xi) After the act of penetration and after being subjected to further violence and threats made in the presence of the boy by [K] and [B], the boy held out his erect penis and [W] was forced to suck it until she became sick.

(xii) The identity of the boy was not established and there was no positive evidence as to his age. In relation to his age the following matters emerged during the course of the case:

(a) In evidence [W] gave the age of the boy as 'around 14 I think'. She described him in relation to another boy as smaller, but thought the other boy 'looked about 18'. She referred to the boy during her evidence as 'the little boy'.

(b) [B] (who was 11 years old at the relevant time) said in her interview by the police that she believed the boy to be 'about 15'.

(c) [K] (who at the relevant time was herself aged 14) said in interview by the police that she considered he was 'about 13'.

(xiii) Given the absence of positive evidence as to age and given the age of all the children and young persons involved in the incident, it was reasonably possible that the boy was aged less than 14.

[Counsel] on behalf of the Director makes a number of submissions arising out of these findings. First, he contends that the respondents K and B were procurers of the offence of rape. As such, they were in reality secondary parties to the offence and were never principals. They did not assist the boy to have sexual intercourse with [W] by, for example holding the girl down. Indeed, they were not physically present when the sexual activity took place. Not being principals but rather accessories before the fact, their gender was irrelevant and the magistrate fell into error in para. 6 of his conclusions. A female can undoubtedly procure the commission of rape by a male.

As a procurer, a female is liable to conviction as a principal but in law is not a principal save when employing an innocent agent. In this case the boy involved could hardly be so described.

Secondly, [counsel for the DPP] contends that the finding of *doli incapax* in the boy or the failure of the Crown to negative it, did not vitiate the conviction of the respondents as procurers. This is the kernel of the appeal.

In my view, [counsel] is right and with all respect to him the magistrate was wrong.

A boy under the age of 10 years cannot commit any criminal offence. Accordingly, no one can procure a boy under the age of 10 years to commit a criminal offence. Whatever the boy does and whatever his state of mind no crime is or can be committed by him.

The position of a boy over 10 years but under 14 years, however, is in my view quite different. He is not by virtue of his tender years incapable of committing a criminal offence. He can do so, but in his case the concept of *doli incapax* raises a rebuttable presumption against the boy having the requisite *mens rea*. What that *mens rea* is will depend upon the nature of the offence and the mental processes of the boy ...

[His Lordship referred to *Walter v Lunt, Cogan and Leak* and *R v Millward* and went on]

In my judgment, the decision of the magistrate in this appeal cannot be supported. There is no doubt whatever that 'W' was the victim of unlawful sexual intercourse without her consent; such was not disputed. The actus reus was proved. The respondents procured the situation which included the sexual intercourse.

It would, in my view, be singularly unattractive to find that because of the absence of a mental element on the part of the principal, the procurers could thereby escape conviction when, as the magistrate found, K and B had the requisite *mens rea* namely, the desire that rape should take place and the procuring of it.

In my judgment, neither authority nor common sense nor justice compels this Court to support the finding of the magistrate.

I would therefore allow this appeal. The magistrate heard all available evidence from both sides. I would remit the case to him with a direction to convict in relation to rape and indecent assault.

A v Director of Public Prosecutions [1997] 1 Cr App R 27 (DC)

Pill LJ: ... The ... Crown Court found that on the evening of July 30, 1993, the complainant, aged 12 years, was approached by a boy named L at a fair. He took her to nearby gardens and struck her. She returned to her friends but when L called her back she returned to him. She rejected his sexual advances.

L took the complainant to the 20th floor of a block of flats. The appellant and another boy C accompanied them. They entered the chute room. L threatened the complainant with violence unless she gave him oral sex. During the sexual act between L and the complainant, the appellant said that it was his turn and put his penis into her mouth. He forced her head backwards and forwards with his hands. She felt scared and sick and was gasping for breath.

The appellant also had sexual intercourse with the complainant, the penetration lasting only a few seconds. He forced her legs open. She was pushing him by the shoulders pleading for him to stop. When the boys heard adults on the landing, they ran downstairs.

When arrested on August 6, 1993 the appellant, on the advice of his mother, said nothing. When interviewed on the same day at the police station in the presence of a solicitor and his mother he declined to answer any questions. At his trial he did not give evidence.

The conclusion of the court was stated as follows:

> We were of the opinion that the evidence suggested that the appellant knew that what he was doing was seriously wrong as opposed to merely naughty and that the presumption of *doli incapax* had been rebutted.

The question posed for the opinion of this Court is 'whether or not there was any, or sufficient evidence to justify the finding of fact made by us, that this particular defendant knew that what he was doing was seriously wrong' ...

In the present case, the only material evidence was that of the complainant. The appellant, on advice, declined to answer questions. This does not appear to be that type of case contemplated by Lord Lowry in which running away in itself indicated guilty knowledge. The case turns upon whether evidence of the surrounding circumstances, which included what the appellant did before and after the act, was such as to enable the trial court to hold that the presumption was in this case rebutted ...

Ward v DPP unreported, (transcript May 22, 1995) was a case where a boy aged almost 14 was convicted of burglary. The justices had relied, *inter alia* on the sophisticated character of the *actus reus* to rebut the presumption. Mitchell J, with whom McCowan LJ agreed, stated that 'What Lord Lowry's speech makes clear beyond doubt is that conduct relied upon as proof of the *actus reus* of the offence is insufficient to rebut the presumption because that approach would, in effect be applying the presumption of normality in favour of the prosecution. The child's age is relevant in one respect only; the older the child the more easily the presumption is rebutted.' Mitchell J concluded that 'the justices were wrong in law to rely upon the child's participating conduct as evidence which was significantly material to the rebuttal of the presumption. Standing alone it was irrelevant'.

In *L & Others v DPP* [1996] 2 Cr App R 501, the Divisional Court upheld convictions upon children. Otton LJ, with whom Newman J agreed, set out principles relevant to the rebuttal of the presumption. These included the principle that 'The conduct of the child before or after the act may go to prove his guilty mind'.

I do not read the speech of Lord Lowry as setting out fresh principles but as affirming the existing law. The passage cited from the summing-up of Erle J in *Smith* (1845) 1 Cox CC 260 dealt with the present point succinctly: 'A guilty knowledge that he was doing wrong – must be proved by the evidence, and cannot be presumed from the mere commission of the act'. It is from the 'mere commission' of that act that guilty knowledge cannot be presumed. The act does not speak for itself but that does not prevent consideration for this purpose of the circumstances in which the act was committed. Consideration of conduct closely associated with the act is permitted for the purpose of deciding whether guilty knowledge is proved. It also emerges from Lord Lowry's reference [in *C v DPP*] to drug offence and Donaldson LJ's reference to forgery [in *JBH and JH (Minors v O'Connell)*] that the nature of the offence charged may be a relevant factor in deciding whether guilty knowledge is in all the circumstances proved ...

The present offence was one of serious violence against the person. It was not, in terms of mental element, a sophisticated offence. The appellant committed it as one of a group of three acting together. The complainant was taken some distance to a remote place where intervention by others was unlikely. The acts were performed against a background of threats and the complainant's distress must have been obvious.

The judges of the Crown Court directed themselves correctly in law. They heard and considered the evidence. On the facts they found, the circumstances surrounding the offence were such that, in my judgment, there was enough material to entitle them to hold that the appellant knew that what he was doing was seriously wrong and that the presumption was rebutted.

I would answer the question posed in the affirmative and dismiss the appeal.

CHAPTER 11

INCHOATE OFFENCES – ATTEMPTS

INCHOATE OFFENCES

Not all criminal offences which are planned actually take place. There may be many reasons why the intended result never comes about. For example, the police may be 'tipped off' about an armed robbery which is planned and may intervene in time to prevent it; a 'contract killing' may be planned, but the victim does not die of the wounds inflicted; where two people are involved, it may be that D2 does not succumb to D1's solicitation to crime.

In situations such as these it would clearly be wrong for those involved to escape punishment, even though their intended aims have not been realised. It is for this reason that the criminal law has a number of 'inchoate' offences.

An inchoate offence is simply an offence which is 'uncompleted'. The criminality of the participants lies in the steps which are taken to bring about the completion of the crime.

There are three types of inchoate offence:

(1) attempts;

(2) conspiracy; and

(3) incitement.

ATTEMPTS

The law relating to attempts is governed by the Criminal Attempts Act 1981.

Sections 1 and 4 of the Criminal Attempts Act 1981

Section 1:

(1) If, with intent to commit an offence to which this section applies, a person does an act which is more than merely preparatory to the commission of the offence, he is guilty of attempting to commit the offence.

(2) A person may be guilty of attempting to commit an offence to which this section applies even though the facts are such that the commission of the offence is impossible.

(3) In any case where:

(a) apart from this subsection a person's intention would not be regarded as having amounted to an intent to commit an offence; but

(b) if the facts of the case had been as he believed them to be, his intention would be so regarded,

then for the purposes of subsection (1) above, he shall be regarded as having an intent to commit that offence.

(4) This section applies to any offence which, if it were completed, would be triable in England and Wales as an indictable offence, other than:

(a) conspiracy (at common law or under s 1 of the Criminal Law Act 1977 or any other enactment);

(b) aiding, abetting, counselling procuring or suborning the commission of an offence;

(c) offences under s 4(1) (assisting offenders) or 5(1) (accepting or agreeing to accept consideration for not disclosing information about an arrestable offence) of the Criminal Law Act 1967.

Section 4:

(3) Where, in proceedings against a person for an offence under s 1 above, there is evidence sufficient in law to support a finding that he did an act falling within subsection (1) of that section, the question whether or not his act fell within that subsection is a question of fact.

Actus reus: an act which is more than merely preparatory

Various tests of what constituted an attempt existed prior to the Criminal Attempts Act 1981. For example, whether the defendant had gone past the point of no return ('crossing the Rubicon'), and the 'uninterrupted series of acts' test set out in *Davey v Lee* [1968] 1 QB 366. However, pre-1981 case law is only persuasive; the correct approach is to give the words of the statute their ordinary and natural meaning. Was the act alleged 'more than merely preparatory to the commission of the offence'? See, for example, *R v Gullefer* [1990] 1 WLR 1063, *R v Jones* [1990] 1 WLR 1057; *Attorney General's Reference (No 1 of 1992)* [1993] 1 WLR 274.

The effect of s 4(3) of the Criminal Attempts Act 1981 is that if there is a *prima facie* case that the defendant did an act which was more than merely preparatory, the jury must be left to decide whether the act was indeed more than merely preparatory.

Davey v Lee [1968] 1 QB 366 (CA)

Lord Parker CJ: ... What amounts to an attempt has been described variously in the authorities, and for my part I prefer to adopt the definition given in Stephen's *Digest of the Criminal Law*, 5th edn, 1894, art 50, where it says that:

> An attempt to commit a crime is an act done with intent to commit that crime, and forming part of a series of acts which would constitute its actual commission if it were not interrupted.

As a general statement that seems to me to be right, although it does not help to define the point of time at which the series of acts begins. That, as Stephen said, depends upon the facts of each case.

A helpful definition is given in paragraph 4104 in the current (36th edition (1966)) of Archbold's *Criminal Pleading, Evidence and Practice*, where it is stated in this form:

> It is submitted that the *actus reus* necessary to constitute an attempt is complete if the prisoner does an act which is a step towards the commission of the specific crime, which is immediately and not merely remotely connected with the commission of it, and the doing of which cannot reasonably be regarded as having any other purpose than the commission of the specific crime.

Diplock LJ: I agree. There are some branches of the criminal law in which it is permitted for justices and juries to use their common sense. I am glad to find that I am not constrained by the authorities to say that the law of attempt is excluded from those branches. I accept the definition which my Lord has taken from the current edition of Archbold as a correct definition of the test to be applied, and the facts of this case fall amply within that definition.

Ashworth J: I agree.

R v Jones (Kenneth Henry) [1990] 1 WLR 1057 (CA)

Taylor LJ: read the following judgment of the court. This case raises a point of law as to the true construction of s 1 of the Criminal Attempts Act 1981 ...

The appellant, a married man, started an affair with a woman named Lynn Gresley in 1985. She lived with him in Australia during 1986. In September 1987, back in England, she began a relationship with the victim, Michael Foreman. She continued, however, to see the appellant to whom she was still very attached. In November 1987 she decided to break off the relationship with the appellant, but he continued to write to her, begging her to come back to him.

On 12 January 1988 the appellant applied for a shotgun certificate, and three days later bought two guns in company with two companions. He bought two more guns a few days later on his own. On 23 January he shortened the barrel of one of them and test fired it twice the following day.

The appellant told a colleague at work that he would be away on Tuesday 26 January. On 24 January he phoned Lynn Gresley in a distraught state. The next day he apologised, but she again refused his invitation to resume their relationship. The appellant then told his wife he had packed a bag as he was going to Spain to do some work on their chalet. On 26 January he left home dressed normally for work, saying he would telephone his wife as to whether he was leaving for Spain that evening.

That same morning, the victim, Michael Foreman, took his daughter to school by car as usual. After the child left the car, the appellant appeared, opened the door and jumped into the rear seat. He was wearing overalls, a crash helmet with the visor down, and was carrying a bag. He and the victim had never previously met. He introduced himself, said he wanted to sort things out and asked the victim to drive on. When they stopped on a grass verge, the appellant handed over a letter he had received from Lynn. Whilst the victim read it, the appellant took the sawn-off shotgun from the bag. It was loaded. He pointed it at the victim at range of some 10 to 12 inches. He said, 'You are not going to like this', or similar words. The victim grabbed the end of the gun and pushed it sideways and upwards. There was a struggle during which the victim managed to throw the gun out of the window. As he tried to get out, he felt a cord over his head pulling him back. He managed to break free and run away, taking the gun with him. From a nearby garage he telephoned the police.

Meanwhile, the appellant drove off in the victim's car. He was arrested jogging away from it carrying his holdall. He said he had done nothing and only wanted to kill himself. His bag contained a hatchet, some cartridges and a length of cord. He also had a sharp kitchen knife which he threw away. In the appellant's car parked near the school was £1,500 sterling together with a quantity of French and Spanish money. The evidence showed that the safety catch of the shotgun had been in the on position. The victim was unclear as to whether the appellant's finger was ever on the trigger. When interviewed, the appellant declined to make any comment.

At the end of the prosecution case, after the above facts had been given in evidence, a submission was made to the judge that the charge of attempted murder should be withdrawn from the jury. It was argued that since the appellant would have had to perform at least three more acts before the full offence could have been completed, ie remove the safety catch, put his finger on the trigger and pull it, the evidence was insufficient to support the charge. There was a discussion as to the proper construction of s 1(1) of the Criminal Attempts Act 1981. After hearing full argument, the judge ruled against the submission and allowed the case to proceed on count 1. Thereafter, the appellant gave evidence. In the result, the jury convicted him unanimously of attempted murder. It follows that they found he intended to kill the victim.

The sole ground of appeal is that the judge erred in law in his construction of s 1(1) and ought to have withdrawn the case.

[His Lordship then quoted s 1(1) and s 4(3) of the Criminal Attempts Act 1981].

[Counsel for the appellant] says that for about a century, two different tests as to the *actus reus* of attempt have been inconsistently applied by the courts. In *R v Eagleton* (1855) Dears CC 515, the defendant was charged with attempting to obtain money from the guardians of a parish by falsely pretending to the relieving officer that he had delivered loaves of bread of proper weight to the poor when in fact the loaves were underweight. In the course of giving the judgment of the court, Parke B said at 538:

> Acts remotely leading towards the commission of the offence are not to be considered as attempts to commit it, but acts immediately connected with it are; and if, in this case, after the credit with the relieving officer for the fraudulent overcharge, any *further step* on the part of the defendant had been necessary to obtain payment, as the making out a further account or producing the vouchers to the board, we should have thought that the obtaining credit in account with the relieving officer would not have been sufficiently proximate to the obtaining the money. But, on the statement in this case, no other act on the part of the defendant would have been required. It was the last act, depending on himself towards the payment of the money, and therefore it ought to be considered as an attempt.

Accordingly, the test deriving from *R v Eagleton* was said to be the 'last act' test. It was adopted in a number of cases, eg *R v Robinson* [1915] 2 KB 342. In *DPP v Stonehouse* [1978] AC 55, 68, Lord Diplock referred to *R v Eagleton* as the locus classicus, adopted some of the words of Parke B and summarised them in the graphic phrase: 'In other words, the offender must have crossed the Rubicon and burnt his boats'.

The other test referred to by [counsel for the appellant] derives from Stephen's Digest of the *Criminal Law*, 9th edn, 1950, chapter 4, art 29 where it was stated, at pp 24–25:

> An attempt to commit a crime is an act done with intent to commit that crime, and forming part of a series of acts, which would constitute its actual commission if it were not interrupted.

Lord Edmund-Davies noted in *Stonehouse's* case at 86, that Stephen's definition has been repeatedly cited with approval. He referred to its adoption in *Hope v Brown* [1954] 1 WLR 250, 253, and *Davey v Lee* [1968] 1 QB 366. It was also applied in *R v Linneker* [1906] 2 KB 99 where *Eagleton's* case was not cited.

In some cases, including three since the Act of 1981, both tests have been considered, and the court has found it unnecessary to decide between them, holding that the result in those cases would have been the same, whichever applied: see *R v Ilyas* (1983) 78 Cr App R 17; *R v Widdowson* (1986) 82 Cr App R 314 and *R v Boyle* (1986) 84 Cr App R 270 ...

... The Act of 1981 is a codifying statute. It amends and sets out completely the law relating to attempts and conspiracies. In those circumstances the correct approach is to look first at the natural meaning of the statutory words, not to turn back to earlier case law and seek to fit some previous test to the words of the section ...

[His Lordship then quoted with approval from the judgment of Lord Lane CJ in *R v Gullefer (Note)* [1990] 1 WLR 1063] ...

... We do not accept [the appellant's] contention that s 1(1) of the Act of 1981 in effect embodies the 'last act' test derived from *R v Eagleton*. Had Parliament intended to adopt that test, a quite different form of words could and would have been used.

It is of interest to note that the Act of 1981 followed a report from the Law Commission on 'Attempt, and Impossibility in Relation to Attempt Conspiracy and Incitement' (1980) Law Com No 102. At paragraph 2.47 the report states:

> The definition of sufficient proximity must be wide enough to cover two varieties of cases; first, those in which a person has taken all steps towards the commission of a crime which he believes to be necessary as far as he is concerned for that crime to result, such as firing a gun at another and missing. Normally such cases cause no difficulty. Second, however, the definition must cover those instances where a person has to take some further step to complete the crime, assuming that there is evidence of the necessary mental element on his part to commit it; for example, when the defendant has raised the gun to take aim at another but has not yet squeezed the trigger. We have reached the conclusion that, in regard to these cases, it is undesirable to recommend anything more complex than a rationalisation of the present law.

In paragraph 2.48 the report states:

> The literal meaning of 'proximate' is 'nearest, next before or after (in place, order, time, connection of thought, causation, etc)'. Thus, were this term part of a statutory description of the *actus reus* of attempt, it would clearly be capable of being interpreted to exclude all but the 'final act'; this would not be in accordance with the policy outlined above.

Clearly, the draftsman of s 1(1) must be taken to have been aware of the two lines of earlier authority and of the Law Commission's report. The words 'an act which is more than merely preparatory to the commission of the offence' would be inapt if they were intended to mean 'the last act which lay in his power towards the commission of the offence'.

Looking at the plain natural meaning of s 1(1) in the way indicated by the Lord Chief Justice [in *R v Gullefer*], the question for the judge in the present case was whether there was evidence from which a reasonable jury, properly directed, could conclude that the appellant had done acts which were more than merely preparatory. Clearly his actions in obtaining the gun, in shortening it, in loading it, in putting on his disguise, and in going to the school could only be regarded as preparatory acts. But, in our judgment, once he had got into the car, taken out the loaded gun and pointed it at the victim with the intention of killing him, there was sufficient evidence for the consideration of the jury on the charge of attempted murder. It was a matter for them to decide whether they were sure those acts were more than merely preparatory. In our judgment, therefore, the judge was right to allow the case to go to the jury, and the appeal against conviction must be dismissed.

R v Gullefer [1990] 1 WLR 1063 (Note)

Lord Lane CJ: On 26 February 1986 before the Crown Court at Snaresbrook the appellant was convicted of attempted theft and sentenced to six months' imprisonment.

The judge certified that the case was fit for appeal on the ground that:

> a submission was made that the action alleged as constituting the attempt (as to which there was no dispute, because his action was filmed on video tape, which the jury and I saw) could not amount to an attempt to steal, even if the jury were satisfied that what the defendant did was done with the object of dishonestly receiving a sum of money equivalent to his stake from a bookmaker ...

The facts were as follows. On 5 March 1985 the appellant attended the Greyhound Racing Stadium at Romford. During the last race, as the dogs rounded the final bend, he climbed the fence on to the track in front of the dogs, waving his arms and attempting to distract them. His efforts were only marginally successful, and the stewards decided that it was unnecessary to declare 'no race'. Had they made such a declaration, by the rules the bookmakers would have been obliged to repay the amount of his stake to any punter, but would not have been liable to pay any winnings to those punters who would have been successful if the race had been valid.

When interviewed by the police the appellant said the reasons for his behaviour were partly that a year earlier he had lost a large bet at the stadium by reason of one of the stadium's staff leaning over the rails and distracting the dog on which he had gambled. He also admitted that he had attempted to stop the race because the dog on which he had staked £18 was losing. He hoped that by his actions the dogs would be distracted, that the stewards would declare 'no race' and that he would therefore recover his stake from the bookmaker ...

[His Lordship quoted s 1(1) and s 4(3) of the Criminal Attempts Act and continued:]

Thus the judge's task is to decide whether there is evidence upon which a jury could reasonably come to the conclusion that the appellant had gone beyond the realm of mere preparation and had embarked upon the actual commission of the offence. If not, he must withdraw the case from the jury. If there is such evidence, it is then for the jury to decide whether the defendant did in fact go beyond mere preparation ...

The first task of the court is to apply the words of the Act of 1981 to the facts of the case. Was the appellant still in the stage of preparation to commit the substantive offence, or was there a basis of fact which would entitle the jury to say that he had embarked on the theft itself? Might it properly be said that when he jumped on to the track he was trying to steal £18 from the bookmaker?

Our view is that it could not properly be said that at that stage he was in the process of committing theft. What he was doing was jumping on to the track in an effort to distract the dogs, which in its turn, he hoped, would have the effect of forcing the stewards to declare 'no race', which would in its turn give him the opportunity to go back to the bookmaker and demand the £18 he had staked. In our view there was insufficient evidence for it to be said that he had, when he jumped on to the track, gone beyond mere preparation.

So far at least as the present case is concerned, we do not think that it is necessary to examine the authorities which preceded the Act of 1981, save to say that the sections we have already quoted in this judgment seem to be a blend of various decisions, some of which were not easy to reconcile with others ...

It seems to us that the words of the Act of 1981 seek to steer a midway course. They do not provide, as they might have done, that the *R v Eagleton* test is to be followed, or that, as Lord Diplock suggested, the defendant must have reached a point from which it was impossible for him to retreat before the *actus reus* of an attempt is proved. On the other hand the words give perhaps as clear a guidance as is possible in the circumstances on the point of time at which Stephen's 'series of acts' begin. It begins when the merely preparatory acts come to an end and the defendant embarks upon the crime proper. When that is, will depend of course upon the facts in any particular case ...

Attorney General's Reference (No 1 of 1992) [1993] 1 WLR 274 (CA)

Lord Taylor of Gosforth CJ: This case comes before the court on a reference by Her Majesty's Attorney General under s 36 of the Criminal Justice Act 1972.

The respondent was charged with attempted rape and was acquitted by direction of the trial judge. In consequence of the judge's ruling, the Attorney General has referred a point of law for the opinion of this court. The point of law is stated thus:

> Whether, on a charge of attempted rape, it is incumbent upon the prosecution, as a matter of law, to prove that the defendant physically attempted to penetrate the woman's vagina with his penis.

... In *R v Jones (Kenneth Henry)* [1990] 1 WLR 1057 and again in *R v Campbell (Tony)* (1991) 93 Cr App R 350, this court made it clear that the words of the Act were to be applied in their plain and natural meaning, as the judge reminded himself in his first ruling. The words are not to be interpreted so as to reintroduce either of the earlier common law tests. Indeed one of the objects of the Act was to resolve the uncertainty those tests created ...

It is not, in our judgment, necessary, in order to raise a *prima facie* case of attempted rape, to prove that the defendant with the requisite intent had necessarily gone as far as to attempt physical penetration of the vagina. It is sufficient if there is evidence from which the intent can be inferred and there are proved acts which a jury could properly regard as more than merely preparatory to the commission of the offence. For example, and merely as an example, in the present case the evidence of the young woman's distress, of the state of her clothing, and the position in which she was seen, together with the respondent's acts of dragging her up the steps, lowering his trousers and interfering with her private parts, and his answers to the police, left it open to a jury to conclude that the respondent had the necessary intent and had done acts which were more than merely preparatory. In short that he had embarked on committing the offence itself.

For the reasons which we have endeavoured to give, we would answer the question posed in the reference, 'No'.

R v Geddes (1996) 160 JP 697 (CA)

Lord Bingham of Cornhill CJ: The background to the case may be shortly summarised. On 20 July 1994 the appellant went into the boys' lavatory block at Dorothy Stringer School, Brighton. He had no connection with the school and had no right to be there. At about midday a teacher saw him in the boys' lavatory and spoke to him. He had a rucksack with him. A woman police officer, who, by chance, was on the premises, saw him and shouted at him, but he left. In a cubicle in the lavatory block there was a cider can which had belonged to the appellant. In the course of leaving the school the appellant discarded his rucksack which was found in some bushes. Its contents included several articles: a large kitchen knife, some lengths of rope and a roll of masking tape. The appellant was arrested three days later. The teacher and some pupils from the school identified him.

The prosecution alleged that the presence of the cider can showed that the appellant had been inside a cubicle in the lavatory block. They further alleged that the contents of the rucksack could be used to catch and restrain a boy who entered the lavatory. The rope could have been used to tie the boy; the knife to frighten him; and the tape to cover his mouth to prevent him screaming.

The defence resisted the charge on the basis that the prosecution case was based on speculation. It was contested that the cider can showed that the appellant had been hiding in the cubicle, since he could well have entered the cubicle for normal purposes and left the cider can there. Alternatively, since the partitions of the lavatory did not extend from the floor to the ceiling, the can could have rolled or been thrown into the position where it was ultimately found. It was argued that there were other explanations for the contents of the rucksack ...

... The cases show that the line of demarcation between acts which are merely preparatory and acts which may amount to an attempt is not always clear or easy to recognise. There is no rule of thumb test. There must always be an exercise of judgment based on the particular facts of the case. It is, we think, an accurate paraphrase of the statutory test and not an illegitimate gloss upon it to ask whether the available evidence, if accepted, could show that a defendant has done an act which shows that he has actually tried to commit the offence in question, or whether he has only got ready or put himself in a position or equipped himself to do so.

In the present case ... there is not much room for doubt about the appellant's intention. Furthermore, the evidence is clearly capable of showing that he made preparations, that he equipped himself, that he got ready, that he put himself in a position to commit the offence charged. We question whether the cider can in the cubicle is of central importance, but would accept that in the absence of any explanation it could lead to the inference that the appellant had been in the cubicle. But was the evidence sufficient in law to support a finding that the appellant had actually tried or attempted to commit the offence of imprisoning someone? Had he moved from the realm of intention, preparation and planning into the area of execution or implementation? ... Here it is true that the appellant had entered the school; but he had never had any contact or communication with any pupil; he had never confronted any pupil at the school in any way ... [The] contents of the rucksack, which gave a clear indication as to what the appellant may have had in mind, but do not throw light on whether he had begun to carry out the commission of the offence [and so must be treated as irrelevant]. On the facts of this case we feel bound to conclude that the evidence was not sufficient in law to support a finding that the appellant did an act which was more than merely preparatory to wrongfully imprisoning a person unknown. In those circumstances we conclude that the appeal must be allowed and the conviction quashed.

Mens rea

The *mens rea* for an attempt is the intention to commit the complete offence; recklessness is not enough: *R v Pearman* (1984) 80 Cr App R 259. It follows that the *mens rea* for an attempt is the same as the *mens rea* for the completed offence:

R v Millard [1987] Crim LR 393; *R v Khan* [1990] 1 WLR 813; *Attorney General's Reference (No 3 of 1992)* [1994] 1 WLR 409.

R v Pearman (1984) 80 Cr App R 259 (CA)

Facts: The appellant was charged with attempting to cause grievous bodily harm. He had driven his car at a police officer. His defence was that he did not intend to harm the police officer and did not foresee that his actions could cause serious injury to anybody.

Stuart-Smith J: ... This court, in the case of *Mohan* [1976] QB 1 dealt with the question of the mental element in an attempt before passing to that Act. It is not necessary to deal with the facts of the case. James LJ gave the judgment of the court. After reviewing the speeches of the House of Lords in *Hyam v DPP*, he said at p 11:

> In our judgment, evidence of knowledge of likely consequences, or from which knowledge of likely consequences can be inferred, is evidence by which intent may be established but it is not in relation to the offence of attempt to be equated with intent. If the jury find such knowledge established, they may, and using common sense, they probably will find intent proved, but it is not the case that they must do so. An attempt to commit crime is itself an offence. Often it is a grave offence. Often it is as morally culpable as the completed offence which is attempted but not in fact committed. Nevertheless it falls within the class of conduct which is preparatory to the commission of the crime and is one step removed from the offence which is attempted. The court must not strain to bring within the offence of attempt conduct which does not fall within the well-established bounds of the offence. On the contrary, the court must safeguard against extension of those bounds save by the authority of Parliament. The bounds are presently set requiring proof of specific intent, a decision to bring about, in so far as it lies within the accused's power, the commission of the offence which it is alleged the accused attempted to commit, no matter whether the accused desired that consequence of his act or not.

The last few words of that sentence, 'no matter whether the accused desired that consequence of his act or not', has given rise to debate amongst textbook writers as to what is meant by it, but it is clear from that passage that if the law is, as stated by James LJ in *Mohan* (*above*), still the same, that foresight of the consequences might be something from which the jury can infer intent, it is not to be equated with intent. We see no reason why the passing of the 1981 Act should have altered the law as to what is meant by the words 'intent'. The purpose of the Act was to deal with other matters rather than the content of the word 'intent'. We can see no reason why the judgment of the court in that case should not still be binding upon this court. It was, to some extent, based on the earlier decision of this court in *Whybrow* (1951) 35 Cr App R 141, where it was held that in the case of attempted murder although the *mens rea* for the completed offence of murder must be intent to kill or to cause really serious bodily harm, that was not sufficient in a case of attempted murder and it was necessary to prove the intent to kill.

As Parker LJ said in the course of argument, it would be an illogical conclusion and one offensive to common sense and offensive to any notion of an attempt if a man, who was in fact trying his best to avoid something coming about, could be guilty of an attempted offence simply because he foresaw that his actions might so involve him in committing it. It is offensive to common sense to suppose that simply because he could foresee it, he would be intending the offence to come about.

The words of James LJ which he used at the end of that passage, namely 'no matter whether the accused desired that consequence of his act of not', are probably designed to deal with a case where the accused has, as a primary purpose, some other object, for example, a man who plants a bomb in an aeroplane which he knows is going to take off, it being his primary intention that he should claim the insurance on the aeroplane when the freight goes down into the sea. The jury would not be put off from saying that he intended to murder the crew simply by saying that he did not want or desire to kill the crew, but that was something that he inevitably intended to do. Similarly, for example, a man who is cornered by the police when he is in a car may have the primary purpose of simply escaping from that situation. If he drives straight at the police officers at high speed, a jury is likely to conclude that he intended to injure a police officer and maybe cause him serious grievous bodily harm.

In the ordinary way, it would seem to this court to be sufficient for the judge to have told the jury that the Crown has to prove intent to cause grievous bodily harm on the part of the accused man ...

R v Millard and Vernon [1987] Crim LR 393 (CA)

Facts: The appellants were convicted of attempting to damage property, contrary to s 1(1) of the Criminal Attempts Act 1981. The particulars of the offence stated that they 'attempted to damage a wooden wall ... intending to damage [it] or being reckless as to whether [it] would be damaged'. They were football supporters who had repeatedly pushed against a wooden wall of a stand at a football ground. The prosecution alleged that they were trying to break the line of planking. The appellants denied pushing in unison and denied intending to damage the wall. The judge directed the jury that recklessness was an alternative to intention as an element of the substantive offence. The appellants appealed against conviction on the ground that recklessness – indifference to a known risk or failure to advert to an obvious risk – was incompatible with the intent required by s 1(1) of the 1981 Act.

Held, allowing the appeal and quashing the convictions, the result which would have been achieved by the full offence was damage to the stand. The prosecution had to show that it was this state of affairs which each appellant had decided to bring about. The judge was misled by the form of the indictment into offering a less stringent test. That was a material misdirection. Two different situations must be distinguished: (1) where the substantive offence consists simply of the act which constitutes the *actus reus*, the 'result', coupled with some element of volition, which may or may not amount to a full intent. The only question is whether the 'intent' to bring about the result called for by s 1(1) is to be watered down to such a degree, if any, as to make it correspond with the *mens rea* of the substantive offence. (2) The substantive offence does not consist of one result and one *mens rea*, but involves not only the underlying intention to produce the result, but also another state of mind directed to some circumstance or act which the prosecution must also establish in addition to proving the result. The substantive offence in the present case was in the first category. There was just one potential result, damage to the fence, and just one state of mind, the one which accompanied the acts said to have constituted the offence. There was no reason why the statutory requirement of an intent should be diluted by reference to the lower standard required by the substantive offence. There was nothing anomalous about a situation where, so far as the mental element is concerned, it is easier to prove the substantive offence than the attempt, eg murder and attempted murder.

Obiter: The problem in the second category could be illustrated by reference to the offence of attempted rape. As regards the substantive offence the 'result' is sexual intercourse with a woman. The offence is not established without proof of an additional circumstance (ie that the woman did not consent) and a state of mind relative to that circumstance (ie that the defendant knew she did not consent or was reckless as to whether she consented). In the offence of attempted rape, must the prosecution prove that the defendant intended the act to be non-consensual or should the jury be directed to consider two different states of mind, intent as to act and recklessness as to the circumstances? A similar problem may also arise where the additional matters to be proved relate not to some additional circumstance but to the method by which the result is achieved. An obvious example was causing death by reckless driving. Is it logically possible to attempt to commit the offence? *Mohan* [1976] QB 1 provided a partial answer; that intent bears its ordinary meaning and that the intent must be directed to the 'result' and not solely to the means of bringing about the result.

R v Khan [1990] 1 WLR 813 (CA)

See Chapter 23.

Attorney General's Reference (No 3 of 1992) [1994] 1 WLR 409 (CA)

Schiemann J: The court has heard a reference made under s 36(1) of the Criminal Justice Act 1972. The point of law which has been referred to us was formulated as follows:

> Whether on a charge of attempted arson in the aggravated form contemplated by s 1(2) of the Criminal Damage Act 1971, in addition to establishing a specific intent to cause damage by fire, it is sufficient to prove that the defendant was reckless as to whether life would thereby be endangered.

The acquittals which have given rise to this reference had the following background according to the prosecution evidence. Following previous attacks upon their property the complainants maintained a night-time watch over their premises from a motor car (a Ford Granada). In the early hours of the morning the respondents came upon the scene in a vehicle. Inside this car, a Sierra, was a milk crate containing a number of petrol bombs, matches, a petrol can and some rags. As the Sierra approached the complainants, four inside their car and two persons on the pavement talking to them, a lighted petrol bomb was thrown towards them from the Sierra. The prosecution's case was that it was thrown at the Granada and its occupants. The petrol bomb in fact passed over the top of the Granada and smashed against the garden wall of a house a pavement's width away from the car. The Sierra accelerated away but crashed, and the respondents were arrested ...

So far as attempting to commit the ... offence [under s 1(1) of the Criminal Damage Act 1971] is concerned, in order to convict on such a charge it must be proved that the defendant: (a) did an act which was more than merely preparatory to the commission of the offence; and (b) did an act intending to damage any property belonging to another.

One way of analysing the situation is to say that a defendant, in order to be guilty of an attempt, must be in one of the states of mind required for the commission of the full offence, and did his best, as far as he could, to supply what was missing from the completion of the offence. It is the policy of the law that such people should be punished notwithstanding that in fact the intentions of such a defendant have not been fulfilled.

If the facts are that, although the defendant had one of the appropriate states of mind required for the complete offence, but the physical element required for the commission of the complete offence is missing, the defendant is not to be convicted unless it can be shown that he intended to supply the physical element. This was the state of affairs in *R v Millard and Vernon* [1987] Crim LR 393, of which we have seen the transcript. There the defendants were convicted of attempting to damage property. The particulars of the offence were that they 'attempted to damage a wooden wall at the ... stadium ... intending to damage the ... wall or being reckless as to whether the ... wall was damaged'. The trial judge directed the jury that recklessness was sufficient. Mustill LJ, delivering the judgment of the Court of Appeal, stated:

> The result which would have been achieved if the offence had been taken to fruition was damage to the stand ... the prosecution had to show ... that it was this state of affairs which each appellant had decided, so far as in him lay, to bring about.

In consequence, mere recklessness was not sufficient and the convictions were quashed.

We turn finally to the attempt to commit the aggravated offence [under s 1(2) of the Criminal Damage Act 1971]. In the present case, what was missing to prevent a conviction for the completed offence was damage to the property referred to in the opening lines of s 1(2) of the Act of 1981, what in the example of a crane, which we gave earlier in this judgment, we referred to as 'the first-named property'. Such damage is essential for the completed offence. If a defendant does not intend to cause such damage he cannot intend to commit the completed offence. At worst he is reckless as to whether the offence is committed. The law of attempt is concerned with those who are intending to commit crimes. If that intent cannot be shown, then there can be no conviction.

However, the crime here consisted of doing certain acts in a certain state of mind in circumstances where the first-named property and the second-named property were the same, in short where the danger to life arose from the damage to the property which the defendant intended to damage. The substantive crime is committed if the defendant damaged property in a state of mind where he was reckless as to whether the life of another would thereby be endangered. We see no reason why there should not be a conviction for attempt if the prosecution can show that he, in that state of mind, intended to damage the property by throwing a bomb at it. One analysis of this situation is to say that although the defendant was in an appropriate state of mind to render him guilty of the completed offence the prosecution had not proved the physical element of the completed offence, and therefore he is not guilty of the completed offence. If, on a charge of attempting to commit the offence, the prosecution can show not only the state of mind required for the completed offence but also that the defendant intended to supply the missing physical element of the completed offence, that suffices for a conviction. That cannot be done merely by the prosecution showing him to be reckless. The defendant must intend to damage property, but there is no need for a graver mental state than is required for the full offence ...

... What was missing in the present case was damage to the first-named property, without which the offence was not complete. The mental state of the defendant in each case contained everything which was required to render him guilty of the full offence. In order to succeed in a prosecution for attempt, it must be shown that the defendant intended to achieve that which was missing from the full offence. Unless that is shown, the prosecution have not proved that the defendant intended to commit the offence. Thus in *R v Khan (Mohammed Iqbal)*

[1990] 1 WLR 813 the prosecution had to show an intention to have sexual intercourse, and the remaining state of mind required for the offence of rape. In the present case, the prosecution had to show an intention to damage the first-named property, and the remaining state of mind required for the offence of aggravated arson ...

We answer [the question posed by the reference] in the affirmative.

We add that, in circumstances where the first-named property is not the same as the second-named property, in addition to establishing a specific intent to cause damage by fire to the first-named property, it is sufficient to prove that the defendant was reckless as to whether any second-named property was damaged and reckless as to whether the life of another would be endangered by the damage to the second-named property.

IMPOSSIBILITY

It is no defence that the facts are such that it is impossible to commit an offence. In *R v Shivpuri* [1987] 1 AC 1 the defendant was convicted of attempting to import a controlled drug (namely heroin) even though the substance was not, in fact, a controlled drug. His belief that the substance was a controlled drug, coupled with acts which were more than merely preparatory to its import, was sufficient to make him guilty of an attempt to import heroin.

Of course, no offence of criminal attempt is committed if the act which the defendant was attempting to commit is not a criminal offence (eg an attempt to import the complete works of Shakespeare into the UK).

R v Shivpuri [1987] 1 AC 1 (HL)

Lord Hailsham of St Marylebone LC: My Lords, I have had the advantage of reading in draft the speech about to be delivered ... by my noble and learned friend, Lord Bridge of Harwich. Save for one relatively minor point I agree with it in its entirety and would dispose of this appeal as he proposes and for the reasons which he gives. I add a few remarks of my own for reasons which will appear ...

I must add, however, that even had I not been able to follow my noble and learned friend in interring *Anderton v Ryan* by using the *Practice Statement* of 1966, I would still have dismissed the instant appeal by distinguishing its facts from that case. Shortly, my reasoning would have been that the appellant was guilty on the clear wording of ss 1(1) and 1(2) of the Act of 1981 and that no recourse was therefore necessary to the wording of s 1(3) which if so would be irrelevant.

I would have arrived at this conclusion by asking myself three simple questions to which the answers could only be made in one form. They are:

Q1: What was the intention of the appellant throughout?

A1: His intention throughout was to evade and defeat the customs authorities of the UK. He had no other intention. His motive was gain (the bribe of £1,000). But as I pointed out in *R v Hyam* [1975] AC 55 at 73 motive is not the same thing as intention.

Q2: Is the knowing evasion of the UK customs in the manner envisaged in the appellant's intent an offence to which s 1 of the Act of 1981 applies?

A2: Yes, see s 1(4).

Q3: Did the appellant do an act which was more than preparatory to the commission of the offence?

A3: Yes, for the reasons stated in the relevant paragraphs of my noble and learned friend's speech.

In this connection I do not feel it would have been necessary to invoke the doctrine of dominant and subordinate intention referred to by my noble and learned friend. The *sole* intent of the instant appellant from start to finish was to defeat the customs prohibition. In *Anderton v Ryan* [1985] AC 560 the only intention of Mrs Ryan was to buy a particular video cassette recorder at a knock-down price, and the fact that she believed it to be stolen formed no part of that intention. It was a belief, assumed to be false and not an intention at all. It was a false belief as to a state of fact, and, if it became an intention it was only the result of the deeming provisions of s 1(3) of the Act of 1981. Whether or not *Anderton v Ryan* was correctly decided, one has to go to s 1(3) to decide whether Mrs Ryan had committed a criminal attempt under the Act as the result of her belief, assumed to be false, that the video cassette recorder had in fact been stolen. Similarly, to my mind, the only intention of the lustful youth postulated by my noble and learned friends, Lord Roskill and Lord Bridge of Harwich, by way of example in *Anderton v Ryan* was to have carnal connection with a particular girl. One has to go to s 1(3) to discover whether or not a criminal attempt had been committed as the result of his false belief that she was under age.

By way of conclusion I have to say that I think it a pity that, as it emerged from Parliament, the Act of 1981 departed from the draft Bill attached to the Law Commission report 'Criminal Law: Attempt, and Impossibility in Relation to Attempt, Conspiracy and Incitement' (1980) Law Commission No 102, which might have saved a lot of trouble. In particular the distinction which I have sought to draw above between the facts in *Anderton v Ryan* and the instant appeal would have been patently obvious and not to some extent controversial. In the second place it may perhaps have been inevitable, but is nonetheless unusual, that, in defining the prohibited act in s 1, the draftsman in both cases was driven to define the act by reference to an intent, instead, as is more usual in criminal jurisprudence, of defining the criminal intent by reference to a separately defined prohibited act. It is this feature of s 1 which, I believe, has caused the trouble, and once this road has been followed it was I believe impossible to avoid the disadvantages pointed out in paragraph 2.97 of the Law Commission's report to which my noble and learned friend has drawn attention.

In the circumstances I am happy that my noble and learned friend's conclusion has enabled the House to arrive at its destination without resorting to these, possibly excessively sophisticated, subtleties.

Lord Elwyn-Jones: My Lords, having had the advantage of reading in draft the speech of my noble and learned friend, Lord Bridge of Harwich, with which I agree, I would dismiss the appeal as he proposes and for the reasons which he gives.

Lord Scarman: My Lords, I have had the advantage of studying in draft the speech to be delivered by my noble and learned friend Lord Bridge of Harwich. I agree with it. For the reasons which he gives I would dismiss the appeal, answering the certified question as he proposes.

Lord Bridge of Harwich: My Lords, on 23 February 1984 the appellant was convicted at the Crown Court at Reading of two attempts to commit offences. The offences attempted were being knowingly concerned in dealing with (count 1) and in harbouring (count 2) a Class A controlled drug namely diamorphine, with intent to evade the prohibition of importation imposed by s 3(1) of the Misuse of Drugs Act 1971, contrary to s 170(1)(b) of the Customs and Excise Management Act 1979. On 5 November 1984 the Court of Appeal (Criminal Division) dismissed his appeal against conviction but certified that a point of law of general public importance was involved in their decision and granted leave to appeal to your Lordships' House.

The certified question granted on 13 November 1984 reads:

> Does a person commit an offence under s 1 of the Criminal Attempts Act 1981 where, if the facts were as that person believed them to be, the full offence would have been committed by him, but where on the true facts of the offence which that person set out to commit was in law impossible, eg because the substance imported and believed to be heroin was not heroin but a harmless substance?

The facts plainly to be inferred from the evidence, interpreted in the light of the jury's guilty verdicts, may be shortly summarised. The appellant, on a visit to India, was approached by a man named Desai, who offered to pay him £1,000 if, on his return to England, he would receive a suitcase which a courier would deliver to him containing packages of drugs which the appellant was then to distribute according to instructions he would receive. The suitcase was duly delivered to him in Cambridge. On 30 November 1982, acting on instructions, the appellant went to Southall Station to deliver a package of drugs to a third party. Outside the station he and the man he had met by appointment were arrested. A package containing a powdered substance was found in the appellant's shoulder bag. At the appellant's flat in Cambridge, he produced to customs officers the suitcase from which the lining had been ripped out and the remaining packages of the same powdered substance. In answer to questions by customs officers and in a long written statement the appellant made what amounted to a full confession of having played his part, as described, as recipient and distributor of illegally imported drugs. The appellant believed the drugs to be either heroin or cannabis. In due course the powdered substance in the several packages was scientifically analysed and found not to be a controlled drug but snuff or some similar harmless vegetable matter ...

The certified question depends on the true construction of the Criminal Attempts Act 1981. That Act marked an important new departure since, by s 6, it abolished the offence of attempt at common law and substituted a new statutory code governing attempts to commit criminal offences. It was considered by your Lordships' House last year in *Anderton v Ryan* [1985] AC 560 after the decision in the Court of Appeal which is the subject of the present appeal. That might seem an appropriate starting point from which to examine the issues arising in this appeal. But your Lordships have been invited to exercise the power under the *Practice Statement (Judicial Precedent)* [1966] 1 WLR 1234 to depart from the reasoning in that decision if it proves necessary to do so in order to affirm the convictions appealed against in the instant case. I was not only a party to the decision in *Anderton v Ryan,* I was also the author of one of the two opinions approved by the majority which must be taken to express the House's ratio. That seems to me to afford a sound reason why, on being invited to re-examine the language of the statute in its application to the facts of this appeal, I should initially seek to put out of mind what I said in *Anderton v Ryan.* Accordingly I propose to approach the issue in the first place as an exercise in statutory construction, applying the language of the Act to the facts of the case, as if the matter were res integra. If this leads me to the conclusion that the appellant was not guilty of any attempt to commit a relevant offence, that will be the end of the matter. But if this initial exercise inclines me to reach a contrary conclusion, it will then be necessary to consider whether the precedent set by *Anderton v Ryan* bars that conclusion or whether it can be surmounted either on the ground that the earlier decision is distinguishable or that it would be appropriate to depart from it under the *Practice Statement.*

[His Lordship quoted s 1 of the Criminal Attempts Act 1981 and continued:]

Applying this language to the facts of the case, the first question to be asked is whether the appellant intended to commit the offences of being knowingly concerned in dealing with and harbouring drugs of Class A or Class B with intent to evade the prohibition on their importation. Translated into more homely language the question may be rephrased, without in any way altering its legal significance, in the following terms: did the appellant intend to receive and store (harbour) and in due course pass on to third parties (deal with) packages of heroin or cannabis which he knew had been smuggled into England from India? The answer is plainly yes, he did. Next, did he in relation to each offence, do an act which was more than merely preparatory to the commission of the offence? The act relied on in relation to harbouring was the receipt and retention of the packages found in the lining of the suitcase. The act relied on in relation to dealing was the meeting at Southall Station with the intended recipient of one of the packages. In each case the act was clearly more than preparatory to the commission of the *intended* offence; it was not and could not be more than merely preparatory to the commission of the *actual* offence, because the facts were such that the commission of the *actual* offence was impossible. Here then is the nub of the matter. Does the 'act which is more than merely preparatory to the commission of the offence' in s 1(1) of the Act of 1981 (the *actus reus* of the statutory offence of attempt) require any more than an act which is more than merely preparatory to the commission of the offence which the defendant intended to commit? S 1(2) must surely indicate a negative answer; if it were otherwise, whenever the facts were such that the commission of the actual offence was impossible, it would be impossible to prove an act more than merely preparatory to the commission of that offence and subsections (1) and (2) would contradict each other.

This is very simple, perhaps oversimple, analysis leads me to the provisional conclusion that the appellant was rightly convicted of the two offences of attempt with which he was charged. But can this conclusion stand with *Anderton v Ryan*? The appellant in that case was charged with an attempt to handle stolen goods. She bought a video recorder believing it to be stolen. On the facts as they were to be assumed it was not stolen. By a majority the House decided that she was entitled to be acquitted. I have re-examined the case with care. If I could extract from the speech of Lord Roskill or from my own speech a clear and coherent principle distinguishing those cases of attempting the impossible which amount to offences under the statute from those which do not, I should have to consider carefully on which side of the line the instant case fell. But I have to confess that I can find no such principle.

Running through Lord Roskill's speech and my own in *Anderton v Ryan* [1985] AC 560 is the concept of 'objectively innocent' acts which, in my speech certainly, are contrasted with 'guilty acts'. A few citations will make this clear. Lord Roskill said at 580:

> My Lords, it has been strenuously and ably argued for the respondent that these provisions involve that a defendant is liable to conviction for an attempt even where his actions are innocent but he erroneously believes facts which, if true, would make those actions criminal, and further, that he is

> liable to such conviction whether or not in the event his intended course of action is completed.

He proceeded to reject the argument. At p 582 I referred to the appellant's purchase of the video recorder and said: 'Objectively considered, therefore, her purchase of the recorder was a perfectly proper commercial transaction'. A further passage from my speech proceeded, at pp 582–83:

> The question may be stated in abstract terms as follows. Does s 1 of the Act of 1981 create a new offence of attempt where a person embarks on and completes a course of conduct which is objectively innocent, solely on the ground that the person mistakenly believes facts which, if true, would make that course of conduct a complete crime? If the question must be answered affirmatively it requires convictions in a number of surprising cases: the classic case, put by Bramwell B in *R v Collins* (1864) 9 Cox CC 497, of the man who takes away his own umbrella from a stand, believing it not to be his own and with intent to steal it; the case of the man who has consensual intercourse with a girl over 16 believing her to be under that age; the case of the art dealer who sells a picture which he represents to be and which is in fact a genuine Picasso, but which the dealer mistakenly believes to be a fake. The common feature of all these cases, including that under appeal, is that the mind alone is guilty, the act is innocent.

I then contrasted the case of the man who attempts to pick the empty pocket, saying:

> Putting the hand in the pocket is the guilty act, the intent to steal is the guilty mind, the offence is appropriately dealt with as an attempt, and the impossibility of committing the full offence for want of anything in the pocket to steal is declared by [subsection (2)] to be no obstacle to conviction.

If we fell into error, it is clear that our concern was to avoid convictions in situations which most people, as a matter of common sense, would not regard as involving criminality. In this connection it is to be regretted that we did not take due note of paragraph 2.97 of the Law Commission's report 'Criminal Law: Attempt, and Impossibility in Relation to Attempt, Conspiracy and Incitement' (1980) Law Com No 102 which preceded the enactment of the Act of 1981, which reads:

> If it is right in principle that an attempt should be chargeable even though the crime which it is sought to commit could not possibly be committed, we do not think that we should be deterred by the consideration that such a change in our law would also cover some extreme and exceptional cases in which a prosecution would be theoretically possible. An example would be where a person is offered goods at such a low price that he believes that they are stolen, when in fact they are not; if he actually purchases them, upon the principles which we have discussed he would be liable for an attempt to handle stolen goods. Another case which has been much debated is that raised in argument by Bramwell B in *R v Collins* (1864) 9 Cox CC 497. If A takes his own umbrella, mistaking it for one belonging to B and intending to steal B's umbrella, is he guilty of attempted theft? Again, on the principles which we have discussed he would in theory be guilty, but in neither case would it be realistic to suppose that a complaint would be made or that a prosecution would ensue.

The prosecution in *Anderton v Ryan* itself falsified the Commission's prognosis in one of the 'extreme and exceptional cases'. It nevertheless probably holds good for other such cases, particularly that of the young man having sexual intercourse with a girl over 16, mistakenly believing her to be under that age, by which both Lord Roskill and I were much troubled.

However that may be, the distinction between acts which are 'objectively innocent' and those which are not is an essential element in the reasoning in *Anderton v Ryan* and the decision, unless it can be supported on some other ground, must stand or fall by the validity of this distinction. I am satisfied on further consideration that the concept of 'objective innocence' is incapable of sensible application in relation to the law of criminal attempts. The reason for this is that any attempt to commit an offence which involves 'an act which is more than merely preparatory to the commission of the offence' but for any reason fails, so that in the event no offence is committed, must *ex hypothesi*, from the point of view of the criminal law, be 'objectively innocent'. What turns what would otherwise, from the point of view of the criminal law, be an innocent act into a crime is the intent of the actor to commit an offence. I say 'from the point of view of the criminal law' because the law of tort must surely here be quite irrelevant. A puts his hand into B's pocket. Whether or not there is anything in the pocket capable of being stolen, if A intends to steal, his act is a criminal attempt; if he does not so intend, his act is innocent. A plunges a knife into a bolster in a bed. To avoid the complication of an offence of criminal damage, assume it to be A's bolster. If A believes the bolster to be his enemy B and intends to kill him, his act is an attempt to murder B; if he knows the bolster is only a bolster, his act is innocent. These considerations lead me to the conclusion that the distinction sought to be drawn in *Anderton v Ryan* between innocent and guilty acts considered 'objectively' and independently of the state of mind of the actor cannot be sensibly maintained.

Another conceivable ground of distinction which was to some extent canvassed in argument, both in *Anderton v Ryan* and in the instant case, though no trace of it appears in the speeches in *Anderton v Ryan*, is a distinction which would make guilt or innocence of the crime of attempt in a case of mistaken belief dependent on what, for want of a better phrase, I will call the defendant's dominant intention. According to the theory necessary to sustain this distinction, the appellant's dominant intention in *Anderton v Ryan* was to buy a cheap video recorder, her belief that it was stolen was merely incidental. Likewise in the hypothetical case of attempted unlawful sexual intercourse, the young man's dominant intention was to have intercourse with the particular girl; his mistaken belief that she was under 16 was merely incidental. By contrast, in the instant case the appellant's dominant intention was to receive and distribute illegally imported heroin or cannabis.

Whilst I see the superficial attraction of this suggested ground of distinction, I also see formidable practical difficulties in its application. By what test is a jury to be told that a defendant's dominant intention is to be recognised and distinguished from his incidental but mistaken belief? But there is perhaps a more formidable theoretical difficulty. If this ground of distinction is relied on to support the acquittal of the appellant in *Anderton v Ryan*, it can only do so on the basis that her mistaken belief that the video recorder was stolen played no significant part in her decision to buy it and therefore she may be acquitted of the intent to handle stolen goods. But this line of reasoning runs into head-on collision with s 1(3) of the Act of 1981. The theory produces a situation where, apart from the subsection, her intention would not be regarded as having amounted to any intent to commit an offence. Section 1(3)(b) then requires one to ask whether, if the video recorder had in fact been stolen, her intention would have been regarded as an intent to handle stolen goods. The answer must clearly be yes, it would. If she had bought the video recorder knowing it to be stolen, when in fact it was, it would have availed her nothing to say that her dominant intention was to buy a video recorder because it was cheap and that her knowledge that it was stolen was merely incidental. This seems to me fatal to the dominant intention theory.

I am thus led to the conclusion that there is no valid ground on which *Anderton v Ryan* can be distinguished. I have made clear my own conviction, which as a party to the decision (and craving the indulgence of my noble and learned friends who agreed in it) I am the readier to express, that the decision was wrong. What then is to be done? If the case is indistinguishable, the application of the strict doctrine of precedent would require that the present appeal be allowed. Is it permissible to depart from precedent under the *Practice Statement (Judicial Precedent)* [1966] 1 WLR 1234 notwithstanding the especial need for certainty in the criminal law? The following considerations lead me to answer that question affirmatively. First, I am undeterred by the consideration that the decision in *Anderton v Ryan* was so recent. The *Practice Statement* is an effective abandonment of our pretention to infallibility. If a serious error embodied in a decision of this House has distorted the law, the sooner it is corrected the better. Second, I cannot see how, in the very nature of the case, anyone could have acted in reliance on the law as propounded in *Anderton v Ryan* in the belief that he was acting innocently and now find that, after all, he is to be held to have committed a criminal offence. Third, to hold the House bound to follow *Anderton v Ryan* because it cannot be distinguished and to allow the appeal in this case would, it seems to me, be tantamount to a declaration that the Act of 1981 left the law of criminal attempts unchanged following the decision in *R v Smith* [1975] AC 476. Finally, if, contrary to my present view, there is a valid ground on which it would be proper to distinguish cases similar to that considered in *Anderton v Ryan*, my present opinion on that point would not foreclose the option of making such a distinction in some future case.

I cannot conclude this opinion without disclosing that I have had the advantage, since the conclusion of the argument in this appeal, of reading an article by Professor Glanville Williams entitled 'The Lords and Impossible Attempts, or *Quis Custodiet Ipsos Custodes?*' [1986] CLJ 33. The language in which he criticises the decision in *Anderton v Ryan* is not conspicuous for it moderation, but it would be foolish, on that account, not to recognise the force of the criticism and churlish not to acknowledge the assistance I have derived from it.

I would answer the certified question in the affirmative and dismiss the appeal.

Lord Mackay of Clashfern: My Lords, I have had the advantage of reading in draft the speeches prepared by my noble and learned friends the Lord Chancellor and Lord Bridge of Harwich. I agree with the disposal of this appeal proposed by my noble and learned friend Lord Bridge. On the relatively minor point referred to in the speech of the Lord Chancellor in which he differs from Lord Bridge I agree with the Lord Chancellor's view. Otherwise I agree with the reasons given by my noble and learned friend, Lord Bridge.

CHAPTER 12

INCHOATE OFFENCES – CONSPIRACY

There are two types of conspiracy: statutory conspiracy and common law conspiracy.

STATUTORY CONSPIRACY

The basis of statutory conspiracy is an agreement between two or more people to embark on a criminal course of conduct. Liability results from one or more of those people acting in accordance with the terms of the agreement.

Sections 1 and 2 of the Criminal Law Act 1977

Section 1:

(1) Subject to the following provisions of this part of this Act, if a person agrees with any other person or persons that a course of conduct shall be pursued which, if the agreement is carried out in accordance with their intentions, either:

(a) will necessarily amount to or involve the commission of any offence or offences by one or more of the parties to the agreement; or

(b) would do so but for the existence of facts which render the commission of the offence or any of the offences impossible,

he shall be guilty of conspiracy to commit the offence or offences in question.

(2) Where liability for any offence may be incurred without knowledge on the part of the person committing it of any particular fact or circumstance necessary for the commission of the offence, a person shall nevertheless not be guilty of conspiracy to commit that offence by virtue of subsection (1) above unless he and at least one other party to the agreement intend or know that the fact or circumstance shall or will exist at the time when the conduct constituting the offence is to take place.

(3) [repealed]

(4) In this part of this Act 'offence' means an offence triable in England and Wales, except that it includes murder notwithstanding that the murder in question would not be so triable if committed in accordance with the intentions of the parties to the agreement.

Section 2:

(1) A person shall not by virtue of s 1 above be guilty of conspiracy to commit any offence if he is an intended victim of that offence.

(2) A person shall not by virtue of s 1 above be guilty of conspiracy to commit any offence or offences if the only other person or persons with whom he agrees are (both initially and at all times during the currency of the agreement) persons of any one or more of the following descriptions, that is to say:

(a) his spouse;

(b) a person under the age of criminal responsibility;

(c) an intended victim of that offence or of each of those offences.

The *actus reus* of statutory conspiracy

The *actus reus* of conspiracy is the agreement: *R v Gill* (1993) 97 Cr App R 215 (CA). This agreement is usually proved by evidence of acts carried out to fulfil the agreement: see *R v Cooper* [1947] 2 All ER 701. Nevertheless, because it is the agreement itself which amounts to the conspiracy, it does not matter if the acts actually carried out differ from those agreed: see *R v Bolton* (1991) 94 Cr App R 74. For people to be conspirators, they must be acting together: see *R v Griffiths* [1966] 1 QB 589.

R v Cooper and Compton [1947] 2 ALL ER 701 (CA)

Humphreys J: These two appellants were tried at the Central Criminal Court on an indictment which contained nine counts. The first count was a charge of conspiracy to steal. The second, third, fourth and fifth counts alleged that in four separate cases the appellants had been guilty of robbing four separate persons, that is, forcing them to give their money or goods as the result of threats and owing to fear. The next four counts charged that in those same cases they had stolen the money of those four persons, simple larceny.

The main ground of this appeal is put well in the grounds of appeal. The jury found a verdict of guilty on the first count. They found a verdict of not guilty on each and all of the remaining counts, and it is argued in support of the appeals that in those circumstances a verdict of not guilty on the substantive counts 2 and 9 leaves the first count unsupported by sufficient, or any, evidence ...

...The jury ... returned the verdict of guilty on the first count and not guilty on each of the others ...

... All we can say is that the jury has said in terms: 'We are not satisfied with the case for the prosecution on counts 2 – 9. We are satisfied with the case for the prosecution on count 1.'

Is it possible that this court can uphold that verdict as being reasonable? In a great many cases there is no doubt that a verdict of guilty of conspiracy, but not guilty of the particular acts charged, is a perfectly proper and reasonable one. In such cases it would be wrong not to insert in the indictment a charge of conspiracy. Criminal lawyers know it often happens that, while a general conspiracy to do such a thing as to steal is likely to be inferred by the jury from the evidence, it may be that the evidence of the particular acts constituting the larcenies charged in the indictment are supported by rather nebulous evidence. That is a case where the jury may say, and very likely will say, not guilty of larceny but guilty of being concerned with others to commit larceny ...

In the present case it appears that to us that there was no necessity from any point of view for the insertion of any charge of conspiracy. A verdict of guilty could only be supported if the jury believed the general story, and the general story was told by four different persons, each of whom, if he was believed, proved conclusively a charge of stealing ...

R v Bolton (1992) 94 Cr App R 74 (CA)

Facts: The defendant was charged with conspiracy to procure the execution of valuable securities by deception. The appeal concerned the question whether it mattered that the defendant expected a cheque but in fact money was transferred by electronic means.

Woolf LJ: ... [His Lordship referred to *R v Siracusa* (1990) 90 Cr App R 340, *R v Anderson* [1986] AC 27 and *R v Reed* [1982] Crim LR 819]. In the latter case Donaldson LJ said:

> ... A and B agree to drive from London to Edinburgh in a time which can be achieved without exceeding the speed limits, but only if the traffic which they encounter is exceptionally light. Their agreement will not necessarily involve the commission of any offence, even if it is carried out in accordance with their intentions, and they do arrive ... within the agreed time. Accordingly the agreement does not constitute the offence of statutory conspiracy.

[Woolf LJ went on to say:] there can be a distinction between the manner in which the conspirators *intend* to achieve their objective and how that objective is in fact achieved. Taking the example given by Donaldson LJ in the case of *Reed*, if A and B agree and intend to drive from London to Edinburgh in excess of the speed limit because they expect heavy traffic, the fact that it proves unnecessary for them to do so because the traffic is light does not avoid them being guilty of conspiracy. Their agreement was to do something which necessarily would involve the commission of an offence, namely exceeding the speed limit and they embarked on the commission of that offence. So in this case, if Roger Bolton and his co-conspirators agree dishonestly etc to procure the building societies to make a mortgage advance by executing a valuable security and this was what they set out to achieve, it would not mean the conspirators were not guilty of conspiracy, if contrary to what they intended, the building societies happened always to use a method of advancing the mortgage moneys which did not involve the use of a valuable security. In the case of conspiracy as opposed to the substantive offence, it is what is agreed to be done and not what was in fact done which is all important ...

R v Griffiths [1966] 1 QB 589 (CA)

Paull J: ... In the opening the case for the prosecution, Mr Morris said: 'This is the story of a large-scale fraud', and a little later said: 'It is the case for the Crown that they each conspired together with Griffiths and Booth in this fraud but not with each other'. Construed strictly, these words mean that there were a number of different conspiracies and not one conspiracy, for in law all must join the one agreement, each with the others, in order to constitute one conspiracy. They may join in at various times, each attaching himself to that agreement; any one of them may not know all the other parties but only that there are other parties; any one of them may not know the full extent of the scheme to which he attaches himself. But what each must know is that there is coming into existence, or is in existence, a scheme which goes beyond the illegal act or acts which he agrees to do ...

The matter can be illustrated quite simply. I employ an accountant to make out my tax return. He and his clerk are both present when I am about to sign the return. I notice an item in my expenses of £100 and say: 'I don't remember incurring this expense'. The clerk says: 'Well, actually I put it in. You didn't incur it, but I didn't think you would object to a few pounds being saved.' The accountant indicates his agreement to this attitude. After some hesitation I agree to let it stand. On those bare facts I cannot be charged with 50 others in a conspiracy to defraud the Exchequer of £100,000 on the basis that this accountant and his clerk have persuaded 500 other clients to make false returns, some being false in one way, some in another, or even all in the same way. I have not knowingly attached myself to a general agreement to defraud. Similarly, the Post Office clerk who agrees to alter a date stamp in a case where a bookmaker has been swindled must know that the alteration is to be used for a fraudulent purpose. He therefore joins a scheme to defraud that bookmaker, of whom he may not have heard, but he cannot be indicted, merely because he has agreed to alter that stamp, on a charge of a conspiracy to alter date stamps and cheat bookmakers all over the country ...

The *mens rea* of statutory conspiracy

According to the House of Lords in *R v Anderson* [1986] AC 27 a person may be guilty of conspiracy even if he never intends that the agreed plan should be carried out.

R v Anderson [1986] AC 27 (HL)

Lord Bridge of Harwich: ... In June 1981 the appellant and Ahmed Andaloussi were both in custody on remand in Lewes prison. Andaloussi was awaiting trial on charges of very serious drug offences and was rightly believed by the appellant to have large sums of money at his disposal. The appellant was on remand in connection with some entirely different matter. He spent one night in the same cell as Andaloussi. The appellant was then confidently expecting that in a short time he would be, as in the event he was, released on bail. During the night they spent together the appellant agreed with Andaloussi to participate in a scheme to effect Andaloussi's escape from prison. Other participants in the scheme were to be Ahmed Andaloussi's brother Mohammed and Mohammed Assou. They were to maintain contact with Ahmed in prison after the appellant's release. The appellant was to be paid £20,000 for his part in the escape scheme. It is not clear, nor is it significant for the purpose of any issue arising in the appeal, how far details of the escape plan were worked out at the initial meeting in prison between the appellant and Ahmed Andaloussi. What is clear is that either at that meeting or after the appellant's release from prison and after one or more meetings between the appellant and Assou, it was agreed that the appellant would purchase and supply diamond wire, a cutting agent capable of cutting through metal bars, to be smuggled into the prison by Assou or Mohammed Andaloussi to enable Ahmed Andaloussi to escape from his cell. Further steps in the escape plan were to include the provision of rope and a ladder to enable Ahmed Andaloussi to climb on to the roof of an industrial building in the prison and thence over the main wall, transport to drive him away from the prison and safe accommodation where he could hide.

What happened in the event was that the appellant received from Assou a payment of £2,000 on account of the agreed fee of £20,000. Shortly after this the appellant was injured in a road accident and thereafter took no further step in pursuance of the escape plan. His admitted intention, however, was to acquire the diamond wire and give it to Assou. His further intention, according to the version of the facts which we must for present purposes accept, was then to insist that before he would proceed further he should be paid a further £10,000 on account, on receipt of which he would have left the country and gone to live in Spain, taking no further part in the scheme to effect Andaloussi's escape ...

The Court of Appeal, having dismissed his appeal, certified that their decision involved a point of law of general public importance in terms which can conveniently be divided into two parts, since, in truth, there are two separate questions involved:

(1) Is a person who 'agrees' with two or more others, who themselves intend to pursue a course of conduct which will necessarily involve the commission of an offence, and who has a secret intention himself to participate in part only

of that course of conduct, guilty himself of conspiracy to commit that offence under s 1(1) of the Criminal Law Act 1977?

(2) If not, is he liable to be indicted as a principal offender under s 8 of the Accessories and Abettors Act 1861? ...

The Criminal Law Act of 1977, subject to exceptions not presently material, abolished the offence of conspiracy at common law. It follows that the elements of the new statutory offence of conspiracy must be ascertained purely by interpretation of the language of s 1(1) of the Act of 1977. For purposes of analysis it is perhaps convenient to isolate the three clauses each of which must be taken as indicating an essential ingredient of the offence as follows: (1) 'if a person agrees with any other person or persons that a course of conduct shall be pursued' (2) 'which will necessarily amount to or involve the commission of any offence or offences by one or more of the parties to the agreement' (3) 'if the agreement is carried out in accordance with their intentions'.

Clause (1) presents, as it seems to me, no difficulty. It means exactly what it says and what it says is crystal clear. To be convicted, the party charged must have agreed with one or more others that 'a course of conduct shall be pursued'. What is important is to resist the temptation to introduce into this simple concept ideas derived from the civil law of contract. Any number of persons may agree that a course of conduct shall be pursued without undertaking any contractual liability. The agreed course of conduct may be a simple or an elaborate one and may involve the participation of two or any larger number of persons who may have agreed to play a variety of roles in the course of conduct agreed.

Again, clause (2) could hardly use simpler language. Here what is important to note is that it is not necessary that more than one of the participants in the agreed course of conduct shall commit a substantive offence. It is, of course, necessary that any party to the agreement shall have assented to play his part in the agreed course of conduct, however innocent in itself, knowing that the part to be played by one or more of the others will amount to or involve the commission of an offence.

It is only clause (3) which presents any possible ambiguity. The heart of the submission for the appellant is that in order to be convicted of conspiracy to commit a given offence the language of clause (3) requires that the party charged should not only have agreed that a course of conduct shall be pursued which will necessarily amount to or involve the commission of that offence by himself or one or more other parties to the agreement, but must also be proved himself to have intended that that offence should be committed. Thus, it is submitted here that the appellant's case that he never intended that Andaloussi should be enabled to escape from prison raised an issue to be left to the jury, who should have been directed to convict him only if satisfied that he did so intend. I do not find it altogether easy to understand why the draftsman of this provision chose to use the phrase 'in accordance with their intentions'. But I suspect the answer may be that this seemed a desirable alternative to the phrase 'in accordance with its terms', or any similar expression, because it is a matter of common experience in the criminal courts that the 'terms' of a criminal conspiracy are hardly ever susceptible of proof. The evidence from which a jury may infer a criminal conspiracy is almost invariably to be found in the conduct of the parties. This was so at common law and remains so under the statute. If the evidence in a given case justifies the inference of an agreement that a course of conduct should be pursued, it is a not inappropriate formulation of the test of the criminality of the inferred agreement to ask whether the further inference can be drawn that a crime would necessarily have been committed if the agreed course of conduct had been pursued in accordance with the several intentions of the parties. Whether that is an accurate analysis or not, I am clearly driven by consideration of the diversity of roles which parties may agree to play in criminal conspiracies to reject any construction of the statutory language which would require the prosecution to prove an intention on the part of each conspirator that the criminal offence or offences which will necessarily be committed by one or more of the conspirators if the agreed course of conduct is fully carried out should in fact be committed. A simple example will illustrate the absurdity to which this construction would lead. The proprietor of a car hire firm agrees for a substantial payment to make available a hire car to a gang for use in a robbery and to make false entries in his books relating to the hiring to which he can point if the number of the car is traced back to him in connection with the robbery. Being fully aware of the circumstances of the robbery in which the car is proposed to be used he is plainly a party to the conspiracy to rob. Making his car available for use in the robbery is as much part of the relevant agreed course of conduct as the robbery itself. Yet, once he has been paid, it will be a matter of complete indifference to him whether the robbery is in fact committed or not. In these days of highly organised crime the most serious statutory conspiracies will frequently involve an elaborate and complex agreed course of conduct in which many will consent to play necessary but subordinate roles, not involving them in any direct participation in the commission of the offence or offences at the centre of the conspiracy. Parliament cannot have intended that such parties should escape conviction of conspiracy on the basis that it cannot be proved against them that they intended that the relevant offence or offences should be committed.

There remains the important question whether a person who has agreed that a course of conduct will be pursued which, if pursued as agreed, will necessarily amount to or involve the commission of an offence, is guilty of statutory conspiracy irrespective of his intention, and, if not, what is the *mens rea* of the offence. I have no hesitation in answering the first part of the question in the negative. There may be many situations in which perfectly respectable citizens, more particularly those concerned with law enforcement, may enter into agreements that a course of conduct shall be pursued which will involve commission of a crime without the least intention of playing any part in furtherance of the ostensibly agreed criminal objective, but rather with the purpose of exposing and frustrating the criminal purpose of the other parties to the agreement. To say this is in no way to encourage schemes by which police act, directly or through the agency of informers, as *agents provocateurs* for the purpose of entrapment. That is conduct of which the courts have always strongly disapproved. But it may sometimes happen, as most of us with experience in criminal trials well know, that a criminal enterprise is well advanced in the course of preparation when it comes to the notice either of the police or of some honest citizen in such circumstances that the only prospect of exposing and frustrating the criminals is that some innocent person should play the part of an intending collaborator in the course of criminal conduct proposed to be pursued. The *mens rea* implicit in the offence of statutory conspiracy must clearly be such as to recognise the innocence of such a person, notwithstanding that he will, in literal terms, be obliged to agree that a course of conduct be pursued involving the commission of an offence.

I have said already, but I repeat to emphasise its importance, that an essential ingredient in the crime of conspiring to commit a specific offence or offences under s 1(1) of the Act of 1977 is that the accused should agree that a course of conduct be pursued which he knows must involve the commission by one or more of the parties to the agreement of that offence or those offences. But, beyond the mere fact of agreement, the necessary *mens rea* of the crime is, in my opinion, established if, and only if, it is shown that the accused, when he entered into the agreement, intended to play some part in the agreed course of conduct in furtherance of the criminal purpose which the agreed course of conduct was intended to achieve. Nothing less will suffice; nothing more is required.

Applying this test to the facts which, for the purposes of the appeal, we must assume, the appellant, in agreeing that a course of conduct be pursued that would, if successful, necessarily involve the offence of effecting Andaloussi's escape from lawful custody, clearly intended, by providing diamond wire to be smuggled into the prison, to play a part in the agreed course of conduct in furtherance of that criminal objective. Nether the fact that he intended to play no further part in attempting to effect the escape, nor that he believed the escape to be impossible, would, if the jury had supposed they might be true, have afforded him any defence.

In the result, I would answer the first part of the certified question in the affirmative and dismiss the appeal. Your Lordships did not find it necessary to hear argument directed to the second part of the certified question and it must, therefore, be left unanswered.

R v Siracusa (1990) 90 Cr App R 340 (CA)

O'Connor LJ: ... The case arises out of the operations of an organisation of smugglers engaged in moving massive quantities of heroin from Thailand and cannabis from Kashmir to Canada via England. The scheme was simple. The drugs were to be housed in secret compartments in selected items of locally produced furniture, which would be included in substantial shipments of furniture. The object of passing the consignments through England was to support the manifests to be presented to the Canadian customs declaring the country of origin of the goods as England.

On 13 December 1984 a consignment of 52 packing cases of furniture from India consigned to Elongate Ltd arrived at Felixstowe. Customs officers found in some articles of furniture cannabis with a street value of £0.5 million in England and £3 million in Canada. They repacked and waited and watched. The consignment was cleared by shipping agents and delivered to a warehouse, Unit 5, Batsworth Road, Mitcham. The customs moved in on 18 December 1984, seized the consignment and arrested Siracusa and a man named Gaultieri. Unit 5 is a spacious warehouse. There was nothing in it except the 52 cases of furniture and a fork-lift truck. The work in hand was the painting out of the Indian shipping marks with black paint.

On 28 May 1985, a consignment of 84 packing cases of furniture from Thailand consigned to Ital Provisions Ltd arrived at Southampton. Customs officers found in some articles of furniture heroin with a street value of £15 million in England and £75 million in Canada. They repacked some of the heroin and waited and watched. The consignment was not delivered in this country, but transshipped and left for Canada on 8 June 1985.

After delivery in Canada on 21 June 1985, enforcement officers moved in, seized the consignment and arrested three men. It was found that they had gone unerringly to the cases containing the pieces in which heroin was concealed. In England, Monteleone, Luciani and Di Carlo were arrested on 21 June 1985 ...

The appellants contend that ... the prosecution had to prove against each defendant that he knew that the Kashmir operation involved cannabis and that the Thailand operation involved heroin ...

[His Lordship referred to the speech of Lord Bridge in *R v Anderson* [1986] AC 27 and commented:]

... We think it obvious that Lord Bridge cannot have been intending that the organiser of a crime who recruited others to carry it out would not himself be guilty of conspiracy unless it could be proved that he intended to play some active part himself thereafter ...

The present case is a classic example of such a conspiracy. It is the hallmark of such crimes that the organisers try to remain in the background and more often than not are not apprehended. Second, the origins of all conspiracies are concealed and it is usually quite impossible to establish when or where the initial agreement was made, or when or where other conspirators were recruited. The very existence of the agreement can only be inferred from overt acts. Participation in a conspiracy is infinitely variable: it can be active or passive. If the majority shareholder and director of a company consents to the company being used for drug smuggling carried out in the company's name by a fellow director and minority shareholder, he is guilty of conspiracy. Consent, that is the agreement or adherence to the agreement, can be inferred if it is proved that he knew what was going on and the intention to participate in the furtherance of the criminal purpose is also established by his failure to stop the unlawful activity. Lord Bridge's *dictum* does not require anything more.

[His Lordship then referred to the *dictum* of Lord Bridge that:]

> an essential ingredient in the crime of conspiring to commit a specific offence or offences under s 1(1) of the Act of 1977 is that the accused should agree that a course of conduct be pursued which he knows must involve the commission by one or more of the parties to the agreement of that offence or those offences.

[and O'Connor LJ went to observe that:]

Lord Bridge plainly does not mean that the prosecution have to prove that persons who agree to import prohibited drugs into this country know that the offence which will be committed will be in contravention of s 170(2) of the Customs and Excise Management Act. He is not to be taken as saying that the prosecution must prove that the accused knew the name of the crime. We are satisfied that Lord Bridge was doing no more than applying the words of s 1 of the Criminal Law Act 1977, namely that when the accused agreed to the course of conduct, he knew that it involved the commission of an offence.

The *mens rea* sufficient to support the commission of a substantive offence will not necessarily be sufficient to support a charge of conspiracy to commit that offence. An intent to cause grievous bodily harm is sufficient to support the charge of murder, but is not sufficient to support a charge of conspiracy to murder or of attempt to murder.

We have come to the conclusion that if the prosecution charge a conspiracy to contravene s 170(2) of the Customs and Excise Management Act by the importation of heroin, then the prosecution must prove that the agreed course of conduct was the importation of heroin. This is because the essence of the crime of conspiracy is the agreement and in simple terms, you do not prove an agreement to import heroin by proving an agreement to import cannabis.

We are confident that in coming to this conclusion, we are not making the enforcement of the anti-drug laws more difficult. If the facts suggest that the agreement was to import prohibited drugs of more than one class that can be appropriately laid because s 1(1) of the Criminal Law Act expressly provides for the agreed course of conduct to involve the commission of more than one offence ...

Yip Chiu-Cheung v The Queen [1994] 3 WLR 514 (PC)

Lord Griffiths: ... The prosecution case was based primarily on the evidence of Philip Needham who was an undercover drug enforcement officer of the United States of America and named in the indictment as a co-conspirator. The other conspirator, referred to in the indictment as a person unknown, was introduced to Needham by the defendant under the name of Hom.

In outline Needham's evidence was that he had a series of meetings in Thailand with the defendant, at one of which Hom also took part, at which it was arranged that Needham would act as a courier to carry five kilos of heroin from Hong Kong to Australia, travelling by air.

The arrangement was that Needham would fly to Hong Kong on 22 October 1989 under the name of Larsen, where he would be met by the defendant. He would then stay at the Nathan Hotel in Kowloon for a few days and then fly on to Australia with five kilos of heroin supplied by the defendant. For this service he would be paid US $16,000. In fact Needham did not fly to Hong Kong on 22 October because the flight was delayed and he missed the rescheduled flight. Needham said he had no way of contacting the defendant in Hong Kong and had been advised by the Hong Kong authorities that the Nathan Hotel would be a dangerous place for him to stay. Needham therefore proceeded no further with the plan, and did not go to Hong Kong.

The defendant was arrested in Hong Kong on 15 November, a piece of paper with the name Larsen was found in the defendant's possession and it was admitted that he had come to the airport to meet Needham's flight on 22 October.

Needham said that throughout his dealings with the defendant and Hom he kept the authorities in Hong Kong and Australia informed of the plans and they agreed that he would not be prevented from carrying the heroin out of Hong Kong and into Australia. It was obviously the intention to try to identify and arrest both the suppliers and the distributors of the drug ...

On the principal ground of appeal it was submitted that the trial judge and the Court of Appeal were wrong to hold that Needham, the undercover agent, could be a conspirator because he lacked the necessary *mens rea* or guilty mind required for the offence of conspiracy. It was urged upon their Lordships that no moral guilt attached to the undercover agent who was at all times acting courageously and with the best of motives in attempting to infiltrate and bring to justice a gang of criminal drug dealers. In these circumstances it was argued that it would be wrong to treat the agent as having any criminal intent, and reliance was placed upon a passage in the speech of Lord Bridge of Harwich in *R v Anderson* [1986] AC 27, 38–39; but in that case Lord Bridge was dealing with a different situation from that which exists in the present case. There may be many cases in which undercover police officers or other law enforcement agents pretend to join a conspiracy in order to gain information about the plans of the criminals, with no intention of taking any part in the planned crime but rather with the intention of providing information that will frustrate it. It was to this situation that Lord Bridge was referring in *R v Anderson*. The crime of conspiracy requires an agreement between two or more persons to commit an unlawful act with the intention of carrying it out. It is the intention to carry out the crime that constitutes the necessary *mens rea* for the offence. As Lord Bridge pointed out, an undercover agent who has no intention of committing the crime lacks the necessary *mens rea* to be a conspirator.

The facts of the present case are quite different. Nobody can doubt that Needham was acting courageously and with the best of motives; he was trying to break a drug ring. But equally there can be no doubt that the method he chose and in which the police in Hong Kong acquiesced involved the commission of the criminal offence of trafficking in drugs by exporting heroin from Hong Kong without a licence. Needham intended to commit that offence by carrying the heroin through the customs and on to the aeroplane bound for Australia.

Neither the police, nor customs, nor any other members of the executive have any power to alter the terms of the ordinance forbidding the export of heroin, and the fact that they may turn a blind eye when the heroin is exported does not prevent it from being a criminal offence ...

Naturally, Needham never expected to be prosecuted if he carried out the plan as intended. But the fact that in such circumstances the authorities would not prosecute the undercover agent does not mean that he did not commit the crime albeit as part of a wider scheme to combat drug dealing.

The judge correctly directed the jury that they should regard Needham as a conspirator if they found that he intended to export the heroin ...

R v Nicholas Reed [1982] Crim LR 819 (CA)

Facts: The appellant was convicted on two counts of conspiring with L to aid and abet suicide and of two substantive offences of aiding and abetting suicide. L was convicted in the same trial on the counts of conspiracy and five substantive counts of aiding and abetting suicide.

The appellant submitted that the summing up had not adequately conveyed the requirements of s 1(1) Criminal Law Act 1977. These, it was said, clearly indicate that a course of conduct agreed upon must necessarily amount to or involve the commission of an offence if the agreement is carried out in accordance with the parties' intentions. The agreement on the relevant course of conduct must therefore not be capable of a successful conclusion without a crime being committed (*cf* Smith and Hogan, *Criminal Law*, 4th edn, pp 226-27). It was argued that the most that could be inferred about the nature of the agreement between L and the appellant was that L would visit individuals and either give them faith healing, consolation and comfort while discouraging suicide or he would actively help them to commit suicide, depending on his assessment of the appropriate course of action. Such an agreement was capable of execution without the law being broken, and therefore should not have attracted the charge of conspiracy. It was argued that the jury should have at least been made aware of such a possible defence in the directions given.

The court held against the applicant on this point. Donaldson LJ considered two examples:

> In the first A and B agree to drive from London to Edinburgh in a time which can be achieved without exceeding the speed limits, but only if the traffic which they encounter is exceptionally light. Their agreement will not necessarily involve the commission of any offence, even if it is carried out in accordance with their intentions, and they do arrive from London to Edinburgh within the agreed time. Accordingly the agreement does not constitute the offence of statutory conspiracy or indeed of any offence. In the second example, A and B agree to rob a bank, if when they arrive at the bank it seems safe to do so. Their agreement will necessarily involve the commission of the offence of robbery if it is carried out in accordance with their intentions. Accordingly, they are guilty of the statutory offence of

conspiracy. The instant case is an example of the latter type of agreement. If circumstances had permitted and the agreement of the appellant and L had been carried out in accordance with their intentions L would have aided, abetted, counselled, and procured a suicide ...

COMMON LAW CONSPIRACY

As well as statutory conspiracy, there remain certain forms of common law conspiracy:

(1) conspiracy to defraud;

(2) conspiracy to corrupt public morals and conspiracy to outrage public decency.

Section 5 of the Criminal Law Act 1977

(1) Subject to the following provisions of this section, the offence of conspiracy at common law is hereby abolished.

(2) Subsection (1) above shall not affect the offence of conspiracy at common law so far as it relates to conspiracy to defraud.

(3) Subsection (1) above shall not affect the offence of conspiracy at common law if and in so far as it may be committed by entering into an agreement to engage in conduct which:

(a) tends to corrupt public morals or outrages public decency; but

(b) would not amount to or involve the commission of an offence if carried out by a single person otherwise than in pursuance of an agreement ...

(7) Incitement to commit the offence of conspiracy (whether the conspiracy incited would be an offence at common law or under s 1 above or any other enactment) shall cease to be an offence.

Conspiracy to defraud

There are two types of conspiracy to defraud. One involves agreeing dishonestly to deprive a person of something to which he is entitled or to which he might be entitled; no actual deception need be proved. See *Scott v Metropolitan Police Commissioner* [1975] AC 819 and *R v Hollinshead* [1985] AC 975.

The other form, which does require proof of deception, consists of dishonestly deceiving a person into acting contrary to his public duty. See, for example, *Welham v DPP* [1961] AC 103 and *R v Moses* [1991] Crim LR 617.

Dishonesty for these purposes is interpreted in the same way as in relation to theft (see Chapter 15).

Scott v Metropolitan Police Commissioner [1975] AC 818 (HL)

Viscount Dilhorne: ... The Court of Appeal certified that a point of law of general public importance was involved in the decision to dismiss the appeal against conviction on count 1, namely:

Whether, on a charge of conspiracy to defraud, the Crown must establish an agreement to deprive the owners of their property by deception; or whether it is sufficient to prove an agreement to prejudice the rights of another or others without lawful justification and in circumstances of dishonesty ...

In this case it is not necessary to decide that a conspiracy to defraud may exist even though its object was not to secure a financial advantage by inflicting an economic loss on the person at whom the conspiracy was directed. But for myself I see no reason why what was said by Lord Radcliffe in relation to forgery should not equally apply in relation to conspiracy to defraud.

In this case the accused bribed servants of the cinema owners to secure possession of films in order to copy them and in order to enable them to let the copies out on hire. By so doing Mr Blom-Cooper conceded they inflicted more than nominal damage to the goodwill of the owners of the copyright and distribution rights of the films. By so doing they secured for themselves profits which but for their actions might have been secured by those owners just as in *R v Button*, 3 Cox CC 229 the defendants obtained profits which might have been secured by their employer. In the circumstances it is, I think, clear that they inflicted pecuniary loss on those owners ...

Reverting to the questions certified by the Court of Appeal, the answer to the first question is in my opinion in the negative. I am not very happy about the way in which the second question is phrased although the word 'prejudice' has been not infrequently used in this connection. If by 'prejudice' is meant 'injure', then I think the answer to that question is yes, for in my opinion it is clearly the law that an agreement by two or more by dishonesty to deprive a person of something which is his or to which he is or would be or might be entitled and an agreement by two or more by dishonesty to injure some proprietary right of his, suffices to constitute the offence of conspiracy to defraud.

In my opinion this appeal should be dismissed.

Lord Diplock: My Lords, I have had the advantage of reading the speech of my noble and learned friend, Viscount Dilhorne. I agree with it. The authorities he cites and others cited in the speeches in this House in the contemporaneous appeal in *R v Withers* [1975] AC 751, in my view, established the following propositions: ...

(2) Where the intended victim of a 'conspiracy to defraud' is a private individual the purpose of the conspirators must be to a cause the victim economic loss by depriving him of some property or right, corporeal or incorporeal, to which he is or would or might become entitled. The intended means by which the purpose is to be achieved must be dishonest. They need not involve fraudulent misrepresentation such as is needed to constitute the civil tort of deceit. Dishonesty of any kind is enough.

(3) Where the intended victim of a 'conspiracy to defraud' is a person performing public duties as distinct from a private individual it is sufficient if the purpose is to cause him to act contrary to his public duty, and the intended means of achieving this purpose are dishonest. The purpose need not involve causing economic loss to anyone.

In the instant case the intended victims of the conspiracy to defraud were private individuals. The facts bring it squarely within proposition 2 above. The dishonest means to be employed were clandestine bribery.

I would dismiss the appeal.

R v Hollinshead [1985] 1 AC 975 (HL)

Lord Roskill: ... The Court of Appeal (Criminal Division) certified two points of law as of general public importance:

1 If parties agree (a) to manufacture devices whose only use is fraudulently to alter electricity meters and (b) to sell those devices to a person who

intends merely to re-sell them and not himself to use them, does that agreement constitute a common law conspiracy to defraud?

2 Alternatively, is such an agreement properly charged as a statutory conspiracy to aid, abet counsel or procure persons unknown to commit offences under s 2 of the Theft Act 1978? ...

[His Lordship quoted from the speech of Lord Bridge of Harwich in *R v Ayres* [1984] AC 447 and continued:]

I therefore turn to consider whether it was necessary for the prosecution in order to secure a conviction on count 2 to aver and prove a dishonest agreement actually to use the black boxes so as to defraud the intended victims, various electricity boards ...

The real question ... is whether in order to secure conviction on count 2 it was necessary to aver and prove a dishonest agreement by the respondents actually to use the black boxes, the submission being that it was not enough to show only an intention that such a dishonest use should follow their dishonest manufacture and sale ...

[His Lordship referred to a number of authorities including *Attorney General's Reference (No 1 of 1982)* [1983] QB 751, concerning a dishonest agreement to produce, label and distribute bottles of whiskey so as to represent them as containing whiskey of a well-known brand which in fact they did not contain, and said:]

In my view the respondents were liable to be convicted of conspiracy to defraud because they agreed to manufacture and sell and thus put into circulation dishonest devices, the sole purpose of which was to cause loss just as the former defendants in the case just referred to would, apart from the jurisdictional problem, have been liable to be convicted to defraud because they agreed dishonestly to produce, label and distribute bottles of whiskey, the sole purpose of the sale of which was to defraud potential purchasers of those bottles ...

In the result I would allow the appeals, answer certified question 1 'Yes' and certified question 2 'No'. I would restore the convictions of the respondents on count 2 ...

Welham v DPP [1961] AC 103 (HL)

Lord Radcliffe: ... Now, I think that there are one or two things that can be said with confidence about the meaning of this word 'defraud'. It requires a person as its object: that is, defrauding involves doing something to someone. Although in the nature of things it is almost invariably associated with the obtaining of an advantage for the person who commits the fraud, it is the effect upon the person who is the object of the fraud that ultimately determines its meaning. This is nonetheless true because since the middle of the last century the law has not required an indictment to specify the person intended to be defrauded or to prove intent to defraud a particular person.

Second, popular speech does not give, and I do not think ever has given, any sure guide as to the limits of what is meant by 'to defraud'. It may mean to cheat someone. It may mean to practise a fraud on someone. It may mean to deprive someone by deceit of something which is regarded as belonging to him or, though not belonging to him, as due to him or his right. It passes easily into metaphor, as does so much of the English natural speech. Murray's *New English Dictionary* instances such usages as defrauding a man of his due praise or his hopes. Rudyard Kipling in the First World War wrote of our 'angry and defrauded young'. There is nothing in any of this that suggests that to defraud is in ordinary speech confined to the idea of depriving a man by deceit of some economic advantage or inflicting upon him some economic loss.

Has the law ever so confined it? In my opinion there is no warrant for saying that it has ...

Of course, as I have said, in 99 cases out of 100 the intent to deceive one person to his prejudice merely connotes the deceiver's intention of obtaining an advantage for himself by inflicting a corresponding loss upon the person deceived. In all such cases the economic explanation is sufficient. But in that special line of cases where the person deceived is a public authority or a person holding a public office, deceit may secure an advantage for the deceiver without causing anything that can fairly be called either a pecuniary or an economic injury to the person deceived. If there could be no intent to defraud in the eyes of the law without an intent to inflict a pecuniary or economic injury, such cases as these could not have been punished as forgeries at common law, in which an intent to defraud is an essential element of the offence, yet I am satisfied that they were regularly so treated ...

Lord Denning: ... If a drug addict forges a doctor's prescription so as to enable him to get drugs from a chemist, he has, I should have thought, an intent to defraud, even though he intends to pay the chemist the full price and no one is a penny the worse off ...

... It has long been ruled that it is no answer to a charge of forgery to say that there was no intent to defraud any particular person, because a general intent to defraud is sufficient to constitute the crime. So also it is no answer to say that there was no intent to defraud the recipient, if there was intent to defraud somebody else: see *R v Taylor* (1779) 1 Leach 214 ...

R v Moses and Ansbro [1991] Crim LR 617 (CA)

Facts: The two appellants were charged with conspiracy to defraud by facilitating applications by immigrants to get work permits, notwithstanding that they were barred from so doing by a passport stamp. The first step was obtaining a National Insurance number, which required attendance with documents for checking and the completion of form CF8. An applicant whose passport bore a stamp prohibiting him from working would be refused a National Insurance number. It was alleged that the appellants conspired to ensure that such applications were not turned down by withholding from the departmental supervisors the existence of the stamp in the applicants' passports. They obtained blank CF8 forms, the first appellant completed them and the second appellant signed them and obtained a countersignature from another member of staff, withholding the evidence that the applicant was barred from working. Thus, the CF8s were successfully introduced into the system and the risk of the applications being turned down avoided. On appeal.

Held, dismissing the appeals, in by-passing the system, they were practising a deception on the department by causing the CF8s to enter the system as though they had been properly processed. It was clear that they intended that the department should treat the applications as regular in form and in compliance with procedure. They recognised that had the proper procedures been followed there was at least a chance that the applications would fail. This was a conspiracy to defraud. Officers of the department who played a part in processing the applications which, on their true facts, ought not to have been processed, were acting contrary to their public duty, and where the intended victim of a conspiracy to defraud was a person performing public duties, it was sufficient if the purpose was to cause him to contravene that duty, and the intended means of achieving it were dishonest. The purpose need not involve causing economic loss to anyone (see the *dictum* in *Scott* (1974) 60 Cr App R 124 at 131) ... The department was entitled to decide how the National Insurance contributions scheme should be administered, both locally and nationally, and it was not accepted that it was not defrauded by the circumvention of the system.

R v Landy [1981] 1 WLR 355 (CA)

Lawton LJ: ... What the prosecution had to prove was a conspiracy to defraud which is an agreement dishonestly to do something which will or may cause loss or prejudice to another. The offence is one of dishonesty. This is the all-important ingredient which must be stressed by the judge in his directions to the jury and must not be minimised in any way. There is always a danger that a jury may think that proof of an irregularity followed by loss is proof of dishonesty. The dishonesty to be proved must be in the minds and intentions of the defendants. It is to their states of mind that the jury must direct their attention. What the reasonable man or the jurors themselves would have believed or intended in the circumstances in which the defendants found themselves is not what the jury have to decide; but what a reasonable man or they themselves would have believed or intended in similar circumstances may help them to decide what in fact individual defendants believed or intended. An assertion by a defendant that throughout a transaction he acted honestly does not have to be accepted but has to be weighed like any other piece of evidence. If that was the defendant's state of mind, or may have been, he is entitled to be acquitted. But if the jury, applying their own notions of what is honest and what is not, conclude that he could not have believed that he was acting honestly, then the element of dishonesty will have been established. What a jury must not do is to say to themselves: 'If we had been in his place we would have known we were acting dishonestly so he must have known he was'. What they can say is: 'We are sure he was acting dishonestly because we can see no reason why a man of his intelligence and experience would not have appreciated, as right-minded people would have done, that what he was doing was dishonest'. In our judgment this is the way *R v Feely* [1973] QB 530 should be applied in cases where the issue of dishonesty arises. It is also the way in which the jury should have been directed in this case but, unfortunately, they were not ...

Wai Yu-Tsang v The Queen [1992] 1 AC 269 (PC)

Lord Goff of Chieveley: ... [*Welham v DPP* [1961] AC 103] establishes that the expression 'intent to defraud' is not to be given a narrow meaning, involving an intention to cause economic loss to another. In broad terms, it means simply an intention to practise a fraud on another, or an intention to act to the prejudice of another man's right ...

[His Lordship then referred to *R v Scott* [1975] AC 819 and to the speech of Lord Diplock and said:]

With the greatest respect to Lord Diplock, their Lordships consider this categorisation to be too narrow. In their opinion, in agreement with the approach of Lord Radcliffe in *Welham v DPP* [1961] AC 103, the cases concerned with persons performing public duties are not to be regarded as a special category in the manner described by Lord Diplock, but rather as exemplifying the general principle that conspiracies to defraud are not restricted to cases of intention to cause the victim economic loss ...

> ... In *R v Allsop* 64 Cr App R 29 what the defendant agreed to do was to present the company with false particulars, in reliance upon which, as he knew, the company would decide whether to enter into hire-purchase transactions. It is then necessary to consider whether that could constitute a conspiracy to defraud, notwithstanding that the defendant's underlying purpose or motive was not to damage any economic interest of the company but to ensure that the transaction went through so that he would earn his commission. Their Lordships can see no reason why such an agreement should not be a conspiracy to defraud the company, substantially for the reasons given by the Court of Appeal. The defendant was, for his own purposes, dishonestly supplying the company with false information which persuaded it to accept risks which it would or might not have accepted if it had known the true facts. Their Lordships cannot see why this was not an agreement to practise a fraud on the company because ... it was a dishonest agreement to employ a deceit which imperilled the economic interests of the company ...
>
> ... Their Lordships are ... reluctant to allow this part of the law to become enmeshed in a distinction, sometimes artificially drawn, between intention and recklessness. The question whether particular facts reveal a conspiracy to defraud depends upon what the conspirators have dishonestly agreed to do, and in particular whether they have agreed to practise a fraud on somebody. For this purpose it is enough for example that, as in *R v Allsop* and in the present case, the conspirators have dishonestly agreed to bring about a state of affairs which they realise will or may deceive the victim into so acting, or failing to act, that he will suffer economic loss or his economic interests will be put at risk. It is however important in such a case, as the Court of Appeal stressed in *R v Allsop*, to distinguish a conspirator's intention (or immediate purpose) dishonestly to bring about such a state of affairs from his motive (or underlying purpose). The latter may be benign to the extent that he does not wish the victim or potential victim to suffer harm; but the mere fact that it is benign will not of itself prevent the agreement from constituting a conspiracy to defraud. Of course, if the conspirators were not acting dishonestly, there will have been no conspiracy to defraud; and in any event their benign purpose (if it be such) is a matter which, if they prove to be guilty, can be taken into account at the stage of sentence ...

Conspiracy to corrupt public morals; conspiracy to outrage public decency

The existence of these offences was confirmed by the House of Lords in *Shaw v DPP* [1962] AC 220 and *Knuller v DPP* [1973] AC 435 and their existence has been preserved by s 5(3) of the Criminal Law Act 1977 (set out *above*).

These offences have been interpreted very restrictively. In essence, 'corrupting public morals' involves undermining the very fabric of society; 'outraging public decency' means going considerably further than shocking reasonable people.

Shaw v DPP [1962] AC 220 (HL)

Lord Tucker: ... The first count charged the appellant in the following terms:

> Statement of offence: Conspiracy to corrupt public morals.
>
> Particulars of offence: Frederick Charles Shaw on divers days between the first day of October 1959 and 23 July 1960, within the jurisdiction of the Central Criminal Court conspired with certain persons who inserted

> advertisements in issues of a magazine entitled 'Ladies Directory' numbered 7, 7 revised, 8, 9, 10 and a supplement thereto, and with certain other persons whose names are unknown, by means of the said magazine and the said advertisements to induce readers thereof to resort to the said advertisers for the purposes of fornication and of taking part in ... other disgusting and immoral acts and exhibitions with intent thereby to debauch and corrupt the morals as well of youth as of divers other liege subjects of Our Lady the Queen and to raise and create in their minds inordinate and lustful desires ...

... It has for long been accepted that there are some conspiracies which are criminal although the acts agreed to be done are not *per se* criminal or tortious if done by individuals. Such conspiracies form a third class in addition to the well-known and more clearly defined conspiracies to do acts which are unlawful, in the sense of criminal or tortious, or to do lawful acts by unlawful means. Assuming that the corruption of public morals by the acts of an individual may not be criminal or tortious, does it follow that a conspiracy by two or more persons to this end is not indictable? The difficulty with regard to this third class of conspiracy has always been to define its limits or give a label which will include all its manifestations ...

It was further contended for the appellant that in any event the particulars in the indictment and the evidence adduced in support thereof were insufficient to support a conviction for conspiring to corrupt public morals. It was said that neither fornication nor prostitution are illegal and that, in any event, there is no precedent for holding that such conduct tends to corrupt and deprave adult males.

My Lords, I think that these were matters for the decision of the jury and that the learned judge was right in ruling that there was a case to be left to them. There was material in this case to support the view that some of the advertisements in the magazines indicated that the advertisers were willing to take part in acts of sexual perversion. This element was, I think, conclusive against the appellant's submission, but I am not to be taken as expressing the view that in the absence of this feature the case should have been withdrawn from the jury, who must be the final arbiters in such matters, as they are on the question of obscenity. They alone can adequately reflect the changing public view on such matters through the centuries ...

Lord Morris of Borth-y-Gest: My Lords, I have had the privilege of reading in advance the speeches which have been delivered by my noble and learned friend on the Woolsack and by my noble and learned friend Lord Tucker, and I am in agreement with them ...

I join ... with those of your Lordships who affirm that the law is not impotent to convict those who conspire to corrupt public morals ... [His Lordship went on to approve a statement in Kenny's *Outlines of Criminal Law*] that agreements by two or more persons may be criminal if they are agreements to do acts which are outrageously immoral or else are in some way extremely injurious to the public. There are certain manifestations of conduct which are an affront to and an attack upon recognised public standards of morals and decency, and which all well-disposed persons would stigmatise and condemn as deserving of punishment. The cases afford examples of the conduct of individuals which has been punished because it outraged public decency or because its tendency was to corrupt the public morals.

It is said that there is a measure of vagueness in a charge of conspiracy to corrupt public morals, and also that there might be peril of the launching of prosecutions in order to suppress unpopular or unorthodox views. My Lords, I entertain no anxiety on these lines. Even if accepted public standards may to some extent vary from generation to generation, current standards are in the keeping of juries, who can be trusted to maintain the corporate good sense of the community and to discern attacks upon values that must be preserved. If there were prosecutions which were not genuinely and fairly warranted juries would be quick to perceive this ...

Lord Hodson: My Lords, I am in full agreement with the speeches by my noble and learned friend on the Woolsack, and by my noble and learned friend Lord Tucker, and wish only to add a few sentences on the first count.

I am wholly satisfied that there is a common law misdemeanour of conspiracy to corrupt public morals. The judicial precedents which have been cited show conclusively to my mind that the courts have never abandoned their function as *custodes morum* by surrendering to the legislature the right and duty to apply established principles to new combinations of circumstances ...

That prostitution is not a punishable offence does not involve that it is regarded as a lawful activity ... I do not see why any reason why a conspiracy to encourage fornication and adultery should be regarded as outside the ambit of conspiracy to corrupt public morals ...

Since a criminal indictment is followed by the verdict of a jury it is true that the function of *custos morum* is in criminal cases ultimately performed by the jury, by whom, on a proper direction, each case will be decided. This I think is consonant with the course of the development of our law. One may take, as an example, the case of negligence where the standard of care of the reasonable man is regarded as fit to be determined by the jury. In the field of public morals it will thus be the morality of the man in the jury-box that will determine the fate of the accused, but this should hardly disturb the equanimity of anyone brought up in the traditions of our common law ...

Knuller (Publishing, Printing and Promotions) Ltd v DPP [1973] AC 435 (HL)

Lord Reid: My Lords, the accused took part in publishing a magazine which contained a wide variety of material thought to be of interest to those holding 'progressive' views. Much of this material is unobjectionable. Some would be distasteful to many people, some is more objectionable. In this case we are only concerned with some columns of advertisements appearing on inner pages of the magazine. These columns are headed 'Males'. In most cases these advertisements were inserted by homosexuals and their express purpose was to attract answers from persons who would indulge in homosexual practices with the advertisers. Sometimes persons answering the advertisements were to communicate directly with the advertisers. Sometimes they were to send their answers to the magazine and the answers were then forwarded to the advertisers ...

The first count charges a conspiracy to corrupt public morals. The particulars given are that between January and May 1969 the accused conspired together and with persons inserting the advertisements by means of the advertisements 'to induce readers thereof to meet those persons inserting such advertisements for the purpose of sexual practices taking place between male persons and to encourage readers thereof to indulge in such practices, with intent thereby to debauch and corrupt the morals as well of youth as of divers other liege subjects of Our Lady the Queen'.

It was decided by this House in *Shaw v DPP* [1962] AC 220 that conspiracy to corrupt public morals is a crime known to the law of England. So if the appellants are to succeed on this count, either this House must reverse that decision or there must be sufficient grounds for distinguishing this case. The appellants' main argument is that we should reconsider that decision; alternatively they submit that it can and should be distinguished.

I dissented in *Shaw's* case. On reconsideration I still think that the decision was wrong and I see no reason to alter anything which I said in my speech. But it does not follow that I should now support a motion to reconsider the decision. I have said more than once in recent cases that our change of practice in no longer regarding previous decisions of this House as absolutely binding does not mean that whenever we think that a previous decision was wrong we should reverse it. In the general interest of certainty in the law we must be sure that there is some very good reason before we so act. We were informed that there had been at least 30 and probably many more convictions of this new crime in the 10 years which have elapsed since *Shaw's* case was decided, and it does not appear that there has been manifest injustice or that any attempt has been made to widen the scope of the new crime. I do not regard our refusal to reconsider *Shaw's* case as in any way justifying any attempt to widen the scope of the decision and I would oppose any attempt to do so. But I think that however wrong or anomalous the decision may be it must stand and apply to cases reasonably analogous unless or until it is altered by Parliament.

I hold that opinion the more strongly in this case by reason of the nature of the subject-matter we are dealing with. I said in *Shaw's* case [1962] AC 220, 275 and I repeat that Parliament and Parliament alone is the proper authority to change the law with regard to the punishment of immoral acts. Rightly or wrongly the law was determined by the decision in *Shaw*. Any alteration of the law as so determined must in my view be left to Parliament ...

Although I would not support reconsidering *Shaw's* case I think that we ought to clarify one or two matters. In the first place conspiracy to corrupt public morals is something of a misnomer. It really means to corrupt the morals of such members of the public as may be influenced by the matter published by the accused.

Next I think that the meaning of the word 'corrupt' requires some clarification. One of my objections to the *Shaw* decision is that it leaves too much to the jury. I recognise that in the end it must be for the jury to say whether the matter published is likely to lead to corruption. But juries, unlike judges, are not expected to be experts in the use of the English language and I think that they ought to be given some assistance ...

... I think that the jury should be told in one way or another that although in the end the question whether matter is corrupting is for them, they should keep in mind the current standards of ordinary decent people.

I can now turn to the appellants' second argument. They say that homosexual acts between adult males in private are now lawful so it is unreasonable and cannot be the law that other persons are guilty of an offence if they merely put in touch with one another two males who wish to indulge in such acts. But there is a material difference between merely exempting certain conduct from criminal penalties and making it lawful in the full sense. Prostitution and gaming afford examples of this difference ...

I find nothing in the Act to indicate that Parliament thought or intended to lay down that indulgence in these practices is not corrupting. I read the Act as saying that, even though it may be corrupting, if people choose to corrupt themselves in this way that is their affair and the law will not interfere. But no licence is given to others to encourage the practice. So if one accepts *Shaw's* case as rightly decided it must be left to each jury to decide in the circumstances of each case whether people were likely to be corrupted. In this case the jury were properly directed and it is impossible to say that they reached a wrong conclusion. It is not for us to say whether or not we agree with it. So I should dismiss the appeal as regards the first count.

The second count is conspiracy to outrage public decency, the particulars, based on the same facts, being that the accused conspired with persons inserting lewd disgusting and offensive advertisements in the magazine 'by means of the publication of the said magazine containing the said advertisements to outrage public decency'.

The crucial question here is whether in this generalised form this is an offence known to the law. There are a number of particular offences well-known to the law which involve indecency in various ways but none of them covers the facts of this case. We were informed that a charge of this character has never been brought with regard to printed matter on sale to the public. The recognised offences with regard to such matter are based on its being obscene, ie likely to corrupt or deprave. The basis of the new offence, if it is one, is quite different. It is that ordinary decent-minded people who are not likely to become corrupted or depraved will be outraged or utterly disgusted by what they read. To my mind questions of public policy of the utmost importance are at stake here.

I think that the objections to the creation of this generalised offence are similar in character to but even greater than the objections to the generalised offence of conspiracy to corrupt public morals.

In upholding the decision in *Shaw's* case we are, in my view, in no way affirming or lending any support to the doctrine that the courts still have some general or residual power either to create new offences or so to widen existing offences as to make punishable conduct of a type hitherto not subject to punishment. Apart from some statutory offences of limited application, there appears to be neither precedent nor authority of any kind for punishing the publication of written or printed matter on the ground that it is indecent as distinct from being obscene. To say that published matter offends against public decency adds nothing to saying that it is indecent. To say, as is said in this charge, that it outrages public decency adds a new factor: it seems to me to mean no more than that the degree of indecency is such that decent members of the public who read material will not merely feel shocked or disgusted but will feel outraged. If this charge is an attempt to introduce something new into the criminal law it cannot be saved because it is limited to what a jury might think to be a high degree of indecency ...

I must now consider what the effect would be if this new generalised crime were held to exist. If there were in any book, new or old, a few pages or even a few sentences which any jury could find to be outrageously indecent, those who took part in its publication and sale would risk conviction. I can see no way of denying to juries the free hand which *Shaw's* case gives them in cases of conspiracy to corrupt public morals. There would be no defence based on literary, artistic or scientific merit. The undertaking given in Parliament with regard to obscene publications would not apply to this quite different crime. Notoriously many old words, commonly regarded as classics of the highest merit, contain passages which many a juryman might regard as outrageously indecent. It has been generally supposed that the days for bowdlerising the classics were long past, but the introduction of this new crime might make publishers of such works think twice. It may be said that no prosecution would ever be brought except in a very bad case. But I have expressed on previous occasions my opinion that a bad law is not defensible on the ground that it will be judiciously administered. To recognise this new crime would go contrary to the whole trend of public policy followed by Parliament in recent times. I have no hesitation in saying that in my opinion the conviction of the accused on the second count must be quashed ...

Lord Morris of Borth-y-Gest: ... The point of law which the Court of Appeal certified as being of general importance was:

> whether an agreement by two or more persons to insert advertisements in a magazine whereby adult male advertisers seek replies from other adult males who are prepared to consent to commit homosexual acts with them in private, is capable of amounting to the offence of conspiracy to corrupt public morals ...

I agree ... with Fenton Atkinson LJ when he said in the Court of Appeal [1972] 2 QB 179, 187 that:

> it was for the jury to say whether by present-day standards, which they were there to represent, these advertisements were in their view corrupting of public morals even though Parliament had provided that acts of this kind between consulting male adults should no longer be a crime.

I pass, then, to consider the second main submission on behalf of the appellants. It was urged that *Shaw's* case [1962] AC 220 should now be reconsidered. I reject this submission primarily because, in my view, *Shaw's* case was correctly decided. Even had I been of a different opinion I would nevertheless consider it wholly inappropriate now to review the decision. Such a course would not, in my view, be warranted or desirable within the ambit of the statement made in this House on 26 July 1966 [*Practice Statement (Judicial Precedent)* [1966] 1 WLR 1234]. That statement drew attention to the especial need for certainty as to the criminal law. It was clearly held in *Shaw's* case that there had been and that there continued to be as part of the criminal law of England the offence of conspiracy to corrupt public morals. The decision established that fact with certainty. If any person had previously had doubts as to this their doubts were removed. There are some who regret that there should be such an offence and who would wish to change the law: their course is to persuade Parliament to change it. Once this House in its judicial capacity was satisfied that the offence was known to and existed as part of the law it would neither have been proper nor would it have been within its judicial province to proclaim or to suggest that the law should be forgotten or ignored or that its force should be denied. The decision in *Shaw's* case was made nearly 11 years ago. We were told that in one period of four years since that time there had been over 30 prosecutions for conspiracy to corrupt public morals: we do not know how many in total there have been. Those prosecutions were for an offence which this House had authoritatively laid down to be a part of our criminal law. It is accepted that all relevant authorities were examined before this House came to its decision. There comes a stage when further disputation should cease ...

It has sometimes been asserted that in his speech in *Shaw's* case Viscount Simonds was proclaiming that the courts had power to extend the sphere of the law by devising new extensions of the operations of the criminal law; his use of the words 'residual power' is pointed to as a basis of what is asserted. In my view, the sustained reasoning of his speech refutes the assertion. In the first place, he expressly and firmly repudiated any notion that there is in the judges a right to create new criminal offences. He held, in agreement with Lord Tucker, that the offence of conspiracy to corrupt public morals was an offence known to the common law. He then proceeded to demonstrate that if offending acts do reveal a conspiracy to corrupt public morals it is not to be said that no offence has been committed merely because the particular acts are novel or unprovided for or are unprecedented. He pointed out that Parliament from time to time by legislative acts alters the common law but that yet there are 'unravished remnants' of it. The residual power to which he referred is the power 'where no statute has yet intervened to supersede the common law, to superintend those offences which are prejudicial to the public welfare' ([1962] AC 220, 268). The reasoning is directed to the enforcement of the common law to the extent that its power may reach: the reasoning disclaims the existence of an arbitrary power to refashion the common law ...

Lord Simon of Glaisdale: ... It follows, in my view, that your Lordships should follow *Shaw v DPP* on the matter as to which it constituted a direct authority: namely, that the offence of conspiracy to corrupt public morals is part of the criminal law of England ... [T]here are some suggestions in the speeches in *Shaw v DPP* that the courts have still some role to play in the way of general superintendence of morals. This was a phrase used in various 18th and 19th century cases, 'superintendence of' meaning 'jurisdiction over'. Whatever may have been the position in the 18th century – and there is more than one clear indication that the courts of common law then assumed that they were fitted for and bound to exercise such a role – I do not myself believe that such is any part of their present function. As will appear, I do not think that 'conspiracy to corrupt public morals' invites a general tangling with codes of morality ... [I]t has [also] been suggested that the speeches in *Shaw v DPP* indicated that the courts retain a residual power to create new offences. I do not think they did so. Certainly, it is my view that the courts have no more power to create new offences than they have to abolish those already established in the law; both tasks are for Parliament. What the courts can and should do (as was truly laid down in *Shaw v DPP*) is to recognise the applicability of established offences to new circumstances to which they are relevant. [Next] I have already indicated my view that *Shaw v DPP* is not authority for the proposition that male homosexualism, or even its facilitation or encouragement, are themselves as a matter of law corrupting of public morals. It is for the jury to decide as a matter of fact whether the conduct alleged to be the subject-matter of the conspiracy charged is in any particular case corrupting of public morals. Last, it was suggested in argument before your Lordships that, if *Shaw v DPP* were not overruled, it would be open to juries to convict if they thought that the conduct in question was liable to 'lead morally astray'. But all that was decided in *Shaw v DPP* was that, in the general context of the whole of the summing up in that case, the use of the phrase 'lead morally astray' was not a misdirection. *Shaw v DPP* must not be taken as an authority that 'corrupt public morals' and 'lead morally astray' are interchangeable expressions. On the contrary, 'corrupt' is a strong word. The Book of Common Prayer, following the Gospel, has '... where rust and moth doth corrupt'. The words 'corrupt public morals' suggest conduct which a jury might find to be destructive of the very fabric of society ...

[Turning to the second count, conspiracy to outrage public decency, Lord Simon said:]

The following questions, therefore, arise on this part of the case: (1) is there a general common law offence of outraging public decency, or only the particular offences which the cases establish? (2) Is there a common law offence of conspiring to outrage public decency? ...

[His Lordship reviewed the authorities and said:]

I think that the authorities establish a common law offence of conduct which outrages public decency.

If there is a common law offence of conduct which outrages public decency, a conspiracy to outrage public decency is also a common law offence, as an agreement to do an illegal act. In *Shaw v DPP* [1962] AC 220, 267, Viscount Simonds seems to have considered that the conduct there in question was indictable also as a conspiracy 'to affront public decency'.

In my view, counsel for the appellants was right to concede that there is a common law offence of conspiring to outrage public decency ...

Lord Kilbrandon: ... My Lords, I have had the advantage of reading in advance the speech prepared by my noble and learned friend, Lord Simon of Glaisdale, and since I find myself in agreement with it I would avoid repeating in detail in my own words the conclusions at which he has arrived ...

R v Gibson [1990] 2 QB 619 (CA)

Lord Lane CJ: ... Richard Norman Gibson and Peter Sebastian Sylveire were convicted ... of outraging public decency, contrary to common law ...

The facts of the case were unusual, but simple, Sylveire ran an art gallery called the Young Unknowns Gallery in the Cut, London, SE1. Displayed in that gallery was an article which had been assembled by Gibson. The article consisted of a model's head to each ear of which was attached an earring. The earring was made out of a freeze-dried human foetus of three or four months' gestation. The foetus was attached to the ear by means of a ring fitting tapped into the skull of the foetus, and the upper end of that fitting was attached to the lobe of the model's ear.

The gallery was in a parade of shops. The general public was invited to and had access to the gallery during the exhibition. No payment was required for entry. Gibson had, apparently unknown to his co-defendant, done some advertising promotion of this particular article, with the result that the police and press were on the scene not long after the exhibition had opened its doors. The gallery charged a commission on any works which were sold to members of the public.

The article in question was one of 41 items which had been selected for display out of a much larger number by Sylveire. It was Exhibit No 9, and was described in the catalogue as 'Human Earrings'. Although it was not suggested that Sylveire had taken active steps to publicise this particular exhibit, there was no doubt that the more people who attended the gallery, the better pleased Sylveire would be, and the greater would be the likelihood of selling exhibits ...

The first question to decide then is whether there is an offence at common law of outraging public decency. The answer to that question is to be found in the speech of Lord Simon of Glaisdale in *Knuller (Publishing, Printing and Promotions) Ltd v DPP* [1973] AC 435, 493:

> Fourth, my noble and learned friend, Lord Morris of Borth-y-Gest, in *Shaw v DPP* [1962] AC 200 where, though there was no count of conspiracy to outrage decency, most of the cases were reviewed, said at 292: 'The cases afford examples of the conduct of individuals which has been punished because it outraged public decency ...' And my noble and learned friend, Lord Reid, though dissenting on the main issue, said at 281: 'I think that they [the authorities] establish that it is an indictable offence to say or do or exhibit anything in public which outrages public decency, whether or not it also tends to corrupt and deprave those who see or hear it'.

Lord Morris of Borth-y-Gest and Lord Kilbrandon seem to have agreed with that view.

The point is not taken before us that no such offence exists. We respectfully agree with their Lordships in *Knuller* that it does ...

... [W]here the charge is one outraging public decency, there is no requirement that the prosecution should prove an intention to outrage ... If the publication takes place, and if it is deliberate, there is, in the words of Lord Russell in *R v Lemon* [1979] AC 617, 657–58: 'no justification for holding that there is no offence when the publisher is incapable for some reason particular to himself of agreeing with the jury on the true nature of the publication' ...

CONSPIRACY TO COMMIT A CRIME ABROAD

Subject to the Sexual Offences (Conspiracy and Incitement) Act 1996, the English courts only have jurisdiction to try a conspiracy if they would have the jurisdiction to try the substantive offence.

Attorney General's Reference (No 1 of 1982) [1983] 1 QB 751

Lord Lane CJ: This is a reference by Her Majesty's Attorney General under s 36 of the Criminal Justice Act 1972. The defendants were charged with conspiracy to defraud. The particulars of the offence were that they had conspired together and with others to defraud such companies and persons, and in particular X Co Ltd, as might be caused loss by unlawful labelling, sale, supply or marketing of whiskey purporting to be that of X label products, the said X Co Ltd being the proprietors of the labelled products and owning the copyright in the label ...

The real question must in each case be what was the true object of the agreement entered into by the conspirators? In our judgment, the object here was to obtain money from prospective purchasers of whiskey in the Lebanon by falsely representing that it was the X company's whiskey. It may well be that if the plan had been carried out, some damage could have resulted to the X company. But that would have been a side effect or incidental consequence of the conspiracy, and not its object. There may be many conspiracies aimed at particular victims which in their execution result in loss or damage to third parties. It would be contrary to principle, as well as being impracticable for the courts to attribute to defendants constructive intentions to defraud third parties based on what the defendants should have foreseen as probable or possible consequences. In each case to determine the object of the conspiracy, the court must see what the defendants actually agreed to do. Had it not been for the jurisdictional problem, we have no doubt the charge against these conspirators would have been conspiracy to defraud potential purchasers of the whiskey, for that was the true object of the agreement ...

SEXUAL OFFENCES (CONSPIRACY AND INCITEMENT) ACT 1996

This Act was passed to deal with the problem of 'child sex tourism', that is the activities of paedophiles who travels overseas (eg to Thailand or the Philippines) to have sex with child prostitutes.

Section 1

Conspiracy to commit certain sexual acts outside the United Kingdom

(1) Where each of the following conditions is satisfied in the case of any agreement, Part I of the Criminal Law Act 1977 (conspiracy) has effect in relation to the agreement as it has effect in relation to an agreement falling within section 1(1) of that Act.

(2) The first condition is that the pursuit of the agreed course of conduct would at some stage involve -

(a) an act by one or more of the parties, or

(b) the happening of some other event,

intended to take place in a country or territory outside the United Kingdom.

(3) The second condition is that that act or other event constitutes an offence under the law in force in that country or territory.

(4) The third condition is that the agreement would fall within section 1(1) of that Act as an agreement relating to the commission of a listed sexual offence but for the fact that the offence would not be an offence triable in England and Wales if committed in accordance with the parties' intentions.

(5) The fourth condition is that -

(a) a party to the agreement, or a party's agent, did anything in England and Wales in relation to the agreement before its formation, or

(b) a party to the agreement became a party in England and Wales (by joining it either in person or through an agent), or

(c) a party to the agreement, or a party's agent, did or omitted anything in England and Wales in pursuance of the agreement.

(6) In the application of Part I of that Act to such an agreement, any reference to an offence is to be read as a reference to what would be the listed sexual offence in question but for the fact that it is not an offence triable in England and Wales.

Note: The term 'listed sexual offence' is defined in the Schedule to the Sexual Offences (Conspiracy and Incitement) Act 1996:

- rape (s 1 of the Sexual Offences Act 1956), but only if the victim has not attained the age of 16.
- intercourse with a girl under the age of 13 (s 5 of the Sexual Offences Act 1956)
- intercourse with a girl under the age of 16 (s 6 of the Sexual Offences Act 1956)
- buggery (s 12 of the Sexual Offences Act 1956), but only if the victim has not attained the age of 16
- indecent assault on a girl (s 14 of the Sexual Offences Act 1956), provided that the victim has not attained the age of 16
- indecent assault on a boy (s 15 of the Sexual Offences Act 1956), provided that the victim has not attained the age of 16.
- indecent conduct towards a young child (s 1 of the Indecency with Children Act 1960).

OVERLAP BETWEEN STATUTORY CONSPIRACY AND CONSPIRACY TO DEFRAUD

The prosecution can choose whether to charge statutory conspiracy or conspiracy to defraud.

Section 12 of the Criminal Justice Act 1987

(1) If:

(a) a person agrees with any other person or persons that a course of conduct shall be pursued; and

(b) the course of conduct will necessarily amount to or involve the commission of any offence or offences by one or more parties to the agreement if the agreement is carried out in accordance with their intentions,

the fact that it will do so shall not preclude a charge of conspiracy to defraud being brought against them in respect of the agreement.

IMPOSSIBILITY AS A DEFENCE TO CONSPIRACY

Section 1(1)(b) of the Criminal Law Act 1977 effectively removes the defence of impossibility. For statutory conspiracy, the key question is whether the agreement of the parties was to commit something which amounts to a criminal offence.

For common law conspiracy, the defence of impossibility remains. The ambit of this defence was considered by the House of Lords in *DPP v Nock* [1978] AC 979.

DPP v Nock [1978] AC 979 (HL)

Lord Scarman: ... Five persons, including the two appellants, David Michael Nock and Kevin Charles Alsford, appeared at the Snaresbrook Crown Court on 5 January 1977, to answer an indictment charging them with a number of drug offences. Nock and Alsford were convicted upon several counts but your Lordships' House is concerned only with their conviction upon the first count in the indictment. It charged them (and others) with conspiracy to contravene s 4 of the Misuse of Drugs Act 1971. The section provides by subsection (1) that subject to regulations (which are of no present relevance) it shall not be lawful for a person to produce a controlled drug and by subsection (2) that it is an offence to produce a controlled drug in contravention of subsection (1). The particulars of offence, after being amended, were as follows:

> Kevin Charles Alsford, David Michael Nock [and three other named defendants] on divers days before 23 September 1975, conspired together and with other persons unknown to produce a controlled drug of Class A, namely cocaine.

The indictment makes plain that the Crown is alleging in this case a conspiracy to commit a crime: and no one has suggested that the particulars fail to disclose an offence known to the law. But the appellants submit, and it is not disputed by the Crown that the agreement as proved was narrower in scope than the conspiracy charged. When the case was before the Court of Appeal, counsel on both sides agreed that the evidence went to prove that the appellants agreed together to obtain cocaine by separating it from the other substance or substances contained in a powder which they had obtained from one of their co-defendants, a Mr Mitchell. They believed that the powder was a mixture of cocaine and lignocaine, and that they would be able to produce cocaine from it. In fact the powder was lignocaine hydrochloride, an anaesthetic used in dentistry, which contains no cocaine at all. It is impossible to produce, by separation or otherwise, cocaine from lignocaine. The agreement between the appellants was correctly summarised by the Court of Appeal, when certifying the point of law, as an agreement 'to pursue a course of action which could never in fact have produced cocaine'.

The appellants made a number of attempts – all of them, of course, unsuccessful – to extract cocaine from their powder. It was not until after they had been arrested and the powder seized by the police and sent for analysis that they learnt to their surprise that there was no way in which cocaine could be produced from it.

The trial judge in his direction to the jury, the Court of Appeal in their judgment dismissing the two appeals, treated this impossibility as an irrelevance. In their view the agreement was what mattered: and there was plain evidence of an agreement to produce cocaine, even though unknown to the two conspirators it could not be done. Neither the trial judge nor the Court of Appeal thought it necessary to carry their analysis of the agreement further. The trial judge described it simply as an agreement to produce cocaine. The Court of Appeal thought it enough that the prosecution had proved 'an agreement to do an act which was forbidden by s 4 of the Misuse of Drugs Act 1971'. Both descriptions are accurate, as far as they go. But neither contains any reference to the limited nature of the agreement proved: it was an agreement upon a specific course of conduct with the object of producing cocaine, and limited to that course of conduct. Since it could not result in the production of cocaine, the two appellants by pursuing it could not commit the statutory offence of producing a controlled drug. The appellants, who did get a chemist to take on the impossible job of extracting cocaine from the powder, may perhaps be treated as having completed their agreed course of conduct: if so, they completed it without committing the statutory offence. Perhaps, however, it would be more accurate to treat them as having desisted before they had completed all that they had agreed to do: but it makes no difference because, had they completed all that they had agreed to do, no cocaine would have been produced.

If, therefore, their agreement, limited as it was to a specific course of conduct which could not result in the commission of the statutory offence, constituted (as the Court of Appeal held) a criminal conspiracy, the strange consequence ensues, that by agreeing upon a course of conduct which was not criminal (or unlawful) the appellants were guilty of conspiring to commit a crime.

Upon these facts the appellants submit that the evidence reveals no 'conspiracy at large', by which they mean an agreement in general terms to produce cocaine if and when they could find a suitable raw material, but only the limited agreement, to which I have referred. Counsel for the appellants concedes that, if two or more persons decide to go into business as cocaine producers, or, to take another example, as assassins for hire (eg 'Murder Incorporated'), the mere fact that in the course of performing their agreement they attempt to produce cocaine from a raw material which could not possibly yield it or (in the second example), stab a corpse, believing it to be the body of a living man, would not avail them as a defence: for the performance of their general agreement would not be rendered impossible by such transient frustrations. But performance of the limited agreement proved in this case could not in any circumstances have involved the commission of the offence created by the statute.

The answer sought to be made by the Crown (and accepted by the Court of Appeal) is that the offence of conspiracy is committed when an agreement to commit, or to try to commit, a crime is reached, whether or not anything is, or can be, done to perform it. It is wrong, upon their view, to treat conspiracy as a 'preliminary' or 'inchoate' crime: for its criminality depends in no way upon its being a step towards the commission of the substantive offence (or, at common law, the unlawful act). Upon this view of the law the scope of agreement is irrelevant: all that is needed to constitute the crime is the intention to commit the substantive offence and the agreement to try to do so.

... In *Board of Trade v Owen* [1957] AC 602, 623-25 Lord Tucker, quoting with approval some observations from R S Wright J's little classic, *The Law of Criminal Conspiracies and Agreements* (1873) and some passages from Sir William Holdsworth's (somewhat larger) work, *The History of English Law*, accepted that the historical basis of the crime of conspiring to commit a crime (the case with which we are now concerned) was that it developed as an 'auxiliary' (R S Wright's word) to the law which creates the crime agreed to be committed. Lord Tucker accepted Holdsworth's comment (at 625) that 'it was inevitable therefore, as Stephen has said, that conspiracy should come to be regarded as a form of attempt to commit a wrong'. Lord Tucker concluded his survey with these words at 626:

> Accepting the above as the historical basis of the crime of conspiracy, it seems to me that the whole object of making such agreements punishable is to prevent the commission of the substantive offence before it has even reached the stage of an attempt ...

Lord Tucker, in whose opinion the other noble and learned Lords sitting with him concurred, by stressing the 'auxiliary' nature of the crime of conspiracy and by explaining its justification as being to prevent the commission of substantive offences, has placed the crime firmly in the same class and category as attempts to commit a crime. Both are criminal because they are steps towards the commission of a substantive offence. The distinction between the two is that, whereas a 'proximate' act is that which constitutes the crime of attempt, agreement is the necessary ingredient in conspiracy. The importance of the distinction is that agreement may, and usually will, occur well before the first step which can be said to be an attempt. The law of conspiracy thus makes possible an earlier intervention by the law to prevent the commission of the substantive offence. But the distinction has no relevance in determining whether the impossibility of committing the substantive offence should be a defence. Indeed upon the view of the law authoritatively explained and accepted in *Owen's* case [1957] AC 602, logic and justice would seem to require that the question as to the effect of the impossibility of the substantive offence should be answered in the same way, whether the crime charged be conspiracy or attempt ...

The Crown's argument, as developed before your Lordships, rests, in my judgment, upon a misconception of the nature of the agreement proved. This is a case not of an agreement to commit a crime capable of being committed in the way agreed upon, but frustrated by a supervening event making its completion impossible, which was the Crown's submission, but of an agreement upon a course of conduct which could not in any circumstances result in the statutory offence alleged, ie the offence of producing the controlled drug, cocaine ...

SUBSTANTIVE OFFENCES AND CONSPIRACY

Practice Note [1977] 2 All ER 540

Lord Widgery CJ at the sitting of the court announced the following practice direction made after consultation with the judges of the Queen's Bench Division:

1 In any case where an indictment contains substantive counts and a related conspiracy count, the judge should require the prosecution to justify the joinder, or, failing justification, to elect whether to proceed on the substantive or on the conspiracy counts.

2 A joinder is justified for this purpose if the judge considers that the interests of justice demands it.

ACQUITTAL OF ANOTHER PARTY TO A CONSPIRACY

Section 5 of the Criminal Law Act 1977

(8) The fact that the person or persons who, so far as appears from the indictment on which any person has been convicted of conspiracy, were the only other parties to the agreement on which his conviction was based has been acquitted of conspiracy by reference to that agreement (whether after being tried with the person convicted or separately) shall not be a ground for quashing his conviction unless under all the circumstances of the case his conviction is inconsistent with the acquittal of the other person or persons in question.

(9) Any rule of law or practice inconsistent with the provisions of subsection (8) above is hereby abolished.

CHAPTER 13

INCHOATE OFFENCES – INCITEMENT

Incitement is a common law offence. It is incitement to encourage another person to commit what would be an offence if the person carried it out.

ACTUS REUS

The act incited must amount to a crime: see *R v Tyrrell* [1894] 1 QB 710; *R v Whitehouse* [1977] QB 868. The encouragement can be express or implied: see *Invicta Plastics Ltd v Clare* [1976] RTR 251.

R v Tyrrell [1894] 1 QB 710 (CCR)

Facts: The question for the opinion of the court was, 'Whether it is an offence for a girl between the ages of 13 and 16 to aid and abet a male person in the commission of the misdemeanour of having unlawful carnal connection with her, or to solicit and incite a male person to commit that misdemeanour'.

Lord Coleridge CJ: The Criminal Law Amendment Act, 1885, was passed for the purpose of protecting women and girls against themselves. At the time it was passed there was a discussion as to what point should be fixed as the age of consent. That discussion ended in a compromise, and the age of consent was fixed at 16. With the object of protecting women and girls against themselves the Act of Parliament has made illicit connection with a girl under that age unlawful; if a man wishes to have such illicit connection he must wait until the girl is 16, otherwise he breaks the law; but it is impossible to say that the Act, which is absolutely silent about aiding or abetting, or soliciting or inciting, can have intended that the girls for whose protection it was passed should be punishable under it for the offences committed upon themselves. I am of opinion that this conviction ought to be quashed.

Mathew J: I am of the same opinion. I do not see how it would be possible to obtain convictions under the statute if the contention for the Crown were adopted, because nearly every section which deals with offences in respect of women and girls would create an offence in the woman or girl. Such a result cannot have been intended by the legislature. There is no trace in the statute of any intention to treat the woman or girl as criminal.

R v Whitehouse [1977] QB 868 (CA)

Scarman LJ: ... The indictment which the defendant faced in 1976 was an indictment charging him with incitement to commit incest, and the particulars of the offence charged were that he, on a date unknown between 1 December 1975, and 10 February 1976, unlawfully incited a girl then aged 15, who was to his and her knowledge his daughter, to have sexual intercourse with him. To that count he pleaded guilty, as also to a second count charging incitement to commit incest, but on a different occasion, and he pleaded guilty to that as well.

When the court saw those two counts framed in the way I have just described, we queried whether it was an offence known to law and we doubted whether it was because a girl aged 15 is incapable of committing the crime of incest. Later in this judgment it will be necessary to look at the terms of s 11 of the Sexual Offences Act 1956 but that shortly is the effect of the section so far as material to the issue in this case ...

We turn now to consider whether the indictment disclosed an offence known to the law. The count standing by itself does disclose such an offence because the count merely alleges incitement to commit incest. But when one goes on to the particulars one sees that the defendant is charged with inciting his daughter, a girl aged 15, to commit incest with him. The Crown recognises that there are difficulties in the drafting of the indictment. The Crown recognises that under s 11 of the Sexual Offences Act 1956 a girl aged 15 cannot commit incest. The relevant subsection is (1) and I read it:

> It is an offence for a woman of the age of 16 or over to permit a man whom she knows to be her ... father ... to have sexual intercourse with her by her consent.

It is of course accepted by the Crown that at common law the crime of incitement consists of inciting another person to commit a crime. When one looks at this incitement in the light of the particulars of the offence pleaded, one sees that it is charging the defendant with inciting a girl to commit a crime which in fact by statute she is incapable of committing. If therefore the girl was incapable of committing the crime alleged, how can the defendant be guilty of the common law crime of incitement? The Crown accepts the logic of that position and does not seek in this court to rely on s 11 of the Act of 1956 or to suggest that this man could be guilty of inciting his daughter to commit incest, to use the old phrase, as a principal in the first degree. But the Crown says that it is open to them upon this indictment to submit that it covers the offence of inciting the girl to aid and abet the man to commit the crime of incest upon her. Section 10 of the Act of 1956 makes it an offence for a man to have sexual intercourse with a woman whom he knows to be his daughter, and the Crown says that upon this indictment it is possible to say that the defendant has committed an offence known to the law, the offence being that of inciting his daughter under the age of 16 to aid and abet him to have sexual intercourse with her.

All this is clearly very strange and we will come to the problem of the substantive law a little later. At this stage, we have to ask ourselves whether the indictment framed in the terms to which I have referred can conceivably encompass the offence which the Crown now says is known to the law, that is to say, the offence of inciting this girl to aid and abet this man to have unlawful sexual intercourse with her. The Crown, accepting that the indictment is most ineptly drafted, nevertheless submits that under the broad principles governing the drafting and amendment of indictments all is cured by the existence of a plea of guilty. It will be obvious from the somewhat tortuous language in which it has been necessary to explain what the offence is that is said to be known to the law, that it would be a very odd-looking indictment indeed, and would certainly bear not even a faint resemblance to the particulars as pleaded.

[Counsel] for the defendant has understandably submitted that, however flexible be the rules allowing amendment, the language of this indictment is too far away from what the Crown says is the offence charged, to be able to encompass it. We think there is much to be said for that submission, but we are prepared to assume, for the purposes of this appeal, that the indictment can be cured, and accordingly we now read the indictment as an indictment charging this man with the offence of inciting a girl of 15 to aid and abet him to commit incest with her.

Is there such an offence known to the law? The difficulty arises from two features of the law to which I have already referred. First, at common law the crime of incitement consists of inciting another person to commit a crime ... The second difficult feature of the law is s 11 of the Act of 1956 to which I have already referred. A woman under the age of 16 cannot commit the crime of incest. But, says the Crown, a man can commit incest, and so they go on to make their submission that a girl of 15 can aid and abet him to do so.

There is no doubt of the general principle, namely that a person, provided always he or she is of the age of criminal responsibility, can be guilty of aiding or abetting a crime even though it be a crime which he or she cannot commit as a principal in the first degree. There are two famous illustrations in the books of this principle. A woman can aid and abet a rape so as herself to be guilty of rape, and a boy at an age where he is presumed impotent can nevertheless aid and abet a rape ...

But what if the person alleged to be aiding and abetting the crime is herself the victim of the crime? This poses the short question with which this appeal is concerned. Before we consider it we would comment that, if indeed it be the law that this girl aged 15 can be guilty of incest as the aider and abettor of a man who is seeking to have intercourse with her, then one has the strange situation that, although she cannot be guilty of the crime of incest under the section which formulates the conditions under which a woman may be found guilty of that crime, yet through this doctrine of aiding and abetting she can be guilty of the offence when it is committed by a man. That is an odd conclusion, but not necessarily to be rejected because of its oddity.

The important matters in our judgment are these. First this girl, aged 15, belongs to a class which is protected, but not punished, by ss 10 and 11 of the Sexual Offences Act 1956, and second the girl is alleged to be the victim of this notional crime. The whole question has an air of artificiality because nobody is suggesting either that the father has committed incest with her or that she has aided and abetted him to commit incest upon her. What is suggested is that the father has committed the crime of incitement because by his words and conduct he has incited her to do that which, of course, she never has done.

The question in our judgment is determined by authority. It is, strictly speaking, persuasive authority only because it deals with a different Act of Parliament, but it is a decision by a strong court which has declared a principle which is as applicable to the statutory provision with which we are concerned as to that with which that case was concerned. The case is *R v Tyrrell* [1894] 1 QB 710. It was a decision of the Court of Crown Cases Reserved and it was a five-judge court, consisting of Lord Coleridge CJ, Mathew, Grantham, Lawrence and Collins JJ. The headnote reads as follows:

> It is not a criminal offence for a girl between the ages of 13 and 16 to aid and abet a male person in committing, or to incite him to commit, the misdemeanour of having unlawful carnal knowledge of her contrary to s 5 of the Criminal Law Amendment Act 1885.

... In our judgment it is impossible, as a matter of principle, to distinguish *R v Tyrrell* from the present case. Clearly the relevant provisions of the Sexual Offences Act 1956 are intended to protect women and girls. Most certainly, s 11 is intended to protect girls under the age of 16 from criminal liability, and the Act as a whole exists, in so far as it deals with women and girls exposed to sexual threat, to protect them. The very fact that girls under the age of 16 are protected from criminal liability for what would otherwise be incest demonstrates that this girl who is said to have been the subject of incitement was being incited to do something which, if she did it, could not be a crime by her.

One can only avoid that conclusion if one can pray in aid the doctrine of aiding and abetting and apply it to the crime committed by a man under s 10. But *R v Tyrrell* makes it clear that to do that would be to impose criminal liability upon the persons whom Parliament has intended should be protected, not punished.

> We have therefore come to the conclusion, with regret, that the indictment does not disclose an offence known to the law because it cannot be a crime on the part of this girl aged 15 to have sexual intercourse with her father, though it is of course a crime, and a very serious crime, on the part of the father. There is here incitement to a course of conduct, but that course of conduct cannot be treated as a crime by the girl. Plainly a gap or lacuna in the protection of girls under the age of 16 is exposed by this decision. It is regrettable indeed that a man who importunes his daughter under the age of 16 to have sexual intercourse with him but does not go beyond incitement cannot be found guilty of a crime ...

[Note: It is now an offence, under s 54(1) of the Criminal Law Act 1977, for a man to incite to have sexual intercourse with him a girl under the age of 16 whom he knows to be his granddaughter, daughter or sister.]

Invicta Plastics Ltd and Another v Clare [1976] RTR 251 (DC)

Park J: These two defendants appeal by way of case stated from Hertfordshire Justices sitting at St Albans against convictions on 15 January 1975 of four offences of incitement to use unlicensed apparatus for wireless telegraphy, contrary to s 1(1) of the Wireless Telegraphy Act 1949. That section, as amended, provides, *inter alia*:

> No person shall ... use any apparatus for wireless telegraphy except under the authority of a licence in that behalf granted by the Secretary of State ... and any person who ... uses any apparatus for wireless telegraphy except under and in accordance with such a licence shall be guilty of an offence ...

The company, Invicta Plastics Ltd, were the manufacturers of a device called 'Radatec', and the defendant, Mr Jones-Fenleigh, was the chairman of the company. According to the case, Radatec is apparatus for wireless telegraphy within the meaning of the Act of 1949. It operates on the frequency range which is allocated to a number of radio services, including radio amateurs and the police in pursuance of their responsibilities in law enforcement.

By regulation 3 of the Wireless Telegraphy (Broadcast Licence Charges and Exemptions) Regulations 1970 the licence is not required for the use of wireless telegraphy apparatus used only for the reception of messages sent from authorised broadcasting stations and licensed amateur stations. Accordingly, s 1(1) of the Act of 1949 prohibits the use of apparatus for wireless telegraphy for the interception of radio communications not intended for the general use of the public except under the authority of a licence. Signals transmitted by the police in pursuance of their responsibility in law enforcement in connection with speeding offences are not intended for reception by the general public and a licence for their reception would not be granted except to authorised members of the public.

The facts giving rise to these charges are that the prosecutor bought a copy of a magazine called *What Car*. It contained an advertisement covering one-third of a page which used the words:

> You ought to know more about Radatec.

We have in fact seen a copy of it. It included a picture taken from behind the driver of a motor car travelling along a road and showed a 40 mph restriction sign immediately ahead of the car; it also showed the Radatec device attached to the top of the windscreen near the driving mirror. That advertisement forms the basis of the first two charges against the defendants. The prosecutor wrote to the address given in the advertisement and received in return two documents: namely, a slip giving the name of the stockist nearest to his address from which he could obtain Radatec, and a leaflet describing the Radatec X band receiver. The contents of the leaflet are fully set out in the case; they form the basis of the other two charges of incitement. I need only refer to some sentences. It begins with the words:

> The Radatec unit gives advance warning of X band transmissions in the vicinity. This band covers transmission from radio amateurs, police radar speed traps, commercial airport radar, military airport radar and commercial shipping navigational radar. The majority of X band transmissions are not intended for public use and, therefore, their deliberate reception is illegal unless licensed by the Post Office. However, no licence is required to receive amateur radio transmissions. As the Radatec is a broadly tuned receiver, it will intercept transmissions from any of the above sources. This need give no cause for concern since accidental reception of other transmissions while listening for amateur radio transmissions is not an offence. It is illegal to employ the Radatec specifically for the reception of, for instance, police radar transmissions. Admission of such an intentional mode of employment would doubtless lead to prosecution. Ownership of a Radatec unit is absolutely legal.

Then, under the heading 'operating features' is this sentence:

> As you approach the transmitting source, the tone of the Radatec will change to a high-pitched whine, diminishing again as you pass out of range.

In the next paragraph are the words:

> Detection ranges of up to half a mile have been noted.

The first question which the justices had to decide was whether a person who used the Radatec in his motor car without a licence from the Secretary of State would be using apparatus for wireless telegraphy contrary to s 1 of the Act of 1949. On the evidence before them they decided that such a person would be committing such an offence. There is no submission to this court that the justices were wrong in coming to that conclusion. So, on the first summons, which concerned the company, the question was whether the company by the advertisement in the magazine incited its readers to commit an offence under the Act.

When summing up to the jury on a case of incitement, judges sometimes use such words as 'incitement involves the suggestion to commit the offence' or 'a proposal to commit the offence' or 'persuasion or inducement to commit the offence' which the defendant is alleged to have incited. But Lord Denning MR considered the meaning of 'incitement' in *Race Relations Board v Applin* [1973] QB 815, 825G, where he said:

> Mr Vinelott suggested that to 'incite' means to urge or spur on by advice, encouragement, and persuasion, and not otherwise. I do not think the word is so limited, at any rate in this context. A person may 'incite' another to do an act by threatening or by pressure, as well as persuasion.

Accordingly, the justices had to decide whether, in the context, the advertisement amounted to an incitement to the readers of the magazine to commit the offence.

It is submitted on behalf of the company that, before the offence of incitement could be committed by means of the advertisement, there had to be in it an incitement to use the device which was advertised; that, if not, any matter in the advertisement would not constitute incitement, as it would not be sufficiently proximate to the offence alleged to have been incited; and that, as the advertisement merely encouraged readers to find out more about the device, it did not amount to incitement in fact or in law.

I think that it is necessary to look at the advertisement as a whole. Approaching it in this way, I have come to the conclusion that the company did incite a breach of the Act by means of the advertisement. I think, therefore, that justices were right to convict the company of this offence.

It is conceded that on the other summons against the company the case is much stronger because it depends upon the view taken by the justices of the pamphlet. [Counsel for the defendants], in the course of his argument, conceded that this pamphlet would amount to incitement except for two sentences, which I have read, which he submits amount to 'disclaimers'. Those two sentences are those where the pamphlet states that the majority of X band transmissions are not intended for public use and, therefore, their deliberate reception is illegal unless licensed by the Post Office, and where it states that it is illegal to employ Radatec specifically for the reception of, for instance, police radar transmissions.

Again, looking at the pamphlet as a whole, as the justices did, it is plain that from the words used readers were being persuaded and incited to use the Radatec device. In my view, therefore, the justices were also right to convict the company on that charge.

I now turn to the position of the other defendant, the chairman of the company. The justices convicted him solely on the basis that he was liable by virtue of s 14(2) of the Wireless Telegraphy Act 1949. That subsection begins with the words:

> Where any offence under this Act

– and I emphasise 'under this Act' –

> has been committed by a body corporate ... a director, general manager ... shall be deemed to be guilty of that offence unless he proves that the offence was committed without his consent or connivance ...'

[Counsel for the defendants] submits that that subsection cannot apply to the common law offence of incitement. [Counsel for the prosecutor] does not seek to support the conviction of the chairman.

In those circumstances, therefore, I would dismiss the appeal by the company and allow the appeal of the chairman.

MENS REA

To be guilty of incitement the defendant must know or believe that the person incited has the necessary *mens rea* to be guilty of committing the offence incited. The defendant must also intend that the offence be committed.

R v Curr [1968] 2 QB 944 (CA)

Fenton Atkinson J: ... The facts shortly were these, that he was in fact a trafficker in family allowance books. His method was to approach some married woman who had a large family of children and lend her money on the security of her family allowance book. A woman would borrow from him, let us say, £6 and would sign three of the vouchers in her family allowance book to the value of, let us say, £9, and hand over the book to him as security. He then had a team of women agents whom he sent out to cash the vouchers, and he would pocket the proceeds in repayment of the loans and thereafter return the books. He admitted quite freely in evidence that he had done, as he put it, 40 to 80 books a week, and he said, in February 1966, he had between three and five women agents assisting him in this matter, and when he was arrested he had about 80 family allowance books in his possession. He agreed quite frankly that he knew he was not legally entitled to receive these payments, and that it could be risky; in dealing with the husband of one of the women concerned he said: 'When you're doing business like this, you should keep your big mouth shut'. So it is quite plain that the dealings of this man were highly objectionable, and the assistant recorder who tried the case clearly had very strong views about it; on two occasions in his summing up he spoke of preying on these women with large families, and he finished up his direction to the jury with words to this effect: 'If you are getting interest at 800% *per annum* it is not bad, is it? That is what the prosecution say here, that the whole system was corrupt', and the language there used was no whit too strong.

But the very nature of the case being bound to arouse strong prejudice in the mind of any right-thinking juror, for that reason it was all the more important to put the law on each count clearly to the jury, and to make sure that the defence was clearly put before them ...

... [The defendant was charged] that on a day unknown [he] unlawfully 'solicited a woman unknown to obtain on his behalf from HM's Postmaster General the sum of £2 18s on account of an allowance knowing that it was not properly receivable by her' ...

[The relevant legislation, the Family Allowances Act 1945, contained a section headed] 'Penalty for obtaining or receiving payment wrongfully' [which provided:]

> If any person: ... (b) obtains or receives any such sum as on account of an allowance, either as in that person's own right or as on behalf of another, knowing that it was not properly payable, or not properly receivable by him or her; that person shall be liable on summary conviction to imprisonment for a term not exceeding three months or to a fine not exceeding £50 or to both such imprisonment and such fine.

[Defence counsel's] argument was that if the woman agent in fact has no guilty knowledge, knowing perhaps nothing of the assignment, or supposing that the defendant was merely collecting for the use and benefit of the woman concerned, then she would be an innocent agent, and by using her services in that way the defendant would be committing the summary offence himself, but would not be inciting her to receive money knowing that it was not receivable by her. He contends that it was essential to prove, to support this charge, that the woman agent in question in this transaction affecting a Mrs Currie knew that the allowances were not properly receivable by her. [Prosecuting counsel's] answer to that submission was that the woman agent must be presumed to know the law, and if she knew the law, she must have known, he contends, that the allowance was not receivable by her ...

The argument is that in no other circumstances may an agent lawfully collect for the use and benefit of the book holder, and [counsel for the prosecution] was ready to contend, for example, that if a mother with, say, eight children to look after at home asks a neighbour to go and collect her allowance for her, and the neighbour does so, the neighbour would be committing an offence under the 1945 Act, and the mother would be guilty of the offence of soliciting. We are by no means satisfied that any agent who collects with the full authority of the book holder and for her use and benefit would commit an offence under that subsection. There appears to be no express prohibition, certainly we were referred to no express prohibition, in the Family Allowance Act 1945, or any orders making such collection unlawful. On the evidence, the Post Office in practice appears to allow this to be done in certain cases; in our view there can be situations, or may be situations, in which an agent, however well she may know the statute and regulations, could properly suppose that her action in receiving an allowance of this kind was lawful.

In our view the prosecution argument here gives no effect to the word 'knowing' in the 1945 Act, and in our view the defendant could only be guilty if the woman solicited, that is, the woman agent sent to collect the allowance, knew that the action she was asked to carry out amounted to an offence. As has already been said, the defendant himself clearly knew that his conduct in the matter was illegal and contrary to the 1945 Act, but it was essential in our view for the jury to consider the knowledge, if any, of the woman agent. The assistant recorder dealt with this count be referring to soliciting as follows: 'Solicited means encouraged or incited another person to go and draw that money which should have been paid, you may think, to Mrs Currie'. He later dealt with ignorance of the law being no excuse. He went on to deal with statutory offences, under the Family Allowances Act 1945, telling the jury in effect that, apart from the case of sickness, nobody else could legally receive these allowances, and then went on to consider the position of the defendant, asking the rhetorical question whether he could be heard to say with his knowledge of this matter and his trafficking in these books that it was not known to be wrong to employ an agent to go and collect the family allowance. But the assistant recorder never followed that with the question of the knowledge of the woman agents, and in the whole of the summing up dealing with this matter he proceeded on the assumption that either guilty knowledge in the woman agent was irrelevant, or, alternatively, that any woman agent must be taken to have known that she was committing an offence under the Act.

If the matter had been left on a proper direction for the jury's consideration, they might well have thought that the woman agents, other than Mrs Nicholson, whom they acquitted, must have known very well that they were doing something wrong; some of them were apparently collecting as many as 10 of these weekly payments. But the matter was never left to them for their consideration, and here again, so it seems to this court, there was a vital matter where the defence was not left to the jury at all and there was no sufficient direction; it would be quite impossible to say that on a proper direction the jury must have convicted on this count ...

IMPOSSIBILITY AS A DEFENCE TO INCITEMENT

The test to be applied is the same as the test laid down for conspiracy in *DPP v Nock* [1978] AC 979: see *R v Fitzmaurice* [1983] QB 1083.

R v Fitzmaurice [1983] QB 1083 (CA)

Neill J: On 22 July 1981, Robert Fitzmaurice was convicted at the Central Criminal Court of unlawfully inciting three men, Terence Bonham, James Brown and Steven Brown to commit robbery by robbing a woman at Bow ...

The facts of the case were unusual. They have been set out in a convenient form in an agreed statement of facts as follows:

(1) On 28 September 1978, Bonham, James Brown and Steven Brown were arrested in Bow in a green van. Bonham was the driver and the Browns were each armed with an imitation firearm. All had sleeve masks and there was a pickaxe handle in the van.

(2) Bonham and the others believed that they were there to carry out a wages snatch from a woman walking from her place of work to the bank. A security

van was due to visit the National Westminster Bank in Bow Road at that time, and police officers had received information from the appellant's father that a robbery on the security van had been planned. All three were subsequently charged with conspiracy to rob a person on the basis of their account that they were there to rob a woman of money on her way to the bank and not the security van. At their trial they pleaded guilty to the conspiracy count and were sentenced to imprisonment.

(3) Subsequent investigations revealed that the three men were victims of a trick by the appellant's father, and had been set up to carry out a robbery by him so that he and his accomplice Skipp could collect the reward money for informing the police of an intended raid on the security van. That information was false and the invention of the appellant's father.

(4) The appellant's father asked the appellant if he could find someone to carry out a robbery. The appellant approached Bonham and informed him of the proposed robbery, describing it as a 'wages snatch'. The appellant brought Bonham to an address where the appellant's father outlined the plan. The plan was to snatch wages from a woman carrying money from a factory to a bank in Bow, east London. The appellant offered to participate, but was excluded. Bonham agreed to the plan. Later Bonham, who had recruited the two Browns, visited Bow with the appellant's father, but not the appellant. They saw a woman, in fact Skipp's girlfriend, walking from the factory to the bank. She was carrying a bag. The following week the appellant's father took Bonham and the two Browns to Bow again and pointed out where the getaway car would be left. On the day appointed, Bonham and the others met the appellant's house. Imitation guns and masks were distributed. Bonham and the others left the premises and were subsequently arrested. The appellant believed throughout that the robbery plan was genuine and agreed to accept £200 and a television for his part.

(5) On 5 June 1981 Bonham had his conviction for conspiracy set aside by the Court of Appeal on the grounds that the crime which he had conspired to commit was impossible of fulfilment. O'Connor LJ said:

> However morally culpable, the truth is that these three men had been fraudulently induced to agree to commit a crime which could not be committed in the strict sense; they were themselves the victims of a different conspiracy to which they were not parties.

In support of the appellant's appeal to this court, [counsel for the appellant] put forward two submissions: (a) that the trial judge had misdirected the jury as to the meaning of 'incitement'; and (b) that the appellant could not be guilty of inciting other men to commit a crime which in fact could not be committed.

On his first submission, [counsel for the appellant] drew our attention to a passage in the summing up where the judge said:

> The word 'incitement' is a word which is used in widely differing circumstances. A person can incite another to envy or hatred. A person can also be incited to loyalty and patriotism. Here, the charge is that the accused incited Mr Bonham to commit a crime. Now, the original approach by the defendant to Mr Bonham is not denied. There is no dispute about the fact that the defendant approached Mr Bonham, and it was an approach to him to commit a crime. There is no question about that. The defendant does not deny that Mr Bonham was an old friend of his, and that he knew at the time that he was out of work and needed money. You may conclude that an approach to Mr Bonham in those circumstances by the defendant, whether it

> was a suggestion, a proposal or a request, was an approach that embodied naturally the promise of reward, that if he engaged in the enterprise he would get money. That prospect, you may think, was the most persuasive factor in the approach. If you take that view, then clearly you may think that there was incitement to commit the crime, in the broad sense I have indicated.

[Counsel for the appellant] criticised this passage on the basis that it provided an unsatisfactory and inadequate definition of incitement because the judge did not sufficiently instruct the jury as to the necessity of proof that the appellant had persuaded or encouraged the commission of the robbery. He submitted that there was a clear distinction between the mere procurement of a crime and incitement. Procuration, he said, did not necessarily involve any persuasion or counselling of a third party by the defendant to commit the crime. Similarly, said [counsel], a person may be liable as an accessory before the fact, for example, by providing the tools for a crime, but, in the absence of any proof of persuasion to commit the crime, he will not be guilty of incitement ...

We have considered this submission in the context of the present case. In our judgment the judge gave a perfectly adequate definition to deal with the facts which the jury had to consider. We are satisfied that in some cases a person who is deputed to collect men together to take part in a crime may well not be guilty of incitement. For example, his role may be limited to informing certain named individuals that the planner of the enterprise would like to see them. But in the present case the judge could point to the fact that Bonham was out of work and needed money. The suggestion, proposal or request was accompanied by an implied promise of reward. Indeed, by using the words 'That proposal, you may think, was the most persuasive factor in the approach', the judge rightly focused the attention of the jury on the element of persuasion which it was necessary for the prosecution to prove. We therefore see no reason to fault the judge's summing up in this respect.

[Counsel's] second submission, however, is at first sight more formidable. Incitement is one of the three inchoate offences, incitement, conspiracy and attempt. [Counsel] argued that there was no logical basis for treating the three offences differently when considering their application in circumstances where the complete offence would be impossible to commit, and that therefore the court should apply the principles laid down by the House of Lords in the case of attempts in *R v Smith (Roger)* [1975] AC 476 and in the case of conspiracy in *DPP v Nock* [1978] AC 979 ...

In our view ... the right approach in a case of incitement is the same as that which was underlined by Lord Scarman in *DPP v Nock* [1978] AC 979 when he considered the offence of conspiracy. In every case it is necessary to analyse the evidence with care to decide the precise offence which the defendant is alleged to have incited. Lord Scarman said, at 995:

> The indictment makes plain that the Crown is alleging in this case a conspiracy to commit a crime: and no one has suggested that the particulars fail to disclose an offence known to the law. But the appellants submit, and it is not disputed by the Crown, that the agreement as proved was narrower in scope than the conspiracy charged. When the case was before the Court of Appeal, counsel on both sides agreed that the evidence went to prove that the appellants agreed together to obtain cocaine by separating it from the other substance or substances contained in a powder which they had obtained from one of their co-defendants, a Mr Mitchell. They believed that the powder was a mixture of cocaine and lignocaine, and that they would be

> able to produce cocaine from it. In fact the powder was lignocaine hydrochloride, an anaesthetic used in dentistry, which contains no cocaine at all. It is impossible to produce, by separation or otherwise, cocaine from lignocaine ...
>
> The trial judge in his direction to the jury, and the Court of Appeal in their judgment dismissing the two appeals, treated this impossibility as an irrelevance. In their view the agreement was what mattered: and there was plain evidence of an agreement to produce cocaine, even though unknown to the two conspirators it could not be done. Neither the trial judge nor the Court of Appeal thought it necessary to carry their analysis of the agreement further. The trial judge described it simply as an agreement to produce cocaine. The Court of Appeal thought it enough that the prosecution had proved 'an agreement to do an act which was forbidden by s 4 of the Misuse of Drugs Act 1971'. Both descriptions are accurate, as far as they go. But neither contains any reference to the limited nature of the agreement proved; it was an agreement upon a specific course of conduct with the object of producing cocaine, and limited to that course of conduct. Since it could not result in the production of cocaine, the two appellants by pursuing it could not commit the statutory offence of producing a controlled drug.

In our view these words suggest the correct approach at common law to any inchoate offence. It is necessary in every case to decide on the evidence what was the course of conduct which was (as the case may be) incited or agreed or attempted. In some cases the evidence may establish that the persuasion by the inciter was in quite general terms whereas the subsequent agreement of the conspirators was directed to a specific crime and a specific target. In such cases where the committal of the specific offence is shown to be impossible it may be quite logical for the inciter to be convicted even though the alleged conspirators (if not caught by s 5 of the Criminal Attempts Act 1981) may be acquitted. On the other hand, if B and C agree to kill D and A, standing beside B and C, though not intending to take any active part whatever in the crime, encourages them to do so, we can see no satisfactory reason, if it turns out later that D was already dead, why A should be convicted of incitement to murder whereas B and C at common law would be entitled to an acquittal on a charge of conspiracy. The crucial question is to establish on the evidence the course of conduct which the alleged inciter was encouraging.

We return to the facts of the instant case. [Counsel for the appellant] submitted that the 'crime' which Bonham and the two Browns were being encouraged to commit was a mere charade. The appellant's father was not planning a real robbery at all and therefore the appellant could not be found guilty of inciting the three men to commit it. In our judgment, however, the answer to [counsel's] argument is to be found in the facts which the prosecution proved against the appellant. As was made clear by [counsel for the Crown], the case against the appellant was based on the steps he took to recruit Bonham. At that stage the appellant believed that there was to be a wages snatch and he was encouraging Bonham to take part in it. As [counsel] put it, 'The appellant thought he was recruiting for a robbery not for a charade'. It is to be remembered that the particulars of offence in the indictment included the words 'by robbing a woman at Bow'. By no stretch of the imagination was that an impossible offence to carry out and it was that offence which the appellant was inciting Bonham to commit.

For these reasons, therefore we are satisfied that the appellant was rightly convicted. The appeal is dismissed.

R v Sirat (1986) 83 Cr App R 41 (CA)

Parker LJ: ... The charges on the indictment were as follows:

> Count 1: soliciting to murder contrary to s 4 of the Offences Against the Person Act 1861.
>
> Particulars of offence: Mohammed Sirat between the 15th and 21st days of August 1984 solicited encouraged persuaded or endeavoured to persuade Mohammed Bashir to murder Raquia Begum by the act of Mohammed Bashir and/or by the acts of another or others.
>
> Count 2: incitement to cause grievous bodily harm.
>
> Particulars of offence: Mohammed Sirat Between the 15th and 21st days of August 1984 unlawfully incited Mohammed Bashir to cause grievous bodily harm to Raquia Begum by the acts of Mohammed Bashir and/or by the acts of another or others.

The facts may be shortly stated. Between Thursday 16 August 1984, and Monday 20 August, both dates inclusive, the appellant had four meetings with Mr Bashir, the last of which was recorded by the police, to whom Mr Bashir had reported after the first two had taken place. It is unnecessary to set out the details of the conversations. It is sufficient to say that they plainly showed that the appellant desired the death of his wife or, if not that, her serious injury, and that he was urging Bashir to (1) either kill or injure her himself, or (2) pay a man who was in fact non-existent to do so, or (3) procure the result, whether by doing the deed himself or by paying someone else, not necessarily the non-existent man, to do so.

At the close of the prosecution case it was submitted on behalf of the appellant that (1) there was no such offence in law as inciting a person to counsel or abet a third person to commit an offence, and (2) there was not sufficient evidence to go to the jury that the appellant had incited Bashir himself to murder or cause grievous bodily harm to the appellant's wife. The judge rightly rejected the second of those two submissions and no complaint is made as to that.

We are now only indirectly concerned with the ruling on the first submission; for what now matters is not the ruling itself but the subsequent direction to the jury which was based on it. Of this complaint is made. In the only ground of appeal which was pursued it is contended that the learned judged erred in law 'in directing the jury that if the defendant urged the witness Bashir to incite a third man to cause grievous bodily harm to the defendant's wife the defendant was guilty of the offence charged in count 2 of the indictment and in rejecting a submission by defence counsel that there was no such offence in law as inciting a person to counsel or abet a third person to commit an offence'.

There is no doubt that at common law incitement to commit a crime is an offence. This being so, it follows logically that if A incites B to incite C to commit a crime, eg to wound D, A is guilty of incitement to commit a crime, namely incitement. This however is subject to the qualification that if C is non-existent, being either dead or fictional, A would not be guilty, because he would be inciting the commission of an impossible crime. B cannot incite C, because C does not exist. On the basis of *Fitzmaurice* [1983] QB 1083, the judge rightly so directed the jury. Hence, since the jury convicted on count 2, it follows that they must have concluded that the appellant had not urged Bashir to get the fictional man and no other to do the deed.

With regard to the remaining possibilities, the essence of the learned judge's directions appears from the following passages in his summing up:

> If a man wants a murder to be committed and he tries to persuade somebody else to commit it or he tries to persuade that second person to get a third person to commit it, then the first man is guilty of the crime of incitement ... incitement to murder.
>
> If you are sure that in reality the effect of what he was saying to Bashir was this, 'I want you to get her seriously injured, do it yourself or get the white man from Leeds to do it', then what Sirat was proposing was a possibility because the white man from Leeds was only one way in which he was making his proposal. Another, on the basis that I am putting it to you, was that Bashir might do it himself and that was obviously possible, so in that event he would be guilty of count 2 and, equally, if the effect of what he was saying was this, 'I want you to get her seriously injured, get the white man from Leeds to do it if you like, get somebody else to do it if you like, so long as you get somebody', if that is the effect of what he was saying, then once again the serious injury which he wanted brought about would be a possibility and he would then be guilty of count 2.
>
> Similarly with count 2, you have to be sure before you can convict him that he desired his wife to be seriously injured and that he tried to persuade Bashir to bring about her serious injury in a way which was, in fact, possible.

In principle there is nothing wrong with these directions, but complication is introduced by the provisions of the Criminal Law Act 1977. Section 1 of that Act created the statutory offence of conspiracy and s 5(1), subject to exceptions which do not matter, abolished the offence of conspiracy at common law. Section 5(7) then provided: 'Incitement and attempt to commit the offence of conspiracy (whether the conspiracy incited or attempted would be an offence at common law or under s 1 above or any other enactment) shall cease to be offences'. If, therefore, A incites B to agree with C that C will wound D, A's incitement of B is by statute not an offence.

There is, in our view, no doubt that one possible view of the evidence was that the appellant was inciting Bashir to agree, with either the non-existent man or anyone else who would do it at the right price, that such person should cause grievous bodily harm to the appellant's wife. It is therefore clearly possible that the jury may have convicted him of something which by statute is no longer an offence. Moreover, as was accepted by the prosecution, they may have convicted him of an offence with which he was not charged, namely incitement to incite to cause grievous bodily harm, whereas the prosecution charged incitement to cause grievous bodily harm.

This being so, we allowed the appeal on two grounds: (a) that the appellant may have been convicted of an offence of which he was not charged, and (b) that he may have been convicted of an offence which does not exist.

Lest there be any doubt, we do not intend to indicate that the common law offence of inciting to incite no longer exists. Where however the facts are that the accused's incitement of B is actually to enter into an agreement with C for the commission of a crime, it would in our judgment be impossible to hold that the accused can be guilty of incitement, on the ground that B must of necessity propose the crime to C on the way to making the agreement. Whether other forms of incitement to incite survive will fall for decision when the question arises. It may appear to be absurd that, where a person is inciting actual agreement to be made for the commission of a crime, he should be guilty of no offence, but that where he does not seek actual agreement but mere encouragement he should be guilty. This however is not necessarily absurd, for there may well be circumstances where there is no question of an agreement being sought but where the particular form of incitement is more effective than any attempt to secure agreement.

R v Pickford [1995] 1 Cr App R 420 (CA)

Laws J: ... The appellant was married to a woman who had three children, two boys and a girl. The elder of the two boys was born on 22 August 1961. On an occasion whose date cannot be precisely specified, the appellant forced this boy to have sexual intercourse with his mother, the appellant's wife. It took place in the presence of his stepdaughter (who was the victim of the offence charged in count 8, to which the application as regards sentence relates). The circumstances of this event, as described in the witness statements, are extremely unpleasant and distressing, but it is not necessary to go into them in order to determine the issues of law upon which the appeal turns.

The particulars of the offence which are pleaded in count 3 are, for reasons which we shall explain, of great importance in the case. They are in these terms:

> John Andrew Pickford on a day between the first day of January 1975 and the 31st day of December 1975 unlawfully incited [L], a male person, to have sexual intercourse with ... a woman whom he knew to be the mother of the said [L].

As we have said, the boy's date of birth was 22 August 1961. It will at once be apparent that his 14th birthday fell between the two dates referred to in the particulars. It was on 22 August 1975 ...

The significance of the date when this very nasty event took place arises because of the law's presumption, now abolished but effective at the time of the appellant's trial, that a boy under 14 is incapable of an offence involving the act of sexual intercourse by him. The appellant's argument, within which the presumption is relied upon, engages the authority of *Whitehouse* [1977] QB 868, which we shall describe shortly.

[Counsel for the appellant] submits that it is a necessary ingredient of the offence of incitement to commit a crime that the person incited was himself legally capable of the crime in question. If the stepson was under 14 when the relevant events took place, he was not capable of committing incest with his mother. Since it is not shown that he was over 14 at the time, it follows that the appellant is not guilty of the offence charged in count 3.

We should first say that if in truth the appellant pleaded guilty to an offence not known to the law, his plea would be no bar to this court entertaining an appeal against conviction, and Mr Hale for the Crown did not submit the contrary. This position is vouchsafed by *Whitehouse* in the court's judgment delivered by Scarman LJ, at 35 and 871.

[Counsel] for the Crown, accepted, by reason of the presumption against capacity in a boy under 14 for a sexual crime involving intercourse, that the boy's age is a critical element, both in the primary offence of incest by a male person, and in the offence of inciting a male person to commit incest. We consider that he was right to do so. It is beyond argument that until the coming into force of the Sexual Offences Act 1993 a male under 14 could be convicted (as the primary offender) neither of rape nor of unlawful sexual intercourse with an underage girl. But the legal presumption was not merely that he was incapable of committing either of these specific offences; it was that he was incapable of committing any crime, one of whose elements was sexual intercourse by him.

... It follows that a boy under 14 could not be convicted of any offence whose *actus reus* involved the act of intercourse with a woman by him. Archbold, *Criminal Pleading, Evidence and Practice*, 1994 edn, Vol 2, expresses the rule thus, at para 20.18: 'A boy under that age was presumed incapable of being a principal in any offence of which sexual intercourse is an ingredient'. The presumption therefore must have applied to the offence of incest by a male person. In addition, since it is a necessary element of the offence of incitement that the person incited be capable of committing the primary crime (as *Whitehouse* demonstrates: see pp 34, 36, 38 and 872, 875), it follows that no person can be guilty of inciting a boy under 14 to commit incest.

The first point which we ought to consider is one not taken by the Crown against the appellant, but one which was put by the court in the course of argument. In order to explain it, it is necessary to examine *Whitehouse* ...

In *Whitehouse* the daughter, alleged on the face of the indictment to have been 15 at the relevant time, was not capable of the offence of incest with her father. For reasons explained at pp 36–38, 872, 873, the court was prepared to assume for the purposes of the appeal that the indictment could be read, or treated as amended, so as to charge the appellant with the offence of inciting a girl of 15 to aid and abet him to commit incest with her. The court proceeded to hold, basing itself on the authority of *Tyrrell* [1894] 1 QB 710, that a girl under 16 was not in law capable of aiding and abetting her father to commit incest upon her. That being so, it was held that the indictment, even in its putative amended form, disclosed no offence known to the law. Once it was shown that the person incited was not capable of committing the principal crime, it followed that the appellant could not be guilty of incitement. The court regarded it as clear law that it is a necessary ingredient of the offence of incitement that the person incited be capable of committing the crime in question.

In *Whitehouse* (*above*), as we have said, the particulars of the offence on their face alleged the fact that the girl was 15, so that the court was able to, and did, arrive at its conclusion by looking no further than the indictment itself. The present case is different. Here lies the point which the court put to counsel in the course of argument. Count 3 alleged, as we have made plain, that the incitement offence was committed in a bracket of time during part of which the stepson was indeed under 14. But for the remaining part of the period specified he was over 14. In those circumstances, the question arises whether this appellant did in truth plead guilty to an offence not known to the law ...

... In contrast to the position in *Whitehouse*, the appellant's case requires the court to go behind the indictment, despite his plea of guilty. If the true ratio of *Whitehouse* is limited to the proposition that a conviction after a plea of guilty will be quashed where no offence known to the law is disclosed on the face of the indictment, it cannot avail [counsel for the appellant] ...

In our judgment the principle that the court may set aside a conviction after a plea of guilty on the footing that the plea was offered to an offence not known to the law is not limited to the class of case where the defect appears on the face of the indictment ...

... The features of the present case upon which [counsel for the appellant's] submissions must turn may be isolated thus. First, although there is no concession that the stepson was under 14 at the material time, the Crown nevertheless accepts, as we have indicated, that it is not demonstrated that he was over that age. Second, in the light of his date of birth it is clear, as we have said, that the indictment covers a period 1 January 1975 to 21 August 1975, in which he was indubitably under 14. In judgment this latter fact is of great importance. It implies that when the charge was framed the prosecutor did not have in mind the significance of the stepson's date of birth. If he had, he would inevitably have drawn the indictment so as to refer only to a period after the boy's fourteenth birthday. When one sets this alongside this inconclusive state of the evidence as to the date of the incident, the inference is that this case was not mounted, nor did the appellant plead guilty, on the basis that it was a necessary ingredient of the offence that the stepson be over 14 when it was committed.

We consider that it follows from these circumstances that there has been 'a wrong decision of [a] question of law' within s 2(1)(b) [of the Criminal Appeal Act 1968 as it was then drafted]. That decision consists in the acceptance of the appellant's plea, and thus his conviction, upon the erroneous assumption that the boy's age did not matter. That assumption was a premise of count 3 in the indictment as it was drafted. But unless it was pleaded and proved (by trial or plea of guilty) that the stepson was over 14 at the material time, the alleged incitement constituted no offence against the criminal law. Here, this necessary fact was neither pleaded nor proved.

The appeal is therefore good unless, as [counsel for the Crown] has submitted to us, we should apply the proviso ...

... [Counsel for the Crown submits] that exactly the same facts (which the appellant undoubtedly admitted) could have been charged differently, with no prejudice to him, and in terms which would have avoided altogether the defect upon which the appeal to this court is founded. He submits that there were two alternatives. Either the appellant could have been charged with inciting the mother to have intercourse with the son, rather than the other way round; or he could have been charged with aiding and abetting the son to have intercourse with the mother, or the mother with the son.

The first of these alternatives depends for its validity upon this proposition of law: that the offence of incest by a woman with her son, under s 11(1) of the Act of 1956, may be committed in circumstances where the son is under 14 at the material time. If that is not the case, this appellant could not have been convicted of inciting the mother to commit incest, since in her turn she could not have been found guilty of the principal offence. In that event the proviso would of course not arise, since the appellant would be no more guilty of an offence known to the law than he was under the indictment as it was in fact drawn. For convenience we set out again the relevant terms of s 11(1):

> It is an offence for a woman of the age of 16 or over to permit a man whom she knows to be her ... son to have sexual intercourse with her by her consent.

[Counsel's] argument on this part of the case would require the court to hold that the presumption of incapacity in a boy under 14 has no application in s 11 ...

... There is ... an obvious difference between s 11 and the other provisions creating sexual offences to which we have referred. It is that under s 11 the woman is the defendant; the male person is the victim of the offence. In the others, the male person is of course himself the criminal. The significance of this distinction is very great. No doubt the general policy of the legislature in enacting the crime constituted by s 11 was the same as that which underpins s 10, and was to the effect that intercourse between any family members, within what one may call the forbidden degrees, is a social and moral evil. But it must at least in part have been the legislative intention in s 11 to protect a son from the sexual advances of his mother, where such a terrible thing might occur, notwithstanding that the section also criminalises incest by a woman with her grandfather, father or brother. In the same way the aims of s 10 include the protection of a daughter from sexual advances of her father.

In the latter case, it is of course undoubted that the section prohibits intercourse by a father with his daughter of any age. The question arises whether, as regards intercourse between mother and son, Parliament in s 11 intended only to protect sons who were over the age of 14. It is surely beyond contention that the potential victims of incest who stand most in need of the law's protection are young children; and that is afforded to daughters, however young, by s 10. In our judgment it is inconceivable that, in enacting s 11, Parliament intended to exclude from its scope the most vulnerable class of potential victims – young sons under 14. We would therefore hold that the offence created by s 11 may be committed by a woman with her son below that age. It follows that another person may commit the offence of inciting a woman to do such an act.

Similar reasoning effectively underpins the decision in *Tyrrell* [1894] 1 QB 710 which, as we have said, was referred to in *Whitehouse* ...

We do not consider that this result in any way contradicts or qualifies the common law presumption of incapacity. The presumption was not that a boy under 14 was incapable of the act of intercourse *simpliciter*, it was that he was incapable *himself of committing an offence* whose *actus reus* included sexual intercourse by him.

The reasons for the presumption, however they may have been articulated in the old cases, cannot begin to justify its application in a case where the boy is not the perpetrator of the offence, but its victim. Accordingly, the appellant in the present case would rightly have been found guilty of inciting the mother to have intercourse with her son, even if it were plain beyond argument that he was under 14 at the time ...

That leaves [counsel for the Crown's] further alternative, which was that the appellant could have been charged with aiding and abetting his stepson to commit incest with his mother, or the mother with the stepson. In view of our conclusion on the first alternative, it is not necessary to go into this for the determination of the appeal; but we should say a few words about it out of deference to the argument and for the assistance of those drafting indictments in cases of this kind which, despite the abolition of the presumption of incapacity in 1993, may arise well into the future, since sexual crimes of this nature are often only disclosed years after they have taken place.

If the charge had been one of aiding and abetting the boy to commit a s 10 offence, the presumption would in our judgment have applied, and the case against the appellant would have foundered on the boy's age, just as it did on the indictment as in fact drawn. We do not consider that either *Bourne* (1952) 36 Cr App R 125 or *Cogan and Leak* [1976] QB 217 is authority to the contrary. In those cases the person who committed the act said to constitute the principal offence, in which the appellant was impleaded as a secondary party, was fully capable at law of committing the offence in question, but had a complete defence on the facts. These authorities do not support the proposition that where the principal offender lacks all legal capacity to commit the crime in question another may nevertheless be guilty of aiding and abetting him.

But if the appellant had been charged with aiding and abetting the mother to commit a s 11 offence upon her son, the presumption of incapacity would have had no application, for the reasons we have given. In such case the son would not have been, even putatively, the principal offender. He would have been the victim of the crime.

We should, however, add that even though a charge of aiding and abetting the mother might on the facts of the case have led to a lawful conviction, the appellant's true criminality is properly represented by the offence of incitement. Neither son nor mother was remotely a willing party to the events which took place. They were both forced to the act of intercourse by this appellant. Had he been charged with inciting the mother, he could in law, and upon his plea of guilty would, on the facts, have been rightly convicted. On that basis, and for the reasons we have given, the proviso falls to be applied and the appeal will be dismissed.

SEXUAL OFFENCES (CONSPIRACY AND INCITEMENT) ACT 1996

Section 2

Incitement to commit certain sexual acts outside the United Kingdom

(1) This section applies where -

(a) any act done by a person in England and Wales would amount to the offence of incitement to commit a listed sexual offence but for the fact that what he had in view would not be an offence triable in England and Wales,

(b) the whole or part of what he had in view was intended to take place in a country or territory outside the United Kingdom, and

(c) what he had in view would involve the commission of an offence under the law in force in that country or territory.

(2) Where this section applies -

(a) what he had in view is to be treated as that listed sexual offence for the purpose of any charge of incitement brought in respect of that act, and

(b) any such charge is accordingly triable in England and Wales.

(3) Any act of incitement by means of a message (however communicated) is to be treated as done in England and Wales if the message is sent or received in England and Wales.

Note: The term 'listed sexual offence' is defined in the Schedule to the Sexual Offences (Conspiracy and Incitement) Act 1996 (set out in Chapter 12).

CHAPTER 14

STRICT LIABILITY

Some offences do not require proof of *mens rea*. All that has to be proved is that the defendant did the act(s) which constitute the offence. Such offences are called offences of 'strict' or 'absolute' liability.

Most examples of strict liability offences are to be found in the area of regulatory law (such as food safety legislation), where the paramount need is to regulate activity in the public interest.

As a general rule, the courts will only construe an offence as being one of strict liability if that is clearly the intention of Parliament.

Sherras v De Rutzen [1895] 1 QB 918 (QBD)

Day J: I am clearly of opinion that this conviction ought to be quashed. This police constable comes into the appellant's public house without his armlet, and with every appearance of being off duty. The house was in the immediate neighbourhood of the police station, and the appellant believed, and he had very natural grounds for believing, that the constable was off duty. In that belief he accordingly served him with liquor. As a matter of fact, the constable was on duty; but does that fact make the innocent act of the appellant an offence? I do not think it does. He had no intention to do a wrongful act; he acted in the *bona fide* belief that the constable was off duty. It seems to me that the contention that he committed an offence is utterly erroneous ...

Wright J: I am of the same opinion. There are many cases on the subject, and it is not very easy to reconcile them. There is a presumption that *mens rea*, an evil intention, or a knowledge of the wrongfulness of the act, is an essential ingredient in every offence; but that presumption is liable to be displaced either by the words of the statute creating the offence or by the subject-matter with which it deals, and both must be considered: *Nichols v Hall* Law Rep 8 CP 322. One of the most remarkable exceptions was in the case of bigamy. It was held by all the judges, on the statute 1 Jac 1, c 11, that a man was rightly convicted of bigamy who had married after an invalid Scotch divorce, which had been obtained in good faith, and the validity of which he had no reason to doubt: *Lolley's* case R & R 237. Another exception, apparently grounded on the language of a statute, is *Prince's Case* Law Rep 2 CC 154, where it was held by 15 judges against one that a man was guilty of abduction of a girl under 16, although he believed, in good faith and on reasonable grounds, that she was over that age. Apart from isolated and extreme cases of this kind, the principal classes of exceptions may perhaps be reduced to three. One is a class of acts which, in the language of Lush J in *Davies v Harvey* Law Rep 9 QB 433, are not criminal in any real sense, but are acts which in the public interest are prohibited under a penalty. Several such instances are to be found in the decisions on the Revenue Statutes, eg *Attorney General v Lockwood* 9 M & W 378, where the innocent possession of liquorice by a beer retailer was held an offence. So under the Adulteration Acts, *R v Woodrow* 15 M & W 404, as to innocent possession of adulterated tobacco; *Fitzpatrick v Kelly* Law Rep 8 QB 337 and *Roberts v Egerton* Law Rep 9 QB 494 as to the sale of adulterated food ...

... Another class comprehends some, and perhaps all, public nuisances: *R v Stephens* Law Rep 1 QB 702 where the employer was held liable on indictment for a nuisance caused by workmen without knowledge and contrary to his orders ...

Last, there may be cases in which, although the proceeding is criminal in form, it is really only a summary mode of enforcing a civil right: see *per* Williams and Willes JJ in *Morden v Porter* 7 CB (NS) 641; 29 LJ (MC) 213, as to unintentional trespass in pursuit of game; *Lee v Simpson* 3 CB 871, as to unconscious dramatic piracy; and *Hargreaves v Diddams* Law Rep 10 QB 582, as to a *bona fide* belief in a legally impossible right to fish. But, except in such cases as these there must in general be guilty knowledge on the part of the defendant, or of someone whom he has put in his place to act for him, generally, or in the particular matter, in order to constitute an offence. It is plain that if guilty knowledge is not necessary, no care on the part of the publican could save him from a conviction ... since it would be as easy for the constable to deny that he was on duty when asked, or to produce a forged permission from his superior officer, as to remove his armlet before entering the public house. I am, therefore, of opinion that this conviction ought to be quashed.

Parker v Alder [1899] 1 QB 20 (DC)

Lord Russell of Killowen CJ: This appeal from the decision of a metropolitan police magistrate, by which he declined to convict the respondent of the offence with which he was charged: namely, that he had committed an offence against s 6 of the Sale of Food and Drugs Act 1875, as amended by s 3 of the Sale of Food and Drugs Act Amendment Act 1879. In my judgment, the learned magistrate ought to have convicted the respondent, and I think that he was wrong in coming to the conclusion that no offence had been committed by him.

The respondent had entered into a contract with an association for the supply to them of considerable quantities of milk, which was to be pure, unskimmed milk, and was to be delivered either at Paddington or at any other railway station served by the Great Western Railway near London; and by the first clause of the contract only milk sent in accordance with the terms of the contract and the quantity actually received were to be paid for, and the association were not to be accountable for loss in transit; and, last, the contract provided that the respondent 'warrants each and every consignment of milk delivered or to be delivered under this contract to be pure and unadulterated milk, and with all its cream as from the cows'.

I say all this because of the erroneous view which was, as it seems to me, taken by the magistrate. It is clear, on the construction of the contract, that the risk of the association only began when the property was delivered to them at Paddington. Up to that time the risk was that of the respondent, the vendor. The liability of the vendor did not cease when he put the milk on the train at Challow Station consigned to Paddington ...

Under those circumstances, the appellant, who is the inspector of nuisances for the parish of Paddington, took a sample of the milk on 1 January 1898, from a churn standing in Paddington Railway Station, and that sample, on being analysed, was found to be adulterated by 9% of added water. An offence, therefore, against the Act had been committed. The learned magistrate on the facts came to the conclusion that the respondent had honestly delivered pure and unadulterated milk to the servants of the railway company at Challow, and that he was no party either directly or indirectly to the adulteration. That adulteration, he finds, must have taken place in the course of the transit of the milk from Challow to Paddington. The question for us is whether on those facts any offence has been committed by the respondent ...

Now, assuming that the respondent was entirely innocent morally, and had no means of protecting himself from the adulteration of this milk in the course of transit, has he committed an offence against the Acts? I think that he has. When the scope and object of these Acts are considered, it will appear that if he were to be relieved from responsibility a wide door would be opened for evading the beneficial provisions of this legislation. It has been decided in *Brown v Foot* 66 LT(NS) 649 in the clearest manner that an innocent vendor of milk is undoubtedly liable for the unauthorised act of his servant in adulterating it. It becomes, therefore, at once apparent that there is really no material difference between this case and that, because a vendor is no more able to prevent the adulteration by a dishonest servant than he is to prevent adulteration by strangers such as the servants of the railway company. This is one of the class of cases in which the legislature has, in effect, determined that *mens rea* is not necessary to constitute the offence ...

Wills J: I am of the same opinion. I was myself a party to the decision in *Brown v Foot*, and I believe that decision to be sound law. It certainly has frequently been acted upon. There is, as it seems to me, no material distinction between the case of adulteration by a servant without the authority, and against the express orders, of his master, and adulteration by the fraudulent act of a stranger. The legislation on the subject was intended to be drastic, and the offence was created quite independently of the moral character of the act. I feel no doubt that Paddington was the place of delivery, and that the railway company were acting in carrying the milk as the agents of the respondent. That really disposes of the case ...

Lim Chin Aik v The Queen [1963] AC 160 (PC)

Lord Evershed: ... What should be the proper inferences to be drawn from the language of the statute or statutory instrument under review – in this case of ss 6 and 9 of the Immigration Ordinance? More difficult, perhaps, still, what are the inferences to be drawn in a given case from the 'subject-matter with which [the statute or statutory instrument] deals'?

Where the subject-matter of the statute is the regulation for the public welfare of a particular activity – statutes regulating the sale of food and drink are to be found among the earliest examples – it can be and frequently has been inferred that the legislature intended that such activities should be carried out under conditions of strict liability. The presumption is that the statute or statutory instrument can be effectively enforced only if those in charge of the relevant activities are made responsible for seeing that they are complied with. When such a presumption is to be inferred, it displaces the ordinary presumption of *mens rea* ...

But it is not enough in their Lordships' opinion merely to label the statute as one dealing with a grave social evil and from that to infer that strict liability was intended. It is pertinent also to inquire whether putting the defendant under strict liability will assist in the enforcement of the regulations. That means that there must be something he can do, directly or indirectly, by supervision or inspection, by improvement of his business methods or by exhorting those whom he may be expected to influence or control, which will promote the observance of the regulations. Unless this is so, there is no reason in penalising him, and it cannot be inferred that the legislature imposed strict liability merely in order to find a luckless victim ...

Where it can be shown that the imposition of strict liability would result in the prosecution and conviction of a class of persons whose conduct could not in any way affect the observance of the law, their Lordships consider that, even where the statute is dealing with a grave social evil, strict liability is not likely to be intended.

Their Lordships apply these general observations to the Ordinance in the present case. The subject-matter, the control of immigration, is not one in which the presumption of strict liability has generally been made. Nevertheless, if the courts of Singapore were of the view that unrestricted immigration is a social evil which it is the object of the Ordinance to control most rigorously, their Lordships would hesitate to disagree. That is a matter peculiarly within the cognisance of the local courts. But [counsel for the Crown] was unable to point to anything that the appellant could possibly have done so as to ensure that he complied with the regulations. It was not, for example, suggested that it would be practicable for him to make continuous inquiry to see whether an order had been made against him. Clearly one of the objects of the Ordinance is the expulsion of prohibited persons from Singapore, but there is nothing that a man can do about it if, before the commission of the offence, there is no practical or sensible way in which he can ascertain whether he is a prohibited person or not.

[Counsel], therefore, relied chiefly on the text of the Ordinance and their Lordships return, accordingly, to the language of the two material sections. It is to be observed that the Board is here concerned with one who is said (within the terms of s 6(3)) to have 'contravened' the subsection by 'remaining' in Singapore (after having entered) when he had been 'prohibited' from entering by an 'order' made by the Minister containing such prohibition. It seems to their Lordships that, where a man is said to have contravened an order or an order of prohibition, the common sense of the language presumes that he was aware of the order before he can be said to have contravened it. Their Lordships realise that this statement is something of an oversimplification when applied to the present case; for the 'contravention' alleged is of the unlawful act, prescribed by subsection (2) of the section, of remaining in Singapore after the date of the order of prohibition. Nonetheless it is their Lordships' view that, applying the test of ordinary sense to the language used, the notion of contravention here alleged is more consistent with the assumption that the person charged had knowledge of the order than the converse. But such a conclusion is in their Lordships' view much reinforced by the use of the word 'remains' in its context. It is to be observed that if the respondent is right a man could lawfully enter Singapore and could thereafter lawfully remain in Singapore until the moment when an order of prohibition against his entering was made; that then, *instanter*, his purely passive conduct in remaining – that is, the mere continuance, quite unchanged, of his previous behaviour, hitherto perfectly lawful – would become criminal. These considerations bring their Lordships clearly to the conclusion that the sense of the language here in question requires for the commission of a crime thereunder *mens rea* as a constituent of such crime; or at least that there is nothing in the language used which suffices to exclude the ordinary presumption. Their Lordships do not forget the emphasis placed by [counsel] on the fact that the word 'knowingly' or the phrases 'without reasonable cause' or 'without reasonable excuse' are found in various sections of the Ordinance (as amended) but find no place in the section now under consideration – see, for example, ss 16(4), 18(4), 19(2), 29, 31(2), 41(2) and 56(d) and (e) of the Ordinance. In their Lordships' view the absence of such a word or phrase in the relevant section is not sufficient in the present case to prevail against the conclusion which the language as a whole suggests. In the first place, it is to be noted that to have inserted such words as 'knowingly' or 'without lawful excuse' in the relevant part of s 6(3) of the Act would in any case not have been sensible. Further, in all the various instances where the word or phrase is used in the other sections of the Ordinance before-mentioned the use is with reference to the doing of some specific act or the failure to do some specific act as distinct from the mere passive continuance of behaviour theretofore perfectly lawful. Finally, their Lordships are mindful that in the *Sherras* case [1895] 1 QB 918 itself the fact that the word 'knowingly' was not found in the subsection under consideration by the court but was found in another subsection in the same section was not there regarded as sufficient to displace the ordinary rule.

Their Lordships have accordingly reached the clear conclusion, with all respect to the view taken in the courts below, that the application of the rule that *mens rea* is an essential ingredient in every offence has not in the present case been ousted by the terms or subject-matter of the Ordinance, and that the appellant's conviction and sentence cannot stand ...

Sweet v Parsley [1970] AC 132 (HL)

Lord Morris of Borth-y-Gest: My Lords, it has frequently been affirmed and should unhesitatingly be recognised that it is a cardinal principle of our law that *mens rea*, an evil intention or a knowledge of the wrongfulness of the act, is in all ordinary cases an essential ingredient of guilt of a criminal offence. It follows from this that there will not be guilt of an offence created by statute unless there is mens rea or unless Parliament has by the statute enacted that guilt may be established in cases where there is no *mens rea*.

To this effect were the words of Wright J in *Sherras v De Rutzen* [1895] 1 QB 918 and in *Derbyshire v Houliston* in [1897] 1 QB 772. In the judgment of the Privy Council in *Lim Chin Aik v The Queen* [1963] AC 160 the principle was amply expressed. It was said, at 172: 'That proof of the existence of a guilty intent is an essential ingredient of a crime at common law is not at all in doubt'.

But as Parliament is supreme, it is open to Parliament to legislate in such a way that an offence may be created of which someone may be found guilty though *mens rea* is lacking. There may be cases in which, as Channell J said in *Pearks, Gunston and Tee Ltd v Ward* [1902] 2 KB 1 at 11:

> ... the legislature has thought it so important to prevent the particular act from being committed that it absolutely forbids it to be done; and if it is done the offender is liable to a penalty whether he had any *mens rea* or not, and whether or not he intended to commit a breach of the law.

Thus in diverse situations and circumstances and for any one of a variety of reasons Parliament may see fit to create offences and make people responsible before criminal courts although there is an absence of *mens rea*. But I would again quote with appreciation (as I did in *Warner's* case [1969] 2 AC 256) the words of Lord Goddard CJ, in *Brend v Wood* (1946) 175 LT 306 at 307, when he said:

> It is of the utmost importance for the protection of the liberty of the subject that a court should always bear in mind that, unless a statute, either clearly or by necessary implication, rules out *mens rea* as a constituent part of a crime, the court should not find a man guilty of an offence against the criminal law unless he has a guilty mind.

The intention of Parliament is expressed in the words of an enactment. The words must be looked at in order to see whether either expressly or by necessary implication they displace the general rule or presumption that *mens rea* is a necessary prerequisite before guilt of an offence can be found. Particular words in a statute must be considered in their setting in the statute and having regard to all the provisions of the statute and to its declared or obvious purpose. In 1842 in *Attorney General v Lockwood* (1842) 9 M & W 378, 398 Alderson B said:

> The rule of law, I take it, upon the construction of all statutes ... is, whether they be penal or remedial, to construe them according to the plain, literal and

> grammatical meaning of the words in which they are expressed, unless that construction leads to a plain and clear contradiction of the apparent purpose of the Act, or to some palpable and evident absurdity.

It must be considered, therefore, whether by the words of a penal statute it is either express or implied that there may be a conviction without *mens rea* or, in other words, whether what is called an absolute offence is created ...

The inquiry must be made, therefore, whether Parliament has used words which expressly enact or impliedly involve that an absolute offence is created. Though sometimes help in construction is derived from noting the presence or the absence of the word 'knowingly', no conclusive test can be laid down as a guide in finding the fair, reasonable and common sense meaning of language. But in considering whether Parliament has decided to displace what is a general and somewhat fundamental rule it would not be reasonable lightly to impute to Parliament an intention to create an offence in such a way that someone could be convicted of it who by all reasonable and sensible standards is without fault ...

The question must always be: what has Parliament enacted? That is the question in the present case and to that I now turn. The wording of s 5 of the Dangerous Drugs Act 1965, is as follows:

> If a person: (a) being the occupier of any premises, permits those premises to be used for the purpose of smoking cannabis or cannabis resin or of dealing in cannabis resin (whether by sale or otherwise); or (b) is concerned in the management of any premises used for any such purpose as aforesaid; he shall be guilty of an offence against this Act.

The words are nearly the same as and presumably were derived from words in s 5 of the Dangerous Drugs Act 1920, concerning opium.

In the present case the appellant was charged with being concerned in the management of certain premises situate at Fries Farm which were used for the purpose of smoking cannabis or cannabis resin. I need not recite the facts which are set out in the case stated.

It was for the prosecution to prove the guilt of the appellant. It was found by the magistrates that the appellant had no knowledge whatsoever that cannabis had been smoked in the house. The prosecution contended that guilt can be established of the offence created by s 5(b) if a person is concerned in the management of premises in which cannabis is in fact smoked. The consequence was acknowledged and indeed asserted that if some person managed a hostel containing, say, 50 – 100 rooms, and if on one day in one room an occupant smoked one cannabis cigarette without the knowledge of the persons managing, they would have no defence to a charge under s 5(b). If Parliament has so enacted, then the law must be enforced. But I am sure that that is not what Parliament has decreed.

If someone is concerned in management there must at least be knowledge of what it is that is being managed: otherwise there could be no concern in it. If someone is concerned in the management of a building containing a number of separately let residential flats the concern in such case would be in the arrangements for the lettings and in the arrangements relating to lifts or staircases or the structure of the building as a whole. The concern would be in the management of premises used for residential purposes. In the ordinary course of things the landlord or the manager would have no right of entry into a flat and would have no concern with any normal, reasonable and lawful activity within a flat. If a tenant, who was a non-smoker, had a guest one day who smoked a pipe of tobacco in the flat, it would be a strained and unnatural use of language to describe the flat which the tenant rented as being premises used for the purpose of smoking. It would be equally strained and unnatural to describe the landlord or his agent as being concerned in the management of premises used for the purpose of smoking. If on an isolated occasion a tenant gave a showing of some cinematograph films to his friends, it would be unreasonable to describe the manager of the flats (who had no occasion to know of the film showing) as being one who was concerned in the management of premises used for the purpose of exhibiting films.

If a tenant took sugar with his tea it would be fanciful to describe the flat as premises used for the purpose of putting sugar into tea.

It seems to me, therefore that the words 'premises ... used for the purpose of smoking cannabis' are not happily chosen if they were intended to denote premises in which at any time cannabis is smoked. In my opinion, the words 'premises ... used for the purpose of ...' denote a purpose which is other than quite incidental or casual or fortuitous: they denote a purpose which is or has become either a significant one or a recognised one though certainly not necessarily an only one. There is no difficulty in appreciating what is meant if it is said that premises are used for the purposes of a dance hall or a billiard hall or a bowling alley or a hairdressing saloon or a cafe. A new or additional use might, however, arise. It might happen that a house let as a private dwelling might come to be used as a brothel or for the purposes of prostitution. A room let for private occupation might come to be the resort of a number of people who wished to smoke opium so that the time would come when the room could rationally be described as a room used for the purpose of smoking opium.

The words 'concerned in the management of any premises used for the purpose of' are, in my view, to be considered together and as one phrase. Even so the phrase may be capable of two meanings. It could denote the management of premises used for a certain purpose in the sense that the management is limited to management in respect of the premises themselves. It could denote the management of premises used for a certain purpose in the sense that the management was concerned either additionally or perhaps separately with the purpose for which the premises were used. Thus, if someone is said so to be concerned in the management of premises used for the purpose of dancing, he could be someone concerned only in the management of the premises themselves, or he could be someone who additionally or possibly separately was concerned with the dancing. On either approach and with an ordinary use of words, it would seem to me that the person would be one who would have and would need to have knowledge of the use of the premises for the particular purpose.

It is said that the intention of Parliament was to impose a duty on all persons concerned in the management of any premises to exercise vigilance to prevent the smoking of cannabis. If that had been the intention of Parliament different words would have been used. It would be possible for Parliament to enact, though it would be surprising if it did, that if anyone should at any time smoke cannabis on any premises, then all those concerned in the management of those premises, whether they knew of the smoking or not, should automatically be guilty of a criminal offence. Yet this is in effect what it is now said that Parliament has enacted. The implications are astonishing. Parliament would not only be indirectly imposing a duty upon persons concerned in the management of any premises requiring them to exercise complete supervision over all persons who enter the premises to ensure that no one of them should smoke cannabis, but Parliament would be enacting that the persons concerned in the management would become guilty of an offence it, unknown to them, someone by surreptitiously smoking cannabis eluded the most elaborately devised measures of supervision. There would not be guilt by reason of anything done nor even by reasons of any carelessness, but by reason of the unknown act of some unknown person whom it had not been found possible to control. When the range of possible punishments is remembered the unlikelihood that Parliament intended to legislate in such way becomes additionally apparent.

For the reasons that I have indicated I consider that on a fair reading of the phrase 'concerned in the management of premises used for the purpose of' a link is denoted between management and user for a purpose. To say that someone is concerned in the management of premises used for the purpose of smoking cannabis involves, in my view, that his management is with knowledge that the premises are so used. The wording of s 5(b) contains positive indications that *mens rea* is an essential ingredient of an offence. Even if, contrary to my view, it is not affirmatively enacted that there must be *mens rea* I cannot read the wording as enacting that there need not be *mens rea*. I find it wholly impossible to say that the statute has either clearly, or by necessary implication, ruled out *mens rea* as a constituent part of guilt.

On the findings of the magistrates it follows that the appellant was not guilty. I would, therefore, allow the appeal. Accordingly, in my view, the case should be remitted to the Divisional Court with a direction to quash the conviction.

Lord Pearce: My Lords, the prosecution contend that any person who is concerned in the management of premises where cannabis is in fact smoked even once, is liable, though he had no knowledge and no guilty mind. This is, they argue, a practical act intended to prevent a practical evil. Only by convicting some innocents along with the guilty can sufficient pressure be put upon those who make their living by being concerned in the management of premises. Only thus can they be made alert to prevent cannabis being smoked there. And if the prosecution have to prove knowledge or *mens rea*, many prosecutions will fail and many of the guilty will escape. I find that argument wholly unacceptable.

The notion that some guilty mind is a constituent part of crime and punishment goes back far beyond our common law. And at common law *mens rea* is a necessary element in a crime. Since the Industrial Revolution the increasing complexity of life called into being new duties and crimes which took no account of intent. Those who undertake various industrial and other activities, especially where these affect the life and health of the citizen, may find themselves liable to statutory punishment regardless of knowledge or intent, both in respect of their own acts or neglect and those of their servants. But one must remember that normally *mens rea* is still an ingredient of any offence. Before the court will dispense with the necessity for *mens rea* it has to be satisfied that Parliament so intended. The mere absence of the word 'knowingly' is not enough. But the nature of the crime, the punishment, the absence of social obloquy, the particular mischief and the field of activity in which it occurs, and the wording of the particular section and its context, may show that Parliament intended that the act should be prevented by punishment regardless of intent or knowledge.

Viewing the matter of these principles, it is not possible to accept the prosecution's contention. Even granted that this were in the public health class of case, such as, for instance, are offences created to ensure that food shall be clean, it would be quite unreasonable. It is one thing to make a man absolutely responsible for all his own acts and even vicariously liable for his servants if he engages in a certain type of activity. But it is quite another matter to make him liable for persons over whom he has no control. The innocent hotel-keeper, the lady who keeps lodgings or takes paying guests, the manager of a cinema, the warden of a hostel, the matron of a hospital, the house-master and matron of a boarding school, all these, it is conceded, are, on the prosecution's argument, liable to conviction the moment that irresponsible occupants smoke cannabis cigarettes. And for what purpose is this harsh imposition laid on their backs? No vigilance by night or day can make them safe. The most that vigilance can attain is advance knowledge of their own guilt. If a smell of cannabis comes from a sitting room, they know that they have committed the offence. Should they then go at once to the police and confess their guilt in the hope that they will not be prosecuted? They may think it easier to conceal the matter in the hope that it may never be found out. For if, though morally innocent, they *are* prosecuted they may lose their livelihood, since thereafter, even though not punished, they are objects of suspicion. I see no real, useful object achieved by such hardship to the innocent. And so wide a possibility of injustice to the innocent could not be justified by any benefit achieved in the determent and punishment of the guilty. If, therefore, the words creating the offence are as wide in their application as the prosecution contend, Parliament cannot have intended an offence to which absence of knowledge or *mens rea* is no defence ...

Lord Wilberforce: My Lords, in my opinion Miss Stephanie Sweet, who was found to have 'no knowledge whatever that [her] house was being used for the purpose of smoking cannabis', ought not to have been convicted.

Her conviction was based upon s 5(b) of the Dangerous Drugs Act, 1965, and upon an interpretation of the words 'concerned in the management of any premises used [for the purpose of smoking cannabis or cannabis resin or of dealing in cannabis or cannabis resin] which makes a person liable to prosecution who lets, or licenses the occupation of premises, upon which cannabis or cannabis resin is smoked or dealt in. It requires no amplification to show how wide a category of persons would thus be brought into the category of potential offenders. So, for this appeal, the essential question is to determine whether this interpretation is correct.

The words 'concerned in the management' are not, on the face of them, very clear, but at least they suggest some technical or acquired meaning, some meaning other than one which refers merely to such common transactions as letting or licensing the occupation of premises. For if it had been intended to penalise anyone who lets or licenses premises on which cannabis comes to be smoked, it would have been easy to do so in simple language. This impression is strengthened when the following words of the subsection are read. They reflect what I would think to be logically correct – namely that one does not 'manage' premises, the inert subject of a conveyance or a lease, but rather some human activity on the premises which the manager has an interest in directing. And so, when the subsection speaks of management of premises, and for a purpose, I would expect the purpose for which the premises are used to be that of the manager: otherwise, what would be the nature and object of the management? ...

Gammon (Hong Kong) Ltd v Attorney General of Hong Kong [1985] 1 AC 1 (PC)

Lord Scarman: ... The issue in the appeal is whether the offences charged are offences of strict liability or require proof of *mens rea* as to their essential facts.

The first appellant, Gammon (Hong Kong) Ltd ('the company') is a contractor registered under the Ordinance and was carrying out building works at a site known as Marine Lot No 3 Queen's Road Central, Hong Kong. The second and third appellants were employees of the company, being respectively the project manager and site agent for the works.

The appellants were charged under subsection (2A) and (2B) of s 40 of the Ordinance. It is necessary to set out in full the two subsections:

> (2A) Any person for whom any building works, street works, lift works or escalator works are being carried out and any authorised person, registered structural engineer, registered contractor, registered lift contractor or registered escalator contactor directly concerned with any such works who: (a) permits or authorises to be incorporated in or used in the carrying out of any such works any material which: (1) are defective or do not comply with the provisions of this Ordinance; (2) have not been mixed, prepared, applied, used, erected, constructed, placed or fixed in the manner required for such material under this Ordinance; (b) diverges or deviates in any material way from any work shown in a plan approved by the Building Authority under this Ordinance; or (c) knowingly misrepresents a material fact in any plan, certificate, form or notice given to the Building Authority under this Ordinance, shall be guilty of an offence and shall be liable on conviction to a fine of $250,000 and to imprisonment for three years.
>
> (2B) Any person (whether or not an authorised person, a registered structural engineer or a registered contractor) directly concerned with any site formation works, piling works, foundation works or other form of building works who: (a) carries out or has carried out such works, or authorises or permits or has authorised or permitted such works to be carried out, in such manner that it causes injury to any person or damage to any property; or (b) carries out or has carried out such works, or authorises or permits or has authorised or permitted such works to be carried out, in such manner as is likely to cause a risk of injury to any person or damage to any property, shall be guilty of an offence and shall be liable on conviction to a fine of $250,000 and to imprisonment for three years.

The company was charged with a material deviation from an approved plan in contravention of subsection (2A)(b), and with carrying out works in a manner likely to cause risk or injury or damage in contravention of subsection (2B)(b). The second and third appellants were charged under subsection (2B)(b): it was charged against the second appellant that, being the company's manager, he carried out the works, and against the third appellant that he permitted the works to be carried out, in a manner likely to cause risk of injury or damage ...

The facts relevant to the issue can be very briefly summarised. The company had delegated the fulfilment of its obligations under the Ordinance on the site to the second and third appellants: it is accepted, therefore, that the company is vicariously responsible if either of them contravened or failed to comply with the provisions of the Ordinance. If either of them committed an offence in the course of his employment, the company has also offended and is liable to the penalties imposed by the Ordinance.

The offending act, which is the basis of all the charges, was the removal of part of the lateral support system on the site; a system which was required in the interest of safety by plans approved by the building authority. The removal was a 'deviation of substance' from the plans; and it is to be assumed for the purpose of the appeal (for it is not admitted by the appellants) that the removal was likely to cause a risk of injury or damage ...

The general law

In *Sweet v Parsley* [1970] AC 132, 149 Lord Reid observed:

> it is firmly established by a host of authorities that *mens rea* is an essential ingredient of every offence unless some reason can be found for holding that that is not necessary.

The question in the appeal is whether the Ordinance, correctly interpreted, provides a sound reason for holding that the offences created by subsection (2A)(b) and (2B)(b) of s 40 of the Ordinance are offences of strict liability. The Attorney General of Hong Kong contends that it does; the appellants contend that it does not.

Before, however, one considers the Ordinance it is necessary to have clearly in mind the applicable principles of the criminal law. Three cases, all of them well-known, bear directly on the issue. In *Sherras v De Rutzen* [1895] 1 QB 918 the court had under consideration the prohibition contained in the Licensing Act 1872 upon the supply by a licensee of liquor to a police constable while on duty. The appellant's case was that he did not know and had no reason to believe that the constable was on duty. The court quashed the conviction. Wright J, in the course of his judgment considered the classes of case in which the presumption of *mens rea* can be displaced in English law. He saw three principle classes of cases in which the presumption can be displaced: two of them are relevant to this appeal, namely: (1) cases where the prohibited acts are not criminal in any real sense but are acts which in the public interest are prohibited under a penalty; and (2) cases of public nuisance.

He prefaced his judgment by a statement of general principle at 921:

> There is a presumption that *mens rea*, an evil intention, or a knowledge of the wrongfulness of the act, is an essential ingredient in every offence; but that presumption is liable to be displaced either by the words of the statute creating the offence or by the subject-matter with which it deals, and both must be considered: ...

In *Lim Chin Aik v The Queen* [1963] AC 160 the Judicial Committee accepted Wright J's formulation of principle as correct, but the Board warned at 173–74, that the adoption of the principle does not dispose of the question whether the presumption is displaced. For the difficulty of applying the principle remains. What should be the proper inferences to be drawn from the language of the statute under review? And what are the inferences to be drawn from the subject-matter with which the statute deals?

The Board went on to state an approach to these two questions which was later approved and accepted by the House of Lords in *Sweet v Parsley* [1970] AC 132. The Board said at 174:

> Where the subject-matter of the statute is the regulation for the public welfare of a particular activity – statutes regulating the sale of food and drink are to be found among the earliest examples – it can be and frequently has been inferred that the legislature intended that such activities should be carried out under conditions of strict liability. The presumption is that the statute or statutory instrument can be effectively enforced only if those in charge of the relevant activities are made responsible for seeing that they are complied with. When such a presumption is to be inferred, it displaces the ordinary presumption of *mens rea*.

But the Board added at 175:

> Where it can be shown that the imposition of strict liability would result in the prosecution and conviction of a class of persons whose conduct could not in any way affect the observance of the law, their Lordships consider that, even where the statute is dealing with a grave social evil, strict liability is not likely to be intended.

However, in *Sweet v Parsley* [1970] AC 132 at 149 Lord Reid refused to accept that in determining the question of *mens rea* or strict liability it is sufficient merely to have regard to the subject-matter of the statute in construing the words of the provision creating the offence. Other considerations have to be borne in mind including the nature of the prohibited act: if it were 'truly criminal', it would be necessary, for example, to consider whether the public interest really required that an innocent person should suffer in order that fewer guilty men might escape.

In the course of his speech in *Sweet v Parsley* [1970] AC 132 Lord Diplock addressed himself directly to the question which their Lordships have to consider in this appeal. He said at 163:

> But where the subject-matter of a statute is the regulation of a particular activity involving potential danger to public health, safety or morals in which citizens have a choice as to whether they participate or not, the court may feel driven to infer an intention of Parliament to impose by penal sanctions a higher duty of care on those who choose to participate and to place upon them an obligation to take whatever measures may be necessary to prevent the prohibited act, without regard to those considerations of cost or business practicability which play a part in the determination of what would be required of them in order to fulfil the ordinary common law duty of care. But such an inference is not lightly to be drawn, nor is there any room for it unless there is something that the person on whom the obligation is imposed can do directly or indirectly, by supervision or inspection, by improvement of his business methods or by exhorting those whom he may be expected to influence or control, which will promote the observance of the obligation (see *Lim Chin Aik v The Queen* [1963] AC 160, 174).

In their Lordships' opinion, the law relevant to this appeal may be stated in the following propositions ...: (1) there is a presumption of law that *mens rea* is required before a person can be held guilty of a criminal offence; (2) the presumption is particularly strong where the offence is 'truly criminal' in character; (3) the presumption applies to statutory offences, and can be displaced only if this is clearly or by necessary implication the effect of the statute; (4) the only situation in which the presumption can be displaced is where the statute is concerned with an issue of social concern, and public safety is such an issue; (5) even where a statute is concerned with such an issue, the presumption of *mens rea* stands unless it can also be shown that the creation of strict liability will be effective to promote the objects of the statute by encouraging greater vigilance to prevent the commission of the prohibited act.

The Ordinance

Their Lordships turn to consider the purpose and subject matter of the Ordinance. Its overall purpose is clearly to regulate the planning, design and construction of the building works to which it relates in the interests of safety. It covers a field of activity where there is, especially in Hong Kong, a potential danger to public safety. And the activity which the Ordinance is intended to regulate is one in which citizens have a choice as to whether they participate or not. Part IV (s 40) of the Ordinance makes it very clear that the legislature intended that criminal sanctions for contraventions of the Ordinance should be a feature of its enforcement. But it is not to be supposed that the legislature intended that any of the offences created by the Ordinance should be offences of strict liability unless it is plain, from a consideration of the subject matter of the Ordinance and of the wording of the particular provision creating the offence, that an object of the Ordinance, eg the promotion of greater vigilance by those having responsibility under the Ordinance, would be served by the imposition of strict liability...

Put in positive terms, the conclusion of the Board is that it is consistent with the purpose of the Ordinance in its regulation of the works to which it applies that at least some of the criminal offences which it creates should be of strict liability. It is a statute the subject-matter of which may properly be described as: 'the regulation of a particular activity involving potential danger to public health [and] safety ... in which citizens have a choice as to whether they participate or not ...': *per* Lord Diplock in *Sweet v Parsley* [1970] AC 132, 163.

Whether, therefore, a particular provision of the statute creates an offence of full *mens rea* or of strict liability must depend upon the true meaning of the words of the particular provision construed with reference to its subject-matter and to the question whether strict liability in respect of all or any of the essential ingredients of the offence would promote the object of the provision ...

Subsection (2A) and (2B)

Their Lordships now turn to consider the two subsections in detail and separately; for it does not follow that, if one subsection should create an offence of strict liability, the other must also do so. But first a few observations on certain features common to both.

The first common feature is that both subsections have a characteristic of which Lord Reid spoke in *Sweet v Parsley* [1970] AC 132, 149. The specific provisions subsections (2A)(b) and (2B)(b) belong to that

> multitude of criminal enactments where the words of the Act simply make it an offence to do certain things but where everyone agrees that there cannot be a conviction without proof of *mens rea* in some form?

Each provision clearly requires a degree of *mens rea*, but each is silent as to whether it is required in respect of all the facts which together constitute the offence created. The issue here is, therefore, a narrow one. Does subsection (2A)(b) require knowledge of the materiality of the deviation? Does subsection (2B)(b) require knowledge of the likelihood of risk of injury or damage?

The second common feature is that each provision appears in a section which creates many other offences, the wording of some, though not all, of which clearly requires full *mens rea*.

A third common feature is that the maximum penalties for the offences which they create are heavy: a fine of $250,000 and imprisonment for three years. There is no doubt that the penalty indicates the seriousness with which the legislature viewed the offences.

The first of these features raises the determinative question in the appeal. Their Lordships will, therefore, consider it later in respect of each subsection.

The second feature, in their Lordships' opinion, proves nothing. One would expect a wide range of very different offences in a statute which establishes a comprehensive system of supervision and control over a great range of complicated works in diverse circumstances. And it can be said with equal force that a feature of s 40 is that in many cases where *mens rea* is required it expressly says so, and that, where a defence of reasonable excuse or lack of knowledge is to be available, it makes express provision to that end: examples may be seen in subsections (1B), (1C), (2A)(c), (2C), (6), (7) and (7A).

The severity of the maximum penalties is a more formidable point. But it has to be considered in the light of the Ordinance read as a whole. For reasons which their Lordships have already developed, there is nothing inconsistent with the purpose of the Ordinance in imposing severe penalties for offences of strict liability. The legislature could reasonably have intended severity to be a significant deterrent, bearing in mind the risks to public safety arising from some contraventions of the Ordinance. Their Lordships agree with the view on this point of the Court of Appeal. It must be crucially important that those who participate in or bear responsibility for the carrying out of works in a manner which complies with the requirements of the Ordinance should know that severe penalties await them in the event of any contravention or non-compliance with the Ordinance by themselves or by anyone over whom they are required to exercise supervision or control.

Subsection (2A)

This provision applies to building owners, authorised persons (ie architects, surveyors, structural engineers), registered structural engineers and registered contractors. It is thus confined to persons bearing responsibility for the decision to undertake works and for their supervision and control. There is plainly an element of *mens rea* in the offences it creates: the wording of subparagraphs (a) and (b) does no make clear how far *mens rea* extends: the wording of subparagraph (c) reveals an offence of full *mens rea* ...

The wording of subparagraph (b) clearly requires knowledge of the approved plan and of the fact of deviation. But in their Lordships' view it would be of little use in promoting public safety if it also required proof of knowledge of the materiality of the deviation. As it was put on behalf of the Attorney General, if the offence requires knowledge of the materiality of the deviation to be proved, the defendant is virtually judge in his own cause. The object of the provision is to assist in preventing material deviations from occurring. If a building owner, an authorised or a registered person is unaware of the materiality of the deviation which he authorises (and knowledge of the deviation is necessary), he plainly ought to be. He is made liable to criminal penalties because of the threat to public safety arising from material deviations from plans occurring within the sphere of his responsibility. The effectiveness of the Ordinance would be seriously weakened if it were open to such a person to plead ignorance of what was material. In the words ... of the Court of Appeal: 'it therefore behoves the incompetent to stay away and the competent to conduct themselves with proper care'.

Subsection (2B)

The construction of subsection (2B)(b) is more difficult, but their Lordships are satisfied that it imposes strict liability for substantially the same reasons as those which have led them to this conclusion in respect of subsection (2A)(b). The offence created clearly requires a degree of *mens rea*. A person cannot carry out works or authorise or permit them to be carried out in a certain manner unless he knows the manner which he is employing, authorising, or permitting. The appellants laid great emphasis on the reference to permitting as an indication of full *mens rea*. They referred their Lordships to *James and Son Ltd v Smee* [1955] 1 QB 78. But their Lordships agree with the answer of the Court of Appeal to this point:

> We would therefore hold that the word 'permitting' in s 40(2B)(b) does not by itself import *mens rea* in the sense of intention to cause a likelihood of risk of injury or knowledge that such likelihood would result but does require that the defendant shall have had a power to control whether the *actus reus* (the carrying out of the works in the manner which in fact causes a likelihood of risk of injury) shall be committed or not ...

Their Lordships find some support for their view that subsection (2B)(b) is an offence of strict liability in the wording of the offence created by (2B)(a). The wording of (a) points to strict liability, once injury or damage has in fact been caused. Anyone who has carried out authorised or permitted work to be carried out in a manner which has in fact caused injury or damage is caught ...

Wings Ltd v Ellis [1985] AC 272 (HL)

Lord Scarman: My Lords, this appeal turns on the construction properly to be put upon a few ordinary English words in the context of s 14 of the Trade Descriptions Act 1968. Put very shortly, the basic issue between the parties is whether upon its proper construction s 14(1)(a) creates an offence of strict, or more accurately, semi-strict, liability or is one requiring the existence of full *mens rea*. The issue has provoked elaborate and subtle legal argument between the parties before the Divisional Court and in your Lordships' House. But the point is, or ought to be, a short one, arising, as it does, upon the words of a statute passed to protect the public in a way the public can understand.

Section 14, so far as material, is in these terms:

> (1) It shall be an offence for any person in the course of any trade or business: (a) to make a statement which he knows to be false; or (b) recklessly to make a statement which is false; as to any of the following matters, that is to say: (1) the provision in the course of any trade or business of any services, accommodation or facilities ...

The respondent company was charged with two offences under the section. The first, to which the appeal relates, was an offence under s 14(1)(a) of making a statement which the company knew to be false as to the provision which it offered to its customers of certain hotel accommodation. The statement was alleged to have been made on 13 January 1982, the date on which a customer, Mr Wade, having read it in a brochure published by the respondent company booked a holiday for his wife and himself in reliance upon it. The second, which is not the subject of an appeal to the House, was an offence under s 14(1)(b) of recklessly making a false statement in respect of the same offer. This charge related to the same booking but arose from a photograph said in the brochure to be a photograph of the hotel bedroom, which it was not. The Plymouth justices convicted the company on both charges. The Divisional Court allowed the company's appeal against both convictions. The prosecutor now, with the leave of the House, appeals only against the quashing of the first conviction.

The Divisional Court certified that the case involved the following point of law of general public importance:

> Whether a defendant may properly be convicted of an offence under s 14(1)(a) of the Trade Descriptions Act 1968 where he had no knowledge of the falsity of the statement at the time of its publication but knew of the falsity at the time when the statement was read by the complainant.

As will later appear, the statement (admittedly false) was contained in a brochure prepared and published without knowledge of its falsity by the respondent company in May 1981, but not read by the complainant until 13 January 1982, by which time (admittedly) the respondent company knew it was false. The two issues, therefore, which arise in the appeal are both points of construction. The first is whether, as the respondent contends, the offence is knowingly to make a false statement or whether the offence can be committed without knowledge of the making of the statement. The second point raises the question: what is meant by the words 'make a statement' in their statutory context? What constitutes a statement upon the proper construction of s 14(1)(a)? Did the respondent company make a statement on 13 January 1982?

The details of the charge laid under s 14(1)(a) were that on 13 January 1982 (the prosecution tied its case to this date) the defendant in the course of its business made a statement, which it knew to be false, as to the nature of the accommodation at the Seashells Hotel, Negombo, Sri Lanka, namely that the bedrooms were air-conditioned, whereas in truth they were not. The statement consisted of the use of two code letters 'AC' in the description of the hotel's accommodation published by the defendant in its brochure 'Wings Faraway Holidays Winter Oct 1981 – April 1982'.

The defendant (hereinafter called the respondent or respondent company) is a body corporate engaged in the business of providing holidays on a package deal basis. The business is entrepreneurial in character, a service industry: the company arranges for the travel to and from the holiday destination and for the accommodation to be provided by others. Business, as between company and holidaymaker, is done on the basis of a written description of what is on offer. The description is usually contained, as in this case, in an attractively written and illustrated brochure published by the company well in advance of the holiday season and widely distributed to travel agents through whom it becomes available and is seen by interested members of the public. The brochure is, therefore, as in this case, the document from which the holidaymaker is invited to choose his holiday and upon the faith of the descriptions contained in which he makes his choice. The print run of a brochure may, as in this case, go into hundreds of thousands of copies. Most inquiries from the public reach the company through travel agents who pass them on to the company, as also in this case, by telephone. The holidaymaker tells the travel agent his selection, and the travel agent phones it through to the company, a member of whose sales staff, as also in this case, makes the booking.

The justices found that the respondent published the brochure containing the false statement relied on in this case in May 1981. At that time no one in the respondent company knew that it was false. It was an innocent error, the source of which has never been traced. The error was, however, discovered before 1 June 1981 by which time the brochure had already been given a wide distribution. The brochure was not however, withdrawn: indeed, it would have been impossible to recall all copies. Nor were *'errata'* slips distributed – again because they would not have reached everyone into whose hands the brochure had come. But the company did prepare and on 1 June 1981 despatched to their sales staff a memorandum instructing them to amend their own copies of the brochure by deleting the code letters 'AC'. The memorandum further instructed the sales staff to inform travel agents and customers of the error whenever a booking was sought to be made for the Seashells Hotel holiday. A letter was also sent in June 1981 to customers who had already booked a Seashells holiday informing them that the bedrooms were not air-conditioned.

The letter, of course, never went to Mr Wade who did not make his booking until 13 January 1982. He made the booking through a Plymouth travel agent who telephoned a member of the respondent company's sales staff who accepted it. Under the instruction of 1 June 1981 the member of staff should have informed the travel agent of the error in description. The justices made no finding as to whether she did or did not do so, although they ventured the comment in their case stated that 'the travel agent might well have known'. It certainly was not found as a fact that he did. But the justices did find unequivocally that Mr Wade was never informed of the lack of air-conditioning at the hotel and that he selected the holiday from the brochure in reliance upon its uncorrected false statement that the bedrooms were air-conditioned. Mr Wade and his wife went on the holiday on 3 March 1982, found to their discomfort that the bedroom was not air-conditioned and, not surprisingly, complained to the trading standards officer on their return home.

It is no exaggeration to say that the social impact of the class of business which I have described and in which the respondent company is engaged has been immense. It has brought about a dramatic change in the lifestyle of millions. People rely on the brochures issued by the companies engaged in this highly competitive business when choosing their annual holidays abroad. Some, like Mr and Mrs Wade in this case, choose to travel great distances to far-away places very different from anything which they have experienced at home upon their faith in a description which they have read in a brochure but which they cannot check.

The Trade Descriptions Act 1968 is plainly a very important safeguard for those members of the public (and they run into millions) who choose their holidays in this way. If the protection is not to be undermined, the Act must be widely known (as indeed it is), easily understood (as, having heard the arguments in this case, I fear that it may not be), and must be of general application save in situations specifically excepted by the statute itself. The Act is not based on the law of contract or tort. It operates by prohibiting false descriptions under the pain of penalties enforced through the criminal courts. But it is not a truly criminal statute. Its purpose is not the enforcement of the criminal law but the maintenance of trading standards. Trading standards, not criminal behaviour, are its concern.

Its prohibitions include false trade descriptions applied to goods (s 1); misleading indications as to the price of goods (s 11); false representations as to royal approval or awards (s 12); and false statements as to the nature of services, accommodation, or facilities provided in the course of business (s 14). It provides for certain defences to be available, two of which could have been relevant in this case. They are defences made available under ss 23 and 24, to which I shall return later. Neither section was invoked at the hearing before the justices, who consequently made no finding upon either of them. Indeed, it was argued by the respondent in your Lordships' House that neither was applicable to an offence charged under s 14.

The Act, of course, to be of any value at all in modern conditions, has to cover trades and businesses conducted on a large scale by individual proprietors, by firms, and by bodies corporate. The day-to-day business activities of large enterprises, whatever their legal structure, are necessarily conducted by their employees, and particularly by their sales staff. It follows that many of the acts prohibited by the Act will be the acts of employees done in the course of the trade or business and without the knowledge at the time of those who direct the business. It will become clear that the Act does cover such acts when one comes to consider the terms of the two statutory defences to which I have already referred. The Act also makes specific provision consistent with this view of its operation in respect of businesses carried on by bodies corporate. Section 20 provides that where an offence has been committed by a body corporate and was committed with the consent or is attributable to the neglect of a director or other officer of the company, he '*as well as the body corporate*' is guilty of the offence ...

My Lords, the subject-matter and structure of the Act make plain that the Act belongs to that class of legislation which prohibits acts which 'are not criminal in any real sense, but are acts which in the public interest are prohibited under a penalty', as Wright J put it in *Sherraz v De Rutzen* [1895] 1 QB 918, 922. In construing the offence-creating sections of the Act it will, therefore, be necessary to bear in mind that it may well have been the intention of the legislature 'in order to guard against the happening of the forbidden thing, to impose a liability upon a principal even though he does not know of, and is not a party to, the forbidden act done by his servant': see *per* Viscount Reading CJ in *Mousell Brothers Ltd v London and North-Western Railway Co* [1917] 2 KB 836, 844.

While, however, the subject-matter of the Act is such that the presumption recognised by Lord Reid in *Sweet v Parsley* [1970] AC 132, 148G as applicable to truly criminal statutes 'that Parliament did not intend to make criminals of persons who were in no way blameworthy in what they did' is not applicable to this Act, it does not necessarily follow that merely because an offence-creating section in the Act is silent as to *mens rea* its silence must be construed as excluding *mens rea*. As Lord Reid said, at 149, in the absence of a clear indication that an offence is intended to be an absolute offence one must examine all relevant circumstances in order to establish the intention of Parliament.

What the relevant circumstances are may now be said to have been settled in a line of cases of which the greatest is *Sweet v Parsley* and the most recent is a decision of the Privy Council in a Hong Kong appeal, *Gammon (Hong Kong) Ltd v Attorney General of Hong Kong* [1985] AC 1. At the end of the day the question whether an offence created by statute requires *mens rea*, guilty knowledge or intention, in whole, in part, or not at all, turns on the subject-matter, the language and the structure of the Act studied as a whole, on the language of the particular statutory provision under consideration construed in the light of the legislative purpose embodied in the Act, and on 'whether strict liability in respect of all or any of the essential ingredients of the offence would promote the object of the provision': *Gammon's* case at 16 and see *Sweet v Parsley* [1970] AC 132, 163, *per* Lord Diplock.

In the light of the foregoing it is now necessary to determine the proper construction to be put upon the words of s 14(1)(a). The necessary ingredients of the offence as formulated in the subsection are that: (1) a person in the course of a trade or business (2) makes a statement (3) which he knows to be false (4) as to the provision in the course of trade or business of any services, accommodation, or facilities. The respondent submits that the essence of the offence is knowingly making a false statement. The appellant submits that it suffices to prove that the statement was made on a person's behalf in the course of his business and that its content was false to the knowledge of the person carrying on the business.

My Lords, I accept the appellant's construction as correct. First, it advances the legislative purpose embodied in the Act, in that it strikes directly against the false statement irrespective of the reason for, or explanation of, its falsity. It involves, of course, construing the offence as one of strict liability to the extent that the offence can be committed unknowingly, ie without knowledge of the act of statement: but this is consistent with the social purpose of a statute in the class to which this Act belongs. And the strictness of the offence does no injustice: the accused, if he has acted innocently, can invoke and prove one of the statutory defences. Second, the appellant's submission has the advantage of following the literal and natural meaning of the words used. The subsection says not that it is an offence knowingly to make the statement but that it is an offence to make the statement.

Respondent's counsel, however, in support of his submission made a number of telling points. None of them is, in my judgment, strong enough to overcome the difficulties in his way. First, he relied on the general principles governing the interpretation of the provisions of a criminal statute. They are, however, for the reasons already developed, not applicable to this statute. Second, he submitted that he who makes a statement must as a matter of common sense know that he is making it. This is not so, however, when one is dealing, as in this statute, with statements made in the course of a trade or business. It would stultify the statute if this submission were to be upheld. Third, he contrasted the wording of s 14(1)(a) with (b). Section 14(1)(b) provides that it should be an offence 'recklessly' to make the false statement. The inference arises, therefore, that the offence under s 14(1)(a) requires proof of a deliberate false statement. This, with respect, I believe to be his best point, but it cannot prevail against all the indications to which I have referred in favour of the interpretation put upon (a) by the appellant.

But this is not the end of the respondent's case. There remains the question: did the respondent make any statement at all as to the air-conditioning of the hotel bedroom on 13 January when Mr Wade read it? The respondent's submission was that such a statement was made only once, on publication of the brochure in May 1981. The importance of the question is not only that the prosecution pinned its case to 13 January 1982 but that in May 1981 the company did not know the statement was false whereas in January 1982 it did know it was false.

This submission was not open to the respondent company before the justices or in the Divisional Court. The Court of Appeal had decided in *R v Thomson Holidays Ltd* [1974] QB 592 that a new statement is made on every occasion that an interested member of the public reads it in a brochure published by a company engaged in attracting his custom. The court considered that communication is the essence of statement. My Lords, I think *Thomson's* case was correctly decided, even though I do not accept the totality of the court's reasoning. A statement can consist of a communication to another: and in the context of this Act and the circumstances of this class of business I have no hesitation in accepting the court's view that communication by an uncorrected brochure of false information to someone who is being invited to do business in reliance upon the brochure is 'to make a statement' within s 14(1)(a). But there can be statements which are not communicated to others. It was unnecessary for the Court of Appeal to hold that communication was of the essence, and to that extent only I think the court erred.

The respondent's case that the company only made one statement, ie on publication of the brochure, is as fallacious in its way as is the view of the Court of Appeal that without communication there is no statement. I have no doubt that a statement as to the air-conditioning in the hotel was made when the brochure was published. But further statements to the same effect were made whenever persons did business with the company on the strength of the uncorrected brochure which so far from being withdrawn continued to be the basis on which the company was inviting business. There is no injustice in this being the effect of the statute. If the company believed that there was no default on its part when the false description was communicated to Mr Wade, it should have admitted that the offence was committed and called evidence to establish a s 23 or s 24 defence. Instead, the company chose to argue that no offence had been committed at all, an argument which for the reasons I have given, I believe to be unsustainable.

Accordingly, I hold that the respondent company did make a statement as to the air-conditioning to Mr Wade on 13 January 1982. This conclusion renders it unnecessary to deal with the ingenious, if far-fetched, analogy which the respondent sought to draw between this case and your Lordships' analysis of a 'result crime' in the arson case of *R v Miller* [1983] 2 AC 161, and which found favour with the Divisional Court. I will say only that to construe the words 'to make a statement which he knows to be false' in the context of this Act as being capable of covering a physical act of statement completed or perfected at a later date by a damaging result when it is read appears to me to be an unhelpful and overelaborate approach to the interpretation of an Act intended to protect the public by provisions which the public can understand without a lawyer at their elbow. Making a statement consists of the act of statement. If it has consequences, so be it: the consequences are not the statement.

For these reasons I would make answer to the certified point of law as follows. A statement which was false was made by the respondent company in the course of its business when it was read by Mr Wade, an interested member of the public doing business with the respondent company upon the basis of the statement. The offence was committed on that occasion because the respondent company then knew that it was false to state that the hotel accommodation was air-conditioned. The fact that the company was unaware of the falsity of the statement when it was published as part of the brochure in May 1981 is irrelevant. If the company believed it was innocent of fault, it was open to it to prove lack of fault. It did not do so ...

Pharmaceutical Society of Great Britain v Storkwain Ltd [1986] 1 WLR 903 (HL)

Lord Goff of Chieveley: My Lords, this appeal is concerned with a question of construction of s 58 of the Medicines Act 1968. Section 58(2)(a) of the Act provides:

> (2) Subject to the following provisions of this section: (a) no person shall sell by retail, or supply in circumstances corresponding to retail sale, a medicinal product of a description, or falling within a class specified in an order under this section except in accordance with a prescription given by an appropriate practitioner ...

By s 67(2) of the Act of 1968, it is provided that any person who contravenes, *inter alia*, s 58 shall be guilty of an offence. The question which has arisen for decision in the present case is whether, in accordance with the well-organised presumption, there are to be read into s 58(2)(a) words appropriate to require *mens rea*, on the principle stated in *R v Tolson* (1889) 23 QBD 168, and *Sweet v Parsley* [1970] AC 132.

The matter has arisen in the following way. On 2 February 1984, informations were preferred by the prosecutor, the Pharmaceutical Society of Great Britain, against the defendants, Storkwain Ltd, alleging that the defendants had on 14 December 1982 unlawfully sold by retail certain medicines. It was alleged that they unlawfully sold by retail, to a person purporting to be Linda Largey, 200 Physeptone tablets and 50 Ritalin tablets; and that they unlawfully sold by retail, to a person purporting to be Thomas Patterson, 50 ampoules of Physeptone and 30 Valium tablets. All these medicines are substances controlled under Article 3(1)(b) of the Medicines (Prescription only) Order 1980 (SI 1980, No 1921); and the informations alleged in each case that the sale was not in accordance with a prescription issued by an appropriate practitioner, contrary to s 58(2) and s 67(2) of the Act of 1968. Before the magistrate, the evidence (which was all agreed) was to the effect that the medicines were supplied under documents which purported to be prescriptions signed by a doctor, Dr Irani, of Queensdale Road, London; but that subsequent inquiries revealed that the prescriptions were both forgeries. It was submitted on behalf of the defendants that the presumption of *mens rea* applied to the prohibition in s 58(2)(a) of the Act of 1981; and that, the medicines having been supplied by the defendants on the basis of prescriptions which they believed in good faith and on reasonable grounds to be valid prescriptions, the informations should be dismissed. The magistrate accepted that submission and accordingly dismissed the informations; but he stated a case for the opinion of the High Court, the question for the opinion of the court being whether or not mens rea was required in the case of a prosecution under ss 58(2) and 67(2) of the Medicines Act 1968. On 2 May 1985, a Divisional Court (Farquharson and Tudor Price JJ) answered the question in the negative, and accordingly allowed the appeal of the prosecutor and directed that the case should be remitted to the magistrate with a direction to convict. The Divisional Court certified the following point of law as being of general public importance:

> Whether the prosecution has to prove *mens rea* where an information is brought under s 58(2)(a) of the Medicines Act 1968, where the allegation is that the supply of prescription only drugs was made by the [defendants] in accordance with a forged prescription and without fault on their part.

From that decision, the defendants now appeal with leave of your Lordships' House, the Divisional Court having refused leave ...

For the defendants, Mr Fisher submitted that there must, in accordance with the well-recognised presumption, be read into s 58(2)(a) words appropriate to require *mens rea* in accordance with *R v Tolson*, (1889) 23 QBD 168; in other words, to adopt the language of Lord Diplock in *Sweet v Parsley* [1970] AC 132, 163, the subsection must be read subject to the implication that a necessary element in the prohibition (and hence in the offence created by the subsection together with s 67(2) of the Act of 1968) is the absence of belief, held honestly and upon reasonable grounds, in the existence of facts which, if true, would make the act innocent. He further submitted, with reference to the speech of Lord Reid in *Sweet v Parsley*, at 149, that the offence created by s 58(2)(a) and s 67(2) of the Act of 1968 was not to be classified as merely an offence of a quasi-criminal character in which the presumption of *mens rea* might more readily be rebutted, because in his submission the offence was one which would result in a stigma attaching to a person who was convicted of it, especially as Parliament had regarded it as sufficiently serious to provide that it should be triable on indictment, and that the maximum penalty should be two years' imprisonment. He also submitted that, if Parliament had considered that a pharmacist who dispensed under a forged prescription in good faith and without fault should be convicted of the offence, it would surely have made express provision to that effect; and that the imposition of so strict a liability could not be justified on the basis that it would tend towards greater efficiency on the part of pharmacists in detecting forged prescriptions. Finally, he referred your Lordships to the Misuse of Drugs Act 1971. Under s 4(1) and (3) of that Act, it is an offence to supply a controlled drug to another; but it is provided in s 28 that (subject to an immaterial exception) it shall be a defence for the accused to prove that he neither knew of nor suspected nor had reason to suspect the existence of some fact alleged by the prosecution which it is necessary for the prosecution to prove if he is to be convicted of the offence charged. Mr Fisher submitted that it would be anomalous if such a defence were available in the case of the more serious offence of supplying a controlled drug to another, but that the presumption of *mens rea* should be held inapplicable in the case of the offence created by s 58(2)(a) and 67(2) of the Act of 1968.

I am unable to accept Mr Fisher's submission, for the simple reason that it is, in my opinion, clear from the Act of 1968 that Parliament must have intended that the presumption of *mens rea* should be inapplicable to s 58(2)(a). First of all, it appears from the Act of 1968 that, where Parliament wished to recognise that *mens rea* should be an ingredient of an offence created by the Act, it has expressly so provided. Thus, taking first of all offences created under provisions of Part II of the Act of 1968, express requirements of *mens rea* are to be found both in s 45(2) and in s 46(1)(2) and (3) of the Act. More particularly, in relation to offences created by Part III and Parts V and VI of the Act of 1968, s 121 makes detailed provision for a requirement of *mens rea* in respect of certain specified sections of the Act, including ss 63 – 65 (which are contained in Part 3), but significantly not s 58, nor indeed ss 52 and 53 ... It is very difficult to avoid the conclusion that, by omitting s 58 from those sections to which s 121 is expressly made applicable, Parliament intended that there should be no implication of a requirement of *mens rea* in s 58(2)(a). This view is fortified by subsections (4) and (5) of s 58 itself. Subsection (4)(a) provides that any order made by the appropriate ministers for the purposes of s 58 may provide that s 58(2)(a) or (b), or both, shall have effect subject to such exemptions as may be specified in the order. From this subsection alone it follows that the ministers, if they think it right, can provide for exemption where there is no *mens rea* on the part of the accused. Subsection (5) provides that any exemption conferred by an order in accordance with subsection (4)(a) may be conferred subject to such conditions or limitations as may be specified in the order. From this it follows that if the ministers, acting under subsection (4), were to confer an exemption relating to sales where the vendor lacked the requisite *mens rea* they may nevertheless circumscribe their exemption with conditions and limitations which render the exemption far narrower than the implication for which Mr Fisher contends should be read into the statute itself. I find this to be very difficult to reconcile with the proposed implication.

It comes as no surprise to me, therefore, to discover that the relevant order in force at that time, the Medicines (Prescription only) Order 1980, is drawn entirely in conformity with the construction of the statute which I favour. It is unnecessary, in the present case, to consider whether the relevant articles of the Order may be taken into account in construing s 58 of the Act of 1968; it is enough, for present purposes, that I am able to draw support from the fact that the ministers, in making the Order, plainly did not read s 58 as subject to the implication proposed by Mr Fisher. So, for example, Article 11 of the order (which is headed 'Exemption in cases involving another's default') reads as follows:

> The restrictions imposed by s 58(2)(a) (restrictions on sale and supply) shall not apply to the sale or supply of a prescription only medicine by a person who, having exercised all due diligence believes on reasonable grounds that the product sold or supplied is not a prescription only medicine, where it is due to the act or default of another person that the product is a product to which s 58(2)(a) applies.

This provision which, by including the words 'having exercised due diligence', provides for a narrower exemption than that which Mr Fisher has submitted should be read by implication into the statute, in the limited circumstances specified in the concluding words of the paragraph, is plainly inconsistent with the existence of any such implication. Likewise, Article 13(1) provides that, for the purposes of s 58(2)(a), a prescription only medicine shall not be taken to be sold or supplied in accordance with a prescription given by a practitioner unless certain specified conditions are fulfilled. Those conditions, which are very detailed, are set out in Article 13(2); and they all presuppose the existence of a valid prescription. Furthermore, Article 13(3) provides:

> The restrictions imposed by s 58(2)(a) (restrictions on sale and supply) shall not apply to a sale or supply of a prescription only medicine which is not in

> accordance with a prescription given by an appropriate practitioner by reason only that a condition specified in paragraph (2) is not fulfilled, where the person selling or supplying the prescription only medicine, having exercised all due diligence believes on reasonable grounds that that condition is fulfilled in relation to that sale or supply.

So here again we find a provision which creates an exemption in narrower terms than that which Mr Fisher submits is to be found, by implication, in s 58(2)(a) itself. It follows that Article 13, like Article 11, of the Order is inconsistent with the existence of any such implication.

For these reasons, which are substantially the same as those which are set out in the judgments of Farquharson and Tudor Price JJ in the *Divisional Court* [1985] 3 All ER 4, I am unable to accept the submissions advanced on behalf of the defendants. I gratefully adopt as my own the following passage from the judgment of Farquharson J, at 10:

> It is perfectly obvious that pharmacists are in a position to put illicit drugs and perhaps other medicines on the market. Happily this rarely happens but it does from time to time. It can therefore be readily understood that Parliament would find it necessary to impose a heavier liability on those who are in such a position, and make them more strictly accountable for any breaches of the Act.

I would therefore answer the certified question in the negative, and dismiss the appeal with costs.

DPP v Waite (1996) 160 JP 726 (DC)

Newman J: The facts of the matter are as follows. The respondent, on the appeal, was driving his motor car at about 11.25 in the evening of 11 January 1995. His car was fitted with a scanning receiver which was located in his dashboard. The scanning receiver was connected to an aerial type of lead and was tuned into the Nuneaton police channel. He owned the receiver; he had purchased it a year before.

On the evening in question, when he was stopped by two police officers, he was not at that time using the receiver, but the scanning receiver had been specifically tuned into the police station. On the facts as found, earlier that evening the respondent had been listening to the police channel with his girlfriend at approximately 11 pm, namely some 25 minutes before he was stopped.

On the material before the magistrates, the magistrates found that the precise purpose he had in tuning to that particular frequency was, as they put it, '... not able to be ascertained on the evidence available'.

The respondent contended, and no doubt contended in the course of the successful submission of no case which was made to the magistrates, as follows:

> In the absence of any evidence to the contrary his purpose in listening to the broadcasts should be seen as for amusement only with no special interest in or intention to obtain, use or act upon any particular information therein.

The magistrates were referred to *Paul v Ministry of Posts and Telecommunications* [1973] Crim LR 322. Having heard submissions and having considered the matter, they dismissed the case because they were of the view that there was not a blanket prohibition on the use of radio scanners, and consideration of the section and the case of *Paul* led them to conclude that simply listening in to particular messages did not give rise to an inference or a conclusion that there had been what the section required, namely 'an intent to obtain information'.

The offence with which this respondent was charged was using his receiver with intent to obtain information as to the contents, sender or addressee of the messages broadcasted, and not being authorised to do so by the Secretary of State. The relevant words which have fallen for consideration in this case, and upon which we have been addressed by both counsel, are 'intent to obtain information'.

Mr Morse, for the DPP (the appellant) submits that the purpose for which any information is put, it having been obtained by listening to a receiver such as this, is irrelevant to the commission of the offence. He says, by way of submission, that what the section of the Act is concerned to prohibit is the intentional obtaining of information; as opposed to the accidental obtaining of information; accidental, in the sense that one may be tuning in to your receiver and in the course of tuning in, with a view to listening to some other channel, in passing hear police messages on the police wavelength. The evidence here, he submits, established according to the findings in the case stated, that this respondent had deliberately tuned into the channel, had settled on the channel and had used his device so as to listen to the messages on the channel. That being the evidence, the case was made out and it was wrong for the magistrate to acquit the respondent.

Miss Taiton, for the respondent, has submitted to us that the word 'obtain' means more than just simply to receive. She submits that there must be some positive act, some act by way of procurement which can be found to fall within the meaning of the section. Just listening for entertainment is not sufficient. Further, she argues that the real distinction between that which the Act is designed to prohibit and that which occurred in this case is that the evidence established no more than that the information would be listened to, that the chances were the information would not be retained, would hardly be present in the mind of the respondent and would dissipate with no consequent use being made of it. Thus, she says, those two arguments drawn together provide the true meaning of the section.

In my judgment, Mr Morse's submission is correct. No question of purpose requires consideration. There does, and will undoubtedly have to be, some positive act or some act of procurement, as Miss Taiton submitted. That will normally be, as in this case, provided by the deliberate tuning in to the programme.

If, having tuned into the programme, the user deliberately and intentionally settles on the channel in order to listen to the messages, in my judgment, it cannot be suggested that in listening the user is not obtaining information within the meaning of the Act. The purpose to which the information may be put may, at the time it is obtained, have been formed. There may be no particular purpose other than the desire to listen to the information. The user does not have to have an improper purpose in mind at the time he obtains the information in order to be guilty of an offence. A person who intentionally and deliberately listens (*Paul v Ministry of Posts and Telecommunications*) to the messages thereby obtains them, and commits the offence. It follows, the magistrates were wrong to acquit the respondent on a submission of no case and thus we shall have to consider what course should now be taken.

Pill LJ: I agree. Miss Taiton submits that the crux of the matter is what was the defendant's state of mind and what 'intent' is required to be proved. Miss Taiton concedes that there must, on the evidence, have been an intent to listen to the broadcast. She concedes, on the authority of *Paul*, that mischievous intent is not necessary. Her submission is that intent to obtain information within the meaning of the section requires more than merely listening to a broadcast, without any intention of making a note, mental or otherwise, of the contents. If the user intends to listen only for amusement or entertainment, Miss Taiton submits that the necessary intent is not established.

Like my Lord, I cannot accept that submission. The proof of an intent to obtain information within the meaning of the section does not require proof that the listener intends to memorise or store the information received from the broadcast. An intent to obtain information merely for the amusement of the listener is sufficient for the purpose of the section.

I agree that the appeal should be allowed.

R v Blake [1997] 1 All ER 963 (CA)

Hirst LJ: [The appellant was convicted of using a station for wireless telegraphy without a licence]

... [T]here was no dispute that [the appellant] knew he was using the broadcasting apparatus in the studio. His defence was that he believed he was making demonstration tapes at the time and so did not know that he was, in fact, transmitting.

The question which the [trial judge] had to decide on ... was whether, as the prosecution contended, the offence created by s 1(1) of the Wireless Telegraphy Act 1949 is an absolute offence of strict liability, or whether, as the defence contended, the prosecution needed to establish *mens rea* ...

Section 1(1) provides, so far as relevant, as follows:

> *Licensing of wireless telegraphy* - No person shall establish or use any station for wireless telegraphy or instal or use any apparatus for wireless telegraphy except under the authority of a licence in that behalf granted under this section ... and any person who establishes or uses any station for wireless telegraphy or instals or uses any apparatus for wireless telegraphy except under and in accordance with such a licence shall be guilty of an offence under this Act...

[His Lordship then quoted from the judgment of Lord Scarman in *Gammon (Hong Kong) Ltd v Attorney-General of Hong Kong* [1985] AC 1 at 14:]

> In their Lordships' opinion, the law relevant to this appeal may be stated in the following propositions ...: (1) there is a presumption of law that *mens rea* is required before a person can be held guilty of a criminal offence; (2) the presumption is particularly strong where the offence is 'truly criminal' in character; (3) the presumption applies to statutory offences, and can be displaced only if this is clearly or by necessary implication the effect of the statute; (4) the only situation in which the presumption can be displaced is where the statute is concerned with an issue of social concern; public safety is such an issue; (5) even where a statute is concerned with such an issue, the presumption of mens rea stands unless it can also be shown that the creation of strict liability will be effective to promote the objects of the statute by encouraging greater vigilance to prevent the commission of the prohibited act.

[His Lordship then noted the creation of additional offences by the Broadcasting Act 1990 and noted that the penalty was increased, from 3 months' imprisonment and/or a fine up to £100, to six months' imprisonment and/or a fine up to the statutory maximum (following summary trial) or 2 years' imprisonment and/or a fine (following trial on indictment).] ...

The solution to this case ... clearly lies in the application of the five principles laid down by Lord Scarman in the *Gammon* case. In our judgment, since throughout the history of s 1(1), an offender has been potentially subject to a term of imprisonment, the offence is 'truly criminal' in character, and it follows ... that the presumption in favour of *mens rea* is particularly strong. However, it seems to us manifest that the purpose behind making unlicensed transmissions a serious criminal offence must have been one of social concern in the interests of public safety ... since undoubtedly the emergency services and air traffic controllers were using radio communications in 1949, albeit in a much more rudimentary form than nowadays. No doubt the much greater sophistication of these modes of communication, and the wider prevalence of pirate radio stations 40 years on, led to the substantial increase in the penalty in 1990.

Clearly, interference with transmissions by these vital public services poses a grave risk to wide sections of the public. We, therefore, consider that the test laid down in para (4) in the *Gammon* case is met.

Furthermore, we are satisfied that the test in para (5) is also met, since the imposition of an absolute offence must surely encourage greater vigilance on the part of those establishing or using a station, or installing or using the apparatus, to avoid committing the offence, eg in the case of users by carefully checking whether they are on air; it must also operate as a deterrent. The case is thus in our judgment, *mutatis mutandis*, comparable with *R v Wells Street Metropolitan Stipendiary Magistrate ex p Westminster City Council* [1986] 1 WLR 1046 [where the Divisional Court applied the principles laid down in *Gammon* and concluded that s 55(1) of the Town and Country Planning Act 1971, which prohibited the execution of various works to a listed building, was an absolute offence], perhaps *a fortiori*, since here public safety is the main consideration and, in our view, a consideration of paramount importance ...

So ... it is incumbent upon the prosecution to establish that the defendant knew he was making use of the apparatus, but they need not show that he was doing it with a guilty mind. Thus, for example, if a remark made by a bystander near the studio was accidentally picked up by the microphone and broadcast, the bystander would not be liable.

In these circumstances, we are satisfied that s 1(1) does create an absolute offence and it follows that this appeal will be dismissed.

In *Harper* (1997), *The Times*, April 16 (news item), the Divisional Court held that insanity is no defence to a charge of driving with excess alcohol, since that offence is one of strict liability. The defendant suffered from manic depression and was found by police 'talking gibberish' and displaying 'a Walter Mitty nature'.

Note: In *R v Sandhu* (1997) *The Times*, 2 January, the Court of Appeal held that where an offence is one of strict liability, evidence which is irrelevant to the elements of the offence is inadmissible. Such evidence must not be adduced where it is also prejudicial to the defendant.

CORPORATE LIABILITY

A limited company is a legal person and so can commit offences for which *mens rea* is not required (ie strict liability offences).

Where *mens rea* is required, a company can still be guilty of the offence, provided that a very senior member of the company's staff, such as director of the company, had the appropriate mens rea. See *R v Robert Millar (Contractors) Ltd* [1970] 2 QB 54 and *R v P&O Ferries* (1991) 93 Cr App R 72.

Some statutes impose liability on individuals who are employed by a company. To be liable for these offences, such individuals must have a governing role in the affairs of the company: see *R v Boal* [1992] 1 QB 591.

A company can be accessory to a crime, even in respect of offences it could not commit as a principal. See, for example, *R v Robert Millar (Contractors) Ltd* [1970] 2 QB 54.

R v I C R Haulage Ltd [1944] KB 551 (CA)

Stable J: The question before us is whether a limited company can be indicted for a conspiracy to defraud. Section 33 of the Criminal Justice Act 1925, removed certain procedural obstacles which had hitherto existed in connection with the trial of criminal offences alleged against corporations. This section did not enlarge the ambit of a company's criminal responsibility, but provided machinery for simplifying its enforcement.

It was conceded by counsel for the company that a limited company can be indicted for some criminal offences, and it was conceded by counsel for the Crown that there were some criminal offences for which a limited company cannot be indicted. The controversy centred round the question where and on what principle the line must be drawn and on which side of the line an indictment such as the present one falls. Counsel for the company contended that the true principle was that an indictment against a limited company for any offence involving as an essential ingredient *mens rea* in the restricted sense of a dishonest or criminal mind, must be bad for the reason that a company, not being a natural person, cannot have a mind honest or otherwise, and that, consequently, though in certain circumstances it is civilly liable for the fraud of its officers, agents or servants, it is immune from criminal process. Counsel for the Crown contended that a limited company, like any other entity recognised by the law, can as a general rule be indicted for its criminal acts which from the very necessity of the case must be performed by human agency and which in given circumstances become the acts of the company, and that for this purpose there was no distinction between an intention or other function of the mind and any other form of activity.

The offences for which a limited company cannot be indicted are, it was argued, exceptions to the general rule arising from the limitations which must inevitably attach to an artificial entity, such as a company. Included in these exceptions are the cases in which, from its very nature, the offence cannot be committed by a corporation, as, for example, perjury, an offence which cannot be vicariously committed, or bigamy, an offence which a limited company, not being a natural person, cannot commit vicariously or otherwise. A further exception, but for a different reason, comprises offences of which murder is an example, where the only punishment the court can impose is corporal, the basis on which this exception rests being that the court will not stultify itself by embarking on a trial in which, if a verdict of guilty is returned, no effective order by way of sentence can be made. In our judgment these contentions of the Crown are substantially sound, and the existence of these exceptions, and it may be that there are others, is by no means inconsistent with the general rule ...

In support of the contention of the Crown we were referred to a number of authorities. The earliest of these to which we think it necessary to refer is *Pharmaceutical Society v London and Provincial Supply Association* 5 App Cas 857, 869. The decision in that case, which was earlier than the Interpretation Act 1889, was that the words 'person' in the Act then under consideration did not include an incorporated company. Lord Blackburn, however, said at 869:

> But I may also say now, in order to avoid coming back to it, that I do not feel the least difficulty arising from what seems to have troubled some of the learned judges in the court below. If this word does include a corporation – I quite agree that a corporation cannot, in one sense, commit a crime – a corporation cannot be imprisoned, if imprisonment be the sentence for the crime; a corporation cannot be hanged or put to death if that be the punishment for the crime; and so, in those senses a corporation cannot commit a crime. But a corporation may be fined, and a corporation may pay damages; and therefore I must totally dissent, notwithstanding what Bramwell LJ said, or is reported to have said, upon the supposition that a body corporate or a corporation that incorporated itself for the purpose of publishing a newspaper could not be tried and fined, or an action for damages brought against it for a libel; or that a corporation which commits a nuisance could not be convicted of the nuisance or the like. I must really say that I do not feel the slightest doubt upon that part of the case. If you could get over the first difficulty of saying that the word 'person' here may be construed to include an artificial person, a corporation, I should not have the least difficulty upon those other grounds which have been suggested.

Lord Blackburn's emphatic expression of opinion that a limited company can be indicted and convicted for publishing a criminal libel was later accepted by the Court of Appeal in *Triplex Safety Glass Co Ltd v Lancegaye Safety Glass Co Ltd* [1939] 2 KB 395, where it was held that a limited company was entitled to object to answering an interrogatory on the ground that the answer would tend to incriminate it. As an actual condition of mind amounting to express malice may be an element in the offence of libel, it is plain that the Court of Appeal decided that, whatever the principle may be that fixes the line between those offences for which a limited company can and those for which it cannot be indicted, it is not the presence or absence in the human agent of a particular condition of mind. It would be unreasonable to suppose that a limited company can be indicted for a criminal libel only in those cases in which express malice is not proved, or that it could defeat a prosecution by proving that its duly authorised agent was, in fact, actuated by malice.

The latest authority is the *DPP v Kent and Sussex Contractors Ltd* [1944] KB 146. A limited company was charged with offences under a Defence of the Realm Regulation which involved an intent to deceive. The justices dismissed the informations on the ground that a body corporate could not be guilty of the offences charged in as much as an act of will or state of mind which could not be imputed to a corporation was implicit in the commission of these offences. On a case stated to a Divisional Court this conclusion of law on the part of the justices was held to be erroneous, and the case was remitted to them to hear and determine. It is clear that the state of mind involved was a dishonest state of mind, namely an intention to deceive and that the state of mind was an essential element in the offence. There is a distinction between that case and the present, in that there the offences were charged under a regulation having the effect of a statute, whereas here the offence is a common law misdemeanour, but, in our judgment, this distinction has no material bearing on the question we have to decide. Lord Caldecote CJ said, at 151: 'the real point we have to decide ... is whether a company is capable of an act of will or of a state of mind, so as to be able to form an intention to deceive or to have knowledge of the truth or falsity of a statement', and after dealing with a number of authorities, he proceeds, at 155:

> The offences created by the regulation are those of doing something with intent to deceive or of making a statement known to be false in a material

> particular. There was ample evidence, on the facts as stated in the special case, that the company, by the only people who could act or speak or think for it, had done both these things, and I can see nothing in any of the authorities to which we have been referred which requires us to say that a company is incapable of being found guilty of the offences with which the respondent company was charged.

In his judgment in the same case MacNaghten J says as follows:

> It is true that a corporation can only have knowledge and form an intention through its human agents, but circumstances may be such that the knowledge and intention of the agent must be imputed to the body corporate ... If the responsible agent of a company, acting within the scope of this authority, puts forward on its behalf a document which he knows to be false and by which he intends to deceive, I apprehend that according to the authorities that my Lord has cited, his knowledge and intention must be imputed to the company.

With both the decision in that case and the reasoning on which it rests, we agree.

In our judgment, both on principle and in accordance with the balance of authority, the present indictment was properly laid against the company, and the learned commissioner rightly refused to quash. We are not deciding that in every case where an agent of a limited company acting in its business commits a crime the company is automatically to be held criminally responsible. Our decision only goes to the invalidity of the indictment on the face of it, an objection which is taken before any evidence is led and irrespective of the facts of the particular case. Where in any particular case there is evidence to go to a jury that the criminal act of an agent, including his state of mind, intention, knowledge or belief is the act of the company, and, in cases where the presiding judge so rules, whether the jury are satisfied that it has been proved, must depend on the nature of the charge, the relative position of the officer or agent, and the other relevant facts and circumstances of the case. It was because we were satisfied on the hearing of this appeal that the facts proved were amply sufficient to justify a finding that the acts of the managing director were the acts of the company and the fraud of that person was the fraud of the company, that we upheld the conviction against the company, and, indeed, on the appeal to this court no argument was advanced that the facts proved would not warrant a conviction of the company assuming that the conviction of the managing director was upheld and that the indictment was good in law.

R v Robert Millar (Contractors) Ltd and Millar [1970] 2 QB 54 (CA)

Fenton Atkinson LJ: These appeals and applications, which will be refused, arise out of a very terrible accident which occurred on Thursday 6 June 1968, when a heavy lorry and trailer laden with 18 tons of bricks was travelling north on the M6 motorway at about 45 mph driven by a man called Hart. At a point in Lancashire near Newton-le-Willows the front offside tyre of the lorry blew out. Hart lost control, his vehicle swung to the right across the central reservation, it crashed into a motor car which was travelling south – that is to say coming from the opposite direction – and all six occupants of that car (the two grandparents, the two parents and the two children, the entire family in fact) were killed.

Examination of Hart's vehicle showed certain quite serious defects in the brakes of the trailer, but those defects could not be said to be a cause of the accident. The examination revealed beyond all doubt that, although five of the tyres on the lorry were in perfectly good condition, the front offside tyre was extremely badly worn: it was manifestly in a dangerous state and should never have been on the road.

Hart was charged with causing death by dangerous driving of all six persons. It was not suggested that the actual manner of his driving was of itself dangerous, or that he could have done any better than he did once the tyre burst. The case against him was founded on *R v Spurge* [1961] 2 QB 205 namely that he was driving a heavy vehicle at speed with a tyre which he must have known (and, indeed, did know very well) was in a dangerous state: and to drive a vehicle of that weight at any speed with that tyre with that knowledge was manifestly dangerous in the view of this court.

His own evidence made it clear that he knew of the defective state of the tyre: he said he had complained about it more than once to his employers with no result, but he had gone on this trip thinking the tyre might stand up to one more trip. His journey on this occasion started from Bridge of Weir, which is about 14 miles west of Glasgow; he travelled down into England to Newark to deliver a load; from there he went to Keele in Staffordshire, where he picked up a load of some 18 tons of bricks; and then he was to travel north back to Bridge of Weir.

He was found guilty by the jury on all six counts, and he was leniently treated by Fisher J by means of a modest fine and disqualification, the trial judge taking the view (as we think rightly) that the real major responsibility for this disaster lay elsewhere. Hart was at the material time employed by the appellant company, Robert Millar (Contractors) Ltd, who owned the vehicle, and that company had three directors. The appellant (Mr Robert Millar) was the managing director. On his own evidence he was a man responsible for the day-to-day running of the business: the other directors were his father (now semi-retired) and an uncle (who still works in the business in some capacity). But, as Robert Millar accepted in evidence, he was the man who gave the orders at the material time.

After a five-day trial at Liverpool Crown Court before Fisher J and a jury Robert Millar and the company were found guilty of counselling and procuring these six offences of causing death by dangerous driving; the case against them being that Robert Millar sent Hart out on this trip with the vehicle knowing full well that the front offside tyre was in a dangerous state ...

So I come at last to Mr Wright's two points of law. His first point logically (although he took it last) is that no such offence as counselling or procuring the causing of death by dangerous driving exists when the dangerous driving alleged is of what for convenience might be called the *Spurge* type of dangerous driving; and, if that is wrong, Mr Wright says that the gist of his clients' offence (ie the counselling and procuring of Hart to set off on this journey) was committed and was complete at the moment the vehicle set off from the garage at Bridge of Weir, and that was (if an offence at all) an offence committed in Scotland and, therefore, not triable in an English court.

As to the first of these submissions, Mr Wright accepts that there is an offence of counselling and procuring in involuntary manslaughter. For example, if a man arranges for a pregnant girl friend to have a back-street abortion and as a result the girl dies, then he accepts that cases such as *R v Buck and Buck* (1960) 44 Cr App R 213 and *R v Creamer* [1966] 1 QB 72 were correctly decided: the basis of the decision being that a man may properly be found guilty of being an accessory before the fact to involuntary manslaughter if he counsels or procures an unlawful act and one likely to do harm to another person and death results, even though the death was neither intended nor foreseen.

He accepts, further, that you may have a counsellor or procurer of the offence of causing death by dangerous driving in certain circumstances. For example, he accepts that if an employer orders his employee to drive a motor vehicle from point A to point B in a very short time so that to obey his orders the driver will have to drive down crowded streets at excessive speed, and the employee in trying to obey his orders does, in fact, drive at a dangerous speed down a crowded street and kills a pedestrian or other road-user, then Mr Wright agrees that the employer could properly be held to have counselled and procured the offence of causing death by dangerous driving. But Mr Wright says that that cannot apply to the *Spurge* type of dangerous driving, where he says, in effect, that driving in a manner dangerous only begins at the moment that the tyre bursts or the failure occurs or whatever it may be that causes the accident.

The members of this court cannot see why exactly the same principle does not apply to a *Spurge* type of case. *R v Spurge* [1961] 2 QB 205 itself was a case of a man being convicted of driving in a manner dangerous to the public, although the disaster was caused by him applying his brake and, because it was a defective brake, it caused his vehicle to swerve dangerously across the road. In our view, if a driver is sent out by his employer to drive a heavy vehicle on a trip extending over some hundreds of miles carrying heavy loads with a dangerously defective front offside tyre, by an employer who knows that the tyre is dangerous, and there is a serious risk of harm resulting to other road-users, then if that tyre does burst and thereby causes an accident killing somebody, the employer is guilty of counselling and procuring death by dangerous driving, and it is no answer to that to say that the driver of the vehicle at the time was said to be doing his best and was steering the vehicle properly, controlling it as well as he could and so on and there would have been no accident but for the bursting of the tyre. In our view, a man is driving in a manner dangerous to the public if he drives at some speed on the road a vehicle with a tyre which he knows is dangerous and defective and liable to burst at any moment.

We now turn to Mr Wright's second point. He has assembled with very great industry a mass of authorities going back 200 years or more; but, in our view, he has been unable to find any case which established his proposition. He has against him at least two statements of the law by very learned authors. I refer first to *Russell on Crime*, 12 edn, 1964, pp 128, 129, where the law is stated in this way:

> A simple but important point is sometimes overlooked, namely that when the law relating to principles and accessories as such is under consideration there is only one crime, although there may be more than one person criminally liable in respect of it; if there is more than one person, then the question arises as to the category in which each one is to be placed, that is, whether he is accessory before the fact, or principal in the first or second degree or an accessory after the fact. There is one crime, and that it has been committed must be established before there can be any question of criminal guilt of participation in it ...
>
> To make a man responsible for a crime, whether felony or misdemeanour, it is not essential that he should be present at the place where the crime takes effect, if he had, in fact, set in motion the agencies by which the crime is effected. But in case of absence from the scene of the crime, to make a man responsible as a principal offender, he must have set in force physical agencies or have employed an innocent agent.

It seems to us that in this case the company and Mr Millar set in motion on the road this vehicle with the known dangerous tyre.

The other statement of law is by Professor Glanville Williams, which appears in an article in (1965) 81 LQR 518 at 530, where he is dealing with secondary parties, accessories and abettors. He says:

> Where a crime is committed in England, a secondary party (accessory or abettor) can be punished even though he was not within British territorial jurisdiction at the time when the crime was committed or when he gave his assistance – at least if he is a citizen of the United Kingdom. [These are the important words:] This is an application of the principle that secondary parties are guilty not of self-subsisting crimes on their own account but of participation in a crime committed by another.

We think the law is correctly stated in the passages that I have read, and here the offence of causing death by dangerous driving was committed in England by Hart; but the appellants are guilty of participating in that crime and not of some self-subsisting crime on their own account and, therefore, they are in the same position as the principal offender and they are liable to be tried in this country. There is a second way of perhaps reaching the same result, and that is to be found set out very clearly in Fisher J's judgment in dealing with this matter at the Crown Court. He says at 64E, *above*:

> The offence of causing death by dangerous driving is plainly not committed until the death occurs, and in the present case the death occurred in England. Where an employer with actual or imputed knowledge of the defective mechanical state of the vehicle permits an employee to take that vehicle out on the road he is, so this indictment alleges, counselling and procuring the employee to drive that vehicle in that state and it seems to me that the common sense of the matter is that counselling and procuring is a continuous act which persists so long as the driver is driving the vehicle in that condition on the road.

We think that is right.

We are quite satisfied that it is not right on the facts of this case to say that the counselling and procuring was complete, over and done with at the moment that Hart drove his lorry out of the garage at Bridge of Weir. The counselling and procuring was a continuing act which persisted so long as Hart in pursuance of his employers' orders was driving the vehicle on this particular trip in its known dangerous condition on the road. In our view, at the moment this accident happened in Lancashire the appellants were still counselling and procuring the dangerous driving by Hart which brought about this disaster. In our view, therefore, the appeals against conviction by the company and Mr Millar must be dismissed.

Tesco Ltd v Nattrass [1972] AC 153 (HL)

Lord Reid: My Lords, the appellants own a large number of supermarkets in which they sell a wide variety of goods. The goods are put out for sale on shelves or stands, each article being marked with the price at which it is offered for sale. The customer selects the articles he wants, takes them to the cashier, and pays the price. From time to time the appellants, apparently by way of advertisement, sell 'flash packs' at prices lower than the normal price. In September 1969 they were selling Radiant washing powder in this way. The normal price was 3s 11d but these packs were marked and sold at 2s 11d. Posters were displayed in the shops drawing attention to this reduction in price.

These prices were displayed in the appellants' shop at Northwich on 26 September. Mr Coane, an old age pensioner, saw this and went to buy a pack. He could only find packs marked 3s 11d. He took one to the cashier who told him that there were none in stock for sale at 2s 11d. He paid 3s 11d and complained to an inspector of weights and measures. This resulted in a prosecution under the Trade Descriptions Act 1968 and the appellants were fined £25 and costs.

Section 11(2) provides:

> If any person offering to supply any goods gives, by whatever means, any indication likely to be taken as an indication that the goods are being offered at a price less than that at which they are in fact being offered he shall, subject to the provisions of this Act, be guilty of an offence.

It is not disputed that that section applies to this case. The appellants relied on s 24(1) which provides:

> In any proceedings for an offence under this Act it shall, subject to subsection (2) of this section, be a defence for the person charged to prove: (a) that the commission of the offence was due to a mistake or to reliance on information supplied to him or to the act or default of another person, an accident or some other cause beyond his control; and (b) that he took all reasonable precautions and exercised all due diligence to avoid the commission of such an offence by himself or any person under his control.

The relevant facts as found by the magistrates were that on the previous evening a shop assistant, Miss Rogers, whose duty it was to put out fresh stock, found that there were no more of the specially marked packs in stock. There were a number of packs marked with the ordinary price so she put them out. She ought to have told the shop manager, Mr Clement, about this, but she failed to do so. Mr Clement was responsible for seeing that the proper packs were on sale, but he failed to see to this although he marked his daily return 'all special offers OK'. The magistrates found that if he had known about this he would either have removed the poster advertising the reduced price or given instructions that only 2s 11d was to be charged for the packs marked 3s 11d.

Section 24(2) requires notice to be given to the prosecutor if the accused is blaming another person and such notice was duly given naming Mr Clement.

In order to avoid conviction the appellants had to prove facts sufficient to satisfy both parts of s 24(1) of the Act of 1968. The magistrates held that they:

> had exercised all due diligence in devising a proper system for the operation of the said store and by securing so far as was reasonably practicable that it was fully implemented and thus had fulfilled the requirements of s 24(1)(b).

But they convicted the appellants because in their view the requirements of s 24(1)(a) had not been fulfilled: they held that Clement was not 'another person' within the meaning of that provision.

The Divisional Court held that the magistrates were wrong in holding that Clement was not 'another person'. The respondent did not challenge this finding of the Divisional Court so I need say no more about it than that I think that on this matter the Divisional Court was plainly right. But that court sustained the conviction on the ground that the magistrates had applied the wrong test in deciding that the requirements of s 24(1)(b) had been fulfilled. In effect that court held that the words 'he took all reasonable precautions ...' do not mean what they say: 'he' does not mean the accused, it means the accused and all his servants who were acting in a managerial or supervisory capacity. I think that earlier authorities virtually compelled the Divisional Court to reach this strange construction. So the real question in this appeal is whether these earlier authorities were rightly decided.

But before examining those earlier cases I think it necessary to make some general observations.

Over a century ago courts invented the idea of an absolute offence. The accepted doctrines of the common law put them in a difficulty. There was a presumption that when Parliament makes the commission of certain acts an offence it intends that *mens rea* shall be a constituent of that offence whether or not there is any reference to the knowledge or state of mind of the accused. And it was and is held to be an invariable rule that where *mens rea* is a constituent of any offence the burden of proving *mens rea* is on the prosecution. Some day this House may have to re-examine that rule, but that is another matter. For the protection of purchasers or consumers Parliament in many cases made it an offence for a trader to do certain things. Normally those things were done on his behalf by his servants and cases arose where the doing of the forbidden thing was solely the fault of a servant, the master having done all he could to prevent it and being entirely ignorant of its having been done. The just course would have been to hold that, once the facts constituting the offence had been proved, *mens rea* would be presumed unless the accused proved that he was blameless. The courts could not, or thought they could not, take that course. But they could and did hold in many such cases on a construction of the statutory provision that Parliament must be deemed to have intended to depart from the general rule and to make the offence absolute in the sense that *mens rea* was not to be a constituent of the offence.

This has led to great difficulties. If the offence is not held to be absolute the requirement that the prosecutor must prove *mens rea* makes it impossible to enforce the enactment in very many cases. If the offence is held to be absolute that leads to the conviction of persons who are entirely blameless: an injustice which brings the law into disrepute. So Parliament has found it necessary to devise a method of avoiding this difficulty. But instead of passing a general enactment that it shall always be a defence for the accused to prove that he was no party to the offence and had done all he could to prevent it, Parliament has chosen to deal with the problem piecemeal, and has in an increasing number of cases enacted in various forms with regard to particular offences that it shall be a defence to prove various exculpatory circumstances.

In my judgment the main object of these provisions must have been to distinguish between those who are in some degree blameworthy and those who are not, and to enable the latter to escape from conviction if they can show that they were in no way to blame. I find it almost impossible to suppose that Parliament or any reasonable body of men would as a matter of policy think it right to make employers criminally liable for the acts of some of their servants but not for those of others and I find it incredible that a draftsman, aware of that intention, would fail to insert any words to express it. But in several cases the courts, for reasons which it is not easy to discover, have given a restricted meaning to such provisions. It has been held that such provisions afford a defence if the master proves that the servant at fault was the person who himself did the prohibited act, but that they afford no defence if the servant at fault was one who failed in his duty of supervision to see that his subordinates did not commit the prohibited act. Why Parliament should be thought to have intended this distinction or how as a matter of construction these provisions can reasonably be held to have that meaning is not apparent.

In some of these cases the employer charged with the offence was a limited company. But in others the employer was an individual and still it was held that he, though personally entirely blameless, could not rely on these provisions if the fault which led to the commission of the offence was the fault of a servant in failing to carry out his duty to instruct or supervise his subordinates.

Where a limited company is the employer difficult questions do arise in a wide variety of circumstances in deciding which of its officers or servants is to be identified with the company so that his guilt is the guilt of the company.

I must start by considering the nature of the personality which by a fiction the law attributes to a corporation. A living person has a mind which can have knowledge or intention or be negligent and he has hands to carry out his intentions. A corporation has none of these: it must act through living persons, though not always one or the same person. Then the person who acts is not speaking or acting for the company. He is acting as the company and his mind which directs his acts is the mind of the company. There is no question of the company being vicariously liable. He is not acting as a servant, representative, agent or delegate. He is an embodiment of the company or, one could say, he hears and speaks through the persona of the company, within his appropriate sphere, and his mind is the mind of the company. If it is a guilty mind then that guilt is the guilt of the company. It must be a question of law whether, once the facts have been ascertained, a person in doing particular things is to be regarded as the company or merely as the company's servant or agent. In that case any liability of the company can only be a statutory or vicarious liability.

In *Lennard's Carrying Co Ltd v Asiatic Petroleum Co Ltd* [1915] AC 705 the question was whether damage had occurred without the 'actual fault or privity' of the owner of a ship. The owners were a company. The fault was that of the registered managing owner who managed the ship on behalf of the owners and it was held that the company could not dissociate itself from him so far as to say that there was no actual fault or privity on the part of the company. Viscount Haldane LC said, at pp 713, 714:

> For if Mr Lennard was the directing mind of the company, then his action must, unless a corporation is not to be liable at all, have been an action which was the action of the company itself within the meaning of s 502 ... It must be upon the true construction of that section in such a case as the present one that the fault or privity is the fault or privity of somebody who is not merely a servant or agent for whom the company is liable upon the footing *respondeat superior*, but somebody for whom the company is liable because his action is the very action of the company itself.

Reference is frequently made to the judgment of Denning LJ in *H L Bolton (Engineering) Co Ltd v T J Graham and Sons Ltd* [1957] 1 QB 159. He said, at 172:

> A company may in many ways be likened to a human body. It has a brain and nerve centre which controls what it does. It also has hands which hold the tools and act in accordance with directions from the centre. Some of the people in the company are mere servants and agents who are nothing more than hands to do the work and cannot be said to represent the mind or will. Others are directors and managers who represent the directing mind and will of the company, and control what it does. The state of mind of these managers is the state of mind of the company and is treated by the law as such.

In that case the directors of the company only met once a year, they left the management of the business to others, and it was the intention of those managers which was imputed to the company. I think that was right. There have been attempts to apply Lord Denning's words to all servants of a company whose work is brain work, or exercise some managerial discretion under the direction of superior officers of the company. I do not think that Lord Denning intended to refer to them. He only referred to those who 'represent the directing mind and will of the company, and control what it does'.

I think that it is right for this reason. Normally the board of directors, the managing director and perhaps other superior officers of a company carry out the functions of management and speak and act as the company. Their subordinates do not. They carry out orders from above and it can make no difference that they are given some measure of discretion. But the board of directors may delegate some part of their functions of management giving to their delegate full discretion to act independently of instructions from them. I see no difficulty in holding that they have thereby put such a delegate in their place so that within the scope of the delegation he can act as the company. It may not always be easy to draw the line but there are cases in which the line must be drawn. *Lennard's* case [1915] AC 705 was one of them.

In some cases the phrase *alter ego* has been used. I think it is misleading. When dealing with a company the word *alter* is I think misleading. The person who speaks and acts as the company is not *alter*. He is identified with the company. And when dealing with an individual no other individual can be his *alter ego*. The other individual can be a servant, agent, delegate or representative but I know of neither principle nor authority which warrants the confusion (in the literal or original sense) of two separate individuals ...

[Where a statute introduces a] defence if the accused proved that 'he used all due diligence' I think that it [means] what it [says]. As a matter of construction I can see no ground for reading in 'he and all persons to whom he has delegated responsibility'. And if I look to the purpose and apparent intention of Parliament in enacting this defence I think that it was plainly intended to make a just and reasonable distinction between the employer who is wholly blameless and ought to be acquitted and the employer who was in some way at fault, leaving it to the employer to prove that he was in no way to blame.

What good purpose could be served by making an employer criminally responsible for the misdeeds of some of his servants but not for those of others? It is sometimes argued – it was argued in the present case – that making an employer criminally responsible, even when he has done all that he could to prevent an offence, affords some additional protection to the public because this will induce him to do more. But if he has done all he can how can he do more? I think that what lies behind this argument is a suspicion that magistrates too readily accept evidence that an employer has done all he can to prevent offences. But if magistrates were to accept as sufficient a paper scheme and perfunctory efforts to enforce it they would not be doing their duty – that would not be 'due diligence' on the part of the employer.

Then it is said that this would involve discrimination in favour of a large employer like the appellants against a small shopkeeper. But that is not so. Mr Clement was the 'opposite number' of the small shopkeeper and he was liable to prosecution in this case. The purpose of this Act must have been to penalise those at fault, not those who were in no way to blame.

The Divisional Court decided this case on a theory of delegation. In that they were following some earlier authorities, but they gave far too wide a meaning to delegation. I have said that a board of directors can delegate part of their functions of management so as to make their delegate an embodiment of the company within the sphere of the delegation. But here the board never delegated any part of their functions. They set up a chain of command through regional and district supervisors, but they remained in control. The shop managers had to obey their general directions and also take orders from their superiors. The acts or omissions of shop managers were not acts of the company itself.

In my judgment the appellants established the statutory defence. I would therefore allow this appeal.

Lord Morris of Borth-y-Gest: ... My Lords, we are here only concerned with the question whether the company committed an offence. If the nature of the offence under s 11(2) was such that, under the perhaps rather exceptional principle already referred to, the company could be held to be guilty of it – it would only be guilty if it failed to prove one of the defences available under s 24(1). If it is accepted that 'the commission of the offence' was due to 'the act or default of another person' then the company would have a defence (and so be entitled to be acquitted) if it further proved that it (ie the company) 'took all reasonable precautions and exercised all due diligence to avoid the commission' of the offence either by itself or by any person under its control. It is here that it is important to remember that it is the criminal liability of the company itself that is being considered. In general criminal liability only results from personal fault. We do not punish people in criminal courts for the misdeeds of others. The principle of *respondeat superior* is applicable in our civil courts but not generally in our criminal courts. So the sole issue in the present case is whether 'the company' took all reasonable precautions and exercised all due diligence. We are not concerned to express any opinion as to whether some other or which other person was by reason of the terms of s 11 and of s 23 guilty of an offence.

How, then, does a company take all reasonable precautions and exercise all due diligence? The very basis of s 24 involves that some contraventions of the Act may take place and may be contraventions by persons under the control of the company even though the company itself has taken all reasonable precautions and exercised all due diligence and that the company will not be criminally answerable for such contraventions. How, then, does a company act? When is some act the act of the company as opposed to the act of a servant or agent of the company (for which, if done within the scope of employment, the company will be civilly answerable)? In *Lennard's Carrying Co Ltd v Asiatic Petroleum Co Ltd* [1915] AC 705 Viscount Haldane LC said, at 713:

> My, Lords, a corporation is an abstraction. It has no mind of its own any more than it has a body of its own; its active and directing will must consequently be sought in the person of somebody who for some purposes may be called an agent but who is really the directing mind and will of the corporation, the very *ego* and centre of the personality of the corporation. That person may be under the direction of the shareholders in general meeting; that person may be the board of directors itself, or it may be, and in some companies it is so, that that person has an authority co-ordinate with the board of directors given to him under the articles of association, and is appointed by the general meeting of the company, and can only be removed by the general meeting of the company.

Within the scheme of the Act now being considered an indication is given (which need not necessarily be an all-embracing indication) of those who may personify 'directing mind and will' of the company. The question in the present case becomes a question whether the company as a company took all reasonable precautions and exercised all due diligence. The magistrates so found and so held. The magistrates found and held that 'they' (ie the company) had satisfied the provisions of s 24(1)(b). The reason why the Divisional Court felt that they could not accept that finding was that they considered that the company had delegated its duty to the manager of the shop. The manager was, they thought, 'a person whom the appellants had delegated in respect of that particular shop their duty to take all reasonable precautions and exercise all due diligence to avoid the commission' of an offence. Though the magistrates were satisfied that the company had set up an efficient system there had been 'a failure by someone to whom the duty of carrying out the system was delegated properly to carry out that function'.

My Lords, with respect I do not think that there was any feature of delegation in the present case. The company had its responsibilities in regard to taking all reasonable precautions and exercising all due diligence. The careful and effective discharge of those responsibilities required the directing mind and will of the company. A system had to be created which could rationally be said to be so designed that the commission of offences would be avoided. There was no delegation of the duty of taking precautions and exercising diligence. There was no such delegation to the manager of a particular store. He did not function as the directing mind or will of the company. His duties as the manager of one store did not involve managing the company. He was one who was being directed. He was one who was employed but he was not a delegate to whom the company passed on its responsibilities. He had certain duties which were the result of the taking by the company of all reasonable precautions and of the exercising by the company of all due diligence. He was a person under the control of the company and on the assumption that there could be proceedings against him, the company would by s 24(1)(b) be absolved if the company had taken all proper steps to avoid the commission of an offence by him. To make the company automatically liable for an offence committed by him would be to ignore the subsection. He was, so to speak, a cog in the machine which was devised: it was not left to him to devise it. Nor was he within what has been called the 'brain area' of the company. If the company had taken all reasonable precautions and exercised all due diligence to ensure that the machine could and should run effectively then some breakdown due to some action or failure on the part of 'another person' ought not to be attributed to the company or to be regarded as the action or failure of the company itself for which the company was to be criminally responsible. The defence provided by s 24(1) would otherwise be illusory ...

Lord Pearson: ... Clearly the Divisional Court's decision was based on the theory of 'delegation'. One has to examine the meaning of the word 'delegation' in relation to the facts of this case and the provision of ss 11(2) and 24 Trade Descriptions Act 1968. In one sense the meaning is as wide as the principle of the master's vicarious liability for the acts and omissions of his servants acting within the scope of their employment. In this sense the master can be said to 'delegate' to every servant acting on his behalf all duties which the servant has to perform. But that cannot be the proper meaning here. If the company 'delegated' to Miss Rogers the duty of filling the fixture with appropriate packets of washing powder, and 'delegated' to Mr Clement the duty of supervising the proper filling of fixtures and the proper exhibition or withdrawal of posters proclaiming reduced prices, then any master whether a company or an individual, must be vicariously liable for all the acts and omissions of all its or his servants acting on its or his behalf. That conclusion would defeat the manifest object of s 24 which is to enable defendants to avoid vicarious liability where they were not personally at fault. Section 24 requires a dividing line to be drawn between the master and any other person. The defendant cannot disclaim liability for an act or omission of his *ego* or his *alter ego*. In the case of an individual defendant, his *ego* is simply himself, but he may have an *alter ego*. For instance, if he has only one shop and he appoints a manager of that shop with full discretion to manage it as he thinks fit, the manager is doing what the employer would normally do and may be held to be the employer's *alter ego*. But if the defendant has hundreds of shops, he could not be expected personally to manage each one of them and the manager of one of his shops cannot in the absence of exceptional circumstances be considered his *alter ego*. In the case of a company, the *ego* is located in several persons, for example, those mentioned in s 20 of the Act or other persons in a similar position of direction or general management. A company may have an *alter ego*, if those persons who are or have its *ego* delegate to some other person the control and management, with full discretionary powers, of some section of the company's business. In the case of a company, it may be difficult, and in most cases for practical purposes unnecessary, to draw the distinction between its *ego* and its *alter ego*, but theoretically there is that distinction.

Mr Clement, being the manager of one of the company's several hundreds of shops, could not be identified with the company's *ego* nor was he an *alter ego* of the company. He was an employee in a relatively subordinate post. In the company's hierarchy there were a branch inspector and an area controller and a regional director interposed between him and the board of directors.

It was suggested in the argument of this appeal that in exercising supervision over the operations in the shop Mr Clement was performing functions of management and acting as a delegate and *alter ego* of the company. But supervision of the details of operations is not normally a function of a higher management: it is normally carried out by employees at the level of foremen, chargehands, overlookers, floor managers and 'shop' managers (in the factory sense of 'shop') ...

Alphacell Ltd v Woodward [1972] AC 824 (HL)

Lord Wilberforce: My Lords, the enactment under which the appellants have been convicted is the Rivers (Prevention of Pollution) Act 1951. The relevant words are '... if he causes or knowingly permits to enter a stream any poisonous, noxious or polluting matter ...' [s 2(1)(a)].

The subsection evidently contemplates two things – *causing*, which must involve some active operation or chain of operations involving as the result the pollution of the stream; *knowingly permitting*, which involves a failure to prevent the pollution, which failure, however, must be accompanied by knowledge. I see no reason either for reading back the word 'knowingly' into the first limb, or for reading the first limb as, by deliberate contrast, hitting something which is unaccompanied by knowledge. The first limb involves causing and this is what has to be interpreted.

In my opinion, 'causing' here must be given a common sense meaning and I deprecate the introduction of refinements, such as *causa causans*, effective cause or *novus actus*. There may be difficulties where acts of third persons or natural forces are concerned but I find the present case comparatively simple. The appellants abstract water, pass it through their works where it becomes polluted, conduct it to a settling tank communicating directly with the stream, into which the polluted water will inevitably overflow if the level rises over the overflow point. They plan, however, to recycle the water by pumping it back from the settling tank into their works: if the pumps work properly this will happen and the level in the tank will remain below the overflow point. It did not happen on the relevant occasion due to some failure in the pumps.

In my opinion, this is a clear case of causing the polluted water to enter the stream. The whole complex operation which might lead to this result was an operation deliberately conducted by the appellants and I fail to see how a defect in one stage of it, even if we must assume that this happened without their negligence, can enable them to say they did not cause the pollution. In my opinion, complication of this case by infusion of the concept of *mens rea*, and its exceptions, is unnecessary and undesirable. The section is clear, its application plain. I agree with the majority of the Divisional Court, who upheld the conviction, except that rather than say that the actions of the appellants were *a cause* of the pollution I think it more accurate to say that the appellants caused the polluting matter to enter the stream ...

Viscount Dilhorne: ... This Act, in my opinion, is one of those Acts to which my noble and learned friends, Lord Reid and Lord Diplock, referred in *Sweet v Parsley* [1970] AC 132, 149, 163 which, to apply the words of Wright J in *Sherras v De Rutzen* [1895] 1 QB 918, 922 deals with acts which 'are not criminal in any real sense, but are acts which in the public interest are prohibited under a penalty'.

What, then, is meant by the word 'caused' in the subsection? If a man, intending to secure a particular result, does an act which brings that about, he causes that result. If he deliberately and intentionally does certain acts of which the natural consequence is that certain results ensue, may he not also be said to have caused those results even though they may not have been intended by him? I think he can, just as he can be said to cause the result if he is negligent, without intending that result ...

We have not here to consider what the position would be if pollution were caused by an inadvertent and unintentional act without negligence. In such case it might be said that the doer of the act had not caused the pollution although the act had caused it. Here the acts done by the appellants were intentional. They were acts calculated to lead to the river being polluted if the acts done by the appellants, the installation and operation of the pumps, were ineffective to prevent it. Where a person intentionally does certain things which produce a certain result, then it can truly be said that he has caused that result, and here in my opinion the acts done intentionally by the appellants causes the pollution ...

Lord Salmon: My Lords, I agree that this appeal should be dismissed and I wish to add only a few observations of my own. It is undisputed that the river on the banks of which stands the appellants' Mount Sion Works was polluted by contaminated effluent which flowed from those works into the river. The vital question is whether the appellants caused that pollution within the meaning of s 2(1) of the Rivers (Prevention of Pollution) Act 1951. The nature of causation has been discussed by many eminent philosophers and also by a number of learned judges in the past. I consider, however, that what or who has caused a certain event to occur is essentially a practical question of fact which can best be answered by ordinary common sense rather than by abstract metaphysical theory.

It seems to me that, giving the word 'cause' its ordinary and natural meaning, anyone may cause something to happen intentionally or negligently or inadvertently without negligence and without intention. For example, a man may deliberately smash a porcelain vase; he may handle it so negligently that he drops and smashes it; or he may without negligence slip or stumble against it and smash it. In each of these examples, no less in the last than in the other two, he has caused the destruction of the vase.

The appellants clearly did not cause the pollution intentionally and we must assume that they did not do so negligently. Nevertheless, the facts so fully and clearly stated by my noble and learned friend Viscount Dilhorne to my mind make it obvious that the appellants in fact caused the pollution. If they did not cause it, what did? There was no intervening act of a third party nor was there any act of God to which it could be attributed. The appellants had been responsible for the design of the plant; everything within their works was under their control; they had chosen all the equipment. The process which they operated required contaminated effluent being pumped round their works until it came to rest in an open tank which they sited on the river bank. If the pumps which they had installed in this tank failed to operate efficiently the effluent would necessarily overflow into the river. And that is what occurred. It seems plain to me that the appellants caused the pollution by the active operation of their plant. They certainly did not intend to cause pollution but they intended to do the acts which caused it ...

The appellants contend that, even if they caused the pollution, still they should succeed since they did not cause it intentionally or knowingly or negligently. Section 2(1)(a) of the Rivers (Prevention of Pollution) Act 1951 is undoubtedly a penal section. It follows that if it is capable of two or more meanings then the meaning most favourable to the subject should be adopted. Accordingly, so the argument runs, the words 'intentionally' or 'knowingly' or 'negligently' should be read into the section immediately before the word 'causes'. I do not agree. It is of the utmost public importance that our rivers should not be polluted. The risk of pollution, particularly from the vast and increasing number of riparian industries, is very great. The offences created by the Act of 1951 seem to me to be prototypes of offences which 'are not criminal in any real sense, but are acts which in the public interest are prohibited under a penalty': *Sherras v De Rutzen* [1895] 1 QB 918, *per* Wright J at 922, referred to with approval by my noble and learned friends, Lord Reid and Lord Diplock, in *Sweet v Parsley* [1970] AC 132, 149 162. I can see no valid reason for reading the word 'intentionally', 'knowingly' or 'negligently' into s 2(1)(a) and a number of cogent reasons for not doing so. In the case of a minor pollution such as the present, when the justices find that there is no wrongful intention or negligence on the part of the defendant, a comparatively nominal fine will no doubt be imposed. This may be regarded as a not unfair hazard of carrying on a business which may cause pollution on the banks of a river. The present appellants were fined £20 and ordered to pay, in all, £24 costs. I should be surprised if the costs of pursuing this appeal to this House were incurred for the purpose of saving these appellants £44.

If this appeal succeeded and it were held to be the law that no conviction could be obtained under the Act of 1951 unless the prosecution could discharge the often impossible onus of proving that the pollution was caused intentionally or negligently, a great deal of pollution would go unpunished and undeterred to the relief of many riparian factory owners. As a result, many rivers which are now filthy would become filthier still and many rivers which are now clean would lose their cleanliness. The legislature no doubt recognised that as a matter of public policy this would be most unfortunate. Hence s 2(1)(a) which encourages riparian factory owners not only to take reasonable steps to prevent pollution but to do everything possible to ensure that they do not cause it.

I do not consider that the appellants can derive any comfort (as they seek to do) from the inclusion in s 2(1)(a) of the words 'knowingly permits' nor from the inclusion in s 2(1)(a) of the words 'knowingly permits' nor from the deeming provision against local authorities in relation to sewage escaping into a river from sewers or sewage disposal units [s 2(1)]. The creation of an offence in relation to permitting pollution was probably included in the section so as to deal with the type of case in which a man knows that contaminated effluent is escaping over his land into a river and does nothing at all to prevent it. The inclusion of the word 'knowingly' before 'permits' is probably otiose and, if anything, is against the appellants, since it contrasts with the omission of the word 'knowingly' before the word 'causes'. The deeming provision was probably included to meet what local authorities might otherwise have argued was a special case and cannot, in my opinion, affect the plain and unambiguous general meaning of the word 'causes'.

For these reasons I would dismiss the appeal with costs.

R v P & O European Ferries (Dover) Ltd (1991) 93 Cr App R 72 (Turner J at Central Criminal Court)

Turner J: ... The main thrust of the argument for the company in support of the submission that the four counts of manslaughter in this indictment should be quashed was not merely that English law does not recognise the offence of corporate manslaughter but that, as a matter of positive English law, manslaughter can only be committed when one natural person kills another natural person. Hence it was no accident that there is no record of any corporation or non-natural person having been successfully prosecuted for manslaughter in any English court. It was, however, accepted that there is no conceptual difficulty in attributing a criminal state of mind to a corporation. The broad argument advanced on behalf of the prosecution was that, there being no all embracing statutory definition of murder or manslaughter there is, in principle, no reason why a corporation, or other non-natural person, cannot be found guilty of most offences in the criminal calendar. The exceptions to such a broad proposition could be found either in the form of punishment, which would be inappropriate for a corporation, or in the very person nature of individual crimes or categories of crime such as offences under the Sexual Offences Act, bigamy and, arguably, perjury. It was further argued that the definitions of homicide to be found in the works of such as Coke, Hale, Blackstone and Stephen, and which were strongly relied upon by the company, were not intended to be exclusive, but reflected the historical fact that, at the dates when these definitions originated, the concept of criminal liability of a corporation, just as their very existence, was not within the contemplation of the courts or the writers of the legal treatises referred to. Before the days when corporate crime was in contemplation, it can be a matter of no surprise to find that the definition of homicide did not include the possibility of a corporation committing such a crime ...

In the years 1943 and 1944, three cases were decided which can be seen to have had a watershed effect on the way in which the law has since developed. The first of these was the *DPP v Kent and Sussex Contractors Ltd* [1944] 1 KB 146, and was a decision of the Divisional Court. The offence in question was one under the Motor Fuel Rationing (No 3) Order 1941 and involved the use of a document which was false in a material particular. The decision of the justices to acquit was based on the proposition that: 'An act of will or state of mind ... could not be imputed to the company'. In the course of his judgment, Lord Caldecote CJ summarising the submissions for the defendant company said at 149:

> Mr Carey Evans submits that a company can only be held to be responsible in respect of the intention or knowledge of its agents, the officers of the company, to the same extent as a private individual is responsible for the acts of his agent, and, therefore, that the respondent company cannot be held to form the intention or to have knowledge necessary to constitute the offences charged. He has not disputed the abstract proposition that a company can have knowledge and can form an intention to do an act. A company cannot be found guilty of certain criminal offences, such as treason or other offences for which it is provided that death or imprisonment is the only punishment, but there are a number of criminal offences of which a company can be

> convicted. In the judgment of Finlay J in *Cory Brothers and Co* [1927] 1 KB 810, 816, there is a convenient citation from the judgment of Patteson J in *Birmingham and Gloucester Ry Co* (1842) 3 QB 223.

The learned Lord Chief Justice then quoted from that case, and continued at p 150:

> Under the Defence (General) Regulations 1939, it is common for offences to be created in which certain ingredients are required to be found and the present case seems to me to fall within that category. They are offences in which it is not material to consider whether there is or is not *mens rea*, which I understand to mean criminal intention, because the ingredients are stated in the regulation creating the offence. For instance, in the present case one of the necessary ingredients of the second offence charged is an intent to deceive. When that intent is stated to be necessary it seems to me idle to enquire whether a mens rea is or is not involved.
>
> In *Chuter v Freeth and Pocock Ltd* [1911] 2 KB 832 to which we were not referred, the question seems to have been similar to the one raised in this case.

He then read from the headnote, and the passage to which I refer is (at 151):

> 'The magistrate, although upon the facts as above stated he would have convicted if the respondents' servants had been principals in the matter, was yet of opinion that, as the exempting clause of the section implied that only such a person could commit the offence as was capable of believing, and as a corporation having no mind could not exercise that faculty, the respondents, being a corporation, were not liable under the section.' Lord Alverstone CJ stated the facts and then said: 'The magistrate has held that, in as much as "the person" who gives a false warranty is made liable unless he proves that when he gave the warranty "he had reason to believe" that the statements or descriptions contained therein were true, therefore "the person" cannot be construed as including a corporation, but must be limited to natural persons capable of belief. In my view that is too narrow a construction. Where a person is capable of giving a warranty that person is liable to a fine. There is no reason why a warranty should not be given by a corporation. It can give a warranty through its agents, it can believe or not believe, as the case may be, that the statements in the warranty are true. A similar point has been raised in cases concerning the liability of a corporation in actions which, in the case of an individual, would involve an enquiry into a state of mind, such as fraud, libel, or malicious prosecution. It is well settled that a corporation may be liable in all those actions. Further, the question in this case has in substance been decided by Channell J in *Pearks, Gunston and Tee Ltd v Ward* [1902] 2 QB 1, 11, 12. Taking the principle of the Act into consideration, there is no reason why in s 20(6), "person" should not include corporation.' There was ample evidence, on the facts as stated in the special case, that the company, by the only people who could act or speak or think for it had done both these things, and I can see nothing in any of the authorities to which we have been referred which requires us to say that a company is incapable of being found guilty of the offences with which the respondent company was charged. The case must go back to the justices with an intimation of our opinion to this effect, and for their determination of the facts.

MacNaghten J, in giving his judgment, having referred to the background of the case, continued [1944] 1 KB at 156:

> It is true that a corporation can only have knowledge and form an intention through its human agents, but circumstances may be such that the knowledge and intention of the agent must be imputed to the body corporate. Mr Carey Evans says that, although a body corporate may be capable of having knowledge and also of forming an intention, it cannot have a *mens rea*. If the responsible agent of a company, acting within the scope of his authority, puts forward on its behalf a document which he knows to be false and by which he intends to deceive, I apprehend that, according to the authorities that my Lord has cited, his knowledge and intention must be imputed to the company. In my opinion, the submission made to the justices that the respondents could not in law be capable of a criminal intention cannot be sustained.

In his judgment, Hallet J, at 157, said:

> With regard to the liability of a body corporate for torts or crimes, a perusal of the case shows, to my mind, that there has been a development in the attitude of the courts arising from the large part played in modern times by limited liability companies. At one time the existence, and later the extent and conditions of such a body's liability in tort was a matter of doubt, due partly to the theoretical difficulty of imputing wrongful acts or omissions to a fictitious person, and it required a long series of decisions to clear up the position. Similarly, the liability of a body corporate for crimes was at one time a matter of doubt, partly owing to the theoretical difficulty of imputing a criminal intention to a fictitious person and partly to technical difficulties of procedure. Procedure has received attention from the legislature, as for instance, in s 33 of the Criminal Justice Act 1925, and the theoretical difficulty of imputing criminal intention is no longer felt to the same extent.

Hallet J then referred to the passage in the speech from Lord Blackburn in the *Pharmaceutical Society* case (1880) 5 App Cas 857, 870, to which I have already referred. He then referred to *Tyler's* case [1891] 2 QB 588, 594, 597 and quoted from the judgment of Bowen LJ in these terms:

> 'I take it, therefore, to be clear that in the ordinary case of a duty imposed by statute, if the breach of the statute is a disobedience to the law, punishable in the case of a private person by indictment, the offending corporation cannot escape from the consequences which would follow in the case of an individual by showing that they are a corporation.' Kay LJ said: 'Therefore, that part of the argument, that, in as much as a criminal act involves a *mens rea*, a corporation which has no *mens rea* at all is not subject to criminal proceedings in any case, is untenable.' Applying the observations of Bowen LJ to the present case, if every person desiring to obtain petrol coupons has a duty imposed by statutory authority to furnish honest information, it seems strange and undesirable that a body corporate desiring to obtain petrol coupons and furnishing dishonest information for that purpose should be able to escape the liability which would be incurred in like case by a private person. In *R v Cory Brothers* Finlay J referred to certain types of crime, in respect of which, according to old authorities by which he considered himself to be bound, a body corporate could not be held to be liable. It may be that those authorities will require reconsideration some day in the light of the development to which I have already referred, but for present purposes it is sufficient to notice that the offences now in question are of a fundamentally different character.

The Kent and Sussex Contractors case was followed in point of time by *I C R Haulage Ltd* [1944] 1 KB 551. The headnote reads: 'An indictment for a common law conspiracy to defraud will lie against a limited company'. In the course of argument, all the cases previously referred to were cited. The judgment of the court was delivered by Stable J who, at 553, said:

> It was conceded by counsel for the company that a limited company can be indicted for some criminal offences, and it was conceded by counsel for the Crown that there were some criminal offences for which a limited company cannot be indicted. The controversy centred round the question where and on what principle the line must be drawn and on which side of the line an indictment such as the present one falls. Counsel for the company contended that the true principle was that an indictment against a limited company for any offence involving as an essential ingredient *mens rea* in the restricted sense of a dishonest or criminal mind, must be bad for the reason that a company, not being a natural person, cannot have a mind honest or otherwise, and that, consequently, though in certain circumstances it is civilly liable for the fraud of its officers, agents or servants, it is immune from criminal process. Counsel for the Crown contended that a limited company, like any other entity recognised by the law, can as a general rule be indicted for its criminal acts which from the very necessity of the case must be performed by human agency and which in given circumstances become the acts of the company, and that for this purpose there was no distinction between an intention or other function of the mind and any form of activity. The offences for which a limited company cannot be indicted are, it was argued, exceptions to the general rule arising from the limitations which must inevitably attach to an artificial entity, such as a company. Included in these exceptions are the cases in which , from its very nature, the offence cannot be committed by a corporation, as, for example, perjury, an offence which cannot be vicariously committed, or bigamy, an offence which a limited company, not being a natural person, cannot commit vicariously or otherwise. A further exception, but for a different reason, comprises offences of which murder is an example, where the only punishment the court can impose is corporal, the basis on which this exception rests being that the court will not stultify itself by embarking on a trial in which, if a verdict of guilty is returned, no effective order by way of sentence can be made. In our judgment these contentions of the Crown are substantially sound, and the existence of these exceptions, and it may be that there are others, is by no means inconsistent with the general rule.

The earlier cases were then reviewed, including the *Cory Brothers* case (*above*) of which Stable J had this to say at 556:

> The learned judge advanced no reasons of his own for quashing the whole indictment, simply expressing the view that he felt compelled by the authorities to which his attention had been called to decide as he did. It is sufficient, in our judgment, to say that, inasmuch as that case was decided before the decision in *DPP v Kent* and *Sussex Contractors* [1944] 1 KB 146, and that *Chuter v Freeth and Pocock Ltd* [1911] 2 KB 832 was not cited at all, if the matter came before the court today, the result might well be different. As was pointed out by Hallet J in the *Kent and Sussex Contractors* case (at 157), this is a breach of the law to which the attitude of the courts has in the passage of time undergone a process of development.

He concluded the judgment of the court at 559 by saying:

> Where in any particular case there is evidence to go to a jury that the criminal act of an agent, including his state of mind, intention, knowledge or belief is the act of the company, and, in cases where the presiding judge so rules,

> whether the jury are satisfied that it has been proved, must depend on the nature of the charge, the relative position of the officer or agent, and the other relevant facts and circumstances of the case.

This passage, as will be seen, was criticised as being too widely stated by Lord Reid in the *Tesco Stores* case, of which more anon. The last of the trio of 1944 cases was *Moore v Bresler* [1944] 2 All ER 515, which again was a decision of the Divisional Court and merely followed the decision in the earlier two cases. While these developments were occurring in the field of criminal law, in a line of civil cases commencing in 1915 the courts were striving to identify the true basis upon which the mind of a corporation might be identified. Those three cases are *Lennard's Carrying Company Limited v Asiatic Petroleum Company Limited* [1915] AC 705, *H L Bolton Engineering Company Limited v T J Graham* [1957] 1 QB 159 and *Tesco Supermarkets Limited v Nattrass* [1972] AC 153. *Lennard's* case concerned an application by the plaintiffs to limit their liability under the terms of s 502 of the Merchant Shipping Act 1894 which might only be achieved if it could be demonstrated that the casualty occurred without the actual fault or privity of the owner or managing agent. *Bolton's* case involved consideration of the intention of the company to occupy certain premises for the purposes of its business and turned on the interpretation of s 30(1)(g) of the Landlord and Tenant Act 1954. The *Tesco Supermarkets* case turned on the interpretation of s 20 of the Trade Descriptions Act 1968 and whether the manager of a particular retail branch of the company was another person for the purposes of its statutory defence under s 24 of the same Act. Although it is no doubt apt to say, as Mr Kentridge submitted, that the decision in each of these cases turned on the construction of the particular statute that was there in question, it is nevertheless possible to deduce from those cases the principles which the mental element that a corporation must possess if it is to be convicted of a crime where a 'mental element' must be found. Indeed, when this was put to Mr Kentridge he was not minded to dissent from that broad proposition, but he sought to qualify the concession by submitting that the principle did not assist in answering the further question whether or not the particular crime was one which could be committed by a corporation. From these three cases, coupled possibly with the *dictum* of Lord Blackburn in the *Pharmaceutical Society* case, the origins of what has become known to writers of jurisprudence as the 'identification doctrine' can be found. The *Tesco* case deserves particular scrutiny for within certain of the speeches in that case are to be found the limits of this doctrine of identification. It is this doctrine which is fundamental to the true basis of corporate criminal liability which has now to be accepted is an integral part of the law of England. At 170D, of the report in the *Tesco* case, Lord Reid said:

> Where a limited company is the employer difficult questions do arise in a wide variety of circumstances in deciding which of its officers or servants is to be identified with the company so that his guilt is the guilt of the company.
>
> I must start by considering the nature of the personality which by a fiction the law attributes to a corporation. A living person has a mind which can have knowledge or intention or be negligent and he has hands to carry out his intentions. A corporation has none of these; it must act through living persons, though not always one or the same person. Then the person who acts is not speaking or acting for the company. He is acting as the company and his mind which directs his acts is the mind of the company. There is no question of the company being vicariously liable. He is not acting as a servant, representative, agent or delegate. He is an embodiment of the company or, one could say, he hears and speaks through the persona of the

company, within his appropriate sphere, and his mind is the mind of the company. If it is a guilty mind then that guilt is the guilt of the company. It must be a question of law whether, once the facts have been ascertained, a person in doing particular things is to be regarded as the company or merely as the company's servant or agent. In that case any liability of the company can only be a statutory vicarious liability.

In *Lennard's Carrying Co Ltd v Asiatic Petroleum Co Ltd* [1915] AC 705 the question was whether damage had occurred without the 'actual fault or privity' of the owner of the ship. The owners were a company. The fault was that of the registered managing owner who managed the ship on behalf of the owners and it was held that the company could not dissociate itself from him so as to say that there was not actual fault or privity on the part of the company. Viscount Haldane said at 713:

For if Mr Lennard was the directing mind of the company, then his action must, unless a corporation is not to be liable at all, have been an action which was the action of the company itself within the meaning of s 502 ... It must be upon the true construction of that section in such a case as the present one that the fault or privity is the fault or privity of somebody who is not merely a servant or agent for whom the company is liable upon the footing *respondeat superior*, but somebody for whom the company is liable because his action is the very action of the company itself.

Reference is frequently made to the judgment of Denning LJ as he then was in *H L Bolton (Engineering) Co Ltd v T J Graham and Sons Ltd* [1957] 1 QB 159. He said, at 172:

A company may in many ways be likened to a human body. It has a brain and nerve centre which controls what it does. It also has hands which hold the tools and act in accordance with directions from the centre. Some of the people in the company are mere servants and agents who are nothing more than hands to do work and cannot be said to represent the mind or will. Others are directors and managers who represent the directing mind and will of the company, and control what it does. The state of mind of these managers is the state of mind of the company and is treated by the law as such.

In that case the directors of the company only met once a year: they left the management of the business to others, and it was the intention of those managers which was imputed to the company. I think that was right. There have been attempts to apply Lord Denning's words to all servants of a company whose work is brain work, or who exercise some managerial discretion under the direction of superior officers of the company. I do not think that Lord Denning intended to refer to them. He only referred to those who 'represent the directing mind and will of the company, and control what it does'.

I think that it is right for this reason. Normally the board of directors, the managing director and perhaps other superior officers of a company carry out the functions of management and speak and act as the company. Their subordinates do not. They carry out orders from above and it can make no difference that they are given some measure of discretion. But the board of directors may delegate some part of their functions of management giving to their delegate full discretion to act independently of instructions from them. I see no difficulty in holding that they have thereby put such a delegate in their place so that within the scope of the delegation he can act as the

> company. It may not always be easy to draw the line but there are cases in which the line must be drawn.

And he cites *Lennard's* case *above*. Later in his judgment at 173 Lord Reid continues:

> In the next two cases a company was accused and it was held liable for the fault of a superior officer. In *DPP v Kent and Sussex Contractors Limited* [1944] KB 146 he was the transport manager. In *I C R Haulage Limited* [1944] KB 551 it was held that a company can be guilty of common law conspiracy. The act of the managing director was held to be the act of the company.

I think that a passage in the judgment, and this is one to which I earlier referred, is too widely stated, at 559 of the report, and he then cites the passage I have already cited and continued:

> This may have been influenced by the erroneous views expressed in the two *Hammett* cases. I think that the true view is that the judge must direct the jury that if they find certain facts proved then as a matter of law they must find that the criminal act of the officer, servant or agent including his state of mind, intention, knowledge or belief is the act of the company. I have already dealt with the considerations to be applied in deciding when such a person can and when he cannot be identified with the company. I do not see how the nature of the charge can make any difference. If the guilty man was in law identifiable with the company then whether his offence was serious or venial his act was the act of the company but if he was not so identifiable then no act of his, serious or otherwise, was the act of the company itself.

Lord Diplock in his speech, at 198H, said:

> A corporation is an abstraction. It is incapable itself of doing any physical act or being in any state of mind. Yet in law it is a person capable of exercising legal rights and of being subject to legal liabilities which may involve ascribing to it not only physical acts which are in reality done by a natural person on its behalf but also the mental state in which that person did them. In civil law, apart from certain statutory duties, this presents no conceptual difficulties. Under the law of agency the physical acts and state of mind of the agent are in law ascribed to the principal, and if the agent is a natural person it matters not whether the principal is also a natural person or a mere legal abstraction. *Qui facit per alium facit per se; qui cogitat per alium cogitat per se.*
>
> But there are some civil liabilities imposed by statute which, exceptionally, exclude the concept of vicarious liability of a principal for the physical acts and state of mind of his agent; and the concept has no general application in the field of criminal law. To constitute a criminal offence, a physical act done by any person must generally be done by him in some reprehensible state of mind. Save in cases of strict liability where a criminal statute, exceptionally, makes the doing of an act a crime irrespective of the state of mind in which it is done, criminal law regards a person as responsible for his own crimes only. It does not recognise the liability of a principal for the criminal acts of his agent; because it does not ascribe to him his agent's state of mind. *Qui peccat per alium peccat per se* is not a maxim of criminal law.
>
> In my view, therefore, the question: what natural persons are to be treated in law as being the company for the purpose of acts done in the course of its business including the taking of precautions and the exercise of due diligence to avoid the commission of a criminal offence, is to be found by identifying those natural persons who by the memorandum and articles of association or as a result of action taken by directors, or by the company in general meeting

> pursuant to the articles, are entrusted with the exercise of the powers of the company.
>
> This test is in conformity with the classic statement of Viscount Haldane LC in *Lennard's Carrying Co Ltd v Asiatic Petroleum Co Ltd* [1915] AC 705. The relevant statute in that case, although not a criminal statute, was in *pari materia,* for it provided for a defence to a civil liability which excluded the concept of vicarious liability of a principal for the physical acts and state of mind of his agent.
>
> There has been in recent years a tendency to extract from Denning LJ's judgment in *H L Bolton (Engineering) Co Ltd v T J Graham and Sons Ltd* [1957] 1 QB 159, 172, 173 his vivid metaphor about the 'brains and nerve centre' of a company as contrasted with its hands, and to treat this dichotomy, and not the articles of association, as laying down the test of whether or not a particular person is to be regarded in law as being the company itself when performing duties which a statute imposes on the company.
>
> In the case in which this metaphor was first used Denning LJ was dealing with acts and intentions of directors of the company in whom the powers of the company were vested under its articles of association.

Since the 19th century there has been a huge increase in the numbers and activities of corporations whether nationalised, municipal or commercial, which enter the private lives of all or most of 'men and subjects' in a diversity of ways. A clear case can be made for imputing to such corporations social duties including the duty not to offend all relevant parts of the criminal law. By tracing the history of the cases decided by the English courts over the period of the last 150 years, it can be seen how, first tentatively and finally confidently, the courts have been able to ascribe to corporations a 'mind' which is generally one of the essential ingredients of common law and statutory offences. Indeed, it can be seen that in many Acts of Parliament the same concept has been embraced. The parliamentary approach is, perhaps, exemplified by s 18 of the Theft Act 1968 which provides for directors and managers of a limited company to be rendered liable to conviction if an offence under s 15, 16 or 17 of the Act are proved to have been committed – and I quote – 'with the consent, connivance of any director, manager, secretary ... purporting to act in such capacity, then such director, manager or secretary shall be guilty of the offence'. Once a state of mind could be effectively attributed to a corporation, all that remained was to determine the means by which that state of mind could be ascertained and imputed to a non-natural person. That done, the obstacle to the acceptance of general criminal liability of a corporation was overcome. *Cessante ratione legis, cessat ipsa lex.* As some of the decisions in other common law countries indicate, there is nothing essentially incongruous in the notion that a corporation should be guilty of an offence of unlawful killing. I find unpersuasive the argument of the company that the old definitions of homicide positively exclude the liability of a non-natural person to conviction of an offence of manslaughter. Any crime, in order to be justiciable must have been committed by or through the agency of a human being. Consequently, the inclusion in the definition of the expression 'human being' as the author of the killing was either tautologous or, as I think more probable, intended to differentiate those cases of death in which a human being played no direct part and which would have led to forfeiture of the inanimate, or if animate non-human, object which caused the death (*deodand*) from those in which the cause of death was initiated by human activity albeit the instrument of death was inanimate or if animate non-human. I am confident that the expression 'human being' in the definition of homicide was not intended to have the effect of words of limitation as might have been the case had it been found in some Act of Parliament or legal deed. It is not for me to attempt to set the limits of corporate liability for criminal offences in English law. Examples of other crimes which may or may not be committed by corporations will, no doubt, be decided on a case by case basis in conformity with the manner in which the common law has adapted itself in the past. Suffice it that where a corporation, through the controlling mind of one of its agents, does an act which fulfils the prerequisites of the crime of manslaughter, it is properly indictable for the crime of manslaughter ...

... Before concluding and because of its topical and potential relevance to the instant prosecution, I should refer to *Her Majesty's Coroner for East Kent, ex p Spooner* (1989) 88 Cr App R 10, a decision of the Divisional Court in relation to proceedings before the coroner arising from the selfsame events as have led to this prosecution. It is only necessary to refer to one short passage in the judgment of Bingham LJ to explain why reference has not been made to it earlier in these reasons. At 16 of the report Bingham LJ said:

> The arguments which were deployed and elaborated before the coroner have, in substance, been repeated with great cogency and skill before us. The first question is whether a corporation can be indicted for manslaughter. The coroner originally ruled that it could not. In the course of argument in this court we indicated at an early stage that we were prepared to assume for the purposes of this hearing that it could. As a result the question has not been fully argued and I have not found it necessary to reach a final conclusion. I am, however, tentatively of opinion that on appropriate facts the *mens rea* required for manslaughter can be established against a corporation. I see no reason in principle why such a charge should not be established. I am therefore tentatively of opinion that the coroner's original ruling was wrong, and indeed I would need considerable persuasion to reach the conclusion that it was correct.
>
> But that is not the end of the matter because the coroner clearly adhered to his substantial ruling even on the assumption that a company could in principle be guilty of manslaughter. The coroner made it clear that he was of opinion that the evidence which he had considered was not capable of supporting the conclusion that those who represented the directing mind and will of the company and controlled what it did had been guilty of conduct amounting to manslaughter.
>
> I am not persuaded that that is a conclusion which is or may be wrong. Nothing was, in my judgment, said by Sheen J of by way of concession before him which undermines that conclusion. It is important to bear in mind an important distinction. A company may be vicariously liable for the negligent acts and omissions of its servants and agents, but for a company to be criminally liable for manslaughter – on the assumption I am making that such a crime exists – it is required that the *mens rea* and the *actus reus* of manslaughter should be established not against those who acted for or in the name of the company but against those who were to be identified as the embodiment of the company itself. The coroner formed the view that there was no such case fit to be left to the jury against the company. I see no reason to disagree. I would add that I see no sustainable case in manslaughter against the directors who are named either ...

R v Boal [1992] 1 QB 591 (CA)

Simon Brown J: The appellant is employed by W & G Foyle Ltd ('Foyles'), the well-known booksellers in Charing Cross Road. He has worked for them now for some 10 years in all. In about November 1988 he was promoted from being senior sales assistant in their technical department to assistant general manager.

On 15 February 1989 the appellant was in charge of the shop: the general manager, Mr Cruickshank, had gone away on a week's holiday. That day officers of the London Fire and Civil Defence Authority inspected the shop following a complaint by a member of the public. They found a number of serious breaches of the premises' fire certificate. To instance but a few, various lighting was defective, certain fire escape routes were narrowed or blocked by an accumulation of boxes and books, a number of doors were bolted and, most serious of all, two sets of double entrance doors were padlocked shut.

On 10 January 1990 both the appellant and Foyles were arraigned before Middlesex Crown Court upon an indictment containing 11 pairs of counts, 22 counts in all. Each even numbered count charged against the appellant an offence contrary to s 7(4) of the Fire Precautions Act 1971, criminal liability on his part being alleged to arise by virtue of s 23 of the Act.

Section 23(1) in its material parts provides:

> Where an offence under this Act committed by a body corporate is proved ... to be attributable to any neglect on the part of, any director, manager, secretary or other similar officer of the body corporate ... he as well as the body corporate shall be guilty of that offence ...

The 11 counts directed against the appellant charged that he was 'a manager' of Foyles when the relevant offences were committed by them and that such offences were attributable to his neglect ...

Mr de Haan who now appears for the appellant advances two central submissions upon this unusual appeal. First, that the appellant, through no fault of his own but rather because of his lawyers' misappreciation of the true scope of s 23, was deprived of a defence which would have had a realistic prospect of succeeding at trial.

Second, that in those circumstances this court should allow his appeal and set aside the conviction even though the appellant pleaded guilty to three counts at trial and never contested this particular element of the offences charged against him ...

... [T]he appellant was only properly to be regarded as imperilled by s 23 if, as the assistant general manager of the shop, he had 'the management of the whole affairs of the company', was 'entrusted with power to transact the whole of the affairs of the company', and was 'managing in a governing role the affairs of the company itself'. The intended scope of s 23 is, we accept, to fix with criminal liability only those who are in a position of real authority, the decision-makers within the company who have both the power and responsibility to decide corporate policy and strategy. It is to catch those responsible for putting proper procedures in place; it is not meant to strike at underlings.

What, then, was the appellant's real position in the company? The fact is that because this whole question went by default, there is scant evidence about this in the documents before us. We are told that the only directors of the company are Miss Christina Foyle and her husband, and that the only other person senior to the appellant was Mr Cruickshank the general manager. In evidence the appellant described his duties thus:

> My primary duty was to be the chief buyer, checking the orders generated by our assistants and presented to me by the representatives. The rest of my work was in the cash office counting the money sent up from the shop floor, making sure that it was sent down to the bank in its correct fashion, and generally anything else required of management. I had to maybe ensure the staff were in when they were supposed to be in. I had to assist them in anything that they required. There were all other managerial functions.

That said, it certainly appears that the appellant was given no management training by the company, least of all in matters of health and safety at work or fire precautions. When, however, asked at trial 'Who is generally responsible on the premises within your organisation for fire safety?' he answered in the broadest terms that he and the general manager 'both have responsibility for the whole thing really', and accepted that he was aware of the general responsibilities imposed by the fire certificate.

Were these admissions sufficient to indicate that, even on the correct, narrow, approach to s 23, the appellant was properly to be regarded as a manager of the company? Mr Pawlak for the prosecuting authority submits that they were. This is not, he contends, a case like *Registrar of Restrictive Trading Agreements v W H Smith and Son Ltd* [1969] 1 WLR 1460 where those in question were merely remote branch managers of a substantial public company; rather Foyles' sole activity is their single large bookshop and, as stated, the appellant was number four in the hierarchy, directors included.

We disagree. Whilst declining to accept the full width of Mr de Haan's submissions – which include the proposition that not even Mr Cruickshank as the general manager could properly be said to fall within s 23 – we are certainly disposed to agree that this appellant could well have been regarded as responsible only for the day-to-day running of the bookshop rather than enjoying any sort of governing role in respect of the affairs of the company itself. Whether or not such a defence, had it been advanced at the trial, must inevitably have prospered, it is frankly not possible to say. The issue would clearly have needed to be explored a good deal further than it was. But we do conclude not merely that such defence would have had a realistic prospect of success but that in all likelihood it would have prevailed ...

CHAPTER 15

THEFT

The eighth commandment in the Bible is 'You shall not steal' (Exodus 20:15). This may appear simple enough. To lawyers, however, the meaning of 'stealing' is far from straightforward.

The Theft Act 1968 sets out the definition of theft in s 1:

Section 1 of the Theft Act 1968: basic definition of theft

(1) A person is guilty of theft if he dishonestly appropriates property belonging to another with the intention of permanently depriving the other of it; and 'thief' and 'steal' shall be construed accordingly.

(2) It is immaterial whether the appropriation is made with a view to gain, or is made for the thief's own benefit.

(3) The five following sections of this Act shall have effect as regards the interpretation and operation of this section (and, except as otherwise provided by this Act, shall apply only for purposes of this section).

From this definition (and from ss 2 – 6 of the Theft Act 1968) it is apparent that there are five elements in the offence of theft. To secure a conviction for theft, the prosecution must establish each and every one of the five elements. Those elements are:

(1) Dishonest ...

(2) ... appropriation ...

(3) ... of property ...

(4) ... belonging to another ...

(5) ... with the intention of permanently depriving that other of the property.

Each of these elements will be considered in turn.

Section 7 of the Theft Act 1968: punishment

A person guilty of theft shall on conviction on indictment be liable to imprisonment for a term not exceeding [seven years].

Section 2 of the Theft Act 1968: 'dishonestly'

(1) A person's appropriation of property belonging to another is not to be regarded as dishonest:

(a) if he appropriates the property in the belief that he has in law the right to deprive the other of it, on behalf of himself or of a third person; or

(b) if he appropriates the property in the belief that he would have the other's consent if the other knew of the appropriation and the circumstances of it; or

(c) (except where the property came to him as trustee or personal representative) if he appropriates the property in the belief that the person to whom the property belongs cannot be discovered by taking reasonable steps.

(2) A person's appropriation of property belonging to another may be dishonest notwithstanding that he is willing to pay for the property.

DISHONESTY

The provisions of s 2 of the Theft Act 1968 are not exhaustive; they provide the answer only in certain cases. In *R v Feely* [1973] QB 530 it was held that the test of whether a person is dishonest or not is a subjective one, and it was said that juries need not be given further directions on the word 'dishonest'. However, there are cases where further definition is needed. The leading case on the general meaning of dishonesty is *R v Ghosh* [1982] QB 1053. Two principles emerge from that case:

(a) Whether a person was dishonest is a question of fact to be decided by the tribunal of fact (ie the magistrates or the jury);

(b) If, by the standards of reasonable and honest people, what the defendant did was not dishonest, then the defendant must be acquitted; if, by the standards of reasonable and honest people, what the defendant did was dishonest, he is only to be regarded as dishonest if he realised that what he was doing was dishonest according to the standards of reasonable and honest people.

In a trial on indictment, it is only necessary for the judge to explain all this if defendant has asserted that he was not dishonest (*R v Roberts* (1985) 84 Cr App R 117; *R v Price* (1989) 90 Cr App R 409).

R v Ghosh [1982] QB 1053 (CA)

Lord Lane CJ: ... At all material times the appellant was a surgeon acting as a *locum tenens* consultant at a hospital. The charges alleged that he had falsely represented that he had himself carried out a surgical operation to terminate pregnancy or that money was due to himself or an anaesthetist for such an operation, when in fact the operation had been carried out by someone else, and/or under the National Health Service provisions.

His defence was that there was no deception; that the sums paid to him were due for consultation fees which were legitimately payable under the regulations, or else were the balance of fees properly payable; in other words that there was nothing dishonest about his behaviour on any of the counts ...

... *R v Feely* [1973] QB 530 ... is often treated as having laid down an objective test of dishonesty for the purpose of s 1 of the Theft Act 1968. But what it actually decided was: (1) that it is for the jury to determine whether the defendant acted dishonestly and not for the judge; (2) that the word 'dishonestly' can only relate to the defendant's own state of mind; and (3) that it is unnecessary and undesirable for judges to define what is meant by 'dishonestly' ...

... Is 'dishonestly' in s 1 of the Theft Act 1968 intended to characterise a course of conduct? Or is it intended to describe a state of mind? If the former, then we can well understand that it could be established independently of the knowledge or belief of the accused. But if, as we think, it is the latter, then the knowledge and belief of the accused are at the root of the problem.

Take for example a man who comes from a country where public transport is free. On his first day here he travels on a bus. He gets off without paying. He never had any intention of paying. His mind is clearly honest; but his conduct, judged objectively by what he has done, is dishonest. It seems to us that in using the word 'dishonestly' in the Theft Act 1968, Parliament cannot have intended to catch dishonest conduct in that sense, that is to say conduct to which no moral obloquy could possibly attach. This is sufficiently established by the partial definition in s 2 of the Theft Act 1968 itself. All the matters covered by s 2(1) relate to the belief of the accused. Section 2(2) relates to his willingness to pay. A man's belief and his willingness to pay are things which can only be established subjectively. It is difficult to see how a partially subjective definition can be made to work in harness with the test which in all other respects is wholly objective.

If we are right that dishonesty is something in the mind of the accused ... then if the mind of the accused is honest, it cannot be deemed dishonest merely because members of the jury would have regarded it as dishonest to embark on that course of conduct. So we would reject the simple uncomplicated approach that the test is purely objective, however attractive from the practical point of view that solution may be.

There remains the objection that to adopt a subjective test is to abandon all standards but that of the accused himself, and to bring about a state of affairs in which 'Robin Hood would be no robber' ... This objection misunderstands the nature of the subjective test. It is no defence for a man to say 'I knew that what I was doing is generally regarded as dishonest; but I do not regard it as dishonest myself. Therefore I am not guilty.' What he is, however, entitled to say is, 'I did not know that anybody would regard what I was doing as dishonest'. He may not be believed; just as he may not be believed if he sets up 'a claim of right' under s 2(1) of the Theft Act 1968, or asserts that he believed in the truth of a misrepresentation under s 15 of the 1968 Act. But if he is believed, or raises a real doubt about the matter, the jury cannot be sure that he was dishonest.

In determining whether the prosecution has proved that the defendant was acting dishonestly, a jury must first of all decide whether according to the ordinary standards of reasonable and honest people what was done was dishonest. If it was not dishonest by those standards, that is the end of the matter and the prosecution fails.

If it was dishonest by those standards, then the jury must consider whether the defendant himself must have realised that what he was doing was by those standards dishonest. In most cases, where the actions are obviously dishonest by ordinary standards, there will be no doubt about it. It will be obvious that the defendant himself knew that he was acting dishonestly. It is dishonest for a defendant to act in a way which he knows ordinary people consider to be dishonest, even if he asserts or genuinely believes that he is morally justified in acting as he did. For example, Robin Hood or those ardent anti-vivisectionists who remove animals from vivisection laboratories are acting dishonestly, even though they may consider themselves to be morally justified in doing what they do, because they know that ordinary people would consider these actions to be dishonest ...

R v Feely [1973] QB 530 (CA)

Facts: The appellant took £30 from his employer's safe. He did not put an IOU in the safe, nor make any record to show what he had done, nor tell his employer what he had done. Four days later a shortfall of £40 was discovered. The appellant then gave an IOU for that amount. When interviewed by the police, the appellant said:

(1) that he would have paid the money back, and
(2) that his employer owed him about £70 and he wanted the employer to take the money which was owing from that.

Lawton LJ: ... The appeal raises an important point of law, namely, can it be a defence *in law* for a man charged with theft and proved to have taken money, to say that when he took the money he intended to repay it and had reasonable grounds for believing and did believe that he would be able to do so? ...

In s 1(1) of the Theft Act 1968 the word 'dishonestly' can only relate to the state of mind of the person who does the act which amounts to appropriation. Whether an accused person has a particular state of mind is a question of fact which has to be decided by the jury when there is a trial on indictment and by the justices when there are summary proceedings. The Crown did not dispute this proposition, but it was submitted that in some cases (and this, it was said, was such a one) it was necessary for the trial judge to define 'dishonestly' and when the facts fell within the definition he had a duty to tell the jury that if there had been an appropriation it must have been dishonestly done. We do not agree that judges should define what 'dishonestly' means.

This word is in common use ... Jurors, when deciding whether an appropriation was dishonest can be reasonably expected to, and should, apply the current standards of ordinary decent people. In their own lives they have to decide what is and what is not dishonest. We can see no reason why, when in a jury box, they should require the help of a judge to tell them what amounts to dishonesty ...

... People who take money from tills and the like without permission are usually thieves; but if they do not admit that they are by pleading guilty, it is for the jury, not the judge, to decide whether they have acted dishonestly.

The provisions of s 2(1)(a)

Under s 2(1)(a) a defendant is not dishonest if she believes that she has a legal right to appropriate the property. All that is required is that the defendant should honestly believe that this is the case; the reasonableness of that belief is relevant only in considering whether that belief was actually held (*R v Holden* [1991] Crim LR 478).

R v Holden [1991] Crim LR 478 (CA)

Facts: The appellant was charged with theft of scrap tyres from Kwik-Fit, where he had worked (although he was not employed there at the time of the offence). He claimed that other people had taken tyres with the permission of a supervisor. The depot manager gave evidence that taking tyres was a sackable offence. The jury had been directed that the test for dishonesty was whether the defendant had a reasonable belief that he had a right to take the tyres.

Held, reasonable belief was not the relevant test of dishonesty. A person was not dishonest if he believed, reasonably or not, that he had a legal right to do what was alleged to constitute an appropriation of property. The question was whether he had, or might have had, an honest belief. However, the reasonableness of the belief might be relevant to the question of whether the defendant could have had an honest belief that he was entitled to take the tyres.

The provisions of s 2(1)(b)

Under s 2(1)(b) a defendant is not dishonest if she believes that the owner of the property would have consented to the appropriation; again the reasonableness of the belief is relevant only to considering whether that belief was actually held.

In *DPP v Gomez* [1993] AC 442 Lord Browne-Wilkinson approved the approach taken by the Court of Appeal in *Attorney General's Reference (No 2 of 1982)*, where the Court of Appeal had had to apply s 2(1)(a) and (b) in the context of appropriation of the property by directors of a limited company. A limited company is a separate legal entity from its directors and shareholders and, said the court, s 2 will not shield directors who know that they are acting dishonestly.

Attorney General's Reference (No 2 of 1982) [1984] QB 624 (CA)

Kerr LJ: On this reference by the Attorney General under s 36 of the Criminal Justice Act 1972, the court is asked to give its opinion on the following point of law:

> Whether a man in total control of a limited liability company (by reason of his shareholding and directorship) is capable of stealing the property of the company; and whether two men in total control of a limited liability company (by reason of their shareholdings and directorships) are (while acting in concert) capable of jointly stealing the property of the company ...

The counts of theft were specimen counts alleging the appropriation by the defendants for their own private purposes of funds of various companies of which they were the sole shareholders and directors. The total amounts involved ran into millions. Some of the counts related to X alone, some to Y alone, and in some of them they were charged jointly. However, it is common ground that, in relation to all of them, each acted with the consent of the other: indeed, all the alleged thefts appear to have been carried out by means of cheques drawn on various accounts of the companies concerned and signed in each case by X and Y jointly. There is no question of X or Y having been the victim of the dishonesty of the other ...

It was submitted that since the defendants were the sole owners of the company and, through their shareholding, the sole owners of all its property, they could not, in effect, be charged with stealing from themselves. In particular, it was submitted that there was no issue to go to the jury on the ingredient of 'dishonestly'. The defendants were the sole will and directing mind of the company. The company was therefore bound to consent to all to which they themselves consented ... Further, the defendants relied on the wide 'objects' clauses of the memorandum of association of the various companies concerned and submitted that the defendants' acts were covered by these and were accordingly *intra vires* ...

... The basic fallacy in the submission on behalf of the defendants is the contention that, in effect, in a situation such as the present a jury is bound to be directed that, when all the members and directors of a company act in concert in appropriating the property of their company, they cannot, as a matter of law, be held to have acted dishonestly; or that, on such facts, any reasonable jury is bound to reach this conclusion. We entirely disagree with both these propositions ...

... In our view there is no substance whatever in the submission that s 2(1)(b) would preclude a jury from concluding, as a matter of law, that the defendants had acted dishonestly in these cases. Nor can we accept for one moment that any jury would be bound to conclude, on the facts alleged that dishonesty had not been established.

... [I]t does not by any means follow that the members and directors of a company which is wholly owned by them cannot properly be charged with theft of the company's property, or that the defendants cannot rely on s 2 of the 1968

Act in answer to such a charge. Their appropriate defence in such cases is provided by s 2(1)(a) of the Act, the belief of a defendant, which must of course be an honest belief, 'that he has in law the right to deprive [the company] of [the property]'.

In effect, the defendants' answer to the charges in the present case, assuming that the prosecution establishes the facts alleged, would have been: 'We honestly believed that we were entitled to do what we did. They were our companies, and we honestly believed that we were entitled to draw all the cheques and expend all the moneys which are now charged as acts of theft'. This is the defence provided by s 2(1)(a). To obtain a conviction, the prosecution would have had to establish the contrary to the satisfaction of the jury ...

... In our view the *vires* of the company may be of evidential relevance to, but not determinative of, the crucial issue as to the defendants' honesty or dishonesty. Of course, in asserting an honest belief in his right to act as he did, a defendant may wish to refer to the objects for which the company was constituted, and to the terms of its memorandum, to assist him in his defence that he had acted honestly ...

The converse equally applies to the case for the prosecution. Thus, although the prosecutor may seek to prove by reference to the company's memorandum that on its true construction the acts charged were *ultra vires*, the prosecution will not thereby inevitably establish that the defendant had acted dishonestly. The defendant would of course be perfectly entitled to assert that in all the circumstances, and especially because he at all times believed his acts to be *intra vires*, he had not acted dishonestly. Whether or not the defendant had acted *ultra vires* is a matter which the jury would then be entitled to take into account, giving it such weight as they thought proper in deciding the ultimate question, namely: has the prosecution proved that the defendant had acted dishonestly?

DPP v Gomez [1993] AC 442 (HL)

Lord Browne-Wilkinson: ... Turning to the company cases, the *dictum* in *R v Morris* [1984] AC 320 has led to much confusion and complication where those in *de facto* control of the company have been charged with theft from it ...

... Where a company is accused of a crime the acts and intentions of those who are the directing minds and will of the company are to be attributed to the company. That is not the law where the charge is that those who are the directing minds and will have themselves committed a crime against the company: see *Attorney General's Reference (No 2 of 1982)* [1984] QB 624 applying *Belmont Finance Corporation Ltd v Williams Furniture Ltd* [1979] Ch 250.

In any event, your Lordships' decision in this case, re-establishing as it does the decision in *R v Lawrence* [1972] AC 626, renders the whole question of consent by the company irrelevant. Whether or not those controlling the company consented or purported to consent to the abstraction of the company's property by the accused, he will have appropriated the property of the company. The question will be whether the other necessary elements are present, *viz* was such appropriation dishonest and was it done with the intention of permanently depriving the company of such property? ...

I am glad to be able to reach this conclusion. The pillaging of companies by those who control them is now all too common. It would offend both common sense and justice to hold that the very control which enables such people to extract the company's assets constitutes a defence to a charge of theft from the company. The question in each case must be whether the extraction of the property from the company was dishonest, not whether the alleged thief has consented to his own wrongdoing.

The provisions of s 2(1)(c)

Section 2(1)(c) covers appropriation of property which the defendant honestly believes to be lost or abandoned property. Again, the reasonableness of the belief goes to whether that belief was genuinely held.

R v Small (1988) 86 Cr App R 170 (CA)

Facts: The appellant was charged with theft of a car; having admitted to the police that he had stolen it, his defence at trial was that he believed the car to have been abandoned.

Henry J: ... The appellant when he was called gave evidence that he lived in a road adjacent to Links Road and that he had seen the car [in Links Road] every day for about two weeks, during which time it had not moved. He said it was parked at an angle on a corner, the doors were unlocked and the keys were in the ignition. According to him the car was in a somewhat forlorn state. The tyre was flat, as was the battery. The petrol tank was empty and the windscreen wipers did not work. He thought it was 'dumped', he said ...

The appellant told the court how he got petrol, bump started the car and drove it round the corner. There it remained for a few days, when he and his co-accused decided to go for a drive with Williams driving. He said that it had not occurred to him until the police flashed their lights that the car was stolen, but it did occur to him then. He then panicked and ran away.

In cross-examination he said that he thought the car had been dumped, abandoned by the true owner. He accepted that he did not have the right to take it. He said he intended to leave it with the keys in it after he had driven it. He said he had initially told the police that he had stolen the car because he had not in fact paid for it. He said that he did not know that the fact that the car was being dumped might offer him a defence at the time when he admitted to the police that he had stolen it.

[Counsel for the appellant contended (1) that one cannot steal abandoned property, and (2) that an honest belief that property was abandoned is a defence.]

In considering whether a belief is honest or not, it seems to us that a belief can, in certain circumstances, be honest or genuinely held, even though it is not reasonably held. The relevance of reasonableness is this. It is certainly relevant as to whether the belief was in fact held, because the fact that such a belief would be objectively viewed as unreasonable is a factor – and a strong factor – for the jury to take into account first in considering whether that belief was held, and second, if held, in considering whether it was honestly held ...

The provisions of s 2(2)

Section 2(2) of the Theft Act 1968 says that an appropriation may be dishonest even if the defendant is willing to pay for the property. In *Boggeln v Williams* [1978] 1 WLR 873 the Divisional Court stressed the word 'may'.

Boggeln v Williams [1978] 1 WLR 873 (DC)

Lloyd J: ... The question for the opinion of the court is whether a person can be convicted of dishonestly abstracting electricity contrary to s 13 of the Theft Act 1968, if he intends to pay for the electricity when payment is due, and that intention is based on a genuine belief that he will be able to do so ...

The facts are these. On 27 October 1976, a representative of the East Midlands Electricity Board had disconnected the defendant's supply of electricity after due warning had been given by reason of the defendant's failure to pay an outstanding amount of £39.65. The defendant thereupon spoke to one of the Board's employees and informed him that he was intending to reconnect the supply himself. Shortly thereafter he broke the seal on the board's main fuse box and reconnected the supply by means of a piece of wire which he inserted in place of the main fuse which the board's employees had removed. The way in which he carried out the re-connection meant that the electricity which he used would continue to be recorded on the meter in the usual way.

There is then this important finding of fact in paragraph 2(5) of the case [stated by the justices]:

> As a result of the said conversation the [defendant] did not believe that the Board consented to reconnection by him. The [defendant] nevertheless did believe that, by giving notice of his intention and by ensuring that consumption was duly recorded through the meter, he was not acting dishonestly in reconnecting.

... There is then another important finding of fact in paragraph 2(8) [of the case stated by the justices]:

> At the time when the [defendant] reconnected the supply, the [defendant] believed, as he asserted, that he would be in a position to pay for the electricity consumed thereafter at the date when payment was due. We were satisfied that this belief was a genuine one and we were not satisfied that it was unreasonable.

There is no specific finding anywhere in the case as to the defendant's intention to pay for the electricity, but it is common ground in this case that that can be inferred. Finally, in paragraph 5 of the case it is stated:

> We were of the opinion that the defendant did believe that, when payment became due, he would be able to pay for the electricity consumed; that this belief was not proved to be unreasonable; and that the defendant's state of mind at the relevant time (ie when reconnecting the supply) was not dishonest.

The question for the opinion of the court is as follows:

> Is an intention to pay for electricity knowingly used without the authority of the Electricity Board capable of affording a defence to a charge under s 13 of the Theft Act 1968, if that intention is based on a genuine belief that the user will be able to pay at the due time for payment?

... The fact that the defendant did not believe at the time he reconnected his supply that he had the consent of the Board does not of itself make the defendant's conduct dishonest in law. It is a question of fact in each case for the tribunal of fact whether the necessary dishonesty is proved or not ...

O'Connor J and **Lord Widgery CJ** delivered concurring judgments.

APPROPRIATION

Section 3 of the Theft Act 1968: 'appropriates'

(1) Any assumption by a person of the rights of an owner amounts to an appropriation, and this includes, where he has come by the property (innocently or not) without stealing it, any later assumption of a right to it by keeping or dealing with it as owner.

(2) Where property or a right or interest in property is or purports to be transferred for value to a person acting in good faith, no later assumption by him of rights which he believed himself to be acquiring shall, by reason of any defect in the transferor's title, amount to theft of the property.

From s 3(1) of the Theft Act 1968, 'to appropriate' means 'to assume the rights of the owner of the property'. This apparently straightforward definition has been the source of enormous difficulty for the courts. The concept of appropriation has been the subject-matter of no less than three decisions of the House of Lords (*Lawrence v Metropolitan Police Commissioner* [1972] AC 626, *R v Morris* [1984]; *R v Gomez* [1993] AC 442 , together with a decision of the Court of Appeal (*Dobson v General Accident Fire and Life Assurance Corp* [1990] 1 QB 274) which tried to reconcile the first two decisions of the House of Lords.

A number of points can be derived from these decisions:

(a) The fact that the owner of the property consents to the appropriation of that property does not prevent the defendant's actions from amounting to an appropriation: see *Lawrence v Metropolitan Police Commissioner* [1972] AC 626; *R v Gomez* [1993] AC 442.

(b) In order to appropriate property, the defendant does not have to assume *all* the rights of the owner; it is sufficient if he appropriates any of the rights of the owner: see *R v Morris* [1984]; *R v Gomez* [1993] AC 442.

(c) To the extent that there is any inconsistency between *Lawrence* and *Morris*, in that *Morris* suggests that consent may prevent an act from being an appropriation, *Lawrence* is to be preferred.

Lawrence v Metropolitan Police Commissioner [1972] AC 626 (HL)

Lord Donovan: My Lords, I have had the advantage of reading the opinion of my noble and learned friend, Viscount Dilhorne. I agree with it and would therefore dismiss this appeal.

Viscount Dilhorne: My Lords, the appellant was convicted on 2 December 1969, of theft contrary to s 1(1) of the Theft Act 1968. On 1 September 1969, a Mr Occhi, an Italian who spoke little English, arrived at Victoria Station on his first visit to this country. He went up to a taxi driver, the appellant, and showed him a piece of paper on which an address in Ladbroke Grove was written. The appellant said that it was very far and very expensive. Mr Occhi got into the taxi, took £1 out of his wallet and gave it to the appellant who then, the wallet being still open, took a further £6 out of it. He then drove Mr Occhi to Ladbroke Grove. The correct lawful fare for the journey was in the region of 10s 6d. The appellant was charged with and convicted of the theft of the £6 ...

I see no ground for concluding that the omission of the words 'without the consent of the owner' [from s 1(1) of the Theft Act 1968] was inadvertent and not deliberate, and to read the subsection as if they were included is, in my opinion, wholly unwarranted. Parliament by the omission of these words has relieved the prosecution of the burden of establishing that the taking was without the owner's consent. That is no longer an ingredient of the offence ...

... That there was appropriation in this case is clear. Section 3(1) states that any assumption by a person of the rights of an owner amounts to an appropriation. Here there was clearly such an assumption. That an appropriation was dishonest may be proved in a number of ways. In this case it was not contended that the appellant had not acted dishonestly. Section 2(1) provides, *inter alia*, that a person's appropriation of property belonging to another is not to be regarded as dishonest if he appropriates the property in the belief that he would have the other's consent if the other knew of the appropriation and the circumstances of it. A *fortiori*, a person is not to be regarded as acting dishonestly if he appropriates another's property believing that with full knowledge of the circumstances that other person has in fact agreed to the appropriation. The appellant, if he believed that Mr Occhi, knowing that £7 was far in excess of the legal fare, had nevertheless agreed to pay him that sum, could not be said to have acted dishonestly in taking it.

... Belief or the absence of belief that the owner had with such knowledge consented to the appropriation is relevant to the issue of dishonesty, not to the question whether or not there has been an appropriation. That may occur even though the owner has permitted or consented to the property being taken. So proof that Mr Occhi had consented to the appropriation of £6 from his wallet without agreeing to paying a sum in excess of the legal fare does not suffice to show that there was not dishonesty in this case. There was ample evidence that there was.

I now turn to the third element, 'property belonging to another' ... [T]he money in the wallet which [the appellant] appropriated belonged to another, to Mr Occhi.

There was no dispute about the appellant's intention being permanently to deprive Mr Occhi of the money.

The four elements of the offence of theft as defined in the Theft Act 1968 were thus clearly established and, in my view, the Court of Appeal was right to dismiss the appeal.

Having done so, they granted a certificate that a point of law of general public importance was involved ...

The first question posed in the certificate was:

> Whether s 1(1) of the Theft Act, 1968, is to be construed as though it contained the words 'without having the consent of the owner' or words to that effect.

In my opinion, the answer is clearly No.

The second question was:

> Whether the provisions of s 15(1) and of s 1(1) of the Theft Act 1968, are mutually exclusive in the sense that if the facts proved would justify a conviction under s 15(1) there cannot lawfully be a conviction under s 1(1) on those facts.

Again, in my opinion, the answer is No. There is nothing in the Act to suggest that they should be regarded as mutually exclusive and it is by no means uncommon for conduct on the part of an accused to render him liable to conviction for more than one offence. Not infrequently there is some overlapping of offences. In some cases the facts may justify a charge under s 1(1) and also a charge under s 15(1).

On the other hand, there are cases which only come within s 1(1) and some which are only within s 15(1). If in this case the appellant had been charged under s 15(1), he would, I expect, have contended that there was no deception, that he had simply appropriated the money and that he ought to have been charged under s 1(1). In my view, he was rightly charged under that section ...

Lord Pearson: My Lords, I have read the opinion of my noble and learned friend, Viscount Dilhorne, and I agree with it; and for the reasons given by him I would dismiss the appeal.

Lord Diplock: My Lords, I agree, for the reasons given by my noble and learned friend, Viscount Dilhorne, that this appeal should be dismissed.

Lord Cross of Chelsea: My Lords, I agree, for the reasons given by my noble and learned friend, Viscount Dilhorne, that this appeal should be dismissed.

Anderton v Wish (1980) 72 Cr App R 23 (DC)

Roskill LJ: ... The facts are these. On the evening of 4 October 1977, the defendant went into Boots at the Royal Exchange in this city: she saw there a back brush. That back brush bore a price ticket of £1.45. She saw another back brush which bore a price ticket of £1.20. She took the £1.20 price ticket and put it over the £1.45 price ticket in order to obscure it. While holding this back brush with the labels one on top of the other, she took the price labels off several of the other cheaper brushes and threw those on the floor. She then took the brush which, by this time, was wholly in her possession, to the cashier and paid the £1.20. She left the store with the brush and was promptly arrested. She denied the theft to the store detective and the police and when she was charged she made no reply ...

... No doubt the brush belonged to Boots and not to Mrs Wish. No doubt she acted dishonestly. The sole question is whether at the relevant time namely when she took that brush into her possession and switched the labels she appropriated that brush.

... [D]ishonesty being conceded, an intention permanently to deprive being conceded, the only question is whether this lady acted in such a way as to assume the rights of an owner. I think that she clearly did ...

[His Lordship referred to *R v McPherson* [1973] Crim LR 191 and said:]

If that decision is right and, with respect, it seems to me plainly right, it completely governs the present case because there was here a dishonest appropriation at the point of time when the defendant switched the labels on the brush ...

R v Morris; Anderton v Burnside [1984] AC 320 (HL)

Lord Fraser of Tullybelton: My Lords, I have had the advantage of reading in draft the speech prepared by my noble and learned friend Lord Roskill. I entirely agree with it, and for the reasons given by him I would answer the certified questions in the way he proposes, and I would dismiss both appeals.

Lord Edmund-Davies: My Lords, having had the advantage of reading in draft form the speech prepared by my noble and learned friend, Lord Roskill, I too would answer the question certified in these appeals in the manner indicated by him and dismiss both appeals.

Lord Roskill: ... The facts giving rise to these appeals are simple. Morris, the appellant from the Court of Appeal (Criminal Division), on 30 October 1981, took goods from the shelves of a supermarket. He replaced the price labels attached to them with labels showing a lesser price than the originals. At the check-out point he was asked for and paid those lesser prices. He was then arrested. Burnside, the appellant from the Divisional Court, was seen to remove a price label from a joint of pork in the supermarket and attach it to a second joint. This action was detected at the check-out point but before he had paid for that second joint which at that moment bore a price label showing a price of £2.73 whereas the label should have shown a price of £6.91. Burnside was then arrested.

The only relevant difference between the two cases is that Burnside was arrested before he had dishonestly paid the lesser price for the joint of pork. Morris was arrested after he had paid the relevant lesser prices ...

... [I]t is enough for the prosecution if they have proved in these cases the assumption by the respondents of any of the rights of the owner of the goods in question, that is to say, the supermarket concerned ...

... In one passage in his judgment in *Morris's* case, the learned Lord Chief Justice ... said.

> ... it seems to us that in taking the article from the shelf the customer is indeed assuming one of the rights of the owner, the right to move the article from its position on the shelf to carry it to the check-out.

With the utmost respect, I cannot accept this statement as correct. If one postulates an honest customer taking goods from a shelf to put in his or her trolley to take to the checkpoint there to pay the proper price, I am unable to see that any of these actions involves any assumption by the shopper of the rights of the supermarket. In the context of s 3(1), the concept of appropriation in my view involves not an act expressly or impliedly authorised by the owner but an act by way of adverse interference with or usurpation of those rights. When the honest shopper acts as I have just described, he or she is acting with the implied authority of the owner of the supermarket to take the goods from the shelf, put them in the trolley, take them to the checkpoint and there to pay the correct price, at which moment the property in the goods will pass to the shopper for the first time. It is with the consent of the owners of the supermarket, be that consent express or implied, that the shopper does these acts and thus obtained at least control if not actual possession of the goods preparatory, at a later stage, to obtaining the property in them on payment of the proper amount at the checkpoint. I do not think that s 3(1) envisages any such act as an 'appropriation', whatever may be the meaning of that word in other fields such as contract or sale of goods law.

If, as I understand all of your Lordships agree, the concept of appropriation in s 3(1) involves an element of adverse interference with or usurpation of some right of the owner, it is necessary next to consider whether that requirement is satisfied in either of these cases. As I have already said, in my view mere removal from the shelves without more is not an appropriation. Further, if a shopper with some perverted sense of humour, intending only to create confusion and nothing more, both for the supermarket and for other shoppers, switches labels, I do not think that that act of label-switching alone is without more an appropriation, though it is not difficult to envisage some cases of dishonest label-switching which could be. In cases such as the present, it is in truth a combination of these actions, the removal from the shelf and the switching of the labels, which evidences adverse interference with or usurpation of the right of the owner. Those acts, therefore, amount to an appropriation and if they are accompanied by proof of the other three elements to which I have referred, the offence of theft is established. Further if they are accompanied by other acts such as putting the goods so removed and re-labelled into a receptacle, whether a trolley or the shopper's own bag or basket, proof of appropriation within s 3(1) becomes overwhelming. It is the doing of one or more acts which individually or collectively amount to such adverse interference with or usurpation of the owner's rights which constitute appropriation under s 3(1) and I do not think it matters where there is more than one such act in which order the successive acts take place, or whether there is any interval of time between them. To suggest that it matters whether the mislabelling precedes or succeeds removal from the shelves is to reduce this branch of the law to an absurdity ...

[His Lordship referred to *R v McPherson* [1973] Crim LR 191 and continued:]

Your Lordships have had the benefit of a transcript of the judgment of Lord Widgery CJ. I quote from the transcript:

> Reducing this case to its bare essentials we have this: Mrs McPherson in common design with the others takes two bottles of whisky from the stand, puts them in her shopping bag; at the time she intends to take them out without paying for them, in other words she intends to steal them from the very beginning. She acts dishonestly as the jury found, and the sole question is whether that is an appropriation of the bottles within the meaning of s 1. We have no hesitation whatever in saying that it is such an appropriation and indeed we content ourselves with a judgment of this brevity because we have been unable to accept or to find any argument to the contrary, to suggest that an appropriation is not effective in those simple circumstances.

That was not, of course, a label-switching case, but it is a plain case of appropriation effected by the combination of the acts of removing the goods from the shelf and of concealing them in the shopping bag. *R v McPherson* is to my mind clearly correctly decided as are all the cases which have followed it. It is wholly consistent with the principles which I have endeavoured to state in this speech.

... The precise moment when dishonest acts, not of themselves amounting to an appropriation, subsequently, because of some other and later acts combined with those earlier acts, do bring about an appropriation within s 3(1) will necessarily vary according to the particular case in which the question arises.

... I understand all your Lordships to agree that *Anderton v Wish* (1980) 72 Cr App R 23 was rightly decided ...

My Lords, it remains briefly to consider any relationship between s 1 and s 15. If the conclusion I have reached that theft takes place at the moment of appropriation and before any payment is made at the checkpoint be correct, it is wrong to assert, as has been asserted, that the same act of appropriation creates two offences, one against s 1(1) and the other against s 15(1), because the two offences occur at different points of time; the s 15(1) offence is not committed until payment of the wrong amount is made at the checkpoint while the theft has been committed earlier. It follows that in cases such as Morris's two offences were committed ...

... I see no reason in principle why, when there is clear evidence of both offences being committed, both offences should not be charged. But where a shoplifter has passed the checkpoint and quite clearly has, by deception, obtained goods either without paying or by paying only a lesser price than he should, those concerned with prosecutions may in future think it preferable ... to charge only an offence against s 15(1) ... Of course when dishonesty is detected before the defendant has reached the checkpoint and he or she is arrested before that point so that no property has been obtained by deception, then theft is properly charged and if appropriation, within the meaning I have attributed to that word in this speech, is proved as well as the other three ingredients of the offence of theft, the defendant is plainly guilty of that offence ...

I would answer the certified questions in this way:

> There is a dishonest appropriation for the purposes of the Theft Act 1968 where by the substitution of a price label showing a lesser price on goods for one showing a greater price, a defendant either by that act alone or by that act in conjunction with another act or other acts (whether done before or after the substitution of the labels) adversely interferes with or usurps the right of the owner to ensure that the goods concerned are sold and paid for at that greater price.

I would dismiss these appeals.

Lord Brandon of Oakbrook: My Lords, I have had the advantage of reading in draft the speech prepared by my noble and learned friend, Lord Roskill. I agree with it, and for the reasons which he gives I would dismiss both appeals.

Lord Brightman: My Lords, I would dismiss these appeals for the reasons given by my noble and learned friend, Lord Roskill.

Dobson v General Accident Fire and Life Assurance Corp plc [1990] 1 QB 274 (CA)

Facts: This was a civil case involving a claim under a home insurance policy which included cover for loss by theft. The Court of Appeal (Civil Division) had to consider the meaning of 'theft' (the meaning of the word in the insurance policy being taken to be the same as the meaning of the word under the Theft Act 1968).

Parker LJ: ... On 19 November 1987 the plaintiff advertised for sale his gold Rolex Oyster wristwatch and a diamond ring at a total price of £5,950. On 20 November he received a telephone call from a person whose identity he did not then and does not now know. I shall refer to him as 'the rogue'. He expressed interest in purchasing the two articles at the advertised price. It was provisionally agreed between them that payment would be by a building society cheque, ie a cheque drawn by a building society in favour of the plaintiff. This the plaintiff believed would be as good as a banker's draft.

On 21 November the rogue came to the plaintiff's premises and the plaintiff handed over the watch and ring, receiving in return what purported to be a Birmingham Midshires Building Society cheque in the agreed amount of £5,950, for which he gave a receipt. This transaction took place at the weekend. On the Monday he paid the cheque into his bank. A few days later he was informed that the cheque had been stolen and was worthless.

... The issue for determination on the appeal is whether the circumstances constituted a theft of the watch and ring by the rogue.

... On the basis of *Lawrence v Commissioner of Police for the Metropolis* [1972] AC 626, the facts of the present case appear to establish that the rogue assumed all the rights of an owner when he took or received the watch and ring from the plaintiff. That he did so dishonestly and with the intention of permanently depriving the plaintiff of them are matters beyond doubt. It was however submitted that the third element was not satisfied because, at the time of appropriation, if there was one, the watch and ring were not property belonging to another. The property had, it was submitted, already passed to the rogue at the time the articles were delivered to him.

This argument is put in two ways. First, it is said that there was an agreement of sale over the telephone and accordingly the property passed to the rogue on 20 November. Alternatively, it is said that an agreement of sale took place on 21 November prior to the rogue receiving the articles in exchange for the cheque, and accordingly the property again passed to him, before delivery and receipt of the articles ...

Having regard to the terms of the contract, the conduct of the parties and the circumstances of the case, I have no doubt that the property was not intended to pass in this case on contract but only in exchange for a valid building society cheque, but even if it may be regarded as intended to pass in exchange for a false, but believed genuine, building society cheque it will not in my view avail the insurers ...

It was further submitted on the part of the insurers that, notwithstanding the emphatic statement of the House of Lords that absence of consent on the part of the owner was not an ingredient of the offence and was not relevant to the question whether there had been an appropriation, the later decision of the House in *R v Morris* [1984] AC 320 at 332, that appropriation 'involves not an act expressly or impliedly authorised by the owner but an act by way of adverse interference with or usurpation of those rights', must lead in the present case to the conclusion that there had been no theft.

The difficulties caused by the apparent conflict between the decision in *Lawrence's* case and *R v Morris* have provided, not surprisingly, a basis for much discussion by textbook writers and contributors of articles to law journals. It is, however, clear that their Lordships in *R v Morris* did not regard anything said in that case as conflicting with *Lawrence's* case for it was specifically referred to in Lord Roskill's speech, with which the other members of the Appellate Committee all agreed, without disapproval or qualification. The only comment made was that, in *Lawrence's* case, the House did not have to consider the precise meaning of 'appropriation' in s 3(1) (see [1984] AC 320 at 331). With respect, I find this comment hard to follow in the light of the first of the questions asked in *Lawrence's* case and the answer to it, the passages from Viscount Dilhorne's speech already cited, the fact that it was specifically argued that '"appropriates" is meant in a pejorative, rather than a neutral, sense in that the appropriation is against the will of the owner' (see [1972] AC 626 at 631 arg), and finally that dishonesty was common ground. I would have supposed that the question in *Lawrence's* case was whether appropriation necessarily involved an absence of consent ...

[His Lordship then cited two passages from the speech of Lord Roskill in *R v Morris* [1984] AC 320 at 332 and 335 and continued:]

In the first passage Lord Roskill, as it seems to me, impliedly envisages that mere label-switching could be an appropriation and that this is so is confirmed by the answer to the certified question which specifically uses the words 'either by that act alone'. What then is it which would make label-switching alone something which adversely affects or usurps the right of the owner? In that passage it appears to be envisaged that it will depend on the question whether the label-switching was dishonest and coupled with the other elements of the offence of theft or was due a perverted sense of humour. This, however, appears to run together the elements of dishonesty and appropriation when it is clear from *Lawrence's* case that they are separate. That the two elements were indeed, at any rate to some extent, run together is plain from the fact that the answer to the certified question begins with the words 'there is a dishonest appropriation'.

Moreover, on general principles, it would in my judgment be a plain interference with or usurpation of an owner's rights by the customer if he were to remove a label which the owner had placed on goods or put another label on. It would be a trespass to goods and it would be usurping the owner's rights, for only he would have any right to do such an act and no one could contend that there was any implied consent or authority to a customer to do any such thing. There would thus be an appropriation. In the case of the customer with a perverted sense of humour there would however be no theft for there would probably be no dishonesty and certainly no intent permanently to deprive the owner of the goods themselves.

The case of the customer who simply removes goods from the shelves is of course different because the basis on which a supermarket is run is that customers certainly have the consent of the owner to take goods from the shelves and take them to the checkout point, there to pay the proper price for them. Suppose, however, that there were no such consent, in, for example, a shop where goods on display were to be taken from the shelves only by the attendant. In such a case a customer who took from the shelves would clearly be usurping the right of the owner. Indeed he would be doing so if he did no more than move an item from one place on a shelf to another. The only difference appears to be that in the one case there is consent and in the other there is not. Since, however, it was held in *Lawrence's* case that consent is not relevant to appropriation there must, one would have supposed, be no difference between the two cases on that aspect of the offence ...

After anxious consideration I have reached the conclusion that whatever *R v Morris* did decide it cannot be regarded as having overruled the very plain decision in *Lawrence's* case that appropriation can occur even if the owner consents, and that *R v Morris* itself makes it plain that it is no defence to say that the property passed under a voidable contract ...

Returning now to the present case, the insurers' contention that there was no theft is based on consent and the fact that there was a clear s 15(1) offence, both of which are negatived as answers to appropriation by *Lawrence's* case, and the fact that the contract of sale between the plaintiff and the rogue was voidable only and not void, which is not relevant according to *R v Morris*.

If, then the insurers are deprived of their arguments to defeat the only element of the offence of theft which was in doubt once the 'belonging to another' argument has been rejected, they cannot in my judgment succeed on the basis of Lord Roskill's statement in *R v Morris* that there must be an act by way of adverse interference with or usurpation of the owner's rights. If consent and the existence of a voidable contract under which property passes are irrelevant, there was in my judgment a plain interference with or usurpation of the plaintiff's rights.

I am fully conscious of the fact that in so concluding I may be said not to be applying *R v Morris*. This may be so, but in the light of the difficulties inherent in the decision, the very clear decision in *Lawrence's* case and the equally clear statement in *R v Morris* that the question whether a contract is void or only voidable is irrelevant, I have been unable to reach any other conclusion. I would therefore dismiss the appeal.

Bingham LJ: ... It ... appears that A commits theft if he dishonestly assumes any of the rights of an owner over B's property intending to deprive B of that property permanently.

This simple analysis may be applied to the everyday example of a customer selecting goods from a supermarket shelf and putting them in the wire basket or trolley provided. The goods on the shelves belong to the supermarket. They continue to belong to the supermarket until paid for by a customer: see *Laci v Cashmarts* [1969] 2 QB 400. The customer assumes some of the rights of an owner when he takes them into his (or her) possession and exercises control over them by putting them in a basket or trolley. The customer, not intending to return the goods to the supermarket, intends to deprive the supermarket of the goods permanently. In the ordinary case the customer will honestly intend to pay the market price for the goods at the cash desk, so no offence of theft will be committed. But a customer who dishonestly intends not to pay the marked price will be guilty of theft, at the time of dishonest appropriation. On this analysis it is irrelevant that the supermarket displays the goods for sale and invites, perhaps even tempts, customers to put them in their baskets or trolleys. The acid test is whether when doing so the customer acts honestly or dishonestly. (I need not discuss the case where a customer initially appropriates goods honestly intending to pay and later forms a dishonest intention to keep the goods without paying) ...

I do not find it easy to reconcile [the] ruling of Viscount Dilhorne [in *Lawrence's* case, that appropriation may occur even though the owner has permitted or consented to the property being taken], which was as I understand central to the answer which the House of Lords gave to the certified question, with the reasoning of the House in *R v Morris*. Since, however, the House in *R v Morris* considered that there had plainly been an appropriation in *Lawrence's* case, this must (I think) have been because the Italian student, although he had permitted or allowed his money to be taken, had not in truth consented to the taxi driver taking anything in excess of the correct fare. This is not a wholly satisfactory reconciliation, since it might be said that a supermarket consents to customers taking goods from its shelves only when they honestly intend to pay and not otherwise. On the facts of the present case, however, it can be said, by analogy with *Lawrence's* case, that although the plaintiff permitted and allowed his property to be taken by the rogue, he had not in truth consented to the rogue becoming owner without giving a valid draft drawn by the building society for the price. On this basis I conclude that the plaintiff is able to show an appropriation sufficient to satisfy s 1(1) of the 1968 Act when the rogue accepted delivery of the articles.

On the facts here the plaintiff has no difficulty in showing dishonesty and an intention permanently to deprive on the part of the rogue. It is, however, argued for the insurers that when the rogue appropriated the ring and the watch they were not property belonging to another because ownership of the goods had already, before delivery, passed to the rogue under the contract of sale.

The courts have been enjoined so far as possible to eschew difficult questions of contract law relating to title to goods: see *R v Morris* [1984] AC 320 at 334. But whether, in the ordinary case to which s 5 of the 1968 Act does not apply, goods are to be regarded as belonging to another is a question to which the criminal law offers no answer and which can only be answered by reference to civil law principles. Applying these principles, I would without much doubt impute an intention to the plaintiff and the rogue that property in the watch and the ring should pass to the rogue on delivery of the goods to him and not before. That would also, as I think, be the moment of appropriation. If, therefore, it were necessary for the plaintiff to show that the goods still belonged to him at the moment of appropriation I would doubt whether he could do so, appropriation and transfer of title being simultaneous. Happily for the plaintiff, the point was raised in *Lawrence v Commissioner of Police for the Metropolis* [1972] AC 626 at 632 and decided in his favour ...

... Just as it is enough to satisfy s 15 that the goods belong to the victim up to the time of obtaining, so it is enough for the plaintiff that the watch and ring belonged to him up to the time of appropriation ...

R v Rader [1992] Crim LR 663 (CA)

Facts: The appellant was convicted of seven counts of theft under s 1(1) of the Theft Act 1968. The victim had paid over to the appellant sums totalling £8,000 on the basis that it would be put to good use and returned to him on a fixed date with some sort of profit. The money was not repaid on the due date and, after reassurance from the appellant, the victim gave him another £1,000. At a later date he handed over a further £994. Cheques tendered by the appellant in repayment were dishonoured and, despite further promises by the appellant of repayment, none of the moneys had ever been repaid.

It was the Crown's case that the appellant had appropriated the money for his own purposes. The appellant's defence was that he had not stolen the victim's money or treated it as his own. His account was that he had offered to invest the money on the victim's behalf, as he had heard of an opportunity, through an acquaintance of his in Miami, which offered a higher rate of return than could be obtained through the bank. He transferred the victim's money to the acquaintance in Miami. When the time for repayment came, the funds he had expected to receive from Miami failed to arrive. The appellant said that he had made repeated efforts to recover the victim's money and had finally travelled to Miami, against his doctor's orders. As a result of this visit, the acquaintance wrote a letter to the appellant's solicitors confirming the appellant's account of events.

The indictment alleged theft between the dates on which the moneys were handed over and the date of the appellant's arrest.

Held: The fact that the appellant had obtained the moneys with the victim's full consent was no bar to conviction for theft: see the answer to the first question in the certificate in *Lawrence*. Section 5(3) of the Theft Act provided that where a person received property from another and was under an obligation to the other to deal with the property in a particular way, the property should be regarded, as against him, as belonging to the other. The court had no doubt that the appellant was under an obligation to invest the money in such a way as to produce a profit for the victim. Nor did the court doubt that when the victim handed over the various sums, they remained his property and there was no appropriation at that stage. In the circumstances, s 3(1) of the Theft Act was entirely apt; it provided that any assumption by a person of the rights of an owner amounted to an appropriation and that this included, where he had come by the property (innocently or not) without stealing it, any later assumption of a right to it by keeping or dealing with it as owner.

R v Gomez [1993] AC 442 (HL)

Lord Keith of Kinkel: My Lords, this appeal raises the question whether two decisions of your Lordships' House upon the proper construction of certain provisions of the Theft Act 1968 are capable of being reconciled with each other, and, if so, in what manner. The two decisions are *R v Lawrence (Alan)* [1972] AC 626 and *R v Morris (David)* [1984] AC 320 ...

The facts of this case are that the defendant, Edwin Gomez was employed as assistant manager at a shop trading by retail in electrical goods. In September 1987 he was asked by an acquaintance called Jit Ballay to supply goods from the shop and to accept payment by two stolen building society cheques, one for

£7,950 and the other for £9,250, which were undated and bore no payee's name. The defendant agreed, and prepared a list of goods to the value of £7,950 which he submitted to the manager, Mr Gilberd, saying that it represented a genuine order by one Johal and asking him to authorise the supply of the goods in return for a building society cheque in that sum. Mr Gilberd instructed the defendant to confirm with the bank that the cheque was acceptable, and the defendant later told him that he had done so and that such a cheque was 'as good as cash'. Mr Gilberd agreed to the transaction, the defendant paid the cheque into the bank, and a few days later Ballay took possession of the goods, the defendant helping him to load them into his vehicle. Shortly afterwards a further consignment of goods to the value of £9,250 was ordered and supplied in similar fashion (apart from one item valued at £1,002.99 which was not delivered), against the second stolen building society cheque. Mr Gilberd agreed to this transaction without further enquiry. Later the two cheques were returned by the bank marked 'Orders not to pay. Stolen cheque.'

[The Court of Appeal certified that a point of law of general public importance was involved, namely:]

> When theft is alleged and that which is alleged to be stolen passes to the defendant with the consent of the owner, but that consent has been obtained by a false representation, has (a) an appropriation within the meaning of s 1(1) of the Theft Act 1968 taken place, or (b) must such a passing of property necessarily involve an element of adverse [interference] with or usurpation of some right of the owner?

... It will be seen that Viscount Dilhorne's speech [in *Lawrence's* case] contains two clear pronouncements, first that it is no longer an ingredient of the offence of theft that the taking should be without the owner's consent and second, that an appropriation may occur even though the owner has permitted or consented to the property being taken ...

In my opinion Lord Roskill [in *R v Morris*] was undoubtedly right when he said ... that the assumption by the defendant of any of the rights of an owner could amount to an appropriation within the meaning of s 3(1), and that the removal of an article from the shelf and the changing of the price label on it constituted the assumption of one of the rights of the owner and hence an appropriation within the meaning of the subsection. But there are observations in the passage which, with the greatest possible respect to Lord Roskill, I must regard as unnecessary for the decision of the case and as being incorrect. In the first place, it seems to me that the switching of price labels on the article is in itself an assumption of one of the rights of the owner, whether or not it is accompanied by some other act such as removing the article from the shelf and placing it in a basket or trolley. No one but the owner has the right to remove a price label from an article or to place a price label upon it. If anyone else does so, he does an act, as Lord Roskill puts it, by way of adverse interference with or usurpation of that right. This is no less so in the case of the practical joker figured by Lord Roskill than in the case of one who makes the switch with dishonest intent. The practical joker, of course, is not guilty of theft because he has not acted dishonestly and does not intend to deprive the owner permanently of the article. So the label-switching in itself constitutes an appropriation and so to have held would have been sufficient for the dismissal of both appeals. On the facts of the two cases it was unnecessary to decide whether, as argued by [counsel for the prosecution], the mere taking of the article from the shelf and putting it in a trolley or other receptacle amounted to the assumption of one of the rights of the owner, and hence an appropriation. There was much to be said in favour of the view that it did, in respect that doing so gave the shopper control of the article and the capacity to exclude any other shopper from taking it. However, Lord Roskill expressed the opinion that it did not, on the ground that the concept of appropriation in the context of s 3(1):

> involves not an act expressly or impliedly authorised by the owner but an act by way of adverse interference with or usurpation of those rights.

While it is correct to say that appropriation for purposes of s 3(1) includes the latter sort of act, it does not necessarily follow that no other act can amount to an appropriation and in particular that no act expressly or impliedly authorised by the owner can in any circumstances do so. Indeed, *R v Lawrence* [1972] AC 626 is a clear decision to the contrary since it laid down unequivocally that an act may be an appropriation notwithstanding that it is done with the consent of the owner. It does not appear to me that any sensible distinction can be made in this context between consent and authorisation.

In the civil case of *Dobson v General Accident and Life Assurance Corporation plc* [1990] 1 QB 274 a Court of Appeal consisting of Parker and Bingham LJJ considered the apparent conflict between *R v Lawrence* and *R v Morris* and applied the former decision.

[His Lordship then quoted extensively from the judgment from of Parker LJ and from the judgment of Bingham LJ in *Dobson* and continued:]

It was argued for the defendant in the present appeal that *Dobson v General Accident Fire and Life Assurance Corporation plc* [1990] 1 QB 274 was wrongly decided. I disagree, and on the contrary find myself in full agreement with those parts of the judgment of Parker LJ to which I have referred. As regards the attempted reconciliation by Bingham LJ of the reasoning in *R v Morris* ... with the ruling in *R v Lawrence,* it appears to me that the suggested basis of reconciliation, which is essentially speculative, is unsound. The actual decision in *Morris* was correct, but it was erroneous, in addition to being unnecessary for the decision, to indicate that an act expressly or impliedly authorised by the owner could never amount to an appropriation. There is no material distinction between the facts in *Dobson* and those in the present case. In each case the owner of the goods was induced by fraud to part with them to the rogue. *Lawrence* makes it clear that consent to or authorisation by the owner of the taking by the rogue is irrelevant. The taking amounted to an appropriation within the meaning of s 1(1) of the Act of 1968. *Lawrence* also makes it clear that it is no less irrelevant that what happened may also have constituted the offence of obtaining property by deception under s 15(1) of the 1968 Act.

... The decision in *Lawrence* was a clear decision of this House upon the construction of the word 'appropriates' in s 1(1) of the 1968 Act, which had stood for 12 years when doubt was thrown upon it by *obiter dicta* in *Morris. Lawrence* must be regarded as authoritative and correct, and there is no question of it now being right to depart from it ...

There were cited to your Lordships a number of cases involving the abstraction of moneys from a limited company by a person who was in a position to give the consent of the company to the abstraction. It is sufficient to say that I agree with what my noble and learned friend, Lord Browne-Wilkinson, has to say about these cases in the speech to be delivered by him and that in my opinion a person who thus procures the company's consent dishonestly and with the intention of permanently depriving the company of the money is guilty of theft contrary to s 1(1) of the Act 1968.

My Lords, for the reasons which I have given I would answer branch (a) of the certified question in the affirmative and branch (b) in the negative, and allow the appeal.

Lord Jauncey of Tullichettle: My Lords, I have had the advantage of reading in draft the speeches of my noble and learned friends, Lord Keith of Kinkel and Lord Browne-Wilkinson, and for the reasons which they give I agree that the appeal should be allowed and the questions answered in the way in which my noble and learned friend, Lord Keith of Kinkel, proposes.

Lord Browne-Wilkinson: My Lords, I have read the speech of my noble and learned friend, Lord Keith of Kinkel, with which I agree ...

The fact that Parliament used that composite phrase 'dishonest appropriation' in my judgment casts light on what is meant by the word 'appropriation'. The views expressed (*obiter*) by this House in *R v Morris* [1984] AC 320 that 'appropriation' involves an act by way of adverse interference with or usurpation of the rights of the owner treats the word appropriation as being tantamount to 'misappropriation'. The concept of adverse interference with or usurpation of rights introduces into the word appropriation the mental state of both the owner and the accused. So far as concerns the mental state of the owner (did he consent?), the 1968 Act expressly refers to such consent when it is a material factor: see ss 2(1)(b), 11(1), 12(1) and 13. So far as concerns the mental state of the accused, the composite phrase in s 1(1) itself indicates that the requirement is dishonesty.

For myself, therefore, I regard the word 'appropriation' in isolation as being an objective description of the act done irrespective of the mental state of either the owner or the accused. It is impossible to reconcile the decision in *Lawrence* (that the question of consent is irrelevant in considering whether there has been an appropriation) with the views expressed in *Morris*, which latter views in my judgment were incorrect.

It is suggested that this conclusion renders s 15 of the Act of 1968 otiose since a person who, by deception, persuades the owner to consent to part with his property will necessarily be guilty of theft within s 1. This may be so though I venture to doubt it. Take for example a man who obtains land by deception. Save as otherwise expressly provided the definitions in ss 4 and 5 of the 1968 Act apply only for the purposes of interpreting s 1 of that Act: see s 1(3). Section 34(1) applies ss 4(1) and 5(1) generally for the purposes of the 1968 Act. Accordingly the other subsections of s 4 and s 5 do not apply to s 15. Suppose that a fraudster has persuaded a victim to part with his house: the fraudster is not guilty of theft of the land since s 4(2) provides that you cannot steal land. The charge could only be laid under s 15 which contains no provisions excluding land from the definition of property. Therefore, although there is a substantial overlap between s 1 and s 15, s 15 is not otiose.

[His Lordship then dealt with the question of the appropriation of company property by directors of the company: see *above*] ...

Lord Slynn of Hadley: My Lords, I agree with my noble and learned friend, Lord Keith of Kinkel, whose draft speech I have had the opportunity to read, that for the reasons he gives the appeal should be allowed and the questions answered in the way he proposes.

Lord Lowry delivered a dissenting speech.

Cheques

Chan Man-Sin v The Queen [1988] 1 WLR 196 (PC)

Facts: This was an appeal from a decision of the Court of Appeal of Hong Kong. The defendant was the accountant for two companies. By means of ten forged cheques he withdrew money from the companies' bank accounts and caused it to be deposited in his personal account or the account of a business of which he was the sole proprietor. The companies' banks debited their accounts, which were overdrawn but not by an amount which exceeded agreed overdraft limits. The defendant was charged (under Hong Kong legislation identical to the Theft Act 1968) with theft of choses in action, namely debts owed by the bank to the companies.

Lord Oliver of Aylmerton: ... It is not disputed that the debt due to the customer from his banker is a chose in action capable of being stolen and this equally applies to the sum which a customer is entitled to overdraw under contractual arrangements which he has made with the bank (see *R v Kohn* (1979) 69 Cr App R 395), though strictly in the latter case the chose in action is the benefit of the contractual arrangement with the bank. What is argued, however, is that, since as between the customer and the bank an unauthorised debit entry in the customer's account is a mere nullity, the customer is deprived of nothing and therefore there has been no appropriation. Equally, it is said that, since the customer whose property is alleged to have been stolen has not in fact been deprived of anything, there cannot have been an intention permanently to deprive him of the property. Thus, it is argued, there were lacking two essential ingredients of the offences with which the defendant was charged and he was entitled to an acquittal.

Their Lordships can deal very briefly with the second submission. The defendant did not elect to give evidence and if there was, as the prosecution contended, an appropriation of the companies' property, there was ample evidence from which the intention permanently to deprive them of it could be inferred. Even if it were possible to infer or assume that the defendant contemplated that the fraud would be discovered and appreciated also that his employers would or might challenge the bank's entitlement to payment of the sums debited, he would fall within [the statutory definition of having an intention permanently to deprive the owner of the property].

Quite clearly here the defendant was purporting to deal with the companies' property without regard to their rights.

Reverting to the defendant's principal ground of appeal, this has an appealing simplicity. The defendant's difficulty, however, is that it entirely ignores the artificial definition of appropriation which is contained in ... s 3(1) [above] of the Act of 1968.

The owner of the chose in action consisting of a credit with his bank or a contractual right to draw on an account has, clearly, the right as owner to draw by means of a properly completed negotiable instrument or order to pay and it is, in their Lordships' view, beyond argument that one who draws, presents and negotiates a cheque on a particular bank account is assuming the rights of the owner of the credit in the account or (as the case may be) of the prenegotiated right to draw on the account up to the agreed figure. Ownership, of course, consists of a bundle of rights and it may well be that there are other rights which an owner could exert over the chose in action in question which are not trespassed on by the particular dealing which the thief chooses to assume. In

R v Morris (David) [1984] AC 320, however, the House of Lords decisively rejected a submission that it was necessary, in order to constitute an appropriation as defined by s 3(1) of the Act of 1968, to demonstrate an assumption by the accused of all the rights of an owner.

Their Lordships are accordingly entirely satisfied that the transactions initiated and carried through by the defendant constituted an assumption of the rights of the owner and, consequently, an appropriation. It is unnecessary, for present purposes, to determine whether that occurred on presentation of the forged cheques or when the transactions were completed by the making of consequential entries in the bank accounts of the companies and the defendant or his business respectively. It is, in their Lordships' view, entirely immaterial that the end result of the transaction may be a legal nullity for it is not possible to read into s [3(1) of the 1968 Act] any requirement that the assumption of rights there envisaged should have a legally efficacious result ...

Several appropriations of the same property or a continuing process?

Where a 'thief' does several acts in respect of a particular item, are the acts of appropriation a continuing process which is complete only when the final act has been done, or can an item be appropriated on more than one occasion? This uncertainty makes it difficult for the prosecution to point to the exact moment when the goods are stolen. In most cases this will not matter (since the jury or magistrates will only have to consider whether the goods were stolen by the defendant on a particular date: the exact time of the appropriation does not matter). However, uncertainty over when the theft is complete creates a particular problem with the regard to the offence of handling stolen goods (s 22 of the Theft Act 1968), since this offence cannot be committed until the goods have been 'stolen'. In *R v Atakpu* [1994] QB 69 the Court of Appeal gave some guidance on when the appropriation takes place, favouring the idea of appropriation as a continuing process.

R v Atakpu and Abrahams [1994] QB 69 (CA)

Ward J: ... The facts of [the appellants'] disreputable endeavour can be quite shortly stated. The prosecution satisfied the jury that these appellants embarked on a simple but audacious scheme to hire expensive motor cars abroad, have them driven into the United Kingdom but then, after ringing the changes to the vehicles, to sell them on to unsuspecting purchasers. Their first step was to create false identities for themselves. That they did by prevailing on a co-accused, Brian Saunders, to apply for British visitor's passports on 12 July 1990, one from a post office in Maida Vale in the false name of Pearce, which was the identity assumed by Abrahams, and the other from a post office at Swiss Cottage in the name of Green, which was the identity assumed by Atakpu. They also procured false driving licences in the names of Pearce and Green ...

On the same day, 12 July 1990, Thomas Cook's travel agency close to the Swiss Cottage post office arranged, at the request of a man named Green, for a luxury motor car to be hired from 'downtown Frankfurt' and the appropriate vouchers were issued. On the same day at Gatwick Airport two return air tickets to Frankfurt were issued in the names of Pearce and Green for an outward flight on the following day and the package included the hiring of two more luxury motor cars to be collected at Frankfurt Airport.

The mythical Messrs Pearce and Green duly flew to Frankfurt on 13 July. At about 8.35 am on 14 July a Mr Green hired a Mercedes 300SE motor car from the Hertz city office, or the so-called 'downtown' office, and at about 8.58 am Hertz at Frankfurt Airport hired a Mercedes 190E to a black man giving the name Pearce. Later that morning that office hired a BMW automatic to an African man whose identity was established by the production of a British visitor's passport in the name of Green, a copy of which passport was kept by Hertz. The prosecution contended, without doubt correctly, that the photograph was one of Atakpu.

It would seem that the Mercedes 300SE was then driven to Brussels but broke down in Belgium and was replaced with a BMW by the Brussels office of Hertz. From there the appellants drove to Ghent where they recruited their co-defendant, de Ligne, to go back with them to Frankfurt to collect the two cars still parked in Frankfurt. On the way they were stopped for speeding and Atakpu, otherwise known as Green, produced his passport and paid an immediate fine. The two cars were duly collected from Frankfurt and the convoy of three returned to Ghent where they recruited the co-defendant, Miss Englen. De Ligne drove the replacement BMW to Ostende, boarded the ferry to Dover, left the car in Dover and returned to Ostende. The co-defendant then collected the remaining two vehicles and boarded the Dover ferry. The four defendants shared a cabin and arrived at Dover in the early hours of 16 July. The appellants left the ferry as foot passengers. Englen drove the Mercedes 190E and de Ligne the BMW into the customs shed but were stopped by customs officers. Their suspicions were aroused by finding four boarding cards with consecutive numbers in Englen's car. De Ligne also aroused suspicion. It was not long before the appellants were arrested. In their possession were excess travel tickets issued by British Rail for the journey between Victoria and Gatwick during the late afternoon of 13 July, the airline tickets and boarding cards, torn British visitor's passports, driving licences and the hire documentation all variously bearing the names of Pearce and Green. Atakpu had in his possession the keys to the BMW which had been left in Dover. It was recovered from the car park. The period of hire of the two vehicles taken in Frankfurt would have expired within a matter of hours and the Brussels BMW not long thereafter ...

We begin by recording that it was common ground that (1) the appellants would only be guilty if they had agreed that a course of conduct should be pursued which, if the agreement had been carried out in accordance with their intentions, necessarily amounted to or involved the commission of an offence which was triable in England and Wales: see *Board of Trade v Owen* [1957] AC 602 and s 1 of the Criminal Law Act 1977, as amended by s 5 of the Criminal Attempts Act 1981; (2) a theft committed abroad is not triable in England and Wales.

Accordingly, the question in this appeal now boils down simply to where the theft of these motor cars was committed – in Germany/Belgium or in England ...

So interesting questions arise in this appeal as to (1) whether the theft committed abroad continued within the jurisdiction so that it could be established here by the retention of the car after the hire period had expired, or by ringing the changes or by some other fresh appropriation; (2) whether cars stolen abroad could be stolen again, and again and again, within the jurisdiction each time an appropriation of them is made.

[His Lordship reviewed a number of authorities and continued:]

[I]t would seem that: (1) theft can occur in an instant by a single appropriation but it can also involve a course of dealing with property lasting longer and involving several appropriations before the transaction is complete; (2) theft is a finite act – it has a beginning and it has an end; (3) at what point the transaction is complete is a matter for the jury to decide upon the facts of each case; (4) though there may be several appropriations in the course of a single theft or several appropriations of different goods each constituting a separate theft ... no case suggests that there can be successive thefts of the same property (assuming of course that possession is constant and not lost or abandoned, later to be assumed again).

Can these conclusions stand in the light of *R v Gomez* [1993] AC 442? Whilst we see the logic of the argument that if there are several appropriations each one can constitute a separate theft, we flinch from reaching that conclusion.

[His Lordship then approves the following passage by Professor Glanville Williams in [1978] Crim LR 69:]

> A man steals a watch, and two weeks later sells it. In common sense and ordinary language he is not guilty of a second theft when he sells it. Otherwise it would be possible, in theory, to convict a thief of theft of a silver teapot every time he uses it to make tea.

[His Lordship then quotes s 3(1) of the Theft Act 1968, *above* and continued:]

If, therefore, he has come by the property by stealing it then his later dealing with the property is by implication not included among the assumptions of the rights of an owner which amount to an appropriation within the meaning of s 3(1). We reject the speculation that he would not have come by the property by stealing it if an indictment for the theft would not lie because the theft occurred abroad. There is no reason to restrict the plain ordinary words of s 3(1) in such a narrow legalistic way. We note that one is guilty of handling stolen property under s 24 and the provisions of the Act apply whether the stealing occurred in England or Wales or elsewhere. 'Stealing' must have the same meaning in s 3(1) as it has in s 24. In our judgment, if goods have once been stolen, even if stolen abroad, they cannot be stolen again by the same thief exercising the same or other rights of ownership over the property.

We find it more difficult to answer the first question we posed as to whether or not theft is a continuous offence. On a strict reading of *R v Gomez* [1993] AC 442 any dishonest assumption of the rights of the owner made with the necessary intention constitutes theft and that leaves little room for a continuous course of action.

We would not wish that to be the law. Such restriction and rigidity may lead to technical anomalies and injustice. We would prefer to leave it for the common sense of the jury to decide that the appropriation can continue for so long as the thief can sensibly be regarded as in the act of stealing or, in more understandable words, so long as he is 'on the job' ... Since the matter is not strictly necessary for our decision we ... will leave it open for further argument. It is not necessary for us to decide because no jury properly directed could reasonably arrive at a conclusion that the theft of these motor cars was still continuing days after the appellants had first taken them. If the jury had been asked when and where these motor cars were stolen they could only have answered that they were stolen in Frankfurt or Brussels. The theft was complete abroad and the thieves could not steal again in England. For these reasons the appeal must be allowed ...

Appropriation of property acquired innocently

Section 3(1) of the Theft Act 1968 provides that where a person comes by property (whether innocently or not) and later assumes the rights of the owner of that property, that subsequent assumption of the rights of the owner is an appropriation.

Purchaser in good faith of stolen goods

Section 3(2) of the Theft Act 1968 provides that where a person assumes the rights of the owner of goods because he has purchased them, for money or money's worth, in good faith, that assumption of rights is not to be regarded as an appropriation. The relevant time when the purchaser must be acting in good faith is the moment when he purchases the goods.

R v Adams [1993] Crim LR 72 (CA)

> *Facts*: The appellant was a motor cycle enthusiast with a garage full of parts. Stolen motor cycle parts were sold to him for £350, for which he issued a proper receipt with his true name and address. He was told that they represented a 'write-off' from an accident. He did not notice that the engine number had been drilled out and did not suspect that the parts were stolen until two or three days after receiving them. He was acquitted of handling but convicted of theft.
>
> *Held*, allowing the appeal: Section 3(2) of the Theft Act 1968 provides that where a person has received property for value in good faith, no later assumption by him of rights which he believed himself to be acquiring would, by reason of a defect in title, amount to theft. The Crown had submitted that the words 'which he believed himself to be acquiring' related to the moment not when he purchased in good faith but when he appropriated the property by deciding to keep it as his own or selling it on. The court was of the view that the relevant moment was when the receiver purchased for value.

PROPERTY

Section 4 of the Theft Act 1968: 'property'

> (1) 'Property' includes money and all other property, real or personal, including things in action and other intangible property.
>
> (2) A person cannot steal land, or things forming part of land and severed from it by him or by his directions, except in the following cases, that is to say:
>
> (a) when he is a trustee or personal representative, or is authorised by power of attorney, or as liquidator of a company, or otherwise, to sell or dispose of land belonging to another, and he appropriates the land or anything forming part of it by dealing with it in breach of the confidence reposed in him; or
>
> (b) when he is not in possession of the land and appropriates anything forming part of the land by severing it or causing it to be severed, or after it has been severed; or
>
> (c) when, being in possession of the land under a tenancy, he appropriates the whole or part of any fixture or structure let to be used with the land.
>
> For purposes of this subsection 'land' does not include incorporeal hereditaments; 'tenancy' means a tenancy for years or any less period and includes an agreement for such a tenancy, but a person who after the end of a tenancy remains in possession as statutory tenant or otherwise is to be treated as having possession under the tenancy, and 'let' shall be construed accordingly.

(3) A person who picks mushrooms growing wild on any land, or who picks flowers, fruit or foliage from a plant growing wild on any land, does not (although not in possession of the land) steal what he picks, unless he does it for reward or for sale or other commercial purpose.

For purposes of this subsection 'mushroom' includes any fungus, and 'plant' includes any shrub or tree.

(4) Wild creatures, tamed or untamed, shall be regarded as property; but a person cannot steal a wild creature not tamed nor ordinarily kept in captivity, or the carcase of any such creature, unless either it has been reduced into possession by or on behalf of another person and possession of it has not since been lost or abandoned, or another person is in course of reducing it into possession.

Property is defined very widely in s 4 of the Theft Act 1968. It should be noted that the statutory definition excludes land but includes 'things in action'. A 'thing (or 'chose') in action' describes 'all personal rights of property which can only be claimed or enforced by [taking legal] action, and not by taking physical possession' (*Torkington v Magee* [1902] 2 KB 427 at 430, *per* Channell J). The best example of a 'thing in action' is a debt. The term therefore includes bank and building society accounts (if my bank account is in credit, then the bank owes me a debt equivalent to the amount of my credit balance). A cheque is a piece of paper and therefore amounts to 'property', and this is so whether or not the account on which the cheque is drawn is in credit.

Electricity cannot be stolen (*Low v Blease* [1975] Crim LR 513), but there is the specific offence of abstracting electricity under s 13 of the Theft Act 1968 (*qv*).

Although s 4 refers to 'intangible property' (which includes patents and copyright), this term does not include confidential information.

Oxford v Moss (1978) 68 Cr App R 183 (DC)

Smith J: ... On 5 May 1976, an information was preferred by the prosecutor against the defendant alleging that the defendant stole certain intangible property, namely confidential information being examination questions for a civil engineering examination to be held in the month of June 1976 at Liverpool University, the information being the property of the Senate of the University, and the allegation being that the respondent intended permanently to deprive the said Senate of the said property.

The facts can be stated very shortly indeed. They were agreed facts. They are set out in the case and they are as follows. In May 1976 the defendant was a student at Liverpool University. He was studying engineering. Somehow (and this court is not concerned precisely how) he was able to acquire the proof of an examination paper for an examination in civil engineering to be held in the University during the following month, that is to say June 1976. Without doubt the proof, that is to say the piece of paper, was the property of the University. It was an agreed fact, as set out in the case, that the respondent at no time intended to steal what is described as 'any tangible element' belonging to the paper; that is to say it is conceded that he never intended to steal the paper itself.

In truth and in fact, and in all common sense, what he was about was this. He was borrowing a piece of paper hoping to be able to return it and not be detected in order that he should acquire advance knowledge of the questions to be set in the examination and thereby, I suppose, he would be enabled to have an unfair advantage as against other students who did not possess the knowledge that he did.

By any standards, it was conduct which is to be condemned, and to the layman it would readily be described as cheating. The question raised is whether it is conduct which falls within the scope of the criminal law ...

... The question for this court, shortly put, is whether confidential information can amount to property within the meaning of the Theft Act 1968 ...

The question for this court is whether confidential information of this sort falls within that definition contained in s 4(1) ...

In my judgment, it is clear that the answer to that question must be no. Accordingly, I would dismiss the appeal.

Wien J: ... [T]he right to confidential information is not intangible property within the meaning of s 4(1) of the Theft Act 1968 ...

Stealing of part can be stealing of whole

Pilgram v Rice-Smith [1977] 2 All ER 659 (DC)

Lord Widgery CJ: ... At the Crown Court the following facts were found. The first respondent was an assistant employed by International Stores, the victims of the alleged theft. She worked in their shop at East Dereham. The second respondent was known to, and I think one can fairly say a friend of, the first respondent.

On the day in question the second respondent went to the counter where the first respondent was serving, and at that time corned beef was 18p a quarter and bacon was 72p a pound. The first respondent, who (it will be remembered) was behind the counter and an employee of the shop, served the second respondent with a quantity of corned beef which appeared to be well over a quarter and marked the price as 20p on the wrapping. She then weighed just over a pound of bacon and marked the price as 38p on the wrapping. Both articles were handed to the second respondent.

The second respondent then went around the store and bought some further articles. At the check-out she paid for all the articles in the total sum of £1.04. This included the 20p for the corned beef and the 38p for the bacon. The appellant alleged that the second respondent should have paid 83p more than that in respect of an undercharge on the bacon and the corned beef.

As the second respondent was leaving the store she was spoken to by the store detective and the usual investigation followed ...

In the result I analyse the case in this way. It seems to me clear that we must treat the two respondents as having been in league with one another from the outset. It is proper to treat the parcel of bacon and corned beef as a single parcel for this purpose. The fraud was inspired from the very beginning and therefore it operated from before the time when the goods were handed over to the purchaser, and accordingly the transaction of sale, or the purported transaction of sale, was a nullity from the start. It was a nullity from the start because from the start the lady behind the counter had no authority on the part of her employer to sell these goods at under value. She just did not have that authority. Consequently no contract of sale was entered into at all. That opens the door immediately for a conviction of theft in respect of the whole of the goods, and it is well established that it matters not in a case such as this that you have charged only the theft of part and proved the whole. You can nevertheless obtain a conviction in respect of what has been charged ...

Section 5 of the Theft Act 1968: 'belonging to another'

(1) Property shall be regarded as belonging to any person having possession or control of it, or having in it any proprietary right or interest (not being an equitable interest arising only from an agreement to transfer or grant an interest).

(2) Where property is subject to a trust, the persons to whom it belongs shall be regarded as including any person having a right to enforce the trust, and an intention to defeat the trust shall be regarded accordingly as an intention to deprive of the property any person having that right.

(3) Where a person receives property from or on account of another, and is under an obligation to the other to retain and deal with that property or its proceeds in a particular way, the property or proceeds shall be regarded (as against him) as belongings to the other.

(4) Where a person gets property by another's mistake, and is under an obligation to make restoration (in whole or in part) of the property or its proceeds or of the value thereof, then to the extent of that obligation the property or proceeds shall be regarded (as against him) as belonging to the person entitled to restoration, and an intention not to make restoration shall be regarded accordingly as an intention to deprive that person of the property or proceeds.

(5) Property of a corporation sole shall be regarded as belonging to the corporation notwithstanding a vacancy in the corporation.

Theft from the owner

The simplest case is where the property is stolen from the owner of that property, who need not be in possession of the property at the time (*R v Hancock* [1990] 2 WLR 640).

R v Hancock [1990] 2 WLR 640 (CA)

Facts: The appellant was charged with theft from the Crown of 16 ancient coins found in an area which appeared to have been the site of a Romano-Celtic temple. If the coins were a treasure trove, they belonged to the Crown.

Auld J: ... [I]t is not necessary for the offence of theft that the property alleged to have been stolen is in the possession, actual or constructive, of the owner at the time when it is appropriated ...

Accordingly, we are of the view that it was for the jury in the trial of this matter to determine as part of their finding on the issue of guilt or innocence of the appellant whether the coins were in fact treasure trove and thus the property of the Crown. In their determination of that issue they had to apply the ordinary criminal burden and standard of proof, namely they could only convict the appellant if they were sure that the coins in question were treasure trove, namely that they had been deposited by someone who had intended to retrieve them ...

Theft from a bailee

Because of the very broad definition of 'belonging to' in s 5 of the Theft Act 1968, property can be regarded as belonging to a bailee. It is for this reason that it is possible to be guilty of stealing one's own property, where that property was in the possession of a bailee who had a lien over it (*R v Turner (No 2)* [1971] 1 WLR 901).

R v Turner (No 2) [1971] 1 WLR 901 (CA)

Lord Parker CJ: ... The defendant was at the material time living in Seymour Road, East Ham, with a Miss Nelson and their children. Three miles away a man called Arthur Edwin Brown ran a garage in Carlyle Road, Manor Park. There is no doubt that at some time prior to 7 March 1969, the defendant took a Sceptre car of which he was the registered owner to Mr Brown's garage for repairs. It was Mr Brown's case that he did those repairs, that as he was short of space he left the car in Carlyle Road some 10 to 20 yards from the garage. The ignition key had been handed to him by the defendant, and this he retained on the keyboard in his office. According to Mr Brown, on 7 March 1969, the defendant called at the garage and asked if the car was ready. On being told that it was except that it might require to be tuned, the defendant said that he would return on the next day, Saturday 8 March, and would pay Mr Brown for the repairs and pick up the car. A few hours later, however, Mr Brown found that the Sceptre car had gone; moreover whoever had taken it had a key, because the key that Mr Brown had was still on the keyboard. He reported the matter to the police.

Apparently night after night thereafter until 16 March Mr Brown, according to him, went round the neighbouring streets to see if he could find the car, and sure enough on Sunday 16 March, he found it parked in a street near the defendant's flat. It was, moreover, his evidence that he did not know the defendant's full name or his address and only knew of him as Frank.

What Mr Brown then did was to take the car back to his garage, to take out the engine and then tow it back less the engine to the place from which he had taken it. Meanwhile, the police made enquiries of the defendant and there is no doubt in the light of what happened afterwards that he, the defendant, told lie after lie to the police. He said that Mr Brown had never had his Sceptre car at all, that the car had never been to the garage, and that the only work that Mr Brown had done was to a Zephyr car on an earlier occasion. However, a time came when he abandoned those denials and agreed that he had taken the car to the garage, and that he had taken it away and had never paid for it. In saying that, however, he emphasised that he had taken it away with the consent of Mr Brown. It was on those short facts that the jury ... found the defendant guilty of the theft of his own car ...

[His Lordship quoted s 5(1) of the Theft Act 1968 and went on:]

The sole question was whether Mr Brown had possession or control.

This court is quite satisfied that there is no ground whatever for qualifying the words 'possession or control' in any way. It is sufficient if it is found that the person from whom the property is taken, or to use the words of the Act, appropriated, was at the time in fact in possession or control ... The only question was whether Mr Brown was in fact in possession or control ...

[His Lordship then turned to the question of dishonesty and said:]

The whole test of dishonesty is the mental element of belief. No doubt, although the defendant may for certain purposes be presumed to know the law, he would not at the time have the vaguest idea whether he did have in law a right to take the car back again, and accordingly when one looks at his mental state, one looks at it in the light of what he believed. The jury were properly told that if he believed that he had a right, albeit there was none, he would nevertheless fall to be acquitted ...

Theft from a company

We have already seen that, since consent does not prevent an appropriation from taking place, a company director cannot say that he can give consent on behalf of the company for the appropriation of the company's property (see *above*). It also follows from the fact that a limited liability company is a separate legal entity from its directors and shareholders, that a director or shareholder takes property 'belonging to another' if she takes property belonging to the company (*cf Attorney General's Reference (No 2 of 1982)* [1984] QB 624, approved in *R v Gomez* [1993] AC 442).

Theft from a partner

A partner may be guilty of theft of property belonging jointly to her and to her partner (*R v Bonner* [1970] 1 WLR 838).

R v Bonner [1970] 1 WLR 838 (CA)

Edmund Davies LJ: ... The view of this court is that in relation to partnership property the provisions in the Theft Act 1968 have the following result: provided there is the basic ingredient of dishonesty, provided there be no question of there being a claim of right made in good faith, provided there be an intention permanently to deprive, one partner can commit theft of partnership property just as much as one person can commit the theft of the property of another to whom he is a complete stranger ...

Section 5(3) of the Theft Act 1968: obligation to deal with property

Under s 5(3) of the Theft Act 1968, where a person receives property from another and is under an obligation to deal with that property in a particular way, the property is to be regarded as belonging to that other person. The obligation to deal with property in a particular way must be a *legal* obligation (ie one which is enforceable by civil proceedings): see *R v Gilks* [1972] 1 WLR 1341 (a case decided under s 5(4) of the Theft Act 1968)

R v Wain [1995] 2 Cr App R 660 (CA)

Facts: The appellant took part in raising money for a 'telethon' organised for charity by Yorkshire Television. He raised £2,833.25, which he paid into a separate bank account. When asked by Yorkshire Television for the money he made a number of excuses. Eventually the company gave him permission to pay the money into his own bank account. The appellant then handed the company a cheque drawn on that account. The cheque was not met. Meanwhile, the appellant withdrew cash from that account.

At trial, it was submitted on the appellant's behalf that, under s 5(3) of the Theft Act 1968, the debt owed to the charity could not be said to be the proceeds of the money which he had been paid, because the proceeds were the things purchased with the money. This unmeritorious submission was rejected by the trial judge and the appellant was convicted. His appeal to the Court of Appeal was dismissed.

McCowan LJ: ... [I]t seems to us that by virtue of s 5(3), the appellant was plainly under an obligation to retain, if not the actual notes and coins, at least their proceeds, that is to say the money credited in the bank account which he opened for the trust with the actual property. When he took the money credited to that account and moved it over to his own bank account, it was still the proceeds of the notes and coins donated which he proceeded to use for his own purposes, thereby appropriating them ...

We would add this. Whether a person in the position of the appellant is a trustee is to be judged on an objective basis. It is an obligation imposed on him by law. It is not essential that he should have realised that he was a trustee, but of course the question remains as to whether he was acting honestly or dishonestly in using the money for his own purposes. That is a matter of fact for the jury.

Section 5(3) of the Theft Act 1968: obligation to restore property

Under s 5(4) of the Theft Act 1968, where A receives money from B as the result of a mistake on B's part, and A is under an obligation return some or all of that money to B, the money which should be returned to B is regarded as belonging to B.

The obligation must be a legally enforceable obligation (*R v Gilks* [1972] 1 WLR 1341). The way s 5(4) works may be seen from *Attorney General's Reference (No 1 of 1983)* [1985] QB 182.

R v Gilks [1972] 1 WLR 1341 (CA)

Cairns LJ: ... The facts were as follows. On 27 March 1971 the appellant went into Ladbrokes' betting shop at North Cheam and placed some bets on certain horses: one of his bets was on a horse called 'Fighting Scot'. 'Fighting Scot' did not get anywhere in the race which was in fact won by a horse called 'Fighting Taffy'. Because of a mistake on the part of the relief manager in the betting shop, the appellant was paid out as if he had backed the successful horse with the result that he was overpaid to the extent of £106.63. He was paid £117.25 when the amount he had won (on other races) was only £10.62. At the very moment when he was being paid the appellant knew that a mistake had been made and that he was not entitled to the money, but he kept it. He refused to consider repaying it, his attitude being that it was Ladbrokes' hard lines ...

The trial judge held that it was unnecessary for the prosecution to rely on s 5(4) [of the Theft Act 1968] because the property in the £106.63 never passed to the appellant. In the view of this court that ruling was right. The subsection introduced a new principle into the law of theft but long before it was enacted it was held in *R v Middleton* (1873) LR 2 CCR 38 that where a person was paid by mistake ... a sum in excess of that properly payable, the person who accepted the overpayment with knowledge of the excess was guilty of theft ...

The gap in the law which s 5(4) was designed to fill was ... that which is illustrated by the case of *Moynes v Cooper* [1956] 1 QB 439. There a workman received a pay packet containing £7 more than was due to him but did not become aware of the overpayment until he opened the envelope some time later. He then kept the £7. This was held not to be theft because there was no *animus furandi* at the moment of taking ...

An alternative ground on which the [trial judge] held that the money should be regarded as belonging to Ladbrokes was that 'obligation' in s 5(4) meant an obligation whether a legal one or not. In the opinion of this court that was an incorrect ruling. In a criminal statute, where a person's criminal liability is made dependant on his having an obligation, it would be quite wrong to construe that word so as to cover a moral or social obligation as distinct from a legal one ...

[The appeal against conviction was dismissed]

Attorney General's Reference (No 1 of 1983) [1985] QB 182 (CA)

Lord Lane CJ: ... The respondent is a woman police officer and she received her pay from the Receiver of the Metropolitan Police. Owing to an error in the Receiver's department she was credited (in a way which will have to be described in more detail in a moment) with the sum of £74.74 for wages and overtime in respect of a day when she was not at work at all. That amount, together with other sums which were properly due to her, was paid into her bank by direct debit by the Receiver's bank. She knew nothing of the error until later, though it was not proved precisely when. There was some evidence before the jury that she had decided to say nothing about this unsolicited windfall which had come her way, and had decided to take no action about it after she discovered the error. No demand for payment of the sum was made by the Receiver of the Metropolitan Police or anyone else ...

The question comes up to this court on the Attorney General's reference in the following form:

> Whether a person who receives overpayment of a debt due to him or her by way of a credit to his or her bank account through the 'direct debit' system operated by the banks and who knowing of that overpayment intentionally fails to repay the amount of the overpayment 'may be' [which is an amendment which counsel for the Attorney General has asked us to make to the reference] guilty of theft of the credit to the amount of the overpayment ...

[W]hat the respondent ... got was simply the debt due to her from her own bank. That is so unless her account was overdrawn or overdrawn beyond any overdraft limit, in which case she did not even get that right to money. That point is made in a decision of this court in *R v Kohn* (1979) 69 Cr App R 395 ...

The property in the present case was the debt owed by the bank to the respondent [his Lordship then quoted the definition of property in s 4(1) of the Theft Act, which includes 'things in action', and continued:] The debt here was a thing in action, therefore the property was capable of being stolen.

It will be apparent that, at first blush, that debt did not belong to anyone except the respondent herself. She was the only person who had the right to go to her bank and demand the handing over of that £74.74 ...

[His Lordship then referred to s 5(4) of the Theft Act 1968]. In order to determine the effect of that subsection on this case one has to take it piece by piece to see what the result is read against the circumstances of this particular prosecution. First of all: did the respondent get property? The word 'get' is about as wide a word as could possibly have been adopted by the draftsman of the Act. The answer is Yes; the respondent in this case did get her chose in action, that is her right to sue the bank for the debt which they owed her, money which they held in their hands to which she was entitled by virtue of the contract between bank and customer.

Second: did she get it by another's mistake? The answer to that is plainly Yes, the Receiver of the Metropolitan Police made the mistake of thinking she was entitled to £74.74 when she was not entitled to that at all.

Was she under an obligation to make restoration of either the property or its proceeds or its value? We take each of those in turn. Was she under an obligation to make restoration of the 'property', the chose in action? The answer to that is No, it was something which could not be restored in the ordinary meaning of the word. Was she under an obligation to make restoration of its proceeds? The answer to that is No, there were no proceeds of the chose in action to restore.

Was she under an obligation to make restoration of the value thereof, the value of the chose in action? The answer to that seems to us to be Yes.

I should say here, in parentheses, that a question was raised during the argument this morning whether 'restoration' is the same as 'making restitution'. We think that, on the wording of s 5(4) as a whole, the answer to that question is Yes. One therefore turns to see whether, under the general principles of restitution, the respondent was obliged to restore or pay for the benefit which she received. Generally speaking the respondent, in these circumstances, is obliged to pay for a benefit received when the benefit has been given under a mistake as to a material fact on the part of the giver. The mistake must be as to a fundamental or essential fact and the payment must have been due to that fundamental or essential fact. The mistake here was that this police officer had been working on a day when she had been at home and not working at all ...

In the present case, applying that principle to the facts of this case, the value of the chose in action (the property) was £74.74 and there was a legal obligation on the respondent to restore that value to the receiver when she found that the mistake had been made. One continues to examine the contents of s 5(4). It follows from what has already been said that the extent of that obligation, the chose in action, has to be regarded as belonging to the person entitled to restoration, that is the Receiver of the Metropolitan Police.

As a result of the provisions of s 5(4) the debt of £74.74 due from the respondent's bank to the respondent notionally belonged to the Receiver of the Metropolitan Police, therefore the prosecution, up to this point, have succeeded in proving (remarkable though it may seem) that the 'property' in this case belonged to another within the meaning of s 1 in the 1968 Act from the moment when the respondent became aware that this mistake had been made and that her account had been credited with the £74.74 and she consequently became obliged to restore the value. Furthermore, by the final words of s 5(4), once the prosecution succeed in proving that the respondent intended not to make restoration, that is notionally to be regarded as an intention to deprive the receiver of that property which notionally belongs to him ...

Section 6 of the Theft Act 1968: 'with the intention of permanently depriving the other of it'

(1) A person appropriating property belonging to another without meaning the other permanently to lose the thing itself is nevertheless to be regarded as having the intention of permanently depriving the other of it if his intention is to treat the thing as his own to dispose of regardless of the other's rights; and a borrowing or lending of it may amount to so treating it if, but only if, the borrowing or lending is for a period and in circumstances making it equivalent to an outright taking or disposal.

(2) Without prejudice to the generality of subsection (1) above, where a person, having possession or control (lawfully or not) of property belonging to another, parts with the property under a condition as to its return which he may not be able to perform, this (if done for purposes of his own and without the other's authority) amounts to treating the property as his own to dispose of regardless of the other's rights.

For a charge of theft to succeed, it must be established that, at the time of the appropriation, the defendant intended permanently to deprive the person to whom the property belongs of that property. The intention permanently to deprive the other person of the property must exist at the time of the appropriation: see *R v Cocks* (1976) 63 Cr App R 79 (CA).

Section 6 of the Theft Act 1968: intention permanently to deprive

The essence of the statutory definition is that to treat something as one's own, to dispose of without regard to the rights of the person to whom it belongs, is to intend permanently to deprive that other person of the property.

In *R v McHugh* (1993) 97 Cr App R 335, the Court of Appeal said that it was a correct statement of law that 'later repayment does not negative an intention at the time of appropriation permanently to deprive the owner of the property' (*per* Lord Taylor CJ).

The commonest situation where this element of theft is in issue is where the defendant says, 'I was only borrowing the property'. In *R v Velumyl* [1989] Crim LR 299 it was held that where money is taken, the defendant does not intend to return the same banknotes or coins, even if he intends to return the same amount of money, and so intends permanently to deprive the owner of those banknotes or coins (so the issue then becomes whether the defendant was acting dishonestly). See also *Halsted v Patel* [1972] 2 All ER 147 (dealt with under 'obtaining property by deception').

Where the defendant intended to return the property on the happening of a particular event, the defendant's estimation of the likelihood of that event is relevant to determining whether he intended permanently to deprive the other of his property (*R v Coffey* [1987] Crim LR 498).

In the vast majority of cases, that is all a jury needs to be told. Section 6 need only be referred to in exceptional cases (*R v Lloyd* [1985] QB 829).

R v Warner (1970) 55 Cr App R 93 (CA)

Facts: The defendant took some tools belonging to another. He said that he intended to return the tools to their owner, but had not decided when he was going to do so.

Edmund Davies LJ: The one point involved in the appeal is whether the Crown established that the appellant intended permanently to deprive the owner of certain goods which he unquestionably took ...

... [T]here can be no theft without the intention of permanently depriving another of his property ...

... [T]he essential question was whether the accused man had ever formed the intention to deprive the owner indefinitely of the use of his tools. If he had, then he could in certain circumstances be regarded as intending to treat the thing as his own to dispose of, regardless of the other's rights, within the meaning of s 6(1). But if this was not so, if, for example, his intention was to deprive the owner of the use of his goods for a limited period, the precise length of which he had not yet decided upon, but fully intending to return them to their owner in due course, this would not necessarily justify conviction for theft and in the majority of cases probably would not do so.

R v Velumyl [1989] Crim LR 299 (CA)

Facts: The appellant, who was employed in a managerial capacity, had taken £1,050 from a safe at work. He did so without authority and in breach of company rules. He said that he had lent the money to a friend on the Saturday preceding its removal and expected to return that sum on the following Monday.

At interview, he declined to name the friend and agreed that he had no legal right to take the money, nor did he think that he had his employer's permission to do so. He further agreed that he had treated the money as if it were his own, and that he had acted dishonestly in acting as he had done. Following arraignment, on a charge of theft, his counsel sought a preliminary ruling from the judge as to whether the appellant would have a defence under the Theft Act 1968 (other than on an issue of dishonesty) if he had intended to pay the money back. Essentially, the submission was that one piece of money was as good as another and if there was an intention to repay the money, albeit not the exact notes or coins taken, then an essential ingredient of theft, namely the intention permanently to deprive the owner of the money, was missing. The judge ruled against the appellant, who changed his plea to 'guilty' and appealed on a point of law to the Court of Appeal.

Held, dismissing the appeal, there had been an appropriation by the appellant's assumption of the rights of the owner of the money. He did have the requisite intention of permanently depriving the owner of the money because he had no intention to return the objects which he had taken. His intention had been to return objects of equivalent value, which intention was relevant to the question of dishonesty which was not in issue.

The point was that the person who had taken the money, albeit intending and reasonably expecting to replace it with an equivalent sum, committed the offence because he had taken something which he was not entitled to take without the consent of the owner and was, in effect, trying to force upon the owner a substitution to which the latter had not consented.

R v Coffey [1987] Crim LR 498 (CA)

Facts: The appellant was convicted of obtaining property by deception. He had obtained machinery using a worthless cheque. At his trial he explained that he had been in dispute with the victim, who refused to negotiate its resolution. He had decided to exert pressure by obtaining and keeping the machinery until he got what he wanted. It was not clear exactly what the appellant wanted or what would happen to the machinery if he did not achieve his purpose. The appellant appealed against conviction on the ground that the judge's summing up did not fully or accurately state the law as to intent and dishonesty.

Held: The court preferred the view that the culpability of the appellant's act depended upon the quality of the intended detention, considered in all its aspects, including in particular the appellant's own assessment at the time as to the likelihood of the victim coming to terms and of the time for which the machinery would have to be retained.

This was one of the rare cases where it was right for the judge to bring s 6(1) before the jury. The judge could usefully have illustrated the first part of s 6(1) by the expression 'equivalent to an outright taking or disposal'. If they thought that the appellant might have intended to return the goods even if the victim did not do what he wanted, they would not convict unless they were sure that he intended that the period of detention should be so long as to amount to an outright taking. Even if they did conclude that the appellant had in mind not to return the goods if the victim failed to do what he wanted, they would still have to consider whether the appellant had regarded the likelihood of this happening as being such that his intended conduct could be regarded as equivalent to an outright taking.

R v Lloyd, Bhuee and Ali [1985] QB 829 (CA)

Lord Lane CJ: ... At all material times the appellant Lloyd was employed as chief projectionist at the Odeon Cinema at Barking. The other two appellants with whom we are concerned, namely Ali and Bhuee, were employed by a man called Mustafa ... They were employed at premises at 3, Plumstead Road, Barking. The case against the appellants was that over a period of months Lloyd had been clandestinely removing feature films which were due to be shown at the Odeon Cinema at Barking and lending them to his co-defendants, who had sophisticated equipment at their premises at 3, Plumstead Road. That sophisticated equipment enabled them to copy the feature films on to a master video tape, and, as a result of the preparation of that master video tape, they or others were enabled to produce a very large quantity of pirated versions of the film. The process of copying was done rapidly. The films were only out of the cinema and out of the hands of Lloyd for a few hours and were always back in time for their projection to take place at the advertised times to those people who attended the cinema to see them.

It was important that the film should be returned rapidly, because if it was not it would soon become apparent that the film had been illegally removed and steps would be taken to prevent a recurrence.

The pirated copies prepared from the master tape would be put on the market to the great financial benefit of the pirates and the great financial detriment of the lawful owners, the film distributors and those who would derive money from the film enterprise. The detriment would occur in a number of different ways, and that indeed was proved before the jury. First of all it would occur through a lowering of cinema attendances to see the particular film, and second, through the legitimate sales of cassettes of the film being undermined by the sale of the pirated copies. The profits apparently, so it was stated in evidence, to the film pirates are enormous and the loss to the legitimate trade is potentially crippling.

In the upshot the appellants were caught red-handed in the process of copying a film called 'The Missionary' onto the master tape.

The trial judge issued his certificate [that the case was fit for appeal] by posing the following question:

> Whether the offence of conspiracy to steal is committed when persons dishonestly agree to take a film from a cinema without authority intending it should be returned within a few hours but knowing that many hundreds of copies will be subsequently made and that the value of the film so returned will thereby be substantially reduced?

... [His Lordship quoted s 6(1) of the Theft Act 1968 and said that it] is abstruse. But it must mean, if nothing else, that there are circumstances in which a defendant may be deemed to have the intention permanently to deprive, even though he may intend the owner eventually to get back the object which has been taken ...

... The first part of s 6(1) seems to us to be aimed at the sort of case where a defendant takes things and then offers them back to the owner for the owner to buy if he wishes. If the taker intends to return them to the owner only on such payment, then, on the wording of s 6(1), that is deemed to amount to the necessary intention permanently to deprive: see, for instance, *R v Hall* (1848) 1 Den 381, where the defendant took fat from a candlemaker and then offered it for sale to the owner. His conviction for larceny was affirmed. There are other cases of similar intent: for instance, 'I have taken your valuable painting. You can have it back on payment to me of £X,000. If you are not prepared to make that payment, then you are not going to get your painting back.'

It seems to us that in this case we are concerned with the second part of s 6(1), namely the words after the semicolon:

> and a borrowing or lending of it may amount to so treating it if, but only if, the borrowing or lending is for a period and in circumstances making it equivalent to an outright taking or disposal.

These films, it could be said, were borrowed by Lloyd from his employers in order to enable him and the others to carry out their 'piracy' exercise.

Borrowing is *ex hypothesi* not something which is done with an intention permanently to deprive. This half of the subsection, we believe, is intended to make it clear that a mere borrowing is never enough to constitute the necessary guilty mind unless the intention is to return the 'thing' in such a changed state that it can truly be said that all its goodness or virtue has gone: for example *R v Beecham* (1851) 5 Cox CC 181, where the defendant stole railway tickets intending that they should be returned to the railway company in the usual way only after the journeys had been completed. He was convicted of larceny. The judge in the present case gave another example, namely the taking of a torch battery with the intention of returning it only when its power is exhausted.

That being the case, we turn to inquire whether the feature films in this case can fall within that category. Our view is that they cannot. The goodness, the virtue, the practical value of the films to the owners has not gone out of the article. The film could still be projected to paying audiences, and, had everything gone according to the conspirator's plans, would have been projected in the ordinary way to audiences at the Odeon Cinema, Barking, who would have paid for their seats. Our view is that those particular films which were the subject of this alleged conspiracy had not themselves diminished in value at all. What had happened was that the borrowed film had been used or was going to be used to perpetrate a copyright swindle on the owners whereby their commercial interests were grossly and adversely affected in the way that we have endeavoured to describe at the outset of this judgment. The borrowing, it seems to us, was not for a period, or in such circumstances, as made it equivalent to an outright taking or disposal. There was still virtue in the film.

R v Fernandes [1996] 1 Cr App R 175 (CA)

Auld LJ: ... In our view, s 6(1) of the Theft Act 1968, which is expressed in general terms, is not limited in its application to the illustrations given by Lord Lane CJ in *R v Lloyd* (1985) 81 Cr App R 182. Nor, in saying that in most cases it would be unnecessary to refer to the provision, did Lord Lane suggest that it should be so limited. The critical notion, stated expressly in the first limb and incorporated by reference in the second, is whether a defendant intended to 'treat the thing as his own to dispose of regardless of the other's rights'. The second limb of subsection (1), and also subsection (2), are merely specific illustrations of the application of that notion. We consider that s 6 may apply to a person in possession or control of another's property who, dishonestly and for his own purpose, deals with that property in such a manner that he knows he is risking its loss.

In the circumstances alleged here, an alleged dishonest disposal of someone else's money on an obviously insecure investment, we consider that the [trial] judge was justified in referring to s 6.

Conditional intent

What if the accused only intends to keep any property which he thinks worth taking? In *R v Easom* [1971] 2 QB 315 it was said that conditional intention is not enough. Thus if the defendant is charged with theft (or attempted theft) of a specific object but the defendant, at the time of the alleged appropriation, had not decided to keep that item, he cannot be convicted of theft. However, if the charge against the defendant is worded generally (ie without reference to specific items), the defendant can be convicted of attempted theft if it can be shown that he intended to steal anything he thought worth taking (see *Attorney General's References (Nos 1 and 2 of 1979)* [1980] QB 180).

R v Easom [1971] 2 QB 315 (CA)

Edmund Davies LJ: ... This is an appeal by the appellant against his conviction ... on an indictment charging him with theft, the particulars of the charge being that, on 27 December 1969, he 'stole one handbag, one purse, one notebook, a quantity of tissues, a quantity of cosmetics and one pen, the property of Joyce Crooks'.

The circumstances giving rise to the charge may be shortly stated. On the evening of 27 December 1969, Woman Police Sergeant Crooks and other plain-clothes officers went to the Metropole Cinema in Victoria. Sergeant Crooks sat in an aisle seat and put her handbag (containing the articles enumerated in the charge) alongside her on the floor. It was attached to her right wrist by a piece of black cotton. Police Constable Hensman sat next to her on the inside seat. When the house lights came on during an interval, it was seen that the appellant was occupying the aisle seat in the row immediately behind Sergeant Crooks and that the seat next to him was vacant. Within a few minutes of the lights being put out, Sergeant Crooks felt the cotton attached to her wrist tighten. She thereupon gave Police Constable Hensman a prearranged signal. The cotton was again pulled, this time so strongly that she broke it off. Moments later the officers could hear the rustle of tissues and the sound of her handbag being closed. Very shortly afterwards the appellant left his seat and went to the lavatory. The officers then turned round and found Sergeant Crook's handbag on the floor behind her seat and in front of that which the appellant had vacated. Its contents were intact. When the appellant emerged from the lavatory and seated himself in another part of the cinema, he was approached by the police officers. When the offence of theft was put to him, he denied it ...

... In every case of theft the appropriation must be accompanied by the intention of permanently depriving the owner of his property. What may be loosely described as a 'conditional' appropriation will not do. If the appropriator has it in mind merely to deprive the owner of such of his property as, on examination, proves worth taking and then, finding that the booty is valueless to the appropriator, leaves it ready to hand to be repossessed by the owner, the appropriator has not stolen. If a dishonest postal sorter picks up a pile of letters, intending to steal any which are registered, but, on finding that none of them are, replaces them, he has stolen nothing, and this is so notwithstanding the provisions of s 6(1) of the Theft Act 1968 ...

But does it follow from all this that the appellant ... has to go scot-free? Can he not, as counsel for the Crown originally submitted, be convicted at least of attempted theft?

... [M]uch depends on the manner in which the charge is framed. Thus, 'if you indict a man for stealing your watch, you cannot convict him of attempting to steal your umbrella' (*per* Cockburn CJ in *R v M'Pherson* (1857) Dears & B 197, 200) – unless, of course, the court of trial has duly exercised the wide powers of amendment conferred by s 5 of the Indictments Act 1915 ... No amendment was sought or effected in the present case, which accordingly has to be considered in relation to the articles enumerated in the theft charge and nothing else. Furthermore, it is implicit in the concept of an attempt that the person acting intends to do the act attempted, so that the *mens rea* of an attempt is essentially that of the complete crime ... That being so, there could be no valid conviction of the appellant of attempted theft on the present indictment unless it were established that he was animated by the same intention permanently to deprive Sergeant Crooks of the goods enumerated in the particulars of the charge as would be necessary to establish the full offence. We hope that we have already made sufficiently clear why we consider that, in the light of the evidence and of the direction given, it is impossible to uphold the verdict on the basis that such intention was established in this case. For these reasons, we are compelled to allow the appeal and quash the conviction.

Section 12 of the Theft Act 1968: taking motor vehicle or other conveyance without authority

(1) Subject to subsections (5) and (6) below, a person shall be guilty of an offence if, without having the consent of the owner or other lawful authority, he takes any conveyance for his own or another's use or, knowing that any conveyance has been taken without such authority, drives it or allows himself to be carried in or on it.

(2) A person guilty of an offence under subsection (1) above shall [be liable on summary conviction to a fine not exceeding level 5 on the standard scale, to imprisonment for a term not exceeding six months, or to both.]

(3) ...

(4) If on the trial of an indictment for theft the jury are not satisfied that the accused committed theft, but it is proved that the accused committed an offence under subsection (1) above, the jury may find him guilty of the offence under subsection (1) [and if he is found guilty of it, he shall be liable as he would have been liable under subsection (2) above on summary conviction].

(5) Subsection (1) above shall not apply in relation to pedal cycles; but, subject to subsection (6) below, a person who, without having the consent of the owner or other lawful authority, takes a pedal cycle for his own or another's use, or rides a pedal cycle knowing it to have been taken without such authority, shall on summary conviction be liable to a fine not exceeding [level 3 on the standard scale].

(6) A person does not commit an offence under this section by anything done in the belief that he has lawful authority to do it or that he would have the owner's consent if the owner knew of his doing it and the circumstances of it.

(7) For purposes of this section:

(a) 'conveyance' means any conveyance constructed or adapted for the carriage of a person or persons whether by land, water or air, except that it does not include a conveyance constructed or adapted for use only under the control of a person not carried in or on it, and 'drive' shall be construed accordingly; and

(b) 'owner', in relation to a conveyance which is the subject of a hiring agreement or hire-purchase agreement, means the person in possession of the conveyance under that agreement.

Section 12A of the Theft Act 1968: aggravated vehicle-taking

(1) Subject to subsection (3) below, a person is guilty of aggravated taking of a vehicle if:

(a) he commits an offence under s 12(1) above (in this section referred to as a 'basic offence') in relation to a mechanically propelled vehicle; and

(b) it is proved that, at any time after the vehicle was unlawfully taken (whether by him or another) and before it was recovered, the vehicle was driven, or injury or damage was caused, in one or more of the circumstances set out in paragraphs (a) to (d) of subsection (2) below.

(2) The circumstances referred to in subsection (1)(b) above are:

(a) that the vehicle was driven dangerously on a road or other public place;

(b) that, owing to the driving of the vehicle, an accident occurred by which injury was caused to any person;

(c) that, owing to the driving of the vehicle, an accident occurred by which damage was caused to any property, other than the vehicle;

(d) that damage was caused to the vehicle.

(3) A person is not guilty of an offence under this section if he proves that, as regards any such proven driving, injury or damage as is referred to in subsection (1)(b) above, either:

(a) the driving, accident or damage referred to in subsection (2) above occurred before he committed the basic offence; or

(b) he was neither in nor on nor in the immediate vicinity of the vehicle when that driving, accident or damage occurred.

(4) A person guilty of an offence under this section shall be liable on conviction on indictment to imprisonment for a term not exceeding two years or, if it is proved that, in circumstances falling within subsection (2)(b) above, the accident caused the death of the person concerned, five years.

(5) If a person who is charged with an offence under this section is found not guilty of that offence but it is proved that he committed a basic offence, he may be convicted of the basic offence.

(6) If by virtue of subsection (5) above a person is convicted of a basic offence before the Crown Court, that court shall have the same powers and duties as a magistrates' court would have had on convicting him of such an offence.

(7) For the purposes of this section a vehicle is driven dangerously if:

(a) it is driven in a way which falls far below what would be expected of a competent and careful driver; and

(b) it would be obvious to a competent and careful driver that driving the vehicle in that way would be dangerous.

(8) For the purposes of this section a vehicle is recovered when it is restored to its owner or to other lawful possession or custody; and in this subsection 'owner' has the same meaning as in s 12 above.

The elements of the offence under s 12 of the Theft Act 1968 are that the defendant:

(a) takes

(b) a conveyance (as defined in s 12(7)(a))

(c) for his own or another's use

(d) without the owner's consent

or

(a) knowing that the conveyance has been taken without the owner's consent

(b) drives it or allows himself to be carried in it.

For an offence under s 12A to be committed, it must be proved that:

(a) an offence under s 12(1) of the Theft Act 1968 has been committed;

(b) the conveyance must be a 'mechanically propelled vehicle';

(c) one of the following has also occurred:

(1) the vehicle was driven dangerously;

(2) as a result of the driving of the vehicle, injury has been caused to someone;

(3) as a result of the driving of the vehicle, property other than the vehicle has been damaged; or

(4) the vehicle has been damaged.

Taking

The word 'taking' requires that the conveyance must be moved, albeit by a small distance. Merely starting the vehicle's engine is not enough (although it may amount to an attempt to commit the full offence)

R v Bogacki and Others [1973] QB 832 (CA)

Roskill LJ: These three young men, the defendants, Bogacki, Tillwach and Cox, were charged ... with attempting, and I venture to underline the word 'attempting', to take a motor vehicle without authority ...

... The evidence for the Crown was to a large extent undisputed. At about 3.45 am on New Year's Day 1972, these three young men, who had been having a lot to drink at a New Year's Eve party, went to Ponders End bus garage. There they tried to change a 50p piece in order to purchase cigarettes from a machine. They were refused change and told to go away. As they went they boarded a single decker bus which was standing on the forecourt of the garage. One of them turned the engine over with the starter as if to start it. It was common ground that after three or four minutes they left the garage quite openly. They walked to the police station where they were given change for the 50p piece which they had been refused at the bus station. Very shortly thereafter they were arrested. According to the police evidence, Cox first of all denied he had ever boarded the bus. Tillwach made a written statement in which he admitted that he had been on the bus and he alleged that Bogacki had sat in the driving seat and tried to start the engine.

There was no doubt, and [counsel] for the defendants has not sought to contend otherwise, that one of those three young men acting in concert with the others got on board that bus and attempted to start the engine. The bus never moved. Indeed the weight of the evidence was that the engine never started and this court deals with the appeal on that assumption ...

... The word 'take' is an ordinary simple English word ...

... [T]he court accepts [the defendants'] submission that there is still built in, if I may use the phrase, to the word 'takes' in the subsection the concept of movement and that before a man can be convicted of the completed offence

> under s 12(1) it must be shown that he took the vehicle, that is to say that there was an unauthorised taking possession or control of the vehicle by him adverse to the rights of the true owner or person otherwise entitled to such possession or control, coupled with some movement, however small ... of that vehicle following such unauthorised taking.
>
> Here, had the judge given the jury a correct direction, there was abundant evidence to justify convictions for attempting to take the bus because what was done must on the verdict of the jury clearly be taken to have been an act to which all these men were joint parties, preparatory to putting the bus into motion after an unauthorised taking of possession or control ...

For his own or another's use

'Use' means use as a conveyance; the defendant's motive is immaterial (*R v Bow* (1976) 64 Cr App R 54). This was further explained in *R v Marchant* (1984) 80 Cr App R 361. Once a conveyance has been 'taken' for the purpose of s 12, subsequent acts by the taker do not amount to a further taking; however, if the first taker abandons the conveyance, it may be 'taken' by another person even though it has not been restored to its owner in the meantime (*DPP v Spriggs* [1994] RTR 1).

R v Bow (1976) 64 Cr App R 54 (CA)

Facts: On Sunday morning 2 November 1975, the appellant, his brother and his father drove in the brother's motor car from their home to a country estate known as the Racton Estate. They were armed with air rifles. The case for the Crown, for which there was, one must say, a good deal of circumstantial support, was that the object of their excursion was to go poaching. That at all events was the view taken by the gamekeepers employed on the estate. They approached the appellant's party and asked for their names and addresses. They were not forthcoming. The head gamekeeper decided to call the police. He also decided to park his Land Rover in such a position as to obstruct the only escape route which could be taken by the appellant's party in the brother's motor car. The head gamekeeper was asked to move the Land Rover but declined to do so. There followed a scuffle between the head gamekeeper and the appellant's brother which resulted in due course in the brother being convicted of common assault. It was during this scuffle that the appellant got into the driving seat of the Land Rover, released the handbrake and coasted down the lane with the engine not switched on, travelling a distance of some 200 yards. The effect of that was to enable the appellant's brother's motor car to be driven off.

Bridge LJ: ... The short answer, we think, is that where as here, a conveyance is taken and moved in a way which necessarily involves its use as a conveyance, the taker cannot be heard to say that the taking was not for that use. If he has in fact taken the conveyance and used it as such, his motive in so doing is ... quite immaterial.

R v Marchant and McCallister (1984) 80 Cr App R 361 (CA)

Facts: Two police officers gave evidence to the effect that they saw the two appellants pushing a car. They said that they saw the two appellants succeeding in moving the car, by pushing it, although moving it only a very short distance, about two or three feet.

The two appellants gave evidence to the effect that they did not know who the car belonged to. They said that they were moving it because it was badly parked and sticking out from the kerb. McCallister however also said that he was looking out for a car like that, and that he thought it was abandoned; and Marchant also gave evidence to the effect that McCallister was looking for a car of this kind.

Robert Goff LJ: ... [Section 12 of the Theft Act 1968] simply provides that the offence is committed if a person takes a conveyance for his own use, without prior consent or lawful authority. So, to be guilty of the offence, the accused must have both taken the vehicle, ie have taken control of it and caused it to be moved, and he must have done so for his own or another's use. The latter requirement has been said to mean 'for his own use or another's as a conveyance': see *R v Bow* (1977) 64 Cr App R 54 at 57, *per* Bridge LJ. Even so, as we see it, if a person takes a vehicle for that use, ie to use it as a conveyance, without the consent of the owner or lawful authority, he commits the offence ... Suppose a man finds a car in the street. He needs a car for a day's expedition. He forms the intent to take the car for that use, though intending to return it later to that place where he found it. He knows he cannot start it then, so he pushes it round the corner to his home with the intention of getting it going for use on his expedition. The police catch up with him and find the car parked in his yard. Has that person committed the offence of taking a conveyance for his own use, without having the necessary consent or authority? In our judgment, he has. He has certainly taken it because he has moved it a certain distance. In my judgment his purpose for taking it is plain. It was for use as a conveyance. So in those circumstances, the offence has been committed.

Director of Public Prosecution v Spriggs [1994] RTR 1 (DC)

Tudor Evans J: ... The car had originally been taken from the car park of a company which owned the car during the course of the afternoon or early evening on 23 November 1990. It was taken without the consent of the owner or other lawful authority. The prosecution did not suggest that the defendant took the vehicle from the car park or that he was in any way involved in the original taking.

The case for the prosecution was that, much later on the day of the original taking, he was seen by police officers at the wheel of the car, that it was being driven very slowly in convoy with another vehicle which drove off at the approach of the police car, and that, when the police car stopped the car, the defendant tried to run away and both he and Mr Staff were arrested. The evidence showed that there were obvious signs of damage to the door and the ignition of the car and the defendant was found with a bent screwdriver in his possession.

The account given by him at interview was that Mr Staff had been giving him a lift home in another vehicle when they came across the car in question which they saw had been left blocking the road with the engine running. The defendant's account was that, whilst he accepted that he should never have got into the car and whilst he accepted that he had driven it for about 200 yards, he was simply moving the car preparatory to notifying the police of what he had found. He accepted that he realised that the car had been stolen when he got into it ...

The question for the opinion of the court is whether a person, not being the person who is responsible for the original and unlawful taking of a vehicle from the place where its lawful owner last left it, is capable in law of committing the offence of taking a conveyance without authority contrary to s 12(1) of the Theft

Act 1968 by reason only of a later and separate taking of the same vehicle from some other place ...

... This is a case in which the car was taken and then possession of it was abandoned, as is quite plain on the facts as found. There was then a fresh assumption of possession and taking within the language of the subsection.

In those circumstances, where a vehicle is abandoned, it seems to me that it must inevitably follow that, if there is a subsequent taking which falls within the language of the first part of s 12(1), then the offence is committed. It cannot be that offences under this subsection are limited only to facts where there has been one taking either by a single person or by his acting jointly with another.

Accordingly, I would answer the question which I have already identified with the answer 'Yes' and I would remit the matter to the Crown Court with a direction to convict. It follows that the appeal must be allowed.

Without the owner's consent

Where the owner is deceived into allowing the defendant to take the conveyance, that consent is not vitiated by the fraud and so no offence is committed under s 12 of the Theft Act 1968 (*Whittaker v Campbell* [1984] QB 318).

Whittaker and Another v Campbell [1984] QB 318 (DC)

Robert Goff LJ: ... The following facts are taken from the case [stated by the Crown Court]: (1) In about June 1981 the defendants, who are brothers aged 27 and 25 years, and who lived in St Helen's Auckland, County Durham, had an opportunity to obtain some coal at an advantageous price from a private colliery quite lawfully. (2) In order to remove the coal the defendants required their own means of transport. At all material times, the defendant Wilson Coglan Whittaker had no driving licence whatsoever and the defendant Stewart Whittaker had a provisional licence only and neither defendant had a vehicle of his own. (3) In about June 1981 the defendants came into possession of a full driving licence belonging to one Derek Dunn. The defendant Wilson Coglan Whittaker said that he had found it near Mr Dunn's place of work. The defendants decided to use the licence to hire a van to remove the coal. (4) On 24 June 1981, the defendants went to a local vehicle hire firm called Stangarths Ltd ... and there hired from a director, one Duncan Stuart Robson, aged 23, a Ford Transit van for a day. (5) The defendant Wilson Coglan Whittaker represented himself as being Derek Dunn of the address shown on the driving licence which he produced to Mr Robson. The same defendant also signed the name 'D Dunn' on the hire agreement form ... The appropriate hire charge was paid by the defendants and the defendant Wilson Coglan Whittaker drove away the Ford Transit van. On five subsequent occasions the defendants did the same thing ... on each occasion the defendant Wilson Coglan Whittaker signing the hire agreement form 'D Dunn'. On the later occasions the driving licence was not produced to Mr Robson who acted in reliance on what had happened on earlier occasions. On each occasion the defendants paid the appropriate hire charge. (6) On 16 October 1981 the defendant Stewart Whittaker was driving the hire van when it was stopped and checked by police officers ... The defendants were questioned and their true identities were established. (7) According, to Mr Robson, the hire company's director, on the occasion of each hire, he was deceived by the defendants into believing that the defendant Wilson Coglan Whittaker was Derek Dunn and that he was the holder of a full driving licence, and had he known that that was not the case the defendant Wilson Coglan

Whittaker would not have been allowed to hire any of his (Robson's) vehicles or drive any of his vehicles (8) ... [I]t was alleged that the defendants jointly on 16 October 1981, without the consent of the owner or other lawful authority took a certain conveyance, namely a motor van, for their own use, contrary to s 12(1) of the Theft Act 1968. The offence alleged referred to the last occasion of hire ...

... There being no general principle that fraud vitiates consent, we see the problem simply as this: can a person be said to have taken a conveyance for his own or another's use 'without having the consent of the owner or other lawful authority' within those words as used in s 12(1) of the Theft Act 1968, if he induces the owner to part with possession of the conveyance by a fraudulent misrepresentation of the kind employed by the defendants in the present case? ...

In circumstances such as those of the present case, the criminality (if any) of the act would appear to rest rather in the fact of the deception, inducing the person to part with the possession of his vehicle, rather than in the fact (if it be the case) that the fraud has the effect of inducing a mistake as to, for example, 'identity' rather than 'attributes' of the deceiver. It would be very strange if fraudulent conduct of this kind has only to be punished if it happened to induce a fundamental mistake; and it would be even more strange if such fraudulent conduct has only to be punished where the chattel in question happened to be a vehicle. If such fraudulent conduct is to be the subject of prosecution, the crime should surely be classified as one of obtaining by deception, rather than an offence under s 12(1) of the Act of 1968, which appears to us to be directed to the prohibition and punishment of a different form of activity ...

Belief in consent of owner (s 12(6))

No offence is committed if, at the time of the taking (and it must be at the time of the taking (*R v Ambler* [1979] RTR 217)), the accused genuinely believed that the owner had consented (or would have consented) to the taking. It is for the prosecution to prove the absence of such a belief, but before the prosecution have to do so the defence must make out a prima facie case that he held this belief.

R v Gannon (1988) 87 Cr App R 254 (CA)

Kenneth Jones J: ... The onus was of course on the prosecution to prove the absence of the belief [that the defendant had lawful authority to take the car] – *R v MacPherson* [1973] RTR 157. But before that stage was reached, it was of course for the appellant to raise the issue. That means that he was required to call evidence or at least be able to point to some evidence which tended to show that he did hold the belief referred to in s 12(6) ...

Allowing himself to be carried

Again, there must have been some movement of the conveyance and it must be proved that the accused knew that the conveyance had been taken without the owner's consent (*R v Diggin* (1980) 72 Cr App R 204).

Aggravating circumstances for s 12A

R v Marsh (1996) 160 JP 721 (DC)

Laws J: ... [The appellant had taken a motor car without the consent of the owner.] During the journey, the [passenger] noticed a figure towards the right of the car

> and it seemed as if it was about to cross towards the footpath on the left. The car continued down. The figure began to run over towards the left-hand side footpath and, unfortunately, it transpired that it was a lady who was running across the road. She was knocked to the ground. The appellant ... stopped to help her. She was not, it seems, seriously injured ...
>
> It is right that we should note that the [passenger] was to state that throughout the journey the appellant drove at around the 30 mph mark and that, had the pedestrian remained to the right of the car, there would have been no accident. There was, therefore, no evidence of fault in the manner in which the car was driven; certainly, the Crown relied on none ...
>
> [His Lordship quoted from ss 12A(1), (2) of the Theft Act 1968 and went on:]
>
> The assertion made in the Crown Court by the defendant was that no liability could attach to him under s 12A(2)(b) unless it were proved that the accident in question had been occasioned by culpable driving on his part ...
>
> ...[I]t is unhelpful, in our judgment, to gloss the statute by referring to the manner or mode of driving: the words are plain and simple. In our view, the question for the court on their proper construction is, was the driving of the vehicle a cause of an accident? Any other approach would require the court to read in words which are not there.
>
> The learned recorder, in our view, was right to hold that the policy of this statute is to impose heavier sanctions on those who take vehicles unlawfully and then cause an accident, whether or not the accident involves any fault in the driving.
>
> Dealing with the statutory words more distinctly, it is to be noted that there is a clear contrast between the words of s 12A(2)(a) that 'the vehicle was driven dangerously on a road' and those in (b) and (c), where the phrase is only 'owing to the driving of the vehicle'. Of course (d), the subparagraph contemplating that damage is caused to the vehicle, has nothing to say about fault at all ...
>
> ... Applying ordinary canons of statutory construction, it is impossible to say that the words of s 12A(2)(b) import a requirement of fault in the driving of the vehicle. No word suggesting fault appears in the statutory language. It seems to us that the ordinary meaning of the words used is simply to point to a requirement that there be a causal connection between the moving of the vehicle on the road and an accident which follows ...

Section 13 of the Theft Act 1968: abstracting of electricity

> A person who dishonestly uses without due authority, or dishonestly causes to be wasted or diverted, any electricity shall on conviction on indictment be liable to imprisonment for a term not exceeding five years.

On dishonesty, see *Boggeln v Williams* [1978] 1 WLR 873. Although electricity is used without due authority if the meter is tampered with so that the amount of electricity used does not register on the meter (as in *Collins v DPP* (1987) Times, 20 October), the offence can also be committed even if the meter is not tampered with (*R v McCreadie* (1992) 96 Cr App R 143).

R v McCreadie and Tume (1992) 96 Cr App R 143 (CA)

Facts: The appellants moved in, as squatters, to an empty property where the electricity supply had originally been disconnected by the Electricity Board but subsequently reconnected to a meter installed illegally, possibly by earlier squatters. The appellants used the electricity but took no steps to inform the Electricity Board of their occupancy or to pay any bills.

Lord Taylor CJ: ... [W]e are unable to accept the submission that without tampering or interference with the meter an offence under s 13 cannot be committed. The three ingredients of the offence [are]: ... first, using a quantity of electricity; second, doing so without authority; and third, doing so dishonestly.

Here there is no doubt that the appellants used electricity. The lights were on when they were there and the police arrived. Equally they were doing so without authority. They were not the registered consumers. The Electricity Board had not authorised them to use electricity and indeed they had withdrawn the supply of electricity from those premises, so far as any use of it was concerned. The Electricity Board had no knowledge of them and no knowledge where to contact them should they wish to send the bill. There was no question here of due authority having been granted to these appellants to use the electricity.

The vital issue therefore is whether dishonesty has been proved ...

The suggestion that the meter had to be tampered with in some way in order to constitute the offence is, in our judgment, quite wrong. [His Lordship then approved a passage from Professor J C Smith's book, *The Law of Theft*, which stated:] '"use" implies some consumption of electricity which would not occur but for the accused's act. If squatters switch on the electricity not intending to pay for it they appear to use it dishonestly.' We agree with that passage ...

The defence was that if a bill had come they would have paid. However, they were moving when the police arrived. They had not apprised the Electricity Board of their arrival, their departure, or their identity. In those circumstances, it was open to the jury to find that they were acting dishonestly and to convict. The jury did so. In our judgment this appeal must be dismissed.

CHAPTER 16

BURGLARY

Section 9 of the Theft Act 1968

(1) A person is guilty of burglary if:

(a) he enters any building or part of a building as a trespasser and with intent to commit any such offence as is mentioned in subsection (2) below; or

(b) having entered any building or part of a building as a trespasser he steals or attempts to steal anything in the building or that part of it or inflicts or attempts to inflict on any person therein any grievous bodily harm.

(2) The offences referred to in subsection (1)(a) above are offences of stealing anything in the building or part of a building in question, of inflicting on any person therein any grievous bodily harm or raping any person therein, and of doing unlawful damage to the building or anything therein.

(3) A person guilty of burglary shall on conviction on indictment be liable to imprisonment for a term not exceeding:

(a) where the offence was committed in respect of a building or part of a building which is a dwelling, 14 years;

(b) in any other case, 10 years.

(4) References in subsections (1) and (2) above to a building, and the reference in subsection (3) above to a building which is a dwelling, shall apply also to an inhabited vehicle or vessel, and shall apply to any such vehicle or vessel at times when the person having a habitation in it is not there as well as at times when he is.

Section 9(1) of the Theft Act 1968 creates two separate offences. In other words, there are two types of burglary. Common to both types are these requirements:

(1) that the defendant must enter a building, or part of a building,

(2) that the defendant must enter the building (or part thereof) as a trespasser (ie a person who does not have permission, whether express or implied, to be on the premises).

For an offence under s 9(1)(a), the defendant must so enter with the intention of committing theft, causing grievous bodily harm, rape or criminal damage.

For an offence under s 9(1)(b), the defendant, having so entered, must actually commit or attempt to commit theft or the infliction of grievous bodily harm.

ENTRY AS A TRESPASSER

Entry must, according to the case of *R v Collins* [1973] QB 100 (the case which does for the Law Reports what *Lady Chatterley's Lover* does for English literature), entry must be 'effective and substantial'.

It is an essential ingredient of the offence of burglary that the defendant should be a trespasser at the time he enters the building. Trespass has the same meaning for the purpose of s 9 of the Theft Act 1968 as it has for the tort of trespass, that is entry onto premises with neither express nor implied permission to be there.

Furthermore, the defendant must not only be a trespasser but must know that he is entering as a trespasser or be reckless whether he is entering as a trespasser (*R v Collins* [1973] QB 100 and *R v Walkington* [1979] 1 WLR 1169; the later authority is dealt with when we come to consider the phrase 'part of a building').

Entry may amount to trespass if a defendant enters the premises for a purpose for which he does not have permission: see *R v Jones* and *Smith* [1976] 1 WLR 672.

R v Collins [1973] QB 100 (CA)

Edmund Davies LJ: This is about as extraordinary a case as my brethren and I have ever heard either on the bench or while at the bar. Stephen William George Collins was convicted ... of burglary with intent to commit rape ...

... At about 2 o'clock in the early morning of Saturday 24 July 1971, a young lady of 18 went to bed at her mother's home in Colchester. She had spent the evening with her boyfriend. She had taken a certain amount of drink, and it may be that this fact affords some explanation of her inability to answer satisfactorily certain crucial questions put to her at the trial.

She has the habit of sleeping without wearing night apparel in a bed which is very near the lattice-type window of her room. At one stage in her evidence she seemed to be saying that the bed was close up against the window which, in accordance with her practice, was wide open. In the photographs which we have before us, however, there appears to be a gap of some sort between the two, but the bed was clearly quite near the window.

At about 3.30 or 4.00 am she awoke and she then saw in the moonlight a vague form crouched in the open window. She was unable to remember, and this is important, whether the form was on the outside of the window sill or on that part of the sill which was inside the room, and for reasons which will later become clear, that seemingly narrow point is of crucial importance.

The young lady then realised several things: first of all that the form in the window was that of a male; second that he was a naked male, and third that he was a naked male with an erect penis. She also saw in the moonlight that his hair was blond. She thereupon leapt to the conclusion that her boyfriend, with whom for some time she had been on terms of regular and frequent sexual intimacy, was paying her an ardent nocturnal visit. She promptly sat up in bed, and the man descended from the sill and joined her in bed and they had full sexual intercourse. But there was something about him which made her think that things were not as they usually were between her and her boyfriend. The length of his hair, his voice as they had exchanged what was described as 'love talk', and other features led her to the conclusion that somehow there was something different. So she turned on the bedside light, saw that her companion was not her boyfriend and slapped the face of the intruder, who was none other than the defendant. He said to her, 'Give me a good time tonight', and got hold of her arm, but she bit him and told him to go. She then went into the bathroom and he promptly vanished.

The complainant said that she would not have agreed to intercourse if she had known that the person entering her room was not her boyfriend. But there was no suggestion of any force having been used on her, and the intercourse which took place was undoubtedly effected with no resistance on her part.

The defendant was seen by the police at about 10.30 am later that same morning. According to the police, the conversation which took place then elicited these points: He was very lustful the previous night. He had taken a lot of drink, and we may here note that drink (which to him is a very real problem) had brought this young man into trouble several times before, but never for an offence of this kind. He went on to say that he knew the complainant because he had worked around her house. On this occasion, desiring sexual intercourse – and according to the police evidence he added that he was determined to have a girl, by force in necessary, although that part of the police evidence he challenged – he went on to say that he walked around the house, saw a light in an upstairs bedroom, and he knew that this was the girl's bedroom. He found a step ladder, leaned it against the wall and climbed up and looked into the bedroom. What he could see inside through the wide-open window was a girl who was naked and asleep. So he descended the ladder and stripped off all his clothes with the exception of his socks, because apparently he took the view that if the girl's mother entered the bedroom it would be easier to effect a rapid escape if he had his socks on than if he was in his bare feet. That is a matter about which we are not called on to express any view, and would in any event find ourselves unable to express one.

Having undressed, he then climbed the ladder and pulled himself up on to the window sill. His version of the matter is that he was pulling himself in when she awoke. She then got up and knelt on the bed, she put her arms around his neck and body, and she seemed to pull him into the bed.

He went on:

> I was rather dazed because I didn't think she would want to know me. We kissed and cuddled for about 10 or 15 minutes and then I had it away with her but found it hard because I had had so much to drink.

The police officer said to the defendant:

> It appears that it was your intention to have intercourse with this girl by force if necessary, and that it was only pure coincidence that this girl was under the impression that you were her boyfriend and apparently that is why she consented to allowing you to have sexual intercourse with her.

It was alleged that he then said, 'Yes, I feel awful about this. It is the worst day of my life, but I know it could have been worse.'

Thereupon the officer said to him – and the defendant challenges this: 'What do you mean, you know it could have been worse?', to which he is alleged to have replied:

> Well, my trouble is drink and I got very frustrated. As I've told you, I only wanted to have it away with a girl and I'm only glad I haven't really hurt her.'

Then he made a statement under caution, in the course of which he said:

> When I stripped off and got up the ladder I made my mind up that I was going to try and have it away with this girl. I feel terrible about this now, but I had too much to drink. I am sorry for what I have done.

In the course of his testimony, the defendant said that he would not have gone into the room if the girl had not knelt on the bed and beckoned him into the room. He said that if she had objected immediately to his being there or to his having sexual intercourse he would not have persisted. While he was keen on having sexual intercourse that night, it was only if he could find someone who was willing. He strongly denied having told the police that he would, if necessary, have pushed over some girl for the purpose of having intercourse ...

Now, one feature of the case which remained at the conclusion of the evidence in great obscurity is where exactly Collins was at the moment when, according to him, the girl manifested that she was welcoming him. Was he kneeling on the sill outside the window or was he already inside the room, having climbed through the window frame, and kneeling on the inner sill? It was crucial matter, for there were certainly three ingredients that it was incumbent on the Crown to establish. Under s 9 of the Theft Act 1968, which renders a person guilty of burglary if he enters any building or part of a building as a trespasser and with the intention of committing rape, the entry of the accused into the building must first be proved. Well, there is no doubt about that, for it is common ground that he did enter this girl's bedroom, second, it must be proved that he entered as a trespasser. We will develop that point a little later. Third, it must be proved that he entered as a trespasser with intent at the time of entry to commit rape therein ...

... We hold that, for the purposes of s 9 of the Theft Act 1968, a person entering a building is not guilty of trespass if he enters without knowledge that he is trespassing or at least without acting recklessly as to whether or not he is unlawfully entering ...

... In the judgment of this court there cannot be a conviction for entering premises 'as a trespasser' within the meaning of s 9 of the Theft Act 1968 unless the person entering does so knowing that he is a trespasser and nevertheless deliberately enters, or, at the very least, is reckless as to whether or not he is entering the premises of another without the other party's consent.

Having so held, the pivotal point of this appeal is whether the Crown established that this defendant at the moment that he entered the bedroom knew perfectly well that he was not welcome there or, being reckless whether he was welcome or not, was nevertheless determined to enter.

That in turn involves consideration as to where he was at the time that the complainant indicated that she was welcoming him into her bedroom. If, to take an example that was put in the course of argument, her bed had not been near the window but was on the other side of the bedroom, and he (being determined to have her sexually even against her will) climbed through the window and crossed the bedroom to reach her bed, then the offence charged would have been established. But in this case, as we have related, the layout of the room was different, and it became a point of nicety which had to be conclusively established by the Crown as to where he was when the girl made welcoming signs, as she unquestionably at some stage did ...

... [W]hat the accused had said was, 'She knelt on the bed, she put her arms around me and then I went in'. If the jury thought he might be truthful in that assertion, they would need to consider whether or not, although entirely surprised by such a reception being accorded to him, this young man might not have been entitled reasonably to regard her action as amounting to an invitation to him to enter. If she in fact appeared to be welcoming him, the Crown do not suggest that he should have realised or even suspected that she was so behaving because, despite the moonlight, she thought he was someone else. Unless the jury were entirely satisfied that the defendant made an effective and substantial entry into the bedroom without the complainant doing or saying anything to cause him to believe that she was consenting to his entering it, he ought not to be convicted of the offence charged. The point is a narrow one, as narrow maybe as the window sill which is crucial to this case. But this is a criminal charge of gravity and, even though one may suspect that his intention was to commit the offence charged, unless the facts show with clarity that he in fact committed it he ought not to remain convicted.

Some question arose whether or not the defendant can be regarded as a trespasser *ab initio*. But we are entirely in agreement with the view ... that the common law doctrine of trespass *ab initio* has no application to burglary under the Theft Act 1968. One further matter that was canvassed ought perhaps to be mentioned. The point was raised that, the complainant not being the tenant or occupier of the dwelling house and her mother being apparently in occupation, this girl herself could not in any event have extended an effective invitation to enter, so that even if she had expressly and with full knowledge of all material facts invited the defendant in, he would nevertheless be a trespasser. Whatever be the position in the law of tort, to regard such a proposition as acceptable in the criminal law would be unthinkable.

We have to say that this appeal must be allowed on the basis that the jury were never invited to consider the vital question whether this young man did enter the premises as a trespasser, that is to say knowing perfectly well that he had no invitation to enter or reckless of whether or not his entry was with permission ...

R v Brown [1985] Crim LR 212 (CA)

Facts: A witness, having heard the sound of breaking glass, saw the appellant partially inside a shop front display. The top half of his body was inside the shop window as though he were rummaging around inside it. The witness assumed that his feet were on the ground outside, although his view was obscured. The appellant appealed against his conviction for burglary on the ground that he had not 'entered' the building, since his body was not entirely within it.

Held: Dismissing the appeal (and applying *R v Collins* [1973] QB 100), the word 'enter' in s 9 of the Theft Act 1968 did not require that the whole of a defendant's body be within a building. His entry had been 'substantial and effective'.

R v Ryan (1996) 160 JP 610 (CA)

Hirst LJ: ... The facts of the burglary are as follows. At about 2.30 am on Sunday 13 November 1994 the appellant was found stuck in a downstairs window by the elderly occupier. The window was 1 ft high and 2 ft 6 ins across. The appellant had his head and right arm inside the window and was trapped by the window itself on his neck. The rest of his body remained outside the window. On being accosted by the householder, the appellant said: 'Have you any Fairy Liquid? I'm stuck in the window?' The occupier demanded to know what he was doing there, to which he replied: 'I'm getting my baseball hat. My mate's put my baseball hat through the window.' The police were called and recovered a knife and a baseball hat from the ground outside the window in which the appellant was stuck. These two items significantly were the same knife and hat which formed the subject matter of the handling charge to which the appellant pleaded guilty. Eventually, the fire brigade had to be summoned to extricate the appellant from the window.

He was interviewed at 2.25 pm on the same day at Swindon police station and maintained his scarcely credible story that the baseball cap had been dropped through the open window by another person. He repeated the same line of defence in his evidence at the trial, which not surprisingly was disbelieved by the jury.

The appeal against conviction raises one point and one point only, namely whether as a matter of law his action was capable of constituting an entry ...

[His Lordship quoted from s 9(1) of the Theft Act 1968 and went on:]

The question is, was this capable of constituting an entry? That point was conclusively decided in *R v Brown* (18 January 1985; Watkins LJ, Peter Pain J and Sir John Thompson). The judgment of the court was given by Watkins LJ. In that case also there was a partial entry through a window. The very same point was taken as in the present case, namely:

> Counsel for the appellant contends there can be no offence committed under the provisions of s 9(1) unless the person accused of the burglary is found upon the facts to have been at the relevant time wholly within the building.

That proposition was rejected by the court and Watkins LJ made it crystal clear in his judgment that a person can enter in the circumstances where only part of his body is actually within the premises.

[Counsel for the appellant] sought to distinguish *Brown's* case from the present case on the footing that in the former the appellant was capable of stealing property within the building, whereas in the present case, since the appellant was stuck firm by his neck in the window, he was incapable. That is a totally irrelevant distinction which in no way affects the principle laid down in *Brown* which is binding on us. There, the partial entry was capable of constituting entry. So here also this partial presence of the appellant within the building, albeit stuck in the window, was capable of constituting entry and it was therefore a matter for the jury to decide, as the learned recorder admirably directed them. The appeal against conviction will therefore be dismissed ...

R v Jones; R v Smith [1976] 1 WLR 672 (CA)

Facts: The appellants were charged with burglary, contrary to s 9(1)(b) of the Theft Act 1968. The prosecution case was that they had entered the house of Smith's father and stolen two television sets. Smith's father had reported the theft to the police at the time, but at the trial of Smith and Jones he gave evidence to the effect that he had given Smith unreserved permission to enter the house, stating that his son, Christopher Smith, 'would not be a trespasser in the house at any time'.

James LJ: [After referring to the civil case of *Hillen and Pettigrew v ICI (Alkali) Ltd* [1936] AC 65 at 69, *per* Lord Atkin, his Lordship continued] ... it is our view that a person is a trespasser for the purpose of s 9(1)(b) of the Theft Act 1968 if he enters premises of another knowing that he is entering in excess of the permission that has been given to him, or being reckless whether he is entering in excess of the permission that has been given to him to enter, providing the facts are known to the accused which enable him to realise that he is acting in excess of the permission given or that he is acting recklessly as to whether he exceeds that permission, then that is sufficient for the jury to decide that he is in fact a trespasser.

In this particular case it was a matter for the jury to consider whether, on all the facts, it was shown by the prosecution that the appellants entered with the knowledge that entry was being effected against the consent or in excess of the consent that had been given by Mr Alfred Smith to his son Christopher ...

BUILDING OR PART OF A BUILDING

To be a building, a structure must have a degree of permanence. So, a freezer trailer (which could be hooked up to a lorry and transported at any time) was held not to be a building (*Norfolk Constabulary v Seekings* [1986] Crim LR 167); but a freezer which was 25 feet long, weighed three tons, was connected to the electricity supply and had been in place for at least two years, was held to be a building (*B v Leathley* [1979] Crim LR 314). The test is that laid down by Byles J in *Stevens v Gourley* (1859) CBNS 99 at 112, that the structure must be 'of considerable size and intended to be permanent or at least to endure for a considerable period'.

That entry into part of a building may amount to burglary means that a person may become a burglar (if the other elements of the offence are satisfied) by going from a part in which he is lawful visitor to a part in which he is not: see *R v Walkington* [1979] 1 WLR 1169.

R v Walkington [1979] 1 WLR 1169 (CA)

Geoffrey Lane LJ: ... It is important at the outset to see what it was that the defendant was charged with precisely. The charge read as follows:

> Statement of offence: Burglary, contrary to s 9(1)(a) of the Theft Act 1968.
>
> Particulars of offence: Terence Walkington on 15 January 1977, entered as a trespasser part of a building known as Debenhams store with intent to steal therein.

... So far as the facts were concerned, there was very little, if any, dispute. On 15 January 1977, shortly before closing time of Debenhams store in Oxford Street, the defendant was seen in the menswear department of that store. He was kept under observation by Mr Rogers, who was a store detective, and two of his colleagues. The store closed at 6.00 pm. At about 20 minutes to six the various counter assistants were cashing up their tills. The evidence given by Mr Rogers was that the defendant seemed to be interested primarily, if not solely, in what was going on at the various tills in the store.

In due course he was observed to travel up on the escalator to the first floor. On that floor was an unattended till in the centre of a three-sided counter, the drawer of the till being partially opened. There was some dispute as to the precise dimensions of this three-sided counter, but what was agreed was that it was a movable counter. It was not static in the sense of being fixed to the floor. One of the descriptions of it showed that what we may call the north side of the counter was about 4 feet in length, the east side was about 12 feet in length and the west side was about 6 feet in length, the till being situated on the north side, the 4 foot length. Other descriptions of the counter gave different dimensions. But in each case it is to be observed that the till was in a corner formed by two of these counters. The evidence was that the area inside that rectangle or partial rectangle was reserved for the staff and it was clear, so it was suggested, that any customer seeing that area would realise that his permission to be in the store did not extend to a permission to be in that area.

The defendant, on the evidence, moved to the opening of the rectangular area described, that is to say to the part thereof which was not filled in by any counter, looked all around him, then bent down and having got to the till pulled the drawer further open. Having looked into the drawer the defendant slammed it to, said something and started making his way out of the shop, when he was stopped by the store detective.

In fact there was nothing in the drawer. The fact that the till drawer was partially open was an indication to anyone in the know that the assistant at that particular counter had cashed up that particular till.

The police were duly called in and the defendant was arrested. He was taken to Marylebone police station where he made a statement in writing, which reads as follows:

> I came up the West End to do some shopping and I went into Debenhams for a tie. I walked around the store for a while and looked at some coats. I went up on the first floor to have a look at the shoes. After a while I noticed a till

> partly open with a drawer beneath it. I thought I might be able to steal something from it so I opened the drawer but there was nothing in it worth stealing which was my intention. I shut the drawer again and walked away. That was when the security bloke stopped me. I don't know why I did it now, it seems so stupid. I would like to take this opportunity of saying how sorry I am and apologise to the store, the police and the court.

The defendant at the trial gave evidence according to his statement, claiming that he had gone to the store originally as a *bona fide* customer. He had gone to look at the dresses on the first floor and had given way to the temptation of opening the drawer. He had no idea that he was trespassing and he had not looked at the tills on the ground floor before he went up to the first floor as the store detective had said ...

What the prosecution had to prove here was that the defendant had entered a part of a building as a trespasser with intent to steal anything in that part of the building ...

[His Lordship then cited with approval two passages, one from Professor Griew's book, *The Theft Acts 1968 and 1978*, and the other from Professor Smith's book, *The Law of Theft*. Those passages read as follows:]

> A licence to enter a building may extend to part of the building only. If so, the licensee will trespass if he enters some other part not within the scope of the licence. To do so with intent to commit in that other part one of the specified offences, or to do so and then to commit or attempt to commit one of those offences therein, will be burglary. [Professor Griew]
>
> ... A customer in a shop who goes behind the counter and takes money from the till during a short absence of the shopkeeper would be guilty of burglary even though he entered the shop with the shopkeeper's permission. The permission did not extend to his going behind the counter. [Professor Smith]

... Here, it seems to us, there was a physical demarcation. Whether it was sufficient to amount to an area from which the public was plainly excluded was a matter for the jury. It seems to us that there was ample evidence on which they could come to the conclusion (a) that the management had impliedly prohibited customers entering that area and (b) that this particular defendant knew of that prohibition ...

Section 9(1)(a) of the Theft Act 1968: theft and 'conditional intent'

A person is guilty of burglary if (assuming the other elements of the offence to have been established) even if he intends to steal only if there is something worth stealing.

R v Walkington [1979] 1 WLR 1169 (CA)

[See *above* for facts.]

Geoffrey Lane LJ: ... [His Lordship turned to the second issue in the appeal, namely that there was no evidence that there was anything capable of being stolen.] In this case there is no doubt that the defendant was not on the evidence in two minds as to whether to steal or not. He was intending to steal when he went to that till and it would be totally unreal to ask oneself, or for the jury to ask themselves, the question, what sort of intent did he have? Was it a conditional intention to steal if there was money in the till or a conditional intention to steal only if what he found there was worth stealing? In this case it was a cash till and what plainly he was intending to steal was the contents of the till, which was cash. The mere fact that the till happened to be empty does not destroy his undoubted intention at the moment when he crossed the boundary between the legitimate part of the store and the illegitimate part of the store ...

... It seems to this court that in the end one simply has to go back to the words of the Act itself which we have already cited, and if the jury are satisfied, so as to feel sure, that the defendant has entered any building or part of a building as a trespasser, and are satisfied that at the moment of entering he intended to steal anything in the building or that part of it, the fact that there was nothing in the building worth his while to steal seems to us to be immaterial. He nevertheless had the intent to steal. As we see it, to hold otherwise would be to make a nonsense of this part of the Act and cannot have been the intention of the legislature at the time when the Theft Act 1968 was passed. Nearly every prospective burglar could no doubt truthfully say that he only intended to steal if he found something in the building worth stealing.

Petition: The Appeal Committee of the House of Lords (**Lord Wilberforce, Lord Edmund-Davies** and **Lord Keith of Kinkel**) refused a petition by the defendant for leave to appeal.

Attorney General's References (Nos 1 and 2 of 1979) [1980] QB 180 (CA)

Roskill LJ: ... The question referred in Reference No 1 is:

> Whether a man who has entered a house as a trespasser with the intention of stealing money therein is entitled to be acquitted of an offence against s 9(1)(a) of the Theft Act 1968 on the grounds that his intention to steal is conditional upon his finding money in the house.

The answer of this court to this question is 'No'.

In the second reference the question is:

> Whether a man who is attempting to enter a house as a trespasser with the intention of stealing anything of value which he may find therein is entitled to be acquitted of the offence of attempted burglary on the ground that at the time of the attempt his said intention was insufficient to amount to 'the intention of stealing anything' necessary for conviction under s 9 of the Theft Act 1968.

The answer of this court to this question is also 'No'.

[His Lordship then referred to *R v Husseyn* (1977) 67 Cr App R 131 and continued:]

The indictment in *R v Husseyn* – the Registrar has supplied the court with copies – was as follows:

> Statement of Offence: Attempted Theft.
>
> Particulars of Offence: Ulus Husseyn and Andrew Demetriou on or about the 27th day of February 1976 in Greater London, attempted to steal a quantity of sub-aqua equipment belonging to David Johnson.

Here therefore the relevant count was of attempted theft and not of theft but the charge related to a specific object. Therefore it was essential, in order to establish guilt on this charge of attempted theft, that the accused's intention had been to steal, not the contents of the parked van in question, but the specific object named in the count, namely the sub-aqua equipment. Lord Scarman's judgment must be understood against the background of that fundamental fact ...

[Lord Scarman in *R v Husseyn* said:]

> ... it cannot be said that one who has it in mind to steal only if what he finds is worth stealing has a present intention to steal.

We were asked to say that either that [that] sentence was wrong or that it was *obiter*. We are not prepared to do either. If we may say so with the utmost deference to any statement of law by Lord Scarman, if this sentence be open to criticism, it is because in the context it is a little elliptical. If one rewrites that sentence, so that it reads: 'It must be wrong, for it cannot be said that one who has it in mind to steal only if what he finds is worth stealing has a present intention to steal *the specific item charged*', (our emphasis added), then the difficulties disappear, because, as already stated, what was charged was attempted theft of a specific object ...

I come back to what Lord Scarman himself said in *Director of Public Prosecutions v Nock* [1978] AC 979 ...

> An intention to steal can exist even though, unknown to the accused, there is nothing to steal: but, if a man be in two minds whether to steal or not, the intention required by the statute is not proved.

Section 9(1)(b) of the Theft Act 1968: theft and appropriation

For there to have been a burglary there must have been a theft, and therefore there must have been an appropriation.

R v Gregory (1981) 77 Cr App R 41 (CA)

Facts: The appellant was charged with burglary of a dwelling house. He gave evidence at his trial that a man called Tony, knowing that the appellant was a general dealer, had told him that his (Tony's) parents had died and that he was clearing out their bungalow. It was agreed that the appellant should visit the bungalow to see if there was anything he wished to purchase. The appellant and Tony went to a bungalow in Broadstairs and the appellant took some jewellery. He said that he did not realise that Tony had told him a pack of lies.

Watkins LJ: ... [His Lordship referred to the judgment of Eveleigh LJ in *R v Hale* (1979) 68 Cr App R 415 at 418 and continued:] Nor do we think that in a given criminal enterprise involving theft there can necessarily be only one 'appropriation' within s 3(1) of the Theft Act 1968. It seems to us that the question of whether, when and by whom there has been an appropriation of property has always to be determined by the jury having regard to the circumstances of the case. The length of time involved, the manner in which it came about and the number of people who can properly be said to have taken part in an appropriation will vary according to those circumstances. In a case of burglary of a dwelling-house and before any property is removed from it, it may consist of a continuing process and involve either a single appropriation by one or more persons or a number of appropriations of the property in the house by several persons at different times during the same incident. If this were not a correct exposition of the law of appropriation, startling and disturbing consequences could arise out of the presence of two or more trespassers in a dwelling-house.

Thus a person who may have more the appearance of a handler than the thief can nevertheless still be convicted of theft, and thus of burglary, if the jury are satisfied that with the requisite dishonest intent he appropriated, or took part in the appropriation, of another person's goods.

AGGRAVATED BURGLARY

Section 10 of the Theft Act 1968

(1) A person is guilty of aggravated burglary if he commits any burglary and at the time has with him any firearm or imitation firearm, any weapon of offence, or any explosive; and for this purpose:

(a) 'firearm' includes an airgun or air pistol, and 'imitation firearm' means anything which has the appearance of being a firearm, whether capable of being discharged or not; and

(b) 'weapon of offence' means any article made or adapted for use for causing injury to or incapacitating a person, or intended by the person having it with him for such use; and

(c) 'explosive' means any article manufactured for the purpose of producing a practical effect by explosion, or intended by the person having it with him for that purpose.

(2) A person guilty of aggravated burglary shall on conviction on indictment be liable to imprisonment for life.

Section 10(1)(b)of the Theft Act 1968: 'weapon of offence'

If the weapon is not 'made or adapted for causing injury to or incapacitating a person', the defendant must intend to use the weapon for such a purpose during the particular burglary with which he is charged.

R v Stones [1989] 1 WLR 156 (CA)

Facts: The appellant was charged with aggravated burglary, contrary to s 10(1) of the Theft Act 1968.

Glidewell LJ: ... The primary facts, which were not in dispute at all, were these. The appellant admitted that he had taken part in a burglary of a dwelling house in Bedlington in the early hours of 29 June 1987. A police officer who was off duty had seen the appellant and another man loading stolen goods into a car. He telephoned the police. The two men ran off, but the appellant was caught running across a field and was arrested. When he was searched, a household knife was found in his pocket. When asked why he had it with him, he replied, 'For self-defence, because some lads from Blyth are after me'.

Since it was a household knife, it was accepted by the prosecution that it was not, to go back to s 10(1) [of the Theft Act 1968], an article made or adapted for use for causing injury to or incapacitating a person. The prosecution accepted that they had to prove that it was intended by the person having it with him (the defendant) for such use ...

It is agreed by counsel that the prosecution must prove that the appellant knew that he had a knife with him at the relevant time. Clearly that is right, because otherwise he cannot have the relevant intent. As I have said, the prosecution submit that if he knowingly had the knife with him at the time of the burglary with the intention of using it to cause injury to or incapacitate the lads from Blyth if he met them, the offence is proved. It is not necessary to prove the intention to use the knife to cause injury etc during the course of the burglary.

In our view that submission is correct. The mischief at which the section is clearly aimed is that if a burglar has a weapon which he intends to use to injure some person unconnected with the premises burgled, he may nevertheless be tempted to use it if challenged during the course of the burglary and put under sufficient pressure ...

Time at which defendant must have with him the firearm, etc

If the allegation of burglary is brought under s 9(1)(a) the prosecution have to prove that *at the time of entering the building* as a trespasser with the intention to commit one of the specified offences (theft, grievous bodily harm, rape, criminal damage) the defendant had with him the firearm or other weapon.

If, on the other hand, the allegation of burglary is brought under s 9(1)(b), the time at which the defendant must be in possession of the firearm or other weapon is *the time at which he commits or attempts to commit one of the specified offences* theft or grievous bodily harm: see *R v O'Leary* (1986) 82 Cr App R 341.

R v O'Leary (1986) 82 Cr App R 341 (CA)

Lord Lane CJ: ... The facts of the case, which are not in dispute, were these. In the early hours of 31 January 1985 the appellant entered a house in South East London, almost certainly in search of money and valuables, though such an intent, namely the intent at the time of entry to steal, was not alleged against him. At the time of that entry he was unarmed. He looked round the house downstairs. It seems he found nothing there which interested him, except a kitchen knife with which he armed himself.

He then went upstairs. The occupants of the house, husband and wife, were disturbed. A struggle ensued in the course of which all three, husband wife and the appellant, received injuries. The appellant demanded and was given, he at that point being armed still with the kitchen knife, some cash and a bracelet ...

... Count 2 of the indictment reads as follows:

> Statement of Offence: Aggravated Burglary contrary to s 10(1) of the Theft Act 1968.
>
> Particulars of Offence: Michael O'Leary on 31st day of January 1985 entered as a trespasser a building known as 104 Lyndhurst Grove, London, SE15, and stole therein a sum of money, a bracelet, a number of keys and a cash card belonging to John Marsh, and at the time of committing the said burglary had with him a weapon of offence, namely a knife.

If he had been charged under subsection (1)(a), the offence of burglary would be completed and committed when he entered and it would be at that point that one would have to consider whether or not he was armed. But in the case of subsection (1)(b), which is the one under which he was charged, the offence is complete when, and not until, the stealing is committed, provided again of course that he has trespassed in the first place. The prosecution did not have to prove an intent to steal at the time of entry as the charge is laid here. Indeed such an intent is irrelevant to the charge as laid.

It follows that under this particular charge, the time at which the defendant must be proved to have had with him a weapon of offence to make him guilty of aggravated burglary was the time at which he actually stole. As already indicated, at that moment, when he confronted the householders and demanded their cash and jewellery, which was the theft, he still had the kitchen knife in his hand ...

The judge ruled, as this court has indicated he should have ruled, namely that the material time in this charge for the possession of the weapon was the time when he confronted the householders and stole ...

R v Kelly (1992) 97 Cr App R 245 (CA)

Potts J: ... The prosecution's case was that on 19 June 1991, in the early hours of the morning, the appellant broke into a house in Brixton using a screwdriver to effect entry. He was surprised by the occupants of the house, a young couple, Mr Sheterline and Ms Matthews, while removing a video recorder from the living room ... The relevant part of [Mr Sheterline's evidence] reads as follows:

> I went back into the living room and looked towards the bar and shouted, 'Oi, what do you want?' On hearing this, a black man sprung up from behind the bar. He looked unshaven with short black hair and was wearing a black hooded anorak with the hood down. He said to me, 'Where's the remote for the video?' I threw my knife over to the TV and video recorder which are in the far left-hand corner of the room and handed both remote control units to him. Whilst I was there, he said, 'Unplug the TV and video.' He had already turned the light off and he had pulled the hood up over his head and I suddenly felt him push something into the left-hand side of my rib cage. I could see it had a brown handle with a blunt metal end to it. It looked like a chisel.
>
> I said to the man, 'Can I turn the light on because I can't see what I'm doing.' He said, 'No.' I said, 'Don't hurt us, just take the stuff and go, we won't say anything.'

The appellant then attempted to leave the house with the video in one hand and the screwdriver in the other, but he was apprehended by the police who had attended in response to information received from a member of the public. When the appellant emerged from the house, a policeman saw him holding the screwdriver in his hand.

... Thus the charge derives from s 9(1)(b) of the Act and the time at which the appellant must be proved to have had with him a weapon of offence to make him guilty of aggravated burglary was the time he actually stole: the screwdriver would become a weapon of offence on proof that the appellant intended to use it for causing injury to, or incapacitating Mr Sheterline or Ms Matthews at the time of the theft, thereby aggravating the burglary: s 10(1)(b). This construction follows from the clear language of s 10 of the Theft Act, and is consistent with its purpose.

Has with him

This phrase connotes a degree of immediate control over the firearm or weapon: see *R v Kelt* [1977] 1 WLR 1365.

R v Kelt [1977] 1 WLR 1365 (CA)

The defendant was charged that he 'had with him a firearm ... with intent to commit an indictable offence' contrary to s 18 of the Firearms Act 1968.

Scarman LJ: ... [T]here must be a very close physical link and a degree of immediate control over the weapon by the man alleged to have the firearm with him ...

... [T]he judge [must] make it clear to the jury that possession of the firearm is not enough, that the law requires the evidence to go a stage further and to establish that the accused had the firearm with him. Of course the classic case of having a gun with you is if you are carrying it. But, even if you are not carrying it, you may yet have it with you, if it is immediately available to you. But if all that can be shown is possession in the sense that it is in your house or in a shed or somewhere where you have ultimate control, that is not enough.

R v Pawlicki [1992] 1 WLR 827 (CA)

The defendant was charged that he 'had with him a firearm' contrary to s 18 of the Firearms Act 1968.

Steyn LJ: ... A man who leaves a shotgun at home while he proceeds to the next town to rob a bank is still in possession of the shotgun but he does not 'have it with him' when he commits the robbery at the bank. Under s 18 [of the Firearms Act 1968] the words 'have it' import an element of propinquity which is not required for possession. [Further] 'having with him a firearm' is a wider concept than carrying the firearm.

CHAPTER 17

ROBBERY

Section 8 of the Theft Act 1968

(1) A person is guilty of robbery if he steals, and immediately before or at the time of doing so, and in order to do so, he uses force on any person or puts or seeks to put any person in fear of being then and there subjected to force.

(2) A person guilty of robbery, or of an assault with intent to rob, shall on conviction on indictment be liable to imprisonment for life.

The offence of robbery, which (unlike the other common Theft Act offences such as burglary and theft) is triable only in the Crown Court, comprises two elements:

(1) Theft (ie the offence created by s 1 of the Theft Act 1968 as defined in ss 2–7 of the Act); and

(2) The use or threat of force by the defendant in order to steal.

THEFT

Since theft is an essential ingredient of robbery, it follows that if the defendant is not guilty of theft he cannot be guilty of robbery (so, in *R v Robinson* [1977] Crim LR 173 it was held that since the defendant had not acted dishonestly he could not be guilty of theft and so could not be guilty of robbery).

However, the prosecution must also prove that force was used immediately before, or at the same time as, the appropriation of the property. There must be a causal link between the theft and the use or threat of force (so a direction to the jury that they can convict of robbery even if they find that the violence is unconnected with the theft is wrong in law: see *R v Shendley* [1970] Crim LR 49). In *R v Clouden* [1987] Crim LR 56 the defendant wrenched the victim's shopping bag from her grasp and ran off with it; this use of force was held to amount to robbery.

It is clear that the courts take a robust attitude to the question of appropriation in the context of robbery, so as to allow the jury to take a common sense approach to the question whether there was a robbery.

R v Hale (1978) 68 Cr App R 415 (CA)

Eveleigh LJ: ... The prosecution alleged that the appellant and one McGuire went to the house of a Mrs Carrett. When she answered the door they rushed in. Each was wearing a stocking mask. The appellant put his hand over Mrs Carrett's mouth to stop her screaming and McGuire went upstairs to search. The appellant subsequently released his hold on Mrs Carrett and she went to the settee. He undid her dressing gown and touched her. He also exposed himself. McGuire then came downstairs with a jewellery box and asked where the rest was. The telephone rang. It was a next-door neighbour who had heard Mrs Carrett scream and wanted to know if everything was all right. Under threat from the appellant she replied everything was all right. All three then went upstairs and Mrs Carrett was asked where her money was. The appellant and McGuire then used the toilet and on their return said that they would tie her up and she was not to telephone the police. They tied her ankles and hands and put socks in her mouth. They went out of the front door warning her not to telephone, saying that they would come back and do something to her little boy if she phoned the police within five minutes ...

Section 8 of the Theft Act 1968 begins: 'A person is guilty of robbery if he steals ...' He steals when he acts in accordance with the basic definition of theft in s 1 of the Theft Act; that is to say when he dishonestly appropriates property belonging to another with the intention of permanently depriving the other of it. It thus becomes necessary to consider what is 'appropriation' or, according to s 3, 'any assumption by a person of the rights of an owner'. An assumption of the rights of an owner describes the conduct of a person towards a particular article. It is conduct which usurps the rights of the owner. To say that the conduct is over and done with as soon as he lays hands upon the property, or when he manifests an intention to deal with it as his, is contrary to common sense and to the natural meaning of words. A thief who steals a motor car first opens the door. Is it to be said that the act of starting up the motor is no more a part of the theft?

In the present case there can be little doubt that if the appellant had been interrupted after the seizure of the jewellery box the jury would have been entitled to find that the appellant and his accomplice were assuming the rights of an owner at the time when the jewellery box was seized. However, the act of appropriation does not suddenly cease. It is a continuous act and it is a matter for the jury to decide whether or not the act of appropriation has finished. Moreover, it is quite clear that the intention to deprive the owner permanently, which accompanies the assumption of the owner's rights was a continuing one at all material times. This court therefore rejects the contention that the theft had ceased by the time the lady was tied up. As a matter of common sense the appellant was in the course of committing theft; he was stealing.

There remains the question whether there was robbery. Quite clearly the jury were at liberty to find the appellant guilty of robbery relying upon the force used when he put his hand over Mrs Carrett's mouth to restrain her from calling for help. We also think that they were entitled to rely upon the act of tying her up provided they were satisfied (and it is difficult to see how they could not be satisfied) that the force so used was to enable them to steal. If they were still engaged in the act of stealing the force was clearly used to enable them to continue to assume the rights of the owner and permanently to deprive Mrs Carrett of her box, which is what they began to do when they first seized it ...

Corcoran v Anderton (1980) 71 Cr App R 104 (DC)

Watkins J: ... At 7.55 pm on 22 February 1979, Mrs Hall was in Conran Street in Manchester. She was carrying a handbag. Two youths came along, one the defendant, Christopher Corcoran, and another his co-accused Peter Partington. They had agreed beforehand to steal Mrs Hall's handbag. They began to carry out their purpose. Partington struck her in the back, took hold of and tugged at her handbag causing her to release it. Corcoran was present and participated. Mrs Hall understandably screamed when this attack was made upon her and fell. At that these two youths ran away. So Mrs Hall managed to recover her handbag. At no time, say the justices, did Partington have sole control of the handbag. They were finally of the opinion ... that the appropriation of the bag was complete when Partington pulled at it so causing Mrs Hall to release it ...

They were asked to state a case. They did and asked this court this question: 'Could the tugging at the handbag, accompanied by force, amount to robbery, notwithstanding the fact that the co-accused did not have sole control of the bag at any time?'

... Robbery, as the Theft Act 1968 provides by s 8(1), is committed if a person steals and immediately before or at the time of doing so and in order to do so force is used on any person.

... [The] circumstances [found by the justices] involve the use of force upon the person of Mrs Hall so that she lost her grip upon her handbag accompanied by the intention in the minds of both the appellant and his companion to steal, that is to say to take the handbag, by force if necessary, away from Mrs Hall and permanently deprive her of that handbag or its contents ...

... [C]onfining myself to the facts as found by the justices in the instant case, I think that an 'appropriation' takes place when an accused snatches a woman's handbag completely from her grasp, so that she no longer has physical control of it because it has fallen to the ground. What has been involved in such activity as that, bearing in mind the dishonest state of mind of the accused, is an assumption of the rights of the owner, a taking of the property of another ... In my judgment there cannot possibly be, save for the instance where a handbag is carried away from the scene of it, a clearer instance of robbery than that which these justices found was committed.

Turning to the actual question posed to this court, 'Could the tugging at the handbag, accompanied by force, amount to robbery, notwithstanding the fact that the co-accused did not have sole control of the bag at any time?' In my opinion, which may be contrary to some notions of what constitutes a sufficient appropriation to satisfy the definition of that word in s 3(1) of the Theft Act the forcible tugging of the handbag of itself could in the circumstances be a sufficient exercise of control by the accused person so as to amount to an assumption by him of the rights of the owner, and therefore an appropriation of the property ...

Eveleigh LJ: I agree. Each, that is to say the lady and the defendant, was trying to exclude the other from exclusive claim to the bag. The lady was treating the bag as hers, as indeed it was, and resisting any efforts of his to deprive her of it. He, on the other hand, was treating the bag as his and seeking to overcome her efforts to retain it. He was thereby exercising the rights which belonged to the owner. She too was doing so. She was doing it lawfully, he was doing it unlawfully. He was, in my view, appropriating that bag ...

FORCE

It has been said by the Court of Appeal that the word 'force' is used in its ordinary sense in the Theft Act and so does not usually require explanation.

R v Dawson and James (1976) 64 Cr App R 170 (CA)

The point at issue was whether 'jostling' amounted to the use of force.

Lawton LJ: [Force] is a word in ordinary use. It is a word which juries understand. The learned judge left it to the jury to say whether jostling a man in the way which the victim described to such an extent that he had difficulty in keeping his balance could be said to be the use of force.

... It was a matter for the jury. They were to use their common sense and knowledge of the word. We cannot say that their decision as to whether force was used was wrong. They were entitled to the view that force was used.

Other points were discussed in the case as to whether the force had been used for the purpose of distracting the victim's attention or whether it was for the purpose of overcoming resistance. Those sorts of refinements may have been relevant under the old law, but so far as the new law is concerned the sole question is whether the accused used force on any person in order to steal. That issue in this case was left to the jury. They found in favour of the Crown.

We cannot say that this verdict was either unsafe or unsatisfactory. Accordingly the appeal is dismissed.

R v Clouden [1987] Crim LR 56 (CA)

Facts: The appellant was seen to follow a woman who was carrying a shopping basket in her left hand. He approached her from behind and wrenched the basket down and out of her grasp with both hands and ran off with it. He was charged in two counts with robbery and theft respectively and convicted on the first count of robbery. He appealed on the grounds (i) that there was insufficient evidence of resistance to the snatching of the bag to constitute force on the person under s 8 of the Theft Act 1968; and (ii) that the learned judge's direction to the jury on the requirement of force on the person was inadequate and confused.

Held ,(dismissing the appeal): the old cases distinguished between force on the actual person and force on the property which in fact causes force on the person but, following *Dawson & James* (1976) 64 Cr App R 170, the court should direct attention to the words of the statute without referring to the old authorities. The old distinctions have gone. Whether the defendant used force on any person in order to steal is an issue that should be left to the jury. The judge's direction to the jury was adequate. He told the jury quite clearly at the outset what the statutory definition was, though thereafter he merely used the word force and did not use the expression 'on the person'.

BLACKMAIL

Section 21 of the Theft Act 1968

(1) A person is guilty of blackmail if, with a view to gain for himself or another or with intent to cause loss to another, he makes any unwarranted demand with menaces; and for this purpose a demand with menaces is unwarranted unless the person making it does so in the belief:

(a) that he has reasonable grounds for making the demand; and

(b) that the use of the menaces is a proper means of reinforcing the demand.

(2) The nature of the act or omission demanded is immaterial, and it is also immaterial whether the menaces relate to action to be taken by the person making the demand.

(3) A person guilty of blackmail shall on conviction on indictment be liable to imprisonment for a term not exceeding 14 years.

Menaces

R v Lawrence and Pomroy (1971) 57 Cr App R 64 (CA)

Facts: Pomroy repaired the roof of the house of one Thorn. Thorn was dissatisfied with the work and withheld £70 from the agreed price for the work. One evening Pomroy went to Thorn's house and said 'Unless you pay me within seven days ... you will have to look over your shoulder before you step out of doors'. A few days later Pomroy again went to Thorn's house. This time, Pomroy was accompanied by Lawrence, who was a big man. When Thorn again refused to pay the balance of £70, Lawrence said 'Step outside the house and we will sort this matter out'. When Thorn refused, Lawrence said menacingly: 'Come on mate, come outside'. At that point, police officers who had been hiding in Thorn's house, emerged and arrested the appellants.

Cairns LJ: ... The word 'menaces' is an ordinary English word which any jury can be expected to understand. In exceptional cases where because of special knowledge in special circumstances what would be a menace to an ordinary person is not a menace to the person to whom it is addressed, or where the converse may be true, it is no doubt necessary to spell out the meaning of the word ...

R v Clear [1968] 1 QB 670 (CA)

Sellers LJ: ... Words or conduct which would not intimidate or influence anyone to respond to the demand would not be menaces ... but threats and conduct of such a nature and extent that the mind of an ordinary person of normal stability and courage might be influenced or made apprehensive so as to accede unwillingly to the demand would be sufficient for a jury's consideration ... [The victim must be] deprived of 'that element of free, voluntary action which alone constitutes consent' in the words used by Wilde B in *R v Walton and Ogden* (1863) Le & Ca 288.

There may be special circumstances unknown to an accused which would make the threats innocuous and unavailing for the accused's demand, but such circumstances would have no bearing on the accused's state of mind and on his intention. If an accused knew that what he threatened would have no effect on the victim it might be different ...

R v Garwood [1987] 1 WLR 319 (CA)

Facts: The appellant was convicted of blackmail, having obtained money from the victim by 'menaces'. The jury found that the victim was rather timid and that other people may not have found the appellant's behaviour menacing.

Lord Lane CJ: ... In our judgment it is only rarely that a judge will need to enter on a definition of the word 'menaces'. It is an ordinary word of which the meaning will be clear to any jury ...

It seems to us that there are two possible occasions on which a further direction on the meaning of the word menaces may be required. The first is where the threats might have affected the mind of an ordinary person of normal stability but did not affect the person actually addressed. In such circumstances that would amount to a sufficient menace: see *R v Clear* [1968] 1 QB 670.

The second situation is where the threats in fact affected the mind of the victim, although they would not have affected the mind of a person of normal stability. In that case, in our judgment, the existence of menaces is proved providing that the accused man was aware of the likely effect of his action upon the victim.

If the recorder had told the jury that [the victim's] undue timidity did not prevent them from finding 'menaces' proved, provided that the appellant realised the effect his actions were having on [the victim], all would have been well ...

Unwarranted demand

It will only be in very rare cases that 'menaces [will be] a proper means of reinforcing the demand' so that the demand becomes a warranted one under s 21(1). It would not be enough that one is demanding back property to which one is entitled, since the making of menaces is not a proper means of achieving that objective: see *R v Lawrence* (1971) 57 Cr App R 64 (*above*); *R v Harvey* (1980) 72 Cr App R 139.

R v Harvey (1980) 72 Cr App R 139 (CA)

Facts: The appellants agreed with one Scott that they would pay him £20,000 to procure a large quantity of cannabis. Scott failed to supply the cannabis. The appellants kidnapped Scott, along with his wife and small child, and they subjected Scott to threats of what would happen to wife and child if he did not give them their money back.

Bingham J: ... [T]wo points emerge with clarity: (1) [s 21(1) of the Theft Act 1968] is concerned with the belief of the individual defendant in the particular case ... It matters not what the reasonable man, or any man other than the defendant, would believe save in so far as that may throw light on what the defendant in fact believed. Thus the factual question of the defendant's belief should be left to the jury ... (2) In order to exonerate a defendant from liability his belief must be that the use of the menaces is a 'proper' means of reinforcing the demand. 'Proper' ... is ... plainly a word of wide meaning, certainly wider than (for example) 'lawful'. But the greater includes the less and no act which was not believed to be lawful could be believed to be proper within the meaning of the subsection. Thus no assistance is given to any defendant, even a fanatic or a deranged idealist, who knows or suspects that his threat, or the act threatened, is criminal, but believes it to be justified by his end or his peculiar circumstances. The test is not what he regards as justified, but what he believes to be proper. And where, as here, the threats were to do acts which any sane man knows to be against the laws of every civilised country, no jury would hesitate long before dismissing the contention that the defendant genuinely believed the threats to be a proper means of reinforcing even a legitimate demand.

... [T]he jury should have been directed that the demand with menaces was not to be regarded as unwarranted unless the Crown satisfied them in respect of each defendant that the defendant did not make the demand with menaces in the genuine belief both: (a) that he had had reasonable grounds for making the demand; and (b) that the use of the menaces was in the circumstances a proper (meaning for present purposes a lawful, and not a criminal) means of reinforcing the demand ...

CHAPTER 18

HANDLING STOLEN GOODS

Section 22 of the Theft Act 1968

(1) A person handles stolen goods if (otherwise than in the course of the stealing) knowing or believing them to be stolen goods he dishonestly receives the goods, or dishonestly undertakes or assists in their retention, removal, disposal or realisation by or for the benefit of another person, or if he arranges to do so.

(2) A person guilty of handling stolen goods shall on conviction on indictment be liable to imprisonment for a term not exceeding 14 years.

STOLEN GOODS

The scope of s 23 is extended beyond the literal words of s 22 by the provisions of s 24 of the Theft Act 1968.

Section 24 of the Theft Act 1968: scope of offences relating to stolen goods

(1) The provisions of this Act relating to goods which have been stolen shall apply whether the stealing occurred in England or Wales or elsewhere, and whether it occurred before or after the commencement of this Act, provided that the stealing (if not an offence under this Act) amounted to an offence where and at the time when the goods were stolen; and references to stolen goods shall be construed accordingly.

(2) For the purposes of those provisions references to stolen goods shall include, in addition to the goods originally stolen and parts of them (whether in their original state or not):

 (a) any other goods which directly or indirectly represent or have at any time represented the stolen goods in the hands of the thief as being the proceeds of any disposal or realisation of the whole or part of the goods stolen or of goods so representing the stolen goods; and

 (b) any other goods which directly or indirectly represent or have at any time represented the stolen goods in the hands of a handler of the stolen goods or any part of them as being the proceeds of any disposal or realisation of the whole or part of the stolen goods handled by him or of goods so representing them.

(3) But no goods shall be regarded as having continued to be stolen goods after they have been restored to the person from whom they were stolen or to other lawful possession or custody, or after that person and any other person claiming through him have otherwise ceased as regards those goods to have any right to restitution in respect of the theft.

(4) For the purposes of the provisions of this Act relating to goods which have been stolen (including subsections (1) to (3) above) goods obtained in England and Wales or elsewhere either by blackmail or in the circumstances described in s 15(1) of this Act shall be regarded as stolen; and 'steal', 'theft' and 'thief' shall be construed accordingly.

Stolen

'Stolen' means that the goods have been the subject of theft (under s 1 of the Theft Act 1968) or (by virtue of the extended definition of theft in s 24(4) of the Act) have been obtained by deception (under s 15 of the Act) or have been obtained by blackmail (under s 21 of the Act).

There can be no conviction under s 23 unless the prosecution can prove that the goods have been stolen. However, where all of the other requirements of handling are satisfied (ie the only one missing is that the goods are stolen), the defendant may be convicted of attempted handling under s 1 of the Criminal Attempts Act 1981 (*cf R v Shivpuri* [1987] AC 1), or the handling may amount to a fresh appropriation (and so theft) of the goods.

A case where the goods were not 'stolen' was *Walters v Lunt* [1951] 2 All ER 645.

Walters v Lunt and Another [1951] 2 All ER 645

Facts: The defendants were charged (under legislation which preceded the Theft Act 1968) with receiving stolen goods. The goods in question had been taken by a child aged seven. A child of that age is conclusively presumed to be incapable of committing a criminal offence (see s 50 of the Children and Young Persons Act 1933).

The Divisional Court held that since the person who took the goods could not be guilty of theft, the goods were not stolen goods. It followed that the defendants could not be guilty of receiving stolen goods. Lord Goddard CJ pointed out, however, that the defendants, by taking possession of the goods and keeping the goods (and thereby appropriating them), could have been charged instead with theft of those goods.

Goods

The word 'goods' is partly defined in s 34(2)(b) of the Theft Act 1968: 'goods', except in so far as the context otherwise requires, includes money and every other description of property except land, and includes things severed from the land by stealing.

Otherwise than in the course of stealing

The 'stealing' to which these words refer is the stealing by which the goods first became stolen goods. Thus, a thief is not also a handler while doing the act or acts which amount to the original theft. So, for example, if two people break into a house and one takes a painting off a wall and hands it to her accomplice, the accomplice is not guilty of an offence under s 22: the original theft is, in effect, still in progress.

In *R v Cash* [1985] QB 801 it was held that, unless there is, on the evidence, doubt as to whether the defendant is the original thief or a subsequent handler, the prosecution does not have to prove that the defendant was innocent of the original theft.

However, if there is, on the evidence, doubt as to whether the defendant is a thief or a handler, he may be convicted of theft: if a person handles stolen goods, that act of handling is also an act of appropriation and therefore (if the other elements of theft are present) also amounts to a theft. Thus, a thief is not a handler in respect of what he does during the course of the original theft, but even a handler is a thief (since his acts amount to a fresh appropriation of the goods): see *Stapylton v O'Callaghan* [1973] 2 All ER 782.

R v Cash [1985] QB 801 (CA)

Lord Lane CJ: ... The point taken by counsel for the appellant is concerned with the words 'otherwise than in the course of the stealing'. He submits that before there can be a conviction for handling, the prosecution has to prove affirmatively that the defendant was not the thief or a party to the theft, and if that is not proved the charge of handling is not made out. It is submitted that the words 'otherwise than in the course of the stealing', constitute an essential ingredient of the offence of handling and that a burden is placed on the prosecution to prove this negative averment ...

... [I]t was open to the jury to infer from the facts that the appellant was the guilty handler. There was no issue whether the receipt of the stolen goods was in the course of the stealing. It was not suggested to or by any witness that the appellant was the thief or that the property came into his possession in the course of the stealing; there was no evidence that the appellant was the burglar. Furthermore, when he went into the dock, there was a presumption that he was innocent of any charge of burglary as well as of handling. There was no evidence to displace that presumption so far as burglary was concerned. The presumption was displaced by evidence so far as dishonest handling was concerned. If, therefore, there was no evidence that the appellant was the burglar or had taken part in the burglary, the jury, as a matter of logic and common sense, were entitled to find that his handling which was not in dispute was a handling otherwise than in the course of the stealing ...

If the appellant's contentions are correct, moreover, it would seem to follow that the prosecution might in some cases have the task of disproving burglary before a charge of handling could be sustained. It is difficult to imagine what evidence could be adduced. Parliament could not have intended that the burglar or burglars should be called to exculpate the defendant, or that the prosecution would have to call evidence, for example, supporting an alibi, in order to demonstrate that the defendant was not a party to the burglary ...

In our judgment, Parliament intended by the words of s 22(1) to make it clear that, despite the wording of the rest of that section and of s 1 and s 3 of the Theft Act 1968, where the evidence shows that a defendant was simply a party to the original theft, he is not to be convicted as a handler and therefore subject to the greater maximum penalty which handling carries ...

For these reasons we are of the view that in the ordinary case there is no burden placed on the prosecution by the words 'otherwise than in the course of the stealing' – which is perhaps why they appear in brackets. Of course they may be important words where ... a jury does have to decide whether a particular defendant was indeed a thief or a handler; but where in reality the defendant must be acquitted if he cannot be shown to have been a handler, the words have little importance and the jury should not even be told about them.

We turn now to [the appellant's] submission that in a 'recent possession' case, the indictment should include counts alleging burglary as alternatives to those of handling and that in the absence of such counts, the judge should invite the jury to consider whether the evidence proves not handling, but burglary, in which case the appellant would have been entitled to a finding of not guilty.

As Lord Goddard CJ made clear in *R v Seymour* [1954] 1 WLR 678 there are circumstances where the defendant is in possession of property so recently after it is stolen that it is the inevitable inference that he was the thief, where, for example, he is found within a few hundred yards of the scene of the theft and minutes after the theft took place. In such circumstances, no doubt, alternative counts might be appropriate. In such cases, if there were only counts of handling in the indictment, the judge would direct the jury that if they took the view that the defendant was the thief, he should be acquitted of the handling.

The instant case was not that type of case at all. The goods were found in the possession of the appellant on 25 February 1983. None of the property was stolen more recently than 16 February 1983. It seems to us that in those circumstances it was not properly open to the jury to infer that the appellant was the burglar rather than the guilty receiver/handler. The judge was right to ignore the suggestion that the appellant might have been the thief or burglar. If there had been alternative counts, it would have been correct for the judge to leave only the handling counts to the jury ...

Petition: The Appeal Committee of the House of Lords (**Lord Fraser of Tullybelton, Lord Roskill** and **Lord Bridge of Harwich**) dismissed a petition by the appellant for leave to appeal.

Ryan and French v DPP [1994] Crim LR 457 (DC)

Facts: A month after a dinghy had been stolen, the loser saw it in the possession of the appellants. They claimed that the appellant French had bought it a year previously. They were charged with both theft and handling of the dinghy. Justices convicted them of the handling and acquitted them of the theft.

On appeal by way of case stated it was argued: (1) that the justices would have had to have found as a fact that the appellants were not the thieves, which they could not have done, as the evidence was equally consistent with theft as handling; (2) the justices should have directed themselves to withdraw the count of handling, the evidence being more consistent with theft.

The question certified was: 'can a conviction of handling be justified on the evidence given, having regard to the fact that the appellants were acquitted on the count of theft?'

Held, dismissing the appeal:

(1) It was well understood that the prosecution did not have to prove that handlers were not thieves.

(2) There are cases where it is appropriate to withdraw a count or charge of handling when both theft and handling are charged. This was not such a case. There was sufficient evidence to support a *prima facie* case on each charge and it was for the justices to decide on the basis of their assessment of the witnesses and the inferences they were prepared to draw if either charge were made out.

R v Fernandez [1997] 1 Cr App R 123 (CA)

Hobhouse LJ: This appeal ... raises points upon the relationship between the offences of theft and handling under the Theft Act 1968...

The appellant was tried ... on an indictment which included eight counts. The counts with which this appeal is concerned were counts 3, 4 and 5. Count 3 charged him with an offence of robbery contrary to s 8(1) of the Theft Act: it alleged that he had robbed an employee of the Allied Irish Bank on November 10, 1994 of a quantity of money. Count 4 charged him with having a firearm with intent to commit an indictable offence, namely theft, on the same occasion, contrary to s 18(1) of the Firearms Act 1968. Count 5 was a count of handling stolen goods contrary to s 22(1) of the Theft Act. The particulars alleged that the appellant had:

> On a day between the 9th day of November 1994 and the 12th day of November 1994 dishonestly received stolen goods, namely a quantity of money belonging to Allied Irish Bank, knowing or believing the same to be stolen goods.

The drafting of count 5 shows that it was intended to be an alternative to count 3 and counsel for the Crown in his opening at the trial so stated to the jury...

The submissions in this Court of [counsel] on behalf of the appellant were:

> (1) A defendant cannot in respect of the same goods commit an offence under both sections 8 and 22 of the Theft Act unless the possession of those goods by another has intervened.
>
> (2) A court cannot lawfully convict a defendant of theft or robbery after a jury has returned a verdict of handling the same goods...

In *Dolan* (1976) 62 Cr App R 36 ... the Court of Appeal ... said (pp 38 to 39):

> ... In the course of his argument [counsel for the appellant] submitted that as a matter of law a man cannot be guilty both of stealing and receiving the same goods... Although strictly the point does not arise in this appeal, it has been argued, and we have reached a view which we propose to state very shortly.
>
> ... The combined effect of the Criminal Law Act 1967, s 1 and the Theft Act 1968, s 22(1) is that, as Professor Smith suggests in paragraph 487 of his *Law of Theft* (1972), a thief 'could be convicted of handling the goods stolen by him by receiving them - *if the evidence warranted this conclusion*' (our italics).
>
> If the defendant's handling of the goods occurs only in the course of the stealing he cannot be found guilty of handling by receiving: see Theft Act 1968 s 22(1). But, if he handles them alter, ie after the stealing, he commits an offence under the subsection. It is, therefore, perfectly possible for a man to be guilty of stealing and receiving the same goods...

In *Shelton* (1986) 83 Cr App R 379 Lawton LJ summarised the law at p 385, saying:

> ... a jury should be told that a handler can be a thief, but he cannot be convicted of being both a thief and a handler.

In the present case, there was no *legal* inconsistency between counts 3 and 4 on the one hand and count 5 on the other. The inconsistency arose simply from the way in which the Crown was, perfectly properly, putting its case. The Crown said that it had proved that the appellant was one of the robbers and that the robbers had been carrying guns. The Crown said that if the jury were not satisfied that he was a robber, they must at least be satisfied that he knew about the robbery and, as the notes had been found in his flat, they must at least be satisfied of his guilt under s 22. The counts, on this presentation, simply represented alternative views of the facts. In the present case the appellant said that at no stage had he had anything to do with the robbery or the currency notes stolen during the robbery ...

There can be no doubt that the judge should have properly directed the jury upon the relationship between counts 5 and 3. He should have explained to them that handling has to be otherwise than in the course of the stealing and, if importance was being attached to it, the implication of the use of the word 'received' in count 5. He should have directed them that count 5 was charged as an alternative to counts 3 and 4 and that he would not take a verdict from them on count 5 until they had concluded their deliberations and decided upon their verdict on counts 3 and 4.

It does not follow however ... that the jury's verdict on count 5 entitled the appellant as a matter of law to verdicts of not guilty on counts 3 and 4. The appellant was in the charge of the jury on counts 3 and 4 and justice required that, if they were able to agree, the jury should return verdicts on those counts. They were undoubtedly the more serious counts. The jury had not been directed to treat the counts as alternatives. The summing-up had not identified for the jury any considerations in relation to count 5 which involved any inconsistency between verdicts of guilty on all three counts. Indeed, the summing-up had been inadequate in relation to count 5 in that it included no adequate direction as to the Crown's case on that count...

Dishonesty

The test of dishonesty for the purpose of s 22 is the same as for theft, as to which see *R v Ghosh* [1982] QB 1053.

R v Roberts (1985) 84 Cr App R 117 (CA)

Facts: Two Renoir paintings, valued at £51,000, were stolen in the course of a burglary. The insurance company offered a 10% reward for their return. Some three months later the appellant telephoned the loss adjuster and told him that he had the paintings. The appellant subsequently handed the paintings over to the loss adjuster and was arrested by the police.

O'Connor LJ: ... [W]e start with the proposition that for the subjective test to arise, somewhere along the line the defendant has to say 'I did not know that anybody would regard what I was doing as dishonest'. We have come to the conclusion that no one can properly say that, if what he is doing is receiving stolen property knowing it to be stolen and then trying to sell it. A person may come into possession of stolen property innocently and the test for that would be normally as to what he did with it. If, for example, he had taken it straight to the police and said 'I have found this in my motor car', then the question would plainly arise because nobody would say that a person acting in that fashion was acting dishonestly if it was true. But for somebody to put forward this kind of assertion is, in our judgment, really not possible. In fact, it is not only not possible, but it was not done. At no stage in the present case did this appellant say on the facts, 'I received the stolen goods and was trying to sell them for my own profit, but I did not know that anybody would think that dishonest'. He had never raised the problem and unless the problem is properly raised it does not seem to us that it is necessary for the trial judge to embark on the full *Ghosh* direction.

Knowing or believing that the goods are stolen

Not only must it proved that the goods were, in fact, stolen (see *above*); it must also be proved that the defendant knew that the goods were stolen or believed them to be stolen.

Two important points have to be made regarding this element of the offence. The first is that mere suspicion that the goods may be stolen falls short of amounting to believing that they are stolen: see *Atwal v Massey* [1976] 3 All ER 881; *R v Grainge* [1974] 1 All ER 928; *R v Hall* (1985) 81 Cr App R 260; *R v Griffiths* (1974) 60 Cr App R 14.

Second, the defendant must have the knowledge or belief that the goods are stolen at the time he carries out the acts which allegedly amount to an offence under s 22: see *R v Brook* [1993] Crim LR 455; *R v Williams* [1994] Crim LR 934

Atwal v Massey [1971] 3 All ER 881 (DC)

Facts: A stolen electric kettle was left by the roadside by the thief for collection by the appellant, who paid the thief £1.50 for it.

Lord Widgery CJ: ... The question the justices have asked us is:

> Whether the fact that the appellant ought to have known that the kettle was stolen is sufficient to render him guilty of an offence under s 22 of the Theft Act 1968 ...

... It is not sufficient to establish an offence under s 22 that the goods were received in circumstances which would have put a reasonable man on his enquiry. The question is a subjective one: was the appellant aware of the theft or did he believe the goods to be stolen or did he, suspecting the goods to be stolen, deliberately shut his eyes to the consequences.

R v Grainge [1974] 1 All ER 928 (CA)

Eveleigh J: ... On 7 March 1973 the appellant, his co-defendant (a man named O'Connor), and a third man, entered a shop in Sheffield which sold office machinery and stationery. During the course of the visit O'Connor stole a pocket calculating machine valued at £59. The loss of the machine was soon noticed and the salesman went out of the shop into the street to search for the three men. Having seen them he noticed that one of the men passed the calculator to the appellant ...

... The summing up as a whole could well have left the jury with the impression that suspicious circumstances, irrespective of whether the accused himself appreciated they were suspicious, imposed a duty as a matter of law to act and enquire and that failure so to do was to be treated as knowledge or belief ...

[Going on to deal with the second ground of appeal, his Lordship said:]

In the judgment of this court the [trial judge] ought to have made it plain that it was at the moment of receipt and not at any time during the handling thereafter that guilty knowledge had to be proved ...

R v Hall (1985) 81 Cr App R 260 (CA)

Boreham J: ... We think that a jury should be directed along these lines. A man may be said to know that goods are stolen when he is told by someone with first-hand knowledge (someone such as the thief or the burglar) that such is the case. Belief, of course, is something short of knowledge. It may be said to be the state of mind of a person who says to himself: 'I cannot say I know for certain that these goods are stolen, but there can be no other reasonable conclusion in the light of all the circumstances, in the light of all that I have heard and seen'. Either of those two states of mind is enough to satisfy the words of the statute. The second is enough (that is, belief) even if the defendant says to himself: 'Despite all that I have seen and all that I have heard, I refuse to believe what my brain tells me is obvious'. What is not enough, of course, is mere suspicion: 'I suspect that these goods may be stolen, but it may be on the other hand that they are not'. That state of mind, of course, does not fall within the words 'knowing or believing'.

R v Griffiths (1974) 60 Cr App R 14 (CA)

Facts: The appellant had been charged with handling a pair of candlesticks stolen from a church in Cheltenham. In evidence, the appellant had said that he might have had suspicions, but the suspicions were not related to any criminal offence.

James LJ: ... To direct the jury that the offence is committed if the defendant, suspecting that the goods were stolen, deliberately shut his eyes to the circumstances as an alternative to knowing or believing the goods were stolen is a misdirection. To direct the jury that, in common sense and in law, they may find that the defendant knew or believed the goods to be stolen because he deliberately closed his eyes to the circumstances is a perfectly proper direction.

R v Brook [1993] Crim LR 455 (CA)

Facts: The defendant was found in possession of a carrier bag containing stolen cheque books and cheque cards. The bag was in his briefcase, which was in his car. His explanation was that his wife had found the bag in a public lavatory, had told him what was in it and, at the defendant's suggestion, put it in the back of the car while he decided what to do with it.

Held: It was clear that a person was guilty of handling only if he believed goods to be stolen at the time he received them: supervening belief or dishonesty after receipt was not enough.

Section 24(1) of the Theft Act 1968: territorial jurisdiction

If a thief steals property in a country other than England & Wales but the defendant receives that stolen property (or its proceeds) in England or Wales, then (assuming the other elements of the offence of handling are made out) the defendant can be convicted of handling those goods provided that the original theft was against the law of the country where that theft took place.

Section 24(2) of the Theft Act 1968: proceeds of stolen goods

Goods come within the definition of stolen goods if either:

(a) they are the goods which were originally stolen; or

(b) they represent the goods which were originally stolen and are in the hands of the original thief or someone who is handling them dishonestly.

So if a car is stolen and is then part-exchanged for a different car, the second car comes within the definition of stolen goods only if it is in the hands of the person who stole the first car or it is in the hands of someone who knows (or believes) that it was acquired in part-exchange for a stolen car.

Section 24(3) of the Theft Act 1968: goods restored to their owner, etc

Goods cease to be 'stolen' if they have been restored to lawful possession; any act after that restoration to lawful possession cannot amount to an offence under s 22 (although since the decision of the House of Lords in *R v Shivpuri* [1987] AC 1 it could amount to an attempt to handle stolen goods under the Criminal Attempts Act 1981).

Attorney General's Reference (No 1 of 1974) [1974] QB 744 (CA)

Lord Widgery CJ: ... The facts of the present case ... are these: a police constable found an unlocked, unattended car containing packages of new clothing which he suspected, and which in fact subsequently proved to be stolen. The officer removed the rotor arm from the vehicle to immobilise it, and kept observation. After about 10 minutes, the accused appeared, got into the van and attempted to start the engine. When questioned by the officer, he gave an implausible explanation, and was arrested.

[The defendant was charged, *inter alia*, with receiving stolen goods, namely the clothing, knowing them to be stolen.]

[His Lordship quoted s 24(3) of the Theft Act 1968 and went on to say:]

We are satisfied that despite the absence of another and perhaps more appropriate verb [than 'restore'], the effect of s 24(3) is to enable a defendant to plead that the goods had ceased to be stolen goods if the facts are that they were taken by a police officer in the course of his duty and reduced into possession by him ...

In our judgment it depended primarily on the intentions of the police officer. If the police officer seeing these goods in the back of the car had made up his mind that he would take them into custody, that he would reduce them into his possession or control, take charge of them so that they could not be removed and so that he would have the disposal of them, then it would be a perfectly proper conclusion to say that he had taken possession of the goods. On the other hand, if the truth of the matter is that he was of an entirely open mind at that stage as to whether the goods were to be seized or not and was of an entirely open mind as to whether he should take possession of them or not, but merely stood by so that when the driver of the car appeared he could ask certain questions of that driver as to the nature of the goods and why they were there, then there is no reason whatever to suggest that he had taken the goods into his possession or control. It may be, of course, that he had both objects in mind. It is possible in a case like this that the police officer may have intended by removing the rotor arm both to prevent the car from being driven away and to enable him to assert control over the woollen goods as such. But if the jury came to the conclusion that the proper explanation of what had happened was that the police officer had not intended at that stage to reduce the goods into his possession or to assume the control of them, and at that stage was merely concerned to ensure that the driver, if he appeared, could not get away without answering questions, then in that case the proper conclusion of the jury would have been to the effect that the goods had not been reduced into the possession of the police and therefore a defence under s 24(3) of the Theft Act 1968 would not be of use to this particular defendant ...

THE FORMS OF HANDLING

Section 22 can, for practical purposes, be regarded as creating two offences:

(1) dishonestly receiving stolen goods (or arranging to do so);

(2) dishonestly undertaking or assisting in their retention, removal, disposal or realisation by or for the benefit of another person (or arranging to do so).

Receiving

The word 'receiving' is not defined in the Theft Act 1968. However, the same word was used under the legislation which preceded the 1968 Act, so the old cases on the meaning of receiving are still good law. The essence of receiving is exercising control over the goods.

R v Frost and Hale (1964) 48 Cr App R 284 (CA)

Lord Parker CJ: ... [Where a defendant is charged with receiving stolen goods, the jury should be directed that] they must be satisfied that the physical possession was such as to give [the defendant] control as against the persons [he was] assisting, or, if not against them, joint control with them ...

Hobson v Impett (1957) 41 Cr App R 138 (DC)

Facts: On 14 January 1957 the appellant helped one George Porritt to unload from a cart a sack which contained some stolen ingots and to take the ingots into Porritt's house. By the time the unloading was finished, the appellant knew that the sack contained ingots and that they were stolen. The next day, the appellant helped Porritt to load some of the ingots into a motor car. The appellant travelled as a passenger in the car, and although there was no evidence that he touched them again or took part in offering them for sale, he was for a time alone in the car with the ingots.

Lord Goddard CJ: ... It is not the law that, if a man knows goods are stolen and puts his hands on them, that in itself makes him guilty of receiving, because it does not follow that he is taking them into his control. The control may still be in the thief or the man whom he is assisting, and the alleged receiver may be only picking the goods up without taking them into his possession, the goods all the time remaining in the possession of the person whom he is helping ... It cannot be the law that merely because a man picks up goods which he knows are stolen he is receiving the goods ...

Arranging to receive

The goods must have been stolen by the time the arrangement to receive them is made (although if they are not, a charge of conspiracy to handle stolen goods may be appropriate): see *R v Park* (1987) 87 Cr App R 164.

R v Park (1988) 87 Cr App R 164(CA)

Woolf LJ: [His Lordship rejected a submission made by counsel for the Crown that if you had an arrangement made before the goods are stolen and if that arrangement is one which has not been terminated, then the consequence of that is that if the goods are subsequently stolen, the person who is a party to the arrangement can be guilty, subject to his knowing or believing that the goods which are to be the subject of the arrangement are to be stolen and he is also acting dishonestly. His Lordship said:] In my view, this interpretation ... is not correct ... [T]he guilty knowledge must exist at the time that the offence is committed ...

[Section 22 of the Theft Act 1968] does not alter the requirement ... that the subject-matter of the handling must in fact be stolen goods. It is not possible to rely upon an activity which took place prior to the theft as in itself amounting to the necessary *actus reus* to create handling, albeit that it may be possible to take advantage of the arrangements previously made when the theft has taken place. The appropriate charge in the circumstances where there is conduct prior to the theft is to lay a count of conspiracy ...

...[T]his court has no doubt that it is not possible to rely on an arrangement made before the theft in order to establish a charge of handling where the goods were only stolen after the arrangement had been made and not before.

Undertaking or assisting in retention, removal, disposal or realisation by or for the benefit of another person

Where a defendant is charged with the second form of handling, the charge or indictment will not differentiate between the various ways in which the second form of handling may be committed (see the specimen indictments in Archbold and in Blackstone's *Criminal Practice*).

Whatever the exact nature of the defendant's actions, for a conviction under the second limb of s 22, those actions must be performed by way of assisting someone else or for someone else's benefit. If the act is done by the accused himself and is for his own benefit, a charge under the second limb of s 22 cannot be sustained.

R v Bloxham [1983] 1 AC 109 (HL)

Lord Bridge of Harwich: My Lords, in January 1977 the appellant purchased a motor car for £1,300. He paid the seller £500 in cash and was to pay the balance when the seller produced the car's registration document, but in the event this never happened. The car had in fact been stolen. It is accepted by the Crown that the appellant did not know or believe this when he acquired the car. In December 1977 he sold the car for £200 to an unidentified third party who was prepared to take the car without any registration document.

The appellant was charged under s 22(1) of the Theft Act 1968 with handling stolen goods, the particulars of the relevant count in the indictment alleging that he:

> Dishonestly undertook or assisted in the disposal or realisation of certain stolen goods, namely a Ford Cortina motor car registered number SJH 606M, by or for the benefit of another, namely the unknown purchaser knowing or believing the same to be stolen goods.

At the trial it was submitted that the count disclosed no offence in that the disposal or realisation of the car had been for the appellant's own benefit, not for the benefit of the unknown purchaser, and that in any event the purchaser was not within the ambit of the categories of 'other person' contemplated by s 22(1). The judge ruled that the purchaser derived a benefit from the transaction, in that, although he got no title, he had the use of the car; that there was no reason to give any restricted construction to the words 'another person' in the subsection; and that, accordingly, on the undisputed facts, the appellant had undertaken the disposal or realisation of the car for the benefit of another person within the meaning of s 22(1) ...

... The [Court of Appeal] certified the following point of law of general public importance as involved in their decision:

> Does a *bona fide* purchaser for value commit an offence of dishonestly undertaking the disposal or realisation of stolen property for the benefit of another if when he sells the goods on he knows or believes them to be stolen.

... It is, I think, now well settled that this subsection creates two distinct offences, but no more than two. The first is equivalent to the old offence of receiving under s 33 of the Larceny Act 1916. The second is a new offence designed to remedy defects in the old law and can be committed in any of the various ways indicated by the words from 'undertakes' to the end of the subsection. It follows that the new offence may and should be charged in a single count embodying in the particulars as much of the relevant language of the subsection, including alternatives, as may be appropriate to the circumstances of the particular case, and that such a count will not be bad for duplicity. It was so held by Geoffrey Lane J delivering the judgment of the Court of Appeal in *R v Willis* [1972] 1 WLR 1605, and approved by the Court of Appeal in *R v Deakin* [1972] 1 WLR 1618. So far as I am aware, this practice has been generally followed ever since.

The critical words to be construed are 'undertakes ... their ... disposal or realisation ... for the benefit of another person'. Considering these words first in isolation, it seems to me that, if A sells his own goods to B, it is a somewhat strained use of language to describe this as a disposal or realisation of the goods for the benefit of B. True it is that B obtains a benefit from the transaction, but it is surely more natural to say that the disposal or realisation is for A's benefit than for B's. It is the purchase not the sale, that is for the benefit of B. It is only when A is selling as agent for a third party C that it would be entirely natural to describe the sale as a disposal or realisation for the benefit of another person.

But the words cannot, of course, be construed in isolation. They must be construed in their context, bearing in mind, as I have pointed out, that the second half of the subsection creates a single offence which can be committed in various ways. I can ignore for present purposes the concluding words 'or if he arranges to do so', which throw no light on the point at issue. The preceding words contemplate four activities (retention, removal, disposal, realisation). The offence can be committed in relation to any one of these activities in one or other of two ways. First, the offender may himself undertake the activity for the benefit of another person. Second, the activity may be undertaken by another person and the offender may assist him. Of course, if the thief or an original receiver and his friend act together in, say, removing the stolen goods, the friend may be committing the offence in both ways. But this does not invalidate the analysis and if the analysis holds good it must follow, I think, that the category of other persons contemplated by the subsection is subject to the same limitations in whichever way the offence is committed. Accordingly, a purchaser, as such, of stolen goods, cannot, in my opinion, be 'another person' within the subsection, since his act of purchase could not sensibly be described as a disposal or realisation of the stolen goods by him. Equally, therefore, even, if the sale to him could be described as a disposal or realisation for his benefit, the transaction is not, in my view, within the ambit of the subsection ...

As a general rule, ambiguities in a criminal statute are to be resolved in favour of the subject, that is in favour of the narrower rather than the wider operation of an ambiguous penal provision. But here there are, in my opinion, more specific and weightier indications which point in the same direction as the general rule.

First, it is significant that the Theft Act 1968, notwithstanding the wide ambit of the definition of theft provided by ss 1 and 3(1), specifically protects the innocent purchaser of goods who subsequently discovers that they were stolen, by s 3(2) [which his Lordship then quoted].

It follows that, though some might think that in this situation honesty would require the purchaser, once he knew the goods were stolen, to seek out the true owner and return them, the criminal law allows him to retain them with impunity for his own benefit. It hardly seems consistent with this that, if he deals with them for the benefit of a third party in some way that falls within the ambit of the activities referred to in the second half of s 22(1), he risks prosecution for handling which carries a heavier maximum penalty (14 years) than theft (10 years). The force of this consideration is not, in my view, significantly weakened by the possibility that the innocent purchaser of stolen goods who sells them after learning they were stolen may commit the quite distinct offences of obtaining by deception (if he represents that he has a good title) or, conceivably, of aiding and abetting the commission by the purchaser of the offence of handling by receiving (if both know the goods were stolen).

Second, it is clear that the words in parentheses in s 22(1) 'otherwise than in the course of the stealing' were designed to avoid subjecting thieves, in the ordinary course, to the heavier penalty provided for handlers. But most thieves realise the goods they have stolen by disposing of them to third parties. If [the ruling of the trial judge, *supra*, was] right, all such thieves are liable to prosecution as principals both for theft and for handling under the second half of s 22(1) ...

For these reasons I have reached the conclusion that any ambiguity in the relevant language of s 22(1) should be resolved in favour of the narrower meaning suggested earlier in this opinion. I would accordingly answer the certified question in the negative and allow the appeal.

Lord Diplock, **Lord Scarman** and **Lord Brandon of Oakbrook** agreed with the speech of **Lord Bridge of Harwich**.

What amounts to 'assisting'

The word 'assisting' connotes active assistance: it follows that providing a place for stolen goods to be hidden (as in *R v Pitchley* (1972) 57 Cr App R 30) or trying to deceive the police that goods are not stolen both fall within s 22 but merely failing to co-operate with a police search does not.

R v Brown [1970] 1 QB 105; [1969] 3 All ER 198 (CA)

Facts: A man called Holden broke into a cafe and stole some food and cigarettes. He took the stolen goods to the appellant's flat and, after hiding the cigarettes, told the appellant about them. Later the police went to the flat. The appellant denied knowledge of the theft but did not impede the search of his flat. After some of the stolen food had been found in the flat, the appellant was warned that he would be arrested. He said to the police officer, 'Get lost'. Later, the cigarettes were found in the flat.

Lord Parker CJ: ... It is urged here that the mere failure to reveal the presence of the cigarettes, with or without the addition of the spoken words 'Get lost', was incapable in itself of amounting to an assisting in the retention of the goods within the meaning of the subsection. The court has come to the conclusion that that is right. It does not seem to this court that the mere failure to tell the police, coupled if you like with the words 'Get lost', amounts in itself to an assisting in their retention. On the other hand, those matters did afford strong evidence of what was the real basis of the charge here, namely that knowing that they had been stolen he permitted them to remain there or, as it has been put, provided accommodation for these stolen goods in order to assist Holden to retain them ...

R v Kanwar [1982] 1 WLR 845 (CA)

Cantley J: ... [The appellant's] husband had brought the stolen goods to their house where the goods were used in the home. It was conceded that the appellant was not present when the goods were brought to the house. She was in hospital at the time.

On 2 November 1978 police officers, armed with a search warrant, came to the house to look for and take away any goods which they found there which corresponded with a list of stolen goods in their possession. The appellant arrived during the search and was told of the object of the search. She replied: 'There's no stolen property here'.

She was subsequently asked a number of questions with regard to specific articles which were in the house and in reply to those questions, she gave answers which were lies [claiming that she had purchased the goods in question] ...

In *R v Thornhill*, decided in this court on 15 May 1981, and in *R v Sanders*, decided in this court on 25 February 1982, both unreported, it was held that merely using stolen goods in the possession of another does not constitute the offence of assisting in their retention. To constitute the offence, something must be done by the offender, and done intentionally and dishonestly, for the purpose of enabling the goods to be retained. Examples of such conduct are concealing or helping to conceal the goods, or doing something to make them more difficult to find or to identify. Such conduct must be done knowing or believing the goods to be stolen and done dishonestly and for the benefit of another.

We see no reason why the requisite assistance should be restricted to physical acts. Verbal representations, whether oral or in writing, for the purpose of concealing the identity of stolen goods may, if made dishonestly and for the benefit of another, amount to handling stolen goods by assisting in their retention within the meaning of s 22 of the Theft Act 1968.

The requisite assistance need not be successful in its object. It would be absurd if a person dishonestly concealing stolen goods for the benefit of a receiver could establish a defence by showing that he was caught in the act ...

The appellant told these lies to the police to persuade them that the picture and the mirror were not the stolen property which they had come to take away but were her lawful property which she had bought. If that was true, the articles should be left in the house. She was, of course, telling these lies to protect her husband, who had dishonestly brought the articles there but, in our view, she was nonetheless, at the time, dishonestly assisting in the retention of the stolen articles.

... In so far as the trial judge's direction [to the jury] suggests that the appellant would be guilty of the offence if she was merely willing for the goods to be kept and used in the house and was thinking that it was nice to have them there, although they were stolen goods, it is a misdirection. We have considered whether on that account the conviction ought to be quashed. However, the offence was established by the uncontradicted evidence of the police officer which, looked at in full, clearly shows that in order to mislead the officer who had come to take away stolen goods, she misrepresented the identity of the goods which she knew or believed to be stolen ...

Retention

R v Pitchley (1972) 57 Cr App R 30 (CA)

Facts: The appellant's son gave him £150 to look after. The appellant put the money in his account at a savings bank. The appellant said that he did not find out that the money had been stolen, by his son, until a few days later. After finding out that the money had been stolen the appellant did nothing.

Cairns LJ: ... [The main point made by counsel for the appellant is that], assuming that the jury were not satisfied that the appellant received the money knowing it to have been stolen ... then there was no evidence after that, that from the time when the money was put into the savings bank, that the appellant had done any act in relation to it. His evidence was, and there is no reason to suppose that the jury did not believe it, that at the time when he put the money into the savings bank he still did not know or believe that the money had been stolen – it was only at a later stage that he did. That was on the Saturday according to his evidence, and the position was that the money had simply remained in the savings bank from the Saturday, to the Wednesday when the police approached the appellant ...

... [T]he question is: Did the conduct of the appellant between the Saturday and the Wednesday amount to an assisting in the retention of this money for the benefit of his son Brian?

[His Lordship referred to the case of *R v Brown* (1969) 53 Cr App R 527 and went on:]

In this present case there was no question on the evidence of the appellant himself, that he was permitting the money to remain under his control in his savings bank book, and it is clear that this court in *R v Brown* regarded such permitting as sufficient to constitute retention within the meaning of [s 22 of the Theft Act 1968] ...

... [T]he dictionary meaning of the word 'retain' [is] – keep possession of, not lose, continue to have. In the view of this court, that is the meaning of the word 'retain' in this section.

CHAPTER 19

OFFENCES INVOLVING DECEPTION

OBTAINING PROPERTY BY DECEPTION

Section 15 of the Theft Act 1968

(1) A person who by any deception dishonestly obtains property belonging to another, with the intention of permanently depriving the other of it, shall on conviction on indictment be liable to imprisonment for a term not exceeding 10 years.

(2) For purposes of this section a person is to be treated as obtaining property if he obtains ownership, possession or control of it, and 'obtain' includes obtaining for another or enabling another to obtain or to retain.

(3) Section 6 above shall apply for purposes of this section, with the necessary adaptation of the reference to appropriating, as it applies for purposes of s 1.

(4) For purposes of this section 'deception' means any deception (whether deliberate or reckless) by words or conduct as to fact or as to law, including a deception as to the present intentions of the person using the deception or any other person.

The elements of the offence created by s 15 of the Theft Act 1968 are that the defendant:

(a) by any deception ...

(b) dishonestly ...

(c) obtains ...

(d) property ...

(e) belonging to another ...

(f) with the intention of permanently depriving the other of it.

Elements (b), (d), (e) and (f) have been dealt with under Theft (see Chapter 15).

Dishonesty

Dishonesty is a separate element from deception. Both have to be proved.

R v Feeny (1991) 94 Cr App R 1 (CA)

Judge J: ... The combined effect of s 15(1) and (4) of the Theft Act is that although any relevant deception may be made recklessly or deliberately, however the deception is made, the offence cannot be committed unless dishonesty is established as a separate and essential ingredient. It is not enough for the Crown merely to establish that the defendant made a deception recklessly and recklessness in relation to the deception does not establish dishonesty in relation to the obtaining.

Halstead v Patel [1972] 2 All ER 147 (DC)

Lord Widgery CJ: ... The respondent was employed by the Post Office for some time, and on 30 October 1970 he opened a National Giro Account, the National Giro headquarters being at Bootle, which was not where he was serving at that time.

The account was duly opened; he arranged to have his wages paid into the account, and so they were paid until unhappily for him there was a strike of Post Office employees which meant that he received no wages for a substantial period, and the money being fed into the account was cut off for that reason. He knew that he was not allowed to overdraw ...

On 14 January 1971 his account was overdrawn by a small sum, £7 6s 11d, and he was sent a letter ... pointing out this overdraft, and asking him to clear the account immediately. However, despite the receipt of that letter, he went on drawing cheques. There was a credit in respect of wages which momentarily brought his account into credit to the tune of about £21, but during January and early February, when no further credits were coming into the account, he proceeded to draw cheques. By 30 January his account was overdrawn to the extent of £48; on 4 February he cashed a further cheque, raising the overdraft to £68. The same thing happened again on 17 February. Then in due course the respondent was interviewed by representatives of the Giro Office, if I may so describe it, and his explanation of what happened became perfectly clear. He was receiving no wages because of the strike; he had to have money to live, so he knowingly and quite deliberately overdrew this account knowing that the money was not there to meet these cheques, and knowing that he had no business to overdraw. His explanation was that he needed the money to live, and he intended to make good the amount which he had overdrawn to the National Giro as soon as the Post Office strike was over and as soon as he was in funds to achieve that ...

There was here clearly a deception within the meaning of [the] definition [of deception approved in *R v Page* [1971] 2 WLR 1308 at 1312]. When the respondent drew these cheques he knew that there was no money in the account; he knew he had no business to draw them, yet he made ... a false representation to the effect that the cheque would be duly honoured in the ordinary course of events. So much for the deception.

The next question is whether it was done with the intention of permanently depriving the Post Office of the money ... There can be no doubt in this case that the actual notes or coins which were handed over the counter to this respondent were leaving the control of the Post Office for ever. There was no doubt at all of an intention permanently to deprive the Post Office of the actual coins or notes which were transferred. Accordingly, the only remaining feature of the offence which justified consideration is the requirement of dishonesty.

So far as dishonesty is concerned, it is quite clearly established on authority that a man who passes a cheque in respect of an account in which there are no immediate funds to meet the cheque does not necessarily act dishonestly if he genuinely believes on reasonable grounds that when the cheque is presented to the paying bank there will be funds to meet it. For example the man who, overdrawn on Saturday, draws a cheque in favour of a third party in the honest and well-founded belief that funds will be put into his bank on Monday, is a man who many juries would undoubtedly acquit of dishonesty, because there he has a genuine and honest belief that the cheque will be met in the ordinary course of events. But that is not this case; this case is the more common case in which there is no suggestion that the drawer of the cheque thought that funds would be available when the cheque in the ordinary course reached Bootle for payment. This is the case of a man who knows perfectly well that there are no funds and there will not be funds to meet the cheque on presentation, but who has the hope and ... the honest intention of repaying the money another day when he acquires funds for the purpose.

[His Lordship then referred to *R v Cockburn* [1968] 1 WLR 281 and *R v Williams* [1953] 1 QB 660 and continued:]

To my mind those authorities make the whole situation in this case crystal clear. When the cheques were presented for payment, the respondent knew that he had no right to overdraw, he knew that he had no funds in the giro account to meet these cheques, and he had no sort of prospect of providing such funds before the cheques were presented in the ordinary course. He had at best the pious hope of repaying the money at some uncertain future date when the Post Office strike was over, and that ... although it may be a matter of mitigation, is no defence to this charge. The element of dishonesty is satisfied on proof that he had no belief based on reasonable grounds that the money would be there when the cheque was presented. It is not enough to meet the allegation of dishonesty to say: 'I honestly meant to pay the money back some day'...

[Note that the latter part of this judgment needs to be seen in the light of *R v Ghosh* [1982] QB 1053, dealt with under 'theft'.]

R v Lightfoot (1993) 97 Cr App R 24 (CA)

McCullough J: ... [The defendant had tried to use a Barclaycard in the name of J Plummer to purchase goods from Woolworths.] When interviewed [by the police] he declined to say how he had come by the card. He admitted, however, that when he acquired it there was no signature on it. He admitted that he had signed it in the name of J Plummer and had used it frequently in that name to obtain goods. He had used the card on some 25 occasions to obtain goods to the value of about £3,000. The card had been sent by Barclaycard through the post on 5 July 1990, to Mr J Plummer, who was a fellow employee of the appellant's. They were fire officers working from the same fire station. The bank's intention had been that Mr J Plummer should sign the card and use it himself in accordance with Barclaycard's conditions ...

Mr Plummer's evidence was that he had never seen the card. His evidence raised the inference that it had been misappropriated before the envelope, in which it was contained, reached him, or just possibly after the envelope reached him, but before he had opened it. He had never, he said, authorised the appellant to use the card or to sign his name, and he knew nothing of the card or its use by the appellant until after the appellant's arrest.

The appellant's own evidence at trial was that, against his better judgment, Plummer had persuaded him to take the card and use it in Plummer's name. Despite his initial reluctance, he decided to do this because he was in debt and his credit rating would have prevented him from having a card of his own. Everything, he said, had been done with Plummer's authority. Indeed, he claimed that in one instance he had used the card to buy a camera for Plummer and had delivered it to him at the fire station. All this Plummer denied.

The appellant's evidence about the camera was supported by two other officers, who said that they had seen Plummer take the camera away from the fire station.

Plummer's credibility was obviously of crucial importance ...

The proof of dishonesty in a case such as this requires that the jury be sure of two things: first, that the defendant acted dishonestly as objectively judged against the ordinary standards of reasonable and honest people, and, second, that the defendant himself realised that what he was doing was by those standards dishonest: see *R v Ghosh* [1982] QB 1053, 1064 D to G. The direction which the learned judge gave did not precisely follow those words but it was to the same effect. As we have said, no complaint is made about it.

> There is a clear distinction between the defendant's knowledge of the law and his appreciation that he is doing something which, by ordinary standards of reasonable and honest people, is regarded as dishonest. His knowledge of the law, whether the criminal law or the law of contract, is irrelevant. Some dishonest behaviour falls foul of the criminal law; much does not. The fact that a man does not know what is criminal and what is not, or that he does not understand the relevant principles of the civil law, if any, cannot save him from conviction if what he does, coupled with the state of his mind, satisfies all the elements of the crime of which he is accused ...

Deception

Section 15(4) of the Theft Act 1968 provides a partial definition of deception. In *Re London and Globe Finance Corporation Ltd* [1903] 1 Ch 728, 732 Buckley J said that 'to deceive is ... to induce a man to believe that a thing is true which is false', and this provides a useful working definition of the word 'deception'.

It need not be the person from whom the property is obtained who is deceived (*Metropolitan Police Commissioner v Charles* [1977] AC 177, dealt with below under 'cheques and cheque cards').

Section 15(4) refers to deception by 'conduct': examples of such deception are to be found in *DPP v Stonehouse* [1978] AC 55 and *R v Williams* [1980] Crim LR 589.

Dishonest overcharging where the customer trusts the provider of the goods or services can also amount to a deception. See *R v King* [1987] 2 WLR 746, *R v Silverman* (1988) 86 Cr App R 214 and *R v Jones* (1993) Times, 15 February.

It is also possible to deceive someone by omission: such omission can amount to an implied representation (see *R v Firth* (1989) 91 Cr App R 217, which see in the commentary of s 2(1)(c) of the Theft Act 1968).

DPP v Stonehouse [1978] AC 55 (HL)

Lord Diplock: By the summer of 1974, [the appellant's] personal finances were in a disastrous state. He decided to fake his death by drowning and to start life afresh under a new identity with money dishonestly obtained and clandestinely transferred to his chosen country of refuge, Australia. He carried out this plan, but was discovered living in Australia under his false identity some five weeks after his pretended death by drowning ...

The facts that gave rise to [the] charges [of attempting to obtain property by deception] can be stated briefly. Mrs Stonehouse was not a party to the accused's plan. She was intended to believe that he had died by drowning. The accused intended to transfer to Australia all the money that he could lay his hands on; so on his death being presumed, his estate would be insolvent. To provide for his wife, ostensibly his widow, after his disappearance, there were taken out between July and September 1974, in Mrs Stonehouse's name, the five policies of insurance to a total amount of £125,000 payable to her on the death of her husband within five years. Active steps in arranging for the issue of the policies to his wife were taken by the accused himself in England. On 20 November 1974, the accused faked his death by accidental drowning in the sea off Miami in Florida, USA, to which city he had gone with a business associate, ostensibly for a business meeting. He had made an appointment for such a meeting later on that day and pending this had told his companion that he was going to the beach to have a swim. When he failed to keep the business appointment, enquiries were set on foot. His clothes, valuables and passport were found to be still in his hotel room and his bathrobe was found in a bathing hut on the beach. Of the accused himself there was no trace. In fact he had left Miami secretly by air, wearing a new suit of clothes which he and secreted and equipped with a false passport to conceal his identity. He eventually reached Australia and remained there undetected until 24 December 1974.

As soon as his disappearance at Miami was discovered in the circumstances summarised above, the hue and cry was raised. The police were brought in and, as was inevitable, the circumstances of his disappearance hit the headlines in the press, and on television and radio, in England. What the accused had done ensured, as he intended, that the news of his death by drowning should be communicated in England to his wife, who he intended should claim the policy moneys, and to the insurance companies who he intended should pay them over to her ...

The physical acts of the accused that are an essential element of any offence under s 15 must amount to a 'deception', ie the making to the person from whom the property is obtained of a representation of fact, law or intention that is false. The essential state of mind of the accused at the time of doing those physical acts is his knowledge of the falsity of the representation or his indifference as to whether it is true or false, and his intentions (1) that the false representation should be communicated to the person from whom the property is to be obtained; (2) that such person should believe the representation to be true; (3) that this belief should induce that person to part with ownership, possession or control of property to the accused himself or to some other person, and (4) that the accused himself or that other person should assume the rights of owner of the property so obtained.

Of these four intentions which must be present in the mind of the accused at the time of his physical acts which constitute the making of the false representation, the last three are directed solely to the consequences of those physical acts; so is the first in those cases in which the communication reaches the person from whom the property is to be obtained through some person, other than the accused himself, as intermediary. On the other hand, the described consequence of those physical acts which is also an essential constituent element in the 'result-crime' of obtaining property by deception, although they will require physical acts to be done by the person from whom the property is obtained, do not necessarily involve the accused in doing any physical acts himself subsequent to the making of the false representation. They do if the intended consequence of the representation is that he should obtain the property for himself, for this will call for further physical acts by him in assuming the rights of an owner of the property. But if the intended consequence is that another person should be enabled to obtain the property, any further physical acts needed to bring this consequence about may be done exclusively by that other person independently of the accused and, as in the instant case, under the influence of the same deception by the accused as induced the person from whom the property was obtained to part with it ...

... The constituent elements of the inchoate crime of an attempt are a physical act by the offender sufficiently proximate to the complete offence and an intention on the part of the offender to commit the complete offence. Acts that are merely preparatory to the commission of the offence such as, in the instant case, the taking out of the insurance policies are not sufficiently proximate to constitute an attempt. They do not indicate a fixed irrevocable intention to go on to commit the complete offence unless involuntarily prevented from doing so. As it was put in the *locus classicus R v Eagleton* (1855) Dears CC 515, 538:

> The mere intention to commit a misdemeanour is not criminal. Some act is required, and we do not think that all acts towards committing a misdemeanour are indictable. Acts remotely leading towards the commission of the offence are not to be considered as attempts to commit it, but acts immediately connected with it are ...

In other words the offender must have crossed the Rubicon and burnt his boats.

In the instant case ... the accused by 20 November 1974 had done all the physical acts lying within his power that were needed to enable Mrs Stonehouse to obtain the policy moneys if all had gone as he had intended. There was nothing left for him to do thereafter except to avoid detection of his real identity. That was the day on which he crossed his Rubicon and burnt his boats.

In my opinion it is quite unarguable that, given the necessary intention, those acts were not sufficiently proximate to the complete offence of obtaining property by deception to be capable in law of constituting an attempt to commit that offence. On the contrary they clearly do constitute such an attempt in law ...

R v Williams [1980] Crim LR 589 (CA)

Facts: The appellant exchanged obsolete foreign currency (knowing it to be obsolete) for sterling at a *bureau de change* in a department store.

Held, dismissing the appeal: When a person went to a foreign exchange counter, as opposed to a numismatic or curio counter, and proffered a banknote for exchange and asked for the notes to be changed for sterling, it was open to a jury to find that he was representing the notes to be genuine and valid as currency in the country of origin.

In the present case, the notes were no longer valid. That was a fundamental mistake operating on the mind of the cashier handing over the money. The contract was void *ab initio*. When the money was handed over it was the property of the store throughout and was appropriated by the appellant when he put it in his pocket. The dishonest intention was plainly to deprive the owner permanently of the money, given the chance. The offence of theft was therefore made out.

R v King; R v Stockwell [1987] 2 WLR 746 (CA)

Neill LJ: ... The case for the prosecution at the trial can be stated quite shortly. On 5 March 1985 the appellants went to the house of Mrs Mitchell, in New Milton. Mrs Mitchell, who had lived in the house all her life, was a widow of 68 years of age. The appellants told her that they were from Streets, a firm of tree surgeons. She knew of the firm, and in answer to her question one of the appellants claimed to be Mr Street. They told her that a sycamore tree in her garden was likely to cause damage. They purported to carry out a test, with a plastic strip placed against the tree, and one of the appellants then said that the tree was dangerous.

They told her that the roots of the tree were growing into the gas main and could cause thousands of pounds in damage. They told her that it would cost £150 to fell the tree, which Mrs Mitchell agreed to pay. They then looked at other trees and told her that another sycamore was dangerous as well as one of her conifers. In addition they told her that the roots of her bay tree were causing damage to the foundations of the house. Mrs Mitchell asked the appellants about the cost of doing all the work, and they told her that to remove the four trees including the bay tree would cost about £500. When Mrs Mitchell told them that she was going to telephone her brother, one of the appellants informed her that they would do the work for £470 if paid in cash. Mrs Mitchell then said that she would have to go and get the money from the bank. In fact, she decided to draw some money from her two building society accounts. From one account she withdrew £100, and she was in the process of withdrawing £200 from her account with a second building society, intending at that stage to go to her bank to draw the balance, when the cashier at the second building society noticed that she seemed very distressed.

Following a conversation between Mrs Mitchell and the cashier, the police were informed ... [and] the appellants were arrested ...

... [I]t is necessary to start by setting out the particulars of offence as stated in the indictment, as amended. The particulars read:

> David King and Jimmy Stockwell on 5 March 1985 in Hampshire, dishonestly attempted to obtain from Nora Anne Mitchell, £470 in money with the intention of permanently depriving the said Nora Anne Mitchell thereof by deception, namely by false oral representations that they were from J F Street, Tree Specialists, Pennington, that essential work necessary to remove trees in order to prevent damage to the gas supply and house foundations would then have to be carried out.

... In our view, the question in each case is: was the deception an operative cause of the obtaining of the property? This question falls to be answered as a question of fact by the jury applying their common sense ...

In the present case there was, in our judgment, ample evidence on which the jury could come to the conclusion that had the attempt succeeded the money would have been paid over by the victim as a result of the lies told to her by the appellants ...

R v Silverman (1988) 86 Cr App R 213 (CA)

Watkins LJ: ... The appellant came to grief, we are told, in consequence of a television programme, in which his dealings with two ladies, to whom I shall refer in a little detail in a moment or so, were ventilated because it was thought that he had treated them dishonestly. The ladies are twins, who are now 63 or 64 years of age. They had lived with their mother from 1929 until March 1983 at a house in Kenton. They are spinsters. Their home was sold in 1983. All the affairs concerning that place were wound up so that no debts remained in respect of it. They moved to a newly acquired maisonette at 36 Magnolia Court. This they purchased for a good deal less than the sum for which they had sold their previous home. The appellant was known to them because he had done work for their mother and for them in the house which they sold. He was employed with a plumbing and central heating firm called Coiley's. By the time of the material events he had become the manager of this firm. He had seen the sisters on a number of occasions, as had other employees of the firm before him. The sisters and their mother had learned to trust these tradesmen to do properly whatever work they were asked to do and to charge fair and reasonable prices for it. One has therefore an impression arising out of the evidence in the case, which the jury must have accepted, of a relationship of trust which had been built up and maintained between customer and tradesman.

Soon after the sisters had moved to Magnolia Court the appellant paid them a visit. According to one of the sisters, he asked if he could see the boiler because, he said, it was leaking. At that time he gave no estimate for repairing the defect, but the sisters were prepared to accept his word and to allow him to put the boiler right. One of the sisters wrote out a cheque for £2,875 and handed it to the appellant for the work to be done to the boiler. She thought that it was rather a lot to charge for what was to be done, but she told the jury that her family had been employing Coiley's for 15 years or more and she believed that what she was asked to pay was a standard charge.

A short while later the appellant looked at the electricity points and told the sisters that the whole of the maisonette needed to be rewired. He said that that work could be done at a cost of £20,000 plus VAT of £3,000. About a week later the sisters agreed to that because, they said, they trusted the appellant and his firm. They thought this was the normal charge and they paid a deposit of £10,000 before the work was begun. Upon its completion the appellant came to the maisonette and asked for £5,000, which one of the sisters paid him. The work of rewiring was to include the redecoration of the maisonette ...

True it is that the work had been done, but it was agreed on all sides at the trial that the prices charged by the appellant on behalf of his firm were grossly excessive. For instance, a new boiler could have been obtained for £700 and the cost of installing it would have been no more than between £100 and £150. But, as we have said, very nearly £3,000 was charged for repairing it. The Electricity Board, on being asked how much they would have charged to rewire the maisonette, said that their charge would have been considerably less than was charged by the appellant. The same applied to the redecoration of the maisonette ...

The charges of which the appellant was convicted were laid under s 15(1) of the Theft Act 1968. The first alleged that between July and November 1984 he dishonestly obtained from Pauline McCleery and Kathleen McCleery a cheque in the sum of £2,875 with the intention of permanently depriving Pauline and Kathleen McCleery by deception, namely by representing that that sum was a fair and proper charge for the work. The other counts in the indictment were similarly framed with specific reference to other cheques the sisters gave to the appellant. It follows from the particulars of the charges that the prosecution had to establish a number of elements to prove that in his transactions with the sisters the appellant committed criminal offences ...

It seems to us that the complainants, far from being worldly wise, were unquestionably gullible. Having left their former home, they relied implicitly upon the word of the appellant about their requirements in their maisonette. In such circumstances of mutual trust, one party depending upon the other for fair and reasonable conduct, the criminal law may apply if one party takes dishonest advantage of the other by representing as a fair charge that which he but not the other knows is dishonestly excessive ...

... There was material for a finding that there had been a false representation although it is true that the appellant had said nothing at the time he made his representations to encourage the sisters to accept the quotations. He applied no pressure upon them, and apart from mentioning the actual prices to be charged was silent as to the other matters that may have arisen for question in their minds.

On the matter of representations we have been referred to *DPP v Ray* [1974] AC 370 which concerned someone leaving a restaurant without paying for a meal. At 379 Lord Reid said:

> So the accused, after he changed his mind, must have done something intended to induce the waiter to believe that he still intended to pay before he left. Deception, to my mind, implies something positive.

[Counsel for the appellant] submits that nothing positive was done in this case. Lord Reid continued (*ibid*):

> It is quite true that a man intending to deceive can build up a situation in which his silence is as eloquent as an express statement.

Here the situation had been built up over a long period of time. It was a situation of mutual trust and the appellant's silence on any matter other than the sums charged were, we think, as eloquent as if he had said: 'What is more, I can say to you that we are going to get no more than a modest profit out of this' ...

[Note: The convictions were, however, quashed because the judge had failed to deal adequately with the defence case when summing up to the jury.]

R v Jones (1993) Times, 15 February (CA)

Facts: The appellant was a self-employed franchised milkman selling milk wholesale and retail to established customers. He had supplied the family business of a Mr Wilford for 20 years. The relationship was casual and informal and Mr Wilford paid by cheque at the end of each week the amount the appellant asked for.

It later transpired that the appellant had been overcharging Mr Wilford by some £180 per week. Mr Wilford in evidence said that he had never considered the amount he was paying for the milk because he trusted the appellant and therefore assumed that the appellant had been charging the proper cost price to a retailer.

The nature of the deception alleged in the indictment was that the appellant had falsely represented to Mr Wilford that he had received goods to the value of a certain amount when in fact the appellant had only delivered goods to the value of one-half of that amount.

Auld J, giving the judgment of the Court of Appeal, said that Mr Wilford had been remarkably stupid or careless and this was stupidity or carelessness of which the appellant was aware. There could be no doubt that Mr Wilford was deceived.

R v Rozeik [1996] 1 WLR 159 (CA)

Leggatt LJ: This appeal raises a point of law about the deception of a company ...

Each of the 12 counts in the indictment related to a dishonest application to a finance company for funds to purchase equipment to be used by limited companies controlled or owned by the appellant. Each such purchase was by way of a hire-purchase agreement. It was the Crown's case that false information was provided to the finance company concerned as to the description, price, and even the existence of particular equipment, and that had the finance companies been aware of the true facts, cheques in payment for the equipment would never have been issued ...

The particulars of offence of each count in the indictment charged the appellant with having on a stated date dishonestly obtained a specified cheque drawn in a specified sum from the relevant finance company with the intention of permanently depriving the finance company thereof by deception, namely by falsely representing that (1) the details contained in a specified hire-purchase agreement were true and (2) the relative invoice was genuine ...

[His Lordship quoted s 15(1) of the Theft Act 1968 and continued:]

In respect of each count in the indictment the property belonging to a finance company which was dishonestly obtained was a cheque. For the purpose of ascertaining whether the cheque was obtained by a deception it is necessary to consider the state of mind of the person by whom it was furnished on behalf of the company. For the purpose of determining whether in entering into the hire-purchase agreements the company was deceived, whose state of mind stood as the state of mind of the company? The person who in each branch most obviously represented the company was the branch manager. [Counsel for the appellant] drew attention to many examples of employees declaring in evidence that they worked under supervision and control of Birch [a branch manager]. Others similarly worked under Wilkinson [another branch manager]. In relation to several of the counts the evidence showed direct implication by one of them. The managers appear to have had the conduct of those transactions, so as to involve their direct endorsement of approval of it. It may also, we think, be said with some force that, once the credit limits had been set by Birch and Wilkinson, all the ensuing transactions within the limits proceeded by their authority. By appointing credit limits Birch and Wilkinson must be taken to have authorised all transactions with the appellant up to and within those limits.

The next question is whether Birch and Wilkinson knew that the invoice in each transaction was false.

... [S]ince the case for the Crown depended on knowledge of the falsity of the invoices not being imputed to the companies, the jury should have been directed ... that they should ignore in this context the knowledge of anyone who they were sure was party to the fraud ... Unless the state of mind of Birch and Wilkinson was excluded, so that their knowledge was not attributed to the companies, it did not avail the Crown to prove that anyone else was deceived by the appellant.

A more difficult question is whether the knowledge of Birch and Wilkinson should not be imputed to their companies ...

... Since Birch and Wilkinson were managers of their respective branches, their knowledge was the knowledge of their companies unless they were shown to be acting dishonestly ...

... [T]he question is not whether any employee of the company was deceived but whether any employee whose state of mind stood as that of the company knew of the falsity of the transaction, since, if he or she did know, the company also knew. If the company knew, it would not matter how many fellow employees were personally deceived. Second, and in any event, a cheque could only be obtained from the company from an employee who had authority to provide it. The deception had to operate on the mind of the employee from whom the cheque was obtained. In no sense could a cheque be 'obtained' from the person who merely typed it out ... What the Crown had to prove was that when the cheque was obtained from the company it was obtained from a person who was deceived. Although in no sense was it obtained from those who checked or typed it, the signatories of the cheques (apart from Birch and Wilkinson) were in a different position. They had a responsibility to ensure that the cheques were not signed unless satisfied that the money should be paid. They were more than mere mechanics and in our judgment, if they were deceived, the company also was, once Birch and Wilkinson were disregarded. That means that (1) where a manager only signed, the offence could not be made out, (2) where a manager signed with another employee, it had to be shown that that other was deceived, and (3) where two employees (other than a manager) signed, it had to be proved either that one was or that both were deceived, and that where one was, the other did not know of the fraud, since if he or she did, the company would not have been deceived ...

Worthless cheques; use of cheque cards; credit cards

The question what representations are involved in the handing over of a cheque, with or without the additional use of a cheque guarantee card, and in the use of a credit card, was considered by the House of Lords in *Metropolitan Police Commissioner v Charles* [1977] AC 177 and *R v Lambie* [1982] AC 449. Post-dated cheques were considered by the Court of Appeal in *R v Gilmartin* [1983] QB 953.

Commissioner of Police for the Metropolis v Charles [1977] AC 177 (HL)

Lord Diplock: My Lords, I have had the advantage of reading in advance the speeches of my noble and learned friends, Viscount Dilhorne and Lord Edmund-Davies. I agree with their conclusions, and with the revision which they suggest is needed to the certified question and with the answer that they propose to the question as revised.

I will accordingly confine my own speech to a brief analysis of the representations made by the drawer of a cheque; first, where he proffers it to the payee without a cheque card as payment for goods or services or in exchange for cash, and second, where the drawer shows to the payee a cheque card and the cheque which he then draws appears to comply with the conditions endorsed upon the card ...

To take first the case in which no cheque card is involved, it is no doubt true to say that all the payee is concerned with is that the cheque should be honoured by the bank, and that to induce the payee to take the cheque all that the drawer is concerned to do is to assure him that as far as can reasonably be foreseen this is what will happen. But payment by the bank cannot reasonably be foreseen as likely unless the fact be that the cheque is one which the bank on which it is drawn is bound, by an existing contract with the drawer, to pay on presentment or, if not strictly bound to do so, could reasonably be expected to pay in the normal course of dealing ...

When a cheque card is brought into the transaction, it still remains the fact that all the payee is concerned with is that the cheque should be honoured by the bank. I do not think that the fact that a cheque card is used necessarily displaces the representation to be implied from the act of drawing the cheque which has just been mentioned. It is, however, likely to displace that representation at any rate as the main inducement to the payee to take the cheque, since the use of the cheque card in connection with the transaction gives to the payee a direct contractual right against the bank itself to payment on presentation, provided that the use of the card by the drawer to bind the bank to pay the cheque was within the actual or ostensible authority conferred on him by the bank.

By exhibiting to the payee a cheque card containing the undertaking by the bank to honour cheques drawn in compliance with the conditions endorsed on the back, and drawing the cheque accordingly, the drawer represents to the payee that he has actual authority from the bank to make a contract with the payee on the bank's behalf that it will honour the cheque on presentation for payment.

... What creates ostensible authority in a person who purports to enter into a contract as agent for a principal is a representation made to the other party that he has the actual authority of the principal for whom he claims to be acting to enter into the contract on that person's behalf. If (1) the other party has believed the representation and on the faith of that belief has acted on it and (2) the person represented to be his principal has so conducted himself towards that other party as to be estopped from denying the truth of the representation, then, and only then, is he bound by the contract purportedly made on his behalf. The whole foundation of liability under the doctrine of ostensible authority is a representation, believed by the person to whom it is made, that the person claiming to contract as agent for a principal has the actual authority of the principal to enter into the contract on his behalf.

That is the representation that the drawer makes to the payee when he uses a cheque card to back a cheque which he draws in compliance with the conditions endorsed on the card. That in the instant case Mr Cersell, the manager of the gaming club, so understood it is implicit from the passages in his evidence to which my noble and learned friend, Lord Edmund-Davies, refers. Mr Cersell may not have known the doctrine of ostensible authority under that name, but he knew what it was all about. He would not have taken the accused's cheques had he not believed that the accused was authorised by the bank to use the cheque card to back them.

Viscount Dilhorne: My Lords, on 31 October 1972, the appellant opened a bank account at the Peckham Rye Branch of the National Westminster Bank. On 23 November, the manager of that branch agreed to allow him to have an overdraft of £100 for one month, a facility which was later extended for a further month. On 19 December 1972, he was given a cheque card headed 'National Westminster Bank £30 for conditions see over' and on its front a space for the appellant's signature. On the back was printed:

> The issuing banks undertake that any cheque not exceeding £30 will be honoured subject to the following conditions: (a) The cheque must be signed in the presence of the payee. (b) The signature on the cheque must correspond with the specimen signature on this card. (c) The cheque must be drawn on a bank cheque form bearing the code number shown on this card. (d) The cheque must be drawn before the expiry date of this card. (e) The card number must be written on the reverse of the cheque by the payee.

These conditions are designed to secure that the cheque is drawn by the customer to whom the bank has given a cheque book and a cheque card. If they are complied with the recipient need not concern himself about the drawer's creditworthiness for he knows the cheque will be honoured on presentment.

On 27 December a cheque drawn by the appellant was presented and returned unpaid. The next day the appellant was notified that he had exceeded his overdraft limit and on 2 January 1973 his overdraft rose to £248 due to the presentation that day of four cheques each for £30 drawn by the appellant with the use of his cheque card. The bank manager tried to get in touch with the appellant immediately and saw him that day. The bank manager knew that a cheque in favour of the appellant for £500 had been paid into a branch of the bank. Payment of that cheque was, however, stopped and it was not met until March.

When he saw the appellant the bank manager did not know, did not ask and was not told what other cheques had been drawn by the appellant and not presented. In fact the appellant had by 2 January drawn a further 14 cheques which had not then been presented. Not knowing this, the bank manager allowed the appellant to be issued with a new cheque book containing 25 cheque forms. He told the appellant that he must not cash more than one cheque a day for £30 at a bank but he gave him no further instructions as to the use of the cheque card.

That evening the appellant went to the Golden Nugget Club, a gaming club, and in the course of the night he used all the cheques in the new cheque book for the purchase of chips for gaming. Each cheque was for £30 made out to the manager of the club, Mr Cersell, and he used his cheque card in relation to each cheque. The bank had consequently to honour all the cheques with the result that they paid out a further £750 ...

The reality is in my view that a man who gives a cheque represents that it will be met on presentation, and if a cheque is accepted by the payee, it is in the belief that it will be met.

That being the position with a cheque, how is it affected by the production and use of a cheque card by the drawer, the authorised holder of the card? The representation that the cheque will be met is unaltered. It is supported by the bank's undertaking and all doubts in the mind of the payee as to the cheque being honoured will be removed if he sees that the stipulated conditions are complied with.

If in this case the appellant had not used his cheque card, none of his cheques would have been taken by the Golden Nugget Club. Mr Cersell made that clear.

Does a cheque card holder by his conduct in producing his cheque card and using it to secure the acceptance of his cheque make any representation additional to that made by him when giving the cheque? Whether or not an additional representation by conduct is made in those circumstances is a question of fact for the jury but whether an additional representation can be inferred from his conduct is a question of law.

His use of a cheque card to secure acceptance of his cheque can in my opinion amount to a representation that he has the authority of the bank to use it in relation to that cheque for that purpose, and as a matter of fact will ordinarily do so. He is authorised by the bank to give their undertaking to pay up to £30 on a cheque if the stipulated conditions are fulfilled. But the authority given to him is not unlimited. By giving him a cheque book and a cheque card the bank has not authorised him to bind them by the use of the card to honour every cheque in the cheque book. He is not authorised to use it to secure the acceptance of a cheque which he knows would not be met by the bank if the cheque card had not been used ...

The Court of Appeal (Criminal Division) dismissed the appellant's appeal but certified that the following point of law was of general public importance and gave leave to appeal to this House:

> When the holder of a cheque card presents a cheque in accordance with the conditions of the card which is accepted in exchange for goods, services or cash, does this transaction provide evidence of itself from which it can or should be inferred (a) that the drawer represented that he then had authority, as between himself and the bank, to draw a cheque for that amount and (b) that the recipient of the cheque was induced by that representation to accept the cheque?

With respect, I do not think that this question was very happily phrased. Whether an inference can be properly drawn is a matter of law; whether it should be drawn is a question of fact for the jury. Whether or not the recipient of a cheque was induced by a representation to accept it, is also a question of fact. It would have been better if the question had been worded as follows:

> When the holder of a cheque card presents a cheque card together with a cheque made out in accordance with the conditions of the card which cheque is accepted in exchange for goods, services or cash, does this transaction provide evidence of itself from which it can be inferred that the drawer represented that he then had authority as between himself and the bank to use the card in order to oblige the bank to honour the cheque?

So phrased the question raises the issue which has to be determined on this appeal and in my opinion the answer to it is in the affirmative ...

Lord Salmon: My Lords, for the reasons stated in the speeches of my noble and learned friends, Lord Diplock, Viscount Dilhorne and Lord Edmund-Davies, I would answer the revised question in the way they propose and I would dismiss the appeal.

Lord Edmund-Davies: ... The 'pecuniary advantage' alleged in the particulars of each of the charges to have been obtained by the accused (based on s 16(2)(c)) was 'increased borrowing by way of overdraft from the National Westminster Bank Ltd', and there is no contest that the appellant did in fact obtain such advantage in the circumstances hereinafter to be described. The sole contest has been whether that advantage was obtained as the charges alleged:

> by deception, namely by deliberately or recklessly representing that he was entitled and authorised to use a cheque card when issuing cheque no .... drawn on the National Westminster Bank Ltd.

It was therefore incumbent on the Crown to establish that in relation to each of the two incidents giving rise to the charges laid (a) the accused had made the representation alleged; (b) that he made it dishonestly; (c) that the person to whom the representation was made was thereby induced to act as he did; and (d) that by such deception the accused obtained the pecuniary advantage alleged ...

... What of the production and use of the cheque card when each of the 25 cheques in the new cheque book was drawn ... Is [counsel for the appellant] right in submitting that the only representation made by its production was the perfectly correct one that 'this cheque, backed by this card, will be honoured without question'? In my judgment, he is not. The accused knew perfectly well that he would not be able to get more chips at the club simply by drawing a cheque. The cheque alone would not have been accepted; it had to be backed by a cheque card. The card played a vital part, for (as my noble and learned friend, Lord Diplock, put it during counsel's submission) in order to make the bank liable to the payee there must be knowledge on the payee's part that the drawer has the bank's authority to bind it, for in the absence of such knowledge the all-important contract between payee and bank is not created; and it is the representation by the drawer's production of the card that he has that authority that creates such contractual relationship and estops the bank from refusing to honour the cheque. By drawing the cheque the accused represented that it would be met, and by producing the card so that the number thereon could be endorsed on the cheque he in effect represented, 'I am authorised by the bank to show this to you and so create a direct contractual relationship between the bank and you that they will honour this cheque'. The production of the card was the badge of the accused's ostensible authority to make such a representation on the bank's behalf. And this emerges with clarity from the evidence of the club manager, Mr Cersell, who repeatedly stressed during his lengthy testimony that the accused's cheque would not have been accepted unless accompanied by a cheque card the signature on which corresponded with that of the accused when making out the cheque.

... There remains to be considered the vitally important question of whether it was established that it was as a result of such dishonest deception that the club's staff were induced to give chips for cheques and so, in due course, caused the accused's bank account to become improperly overdrawn ...

Whether a party was induced to act as he did because of the deception to which he was dishonestly subjected is a question of fact to be decided on the evidence adduced in each case ...

... [I]n this context it has again to be borne in mind that the witness made clear that the accused's cheques were accepted *only* because he produced a cheque card, and he repeatedly stressed that, had he been aware that the accused was using his cheque book and cheque card 'in a way in which he was not allowed or entitled to use [them]' no cheque would have been accepted. The evidence of that witness, taken as a whole, points irresistibly to the conclusions (a) that by this dishonest conduct the accused deceived Mr Cersell in the manner averred in the particulars of the charges and (b) that Mr Cersell was thereby induced to accept the cheques because of his belief that the representations as to both cheque and card were true ...

Lord Fraser of Tullybelton: My Lords, I have had the advantage of reading in advance the speeches of my noble and learned friends, Viscount Dilhorne, and Lord Diplock and Lord Edmund-Davies. I agree with their reasoning and conclusions. I would answer the question (as revised) in the way proposed by them, and I would dismiss the appeal.

R v Lambie [1982] AC 449 (HL)

Lord Diplock: My Lords, I have had the advantage of reading in draft the speech prepared by my noble and learned friend, Lord Roskill. I agree with it and would allow the appeal.

Lord Fraser of Tullybelton: My Lords, I have had the advantage of reading in draft the speech prepared by my noble and learned friend, Lord Roskill. I agree with it and for the reasons stated therein I would answer the certified question in the negative and allow this appeal.

Lord Russell of Killowen: My Lords, I have had the advantage of reading in draft the speech prepared by my noble and learned friend, Lord Roskill. I agree with it and that this appeal should be allowed.

Lord Keith of Kinkel: My Lords, for the reasons given in the speech of my noble and learned friend, Lord Roskill, which I have had the opportunity of reading in draft and with which I entirely agree, I too would allow the appeal.

Lord Roskill: My Lords, on 20 April 1977, the respondent was issued by Barclays Bank Ltd ('the bank') with a Barclaycard ('the card'). That card was what today is commonly known as a credit card. It was issued subject to the Barclaycard current conditions of use, and it was an express condition of its issue that it should be used only within the respondent's credit limit. That credit limit was £200 as the respondent well knew, since that figure had been notified to her in writing when the card was issued. The then current conditions of use included an undertaking by the respondent, as its holder, to return the card to the bank on request. No complaint was, or indeed could be, made of the respondent's use of the card until 18 November 1977. Between that date and 5 December 1977, she used the card for at least 24 separate transactions, thereby incurring a debt of some £533. The bank became aware of this debt and thereupon sought to recover the card. On 6 December 1977, the respondent agreed to return the card on 7 December 1977. She did not, however, do so. By 15 December 1977, she had used the card for at least 43 further transactions, incurring a total debt to the bank of £1,005.26.

My Lords, on 15 December 1977 [before the coming into force of the Theft Act 1978] the respondent entered into the transaction out of which this appeal arises. She visited a Mothercare shop in Luton. She produced the card to a departmental manager at Mothercare named Miss Rounding. She selected goods worth £10.35. Miss Rounding completed the voucher and checked that the card was current in date, that it was not on the current stop list and that the respondent's signature on the voucher corresponded with her signature on the card. Thereupon, the respondent took away the goods which she had selected. In due course, Mothercare sent the voucher to the bank and were paid £10.35 less the appropriate commission charged by the bank. On 19 December 1977, the respondent returned the card to the bank.

[The defendant was charged under s 16(1) of the Theft Act 1968 with obtaining for herself a pecuniary advantage, namely the evasion of a debt (a form of pecuniary advantage under s 16(2)(a) Theft Act 1968, subsequently replaced by s 2 of the Theft Act 1978) for which she then made herself liable, by deception, namely by representing that she was authorised to use a Barclaycard to obtain goods to the value of £10.35.] ...

[The Court of Appeal] certified the following point of law as of general public importance, namely:

> In view of the proved differences between a cheque card transaction and a credit card transaction, were we right in distinguishing this case from that of *R v Charles* [1977] AC 177 upon the issue of inducement?

... Following the decision of this House in *R v Charles*, it is in my view clear that the representation arising from the presentation of a credit card has nothing to do with the respondent's credit standing at the bank but is a representation of actual authority to make the contract with, in this case, Mothercare on the bank's behalf that the bank will honour the voucher on presentation. On that view, the existence and terms of the agreement between the bank and Mothercare are irrelevant, as is the fact that Mothercare, because of that agreement, would look to the bank for payment.

That being the representation to be implied from the respondent's actions and use of the credit card, the only remaining question is whether Miss Rounding was induced by that representation to complete the transaction and allow the respondent to take away the goods. My Lords, if she had been asked whether, had she known the respondent was acting dishonestly and, in truth, had no authority whatever from the bank to use the credit card in this way, she (Miss Rounding) would have completed the transaction, only one answer is possible – no. Had an affirmative answer been given to this question, Miss Rounding would, of course, have become a participant in furtherance of the respondent's fraud and a conspirator with her to defraud both Mothercare and the bank ...

... My Lords, credit card frauds are all too frequently perpetrated, and if conviction of offenders for offences against ss 15 or 16 of the Act of 1968 can only be obtained if the prosecution are able in each case to call the person on whom the fraud was immediately perpetrated to say that he or she positively remembered the particular transaction and, had the truth been known, would never have entered into that supposedly well-remembered transaction, the guilty would often escape conviction. In some cases, of course, it may be possible to adduce such evidence if the particular transaction is well remembered. But where as in the present case no one could reasonably be expected to remember a particular transaction in detail, and the inference of inducement may well be in all the circumstances quite irresistible, I see no reason in principle why it should not be left to the jury to decide, on the evidence in the case as a whole, whether that inference is in truth irresistible as to my mind it is in the present case. In this connection it is to be noted that the respondent did not go into the witness box to give evidence from which that inference might conceivably have been rebutted.

My Lords, in this respect I find myself in agreement with what was said by Humphreys J giving the judgment of the Court of Criminal Appeal in *R v Sullivan* (1945) 30 Cr App R 132, 136:

> It is, we think, undoubtedly good law that the question of the inducement acting upon the mind of the person who may be described as the prosecutor is not a matter which can only be proved by the direct evidence of the witness. It can be, and very often is, proved by the witness being asked some question which brings the answer: 'I believed that statement and that is why I parted with my money'; but it is not necessary that there should be that question and answer if the facts are such that it is patent that there was only one reason which anybody could suggest for the person alleged to have been defrauded parting with his money, and that is the false pretence, if it was a false pretence.

[His Lordship then referred briefly to *R v Laverty* (1970) 54 Cr App R 495 and continued:]

Of course, the Crown must always prove its case and one element which will always be required to be proved in these cases is the effect of the dishonest representation on the mind of the person to whom it is made. But I see no reason why in cases such as the present, where what Humphreys J called the direct evidence of the witness is not and cannot reasonably be expected to be available, reliance on a dishonest representation cannot be sufficiently established by proof of facts from which an irresistible inference of such reliance can be drawn.

My Lords, I would answer the certified question in the negative and would allow the appeal and restore the conviction of the respondent ...

[Note: A simpler course for the prosecution to have followed would have been to charge the defendant with obtaining *property* by deception, contrary to s 15 of the Theft Act 1968.]

R v Gilmartin [1983] QB 953 (CA)

Robert Goff LJ: ... Each of the four counts in the indictment alleges that the relevant deception by the appellant consisted of a false representation that the cheque in question was a good and valid order for the payment of the sum specified in the cheque. All the cheques in question were post-dated cheques ... The submission for the defence before the judge, which was repeated before this court, was that by giving a post-dated cheque the drawer impliedly represents no more than that he (or any company on whose behalf he draws the cheque) is a customer of the bank on which the cheque is drawn, and makes no implied representation concerning the honouring of the cheque ...

... We can see no reason why in the case of a post-dated cheque the drawer does not impliedly represent that the existing facts at the date when he gives the cheque to the payee or his agent are such that in the ordinary course the cheque will, on presentation on or after the date specified in the cheque, be met.

Take the case where, as in this instance, a post-dated cheque is issued when the account is heavily overdrawn and there is, as the drawer well knows, no prospect of any future funds being paid into the account before the date when the cheque matures or of the bank providing other overdraft facilities before that date. In such a case it appears to us the drawer is as much guilty of deception as he would be in the case of a cheque which is not post-dated. Indeed, where the drawer gives a cheque which is not post-dated his account may be overdrawn and he may have no arrangement with his bank for further overdraft facilities, but he may have in his pocket another cheque payable to him which he intends to pay into his account immediately and which when paid in will enable the cheque which he himself has drawn to be paid on presentation; if so it is difficult to see that he has made any misrepresentation. In these circumstances, we can see no relevant distinction between the case of a cheque which has not been post-dated and one which has.

For the sake of clarity, we consider that in the generality of cases under s 15 and 16 of the Theft Act 1968, the courts should proceed on the basis that by the simple giving of a cheque, whether post-dated or not, the drawer impliedly represents that the state of facts existing at the date of handing over the cheque is such that in the ordinary course the cheque will, on presentation for payment on or after the date specified in the cheque be met ...

Causation

The deception must be the operative cause of the obtaining of the property. If a motorist fills up the petrol tank of her car and *then* deceives the attendant in some way so as to avoid paying for the petrol, it cannot be said that the property (the petrol) was obtained 'by' (ie as a result of) deception (see *R v Collis-Smith* [1971] Crim LR 716; hence the need for the offence of 'making off without payment' under s 3 of the Theft Act 1978). On the requirement of a causal link between the deception and the obtaining, see *R v Clucas* [1949] 2 KB 226, *R v Laverty* [1970] 3 All ER 432, *R v Rashid* [1977] 1 WLR 298, *R v Doukas* [1978] 1 WLR 372 and *R v Miller* (1992) 95 Cr App R 421. *Rashid* and *Doukas* are both cases involving s 25 of the Theft Act 1968 ('going equipped', *qv*), but in both cases the court had to consider whether an offence of obtaining property by deception would have been committed had the articles in question been used.

R v Clucas [1949] 2 KB 226 (CA)

Facts: The appellant and another man induced bookmakers to bet with them by representing that they were commission agents acting on behalf of a large number of workmen who were putting small bets on various races, whereas in fact they were making bets in considerable sums of money for themselves alone.

Lord Goddard CJ: ... In the opinion of the court it is impossible to say that there was an obtaining of the money by the false pretences which were alleged, because the money was obtained not by reason of the fact that the people falsely pretended that they were somebody else or acting in some capacity which they were not; it was obtained because they backed a winning horse and the bookmaker paid because the horse had won. No doubt the bookmaker might never have opened an account with these men if he had known the true facts, but we must distinguish in this case between one contributing cause and the effective cause which led the bookmaker to pay the money.

The effective cause which led the bookmaker to pay the money was the fact that these men had backed a winning horse ... Although these two men induced the bookmaker to bet with them by means of a false pretence, what the court cannot see is that that false pretence was the false pretence which led to the payment of the money. What led to the payment of the money was the fact that these men backed a winning horse by inducing the bookmaker to bet with them ...

[Note: The deception practised in this case would now amount to an offence under s 16(2)(c) of the Theft Act 1968, as to which see below.]

R v Laverty [1970] 3 All ER 432 (CA)

Lord Parker CJ: ... The facts are in a very short compass. The car bearing number plates DUV 111C, a Hillman Imp, was bought by a Mr Bedborough from the appellant, and a cheque was given as part of the price. In fact that car bearing those number plates was a car originally bearing number plates JPA 945C, which had been stolen. According to the appellant when he got the car, and there was no question of his having stolen it, it was in a bad condition, he repaired it and he put onto it the ... number plates of DUV 111C, those plates having been obtained from another source relating of course to another car.

The charge made in the indictment ... took the form of alleging a false representation which here was by conduct. It was not a false representation that the appellant was the owner and had a good title to sell but the false representation was by purporting that a Hillman Imp motor car which the appellant sold to Roy Clinton Bedborough was the original Hillman Imp motor car, index number DUV 111C.

Although it was contested at the trial, it was conceded in this court that there was a representation by conduct that the car being sold to Mr Bedborough was the original Hillman Imp to which the [number] plate[s] which it bore had been assigned. It is conceded that such a representation was made by conduct; it is clear that that was false, and false to the knowledge of the appellant. The sole question was whether this false representation operated on Mr Bedborough's mind so as to cause him to hand over this cheque.

As sometimes happens, in this case Mr Bedborough did not give the answers which were helpful to the prosecution, and no leading questions could be put. The nearest answer was 'I bought this because I thought the appellant was the owner'. In other words, Mr Bedborough was saying: 'What induced me to part with my money was the representation by conduct that the appellant had a title to sell' ...

... It is axiomatic that it is for the prosecution to prove that the false representation acted on the mind of the purchaser; and in the ordinary way, and the court emphasises this, the matter should be proved by direct evidence. However, it was said in *R v Sullivan* (1945) 30 Cr App Rep 132 that the inducement need not be proved by direct evidence, and I quote from the headnote:

> if the facts are such that the alleged false pretence is the only reason that could be suggested as having been the operative inducement.

... This court is very anxious not to extend the principle in *R v Sullivan* more than is necessary. The proper way of proving these matters is through the mouth of the person to whom the false representation is conveyed, and further it seems to the court in the present case that no jury could say that the only inference here was that Mr Bedborough parted with his money by reason of this false representation. Mr Bedborough may well have been of the mind as he stated he was, namely that what operated on his mind was the belief that the appellant was the owner. Provided that the appellant was the owner it may well be that Mr Bedborough did not mind that the car did not bear its original number plates. At any rate as it seems to the court it cannot be said that the only possible inference here is that it actuated on Mr Bedborough's mind ...

R v Rashid [1977] 1 WLR 298 (CA)

Bridge LJ: [T]his defendant was convicted of having with him articles for use in the course of or in connection with cheat [contrary to s 25(1) of the Theft Act 1968] ...

... The particular articles of which the defendant was convicted of having possession, not at his place of abode and for use in connection with cheat, were two loaves of sliced bread and one bag of tomatoes. The facts were that the defendant was a steward employed by British Rail and the offence was said to have been committed when at Euston Station early one morning he was about to board a train for Glasgow. The prosecution case was that his intention was to use his own bread and tomatoes in the making of sandwiches which would then be sold by him to passengers on the train for, no doubt, the same price as would be charged for a British Rail sandwich and that the defendant would pocket the proceeds ...

... [I]t does not follow that in the circumstances of this case this defendant could be convicted of the offence under s 25. At all events, before he could be ... convicted [of an offence under s 25], if he could be convicted at all which the court doubts, at the very least it was necessary that the judge in summing up should have made it abundantly clear to the jury what were the elements of the offence of deception under s 15 which constituted the basis of the intended cheat, and what would be the necessary state of mind of the defendant with regard to the intended commission of that offence under s 15 in order to sustain a conviction for the offence charged under s 25 ...

... At the very least what would have been necessary would have been a direction to the effect that the offence intended to be committed would have been the obtaining of property by deception from the passenger and that a necessary element in the defendant's *mens rea* on which the jury would have to be satisfied would be that he believed the passenger, if he knew that the sandwich offered him was made with bread and tomatoes belonging to the defendant and not belonging to British Rail, would have declined to purchase. Unless that was his state of mind then he had not the necessary *mens rea* to found a conviction under s 25, having articles in his possession in connection with an intended offence under s 15.

R v Doukas [1978] 1 WLR 372 (CA)

Geoffrey Lane LJ: ... The facts of the case are these. On 9 January 1976 Doukas was engaged as a casual wine waiter at the Cunard International Hotel at Hammersmith and it seems that on that engagement he gave certainly a false name and possibly also a false address to his employers. Not very long after his engagement, he was found on the fire escape of the hotel by one of the assistant managers of the hotel. It was against the rules for him to be on the fire escape but that was not the real gravamen of his offence, because found in his coat pocket were six bottles of wine ...

[His Lordship referred to the summing up which noted that when interviewed by the police the appellant had said:]

> I take the wine in. If a carafe is ordered I substitute my own wine and make out a separate bill for the customer from the hotel's bill and I keep the money.

[The summing up continued:]

There, the prosecution say, is a confession of an intended deliberate deception ...

... [T]he following items have to be proved. First of all that there was an article for use in connection with the deception: here the bottles. Second, that there was a proposed deception: here the deception of the guests into believing that the proffered wine was hotel wine and not the waiter's wine. Third, an intention to obtain property by means of the deception, and the property here is the money of the guests which he proposes to obtain and keep. Fourth, dishonesty. There is twofold dishonesty in the way the Crown put the case. First of all the dishonesty in respect of his employers, namely putting into his pocket the money which really should go to the hotel and, more important, the second dishonesty, *vis-à-vis* the guests, the lying to or misleading of the guests into believing that the wine which had been proffered was the hotel wine and not the waiter's wine. Fifth, there must be proof that the obtaining would have been, wholly or partially, by virtue of the deception.

The prosecution must prove that nexus between the deception and obtaining. It is this last and final ingredient which, as we see it in the present case, is the only point which raises any difficulty. Assuming, as we must, and indeed obviously was the case, that the jury accepted the version of the police interviews and accepted that this man had made the confession to which I have referred, then the only question was, would this obtaining have in fact been caused by the deception practised by the waiter? ...

Of course each case of this type may produce different results according to the circumstances of the case and according, in particular, to the commodity which is being proffered. But, as we see it, the question has to be asked of the hypothetical customer: why did you buy this wine? or, if you had been told the truth, would you or would you not have bought the commodity? It is, at least in theory, for the jury in the end to decide that question.

... Certainly so far as the wine is concerned, we have no doubt at all that the hypothetical customer faced with the waiter saying to him: 'This of course is not hotel wine, this is stuff which I imported into the hotel myself and I am going to put the proceeds of the wine, if you pay, into my own pocket', would certainly answer, so far as we can see, 'I do not want your wine, kindly bring me the hotel carafe wine'. Indeed it would be a strange jury that came to any other conclusion, and a stranger guest who gave any other answer, for several reasons. First of all the guest would not know what was in the bottle which the waiter was proffering. True he may not know what was in the carafe which the hotel was proffering, but he would at least be able to have recourse to the hotel if something was wrong with the carafe wine, but he would have no such recourse with the waiter; if he did, it would be worthless.

It seems to us that the matter can be answered on a much simpler basis. The hypothetical customer must be reasonably honest as well as being reasonably intelligent and it seems to us incredible that any customer, to whom the true situation was made clear, would willingly make himself a party to what was obviously a fraud by the waiter on his employers. If that conclusion is contrary to the *obiter dicta* in *R v Rashid* [1977] 1 WLR 298 at 302 *per* Bridge LJ, then we must respectfully disagree with those *dicta* ...

R v Miller (1992) 95 Cr App R 421 (CA)

Lord Chief Justice: ... The facts of the case are these. The applicant operated as an unlicensed taxi driver from both Heathrow and Gatwick Airports from time to time. The prosecution alleged, as the indictment which has been read indicates, that he obtained from various foreign persons coming to this country extortionate fares in respect of journeys which he carried out with those people as his passengers ...

In our judgment ... it is really not legitimate to isolate the moment when the money is handed over from the rest of the story. If on the whole of the story it can legitimately be said that the various deceptions alleged in the indictment were the cause for the money being handed over, it is, or may be, irrelevant that at the final moment the victim suspected or even believed that he or she had been swindled.

This is such a case. The passenger in each case was initially inveigled into agreeing to ride in the car by the lie that it was a proper taxi, and also by the inference that the charges levied by this applicant would be reasonable. By the end of the journey the victim realised, or partially realised in some cases, that the applicant had probably been lying. But by that time in each case the victim feels that he or she is under a compulsion or obligation to pay the extortionate sum requested ...

... [The applicant] had not charged a reasonable fare. He charged in one case 10 times more than the reasonable fare. All of that stemmed from the fact that he was not a taxi driver. The passenger, feeling a compulsion or obligation to pay, and fearing the consequences if he or she did not, handed over the money ...

There is, in our judgment, ample evidence arising from the facts which we have endeavoured to detail, upon which the jury could properly conclude that what was the effective cause of the transfer of this money were the various false assertions which this man made as laid in the indictment. That being the case, it was a question of fact for the jury to decide whether or not the prosecution had made out their case. They had to answer the question what was the effective cause of the transfer of this money. In the light of the fact that there is no complaint, and indeed there could be no complaint, about the direction to the jury, they were left the proper problem to decide. There was ample evidence upon which they could come to the conclusion which they did, and came to very rapidly ...

OBTAINING A MONEY TRANSFER BY DECEPTION

In *R v Preddy* [1996] 3 All ER 481 the House of Lords held that although the appellants had obtained mortgages by giving false information, the transfer of money between bank accounts was not illegal because no 'property' had passed from the payer to the payee. This decision was reversed by s 1 of the Theft (Amendment) Act 1996, which inserted a s 15A into the Theft Act 1968. This section creates a new offence of obtaining a money transfer by deception.

Section 15A of the Theft Act 1968

(1) A person is guilty of an offence if by any deception he dishonestly obtains a money transfer for himself or another.

(2) A money transfer occurs when:

  (a) a debit is made to one account;

  (b) a credit is made to another; and

  (c) the credit results from the debit or the debit results from the credit.

(3) References to a credit and to a debit are to a credit of an amount of money and to a debit of an amount of money.

(4) It is immaterial (in particular):

  (a) whether the amount credited is the same as the amount debited;

  (b) whether the money transfer is effected on presentment of a cheque or by another method;

  (c) whether any delay occurs in the process by which the money transfer is effected;

(d) whether any intermediate credits or debits are made in the course of the money transfer;

(e) whether either of the accounts is overdrawn before or after the money transfer is effected.

(5) A person guilty of an offence under this section shall be liable on conviction on indictment to imprisonment for a term not exceeding 10 years.

Section 15B of the Theft Act 1968

(1) The following provisions have effect for the interpretation of s 15A of this Act.

(2) 'Deception' has the same meaning as in s 15 of this Act.

(3) 'Account' means an account kept with:

(a) a bank; or

(b) a person carrying on business which falls within subsection (4) below.

(4) A business falls within this subsection if:

(a) in the course of the business money received by way of deposit is lent to others; or

(b) any other activity of the business is financed, wholly or to any material extent, out of the capital of or the interest on money received by way of deposit;

and 'deposit' here has the same meaning as in s 35 of the Banking Act 1987 ...

(5) For the purposes of subsection (4) above:

(a) all the activities which a person carries on by way of business shall be regarded as a single business carried on by him; and

(b) 'money' includes money expressed in a currency other than sterling or in the European Currency Unit (as defined in Council Regulation No 3320/94/EC or any Community instrument replacing it).

[Note that nothing in s 15A has effect in relation to anything done before the commencement of the Theft (Amendment) Act 1996 (18 December 1996).]

DISHONESTLY RETAINING A WRONGFUL CREDIT

Section 2 of the Theft (Amendment) Act 1996 adds a new section, s 24A, to the Theft Act 1968. This creates a new offence of dishonestly retaining wrongful credits, which covers instances where transfers of money obtained by deception (an offence under s 15A of the Theft Act 1968) are credited to another account.

Section 24A of the Theft Act 1968

(1) A person is guilty of an offence if:

(a) a wrongful credit has been made to an account kept by him or in respect of which he has any right or interest;

(b) he knows or believes that the credit is wrongful; and

(c) he dishonestly fails to take such steps as are reasonable in the circumstances to secure that the credit is cancelled.

(2) References to a credit are to a credit of an amount of money.

(3) A credit to an account is wrongful if it is the credit side of a money transfer obtained contrary to s 15A of this Act.

(4) A credit to an account is also wrongful to the extent that it derives from:

(a) theft;

(b) an offence under s 15A of this Act;

(c) blackmail; or

(d) stolen goods.

(5) In determining whether a credit to an account is wrongful, it is immaterial (in particular) whether the account is overdrawn before or after the credit is made.

(6) A person guilty of an offence under this section shall be liable on conviction on indictment to imprisonment for a term not exceeding 10 years.

(7) Subsection (8) below applies for purposes of provisions of this Act relating to stolen goods (including subsection (4) above).

(8) References to stolen goods include money which is dishonestly withdrawn from an account to which a wrongful credit has been made, but only to the extent that the money derives from the credit.

(9) In this section 'account' and 'money' shall be construed in accordance with s 15B of this Act.

[Note that s 24A only applies to wrongful credits made on or after 18 December 1996.]

OBTAINING PECUNIARY ADVANTAGE BY DECEPTION

Section 16 of the Theft Act 1968

(1) A person who by any deception dishonestly obtains for himself or another any pecuniary advantage shall on conviction on indictment be liable to imprisonment for a term not exceeding five years.

(2) The cases in which a pecuniary advantage within the meaning of this section is to be regarded as obtained for a person are cases where:

(a) [repealed by s 5(5) of the Theft Act 1978];

(b) he is allowed to borrow by way of overdraft, or to take out any policy of insurance or annuity contract, or obtains an improvement of the terms on which he is allowed to do so; or

(c) he is given the opportunity to earn remuneration or greater remuneration in an office or employment, or to win money by betting.

(3) For purposes of this section 'deception' has the same meaning as in s 15 of this Act.

The elements of the offence created by s 16 of the Theft Act 1968 are that the defendant:

(a) by any deception ...

(b) dishonestly ...

(c) obtains ...

(d) for himself or another ...

(e) any pecuniary advantage ...

Deception; dishonesty; obtains

See commentary on s 15 of the Theft Act 1968.

It does not matter if the person actually deceived is not the person who provides the pecuniary advantage.

R v Kovacs [1974] 1 WLR 370 (CA)

Facts: The prosecution case was that by the end of November 1972 the appellant's account at the Tring branch of the National Westminster Bank was overdrawn in the sum of £572. By letter dated 30 November 1972, the bank told her the extent of her indebtedness and that no more cheques drawn by her would be met. Shortly afterwards a bank official named Hedges called on her and asked her for her cheque book and the cheque card which had been issued to her. She said they were not in her possession. On 1 February 1973, she used a cheque drawn on the Tring branch of her bank and her cheque card to obtain at Berkhamsted Station a railway ticket costing £2.89. On 5 February 1973, she used the same means to obtain a Pekingese dog costing £42 from a pet shop.

> **Lawton LJ**: ... When the bank issued the cheque card to the appellant, they put her into possession of a document which was an undertaking by them to any person to whom she showed it that they would honour her cheque subject to certain conditions. No question arises in this case as to whether these conditions have been complied with. This meant that, if she was overdrawn on her account when she used her cheque card, she would be allowed by the bank to overdraw further to the extent of the cheque covered by it. She was obtaining a pecuniary advantage as defined by s 16(2)(b) of the Theft Act 1968.
>
> The next question is – how did she obtain pecuniary advantage? On the facts the answer is clear, namely by inducing the railway booking clerk and the pet shop owner to believe that she was entitled to use the cheque card when she was not. As a result of this deception they both accepted payment by cheques which the bank were bound to honour pursuant to their undertaking as set out on the face of the cheque card.
>
> In our judgment, the loss suffered by the bank was the result of the appellant's deception of the railway booking clerk and the pet shop owner. Section 16(1) does not provide either expressly or by implication that the person deceived must suffer any loss arising from the deception. What does have to be proved is that the accused by deception obtained for himself or another a pecuniary advantage. What there must be is a causal connection between the deception used and the pecuniary advantage obtained. There was such a connection in this case ...

Pecuniary advantage

If the defendant has obtained money, then the appropriate charge is 'obtaining property', since cash is not within the definition of 'pecuniary advantage'.

The definition of 'pecuniary advantage' in s 16(2) is exhaustive. If he has obtained one of the 'advantages' listed in s 16(2), it does not matter whether the defendant actually acquired any real benefit.

DPP v Turner [1974] AC 357 (HL)

Lord Reid: ... The first part [of s 16(2) of the Theft Act 1968] is drafted in an unusual way. Does it mean that in the cases set out in heads ... (b) and (c) a pecuniary advantage is to be deemed to have been obtained, so that it is irrelevant to consider whether in fact any such advantage was obtained, and equally irrelevant to prove that nothing in the nature of pecuniary advantage was in fact obtained by the accused? I think that that must be its meaning though I am at a loss to understand why that was not clearly stated. 'Is to be regarded as obtained' must, I think, mean 'is to be deemed to have been obtained' even if in fact there was none.

[Note: The rest of Lord Reid's speech deals with the interpretation of s 16(2)(a) of the Theft Act 1968, which was repealed, and replaced by ss 1 and 2 of the Theft Act 1978.]

Section 16(2)(b) of the Theft Act 1968: being allowed to borrow by way of overdraft, etc

The word 'allow' is construed loosely, so as to include the situation where a bank has to honour a cheque because of the use of a cheque card (*R v Waites* [1982] Crim LR 369 and *R v Bevan* (1986) 84 Cr App R 143). It does not matter whether the defendant has actually availed himself of the overdraft facility, since the facility itself is the pecuniary advantage (*R v Watkins* [1976] 1 All ER 578).

R v Waites [1982] Crim LR 369 (CA)

Facts: The appellant opened an account with a bank and was issued with a personalised cheque book and, later, with a cheque card whereby the bank guaranteed to meet a cheque up to £50. She made no arrangements to overdraw her account and used the cheques and card to make many purchases, creating an overdraft of more than £850. She was charged on several counts with obtaining a pecuniary advantage by deception, contrary to s 16(1) of the Theft Act 1968. It was argued in her defence that there was no case to answer because it could not be said that she had been 'allowed' to borrow by way of overdraft within the meaning of s 16(2)(b), since the bank would have been trying to stop her from doing so.

Held, dismissing the appeal against conviction: The definitions in s 16(2) are exclusive and, if the actions do not fall within them, there is no obtaining of a pecuniary advantage. There is no proper doubt as to the meaning of the verb 'allow' in the circumstances of s 16(2)(b). Permission to use the card carried with it the power in the cardholder, albeit in breach of contract with the bank, to use the card beyond the limits imposed knowing that the bank would be obliged to meet the debt created with the shopkeeper. That was, within the ordinary meaning of the words, to allow borrowing by way of overdraft.

R v Bevan (1986) 84 Cr App R 143 (CA)

Staughton J: ... [I]s a person 'allowed to borrow by way of overdraft', in terms of s 16 of the Theft Act 1968, when he uses a cheque card in excess of the limits permitted by the bank that issued it?

... The particulars [alleged in the indictment] were ... that the appellant had 'dishonestly obtained for himself a pecuniary advantage namely a borrowing by way of overdraft from Lloyds Bank plc by deception namely by falsely representing that he was then entitled and authorised to use a cheque card when issuing cheque number ... drawn on Lloyds Bank plc ...'

... In April 1982 the appellant opened an account with Lloyds Bank plc at one of their branches in London. He was provided with cheque books and a cheque card. [He did not obtain permission] to overdraw on his account; and it was specifically stated that the cheque card did not entitle him to overdraw his account if no overdraft arrangements had been made, or to overdraw in excess of any overdraft limit that might be agreed.

Nevertheless the appellant did [on a number of occasions draw £50 in cash from another bank when his account at Lloyd's Bank was overdrawn] ...

... [I]t is not suggested that any deception operated on Lloyd's Bank. When called upon to reimburse the paying bank they no doubt appreciated that the appellant's account was overdrawn. They were no doubt displeased. But they were obliged to honour their obligation to the paying bank, founded upon the use of the cheque card which they had issued.

... The question [is] ... whether the appellant had been allowed to borrow by way of overdraft when he had not negotiated and agreed an overdraft limit, but merely used his card in such a way that his bank felt itself obliged to reimburse the paying bank. [In *R v Waites* [1982] Crim LR 369] this court held that he had been allowed to borrow by way of overdraft.

In those circumstances we consider that we are bound by the authority of *Waites* ... When the appellant's bank received a request by the paying bank for reimbursement in respect of a cheque drawn by the appellant, it of course readily complied. The bank's motive was no doubt the protection of its own reputation, as well as its contractual obligation owed directly to the paying bank ... But reimbursement by the appellant's bank was nevertheless an act of will; when it took place the appellant was allowed by the bank to borrow money on overdraft; and the overdraft was consensual, since the appellant had impliedly requested it and the bank had, albeit reluctantly, agreed ...

R v Watkins [1976] 1 All ER 578

HHJ Paul Clarke (sitting at Warwick Crown Court): ... I interpret the subsection in question as sufficiently proved if the deception caused only the granting of facilities for drawing on an overdraft ... I think that s 16(2)(b) is necessary because when facilities for an overdraft are granted a customer gets a very real advantage in thereafter being able to go to the counter and draw on his overdraft. The opportunities for a deception arise when he goes to the manager and gets the facility, not when he draws on that facility.

Section 16(2)(c) of the Theft Act 1968: opportunity to earn remuneration, etc

The reference to obtaining an opportunity to win money by betting means that the deception practised in *R v Clucas* [1949] 2 KB 226 (see under s 15, *above*) would fall under s 16(2)(c).

A false claim to have professional qualifications can amount to an offence under s 16(2)(c).

R v Callender [1992] 3 WLR 501 (CA)

Wright J: ... The facts of the matter are relatively simple. The applicant described himself as a self-employed accountant. In or about June 1987 Mr Burt met the appellant, whom he said he had heard of from doing accountancy work for others, and he understood from the appellant, having been shown a *curriculum vitae* and other documents, that he was an associate member of the Chartered Institute of Management Accountants, and a graduate or member of the Institute of Marketing. Mr Burt said in evidence that he had relied upon these representations and that he would not have 'employed' him – the word he used in evidence – had he known that he was not qualified. In truth and in fact, the appellant had not obtained the qualifications referred to and his *curriculum vitae* was false in those respects ...

We have come to the clear conclusion that Parliament in adopting the phrase 'office or employment' intended s 16(1) of the 1968 Act to have a wider impact than one confined to the narrow limits of a contract of service ... We take the view that the interpretation of the words in question involves the consideration of their meaning as a matter of ordinary language. That meaning, in our judgment, is not to be arrived at by reference to the more limited and technical interpretation given to those words in the context of the law of master and servant ... or in the context of pensions and national insurance law ... or in the context of income tax.

... The *Shorter Oxford English Dictionary* defines ... 'employment' ... as: 'That on which [one] is employed; business; occupation; a commission'. It seems to us that it is a perfectly proper use of ordinary language and as such to be readily understood by ordinary literate men and women to say of a person in this appellant's position that his services as an accountant were 'employed' by his customers, and that this state of affairs is properly to be described by the word 'employment'. As such the facts in this case fall within the ambit of the section ...

FALSE ACCOUNTING

Section 17 of the Theft Act 1968

(1) Where a person dishonestly, with a view to gain for himself or another or with intent to cause loss to another:

(a) destroys, defaces, conceals or falsifies any account or any record or document made or required for any accounting purpose; or

(b) in furnishing information for any purpose produces or makes use of any account, or any such record or document as aforesaid, which to his knowledge is or may be misleading, false or deceptive in a material particular;

he shall, on conviction on indictment, be liable to imprisonment for a term not exceeding seven years.

(2) For purposes of this section a person who makes or concurs in making in an account or other document an entry which is or may be misleading, false or deceptive in a material particular or who omits or concurs in omitting a material particular from an account or other document, is to be treated as falsifying the account or document.

OBTAINING SERVICES BY DECEPTION

Section 1 of the Theft Act 1978

(1) A person who by any deception dishonestly obtains services from another shall be guilty of an offence.

(2) It is an obtaining of services where the other is induced to confer a benefit by doing some act, or causing or permitting some act to be done, on the understanding that the benefit has been or will be paid for.

(3) Without prejudice to the generality of subsection (2) above, it is an obtaining of services where the other is induced to make a loan, or to cause or permit a loan to be made, on the understanding that any payment (whether by way of interest or otherwise) will be or has been made in respect of the loan.

Section 5 of the Theft Act 1968

(1) For the purpose of ss 1 and 2 above 'deception' has the same meaning as in s 15 of the Theft Act 1968, that is to say, it means any deception (whether deliberate or reckless) by words or conduct as to fact or as to law, including a deception as to the present intentions of the person using the deception or any other person ...

The elements of the offence created by s 1 of the Theft Act 1978 are that the defendant:

(a) by any deception ...

(b) dishonestly ...

(c) obtains ...

(d) services ...

(e) from another.

Deception; dishonesty; obtains

These words have all been considered under s 15 of the Theft Act 1968 (see *above*).

The scope of the offence

The deception must occur *before* the services are obtained, otherwise the services cannot be said to be obtained 'by' (ie as a result of) deception.

Section 1 of the Theft Act 1978 covers situations such as the following:

(a) the defendant hands over a worthless cheque to the provider of the service, claiming thereby to be paying in advance);

(b) the defendant, by means of some deception, persuades the provider of the service to agree to a lesser payment than would otherwise have been the case;

(c) the defendant, by means of some deception, persuades the provider of the service to agree to payment at a later time than would otherwise be the case.

An example of (b) would be as follows: a hairdresser offers a 10% discount to students at the local college. I falsely claim to be such a student (before my hair is cut) and I duly get a 10% discount to which I am not entitled.

It must be stressed that s 1(2) requires that there be an 'understanding that the [service] has been or will be paid for'. It follows that s 1 does not cover the situation where the defendant, by means of some deception, persuades the provider of the service to forgo payment altogether. That situation would be covered by s 2(1)(c) of the Theft Act 1978 (see *below*).

On the overlap between s 1 of the Theft Act 1978 and other offences involving deception, see *R v Widdowson* (1985) 82 Cr App R 314.

Section 1(3) of the Theft Act 1968 was added by the Theft (Amendment) Act 1996. The effect is to reverse the decision in *R v Halai* [1983] Crim LR 624, where it had been held (probably *per incuriam*) that the making of a loan did not come within the definition of a 'service'.

R v Widdowson (1985) 82 Cr App R 314 (CA)

Saville J: ... At the trial the case for the prosecution was that on 14 July 1984, the appellant had gone to a garage with a view to buying a Ford Escort van on hire-purchase. He was said to have told the salesman (a Mr Wilson) that he had looked at the Escort van for sale there, was happy with it and that it would all be subject to finance being arranged. Mr Wilson said that the appellant was satisfied that his own van would cover the initial deposit and that if the finance had been cleared by the finance company the vehicle would have been the appellant's. Mr Wilson gave evidence that the appellant then completed a hire-purchase form putting the name Steven Pitman and an address, 15 Edinburgh Way, Thetford, as the name and address of the hirer. That address was in fact where a Mr Pitman lived next door to the appellant. Mr Wilson said that had he known that this name and address was not that of the appellant, he would not have taken the matter any further and would not have put it forward to the finance company as he did. He agreed that he did not intend that the form should constitute the actual hire-purchase deal, and said it was used so that enquiries could be made whether the person named as hirer was creditworthy. He further agreed that in fact a proposal form rather than a hire-purchase form should have been used for this purpose, but explained that the garage had run out of the latter forms at the time in question. It should also be mentioned that the appellant had in fact signed the form at the end in his own name, something which Mr Wilson only discovered later, apparently from the finance company itself. According to evidence from the police, the appellant stated on being interviewed that he had put his own telephone number on the form and explained that he had put the name Steven Pitman on the form because he could not get credit if it was known who he really was. His explanation for signing the form in his own name was simply that he had not been thinking.

According to the defence, the appellant, being himself unable to obtain credit, completed the form solely in order to enquire into the creditworthiness of Pitman. He said he had earlier agreed with Pitman that on being given clearance by the finance company Pitman should thereby obtain the vehicle on his behalf pending the appellant's receipt of funds to pay the outstanding balance of the purchase price. This explanation had not apparently been given to the police on the occasion of his interview ...

We deal first with the point not canvassed before the learned judge. It seems to us, on the authority of *R v Garlick* (1958) 42 Cr App R 141 and *R v Miller (Simon)*

[1977] 3 All ER 986, that a hire-purchase agreement in ordinary form (and there was no suggestion that any different form might have been used in this case) cannot properly be described as credit facilities, for the simple reason that on making such a hire-purchase agreement the finance company does not give any credit to the hirer. All it does is to hire out the goods to the hirer, who usually has options either to purchase on paying all the instalments, or to terminate the agreement at any time. Thus the words in the particulars to the indictment, 'credit facilities to assist in the purchase' were not supported by any evidence led at the hearing; and since no application to amend the indictment was made, it is conceded that if this is the correct analysis (as we so hold) then the indictment was bad and the conviction on it cannot stand.

We should add that we reject the suggestion that the obtaining of a hire-purchase agreement cannot amount to the obtaining of services. In *R v Halai* [1983] Crim LR 624 this court held that a mortgage advance cannot be described as a service. It is suggested that a hire-purchase agreement is indistinguishable. We disagree. As we have just said, a hire-purchase agreement (at least in the ordinary form) is the hiring of goods with various options given to the hirer, who in return agrees to pay the instalments, maintain the vehicle and so on. In our view the hire-purchasing of a vehicle on some such terms can be regarded as the conferring of some benefit by doing some act, or causing or permitting an act to be done, on the understanding that the benefit has been or will be paid for, this being the definition of services in s 1(2) of the Theft Act 1978. The finance company confers a benefit by delivering possession of the vehicle to the hirer (or by causing or permitting the garage to do so) on the understanding that the hirer has paid or will pay a deposit and subsequent instalments.

There remains the question of attempt. In our judgment there was no evidence of an attempt to commit the crime alleged within the meaning of s 1(1) of the Criminal Attempts Act 1981. It seems to us that at most all the appellant had actually done was to attempt to ascertain whether or not Steven Pitman was creditworthy, in the sense of being acceptable to the finance company as a prospective hire-purchaser. It was not suggested that a favourable reply from the finance company could have constituted the obtaining of services within the meaning of the Theft Act 1978, if only because there was no question of payment being made for such a reply. Thus the question is whether this appellant's act in giving the false particulars on the form can reasonably be said to have been more than merely preparatory to the obtaining of hire-purchase facilities. In our view this cannot be said. Assuming that the finance company had responded favourably to the proposal, it still remained for the appellant to seek a hire-purchase deal from them. To our minds it is that step which would constitute an attempt to obtain the services relied upon in this case. If one asks whether this appellant had carried out every step which it was necessary for him to perform to achieve the consequences alleged to have been attempted, the answer must be that he did not.

Equally, it seems to us, this appellant's acts cannot be described as immediately rather than merely remotely connected with the specific offence alleged to have been attempted. Thus whichever of the tests described in *R v Ilyas* (1984) 78 Cr App R 17 is applied, what the appellant did cannot reasonably be described as more than merely preparatory.

... [I]t would appear that the learned judge was influenced by the suggested inevitability of the transaction going ahead, ie that the appellant's intentions would have remained the same. That, with great respect, ignores the fact that dishonest intentions alone do not constitute criminal attempts and that in addition it is necessary to establish, to use the words of Lord Diplock, that the offender has crossed the Rubicon and burned his boats. He had not done so (as the learned judge himself held) in the sense of attempting to obtain the vehicle. In our judgment, he equally had not done so in attempting to obtain the hire-purchase of the vehicle.

EVASION OF LIABILITY BY DECEPTION

Section 2 of the Theft Act 1978

(1) Subject to subsection (2) below, where a person by any deception:

(a) dishonestly secures the remission of the whole or part of any existing liability to make a payment, whether his own liability or another's; or

(b) with intent to make permanent default in whole or in part on any existing liability to make a payment, or with intent to let another do so, dishonestly induces the creditor or any person claiming payment on behalf of the creditor to wait for payment (whether or not the due date for payment is deferred) or to forgo payment; or

(c) dishonestly obtains any exemption from or abatement of liability to make a payment;

he shall be guilty of an offence.

(2) For purposes of this section 'liability' means legally enforceable liability; and subsection (1) shall not apply in relation to a liability that has not been accepted or established to pay compensation for a wrongful act or omission.

(3) For purposes of subsection (1)(b) a person induced to take in payment a cheque or other security for money by way of conditional satisfaction of a pre-existing liability is to be treated not as being paid but as being induced to wait for payment.

(4) For purposes of subsection (1)(c) 'obtains' includes obtaining for another or enabling another to obtain.

Section 5 of the Theft Act 1978

(1) For the purpose of ss 1 and 2 above 'deception' has the same meaning as in s 15 of the Theft Act 1968, that is to say, it means any deception (whether deliberate or reckless) by words or conduct as to fact or as to law, including a deception as to the present intentions of the person using the deception or any other person ...

Section 2 of the Theft Act 1978 creates three forms of 'evasion of liability'. In each case there must be a deception (as defined for the purposes of s 15 of the Theft Act 1968, as to which see *above*).

In all three cases the liability which is evaded must be legally enforceable: see s 2(2) of the Theft Act 1978 and *R v Modupe* [1991] Crim LR 530. Furthermore, offences can only committed under s 2(1)(a) or (b) in respect of an 'existing liability', but an offence under s 2(1)(c) can be committed before any liability to pay has come into existence.

Section 2(1)(a)

The elements of this offence are:

(1) by any deception ...

(2) dishonestly ...

(3) securing the remission of the whole or part of an existing liability to make a payment.

The subsection makes it clear that it does not matter whether or not the liability is that of the person practising the deception. The word 'remission' means 'release' from the liability to make payment. An example of a situation which falls within s 2(1)(a) is as follows: the defendant borrows a sum of money from someone. Later, the defendant tells the lender a false story which induces the lender to write off some or all of the debt. If the lender is merely induced to wait for payment (ie gives the debtor more time rather than writing off the debt), that may be an offence under s 2(1)(b).

In *R v Jackson* [1983] Crim LR 617 it was held that where someone is induced to accept a stolen credit card in payment for goods, the defendant's debt is remitted in that the supplier of the goods will look to the credit card company for payment, not to the defendant. Presumably, the same would apply where the supplier accepts a cheque supported by a cheque guarantee card: the supplier will look to the bank to honour the cheque in accordance with the terms of the cheque guarantee card.

R v Jackson [1983] Crim LR 617 (CA)

Facts: A stolen credit card was presented by occupants of the appellant's car at petrol stations and accepted in satisfaction of payment for petrol and other goods. The appellant was charged, *inter alia*, with evading liability by deception by dishonestly securing the remission of an existing liability, contrary to s 2(1)(a) of the Theft Act 1978.

Held, dismissing the appeal, that although in *R v Holt* [1981] 1 WLR 1000 it was held that the element under s 2(1)(b) of an intent to make permanent default on the whole or part of an existing liability was unique to subparagraph (b), that judgment was not authority for the proposition that the elements in subparagraphs (a), (b) and (c) of s 2(1) were mutually exclusive. The transaction of tendering a stolen credit card and having it accepted by a trader who forthwith would look to the authority issuing the card for payment and not to the person tendering the card, meant that that person had dishonestly secured the remission of an existing liability. It was not necessary to consider whether a charge in respect of that transaction could be brought under s 2(1)(b). In the circumstances the matter was not wrongly charged under s 2(1)(a).

Section 2(1)(b)

The elements of this offence are:

(1) by any deception ...

(2) with intent to make permanent default on all or part of an existing liability to make a payment (or with intent to let another do so) ...

(3) dishonestly ...

(4) induces the creditor to wait for payment or to forgo payment.

This covers the situation where the defendant borrows a sum of money from someone and later the defendant (who, by this time, does not intend to repay the money), by means of some deception, persuades the creditor to wait longer for payment than had originally been agreed or even to forgo payment altogether. Note that s 2(3) says that, for the purpose only of s 2(1)(b), inducing a creditor to accept a cheque (which is a way of postponing payment) is to be regarded as inducing the creditor to wait for payment.

This is the only one of the three offences where an intention to make permanent default has to be proved. The fact that s 2(1)(b) covers situations where the creditor is induced to forgo payment means that there is an overlap with s 2 (1)(a), securing the remission of an existing liability. This overlap was considered in *R v Jackson* [1983] Crim LR 617 (see *above*) and *R v Holt* [1981] 1 WLR 1000.

The phrase 'or with intent to let another do so' was considered in *R v Attewell-Hughes* [1991] 1 WLR 955.

R v Holt and Another [1981] 1 WLR 1000 (CA)

Lawson J: ... The charge on which the appellants were convicted was as follows. The statement of the offence was attempted evasion of liability by deception, contrary to common law. The particulars of the offence were that the defendants, on 9 December 1979, by deception with intent to make permanent default on an existing liability, did attempt to induce Philip Parkinson, servant of Pizzaland Restaurants Ltd, to forgo payment of £3.65 by falsely representing that payment had been made by them to another servant of the said Pizzaland Restaurants Ltd.

From the use of the expressions 'with intent to make permanent default' and 'to induce [the creditor's agent] to forgo payment', it is clear that the attempt charged was one to commit the offence defined by s 2(1)(b) of the 1978 Act. [NB This case precedes the coming into force of the Criminal Attempts Act 1981 and so the attempt is charged as an offence under the common law.]

The facts of the case were that in the evening of 9 December 1979, the defendants consumed meals costing £3.65 in the Pizzaland Restaurant in Southport. There was a police officer off duty also having a meal in the restaurant and he overheard the defendant planning to evade payment for their meals by the device of pretending that a waitress had removed a £5 note which they had placed on the table. When presented with their bill, the defendants advanced this deception and declined payment. The police officer concerned prevented them from leaving the restaurant and they were shortly afterwards arrested and charged ...

The elements of the offence defined by s 2(1)(b) of the Act of 1978 relevant to the present case are clearly these: first, the defendant must be proved to have the intent to make permanent default on the whole or part of an existing liability. This element is unique to s 2(1)(b); it has no application to the offences defined in s 2(1)(a) or (c). Second, given such intent, he must use deception. Third, his deception must be practised dishonestly to induce the creditor to forgo payment.

It must always be remembered that in the present case, whatever offence was being attempted, the attempt failed. The creditor was not induced by the dishonest deception and did not forgo payment. It is clear on the evidence that the defendants' conduct constituted an attempt to evade liability by deception, and the jury, who were properly directed, clearly concluded that the defendants' conduct was motivated by the intent to make permanent default on their supper bill. Thus, all the elements needed to enable an attempt to commit the offence defined in s 2(1)(b) were found to be present, so that the defendants were rightly convicted as charged.

Reverting to the construction of s 2(1) of the Act of 1978, as to which the commentators are not at one, we are not sure whether the choice of expressions describing the consequences of deception employed in each of its paragraphs, namely in paragraph (a) 'secures the remission of ... any existing liability', in paragraph (b) 'induces the creditor ... to forgo payment' and in paragraph (c) 'obtains any exemption from ... liability' are simply different ways of describing the same end result or represent conceptual differences.

Whilst it is plain that there are substantial differences in the elements of the three offences defined in s 2(1), they show these common features: first, the use of deception to a creditor in relation to a liability; second, dishonesty in the use of deception; and third, the use of deception to gain some advantage in time or money. Thus the differences between the offences relate principally to the different situations in which the debtor-creditor relationship has arisen ...

R v Attewell-Hughes [1991] 4 All ER 810 (CA)

Facts: The appellant was employed as the manager of a hotel by the owner, who lived abroad. The owner gave the appellant authority to act on his behalf and to operate his bank account in relation to the running of the hotel. The appellant opened an account in the name of the hotel at a bank, which made it clear that it would not grant an overdraft facility on the account. However, the appellant wrote a number of cheques on that account for goods and services supplied to the hotel, and to pay VAT due from the hotel to HM Customs and Excise, when the funds available in the account were not sufficient to cover the cheques.

Bingham LJ: ... The case against the appellant was that between about April and November 1986 he was running the Dean House Hotel on the Isle of Wight and that, while doing so, in a number of ways he was systematically defrauding those who were supplying, or had previously supplied, the hotel with various goods. It was alleged that the charges preferred against the appellant were a selection of those which could have been brought.

The essence of the counts of obtaining property by deception was that he persuaded suppliers to provide goods or services by telling lies, causing the suppliers to believe that they would be paid when he knew that they would not. The counts of evading liability by deception depended on the appellant having fobbed off suppliers of goods or services, making them wait for payment by the deception that cheques he was giving them were good and valid orders for payment and that he had authority to draw on the bank account for those amounts ...

[His Lordship then quoted one of the counts in the indictment, which charged the appellant with an offence under s 2(1)(b) of the Theft Act 1978, namely that:]

> ... with intent to make permanent default in whole or in part of an existing liability to pay £6,347 to Geoffrey Arnold Malone on behalf of HM Customs and Excise [he] dishonestly induced the said Geoffrey Arnold Malone on behalf of HM Customs and Excise to wait for payment of the said sum by deception, namely by a false implied representation that cheque number 224358 for £6,347 drawn of the account of Dean House Hotel was a good and valid order for the payment of £6,347 and that he had authority to draw upon the account with Midland Bank Limited for that amount.

We pause to reiterate that, so far as this liability is concerned, it is plain, and indeed not in dispute, that the liability was not that of the appellant but was that of Mr Nicholson [the owner of the hotel] ...

> ...It seems to us that the opening words 'with intent to make permanent default' and the absence of any reference to procuring a default by another clearly suggest a default by the party whose liability it is. We notice the absence of any qualification, 'whether his own or another's', such as exists in s 2(1)(a) and we find the express reference ... 'or with intent to let another do so', which in our judgment clearly indicates an intention on the part of the draftsman to differentiate between these two modes of committing the offence.

Section 2(1)(c)

The elements of this offence are that the defendant:

(1) by any deception ...

(2) dishonestly ...

(3) obtains exemption from or abatement of liability to make a payment.

An example of a situation where this provision applies would be where the defendant persuades the seller of goods that he (the defendant) is entitled to a discount to which he is not, in fact, entitled. For example, a person falsely claims to be a student in order to get a discount at a shop which gives a discount on its goods to students.

Another example is to be found in *R v Firth* (1990) 91 Cr App R 217.

R v Firth (1990) 91 Cr App R 217 (CA)

The Lord Chief Justice: ... The prosecution allegation in these various counts was that the appellant [who was a consultant gynaecologist/obstetrician], by failing dishonestly to inform the hospital of the private patient status of [two of his patients], had caused either them or himself not to be billed for services which should have been charged against them.

If, as was alleged, it was incumbent upon him to give the information to the hospital and he deliberately and dishonestly refrained from doing so, with the result that no charge was levied either upon the patients or upon himself, in our judgment the wording of the section and subsection which I have just read is satisfied. It matters not whether it was an act of commission or an act of omission ...

... The words [of s 2(1)(c) of the Theft Act 1978] as they stand are apt to cover an expected liability or future liability, even if the deception alleged is not in truth a continuing deception. The omission of the word 'existing' was, it seems clear to us, purposeful, and not a matter of chance ...

MAKING OFF WITHOUT PAYMENT

Section 3 of the Theft Act 1978

(1) Subject to subsection (3) below, a person who, knowing that payment on the spot for any goods supplied or service done is required or expected from him, dishonestly makes off without having paid as required or expected and with intent to avoid payment of the amount due shall be guilty of an offence.

(2) For purposes of this section 'payment on the spot' includes payment at the time of collecting goods on which work has been done or in respect of which service has been provided.

(3) Subsection (1) above shall not apply where the supply of the goods or the doing of the service is contrary to law, or where the service done is such that payment is not legally enforceable.

(4) Any person may arrest without warrant anyone who is, or whom he, with reasonable cause, suspects to be, committing or attempting to commit an offence under this section.

The elements of the offence created by s 3 of the Theft Act 1978 are that the defendant:

(1) knowing that payment on the spot (for goods already supplied or services already done) is required or expected ...

(2) dishonestly ...

(3) makes off without having paid ...

(4) with intent to avoid payment of the amount due.

This section was enacted because of a loophole in s 15 of the Theft Act 1968 (obtaining services by deception). In *Edwards v Ddin* [1976] 1 WLR 942 the defendant filled up the tank of his car with petrol at a garage and then drove off without paying. The prosecution failed to secure a conviction under s 15 of the Theft Act 1968 because they were unable to prove that the defendant had intended from the outset not to pay for the petrol. For s 15 to apply, the deception must occur before the property is handed over.

Hence the need for s 3 of the Theft Act 1978, to cover cases where the defendant says that he formed the intention not to pay for the goods or services *after* he had obtained them. This section therefore covers situations such as:

(1) the diner who leaves the restaurant without paying;

(2) the passenger who fails to pay his taxi fare at the end of the journey;

(3) the motorist who fills up his petrol tank and leaves the garage without paying for the petrol.

Payment on the spot

This term is partially defined by s 3(2). It means little more than 'immediate payment'. Under s 3(3) payment must be legally enforceable (so failing to pay a prostitute after intercourse has taken place would not be an offence under s 3, although it could be an offence under s 1 of the Theft Act 1978). See also *Troughton v Metropolitan Police* [1987] Crim LR 138 and *R v Aziz* [1993] Crim LR 708.

Troughton v The Metropolitan Police [1987] Crim LR 138 (DC)

Facts: A taxi driver agreed to take the appellant to his home somewhere in Highbury. The appellant, having had a great deal to drink, had not told the driver his address. The driver had to stop to obtain directions from the appellant at some point. There was an argument, the appellant accusing the driver of making an unnecessary diversion. The taxi driver, being unable to get an address from the appellant, drove to the nearest police station to see if someone else could help.

Held: The basis for allowing this appeal was that the journey had not been completed and the consequence of that was a breach of contract by the taxi driver. Instead of resolving the argument about further instructions during the journey the driver broke away from the route which would have taken the appellant home and in order to go to the police station. The driver being in breach of contract was not lawfully able to demand the fare at any time thereafter. For that reason, among others the appellant was never in a situation in which he was bound to pay or even tender the money for the journey, and thus it could not be contended that he made off without payment.

R v Aziz [1993] Crim LR 708 (CA)

Facts: Two people requested a taxi to take them to a particular address. On arrival at that address the taxi driver asked for a fare of £15. The passengers declined to pay that much and offered £4 instead. The radio controller confirmed that the fare was £15 but the passengers still refused to pay. The driver started to drive them back to the address from which he had collected them but, en route, decided to drive to a police station. However, the two passengers forced the car to stop and ran off. The taxi driver managed to catch one of the men. The defendant argued that the requirement for payment had ceased because the driver had announced his intention of taking the passengers back to the place from where the journey had started.

Held: 'on the spot' means 'there and then'. The words 'makes off' involve a departure without paying from the place where payment would normally be made. In the case of a taxi, payment might be made while sitting in the taxi or standing by the window. In the present case, payment was requested while the passengers were still in the taxi. It became apparent to the driver that they were disputing the fare. The fact that the driver, realising that there was a prospect that they would not pay their fare, drove off somewhere else, did not mean that when the defendant ran off he could not, as a matter of law, be making off without payment. It was the time at which he made off which was critical. When this defendant made off, he had formed the intention to avoid payment of a fare which was still due and owing.

Making off

In most cases, no further explanation of these words is necessary. They simply mean that the customer leaves without paying. However, the offence can be committed where the supplier of the goods or services allows the customer to leave as the result of some deception (although a charge of evading liability may be more appropriate).

Handing over a worthless cheque and then making off could, in principle, be an offence under s 3. However, s 2(1)(b) would be the more appropriate charge: see *R v Hammond* [1982] Crim LR 611.

'Making off' normally entails leaving the premises. Thus, if the customer starts to leave but is prevented from doing so, he is guilty only of an attempt to make off: see *R v McDavitt* [1981] Crim LR 843; *R v Brooks* (1982) 76 Cr App R 66.

R v McDavitt [1981] Crim LR 843 (Croydon Crown Court: Mr Recorder M Mann QC)

Facts: The defendant had a meal with three friends in a restaurant. At the end of the meal his friends left the restaurant and the defendant remained at the table where they had all been sitting. The bill was brought on a saucer to his table and an argument ensued between the defendant and the owner of the restaurant which ended with the defendant refusing to pay any of the bill. He went towards the door whereupon someone standing by the door advised him not to leave as the police were being called. The defendant then went to the toilet in the restaurant where he remained until the police arrived. He was arrested and taken to a police station where he later made a statement under caution in which he admitted the above facts saying that it was his intention to leave without paying for the meal but that he decided to stay on being told about the police being summoned. He was subsequently indicted under s 3 of the Theft Act 1978 with making off from the restaurant without paying for the food and wine which had been consumed. On a submission of no case to answer:

Held: 'Makes off' refers to making off from the spot where payment is required or expected. What is the spot depends on the circumstances of each case. In this case the spot was the restaurant. The jury would be directed that it was not open to them to find the defendant guilty of the offence on the indictment but that it was open to them to find him guilty of an attempt to commit the offence.

R v Brooks and Brooks (1982) 76 Cr App R 66 (CA)

Facts: The appellants, father and daughter, along with a person named Smith, had a meal together one evening in the upstairs room of a restaurant. At 10.30 pm the daughter was seen leaving the premises in haste. The manager went upstairs and saw the two men were not there but found Smith downstairs waiting outside the men's lavatory.

Nearby was a door inside the premises which led into the yard. Smith made no comment when asked about the unpaid bill but, after entering the lavatory, later made off through the outer door. The manager chased after him and asked him to come back. While they were re-entering the restaurant, the father came out of it. All three then went back inside. All the father could offer for payment for the bill of £8.52 was a cheque for £130 in his favour, which later turned out to be valueless. Smith said in the father's hearing that the payment was not due from him, Smith. When the daughter was later interviewed by the police she maintained that Smith had met them earlier that night for the first time and had generously offered to treat her and her father to a meal.

Both father and daughter were charged with making off without payment contrary to s 3(1) of the Theft Act 1978.

Kilner Brown J: ... In our opinion, the words 'dishonestly makes off' are words easily understandable by any jury which, in the majority of cases, require no elaboration in a summing up. The jury should be told to apply the words in their ordinary natural meaning and to relate them to the facts of the case. We agree with the decision in *R v McDavitt* [1981] Crim LR 843 that 'making off' involves a departure from the spot where payment is required ...

On the facts of this case, it was not necessary to elaborate on the necessity to establish that there was a departure from the spot. The evidence of this was there. Both went outside the premises. However, in a case where the accused is stopped before passing the spot where payment is required, a jury should be directed that that may constitute an attempt to commit the offence, rather than the substantive offence, provided that the other ingredients are established ...

In the case of the appellant Julie Brooks, there is a further and different consideration ...

... [T]he jury were never told that upon the evidence that she left earlier and in haste and her defence that she went to the restaurant at the other man's invitation believing that he would pay, they would have to draw the inference that at the time she left she intended dishonestly to evade payment, before she could be convicted. If the jury had been alerted to this necessity, it is quite possible that they may not have been satisfied of her guilt ...

Intent to avoid payment

In addition to proving dishonesty (a separate element of the offence), the prosecution must also prove that the defendant intended to make permanent default, in other words, never to pay for the goods or services supplied. If the defendant is merely trying to postpone payment, then an offence under s 3 is not committed.

R v Allen [1985] AC 1029 (HL)

Lord Hailsham of St Marylebone LC: ... Count 2 of the indictment, which resulted in the conviction appealed from, read as follows:

> Statement of Offence: Making off without payment, contrary to s 3 of the Theft Act 1978.
>
> Particulars of Offence: Christopher Allen, on a day between 8 and 11 February 1983, knowing that payment on the spot for goods supplied and services done was required or expected from him, dishonestly made off without having paid as required or expected and with intent to avoid payment of the £1,286.94 due.

The facts, which are not disputed ... were as follows. The respondent, Christopher Allen, booked a room at a hotel for 10 nights from 15 January 1983. He stayed on thereafter and finally left on 11 February 1983 without paying his bill in the sum of £1,286.94. He telephoned two days later to explain that he was in financial difficulties because of some business transactions and arranged to return to the hotel on 18 February 1983 to remove his belongings and leave his Australian passport as security for the debt. He was arrested on his return and said that he genuinely hoped to be able to pay the bill and denied he was acting dishonestly. On 3 March 1983, he was still unable to pay the bill and provided an explanation to the police of his financial difficulties. The respondent's defence was that he had acted honestly and had genuinely expected to pay the bill from the proceeds of various business ventures ...

The judgment of the Court of Appeal, with which I agree, was delivered by Boreham J. He said [1985] 1 WLR 50, 57:

> To secure a conviction under s 3 of the 1978 Act the following must be proved: (1) that the defendant in fact made off without making payment on the spot; (2) the following mental elements: (a) knowledge that payment on the spot was required or expected of him; and (b) dishonesty; and (c) intent to avoid payment [that is 'of the amount due'].

I agree with this analysis. To this the judge adds the following comment:

> If (c) means, or is taken to include, no more than an intention to delay or defer payment of the amount due it is difficult to see what it adds to the other elements. Anyone who knows that payment on the spot is expected or required of him and who then dishonestly makes off without paying as required or expected must have at least the intention to delay or defer

> payment. It follows, therefore, that the conjoined phrase 'and with intent to avoid payment of the amount due' adds a further ingredient – an intention to do more than delay or defer – an intention to evade payment altogether.

My own view, for what it is worth, is that the section thus analysed is capable only of this meaning ... Even on the assumption that, in the context, the word 'avoid' without the addition of the word 'permanently' is capable of either meaning, which Boreham J was inclined to concede, I find myself convinced by his final paragraph, which reads:

> Finally, we can see no reason why, if the intention of Parliament was to provide, in effect, that an intention to delay or defer payment might suffice, Parliament should not have said so in explicit terms. This might have been achieved by the insertion of the word 'such' before 'payment' in the phrase in question. It would have been achieved by a grammatical reconstruction of the material part of s 3(1) thus, 'dishonestly makes off without having paid and with intent to avoid payment of the amount due as required or expected'. To accede to the Crown's submission would be to read the section as if it were constructed in that way. That we cannot do. Had it been intended to relate the intention to avoid 'payment' to 'payment as required or expected' it would have been easy to say so. The section does not say so. At the very least it contains an equivocation which should be resolved in favour of the appellant.

There is really no escape from this argument ...

Lord Scarman, Lord Diplock, Lord Bridge of Harwich and **Lord Brightman** all agreed with **Lord Hailsham LC**.

Section 4 of the Theft Act 1978: punishments

(1) Offences under this Act shall be punishable either on conviction on indictment or on summary conviction.

(2) A person convicted on indictment shall be liable:

- (a) for an offence under s 1 or s 2 of this Act, to imprisonment for a term not exceeding five years; and
- (b) for an offence under s 3 of this Act, to imprisonment for a term not exceeding two years.

(3) A person convicted summarily of any offence under this Act shall be liable:

- (a) to imprisonment for a term not exceeding six months; or
- (b) to a fine not exceeding the prescribed sum ... [currently £5,000]

GOING EQUIPPED FOR STEALING, ETC

Section 25 of the Theft Act 1968

(1) A person shall be guilty of an offence if, when not at his place of abode, he has with him any article for use in the course of or in connection with any burglary, theft or cheat.

(2) A person guilty of an offence under this section shall on conviction on indictment be liable to imprisonment for a term not exceeding three years.

(3) Where a person is charged with an offence under this section, proof that he had with him any article made or adapted for use in committing a burglary, theft or cheat shall be evidence that he had it with him for such use.

(4) Any person may arrest without warrant anyone who is, or whom he, with reasonable cause, suspects to be, committing an offence under this section.

(5) For the purposes of this section an offence under s 12(1) of this Act of taking a conveyance shall be treated as theft, and 'cheat' means an offence under s 15 of this Act.

The elements of the offence of 'going equipped' are:

(1) That the defendant is not at his 'place of abode'; and

(2) That he 'has with him' (ie has in his possession) certain articles; and

(3) That those articles are for use to commit burglary, theft or obtaining by deception.

Place of abode

R v Bundy [1977] 1 WLR 914 (CA)

Lawton LJ: ... The particulars of the offence ... were as follows: that the defendant and a man called Evans 'on 21 April 1975, when not in their places of abode, had with them a piece of piping, a hammer, a pipe threader and three pieces of stocking for use in the course of or in connection with theft'.

... On arresting the defendant and his passenger, the police searched the motor car [which the defendant had been driving]. In it they found the articles referred to in the particulars of offence. It was accepted in this court that there was evidence on which the jury could properly have decided that all the articles were articles for use in the course of or in connection with theft ...

At the trial, in the witness box, [the defendant's] evidence was that about four or five weeks before his arrest, he had borrowed the motor car in which he was arrested from a friend, and that he had lived in that motor car, travelling around in it ...

... [I]t is manifest that no offence is committed if a burglar keeps the implements of his criminal trade in his place of abode. He only commits an offence when he takes them from his place of abode. The phrase 'place of abode', in our judgment, connotes, first of all, a site. That is the ordinary meaning of the word 'place'. It is a site at which the occupier intends to abide. So, there are two elements in the phrase 'place of abode' – the element of site and the element of intention. When the defendant took the motor car to a site with the intention of abiding there, then his motor car on that site could be said to be his 'place of abode', but when he took it from that site to move it to another site where he intended to abide, the motor car could not be said to be his 'place of abode' during transit.

When he was arrested by the police he was not intending to abide on the site where he was arrested. It follows that he was not then at his place of abode. He may have had a place of abode the previous night, but he was away from it at the time of his arrest when in possession of articles which could be used for the purpose of theft ...

Has with him

This phrase, which also appears in s 10 of the Act (aggravated burglary), connotes a 'degree of immediate control': see *R v Kelt* [1977] 1 WLR 1365; *R v Pawlicki* [1992] 1 WLR 827. These authorities are dealt with in Chapter 16.

For use for burglary, theft or cheat

'Burglary' means burglary for the purposes of s 9 of the Act; 'theft' means theft for the purposes of s 1 of the Act or taking a conveyance contrary to s 12 of the Act; 'cheat' means obtaining property by deception contrary to s 15 of the Act.

It can be proved that the defendant had the requisite intention in either of two ways:

(1) If the article in question is 'made or adapted' for use in burglary, theft or cheat (eg a jemmy or a bunch of skeleton keys), this very fact is evidence that the defendant intended to use the article for such purpose (so, effectively, a burden of proof is placed on the defendant to show that he had the article with him for an innocent purpose; or

(2) If the article is innocuous in itself (eg a screwdriver), the prosecution have to prove that the defendant intended to use it for burglary, theft or cheat (much will depend, of course, on the circumstances in which the defendant is found to be in possession of the article).

The defendant must have intended to use the article at some time in the future (in other words for an offence of burglary, theft or cheat which has not yet been committed). It is not enough that the article has been used in an offence of burglary, theft or cheat which has already been committed.

R v Ellames [1974] 1 WLR 1391 (CA)

Facts: A robbery took place in the course of which certain articles, including a sawn-off shotgun, were used. The appellant was charged with robbery and with going equipped for stealing contrary to s 25(1) of the Theft Act 1968. The case against the appellant was that, although he might not have been present at the robbery, he had helped with the planning of it, and that afterwards he had helped the robbers to escape, and in particular that he had helped in hiding the articles used in the robbery.

Browne J: ... In our judgment, the words in s 25(1) of the 1968 Act: 'has with him any article for use' mean 'has with him for the purpose' (or 'with the intention') 'that they will be used'. The effect of s 25(3) is that if the article is one 'made or adapted for use in committing a burglary, theft or cheat', that is evidence of the necessary intention, though not of course conclusive evidence. If the article is not one 'made or adapted' for such use, the intention must be proved on the whole of the evidence – as it must be in the case of an article which is so made or adapted, if the defendant produces some innocent explanation. We agree with the learned authors of Smith and Hogan's *Criminal Law* that s 25 is directed against acts preparatory to burglary, theft or cheat; that:

> Questions as to D's knowledge of the nature of the thing can hardly arise here, since it must be proved that he intended to use it in the course of or in connection with [burglary, theft or cheat];

and that the *mens rea* for this offence includes 'an intention to use the article in the course of or in connection with any of the specified crimes'.

An intention to use must necessarily relate to use in the future. ... It seems to us impossible to interpret s 25(1) of the 1968 Act as if it read: 'has with him any article for use or *which has been used* in the course of or in connection with any burglary, theft or cheat'. Equally, it is impossible to read s 25(3) as if it said: 'had it with him for or *after* such use'.

> In our judgment the words 'for use' govern the whole of the words which follow. The object and effect of the words 'in connection with' is to add something to 'in the course of'. It is easy to think of cases where an article could be intended for use 'in connection with' though not 'in the course of' a burglary etc, eg articles intended to be used while doing preparatory acts or while escaping after the crime ...
>
> In our view, to establish an offence under s 25(1) the prosecution must prove that the defendant was in possession of the article, and intended the article to be used in the course of or in connection with some future burglary, theft or cheat. But it is not necessary to prove that he intended it to be used in the course of or in connection with any *specific* burglary, theft or cheat; it is enough to prove a general intention to use it for *some* burglary, theft or cheat; we think that this view is supported by the use of the word 'any' in s 25(1). Nor, in our view, is it necessary to prove that the defendant intended to use it himself; it will be enough to prove that he had it with him with the intention that it should be used by someone else. For example, if in the present case it had been proved that the defendant was hiding away these articles, which had already been used for one robbery, with the intention that they should later be used by someone for some other robbery, he would be guilty of an offence under s 25(1).

Scope of s 25(1)

Reference may be made to *R v Doukas* [1978] 1 WLR 372 and *R v Rashid* [1977] 1 WLR 298 for two instances involving allegation of possession of articles for use to obtain property by deception (wine and spirits in the first case, bread and tomatoes in the other!).

CHAPTER 20

CRIMINAL DAMAGE

Section 1 of the Criminal Damage Act 1971: destroying or damaging property

(1) A person who without lawful excuse destroys or damages any property belonging to another intending to destroy or damage any such property or being reckless as to whether any such property would be destroyed or damaged shall be guilty of an offence.

(2) A person who without lawful excuse destroys or damages any property, whether belonging to himself or another:

(a) intending to destroy or damage any property or being reckless as to whether any property would be destroyed or damaged; and

(b) intending by the destruction or damage to endanger the life of another or being reckless as to whether the life of another would be thereby endangered;

shall be guilty of an offence.

(3) An offence committed under this section by destroying or damaging property by fire shall be charged as arson.

Section 5 of the Criminal Damage Act 1971: 'without lawful excuse'

(1) This section applies to any offence under s 1(1) above and any offence under s 2 or 3 above other than one involving a threat by the person charged to destroy or damage property in a way which he knows is likely to endanger the life of another or involving an intent by the person charged to use or cause or permit the use of something in his custody or under his control so to destroy or damage property.

(2) A person charged with an offence to which this section applies shall, whether or not he would be treated for the purposes of this Act as having a lawful excuse apart from this subsection, be treated for those purposes as having a lawful excuse:

(a) if at the time of the act or acts alleged to constitute the offence he believed that the person or persons whom he believed to be entitled to consent to the destruction of or damage to the property in question had so consented, or would have so consented to it if he or they had known of the destruction or damage and its circumstances; or

(b) if he destroyed or damaged or threatened to destroy or damage the property in question or, in the case of a charge of an offence under s 3 above, intended to use or cause or permit the use of something to destroy or damage it, in order to protect property belonging to himself or another or a right or interest in property which was or which he believed to be vested in himself or another, and at the time of the act or acts alleged to constitute the offence he believed:

(i) that the property, right or interest was in immediate need of protection; and

(ii) that the means of protection adopted or proposed to be adopted were or would be reasonable having regard to all the circumstances.

(iii) For the purposes of this section it is immaterial whether a belief is justified or not if it is honestly held.

(iv) For the purposes of subsection (2) above a right or interest in property includes any right or privilege in or over land, whether created by grant, licence or otherwise.

(v) This section shall not be construed as casting doubt on any defence recognised by law as a defence to criminal charges.

Section 10 of the Criminal Damage Act 1971: interpretation

(1) In this Act 'property' means property of a tangible nature, whether real or personal, including money and:

(a) including wild creatures which have been tamed or are ordinarily kept in captivity, and any other wild creatures or their carcasses if, but only if, they have been reduced into possession which has not been lost or abandoned or are in the course of being reduced into possession; but

(b) not including mushrooms growing wild on any land or flowers, fruit or foliage of a plant growing wild on any land.

For the purposes of this subsection 'mushroom' includes any fungus and 'plant' includes any shrub or tree.

(2) Property shall be treated for the purposes of this Act as belonging to any person:

(a) having the custody or control of it;

(b) having in it any proprietary right or interest (not being an equitable interest arising only from an agreement to transfer or grant an interest); or

(c) having a charge on it.

(3) Where property is subject to a trust, the persons to whom it belongs shall be so treated as including any person having a right to enforce the trust.

THE OFFENCES

Section 1 of the Criminal Damage Act creates two offences:

(1) Criminal damage (s 1(1)); and

(2) Aggravated criminal damage (s 1(2)).

Section 1(1) of the Criminal Damage Act 1971: criminal damage

The elements of 'ordinary' criminal damage are that the defendant:

(1) without lawful excuse ...

(2) destroys or damages ...

(3) property belonging to another ...

(4) intending to destroy or damage that property or being reckless as whether that property would be destroyed or damaged.

Aggravated criminal damage

The elements of 'aggravated' criminal damage are that the defendant:

(1) without lawful excuse ...

(2) destroys or damages ...
(3) any property (whether belonging to himself or another) ...
(4) intending to destroy or damage *any* property *or* being reckless as to whether any property would be destroyed or damaged ...
(5) intending that the damage to, or destruction of, that property will endanger the life of another *or* being reckless as to whether the life of another would be endangered by the damage or destruction.

The two offences compared

For the first offence, the key element is that property belonging to another is destroyed or damaged. For the second offence, the key element is that property (whether belonging to the defendant or to someone else) is destroyed or damaged *and* the life of another is endangered.

The two offences: the common elements

Damage

Damage need not be permanent: it is enough if taking remedial steps costs time, labour and expense, or if the value or usefulness of the property has been damaged.

Hardman and Others v The Chief Constable of Avon and Somerset Constabulary [1986] Crim LR 330 (HHJ Llewellyn-Jones sitting at Bristol Crown Court)

Facts: The appellants were members of the Campaign for Nuclear Disarmament. On 6 August 1985 (which was the 40th anniversary of the Hiroshima bombing) they painted human silhouettes on an asphalt pavement to represent vaporised human remains. The 'paint' was a fat-free unstable whitewash, which was soluble in water. It was specially mixed in the expectation that rainwater would wash away the markings. The evidence suggested that this was correct and that rainwater and pedestrian traffic would eventually eradicate the markings. However, the local authority had acted before this happened and a 'Graffiti Squad' was employed to clean the pavement using high pressure water jets.

Held: Notwithstanding the fact that the markings could be washed away there had nonetheless been damage, which had caused expense and inconvenience to the local authority. The word 'damage' may be used in the sense of 'mischief done to property'.

Roe v Kingerlee [1986] Crim LR 735 (DC)

Facts: The respondent was charged with criminal damage to the wall of a police cell. He had smeared mud graffiti on the wall. It cost £7 to clean the wall.

Held: It is not necessary that the damage caused should be permanent before an act can constitute criminal damage. In the circumstances of the present case, what occurred so far as the walls of the cell were concerned could amount to criminal damage. The justices were wrong to take the view that as a matter of law it could not. The application of graffiti to a structure will not necessarily amount to causing criminal damage. That must be a question of fact and degree for the tribunal of fact.

Cox v Riley (1986) 83 Cr App R 54 (DC)

Stephen Brown LJ: ... The justices in the case state that they found the following facts: (1) the defendant was employed by Hi-Tech Profiles Limited to work on a computerised saw owned by that company; (2) that the computerised saw relied for its operation on a printed circuit card being inserted into it, containing programs which enabled the saw to be operated so that it could cut window frame profiles of different designs; (3) that the printed circuit card was of no use to the company unless it contained programs which enabled it to cause the saw to operate as (2) above; (4) that on 30 July 1984 the defendant blanked the computerised saw of all its 16 programs thereby erasing the said programs from the printed circuit card by operating the program cancellation facility, contained within the computerised saw, once for each individual program removed; (5) that the defendant's action rendered the computerised saw inoperable, save for limited manual operation, which would cause production to be slowed dramatically ...

They ask this court the following question: can the erasing of a program from printed circuit card which is used to operate a computerised saw constitute damage within the meaning of the Criminal Damage Act 1971? ...

The question of damage has been considered by the Court of Appeal, Criminal Division, on 29 November 1984 in the unreported case of *Henderson & Battley*. The court was presided over by Lawton LJ and he was sitting with Cantley J and Sir John Thompson. Cantley J gave the judgment of the court.

In that case the facts were different, but it is relevant on the meaning of damage. In that case the charge was one of damaging a development land site, intending to damage that property or being reckless as to whether it would be damaged. The facts concerned a development site in the Isle of Dogs which had been cleared for development. It was flat except for a pile of crushed concrete which was kept there intentionally so that it could be used eventually in the laying of temporary roads whilst the development was carried on.

On the occasion in question 30 lorry loads of soil and rubble and mud were tipped on to the site. The appellants in that case, pretending to act with authority, had been operating the site, as Cantley J said, impudently as a public tip and charging their customers for the rubbish which was tipped. There was a submission before the trial judge which was repeated before the Court of Appeal that what they had done could not be said to have damaged the land, bearing in mind that this was a site cleared for building development. The argument was that the land was not damaged because the land beneath the piles of rubbish which had been tipped upon it was in the same condition as it was before the rubbish was tipped upon it. It was argued that there must be a distinction between the cost of putting something right and actual damage.

Cantley J said in the course of this judgment at 3B of the transcript:

> There is of course such a distinction, but if as here there is evidence that the owner of the land reasonably found it necessary to spend about £2,000 to remove the results of the appellants' operations it is not irrelevant to the question of whether this land, as a building site, was damaged. Ultimately whether damage was done to this land was a question of fact and degree for the jury. Damage can be various kinds. In the *Concise Oxford Dictionary* 'damage' is defined as 'injury impairing value or usefulness'. That is a

definition which would fit in very well with doing something to a cleared building site which at any rate for the time being impairs its usefulness as such. In addition, as it necessitates work and the expenditure of a large sum of money to restore it to its former state, it reduces its present value as a building site. This land was a perfectly good building site which did not need £2,000 spending on it in order to sell or use it as such until the appellants began their operations.

... It seems to me that the principle as explained by Cantley J applies in full measure to the present case. Undoubtedly ... the defendant in this instance for some reason, perhaps a grudge, wished to put out of action, albeit temporarily, the computerised saw, and he was able to do that by operating the computer blanking mechanism in order to erase from the printed circuit card the relevant programs. That made it necessary for time and labour and money to be expended in order to replace the relevant programs on the printed circuit card ...

It seems to me to be quite untenable to argue that what this defendant did on this occasion did not amount to causing damage to property, and for this reason I would dismiss the appeal.

I would answer the question posed by the justices ... with the emphatic answer yes.

R v Whiteley (1991) 93 Cr App R 25 (CA)

Facts: The appellant was a 'computer hacker'. He gained unauthorised access to a computer network ('JANET') and altered data contained on disks in the system, thereby causing the computers in question to fail and to be unable to operate properly; the computers had to be shut down for periods of time.

Lord Lane CJ: ... The prosecution case was twofold. First, that the appellant caused criminal damage to the computers by bringing about temporary impairment of usefulness of them by causing them to be shut down for periods of time preventing them from operating properly; second, that he caused criminal damage to the disks by way of alteration to the state of the magnetic particles on them so as to delete and add files; the disks and the magnetic particles on them containing the information being one entity and capable of being damaged.

The jury acquitted the appellant on those counts which were based upon the first leg of the prosecution case, namely criminal damage to the computers. The counts on which they convicted were based upon the second leg, namely the allegation of damage to the disks ...

The evidence before the jury was that the disks are so constructed as to contain upon them thousands, if not millions, of magnetic particles. By issuing commands to the computer, impulses are produced which magnetise or demagnetise those particles in a particular way. By that means it is possible to write data or information on the disks and to program them to fulfil a variety of functions. By the same method it is possible to delete or alter data, information or instructions which have previously been written on to the disk ...

... What the Act requires to be proved is that tangible property has been damaged, not necessarily that the damage itself should be tangible. There can be no doubt that the magnetic particles upon the metal discs were a part of the disks and if the appellant was proved to have intentionally and without lawful excuse altered the particles in such a way as to cause an impairment of the value or usefulness of the disk to the owner, there would be damage within the meaning of s 1. The fact that the alteration could only be perceived by operating the computer did not make the alterations any the less real, or the damage, if the alteration amounted to damage, any the less within the ambit of the Act ...

> ... Any alteration to the physical nature of the property concerned may amount to damage within the meaning of the section. Whether it does so or not will depend upon the effect that the alteration has had upon the legitimate operator (who for convenience may be referred to as the owner). If the hacker's actions do not go beyond, for example, mere tinkering with an otherwise 'empty' disk, no damage would be established. Where, on the other hand, the interference with the disk amounts to an impairment of the value or usefulness of the disk to the owner, then the necessary damage is established ...

[Note: Although *Cox v Riley* and *R v Whiteley* remain good law on the interpretation of the Criminal Damage Act 1971, and so the general principles they lay down remain valid, damage to computers is now governed by the Computer Misuse Act 1990, the detail of which is outside the scope of this book.]

Property

Note that the definition of property in s 10(1) of the Criminal Damage Act 1971 (unlike the definition of property under the Theft Act 1968) includes land.

Without lawful excuse: the general defence

The offences under s 1(1) and s 1(2) of the Criminal Damage Act 1971 can only be committed if the defendant acts 'without lawful excuse'. Section 5(2) provides a partial definition of 'lawful excuse' but s 5 only applies to offences under s 1(1) and so the provisions of s 5 are considered later. Now, we will consider only the 'general defence' of lawful excuse.

Lloyd v Director of Public Prosecutions [1992] 1 All ER 982 (DC)

Nolan LJ: ... The information laid against [the defendant] alleged that at Southampton on 17 March 1990 without lawful excuse he destroyed or damaged two padlocks belonging to South Coast Securities intending to destroy or damage them or being reckless as to whether they would be destroyed or damaged contrary to s 1(1) of the Criminal Damage Act 1971. The appellant formally admitted before the justices that he had damaged the padlocks by cutting them with a disc cutter. He had done so because they secured clamps which were immobilising his motor car. His defence was that he had a lawful excuse for his actions.

On the evening of 16 March 1990, some time before 7.25 pm, the appellant parked his car in a private car park outside Overline House, Southampton. He was not entitled to use the car park because he was not an employee of Overline House nor had he any authorisation to park it there. No less than five large noticeboards were located at the entrance to and exit of this private car park, positioned at eye level to car drivers. They read as follows:

Overline House
Private Car Park
Unauthorised or unlawfully parked vehicles will be immobilised and a levy of £25 charged for release.
South Coast Securities
Agents to the owners.

The appellant did not dispute that those signs were there or that they were clearly visible. At about 7.25 pm that same evening two employees of South Coast Securities, which is a private security firm employed by the owners, went to the car park. Carrying out the instructions of their employers, they immobilised, by use of wheel clamps, any motor vehicle parked in the car park which was not displaying a pass authorising the parking. Six cars were so immobilised, including the appellant's Volvo. Each car that was clamped had a large yellow sticker affixed to its windscreen alerting the driver to the fact that the car had been restrained by a wheel clamping device and warning him that no attempt should be made to drive the vehicle before the clamp had been removed. Information was also provided in a plastic container secured under the windscreen wiper blade telling the driver what steps should be taken to contact South Coast Securities in order to have the vehicle released.

At about 10.00 pm the same evening the employees of South Coast Securities returned to the car park at the request of someone whose vehicle had been clamped. The appellant by that time was also in the car park. The justices find that he was very agitated and argued with the employee who had clamped his car. The appellant refused to pay the £25 levy. He left the car park by taxi, leaving his car there.

The next day, 17 March 1990, the employees of South Coast Securities returned to the car park. The appellant's vehicle had been removed and the two wheel clamps and two padlocks which had been securing it were on the ground. These were the circumstances in which the appellant made his formal admission, pursuant to s 10 of the Criminal Justice Act 1967, that he was responsible for removing the wheel clamps by cutting the two padlocks with a disc cutter ...

The question which the justices pose for the opinion of this court is:

> Whether, having found that the appellant intentionally caused damage to the two padlocks which belonged to South Coast Securities, we were correct to conclude that he did so without lawful excuse.

... [A]s a general rule, if a motorist parks his car without permission on another person's property knowing that by doing so he runs the risk of it being clamped, he has no right to damage or destroy the clamp. If he does so he will be guilty of a criminal offence.

CRIMINAL DAMAGE (SECTION 1(1))

Ordinary criminal damage: property belonging to another

The offence under s 1(1) of the Criminal Damage Act 1971 requires the destruction or damage of property 'belonging to another'. It is, however, possible to be guilty of an offence under s 1(1) even though the property damaged belongs to the defendant, provided that someone else also has a proprietary right in the property. We have already seen that for the offence of aggravated criminal damage under s 1(2) of the Criminal Damage Act 1971 it does not matter to whom the property belongs.

Lawful excuse: the specific statutory defences

In addition to the general defence of 'lawful excuse', s 5(2) of the Criminal Damage Act 1971 creates two specific statutory defences, which apply only to offences under s 1(1):

(a) Belief that the damage is done with the consent of the owner of the property (or that the owner would consent);

(b) Belief that the damage is necessary to protect other property, provided that there is an immediate threat to that other property and that the means of protection taken are reasonable.

Section 5(3) effectively provides that the reasonableness of the belief is only relevant to the extent that it is evidence of whether the belief was actually held or not.

Johnson v DPP [1994] Crim LR 673 (DC)

Facts: The appellant was a squatter who had damaged the door frame of a house he was occupying, by chiselling off the locks and replacing them with a lock of his own. He claimed that he had a lawful excuse under s 5(2)(b) of the Criminal Damage Act 1971 on the grounds that he had caused the damage in order to protect his own property, that he believed his property to be in immediate need of protection, and that the means which he had adopted were reasonable in all the circumstances.

Held: dismissing the appellant's appeal against conviction: that the damage to the door was not done to protect property and that the appellant had no belief that his property was in immediate need of protection.

The court had reached this conclusion by asking itself first the objective question of whether the act of damage was done in order to protect property. Then, there was the subjective question of whether the appellant believed that his property was in immediate need of protection and that the means adopted were reasonable. The test to be applied was whether he believed that immediate action had to be taken to do something which would otherwise be a crime, in order to prevent the immediate risk of something worse happening.

R v Denton [1981] 1 WLR 1446 (CA)

Lord Lane CJ: [The defendant was charged with] arson contrary to s 1(1) and (3) of the 1971 Act, the particulars being that the defendant:

> on the 3rd day of January 1980 without lawful excuse damaged by fire a building known as Barnfield Mill belonging to Leslie Fink & Co Ltd and the contents thereof belonging to Albus Products Ltd intending to damage such property or being reckless as to whether such property would be damaged.

The facts of the case are somewhat unusual. There is no dispute that on 3 January 1980 the defendant set light to some machinery in the cotton mill. The machinery was very badly damaged, and as a result of that conflagration damage was also done, to a much lesser degree it is true, to the building itself. The total damage to stock and building was said to be some £40,000.

On Monday 17 March 1980, the defendant presented himself at the police station and told the police that he had in fact started that fire. He described how he had done it, and he then made a statement under caution, in which he gave his reason for having started the fire: that it was for the benefit of the business, because the business was in difficulties, and, although he was going to get no direct benefit from it himself, he thought he would be doing a good turn to the financial status of the company if he were to set light to the premises and goods as he did ...

When it came to the trial ... he gave evidence that his employer, whom we will refer to as 'T' for obvious reasons, had asked him to put the machines out of action and he had agreed to set light to it. The reason given to him by the

> employer for that request was because the company was in difficulties; the way that T put it was: 'There is nothing like a good fire for improving the financial circumstances of a business'.
>
> ... It was agreed on all hands for the purpose of this case that T was the person who, any evil motives apart, was entitled to consent to the damage. It was likewise conceded that the defendant honestly believed that T occupied that position and was entitled to consent.
>
> ... It is quite apparent ... that in so far as the 1971 Act is concerned it is not an offence for a man to damage or injure or destroy to set fire to his own premises.
>
> One therefore turns to see what the situation would have been had T made a confession in the same, or similar, terms as that made by the defendant, and to see what would have happened to the Crown's argument if the two of them, T and the defendant, stood charged under s 1(1) of the 1971 Act in the Crown Court. It is not an offence for a man to set light to his own property. So T would have been acquitted. But if the Crown is correct, the defendant, the man who had been charged with the task of actually putting the match to the polystyrene, and setting the fire alight, would have been convicted.
>
> Quite apart from any other consideration, that is such an anomalous result that it cannot possibly be right. The answer is this: that one has to decide whether or not an offence is committed at the moment that the acts are alleged to be committed. The fact that somebody may have had a dishonest intent which in the end he was going to carry out, namely to claim from the insurance company, cannot turn what was not originally a crime into a crime. There is no unlawfulness under the 1971 Act in burning a house. It does not become unlawful because there may be an inchoate attempt to commit fraud contained in it; that is to say it does not become a crime under the 1971 Act, whatever may be the situation outside of the Act.
>
> ... Indeed it seems to us, if it is necessary to go as far as this, that it was probably unnecessary for the defendant to invoke s 5 of the 1971 Act at all, because he probably had a lawful excuse without it, in that T was lawfully entitled to burn the premises down. The defendant believed it. He believed that he was acting under the directions of T and that on its own, it seems to us, may well have provided him with a lawful excuse without having resort to s 5 ...

[Note: Strictly speaking, the owner of the property was the limited company, not T. However, the decision of the court is sustainable on the basis that the defendant believed that T was entitled to authorise the destruction of the property. The present case may be contrasted with *R v Appleyard* where the managing director was convicted of destroying property belonging to his company; it was said that the company was a separate legal entity and so the defendant could not consent to the destruction of its property.]

AGGRAVATED CRIMINAL DAMAGE (SECTION 1(2))

Danger to life

We have already seen that an offence under s 1(2) can be committed whether or not the property damaged belonged to the accused and that the specific statutory defences contained in s 5(2) of the Act do not apply. The key element of the offence under s 1(2) is the endangerment of life. The prosecution have to prove, not only that the defendant intended to endanger life or was reckless as to the endangerment of life, but also that the danger to life arose from the damage caused by the defendant.

R v Steer [1988] AC 111 (HL)

Lord Bridge of Harwich: My Lords, in the early hours of 8 June 1985 the respondent went to the bungalow of his former business partner, David Gregory, against whom he bore some grudge. He was armed with an automatic .22 rifle. He rang the bell and woke Mr and Mrs Gregory, who looked out of their bedroom window. The respondent fired a shot aimed at the bedroom window. He then fired two further shots, one at another window and one at the front door. Fortunately no one was hurt. It was never suggested that the first shot had been aimed at Mr or Mrs Gregory.

[The defendant was charged with possession of a firearm with intent to endanger life (s 16 of the Firearms Act 1968), along with criminal damage to the bedroom window (s 1(1) of the Criminal Damage Act 1971) and with criminal damage with intent to endanger the lives of Mr and Mrs Gregory or being reckless whether their lives would be endangered (s 1(2) of the Criminal Damage Act 1971)] ...

It is to be observed that the offence created by subsection (2), save that it may be committed by destroying or damaging one's own property, is simply an aggravated form of the offence created by subsection (1), in which the prosecution must prove, in addition to the ingredients of the offence under subsection (1), the further mental element specified by subsection (2)(b) ...

We must, of course, approach the matter on the footing, implicit in the outcome of the trial, that the respondent, in firing at the bedroom window, had no intent to endanger life, but accepts that he was reckless whether life would be endangered.

Under both limbs or s 1 of the Act of 1971 it is the essence of the offence which the section creates that the defendant has destroyed or damaged property. For the purpose of analysis it may be convenient to omit the reference to destruction and to concentrate on the references to damage, which was all that was here involved. To be guilty under subsection (1) the defendant must have intended or been reckless as to the damage to property which he caused. To be guilty under subsection (2) he must additionally have intended to endanger life or been reckless whether life should be endangered 'by damage' to property which he caused. This is the context in which the words must be construed and it seems to me impossible to read the words 'by the damage' as meaning 'by the damage or by the act which caused the damage' ...

I would accordingly dismiss the appeal. The certified question should be answered as follows:

> On the true construction of s 1(2)(b) of the Criminal Damage Act 1971 the prosecution are required to prove that the danger to life resulted from the destruction of or damage to property; it is not sufficient for the prosecution to prove that it resulted from the act of the defendant which caused the destruction or damage.

Lord Griffiths: My Lords, I have had the advantage of reading in draft the speech delivered by my noble and learned friend Lord Bridge of Harwich. For the reasons which he has given I agree that the appeal should be dismissed and I would answer the certified question in the way which he has suggested.

Lord Ackner: My Lords, I have had the advantage of reading in draft the speech delivered by my noble and learned friend Lord Bridge of Harwich. For the reasons which he has given I also agree that the appeal should be dismissed and the certified question answered in the manner indicated by him.

Lord Oliver of Aylmerton: My Lords, I have had the advantage of reading in draft the speech delivered by my noble and learned friend Lord Bridge of Harwich. For the reasons which he has given I agree that the appeal should be dismissed and the certified question answered in the sense which he has indicated.

Lord Goff of Chieveley: My Lords, I have had the advantage of reading in draft the speech delivered by my noble and learned friend Lord Bridge of Harwich. For the reasons which he has given I also agree that the appeal should be dismissed and the certified question answered in the manner indicated by him.

R v Dudley [1989] Crim LR 57 (CA)

Facts: Dudley, who had a grievance against a particular family, consumed drink and drugs, went to their house and, using an accelerant, threw a fire bomb at the house, causing a high sheet of flame outside the glass door. The fire was extinguished by the family and only trivial damage was caused.

Held (distinguishing *R v Steer* [1988] AC 111): The words 'destruction or damage' in s 1(2)(b) of the Act (endangering life) referred back to the destruction or damage intended, or as to which there was recklessness, in s 1(2)(a) (damaging property). The words did not refer to the destruction or damage actually caused; if they did, injustice would be done in the converse case where someone was reckless only as to trivial damage but by some mishap caused danger to life.

R v Webster and Others; R v Warwick [1995] 2 All ER 168 (CA)

Lord Taylor of Gosforth CJ: ... Two points must be stressed. First, what has to be proved under s 1(2)(b) is not whether and how life was in fact endangered (if it was) but whether and how it was intended to be endangered or there was an obvious risk of it being endangered.

Second, an issue has been argued before us as to the meaning of 'the destruction or damage' in s 1(2)(b) ... This very point was decided by this court in *R v Dudley* [1989] Crim LR 57 ...

... Staughton LJ [in *R v Dudley*] stated that the House of Lords had not had to deal with this point in *R v Steer* [1988] AC 111. He said:

> It would seem to us, on a mere reading of the section, that the words 'destruction or damage' in s 1(2)(b) refer back to the destruction or damage which has to have been intended by the defendant in s 1(2)(a) or as to which he has to have been reckless, and that they do not refer to the destruction or damage which in fact occurred.

We agree ... In our view, the true construction of s 1(2) is that the *actus reus* is defined in the first two lines of the subsection, while paras (a) and (b) deal with *mens rea* and are conjunctive in the way described by Staughton LJ. Otherwise, the gravamen of an offence involving damage by missile would depend not on the defendant's intention but on whether he was a good shot in seeking to carry it out.

Thus, if a defendant throws a brick at the windscreen of a moving vehicle, given that he causes some damage to the vehicle, whether he is guilty under s 1(2) does not depend on whether the brick hits or misses the windscreen, but whether he intended to hit it and intended that the damage therefrom should endanger life or whether he was reckless as to that outcome. As to the dropping of stones from bridges, the effect of the statute may be thought strange. If the defendant's intention is that the stone itself should crash through the roof of a train or motor vehicle and thereby directly injure a passenger, or if he was reckless only as to that outcome, the section would not bite. That would follow from the ratio in *R v Steer* and is no doubt why Lord Bridge made the comment he did about missiles from motorway bridges. If, however, the defendant intended or was reckless that the stone would smash the roof of the train or vehicle so that metal or wood struts from the roof would or obviously might descend upon a passenger endangering life, he would surely be guilty. This may seem to many a dismal distinction.

We proceed to consider the two cases before us individually.

R v Asquith, Webster and Seamans

... Briefly, the facts were that at about 8.25 pm on 18 May 1992 the appellants pushed a coping stone weighing 1 to 2 cwt from the parapet of a railway bridge in the Burnley area onto a two-carriage passenger train passing below. The stone landed on the first carriage, showering the passengers with glass fibre and polystyrene-type material from the roof. Had it not landed on the carriage's rear bulkhead, the stone would have fallen into the compartment. As it was, only a corner of the stone penetrated the roof. Nobody received any physical injury, although passengers were shocked and affected for some time thereafter ...

... If the intention was that the stone itself should endanger the life of the passengers, then the 'pusher' would not be guilty of this offence ... In our view, by convicting each of the appellants ... the jury must be taken to have found ... that each of them intended the stone itself to crash through the roof and endanger life. The conviction on that basis alone cannot be sustained. However, the jury's finding of an intent by each appellant to endanger life by causing the stone itself to penetrate the roof must, in common sense, carry the implication that they were each reckless as to endangering life by whatever damage the stone might do when it fell. If the intention was for the stone to penetrate the roof, there was clearly an obvious risk that it might endanger life by bringing parts of the roof down into the compartment, quite apart from other obvious risks such as derailment if it fell in front of the train or struck the driver's cab, incapacitating him or the controls.

In the circumstances, we consider the proper course is for us to ... substitute in each case a conviction ... of 'being reckless as to whether the life of another would thereby be endangered'. This we do.

R v Warwick

About 3.30 pm [on 21 February 1992], two police constables, PC Tams and PC McCabe, driving a police van, saw the stolen Fiesta parked outside the appellant's mother's house. They drew alongside it and stopped, intending to arrest the occupant. Both officers recognised the driver as the appellant, whom they knew. He drove off and the officers followed but lost sight of the Fiesta.

About 4.20 pm two other police officers, PC Butcher and PC Davies, in a marked police car, saw the stolen Fiesta in another road at Teesside. The vehicle was stationary and facing away from them. As they drew near to it, a youth wearing a black balaclava emerged through its sunroof with a large brick in his hand, making as if to throw it. PC Butcher reversed his car away from the Fiesta but it reversed towards him. The youth threw the brick at the police car but missed. The Fiesta then reversed into a driveway and emerged, accelerating forwards in the direction of the police car as if about to ram it. PC Davies shouted a warning to PC Butcher who swerved, hitting a bus at a road junction. PC Davies was meanwhile radioing for assistance and recognised the driver of the Fiesta as the appellant, whom he knew. After hitting the bus, PC Butcher drove on and the youth standing up through the Fiesta's sunroof threw a brick at the police car. The brick smashed the rear window, showering the officers with broken glass. At that moment, PC Butcher was accelerating up to 30 mph, the road was busy and cars were passing in both directions. PC Butcher increased his speed, but the Fiesta rammed his vehicle so that he had great difficulty in retaining control of it. Another brick was thrown through the broken rear window, hitting PC Davies on the head, and landing in the footwell. An ice cream van was turning into the road. PC Butcher turned to avoid being pushed into it by the Fiesta, which was close up behind him. The Fiesta then rammed into the police car a second time, causing it to strike a glancing blow to the ice cream van. Further on, as PC Butcher reduced his speed because of parked cars and the number of children who were about, his vehicle was rammed a third time from behind by the Fiesta, which subsequently turned off onto a side road ...

At 4.25 pm two more police constables, PC Cane and PC Mitchinson, were in another marked police car near Eston, a mile or so from the earlier rammings. The stolen Fiesta came into the road where these officers were and accelerated towards their car as if to ram it. PC Cane went into reverse and backed his car some way down the road. The Fiesta reappeared shortly afterwards out of another side road, only 12 feet away from the police car. The officers saw that apart from the driver there was a front seat passenger wearing a balaclava and a youth in the back with a white baseball cap. The Fiesta reversed towards the police car, which reversed away. The youth with the balaclava stood up again through the sunroof and threw a large stone towards the front of the police car, hitting and damaging its bonnet ...

... If the intention was to break the windscreen or window by hurling a brick or stone, the jury would be entitled to infer that there was an intention to shower the driver with broken glass. If as a result of being so showered he were to lose control of the vehicle so that his life and that of his passengers or other road users were endangered, a jury could properly find that that danger was caused and intended to be caused by the broken glass, ie the damage to the vehicle. Clearly ... an intention to render the windscreen opaque, or recklessness as to its becoming so, could invoke the section. Likewise, if a defendant deliberately rams a vehicle in moving traffic, it would be open to a jury to infer an intention to disable the vehicle, for example by damaging the suspension, by damaging the steering, by buckling the bodywork onto the tyres and thereby causing a blowout. Any of these forms of damage in moving traffic could well endanger life and in our judgment it would be open to a jury, hearing evidence of deliberate ramming of a police car, to infer that the intention was to endanger life by damaging the vehicle.

The circumstances in this case are clearly distinguishable from those in *R v Steer*. To shower the driver of a moving vehicle with broken glass or ram his vehicle in moving traffic are clearly distinguishable from merely piercing the window or door of a stationary house by discharging and air rifle ...

ARSON

Under s 1(3) of the Criminal Damage Act 1971, where property is destroyed or damaged by fire, the offence is called 'arson'. The prosecution have to specify, however, whether the offence of criminal damage falls under s 1(1) or s 1(2) of the Act.

THE MENTAL ELEMENT: INTENTION OR RECKLESSNESS

The Criminal Damage Act uses the words 'intending' and 'being reckless' in several places. It is the term 'reckless' which has generated the greatest weight of authority. The starting point for any discussion of 'recklessness' must be the speech of Lord Diplock in *R v Caldwell* [1982] AC 341: a person is reckless if she either:

(a) gives no thought to an obvious risk; or

(b) recognises that there is a risk but goes on regardless of that risk.

A risk is an obvious one for the purpose of (a) if it would be obvious to the reasonable person; it does not have to be obvious to someone of the accused's age and mental capacity: see *R v Miller* [1983] 2 AC 161; *Elliott v C* [1983] 1 WLR 939; *R v R* (1984) 79 Cr App R 334; *R v Sangha* [1988] 1 WLR 519; *R v Coles* [1995] 1 Cr App R 157.

Metropolitan Police Commissioner v Caldwell [1982] AC 343; [1981] 1 All ER 961 (HL)

Lord Diplock: My Lords, the facts that gave rise to this appeal are simple. The respondent had been doing work for the proprietor of a residential hotel. He considered that he had a grievance against the proprietor. One night he got very drunk and in the early hours of the morning he decided to revenge himself on the proprietor by setting fire to the hotel, in which some 10 guests were living at the time. He broke a window and succeeded in starting a fire in a ground floor room; but fortunately it was discovered and the flames were extinguished before any serious damage was caused. At his trial he said that he was so drunk at the time that the thought that there might be people in the hotel whose lives might be endangered if it were set on fire had never crossed his mind ...

The question of law certified for the opinion of this House was:

> Whether evidence of self-induced intoxication can be relevant to the following questions: (a) whether the defendant intended to endanger the life of another; and (b) whether the defendant was reckless as to whether the life of another would be endangered, within the meaning of s 1(2)(b) of the Criminal Damage Act 1971.

The question recognises that under s 1(2)(b) there are two alternative states of mind as respects endangering the life of another, and that existence of either of them on the part of the accused is sufficient to constitute the *mens rea* needed to convert the lesser offence under s 1(1) into the graver offence under s 1(2). One is intention that a particular thing should happen in consequence of the *actus reus*, *viz*, that the life of another person should be endangered (this was not relied on by the prosecution in the instant case). The other is recklessness whether that particular thing should happen or not. The same dichotomy of *mentes reae*, intention and recklessness, is to be found throughout the section; in subsection (1) and paragraph (a) of subsection (2) as well as in paragraph (b); and 'reckless' as descriptive of a state of mind must be given the same meaning in each of them ...

My Lords, the restricted meaning that the Court of Appeal in *R v Cunningham* had placed upon the adverb 'maliciously' in the Malicious Damage Act 1861 in cases where the prosecution did not rely upon an actual intention of the accused to cause the damage that was in fact done, called for a meticulous analysis by the jury of the thoughts that passed through the mind of the accused at or before the time he did the act that caused the damage, in order to see on which side of a narrow dividing line they fell. If it had crossed his mind that there was a risk that someone's property might be damaged but, because his mind was affected by rage or excitement or confused by drink, he did not appreciate the seriousness of the risk or trusted that good luck would prevent its happening, this state of mind would amount to malice in the restricted meaning placed upon that term by the Court of Appeal; whereas if, for any of these reasons, he did not even trouble to give his mind to the question whether there was any risk of damaging the property, this state of mind would not suffice to make him guilty of an offence under the Malicious Damage Act 1861.

Neither state of mind seems to me to be less blameworthy than the other; but if the difference between the two constituted the distinction between what does and what does not in legal theory amount to a guilty state of mind for the purposes of a statutory offence of damage to property, it would not be a practicable distinction for use in a trial by jury. The only person who knows what the accused's mental processes were is the accused himself – and probably not even he can recall them accurately when the rage or excitement under which he acted has passed, or he has sobered up if he were under the influence of drink at the relevant time. If the accused gives evidence that because of his rage, excitement or drunkenness the risk of particular harmful consequences of his acts simply did not occur to him, a jury would find it hard to be satisfied beyond reasonable doubt that his true mental process was not that, but was the slightly different mental process required if one applies the restricted meaning of 'being reckless as to whether' something would happen, adopted by the Court of Appeal in *R v Cunningham*.

My Lords, I can see no reason why Parliament when it decided to revise the law as to offences of damage to property should go out of its way to perpetuate fine and impracticable distinctions such as these, between one mental state and another. One would think that the sooner they were got rid of, the better ...

... 'Reckless' as used in the new statutory definition of the *mens rea* of these offences is an ordinary English word. It had not by 1971 become a term of legal art with some more limited esoteric meaning than that which it bore in ordinary speech, a meaning which surely includes not only deciding to ignore a risk of harmful consequences resulting from one's acts that one has recognised as existing, but also failing to give any thought to whether or not there is any such risk in circumstances where, if any thought were given to the matter, it would be obvious that there was.

If one is attaching labels, the latter state of mind is neither more nor less 'subjective' than the first. But the label solves nothing. It is a statement of the obvious; *mens rea* is, by definition, a state of mind of the accused himself at the time he did the physical act that constitutes the *actus reus* of the offence; it cannot be the mental state of some non-existent, hypothetical person.

Nevertheless, to decide whether someone has been 'reckless' as to whether harmful consequences of a particular kind will result from his act, as distinguished from his actually intending such harmful consequences to follow, does call for some consideration of how the mind of the ordinary prudent individual would have reacted to a similar situation. If there were nothing in the circumstances that ought to have drawn the attention of an ordinary prudent individual to the possibility of that kind of harmful consequence, the accused would not be described as 'reckless' in the natural meaning of that word for failing to address his mind to the possibility; nor, if the risk of the harmful consequences was so slight that the ordinary prudent individual on due consideration of the risk would not be deterred from treating it as negligible, could the accused be described as 'reckless' in its ordinary sense if, having considered the risk, he decided to ignore it. (In this connection the gravity of the possible harmful consequences would be an important factor. To endanger life must be one of the most grave.) So to this extent, even if one ascribes to 'reckless' only the restricted meaning, adopted by the Court of Appeal in *R v Stephenson* [1979] QB 695 and *R v Briggs (Note)* [1977] 1 WLR 605, of foreseeing that a particular kind of harm might happen and yet going on to take the risk of it, it involves a test that would be described in part as 'objective' in current legal jargon. Questions of criminal liability are seldom solved by simply asking whether the test is subjective or objective.

In my opinion, a person charged with an offence under s 1(1) of the Criminal Damage Act 1971 is 'reckless as to whether or not any such property would be destroyed or damaged' if (1) he does an act which in fact creates an obvious risk that property will be destroyed or damaged and (2) when he does the act he either has not given any thought to the possibility of there being any such risk or has recognised that there was some risk involved and has nonetheless gone on to do it. That would be a proper direction to the jury; cases in the Court of Appeal which held otherwise should be regarded as overruled.

Where the charge is under s 1(2) the question of the state of mind of the accused must be approached in stages, corresponding to paragraphs (a) and (b). The jury must be satisfied that what the accused did amounted to an offence under s 1(1), either because he actually intended to destroy or damage the property or because he was reckless (in the sense that I have described) as to whether it might be destroyed or damaged. Only if they are so satisfied must the jury go on to consider whether the accused also either actually intended that the destruction or damage of the property should endanger someone's life or was reckless (in a similar sense) as to whether a human life might be endangered.

Turning now to the instant case, the first stage was eliminated by the respondent's plea of guilty to the charge under s 1(1). Furthermore he himself gave evidence that his actual intention was to damage the hotel in order to revenge himself on the proprietor. As respects the charge under s 1(2) the prosecution did not rely on an actual intent of the respondent to endanger the lives of the residents but relied on his having been reckless whether the lives of any of them would be endangered. His act of setting fire to it was one which the jury were entitled to think created an obvious risk that the lives of the residents would be endangered; and the only defence with which your Lordships are concerned is that the respondent had made himself so drunk as to render him oblivious of that risk. If the only mental state capable of constituting the necessary *mens rea* for an offence under s 1(2) were that expressed in the words 'intending by the destruction or damage to endanger the life of another', it would have been necessary to consider whether the offence was to be classified as one of 'specific' intent for the purposes of the rule of law which this House affirmed and applied in *R v Majewski* [1977] AC 443; and this it plainly is. But this is not, in my view, a relevant inquiry where 'being reckless as to whether the life of another would be thereby endangered' is an alternative mental state that is capable of constituting the necessary *mens rea* of the offence with which he is charged.

The speech of Lord Elwyn-Jones LC in *R v Majewski* [1977] AC 443, 475, with which Lord Simon, Lord Kilbrandon and I agreed, is authority that self-induced intoxication is no defence to a crime in which recklessness is enough to constitute the necessary *mens rea*. The charge in Majewski was of assault occasioning actual bodily harm and it was held by the majority of the House, approving *R v Venna* [1976] QB 421 at 428, that recklessness in the use of force was sufficient to satisfy the mental element in the offence of assault. Reducing oneself by drink or drugs to a condition in which the restraints of reason and conscience are cast off was held to be a reckless course of conduct and an integral part of the crime. Lord Elwyn-Jones LC accepted at 475 as correctly stating English law the provision in s 2.08 (2) of the American Model Penal Code:

> When recklessness establishes an element of the offence, if the actor, due to self-induced intoxication, is unaware of a risk of which he would have been aware had he been sober, such unawareness is immaterial.

So, in the instant case, the fact that the respondent was unaware of the risk of endangering the lives of residents in the hotel owing to his self-induced intoxication, would be no defence if that risk would have been obvious to him had he been sober ...

I would give the following answers to the certified question: (a) If the charge of an offence under s 1(2) of the Criminal Damage Act 1971 is framed so as to charge the defendant only with 'intending by the destruction or damage [of the property] to endanger the life of another', evidence of self-induced intoxication can be relevant to his defence. (b) If the charge is, or includes, a reference to his 'being reckless as to whether the life of another would thereby be endangered', evidence of self-induced intoxication is not relevant.

Lord Keith of Kinkel: My Lords, I am in entire agreement with the reasoning contained in the speech of my noble and learned friend, Lord Diplock, which I have had the benefit of reading in draft. I would answer the certified questions in the manner which he proposes, and dismiss the appeal.

Lord Roskill: My Lords, I had prepared an opinion of my own in this appeal but, having had the advantage of reading in draft the speech of my noble and learned friend, Lord Diplock, I am satisfied that no useful purpose would be served by delivering that speech. I agree in every respect with what my noble and learned friend has said in his speech and with his proposed answers to the questions certified. For the reasons he gives I agree that this appeal should be dismissed.

[**Lord Edmund Davies** and **Lord Wilberforce** agreed that the appeal should be dismissed but disagreed with the reasoning of the majority of the relevance of the defendant's intoxication to the issue of recklessness.]

R v Miller [1983] 2 AC 161 (HL)

Lord Diplock: My Lords, the facts which give rise to this appeal are sufficiently narrated in the written statement made to the police by the appellant Miller. That statement ... reads:

> Last night I went out for a few drinks and at closing time I went back to the house where I have been kipping for a couple of weeks. I went upstairs into the back bedroom where I've been sleeping. I lay on my mattress and lit a

> cigarette. I must have fell to sleep because I woke up to find the mattress on fire. I just got up and went into the next room and went back to sleep. Then the next thing I remember was the police and fire people arriving. I hadn't got anything to put the fire out with so I just left it.

He was charged on indictment with the offence of 'arson contrary to s 1(1) and (3) of the Criminal Damage Act 1971'; the particulars of offence were that he:

> on a date unknown between 13 and 16 August 1980 without lawful excuse damaged by fire a house known as No 9, Grantham Road, Sparkbrook, intending to do damage to such property or recklessly as to whether such property would be damaged ...

... [T]he Court of Appeal ... certified that the following question of law of general public importance was involved:

> Whether the *actus reus* of the offence of arson is present when a defendant accidentally starts a fire and thereafter, intending to destroy or damage property belonging to another or being reckless as to whether any such property would be destroyed or damaged, fails to take any steps to extinguish the fire or prevent damage to such property by that fire?

The question speaks of *actus reus*. This expression is derived from Coke's brocard (3 Co Inst ch 1, fo 10), *actus non facit reum, nisi mens sit rea*, by converting incorrectly into an adjective the word *reus* which was there used correctly in the accusative case as a noun. As long ago as 1889 in *R v Tolson* 23 QBD 168 at 185–87, [1886–90] All ER Rep 26 at 36–37 Stephen J when dealing with a statutory offence, as are your Lordships in the instant case, condemned the phrase as likely to mislead, though his criticism in that case was primarily directed to the use of the expression *mens rea*. In the instant case, as the argument before this House has in my view demonstrated, it is the use of the expression *actus reus* that is liable to mislead, since it suggests that some positive act on the part of the accused is needed to make him guilty of a crime and that a failure or omission to act is insufficient to give rise to criminal liability unless some express provision in the statute that creates the offence so provides.

My Lords, it would I think be conducive to clarity of analysis of the ingredients of a crime that is created by statute, as are the great majority of criminal offences today, if we were to avoid bad Latin and instead to think and speak (as did Stephen J in those parts of his judgment in *R v Tolson* to which I referred at greater length in *Sweet v Parsley* [1970] AC 132 at 162–63) about the conduct of the accused and his state of mind at the time of that conduct, instead of speaking of *actus reus* and *mens rea*.

The question before your Lordships in this appeal is one that is confined to the true construction of the words used in particular provisions in a particular statute, *viz* s 1(1) and (3) of the Criminal Damage Act 1971. Those particular provisions will fall to be construed in the light of general principles of English criminal law so well established that it is the practice of parliamentary draftsmen to leave them unexpressed in criminal statutes, on the confident assumption that a court of law will treat those principles as intended by Parliament to be applicable to the particular offence unless expressly modified or excluded. But this does not mean that your Lordships are doing any more than construing the particular statutory provisions. These I now set out:

> (1) A person who without lawful excuse destroys or damages any property belonging to another intending to destroy or damage any such property or being reckless as to whether any such property would be destroyed or damaged shall be guilty of an offence ...

(3) an offence committed under this section by destroying or damaging property by fire shall be charged as arson.

This definition of arson makes it a 'result-crime' in the classification adopted by Professor Gordon in his work *The Criminal Law of Scotland*, 2nd edn, 1978. The crime is not complete unless and until the conduct of the accused has caused property belonging to another to be destroyed or damaged.

In the instant case property belonging to another, the house, was damaged; it was not destroyed. So in the interest of brevity it will be convenient to refer to damage to property and omit reference to destruction. I should also mention, in parentheses, that in this appeal your Lordships are concerned only with the completed crime of arson, not with related inchoate offences such as attempt or conspiracy to destroy or damage property belonging to another, to which somewhat different considerations will apply. Nor does this appeal raise any question of 'lawful excuse'. None was suggested.

The first question to be answered where a completed crime of arson is charged is: 'Did a physical act of the accused start the fire which spread and damaged property belonging to another (or did his act cause an existing fire, which he had not started but which would otherwise have burnt itself out harmlessly, to spread and damage property belonging to another)?' I have added the words in brackets for completeness. They do not arise in the instant case; in cases where they do, the accused, for the purposes of the analysis which follows, may be regarded as having started a fresh fire.

The first question is a pure question of causation; it is one of fact to be decided by the jury in a trial on indictment. It should be answered 'No' if, in relation to the fire during the period starting immediately before its ignition and ending with its extinction, the role of the accused was at no time more than that of a passive bystander. In such a case the subsequent questions to which I shall be turning would not arise. The conduct of the parabolical priest and Levite on the road to Jericho may have been indeed deplorable, but English law has not so far developed to the stage of treating it as criminal; and if it ever were to do so there would be difficulties in defining what should be the limits of the offence.

If, on the other hand the question, which I now confine to: 'Did a physical act of the accused start the fire which spread and damaged property belonging to another?' is answered 'Yes', as it was by the jury in the instant case, then for the purpose of the further questions the answers to which are determinative of his guilt of the offence of arson, the conduct of the accused, throughout the period from immediately before the moment of ignition to the completion of the damage to the property by the fire, is relevant; so is his state of mind throughout that period.

Since arson is a result-crime the period may be considerable, and during it the conduct of the accused that is causative of the result may consist not only of his doing physical acts which cause the fire to start or spread but also of his failing to take measures that lie within his power to counteract the danger that he has himself created. And if his conduct, active or passive, varies in the course of the period, so may his state of mind at the time of each piece of conduct. If at the time of any particular piece of conduct by the accused that is causative of the result, the state of mind that actuates his conduct falls within the description of one or other of the states of mind that are made a necessary ingredient of the offence of arson by s 1(1) of the Criminal Damage Act 1971 (ie intending to damage property belonging to another or being reckless as to whether such property would be damaged) I know of no principle of English criminal law that would prevent his being guilty of the offence created by that subsection. Likewise I see no rational ground for excluding from conduct capable of giving rise to criminal liability, conduct which consists of failing to take measures that lie within one's power to counteract a danger that one has oneself created, if at the time of such conduct one's state of mind is such as constitutes a necessary ingredient of the offence. I venture to think that the habit of lawyers to talk of *actus reus*, suggestive as it is of action rather than inaction, is responsible for any erroneous notion that failure to act cannot give rise to criminal liability in English law.

No one has been bold enough to suggest that if, in the instant case, the accused had been aware at the time that he dropped the cigarette that it would probably set fire to his mattress and yet had taken no steps to extinguish it he would not have been guilty of the offence of arson, since he would have damaged property of another being reckless whether any such property would be damaged.

I cannot see any good reason why, so far as liability under criminal law is concerned, it should matter at what point of time before the resultant damage is complete a person becomes aware that he has done a physical act which, whether or not he appreciated that it would at the time when he did it, does in fact create a risk that property of another will be damaged; provided that, at the moment of awareness, it lies within his power to take steps, either himself or by calling for the assistance of the fire brigade if this be necessary, to prevent or minimise the damage to the property at risk.

Let me take first the case of the person who has thrown away a lighted cigarette expecting it to go out harmlessly, but later becomes aware that, although he did not intend it to do so, it has, in the event, caused some inflammable material to smoulder and that unless the smouldering is extinguished promptly, an act that the person who dropped the cigarette could perform without danger to himself or difficulty, the inflammable material will be likely to burst into flames and damage some other person's property. The person who dropped the cigarette deliberately refrains from doing anything to extinguish the smouldering. His reason for so refraining is that he intends that the risk which his own act had originally created, though it was only subsequently that he became aware of this, should fructify in actual damage to that other person's property; and what he so intends, in fact occurs. There can be no sensible reason why he should not be guilty of arson. If he would be guilty of arson, having appreciated the risk of damage at the very moment of dropping the lighted cigarette, it would be quite irrational that he should not be guilty if he first appreciated the risk at some later point in time but when it was still possible for him to take steps to prevent or minimise the damage.

In that example the state of mind involved was that described in the definition of the statutory offence as 'intending' to damage property belonging to another. This state of mind necessarily connotes an appreciation by the accused that the situation that he has by his own act created involves the risk that property belonging to another will be damaged. This is not necessarily so with the other state of mind, described in the definition of the statutory offence as 'being reckless as to whether any such property would be damaged'. To this other state of mind I now turn; it is the state of mind which is directly involved in the instant case. Where the state of mind relied on by the prosecution is that of 'intending', the risk of damage to property belonging to another created by the physical act of the accused need not be such as would be obvious to anyone who took the trouble to give his mind to it; but the accused himself cannot form the intention that it should fructify in actual damage unless he himself recognises the existence of some risk of this happening. In contrast to this, where the state of mind relied on is 'being reckless', the risk created by the physical act of the accused that property belonging to another would be damaged must be one that would be obvious to anyone who had given his mind to it at whatever is the relevant time for determining whether the state of mind of the accused fitted the description 'being reckless whether such property would be damaged': see *R v Caldwell* [1982] AC 341, 352; see also *R v Lawrence* [1982] AC 510 at 526 for a similar requirement in the mental element in the statutory offence of reckless driving.

In *R v Caldwell* this House was concerned with what was treated throughout as being a single act of the accused, viz starting a fire in the ground floor room of a residential hotel which caused some damage to it; although, if closer analysis of his conduct, as distinct from his state of mind, had been relevant, what he did must have been recognised as consisting of a series of successive acts. Throughout that sequence of acts, however, the state of mind of Caldwell remained unchanged, his acknowledged intention was to damage the hotel and to revenge himself on its owner, and he pleaded guilty to an offence under s 1(1) of the 1971 Act; the question at issue in the appeal was whether in carrying out this avowed intention he was reckless whether the life of another would be thereby endangered, so as to make him guilty also of the more serious offence under s 1(2). This House did not have to consider the case of an accused who although he becomes aware that, as the result of an initial act of his own, events have occurred that present an obvious risk that property belonging to another will be damaged, only becomes aware of this at some time after he has done the initial act. So the precise language suggested in *Caldwell* as appropriate in summing up to a jury in the ordinary run of cases under s 1(1) of the Criminal Damage Act 1971 requires some slight adaptation to make it applicable to the particular and unusual facts of the instant case.

My Lords, just as in the first example that I took the fact that the accused's intent to damage the property of another was not formed until, as a result of his initial act in dropping the cigarette, events had occurred which presented a risk that another person's property would be damaged, ought not under any sensible system of law to absolve him from criminal liability, so too in a case where the relevant state of mind is not intent but recklessness I see no reason in common sense and justice why, *mutatis mutandis*, a similar principle should not apply to impose criminal liability on him. If in the former case he is criminally liable because he refrains from taking steps that are open to him to try to prevent or minimise the damage caused by the risk he has himself created and he so refrains because he intends such damage to occur, so in the latter case, when, as a result of his own initial act in dropping the cigarette, events have occurred which would have made it obvious to anyone who troubled to give his mind to them that they presented a risk that another person's property would be damaged, he should likewise be criminally liable if he refrains from taking steps that lie within his power to try and prevent the damage caused by the risk that he himself has created, and so refrains either because he has not given any thought to the possibility of there being any such risk or because, although he has recognised that there was some risk involved, he has nonetheless decided to take that risk.

My Lords, in the instant case the prosecution did not rely on the state of mind of the accused as being reckless during that part of his conduct that consisted of his lighting and smoking a cigarette while lying on his mattress and falling asleep without extinguishing it. So the jury were not invited to make any finding as to this. What the prosecution did rely on as being reckless was his state of mind during that part of his conduct after he awoke to find that he had set his mattress on fire and that it was smouldering, but did not then take any steps either to try to extinguish it himself or to send for the fire brigade, but simply went into the other room to resume his slumbers, leaving the fire from the already smouldering mattress to spread and to damage that part of the house in which the mattress was.

The recorder, in his lucid summing up to the jury (they took 22 minutes only to reach their verdict), told them that the accused, having by his own act started a fire in the mattress which, when he became aware of its existence, presented an obvious risk of damaging the house, became under a duty to take some action to put it out. The Court of Appeal upheld the conviction, but its *ratio decidendi* appears to be somewhat different from that of the recorder. As I understand the judgment, in effect it treats the whole course of conduct of the accused, from the moment at which he fell asleep and dropped the cigarette onto the mattress until the time the damage to the house by fire was complete, as a continuous act of the accused, and holds that it is sufficient to constitute the statutory offence of arson if at any stage in that course of conduct the state of mind of the accused, when he fails to try to prevent or minimise the damage which will result from his initial act, although it lies within his power to do so, is that of being reckless whether property belonging to another would be damaged.

My Lords, these alternative ways of analysing the legal theory that justifies a decision which has received nothing but commendation for its accord with common sense and justice have, since the publication of the judgment of the Court of Appeal in the instant case, provoked academic controversy. Each theory has distinguished support. Professor J C Smith espouses the 'duty theory' (see [1982] Crim LR 526 at 528); Professor Glanville Williams who, after the decision of the Divisional Court in *Fagan v Metropolitan Police Comr* [1969] 1 QB 439 appears to have been attracted by the duty theory, now prefers that of the continuous act (see [1992] Crim LR 773). When applied to cases where a person has unknowingly done an act which sets in train events that, when he becomes aware of them, present an obvious risk that property belonging to another will be damaged, both theories lead to an identical result; and, since what your Lordships are concerned with is to give guidance to trial judges in their task of summing up to juries, I would for this purpose adopt the duty theory as being the easier to explain to a jury; though I would commend the use of the word 'responsibility', rather than 'duty' which is more appropriate to civil than to criminal law since it suggests an obligation owed to another person, ie the person to whom the endangered property belongs, whereas a criminal statute defines combinations of conduct and state of mind which render a person liable to punishment by the state itself.

While in the general run of cases of destruction or damage to property belonging to another by fire (or other means) where the prosecution relies on the recklessness of the accused, the direction recommended by this House in *R v Caldwell* [1982] AC 341 is appropriate, in the exceptional case, (which is most likely to be one of arson and of which the instant appeal affords a striking example) where the accused is initially unaware that he has done an act that in fact sets in train events which, by the time the accused becomes aware of them, would make it obvious to anyone who troubled to give his mind to them that they present a risk that property belonging to another would be damaged, a suitable direction to the jury would be: that the accused is guilty of the offence under s 1(1) of the Criminal Damage Act 1971 if, when he does become aware that the events in question have happened as a result of his own act, he does not try to prevent or reduce the risk of damage by his own efforts or if necessary by sending for help from the fire brigade and the reason why he does not is either because he has not given any thought to the possibility of there being any such risk or because having recognised that there was some risk involved he has decided not to try to prevent or reduce it.

So, while deprecating the use of the expression *actus reus* in the certified question, I would answer that question 'Yes' and would dismiss the appeal.

Lord Keith of Kinkel, Lord Bridge of Harwich, Lord Brandon of Oakwood and **Lord Brightman** all agreed with **Lord Diplock**.

Elliott v C [1983] 1 WLR 939 (DC)

Glidewell J: This is an appeal by way of case stated from Kent Justices ... who ... found the defendant not guilty of a charge ... that she on 16 June 1982, without lawful excuse had destroyed by fire a shed and its contents, intending to destroy such property or being reckless as to whether such property would be destroyed, contrary to s 1(1) of the Criminal Damage Act 1971.

The shed was the property of a Mr Walter Davies. It was a large wooden shed, and stood at the bottom of the garden of Mr Davies's home. In it he stored tools, various paints, and turpentine or white spirit.

The defendant was a schoolgirl who had reached the age of 14 years in May 1982. She lived with her foster-mother and was in a remedial class at school. On the evening of 15 June 1982, the defendant went out with an older girl friend. She hoped to stay the night in the friend's home, but was not able to do so. The defendant did not return to her own home but stayed out all night, not sleeping for the whole night.

At about 5 am on 16 June 1982, the defendant entered Mr Davies's garden shed. She found the white spirit in its plastic container. She poured white spirit onto the carpet on the floor of the shed and threw two lighted matches onto the spirit, the second of which ignited. The fire immediately flared up out of control and the defendant left the shed.

A Mr Hubbard, who was delivering milk in the area, saw the defendant in the vicinity at about 5.40 am, and a few minutes later saw the shed on fire and raised the alarm.

The police arrested the defendant at her home at 8 am on 16 June 1982, on suspicion of arson and two offences of burglary. She was cautioned in the presence of her foster-mother and made no reply. She was taken to Whitstable Police Station and placed in the cells, where she slept until about 3 pm on the afternoon of the same day.

At 3 pm on 16 June 1982, the defendant was interviewed by two police officers in the presence of her foster-mother. After caution she admitted that she had entered the shed, put spirit on the floor, and set fire to it. She said that she did not know why she had set fire to the shed and that she had 'just felt like it'. She said that she had had the matches with her when she entered the shed, and that after she had set fire to the shed she had run out into the road and had been seen by the milkman. She agreed to make a written statement under caution, in which she admitted entering the shed and setting fire to it.

Although the wording of the information, following the wording of s 1(1) of the Criminal Damage Act 1971, alleged that the defendant destroyed by fire the shed 'intending to destroy such property or being reckless as to whether such property would be destroyed', at the hearing before the justices the contention on behalf of the prosecutor, was not that the evidence proved an intention to destroy the property but that it did prove that the defendant was reckless as to whether the property would be destroyed ...

... [Counsel for the prosecutor] submits that the phrase [in *R v Caldwell* [1982] AC 341] 'creates an obvious risk' means that the risk is one which must have been obvious to a reasonably prudent man, not necessarily to the particular defendant if he or she had given thought to it. It follows, says [counsel], that if the risk is one which would have been obvious to a reasonably prudent person, once it has also been proved that the particular defendant gave no thought to the possibility of there being such a risk, it is not a defence that because of limited intelligence or exhaustion she would not have appreciated the risk even if she had thought about it ...

That [this] submission is correct is to my mind ... put beyond a peradventure by two later decisions of the House of Lords. [His Lordship then referred to *R v Lawrence (Stephen)* [1982] AC 510 and to *R v Miller* [1983] 2 AC 161 and continued.]

In the light of these last two authorities, we are in my judgment bound to hold that the word 'reckless' in s 1 of the Criminal Damage Act 1971 has the meaning ascribed to it by [counsel for the prosecutor] ...

The questions posed [by the justices] in the case are:

1 Whether properly directing ourselves and upon a true construction of s 1(1) of the Criminal Damage Act 1971 we were correct in our interpretation of the meaning of reckless, namely that a defendant should only be held to have acted recklessly by virtue of his failure to give any thought to an obvious risk that property would be destroyed or damaged, where such risk would have been obvious to him if he had given any thought to the matter?

2 Whether properly directing ourselves on the evidence we could properly have come to our decision that the [defendant] had acted neither intentionally nor recklessly in destroying by fire the shed and its contents?

I would answer 'No' to both questions, and allow the appeal.

Robert Goff LJ: I agree with the conclusion reached by Glidewell J, but I do so simply because I believe myself constrained to do so by authority ...

[His Lordship summarised the facts and noted that the defendant] gave no thought at the time when she started the fire to the possibility of there being a risk that the shed and its contents would be destroyed [and that this] risk would not have been obvious to her or have been appreciated by her if she had given thought to the matter. I add that these conclusions were reached by the justices, having regard to the age and understanding of the defendant, her lack of experience of dealing with inflammable spirit, and the fact that she must have been tired and exhausted at the time ...

Plainly, she did destroy the shed and its contents by fire; plainly, too, she did so without lawful excuse. But was she reckless as to whether the shed and its contents would be destroyed?

[His Lordship then refers to *R v Caldwell* [1982] AC 341 and cites the *dictum* of Lord Diplock at 354]

Now, if that test is applied literally in the present case, the conclusion appears inevitable that, on the facts found by the justices, the defendant was reckless whether the shed and contents would be destroyed; because first she did an act which created an obvious risk that the property would be destroyed, and second she had not given any thought to the possibility of there being any such risk.

Yet, if I next pause ... and ask myself the question: would I, having regard only to the ordinary meaning of the word, consider this girl to have been, on the facts found, reckless whether the shed and contents would be destroyed, my answer would, I confess, be in the negative. This is not a case where there was a deliberate disregard of a known risk of damage or injury of a certain type or degree; nor is it a case where there was mindless indifference to a risk of such damage or injury ... nor is it even a case where failure to give thought to the possibility of the risk was due to some blameworthy cause, such as intoxication. This is a case where it appears that the only basis on which the accused might be held to have been reckless would be if the appropriate test to be applied was purely objective – a test which might in some circumstances be thought justifiable in relation to certain conduct (eg reckless driving) ... But such a test does not appear at first sight to be appropriate to a crime such as that under consideration in the present case, especially as recklessness in that crime has to be related to a particular consequence. I therefore next ask myself the question whether I can, consistently with the doctrine of precedent, sensibly interpreted, legitimately construe or qualify the principle stated by Lord Diplock in *R v Caldwell* [1982] AC 341 so as to accommodate what I conceive to be the appropriate result on the facts of the present case, bearing in mind that those facts are very different from the facts under consideration by the House of Lords in *R v Caldwell*, where the defendant had set fire to a hotel when in a state of intoxication.

... I find it striking that the justices, in reaching their conclusion in the present case, have done so ... by imposing on Lord Diplock's statement of principle a qualification ... that a defendant should only be regarded as having acted recklessly by virtue of his failure to give any thought to an obvious risk that property would be destroyed or damaged, where such risk would have been obvious to him if he had given any thought to the matter. However, having studied Lord Diplock's speech, I do not think it would be consistent with his reasoning to impose any such qualification. I say that not only because this qualification does not appear in terms in his conclusion ... but also because ... earlier in his speech ... Lord Diplock expressly adverted to the fact that [Professor Kenny's] definition presupposed that 'if thought were given to the matter by the doer before the act was done, it would have been apparent to him that there was a real risk of its having the relevant harmful consequences'. It seems to me that, having expressly considered that element in Professor Kenny's test, and having (as I think) plainly decided to omit it from his own formulation of the concept of recklessness, it would not now be legitimate for an inferior court, in a case under this particular subsection, to impose a qualification which had so been rejected by Lord Diplock himself. It follows that for that reason alone I do not feel able to uphold the reasoning of the justices in the present case. But I wish to add that, for my part, I doubt whether this qualification can be justified in any event. Where there is no thought of the consequences, any further enquiry necessary for the purposes of establishing guilt should *prima facie* be directed to the question why such thought was not given, rather than to the purely hypothetical question of what the particular person would have appreciated had he directed his mind to the matter ...

In these circumstances, I agree that the questions must be answered as proposed by Glidewell J, and that the appeal must be allowed.

Petition: The Appeal Committee of the House of Lords (**Lord Fraser of Tullybelton**, **Lord Roskill** and **Lord Brightman**) dismissed a petition by the defendant for leave to appeal.

R v R (Stephen Malcolm) (1984) 79 Cr App R 334 (CA)

Ackner LJ: ... At about 11.20 pm on 13 December, Mrs Galler and her daughter were in their flat at 35 Coomber Close. That is a ground floor flat, which is a particularly relevant fact. Mrs Galler was in the sitting room and Simone was in the bedroom, reading. They both heard three loud bangs and the girl saw sheets of flame at her bedroom window. She thought her room was on fire and she ran screaming to her mother. They found that the fire was coming from the wall outside and blowing across the window. There were three separate fires coming from three milk bottles on the grass close to the window. The police found blackened areas on the wall in close proximity to the girl's window. There was a mark on the wall indicating that a petrol bomb had been thrown as close as some 18 inches to the girl's bedroom window. The police went immediately to the appellant's house. It smelt of petrol and a pair of gloves belonging to him were soaked in petrol. When he was asked whether they were his gloves, he challenged the police to prove it.

The appellant was interviewed on 14 December and told the police that at about 4.30 pm the previous day he was at Thomson's house and from what was said there he and Thomson formed the opinion that Simone had 'grassed' upon them, given the information that led to their arrest at her flat on 9 December. They therefore decided to do something to her and later at the appellant's house Thomson suggested making petrol bombs. He, the appellant, already had petrol. They inserted petrol-soaked rags into the bottle necks to act as wicks. They – himself, Thomson and Franklin (Thomson's friend) – then went to the rear of Simone's flat, lit the wicks, threw the bottles at the wall and ran. Each threw one bottle. There had been no discussion as to whether the bottles should be thrown through the window or at the wall, but he said he threw his at the wall and in fact all the bottles hit the wall. He said that he thought that the petrol would go out after it had burned for only a few minutes. They did not intend to cause Simone any injury but only to frighten her. He had considered beating her up, but then he thought that if he did that he might lose his temper and hurt her, and he did not want to do that. He said he did not realise at the time that if the petrol bomb had gone through the window it might have killed her. He had only just realised when he was interviewed by the police that that danger existed ...

[Counsel for the appellant] sought to induce us to adopt a *via media*. He said he accepted it would be wrong to ask the question whether the defendant himself was aware of the risk, but it would be right to enquire whether a person of the age of the defendant and with his characteristics which might be relevant to his ability to foresee the risk, would have appreciated it ...

We do not think that that *via media* was for one moment in the mind of Lord Diplock. The opportunity to so ingraft this important modification on the principle which he had enunciated had arisen in the subsequent cases and would have been just the sort of point (if it was a valid one) which we would have expected the House of Lords to have desired to have dealt with, thus clearing up the position, when they had the opportunity to do so when considering whether or not to give leave [to appeal] in *Elliott v C* [1983] 1 WLR 939. If they had desired to say, for instance, that the age of the defendant was a factor to which particular regard must be had in applying the test, then *Elliott v C* was just the sort of case to do that, excising, if appropriate, any reference to any other ephemeral characteristics such as exhaustion from which the girl was said to be suffering. But they did not take that opportunity. We do not think that we should seek by this subtlety to avoid applying principles which we also have difficulty accepting.

We respectfully share the regrets voiced by Robert Goff LJ that in essence 'recklessness' has now been construed synonymously with 'carelessness' ...

Chief Constable of Avon and Somerset v Shimmen (1986) 84 Cr App R 7 (DC)

Taylor J: ... The charge against the defendant was that on 15 February 1985, in the City of Bristol, without lawful excuse, he destroyed property belonging to Maskreys Ltd, namely a plate-glass window of the value of £495, intending to destroy such property or being reckless as to whether such property would be destroyed, contrary to s 1(1) of the Criminal Damage Act 1971. The justices found the following facts, *inter alia*.

The defendant had, on the relevant evening, been in the company of four friends. They had been in a public house and later they went to a club. During the evening, the defendant consumed a quantity of alcohol. He and his four friends left the club together and made their way along the road to a position outside Maskrey's shop. There the defendant and one of his friends, David Woodhouse, were laughing, joking, and larking around. Woodhouse pushed the defendant who then started flailing his arms and legs, contriving not to make any contact with Mr Woodhouse. Mr Woodhouse issued a warning to the defendant that he might one day hurt someone. The defendant assured Woodhouse that he had everything under control and, to prove it, he made as if to strike the window with his foot. His foot, however, did make contact with the window and broke it. The defendant was the holder of a green belt and yellow belt in the Korean art of self-defence. He was a skilled and experienced practitioner of that art.

It was conceded that he had no intent to break the window. But the prosecutor's contention was that his act amounted to recklessness and that he ought to be convicted on that ground. The defendant contended that by reason of the skill which he had, he had satisfied himself that the window would not break and that he was, in those circumstances, not reckless. The court was, as one would expect, referred to the leading authorities on the nature of recklessness. They are two decisions of the House of Lords. The first is *R v Caldwell* [1982] AC 341. The second is *R v Lawrence* [1982] AC 510 ...

The justices were of the opinion that an obvious and serious risk was created by the defendant's conduct. They accepted the argument that the inference that he was in one or other of the necessary states of mind required to constitute the offence could be displaced in his case by virtue of his evidence relating to his expertise in the science of martial arts ... They made the finding that the defendant perceived there could be a risk of damage, but after considering such risk concluded that no damage would result. They therefore dismissed the charge.

The question posed for this court is as follows: were we correct in law to decide that the defendant should not be regarded as reckless as to whether or not property would be destroyed or damaged if he does an act which in fact creates an obvious risk that property will be destroyed or damaged and having considered the circumstances subjectively concludes that no damage will result from that act?

... [I]t seems to me that on the findings of the justices and more particularly, as I shall indicate in a moment, on the evidence which they exhibited to their case, this defendant did recognise the risk. It was not a case of his considering the possibility and coming to the conclusion that there was no risk. What he said to the justices in cross-examination should be quoted. He said: 'I thought I might break the window but then I thought I will not break the window ... I thought to myself, the window is not going to break'. A little later on he said: 'I weighed up the odds and thought I had eliminated as much risk as possible by missing by two inches instead of two millimetres'.

The specific finding of the justices ... was as follows:

> ... the defendant perceived there could be a risk of damage but after considering such risk concluded that no damage would result.

It seems to me that what this case amounts to is as follows; that this defendant did perceive, which is the same as Lord Diplock's word 'recognise', [in *Caldwell*] that there could be a risk, but by aiming off rather more than he normally would in this sort of display, he thought he had minimised it and therefore no damage would result. In my judgment, that is far from saying that he falls outside the state of mind described by Lord Diplock in these terms: '... has recognised that there was some risk involved and has nonetheless gone on to do it' ...

R v Sangha [1988] 1 WLR 519 (CA)

Tucker J: ... The events which gave rise to this case occurred on the late afternoon of 22 October 1986 at a council flat, 26 Swift Road, Southall. At that time it was being unlawfully occupied by three women and the children of two of them. They were squatters: Marion Abbott, her sister Amanda and Toni Griffin. There was not much furniture, but there were two armchairs and there was a mattress on which one of the women slept. They had neighbours who had been kind to them. At 24 Swift Road there was a woman called Pauline, and also living at that address were the appellant, known as Suki, and Chana, known as Jimmy.

That afternoon the two men went to No 26 Swift Road at about 4 pm. According to Marion Abbott they were paralytically drunk. They ripped a mattress and the appellant slapped her and called her a bitch. They then left. An hour later they returned. The appellant swore at her again. He had a knife and cut the mattress. He then asked Chana to set the mattress on fire, saying, 'Get the matches out and set it on fire'. Chana did so, while the appellant watched. That was what she said in chief. But when she was cross-examined, she was referred to a statement. She said that statement was correct, and in fact it was the appellant, not Chana, who set fire to the mattress. He got the matches out of his pocket. In the light of this turnabout in her evidence, the judge in summing up asked the jury what weight, if any, they could put on her evidence.

Her sister Amanda gave evidence. She said that first of all the appellant came to the flat and behaved aggressively. Then Chana came in, also very drunk. Then the appellant started ripping the mattress with a knife and pulling the stuffing out. He told Chana to fetch some matches, and Chana did so. He handed them to the appellant, who used three or four of them The mattress began to smoulder. The appellant and Chana left. Toni Griffin tried to put the fire out. A few minutes later they returned and the appellant started the fire again. Eventually they left. The women – certainly Amanda Abbott – went to the police station, not about the fire but because of her child. When she returned the flat was burnt out.

PC Fielding went next door, to Pauline's flat at No 24, where he found Chana in the lounge. He called for the appellant and got no response. The police constable found him in the darkened kitchen. The judge told the jury that they might think it rather odd that he was there in the dark when there was a police officer in the flat calling his name. The two men were arrested. The police officers described them both as being the worse for wear because of drink.

When interviewed the appellant said that he had been to the women's flat once that afternoon to see them and play with the children. He only stayed a short time and then went home. He then visited an off-licence with Chana and then went home again. He denied returning to No 26 or cutting or setting fire to the mattress. No motive was alleged.

The scientific evidence at the trial was to the effect that there were probably three seats of fire corresponding to the positions of the two armchairs and the mattress.

The prosecution case was that there had been a setting fire to the mattress and then, by inference, after the occupants had left, the starting of fires in other places. The danger to life was to anybody in the lounge or the kitchen, who would have to get out through the lounge. There was no flat above and there was no danger of the fire spreading to flats on either side because of the way they were constructed. There was only negligible danger to people living in adjoining flats ...

I will first read the particulars of offence:

> Sukhvinder Singh Sangha and Joginder Singh Chana on 22 October 1986 damaged by fire a dwelling at 26, Swift Road, Southall, Middlesex, being reckless as to whether such property would be damaged and being reckless as to whether the life of another would be thereby endangered.

... It is clear that in the present case the relevant time is the time when the two armchairs were set alight. That is the point at which the ordinary prudent man would recognise that some risk of danger to life would be created.

There may of course be cases of arson where the lives not only of the occupants would be endangered, but also of those who might come to their rescue, or of firemen who might have to put out the blaze. But in the present case counsel for the Crown did not stress that aspect.

In our judgment, when consideration is given whether an act of setting fire to something creates an obvious and serious risk of damaging property and thereby endangering the life of another, the test to be applied is this: Is it proved that an ordinary prudent bystander would have perceived an obvious risk that property would be damaged and that life would thereby be endangered? The ordinary prudent bystander is not deemed to be invested with expert knowledge relating to the construction of the property, nor to have the benefit of hindsight. The time at which his perception is material is the time when the fire is started.

Section 1(2) of the 1971 Act uses the word 'would' in the context of recklessness whether property would be destroyed or damaged, and whether the life of another would be thereby endangered. We interpret this word 'would' as going to the expectations of the normal prudent bystander.

Applying this test to the facts of the case before us, it is clear that in setting fire to these armchairs (as the jury found the appellant did), he created a risk which was obvious and serious that property would be damaged and that the life of another would thereby be endangered. The fact that there were special features here which prevented that risk from materialising is irrelevant.

In our judgment there was evidence here which it was proper to leave to the jury and for them to consider. The judge was right to leave the case to them.

R v Merrick [1995] Crim LR 802 (CA)

Facts: The appellant was convicted of damaging property being reckless as to whether life was endangered contrary to s 1(2) of the Criminal Damage Act

1871. It was the appellant's practice to visit householders to whose property certain old cable television cabling was attached, and ask if they were receiving wayleave payments from the owner of the cables, with whom he had fallen out. If they were not, he offered to collect payments, and if they were not made, he would, with the householder's consent, remove the cable and ancillary equipment. A number of counts of criminal damage relating to such cabling and equipment were withdrawn from the jury, the appellant's defence being reasonable excuse in the form of the householder's consent. In respect of the count on which he was convicted, he had, with the householder's written consent, removed a piece of equipment known as a repeater box. In doing so, he inevitably left a live electrical cable exposed. He then proceeded to put the cable in plastic bags, buried it under rubble and cemented it over.

At trial, he said in his evidence that he knew that the repeater box was attached to the mains and had come prepared with material to make good the damage. To leave the cable exposed would, he knew, have been dangerous. The cable had been left entirely exposed for a period of six minutes. He did not believe there was any risk of endangering life at any stage, and he would not have undertaken the work if he had not been competent to do so. The judge ruled that as a matter of law, any precautions designed to eliminate the risk of endangering life must, to provide a defence, be taken before the damage was caused. As a result of the ruling the appellant changed his plea to guilty.

On appeal, it was argued that the defendant fell outside the definition of recklessness set out in *Caldwell* [1982] AC 341. He had not failed to consider the risk (he had thought about it), and nor had he acted recognising the existence of a risk (he had decided there was no risk). Counsel relied on *Chief Constable of Avon and Somerset v Shimmen* (1987) 84 Cr App R 7.

Held, dismissing the appeal, there is a clear distinction between avoiding a risk and taking steps to remedy a risk which has already been created. If a defendant is to successfully contend that the taking of certain steps has prevented him from falling within the definition of recklessness, then those steps must be directed towards preventing the risk at all, rather than at remedying it once it has arisen. The appellant accepted that he had created a risk by exposing the cable, and that it remained exposed for six minutes. Although he said he took reasonable precautions to eliminate the danger, by then he was inevitably remedying a risk that he had already created rather than preventing the risk which arose when the live wire was exposed.

R v Coles [1995] 1 Cr App R 157 (CA)

Hobhouse LJ: ... Lee Henry Coles was tried ... on two counts alleging arson contrary to s 1 of the Criminal Damage Act 1971. One count (count 2) was a count of arson being reckless as to whether life was endangered, with the particulars:

> Lee Henry Coles on the 13th day of August 1992 without lawful excuse damaged by fire a hay barn and hay bales belonging to Barry David Campion intending to destroy or damage such property or being reckless as to whether such property would be destroyed or damaged and being reckless as to whether the lives of Asa Bianju Antonio and Jennifer Anne Tyson would thereby be endangered.

... After the prosecution evidence had been given and the defendant Lee Coles had himself given evidence, Mr Maynard, counsel for Lee Coles, applied to adduce the expert evidence of a psychologist, Mr Kirby Turner. Coupled with that application, he submitted that it was relevant what was, at the material time, the capacity of Lee Coles to foresee the risks which would arise from his setting fire to hay in a barn and that the judge should depart from the classical direction on recklessness formulated by Lord Diplock in *R v Caldwell* [1982] AC 341 at 354 ...

[The trial judge] refused to admit the evidence of the psychologist on two grounds: first that it was not relevant to any issue which the jury had to consider; second that since the psychological evidence was not evidence of any mental abnormality, merely that the defendant was of low average mental capacity, expert evidence was not admissible ...

... Lee Coles has no basis to dispute that he intended to damage property. The point he was disputing was that he was being reckless whether the lives of his two friends would be endangered by his setting fire to the hay upon which they were sleeping.

The Crown evidence was that Lee Coles, who was aged 15, went to Hassocks with four others, Asa who was 15, Jenny and Leah who were each 14, and Mark Poole who was 18. They went to a hay barn which was known to some of them. They arrived there sometime between 11 pm and midnight. During the course of the night they visited a nearby petrol station which was open all night. On one of these visits a box of matches was bought. Later on, around dawn, when the five of them were all on top of the hay in the barn, Lee started playing with the matches, setting fire to pieces of hay. He even went so far as to pull a bale to pieces so as better to get hay to light. At this time only Leah and Mark were awake. Asa and Jenny were asleep less than 10 feet away from where Lee was setting fire to the hay. It was the evidence of Leah that at no time did Lee make any attempt to put out the fire he had started or to wake up Asa or Jenny. Leah herself woke up Jenny and Jenny with difficulty succeeded in waking up Asa. Asa and Mark, and possibly Jenny, attempted to put out the flames by stamping on the burning hay but without success. Indeed at one stage Lee put more hay upon the fire in order to encourage it to burn. All five of them eventually made their escape successfully from the top of the hay leaving it to burn. The evidence of Leah, of which we have a transcript, was that she herself was at risk from being trapped by the fire when she was waking up Jenny.

In interview Lee admitted starting the fire and that Asa and Jenny were sleeping a short distance away but he suggested that he and the others succeeded in putting it out and then it was relit by Asa when Asa put fresh hay upon the embers. He accepted that it was dangerous – 'highly dangerous' – to start a fire when others were sleeping close by on top of the hay.

In cross-examination at the trial and in his evidence, Lee again sought to implicate Asa in the ultimate fire and to exonerate himself on the ground that he believed that any fire that he started would be put out before it got serious and, indeed, he said that that is what he himself did. He was asked by his own counsel:

> *Q*: Did you think about what would happen to the hay in the barn if you did not put the fire out?
>
> *A*: Yes.
>
> *Q*: And what was that?
>
> *A*: It would have burnt.

Q: You said you intended to put the fire out. Did you think that you could?

A: Yes.

Q: What did you think you could do which would be effective to put the fire out?

A: Just stamp on it.

Earlier he had said in answer to the question what he thought would happen if the lit hay with a match: 'I knew it would burn'. Asked what he was going to do about the burning, he answered: 'Stamp it out'. Asked: 'Did you think what would happen if you did not stamp it out?' he answered: 'Yes'. *Q*: 'What?' *A*: 'It would burn'. He gave varying answers both in his examination-in-chief, cross-examination and re-examination about risk. At the conclusion of his cross-examination he was asked:

Q: You took the risk, though, did you not?

A: Yes.

Q: And you took the risk that Jenny and Asa might not have woken up in time and got up? You took that risk, did you not?

A: Yes.

Whilst Lee Coles was giving evidence, his experience and his assessment of the risks involved in his conduct that night were expressly dealt with and explored in each part of his evidence. Which part of his evidence the jury would have preferred and what conclusions of fact they would have come to, taking into account both his evidence and the evidence adduced on behalf of the Crown, would have been a matter for the jury if the defendant had not chosen to change his plea to one of guilty. They would have been at liberty to conclude that he did actually appreciate the risk to Asa and Jenny and that he chose to disregard that risk.

The evidence of Mr Kirby Turner which was tendered on behalf of Lee Coles was based upon a report and interview with Lee and (it appears) a subsequent reading of the committal papers and certain psychometric assessments which had been made of Lee on two occasions in connection with his educational requirements. The report purports to express opinions about precisely those matters which were explored in evidence at the trial with Lee Coles himself. It inevitably was based upon assumptions about the veracity of what Lee had told Mr Kirby Turner. It accepted that part of Mr Kirby Turner's opinion would not be admissible. However, it is suggested that the opinion he expresses based upon the psychometric assessment of Lee's 'verbal comprehension factor' and 'perceptual organisational factor', that 'Lee operates in the low average range of intellectual functioning' were admissible. At another point in his report he describes Lee as being in 'the low average range of ability' or in 'the range of thinking characteristic of pre-adolescent children'. Elsewhere his IQ results were given in terms which whilst below the average were well within the range of normality. He reports that Lee saw himself as the 'ideas man' in the group and that Lee needed to impress both others and himself; Lee 'was locked into the excitement-seeking in rather a thoughtless way'. It was suggested by counsel for Lee that this evidence provided a possible basis for a conclusion that he lacked a capacity for foresight ...

... The classic definition of recklessness is that of Lord Diplock in *R v Caldwell* [1982] AC 341 at 354:

> In my opinion a person charged with an offence under s 1(1) of the Criminal Damage Act 1971 is 'reckless as to whether any such property would be

destroyed or damaged' if (1) he does an act which in fact creates an obvious risk that property will be destroyed or damaged and (2) when he does the act he either has not given any thought to the possibility of there being any such risk or has recognised that there was some risk involved and has nevertheless gone on to do it.

Part (1) of this direction relates to the criminal act and part (2) relates to the defendant's state of mind. Under each head there are additional elements introduced by the use of the word 'reckless' to the more basic elements in the crime. Thus, in the context of arson, the primary act is starting, or failing to control (see *R v Miller* [1983] AC 161), a fire and the first head of the *Caldwell* direction requires that that act should meet an objective factual criterion: does it create the obvious risk? At this stage only the defendant's act is relevant, not his state of mind.

Still in the context of arson, the mental element in the crime is satisfied if the act of starting (or failing to control) the fire was an intentional act and the defendant's state of mind meets one or other of the two criteria in the second leg of the *Caldwell* direction ...

The first leg of the *Caldwell* direction provides an objective criterion which the act the defendant is accused of committing must fulfil. The actual state of mind of the defendant is at that point irrelevant ...

... The second leg of Lord Diplock's formulation is designed to define the mental element which must be proved in a crime involving recklessness. It requires more than the mere proof of the commission of the relevant act. The inferences to be drawn from the intentional commission of the act will normally provide the primary proof of the relevant mental state ... In any given case, other evidence may confirm or detract from the inference. But the proof of one or other of the mental state included in the second leg of the *Caldwell* direction remains an essential part of the proof of the defendant's guilt. It is open to the defendant in any case to destroy or rebut the inference which the Crown seeks to rely upon ...

The case of *R v R (Stephen Malcolm)* (1984) 79 Cr App R 334 is binding upon us and in our judgment is indistinguishable ...

... The other ground of appeal advanced on behalf of the appellant related to the exclusion of the evidence of Mr Kirby Turner. The judge rightly refused to admit this evidence. It was not evidence of any abnormality of the mind of the defendant. It related to characteristics of the defendant which could be competently evaluated by a jury by reference to the facts of the actual case without the assistance of expert evidence. Adolescents of varying stages of maturity and brightness are all within the common experience of jurors ...

... Unless some factor of the mental health or psychiatric state of the defendant is raised, such evidence is not admissible ...

MISTAKEN BELIEF

R v Smith (David Raymond) [1974] QB 354 (CA)

James LJ: ... The question of law in this appeal arises in this way. In 1970 the appellant became the tenant of a ground floor flat at 209 Freemasons Road, London, E16. The letting included a conservatory. In the conservatory the appellant and his brother, who lived with him, installed some electrical wiring for use with stereo equipment. Also, with the landlord's permission, they put up roofing material and asbestos wall panels and laid floorboards. There is no dispute that the roofing, wall panels and floorboards became part of the house and, in law, the property of the landlord. Then in 1972 the appellant gave notice to quit and asked the landlord to allow the appellant's brother to remain as tenant of the flat. On 18 September 1972 the landlord informed the appellant that his brother could not remain. On the next day the appellant damaged the roofing, wall panels and floor boards he had installed in order – according to the appellant and his brother – to gain access to and remove the wiring. The extent of the damage was £130. When interviewed by the police, the appellant said, 'Look, how can I be done for smashing my own property. I put the flooring and that in, so if I want to pull it down it's a matter for me' ...

[The appellant was charged with criminal damage of the landlord's property, contrary to s 1(1) of the Criminal Damage Act 1971.]

The appellant's defence was that he honestly believed that the damage he did was to his own property, that he believed that he was entitled to damage his own property and therefore that he had a lawful excuse for his actions causing the damage ...

[His Lordship quoted from s 1 of the Criminal Damage Act 1971 and then considered a number of arguments raised by counsel for the appellant. His Lordship concluded:]

Construing the language of s 1(1) we have no doubt that the *actus reus* is 'destroying or damaging any property belonging to another'. It is not possible to exclude the words 'belonging to another' which describe the 'property'. Applying the ordinary principles of *mens rea*, the intention and recklessness and the absence of lawful excuse are required to constitute the offence have reference to property belonging to another. It follows that in our judgment no offence is committed under this section if a person destroys or causes damage to property belonging to another if he does so in the honest though mistaken belief that the property is his own, and provided that the belief is honestly held it is irrelevant to consider whether or not it is a justifiable belief ...

INTOXICATION

Jaggard v Dickinson [1981] QB 527 (CA)

Mustill J: ... The facts set out in the case [stated by the justices who convicted the defendant] are short but striking. On the evening of 11 October 1978, the defendant had been drinking. At 10.45 pm she engaged a taxi to take her to 67, Carnach Green, South Ockendon, a house occupied by Mr Heyfron, a gentleman with whom she had a relationship such that, in the words of the justices, she had his consent at any time to treat his property as if it were her own. Alighting from the taxi, she entered the garden, but was asked to leave by a Mrs Raven, who was a stranger to her. Persisting, she broke the glass in the hallway of the house. She then went to the back door, where she broke another window, and gained entry to the house, damaging a net curtain in the process. At some time thereafter, in circumstances not described by the justices, it became clear that the house was not 67, Carnach Green, but 35, Carnach Green, a house of identical outward appearance, occupied by Mrs Raven. The justices have found that the defendant did believe that she was breaking into the property of Mr Heyfron, but that this mistake was brought about by a state of self-induced intoxication.

[His Lordship quoted ss 1(1) and 5(2) of the Criminal Damage Act 1971 and went on:]

It is convenient to refer to the exculpatory provisions of s 5(2) as if they created a defence, whilst recognising that the burden of disproving the facts referred to by the subsection remains on the prosecution.

The justices held that the defendant was not entitled to rely on s 5(2) of the Act of 1971, since the belief relied upon was brought about by a state of self-induced intoxication.

In support of the conviction [counsel for the prosecutor] advanced an argument which may be summarised as follows: (1) Where an offence is one of 'basic intent', in contrast to one of 'specific intent', the fact that the accused was in a state of self-induced intoxication at the time when he did the acts constituting the *actus reus* does not prevent him from possessing the *mens rea* necessary to constitute the offence: see *R v Morgan* [1976] AC 182 and *R v Majewski* [1977] AC 443. (2) Section 1(1) of the Act of 1971 creates an offence of basic intent: *R v Stephenson* [1979] QB 695. (3) Section 5(3) has no bearing on the present issue. It does not create a separate defence, but is no more than a partial definition of the expression 'without lawful excuse' in s 1(1). The absence of lawful excuse forms an element in the *mens rea*: see *R v Smith (David)* [1974] QB 354, 360. Accordingly, since drunkenness does not negative *mens rea* in crimes of basic intent, it cannot be relied on as part of a defence based on s 5(2).

Whilst this is an attractive submission, we consider it to be unsound, for the following reasons. In the first place, the argument transfers the distinction between offences of specific and of basic intent to a context in which it has no place. The distinction is material where the accused relies on his own drunkenness as a ground for denying that he had the degree of intention or recklessness required in order to constitute the offence. Here, by contrast, the defendant does not rely on her drunkenness to displace an inference of intent or recklessness; indeed she does not rely on it at all. Her defence is founded on the state of belief called for by s 5(2). True, the fact of the defendant's intoxication was relevant to the defence under s 5(2), for it helped to explain what would otherwise have been inexplicable, and hence lent colour to her evidence about the state of her belief. This is not the same as using drunkenness to rebut an inference of intention or recklessness. Belief, like intention or recklessness, is a state of mind: but they are not the same states of mind.

Can it nevertheless be said that, even if the context is different, the principles established by *R v Majewski* [1977] AC 443 ought to be applied to this new situation? If the basis of the decision in *R v Majewski* had been that drunkenness does not prevent a person from having an intent or being reckless, then there would be grounds for saying that it should equally be left out of account when deciding on his state of belief. But this is not our view what *R v Majewski* decided. The House of Lords did not conclude that intoxication was irrelevant to the fact of the accused's state of mind, but rather that, whatever might have been his actual state of mind, he should for reasons of policy be precluded from relying on any alteration in that state brought about by self-induced intoxication. The same considerations of policy apply to the intent or recklessness which is the *mens rea* of the offence created by s 1(1), and that offence is accordingly regarded as one of basic intent: see *R v Stephenson* [1979] QB 695. It is indeed essential that this should be so, for drink so often plays a part in offences of criminal damage; and to admit drunkenness as a potential means of escaping liability would provide much too ready a means of avoiding conviction. But these considerations do not apply to a case where Parliament has specifically required the court to consider the accused's actual state of belief, not the state of belief which ought to have existed. This seems to us to show that the court is required by s 5(3) to focus on the existence of the belief, not its intellectual soundness; and a belief can be just as much honestly held if it is induced by intoxication, as if it stems from stupidity, forgetfulness or inattention. It was, however, urged that we could not properly read s 5(2) in isolation from s 1(1), which forms the context of the words, 'without lawful excuse', partially defined by s 5(2). Once the words are put in context, so it is maintained, it can be seen that the law must treat drunkenness in the same way in relation to lawful excuse (and hence belief) as it does to intention and recklessness; for they are all part of the *mens rea* of the offence. To fragment the *mens rea*, so as to treat one part of it as affected by drunkenness in one way, and the remainder as affected in a different way, would make the law impossibly complicated to enforce.

If it had been necessary to decide whether, for all purposes, the *mens rea* of an offence under s 1(1) extends as far as an intent (or recklessness) as to the existence of a lawful excuse, I should have wished to consider the observations of James LJ delivering the judgment of the Court of Appeal in *R v Smith (David)* [1974] QB 354, 360. I do not however find it necessary to reach a conclusion on this matter, and will only say that I am not at present convinced that, when these observations are read in the context of the judgment as a whole, they have the meaning which the prosecutor has sought to put upon them. In my view, however, the answer to the argument lies in the fact that any distinction which has to be drawn as to the effect of drunkenness arises from the scheme of the Act of 1971 itself. No doubt the *mens rea* is in general indivisible, with no distinction being possible as regards the effect of drunkenness. But Parliament has specifically isolated one subjective element, in the shape of honest belief, and has given it separate treatment, and its own special gloss in s 5(3). This being so, there is nothing objectionable in giving it special treatment as regards drunkenness, in accordance with the natural meaning of its words.

In these circumstances, I would hold that the justices were in error when they decided that the defence furnished to the defendant by s 5(2) was lost because the defendant was drunk at the time. I would therefore allow the appeal.

Donaldson LJ: I agree ... The law in relation to self-induced intoxication and crimes of basic intent is without doubt an exception to the general rule that the prosecution must prove the actual existence of the relevant intent, be it basic or specific: see *R v Stephenson* [1979] QB 695, 704 *per* Lane LJ. And in s 5 Parliament has very specifically extended what would otherwise be regarded as 'lawful excuse' by providing that it is immaterial whether the relevant belief is justified or not provided that it is honestly held. The justification for what I may call the *Majewski* exception, although it is much older than that decision, is said to be that the course of conduct inducing the intoxication supplies the evidence of *mens rea*: see *R v Majewski* [1977] AC 443, 474–75, *per* Lord Elwyn-Jones LC. It seems to me that to hold that this substituted *mens rea* overrides so specific a statutory provision, involves reading s 5(2) as if it provided that 'for the purposes of this section it is immaterial whether a belief is justified or not if it is honestly held and the honesty of the belief is not attributable only to self-induced intoxication'. I cannot so construe the section and I too would therefore allow the appeal.

AGGRAVATED CRIMINAL DAMAGE: *MENS REA*

We have already seen that the definition of recklessness applies equally to s 1(1) and s 1(2). The same applies where an attempt to commit aggravated criminal damage is charged.

Attorney General's Reference (No 3 of 1992) [1994] 1 WLR 409 (CA)

Schiemann J: ... The point of law which has been referred to us was formulated as follows:

> Whether on a charge of attempted arson in the aggravated form contemplated by s 1(2) of the Criminal Damage Act 1971, in addition to establishing a specific intent to cause damage by fire, it is sufficient to prove that the defendant was reckless as to whether life would thereby be endangered.

The acquittals which have given rise to this reference had the following background according to the prosecution evidence. Following previous attacks upon their property the complainants maintained a night-time watch over their premises from a motor car (a Ford Granada). In the early hours of the morning the respondents came upon the scene in a vehicle. Inside this car, a Sierra, was a milk crate containing a number of petrol bombs, matches, a petrol can and some rags. As the Sierra approached the complainants, four inside their car and two persons on the pavement talking to them, a lighted petrol bomb was thrown towards them from the Sierra. The prosecution's case was that it was thrown at the Granda and its occupants. The petrol bomb in fact passed over the top of the Granada and smashed against the garden wall of a house a pavement's width away from the car. The Sierra accelerated away but crashed, and the respondents were arrested.

At the trial count 1 of the indictment alleged attempted aggravated arson, specifying in the particulars of offence, *inter alia*, an intent to endanger life. Count 2 alleged attempted aggravated arson, specifying in the particulars of offence, *inter alia*, recklessness as to whether life would be endangered ...

[The trial judge directed acquittal on both counts; the present appeal is concerned only with the acquittal on count 2] ...

... [A]lthough in the present reference the question is posed in relation to arson, it has not been submitted that the presence or absence of fire makes any difference to the answer to the question posed which applies to any form of attempted criminal damage. So we omit any further reference to the element of fire in this judgment ...

So far as the completed simple offence is concerned, the prosecution needs to prove (1) property belonging to another was damaged by the defendant; (2) the state of mind of the defendant was one of the following, (a) he intended to damage such property, or (b) he was reckless as to whether any such property would be damaged.

In the case of the completed aggravated offence the prosecution needs to prove (1) the defendant in fact damaged property, whether belonging to himself or another; (2) that the state of mind of the defendant was one of the following, (a) he intended to damage property, and intended by the damage to endanger the life of another, or (b) he intended to damage property and was reckless as to whether the life of another would be thereby endangered, or (c) he was reckless as to whether any property would be damaged and was reckless as to whether the life of another would be thereby endangered.

It is to be noted that the property referred to under (1) (to which we shall hereafter refer as 'the first-named property') is not necessarily the same property as that referred to in (2) (to which we shall refer as 'the second-named property'), although it normally will be.

Thus a man who (1) owns a crane from which is suspended a heavy object and (2) cuts the rope (the first-named property) which holds the object with the result that (3) the object falls and hits the roof of a passing car (the second-named property) which roof (4) collapses killing the driver, would be guilty if it could be shown that he damaged the rope, was reckless as to whether this would damage the car, and was reckless as to whether the life of the driver of the car would be endangered by the damage to the car.

All the foregoing is common ground. The problem which has given rise to this reference relates to an attempt to commit the aggravated offence in circumstances where the first-named property is the same as the second-named property – in the instant case a car. It amounts to this: whether, if the state of mind of the defendant was that postulated in (2)(b) above, namely that he intended to damage property and was reckless as to whether the life of another would thereby be endangered, and whilst in that state of mind he did an act which was more than merely preparatory to the offence, he is guilty of attempting to commit that offence ...

So far as attempting to commit the simple offence is concerned, in order to convict on such a charge it must be proved that the defendant (a) did an act which was more than merely preparatory to the commission of the offence and (b) did an act intending to damage any property belonging to another.

One way of analysing the situation is to say that a defendant, in order to be guilty of an attempt, must be in one of the states of mind required for the commission of the full offence, and did his best, as far as he could, to supply what was missing from the completion of the offence. It is the policy of the law that such people should be punished notwithstanding that in fact the intentions of such a defendant have not been fulfilled.

If the facts are that, although the defendant had one of the appropriate states of mind required for the complete offence, but the physical element required for the commission of the complete offence is missing, the defendant is not to be convicted unless it can be shown that he intended to supply that physical element ...

We turn finally to the attempt to commit the aggravated offence. In the present case, what was missing to prevent a conviction for the completed offence was damage to the property referred to in the opening lines of s 1(2) of the 1981 Act, what in the example of a crane, which we gave earlier in this judgment, we referred to as 'the first-named property'. Such damage is essential for the completed offence. If a defendant does not intend to cause such damage he cannot intend to commit the completed offence. At worst he is reckless as to whether the offence is committed. The law of attempt is concerned with those who are intending to commit crimes. If that intent cannot be shown, then there can be no conviction.

However, the crime here consisted of doing certain acts in a certain state of mind in circumstances where the first-named property and the second-named property were the same, in short where the danger to life arose from the damage to the property which the defendant intended to damage. The substantive crime is committed if the defendant damaged property in a state of mind where he was reckless as to whether the life of another would thereby be endangered. We see no reason why there should not be a conviction for attempt if the prosecution can show that he, in that state of mind, intended to damage the property by throwing a bomb at it. One analysis of this situation is to say that although the defendant was in an appropriate state of mind to render him guilty of the completed offence the prosecution had not proved the physical element of the completed offence, and therefore he is not guilty of the completed offence. If, on a charge of attempting to commit the offence, the prosecution can show not only the state of mind required for the completed offence but also that the defendant intended to supply the missing physical element of the completed offence, that suffices for a conviction. That cannot be done merely by the prosecution showing him to be reckless. The defendant must intend to damage property, but there is no need for a graver mental state than is required for the full offence ...

We answer [the referred question] in the affirmative.

We add that, in circumstances where the first-named property is not the same as the second-named property, in addition to establishing a specific intent to cause damage by fire to the first named property, it is sufficient to prove that the defendant was reckless as to as to whether any second-named property was damaged and reckless as to whether the life of another would be endangered by the damage to the second-named property.

OTHER OFFENCES UNDER THE CRIMINAL DAMAGE ACT 1971

Section 2 of the Criminal Damage Act 1971: threats to destroy or damage property

A person who without lawful excuse makes to another a threat, intending that that other would fear it would be carried out:

(a) to destroy or damage any property belonging to that other or a third person; or

(b) to destroy or damage his own property in a way which he knows is likely to endanger the life of that other or a third person,

shall be guilty of an offence.

Section 3 of the Criminal Damage Act 1971: possessing anything with intent to destroy or damage property

A person who has anything in his custody or under his control intending without lawful excuse to use it or cause or permit another to use it:

(a) to destroy or damage any property belonging to some other person; or

(b) to destroy or damage his own or the user's property in a way which he knows is likely to endanger the life of some other person,

shall be guilty of an offence.

Punishment

Section 4 of the Criminal Damage Act 1971: punishment of offences

(1) A person guilty of arson under s 1 above or of an offence under s 1(2) above (whether arson or not) shall on conviction on indictment be liable to imprisonment for life.

(2) A person guilty of any other offence under this Act shall on conviction on indictment be liable to imprisonment for a term not exceeding 10 years.

CHAPTER 21

MURDER AND MANSLAUGHTER

THE DEFINITION OF MURDER

The classic definition of murder is set out in Coke's *Institutes* (3 Co Inst 47): 'Murder is when a [person] ... unlawfully killeth ... any reasonable creature *in rerum natura* under the Queen's peace, with malice aforethought ... so as the party wounded or hurt, etc dies of the wound or hurt'.

A more modern definition can be found in *Attorney General's Reference (No 3 of 1994)* [1996] 2 All ER 11.

Attorney General's Reference (No 3 of 1994) [1996] 2 All ER 10 (CA)

Lord Taylor CJ: ... [To obtain a conviction for murder] the prosecution must prove the following elements:

(1) that the defendant did an act;

(2) that the act was deliberate and not accidental;

(3) that the act was unlawful;

(4) that the act was a substantial cause of a death;

(5) that the death was of a person in being;

(6) ...; and

(7) that at the time of doing the act the defendant intended either to kill or to cause really serious bodily injury to the victim or, subject to the extent of the doctrine of transferred malice, to some other person.

THE 'YEAR AND A DAY' RULE

It used to be the case that, for a person to be convicted of murder, the death of the victim had to occur within a year and a day of the act or omission which caused the death [ie the sixth element in the definition put forward by Lord Taylor CJ]. However, s 1 of the Law Reform (Year and a Day Rule) Act 1996 abolishes this rule. Section 2 of the Act provides instead:

Section 2 of the Law Reform (Year and a Day) Act 1996

(1) Proceedings to which this section applies may only be instituted by or with the consent of the Attorney General.

(2) This section applies to proceedings against a person for a fatal offence if:

(a) the injury alleged to have caused the death was sustained more than three years before the death occurred; or

(b) the person has previously been convicted of an offence committed in circumstances alleged to be connected with the death.

(3) In subsection (2) 'fatal offence' means:

(a) murder, manslaughter, infanticide or any other offence of which one of the elements is causing a person's death; or

(b) the offence of aiding, abetting, counselling or procuring a person's suicide.

An example of the operation of s 2(2)(b) would be where a person is convicted of causing grievous bodily harm and, after the conviction, the victim dies; in such a case, the consent of the Attorney General must be obtained before the person is prosecuted for murder (even if three years have not elapsed since the date of the assault).

Unlawfulness

The inclusion of the word 'unlawful' in the definition of murder is to exclude from the ambit of murder killings which are justified. An example of lawful killings is where one person, acting in reasonable self-defence, kills someone. Similarly, a doctor who withdraws treatment from a patient in a persistent vegetative state is not guilty of murder: see *Airedale NHS Trust v Bland* [1993] 1 All ER 821).

The inclusion of the phrase 'under the Queen's peace' in Coke's definition serves to exclude from the scope of murder killings in the course of warfare.

Death of a person in being

Coke's phrase 'reasonable creature' means a creature capable of reasoning: that is, any human being. The Latin phrase *in rerum natura* means a human being fully expelled from its mother's body and capable of existence independent of its mother.

The situation where a foetus is killed was considered by the Court of Appeal in *Attorney General's Reference (No 3 of 1994)* [1996] 2 All ER 11.

Attorney General's Reference (No 3 of 1994) [1996] 2 All ER 10 (CA)

Lord Taylor CJ: ... The respondent was charged with murder and was acquitted by direction of the trial judge. In consequence of the judge's ruling the Attorney General has referred a point of law for the opinion of this court. The point of law is formulated as follows:

1 Subject to proof by the prosecution of the requisite intent in either case: whether the crimes of murder or manslaughter can be committed where unlawful injury is deliberately inflicted:

(1) to a child *in utero;*

(2) to a mother carrying a child in utero where the child is subsequently born alive, enjoys an existence independent of the mother, thereafter dies and the injuries inflicted while *in utero* either caused or made a substantial contribution to the death.

2 Whether the fact that the death of the child is caused solely as a consequence of injury to the mother rather than as a consequence of direct injury to the foetus can negative any liability for murder or manslaughter in the circumstances set out in question 1.

The facts that led to the charge of murder were that on 26 May 1990 the respondent stabbed his girlfriend, who was to his knowledge pregnant with his child. The stab wounds included one to the left lower abdomen which penetrated the uterus and the abdomen of the foetus. [The child was born prematurely but survived for only 120 days] ...

[His Lordship set out the elements of the crime of the murder, and dealing with the requirement that the act which causes the death must be an unlawful one, he said:]

> In law the foetus is treated as part of the mother until it has a separate existence of its own. Thus to cause injury to the foetus is just as unlawful as any assault upon any other part of the mother ...
>
> The fifth element is that the death must be of a person in being. In its simplest form this means that to cause the death of a foetus in the womb cannot be murder. However, the situation under consideration raises the question whether the child needs to be in being at the time when the act causing death is done by the defendant. Clearly, when the respondent stabbed his girlfriend the child was not a person in being ...
>
> We have concluded that there is no requirement that the person who dies needs to be a person in being at the time that the act causing death is perpetrated ...

[His Lordship rejected the idea that a person who intends to kill or cause serious harm to an unborn child could have the *mens rea* for murder, since such a person does not intend to kill or cause serious harm to a person in being. His Lordship went on to say:]

> That is not to say that we think if an intention is directed towards the foetus a charge of murder must fail. In the eyes of the law the foetus is taken to be a part of the mother until it has an existence independent of the mother. Thus an intention to cause serious bodily injury to the foetus is an intention to cause serious bodily injury to a part of the mother just as an intention to injure her arm or her leg would be so viewed. Thus consideration of whether a charge of murder can arise where the focus of the defendant's intention is exclusively the foetus falls to be considered under the head of transferred malice, as is the case where the intention is focused exclusively or partially upon the mother herself.
>
> It is, therefore, necessary to consider the concept of transferred malice in order to answer the questions posed in this reference. At its simplest the concept is that if a defendant intends to kill or cause really serious bodily injury to A but instead kills B, he is as guilty of the murder of B as if the object of his intentions had been B rather than A ...
>
> ... It is important to observe that malice cannot in any event be transferred until such time as the act affects the victim. For example, if a defendant sends a box of poisoned chocolates to A but B eats them and dies, it can only be at the moment when B places the chocolate in his mouth that any question of transfer of malice can arise. That time would in such circumstances of necessity be significantly after the act done by the sender.
>
> We can see no reason to hold that malice can only be transferred where the person to whom it is transferred was in existence at the time of the act causing death. It is perhaps pertinent to observe that a sufficient intention may be directed at no individual but rather there may be an indiscriminate intention which will suffice. Thus a defendant who introduces poison into baby food on a supermarket shelf with an intention to kill some wholly unidentified child is clearly guilty of murder if a child later dies from eating the poisoned food. It would be a remarkable state of affairs if such a person was only guilty of murder if the child had already been born at the date when the poison was introduced to the food ...

[Turning to the question of causation, the Lord Chief Justice said:]

... It is clear from *R v Mitchell* [1983] QB 741 that it is unnecessary for the precise mechanism of death to be foreseen in manslaughter and we are satisfied that the same is true for murder. We do not think it is right or necessary to reintroduce any question of causation at the stage when *mens rea* falls to be considered. Provided that the jury are satisfied that the death was caused by the defendant's act, then we see no reason why the concept of transferred malice should not operate.

Obviously, if the mode of death is utterly remote, there may be circumstances in which this could be regarded as severing the chain of causation, but in the instant case we cannot see that it should matter whether the child dies after birth as a result of a stab wound suffered by the foetus before birth or as a result of premature birth induced by the stabbing.

[Turning to the question of manslaughter, his Lordship said:]

In the light of our conclusions relating to murder, we cannot see that any different approach is required ... Clearly, the intention required for manslaughter will be less than that required to establish murder but, with appropriate adjustment, we can see no reason to reach a different conclusion ...

It follows from the above that in our opinion the two questions posed in the reference should be answered in the following way:

(1) Yes. Murder or manslaughter can be committed where unlawful injury is deliberately inflicted either to a child *in utero* or to a mother carrying a child *in utero* in the circumstances postulated in the question. The requisite intent to be proved in the case of murder is an intention to kill or cause really serious bodily injury to the mother, the foetus before birth being viewed as an integral part of the mother. Such intention is appropriately modified in the case of manslaughter.

(2) No. The fact that the death of the child is caused solely in consequence of injury to the mother rather than as a consequence of injury to the foetus does not negative any liability for murder and manslaughter provided that the jury are satisfied that causation is proved.

Malice aforethought

The *mens rea* required in order to be guilty of murder is either:

(a) intention to kill; or

(b) intention to cause grievous bodily harm (ie really serious bodily harm: see *DPP v Smith* [1961] AC 290): *R v Cunningham* [1982] AC 566.

From this definition of the *mens rea* for murder, it is clear that the prosecution must establish intention; recklessness is not enough.

In considering whether the defendant did *intend* to cause death or grievous bodily harm, regard must be had to s 8 of the Criminal Justice Act 1967.

Particular care has to be taken where death or serious injury is the natural and probable consequence of what the defendant did. Because of the effect of s 8, the jury must not take it for granted that the defendant intended death or serious injury merely because such a result was the natural and probable consequence of the defendant's actions. However, the jury is entitled to *infer* that the defendant intended death or serious injury to occur. This vexed question has been considered at length by the House of Lords in *R v Moloney* [1985] AC 905, *R v Hancock* [1986] AC 455 and by the Court of Appeal in *R v Nedrick* [1986] 1 WLR 1025 and *R v Walker* (1990) 90 Cr App R 226.

R v Moloney [1985] 1 AC 905 (HL)

Lord Bridge of Harwich: ... My Lords, in the early hours of 22 November 1981, the appellant fired a single cartridge from a 12-bore shotgun. The full blast of the shot struck the appellant's stepfather, Patrick Moloney, in the side of the face at a range of about six feet and killed him instantly ...

There is no doubt that the appellant was one of a united, happy family ... The undisputed evidence at the appellant's trial was that the stepfather and stepson enjoyed a happy and loving relationship with each other ...

... [The appellant made a statement to the police and] has, in all essentials, adhered to that account ever since. The material part of the [appellant's] statement [to the police] reads as follows:

> It started with a dinner party which was thrown for my grandparents' 40th wedding anniversary. Towards the end, we all had a lot to drink and our guests had left and I told me Dad I wanted to leave the army. He disagreed with me and started to outline his reasons for disagreeing with me. It was obviously set for being a long discussion so my mother, my sister and grandparents went to bed. We had a couple more drinks while the discussion went on and I was very drunk, and I suspect he was as well. At this point I have to become vague because the conversation came round to personal prowess and in particular with a shotgun. Me Dad claimed that he could not only outshoot me but outload me, outdraw me, ie he was faster then me, and claimed even with a crippled left arm he was still faster than me. I disagreed with him and said: 'Don't be silly' or words to that effect. In fact we were swearing at each other at this time. So he said: 'We'll prove it. Go and get two of the shotguns.' He has four, I have one. So I went upstairs and got my shotgun and I got his shotgun. I gave him his shotgun and he told me to get two cartridges out of a box in the cupboard. I gave him one and took the other myself. He opened his gun and started to remove his snap caps. I opened my gun and removed two empty cartridges which I use as snap caps as I don't have any. I inserted the cartridge in the right hand barrel, closed the gun, took off the safety catch and pulled the trigger of the left hand barrel, and told him he'd lost. By this time I don't think he'd even cleared his barrel of the snap caps. He looked at me and said: 'I didn't think you'd got the guts, but if you have pull the trigger'. I didn't aim the gun. I just pulled the trigger and he was dead. I then went and called the police and told the operator I had just murdered my father, and that's the story.

... The [Court of Appeal] certified that a point of law of general public importance was involved in their decision in the following terms:

> Is malice aforethought in the crime of murder established by proof that when doing the act which causes the death of another the accused either: (a) intends to kill or do serious harm; or (b) foresees that death or serious harm will probably occur, whether or not he desires either of those consequences?

... The true and only basis of the appellant's defence that he was guilty, not of murder, but of manslaughter, was encapsulated in the two sentences in his statement: 'I didn't aim the gun. I just pulled the trigger and he was dead.' The appellant amplified this defence in two crucial passages in his evidence. He said: 'I never deliberately aimed at him and fired at him intending to hurt him or to aim close to him intending to frighten him'. A little later, he said he had no idea in discharging the gun that it would injure his father. 'In my state of mind I never considered that the probable consequence of what I might do might result in injury to anybody. It was just a lark.'

This being the evidence, the issue for the jury was a short and simple one. If they were sure that, at the moment of pulling the trigger which discharged the live cartridge, the appellant realised that the gun was pointing straight at his stepfather's head, they were bound to convict him of murder. If, on the other hand, they thought it might be true that, in the appellant's drunken condition and in the context of this ridiculous challenge, it never entered the appellant's head when he pulled the trigger that the gun was pointing at his father, he should have been acquitted of murder and convicted of manslaughter ...

... The fact that, when the appellant fired the gun, the gun was pointing directly at his stepfather's head at a range of about six feet was not, and could not be, disputed. The sole issue was whether, when he pressed the trigger, this fact and its inevitable consequence were present to the appellant's mind. If they were, the inference was inescapable, using words in their ordinary, everyday meaning, that he intended to kill his stepfather. The undisputed facts that the appellant loved his stepfather and that there was no premeditation or rational motivation, could not, as any reasonable juror would understand, rebut this inference. If, on the other hand, as the appellant was in substance asserting, it never crossed his mind, in his more or less intoxicated condition and when suddenly confronted by his stepfather's absurd challenge, that by pulling the trigger he might injure, let alone kill, his stepfather, no question of foresight of consequences arose for consideration. Whatever his state of mind, the appellant was undoubtedly guilty of a high degree of recklessness. But, so far as I know, no one has yet suggested that recklessness can furnish the necessary element in the crime of murder ...

... I must turn to consider *R v Hyam* [1975] AC 55 and discover, if I can, just what it decided. Mrs Hyam was jealous of a Mrs Booth. Mrs Hyam feared that Mr Jones, her former lover, was about to marry Mrs Booth. Mrs Hyam went to Mrs Booth's house at night (having first assured herself that Mr Jones would not be there) where Mrs Booth and her three children were sleeping. Taking care to disturb no one, Mrs Hyam set the house on fire with petrol. Mrs Booth and one of her children escaped, the other two children died in the fire. Mrs Hyam was tried for murder ... She was convicted ...

The Court of Appeal (Criminal Division) dismissed Mrs Hyam's appeal but gave her leave to appeal to this House and certified that the following point of law of general public importance was involved in their decision:

> Is malice aforethought in the crime of murder established by proof beyond reasonable doubt that when doing the act which led to the death of another the accused knew that it was highly probable that that act would result in death or serious bodily harm?

Your Lordship's House dismissed [Mrs Hyam's] appeal [against conviction] by a majority of three (Lord Hailsham of St Marylebone LC, Viscount Dilhorne and Lord Cross of Chelsea) to two (Lord Diplock and Lord Kilbrandon). Lord Hailsham of St Marylebone LC gave a qualified negative answer to the certified question expressed in the following propositions [1975] AC 55 at 79:

(1) Before an act can be murder it must be 'aimed at someone' as explained in *DPP v Smith* [1961] AC 290 at 327, and must in addition be an act committed with one of the following intentions, the test of which is always subjective to the actual defendant: (1) The intention to caused death; (2) The intention to

cause grievous bodily harm in the sense of that term explained in *Smith*, at 335, ie really serious injury; (3) Where the defendant knows that there is a serious risk that death or grievous bodily harm will ensue from his acts, and commits those acts deliberately and without lawful excuse, the intention to expose a potential victim to that risk as the result of those acts. It does not matter in such circumstances whether the defendant desires those consequences to ensue or not, and in none of these cases does it matter that the act and the intention were aimed at a potential victim other that the one who succumbed.

(2) without an intention of one of these three types the mere fact that the defendant's conduct is done in the knowledge that grievous bodily harm is likely or highly likely to ensue from his conduct is not by itself enough to convert a homicide into the crime of murder.

Viscount Dilhorne said at 80:

> It is to be observed that Ackner J [the trial judge] in his direction to the jury said that such knowledge [that is that it was highly probable that the act would cause death or serious bodily harm] established the necessary intent. The question certified asked whether it constituted malice aforethought. If it did, it does not follow that it established an intent to do grievous bodily harm.

He went on to express the opinion that the question certified should be answered in the affirmative. He added, however at 82:

> I think, too, that if Ackner J had left the question of intent in the way in which it is left in the vast majority of cases, namely was it proved that the accused had intended to kill or to do grievous bodily harm, no reasonable jury could on the facts of this case have come to any other conclusion than that she had intended to do grievous bodily harm, bearing in mind her knowledge and the fact that, before she set fire to the house, she took steps to make sure that Mr Jones was not in it as she did not want to harm him. If the normal direction had been given, much litigation would have been avoided.

[Lord Bridge went on to quote from the dissenting speeches of Lord Diplock and Lord Kilbrandon in *R v Hyam* and then continued:]

Lord Cross of Chelsea, although voting with the majority, effectively sat on the fence on the main issue which divided the rest of their Lordships. Having reviewed their differences he concluded his speech by saying, at 97–98:

> All that I am certain of is that I am not prepared to decide between them without having heard the fullest possible argument on the point from counsel on both sides – especially as a decision that *R v Vickers* [1957] 2 QB 664 was wrongly decided might have serious repercussions since the direction approved in that case must have been given in many homicide cases in the last 17 years. For my part, therefore, I shall content myself with saying that *on the footing that R v Vickers was rightly decided* the answer to the question put to us should be 'Yes' and that this appeal should be dismissed ...

[His Lordship referred to the Fourteenth Report of the Criminal Law Revision Committee, entitled Offences Against the Person (1980) and went on:]

The golden rule should be that, when directing a jury on the mental element necessary in a crime of specific intent, the judge should avoid any elaboration or paraphrase of what is meant by intent, and leave it to the jury's good sense to decide whether the accused acted with the necessary intent, unless the judge is convinced that, on the facts and having regard to the way the case has been presented to the jury in evidence and argument, some further explanation or elaboration is strictly necessary to avoid misunderstanding. In trials for murder or wounding with intent, I find it very difficult to visualise a case where any such explanation or elaboration could be required, if the offence consisted of a direct attack on the victim with a weapon, except possibly the case where the accused shot at A and killed B, which any first-year law student could explain to a jury in the simplest of terms. Even where the death results indirectly from the act of the accused, I believe the cases that will call for a direction by reference to foresight of consequences will be of extremely rare occurrence. I am in full agreement with the view expressed by Viscount Dilhorne that, in *R v Hyam* [1975] AC 55 at 82 itself, if the issue of intent had been left without elaboration, no reasonable jury could have failed to convict. I find it difficult to understand why the prosecution did not seek to support the conviction, as an alternative to their main submission, on the ground that there had been no actual miscarriage of justice.

I do not, of course, by what I have said in the foregoing paragraph, mean to question the necessity, which frequently arises, to explain to a jury that intention is something quite distinct from motive or desire. But this can normally be quite simply explained by reference to the case before the court or, if necessary, by some homely example. A man who, at London Airport, boards a plane which he knows to be bound for Manchester, clearly intends to travel to Manchester, even though Manchester is the last place he wants to be and his motive for boarding the plane is simply to escape pursuit. The possibility that the plane may have engine trouble and be diverted to Luton does not affect the matter. By boarding the Manchester plane, the man conclusively demonstrates his intention to go there, because it is a moral certainty that that is where he will arrive ...

In one sense I should be happy to adopt in its entirety the qualified negative answer proposed by my noble and learned friend on the Woolsack to the certified question in *R v Hyam* [1975] AC 55 at 79, because, if I may say so, it seems to me to be supported by the most convincing jurisprudential and philosophical arguments to be found in any of the speeches in *R v Hyam*. But I have to add at one that there are two reasons why I cannot regard it as providing practical guidance to judges who have to direct juries in the rare cases where foresight of probable consequences must be canvassed with the jury as an element which should affect their conclusion on the issue of intent.

First, I cannot accept that the suggested criterion that the act of the accused, to amount to murder, must be 'aimed at someone' as explained in *DPP v Smith* [1961] AC 290 by Viscount Kilmuir LC at 327 is one which would be generally helpful to juries. The accused man in *DPP v Smith* was driving a car containing stolen goods. When told to stop by a police constable he accelerated away. The constable clung to the side of his car and the accused, in busy traffic, pursued an erratic course in order to shake the constable off. When finally shaken off, the constable fell in front of another car and was killed. In this context it was, no doubt, entirely apposite to say, as Viscount Kilmuir LC did, at 327, 'The unlawful and voluntary act must clearly be aimed at someone in order to eliminate cases of negligence or of careless or dangerous driving. But what of the terrorist who plants a time bomb in a public building and gives timely warning to enable the public to be evacuated? Assume that he knows that, following evacuation, it is virtually certain that a bomb disposal squad will attempt to defuse the bomb. In the event the bomb explodes and kills a bomb disposal expert ... Can it ... be said that in this case the bomb was 'aimed' at the bomb disposal expert? ... I believe this criterion would create more doubts than it would resolve.

Second, I believe that my noble and learned friend, Lord Hailsham of St. Marylebone LC's inclusion in the mental element necessary to a conviction of murder of 'the intention to expose a potential victim', *inter alia*, to 'a serious risk that ... grievous bodily harm will ensue from his acts' ([1975] AC 55, 79) comes dangerously near to causing confusion with at least one possible element in the crime of causing death by reckless driving, and by inference equally of motor manslaughter, as identified by Lord Diplock in the later case of *R v Lawrence* [1982] AC 510, 526, 527, where the driving was such 'as to create an obvious and serious risk of causing physical injury to some other person' and the driver 'having recognised that there was some risk involved, had nonetheless gone on to take it'. If the driver, overtaking in a narrow country lane in the face of an oncoming cyclist, recognises and takes not only 'some risk' but a serious risk of hitting the cyclist, is he to be held guilty of murder?

Starting from the proposition established by *R v Vickers* [1957] 2 QB 664, as modified by *DPP v Smith* [1961] AC 290 that the mental element in murder requires proof of an intention to kill or cause really serious injury, the first fundamental question to be answered is whether there is any rule of substantive law that foresight by the accused of one of those eventualities as a probable consequence of his voluntary act, where the probability can be defined as exceeding a certain degree, is equivalent or alternative to the necessary intention. I would answer this question in the negative. Here I derive powerful support from the speech of my noble and learned friend, Lord Hailsham of St. Marylebone LC in *R v Hyam* [1975] AC 55. He said at 75:

> I do not, therefore, consider, as was suggested in argument, that the fact that a state of affairs is correctly foreseen as a highly probable consequence of what is done is the same thing as the fact that the state of affairs is intended.

And again at 77:

> I do not think that foresight as such of a high degree of probability is at all the same thing as intention, and, in my view, it is not foresight but intention which constitutes the mental element in murder.

The irrationality of any such rule of substantive law stems from the fact that it is impossible to define degrees of probability, in any of the infinite variety of situations arising in human affairs, in precise or scientific terms. As Lord Reid said in *Southern Portland Cement Ltd v Cooper* [1974] AC 623, 640:

> Chance probability or likelihood is always a matter of degree. It is rarely capable of precise assessment. Many different expressions are in common use. It can be said that the occurrence of a future event is very likely, rather likely, more probable than not, not unlikely, quite likely, not improbable, more than a mere possibility, etc. It is neither practicable nor reasonable to draw a line at extreme probability.

I am firmly of opinion that foresight of consequences, as an element bearing on the issue of intention in murder, or indeed any other crime of specific intent, belongs, not to the substantive law, but to the law of evidence. Here again I am happy to find myself aligned with my noble and learned friend, Lord Hailsham of St Marylebone LC in *R v Hyam* [1975] AC 55, where he said at 65: 'Knowledge or foresight is at best material which entitles or compels a jury to draw the necessary inference as to intention' ...

... I know of no clearer exposition of the law than that in the judgment of the Court of Criminal Appeal (Lord Goddard CJ, Atkinson and Cassels JJ) delivered by Lord Goddard CJ in *R v Steane* [1947] KB 997 where he said at 1004:

> No doubt, if the prosecution prove an act the natural consequence of which would be a certain result and no evidence or explanation is given, then a jury may, on a proper direction, find that the prisoner is guilty of doing the act with the intent alleged, but if on the totality of the evidence there is room for more than one view as to the intent of the prisoner, the jury should be directed that it is for the prosecution to prove the intent to the jury's satisfaction, and if, on a review of the whole evidence, they either think that the intent did not exist or they are left in doubt as to the intent, the prisoner is entitled to be acquitted.

In the rare cases in which it is necessary to direct a jury by reference to foresight of consequences, I do not believe it is necessary for the judge to do more than invite the jury to consider two questions. First, was death or really serious injury in a murder case (or whatever relevant consequence must be proved to have been intended in any other case) a natural consequence of the defendant's voluntary act? Second, did the defendant foresee that consequence as being a natural consequence of his act? The jury should then be told that if they answer yes to both questions it is a proper inference for them to draw that he intended that consequence.

My Lords, I would answer the certified question in the negative. I would allow the appeal, set aside the verdict of murder, and substitute a verdict of manslaughter ...

R v Hancock and Shankland [1986] 1 AC 455 (HL)

Lord Scarman: ... In the dark hours of the early morning of 30 November 1984 Mr David Wilkie was driving his taxi along the Heads of the Valley Road. As he approached the bridge over the road at Rhymney he was killed when two lumps of concrete hit the car. The two lumps, a block and a post, had been dropped from the bridge as he approached it.

Mr Wilkie's passenger was a miner going to work. Mr Hancock and Mr Shankland were miners on strike, and strongly objected to Mr Wilkie's passenger going to work. That morning they had collected the block and the post from nearby, had brought them to the bridge under which the Heads of the Valley Road runs through a cutting, and had placed them on the parapet on the side facing towards the Rhymney roundabout. They then awaited the arrival of a convoy escorting the miner on his way to work ... As the convoy neared the bridge, the concrete block struck the taxi's windscreen. The post struck the carriageway some 4ft 8in from the nearside verge. Before, however, the post subsided on the ground, it was hit by the taxi. The taxi skidded out of control, coming to rest on the embankment. Mr Wilkie died from the injuries he received in the wrecking of the taxi by the two lumps of concrete.

The case for the prosecution was that the two concrete objects were either thrown from the bridge or pushed over its parapet in the path of the taxi at a time when the taxi could not avoid being struck by one or both of them. And, as the trial judge told the jury, the prosecution case could be compressed into one question and answer, the question being 'what else could a person who pushed or threw such objects have intended but to cause really serious bodily harm to the occupants of the car?' The answer in the prosecution's submission was that a person acting in that way could in the circumstances have intended nothing less.

The defence was simple enough: that the two men intended to block the road, to stop the miner going to work, but not to kill or to do serious bodily harm to anyone ... At a later interview Hancock admitted 'shoving' the block of concrete over the parapet of the bridge, but declared that he believed when he did so that he was standing 'over the middle lane', ie not over the nearside lane, along which the convoy was moving. He said that he did not mean to do anyone damage – 'just to frighten him [ie the miner going to work] more than anything'. Shankland admitted that he was party to the plan to obstruct the road but denied that they intended to hurt anyone. Like Hancock, he emphasised that their plan was to drop the objects in the middle lane of the carriageway, ie clear of the lane along which the convoy was travelling, and that they believed that this was what they did.

Hancock and Shankland were prepared to plead guilty to manslaughter but the Crown decided to pursue the charge of murder. The issue was ultimately one of intention. Did they (or either of them) intend to kill or cause anyone serious bodily harm?

[The trial judge directed the jury in accordance with the guidelines given by the House of Lords in *R v Moloney* [1985] AC 905. The Court of Appeal expressed disquiet over those guidelines, in that they offered the jury no assistance as to the relevance or weight of the probability factor in determining whether they should, or could properly, infer from foresight of a consequence the intent to bring about that consequence.]

The question for the House is, therefore, whether the *Moloney* guidelines are sound. In *Moloney* the *ratio decidendi* was that the judge never properly put to the jury the defence, namely that the accused was unaware that the gun was pointing at his stepfather. The House, however, held it necessary in view of the history of confusion in this branch of the law to attempt to clarify the law relating to the establishment of the mental element necessary to constitute the crime of murder and to lay down guidelines for assisting juries to determine in what circumstances it is proper to infer intent from foresight. The House certainly clarified the law. First, the House cleared away the confusions which had obscured the law during the last 25 years laying down authoritatively that the mental element in murder is a specific intent, the intent to kill or to inflict serious bodily harm. Nothing less suffices: and the jury must be sure that the intent existed when the act was done which resulted in death before they can return a verdict of murder.

Second, the House made it absolutely clear that foresight of consequences is no more than evidence of the existence of the intent; it must be considered, and its weight assessed, together with all the evidence in the case. Foresight does not necessarily imply the existence of intention, though it may be a fact from which when considered with all the other evidence a jury may think it right to infer the necessary intent ...

Third, the House emphasised that the probability of the result of an act is an important matter for the jury to consider and can be critical in their determining whether the result was intended ...

It is only when Lord Bridge of Harwich turned to the task of formulating guidelines that difficulty arises. It is said by the Court of Appeal that the guidelines by omitting any express reference to probability are ambiguous and may well lead a jury to a wrong conclusion. The omission was deliberate. Lord Bridge omitted the adjective 'probable' from the time-honoured formula 'foresight of the natural and probable consequences of his acts' because he thought that 'if a consequence is natural, it is really otiose to speak of it as also being probable' [1985] AC 905 at 929B. But is it? ...

... My Lords, I very much doubt whether a jury without further explanation would think that 'probable' added nothing to 'natural'. I agree with the Court of Appeal that the probability of a consequence is a factor of sufficient importance to be drawn specifically to the attention of the jury and to be explained. In a murder case where it is necessary to direct a jury on the issue of intent by reference to foresight of consequences the probability of death or serious injury resulting from the act done may be critically important. Its importance will depend on the degree of probability: if the likelihood that death or serious injury will result is high, the probability of that result may, as Lord Bridge of Harwich noted and the Lord Chief Justice emphasised, be seen as overwhelming evidence of the existence of the intent to kill or injure. Failure to explain the relevance of probability may, therefore, mislead a jury into thinking that it is of little or no importance and into concentrating exclusively of the causal link between the act and its consequence. In framing his guidelines Lord Bridge of Harwich [1985] AC 905, 929G, emphasised that he did not believe it necessary to do more than to invite the jury to consider his two questions. Neither question makes any reference (beyond the use of the word 'natural') to probability. I am not surprised that when in this case the judge faithfully followed this guidance the jury found themselves perplexed and unsure. In my judgment, therefore, the *Moloney* guidelines as they stand are unsafe and misleading. They require a reference to probability. They also require an explanation that the greater the probability of a consequence the more likely it is that the consequence was foreseen and that if that consequence was foreseen the greater the probability is that that consequence was also intended. But juries also require to be reminded that the decision is theirs to be reached upon a consideration of all the evidence.

Accordingly, I accept the view of the Court of Appeal that the *Moloney* guidelines are defective. I am, however, not persuaded that guidelines of general application, albeit within a limited class of case, are wise or desirable ...

I fear that their elaborate structure may well create difficulty. Juries are not chosen for their understanding of a logical and phased process leading by question and answer to a conclusion but are expected to exercise practical common sense. They want help on the practical problems encountered in evaluating the evidence of a particular case and reaching a conclusion. It is better, I suggest, notwithstanding my respect for the comprehensive formulation of the Court of Appeal's guidelines, that the trial judge should follow the traditional course of a summing up. He must explain the nature of the offence charged, give directions as to the law applicable to the particular facts of the case, explain the incidence and burden of proof, put both sides' cases making especially sure that the defence is put; he should offer help in understanding and weighing up all the evidence and should make certain that the jury understand that whereas the law is for him the facts are for them to decide. Guidelines, if given, are not to be treated as rules of law but as a guide indicating the sort of approach the jury may properly adopt to the evidence when coming to their decision on the facts.

In a case where foresight of a consequence is part of the evidence supporting a prosecution submission that the accused intended the consequence, the judge, if he thinks some general observations would help the jury, could well, having in mind s 8 of the Criminal Justice Act 1967, emphasise that the probability, however high, of a consequence is only a factor, though it may in some cases be a very significant factor, to be considered will all the other evidence in determining whether the accused intended to bring it about. The distinction between the offence and the evidence relied on to prove it is vital. Lord Bridge's speech in

Moloney made the distinction crystal clear: it would be a disservice to the law to allow his guidelines to mislead a jury into overlooking it.

For these reasons I would hold that the *Moloney* guidelines are defective and should not be used as they stand without further explanation. The laying down of guidelines for use in directing juries in cases of complexity is a function which can be usefully exercised by the Court of Appeal. But it should be done sparingly, and limited to cases of real difficulty. If it is done, the guidelines should avoid generalisation so far as is possible and encourage the jury to exercise their common sense in reaching what is their decision on the facts. Guidelines are not rules of law: judges should not think that they must use them. A judge's duty is to direct the jury in law and to help them upon the particular facts of the case.

Accordingly, I would answer the certified question in the affirmative and would dismiss the appeal ...

Lord Keith of Kinkel, Lord Roskill, Lord Brightman and **Lord Griffiths** agreed with **Lord Scarman**.

R v Nedrick [1986] 1 WLR 1025 (CA)

Lord Lane CJ: ... The case for the Crown was that the appellant had a grudge against a woman called Viola Foreshaw, as a result of which, after threats that he would 'burn her out', he went to her house in the early hours of 15 July 1984, poured paraffin through the letter-box and on to the front door and set it alight. He gave no warning. The house was burnt down and one of Viola Foreshaw's children, a boy aged 12 called Lloyd, died of asphyxiation and burns.

After a number of interviews during which he denied any responsibility, the appellant eventually confessed to the police that he had started the fire in the manner described, adding, 'I didn't want anyone to die, I am not a murderer; please tell the judge; God knows I am not a murderer'. When asked why he did it, he replied, 'Just to wake her up and frighten her'.

The appellant's defence, rejected by the jury, was that he had neither started the fire nor made any admissions to that effect.

The sole effective ground of appeal is that the judge misdirected the jury on the intent necessary to establish a charge of murder ...

What then does a jury have to decide so far as the mental element in murder is concerned? It simply has to decide whether the defendant intended to kill or do serious bodily harm. In order to reach that decision the jury must pay regard to all the relevant circumstances, including what the defendant himself said and did.

In the great majority of cases a direction to that effect will be enough, particularly where the defendant's actions amounted to a direct attack upon his victim, because in such cases the evidence relating to the defendant's desire or motive will be clear and his intent will have been the same as his desire or motive. But in some cases, of which this is one, the defendant does an act which is manifestly dangerous and as a result someone dies. The primary desire or motive of the defendant may not have been to harm that person, or indeed anyone. In that situation what further directions should a jury be given as to the mental state which they must find to exist in the defendant if murder is to be proved?

We have endeavoured to crystallise the effect of their Lordships' speeches in *R v Moloney* and *R v Hancock* in a way which we hope may be helpful to judges who have to handle this type of case.

It may be advisable first of all to explain to the jury that a man may intend to achieve a certain result whilst at the same time not desiring it to come about. In *R v Moloney* [1985] AC 905 at 926 Lord Bridge gave an illustration of the distinction:

> A man who, at London Airport, boards a plane which he knows to be bound for Manchester, clearly intends to travel to Manchester, even though Manchester is the last place he wants to be and his motive for boarding the plane is simply to escape pursuit.

The man who knowingly boards the Manchester aircraft wants to go there in the sense that boarding it is a voluntary act. His desire to leave London predominates over his desire not to go to Manchester. When he decides to board the aircraft, if not before, he forms the intention to travel to Manchester.

In *R v Hancock* the House decided that the *R v Moloney* guidelines require a reference to probability. Lord Scarman said ([1986] AC 455 at 473):

> They also require an explanation that the greater the probability of a consequence the more likely it is that the consequence was foreseen and that if that consequence was foreseen the greater the probability is that that consequence was also intended.

When determining whether the defendant had the necessary intent, it may therefore be helpful for a jury to ask themselves two questions:

(1) How probable was the consequence which resulted from the defendant's voluntary act?

(2) Did he foresee that consequence?

If he did not appreciate that death or serious harm was likely to result from his act, he cannot have intended to bring it about. If he did, but thought that the risk to which he was exposing the person killed was only slight, then it may be easy for the jury to conclude that he did not intend to bring about that result. On the other hand, if the jury are satisfied that at the material time the defendant recognised that death or serious harm would be virtually certain (barring some unforeseen intervention) to result from his voluntary act, then that is a fact from which they may find it easy to infer that he intended to kill or do serious bodily harm, even though he may not have had any desire to achieve that result.

As Lord Bridge of Harwich said in *R v Moloney* [1985] AC 905 at 925:

> ... the probability of the consequence taken to have been foreseen must be little short of overwhelming before it will suffice to establish the necessary intent.

At p 926 he uses the expression 'moral certainty'; he said at 929 'will lead to a certain consequence unless something unexpected supervenes to prevent it'.

Where the charge is murder and in the rare cases where the simple direction is not enough, the jury should be directed that they are not entitled to infer the necessary intention, unless they feel sure that death or serious bodily harm was a virtual certainty (barring some unforeseen intervention) as a result of the defendant's actions and that the defendant appreciated that such was the case.

Where a man realises that it is for all practical purposes inevitable that his actions will result in death or serious harm, the inference may be irresistible that he intended that result, however little he may have desired or wished it to happen. The decision is one for the jury to be reached upon a consideration of all the evidence.

R v Walker and Hayles (1990) 90 Cr App R 226 (CA)

Lloyd LJ: ... The facts were that Walker's sister, Christine, was having an affair with a man called Royston John, the victim. A week or so before 20 September 1987, there had been a violent quarrel between Christine and John. Christine received two black eyes and a torn fingernail.

On the evening in question (20 September), the two appellants visited Christine's flat. The appellant Hayles was living with another of Walker's sisters. Christine's flat was on the third floor of a block of flats in Battersea Park Road. Royston John was there. He had a key to Christine's flat. He was asked to hand over the key to Christine. He refused. There was then a fight. John ran out onto the balcony, which led towards the central staircase. The appellants followed him.

According to the prosecution case, the appellants caught him up, lifted him over the balcony, and dropped him horizontally to the ground. Somehow or other he survived, perhaps because he landed on some grass. In the course of the fight the appellants had banged the victim's head against the wall, saying that they were going to kill him. There were bloodstains found on the wall. One of the appellants produced a knife and threatened the victim's throat. Just before they threw the victim over the balcony, he said: 'You deserve to die. I am going to kill you. We don't like you.'

The defence case was that as John ran along the balcony, he climbed over the rail in order to make good his escape and fell ...

... Since the charge was attempted murder, the prosecution had to prove an intention to kill. Intention to cause really serious harm would not have been enough ...

... Moreover the position is not quite the same in a case of attempted murder as it is in murder. In the great majority of murder cases, as the court pointed out in *R v Nedrick* (1986) 83 Cr App R 267, the defendant's desire goes hand in hand with his intention. If he desires serious harm, and death results from his action, he is guilty of murder. A simple direction suffices in such cases. The rare and exceptional case is where the defendant does not desire serious harm, or indeed any harm at all. But where a defendant is charged with attempted murder, he may well have desired serious harm, without desiring death. So the desire of serious harm does not provide the answer. It does not go hand in hand with the relevant intention, as it does in the great majority of murder cases, since in attempted murder the relevant intention must be an intention to kill ...

... We agree with counsel this far, that in the rare cases where an expanded direction is required, it is better that the judge should continue to use the term 'virtual certainty', which has the authority of this court in *Nedrick*. We also agree that there is no difference in this respect between the kind of case considered in *Nedrick*, where the question was whether serious harm was intended, even though it was not desired, and the present case, where serious harm was clearly desired and the only question is whether death was intended. In the rare cases where a foresight direction is required, the same language should be used.

But we do not accept that the reference to 'very high degree of probability' was a misdirection. The truth is ... that once one departs from absolute certainty, there is bound to be a question of degree. We do not regard the difference of degree, if there is one, between very high degree of probability on the one hand and virtual certainty on the other as being sufficient to render what the recorder said a misdirection ...

... [W]e are not persuaded that it is only when death is a virtual certainty that the jury can infer intention to kill. Providing the dividing line between intention and recklessness is never blurred, and provided it is made clear, as it was here, that it is a question for the jury to infer from the degree of probability in the particular case whether the defendant intended to kill, we would not regard the use of the words 'very high degree of probability' as a misdirection.

To avoid any misunderstanding, we repeat that in the great majority of cases of attempted murder, as in murder, the simple direction will suffice, without any reference to foresight. In the rare case where an expanded direction is required in terms of foresight, courts should continue to use virtual certainty as the test, rather than high probability ...

R v Woollin [1997] 1 Cr App R 97 (CA)

Roch LJ: The appellant was charged that on 18 August 1994 he murdered Carl James Roper. Carl James Roper was the appellant's son. He was born on 16 May 1994 and was therefore a baby of three months on 18 August ...

At 1.17 pm the appellant called the emergency services. An ambulance took the baby to the neo-natal clinic at Leeds General Infirmary. The baby was found to have sustained a severe head injury with an underlying skull fracture. Two days later, despite surgical and other treatment, Carl died.

A post mortem performed by Professor Green showed that there was a four-and-a-half inch long gaping fracture on the right side of the skull extending from the centre back of the head over the right ear, which was gaping to the extent of some quarter of an inch. There was an area of swelling of some three to four inches in diameter over the site of the fracture, and there had been severe haemorrhaging under the dura. The brain was extensively damaged, although some of the damage was due to surgical intervention. In addition there was haemorrhaging in the retinas of the baby's eyes which, in the view of Professor Green, was probably a result of the baby being violently shaken.

Professor Green, in evidence, expressed the opinion that a heavy impact would have been necessary to cause the fracture which he found on his post mortem examination. There was nothing to indicate with what the impact had been. On balance, Professor Green thought that the impact had been with a flat, hard surface, such as a wall or a table top or possibly the hard part of a sofa which was in the living room of the appellant's home, which is the room where the incident occurred.

The appellant gave differing explanations to account for the baby's injuries ...

Following his arrest on the evening of 16 August the appellant was interviewed on four occasions. In the first interview he claimed that the baby had injured himself by jumping backwards. He then said that he had been handling the baby in a clumsy manner and in the course of turning the baby over had allowed the baby to bang his head on the edge of the coffee table. He had heard a very distinct chilling crack. The appellant repeated that explanation in his second interview.

In his third interview he told police officers that he 'lost his cool' when the baby started to choke on his food. He had taken him out of his chair, sworn at him and shaken him about a bit. He described the baby's head as 'going all over the place'. He had then, in a fit of rage or frustration, thrown the baby in the direction of his pram some four or five feet away, where it stood against the wall, and he admitted using considerable force to do so. He knew that the baby's head had hit something hard, but could not say whether it was the edge of the pram, the door of the room or the floor. However, he said that he knew it was something hard, 'It was something very chilling when I heard that noise'. He denied having any intention of throwing the baby against the wall. He accepted that in throwing the child there was a risk of serious injury.

In his fourth interview, shortly after he had been informed of his son's death, he purported to remember that the baby had landed quite hard on the floor in the gap between the sofa and the carrycot. When asked what was going through his head at the time he threw the baby, he replied, 'I just did not want to know him'. He also said, 'I didn't think it would kill him', and right at the end of the interview, 'I didn't want him to die'.

...The prosecution case [at trial] was that the appellant must have realised when throwing or hitting the baby against whatever object the baby's head struck that what he, the appellant, was doing was virtually certain to cause some serious injury to the baby because the jury would know, and the appellant must have known, how vulnerable babies are. Therefore the jury could safely conclude that when the appellant did this act he intended to do serious bodily harm to the child. It was done in temper by a person aware of the vulnerability of this baby.

The case for the appellant was mounted on two fronts. First, that the appellant had not intended that the baby should suffer serious physical harm and therefore had not had the intent required for this to be an offence of murder. Second, that if the jury concluded that the appellant had intended that the baby should suffer serious physical harm, and therefore had had the intent required for this to be a case of murder, nevertheless the proper verdict was one of manslaughter because the prosecution's evidence did not exclude the partial defence of provocation ...

[No criticism was made of the trial judge's direction to the jury as regards provocation. The basis of the appeal was that the judge had misdirected the jury] for the following reasons:

1 The direction incorrectly stated that the jury might infer intention if they were satisfied that when the defendant threw the child he appreciated that there was a substantial risk that he would cause serious harm to it.

2 The terms of the direction might therefore have served to confuse or mislead the jury as to the degree of foresight required ...

The submission that is relied upon [by the appellant] is that the judge should, in the passage:

> If, on the other hand, you reject that interpretation and are quite satisfied that he was aware of what he was doing and must have realised and appreciated when he threw that child that there was a substantial risk that he would cause serious injury to it, then it would be open to you to find that he intended to cause injury to the child and you should convict him of murder.

have said 'that there was a virtual certainty he would cause serious injury to the baby' and the [judge] should not have used the phrase 'substantial risk', which is a test of recklessness and not of intent. The [judge] in this passage has substituted the test of recklessness for that of intent, or if that is not strictly so he has blurred the distinction between recklessness and intent and there is a danger that the jury could have concluded that the appellant intended to cause the baby serious injury merely because the appellant ignored a substantial risk that what he intended to do, namely throw the baby, would cause the baby serious injury ...

... His Lordship referred to *R v Nedrick* (1986) 83 Cr App R 267 and went on:]

It is important, when considering the case of *Nedrick*, to keep in mind the direction which the trial judge gave the jury based on the case law prior to the House of Lords decision in *Moloney* [1985] AC 905 ...

The jury [in *Nedrick*] were being directed that if, at the moment of acting, the accused knew it was highly probable that the act would result in serious bodily injury, then that in law was the intent required for murder, and not that that was merely evidence from which the jury might infer that the accused had had the intent to cause really serious bodily harm. In *Nedrick*, the first time the court refers to 'virtually certain (barring some unforeseen intervention)', this court then went on to say that the fact that

> ... the defendant recognised that death or serious harm would be virtually certain ... to result from his voluntary act, then that is a fact from which the jury may find it easy to infer that [the defendant] intended to kill or do serious bodily harm, even though he may not have had any desire to achieve that result.

...[In *Nedrick*] this court [is saying] that the jury should be directed that they are not entitled to infer the necessary intent, in the rare case where the simple direction was not enough, unless the jury felt sure that death or really serious bodily harm was a virtual certainty as a result of the defendant's actions and that the defendant appreciated that such was the case ...

We accept that such a direction should be given in cases where the only evidence of the defendant's intention is the evidence of the actions of the defendant and their consequences to the victim. When that is the only evidence that the jury have, then we respectfully agree that the jury are not entitled to infer the necessary intent in the rare cases where the defendant may not have purposed the death or serious injury unless the jury are sure that death or serious bodily injury was virtually a certain result of the defendant's actions and the defendant must have appreciated that such was the case.

We do not accept that a jury is not entitled to infer the necessary intention, in those rare cases, where there is evidence in addition to the evidence of the defendant's actions and their effects on the victim; or that the direction to the jury has to be couched in terms of 'moral' or 'virtual certainty' or of an 'overwhelming probability'.

[His Lordship then quoted s 8 of the Criminal Justice Act 1967 and went on:]

Two points emerge from the wording of that section in our opinion. First, Parliament recognised that a court or jury could infer that a defendant intended a result of his actions by reason of its being a natural and probable result of those actions, but was not bound to do so. Second, in deciding whether the defendant intended the natural and probable consequences of his actions, the court or jury was to take into account all the evidence, drawing such inferences from the evidence as appeared proper. We respectfully suggest that the direction formulated in *Nedrick* prevents the jury from performing its task as Parliament intended if it is given in cases where there is admissible evidence from which inferences relevant to the defendant's intent can be drawn in addition to evidence of the defendant's actions and their consequences on the victim.

This court has, in *Walker and Hayles* (1990) 90 Cr App R 226, indicated that the use of a phrase other than 'virtually certain' does not amount to a misdirection, provided the dividing line between intention and recklessness is never blurred, and it is made clear that it is a question for the jury to infer from the degree of probability in the particular case whether the defendant had the intention needed to constitute the offence charged (see the judgment of the court delivered by Lloyd LJ, as he then was at 233). True it is that the court in that case recommended the use of the phrase 'virtual certainty'. At p 232 the court said:

> Counsel submitted that virtual certainty is the correct test in all cases where the simple direction is not enough, and that to substitute high degree of probability is to water down that test. We agree with counsel this far, that in the rare cases where an expanded direction is required, it is better that the judge should continue to use the term 'virtual certainty', which has the authority of this court in *Nedrick*. We also agree that there is no difference in

> this respect between the kind of case considered in *Nedrick*, where the question was whether serious harm was intended, even though it was not desired, and the present case, where serious harm was clearly desired and the only question is whether death was intended. In the rare cases where a foresight direction is required, the same language should be used.
>
> But we do not accept that the reference to 'very high degree of probability' was a misdirection. The truth is, as Messrs Smith and Hogan point out in *Criminal Law*, 6th edn, p 59, that once one departs from absolute certainty, there is bound to be a question of degree. We do not regard the difference of degree, if there is one, between very high degree of probability on the one hand and virtual certainty on the other as being sufficient to render what the recorder said a misdirection ... Whatever the direction, we suspect that in practice juries will continue to use their common sense.

We go on to consider the speech of Lord Scarman in *Hancock* [1986] AC 455. At 473F Lord Scarman said:

> In my judgment, therefore, the *Moloney* guidelines as they stand are unsafe and misleading. They require a reference to probability. They also require an explanation that the greater the probability of a consequence the more likely it is that the consequence was foreseen and that if that consequence was foreseen the greater the probability is that that consequence was also intended. But juries also require to be reminded that the decision is theirs to be reached upon a consideration of all the evidence.

Lord Scarman was not suggesting that the jury should be directed that they could only infer intention in respect of those consequences of the defendant's actions which were 'virtual certainties'.

A consequence may not be a virtual certainty, but the jury who have seen and heard the defendant may conclude that a substantial probability that the consequence would follow the defendant's actions is enough for them to conclude that the defendant they are trying foresaw and intended the consequence – for example, because of that defendant's intelligence and experience – whereas the same jury might not have drawn the same conclusion in the case of another defendant. An example would be severe injury caused to a small baby by violent shaking. The conclusion that the jury might draw about the defendant's intention could be different in a case where a defendant is simple minded and the case of a defendant who was a paediatrician. The physical probability of serious injury resulting from a shaking would be the same in both cases. The different inferences would flow from the other evidence referred to the jury.

At 474C Lord Scarman said:

> In a case where foresight of a consequence is part of the evidence supporting a prosecution submission that the accused intended the consequence, the judge, if he thinks some general observations would help the jury, could well, having in mind s 8 of the Criminal Justice Act 1967, emphasise that the probability, however high, of a consequence is only a factor, though it may in some cases be a very significant factor, to be considered with all the other evidence in determining whether the accused intended to bring it about. The distinction between the intention and the evidence relied on to prove it is vital.

This passage in Lord Scarman's speech and s 8 of the 1967 Act make it clear that the probability of serious physical harm to the victim, resulting from the admitted acts of the appellant, was no more than evidence which the jury were entitled to consider when deciding what was the appellant's intention in this case. The actions of a defendant, and the consequences of those actions to the victim, will rarely be the only evidence that the jury have to consider, and the jury must consider all the evidence when deciding whether the prosecution have proved the intent required for the offence charged.

Thus the degree of probability that the consequence to the victim (in this case serious harm to his three-month-old baby) would be caused by the admitted actions of the appellant – violently shaking the baby and then throwing him across the room – was one factor, and no doubt a very important one, to be considered by the jury with all the other evidence in determining whether the appellant had, at the material time, an intent to cause serious harm to the child.

In our judgment, although the use of the phrase 'a virtual certainty' may be desirable and may be necessary, it is only necessary where the evidence of intent is limited to the admitted actions of the accused and the consequences of those actions. It is not obligatory to use that phrase or one that means the same thing in cases such as the present where there is other evidence for the jury to consider. We are fortified in this view by the judgment of this Court in *Walker and Hayles* (*above*).

The questions for this court in this appeal are:

1 Whether this passage in the summing up could have led the jury to confuse foresight with intention; and

2 Whether this passage could have caused the jury to forget that one of the matters the prosecution had to prove was that at the time of throwing the baby the appellant intended to cause him serious physical harm?

[His Lordship quoted extensively from the trial judge's summing up and concluded:]

The conclusion that we have reached is that the answer to the second question which we posed is that the jury could not have forgotten that the first matter the prosecution had to prove, because it was disputed, was that at the time of throwing the baby the defendant intended to cause him serious harm. It is important that in the passage about which complaint is made, the [judge] was directing the jury that they had to be satisfied that the appellant had been aware of what he was doing when he threw the child and that he was not acting spontaneously and on impulse and without thought of what he was doing or the consequence of what he was doing. Further, the jury were being directed that when he threw the child they had to be satisfied that the appellant appreciated that there was a substantial risk that he would cause serious injury to him. The jury were therefore being directed to look at the appellant's state of mind, to consider the matter subjectively, and were not being directed to look at the question of risk objectively. The jury were not being directed that if there was a substantial risk of serious injury to the baby, by the way in which the baby had been thrown, they should from that conclude that the appellant intended to cause serious injury. The jury were being directed that it was only if they were sure that the appellant was aware that there was such a risk that it would be open to them to find that he intended to cause really serious injury to the child.

It is of the greatest importance, in our judgment, that the [judge] used the words 'then it would be open to you to find'. Here the [judge] was dealing with matters of evidence as the use of these words made abundantly clear. As this court observed in the case of *Walker and Hayles* (*above*) at 231:

> It may be that that could have been better expressed. Few summings up are perfect. But the message is clear enough. What the [judge] was saying was: 'If

> you are sure of (1) and (2), you would be entitled to draw the inference that they were intending or trying to kill the victim'. It is important to note that the recorder said that the jury would be *entitled* to draw the inference: he was not saying that they must draw the inference. By the use of the word 'entitled', he was making it sufficiently clear to the jury that the question whether they drew the inference or not was a question for them ...
>
> So we reject the submission that the recorder was equating foresight with intent, or that he may have given that impression to the jury.

We gratefully adopt those words ...

Having said that, we have given careful and earnest consideration to this case, a case in which there was no suggestion of any other ill-treatment of this baby, a case in which this appellant lost his temper and behaved in a moment of anger and frustration in a way which we have no doubt he now bitterly regrets. Having considered all the evidence, we have reached the conclusion that the jury came to what was the only proper verdict, and that had the [judge], in the passage about which complaint is made, used the phrase 'virtual certainty' instead of the phrase 'a substantial risk', the verdict would still have been the same. There is, in our judgment, no basis for saying that this verdict is unsafe and consequently this appeal will be dismissed.

DEFENCES UNIQUE TO MURDER

Two defences apply only to charges of murder. They are:

(1) diminished responsibility; and

(2) provocation.

Both these defences have the effect of reducing the defendant's guilt from murder to manslaughter. It must be remembered that for offences other than murder, provocation is a matter of mitigation (ie resulting in a lighter sentence), not a complete defence.

Diminished responsibility

This is a statutory defence, contained in s 2 of the Homicide Act 1957. Its effect is to reduce the crime from murder to manslaughter.

Section 2 of the Homicide Act 1957

(1) Where a person kills or is party to the killing of another, he shall not be convicted of murder if he was suffering from such abnormality of mind (whether arising from a condition of arrested or retarded development of mind or any inherent causes or induced by disease or injury) as substantially impaired his mental responsibility for his acts or omissions in doing or being a party to the killing.

(2) On a charge of murder, it shall be for the defence to prove that the person charged is by virtue of this section not liable to be convicted of murder.

(3) A person who but for this section would be liable, whether as principal or as accessory, to be convicted of murder shall be liable instead to be convicted of manslaughter.

(4) The fact that one party to a killing is by virtue of this section not liable to be convicted of murder shall not affect the question whether the killing amounted to murder in the case of any other party to it.

It should be noted that s 2(2) puts the burden of proof on the defence; this burden has to be satisfied according to the civil standard of proof (ie on the balance of probabilities), not the criminal standard (beyond reasonable doubt): see *R v Dunbar* [1958] 1 QB 1.

The two ingredients of the defence of diminished responsibility are:

(1) abnormality of mind; and

(2) substantial impairment of the defendant's mental responsibility.

These two ingredients were considered by the Court of Appeal in the case of *R v Byrne* [1960] 2 QB 396.

The word 'substantial' means more than trivial but less than total impairment of the defendant's mental responsibility: see *R v Lloyd* [1967] 1 QB 175.

Although the cause of the abnormality of mind has to be one of the causes set out in s 2(1), these causes have been interpreted liberally by the courts. For example, in *R v Reynolds* [1988] Crim LR 679 postnatal depression and premenstrual tension were accepted to be within s 2(1).

Voluntary intoxication is not regarded as a cause of abnormality falling within s 2(1). However, where the defendant is an alcoholic, the position is a little more complicated. Where the defendant is able to choose whether or not to take 'the first drink of the day', that day's drinking is not to be regarded as involuntary. However, where the defendant has no control over whether to take that first drink, the intoxication should be regarded as involuntary. Where the alcoholism has reached a level where damage to the brain has occurred, impairing the defendant's judgment, this is to be regarded as a cause of abnormality to which s 2(1) applies: see *R v Tandy* [1989] 1 WLR 350.

Where the defendant is suffering from voluntary intoxication and from abnormality of mind resulting from a cause to which s 2(1) applies, the jury should be directed to disregard the effect of the alcohol and consider whether the cause to which s 2(1) applies was, on its own, sufficient to impair the defendant's mental responsibility: see *R v Gittens* [1984] QB 698; *R v Egan* [1992] 4 All ER 470.

R v Byrne [1960] 2 QB 396 (CA)

Lord Parker CJ: The appellant was convicted of murder ... The victim was a young woman whom he strangled in the YWCA hostel, and after her death he committed horrifying mutilations upon her dead body. The facts as to the killing were not disputed, and were admitted in a long statement made by the accused. The only defence was that in killing his victim the accused was suffering from diminished responsibility as defined by s 2 of the Homicide Act 1957, and was accordingly, guilty not of murder but of manslaughter.

Three medical witnesses were called by the defence, the senior medical officer at Birmingham Prison and two specialists in psychological medicine. Their uncontradicted evidence was that the accused was a sexual psychopath, that he suffered from abnormality of mind, as indeed was abundantly clear from the other evidence in the case, and that such abnormality of mind arose from a condition of arrested or retarded development of mind or inherent causes. The nature of the abnormality of mind of a sexual psychopath, according to the medical evidence, is that he suffers from violent perverted sexual desires which he finds it difficult or impossible to control. Save when under the influence of his perverted sexual desires he may be normal. All three doctors were of opinion that the killing was done under the influence of his perverted sexual desires, and although all three were of opinion that he was not insane in the technical sense of insanity laid down in the M'Naghten Rules it was their view that his sexual psychopathy could properly be described as partial insanity ...

Section 2 of the Homicide Act 1957, is dealing with the crime of murder in which there are at common law two essential elements:

(1) the physical act of killing another person; and

(2) the state of mind of the person who kills or is a party to the killing, namely his intention to kill or to cause grievous bodily harm. Subsection (1) of s 2 does not deal with the first element. It modified the existing law [when the only defences to murder were insanity and provocation] as respects the second element, that is, the state of mind of the person who kills or is a party to the killing ...

...To satisfy the requirements of s 2(1) of the Homicide Act 1957 the accused must show:

(a) that he was suffering from an abnormality of mind; and

(b) that such abnormality of mind

  (1) arose from a condition of arrested or retarded development of mind or any inherent causes, or was induced by disease or injury; and

  (2) was such as substantially impaired his mental responsibility for his acts in doing or being a party to the killing.

'Abnormality of mind', which has to be contrasted with the time-honoured expression in the M'Naghten Rules 'defect of reason', means a state of mind so different from that of ordinary human beings that the reasonable man would term it abnormal. It appears to us to be wide enough to cover the mind's activities in all its aspects, not only the perception of physical acts and matters, and the ability to form a rational judgment as to whether an act is right or wrong, but also the ability to exercise will power to control physical acts in accordance with that rational judgment. The expression 'mental responsibility for his acts' points to a consideration of the extent to which the accused's mind is answerable for his physical acts which must include a consideration of the extent of his ability to exercise will power to control his physical acts.

Whether the accused was at the time of the killing suffering from any 'abnormality of mind' in the broad sense which we have indicated above is a question for the jury. On this question medical evidence is no doubt of importance, but the jury are entitled to take into consideration all the evidence, including the acts or statements of the accused and his demeanour. They are not bound to accept the medical evidence if there is other material before them which, in their good judgment, conflicts with it and outweighs it.

The aetiology of the abnormality of mind (namely whether it arose from a condition of arrested or retarded development of mind or any inherent causes, or was induced by disease or injury) does, however, seem to be a matter to be determined on expert evidence.

Assuming that the jury are satisfied on the balance of probabilities that the accused was suffering from 'abnormality of mind' from one of the causes specified in parentheses in the subsection, the crucial question nevertheless arises: was the abnormality such as substantially impaired his mental responsibility for his acts in doing or being a party to the killing? This is a question of degree and essentially one for the jury. Medical evidence is, of course, relevant, but the question involves a decision not merely as to whether there was some impairment of the mental responsibility of the accused for his acts but whether such impairment can properly be called 'substantial', a matter upon which juries may quite legitimately differ from doctors.

Furthermore, in a case where the abnormality of mind is one which affects the accused's self-control the step between 'he did not resist his impulse' and 'he could not resist his impulse' is, as the evidence in this case shows, one which is incapable of scientific proof. A *fortiori* there is no scientific measurement of the degree of difficulty which an abnormal person finds in controlling his impulses. These problems which in the present state of medical knowledge are scientifically insoluble, the jury can only approach in a broad, common sense way. This court has repeatedly approved directions to the jury which have followed directions given in Scots cases where the doctrine of diminished responsibility forms part of the common law. We need not repeat them. They are quoted in *R v Spriggs* [1958] 1 QB 270. They indicate that such abnormality as 'substantially impairs his mental responsibility' involves a mental state which in popular language (not that of the M'Naghten Rules) a jury would regard as amounting to partial insanity or being on the borderline of insanity ...

... Inability to exercise will power to control physical acts, provided that it is due to abnormality of mind from one of the causes specified in parentheses in the subsection is, in our view, sufficient to entitle the accused to the benefit of the section; difficulty in controlling his physical acts depending on the degree of difficulty, may be. It is for the jury to decide on the whole of the evidence whether such inability or difficulty has, not as a matter of scientific certainty but on the balance of probabilities, been established, and in the case of difficulty whether the difficulty is so great as to amount in their view to a substantial impairment of the accused's mental responsibility for his acts. The direction in the present case thus withdrew from the jury the essential determination of fact which it was their province to decide ...

R v Lloyd [1967] 1 QB 175 (CA)

Edmund Davies J: ... The evidence in relation to this issue of diminished responsibility can be summarised, I hope, adequately but briefly; a squadron leader who was an RAF medical officer said that in November 1955, the appellant, who was then an airman, was in hospital for a fortnight, having had three fainting attacks. The possibility was then canvassed of there being some mental explanation for these attacks, but such connection was not established. In 1962, he made two unsuccessful attempts at suicide by coal-gas poisoning. The evidence in relation to his present state was given by two doctors called by the defence. Dr Angus, who was the prison medical officer at Birmingham, said that this appellant was abnormal, his abnormality being due to mental illness, namely reactive recurrent depressions, that his mental responsibility was at the material time impaired by that abnormality to some extent, but that he could not go so far as to say that it was diminished to any substantial degree. Then Dr Conlan, a consultant in psychiatry in Birmingham, said that the appellant was suffering from an abnormality of mind, namely depressive illness, and that such illness affected his mental responsibility to a degree; he could not say to what degree; it was not as low as minimal, but on the other hand it was not substantial ...

[His Lordship went on to approve the direction given to the jury by Ashworth J, the trial judge:]

Fourth, this word 'substantial', members of the jury. I am not going to try to find a parallel for the word 'substantial'. You are the judges, but your own common sense will tell you what it means. This far I will go. Substantial does not mean total, that is to say, the mental responsibility need not be totally impaired, so to speak, destroyed altogether. At the other end of the scale substantial does not mean trivial or minimal. It is something in between and Parliament has left it to you and other juries to say on the evidence, was the mental responsibility impaired, and, if so, was it substantially impaired?

R v Reynolds [1988] Crim LR 679 (CA)

The appellant was convicted of murder. On her appeal against conviction, evidence was adduced that at the time of the offence she was suffering from premenstrual syndrome and postnatal depression of sufficient severity to lead to temporary loss of control and this abnormality of mind was such that substantially impaired her mental responsibility for the killing. Counsel for the Crown indicated that in the event of a retrial he would accept a plea of guilty to manslaughter on the basis of diminished responsibility. The Court of Appeal accordingly allowed the appeal and substituted a conviction for manslaughter.

R v Tandy [1989] 1 WLR 350 (CA)

The appellant was an alcoholic. She normally drank Cinzano. On one occasion, however, she consumed 90% of a bottle of vodka (which contains more alcohol than Cinzano). Later that day, she strangled her 11-year-old daughter.

Watkins LJ: ... So in this case it was for the appellant to show:

(1) that she was suffering from an abnormality of mind at the time of the act of strangulation;

(2) that that abnormality of mind was induced by disease, namely the disease of alcoholism; and

(3) that the abnormality of mind induced by the disease of alcoholism was such as substantially impaired her mental responsibility for her act of strangling her daughter.

The principles involved in seeking answers to these questions are, in our view, as follows. The appellant would not establish the second element of the defence unless the evidence showed that the abnormality of mind at the time of the killing was due to the fact that she was a chronic alcoholic. If the alcoholism had reached the level at which her brain had been injured by the repeated insult from intoxicants so that there was gross impairment of her judgment and emotional responses, then the defence of diminished responsibility was available to her, provided that she satisfied the jury that the third element of the defence existed. Further, if the appellant were able to establish that the alcoholism had reached the level where although the brain had not been damaged to the extent just stated, the appellant's drinking had become involuntary, that is to say she was no longer able to resist the impulse to drink then the defence of diminished responsibility would be available to her, subject to her establishing the first and third elements, because if her drinking was involuntary, then her abnormality of mind at the time of the act of strangulation was induced by her condition of alcoholism.

On the other hand, if the appellant had simply not resisted an impulse to drink and it was the drink taken on the [day of the killing] which brought about the impairment of judgment and emotional response, then the defence of diminished responsibility was not available to the appellant.

... The appellant had chosen to drink vodka on the Wednesday rather than her customary drink of Cinzano. Her evidence was that she might not have had a drink at all on the Tuesday. She certainly did not tell the jury that she must have taken drink on the Tuesday or Wednesday because she could not help herself. She had been able to stop drinking at 6.30 pm on the Wednesday evening although her supply of vodka was not exhausted. Thus her own evidence indicated that she was able to exercise some control even after she had taken the first drink, contrary to the view of the doctors. There was the evidence of Dr Lawson that the appellant would have had the ability on that Wednesday to abstain from taking the first drink of the day ...

The three matters on which the appellant relies in the perfected grounds of appeal for saying that there was a misdirection can be dealt with shortly. As to the first, in our judgment the judge was correct in telling the jury that if the taking of the first drink was not involuntary, then the whole of the drinking on the Wednesday was not involuntary. Further, as we have pointed out, the appellant's own evidence indicated that she still had control over her drinking on that Wednesday after she had taken the first drink.

As to the second, the jury were told correctly that the abnormality of mind with which they were concerned was the abnormality of mind at the time of the act of strangulation and as a matter of fact by that time on that Wednesday the appellant had drunk 90% of the bottle of vodka.

On the third point, we conclude that for a craving for drinks or drugs in itself to produce an abnormality of mind within the meaning of s 2(1) of the Act of 1957, the craving must be such as to render the accused's use of drink or drugs involuntary ...

R v Gittens [1984] 1 QB 698 (CA)

The essential issue in this case was whether the abnormality of mind from which the appellant suffered when he killed his wife and stepdaughter was caused by the alcohol and drugs which he taken prior to the killing or whether it was due to inherent causes coupled with the drink and drugs.

Lord Lane CJ: ... Where alcohol or drugs are factors to be considered by the jury, the best approach is that adopted by the judge and approved by this court in *R v Fenton* (1975) 61 Cr App R 261. The jury should be directed to disregard what, in their view, the effect of the alcohol or drugs upon the defendant was, since abnormality of mind induced by alcohol or drugs is not (generally speaking) due to inherent causes and is not therefore within the section. Then the jury should consider whether the combined effect of the other matters which do fall within the section amounted to such abnormality of mind as substantially impaired the defendant's mental responsibility within the meaning of 'substantial' set out in *R v Lloyd* [1967] 1 QB 175.

R v Egan [1992] 4 All ER 470 (CA)

The appellant, whose mentality was said to approach the border of the subnormal, entered the home of an elderly widow after a night of heavy drinking; he attacked and killed her.

Watkins LJ: ... [His Lordship quoted from s 2(1) and s 2(3) of the Homicide Act 1957 and went on:] As is very clear from those provisions the defence [of diminished responsibility] has two elements, namely:

(1) abnormality of mind arising from:
   (a) arrested development; or
   (b) inherent causes; or

(c) disease or injury; and

(2) resulting substantial impairment of mental responsibility.

[His Lordship went on to quote from the judgment of Lord Lane CJ in *R v Atkinson* [1985] Crim LR 314, in which the Lord Chief Justice cited with approval the commentary written by Professor J C Smith in [1984] Crim LR 553 at 554 on *R v Gittens* [1984] QB 698:]

This accords with the opinion in *Fenton* ((1975) 61 Cr App R 261) and the present case that the effect of intoxication is to be disregarded. So the two questions for the jury, in logical sequence, would seem to be: Have the defence satisfied you on the balance of probabilities, that if the defendant had not taken drink: (1) he would have killed as he in fact did? and (2) he would have under diminished responsibility when he did so? We would like respectfully and gratefully to adopt that analysis by Professor Smith, which seems to us to put the matter very clearly and in a way which can be understood by all.

[His Lordship then went on to approve the direction given to the jury in the present case by French J:]

The second point is this, you must disregard the effects produced by alcohol, you look solely at the evidence which bears upon the abnormality of mind. If you conclude that his responsibility was substantially reduced, drink or no drink, then the defence is made out. But if you conclude that the abnormality of mind would not on the balance of probabilities have diminished his responsibility substantially without the drink then the defence is not made out ...

R v Campbell [1997] 1 Cr App R 199 (CA)

Lord Bingham CJ: ...

Diminished responsibility

The correct approach to a defence of diminished responsibility was helpfully stated by this Court when the present case was last before it (at (1987) 84 Cr App R 255):

> So diminished responsibility is something which the defence has to prove on a balance of probabilities. Where, as here, the killing is admitted, what the defence has to prove is that the accused was suffering from such abnormality of mind of the relevant type as substantially impaired his mental responsibility for his acts and omissions in doing the killing. So it is necessary first to identify those acts and omissions, then to consider what evidence there is to suggest that:
>
> (a) the accused was suffering from an abnormality of mind (arising in the way envisaged by the statute), and
>
> (b) the abnormality was such as substantially to impair his mental responsibility for his acts or omissions in doing the killing.

The Court identified the relevant acts and omissions of the appellant in a passage which it is convenient to repeat:

> *'How did the girl come to die?'*
>
> On December 22, 1984, she was hitch-hiking in London seeking a lift to Oxford. The appellant, who had been playing hockey, stopped and picked her up. According to his account to the police he drove his car for a little way, then stopped it in Osterley Lane, and made advances towards her. She struck him across the eye with her hand. He then punched her. He thought that the punch must have hit her in the throat, because she began gurgling and blood poured from her mouth.

The appellant later told the police that she then passed out and collapsed straight forwards. He put the sear belt onto her. He did not throw her out of the car because he had already told her his name and he thought she might report him. Then he drove off. Asked where he went, he said, 'I don't remember, she came to as I was driving around. She was gurgling and blood was coming out of her mouth. I was frightened. I wasn't thinking clearly. I tried to strangle her.'

A little later he said, 'I don't know how many times I kept doing that'. The police officer asked, 'Doing what?', to which the appellant replied, 'Trying to strangle her. It seems like an eternity, there was blood everywhere'.

He was asked to explain how he had strangled her, and he said, 'She struggled a couple of times, I hit her and she passed out and I strangled her with my hands. Everything that happened got worse. It was something that I did not intend'. He was asked, 'At what stage did you know you had killed her?' and he replied, 'When I left her. She was still making a noise. I pushed her in the back and threw some things on top of her. She was too badly hurt to help. I hit her with the hockey stick across the throat. I think I knew she was dead then. I just wanted to get rid of her'.

The officer said, 'For some reason you went berserk and attacked her?'. The appellant replied, 'The first time I hit her I didn't mean to, it was spontaneous; but after that, yes, I went berserk with panic'. A little later on the police officer said to the appellant, 'So basically you strangled her to cover up for the injury you had caused by hitting her in the throat?' The appellant replied, 'Yes'. The officer asked, 'Can you offer any explanation as to why you killed that girl?' and the appellant replied, 'Panic, blind panic' ...

Although the main events in this narrative are not the subject of dispute, the parties interpret them in a very different way. The Crown pointed out that the events took place over a considerable period, and that the appellant was himself able to give a reasonably clear and coherent account of what had happened and where. The Crown suggested that the appellant, having struck his first and highly injurious blow on the deceased, had resorted to ever more desperate steps to cover up his crime and avoid detection, steps which (however criminal) were entirely rational. For the appellant, emphasis was laid on a number of statements made by him, particularly in his initial interviews, which suggested that his memory of certain events was imperfect and that he had at the relevant time been quite unable to control his conduct or measure his responses in anything approaching a rational way. This Court cannot choose between those two competing interpretations.

At the time of the trial and of the first appeal there was clear evidence that the appellant had at the relevant time suffered from an abnormality of mind in the form of epilepsy. The psychiatrist called by the defence had, however, been unable to suggest that this abnormality had been such as substantially to impair the appellant's mental responsibility for his acts and omissions in doing the killing. The nature and extent of this abnormality was accordingly not explored in any depth. As a result of the investigations made on behalf of the appellant since dismissal of his appeal, we were asked to receive the written and oral evidence of two eminent psychiatrists with special expertise in the field of epilepsy, Dr Fenwick and Professor Fenton ...

The evidence given by Dr Fenwick, with which Professor Fenton was in broad agreement, was to the following effect: the appellant suffers (and has at all material times suffered) from epilepsy and frontal lobe damage. This is demonstrated by tests conducted in June 1985 before the trial and repeated this summer. The effect of this frontal lobe epilepsy is to affect the functions of judgment, control of the emotions, control of impulses, and forward planning. The appellant has over the years suffered from generalised seizures and partial complex seizures, but infrequently. More important is the fact that the appellant has suffered from absence seizures, lasting for anything from a few seconds to about half a minute, almost continuously. These seizures can be shown to occur most frequently, and to last longest, when the appellant is for any reason excited or aroused and so inclined to over-breathe. Such seizures lead to a change in the intellect and a reduction of the patient's ability to appreciate the circumstances surrounding him and to process information. While there will be gaps between these seizures, the patient will have a very imperfect understanding of what is happening around him while he is subject to one of them. The effect of the electrical discharges of the brain which occur during such seizures is to interrupt conscious thought processes and affect emotional control in a profound way. The events which preceded and accompanied this killing were, in the doctor's judgment, just such as would lead to a state of excitement and arousal, over-breathing and high levels of electrical discharge. Having studied the available evidence of what the appellant did and said at the time, both doctors were of the clear opinion that at the time of the killing the appellant had been suffering an abnormality of mind of such significance as seriously to diminish his responsibility for the act he carried out.

Having received this new evidence and considered all the material drawn to our attention and all the arguments addressed to us on both sides, we are of opinion that a defence of diminished responsibility, if based on the evidence now available, might well succeed, and might well have succeeded at the trial if then advanced along the present lines. It follows that in our judgment this conviction is unsafe and we must allow the appeal.

...We accordingly order that the appellant be retried on an indictment charging him with murder... [T]he appellant cannot achieve a verdict which will lead to his acquittal. He can at best secure a verdict of not guilty of murder but guilty of manslaughter on the ground of diminished responsibility...

Provocation

Provocation has long been recognised as a common law defence to a charge of murder. The classic definition of provocation is to be found in *R v Duffy* [1949] 1 All ER 932. However, this common law definition has to be seen in the light of the alterations made by s 3 of the Homicide Act 1957.

The essence of provocation is twofold:

(1) The defendant lost his or her self-control; and

(2) The reasonable person would have done what the defendant did.

Unlike diminished responsibility, where the burden of proof rests on the defence, in the case of provocation it is for the prosecution to prove (beyond reasonable doubt) that the accused was *not* provoked. However, the defence do bear an evidential burden in the sense that the prosecution only have the burden of disproving provocation if there is some evidence which is capable of supporting a finding that the accused was provoked: see *R v Cascoe* [1970] 2 All ER 833.

R v Duffy [1949] 1 All ER 932 (Note) (CA)

Lord Goddard CJ: [His Lordship quoted with approval the direction given to the jury by Devlin J:]

> Provocation is some act, or series of acts, done by the dead man to the accused which would cause in any reasonable person, and actually causes in the accused, a sudden and temporary loss of self-control, rendering the accused so subject to passion as to make him or her for the moment not master of his mind ...

Section 3 of the Homicide Act 1957

> Where on a charge of murder there is evidence on which a jury can find that the person charged was provoked (whether by things done or by things said or by both together) to lose his self-control, the question whether the provocation was enough to make a reasonable man do as he did shall be left to be determined by the jury; and in determining that question the jury shall take into account everything both done and said according to the effect which, in their opinion, it would have on a reasonable man.

The effect of s 3 of the Homicide Act 1957

One of the effects of the 1957 Act is to extend provocation so that it includes not only deeds but also words. It follows that words alone can now constitute provocation. For the purposes of s 3, the reasonable man should be regarded as sharing such of the accused's characteristics as the jury thinks would affect the gravity of the provocation as far as the accused is concerned: see *DPP v Camplin* [1978] AC 705. In *Luc Thiet Thuan v R* [1997] AC 131 the Privy Council tried to introduce a more objective test by occluding evidence of mental infirmity. In *R v Campbell* [1997] 1 Cr App R 199, however, the Court of Appeal declined to follow this approach.

An act may amount to provocation even though it is directed at someone other than the accused, as in *R v Pearson* [1992] Crim LR 193.

Furthermore, it has also been held that the provocation can come from someone other than the deceased. In *R v Davies* [1975] QB 691, for example, the provocation emanated from the victim's lover.

In *R v Ahluwalia* [1992] 4 All ER 894, Lord Taylor CJ pointed out that Devlin J's formulation needed re-wording in the light of s 3 of the Homicide Act 1957. His Lordship added the phrase 'or words spoken' and deleted the phrase 'done by the dead man to the accused', in order to reflect the changes made by the Homicide Act 1957. According to this reformulation, Devlin J's direction would now read as follows:

> Provocation is some act, or series of acts, done [or words spoken] ... which would cause in any reasonable person, and actually causes in the accused, a sudden and temporary loss of self-control, rendering the accused so subject to passion as to make him or her for the moment not master of his [or her] mind.

R v Camplin [1978] AC 705 (HL)

Lord Diplock: ... The respondent, Camplin, who was 15 years of age, killed a middle-aged Pakistani, Mohammed Lal Khan, by splitting his skull with a chapati pan, a heavy kitchen utensil like a rimless frying pan. At the time, the two of them were alone together in Khan's flat. At Camplin's trial for murder before Boreham J his only defence was that of provocation so as to reduce the offence to manslaughter. According to the story that he told in the witness box but which differed materially from that which he had told to the police, Khan had buggered him in spite of his resistance and had then laughed at him. Whereupon Camplin had lost his self-control and attacked Khan fatally with the chapati pan ...

The point of law of general public importance involved in the case has been certified as being:

> Whether on the prosecution for murder of a boy of 15, where the issue of provocation arises, the jury should be directed to consider the question under s 3 of the Homicide Act 1957 whether the provocation was enough to make a reasonable man do as he did by reference to a 'reasonable adult' or by reference to a 'reasonable boy of 15'.

My Lords, the doctrine of provocation in crimes of homicide has always represented an anomaly in English law. In crimes of violence which result in injury short of death, the fact that the act of violence was committed under provocation which had caused the accused to lose his self-control does not affect the nature of the offence of which he is guilty. It is merely a matter to be taken into consideration in determining the penalty which it is appropriate to impose. Whereas in homicide provocation effects a change in the offence itself from murder for which the penalty is fixed by law (formerly death and now imprisonment for life) to the lesser offence of manslaughter for which the penalty is in the discretion of the judge ...

... [F]or the purposes of the law of provocation the 'reasonable man' has never been confined to the adult male. It means an ordinary person of either sex, not exceptionally excitable or pugnacious, but possessed of such powers of self-control as everyone is entitled to expect that his fellow citizens will exercise in society as it is today ... [N]ow that the law has been changed so as to permit of words being treated as provocation even though unaccompanied by any other acts, the gravity of verbal provocation may well depend upon the particular characteristics or circumstances of the person to whom a taunt or insult is addressed. To taunt a person because of his race, his physical infirmities or some shameful incident in his past may well be considered by the jury to be more offensive to the person addressed, however equable his temperament, if the facts on which the taunt is founded are true than it would be if they were not ...

In my opinion a proper direction to a jury on the question left to their exclusive determination by s 3 of the Act of 1957 would be on the following lines. The judge should state what the question is using the very terms of the section. He should then explain to them that the reasonable man referred to in the question is a person having the power of self-control to be expected of an ordinary person of the sex and age of the accused, but in other respects sharing such of the accused's characteristics as they think would affect the gravity of the provocation to him; and that the question is not merely whether such a person would in like circumstances be provoked to lose his self-control but also whether he would react to the provocation as the accused did ...

Lord Morris of Borth-y-Gest: ... It will first be for the court to decide whether, on a charge of murder, there is evidence on which a jury can find that the person charged was provoked to lose his self-control; thereafter, as it seems to me, all questions are for the jury. It will be for the jury to say whether they think that whatever was or may have been the provocation, such provocation was in their view enough to make a reasonable man do as the accused did: the jury must take into account everything both done and said according to the effect which they think there would have been on a reasonable man. Who then or what then is the 'reasonable man' who is referred to in the section? It seems to me that the courts are no longer entitled to tell juries that a reasonable man has certain stated and defined features. It is for the jury to consider all that the accused did: it is for them to say whether the provocation was enough to make a 'reasonable man' do as the accused did. The jury must take into account 'everything both done and said'. What do they think would have been the effect on a reasonable man? They must bring their 'collective good sense' to bear. As Lord Goddard CJ said in *R v McCarthy* [1954] 2 QB 105 at 112:

> No court has ever given, nor do we think ever can give, a definition of what constitutes a reasonable or an average man. That must be left to the collective good sense of the jury, and what no doubt would govern their opinion would be the nature of the retaliation used by the provoked person.

... If an impotent man were taunted about his impotence the jury would not today be told that an impotent man could not be a reasonable man as contemplated by the law. The jury would be entitled to decide that the accused man acted as 'a reasonable man' in being provoked as he was and in doing as he did.

It seems to me that as a result of the changes effected by s 3 a jury is fully entitled to consider whether an accused person, placed as he was, only acted as even a reasonable man might have acted if he had been in the accused's situation. There may be no practical difference between, on the one hand, taking a notional independent reasonable man but a man having the attributes of the accused and subject to all the events which surrounded the accused and then considering whether what the accused did was only what such a person would or might have done, and, on the other hand, taking the accused himself with all his attributes and subject to all the events and then asking whether there was provocation to such a degree as would or might make a reasonable man do what he (the accused) in fact did.

In my view it would now be unreal to tell a jury that the notional 'reasonable man' is someone without the characteristics of the accused: it would be to intrude into their province. A few examples may be given. If the accused is of particular colour or particular ethnic origin and things are said which to him are grossly insulting it would be utterly unreal if the jury had to consider whether the words would have provoked a man of different colour or ethnic origin, or to consider how such a man would have acted or reacted. The question would be whether the accused if he was provoked only reacted as even any reasonable man in his situation would or might have reacted. If the accused was ordinarily and usually a very unreasonable person, the view that on a particular occasion he acted just as a reasonable person would or might have acted would not be impossible of acceptance.

It is not disputed that the 'reasonable man' in s 3 could denote a reasonable person and so a reasonable woman. If words of grievous insult were addressed to a woman, words perhaps reflecting on her chastity or way of life, a consideration of the way in which she reacted would have to take account of how other women being reasonable women would or might in like circumstances have reacted. Would or might she, if she had been a reasonable woman, have done what she did?

In the instant case the considerations to which I have been referring have application to a question of age. The accused was a young man ... The jury had to consider whether a young man of about the same age as the accused but placed in the same situation as that which befell the accused could, had he been a reasonable young man, have reacted as did the accused and could have done what the accused did. For the reasons which I have outlined the question so to be considered by the jury would be whether they considered that the accused, placed as he was, and having regard to all the things that they found were said, and all the things that they found were done, only acted as a reasonable young man might have acted, so that, in compassion, and having regard to human frailty, he could to some extent be excused even though he had caused a death ...

Lord Simon of Glaisdale: ... In my judgment the reference to 'a reasonable man' at the end of [s 3 of the Homicide Act 1957] means 'a man of ordinary self-control'. If this is so the meaning satisfies what I have ventured to suggest as the reason for importing into this branch of the law the concept of the reasonable man – namely to avoid the injustice of a man being entitled to rely on his exceptional excitability or pugnacity or ill-temper or on his drunkenness ...

I think that the standard of self-control which the law requires before provocation is held to reduce murder to manslaughter is still that of the reasonable person (hence his invocation in s 3); but that, in determining whether a person of reasonable self-control would lose it in the circumstances, the entire factual situation, which includes the characteristics of the accused, must be considered ...

R v Dryden [1995] 4 ALL ER 987 (CA)

Lord Taylor of Gosforth CJ: ... The case attracted national notoriety since the offences were committed and recorded in a dramatic scene before the press and two film crews. On 29 June 1991, following a planning dispute, local authority employees went to the appellant's land in County Durham to demolish some buildings which he had erected. He shot and killed the principal planning officer of the local authority. He then attempted to kill the solicitor who had acted at various stages for the local authority, and in trying to do that he shot and wounded a BBC newsman and a police officer, wounding them with intent. There was, and could be, no dispute that the appellant had committed those acts since his actions were captured on film. However, there was disagreement between the Crown and the defence as to the appellant's responsibility for his acts. There were a number of doctors called to support, and in one instance reject, a defence of diminished responsibility. The jury were also invited to consider the defence of provocation ...

... [Counsel for the appellant] submits that, by using [the words 'You may think that a reasonable man is not exceptionally excitable or exceptionally eccentric – or indeed eccentric at all – or obsessed'] the judge not only failed to put forward eccentricity and obsession as characteristics which the jury ought to take into account; she excluded them from their consideration. He submits that they were characteristics which the judge ought to have referred specifically to the jury ...

... [Counsel for the appellant says] here one has somebody who was clearly marked off from the rest of the community; he was a man who was obsessive about particular things, and especially about the dispute over his land, which was central to his whole way of life, and he was, as one of the doctors indicated, vulnerable in regard to that matter. [Counsel] therefore submits that this was a characteristic which was permanent. It was something which marked off this appellant and distinguished him from the ordinary man of the community, and it was a factor which was specifically relevant to what happened in this case. It was in regard to his obsession with his property and this dispute that the conduct of bringing the excavator to the scene was 'the last straw' in the build-up of stress upon the appellant.

We have come to the conclusion that this was a characteristic – the obsessiveness on the part of the appellant and his eccentric character – which ought to have been left to the jury for their consideration. We consider that they were features of his character or personality which fell into the category of mental characteristics and which ought to have been specifically left to the jury ...

Luc Thiet Thuan v R [1997] AC 131 (PC)

Lord Goff of Chieveley: ... It has, of course, been pointed out many times that the 1957 Act does not codify the common law, but amends it. Even so, it is clear that the statute has not only retained the objective test, but has recognised the test to be whether the provocation was enough to make a reasonable man do as the defendant did, and that 'in determining that question the jury shall take into account everything both done and said according to the effect which, in [the jury's] opinion, it would have on a reasonable man'. It is not therefore open to the courts either to discard the objective test, or to interpret it in a manner inconsistent with the statute ...

Their Lordships have taken the exceptional course of quoting a substantial part of Lord Diplock's judgment to emphasise that, on the basis that a 'reasonable man' in the section means a 'person having the power of self-control to be expected of an ordinary person', everything that Lord Diplock said was entirely consistent with the words of the section. In particular, to take into account the gravity of taunts or insults when applied to the person to whom they are addressed is consistent with the hypothetical person having such power of self-control, as is the fact that the sex and age of the defendant may be taken into account, so that the hypothetical person is treated as having the power of self-control to be expected, where appropriate, of an ordinary man or woman or an ordinary young person ... But it is an entirely different question whether the mental infirmity of the defendant which impairs his power of self-control should be taken into account; and indeed it is difficult to see how it can be consistent with a person having the power of self-control of an ordinary person.

It is of some interest to refer at this stage to Professor A J Ashworth's article 'The Doctrine of Provocation' [1976] CLJ 292, to which their Lordships wish to express their indebtedness. In this article Professor Ashworth observed of the common law that 'the law's paramount concern is to ascertain whether the accused showed a reasonable amount of self-restraint' (see [1976] CLJ 292 at 299). He went on to observe that provocation can rarely be described as 'grave' *per se*; in general, this can only be so in relation to persons of a particular class. From this he concluded (at 300):

> the proper distinction ... is that individual peculiarities which bear on the gravity of the provocation should be taken into account, whereas individual peculiarities bearing on the accused's level of self-control should not.

... Professor Ashworth's article was published in 1976, and *Camplin* was decided by the House of Lords only two years later. The similarity between the approach recommended by Professor Ashworth, and that adopted by the House of Lords in *Camplin*, is so great that it is difficult to believe that his article did not, at least indirectly, influence the reasoning and the conclusion in that case.

Their Lordships wish to add that the recent decision of the House of Lords in *R v Morhall* [1996] 1 AC 90 is in no way inconsistent with the reasoning in *Camplin* ... [T]he House invoked Lord Diplock's statement that the 'reasonable man' in the section should be understood to be a person with the *ordinary* person's power of self-control, but in other respects sharing such of the defendant's characteristics as the jury might think would affect the gravity of the provocation to him.

... [T]heir Lordships return to the interpretation placed on the English statute in *Camplin* for guidance in answering the question posed for their consideration in the present case. Their conclusion is that, on the principles there stated, there is no basis upon which mental infirmity on the part of the defendant which has the effect of reducing his powers of self-control below that to be expected of an ordinary person can, as such be attributed to the ordinary person for the purposes of the objective test in provocation.

First of all, for mental infirmity of the defendant so to be taken into account would be inconsistent with the statute as interpreted in *Camplin*, in which it was held that the reasonable man referred to in the statute means a person having the power of self-control to be expected of an ordinary person. But their Lordships wish to state that, in holding, they are not simply treating the matter as one of literal application of the principle stated in *Camplin*. That principle is, in their respectful opinion, well-founded in law. It is widely accepted that s 3 of the 1957 Act is not a codifying Act, but an amending Act which expressly recognised and retained the objective test as established in the common law, subject to the amendments provided for in the section. Having regard to the principles of common law then applicable, the intention must, as Professor Ashworth has convincingly demonstrated in his article ([1976] CLJ 292 at 299–300), have been that individual peculiarities of the defendant affecting his power of self-control should not, as such, be taken into account for the purposes of the objective test ...

It is, of course, consistent with Lord Diplock's analysis in *Camplin*, and indeed with the decision of the House of Lords in *Morhall*, that mental infirmity of the defendant, if itself the subject of taunts by the deceased, may be taken into account as going to the gravity of the provocation as applied to the defendant ...

Their Lordships wish to add, as a footnote, that it may be open to a defendant to establish provocation in circumstances in which the act of the deceased, though relatively unprovocative if taken in isolation, was the last of a series of acts which finally provoked the loss of self-control by the defendant and so precipitated his extreme reaction which led to the death of the deceased ...

Lord Steyn (dissenting): I regret I am unable to agree that, on the central point in this case, the law of provocation of England ... is as stated in the judgment of the majority ...

The nature of the difference of opinion can be illustrated by a few simple examples. Let me imagine the case where a woman shortly after giving birth to a child stabs and kills her husband during an argument. She wishes to put to the jury as part of her defence of provocation that she was suffering from postnatal depression, which rendered her more prone to loss of self-control. a second example is the case where there is evidence that a woman, as a result of ill-treatment by her husband, suffers from 'battered woman syndrome'. When taunted by her lover she stabs and kills him. She wants to rely on evidence of battered woman syndrome as part of her defence of provocation. The third example is a woman who suffers from a personality disorder which makes her more prone to loss of self-control. During a quarrel she stabs and kills her husband. She wants to rely on the personality disorder as part of her defence of provocation. A common feature of the three examples is that in none of them can the woman in any way be said to be at fault in inducing her condition. None of these cases can be explained away on a broad view of the provocative conduct of the husband or lover, ie the 'last straw' argument. In all three cases, the merits or demerits of the woman's argument cannot be determined on *a priori* grounds: in the context of provocation it is a matter of fact for exploration in evidence. But in all three cases the particular characteristic of the defendant is potentially relevant only in as much as it affects the degree of self-control of the defendant.

It is trite law that in all three cases relevant evidence of the woman's condition may be placed before the jury. To the extent that the particular condition falls beyond the experience of ordinary men and women, such evidence may include opinion evidence by experts (see R D Mackay and Andrew M Colman,

'Equivocal Rulings on Expert Psychological and Psychiatric Evidence: Turning a Muddle into Nonsense' [1996] Crim LR 88). Such evidence by witnesses of fact or experts may be relevant and admissible on the subjective issue whether the woman had in fact lost her self-control. Moreover, the trial judge would as a matter of fairness be bound to direct the jury that in regard to the subjective enquiry they ought to take into account the evidence as to the woman's condition at the time of the killing. But in my view the logic of the position of the majority is that in all three cases, whatever the strength of the evidence, the judge is as a matter of settled legal principle entitled, and indeed obliged, to direct the jury to ignore the evidence of postnatal depression, battered woman syndrome, and personality disorder when they consider the objective issue ...

R v Campbell [1997] 1 Cr App R 199 (CA)

Lord Bingham CJ: ...

[The first part of the judgment is set out under Diminished Responsibility]

Provocation

If the Crown maintain their challenge to the appellant's defence of diminished responsibility, so that a new trial takes place, on that issue, and if the appellant at that trial advances a defence of provocation in addition to that of diminished responsibility, the trial judge will necessarily be obliged to give the jury an appropriate direction. Until recently, the judge's duty would clearly have been to direct the jury on provocation in accordance with the authoritative decisions of the House of Lords and this Court given since the enactment of s 3 of the 1957 Act. Whether this remains the duty of the judge has been the subject of argument on this appeal. The foundation of the argument is the recent decision of the Judicial Committee of the Privy Council in *Luc Thiet Thuan v R* [1997] AC 131. This was an appeal from the Court of Appeal of Hong Kong, and the issue was whether, in applying the test of the reasonable man, account could be taken of brain damage which would render a defendant more likely to respond violently to an act of provocation than another person of the same age and gender not suffering from such brain damage. Both the trial judge and the Court of Appeal of Hong Kong ruled that such brain damage was irrelevant to the defence of provocation. The Privy Council, by a majority, took the same view. In the majority advice given by Lord Goff of Chieveley doubt was cast on several leading cases decided in this Court. Lord Steyn dissented, expressing support for these Court of Appeal authorities and reaching the conclusion that the trial judge had misdirected the jury by failing to direct them that the evidence of the defendant's brain damage and its impact on his response to provocation was relevant to the objective requirement of provocation. [Counsel] for the Crown submits that the trial judge [at the re-trial of the present case] should direct the jury in accordance with the view of the majority of the Privy Council. [Counsel for the appellant], on the other hand, submits that the view of Lord Steyn is to be preferred.

If we were entitled to choose between the competing views expressed in the Privy Council decision, we should have a difficult task. The legislation in Hong Kong and this country is to the same effect. There is compelling force in the construction which the majority have put on a section which makes reference to the reasonable man and gives no express warrant for elaborating or qualifying that concept. We are, however, conscious that the body of Court of Appeal authority which is in doubt represents a judicial response, born of everyday experience in criminal trials up and down the country, to what fairness seems to require. If the concept of the reasonable man expressed in s 3 were accepted without any qualification, successful pleas of provocation would be rare indeed, since it is not altogether easy to imagine circumstances in which a reasonable man would strike a fatal blow with the necessary mental intention, whatever the provocation. It is in recognition of human frailty that the scope of the defence of provocation has, to a very limited extent, been enlarged. As Lord Steyn put it:

> But even more important than the promptings of legal logic is the dictates of justice. Justice underpinned these decisions.

We do not, however, conceive that it is open to us to choose between these competing views. The previous decisions of this Court are binding upon us. The decision of the Privy Council is not. It appears to us that unless and until the previous decisions of this Court are authoritatively overruled, our duty and that of trial judges bound by the decisions of this Court is to apply the principles which those cases lay down. If there is an effective retrial in this case, and if provocation is an issue, it will be the duty of the trial judge to apply the law binding upon him as it then stands.

R v Pearson [1992] Crim LR 193 (CA)

Facts: William Pearson (aged 17) and his brother Malcolm (aged 16) were charged with the murder of their father. Their parents were divorced in 1982; William went to live with his mother and Malcolm with his father. William and Malcolm both suffered violence at the hands of their father, although Malcolm (who spent more time with his father) suffered more. One day, the father threatened both William and Malcolm with violence. That evening, William struck his father with a sledgehammer. Malcolm then picked up the sledgehammer and delivered further blows.

Held, It was held by the Court of Appeal that the trial judge should have directed the jury that in deciding whether William had reasonably lost his self-control they could have regard to the father's words and conduct not only against him but also against Malcolm.

R v Davies [1975] 1 QB 691 (CA)

Lord Widgery CJ: ... The defendant killed his wife by shooting in the presence of her lover. The only issue in the [Crown Court] was whether the charge should have been reduced to manslaughter on account of provocation. The contention of the defendant is that in directing the jury as to provocation the [trial] judge excluded provocation from any source other than from the victim, that is to say, other than the wife. The question is whether that exclusion was justified or not ...

[His Lordship quoted s 3 of the Homicide Act 1957 and went on:]

... It is to be observed that the reasonable man test, if one may so describe it, prescribed by the section is quite different from the reasonable man test prescribed by Devlin J. In *R v Duffy (Note)* [1949] 1 All ER 932 in Devlin J's direction, both in regard to the particular defendant and in regard to the hypothetical reasonable man, the question was whether the provocation did or would cause a loss of self-control which would prevent the individual from being the master of his mind.

Reading s 3 of the Homicide Act 1957, it is quite apparent that a different test is applied because there one has to consider whether a reasonable man would act as he did, that is to say, would act as the accused had done. [His Lordship then said that in *R v Brown* [1972] 2 QB 229 the Court of Appeal] accepted that the reasonable man test prescribed by the 1957 Act was a new test intended to reflect not only whether the reasonable man would lose his self-control, but also whether the reasonable man would have retaliated in a similar way ...

... [W]e come to the conclusion that ... the situation since 1957 has been that acts or words otherwise to be treated as provocative for present purposes are not excluded from such consideration merely because they emanate from someone other than the victim ...

Sudden and temporary loss of self-control

Where a killing is planned or premeditated, the defence of provocation is not available: see *R v Ibrams* (1981) 74 Cr App R 154. This is so even if the defendant has had to endure a long period of, for example, domestic violence: see *R v Ahluwalia* [1992] 4 All ER 889; *R v Thornton* [1992] 1 All ER 306.

However, cases of planned killings following a long period of provocation should be distinguished from cases where the provocation has been going on for a long time and, immediately after a relatively minor act of provocation, the accused kills the perpetrator of the provocation. The background of provocation is relevant in determining whether the final act of provocation caused the accused to lose self control (and would have caused the reasonable person to do so). See, for example, *R v Pearson* [1992] Crim LR 193 (*above*) and *R v Thorntorn (No 2)* [1996] 2 All ER 1023.

Intoxication is to be disregarded in deciding whether the accused was provoked unless the provocation is directly connected with the intoxication (as where the accused was taunted with the fact that he was intoxicated): see *R v Morhall* [1996] 3 WLR 330.

R v Ibrams and Gregory (1981) 74 Cr App R 154 (CA)

Facts: Ibrams was sharing a flat with his fiancée, Laura Adronik. An ex-boyfriend of Laura's, John Monk, was released from borstal and regularly visited the flat to bully and terrorise Ibrams and Adronik. On some occasions Gregory was also at the flat. On Sunday 7 October 1979 the police were contacted twice but did nothing. As it seemed that the police were not going to protect them, Ibrams, Adronik and Gregory felt that they had to protect themselves. On Wednesday 10 October they met together and drew up a plan for dealing with Monk. In essence, the plan was that they would get Monk drunk and he would be encouraged to go to bed with Adronik. Ibrams and Gregory would then enter the flat and attack Monk whilst he was in bed. This plan was carried out on Friday 12 October. The injuries inflicted by Ibrams and Gregory were so serious that Monk died of his injuries.

The trial judge, McNeill J, held that there was no evidence of provocation for the jury to consider. The Court of Appeal upheld this decision on the basis that the final incident of provocation had taken place several days before the attack on the deceased and that the attack had been planned in advance; accordingly, there was no evidence of the sudden and temporary loss of self-control necessary to establish provocation.

Lawton LJ: ... [His Lordship referred to the speech of Lord Diplock in *DPP v Camplin* [1978] AC 705 where Lord Diplock sets out the history of the law relating to provocation.] That history shows that, in the past at any rate, provocation and loss of self-control tended to be regarded by the courts as taking place with a very short interval of time between the provocation and the loss of self-control ...

In our judgment, Lord Diplock clearly thought that the loss of self-control must occur at or about the time of the act of provocation ...

[His Lordship then cited with approval part of the direction of Devlin J in *R v Duffy* [1949] 1 All ER 932:]

> Indeed, circumstances which induce a desire for revenge are inconsistent with provocation, since the conscious formulation of a desire for revenge means that a person has had time to think, to reflect, and that would negative a sudden temporary loss of self-control, which is of the essence of provocation ...

... [The appellants] were masters of their minds when carrying [their plan] out, because they worked out the details with considerable skill; and in pursuing the plan as they did on the Friday night they were still masters of their own minds. They were doing what they had planned to do ... It follows ... that McNeill J was right in ruling that there was no evidence of loss of self-control ...

R v Ahluwalia [1992] 4 All ER 889 (CA)

Facts: The appellant, an Asian woman entered into an arranged marriage with the deceased. She had to endure several years of violence and abuse. Her husband regularly assaulted her; he had threatened to kill her; he taunted her with the fact that he was having an affair with another woman. During the evening of 8 May 1989 her husband threatened to beat her up and threatened to burn her face with an iron. That night, the appellant poured some petrol, which she had previously purchased, into a bucket (to make it easier to throw); she lit a candle on the gas cooker and carried the bucket and the candle upstairs, taking an oven glove for self protection, and a stick. She went into her husband's bedroom, threw in some petrol, lit the stick with the candle and threw it into the room. Her husband suffered severe burns from which he died a few days later.

Lord Taylor CJ: ... Section 3 of the Homicide Act 1957 did not provide a general or fresh definition of provocation which remains a common law not a statutory defence. The changes effected by the 1957 Act are conveniently summarised in Smith and Hogan, *Criminal Law*, 6th edn, 1988:

> (1) It made it clear that 'things said' alone may be sufficient provocation, if the jury should be of the opinion that they would have provoked a reasonable man ...
>
> (2) It took away the power of the judge to withdraw the defence from the jury on the ground that there was no evidence on which the jury could find that a reasonable man would have been provoked to do as the defendant did ...
>
> (3) It took away the power of the judge to dictate to the jury what were the characteristics of the reasonable man ...

The phrase 'sudden and temporary loss of self-control' encapsulates an essential ingredient of the defence of provocation in a clear and readily understandable phrase. It serves to underline that the defence is concerned with the actions of an individual who is not, at the moment when he or she acts violently, master of his or her own mind ...

... [I]t is open to the judge, when deciding whether there is any evidence of provocation to be left to the jury and open to the jury when considering such evidence, to take account of the interval between the provocative conduct and the reaction of the defendant to it. Time for reflection may show that after the provocative conduct made its impact on the mind of the defendant, he or she kept or regained self-control. The passage of time following the provocation may also show that the subsequent attack was planned or based on motives such as revenge or punishment, inconsistent with the loss of self-control and therefore with the defence of provocation. In some cases, such an interval may wholly undermine the defence of provocation; that, however, depends entirely on the facts of the individual case and is not a principle of law.

[Counsel for the appellant] referred to the phrase 'cooling-off period' which has sometimes been applied to an interval of time between the provocation relied upon and the fatal act. He suggests that although in many cases such an interval may indeed be a time for cooling and regaining self-control so as to forfeit the protection of the defence, in others the time lapse has an opposite effect. He submits, relying on expert evidence not before the trial judge, that women who have been subjected frequently over a period to violent treatment may react to the final act or words by what he calls a 'slow-burn' reaction rather than by an immediate loss of self-control.

We accept that the subjective element in the defence of provocation would not as a matter of law be negatived simply because of the delayed reaction in such cases, provided that there was at the time of the killing a 'sudden and temporary loss of self-control' caused by the alleged provocation. However, the longer the delay and the stronger the evidence of deliberation on the part of the defendant, the more likely it will be that the prosecution will negative provocation ...

R v Thornton (No 2) [1996] 2 ALL ER 1023 (CA)

Lord Taylor of Gosforth CJ: ... [S]ince reliance *is* placed upon the appellant's suffering from a 'battered woman syndrome', we think it right to reaffirm the principle. A defendant, even if suffering from that syndrome, cannot succeed in relying on provocation unless the jury consider she suffered or may have suffered a sudden and temporary loss of self-control at the time of the killing.

That is not to say that a battered woman syndrome has no relevance to the defence of provocation. The severity of such a syndrome and the extent to which it may have affected a particular defendant will no doubt vary and is for the jury to consider. But it may be relevant in two ways. First, it may form an important background to whatever triggered the *actus reus*. A jury may more readily find there was a sudden loss of control triggered by even a minor incident, if the defendant has endured abuse over a period, on the 'last straw' basis. Second, depending on the medical evidence, the syndrome may have affected the defendant's personality so as to constitute a significant characteristic relevant (as we shall indicate) to the second question [ie whether the hypothetical reasonable woman possessing the appellant's characteristics would have reacted to the provocative conduct so as to do what the appellant did] the jury has to consider in regard to provocation.

R v Morhall [1996] 3 WLR 330 (HL)

Lord Goff of Chieveley: ... The circumstances in which the defendant killed the deceased are [as follows]:

> During the daytime on 7 June 1991 the deceased and one Donnellan had been taking the [defendant] to task over his glue-sniffing. At about 5 pm they were at his flat during an argument between the deceased and his girlfriend, also over his glue-sniffing of which she disapproved. She left. Later, the deceased and Donnellan went out a couple of times. The [defendant] was sniffing glue when they left and when they returned. By 10 pm, when they came back

> with some cider and beer, the [defendant] was 'high'. He was unsteady and his speech was affected. The deceased resumed nagging him about his glue-sniffing. At about 2 am the deceased went out and brought some food. Whilst the other two ate, the [defendant] carried on glue-sniffing. The deceased chided him again and then head-butted him. The [defendant] picked up a hammer and hit the deceased on the head. A fight ensued. It was broken up by Donnellan, who got the [defendant] to go to his bedroom. However, the deceased would not stop. He said, 'I am not having that, I am going to do him'. He went to the [defendant's] bedroom and Donnellan heard crashing and banging. When he went in the [defendant] was holding the commando dagger and the deceased said, 'The bastard has stabbed me'. Donnellan wrestled with the [defendant]. Meanwhile, the deceased had gone down to the next landing where he fell to the floor. He had been fatally stabbed.

... The Court of Appeal gave leave to appeal to your Lordship's House, certifying that the following point of law of general public importance was involved in the decision:

> When directing a jury on provocation under s 3 of the Homicide Act 1957, and explaining to them in accordance with the model direction of Lord Diplock in *R v Camplin* [1978] AC 705, 718: 'the reasonable man referred to in the question is a person having the power of self-control to be expected of an ordinary person of the sex and age of the accused, but in other respects sharing such of the accused's characteristics as they think would affect the gravity of the provocation to him'; should the judge exclude from the jury's consideration characteristics and past behaviour of the defendant, at which the taunts are directed, which in the judge's view are inconsistent with the concept of a reasonable man?

... Judging from the speeches in *R v Camplin*, it should indeed have been taken into account. Indeed, it was a characteristic of particular relevance, since the words of the deceased which were said to constitute provocation were directed towards the defendant's shameful addiction to glue-sniffing and his inability to break himself of it. Furthermore, there is nothing in the speeches in *R v Camplin* to suggest that a characteristic of this kind should be excluded from consideration. On the contrary, in [*R v Camplin*] Lord Diplock spoke of the jury taking into consideration 'all those factors' which would affect the gravity of the taunts or insults when applied to the defendant. Likewise, Lord Simon of Glaisdale said ...

> in determining whether a person of reasonable self-control would lose it in the circumstances, the entire factual situation, which includes the characteristics of the accused, must be considered.

... In truth the expression 'reasonable man' or 'reasonable person' in this context can lead to misunderstanding. Lord Diplock described it (in *R v Camplin* at 716G) as an 'apparently inapt expression'. This is because the 'reasonable person test' is concerned not with ratiocination, nor with the reasonable man whom we know so well in the law of negligence (where we are concerned with reasonable foresight and reasonable care), nor with reasonable conduct generally. The function of the test is only to introduce, as a matter of policy, a standard of self-control which has to be complied with if provocation is to be established in law ... Lord Diplock himself spoke of 'the reasonable or ordinary person', and indeed to speak of the degree of self-control attributable to the ordinary person is (despite the express words of the statute) perhaps more apt, and certainly less likely to mislead, than to do so with reference to the reasonable person ... In my opinion it would be entirely consistent with the law as stated in s 3 of the Act of 1957, as properly understood, to direct the jury simply with reference to a hypothetical person having the power of self-control to be expected of an *ordinary* person of the age and sex of the defendant, but in other respects sharing such of the defendant's characteristics as they think would affect the gravity of the provocation to him ...

In truth, the mere fact that a characteristic of the defendant is discreditable does not exclude it from consideration, as was made plain by Lord Diplock in *R v Camplin* when he referred to a shameful incident in a man's past as a relevant characteristic for present purposes. Indeed, even if the defendant's discreditable conduct causes a reaction in another, which in turn causes the defendant to lose his self-control, the reaction may amount to provocation: see *Edwards v The Queen* [1973] AC 648, a case concerned with a hostile reaction to his blackmailer by a man whom he was trying to blackmail, and *R v Johnson (Christopher)* [1989] 1 WLR 740 in which *Edwards v The Queen* was followed and applied by the Court of Appeal ...

Of course glue-sniffing (or solvent abuse), like indulgence in alcohol or the taking of drugs, can give rise to a special problem in the present context, because it may arise in more than one way. First, it is well established that, in considering whether a person having the power of self-control to be expected of an ordinary person would have reacted to the provocation as the defendant did, the fact (if it be the case) that the defendant was the worse for drink at the time should not be taken into account, even though the drink would, if taken by him, have the effect of reducing an ordinary person's power of self-control. It is sometimes suggested that the reason for this exclusion is that drunkenness is transitory and cannot therefore amount to a characteristic. But I doubt whether that is right. Indeed some physical conditions (such as eczema) may be transitory in nature and yet can surely be taken into account if the subject taunts. In *R v Camplin* [1978] AC 705 at 726F, Lord Simon of Glaisdale considered that drunkenness should be excluded as inconsistent with the concept of the reasonable man in the sense of a man of ordinary self-control; but it has to be recognised that, in our society, ordinary people do sometimes have too much to drink. I incline therefore to the opinion that the exclusion of drunkenness in this context flows from the established principle that, at common law, intoxication does not of itself excuse a man from committing a criminal offence, but on one or other of these bases it is plainly excluded. At all events it follows that, in a case such as the present, a distinction may have to be drawn between two different situations. The first occurs where the defendant is taunted with his addiction (for example, that he is an alcoholic, or a drug addict, or a glue-sniffer), or even with having been intoxicated (from any cause) on some previous occasion. In such a case, however discreditable such a condition may be, it may where relevant be taken into account as going to the gravity of the provocation. The second is the simple fact of the defendant being intoxicated – being drunk, or high with drugs or glue – at the relevant time, which may not be so taken into account, because that, like displaying a lack of ordinary self-control, is excluded as a matter of policy ...

When should the jury be directed on the issue of provocation?

R v Stewart [1995] 4 All ER 999 (CA)

Stuart-Smith LJ: ... It is now well established that even if the defence do not raise the issue of provocation, and even if they would prefer not to because it is inconsistent with and will detract from the primary defence, the judge must leave the issue for the jury to decide if there is evidence which suggests that the accused may have been provoked; and this is so even if the evidence of provocation is slight or tenuous in the sense that the measure of the provocative acts or words is slight: see *R v Rossiter* [1994] 2 All ER 752 and *R v Cambridge* [1994] 2 All ER 760, [1994] 1 WLR 971 ...

In our judgment, where the judge must, as a matter of law, leave the issue of provocation to the jury, he should indicate to them, unless it is obvious, what evidence might support the conclusion that the appellant lost his self-control ...

R v Acott [1997] 1 All ER 706 (HL)

Lord Steyn: ... The Court of Appeal (Criminal Division) certified that there was a point of law of general public importance involved in the decision to dismiss the appeal, namely:

> In a prosecution for murder, before the judge is obliged to leave the issue of provocation to the jury, must there be some evidence, either direct or inferential, as to what was either done or said to provoke the alleged loss of self-control? ...

The trial

... The prosecution case was as follows. In 1993 the appellant lived with his mother. He was 48 years old and his mother was 78 years of age. At 9.15 pm on 17 February 1993 the appellant, in a state of agitation, telephoned for an ambulance. He said that his mother had been injured as the result of a fall. The ambulance men met the appellant in his mother's bungalow and found the deceased dead on the floor of the hallway. An examination showed that the deceased had sustained multiple injuries, particularly in the area of the head, face and neck.

The appellant was of good character. He was a mild man. He worked until 1991 when he gave up his job and moved to Rainham to live with his mother. The appellant tried to obtain another job but he was unsuccessful. After exhausting his savings he became financially dependent on his mother. He found his dependence on his mother somewhat irksome. But in his [police] interviews and at the trial he repeatedly said he was very fond of his mother. There was other evidence to the same effect. In accordance with a recent will of his mother he was her sole beneficiary.

When questioned by the police, and at the trial, the appellant consistently denied that he was responsible for his mother's death. He said his mother had come to his bedroom to say 'goodnight' and almost immediately afterwards he heard her fall. He said he tried to help her but she fell again. He tried to pick her up and she again fell heavily. He tried to resuscitate her, he thumped her chest and slapped her face in an effort to bring her round. He said her injuries had been caused by her falls and his unskilled efforts to resuscitate her.

Three pathologists testified: two pathologists, with varying degrees of emphasis, said that the deceased died as a result of a sustained attack; and a third pathologist testifying on behalf of the defence said that the injuries were explicable on the basis of the defendant's account.

The appellant's case at trial was therefore that he had not attacked his mother and that he was entitled to a complete acquittal. Counsel in their speeches and the [trial judge] in his summing up treated it as a case involving a single issue. The [trial judge] directed the jury that 'This is murder or nothing'. The jury rejected the appellant's explanation...

The evidence said to justify a direction on provocation

It is now possible to summarise the materials relied on by the appellant in support of the argument before the Court of Appeal, which was repeated before your Lordships' House, that the judge ought to have left provocation as an issue to the jury. First, counsel for the appellant pointed out correctly that leading counsel for the Crown had repeatedly put to the appellant in cross-examination that he had lost his self-control and attacked his mother. Counsel for the Crown cross-examined on the basis that the appellant had been angered by his mother treating him like a little boy and berating him. Counsel for the appellant submitted that the Crown had made provocation an issue and that accordingly the judge should have summed up on provocation. Instead, counsel for the appellant said, the judge reminded the jury of these passages in the evidence but failed to leave the issue of provocation to the jury.

Counsel for the appellant further argued that the extent of the injuries to the deceased was testimony to a frenzied attack which was prima facie indicative of a loss of self-control. Moreover, counsel argued that this inference was reinforced by the cumulative effect of the following factors: the appellant was unemployed; he was in the humiliating position of having to ask his mother for money; the evidence was that she sometimes treated him like a little boy; she was given to black moods; and apparently sometimes she drank excessively ...

The general principles

[His Lordship quoted s 3 of the Homicide Act 1957 and went on:]

Section 3 moderated the strict requirements of the common law defence of provocation. Section 3 can be divided into three parts: (1) the provoking conduct; (2) causatively relevant loss of self-control; and (3) the objective criterion whether the provocation was enough to make a reasonable man do as the defendant did. For the purposes of examining the constituent elements of provocation it is only necessary to consider the classic case of provocation of an accused person *by the deceased*. First, in respect of the provoking conduct s 3 abolished the common law rule that words alone could not amount to provocation. It did so by using the general words 'whether by things done or by things said or by both together'. The meaning of these words is plain and by using the shorthand expression 'provoking conduct' I do not intend to put a gloss on the words of the statute. Secondly, the question is whether the provoking conduct of the deceased caused the defendant to lose his self-control. This is usually called the subjective condition. In the absence of any evidence, emerging from whatever source, suggestive of the reasonable possibility that the defendant might have lost his self-control due to the provoking conduct of the deceased, the question of provocation does not arise. Thirdly, the section provides that the question whether the provocation was enough to make a reasonable man do as he did shall be left to be determined by the jury. This part of the section provides for an external or objective standard. This provision is explained by the concluding provision that in determining the objective question the jury shall take into account everything done and said according to the effect which, in their opinion, it would have on a reasonable man. The purpose of this part of the section is well settled. After the adoption of the reasonable man test in the second half of the last century, judges withdrew cases where the defendant wished to rely on provocation on the basis of rules or supposed rules which were judicially developed. By converting commonsense criteria into fixed rules of law judges empowered themselves to invoke those rules to withdraw cases from the jury. Thus the rule was laid down that disproportionate retaliation may bar the defence, or, as it was later put, that the retaliation must bear a reasonable relationship to the provocation received: see *Mancini v DPP* [1942] AC 1 and *R v Duffy* [1949] 1 All ER 932; see also generally *Logan v R* [1996] AC 871 at 887. Plainly proportionality was a highly relevant matter to a defence of provocation. But the perceived mischief was that judges withdrew cases from the jury on the ground of fixed rules of law. In *DPP v Camplin* [1978] AC 705 the House of Lords held that s 3 abolished all previous rules linked with the objective requirement as to what can or cannot amount to provocation (see p 716 per Lord Diplock). At the same time s 3 abolished the power of the judge to withdraw provocation as an issue on the ground that there was no evidence on which the jury could find that a reasonable man would have been provoked as the defendant was: *DPP v Camplin*. Henceforth the objective requirement was to be regarded as an issue of fact, or, more realistically as a matter of opinion, within the sole province of the jury. But importantly, in the context of the present appeal, it remained the duty of the judge to decide whether there was evidence of provoking conduct, which resulted in the defendant losing his self-control. If in the opinion of the judge, even on a view most favourable to the accused, there is insufficient material for a jury to find that it is a reasonable possibility that there was specific provoking conduct resulting in a loss of self-control, there is simply no issue of provocation to be considered by the jury (see *Lee Chun-Chuen v R* [1963] AC 220 at 229 per Lord Devlin).

Standing back from the minutiae of s 3, AJ Ashworth (now Professor Ashworth) in *The Doctrine of Provocation* [1976] CLJ 292 at 317-318 described the core features of the modern law of provocation in terms which are helpful in the context of the present appeal. He said:

> Provocation mitigates moral culpability to the extent that a person acted in a less-than-fully-controlled manner in circumstances in which there was reasonable justification for him to feel aggrieved at the conduct of another. The law's subjective condition operates to ensure that it was not a revenge killing, but rather a sudden and uncontrolled reaction to perceived injustice. The objective condition looks to the element of partial justification and, inevitably, to the conduct of the provoking party. It requires of the jury an assessment of the seriousness of the provocation, and a judgment as to whether the provocation was grave enough to warrant a reduction of the crime from murder to manslaughter. This question of sufficiency is one of degree, and the legal rules, although they can take the court so far, cannot determine this ultimate question. Of course there will be clear cases – as, for example, where a teenage son loses control and attacks his bullying father – and there will be doubtful cases – as, for example, where a husband kills his wife during a quarrel over infidelity, which the parties had more or less accepted for a considerable time. Each case is for the decision of the jury, properly directed as to the law.

This passage emphasises that it is an integral part of the idea of provocation that the deceased aroused the anger of the defendant and made him lose his self-control. It explains how the jury cannot determine either the subjective or the objective condition without some evidence of the nature of the provocation.

The proposition that the Crown made provocation an issue

Counsel for the appellant argued that the Crown made provocation an issue by putting to him in cross-examination that he attacked his mother as a result of a loss of self-control caused by momentary anger at the way in which his mother treated him. The appellant throughout denied these suggestions, and he insisted that his relationship with his mother was good and that she had done nothing to anger him. The cross-examination produced no evidence of provoking conduct or of a loss of self-control. In deciding what issues must be left to the jury a judge must be guided by the state of the evidence. Suggestions in cross-examination cannot by themselves raise an issue of provocation where the evidence, on the most favourable view for the defendant, reveals no issue. It follows that I would reject this way of putting the appellant's case.

The relevant evidence

The disposal of the appeal therefore depends on the state of the evidence. Like Rougier J [in the Court of Appeal] I am willing to infer from the injuries of the deceased that there was a reasonable possibility that the appellant lost his self-control and attacked his mother in anger. But by itself that is not enough. The question is whether there is any evidence of specific provoking conduct. As the issues became refined during the helpful oral submissions of both counsel, it became clear that counsel for the appellant was submitting in this part of his argument that from the fact of loss of self-control and the evidence that the appellant was sometimes treated by his mother as a little boy, it is a rational inference that the appellant's loss of self-control might have followed upon a specific provoking element albeit perhaps of a trivial and 'last straw' variety. Subject to his earlier argument already discussed, counsel for the appellant accepted that if such an inference is not justified, the appeal must fail. In my judgment that concession was rightly made. It is a short point not of law but of logic and common sense. The [trial judge] plainly took the view that the evidence did not justify an inference of a specific provoking event. In my view the evidence was insufficient to support the suggested inference. It was not a reasonable possibility arising on the evidence: it was mere speculation. In these circumstances the appeal must fail on the facts.

The certified question

Strictly, the certified question need not be answered in order to dispose of the appeal. But it seems possible to summarise the legal position in terms which might be helpful. Section 3 is only applicable 'if there is evidence ... that the person charged was provoked (whether by things done or things said or by both together) to lose his self-control'. A loss of self-control caused by fear, panic, sheer bad temper or circumstances (eg a slow down of traffic due to snow) would not be enough. There must be some evidence tending to show that the killing might have been an uncontrolled reaction to provoking conduct rather than an act of revenge. Moreover, although there is no longer a rule of proportionality as between provocation and retaliation, the concept of proportionality is nevertheless still an important factual element in the objective inquiry. It necessarily requires of the jury an assessment of the seriousness of the provocation. It follows that there can only be an issue of provocation to be considered by the jury if the judge considers that there is some evidence of a specific act or words of provocation resulting in a loss of self-control. It does not matter from what source that evidence emerges or whether it is relied on at trial by the defendant or not. If there is such evidence, the judge must leave the issue to the jury. If there is no such evidence, but merely the speculative possibility that there had been an act of provocation, it is wrong for the judge to direct the jury to consider provocation. In such a case there is simply no triable issue of provocation...

Counsel for the appellant invited your Lordships to go further and state what would be sufficient evidence of provocation to justify a trial judge in leaving the issue of provocation for the jury to consider. The invitation was attractively put. But it must be rejected. What is sufficient in this particular context is not a question of law. Where the line is to be drawn depends on a judgment involving logic and common sense, the assessment of matters of degree and an intense focus on the circumstances of a particular case. It is unwise to generalise on such matters: it is a subject best left to the good sense of trial judges. For the same reason it is not useful to compare the facts of decided cases on provocation with one another.

For my part the certified question can be answered in the general way in which I have indicated. But the reasoning in this judgment is subject to the overriding principle that the legal burden rests on the Crown to disprove provocation on a charge of murder to the required standard of proof. In *Lee Chun-Chuen v R* [1963] AC 220 at 229 Lord Devlin summed up the legal position as follows:

> It is not of course for the defence to make out a *prima facie* case of provocation. It is for the prosecution to prove that the killing was unprovoked. All that the defence need do is to point to material which could induce a reasonable doubt.

That remains the position.

I would dismiss the appeal.

Proportionality

There is no rule that the act of the accused must bear a reasonable relationship to the provocation. However, the jury is entitled to take account of the question of proportionality in deciding the question posed by s 3 of the Homicide Act 1957, 'whether the provocation was enough to make the reasonable man do as the accused did': see *Phillips v The Queen* [1969] 2 AC 130.

Phillips v The Queen [1969] 2 AC 130 (PC)

Lord Diplock: ... The test of provocation in the law of homicide is twofold. The first, which has always been a question of fact for the jury assuming that there is any evidence upon which they can so find, is 'Was the defendant provoked into losing his self-control?' The second, which is one not of fact but of opinion, 'Would a reasonable man have reacted to the same provocation in the same way as the defendant did?'

... In their Lordships' view [s 3 of the Homicide Act 1957], in referring to the question to be left to be determined by the jury as being 'whether the provocation was enough to make a reasonable man do as he [that is, the person charged] did' explicitly recognises that what the jury have to consider, once they have reached the conclusion that the person charged was in fact provoked to lose his self-control is not merely whether in their opinion the provocation would have made a reasonable man lose his self-control but also whether, having lost his self-control, he would have retaliated in the same way as the person charged in fact did.

... Since the passing of the legislation it may be prudent to avoid the use of the precise words of Viscount Simon in *Mancini v DPP* [1942] AC 1 'the mode of resentment must bear a reasonable relationship to the provocation' unless they are used in a context which makes it clear to the jury that this is not a rule of law which they are bound to follow, but merely a consideration which may or may not commend itself to them ...

Self-induced provocation

The defendant may rely on the defence of provocation even if he or she has been partly responsible for bringing that provocation about: see *Edwards v The Queen* [1973] AC 648, followed in *R v Johnson* [1989] 1 WLR 740.

Edwards v The Queen [1973] AC 648 (PC)

Lord Pearson: ... On principle it seems reasonable to say that:

(1) a blackmailer cannot rely on the predictable results of his own blackmailing conduct as constituting provocation sufficient to reduce his killing of the victim from murder to manslaughter, and the predictable results may include a considerable degree of hostile reaction by the person sought to be blackmailed, for instance vituperative words and even some hostile action such as blows with a fist;

(2) but if the hostile reaction by the person sought to be blackmailed goes to extreme lengths it might constitute sufficient provocation even for the blackmailer;

(3) there would in many cases be a question of degree to be decided by the jury ...

R v Johnson [1989] 1 WLR 740 (CA)

Watkins LJ: ... [His Lordship referred to the judgment of Lord Pearson in *Edwards v The Queen* [1973] AC 648 at 658 and continued:] Those words cannot, we think, be understood to mean, as was suggested to us, that provocation which is 'self-induced' ceases to be provocation for the purposes of s 3 of the 1957 Act.

The relevant statutory provision being considered by the Privy Council was in similar terms to s 3. In view of the express wording of s 3, as interpreted in *DPP v Camplin*, which was decided after *Edwards v R*, we find it impossible to accept that the mere fact that a defendant caused a reaction in others, which in turn led him to lose his self-control, should result in the issue of provocation being kept outside a jury's consideration. Section 3 clearly provides that the question is whether things done or said or both provoked the defendant to lose his self-control. If there is any evidence that it may have done, the issue must be left to the jury. The jury would then have to consider all the circumstances of the incident, including all the relevant behaviour of the defendant, in deciding (a) whether he was in fact provoked and (b) whether the provocation was enough to make a reasonable man do what the defendant did ...

MANSLAUGHTER

We have already seen that the defences of diminished responsibility and provocation serve to reduce murder to manslaughter. Such instances of manslaughter are sometimes called 'voluntary manslaughter'. These offences are called 'voluntary' because the accused has the *mens rea* necessary to be guilty of murder.

The term 'involuntary manslaughter' may be applied to cases where the accused has killed someone but lacks the *mens rea* for murder. There are two types of involuntary manslaughter:

(a) where death results from an unlawful act which is likely to cause bodily harm (sometimes called 'constructive manslaughter');

(b) where death results from an act of gross negligence.

Constructive manslaughter

The elements of this form of manslaughter are:

(a) the accused does an unlawful act;

(b) the accused has the requisite *mens rea* for that unlawful act;

(c) the act is a dangerous one;

(d) the act results in the death of the victim.

An unlawful act

To be guilty of this form of manslaughter, the accused's act must be unlawful, in the sense that it constitutes a criminal offence in its own right. Typical acts include assault, arson (as in *R v Goodfellow* (1986) 83 Cr App R 23), criminal damage and even burglary (as in *R v Watson* [1989] 1 WLR 684).

A person who uses excessive force in circumstances where the use of force would otherwise be lawful (eg a publican ejecting someone from his public house or a person acting in self-defence) may be guilty of manslaughter: see *R v Scarlett* [1993] 4 All ER 629. However, there is no rule that in every case where the defendant is charged with murder and an issue of self-defence has arisen, the jury must be directed to return a verdict of manslaughter if they find that the plea of self-defence fails because the defendant used excessive force. Self-defence only fails if the prosecution can show beyond reasonable doubt that the defendant was not acting in self-defence: see *Palmer v The Queen* [1971] AC 814.

R v Scarlett [1993] 4 All ER 629 (CA)

Beldam LJ: ... The appellant was charged with unlawfully causing the death of a Mr Larkin. The events which gave rise to the charge were that the appellant, now 40 years of age, was the licensee of the Queen's Road Tavern public house in Halifax. Ten minutes after closing time on 12 June 1991 the deceased, Mr Larkin, a large, heavily built man, entered the public house the worse for drink and approached the bar. He indicated he wanted to be served and the appellant, who was behind the bar cleaning up, said 'you've no chance'. The deceased then said to the appellant: 'What are you talking to me like that for? I haven't asked you a question yet.' The appellant repeated that there was no chance of his being served. Still the deceased persisted and eventually the appellant said: 'Look get out now or I'll put you out'. The deceased replied: 'You and who else?' The appellant came from behind the bar through the gap in the counter moving towards the deceased, who said: 'You're not going to put me out', indicating to at least one of those present in the bar that he was not going to leave voluntarily.

The appellant went to take hold of the deceased's right arm to escort him from the bar but with a wide, sweeping movement the deceased threw his right arm round in an arc. The appellant said that he thought that the deceased might strike him, though in fact he did not, so he placed himself behind the deceased and put his arms around his body restraining him by pinning both arms to his side. It was a manoeuvre that the appellant had learnt from his service in the army and in his view it had the advantage that neither of them could come to any harm. It prevented a potential assailant from striking any blows. The appellant was of smaller build than the deceased who struggled and resisted as the appellant tried to get him to the door. The only witnesses on whom reliance was placed described the appellant as 'bundling the deceased towards the door'. On the way to the door the deceased and the appellant bumped into the door by a cigarette machine.

The entrance to the public house is somewhat awkwardly placed. The door into the bar is a swing door hinged upon the right-hand side when facing it, which opens out across a lobby. The lobby, which is 5 feet by 4 feet, gives onto a flight of five steps leading down to the street. On either side of the steps are substantial handrails. The steps are not particularly steep and there is an outer door separating the lobby from the steps but it is normally held back against the wall until the public house is closed for the night.

Due to the position of the door the appellant had to turn sideways still holding onto the deceased in order to push it open with his body, turning as he did so through an angle of 90 degrees to place the deceased in the lobby. The appellant pushed open the door with his body and moved into the lobby, the door closing behind him. Apart from the appellant's account, there was no evidence of what then happened in the lobby. According to the appellant, he placed the deceased with his back against the wall and the frame of the outer door. In the lobby against the wall was an advertisement board of a kind frequently seen advertising snacks, etc. Having placed the deceased in the lobby, the appellant turned to re-enter the bar and had his right hand on the inner door handle when the deceased called out: 'Well you haven't thrown me out yet'.

At that moment the advertisement board came over on top of the appellant's legs and he saw the deceased fall from the top step. A passer-by also saw the deceased fall from the top step backwards into the street, apparently striking his head. The appellant then went down and spoke to the deceased, who did not move. The appellant re-entered the bar and was heard to say: 'He's fallen down the steps'.

The appellant said that he was quite worried and flustered and that he had intended to go to call an ambulance, but he then went back to have another look at the deceased and saw that he was apparently seriously injured, having struck his head. He was unconscious. As he was lying across the pavement, the appellant moved him into a small alleyway at the side of the public house and placed him in the recovery position. He then returned to the public house and telephoned for the ambulance. The ambulance arrived and the deceased was taken to hospital, where it was found that he had sustained a serious injury to his head from which he later died.

... The appellant understandably was shocked and terrified. He was interviewed on three occasions ... in the course of those interviews he consistently denied the use of excessive force on the deceased. On the contrary, it was clear that throughout he was denying any intention to cause harm to the deceased.

The case advanced for the prosecution was that the appellant was guilty of manslaughter because when bundling the deceased towards the door of the bar the appellant had used excessive force and thus had committed an unlawful act. The prosecution disclaimed any suggestion that the appellant had pushed the deceased towards the top of the steps or that he had recklessly placed him in a position from which there was a serious risk of his falling and sustaining injury. The case was based solely on the assertion that by his unlawful act of using excessive force in the bar he had imparted such a momentum to the deceased that the deceased's fall was a consequence of the unlawful act, and his death consequently manslaughter ...

The whole tenor of the judge's directions was that if the jury concluded that the appellant had used more force than was necessary in the circumstances in the bar, and if they were satisfied that that caused the deceased to fall and strike his head, he was guilty of manslaughter ...

[His Lordship referred to a number of cases, including *DPP v Newbury*, *DPP v Jones* [1977] AC 500 and *R v Williams* [1987] 3 All ER 411 and went on:]

The issue in *R v Williams* was whether the accused was entitled to be acquitted if he mistakenly believed that he was justified in using force. The court held that, even if the jury came to the conclusion that the mistake was an unreasonable one, if the defendant may genuinely have been labouring under it, he was entitled to rely upon it. The reason why he was entitled to be acquitted is because he did not intend to apply unlawful force. The principle we have quoted that the mental element necessary to constitute guilt of an assault is the intent to apply unlawful force to the victim was approved by the Board of the Privy Council in *Beckford v R* [1988] AC 130 at 143.

If the mental element necessary to prove an assault is an intention to apply unlawful force to the victim, and the accused is to be judged according to his mistaken view of the facts whether that mistake was on an objective view reasonable or not, we can see no logical basis for distinguishing between a person who objectively is not justified in using force at all but mistakenly believes he is and another who is in fact justified in using force but mistakenly believes that the circumstances call for a degree of force objectively regarded as unnecessary.

Where, as in the present case, an accused is justified in using some force and can only be guilty of an assault if the force used is excessive, the jury ought to be directed that he cannot be guilty of an assault unless the prosecution prove that he acted with the mental element necessary to constitute his action an assault, that is 'that the defendant intentionally or recklessly applied force to the person of another' (see *R v Venna* [1976] 1 QB 421 at 429 *per* James LJ).

Further they should be directed that the accused is not to be found guilty merely because he intentionally or recklessly used force which they consider to have been excessive. They ought not to convict him unless they are satisfied that the degree of force used was plainly more than was called for by the circumstances as he believed them to be and, provided he believed the circumstances called for the degree of force used, he is not to be convicted even if his belief was unreasonable.

In this case the learned judge gave no direction to the jury that the prosecution, to establish an assault, had to prove that the appellant intentionally or recklessly applied excessive force in seeking to evict the deceased. On the contrary the jury were simply left to say what in the circumstances they considered was reasonable force and directed that if they concluded that what was done involved an unnecessary and unreasonable degree of force they then only had to consider whether the act of unlawful and unnecessary force actually caused the deceased to fall down the steps ...

We are of the opinion that the directions to the jury in the circumstances of this case were inadequate to support a verdict of guilty of manslaughter. The appellant had given clear evidence that he only intended to use sufficient force to remove the deceased from the bar, an act he was lawfully entitled to do. It was not contended, nor were submissions made to the jury on the basis, that he acted recklessly. The direction to the jury was based on the assertion that it was sufficient if they found the force used by the appellant excessive in the circumstances. The learned judge seems to have assumed that this was sufficient to prove that what the appellant did amounted to an assault.

The expression used by the witnesses that the appellant 'bundled' the deceased towards the door certainly provided no basis for saying the appellant was reckless, nor by itself did it imply that the force used was excessive in the circumstances. Because of the dire consequences of the deceased's fall, there was a real risk that the jury might be persuaded not only that the force applied was excessive but that the appellant's actions were likely to cause injury. It is important to emphasise that the question whether the action of the appellant was unlawful and the question whether it was dangerous have to be considered separately ...

Palmer v The Queen [1971] AC 814 (PC)

See Chapter 8.

R v Lamb [1967] 2 QB 981 (CA)

Sachs LJ: ... The defendant, Terence Walter Lamb, aged 25, had become possessed of a Smith & Wesson revolver. It was a revolver in the literal old-fashioned sense, having a five-chambered cylinder which rotated clockwise each time the trigger was pulled. The defendant, in jest, with no intention to do any harm, pointed the revolver at the deceased, his best friend, when it had two bullets in the chambers, but neither bullet was in the chamber opposite the barrel. His friend was similarly treating the incident as a joke. The defendant then pulled the trigger and thus killed his friend, still having no intention to fire the revolver. The reason why the pulling of the trigger produced that fatal result was that its pulling rotated the cylinder and so placed a bullet opposite the barrel so that it was struck by the striking pin or hammer.

The defendant's defence was that, as neither bullet was opposite the barrel, he thought they were in such chambers that the striking pin could not hit them; that he was unaware that the pulling of the trigger would bring one bullet into the firing position opposite the barrel; and that the killing was thus an accident. There was not only no dispute that that was what he in fact thought, but the mistake he made was one which three experts agreed was natural for somebody who was not aware of the way the revolver mechanism worked ...

The defence of accident was, however, in effect withdrawn from the jury by the trial judge ... [who] made no mention of the word 'accident' in his summing up nor of the evidence of the experts save that he at one stage directed the jury that their evidence was not relevant ...

[Dealing with manslaughter in the sense of an unlawful act resulting in death his Lordship said:]

... The trial judge took the view that the pointing of the revolver and the pulling of the trigger was something which could of itself be unlawful even if there was no attempt to alarm or intent to injure ...

[Counsel for the Crown] however, had at all times put forward the correct view that for the act to be unlawful it must constitute at least what he then termed 'a technical assault'. In this court moreover he rightly conceded that there was no evidence to go to the jury of any assault of any kind. Nor did he feel able to submit that the acts of the defendant were on any other ground unlawful in the criminal sense of that word. Indeed no such submission could in law be made: if, for instance, the pulling of the trigger had had no effect because the striking mechanism or the ammunition had been defective no offence would have been committed by the defendant.

Another way of putting it is that *mens rea*, being now an essential ingredient in manslaughter (compare *Andrews v DPP* [1937] AC 576 and *R v Church* [1966] 1 QB 59), that could not in the present case be established in relation to the first ground except by proving that element of intent without which there can be no assault.

It is perhaps as well to mention that when using the phrase 'unlawful in the criminal sense of that word' the court has in mind that it is long settled that it is not in point to consider whether an act is unlawful merely from the angle of civil liabilities ...

[Dealing with manslaughter on the ground of criminal negligence, his Lordship said:]

... Nowhere in that part of the summing up relating to the second ground is any mention made of the view the defendant had formed as to being able to pull the trigger without firing a bullet, nor of the experts' unanimous evidence that his mistake was understandable and indeed one which could be expected ...

The general effect of the summing up was thus to withdraw from the jury the defence put forward on behalf of the defendant. When the gravamen of a charge is criminal negligence – often referred to as recklessness – of an accused, the jury have to consider among other matters the state of his mind, and that includes the question of whether or not he thought that that which he was doing was safe. In the present case it would, of course, have been fully open to a jury, if properly directed, to find the defendant guilty because they considered his view as to there being no danger was formed in a criminally negligent way. But he was entitled to a direction that the jury should take into account the fact that he had undisputedly formed that view and that there was expert evidence as to this being an understandable view.

Strong though the evidence of criminal negligence was, the defendant was entitled as of right to have his defence considered, but he was not accorded this right and the jury was left without a direction on an essential matter ... [Therefore] the verdict cannot stand ...

R v Lipman [1970] 1 QB 152 (CA)

Widgery LJ: ... Both the defendant and the victim were addicted to drugs, and on the evening of 16 September 1967, both took a quantity of a drug known as LSD. Early on the morning of 18 September, the defendant, who is a United States citizen, hurriedly booked out of his hotel and left the country. On the following day, 19 September, the victim's landlord found her dead in her room. She had suffered two blows on the head causing haemorrhage of the brain, but she had died of asphyxia as a result of some eight inches of sheet having been crammed into her mouth.

The defendant was returned to this country by extradition proceedings, and at the trial he gave evidence of having gone with the victim to her room and there experienced what he described as an LSD 'trip'. He explained how he had the illusion of descending to the centre of the earth and being attacked by snakes, with which he had fought. It was not seriously disputed that he had killed the victim in the course of this experience, but he said he had no knowledge of what he was doing and no intention to harm her. He was charged with murder, but the jury evidently accepted that he lacked the necessary intention to kill or to do grievous bodily harm ...

For the purposes of criminal responsibility we see no reason to distinguish between the effect of drugs voluntarily taken and drunkenness voluntarily induced. [His Lordship then quoted from the speech of Lord Birkenhead in *DPP v Beard* [1920] AC 479, 499, 500 and from the speeches of Lord Denning in *Bratty v Attorney General for Northern Ireland* [1963] AC 386, 410 and *Attorney General for Northern Ireland v Gallagher* [1963] AC 349, 381. His Lordship went on to hold:] Those authorities show quite clearly, in our opinion, that it was well established that no specific intent was necessary to support a conviction for manslaughter based upon a killing in the course of an unlawful act and that, accordingly, self-induced drunkenness was no defence to such a charge.

In the case of manslaughter by neglect, however, it has been recognised that some mental element must be established ...[His Lordship quoted from the

> speech of Lord Atkin in *Andrews v DPP* [1937] AC 576, 582, 583 and from the judgment of Edmund Davis J in *R v Church* [1966] 1 QB 59, 69. His Lordship continued:] All that the judgment in *Church's* case says in terms is that whereas, formerly, a killing by any unlawful act amounted to manslaughter, this consequence does not now inexorably follow unless the unlawful act is one in which ordinary sober and responsible people would recognise the existence of risk.
>
> The development recognised by *R v Church* relates to the type of act from which a charge of manslaughter may result, not in the intention (real or assumed) of the prisoner ...
>
> The decision in *R v Church* was referred to in this court later in *R v Lamb* [1967] 2 QB 981, where the prisoner had pointed a revolver at the victim in the belief, as he said, that there was no round in the chamber, but the revolver had fired and the victim was killed. It was pointed out in this court that no unlawful act on the part of the prisoner had been proved in the absence of the necessary intent to constitute an assault. But this is intention of a different kind. Even if intent has to be proved to constitute the unlawful act, no specific further intent is required to turn that act into manslaughter ...
>
> We can dispose of the present application by reiterating that when the killing results from an unlawful act of the prisoner no specific intent has to be proved to convict of manslaughter, and self-induced intoxication is accordingly no defence. Since in the present case the acts complained of were obviously likely to cause harm to the victim (and did, in fact, kill her) no acquittal was possible and the verdict of manslaughter, at the least, was inevitable ...

4 November 1969: The Appeal Committee of the House of Lords (**Lord Wilberforce**, **Viscount Dilhorne** and **Lord Pearson**) refused leave to appeal.

The act must be a dangerous one

The act must be a dangerous one in the sense that it is an act which a reasonable person would regard as being likely to cause bodily harm (in other words, an objective test). See *R v Church* [1966] 1 QB 59 and *DPP v Newbury* [1977] AC 500. The harm likely to result from the unlawful act must be physical harm and the physical harm must be foreseeable: see *R v Dawson* (1985) 81 CR App R 150; *R v Watson* [1989] 1 WLR 684.

Where the accused believes that the act is not dangerous but the belief is mistaken the act will still be regarded as a dangerous one. For example, firing a gun at someone with the intention of frightening them, and hence committing an assault, but in the mistaken belief that the gun contains only blank cartridges: see *R v Ball* [1989] Crim LR 730.

The act must be one which is likely to cause immediate injury. Supplying dangerous drugs to someone else is not a dangerous act in this sense, because the mere act of supply does not result in danger; danger only arises if the recipient ingests or injects the drugs: see *R v Dalby* [1982] 1 WLR 425.

Although in *Dalby* Waller LJ says that the act must be directed at the victim, this need not be the case. For example, in *R v Mitchell* [1983] QB 741 the defendant assaulted one person, who fell on top of an elderly woman; the woman died and the defendant was convicted of manslaughter. Similarly, in *R v Goodfellow* (1986) 83 Cr App R 23 the defendant's act – arson – was directed at property and not at the people who died in the fire; nonetheless he was held guilty of manslaughter.

R v Church [1966] 1 QB 59 (CA)

Facts: On Sunday 31 May 1964 the dead body of Sylvia Jeannette Nott was found in the River Ouse within a few yards of the appellant's van, which stood near the river bank. The corpse bore the marks of grave injuries. There had been some degree of manual strangulation. Those injuries were likely to have caused unconsciousness and eventually death, but they had been inflicted about an hour or half an hour before death took place and did not in fact cause death. According to the medical evidence, the deceased's injuries were inflicted not long before she was thrown into the river, but she was alive when that was done. She continued to breathe for an appreciable time afterwards and the eventual cause of death was drowning. When interviewed by the police, the appellant said that he had taken the woman to his van to have sex with her, that he was unable to satisfy her, that she reproached him and slapped his face. They then had a fight, in the course of which he knocked her out. He said, 'I tried shaking her to wake her up for about half an hour, but she didn't wake up, so I panicked and dragged her out of the van and put her in the river'. At his trial he repeated this account and added, for the first time, 'I thought she was dead'.

Edmund Davies J: ... The gravity of the injuries inflicted during life clearly pointed to an intention by the appellant to cause grievous bodily harm to or the death of Mrs Nott. Her death was in fact brought about by the action of the appellant in shortly thereafter throwing her still-living body into the river. Did it make any difference, as far as the murder charge was concerned, whether or not the appellant believed she was then already dead?

[His Lordship then quoted from the summing up and went on:]

The jury were thus told in plain terms that they could not convict of murder unless it had been proved that the appellant knew that Mrs Nott was still alive when he threw her into the river or (at least) that he did not believe she was dead. We venture to express the view that such a direction was unduly benevolent to the appellant and that the jury should have been told that it was still open to them to convict of murder, notwithstanding that the appellant may have thought his blows and attempt at strangulation had actually produced death when he threw the body into the river, if they regarded the appellant's behaviour from the moment he first struck her to the moment when he threw her into the river as a series of acts designed to cause death or grievous bodily harm. See *Thabo Meli v The Queen* [1954] 1 WLR 228. In the present case, the jury, directed as they were, acquitted of murder ...

... Stressing that we are here leaving entirely out of account those ingredients of homicide which might justify a verdict of manslaughter on the grounds of (a) criminal negligence, or (b) provocation or (c) diminished responsibility, the conclusion of this court is that an unlawful act causing the death of another cannot, simply because it is an unlawful act, render a manslaughter verdict inevitable. For such a verdict inexorably to follow, the unlawful act must be such as all sober and reasonable people would inevitably recognise must subject the other person to, at least, the risk of some harm resulting therefrom, albeit not serious harm ...

... In the light of *Thabo Meli v The Queen* it is conceded on behalf of the appellant that, on the murder charge, the trial judge was perfectly entitled to direct the jury, as he did: 'Unless you find that something happened in the course of this evening between the infliction of the injuries and the decision to throw the body into the water, you may undoubtedly treat the whole course of conduct of the accused as one'.

But for some reason not clear to this court, appellant's counsel denies that such an approach is possible when one is considering a charge of manslaughter. We fail to see why. We adopt as sound Dr Glanville Williams's view in his book, *Criminal Law*, 1961 that, 'If a killing by the first act would have been manslaughter, a later destruction of the supposed corpse should also be manslaughter'. Had Mrs Nott died of her initial injuries a manslaughter verdict might quite conceivably have been returned on the basis that the accused inflicted them under the influence of provocation or that the jury were not convinced that they were inflicted with murderous intent. All that was lacking in the direction given in this case was that, when the judge turned to consider manslaughter, he did not again tell the jury that they were entitled (if they thought fit) to regard the conduct of the appellant in relation of Mrs Nott as constituting throughout a series of acts which culminated in her death, and that, if that was how they regarded the accused's behaviour, it mattered not whether he believed her to be alive or dead when he threw her in the river ...

DPP v Newbury and Jones [1977] AC 500 (HL)

Lord Salmon: My Lords, on 11 October 1974, the train travelling from Pontypridd to Cardiff was approaching a bridge which crossed the railway line. The guard was sitting next to the driver of the train in the front cab. The driver noticed the heads of three boys above the parapet of the bridge. He saw one of the boys push something off the parapet towards the oncoming train. This proved to be part of a paving stone which some workmen had left on the parapet. It came through the glass window of the cab in which the driver and the guard were sitting, struck the guard and killed him. There was ample evidence that just as the train was about to reach the bridge the two appellants, who were each about 15 years of age, were jointly concerned in pushing over the parapet the piece of paving stone which killed the guard. They were jointly charged with manslaughter ... The point of law certified to be of general public importance is 'can a defendant be properly convicted of manslaughter, when his mind is not affected by drink or drugs, if he did not foresee that his act might cause harm to another?'

The learned trial judge did not direct the jury that they should acquit the appellants unless they were satisfied beyond a reasonable doubt that the appellants had foreseen that they might cause harm to someone by pushing the piece of paving stone off the parapet into the path of the approaching train. In my view the learned trial judge was quite right not to give such a direction to the jury ... In *R v Larkin* (1942) 29 Cr App R 18, Humphreys J said at 23:

> Where the act which a person is engaged in performing is unlawful, then if at the same time it is a dangerous act, that is, an act which is likely to injure another person, and quite inadvertently the doer of the act causes the death of that other person by that act, then he is guilty of manslaughter.

... [T]hat is an admirably clear statement of the law which has been applied many times. It makes it plain (a) that an accused is guilty of manslaughter if it is proved that he intentionally did an act which was unlawful and dangerous and that that act inadvertently caused death and (b) that it is unnecessary to prove that the accused knew that the act was unlawful or dangerous. This is one of the reasons why cases of manslaughter vary so infinitely in their gravity. They may amount to little more than pure inadvertence and sometimes to little less than murder ...

> ... In judging whether the act was dangerous the test is not did the accused recognise that it was dangerous but would all sober and reasonable people recognise its danger ...

Lord Edmund Davies delivered a concurring speech.

R v Dawson, Nolan and Walmsley (1985) 81 Cr App R 150 (CA)

Facts: The three appellants attempted to rob a petrol filling station but fled when the attendant pressed an alarm button. The attendant, who suffered from a heart condition, collapsed and died shortly afterwards. The appellants were convicted of manslaughter. At their trial, medical experts were of the opinion that the attempted robbery was responsible for the attendant's death; but they could not rule out the possibility of a heart attack having occurred before the attempted robbery.

Watkins LJ: ... It has, in our experience, been generally understood that the harm referred to in the second element of the offence of manslaughter, namely the unlawful act, must be one that all sober and reasonable people would realise was likely to cause some, albeit not serious, harm, means physical harm ...

... [T]here seems to us to be no sensible reason why shock produced by fright should not come within the definition of harm in this context ... Shock can produce devastating and lasting effects, for instance upon the nervous system. That is surely harm, ie injury to the person. Why not harm in this context?

... We shall assume without deciding the point, although we incline to favour the proposition, that harm in the context of manslaughter includes injury to the person through the operation of shock emanating from fright ...

... In our judgment, a proper direction would have been that the requisite harm is caused if the unlawful act so shocks the victim as to cause him physical injury.

... [The] test [of knowledge] can only be undertaken upon the basis of the knowledge gained by a sober and reasonable man as though he were present at the scene of and watched the unlawful act being performed and who knows that, as in the present case, an unloaded replica gun was in use, but that the victim may have thought it was a loaded gun in working order. In other words, he has the same knowledge as the man attempting to rob and no more. It was never suggested that any of these appellants knew that their victim had a bad heart. They knew nothing about him ...

R v Watson [1989] 1 WLR 684 (CA)

Lord Lane CJ: ... The facts of the case, in so far as they are relevant, were as follows. Late at night on 11 December 1986 two men, one of whom was the appellant, broke into the home of a man called Harold Moyler. Mr Moyler was 87 years old and suffered from a serious condition of the heart. He lived alone. The two men first threw a brick through the window and, having made entry to the house, confronted Mr Moyler as he woke up, abused him verbally and then made off without stealing anything.

Mr Moyler died an hour and a half later as the result of a heart attack. The case for the Crown was that the heart attack was a direct consequence of the unlawful actions of the appellant and his colleague ...

It was accepted that the judge correctly defined the offence of manslaughter as it applied to the circumstances as follows:

> Manslaughter is the offence committed when one person causes the death of another by an act which is unlawful and which is also dangerous, dangerous

> in the sense that it is an act which all sober and reasonable people would inevitably realise must subject the victim to the risk of some harm resulting whether the defendant realised that or not.

The first point taken on behalf of the appellant is this. When one is deciding whether the sober and reasonable person (the bystander) would realise the risk of some harm resulting to the victim, how much knowledge of the circumstances does one attribute to the bystander? The appellant contends that the unlawful act here was the burglary as charged in the indictment.

The charge was laid under s 9(1)(a) of the Theft Act 1968, the allegation being that the appellant had entered the building as a trespasser with intent to commit theft. Since that offence is committed at the first moment of entry, the bystander's knowledge is confined to that of the defendant at that moment. In the instant case there was no evidence that the appellant, at the moment of entry, knew the age or physical condition of Mr Moyler or even that he lived there alone.

The judge clearly took the view that the jury were entitled to ascribe to the bystander the knowledge which the appellant gained during the whole of his stay in the house and so directed them. Was this a misdirection? In our judgment it was not. The unlawful act in the present circumstances comprised the whole of the burglarious intrusion and did not come to an end upon the appellant's foot crossing the threshold or window sill. That being so, the appellant (and therefore the bystander) during the course of the unlawful act must have become aware of Mr Moyler's frailty and approximate age, and the judge's directions were accordingly correct ...

R v Ball [1989] Crim LR 730 (CA)

Facts: The defendant shot a neighbour. At his trial, the defendant's defence was lack of intention to kill or cause harm: he thought he had loaded the gun with a blank cartridge. It appeared that he had previously attempted to fire two such blanks to scare and frighten the deceased from his land. For reasons which were not clear they had not detonated. He said that he kept live and blank cartridges together in the pocket of his overalls in the house. He had grabbed a handful when he had picked up the gun, intending only to frighten the deceased.

Held, dismissing the appeal: *R v Dawson* 81 Cr App R 150 went no further than showing that the sober and reasonable man must look at the unlawful act to see if it was dangerous and not at peculiarities of the victim; in that case the victim had a heart condition. In cases of involuntary manslaughter, there was a distinction between unlawful and lawful acts resulting in death. Where the act was unlawful, the question for the jury was whether it was also dangerous in the sense that all sober and reasonable people would inevitably realise that it would subject the victim to the risk of some harm, albeit not serious harm. Questions of gross or criminal negligence were not material. In many cases the judge might have to give a direction on the question of a lawful act and gross or criminal negligence because the jury might not accept that an accused deliberately did an unlawful act. But in this case it was accepted on behalf of the appellant that he had unlawfully assaulted the deceased. His act in firing at the deceased was 'an act directed at the victim' (*per* Waller LJ in *R v Dalby* 74 Cr App R 348 at 352), with 'no fresh intervening cause between the act and the death' (*per* Lord Lane CJ in *R v Goodfellow* 83 Cr App R 23). He had used his own cartridges and loaded the gun himself; no other agency was involved. In manslaughter arising from an unlawful and dangerous act, the accused's state of mind was relevant only to establish (a) that the act was committed intentionally; and (b) that it was an unlawful act (*DPP v Newbury* 62 Cr App R 291). Once (a) and (b) were established, the question whether the act was dangerous was to be judged not by the appellant's appreciation but by that of the sober reasonable man, and it was impossible to impute into his appreciation the mistaken belief that what he was doing was not dangerous because he thought he had a blank cartridge in the chamber. At that stage, his intention, foresight or knowledge was irrelevant.

R v Dalby [1982] 1 WLR 425 (CA)

Facts: The appellant was a drug addict. He lawfully obtained upon prescription a number of tablets of a class A controlled drug. He then supplied some tablets to Stefan O'Such, a friend with whom he was staying, who was also a drug addict. The two of them injected themselves intravenously before they parted company for the evening. During that evening O'Such injected himself intravenously twice more with the help of another person. When the appellant returned to O'Such's flat, O'Such was asleep in the living room; in the morning he could not be woken. At 3 pm O'Such's wife called an ambulance. When the ambulance attendants arrived they found that he was dead.

Waller LJ: ... It was submitted on behalf of the appellant: (1) that the unlawful act must be one directed at the victim; the supply of drugs in this case was not such a direct act; (2) that the supply of drugs can be harmless or extremely harmful according to the manner in which the victim deals with them; (3) that the drugs in this case were taken voluntarily by the victim in a form, ie intravenously, and in a quantity which together made them extremely dangerous and resulted in death; the line of causation was therefore broken between the unlawful act of supplying drugs and the death resulting from intravenous injection of too great a quantity of them ...

...[I]n all of the reported cases of manslaughter by an unlawful and dangerous act, the researches of counsel have failed to find any case where the act was not a direct act.

The difficulty in the present case is that the act of supplying a controlled drug was not an act which caused direct harm. It was an act which made it possible, or even likely, that harm would occur subsequently, particularly if the drug was supplied to somebody who was on drugs. In all the reported cases, the physical act has been one which inevitably would subject the other person to the risk of some harm from the act itself. In this case, the supply of drugs would itself have caused no harm unless the deceased had subsequently used the drugs in a form and quantity which was dangerous ...

In the judgment of this court, the unlawful act of supplying drugs was not an act directed against the person of O'Such and the supply did not cause any direct injury to him. The kind of harm envisaged in all the reported cases of involuntary manslaughter was physical injury of some kind as an immediate and inevitable result of the unlawful act, eg a blow on the chin which knocks the victim against a wall causing a fractured skull and death, or threatening with a loaded gun which accidentally fires, or dropping a large stone on a train (*DPP v Newbury* [1977] AC 500) or threatening another with an open razor and stumbling with death resulting: see *R v Larkin* 29 Cr App R 18.

In the judgment of this court, where the charge of manslaughter is based on an unlawful and dangerous act, it must be an act directed at the victim and likely to cause immediate injury, however slight ...

4 March 1982: The Appeal Committee of the House of Lords (**Lord Wilberforce**, **Lord Scarman** and **Lord Bridge of Harwich**) dismissed a petition by the Crown for leave to appeal.

R v Mitchell [1983] QB 741 (CA)

Staughton J: ... The facts alleged by the prosecution at the trial were briefly as follows. On 26 March 1981, the appellant, who was aged 22 at the time, was in a busy post office at Tottenham. An altercation arose when he tried to force himself into a queue or in some other way to be served before those who had been waiting longer than he had. Mr Edward Smith, who was aged 72, spoke to him about his behaviour. There was some argument, and the appellant hit Mr Smith in the mouth, causing him to stagger back and hit the back of his head against a glass panel above the post office counter. The glass panel shattered. Mr Smith recovered and moved forward. The appellant then either hit Mr Smith again or else threw him, so that he fell into other people who were waiting in the post office, Mr Smith fell against Mrs Anne Crafts, a lady aged 89. Both Mr Smith and Mrs Crafts fell to the ground. Mr Smith suffered a bruise in the back of his head, and his lower lip was cut and swollen. Mrs Crafts suffered a broken femur. She was taken to hospital, and on 31 March 1981, an operation was performed to replace her hip joint. She appeared to make a satisfactory recovery, but on 2 April 1981, she died suddenly. The cause of death was pulmonary embolism caused by thrombosis of the left leg veins, which in turn was caused by fracture of the femur ...

Both counsel were agreed that there are four elements in this class of manslaughter, as follows: first, there must be an act which is unlawful; second, it must be a dangerous act, in the sense that a sober and reasonable person would inevitably recognise that it carried some risk of harm, albeit not serious harm (that being an objective test): third, the act must be a substantial cause of death; fourth, the act itself must be intentional. No question relating to any other class of manslaughter (such as manslaughter by gross negligence) arose in this case.

The main question argued was whether the person at whom the act is aimed must also be the person whose death is caused ...

We can see no reason of policy for holding that an act calculated to harm A cannot be manslaughter if it in fact kills B. The criminality of the doer of the act is precisely the same whether it is A or B who dies. A person who throws a stone at A is just as guilty if, instead of hitting and killing A, it hits and kills B. Parliament evidently held the same view in relation to the allied offence of unlawful and malicious wounding contrary to s 20 of the Offences Against the Person Act 1861: see *R v Latimer* (1886) 17 QBD 359. We accordingly reject the argument of counsel for the appellant that, because the appellant's acts were aimed at Mr Smith, it cannot have been manslaughter when they caused the death of Mrs Crafts.

The second limb of the [appellant's] argument was based wholly on *R v Dalby* [1982] 1 WLR 425. It was argued that for manslaughter to be established the act of the defendant must be shown to have caused direct harm to the victim. On that ground, although it would be manslaughter to throw a stone at A which hits and kills B, it was submitted that there was no manslaughter in the present case, because there was no physical contact between the appellant and Mrs Crafts.

... Here, however ... [a]lthough there was no direct contact between the appellant and Mrs Crafts, she was injured as a direct and immediate result of his act. Thereafter her death occurred. The only question was one of causation: whether her death was caused by the appellant's acts. It was open to the jury to conclude that it was so caused; and they evidently reached that conclusion.

Since the conclusion of the argument we have seen a transcript of the judgment of this court in *R v Pagett* (1983) Times, 4 February. This supports the views we have expressed in two respects. Robert Goff LJ, delivering the judgment of the court, said:

> If, as the jury must have found to have occurred in the present case, the appellant used Gail Kinchin by force and against her will as a shield to protect him from any shots fired by the police, the effect is that he committed not one but two unlawful acts, both of which were dangerous: the act of firing at the police, and the act of holding Gail Kinchen as a shield in front of him when the police might well fire shots in his direction in self-defence. Either act could, in our judgment ... constitute the *actus reus* of the manslaughter.

In the case of the first act mentioned – firing at the police – it could scarcely be said to have been *aimed* at the ultimate victim, Gail Kinchen; nor could it be said by itself to have caused harm to the victim by direct physical contact. We agree that neither requirement exists for manslaughter. Granted an unlawful and dangerous act, the test is one of causation. That is clear from the transcript, where Robert Goff LJ said:

> The question whether an accused person can be guilty of homicide, either murder or manslaughter, of a victim the immediate cause of whose death is the act of another person must be determined on the ordinary principles of causation ...

... [I]t was [also] argued [by the appellant] that the judge failed to direct the jury that the appellant's act had to be a deliberate act, in the sense that he intended to do it ...

...There need not be any intention to injure or kill, or any foresight that injury or death would be caused, provided that all sober and reasonable people would have recognised the act to be dangerous ...

... All of the appellant's actions ... were obviously and admittedly deliberate actions. There was no suggestion of inadvertence, or even automation, in any part of his conduct ...

R v Goodfellow (1986) 83 Cr App R 23 (CA)

The Lord Chief Justice: ... On 14 August 1984 in the early hours of the morning, the appellant set light to the council house he occupied at 24, Cossock Terrace, Pallion. He poured petrol over the sideboard, chair and walls of the downstairs living room, and then set the house on fire by igniting the petrol. In the ensuing blaze three people died: his wife Sarah aged 22, another young woman named Jillian Stuart with whom the appellant was having a liaison, who was in the house that night, and the appellant's two-year-old son Darren.

The background to these events was as follows. The appellant had been having difficulties with two men in the locality. One of them had been fined for damaging the front door of No 24. Hence the appellant wanted to move. He had no chance of exchanging his council house for another because he was some '£300 in arrears with his rent'. He therefore conceived the idea of setting No 24 on fire and making it look as though the fire had been caused by a petrol bomb thrown through the window by one of the men. This story was what he initially told the police when they started to make enquiries ...

It seems to us that this was a case which was capable of falling within either or both types of manslaughter. On the *Lawrence* aspect, the jury might well have been satisfied that the appellant was acting in such a manner as to create an obvious and serious risk of causing physical injury to some person, and second that he, having recognised that there was some risk involved, had nevertheless gone on to take it.

> This was equally, in our view, a case for the 'unlawful and dangerous act' direction. Where the defendant does an unlawful act of such a kind as all sober and reasonable people would inevitably recognise must subject another person to, at least, the risk of some harm resulting therefrom, albeit not serious harm and causes death thereby, he is guilty of manslaughter: see *R v Church* [1966] 1 QB 59 ...
>
> The questions which the jury have to decide on the charge of manslaughter of this nature [ie the unlawful act form] are (1) Was the act intentional? (2) Was it unlawful? (3) Was it an act which any reasonable person would realise was bound to subject some other human being to the risk of physical harm, albeit not necessarily serious harm? (4) Was that act the cause of death? ...

Manslaughter by gross negligence

The elements of this form of manslaughter are set out comprehensively in *R v Adomako* [1995] 1 AC 171 (in which the House of Lords applied the principles laid down in *R v Bateman* (1925) 19 Cr App R 8 and *Andrews v DPP* [1937] AC 576.

Those elements are:

(1) The accused must have been negligent, in the tortious sense of having breached a duty of care owed to the victim;

(2) That breach must have caused the death of the victim;

(3) The negligence must be so serious that is can be characterised as 'gross negligence', and therefore a crime.

Whether the defendant's breach of duty amounts to gross negligence depends on the seriousness of that breach of duty and whether the defendant's conduct was so bad, in all the circumstances, as to amount to a criminal act or omission.

R v Adomako [1995] 1 AC 171 (HL)

Facts: The defendant was an anaesthetist. He failed to notice that the endotracheal tube had become disconnected. The patient suffered a cardiac arrest and died.

Lord Mackay of Clashfern LC: ... The Court of Appeal (Criminal Division) ... certified that a point of law of general public importance was involved in the decision to dismiss the appeal, namely:

> In cases of manslaughter by criminal negligence not involving driving but involving a breach of duty is it a sufficient direction to the jury to adopt the gross negligence test set out by the Court of Appeal in the present case following *R v Bateman* (1925) 19 Cr App R 8 and *Andrews v DPP* [1937] AC 576, without reference to the test of recklessness as defined in *R v Lawrence (Stephen)* [1982] AC 510 or as adapted to the circumstances of the case?

... I begin with *R v Bateman* 19 Cr App R 8 and the opinion of Lord Hewart CJ, where he said, at 10–11:

> In expounding the law to juries on the trial of indictments for manslaughter by negligence, judges have often referred to the distinction between civil and criminal liability for death by negligence. The law of criminal liability for negligence is conveniently explained in that way. If A has caused the death of B by alleged negligence, then in order to establish civil liability, the plaintiff must prove (in addition to pecuniary loss caused by the death) that

> A owed a duty to B to take care, that that duty was not discharged, and that the default caused the death of B. To convict A of manslaughter, the prosecution must prove the three things above-mentioned and must satisfy the jury, in addition, that A's negligence amounted to a crime. In the civil action, if it is proved that A fell short of the standard of reasonable care required by law, it matters not how far he fell short of that standard. The extent of his liability depends not on the degree of negligence, but on the amount of damage done. In a criminal court, on the contrary, the amount and degree of negligence are the determining question. There must be *mens rea.*

Later he said, at 11–12:

> In explaining to juries the test which they should apply to determine whether the negligence, in the particular case, amounted or did not amount to a crime, judges have used many epithets, such as 'culpable', 'criminal', 'gross', 'wicked', 'clear', 'complete'. But, whatever epithet be used and whether an epithet be used or not, in order to establish criminal liability the facts must be such that, in the opinion of the jury, the negligence of the accused went beyond a mere matter of compensation between subjects and showed such disregard for the life and safety of others as to amount to a crime against the state and conduct deserving punishment.

After dealing with a number of authorities Lord Hewart CJ went on, at 12–13:

> The law as laid down in these cases may be thus summarised: If a person holds himself out as possessing special skill and knowledge and he is consulted, as possessing such skill and knowledge, by or on behalf of a patient, he owes a duty to the patient to use due caution in undertaking the treatment. If he accepts the responsibility and undertakes the treatment and the patient submits to his direction and treatment accordingly, he owes a duty to the patient to use diligence, care, knowledge, skill and caution in administering the treatment. No contractual relation is necessary, nor is it necessary that the service be rendered for reward. It is for the judge to direct the jury what standard to apply and for the jury to say whether that standard has been reached. The jury should not exact the highest, or a very high, standard, nor should they be content with a very low standard. The law requires a fair and reasonable standard of care and competence. This standard must be reached in all the matters above mentioned. If the patient's death has been caused by the defendant's indolence or carelessness, it will not avail to show that he had sufficient knowledge; nor will it avail to prove that he was diligent in attendance, if the patient has been killed by his gross ignorance and unskilfulness. No further observation need be made with regard to cases where the death is alleged to have been caused by indolence or carelessness. As regards cases where incompetence is alleged, it is only necessary to say that the unqualified practitioner cannot claim to be measured by any lower standard than that which is applied to a qualified man. As regards cases of alleged recklessness, juries are likely to distinguish between the qualified and the unqualified man. There may be recklessness in undertaking the treatment and recklessness in the conduct of it. It is, no doubt, conceivable that a qualified man may be held liable for recklessly undertaking a case which he knew, or should have known, to be beyond his powers, or for making his patient the subject of reckless experiment. Such cases are likely to be rare. In the case of the quack, where the treatment has been proved to be incompetent and to have caused the patient's death, juries are not likely to hesitate in finding liability on the ground that the defendant undertook, and continued to treat, a case involving the gravest risk to his

> patient, when he knew he was not competent to deal with it, or would have known if he had paid any proper regard to the life and safety of his patient.

The foregoing observations deal with civil liability. To support an indictment for manslaughter the prosecution must prove the matters necessary to establish civil liability (except pecuniary loss), and, in addition, must satisfy the jury that the negligence or incompetence of the accused went beyond a mere matter of compensation and showed such disregard for the life and safety of others as to amount to a crime against the state and conduct deserving punishment.

Next I turn to *Andrews v DPP* [1973] AC 576 which was a case of manslaughter through dangerous driving of a motor car. In a speech with which all the other members of this House who sat agreed, Lord Atkin said at 581–82:

> of all crimes manslaughter appears to afford most difficulties of definition, for it concerns homicide in so many and so varying conditions. From the early days when any homicide involved penalty the law has gradually evolved 'through successive differentiations and integrations' until it recognises murder on the one hand, based mainly, though not exclusively, on an intention to kill, and manslaughter on the other hand, based mainly, though not exclusively, on the absence of intention to kill but with the presence of an element of 'unlawfulness' which is the elusive factor. In the present case it is only necessary to consider manslaughter from the point of view of an unintentional killing caused by negligence, that is, the omission of a duty to take care ...

Lord Atkin then referred to the judgment of Lord Hewart CJ from which I have already quoted and went on at 583:

> Here again I think with respect that the expressions used are not, indeed they were probably not intended to be, a precise definition of the crime. I do not myself find the connotations of *mens rea* helpful in distinguishing between degrees of negligence, nor do the ideas of crime and punishment in themselves carry a jury much further in deciding whether in a particular case the degree of negligence shown is a crime and deserves punishment. But the substance of the judgment is most valuable, and in my opinion is correct. In practice it has generally been adopted by judges in charging juries in all cases of manslaughter by negligence, whether in driving vehicles or otherwise. The principle to be observed is that cases of manslaughter in driving motor cars are but instances of a general rule applicable to all charges of homicide by negligence. Simple lack of care such as will constitute civil liability is not enough: for purposes of the criminal law there are degrees of negligence: and a very high degree of negligence is required to be proved before the felony is established. Probably of all the epithets that can be applied 'reckless' most nearly covers the case. It is difficult to visualise a case of death caused by reckless driving in the connotation of that term in ordinary speech which would not justify a conviction for manslaughter: but it is probably not all-embracing, for 'reckless' suggests an indifference to risk whereas the accused may have appreciated the risk and intended to avoid it and yet shown such a high degree of negligence in the means adopted to avoid the risk as would justify a conviction. If the principle of *Bateman's* case 19 Cr App R 8 is observed it will appear that the law of manslaughter has not changed by the introduction of motor vehicles on the road. Death caused by their negligent driving, though unhappily much more frequent, is to be treated in law as death caused by any other form of negligence: and juries should be directed accordingly.

In my opinion the law as stated in these two authorities is satisfactory as providing a proper basis for describing the crime of involuntary manslaughter. Since the decision in *Andrews* was a decision of your Lordships' House, it remains the most authoritative statement of the present law which I have been able to find ... On this basis in my opinion the ordinary principles of the law of negligence apply to ascertain whether or not the defendant has been in breach of a duty of care towards the victim who has died. If such breach of duty is established the next question is whether that breach of duty caused the death of the victim. If so, the jury must go on to consider whether that breach of duty should be characterised as gross negligence and therefore as a crime. This will depend on the seriousness of the breach of duty committed by the defendant in all the circumstances in which the defendant was placed when it occurred. The jury will have to consider whether the extent to which the defendant's conduct departed from the proper standard of care incumbent upon him, involving as it must have done a risk of death to the patient, was such that it should be judged criminal.

It is true that to a certain extent this involves an element of circularity, but in this branch of the law I do not believe that is fatal to its being correct as a test of how far conduct must depart from accepted standards to be characterised as criminal. This is necessarily a question of degree and an attempt to specify that degree more closely is I think likely to achieve only a spurious precision. The essence of the matter which is supremely a jury question is whether having regard to the risk of death involved, the conduct of the defendant was so bad in all the circumstances as to amount in their judgment to a criminal act or omission ...

For these reasons I am of the opinion that this appeal should be dismissed and that the certified question should be answered by saying:

> In cases of manslaughter by criminal negligence involving a breach of duty, it is a sufficient direction to the jury to adopt the gross negligence test set out by the Court of Appeal in the present case following *R v Bateman* 19 Cr App R 8 and *Andrews v DPP* [1937] AC 576 and that it is not necessary to refer to the definition of recklessness in *R v Lawrence* [1982] AC 510, although it is perfectly open to the trial judge to use the word 'reckless' in its ordinary meaning as part of his exposition of the law if he deems it appropriate in the circumstances of the particular case.

CHAPTER 22

NON-FATAL OFFENCES AGAINST THE PERSON

In this chapter we examine some of the more common offences of violence against the person contained in the Offences Against the Person Act 1861, as well as the offence of common assault.

THE OFFENCES AGAINST THE PERSON ACT 1861

Section 18: shooting or attempting to shoot, or wounding, with intent to do grievous bodily harm, or to resist apprehension

> Whosoever shall unlawfully and maliciously by any means whatsoever wound or cause any grievous bodily harm to any person ... with intent ... to do some ... grievous bodily harm to any person, or with intent to resist or prevent the lawful apprehension or detainer of any person, shall be guilty of [an offence], and being convicted thereof shall be liable ... to [imprisonment] for life ...

Section 20: inflicting bodily injury, with or without weapon

> Whosoever shall unlawfully and maliciously wound or inflict any grievous bodily harm upon any other person, either with or without any weapon or instrument, shall be guilty of [an offence], and being convicted thereof shall be liable ... to [imprisonment for not more than five years] ...

Section 47: assault occasioning actual bodily harm

> Whosoever shall be convicted upon an indictment of any assault occasioning actual bodily harm shall be liable ... to [imprisonment for five years]

CRIMINAL JUSTICE ACT 1988

Section 39: common assault

Common assault is triable only summarily. Charges of common assault, which was originally a common law offence, must be brought under s 39: see *DPP v Taylor* [1992] 1 QB 645.

Common assault is charged where there is an assault, in the sense of causing fear of violence, but no actual injury is caused. If some injury is caused, then a charge under s 47 of the Offences Against the Person Act 1861 is appropriate.

Assault

Although strictly speaking an 'assault' means to cause a person to apprehend use of violence and the actual blow is called a 'battery', the term 'common assault' encompasses assault and/or battery: see *R v Lynsey* [1995] 2 All ER 654 (CA).

Thus, the essence of an assault is causing another to fear violence. So, in *Logdon v DPP* [1976] Crim LR 121 the defendant threatened the victim with an imitation firearm. The defendant did not intend to use any violence, but the victim believed that force was about to be used. The defendant's actions therefore amounted to an assault.

An assault has to be proved if the charge is one of common assault (s 39 of the Criminal Justice Act 1988) or one of assault occasioning actual bodily harm (s 47 of the Offences Against the Person Act 1861).

Fagan v Metropolitan Police Commissioner [1969] 1 QB 439 (DC)

Facts: On 31 August 1967 the appellant was reversing a motor car in Fortunegate Road, London, NW10, when Police Constable David Morris directed him to drive the car forwards to the kerbside and, standing in front of the car, pointed out a suitable place in which to park. At first the appellant stopped the car too far from the kerb for the officer's liking. Morris asked him to park closer and indicated a precise spot. The appellant drove forward towards him and stopped the car with the offside wheel on Morris's left foot. 'Get off, you are on my foot', said the officer. 'Fuck you, you can wait', said the appellant. The engine of the car stopped running. Morris repeated several times 'Get off my foot'. The appellant said reluctantly, 'OK, man, OK' and then slowly turned on the ignition of the vehicle and reversed it off the officer's foot. The appellant had either turned the ignition off to stop the engine or turned it off after the engine had stopped running.

The justices at quarter sessions on those facts were left in doubt as to whether the mounting of the wheel on to the officer's foot was deliberate or accidental. They were satisfied, however, beyond all reasonable doubt that the appellant 'knowingly, provocatively and unnecessarily allowed the wheel to remain on the foot after the officer said, "Get off, you are on my foot"'. They found that on those facts an assault was proved.

James J: ... The sole question is whether the prosecution proved facts which in law amounted to an assault.

[Counsel for the appellant]... contends that on the finding of the justices the initial mounting of the wheel could not be an assault and that the act of the wheel mounting the foot came to an end without there being any *mens rea*. It is argued that thereafter there was no act on the part of the appellant which could constitute an *actus reus* but only the omission or failure to remove the wheel as soon as he was asked. That failure, it is said, could not in law be an assault, nor could it in law provide the necessary *mens rea* to convert the original act of mounting the foot into an assault.

[Counsel for the Crown] argues that the first mounting of the foot was an *actus reus* which act continued until the moment of time at which the wheel was removed. During that continuing act, it is said, the appellant formed the necessary intention to constitute the element of *mens rea* and once that element was added to the continuing act, an assault took place ...

In our judgment, the question arising, which has been argued on general principles, falls to be decided on the facts of the particular case. An assault is any act which intentionally – or possibly recklessly – causes another person to apprehend immediate and unlawful personal violence. Although 'assault' is an independent crime and is to be treated as such, for practical purposes today 'assault' is generally synonymous with the term 'battery', and is a term used to mean the actual intended use of unlawful force to another person without his consent. On the facts of the present case, the 'assault' alleged involved a 'battery'. Where an assault involved a battery, it matters not, in our judgment, whether the battery is inflicted directly by the body of the offender or through the medium of some weapon or instrument controlled by the action of the offender. An assault may be committed by the laying of a hand on another, and the action does not cease to be an assault if it is a stick held in the hand and not the hand itself which is laid on the person of the victim. So, for our part, we see no difference in principle between the action of stepping on to a person's toe and maintaining that position and the action of driving a car on to a person's foot and sitting in the car while its position on the foot is maintained.

To constitute this offence, some intentional act must have been performed; a mere omission to act cannot amount to an assault. Without going into the question whether words alone can constitute an assault, it is clear that the words spoken by the appellant could not alone amount to an assault; they can only shed light on the appellant's action. For our part, we think that the crucial question is whether, in this case, the act of the appellant can be said to be complete and spent at the moment of time when the car wheel came to rest on the foot, or whether his act is to be regarded as a continuing act operating until the wheel was removed. In our judgment, a distinction is to be drawn between acts which are complete, though results may continue to flow, and those acts which are continuing. Once the act is complete, it cannot thereafter be said to be a threat to inflict unlawful force on the victim. If the act, as distinct from the results thereof, is a continuing act, there is a continuing threat to inflict unlawful force. If the assault involves a battery and that battery continues, there is a continuing act of assault. For an assault to be committed, both the elements of *actus reus* and *mens rea* must be present at the same time. The *actus reus* is the action causing the effect on the victim's mind: see the observations of Parke B, in *R v St George* (1840) 9 C & P 483. The *mens rea* is the intention to cause that effect. It is not necessary that *mens rea* should be present at the inception of the *actus reus*; it can be superimposed on an existing act. On the other hand, the subsequent inception of *mens rea* cannot convert an act which has been completed without *mens rea* into an assault.

In our judgment, the Willesden magistrates and quarter sessions were right in law. On the facts found, the action of the appellant may have been initially unintentional, but the time came when, knowing that the wheel was on the officer's foot, the appellant (1) remained seated in the car so that his body through the medium of the car was in contact with the officer, (2) switched off the ignition of the car, (3) maintained the wheel of the car on the foot, and (4) used words indicating the intention of keeping the wheel in that position. For our part, we cannot regard such conduct as mere omission or inactivity.

There was an act constituting a battery which at its inception was not criminal because there was no element of intention, but which became criminal from the moment the intention was formed to produce the apprehension which was flowing from the continuing act. The fallacy of the appellant's argument is that it seeks to equate the facts of this case with such a case where a motorist has accidentally run over a person and, that action having been completed, fails to assist the victim with the intent that the victim should suffer ...

Lord Parker CJ expressed agreement with **James J**; **Bridge J** delivered a dissenting judgment.

Smith v Chief Superintendent, Woking Police Station (1983) 76 Cr App R 234 (DC)

Kerr LJ: ... In view of the question of law I must also refer shortly to the evidence on the basis of which the justices convicted. The incident happened at about 11 pm, when Miss Mooney was in her room wearing a pink, knee-length nightie. There was a bay window and a side window. The curtains were drawn but they left a gap. She saw the defendant peering in and stated that he was right up against the window. She said: 'I instantly recognised him. I was very scared, very shocked. He was there about three or four seconds. I walked backwards and could no longer see him. I turned and he was at the other window, again right against the glass. I just stood and stared at him, didn't know what to do. He was just standing there, didn't seem he was going to go away. I jumped across the bed towards the window and screamed. I was terrified, absolutely terrified. He must have seen me look at him. He moved away when I went across the bed. I looked at him for about 20 seconds at the side window. I called the police.'

Then she says that she was scared and after the incident she was very jumpy and shocked. The defendant, having first denied the incident, later admitted it and agreed that he would be scared stiff in the situation in which Miss Mooney found herself ...

It is ... common ground that the definition of an assault ... [is] 'any act which intentionally – or recklessly – causes another to apprehend immediate and unlawful violence' ... [T]here must be, on the part of the defendant, a hostile intent calculated to cause apprehension in the mind of the victim.

In the present case, on the findings which I have summarised, there was quite clearly an intention to cause fear, an intention to frighten, and that intention produced the intended effect as the result of what the defendant did, in that it did frighten and indeed terrify Miss Mooney to the extent that she screamed. It is not a case where she was merely startled or surprised or ashamed to be seen in her nightclothes; she was terrified as the result of what the defendant deliberately did, knowing and either intending or being reckless as to whether it would cause that fear in her ...

When one is in a state of terror one is very often unable to analyse precisely what one is frightened of as likely to happen next. When I say that, I am speaking of a situation such as the present, where the person who causes one to be terrified is immediately adjacent, albeit on the other side of the window ...

In the present case the defendant intended to frighten Miss Mooney and Miss Mooney was frightened. As it seems to me, there is no need for a finding that what she was frightened of, which she probably could not analyse at that moment, was some innominate terror of some potential violence. It was clearly a situation where the basis of the fear which was instilled in her was that she did not know what the defendant was going to do next, but that, whatever he might be going to do next, and sufficiently immediately for the purposes of the offence, was something of a violent nature. In effect, as it seems to me, it was wholly open to the justices to infer that her state of mind was not only that of terror, which they did find, but terror of some immediate violence ...

ASSAULT OCCASIONING ACTUAL BODILY HARM (SECTION 47)

The elements of the s 47 offence are:

(1) an assault ...

(2) resulting in actual bodily harm.

Actual bodily harm

Actual bodily harm means harm which is more than trivial but less than that required for the more serious offences under ss 18 and 20 of the 1861 Act. There must be a causal link between the assault and the harm: see *R v Roberts* (1971) 56 Cr App R 95). Actual bodily harm includes, in rare cases, psychiatric damage.

R v Roberts (1971) 56 Cr App R 95 (CA)

Facts: The victim of the alleged assault had been at a party. She left the party at about 3 am, having agreed to travel with the appellant in his car to what he said was another party in Warrington. After they had driven out of Warrington in the direction of Liverpool, she asked the appellant where the party was, and he said that they were going to Runcorn. They took a curious route to Runcorn, and eventually, she said, they stopped on what seemed like a big cinder track. The time by then was apparently about 4 am. Then, she said, 'He just jumped on me. He put his hands up my clothes and tried to take my tights off. I started to fight him off, but the door of the car was locked and I could not find the catch. Suddenly he grabbed me and then he drove off and I started to cry and asked him to take me home. He told me to take my clothes off and, if I did not take my clothes off, he would let me walk home, so I asked him to let me do that. He said, that if he did, he would beat me up before he let me go. He said that he had done this before and had got away with it and he started to pull my coat off. He was using foul language.' And then she said that she told him, 'I am not like that', and he said something like, 'You are all like that'. Then he drove on. 'Again', said the girl, 'he tried to get my coat off, so I got hold of my handbag and I jumped out of the car. When I opened the door, he said something and revved the car up and I jumped out. The next thing I remember he was backing towards me and so I ran to the nearest house. He backed and shouted and then he drove off', and then she remembered being in the lady's house. She said she was taken to hospital, where she was treated for some concussion and for some grazing, and was detained in hospital for three days. The defendant was charged with assault occasioning actual bodily harm.

Stephenson LJ: ... [The jury] had to consider: was the appellant guilty of occasioning [the victim] actual bodily harm? Of course, for that to be established, it had to be established that he was responsible in law and in fact for her injuries caused by leaving in a hurry the moving car...

We have been ... referred to ... *Beech* (1912) 7 Cr App R 197, which was a case of a woman jumping out of a window and injuring herself ... In that case the Court of Criminal Appeal (at p 200) approved the direction given by the trial judge in these terms: 'Will you say whether the conduct of the prisoner amounted to a threat of causing injury to this young woman, was the act of jumping the natural consequence of the conduct of the prisoner, and was the grievous bodily harm the result of the conduct of the prisoner?' That, said the Court, was a proper direction as far as the law went, and they were satisfied that there was evidence before the jury of the prisoner causing actual bodily harm to the woman. 'No-one could say' said Darling J when giving the judgment of the Court, 'that if she jumped from the window it was not a natural consequence of the prisoner's conduct. It was a very likely thing for a woman to do as the result of the threats of a man who was conducting himself as this man indisputably was.'

This Court thinks that that correctly states the law...

... The test is: Was it [the action of the victim which resulted in actual bodily harm] the natural result of what the alleged assailant said and did, in the sense that it was something that could reasonably have been foreseen as the consequence of what he was saying or doing? As it was put in one of the old cases, it had got to be shown to be his act, and if of course the victim does something so 'daft', in the words of the appellant in this case, or so unexpected, not that this particular assailant did not actually foresee it but that no reasonable man could be expected to foresee it, then it is only in a very remote and unreal sense a consequence of his assault, it is really occasioned by a voluntary act on the part of the victim which could not reasonably be foreseen and which breaks the chain of causation between the assault and harm or injury.

R v Chan-Fook [1994] 1 WLR 689 (CA)

Hobhouse LJ: ... [The words 'actual bodily harm'] are three words of the English language which require no elaboration and in the ordinary course should not receive any. The word 'harm' is a synonym for injury. The word 'actual' indicates that the injury (although there is no need for it to be permanent) should not be so trivial as to be wholly insignificant. The purpose of the definition in s 47 is to define an element of aggravation in the assault. It must be an assault which besides being an assault (or assault and battery) causes to the victim some injury ...

In certain cases an explanation may be required of what is involved in the word 'bodily' ...

The first question on the present appeal is whether the inclusion of the word 'bodily' in the phrase 'actual bodily harm' limits harm to harm to the skin, flesh and bones of the victim. Lynskey J in *R v Miller* [1954] 2 QB 282 rejected this submission. In our judgment he was right to do so. The body of the victim includes all parts of his body, including his organs, his nervous system and his brain. Bodily injury therefore may include injury to any of those parts of his body responsible for his mental and other faculties. The matter was well summarised by Lord Wilberforce in *McLoughlin v O'Brian* [1983] 1 AC 410 at 418:

> Whatever is unknown about the mind-body relationship (and the area of ignorance seems to expand with that of knowledge), it is now accepted by medical science that recognisable and severe physical damage to the human body and system may be caused by the impact, through the senses, of external events on the mind. There may thus be produced what is as identifiable an illness as any that may be caused by direct physical impact.

As is pointed out by Lord Wilberforce earlier in his speech the conventional phrase 'nervous shock' is now inaccurate and inappropriate. Observations to the like effect are to be found in *Attia v British Gas Plc* [1988] QB 304 and *Alcock v Chief Constable of South Yorkshire Police* [1992] 1 AC 310. In *Attia* the Court of Appeal discussed where the borderline should be drawn between on the one hand the emotions of distress and grief and on the other hand some actual psychiatric illness such as anxiety, neurosis or a reactive depression. The authorities recognised that there is a line to be drawn and whether any given case falls on one side or the other is a matter for expert evidence. The civil cases are also concerned with a broader question of the boundaries of the law of negligence and the duty of care, which do not concern us.

Accordingly the phrase 'actual bodily harm' is capable of including psychiatric injury. But it does not include mere emotions such as fear or distress or panic nor does it include, as such, states of mind that are not themselves evidence of some identifiable clinical condition. The phrase 'state of mind' is not a scientific one and should be avoided in considering whether or not a psychiatric injury has been caused; its use is likely to create in the minds of the jury the impression that something which is no more than a strong emotion, such as extreme fear or panic, can amount to actual bodily harm. It cannot. Similarly juries should not be directed that an assault which causes a hysterical and nervous condition is an assault occasioning actual bodily harm. Where there is evidence that the assault has caused some psychiatric injury, the jury should be directed that that injury is capable of amounting to actual bodily harm; otherwise there should be no reference to the mental state of the victim following the assault unless it be relevant to some other aspect of the case, as it was in *R v Roberts*, 56 Cr App R 95. It is also relevant to have in mind the relationship between the offence of aggravated assault comprised in s 47 and simple assault. The latter can include conduct which causes the victim to apprehend immediate and unlawful violence; *Fagan v Metropolitan Police Commissioner* [1969] 1 QB 439. To treat the victim's fear of such unlawful violence, without more, as amounting to actual bodily harm would be to risk rendering the definition of the aggravated offence academic in many cases.

In any case where psychiatric injury is relied upon as the basis for an allegation of bodily harm, and the matter has not been admitted by the defence, expert evidence should be called by the prosecution. It should not be left to be inferred by the jury from the general facts of the case. In the absence of appropriate expert evidence a question whether or not the assault occasioned psychiatric injury should not be left to the jury. Cases where it is necessary to allege that psychiatric injury has been caused by an assault will be very few and far between ...

R v Ireland [1997] QB 114 (CA)

Swinton Thomas LJ: ... The charges [of assault occasioning actual bodily harm, contrary to s 47 of the Offences Against the Person Act 1861] arose as a result of the appellant making a large number of unwanted telephone calls to the three women. The telephone calls occurred very frequently between the dates set out in the counts in the indictment. When the women answered the telephone there was silence. The calls lasted sometimes for a minute or so, and sometimes for several minutes. On occasions there were repeated calls over a relatively short period. For example, one complainant said that she received no less than 14 telephone calls within an hour on 9 September 1994. The other complainants had similar experiences. Each of the complainants was examined by a psychiatrist, who said in his witness statement that the result of the repeated telephone calls was that each of them suffered significant psychological symptoms. For example, one of the complainants suffered from palpitations, difficulty breathing and cold sweats of an intensity which made it difficult for her to leave home or to answer the telephone. Another of the complainants suffered anxiety, inability to sleep, tearfulness, headaches, tingling in her fingers, dizziness and a constant feeling of being on edge. The third complainant suffered from stress, inability to sleep, and a skin condition brought about by her nervousness.

The issue that arises on this appeal is whether a telephone call, followed by silence, can constitute an assault for the purposes of s 47 of the Offences Against the Person Act 1861 ...

An assault is any act by which a person intentionally or recklessly causes another to apprehend immediate and unlawful violence. This definition ... has received judicial approval in a number of cases, most recently in *R v Savage* [1992] 1 AC 699 at 740. [Counsel for the appellant] submits that the facts relied upon by the prosecution to not disclose an apprehension on the part of the victims of immediate unlawful violence. He submits that violence cannot include psychological harm ...

It was held in *R v Mike Chan-Fook* (1994) 99 Cr App R 147 that 'actual bodily harm' may include harm to any part of the body, including internal organs, the nervous system and the brain. It is capable of including psychiatric injury, but not mere emotion such as fear, distress or panic. In the present case there was abundant evidence that the victims have suffered psychiatric damage ...

... In our judgment, if the Crown can prove that the victims have sustained actual bodily harm, in this case psychological harm, and that the accused must have intended the victims to sustain such harm, or have been reckless as to whether they did sustain such harm, and that harm resulted from an act or acts of the appellant, namely telephone calls followed by silence, it is open to the jury to find that he has committed an assault. As to immediacy, by using the telephone the appellant put himself in immediate contact with the victims, and when the victims lifted the telephone they were placed in immediate fear and suffered the consequences to which we have referred ...

In our judgment the making of a telephone call followed by silence, or a series of telephone calls, is capable of amounting to a relevant act for the purposes of s 47. The act consists in the making of the telephone call, and it does not matter whether words or silence ensue. There is no doubt that the telephone calls made the victims apprehensive. Equally, there is no doubt that they caused them psychological damage. In our judgment, once the fear and the damage are established, then when a telephone call is made by the appellant and the victim lifts the telephone and then knows that the man is telephoning them yet again, they will be apprehensive of suffering the very psychological damage from which they did suffer, namely palpitations, difficulty in breathing, cold sweats, anxiety, inability to sleep, dizziness, stress, and the like. As in the case of *Smith* (1983) 76 Cr App R 234, these victims would not know what the appellant was going to do next. In most cases an assault is likely to involve direct physical violence to the body. However, the fact that the violence is inflicted indirectly, causing psychological harm, does not render the act to be any less an act of violence. Nor, in our judgment, is it necessary that there should be an immediate proximity between defendant and victim. Fear can be instilled as readily over the telephone as it can through the window. In our judgment, repetitious telephone calls of this nature are likely to cause the victims to apprehend immediate and unlawful violence. That the appellant so intended was inherent in his pleas of guilty ...

In *R v Constanza* (1997), *The Times*, March 31, a 'stalker' was convicted of assault occasioning actual bodily harm. It was held by the Court of Appeal that:

(1) It is enough for the prosecution to prove a fear of violence at some time not excluding the immediate future.

(2) An assault can be committed by words alone.

On the topic of 'stalking', reference may also be made to the Protection from Harassment Act 1997. Section 1 of this Act prohibits a person from pursuing a course of conduct which he knows or ought to know amounts to harassment of another person. This offence is punishable with up to 6 months' imprisonment. Section 4 creates the offence of aggravated harassment, where the victim is placed in fear of violence. This offence is punishable with up to 5 years' imprisonment. Section 3 of the Act creates a new tort of harassment (which includes apprehended harassment where the relevant acts have not yet been perpetrated); breach of an injunction granted by a civil court to restrain harassment is made a criminal offence under s 3(3) of the Act. Section 5 of the Act enables a criminal court to make a restraining order on a convicted defendant to prohibit him from conduct which might be injurious to the victim.

Section 47: recklessness as to consequences

R v Venna [1976] QB 421 (CA)

James LJ: ... The four defendants and another youth called Patterson, who was not arrested, were creating a disturbance in the public street by shouting and singing and dancing. At one stage there was a banging of dustbin lids. The local residents were disturbed and at least one complaint of the noise was made to the police. A police officer named Leach went to investigate. What took place between him and the youths was described in evidence by three taxi drivers. Leach patiently and tactfully tried to persuade the four youths to be quiet and to go home. The response was a remark by Robinson, 'Fuck off', and the continuation of the noise and dancing. Leach told them there had already been a complaint about their unruly behaviour and ordered them on their way. Robinson thereafter stood apart from the others and did nothing. That was the foundation of his subsequent acquittal. The others continued a sort of war dance and went on singing. Leach told them that if they continued to create a disturbance and obstruct the pavement they would be arrested. Allison in defiance sat down on the pavement. Leach moved towards him to arrest him and the appellant, Edwards and Patterson crowded round. As he placed his hand on Allison, Leach said 'You are all under arrest'.

The appellant's evidence at the trial was that he did not hear these words and did not appreciate that he was being arrested until a later stage of the incident. As Leach picked Allison up, Allison struggled to free himself and the appellant, Edwards and Patterson tried to pull Allison out of the officer's grip. Leach held on to Allison and called for help on his pocket radio. The scene was such that the taxi drivers were about to intervene. A passer-by, referred to as 'the fat man', did intervene on the officer's behalf. The appellant in evidence surmised that he did so because 'he thought the copper's head might be bashed in'. Other police officers arrived and assisted Leach in the arrest of the appellant and the co-defendants. Before those who were resisting arrest were finally overpowered, Allison had torn Leach's uniform, Edwards had seized Leach's left thumb and bent it forcibly backwards causing physical injury, and the appellant had fought so violently that four officers were required to restrain him. In the course of the appellant's struggles he was knocked or fell to the ground. Two police officers held him by the arms. On the appellant's own admission, he then knew he was being arrested and he continued to 'lash out' wildly with his legs. In doing so he kicked the hand of a police officer who was trying to pick him up. The kick caused a fracture of a bone and was the subject of the charge of assault occasioning actual bodily harm.

The appellant's evidence was to the effect that he and his friends were not told that they were creating a disturbance and that all he done was to tell Leach that he could not arrest Allison. He said that he had been struck on the chin and knocked to the ground and that he had lashed out with his feet in an effort to get up. He did not know or suspect that there was a police officer in the way or that his foot might strike a police officer's hand ...

... In our view the element of *mens rea* in the offence of battery is satisfied by proof that the defendant intentionally or recklessly applied force to the person of another. If it were otherwise, the strange consequence would be that an offence of unlawful wounding contrary to s 20 of the Offences Against the Person Act 1861 could be established by proof that the defendant wounded the victim either intentionally or recklessly, but if the victim's skin was not broken and the offence was therefore laid as an assault occasioning actual bodily harm contrary to s 47 of 1861 Act, it would be necessary to prove that the physical force was intentionally applied.

Director of Public Prosecutions v K (A Minor) [1990] 1 WLR 1067 (DC)

Parker LJ: The facts are unusual. The defendant was, on 14 November 1988, aged 15 years and was attending a chemistry class in the first-floor laboratory of the science block at Stowe School, at which he was a pupil. The lesson began at 11.30 am and was due to end at 12.50 pm. The lesson included observation of the effects of putting concentrated sulphuric acid into chlorine, water and ammonia. Pupils were provided at the outset with an instruction sheet emphasising the need for great care when carrying out the experiments and were orally warned of the dangers of working with acid. The experiments were carried out in the fume cupboard. During the course of them the defendant splashed acid on to his hand and poured alkaline on to it in order to neutralise the acid before continuing with the experiments.

The defendant later asked permission to go to the ground floor toilet to wash his hand because it was sore and hurting. He was given permission. Unknown to the science tutor in charge, he took with him a boiling tube of concentrated acid. On reaching the toilet he went into one of the cubicles and poured some of the acid on to some toilet paper in order to test its reaction. It turned the paper brown. The defendant then heard footsteps in the corridor outside the toilet, turned from the cubicle towards the sinks area where there was a hot air hand/face drier machine, panicked and poured the rest of the acid into the machine, the nozzle of which was pointing upwards. When the footsteps receded the defendant left the toilet taking with him the empty boiling tube. This he discarded on this way upstairs to rejoin the chemistry lesson. He intended to return later to deal with the acid in the drier. The lesson was finished by the time he returned to the laboratory.

Some time later – the case stated does not reveal how much later – another pupil, Julian Barnbrook, went to the toilet to wash his hands. He turned on the drier. The acid was ejected onto his forehead and trickled down the right side of his nose. It caused a permanent scar. The defendant was thus too late to carry out his intention of emptying and washing out the vent. He was later questioned. After an initial denial he made a statement to his housemaster admitting what had happened. The justices concluded their findings of fact ... with the following finding: 'The defendant panicked and had not intended to harm Julian Barnbrook or anyone else'.

[The defendant was charged with assault occasioning actual bodily harm contrary to s 47 of the Offences Against the Person Act 1861.]

... [T]he justices' findings make it abundantly clear that the defendant knew full well that he had created a dangerous situation and the inescapable inference appears to me to be that he decided to take the risk of someone using the machine before he could get back and render it harmless or gave no thought to that risk. Moreover, although it was, on the findings, panic which led him to pour the acid into the machine, that panic had been engendered by footsteps which had disappeared before he left the machine. There is no finding that panic caused him to abandon the machine in its dangerous condition.

Assault occasioning actual bodily harm: foreseeability of harm

The consequences of the assault need not be foreseen or foreseeable.

R v Savage; R v Parmenter [1992] 1 AC 699 (HL)

Lord Ackner (with whom **Lord Keith of Kinkel, Lord Brandon of Oakbrook, Lord Jauncey of Tullichettle** and **Lord Lowry** agreed):

R v Savage

... [T]he appellant, Mrs Savage, was indicted and convicted ... of unlawful wounding contrary to s 20 of the 1861 Act, the particulars of the offence being that on 31 March 1989 she unlawfully and maliciously wounded Miss Beal ... The victim, Miss Beal, was a former girlfriend of Mrs Savage's husband. There had been some bad feeling between these two young women, although they had never previously met. On the evening of 31 March 1989 they were both in the same public house, but not together. Mrs Savage pushed her way through to the table where Miss Beal was sitting with some friends. She had in her hand a pint glass which was nearly full of beer. Having said 'Nice to meet you darling', she then threw the contents of the glass over Miss Beal. Unfortunately, not only was Miss Beal soaked by beer, but, contrary to Mrs Savage's evidence, she must have let go of the glass, since it broke and a piece of it cut Miss Beal's wrist. The jury, by their verdict, concluded either that the appellant had deliberately thrown not only the beer but also the glass at Miss Beal or, alternatively, while deliberately throwing the beer over Miss Beal, the glass had accidentally slipped from her grasp and it, or a piece of it, had struck Miss Beal's wrist, but with no intention that the glass should hit or cut Miss Beal ...

... On 28 November 1990 the Court of Appeal gave leave to appeal, certifying the following points of law to be of general public importance:

(1) Whether a verdict of guilty of assault occasioning actual bodily harm is a permissible alternative verdict on a count alleging unlawful wounding contrary to s 20 of the Offences Against the Persons Act 1861.

(2) Whether a verdict of guilty of assault occasioning actual bodily harm can be returned upon proof of an assault and of the fact that actual bodily harm was occasioned by that assault.

(3) If it is proved that an assault has been committed and that actual bodily harm has resulted from that assault, whether a verdict of assault occasioning actual bodily harm may be returned in the absence of proof that the defendant intended to cause some actual bodily harm or was reckless as to whether such harm would be caused.

It is perhaps convenient at this stage to observe that in order for Mrs Savage to succeed in relation to the first certified question your Lordships must conclude that the decision of this House in *R v Wilson (Clarence)* [1984] AC 242 was wrong. As regards the second certified question, that the intent required in s 47 relates not only to the assault, but also to the consequences of the assault, this clearly overlaps with the third certified question.

R v Parmenter

Paul Parmenter was born on 8 February 1988. Between that date and 11 May 1988 his father, the appellant, Philip Mark Parmenter caused his baby son to suffer injuries to the bony structures of the legs and right forearm ... The only issue before the jury was whether Mr Parmenter had acted with the relevant intent, his case being that he did not realise that the way he handled the child would cause injury ... Mr Parmenter was ... convicted of four s 20 offences ...

The Court of Appeal ... quashed the convictions on the four counts under s 20 ... The court then had to consider whether it could and should substitute for the convictions which it had quashed, alternative verdicts of guilty under s 47 of the 1861 Act.

It was then discovered that a curious situation had emerged, namely that two different divisions of the Court of Appeal (Criminal Division) had, contemporaneously but unwittingly, delivered judgments on the necessary intent in s 47, but had unfortunately reached opposite conclusions. *Savage* was one of those cases and the other is *R v Spratt* [1990] 1 WLR 1073.

In *R v Spratt* a young girl was struck twice whilst playing in the forecourt of a block of flats by two airgun pellets, which had been fired from a window by the appellant. He admitted to the police that he had fired a few shots out of the window, not in order to hit anyone, but to see how far the pellets would go. He was duly charged with an offence under s 47 of the 1861 Act to which he pleaded guilty. The basis of that plea, as was explained to the trial judge, was that the appellant accepted that he had been reckless, and that his recklessness took the shape of a failure to give any thought to the possibility of a risk. However, it was contended on his behalf that if he had known there were children in the area, he would not have fired the shots ... When the [the defendant's appeal against sentence] came before the full [Court of Appeal], the court itself raised the question whether, if the facts asserted on the appellant's behalf were true, he had in law committed the offence to which he had pleaded guilty. Subsequently leave was given to pursue an appeal against conviction ... The court ... concluded that the 'subjective type of recklessness' furnished the test for ss 20 and 47 alike ...

On 6 November 1990 the Court of Appeal granted leave to appeal to your Lordships' House and certified the following points of law to be of general public importance:

(1)(a) Whether in order to establish an offence under s 20 of the Offences Against the Person Act 1861 the prosecution must prove that the defendant actually foresaw that his act would cause the particular kind of harm which was in fact caused, or whether it is sufficient to prove that (objectively) he ought so to have foreseen.

(b) The like question in relation to s 47 of the Act.

(2)(a) For the purposes of the answer to question (1)(a), whether the particular kind of harm to be foreseen may be any physical harm, or harm of:

(1) the nature, or

(2) the degree, or

(3) the nature and the degree of the harm which actually occurred.

(b) The like question in relation to s 47 of the Act.

It will be observed that some of the certified questions in *Parmenter* overlap with those in *Savage*.

My Lords, I will now seek to deal with the issues raised by these appeals *seriatim* ...

Can a verdict of assault occasioning actual bodily harm be returned upon proof of an assault together with proof of the fact that actual bodily harm was occasioned by the assault, or must the prosecution also prove that the defendant intended to cause some actual bodily harm or was reckless as to whether such harm would be caused?

Your Lordships are concerned with the mental element of a particular kind of assault, an assault 'occasioning actual bodily harm'. It is common ground that the mental element of assault is an intention to cause the victim to apprehend immediate and unlawful violence or recklessness whether such apprehension be caused: see *R v Venna* [1976] QB 421. It is of course common ground that Mrs Savage committed an assault upon Miss Beal when she threw the contents of her glass of beer over her. It is also common ground that however the glass came to be broken and Miss Beal's wrist thereby cut, it was, on the finding of the jury, Mrs Savage's handling of the glass which caused Miss Beal 'actual bodily harm'. Was the offence thus established or is there a further mental state that has to be established in relation to the bodily harm element of the offence? Clearly the section, by its terms, expressly imposes no such a requirement. Does it do so by necessary implication? It neither uses the word 'intentionally' nor the word 'maliciously'. The words 'occasioning actual bodily harm' are descriptive of the word 'assault', by reference to a particular kind of consequence ...

... [O]nce the assault was established, the only remaining question was whether the victim's conduct was the natural consequence of that assault. The word 'occasioning' raised solely a question of causation, an objective question which does not involve enquiring into the accused's state of mind ...

... The decision in *R v Roberts* 56 Cr App R 95 was correct. The verdict of assault occasioning actual bodily harm may be returned upon proof of an assault together with proof of the fact that actual bodily harm was occasioned by the assault. The prosecution are not obliged to prove that the defendant intended to cause some actual bodily harm or was reckless as to whether such harm would be caused ...

WOUNDING OR INFLICTING GRIEVOUS BODILY HARM (SECTION 20)

Wounding

A 'wound' means a break in the continuity of the skin.

C (a minor) v Eisenhower also sub nom JJC v Eisenhower [1983] 3 WLR 537 (CA)

Facts: The defendant, a juvenile, had been charged (together with another juvenile) with unlawful and malicious wounding contrary to s 20 of the Offences Against the Person Act 1861. The only point at issue was whether the victim's injuries constituted a 'wound'.

Robert Goff LJ: ... The offence arose in the following circumstances. These two boys were both 15 at the relevant time. The defendant's co-accused, in company with the defendant, purchased an air pistol and some pellets from a shop. A few days later, on 21 January 1982, they were walking together along Flexmere Road, Tottenham, when they became aware of a young man called Martin Cook, together with another young man and two girls, on the opposite side of the road. As the defendant and his co-accused walked along, the co-accused aimed the air pistol in the direction of those four young people. He fired once. A little later he fired again. Martin Cook was hit in the area of the left eye by a pellet from the air pistol.

The justices in the case found that the injuries sustained by Martin Cook amounted to a bruise just below the left eyebrow and that fluid filling the front part of his left eye for a time afterwards abnormally contained red blood cells ...

The question stated by the justices is as follows:

> The question for the opinion of the High Court is whether in the light of the facts as we found them and the law applied to those facts we were right to find the [defendant] guilty of the offence with which he had been charged.

... In *R v M'Loughlin* (1838) 8 Car & P 635, it was held by Coleridge J, other judges being present, that it must be the whole skin that is broken. He, of course, was referring to the fact that the human skin has two layers, an outer layer called the epidermis or the cuticle, and an underlayer which is sometimes called the dermis or the true skin. In that case there was evidence of an abrasion of the skin, with blood issuing from it. It was made plain to the jury by Coleridge J that:

> if it is necessary to constitute a wound, that the skin should be broken, it must be the whole skin, and it is not sufficient to show a separation of the cuticle only.

It was therefore not enough that there had been an abrasion affecting only the cuticle. There had to be a break in the continuity of the whole skin.

[His Lordship then referred to two more old cases: see *R v Shadbolt* (1833) 5 Car & P 504 and *R v Waltham* (1849) 3 Cox CC 442; his Lordship went on:]

These cases show that there can be a break in the continuity of the skin sufficient to constitute a wound if the skin which was broken is the skin of an internal cavity of the body, being a cavity from the outer surface of the body where the skin of the cavity is continuous with the outer skin of the body. So, for example, in *Shadbolt* it was held that it was sufficient if there had been a break in the skin of the internal surface of the lips inside the mouth. In *Waltham*, which is possibly the most extreme of the cases cited to us, it was held by Cresswell J that there would be a wounding if there had been a rupture of the lining membrane of the urethra causing a small flow of blood into the urine, because that membrane was of precisely the same character as that which lined the cheek and the internal skin of the lip.

So we can see a picture emerging. There must be a break in the continuity of the skin. It must be a break in the continuity of the whole skin, but the skin may include not merely the outer skin of the body but the skin of an internal cavity of the body where the skin of the cavity is continuous with the outer skin of the body ...

In my judgment, having regard to the cases there is a continuous stream of authority – to which I myself can find no exception at all – which does establish that a wound is, as I have stated, a break in the continuity of the whole skin ... This has become such a well-established meaning of the word 'wound' that in my judgment it would be very wrong for this court to depart from it.

We now turn to the case stated for our consideration by the justices. The justices concluded that there was a wound because, although they described the injury as a bruise just below the left eyebrow with fluid filling the front part of his left eye for a time afterwards which abnormally contained red blood cells, they thought that the abnormal presence of red blood cells in the fluid in Martin Cook's left eye indicated at least the rupturing of a blood vessel or vessels internally; and this they thought was sufficient to constitute a wound for the purposes of s 20 of the Offences Against the Person Act 1861.

In my judgment, that conclusion was not in accordance with the law. It is not enough that there has been a rupturing of a blood vessel or vessels internally for there to be a wound under the statute because it is impossible for a court to conclude from that evidence alone whether or not there has been any break in the continuity of the whole skin. There may have simply been internal bleeding of some kind or another, the cause of which is not established. Furthermore, even if there had been a break in some internal skin, there may not have been a break in the whole skin. In these circumstances, the evidence is not enough, in my judgment, to establish a wound within the statute. In my judgment, the justices erred in their conclusion on the evidence before them. The question posed for the opinion of this court is whether, in the light of the facts found by the justices and the law applied to those facts, they were right to find the defendant guilty of the offence with which he had been charged, *viz*, the unlawful and malicious wounding of Martin Cook contrary to s 20 of the Offences Against the Person Act 1861. I would answer that question in the negative.

[*Note*: Since the definition of 'grievous bodily harm' is rather wider than that of a 'wound', the best practice is to charge the defendant with inflicting grievous bodily harm if there is doubt whether the injury constitutes a wound or not, for example in the case of internal injuries.]

Grievous bodily harm

Grievous bodily harm means really serious harm, although it not a misdirection to tell a jury that it means 'serious' harm.

Director of Public Prosecutions v Smith [1961] AC 290 (HL)

Facts: The respondent was driving a car in which there was stolen property. The car was stopped by a police officer on point duty in the normal course of traffic control and, while so stopped, another policeman, who was acquainted with the respondent, came to the driver's window and spoke to the respondent. As a result of what the police constable saw in the back of the car, he told the respondent to draw in to his nearside. The respondent began to do so, and the constable walked beside the car. However, the respondent suddenly accelerated and made off down an adjoining road. The constable began to run with the car, and, despite the fact that it had no running board, succeeded in hanging on to the car. The car pursued an erratic course, and eventually the constable was thrown off in the path of another vehicle which ran over him, causing fatal injuries.

Viscount Kilmuir LC: ... My Lords, I confess that, whether one is considering the crime of murder or the statutory offence, I can find no warrant for giving the words 'grievous bodily harm' a meaning other than that which the words convey in their ordinary and natural meaning. 'Bodily harm' needs no explanation and 'grievous' means no more and no less than 'really serious' ...

Lord Goddard, Lord Tucker, Lord Denning and **Lord Parker of Waddington** agreed with the **Lord Chancellor**.

R v Saunders (Ian) [1985] Crim LR 230 (CA)

Facts: The appellant, on a road at night, approaching a stranger who was sitting resting at the roadside, asked him what the problem was and, when the victim said that there was no problem, the appellant said that he would give him one and punched him in the face. The victim suffered a broken nose and other injuries. The appellant desisted when a passer-by approached. The appellant was tried on, *inter alia*, a count of inflicting grievous bodily harm, contrary to s 20 of the Offences Against the Person Act 1861. The judge directed the jury that grievous bodily harm meant 'serious injury'. The appellant was convicted. He appealed on the ground that the judge had misdirected the jury failing to direct them that the injury had to be 'really serious'.

Held: The question had already been considered by the Court of Appeal in *R v McMillan* (unreported, 8 October 1984). The conclusion reached in that case was equally applicable to the present case, in which there was no need to use the phrase 'really' serious harm; the omission of the word 'really' was not significant. The victim had suffered a broken nose, which was clearly grievous bodily harm.

R v Burstow [1997] 1 Cr App R 144 (CA)

Lord Bingham of Cornhill CJ: At the heart of this application lies a short but difficult question of law: may an offence of unlawfully and maliciously inflicting grievous bodily harm contrary to s 20 of the Offences Against the Person Act 1861 be committed where no physical violence has been applied directly or indirectly to the body of the victim? ...

In about April 1992, the applicant was a Petty Officer serving in HMS Collingwood at Fareham in Hampshire ... The applicant became acquainted with Mrs Tracey Sant, a civilian employee at the base, and they enjoyed a social relationship for a time. There came a time when Mrs Sant felt that the relationship had gone far enough, and she was determined to put an end to it. Unfortunately, the applicant refused to accept that the relationship had come to an end. He started following her to work, turning up unexpectedly at places where she happened to be.

In January 1993, she made her first complaint to the police about his behaviour. They warned the applicant about it, but later on in the same month he was arrested for breach of the peace [and was bound over] for two years to be of good behaviour and keep the peace. In February 1993, he was brought back before the court for breach of the bind-over, but the case did not proceed since Mrs Sant was unwilling to give evidence.

In July 1993 he appeared before the ... magistrates' court for breach of his bind-over and in August 1993 he pleaded guilty to an offence under the Offences Against the Person Act 1861. He was conditionally discharged. He continued to persecute Mrs Sant. On 17 September 1993, he was sentenced to a term of imprisonment for pouring solvent on Mrs Sant's car, and he was also sentenced for a series of offences involving the making of malicious communications to Mrs Sant and the persistent making of nuisance telephone calls.

On 27 April 1994 he was sentenced to 18 months' imprisonment for burglary and on 20 February 1995 to three terms of 12 months' imprisonment concurrent on a further three counts of burglary. All this conduct was directed at Mrs Sant. When sentence was passed on 20 February 1995, the applicant was immediately released, because of time that he had spent in custody before sentence. But his obsessional pursuit of Mrs Sant continued. He wrote her letters; he made telephone calls; he made visits; he distributed insulting cards. This conduct was in breach of an injunction made by ... the county court, and on 29 September 1995 he was sentenced to 12 months' imprisonment for contempt.

The applicant's conviction was based on his conduct between February and July 1995, including the telephone calls, letters and photographs already mentioned and frequent visits to Mrs Sant's home. It is unnecessary to recount the details.

[His Lordship then quoted from one of the letters written by the applicant to Mrs Sant and went on:]

The court is satisfied that this note was, and was understood to be, menacing. It was intended to prey on Mrs Sant's mind, as did the other elements of the applicant's conduct, and did so.

There was clear evidence to this effect. Before the trial court was a report by a consultant psychiatrist who had first interviewed Mrs Sant in September 1994 and who had reviewed her mental state through the autumn of 1994 and the winter of 1994–95. He interviewed her again in August 1995. He found her:

> extremely distressed and tearful, reporting a depressed mood and very poor sleep. She had lost weight. She had panic attacks at night. I asked her about her content of thought. She told me that she was continually frightened – that Burstow had contacted her by post and telephone – saying that he hated her and called her a 'lying slut', a 'stupid bitch' and a 'prostitute'. He had left condoms in her parents' garden and distributed them in the gardens of neighbours of her parents. He had threatened personal violence and attack on Tracey. She became extremely distressed describing this to me. She was beginning to lose hope for the future and at times felt that her life was not worth living. I made the diagnosis of severe depressive illness with noticeable deterioration since I last interviewed her on 8 February 1995.

The consultant diagnosed that Mrs Sant was suffering from severe endogenous depression with marked features of anxiety. He regarded this as grievous harm of a psychiatric nature. His judgment was that every contact of the applicant direct or indirect by any means with Mrs Sant caused her psychiatric injury and in his opinion the accumulation of incidents had caused a serious depressive illness such that Mrs Sant feared for her life at the hands of the applicant.

It was accepted by both sides in argument before the court that the expression 'grievous bodily harm' in s 20 could include psychiatric injury of the kind suffered by Mrs Sant. The argument for the applicant rested on the use of the word 'inflict' in s 20. Had the section used the word 'cause' counsel [for the applicant] accepted that he would have no argument. But he submitted that the term 'inflict' necessarily required the application of physical force directly or indirectly to the body of the victim ...

Were the question free from authority, we should entertain some doubt whether the Victorian draftsman of the 1861 Act intended to embrace psychiatric injury within the expressions 'grievous bodily harm' and 'actual bodily harm'. If he did, it is not obvious why he used the expression 'bodily' in a statute concerned with offences against the person and in no way concerned with damage to reputation or economic interests. But there is clear and (in this court) unchallenged authority that actual bodily harm is capable of including psychiatric injury: *R v Mike Chan-Fook* (1994) 99 Cr App R 147. There can in this respect be no meaningful distinction between actual bodily harm and grievous bodily harm. Whatever the intention of the original draftsman, this ruling is to be welcomed since it is now accepted that the distinction between physical and mental injury is by no means clear-cut, and psychiatric injury may often be manifested by physical symptoms, as in the present case where Mrs Sant suffered, as a direct result of the applicant's conduct, a loss of weight. The question posed at the outset of this judgment must accordingly be answered by this court on the premise that 'grievous bodily harm' can include psychiatric injury ...

Counsel for the applicant would, as we understand, accept that if the applicant had caused the harm actually caused to Mrs Sant with intent to cause such harm, he would be guilty of an offence under s 18 of the 1861 Act. His argument that the applicant is not guilty of an offence [under s 20] depends on the fact that s 20 uses the verb 'inflict' in contrast with the use of the verb 'cause' in s 18. This puts great weight on the difference between the meaning of the two verbs. It may be questioned whether in this context this is justified. In R v *Mandair* [1995] 1 AC 208 at 215 Lord Mackay of Clashfern LC said:

> In my opinion, as I have said, the word 'cause' is wider or at least not narrower than the word 'inflict'.

This observation, with which a majority of the House of Lords agreed, would not suggest any radical divergence between the meaning of the two words. The word 'inflict' may primarily suggest a corporal blow, but accepted dictionary definitions include such meanings as 'impose' or 'cause to be borne'. It is not straining language to speak of one person inflicting psychiatric injury on another. It would, in our judgment, be an affront to common sense to distinguish between s 18 and s 20 in the way contended for by the applicant. It would also, we think, introduce extreme and undesirable artificiality into what should be a very practical area of the law if we were to hold that, although grievous bodily harm includes psychiatric injury, no offence against s 20 is committed unless such psychiatric injury is the result of physical violence applied directly or indirectly to the body of the victim. The decision in *R v Mike Chan-Fook* is in our view fatal to the applicant's submission ...

Section 20: foreseeability of consequences

The defendant must foresee the risk of *some* injury (whereas to be guilty of an offence under s 18 the defendant must foresee serious injury).

R v Mowatt [1968] 1 QB 421 (CA)

Diplock LJ: ... The learned judge in summing up explained to the jury the meaning of 'unlawfully' ... but nowhere in the summing up did the judge mention the word 'maliciously' or give the jury any directions as to its meaning ...

... In s 18 the word 'maliciously' adds nothing. The intent expressly required by that section is more specific than such element of foresight of consequences as is implicit in the word 'maliciously' and in directing a jury about an offence under this section the word 'maliciously' is best ignored. In the offence under s 20, and in the alternative verdict which may be given on a charge under s 18 – for neither of which is any specific intent required – the word 'maliciously' does import on the part of the person who unlawfully inflicts the wound or other grievous bodily harm an awareness that his act may have the consequence of causing some physical harm to some other person ... It is quite unnecessary that the accused should have foreseen that his unlawful act might cause physical harm of the gravity described in the section ie a wound or serious physical injury. It is enough that he should have foreseen that some physical harm to some person, albeit of a minor character, might result ...

... There may, of course, be cases where the accused's awareness of the possible consequences of his act is genuinely in issue. *R v Cunningham* [1957] 2 QB 396 is a good example. But where the evidence for the prosecution, if accepted, shows that the physical act of the accused which caused the injury to another person was a direct assault which any ordinary person would be bound to realise was likely to cause some physical harm to the other person (as, for instance, an assault with a weapon or the boot or violence with the hands) and the defence put forward on behalf of the accused is not that the assault was accidental or that he did not realise that it might cause some physical harm to the victim, but is some other defence such as that he did not do the alleged act or that he did it in self-defence, it is unnecessary to deal specifically in the summing up with what is meant by the word 'maliciously' in the section. It can only confuse the jury to invite them in the summing up to consider an improbability not previously put forward and to which no evidence has been directed, to wit, that the accused did not realise what any ordinary person would have realised was a likely consequence of his act, and to tell the jury that the onus lies, not on the accused to establish, but on the prosecution to negative, that improbability, and to go on to talk about presumptions. To a jury who are not jurisprudents that sounds like jargon. In the absence of any evidence that the accused did not realise that it was a possible consequence of his act that some physical harm might be caused to the victim, the prosecution satisfy the relevant onus by proving the commission by the accused of an act which any ordinary person would realise was likely to have that consequence. There is no issue here to which the jury need direct their minds and there is no need to give to them any specific directions about it. In such a case, and these are the commonest of cases under s 18, the real issues of fact on which the jury have to make up their minds are: (1) Are they satisfied that the accused did the act? (2) If so, are they satisfied that the act caused a wound or other serious physical injury? (3) If the defence of self-defence is raised or there is any evidence to support it, do they think that the accused may have done the act in self-defence? (4) If the answer to (1) and (2) is Yes and to (3), if raised, is No, are they satisfied that when he did the act he intended to cause a wound or other really serious physical injury? If (3), (if raised) is answered No and (1) and (2) are answered Yes, the lesser offence under s 20 is made out; and if (4) is also answered Yes, the graver offence under s 18 is made out. In any case under s 18 where the physical act of the accused was a direct assault which any ordinary person would have realised was likely to cause some physical harm to the victim and there is no evidence that the accused himself did not realise that it might do so, if those issues, which we have stated, are put fairly and squarely to the jury it is the view of this court that the summing up is not open to criticism. There is no need for any general dissertation about the meaning of the word 'maliciously'. The less said about it in such a case the better.

The only remaining issue is whether the present case is one of this kind. The relevant evidence for the prosecution was that of the complainant and the two police officers. The complainant, in the early hours of the morning of 30 September, was returning home, according to his evidence, and was stopped in a street by two men, one of whom was the appellant. They asked him if there was a club anywhere about, and then one of them, not the appellant, snatched a £5 note from the complainant's breast pocket and ran off. The complainant said that he chased him without success, returned to the appellant, grasped him by his lapels and demanded to know the whereabouts of his mate. The appellant then (and this was common ground) hit out at the complainant and knocked him down. That was the first assault. Two off-duty police officers then saw the appellant, according to their evidence, sitting astride the complainant, and they saw the appellant strike him several violent blows in the face with his fist and pull him to his feet, strike him again in the face, knocking him down and making him virtually unconscious. The appellant was, according to the police, trying to pull up the complainant again when the police arrested the appellant. When the appellant was taken to the station, he was found to be concealing a £5 note in his hand ... In the view of this court, this was clearly a case where in relation to the lesser offence of which the appellant was convicted it was quite unnecessary for the learned judge to give the jury any instructions on the meaning of the word 'maliciously' ...

R v Sullivan [1981] Crim LR 46 (CA)

Facts: The appellant was tried of charges of causing grievous bodily harm with intent, contrary to s 18 of the Offences Against the Person Act 1861 and with unlawfully and maliciously inflicting grievous bodily harm on the victim, contrary to s 20. The victim's evidence was that the appellant and a companion were undoubtedly drunk and, while the victim was in a street only eight feet wide with a narrow pavement, the appellant drove his car through the street at 25 – 30 mph, mounted the pavement and injured the victim. The appellant was acquitted of the s 18 offence but convicted of offences under s 20. He appealed.

Held: Section 8 of the Criminal Justice Act 1967 in effect enacted that there was no presumption of law that a man intended or foresaw the natural consequences of his act, and removed the whole basis of the argument that an intent to frighten was enough to constitute the necessary *mens rea* under s 20. However, a jury might be convinced from the evidence relating to intent to frighten that the person charged was aware that his act was likely to have the result of causing some sort of injury to the victim. Nevertheless, since s 8, mere intention to frighten without more was insufficient; the person charged must be proved to have been aware that probable consequences of his voluntary act would be to cause some injury to the victim, but not necessarily grievous bodily harm.

In the circumstances a properly directed jury could not have come to any other conclusion than that the appellant must have been aware that what he was doing was likely to cause physical injury to the victim.

R v Savage; R v Parmenter [1992] 1 AC 699 (HL)

Lord Ackner (with whom **Lord Keith of Kinkel**, **Lord Brandon of Oakbrook**, **Lord Jauncey of Tullichettle** and **Lord Lowry** agreed):

[Note: For facts, see *above*] ...

3. In order to establish an offence under s 20 of the 1861 Act, must the prosecution prove that the defendant actually foresaw that his act would cause harm, or is it sufficient to prove that the ought so to have foreseen?

[His Lordship quoted at length from the speech of Lord Diplock in *R v Caldwell* [1982] AC 341 and continued:]

A few weeks after hearing the argument in *R v Caldwell* [1982] AC 341, your Lordships in *R v Lawrence (Stephen)* [1982] AC 510 had to consider the word 'recklessly' in ss 1 and 2 of the Road Traffic Act 1972 as amended. Judgment in that appeal was in fact given on the same day as judgment in the *Caldwell* case. It was a unanimous decision of the House, the leading speech again being given by Lord Diplock. I need not trouble your Lordships with the facts of that case. Lord Diplock in referring to *R v Caldwell* [1982] AC 341 said that the conclusion reached by the majority of your Lordships was that the adjective 'reckless' when used in a criminal statute, ie the Criminal Damage Act 1971, had not acquired a special meaning as a term of legal art, but bore its popular or dictionary meaning of careless, regardless or heedless of the possible harmful consequences of one's acts. The same must be true of the adverbial derivative 'recklessly' when used in relation to driving a motor vehicle. As to the *mens rea* of the offence, he said [1982] AC 510 at 526–27:

> I turn now to the *mens rea*. My task is greatly simplified by what has already been said about the concept of recklessness in criminal law in *R v Caldwell* [1982] AC 341. Warning was there given against adopting the simplistic approach of treating all problems of criminal liability as soluble by classifying the test of liability as being either 'subjective' or 'objective'. Recklessness on the part of the doer of an act does presuppose that there is something in the circumstances that would have drawn the attention of an ordinary prudent individual to the possibility that his act was capable of causing the kind of serious harmful consequences that the section which creates the offence was intended to prevent, and that the risk of those harmful consequences occurring was not so slight that an ordinary prudent individual would feel justified in treating them as negligible. It is only when this is so that the doer of the act is acting 'recklessly' if before doing the act, he either fails to give any thought to the possibility of there being any such risk or, having recognised that there was such risk, he nevertheless goes on

to do it. In my view, an appropriate instruction to the jury on what is meant by driving recklessly would be that they must be satisfied of two things: first, that the defendant was in fact driving the vehicle in such a manner as to create an obvious and serious risk of causing physical injury to some other person who might happen to be using the road or of doing substantial damage to property; and second, that in driving in that manner the defendant did so without having given any thought to the possibility of there being any such risk or, having recognised that there was some risk involved, had nonetheless gone on to take it.

... [Counsel for Parmenter] submitted that in *Caldwell's* case your Lordships' House could have followed either of two possible paths to its conclusion as to the meaning of 'recklessly' in the Act of 1971. These were: (a) to hold that *R v Cunningham* [1957] 2 QB 396 (and *R v Mowatt* [1968] 1 QB 421) were wrongly decided and to introduce a single test, wherever recklessness was an issue; or (b) to accept that *Cunningham*, (subject to the *Mowatt* 'gloss' to which no reference was made), correctly states the law in relation to the Offences Against the Person Act 1981, because the word 'maliciously' in that statute was a term of legal art which imported into the concept of recklessness a special restricted meaning, thus distinguishing it from 'reckless', or 'recklessly' in modern 'revising' statutes then before the House, where those words bore their then popular or dictionary meaning.

I agree with [counsel for Parmenter] that manifestly it was the latter course which the House followed. Therefore in order to establish an offence under s 20 the prosecution must prove either that the defendant intended or that he actually foresaw that his act would cause harm.

4. In order to establish an offence under s 20 is it sufficient to prove that the defendant intended or foresaw the risk of some physical harm or must he intend or foresee either wounding or grievous bodily harm?

... My Lords, I am satisfied that the decision in *R v Mowatt* [1968] 1 QB 421 was correct and that it is quite unnecessary that the accused should either have intended or have foreseen that his unlawful act might cause physical harm of the gravity described in s 20, ie a wound or serious physical injury. It is enough that he should have foreseen that some physical harm to some person, albeit of a minor character, might result.

In the result I would dismiss the appeal in *Savage's* case but allow the appeal in *Parmenter's* case, but only to the extent of substituting, in accordance with the provisions of s 3(2) of the Criminal Appeal Act 1968, verdicts of guilty of assault occasioning actual bodily harm contrary to s 47 of the 1861 Act for the four s 20 offences of which he was convicted.

R v Rushworth (1992) 95 Cr App R 252 (CA)

Mann LJ: ... The circumstances of the case are unusual. The complainant was a 31-year-old woman who was mentally handicapped, but it was not suggested that the appellant had in any way taken advantage of her simplicity. On the evening of 4 April 1990 the complainant went to a public house in order to have a drink. There she met Mary Wright and they had a drink and chatted together. Also in the public house was the appellant, who was known to Mrs Wright and with whom she had had sexual intercourse on a number of occasions. On one of those occasions the appellant had used a vibrator but Mrs Wright refused to allow him to insert the device into her vagina. On the evening of 4 April there came a time when the complainant and Mrs Wright left the public house. The appellant had left shortly before but the two women encountered him outside the public house and all three went back to the appellant's flat which was nearby. The flat was sparsely furnished and the main item of furnishing was a mattress with a duvet on top of it. Upon arrival at the flat the appellant undressed himself and the two women then did likewise. They engaged in sexual activity upon the mattress. The first engagement was between the appellant and Mrs Wright. That did not last for very long before the appellant turned his attention to the complainant.

At some point, after the diversion of attention from herself, Mrs Wright left the room in order to visit the lavatory. She said that when she left the appellant was kneeling over the complainant, who was giggling and had hold of the appellant's private parts. Mrs Wright assumed, not unreasonably, that sexual intercourse was about to occur.

The complainant described what did occur. She said that she was lying on the mattress with the appellant on top of her when she heard a humming sound like that of a hair dryer or an electric razor. She felt something sharp between her legs and then in her vagina. That something must have been the bloodstained vibrating dildo which was subsequently found on the floor near the mattress. The complainant experienced pain and cried out. At that moment Mrs Wright re-entered the room and saw blood on the mattress and the appellant holding something over the pubic area of the complainant. Apparently he said words like, 'it must have slipped', and, 'I did not mean to do it'.

The appellant suggested calling an ambulance but the complainant refused this and said she wanted to go home. The appellant walked with her part of the way when she said that she would be all right and she completed her journey alone.

Unfortunately she was not all right. She had to be admitted to hospital in the early morning of 5 April, where she was discovered to have a split in the left side of the vulva in the groove between the lips. It was about two and a half centimetres in length and it was a penetrating wound that tracked through to the bowel. The injury was repaired and the complainant left hospital five days later. Fortunately she has apparently made a complete physical recovery.

The appellant did not give evidence at the trial. The case put on his behalf was that he was seeking to excite the complainant by inserting his fingers or the vibrator into her vagina and that in doing so a loss or shift of balance accidentally caused his body weight to bear on to his arm at the moment of insertion of the finger or vibrator. He called on his behalf to demonstrate the possibility of accident a pathologist named Dr Denmark. A consultant gynaecologist called by the Crown prior to the evidence of Dr Denmark said that the injury could have been caused by the vibrator, but if it had, very considerable force would have been used ...

[His Lordship considered the speech of Lord Ackner in *R v Parmenter* [1991] 2 WLR 914 and went on:]

... We think that the matter would be accurately expressed in these terms: 'In order to establish an offence under s 20 the prosecution must prove either that the defendant intended to, or that he actually foresaw his act might cause physical harm to some person, albeit harm of a minor character'. For those reasons this appeal is dismissed.

Section 47 as an alternative verdict to s 20

R v Savage; R v Parmenter [1992] 1 AC 699 (HL)

Lord Ackner (with whom **Lord Keith of Kinkel**, **Lord Brandon of Oakbrook**, **Lord Jauncey of Tullichettle** and **Lord Lowry** agreed):

[Note: For facts, see *above*]

1. Is a verdict of guilty of assault occasioning actual bodily harm a permissible alternative verdict on a count alleging unlawful wounding contrary to s 20 of the 1861 Act?

... Having reviewed the relevant authorities Lord Roskill [in *R v Wilson* [1984] AC 242] was content to accept that there can be an infliction of grievous bodily harm contrary to s 20 without an assault being committed. For example, grievous bodily harm could be inflicted by creating panic. Another example provided to your Lordships in the course of the argument in the current appeals was interfering with the braking mechanism of a car, so as to cause the driver to be involved in an accident and thus suffer injuries. These are somewhat far-fetched examples. The allegation of inflicting grievous bodily harm or for that matter wounding ... inevitably imports or includes an allegation of assault, unless there are some quite extraordinary facts.

The critical question remained: do the allegations in a s 20 charge 'include either expressly or by implication' allegations of assault occasioning actual bodily harm. As to this, Lord Roskill concluded [1984] AC 242 at 261:

> If 'inflicting' can, as the cases show, include 'inflicting by assault', then even though such a charge may not necessarily do so, I do not for myself see why on a fair reading of s 6(3) [of the Criminal Law Act 1967] these allegations do not at least *impliedly* include 'inflicting by assault'. That is sufficient for present purposes though I also regard it as also a possible view that those former allegations *expressly* include the other allegations.

I respectfully agree with this reasoning and accordingly reject the submission that *R v Wilson* was wrongly decided. I would therefore answer the first of the certified questions in the *Savage* case in the affirmative. A verdict of guilty of assault occasioning actual bodily harm is a permissible alternative verdict on a count alleging unlawful wounding contrary to s 20 of the Offences Against the Person Act 1861.

WOUNDING OR CAUSING GRIEVOUS BODILY HARM WITH INTENT (SECTION 18)

We have already seen that wounding connotes a break in the skin and that grievous bodily harm means (really) serious harm.

The main difference between s 20 and s 18 is that, whereas under s 20 it is enough for the defendant to foresee the risk of *some* injury, to be guilty under s 18 the defendant must have foreseen that *really serious injury would occur*.

Section 20 as an alternative verdict to s 18

Where a defendant is charged only with an offence under s 18, it is open to the jury to acquit the defendant of that offence but return a verdict of guilty to an offence under s 20.

R v Mandair [1994] 2 WLR 700 (HL)

Lord Mackay of Clashfern LC: The indictment contained a single count alleging causing grievous bodily harm with intent, contrary to s 18 of the Offences Against the Person Act 1861. The particulars of offence were that the defendant on 31 January 1991 unlawfully caused grievous bodily harm to Amarjit Mandair with intent to do her grievous bodily harm.

The recorder, applying s 6(3) of the Criminal Law Act 1967, left open to the jury the option of returning a lesser verdict under s 20 of the Offences Against the Person Act 1861. After sundry procedure the jury returned a verdict of not guilty on the charge against the defendant of causing grievous bodily harm with intent contrary to s 18 and a verdict of guilty on the alternative charge against the defendant of causing grievous bodily harm contrary to s 20 ...

In my view 'cause' in s 18 is certainly sufficiently wide to embrace any method by which grievous bodily harm could be inflicted under s 20 and since causing grievous bodily harm in s 18 is an alternative to wounding I regard it as clear that the word 'cause' in s 18 is wide enough to include any action that could amount to inflicting grievous bodily harm under s 20 where the word 'inflict' appears as an alternative to 'wound'. For this reason, in my view, following the reasoning of this House in *R v Wilson (Clarence)* [1984] AC 242 an alternative verdict under s 20 was open on the terms of this indictment ...

Lord Templeman: My Lords, the criminal law is already overburdened with technicalities. In my opinion: (1) an allegation of causing grievous bodily harm includes an allegation of inflicting grievous bodily harm. (2) A jury may convict of an offence under s 20 of the Offences Against the Person Act 1861 as an alternative to a charge of convicting of an offence under s 18 of that Act. (3) The Court of Appeal may substitute a conviction under s 20 for a conviction under s 18 ...

I agree, therefore, with the order proposed by my noble and learned friend, Lord Mackay of Clashfern LC.

Lord Goff of Chieveley: My Lords, I have had the opportunity of reading in draft the speech of my noble and learned friend, Lord Mackay of Clashfern LC, and I agree with him that, for the reasons he gives, the appeal should be allowed ...

Lord Browne-Wilkinson: My Lords, I have read in draft the speech prepared by my noble and learned friend, Lord Mackay of Clashfern LC. I agree with it and for the reasons which he gives I would make the order which he proposes.

Lord Mustill: ... The reappearance of s 20 before your Lordships' House barely two years after it was minutely examined in *R v Parmenter* [1992] 1 AC 699 demonstrates once again that this unsatisfactory statute is long overdue for repeal and replacement by legislation which is soundly based in logic and expressed in language which everyone can understand. Meanwhile we must make of ss 18 and 20, those staples of the Crown Court, the best that we can ...

GENERAL DEFENCES

Honest belief in need to use force

An honest belief in the need to use force (eg in self-defence) is a defence, provided that the force used is reasonable. Where self-defence is raised, the burden is on the prosecution to prove that the defendant was not acting in self-defence. To be acting in self-defence, the defendant must have been experiencing or must have reasonably feared an unlawful attack and the action taken by the defendant must have been proportionate to the threat that the action was meant to counter. The defendant's belief that he needs to resort to violence to protect himself need not be based on reasonable grounds, but the reasonableness (or otherwise) of that belief may be used as evidence showing whether or not he actually held that belief.

R v Williams [1987] 3 All ER 411 (CA)

Lord Lane CJ: ... The facts were somewhat unusual and were as follows. On the day in question the alleged victim, a man called Mason, saw a black youth seizing the handbag belonging to a woman who was shopping. He caught up with the youth and held him, he said with a view to taking him to a nearby police station, but the youth broke free from his grip. Mason caught the youth again and knocked him to the ground, and he then twisted one of the youth's arms behind his back in order to immobilise him and to enable him, Mason, so he said, once again to take the youth to the police station. The youth was struggling and calling for help at this time, and no one disputed that fact.

On the scene then came the appellant, who had only seen the latter stages of this incident. According to Mason he told the appellant first of all that he was arresting the youth for mugging the lady, and second, that he, Mason, was a police officer. That was not true. He was asked for his warrant card, which obviously was not forthcoming, and thereupon something of a struggle ensued between Mason on the one hand and the appellant and others on the other hand. In the course of these events Mason sustained injuries to his face, loosened teeth and bleeding gums.

The appellant put forward the following version of events. He said he was returning from work by bus when he saw Mason dragging the youth along and striking him again and again. He was so concerned about the matter that he rapidly got off the bus and made his way to the scene and asked Mason what on earth he was doing. In short he said that he punched Mason because he thought if he did so he would save the youth from further beating and what he described as torture ...

... [I]t is for the prosecution to eliminate the possibility that the appellant was acting under a genuine mistake of fact ...

One starts off with the meaning of the word 'assault'. 'Assault' in the context of this case, that is to say, using the word as a convenient abbreviation for assault and battery, is an act by which the defendant, intentionally or recklessly, applies unlawful force to the complainant. There are circumstances in which force may be applied to another lawfully. Taking a few examples: first, where the victim consents, as in lawful sports, the application of force to another will, generally speaking, not be unlawful. Second, where the defendant is acting in self-defence the exercise of any necessary and reasonable force to protect himself from unlawful violence is not unlawful. Third, by virtue of s 3 of the Criminal Law Act 1967, a person may use such force as is reasonable in the circumstances in the prevention of crime or in effecting or assisting in the lawful arrest of an offender or suspected offender or persons unlawfully at large. In each of those cases the defendant will be guilty if the jury are sure that first of all he applied force to the person of another, and secondly that he had the necessary mental element to constitute guilt.

The mental element necessary to constitute guilt is the intent to apply unlawful force to the victim. We do not believe that the mental element can be substantiated by simply showing an intent to apply force and no more.

What then is the situation if the defendant is labouring under a mistake of fact as to the circumstances? What if he believes, but believes mistakenly, that the victim is consenting, or that it is necessary to defend himself, or that a crime is being committed which he intends to prevent? He must then be judged against the mistaken facts as he believes them to be. If judged against those facts or circumstances the prosecution fail to establish his guilt, then he is entitled to be acquitted.

The next question is: does it make any difference if the mistake of the defendant was one which, viewed objectively by a reasonable onlooker, was an unreasonable mistake? In other words should the jury be directed as follows: 'Even if the defendant may have genuinely believed that what he was doing to the victim was either with the victim's consent or in reasonable self-defence or to prevent the commission of crime, as the case may be, nevertheless if you, the jury, come to the conclusion that the mistaken belief was unreasonable, that is to say that the defendant as a reasonable man should have realised his mistake, then you should convict him' ...

... The reasonableness or unreasonableness of the defendant's belief is material to the question of whether the belief was held by the defendant at all. If the belief was in fact held, its unreasonableness, so far as guilt or innocence is concerned, is neither here nor there. It is irrelevant. Were it otherwise, the defendant would be convicted because he was negligent in failing to recognise that the victim was not consenting or that a crime was not being committed and so on. In other words, the jury should be directed, first of all, that the prosecution have the burden or duty of proving the unlawfulness of the defendant's actions, second, that if the defendant may have been labouring under a mistake as to the facts he must be judged according to his mistaken view of the facts and, third, that that is so whether the mistake was, on an objective view, a reasonable mistake or not.

In a case of self-defence, where self-defence or the prevention of crime is concerned, if the jury come to the conclusion that the defendant believed, or may have believed, that he was being attacked or that a crime was being committed, and that force was necessary to protect himself or to prevent the crime, then the prosecution have not proved their case. If, however, the defendant's alleged belief was mistaken and if the mistake was an unreasonable one, that may be a powerful reason for coming to the conclusion that the belief was not honestly held and should be rejected.

Even if the jury come to the conclusion that the mistake was an unreasonable one, if the defendant may genuinely have been labouring under it, he is entitled to rely on it ...

R v Ball [1989] Crim LR 579 (CA)

Facts: The appellant's brother was arrested under the Public Order Act 1986. There was a struggle in which the appellant grabbed a police officer round the neck from behind, causing bruising and grazing. The appellant was charged with assault occasioning actual bodily harm. He maintained that his brother's arrest was unlawful and so his actions, in intervening, were therefore lawful.

Held: Honest belief on reasonable grounds in the unlawfulness of an arrest was not a defence to assault (*R v Fennell* (1970) 54 Cr App R 451) and it was logical that a similar belief in excessive force by the police in executing a lawful arrest would also not afford a defence.

Consent

Consent of the victim prevents an act from amounting to a common assault. However, if any injury is sustained, then the consent of the victim is irrelevant.

Attorney General's Reference (No 6 of 1980) [1981] QB 715 (CA)

Lord Lane CJ: ... The point of law on which the court is asked to give its opinion is as follows:

> Where two persons fight (otherwise than in the course of sport) in a public place can it be a defence for one of those persons to a charge of assault arising out of the fight that the other consented to fight?

The facts out of which the reference arises are these. The respondent, aged 18, and a youth aged 17, met in a public street and argued together. The respondent and the youth decided to settle the argument there and then by a fight. Before the fight the respondent removed his watch and handed it to a bystander for safe keeping and the youth removed his jacket. The respondent and the youth exchanged blows with their fists and the youth sustained a bleeding nose and bruises to his face caused by blows from the respondent ...

We think that it can be taken as a starting point that it is an essential element of an assault that the act is done contrary to the will and without the consent of the victim; and it is doubtless for this reason that the burden lies on the prosecution to negative consent. Ordinarily, then, if the victim consents, the assailant is not guilty.

But the cases show that the courts will make an exception to this principle where the public interest requires: see *R v Coney* (1882) 8 QBD 534 ('the prize fight case') ...

The answer to this question, in our judgment, is that it is not in the public interest that people should try to cause, or should cause, each other actual bodily harm for no good reason. Minor struggles are another matter. So, in our judgment, it is immaterial whether the act occurs in private or in public; it is an assault if actual bodily harm is intended and/or caused. This means that most fights will be unlawful regardless of consent.

Nothing which we have said is intended to cast doubt on the accepted legality of properly conducted games and sports, lawful chastisement or correction, reasonable surgical interference, dangerous exhibitions, etc. These apparent exceptions can be justified as involving the exercise of a legal right, in the case of chastisement or correction, or as needed in the public interest, in the other cases.

Our answer to the point of law is 'No', but not, as the reference implies, because the fight occurred in a public place, but because, wherever it occurred, the participants would have been guilty of assault, subject to self-defence, if, as we understand was the case, they intended to and/or did cause actual bodily harm ...

R v Brown and Others [1994] 1 AC 212 (HL)

Lord Templeman: My Lords, the appellants were convicted of assaults occasioning actual bodily harm contrary to s 47 of the Offences Against the Person Act 1861. Three of the appellants were also convicted of wounding contrary to s 20 of the 1861 Act. The incidents which led to each conviction occurred in the course of consensual sado-masochistic homosexual encounters. The Court of Appeal upheld the convictions and certified the following point of law of general public importance:

> Where A wounds or assaults B occasioning him actual bodily harm in the course of a sado-masochistic encounter, does the prosecution have to prove lack of consent on the part of B before they can establish A's guilt under s 20 or s 47 of the Offences Against the Person Act 1861?

... In *R v Donovan* [1934] 2 KB 498 Swift J delivering the judgment of the Court of Criminal Appeal said at 509:

> 'Bodily harm' has its ordinary meaning and includes any hurt or injury calculated to interfere with the health or comfort of the prosecutor. Such hurt or injury need not be permanent, but must, no doubt, be more than merely transient and trifling.

In the present case each appellant pleaded guilty to an offence under [s 47 of the 1861 Act] when the trial judge ruled that consent of the victim was no defence.

[His Lordship then quoted s 20 of the 1861 Act and continued:]

To constitute a wound for the purposes of the section the whole skin must be broken and not merely the outer layer called the epidermis or the cuticle: see *J J C (A Minor) v Eisenhower* [1983] 3 All ER 230.

'Grievous bodily harm' means simply bodily harm that is really serious and it has been said that it is undesirable to attempt a further definition: see *DPP v Smith* [1961] AC 290.

In s 20 the word 'unlawfully' means that the accused had no lawful excuse such as self-defence. The word 'maliciously' means no more than intentionally for present purposes: see *R v Mowatt* [1968] 1 QB 421.

Three of the appellants pleaded guilty to charges under s 20 when the trial judge ruled that the consent of the victim afforded no defence.

In the present case each of the appellants intentionally inflicted violence upon another (to whom I shall refer as 'the victim') with the consent of the victim and thereby occasioned actual bodily harm or in some cases wounding or grievous bodily harm. Each appellant was therefore guilty of an offence under s 47 or s 20 of the Act of 1861 unless the consent of the victim was effective to prevent the commission of the offence or effective to constitute a defence to the charge.

In some circumstances violence is not punishable under the criminal law. When no actual bodily harm is caused, the consent of the person affected precludes him from complaining. There can be no conviction for the summary offence of common assault if the victim has consented to the assault. Even when violence is intentionally inflicted and results in actual bodily harm, wounding or serious bodily harm the accused is entitled to be acquitted if the injury was a foreseeable incident of a lawful activity in which the person injured was participating. Surgery involves intentional violence resulting in actual or sometimes serious bodily harm but surgery is a lawful activity. Other activities carried on with consent by or on behalf of the injured person have been accepted as lawful notwithstanding that they involve actual bodily harm or may cause serious bodily harm. Ritual circumcision, tattooing, ear-piercing and violent sports including boxing are lawful activities ...

My Lords, the authorities dealing with the intentional infliction of bodily harm do not establish that consent is a defence to a charge under the Act of 1861. They establish that the courts have accepted that consent is a defence to the infliction of bodily harm in the course of some lawful activities. The question is whether the defence should be extended to the infliction of bodily harm in the course of sado-masochistic encounters ...

[His Lordship set out some of the dangers inherent in the activities in which the defendants had participated and went on:]

In principle there is a difference between violence which is incidental and violence which is inflicted for the indulgence of cruelty. The violence of sado-masochistic encounters involves the indulgence of cruelty by sadists and the degradation of victims. Such violence is injurious to the participants and unpredictably dangerous. I am not prepared to invent a defence of consent for sado-masochistic encounters which breed and glorify cruelty and result in offences under ss 47 and 20 of the Act of 1861.

... Society is entitled and bound to protect itself against a cult of violence. Pleasure derived from the infliction of pain is an evil thing. Cruelty is uncivilised. I would answer the certified question in the negative and dismiss the appeals of the appellants against conviction.

Lord Jauncey of Tullichettle: ... It was accepted by all the appellants that a line had to be drawn somewhere between those injuries to which a person could consent to infliction upon himself and those which were so serious that consent was immaterial ...

... In my view the line properly falls to be drawn between assault at common law and the offence of assault occasioning actual bodily harm created by s 47 of the Offences Against the Person Act 1861, with the result that consent of the victim is no answer to anyone charged with the latter offence or with a contravention of s 20 unless the circumstances fall within one of the well-known exceptions such as organised sporting contests and games, parental chastisement or reasonable surgery. There is nothing in ss 20 and 47 of the Act of 1861 to suggest that consent is either an essential ingredient of the offences or a defence thereto. If consent is to be an answer to a charge under s 47 but not to one under s 20, considerable practical problems would arise ... These problems would not arise if consent is an answer only to common assault. I would therefore dispose of these appeals on the basis that the infliction of actual or more serious bodily harm is an unlawful activity to which consent is no answer ...

... Without going into details of all the rather curious activities in which the appellants engaged it would appear to be good luck rather than good judgment which has prevented serious injury from occurring. Wounds can easily become septic if not properly treated, the free flow of blood from a person who is HIV positive or who has Aids can infect another and an inflicter who is carried away by sexual excitement or by drink or drugs could very easily inflict pain and injury beyond the level to which the receiver had consented ...

... If it is to be decided that such activities as the nailing by A of B's foreskin or scrotum to a board or the insertion of hot wax into C's urethra followed by the burning of his penis with a candle or the incising of D's scrotum with a scalpel to the effusion of blood are injurious neither to B, C and D nor to the public interest then it is for Parliament with its accumulated wisdom and sources of information to declare them to be lawful.

... There was argument as to whether lack of consent was a necessary ingredient of the offence of assault or whether consent, where available [ie in the case of common assault], was merely a defence ... If it were necessary, which it is not in this appeal, to decide which argument was correct, I would hold that consent could be a defence to assault but that lack of consent was not a necessary ingredient in assault.

Lord Lowry: My Lords, I have had the advantage of reading in draft the speeches of your Lordships. I agree with the reasoning and conclusions of my noble and learned friends, Lord Templeman and Lord Jauncey of Tullichettle, and I, too, would answer the certified question in the negative and dismiss the appeals.

In stating my own further reasons for this view I shall address myself exclusively to the cases in which, as has been informally agreed, one person has acted upon another in private, occasioning him actual bodily harm but nothing worse ...

... Everyone agrees that consent remains a complete defence to a charge of common assault and nearly everyone agrees that consent of the victim is not a defence to a charge of inflicting really serious personal injury (or 'grievous bodily harm'). The disagreement concerns offences which occasion actual bodily harm: the appellants contend that the consent of the victim is a defence to one charged with such an offence, while the respondent submits that consent is not a defence. I agree with the respondent's contention for reasons which I now explain ...

I suggest that the following points should be noted ...

(3) Wounding is associated in ss 18 and 20 with the infliction of grievous bodily harm and is naturally thought of as a serious offence, but it may involve anything from a minor breaking or puncture of the skin to a near fatal injury. Thus wounding may simply occasion actual bodily harm or it may inflict grievous bodily harm. If the victim's consent is a defence to occasioning actual bodily harm, then, so far as concerns the proof of guilt, the line is drawn, as my noble and learned friend Lord Jauncey of Tullichettle puts it ... 'somewhere down the middle of s 20', which I would regard as a most unlikely solution.

(4) According to the appellants' case, if an accused person charged with wounding relies on consent as a defence, the jury will have to find whether anything more than actual bodily harm was occasioned, something which is not contemplated by s 20.

(5) The distinction between common assault and all other attacks on the person is that common assault does not necessarily involve significant bodily injury. It is much easier to draw the line between no significant injury and some injury than to differentiate between degrees of injury. It is also more logical, because for one person to inflict any injury on another without good reason is an evil in itself (malum in se) and contrary to public policy.

(6) That consent is a defence to a charge of common assault is a common law doctrine which the Act of 1861 has done nothing to change.

... If, as I, too, consider, the question of consent is immaterial, there are *prima facie* offences against s 20 and 47 and the next question is whether there is good reason to add sado-masochistic acts to the list of exceptions contemplated in the *Attorney General's Reference*. In my opinion, the answer to that question is 'No'.

In adopting this conclusion I follow closely my noble and learned friends, Lord Templeman and Lord Jauncey. What the appellants are obliged to propose is that the deliberate and painful infliction of physical injury should be exempted from the operation of statutory provisions the object of which is to prevent or punish that very thing, the reason for the proposed exemption being that both those who will inflict and those who will suffer the injury wish to satisfy a perverted and depraved sexual desire. Sado-masochistic homosexual activity cannot be regarded as conducive to the enhancement or enjoyment of family life or conducive to the welfare of society. A relaxation of the prohibitions in ss 20 and 47 can only encourage the practice of homosexual sado-masochism, with the physical cruelty that it must involve (which can scarcely be regarded as a 'manly diversion'), by withdrawing the legal penalty and giving the activity a judicial imprimatur. As well as all this, one cannot overlook the physical danger to those who may indulge in sado-masochism. In this connection, and also generally, it is idle for the appellants to claim that they are educated exponents of 'civilised cruelty'. A proposed general exemption is to be tested by considering the likely general effect. This must include the probability that some sado-masochistic activity, under the powerful influence of the sexual instinct, will get out of hand and result in serious physical damage to the participants and that some activity will involve a danger of infection such as these particular exponents do not contemplate for themselves ...

Lord Mustill and **Lord Slynn of Hadley** delivered dissenting speeches.

R v Wilson [1996] 3 WLR 125 (CA)

Russell LJ: ... The charge was one of assault occasioning actual bodily harm contrary to s 47 of the Offences Against the Person Act 1861, the particulars being that on

14 May 1994 the appellant assaulted Julie Anne Wilson, thereby occasioning her actual bodily harm. The so-called victim was the wife of the appellant.

The facts were not in dispute ...

The police informed the appellant that his wife had been medically examined and that marks had been observed on both her buttocks. On the right buttock, as the photographs before the court disclose, there was a fading scar in the form of a capital letter 'W', and on the left buttock, a more pronounced and more recent scar in the form of a capital letter 'A'. The two letters 'A' and 'W' were the initials of the appellant.

He at once admitted that he was responsible for the marks. He told the police:

> I put them there ... She wanted a tattoo and I didn't know how to do a tattoo, but she wanted my name tattooing on her bum and I didn't know how to do it; so I burned it on with a hot knife. It wasn't life threatening, it wasn't anything, it was done for love. She loved me. She wanted me to give her – put my name on her body. As I say, she asked me originally if I would tattoo my name on her. She wanted me to do it on her breasts and I talked her out of that because I didn't know how to do a tattoo. Then she said, 'Well, there must be some way. If you can't do a tattoo, there must be some way', she says. I think her exact words were summat like, 'I'm not scared of anybody knowing that I love you enough to have your name on my body', something of that nature, and between us we hit on this idea of using a hot knife of her bum. I wouldn't do it on her breasts.

The medical evidence simply commented upon the existence of the letter 'A' on the left buttock as having been branded on Mrs Wilson a few days before 20 May 1994. Dr McKenna added: 'There was associated bruising around the burn and the skin hadn't fully healed'. No reference was made by the doctor to a faded scar on the right buttock.

At the conclusion of the evidence called by the prosecution, defence counsel submitted that his client had no case to answer. The judge, in a ruling of which we have a transcript, after reviewing the facts and authority, concluded as follows:

> The reality that I have to deal with is that on the face of it the majority in the House of Lords in *R v Brown (Anthony)* [1994] 1 AC 212 approved of the *dicta* in *R v Donovan* [1934] 2 KB 498 and that accordingly until such time as the legislature or the European Court do something about it we are now saddled with a law that means that anyone who injures his partner, spouse, or whatever, in the course of some consensual activity is at risk of having his or her private life dragged before the public to no good purpose. Sadly, I take the view that I am bound by the majority in *R v Brown* and that I would have to, in those circumstances, direct this jury to convict.

Counsel for the defendant, in the light of that ruling, did not call his client and did not make any submissions to the jury, who in due course convicted the appellant. The judge conditionally discharged him for a period of 12 months.

It is effectively against that ruling of the judge that the appeal is brought to this court. In the court below, and before us, reference was predictably made to *R v Donovan* [1934] 2 KB 498, a decision of the Court of Criminal Appeal, and to *R v Brown (Anthony)* [1994] 1 AC 212, a decision of the House of Lords. They are the two authorities to which the trial judge referred in the observations we have cited ...

We are abundantly satisfied that there is no factual comparison to be made between the instant case and the facts of either *R v Donovan* [1934] 2 KB 498 or *R v Brown* 1 AC 212: Mrs Wilson not only consented to that which the appellant did, she instigated it. There was no aggressive intent on the part of the appellant. On the contrary, far from wishing to cause injury to his wife, the appellant's desire was to assist her in what she regarded as the acquisition of a desirable piece of personal adornment, perhaps in this day and age no less understandable than the piercing of nostrils or even tongues for the purposes of inserting decorative jewellery.

In our judgment *R v Brown* is not authority for the proposition that consent is no defence to a charge under s 47 of the Act of 1861, in all circumstances where actual bodily harm is deliberately inflicted. It is to be observed that the question certified for their Lordships in *R v Brown* related only to a 'sado-masochistic encounter'. However, their Lordships recognised in the course of their speeches, that it is necessary that there must be exceptions to what is no more than a general proposition. The speeches of Lord Templeman at 231, Lord Jauncey of Tullichettle at 245, and the dissenting speech of Lord Slynn of Hadley at 277, all refer to tattooing as being an activity which, if carried out with the consent of an adult, does not involve an offence under s 47, albeit that actual bodily harm is deliberately inflicted.

For our part, we cannot detect any logical difference between what the appellant did and what he might have done in the way of tattooing. The latter activity apparently requires no state authorisation, and the appellant was as free to engage in it as anyone else. We do not think that we are entitled to assume that the method adopted by the appellant and his wife was any more dangerous or painful than tattooing. There was simply no evidence to assist the court on this aspect of the matter.

Does public policy or the public interest demand that the appellant's activity should be visited by the sanctions of the criminal law? The majority in *R v Brown* clearly took the view that such considerations were relevant. If that is so, then we are firmly of the opinion that it is not in the public interest that activities such as the appellant's in this appeal should amount to criminal behaviour. Consensual activity between husband and wife, in the privacy of the matrimonial home, is not, in our judgment, normally a proper matter for criminal investigation, let alone criminal prosecution. Accordingly we take the view that the judge failed to have full regard to the facts of this case and misdirected himself in saying that *R v Donovan* [1934] 2 KB 498 and *R v Brown* [1994] 1 AC 212 constrained him to rule that consent was no defence.

In this field, in our judgment, the law should develop upon a case-by-case basis rather than upon general propositions to which, in the changing times in which we live, exceptions may arise from time to time not expressly covered by authority.

We shall allow the appeal and quash the conviction ...

OTHER OFFENCES INVOLVING VIOLENCE

Offences Against the Person Act 1861

Section 38: assault with intent to resist or prevent arrest

Whosoever ... shall assault any person with intent to resist or prevent the lawful apprehension or detainer of himself or of any other person for any offence, shall be guilty of [an offence], and being convicted thereof shall be liable ... to be imprisoned for any term not exceeding two years ...

For this offence to be made out, the arrest must be a lawful one. Where the arrest is carried out by a member of the public (not a police officer), this means that an arrestable offence must have been committed.

R v Self [1992] 1 WLR 657 (CA)

Garland J: ... [T]his appellant was tried on an indictment which contained three counts. Count 1 alleged that he stole a bar of chocolate (value 79p) belonging to F W Woolworth plc. Count 2 alleged that, contrary to s 38 of the Offences Against the Person Act 1861, he assaulted Stuart Michael Frost with intent to resist or prevent the lawful apprehension or detainer of himself. Count 3 alleged a similar offence against Jonathan George Mole ...

The facts quite briefly stated were as follows. The appellant was a serving police officer, a detective constable. He had been in the police force for some 17 years. On the afternoon in question in October 1990 a Mrs Stanton, who is a store detective in Woolworths in Kingston, saw the appellant pick up a bar of chocolate. He then moved on and apparently picked up some Christmas cards using both hands. The chocolate had disappeared; in fact, he had put it in his trouser pocket. He then left the store without paying.

Mrs Stanton asked Mr Frost the young sales assistant to help her. They followed the appellant out into the street and along Church Street. Mrs Stanton saw him put his hand in his pocket, take out the chocolate and throw it under a car. She actually retrieved it and said to him: 'I do not want to call the police for a bar of chocolate. Come here and come back to the store.' Mr Frost approached the appellant and said: 'You have been seen shoplifting'. The appellant became agitated, tried to leave, grabbed Mr Frost's arm and scratched it, punched him on the cheek, kicked him on the shin and then ran off with Mr Frost in pursuit.

Mr Mole came into the picture because he was in his car and saw what had happened between the appellant and Mr Frost. He got out of his car and asked Mrs Stanton if she needed any help. She said: 'Yes', so Mr Mole also ran after the appellant. During the chase the appellant jumped down a steep drop, some 10 feet or more, from a churchyard to the street below. When Mr Mole caught up with him he took hold of his wrist and there was a minor struggle. He told the appellant that he was making a citizen's arrest because he believed he had been shoplifting. The appellant struggled and apparently kicked Mr Mole just above his knee and tried to run away again. Mr Mole and Mr Frost caught up with him, there was a further struggle but in the end the appellant quietened down and there was some conversation between the persons involved. Mr Frost did say the appellant was in a very distressed condition, both physically and mentally.

When the appellant came to give his account of these matters before the jury he said that he recalled picking up the bar of chocolate in Woolworths but had no recollection of what had happened afterwards, save that he remembered looking at the Christmas cards. The chocolate was undoubtedly in his pocket when he left the store. He had forgotten about it. He had no intention of stealing it and had set off towards a bookshop. But on the way he put his hand in his pocket and realised that he had not paid for the chocolate that he found there. He then heard people running behind him and saw Mrs Stanton and Mr Frost coming and shouting and then everything closed in on him. He panicked and thought the situation looked very grave indeed. He threw the chocolate away and ran. Then Mr Frost intervened and the two scuffles with Mr Frost and Mr Mole followed.

He could not explain his actions. He felt sorry for Mr Frost and Mr Mole, who he thought had acted very properly. It should be mentioned in passing that a doctor confirmed that the appellant was at the time suffering from some degree of stress.

... There is one point central to the appeal. It is this. Since the appellant was acquitted of theft neither Mr Frost nor Mr Mole were entitled by virtue of s 24 of the Police and Criminal Evidence Act 1984 to effect a citizen's arrest. If they were not entitled to do that then this appellant could not be convicted of an assault with intent to resist or prevent the lawful apprehension or detainer of himself, that is to say his arrest.

In order to examine this proposition it is necessary of course to look closely at s 24 of the Act of 1984 ...

... Section 24 deals with powers of arrest without warrant. Subsection (1) sets out to define arrestable offences in respect of which powers of summary arrest can be exercised. Subsections (2) and (3) deal with the other qualifying offences, subsection (4) begins to set out powers of arrest in the following terms:

> Any person [and of course 'any person' means both a citizen and a constable] may arrest without a warrant: (a) anyone who is in the act of committing an arrestable offence; (b) anyone whom he has reasonable grounds for suspecting to be committing such an offence.

It is immediately apparent that that subsection is dealing with the present continuous, that is somebody in the act of committing the offence or someone that the arrester has reasonable grounds for suspecting to be committing such an offence. Subsection (5) moves on to the past, indeed the perfect, tense:

> Where an arrestable offence has been committed, any person [both citizen and constable] may arrest without a warrant: (a) anyone who is guilty of the offence; (b) anyone whom he has reasonable grounds for suspecting to be guilty of it.

One asks, guilty of what? The answer is, guilty of the arrestable offence which has been committed.

Then by contrast subsection (6) deals with a constable's powers of arrest which are very much wider than those of the citizen. It provides:

> Where a constable has reasonable grounds for suspecting that an arrestable offence has been committed, he may arrest without a warrant anyone whom he has reasonable grounds for suspecting to be guilty of the offence.

Thus there are doubly reasonable grounds for suspecting, both as to the commission of the offence and the person who has committed it.

Subsection (7) again deals with constables' powers and this is in anticipation of an offence. It provides:

> A constable may arrest without a warrant: (a) anyone who is about to commit an arrestable offence; (b) anyone whom he has reasonable grounds for suspecting to be about to commit an arrestable offence.

Then s 25 goes on to deal with general arrest conditions otherwise than for arrestable offences ...

... [I]n the judgment of this court, the words of s 24 do not admit of argument. Subsection (5) makes it abundantly clear that the powers of arrest without a warrant where an arrestable offence has been committed require as a condition precedent an offence committed. If subsequently there is an acquittal of the alleged offence no offence has been committed. The power to arrest is confined to the person guilty of the offence or anyone who the person making the arrest has reasonable grounds for suspecting to be guilty of it. But of course if he is not guilty there can be no valid suspicion ...

If it is necessary to go further, one contrasts the words of subsection (5) with subsection (6), the very much wider powers given to a constable who has reasonable grounds for suspecting that an arrestable offence has been committed ...

> ... The words of the statute are clear and applying those words to this case there was no arrestable offence committed. It necessarily follows that the two offences under s 38 of the Offences Against the Person Act 1861 could not be committed because there was no power to apprehend or detain the appellant ...

Assaulting a police officer in the execution of his duty; obstructing a police officer in the execution of his duty

Section 89 of the The Police Act 1996

(1) Any person who assaults a constable in the execution of his duty, or a person assisting a constable in the execution of his duty, shall be guilty of an offence and liable on summary conviction to imprisonment for a term not exceeding six months or to a fine not exceeding [£5,000] or to both.

(2) Any person who resists or wilfully obstructs a constable in the execution of his duty, or a person assisting a constable in the execution of his duty, shall be guilty of an offence and liable on summary conviction to imprisonment for a term not exceeding one month or to a fine not exceeding [£1,000] or to both.

The provisions of the Police Act 1996 consolidate provisions in the Police Act 1964. The elements of the offence under s 89(1) are:

(a) an assault ...

(b) on a police officer ...

(c) who is acting in the execution of his duty.

It does not matter that the defendant did not realise that the person he assaulted was a police officer, although this would be good mitigation and would result in a lesser punishment for the assault.

The elements of the offence under s 89(2) are:

(a) obstruction ...

(b) of a police officer ...

(c) who is acting in the execution of his duty.

Assault

Assault is defined above.

Obstruction

Obstruction means making it more difficult for the police to do their job.

Hinchliffe v Sheldon [1955] 1 WLR 1207 (DC)

Facts: The appellant was the son of the licensee of an inn. On returning to the inn one night, at about 11.17 pm, he found that police officers wished to enter the premises as they suspected that the licensee was committing an offence against s 100 of the Licensing Act 1953. The appellant thereupon shouted warnings to the licensee, who did not open the door to the police officers until 11.25 pm. The licensee was not found to be committing any offence. The appellant was charged with wilfully obstructing a constable when in the execution of his duty.

Lord Goddard CJ: ... 'Obstructing' means, for this purpose, making it more difficult for the police to carry out their duties. It is quite obvious that the appellant was detaining the police while giving a warning; he was making it more difficult for the police to get certain entry into the premises, and the justices were entitled to find as they did ...

For an offence under s 89 of the Police Act 1996, the police officer must have been acting in the execution of his or her duty.

Rice v Connolly [1966] 2 QB 414 (DC)

Facts: The defendant appeared to a police constable to have been acting suspiciously in an area where there had been a number of break-ins during the same night. He was asked several times for his full name and address, which he refused to give, and when asked to accompany the police constable to a police box, declined to do so, unless arrested.

Lord Parker CJ: ... What the prosecution have to prove is that there was an obstructing of a constable; that the constable was at the time acting in the execution of his duty and that the person obstructing did so wilfully. To carry the matter a little further, it is in my view clear that 'obstruct' under [s 89(2) of the Police Act 1996], is the doing of any act which makes it more difficult for the police to carry out their duty. That description of obstructing I take from *Hinchcliffe v Sheldon* [1955] 1 WLR 1207. It is also in my judgment clear that it is part of the obligations and duties of a police constable to take all steps which appear to him necessary for keeping the peace, for preventing crime or for protecting property from criminal injury. There is no exhaustive definition of the powers and obligations of the police, but they are at least those, and they would further include the duty to detect crime and to bring an offender to justice.

Pausing there, it seems to me quite clear that the defendant was making it more difficult for the police to carry out their duties, and that the police at the time and throughout were acting in accordance with their duties. The only remaining ingredient, and the one upon which in my judgment this case revolves, is whether the obstructing of which the defendant was guilty was a wilful obstruction. 'Wilful' in this context not only in my judgment means 'intentional' but something which is done without lawful excuse, and that indeed is conceded by Mr Skinner, who appears for the prosecution case. Accordingly, the sole question here is whether the defendant had a lawful excuse for refusing to answer the questions put to him. In my judgment he had. It seems to me quite clear that though every citizen has a moral duty or, if you like, a social duty to assist the police, there is no legal duty to that effect, and indeed the whole basis of the common law is the right of the individual to refuse to answer questions put to him by persons in authority, and to refuse to accompany those in authority to any particular place; short, of course, of arrest ...

In my judgment there is all the difference in the world between deliberately telling a false story – something which on no view a citizen has a right to do – and preserving silence or refusing to answer – something which he has every right to do. Accordingly, in my judgment, looked upon in that perfectly general way, it was not shown that the refusal of the defendant to answer the questions or to accompany the police officer in the first instance to the police box was an obstruction without lawful excuse ...

In the execution of his duty

R v Fennell (1970) 54 Cr App R 451 (DC)

Facts: The appellant was convicted of assaulting a constable in the execution of his duty contrary to [s 89(1) of the Police Act 1996]. His defence was that he had used force to rescue his son from police custody, which was in fact lawful but which the appellant honestly and reasonably believed to be unlawful.

Widgery LJ: ... It was accepted in the court below that, if the arrest had been, in fact, unlawful, the appellant would have been justified in using reasonable force to secure the release of his son. This proposition has not been argued before us and we will assume, without deciding it, that it is correct ... [Counsel for the appellant] then contended that ... a father who used force to effect the release of his son from custody was justified in so doing if he honestly believed on reasonable grounds that (contrary to the fact) the arrest was unlawful.

We do not accept that submission. The law jealously scrutinises all claims to justify the use of force and will not readily recognise new ones. Where a person honestly and reasonably believes that he or his child is in imminent danger of injury, it would be unjust if he were to be deprived of the right to use reasonable force by way of defence merely because he had made some genuine mistake of fact. On the other hand, if the child is in police custody and not in imminent danger of injury there is no urgency of the kind which requires an immediate decision and a father who forcibly releases the child does so at his peril. If in fact the arrest proves to be lawful, the father's use of force cannot be justified ...

Coffin and Another v Smith and Another (1980) 71 Cr App R 221 (DC)

Donaldson LJ: ... The defendants were both teenagers. The offence is alleged to have taken place in February 1978 ...

The main facts emerge from the evidence of Police Constable Coffin. He stated that at 11.45 pm on 3 February 1978, he went to Newhaven Boys' Club with Woman Police Constable Whitney. He requested people to leave the premises. Some did so, but congregated outside the premises by the front door. The defendants were amongst them. He asked them to move on two occasions. He said that the defendant Smith made no attempt to move and was unsteady, his eyes were glazed. The witness believed him to be drunk. He again told Smith to move and Smith replied 'Fuck off, pig'. The defendant Hogsden intervened and said 'Fuck off, bastards. Leave him alone.' Both defendants then walked off. But Smith came back in an aggressive manner. The witness stated that the defendant Smith aimed a punch at him which struck him in the chest. The witness then arrested Smith for assault and put him in the police car. Whilst he was in the police car the defendant Hogsden opened the car door and attempted to remove Smith from the car. Hogsden lashed out with her foot at Woman Police Constable Whitney who was attempting to control her. Smith was then put into another car. Hogsden then struggled with Police Constable Coffin, tore buttons from his jacket and kicked him twice in the chest.

The police had been called to the boys' club by the youth leader who wished to ensure that various boys left, because there was to be some form of entertainment later in the evening to which only a limited number were invited.

The justices considered the question whether these police officers were acting in the execution of their duty, that being the essential ingredient of the offence under [s 89 of the Police Act 1996] and they decided that there was no case to answer ...

In a word a police officer's duty is to be a keeper of the peace and to take all necessary steps with that in view. These officers, just like the ordinary officer on the beat, were attending a place where they thought that their presence would assist in the keeping of the peace ...

... Let me answer the specific questions which the justices ask in their case, which are numerous: 'Were we right in holding that when assisting the youth leader to eject the defendants and others from the Youth Club the police officers were not acting in the execution of their duty?' My answer is that they were wrong, but it is irrelevant, because there was a break, and this was a separate incident.

'Were we right in holding that when the police officers requested the defendant Smith to "move on" they were not acting in the execution of their duty?' I think they were wrong, the officers were plainly acting in the execution of their duty, their duty being to keep the peace.

'Were we right in holding that when the defendant Smith punched Police Constable Coffin, the said constable was not acting in the execution of his duty?' They were wrong for the same reason.

'Were we right in holding that when Police Constable Coffin arrested the defendant Smith he was not acting in the execution of his duty?' They were not right. There had been a very plain breach of the peace personally experienced by the police constable. He was fully entitled to arrest and he was doing so in the execution of his duty.

'Were we right in holding that when Woman Police Constable Whitney was kicked by the defendant Hogsden, the said constable was not acting in the execution of her duty?' No, they were wrong, for the same reasons.

'Were we right in holding that when Police Constable Coffin was kicked by the defendant Hogsden, the said constable was not acting in the execution of his duty?' No, they were wrong, for the same reasons ...

Riley v DPP (1989) 91 Cr App R 14 (DC)

Facts: Extract from case stated : The justices found the following facts: (a) at about 6.10 pm on 19 February 1988 officers McDade, Farndon, Martin, Barnett and Nicholas were summoned to the home of the defendant at 31 Walton Road Manor Park London E12 to search for and arrest one Andrew Riley the younger brother of the defendant; (b) the door of the house was opened by the defendant. The officers explained that they believed that Andrew Riley was hiding in the house and that they wanted to enter and arrest him. They were allowed in without any protestation by the defendant; (c) McDade and Barnett wished to search the bedrooms which were located on the first floor of the house. They were accompanied by the defendant who imposed a condition that only one officer could enter any of the bedrooms to conduct the search as he feared that any more would leave the rooms in a state of disarray. Other officers searched the remaining bedrooms, namely those of Andrew Riley and Stanley Riley senior (the father of the defendant). Apart from expressing his concern that the officers should leave the bedrooms in a tidy condition Stanley Riley senior did not object to the officers continuing their search of his house. The remaining officers who had accompanied McDade and Barnett and officers who had not been identified at the trial searched the ground floor; (d) McDade was allowed to search the defendant's bedroom and while he was doing so the defendant stood in the entrance of the doorway facing the landing and face to face with Barnett. At that moment an officer on the ground floor shouted that

Andrew Riley had been found. On hearing this the defendant pushed past Barnett and made his way to the stairs only to be confronted by Farndon who stood in his way. The other officers and Stanley Riley senior stopped whatever they were doing and made their way to the landing area of the first floor and generally stood there observing as they did the arrest of Andrew Riley; (e) the defendant then attempted to get past Farndon and in so doing he caused Farndon to momentarily lose his balance. Farndon quickly regained his balance and was then joined by McDade who had squeezed past the defendant and positioned himself alongside Farndon. The defendant became agitated and shouted, 'Where are you fucking taking him?' McDade said, 'You can't go down there. Andrew has been arrested, just stay there for a moment.' The defendant ignored this instruction and attempted to get between the officers and was promptly arrested for obstruction. He was then taken into the street where he was cautioned but made no intelligible reply; (f) Martin then appeared on the scene and assisted McDade in ushering the defendant to the waiting police van. As they attempted to get him into the van he raised his foot and wedged it on the step of the van and pushed back. After much pushing and shoving the defendant was forced into the van falling on his stomach as he entered. McDade got into the van while Martin remained on the ground leaning forward but retaining his grip on the defendant; (g) as a consequence of this thrashing about the defendant's elbow struck McDade's upper arm which resulted in McDade suffering a bruise. Martin got into the van and attempted to take a firmer hold of the defendant whereupon the defendant deliberately bit his left thumb. The defendant was restrained from further movement and conveyed to Forest Gate police station where he was formally charged with the offences.

Watkins LJ: ... If police officers are invited into premises by an occupier or other person authorised so to do, who has been told by them the reason for their entry, as was undoubtedly the fact here, then in our view they are lawfully on the premises. If, whilst there, they effect an arrest, that may or may not be lawful, depending on whether the officers have a warrant or can bring themselves within the provisions of s 24, or possibly s 25, of the 1984 Act. These sections provide for arrest without warrant for arrestable and other offences, and general arrest conditions. Reverting to s 17, it is our opinion that its provisions give a right to police officers to enter and search a house in the absence of consent by the occupier, subject of course to compliance with the terms of that section by the police officers concerned.

In the present case the justices found, and in our judgment were entitled to, that the officers were lawfully in the house. Logically the next question is, was the arrest of Andrew Riley lawful, and the officers engaged in it therefore acting in execution of their duty? If the arrest was lawful, it simply could not be argued, as in fact it was, that the appellant's intervention was in opposition to an unlawful arrest. Unfortunately there is nothing in the case stated which informs us as to whether or not the justices were told of the reason for the arrest of Andrew Riley. True it is that the defendant was not told.

If, as we must assume from what the case stated both does and does not inform us, the justices were not told of the reason for the arrest of Andrew Riley, it follows that they could not have known whether the officers were executing a warrant for his arrest, that he was alleged to be guilty of an arrestable offence or that the officers had reasonable grounds for suspecting that he was guilty of an arrestable offence. It may have been, had the facts been known, that the officers had grounds for effecting a general arrest within s 25. But there is, as we have said, simply no evidence of the officers' reasons, whatever they were, for arresting Andrew Riley. Thus plainly the justices were in no position to tell whether the arresting officers were, in the course of arrest, acting in the execution of their duty.

The Crown's failure to lead evidence as to that inevitably caused a failure by them, in our view, to establish the lawfulness of the arrest of Andrew Riley and consequently that the officers were acting in the execution of their duty.

In the light of that can it nevertheless be said that Farndon and McDade lawfully arrested the defendant, and whether Martin was in any event acting in the execution of his duty when his thumb was bitten by the defendant?

In order for there to be a lawful arrest for wilful obstruction of a constable in the execution of his duty, the Crown has to prove, in addition to the fact that he was so acting, the physical and mental element of the obstruction and further that the constable reasonably believed that if he did not make an arrest there would, or might be, a breach of the peace or an attempt to impede a lawful arrest.

In the present case, for the reasons we have already given, it cannot be said there was an attempt to impede a lawful arrest. Moreover there is no finding of fact in the case stated that any one of the officers had a reasonable apprehension that a breach of the peace might follow. That leads us to the conclusion that, although it could be and was properly said that the officers were lawfully on the premises, Andrew Riley's arrest was not proved to be lawful, so the arrest of the defendant must have been unlawful.

That leaves the question of what happened in the street and near and in the police van. Seeing that the arrest of Andrew Riley was not proved to be lawful, Martin, unwittingly, in going to the assistance of McDade was, in our judgment, acting in furtherance of an unlawful arrest of the defendant and could not consequently have been acting in the execution of his duty when he was bitten. That means that an essential element of the offence under [s 89(1)] was not established by the Crown. So the conviction of the defendant simply cannot stand. It has to be quashed. Thus the appeal is allowed ...

Edwards v Director of Public Prosecutions (1993) 97 Cr App R 301 (DC)

Evans LJ: Late on a Saturday night, 19 October 1991, three police officers were on plain clothes duty in the Piccadilly area of London. They saw three men huddled together by a dustbin in Shaftesbury Avenue and they had ample grounds for suspecting that those men were in possession of cannabis. One of the police officers, PC Rowe, produced his identity card and said:

> Police – that's drugs [pointing to the substances]. I am going to search you.

The finding as to what happened next is as follows. The man to whom PC Rowe had spoken was named Fox:

> Fox clenched his right hand and turned away. PC Rowe said, 'give the contents to me'. Fox pushed PC Rowe's hand away, put the contents in his mouth when the officer went to take them and struggled violently. PC Rowe said 'You are nicked for obstruction'.

Then a lady called Prendergast intervened and was arrested. The appellant, Deborah Edwards, then intervened and she, herself, was arrested for obstructing the officers in their arrest of Prendergast. The charge brought against Miss Edwards was that on 19 October 1991, at Piccadilly Circus, she did wilfully obstruct Susan MacSpadden, a constable of the Metropolitan Police, in the execution of her duty contrary to [s 89(2) of the Police Act 1996].

> ... The issue in the case [is:] Was PC Rowe acting in the execution of his duty when he arrested or purported to arrest Fox? In the context, the question becomes: Was his arrest of Fox lawful or not? ...
>
> On that basis, the position in the present case is that we have the finding, but only the finding, of what PC Rowe said to Fox at the time when he was arrested. There was no reference to s 25 or to any of the general arrest conditions and indeed it is not suggested that there was any evidence to the effect that PC Rowe did have those arrest conditions in mind at the time when this incident took place ...
>
> In the present case it seems to me that even if it is permissible for the court to infer in appropriate circumstances what the state of mind of the arresting officer must have been, that that is not open to the court in the present case. That is for the simple reason that the express finding that PC Rowe arrested by reference to the offence of obstruction, with no regard to the possible justification for an arrest under s 25, makes it quite impossible to infer in my judgment that PC Rowe had something quite different in mind at that time, something which he mentioned neither then nor subsequently. That fact alone means that, in my judgment, in the present case the arrest of Fox is not shown to have been lawful in reliance upon s 25 of PACE ...
>
> ... PC Rowe gave a reason. He gave a reason which was not a valid reason. It follows, in my judgment, that the arrest itself, that is the arrest of Fox, must be regarded as invalid. It follows, for the reasons I indicated at the outset, that the charge against Miss Edwards should have been dismissed and that this appeal should be allowed ...

[Note: The police officer could have arrested Fox for possession of cannabis and the police had power to detain and search Fox under the Misuse of Drugs Act 1971. However, when stating the reason for the arrest, the officer relied on 'obstruction' and not on any powers conferred by the 1971 Act. In this case, the prosecution sought to rely on the general powers of arrest contained in s 25 of the Police and Criminal Evidence Act 1984 but were unsuccessful because (as is apparent from the judgment of Evans LJ) the officer did not give any of the reasons set out in s 25 as the reason for the arrest. Accordingly, the arrest was unlawful.]

KIDNAPPING

Regina v D [1984] AC 778 (HL)

Lord Hailsham of St Marylebone LC: My Lords, having read in advance the draft speech about to be delivered by my noble and learned friend, Lord Brandon of Oakbrook, I need only say that I agree with him ...

Lord Fraser of Tullybelton: My Lords, I have had the advantage of reading in draft the speech of my noble and learned friend, Lord Brandon of Oakbrook. I agree with it, and for the reasons stated in it I would answer the certified questions in the affirmative and allow the appeal.

Lord Scarman: My Lords, I have had the advantage of reading in draft the speech to be delivered by my noble and learned friend, Lord Brandon of Oakbrook. I agree with it, and for the reasons he gives I would allow the appeal.

Lord Bridge of Harwich: My Lords, for the reasons given in the speech of my noble and learned friend, Lord Brandon of Oakbrook, I would allow this appeal ...

Lord Brandon of Oakbrook: ... In this appeal your Lordships are called on, for the first time, to examine the nature, ingredients and scope of [kidnapping] ...

... [T]he offence contains four ingredients as follows: (1) the taking or carrying away of one person by another; (2) by force or by fraud; (3) without the consent of the person so taken or carried away; and (4) without lawful excuse ...

... That third ingredient ... consists of the absence of consent on the part of the person taken or carried away. I see no good reason why, in relation to the kidnapping of a child, it should not in all cases be the absence of the child's consent which is material, whatever its age may be. In the case of a very young child, it would not have the understanding or the intelligence to give its consent, so that absence of consent would be a necessary inference from its age. In the case of an older child, however, it must, I think be a question of fact for a jury whether the child concerned has sufficient understanding and intelligence to give its consent; if, but only if, the jury considers that a child has these qualities, it must then go on to consider whether it has been proved that the child did not give its consent. While the matter will always be for the jury alone to decide, I should not expect a jury to find at all frequently that a child under 14 has sufficient understanding and intelligence to give its consent.

I should add that, while the absence of the consent of the person having custody or care or control of a child is not material to what I have stated to be the third ingredient of the common law offence of kidnapping, the giving of consent by such a person may be very relevant to the fourth ingredient, in that, depending on all the circumstances, it might well support a defence of lawful excuse ...

[Note: Reference may also be made to the Child Abduction Act 1984 which was going through Parliament when this case was being considered by the House of Lords. The contents of the Act are outside the scope of the present work.]

FALSE IMPRISONMENT

R v Rahman (1985) 81 Cr App R 349 (CA)

The Lord Chief Justice: We turn ... to consider what it is that has to be proved in order to bring home a charge of false imprisonment. False imprisonment consists in the unlawful and intentional or reckless restraint of a victim's freedom of movement from a particular place. In other words it is unlawful detention which stops the victim moving away as he would wish to move ...

There are many ways in which the prosecution may prove unlawfulness. The existence of a court order, as already mentioned in this judgment, may perhaps be one, by showing that the parental control had by order been given to someone other than the parent himself, and that the detention by the parent was contrary to that order. In this case there was no such order. But there are other ways of proving unlawfulness. The detention may be for such a period or in such circumstances as to take it out of the realms of reasonable parental discipline ...

Whether that stage has been reached, namely the stage of unreasonableness, is a matter for the jury to decide, if there is evidence which it is proper to go before the jury for them to consider ...

CHAPTER 23

SEXUAL OFFENCES

In this chapter we look at rape, indecent assault, and a number of offences dependent on the age of the victim. We start with rape.

RAPE

Until November 1994, rape could only be committed if a man had sexual intercourse with a woman without her consent. Section 142 of the Criminal Justice and Public Order Act 1994 amended s 1 of the Sexual Offences Act 1956 so that it now reads as follows:

Section 1 of the Sexual Offences Act 1956

> (1) It is an offence for a man to rape a woman or another man.
>
> (2) A man commits rape if:
>
> (a) he has sexual intercourse with a person (whether vaginal or anal) who at the time of the intercourse does not consent to it; and
>
> (b) at the time he knows that the person does not consent to the intercourse or is reckless as to whether that person consents to it.

Punishment

The maximum sentence for rape is life imprisonment: s 37 of the Sexual Offences Act 1956.

The elements of rape are thus:

(1) a man has intercourse (anal or vaginal) with a woman, or a man has anal intercourse with another man; and

(2) the victim does not consent to sexual intercourse taking place; and

(3) the defendant knows that the victim is not consenting or is reckless as to whether he or she consents or not.

It had been assumed for many years that a man could not, as a matter of law, be guilty of raping his wife. However, in *R v R* [1992] 1 AC 599, the House of Lords held that a man can be guilty of raping his wife.

We now turn to consider each of the three elements of rape in more detail.

Intercourse

Sexual intercourse in this context means that the defendant's penis must penetrate the victim's vagina or anus, as the case may be.

It follows from this that the term 'intercourse' does not include oral sex (fellatio or cunnilingus); if activities such as these take place without the consent of the victim, the appropriate charge is one of indecent assault.

Furthermore, since 'intercourse' is synonymous with 'penetration', the offence of rape is complete at the moment of initial penetration. It is not necessary that the defendant should ejaculate in order for the offence to be complete. This is made clear in s 44 of the 1956 Act.

Section 44 of the Sexual Offences Act 1956

Where, on the trial of any offence under this Act, it is necessary to prove sexual intercourse (whether natural or unnatural), it shall not be necessary to prove the completion of the intercourse by the emission of seed [ie semen], but intercourse shall be deemed complete upon proof of penetration only.

Lack of consent: physical resistance

The victim does not have to offer physical resistance in order to demonstrate lack of consent (although, of course, the lack of physical resistance may be relevant to whether the defendant knows the victim is not consenting or is reckless whether the victim is consenting or not).

R v Olugboja [1982] QB 320 (CA)

Dunn LJ: ... The question of law raised by this appeal is whether to constitute the offence of rape it is necessary for the consent of the victim of sexual intercourse to be vitiated by force, the fear of force, or fraud; or whether it is sufficient to prove that in fact the victim did not consent ...

The appellant, who is a Nigerian, aged 20 at the time and studying at Oxford, had sexual intercourse with Jayne, then aged 16, on 8 March 1979, at the bungalow of his co-accused Lawal. She had been taken there with her friend Karen (aged 17) with Lawal in a car driven by the appellant from a discotheque in Oxford where they had all been dancing. Lawal had offered the girls a lift home, but the appellant had driven them to the bungalow which was virtually in the opposite direction from where they lived. This was a deliberate trick to get them to the bungalow. When they got there both girls refused to go in, and started walking away. They did not know where they were. Lawal followed them in the car, and after some argument they got in. After a further argument Karen again got out, and, as she was trying to get Jayne out, Lawal drove off, stopped in a lane, and raped Jayne.

Lawal then drove back to the bungalow, picking Karen up on the way, and the three of them went inside. The appellant was there lying on the sofa asleep, and saw them arrive. Jayne was the last to come in. She was either crying, or obviously had been. Music was put on. Jayne declined to dance. She went to the lavatory and returned to find Lawal dragging Karen into the bedroom. The defendant switched the sitting-room lights off and told Jayne that he was going to fuck her. She told him that Lawal had had her in the car and asked why could the appellant not leave her alone. He told her to take her trousers off and she did because she said she was frightened. She was still crying and the room was in darkness. The appellant pushed her on the settee and had intercourse with her. It did not last long. She did not struggle; she made no resistance; she did not scream or cry for help. She did struggle when she thought after penetration that the defendant was going to ejaculate inside her, and he withdrew. She put her clothes on and the other two emerged from the bedroom, where Lawal had raped Karen. The appellant and Jayne then went into the bedroom. She told him she was going to call the police. He said that if she opened her big mouth he would not take her home. He later did.

Once home Jayne made a complaint to her mother about Lawal but not about the appellant. She said later she did not know why she did not complain to her mother about the appellant. She supposed that she was more upset 'about the first one', meaning Lawal. After she had made her complaint to her mother about Lawal she saw the police and a doctor, with whom she spent a total of eight hours. She made no complaint against the appellant; indeed she said he had not touched her.

The police initially saw the appellant as a witness to the complaints by both Jayne and Karen with regard to the rapes on each of them by Lawal. In the course of the interview the police said to the appellant that Lawal had said that he, the appellant, had had sexual intercourse with Jayne. When they put that to him, Jayne had made no complaint against him. The appellant at once admitted he had had sexual intercourse with Jayne and in answer to the question: 'Did she consent?' he replied: 'Well not at first but I persuaded her'. At the end of the interview the appellant made a written statement. The police then saw Jayne who said that the defendant had indeed had intercourse with her against her will. The police then went back to see the defendant and put to him what Jayne had said. There followed a further long and detailed interview ...

... [I]n so far as the *actus reus* is concerned the question now is simply: 'At the time of the sexual intercourse did the woman consent to it?' It is not necessary for the prosecution to prove that what might otherwise appear to have been consent was in reality merely submission induced by force, fear or fraud, although one or more of these factors will no doubt be present in the majority of cases of rape ...

The jury ... should be directed that consent, or the absence of it, is to be given its ordinary meaning and if need be, by way of example, that there is a difference between consent and submission; every consent involves a submission, but it by no means follows that a mere submission involves consent ... In the majority of cases, where the allegation is that the intercourse was had by force or by the fear of force, such a direction coupled with specific references to, and comments on, the evidence relevant to the absence of real consent will clearly suffice. In the less common type of case where intercourse takes place after threats not involving violence or the fear of it ... we think that an appropriate direction to a jury will have to be fuller. They should be directed to concentrate on the state of mind of the victim immediately before the act of sexual intercourse, having regard to all the relevant circumstances; and in particular; the events leading up to the act and her reaction to them showing their impact on her mind. Apparent acquiescence after penetration does not necessarily involve consent, which must have occurred before the act takes place. In addition to the general direction about consent which we have outlined, the jury will probably be helped in such cases by being reminded that in this context consent does comprehend the wide spectrum of states of mind to which we earlier referred, and that the dividing line in such circumstances between real consent on the one hand and mere submission on the other may not be easy to draw. Where it is to be drawn in a given case is for the jury to decide, applying their combined good sense, experience and knowledge of human nature and modern behaviour to all the relevant facts of that case ...

Petition: The Appeal Committee of the House of Lords (**Lord Diplock**, **Lord Keith of Kinkel** and **Lord Bridge of Harwich**) dismissed a petition by the appellant for leave to appeal.

Lack of consent: consent obtain by fraud

Section 1(3) of the Sexual Offences Act 1956 provides that 'A man also commits rape if he induces a married woman to have sexual intercourse with him by impersonating her husband'. Such cases are, needless to say, very rare. Generally, the courts are reluctant to find that the victim's consent is vitiated by deception on the part of the defendant. One case where deception did vitiate consent was *R v Williams* [1923] 1 KB 320, where the defendant deceived the victim as to what he was doing. However, most forms of deception will not vitiate consent. So a man is not guilty of rape if he procures consent by falsely representing that he intends to marry the victim (see *Papadimitropoulos v R* (1957) 98 DLR 249), nor if he procures consent by falsely representing that he intends to pay for the sexual intercourse (see *R v Linekar* [1995] 3 All ER 69).

The King v Williams [1923] 1 KB 340 (CA)

The facts: The appellant was a choirmaster of a Presbyterian church. In that capacity, he became acquainted with one Vera Howley, a girl of 16 years of age. It was arranged by her parents that she should take lessons in singing and voice production from him. At the second singing lesson, the appellant said that Vera was not singing as she should and was not getting her notes properly. He told her to lie down on a settee. He then removed some of her clothing and placed upon the lower part of her body some sort of instrument which, according to the evidence, would not have been affected by her breathing, and he then told her to take a deep breath three times. He looked at the instrument and purported to write something in a book. He then dropped on to her and proceeded to have sexual intercourse with her. She said: 'What are you going to do?' He said: 'It is quite all right; do not worry. I am going to make an air passage. This is my method of training. Your breathing is not quite right and I have to make an air passage to make it right. Your parents know all about it, it has all been arranged; before God, Vera, it is quite right. I will not do you any harm.' The girl made no resistance, as she believed what he told her and did not know that what he did was wrong – nor did she realise that he was having sexual intercourse with her. The appellant had sexual intercourse with Vera a second time three months later.

The appellant also, on two occasions, indecently assaulted one Ada Mary Cannell, a girl of 19 years of age, to whom he was also giving lessons in singing and voice production. Upon the pretence that her breathing was not right, he put his finger into her vagina, saying that he was making an opening for the air to pass up.

Lord Hewart CJ: [His Lordship referred to words from Stephen's *Digest of the Criminal Law*:] 'A consent or submission obtained by fraud is, it would seem, no defence to a charge of rape ... ' In the opinion of this court that is a true proposition ... The appeal must therefore be dismissed.

R v Linekar [1995] 3 All ER 69 (CA)

Morland J: ... The complainant was a woman of 30 who worked occasionally as a prostitute to supplement her social security benefit. On 21 March 1993 she was working as such outside the Odeon cinema in Streatham. Some time after midnight she was approached by the appellant, who was then aged 17. There was negotiation between the two of them and the sum of £25 was agreed for sexual services. The appellant and the complainant went off to find a suitable place where they could have sexual intercourse. This proved difficult but eventually, after a long period of time, sexual intercourse took place between them on the balcony of a block of flats. After sexual intercourse had taken place the appellant, in breach of the agreement he had made with the complainant, made off without paying.

Immediately the complainant knocked on the door of a neighbouring house. She was distressed, nearly naked and complained that she had been raped. The police were called. The appellant was arrested and, when interviewed, told a number of lies.

The Crown case, based on the evidence of the complainant, was that the act of sexual intercourse took place as a result of a forced violent assault upon her and did not take place with her consent. She said in evidence that she would not have agreed to sexual intercourse until she had been paid in advance and unless the man wore a condom. The case for the Crown was what might be described, if one can describe rape as such, an ordinary rape: that is, forcible penetration of the woman without her consent.

The appellant did not give evidence on his own behalf, but cross-examination of the complainant was on the lines that the act of sexual intercourse had been done with the complainant's consent, and that what had happened was that afterwards the appellant had broken his promise to pay her the £25. It seemed clear that the appellant did not in fact have £25 and, as the jury were to find by a verdict, which was in the nature of a special verdict, at the time of sexual intercourse, he did not have any intention of paying even if he had the money to pay ...

An essential ingredient of the offence of rape is the proof that the woman did not consent to the actual act of sexual intercourse with the particular man who penetrated her. If the Crown prove that she did not consent to sexual intercourse, rape is proved. That ingredient is proved in the so-called 'medical cases'. The victim did not agree in those cases to sexual intercourse. In *R v Flattery* (1877) 2 QBD 410 she agreed to a surgical procedure which she hoped would cure her fits. In *R v Williams* [1923] 1 KB 340 she agreed to a physical manipulation which would provide her with extra air supply to improve her singing.

In our judgment, it is the non-consent to sexual intercourse rather than the fraud of the doctor or choirmaster that makes the offence rape ...

... [T]here is the highly persuasive authority of *Papadimitropoulos v R* (1957) 98 CLR 249, a decision of the High Court of Australia. The court was presided over by Dixon CJ, and consisted of McTiernan, Webb, Kitto and Taylor JJ.

... The facts of that case were that the complainant believed that she had gone through a marriage with the appellant.

In its judgment the court said (at 260–61):

> It must be noted that in considering whether an apparent consent is unreal it is the mistake or misapprehension that makes it so. It is not the fraud producing the mistake which is material so much as the mistake itself. But if the mistake or misapprehension is not produced by the fraud of the man, there is logically room for the possibility that he was unaware of the woman's mistake so that a question of his *mens rea* may arise. So in *R v Lambert* ((1919) VLR 205 at 213) Cussen J says: 'It is plain that, though in these cases the question of consent or non-consent is primarily referable to the mind of the woman, if she has really a mind, yet the mind of the man is also affected by the facts which indicate want of consent or possible want of capacity to consent'. For that reason it is easy to understand why the stress has been on the fraud. But that stress tends to distract the attention from the essential enquiry, namely, whether the consent is no consent because it is not directed to the nature and character of the act. The identity of the man and the character of the physical act that is done or proposed seem now clearly to be regarded as forming part of the nature and character of the act to which the woman's consent is directed. That accords with the principles governing mistake vitiating apparent manifestations of will in other chapters of the law. In the present case the decision of the majority of the Full Court extends this

> conception beyond the identity of the physical act and the immediate conditions affecting its nature to an antecedent inducing cause – the existence of a valid marriage. In the history of bigamy that has never been done. The most heartless bigamist has not been considered guilty of rape. Mock marriages are no new thing. Before the Hardwicke Marriage Act it was a fraud easily devised and readily carried out. But there is no reported instance of an indictment for rape based on the fraudulent character of the ceremony. No indictment of rape was founded on such a fraud. Rape, as a capital felony, was defined with exactness, and although there has been some extension over the centuries in the ambit of the crime, it is quite wrong to bring within its operation forms of evil conduct because they wear some analogy to aspects of the crime and deserve punishment. The judgment of the majority of the Full Court of the Supreme Court goes upon the moral differences between marital intercourse and sexual relations without marriage. The difference is indeed so radical that it is apt to draw the mind away from the real question which is carnal knowledge without consent. It may well be true that the woman in the present case never intended to consent to the latter relationship. But, as was said before, the key to such a case as the present lies in remembering that it is the penetration of the woman's body without her consent to such penetration that makes the felony. The capital felony was not directed to fraudulent conduct inducing her consent. Frauds of that kind must be punished under other heads of the criminal law or not at all: they are not rape. To say that in the present case the facts which the jury must be taken to have found amount to wicked and heartless conduct on the part of the applicant is not enough to establish that he committed rape. To say that in having intercourse with him she supposed that she was concerned in a perfectly moral act is not to say that the intercourse was without her consent. To return to the central point; rape is carnal knowledge of a woman without her consent; carnal knowledge is the physical fact of penetration; it is the consent to that which is in question; such a consent demands a perception as to what is about to take place, as to the identity of the man and the character of what he is doing. But once the consent is comprehending and actual the inducing causes cannot destroy its reality and leave the man guilty of rape.

Respectfully applying those *dicta* to the facts of the present case, the prostitute here consented to sexual intercourse with the appellant. The reality of that consent is not destroyed by being induced by the appellant's false pretence that his intention was to pay the agreed price of £25 for her services. Therefore, he was not guilty of rape ...

Lack of consent: intoxication

It is rape to have sexual intercourse with a woman who is too drunk to give her consent (provided that the defendant has the appropriate *mens rea*). In such a case, 'the critical question is whether she understood her situation and was capable of making up her mind'; if she was not, then she could not consent to intercourse (see *R v Lang* (1975) 62 Cr App R 50, *per* Scarman LJ at 52).

Lack of consent: withdrawal of consent during intercourse

Where there is initial consent to intercourse but that consent is withdrawn while intercourse is taking place, it is rape to continue with the intercourse: see *Kaitamaki v The Queen* [1985] AC 147 (PC) and *R v Cooper and Schaub* [1994] Crim LR 531.

R v Cooper and Schaub [1994] Crim LR 531 (CA)

Facts: While they were considering their verdict, the jury sent a note to the judge asking whether it was rape if a woman consented at the start of the intercourse but then withdrew her consent and the man carried on nonetheless. The main issue in the case was that this point had not been raised during the trial, and so the judge should have told the jury not to consider it. However, the Court of Appeal also held (*obiter*) that penetration is a continuing act. So, where a man continues to penetrate a woman after she has withdrawn her consent to that penetration, then (if the other elements of rape are present) he commits rape by carrying on with the intercourse without her consent.

Mens rea: knowing that the victim does not consent or recklessness as to consent

Belief that the victim is consenting does not have to be based on reasonable grounds, although the jury is entitled to take account of the reasonableness (or otherwise) of the belief in deciding whether the defendant actually held that belief.

Section 1(2) of the Sexual Offences (Amendment) Act 1976

> It is hereby declared that if at a trial for a rape offence the jury has to consider whether a man believed that a woman or man was consenting to sexual intercourse, the presence or absence of reasonable grounds for such a belief is a matter to which the jury is to have regard, in conjunction with any other relevant matters, in considering whether he so believed.

R v Thomas (1983) 77 Cr App R 63 (CA)

Lord Lane CJ: ... [T]he judge should have spelt out in terms [to the jury] that a mistaken belief that the woman was consenting, however unreasonable it may appear to have been, is an answer to the charge, and that it is for the prosecution to eliminate the possibility of such a mistake if they are to succeed. He should then have gone on to deal with the matters set out in s 1(2) of the 1976 Act ...

R v Gardiner [1994] Crim LR 455 (CA)

Facts: The defendant, a factory owner, was charged with the attempted rape of a young girl employee. He had attempted to have sexual intercourse but they were disturbed. He suggested that they should meet again to take up where they had left off and she gave him her telephone number. His defence was that he believed that she had consented to sexual intercourse. She said that she was not consenting but was frightened not to do what he asked because of her junior status in his company.

It was held that even though it was the defendant who was asserting mistaken belief that the complainant was consenting, the burden of proof lay on the Crown to negative that defence. The Court of Appeal went on to hold that it must be the state of mind of the actual defendant on the occasion in question, not some hypothetical reasonable person.

Mens rea: recklessness

The definition of recklessness applicable to the *mens rea* of rape is that laid down by Lord Diplock in *R v Caldwell* [1982] AC 341.

R v Pigg [1982] 1 WLR 762 (CA)

Lord Lane CJ: ... [His Lordship referred to *R v Caldwell* [1982] AC 341 and *R v Lawrence* [1982] AC 510 and continued:] ... [S]o far as rape is concerned, a man is reckless if either he was indifferent and gave no thought to the possibility that the woman might not be consenting in circumstances where if any thought had been given to the matter it would have been obvious that there was a risk that she was not, or he was aware of the possibility that she might not be consenting but nevertheless persisted regardless of whether she consented or not ...

Petition: The Appeal Committee of the House of Lords (**Lord Diplock, Lord Fraser of Tullybelton** and **Lord Bridge of Harwich**) dismissed a petition by the appellant for leave to appeal.

[Note: The Court of Appeal gave leave to the Crown to appeal against its ruling on an unrelated matter (the procedure for taking majority verdicts from a jury); the House of Lords reversed the decision of the Court of Appeal on this matter.]

R v Thomas (1983) 77 Cr App R 63 (CA)

Lord Lane CJ: ... A man is reckless if either he was indifferent and gave no thought to the possibility that the woman might not be consenting, in circumstances where, if any thought had been given to the matter, it would have been obvious that there was a risk she was not, or, he was aware of the possibility that she might not be consenting but nevertheless persisted, regardless of whether she consented or not ...

R v Breckenridge (1983) 79 Cr App R 244 (CA)

Facts: The prosecution's case was the appellant followed the complainant, whom he had not known prior to the evening in question, forced her into a churchyard, where there was a struggle. She fell and broke her ankle. In attempting to overpower her, the defendant held her by the throat. He then raped her. The defence was that the complainant had consented to all the sexual activity; that she had gone into the churchyard with the defendant of her own volition; and that the broken ankle resulted from an accidental fall. Both had consumed a considerable amount of alcohol.

Boreham J: ... [W]hat has to be central to any direction [on the issue of whether the defendant was reckless whether the complainant was consenting or not] is to convey clearly to the jury that they will only find the defendant guilty of what is for convenience called 'reckless rape', if they conclude that his attitude as to whether or not the complainant was consenting was that he could not care less ...

R v S (Satnam) and S (1983) 78 Cr App R 149 (CA)

Bristow J: ... Two grounds of appeal were relied on in this court. (1) That the judge should have directed the jury that a genuine though mistaken belief that the girl was consenting offered a defence to a charge of reckless rape; (2) that the judge erred in referring to an 'ordinary observer' in his direction as to recklessness, and that he should have directed the jury that it was necessary to prove that each appellant was actually aware of the possibility that the girl was not consenting before they could find him reckless.

So far as the first ground was concerned, it was accepted by [counsel] for the Crown that he could not support the summing up in the absence of a direction as to belief. In *Thomas* (1983) 77 Cr App R 63 Lord Lane CJ said at 65: 'In this particular case, the judge should have spelt out in terms that a mistaken belief that the woman was consenting, however unreasonable it may appear to have been, is an answer to the charge, and that it is for the prosecution to eliminate the possibility of such a mistake if they are to succeed. He should then have gone on to deal with the matters set out in s 1(2) of the 1976 Act. As it was the jury were left without any guidance on the matter.' The same situation arose here. The jury were left without any guidance on the matter of belief and on that ground alone we would allow the appeal.

We turn now to consider the second ground, ie the direction as to recklessness. Strictly it may be said that this point has already been decided in *Bashir* (1983) 77 Cr App R 59 at 62 where Watkins LJ said:

> As recently as the fifth of this month, Lord Lane CJ in *Thomas* restated the definition of 'reckless' as applied to the offence of rape. He said (1983) 77 Cr App R 63, 66: 'A man is reckless if either he was indifferent and gave no thought to the possibility that the woman might not be consenting, in circumstances where, if any thought had been given to the matter, it would have been obvious that there was a risk she was not, or, he was aware of the possibility that she might not be consenting but nevertheless persisted, regardless of whether she consented or not.' He was in almost exact form repeating the definition of 'reckless' in relation to rape which he had provided in the case of *Pigg* (1982) 74 Cr App R 352. It will be noted that that definition allows of none other than a subjective approach to the state of mind of a person of whom it is said he acted recklessly in committing a crime. It was incumbent therefore on the trial judge in the present case to ensure that he provided the jury with this kind of definition of the word 'reckless'.

[Counsel] on behalf of the appellants submitted, in his able argument, that the use of the word 'obvious' in its context in both *Pigg* and *Thomas* gives rise to a possible ambiguity. 'Obvious' to whom? If it meant obvious to any reasonable person, that would introduce an objective test, and [counsel] submitted that the authorities properly understood do not warrant such a conclusion. He invited us in effect to clarify the situation which has developed since *Caldwell* and *Lawrence*, as he said that judges up and down the country are now in a state of some confusion as to the state of the law. He submitted that the direction of recklessness in *Pigg* was in any event *obiter*.

As Robert Goff LJ said in *Elliott v C (A Minor)* [1983] 1 WLR 939 at 950, with reference to the suggested direction in *Pigg*:

> Now it cannot be disguised that the addition of the words 'was indifferent and' constituted a gloss upon the definition of recklessness proposed by Lord Diplock in *R v Caldwell*. Furthermore, if it were legitimate so to interpret Lord Diplock's speech in relation to a case arising not under s 1 of the Sexual Offences (Amendment) Act 1976, but under s 1(1) of the Criminal Damage Act 1971, the effect would be that the second question posed by the magistrates in the case now before this court would be answered in the affirmative, and the appeal would be dismissed; because there is no finding of fact that this defendant in the case before us was indifferent to the risk of destruction by fire of the shed and its contents. This is an approach which I would gladly adopt, if I felt that I were free to do so. However, I do not consider that it is open to this court, in a case arising under the very subsection to which Lord Diplock's speech was expressly directed, to impose this qualification, which I feel would in this context constitute too substantial a departure from the test proposed by him.

The instant case, unlike *Elliot*, is not concerned with the Criminal Damage Act 1971 but with the Sexual Offences (Amendment) Act 1976, and the court is considering recklessness in the context of rape and not in the context of criminal damage. We feel we are therefore free to review the situation so far as it is governed by relevant authority, and accepting as we do that there is an ambiguity in the suggested direction in *Pigg*, which was in any event *obiter*.

[Counsel for the appellants] took as his starting point DPP *v Morgan* [1976] AC 182, a decision of the House of Lords on the very question of rape, which was not overruled by either *Caldwell* or *Lawrence* and is binding on this court. Lord Hailsham said at 151 and 215 of the respective reports:

> I am content to rest my view of the instant case on the crime of rape by saying that it is my opinion that the prohibited act is and always has been intercourse without consent of the victim and the mental element is and always has been the intention to commit that act, or the equivalent intention of having intercourse willy-nilly not caring whether the victim consents or not. A failure to prove this involves an acquittal because the intent, an essential ingredient, is lacking. It matters not why it is lacking if only it is not there, and in particular it matters not that the intention is lacking only because of a belief not based on reasonable grounds.

In the Report of the Advisory Group on the Law of Rape (The Heilbron Committee) Command Paper 6352, 1975, the following 'Recommendations for declaratory legislation' were made:

> 81. Notwithstanding our conclusions that *Morgan's* case is right in principle, we nevertheless feel that legislation is required to clarify the law governing intention in rape cases, as it is now settled. We think this for two principal reasons. The first is that it would be possible in future cases to argue that the question of recklessness did not directly arise for decision in *Morgan's* case, in view of the form of the question certified; to avoid possible doubts the ruling on recklessness needs to be put in statutory form. 82. Second, it would be unfortunate if a tendency were to arise to say to the jury 'that a belief, however unreasonable, that the woman consented, entitled the accused to acquittal'. Such a phrase might tend to give an undue or misleading emphasis to one aspect only and the law, therefore, should be statutorily restated in a fuller form which would obviate the use of those words. 83. We think that there would be advantage if this matter could also be dealt with by a statutory provision which would: (1) declare that (in cases where the question of belief is raised) the issue which the jury have to consider is whether the accused at the time when sexual intercourse took place believed that she was consenting, and (2) make it clear that, while there is no requirement of law that such belief must be based on reasonable grounds, the presence or absence of such grounds is a relevant consideration to which the jury should have regard, in conjunction with all other evidence, in considering whether the accused genuinely had such a belief.

There followed the Sexual Offences (Amendment) Act 1976, s 1 of which is in the following terms:

> (1) For the purposes of s 1 of the Sexual Offences Act 1956 (which relates to rape) a man commits rape if: (a) he has unlawful sexual intercourse with a woman who at the time of the intercourse does not consent to it; and (b) at that time he knows that she does not consent to the intercourse or he is reckless as to whether she consents to it ... (2) It is hereby declared that if at a trial for a rape offence the jury has to consider whether a man believed that a woman was consenting to sexual intercourse, the presence or absence of

> reasonable grounds for such a belief is a matter to which the jury is to have regard, in conjunction with any other relevant matters, in considering whether he so believed.

We think that in enacting those provisions Parliament must have accepted the recommendations of the Heilbron Committee, so that the provisions are declaratory of the existing law as stated in *DPP v Morgan*.

Any direction as to the definition of rape should therefore be based upon s 1 of the 1976 Act and upon *DPP v Morgan*, without regard to *R v Caldwell* or *R v Lawrence*, which were concerned with recklessness in a different context and under a different statute.

The word 'reckless' in relation to rape involves a different concept to its use in relation to malicious damage or, indeed, in relation to offences against the person. In the latter cases the foreseeability, or possible foreseeability, is as to the consequences of the criminal act. In the case of rape the foreseeability is as to the state of mind of the victim.

A practical definition of recklessness in sexual offences was given in *Kimber* [1983] 1 WLR 1118, where the court was concerned with how far an honest belief in consent constituted a defence to a charge of indecent assault. The defendant said in evidence: 'I was not really interested in Betty's [the victim's] feelings at all'. Lawton LJ said at 230 and 1123 of the respective reports:

> We have already set out in this judgment the admissions which he is alleged to have made to the police and relevant parts of his own evidence. In our judgment a reasonable jury would inevitably have decided that he had no honest belief that Betty was consenting. His own evidence showed that his attitude to her was one of indifference to her feelings and wishes. This state of mind is aptly described in the colloquial expression, 'couldn't care less'. In law this is recklessness.

In summing up a case of rape which involves the issue of consent, the judge should, in dealing with the state of mind of the defendant, first of all direct the jury that before they could convict of rape the Crown had to prove either that the defendant knew the woman did not want to have sexual intercourse, or was reckless as to whether she wanted to or not. If they were sure he knew she did not want to they should find him guilty of rape knowing there to be no consent. If they were not sure about that, then they would find him not guilty of such rape and should go on to consider reckless rape. If they thought he might genuinely have believed that she did want to, even though he was mistaken in his belief, they would find him not guilty. In considering whether his belief was genuine, they should take into account all the relevant circumstances (which could at that point be summarised) and ask themselves whether, in the light of those circumstances, he had reasonable grounds for such a belief. If, after considering those circumstances, they were sure he had no genuine belief that she wanted to, they would find him guilty. If they came to the conclusion that he could not care less whether she wanted to or not, but pressed on regardless, then he would have been reckless and could not have believed that she wanted to, and they would find him guilty of reckless rape ...

Mens rea: knowledge/recklessness: intoxication

Where the defendant mistakenly believes that the victim is consenting but that mistaken belief is the result of voluntary intoxication, the defendant cannot rely on that mistaken belief.

R v Fotheringham (1989) 88 Cr App R 206 (CA)

Facts: The appellant had been convicted of the rape of a 14-year-old girl who had been baby-sitting for the appellant and his wife. The baby-sitter had been sleeping in the matrimonial bed. The defendant, who was drunk, got into bed with her and had sexual intercourse with her.

Watkins LJ: ... [The appellant's] defence, to put it as shortly as possible, was simply that he made an honest mistake. He mistook the 14-year-old girl for his wife, entirely because he was so much under the influence of alcohol that he could not appreciate the difference ...

The ground of appeal is that the learned judge, when summing the matter up to the jury, was wrong in law to direct them to disregard the appellant's self-induced intoxication. In the circumstances this, it was submitted, left him with no real defence. He had admitted that his self-induced intoxication caused his mistake.

... The point of law which ... comes before us for resolution is whether it is a defence to a charge of rape ... that a defendant, as a result of self-induced intoxication, has an honest but mistaken belief that he was having conjugal relations ...

Counsel [for the appellant] had to recognise, as in fact he did, that where the issue in rape is consent, a defendant's self-induced intoxication is not a relevant matter which a jury are entitled to take into account in deciding whether there were reasonable grounds for the defendant's belief that the woman consented: see *R v Woods* (1982) 74 Cr App R 312 [NB the relevance of whether there are reasonable grounds for the defendant's belief is confined to the issue whether he in fact held that belief: s 1(2) Sexual Offences (Amendment) Act 1976]. Likewise he had to face the law, which is that 'self-induced intoxication is no defence to a crime in which recklessness is enough to constitute the necessary *mens rea*': see as to that the speech of Lord Diplock in *R v Caldwell* [1982] AC 341, 355, where Lord Diplock refers to *DPP v Majewski* [1977] AC 443, where it was held that rape is a crime of basic intent to which self-induced intoxication is no defence ...

[Counsel for the appellant] says that the mistake was as to the identification of the person with whom the appellant was having sexual intercourse ... But we are firmly of the view that mistake, as is consent, being a question of fact cannot be raised as a defence if, as here, it arises from self-induced intoxication. For that *O'Grady* [1987] QB 995 is very clear authority in our view ...

... [I]n rape self-induced intoxication is no defence, whether the issue be intention, consent or, as here, mistake as to the identity of the victim ...

In our judgment the judge was correct to rule as he did, namely ... 'But I must stress that ... you must ignore the effects of the drink that [the defendant] had taken, the seven or eight pints of lager which he has spoken about. The reasonable grounds are grounds which would be reasonable to a sober man.' In other words a mistake arising from self-induced intoxication is no defence in rape ...

ATTEMPTED RAPE

Mens rea

The *mens rea* for attempted rape is the same as for the completed offence.

R v Khan [1990] 1 WLR 813 (CA)

Russell LJ: ... These appeals raise the short but important point of whether the offence of attempted rape is committed when the defendant is reckless as to the woman's consent to sexual intercourse. The appellants submit that no such offence is known to the law ...

In our judgment an acceptable analysis of the offence of rape is as follows: (1) the intention of the offender is to have sexual intercourse with a woman; (2) the offence is committed if, but only if, the circumstances are that: (a) the woman does not consent; *and* (b) the defendant knows that she is not consenting or is reckless as to whether she consents.

Precisely the same analysis can be made of the offence of attempted rape: (1) the intention of the offender is to have sexual intercourse with a woman; (2) the offence is committed if, but only if, the circumstances are that: (a) the woman does not consent; *and* (b) the defendant knows that she is not consenting or is reckless as to whether she consents.

The only difference between the two offences is that in rape sexual intercourse takes place whereas in attempted rape it does not, although there has to be some act which is more than preparatory to sexual intercourse. Considered in that way, the intent of the defendant is precisely the same in rape and in attempted rape and the *mens rea* is identical, namely an intention to have intercourse plus a knowledge of or recklessness as to the woman's absence of consent. No question of attempting to achieve a reckless state of mind arises; the attempt relates to the physical activity; the mental state of the defendant is the same. A man does not recklessly have sexual intercourse, nor does he recklessly attempt it. Recklessness in rape and attempted rape arises not in relation to the physical act of the accused but only in his state of mind when engaged in the activity of having or attempting to have sexual intercourse.

If this is the true analysis, as we believe it is, the attempt does not require any different intention on the part of the accused from that for the full offence of rape. We believe this to be a desirable result which in the instant case did not require the jury to be burdened with different directions as to the accused's state of mind, dependant on whether the individual achieved or failed to achieve sexual intercourse.

We recognise, of course, that our reasoning cannot apply to all offences and all attempts. Where, for example, as in causing death by reckless driving or reckless arson, no state of mind other than recklessness is involved in the offence, there can be no attempt to commit it.

In our judgment, however, the words 'with intent to commit an offence' to be found in s 1 of the 1981 Act mean, when applied to rape, 'with intent to have sexual intercourse with a woman in circumstances where she does not consent and the defendant knows or could not care less about her absence of consent'. The only 'intent', giving that word its natural and ordinary meaning, of the rapist is to have sexual intercourse. He commits the offence because of the circumstances in which he manifests that intent – ie when the woman is not consenting and he either knows it or could not care less about the absence of consent ...

Petition: The Appeal Committee of the House of Lords (**Lord Keith of Kinkel**, **Lord Brandon of Oakbrook** and **Lord Lowry**) dismissed petitions by Khan, Dhokia and Faiz for leave to appeal.

Actus reus

To be guilty of attempted rape, the defendant need not have got as far as attempting physical penetration of the victim. It is sufficient if he does an act which is more than merely preparatory to penetration.

Attorney General's Reference (No 1 of 1992) [1993] 1 WLR 274 (CA)

Lord Taylor of Gosforth CJ: ... The point of law is stated thus:

> Whether, on a charge of attempted rape, it is incumbent upon the prosecution, as a matter of law, to prove that the defendant physically attempted to penetrate the woman's vagina with his penis.

The effect of the evidence for the prosecution is not entirely clear, but the following facts were, it seems, proved.

During the evening of Friday 30 November 1990, the complainant, a young woman aged 17, was drinking at various clubs in the company of her boyfriend and others. During the early hours of the following morning she lost contact with them, but began talking to the respondent, a young man of 20, whom she had known as a friend for several years. She indicated she wanted to walk home and began to do so. The respondent accompanied her.

On the way they stopped by a gap in a hedge where there were steps leading to a shed. It is not clear how long they were there, the respondent contending that it was about an hour. However, at some stage the respondent asked the complainant to wait while he relieved himself. When he re-emerged she alleged that he grabbed her, pulled her behind the hedge, forced her to the ground and lay full length on top of her. He put his hand over her mouth and threatened to kill her if she did not stop screaming. At that stage the young woman became extremely frightened and lost consciousness.

Although her account was challenged, there was independent evidence to the following effect. An occupier of a nearby house heard a muffled moaning sound. She looked out of her window and saw the respondent on top of the complainant, the complainant's knickers being around her ankles. The respondent then got up and pulled the complainant roughly up the stone steps away from the road. She was clearly distressed, crying and trying to scream.

The police were called. They arrived within minutes. Two officers heard muffled screams and crying. The complainant was on her back, her skirt pulled up to waist level and her breasts exposed. She was barefoot and without her knickers, which were subsequently found in the undergrowth nearby. At the time the police arrived at the scene the respondent was kneeling near to the girl, although it is contended on his behalf that there was some six feet between them.

The respondent immediately stood up when the police arrived. His trousers were round his ankles and he pulled them up. At that stage one of the officers observed that his penis was flaccid. He was questioned as follows: '*Q*: What have you been doing? *A*: What do you think? *Q*: This girl appears very upset and distressed. Did she agree to you having sex with her? *A*: I don't know. I didn't ask her.'

The young woman was medically examined. She had two love bites on her neck and an area of redness on her left breast. There were superficial injuries to her left shoulder-blade, both elbows, left ankle and right calf, together with mud and grass stains on both heels. As to her private parts, there was a recent bruise just outside the hymen but inside the labia which, in the doctor's opinion, could have been caused by finger pressure, 'someone using fingers clumsily, like a drunken man, that was more likely than a penis to cause it'.

The respondent was also examined. He had superficial cuts and bruises to both knees and recent bruising on the shaft of the penis, consistent either with attempted intercourse or vigorous masturbation. The bruising of the complainant's private parts corresponded to the bruising of the respondent's penis.

On interview the respondent admitted touching the complainant's breasts and putting his hand up her skirt. He claimed that she did not protest or make any noise. He accepted that she was in no fit state owing to drink to give consent. He said he never asked. He denied having an erection, but he admitted that his trousers were down. He was asked:

> *Q*: Surely, There is only one reason to have your trousers down isn't there, what's that?
>
> *A*: To have intercourse but I didn't have intercourse though.
>
> *Q*: Why didn't you have intercourse with her?
>
> *A*: I don't know, I just didn't.

It was then put to him that to have intercourse would be the natural conclusion, and his answer was, 'But I couldn't, cause I was drunk, so I couldn't, could I?' He was unable to recall how the complainant's knickers were removed, but denied that he was responsible ...

[His Lordship then quoted ss 1(1) and 4(3) of the Criminal Attempts Act 1981.]

... It is not, in our judgment, necessary, in order to raise a *prima facie* case of attempted rape, to prove that the defendant with the requisite intent had necessarily gone as far as to attempt physical penetration of the vagina. It is sufficient if there is evidence from which the intent can be inferred and there are proved acts which a jury could properly regard as more than merely preparatory to the commission of the offence. For example, and merely as an example, in the present case the evidence of the young woman's distress, of the state of her clothing, and the position in which she was seen, together with the respondent's acts of dragging her up the steps, lowering his trousers and interfering with her private parts, and his answers to the police, left it open to a jury to conclude that the respondent had the necessary intent and had done acts which were more than merely preparatory. In short that he had embarked on committing the offence itself.

For the reasons which we have endeavoured to give, we would answer the question posed in the reference, 'No'.

INDECENT ASSAULT

Section 14(1) of the Sexual Offences Act 1956: indecent assault on a woman

It is an offence ... for a person to make an indecent assault on a woman.

Section 15(1) of the Sexual Offences Act 1956: indecent assault on a man

It is an offence for a person to make an indecent assault on a man.

Punishment

Punishment for offences under ss 14 and 15: up to 10 years' imprisonment following conviction on indictment; up to 6 months' imprisonment and/or a fine of up to £5,000 following summary conviction (s 37 and Schedule 2 of the Sexual Offences Act 1956).

There are essentially two ingredients to the offence of indecent assault:

(1) There must be what in law amounts to an assault; and

(2) That assault must take place in circumstances of indecency.

Director of Public Prosecutions v Rogers [1953] QB 644 (DC)

Facts: At all material times, the respondent lived with his wife and daughter. On two occasions between 27 October 1952, and 7 November 1952, he put his arm round his daughter's shoulders and led her upstairs. She made no objection or resistance, and no force or compulsion was used. He then exposed his person to the child and told her to masturbate him. On both occasions the child obeyed him although she did not wish to do so. On both occasions he was alone in the house with the child. On the first occasion he committed the indecent conduct on the landing and on the second occasion in his bedroom. On both occasions when he put his arm round his daughter's shoulders he did so to lead her upstairs, intending to conduct himself indecently towards her. On the first occasion the child neither minded nor objected to his putting his arm round her shoulders, but on the second occasion, knowing the nature of his intention towards her, she did not wish to accompany him upstairs, but, nevertheless, she neither objected nor resisted, but submitted to his request.

Lord Goddard CJ: ... Before you can find that a man has been guilty of an indecent assault, you have to find that he was guilty of an assault, for an indecent assault is an assault accompanied by indecency, and, if it could be shown here that the respondent had done anything towards this child which, by any fair use of language could be called compulsion, or had acted, as I have said in other cases, in a hostile manner towards her – that is, with a threat or a gesture which could be taken as a threat, or by pulling a reluctant child towards him – that would, undoubtedly, be assault, and, if it was accompanied by an act of indecency, it would be an indecent assault.

Assault

Fairclough v Whipp [1951] 2 All ER 834 (DC)

Lord Goddard CJ: ... The question is whether there was an assault. The respondent was making water by the bank of a river where there were some four young girls varying in age from six to nine. As he did so one of the girls passed him. He, with his person exposed, said to her, 'Touch it', and she did so. He then went away. The question for decision is whether that conduct amounts to an indecent assault.

An assault can be constituted, without there being battery, for instance, by a threatening gesture or a threat to use violence against a person, but I do not know any authority which says that where one person invites another person to touch him that can be said to be an assault. The question of consent or non-consent only arises if there is something which can be called an assault and, without consent, would be an assault. If that which was done to this child was of an indecent nature and would have been an assault if done against her will, it would also be an assault if it was done with her consent because she could not consent to an indecent assault [in the light of her age]. Before we decide whether there has been an indecent assault we must decide whether there has been an assault, and I cannot hold that an invitation to somebody to touch the invitor can amount to an assault on the invitee.

Indecency

Three situations have to be distinguished:

(1) An act which ordinary, right-thinking members of the public could not regard as indecent: that act cannot amount to an indecent assault;

(2) An act which ordinary, right-thinking members of the public would regard as indecent: that act (provided that it amounts to an assault) will be an indecent assault;

(3) An act which ordinary, right-thinking members of the public would regard as ambivalent, in the sense that it is only *capable* of being indecent: that act will only be indecent if the perpetrator intended it to be so.

An example of a case involving the second category is *R v Culyer* (1992) Times, 17 April and an example of a case involving the third category (where evidence of the defendant's motive is important evidence) is *R v Court* [1989] AC 28.

R v Culyer (1992) Times, 17 April

Lord Justice Woolf (giving the judgment of the Court of Appeal) said that while in *R v Court* [1989] AC 28 whether what had happened amounted to an indecent assault or not turned on the motive and therefore the specific intent had been necessary to the verdict, in the instant case, there was no question as to whether what had occurred was indecent or not so that the basic intent was sufficient. Since the assault was indecent in itself, the issue was simply whether the appellant did what was alleged.

R v Court [1989] AC 28 (HL)

Facts: The appellant, an assistant in a shop, struck a 12-year-old girl visitor some 12 times, for no apparent reason as she thought, outside her shorts on her buttocks. In response to a question by the police as to why the appellant had done so he said, 'I don't know – buttock fetish'.

Lord Keith of Kinkel: My Lords, I have had the opportunity of considering in draft the speech to be delivered by my noble and learned friends Lords Griffiths and Lord Ackner. I agree with them entirely, and will add only a few observations of my own.

A wicked intention is an essential ingredient of the offence of indecent assault, as indeed it is of most other crimes against the person. For the most part, the wicked intention can readily be inferred from the facts found proved as to the circumstances of the assault, unless there are indications that those features of the circumstances which are capable of being considered indecent were not intended – as in the instance put of a common assault accidentally involving damage to a woman's clothing. In a narrow range of cases, however, the circumstances may not point unequivocally to the requisite wicked intention. The delivery of chastisement to the buttocks of a child is capable of presenting a case of that nature, since such chastisement is not necessarily indicative of an intention to do something indecent. Where, however, there is direct evidence, as there was in the present case in the shape of the appellant's statement about buttock fetish, that it was the assailant's intention to use the victim for the purpose of gratifying a peculiar sexual instinct, and that his action did in fact amount to a using of her for that purpose, such evidence can, in my opinion, properly be taken into account so as to resolve any ambiguity about the nature of the act. The contrary view seems to me to fly in the face of all common sense ...

Lord Fraser of Tullybelton: My Lords, I have had the advantage of reading in draft the speeches of my noble and learned friends Lord Keith of Kinkel, Lord Griffiths, and Lord Ackner. I agree that, for the reasons given by them, the evidence of the appellant is admissible and that this appeal should be dismissed.

Lord Griffiths: My Lords, this appeal turns on the answer to the following question. On a trial of indecent assault arising out of a spanking delivered by a man to the buttocks of a young girl, is the evidence that he told the police that he did it because of a 'buttock fetish' admissible evidence which the jury may consider when deciding whether the assault was indecent? I am bound to say my instinctive answer was, yes of course it is. I have now had the advantage of reading the speeches of my noble and learned friends, Lord Ackner and Lord Goff. My answer remains the same. I agree that for the reasons given by my noble and learned friend, Lord Ackner, the evidence is admissible and that his appeal should be dismissed ...

The gravamen of the offence of indecent assault is the element of indecency. It is this element of indecency that distinguishes the offence from common assault and makes it such a potentially serious offence carrying a maximum term of imprisonment of 10 years. By indecency is meant conduct that right-thinking people will consider an affront to the sexual modesty of a woman.

Although the offence of indecent assault may vary greatly in its gravity from an unauthorised teenage sexual groping at one end of the scale to near rape at the other, it is in any circumstances a nasty, unpleasant offence for which a conviction is likely to carry a far greater social stigma than a conviction for common assault. There is agreement that the offence cannot be committed accidentally as, for instance, in the example given by Lord Ackner of ripping a woman's clothing while attempting to force an exit from a tube train. Once this concession is made it is apparent that some extra mental element is required than that necessary for common assault, for, in the example given, a person using unnecessary violence to push through the crowd would have the necessary intent to commit an assault. It seems natural to me that this extra mental element should be that which constitutes the essence of the offence, namely, an intent to do something indecent to the woman in the sense of an affront to her sexual modesty or, in other words, an intent to do that which the jury find indecent. Indecent assault is after all a sexual offence appearing in the Sexual Offences Act 1956 and one should on general principle look for a sexual element as an ingredient of the offence ...

I turn now to consider whether the evidence of the accused's explanation for his conduct as a 'buttock fetish' was admissible. There is a distinction to be drawn in criminal law between motive and intent although it will very rarely be necessary to enter on a discussion of this distinction with a jury and any unnecessary attempt to do so is likely to cause confusion and do more harm than good. But to illustrate what I mean in the context of indecent assault, the necessary intent is to commit an assault which the jury as right-thinking people consider to be sexually indecent. The motive for such an act will usually be to obtain sexual gratification but it need not necessarily be so. A man might strip a woman in public with the motive of obtaining sexual gratification or, alternatively, with the motive of revenge to humiliate her; but whichever his motive he would undoubtedly be guilty of indecent assault because his intentional stripping of her clothing is an indecent affront to her sexual modesty. Motive generally throws light on intention and is therefore generally admissible to prove intention.

The appellant admitted that he had assaulted the girl and the jury had to decide whether his behaviour was indecent. Whether or not right-thinking people will consider an action indecent will sometimes depend on the purpose with which the action is carried out. An obvious example is the examination of an unconscious woman's private parts. If carried out by a doctor for a proper medical purpose no one would consider such an examination indecent. If carried out by a stranger for a prurient interest everyone would consider it indecent.

Spanking a girl's bottom is an equivocal action. The buttocks are an intimate part of the body in close proximity to the sexual organs and unauthorised handling of that part of the body is certainly capable of being indecent. But the buttocks are also a part of the body on which it is possible to inflict pain without the risk of serious physical damage and have long been recognised as an area of the body to which chastisement may be administered by those having proper authority to do so without anyone thinking it indecent. If a juryman is asked to decide whether a man beating a young girl's bottom is acting indecently, the first question he is likely to ask is – why was he doing it? If the answer is that she had been naughty and he was punishing her, the juryman may well consider that if the man was a stranger he should not have laid hands on the girl and was guilty of assault, but I doubt if he would consider the man's action to be indecent. On the other hand, if the juryman was told that the man was spanking the girl to satisfy a buttock fetish, I would be surprised indeed if he did not think that it was indecent.

The fact is that right-thinking people do take into account the purpose or intent with which an act is performed in judging whether or not it is indecent. If evidence of motive is available that throws light on the intent it should be before the jury to assist them in their decision. Suppose, in the present case, the appellant had said to the police, 'I thought the girl had been stealing and I beat her to stop her doing it again'. Such evidence would surely have been admissible to attempt to persuade the jury that this was an act of chastisement and therefore they should not regard it as indecent. If, on the other hand, evidence is available that shows the spanking was not an act of chastisement but carried out with the intention of obtaining perverted sexual gratification, it would, in my view, be an affront to common sense to withhold that evidence from the jury when asking them to decide if this man had behaved indecently. Accordingly, I agree with the judge that the evidence was admissible.

Lord Ackner: ... It cannot, in my judgment, have been the intention of Parliament that an assault can, by a mere mistake or mischance, be converted into an indecent assault, with all the opprobrium which a conviction for such an offence carries. To take one of the less imaginative examples discussed in the course of the arguments, it may be a common occurrence during travel on the London tube during rush hours, for a person suddenly to realise belatedly that the train has stopped at the very station where he wishes to alight, without his having taken the wise precaution of getting close to its doors. Such a person may well in his anxiety to get out, rather than be carried on to the next stop, use unnecessary force in pushing his way through his fellow passengers. If he thus came into contact with a woman, then he would be guilty of having assaulted her. If something that he was carrying, such as an umbrella, became caught up, as it might well do, in her dress as he pushed past, thus tearing away her upper clothing, he would, in my judgment, be guilty only of an assault. He would not be guilty of an indecent assault ...

It was common ground before your Lordships, and indeed it is self evident, that the first stage in the proof of the offence is for the prosecution to establish an assault. The 'assault' usually relied on is a battery, the species of assault conveniently described by Lord Lane CJ in *Faulkner v Talbot* [1981] 1 WLR 1528, 1534 as 'any intentional touching of another person without the consent of that person and without lawful excuse. It need not necessarily be hostile or rude or aggressive, as some of the cases seem to indicate'. But the 'assault' relied on need not involve any physical contact but may consist merely of conduct which causes the victim to apprehend immediate and unlawful personal violence. In the case law on the offence of indecent assault, both categories of assault feature.

... A simpler way of putting the matter to the jury is to ask them to decide whether 'right-minded persons would consider the conduct indecent or not'. It is for the jury to decide whether what occurred was so offensive to contemporary standards of modesty and privacy as to be indecent ...

It also was common ground before your Lordships ... that if the circumstances of the assault are *incapable* of being regarded as indecent, then the undisclosed intention of the accused could not make the assault an indecent one. The validity of this proposition is well illustrated by *R v George* [1956] Crim LR 52. The basis of the prosecution's case was that the defendant on a number of occasions removed a shoe from a girl's foot and that he did so, as indeed he admitted, because it gave him a kind of perverted sexual gratification ... Streatfeild J ruled that an assault became indecent only if it was accompanied by circumstances of indecency towards the person alleged to have been assaulted, and that none of the assaults (the removal or attempted removal of the shoes) could possibly amount to an indecent assault.

Again it was common ground that if, as in this case, the assault involved touching the victim, it was not necessary to prove that she was aware of the circumstances of indecency or apprehended indecency. An indecent assault can clearly be committed by the touching of someone who is asleep or unconscious ...

The assault which the prosecution seek to establish may be of a kind which is inherently indecent. The defendant removes, against her will, a woman's clothing. Such a case, to my mind, raises no problem. Those very facts, devoid of any explanation, would give rise to the irresistible inference that the defendant intended to assault his victim in a manner which right-minded persons would clearly think was indecent. Whether he did so for his own personal sexual gratification or because, being a misogynist or for some other reason, he wished to embarrass or humiliate his victim, seems to me to be irrelevant. He has failed, *ex hypothesi*, to show any lawful justification for his indecent conduct. This, of course, was not such a case. The conduct of the appellant in assaulting the girl by spanking her was only capable of being an indecent assault. To decide whether or not right-minded persons might think that assault was indecent, the following factors were clearly relevant – the relationship of the defendant to his victim – were they relatives, friends, or virtually complete strangers? How had the defendant come to embark on this conduct and why was he behaving in this way? Aided by such material, a jury would be helped to determine the quality of the act, the true nature of the assault and to answer the vital question – were they sure that the defendant not only intended to commit an assault on the girl, but an assault which was indecent – was such an inference irresistible? For the defendant to be liable to be convicted of the offence of indecent assault, where the circumstances of the alleged offence can be given an innocent as well as an indecent interpretation, without the prosecution being obliged to establish that the defendant intended to commit both an assault and an indecent one, seems to me quite unacceptable and not what Parliament intended ...

The jury in their question to the judge were concerned with the position of a doctor who carried out an intimate examination on a young girl. Mars-Jones J dealt with their point succinctly by saying:

> In that situation what is vital is whether the examination was necessary or not. If it was not necessary, but indulged in by the medical practitioner it would be an indecent assault. But if it was necessary, even though he got sexual satisfaction out of it, that would not make it an indecent assault.

I entirely agree. If it could be proved by the doctor's admission that the consent of the parent, or if over 16 of the patient, was sought and obtained by the doctor falsely representing that the examination was necessary, then, of course, no true consent to the examination had ever been given. The examination would be an assault and an assault which right-minded persons could well consider was an indecent one. I would not expect that it would make any difference to the jury's decision whether the doctor's false representations were motivated by his desire for the sexual gratification which he might achieve from such an examination, or because he had some other reason, entirely of his own, unconnected with the medical needs or care of the patient, such as private research, which had caused him to act fraudulently. In either case the assault could be, and I expect would be, considered as so offensive to contemporary standards of modesty or privacy as to be indecent. A jury would therefore be entitled to conclude that he, in both cases, intended to assault the patient and to do so indecently. I can see nothing illogical in such a result. On the contrary, it would indeed be surprising if in such circumstances the only offence that could properly be charged would be that of common assault. No doubt the judge would treat the offence which had been motivated by the indecent motive as the more serious ...

I, therefore, conclude that on a charge of indecent assault the prosecution must not only prove that the accused intentionally assaulted the victim, but that in so doing he intended to commit an indecent assault, ie an assault which right-minded persons would think was indecent. Accordingly, any evidence which tends to explain the reason for the defendant's conduct, be it his own admission or otherwise, would be relevant to establish whether or not he intended to commit, not only an assault, but an indecent one. The doctor's admissions in the two contrasting examples which I have given would certainly be so relevant. The appellant's admission of 'buttock fetish' was clearly such material. It tended to confirm, as indeed did the events leading up to the assault and the appellant's conduct immediately thereafter, that what he did was to satisfy his peculiar sexual appetite. It was additional relevant evidence. It tended to establish the sexual undertones which gave the assault its true cachet ...

I would accordingly dismiss the appeal and answer the certified question as follows:

> On a charge of indecent assault the prosecution must prove: (1) that the accused intentionally assaulted the victim (2) that the assault, or the assault and the circumstances accompanying it, are capable of being considered by right-minded persons as indecent; (3) that the accused intended to commit such an assault as is referred to in (2) above.

... I would add that evidence, if any, of the accused's explanation for assaulting the victim, whether or not it reveals an indecent motive, is admissible both to support or to negative that the assault was an indecent one and was so intended by the accused.

Lord Goff delivered a dissenting speech.

R v Sargeant (1997) 161 JP 127 (CA)

Hutchison LJ: ....[T]his appellant was convicted of indecent assault on a male person contrary to s 15(1) of the Sexual Offences Act 1956 ...

At the trial the complainant's evidence was given by means of a video link. He said that he was approached by a man near some steps and grabbed by the shoulder. The man asked him where he was going and when he replied that he was going home the man said, "No you're not. You've got to come with me", and started pulling him towards the canal. The complainant tried to walk away saying that he had to go home but the man dragged him back and forced him to masturbate into a condom. He said that he was terrified of the man and he was too close to him to be able to escape. After he had masturbated, according to the complainant, the man asked him if he did drugs and whether he was queer. The man himself claimed that he took drugs and was in an angry condition because he had not taken any. He also asked if he had ever been touched by a man. His hands moved towards the complainant but he never touched him in a sexual manner, although he had earlier grabbed hold of him in what was plainly an assault.

... What is submitted by [counsel for the appellant] is that there was here no evidence capable of constituting an indecent assault and ... the essence of his submission comes to this. While, on this boy's evidence, there was in law an assault in that a threat of violence was implied or uttered, there was no indecent touching and no threat of indecent touching and ... for there to be an indecent assault in law the threat must be one of indecent touching. Accordingly, in a case where there is no actual touching, it is only if there is a threat of indecent touching by the defendant that the assault is complete ...

[His Lordship then referred to the 7th edition of *Smith and Hogan's Criminal Law*, which contains a summary of the decision in *R v Court* [1989] AC 28 as follows:]

(i) Where the manner or the external circumstances of the assault include no element of indecency, the assault is not an indecent assault, however indecent the purpose of the offender.

(ii) Where the manner or the circumstances of the assault are unambiguously indecent, the assault is an indecent assault, whether the offender has an indecent purpose or not, provided only that he is aware of the external circumstances.

(iii) Where the manner or the external circumstances of an assault are ambiguous, the assault is an indecent assault only if the offender has an indecent purpose.

... In our judgment, the submissions made on behalf of the appellant ... are not correct. In our judgment, if a man, without touching the victim, were to require him at knife-point to remove his clothing for the purposes of the assaulter's gratification, there can be no doubt that that would be an indecent assault. In such a case of course the demand to strip might be explicable, as in the analogous case of [*R v Pratt* [1984] Crim LR] on some other ground than a sexual one, for example, that the assaulter wished to possess himself of the clothing in order to make good his escape in disguise. Where, however, as in the present case, the act required of the victim admits of no interpretation other than that it is an indecent act, the proof of the threat to secure compliance (which is the assault) establishes the only other necessary ingredient of the offence...

... The boy's account was one which admits of no interpretation other than that it was indecent, apart altogether from whatever may have been the degree of sexual gratification, if any, which the appellant attained from the conduct which he compelled. It seems to us that to compel someone to masturbate in a public place is an indecent act and that accordingly there was here a coincidence of the two ingredients required to establish indecent assault. First, an assault, namely the threat of violence, and secondly, the performance under compulsion of that threat of an indecent act thereby providing the accompanying circumstances of indecency.

We see no reason to accept [counsel's] submission that there must be touching in an indecent manner or the threat of touching in an indecent manner. It is sufficient if the threat procures an act which is plainly indecent and that constitutes, as we have said, circumstances of indecency.

It is accordingly the view of this court that the evidence of the boy, if accepted by the jury, was capable of constituting an indecent assault...

Consent

If the victim consents to the indecent assault, that consent prevents the assault from being an indecent one.

R v Donovan [1934] 2 KB 498 (CA)

Swift J: It was established by the evidence, and was not in dispute, that on 8 March last, in the evening, the appellant induced Norah Eileen Harrison, a girl 17 years of age, to go with him to a garage at Morden, and there he beat her with a cane in circumstances of indecency. The defence was that it lay upon the prosecution to prove absence of consent, and that in fact the girl had consented to everything that was done by the appellant. It is not necessary to narrate the facts in detail. It appeared that the appellant was addicted to a form of sexual perversion, and there was no doubt that during a series of telephone conversations he had made suggestions to the prosecutrix which, if they were taken seriously, meant that he intended or desired to beat her. According to the evidence of the appellant, and of a young woman who said that she had overheard some of the telephone conversations, there was talk between the appellant and the prosecutrix which left no doubt that she had expressed her willingness to submit herself to the kind of conduct to which he was addicted ...

... In *R v May* [1912] 3 KB 572,575 the principle applicable to cases of this kind was laid down by this court in these words: 'The court is of opinion that if the facts proved in evidence are such that the jury can reasonably find consent, there ought to be a direction by the judge on that question, both as to the onus of negativing consent being on the prosecution and as to the evidence in the particular case bearing on the question'.

We have no doubt that the facts proved in the present case were such that the jury might reasonably have found consent; it is, indeed, difficult to reconcile some of the admitted facts with absence of consent. It was therefore of importance (if consent was in issue) that there should be no possibility of doubt in the minds of the jury upon the question whether it was for the Crown to negative consent, or for the defence to prove it. A second observation which may fairly be made is that consent, being a state of mind, is to be proved or negatived only after a full and careful review of the behaviour of the person who is alleged to have consented. Unless a jury is satisfied beyond reasonable doubt that the conduct of the person has been such that, viewed as a whole, it shows that she did not consent, then the prisoner is entitled to be acquitted ...

[The jury asked the judge this question:

> If a man has reason to think that consent has been given, does that constitute consent?' ...

The proper answer to the jury's question would have been that if they as reasonable persons thought that the conduct of the prosecutrix, viewed as a whole, was consistent with consent, they ought not to find that the prosecution had negatived consent ...]

If an act is unlawful in the sense of being in itself a criminal act, it is plain that it cannot be rendered lawful because the person to whose detriment it is done consents to it. No person can license another to commit a crime. So far as the criminal law is concerned, therefore, where the act charged is in itself unlawful, it can never be necessary to prove absence of consent on the part of the person wronged in order to obtain the conviction of the wrongdoer. There are, however, many acts in themselves harmless and lawful which become unlawful only if they are done without the consent of the person affected. What is, in one case, an innocent act of familiarity or affection, may, in another, be an assault, for no other reason than that, in the one case there is consent, and in the other consent is absent. As a general rule, although it is a rule to which there are well-established exceptions, it is an unlawful act to beat another person with such a degree of violence that the infliction of bodily harm is a probable consequence, and when such an act is proved, consent is immaterial.

... Always supposing, therefore, that the blows which he struck were likely or intended to do bodily harm, we are of opinion that [the appellant] was doing an unlawful act, no evidence having been given of facts which would bring the case within any of the exceptions to the general rule. In our view, on the evidence given at the trial, the jury should have been directed that, if they were satisfied that the blows struck by the prisoner were likely or intended to do bodily harm to the prosecutrix, they ought to convict him, and that it was only if they were not so satisfied, that it became necessary to consider the further question whether the prosecution had negatived consent. For this purpose we think that 'bodily harm' has its ordinary meaning and includes any hurt or injury calculated to interfere with the health or comfort of the prosecutor. Such hurt or injury need not be permanent, but must, no doubt, be more than merely transient and trifling.

R v Kimber [1983] 1 WLR 1118 (CA)

Lawton LJ: ... [T]he appellant was convicted of an indecent assault on a woman ...

The appeal raises these points. First, can a defendant charged with indecent assault on a woman raise the defence that he believed she had consented to what he did? ... Second, if he could, did the jury have to consider merely whether his belief was honestly held or, if it was, did they have to go on to consider whether it was based on reasonable grounds? Another way of putting these points is to ask whether the principles upon which the House of Lords decided *R v Morgan* [1976] AC 182 should be applied to a charge of indecent assault on a woman.

The victim was a female patient in a mental hospital. Her mental disorder had been diagnosed as schizophrenia ... Although she was not a defective within the meaning of ss 7 and 45 of the Sexual Offences Act 1956 ... she was suffering from a severe degree of mental disorder ... [T]he appellant admitted trying to have sexual intercourse with [the victim] but said he had not succeeded ... and that he had interfered with her in a way which clearly amounted to an indecent assault if it had been done without her consent ...

[In evidence, the appellant had said that he thought the victim was 'unstable' but he 'thought she was giving consent to have sexual intercourse'; he also said that he 'was not really interested in [her] feelings at all'.]

... At the close of the prosecution's case the [trial judge] ruled that the sole issue for the jury was whether [the victim] had given her real and genuine consent ... He said:

> It is no defence that the defendant thought or believed [the victim] was consenting. The question is: was she consenting? It does not matter what he thought or believed.

Before this court it was accepted by counsel for the prosecution ... that this direction was wrong. The [trial judge] had not had his attention drawn to *R v Tolson* (1889) 23 QBD 168. Before us [counsel for the prosecution] submitted that the jury should have been directed that the appellant had a defence if he had believed that [the victim] was consenting and he had had reasonable grounds for thinking so. On the facts the appellant could not have had any such grounds ... We agree that on the evidence the appellant had no reasonable grounds for thinking that [the victim] was consenting and no jury other than a perverse one could have thought he had.

[Counsel for the appellant] argued, relying on the decision in *R v Morgan* [1976] AC 182, that the sole issue was whether the appellant had honestly believed that [the victim] was consenting. Unless the jury was sure that he had not so believed, he was entitled to be acquitted. The grounds for his belief were irrelevant save in so far as they might have assisted the jury to decide whether he did believe what he said he did ...

The offence of indecent assault is now statutory: see s 14 of the Sexual Offences Act 1956. The prosecution had to prove that the appellant made an indecent assault on [the victim]. As there are no words in the section to indicate that Parliament intended to exclude *mens rea* as an element in this offence, it follows that the prosecution had to prove that the appellant intended to commit it. This could not be done without first proving that the appellant intended to assault [the victim]. In this context assault clearly includes battery. As assault is an act by which the defendant intentionally or recklessly causes the complainant to apprehend, or to sustain, unlawful personal violence: see *R v Venna* [1976] QB 421 at 428–29. In this case the appellant by his own admissions did intentionally lay his hands on [the victim]. That would not, however, have been enough to prove the charge. There had to be evidence that the appellant had intended to do what he did unlawfully. When there is a charge of indecent assault on a woman, the unlawfulness [of the assault] can be proved, as was sought to be done in *R v Donovan* [1934] 2 KB 498, by evidence that the defendant intended to cause bodily harm. In most cases, however, the prosecution tries to prove that the complainant did not consent to what was being done. The burden of proving lack of consent rests on the prosecution: see *R v May* [1912] 3 KB 572 at 575 *per* Lord Alverstone CJ. The consequence is that the prosecution has to prove that the defendant intended to lay hands on his victim without her consent. If he did not intend to do this, he is entitled to be found not guilty; and if he did not so intend because he believed she was consenting, the prosecution will have failed to prove the charge. It is the defendant's belief, not the grounds on which it was based, which goes to negative the intent.

In analysing the issue in this way we have followed what was said by the majority in *R v Morgan* [1976] AC 182: see Lord Hailsham of St Marylebone at 214F–H and Lord Fraser of Tullybelton at 237E–G. If, as we adjudge, the prohibited act in indecent assault is the use of personal violence to a woman without her consent, then the guilty state of mind is the intent to do it without her consent. Then, as in rape at common law, the inexorable logic, to which Lord Hailsham referred in *R v Morgan*, takes over and there is no room either for a 'defence' of honest belief or mistake, or of a 'defence' of honest and reasonable belief or mistake: see [1976] AC 182 at 214F–H.

[His Lordship then went on to criticise the decisions of the Divisional Court in *Albert v Lavin* [1982] AC 546 and *R v Phekoo* [1981] 1 WLR 1117.]

[His Lordship concluded:]

In our judgment the [trial judge] should have directed the jury that the Crown had to make them sure that the appellant never had believed that [the victim] was consenting. [However, despite the judge's failure to so direct the jury] a reasonable jury would inevitably have decided that he had no honest belief that [the victim] was consenting. His own evidence showed that his attitude to her was one of indifference to her feelings and wishes. This state of mind is aptly described in the colloquial expression, 'couldn't care less'. In law this is recklessness. Had the jury been directed on recklessness we are sure they would have found that [the appellant] had acted recklessly. That would have been enough to support a conviction of the offence charged ...

Consent: the age of the victim

Section 14 of the Sexual Offences Act 1956: indecent assault on a woman

(2) A girl under the age of 16 cannot in law give any consent which would prevent an act being an assault for the purposes of this section.

(4) A woman who is a defective cannot in law give any consent which would prevent an act being an assault for the purposes of this section, but a person is only to be treated as guilty of an indecent assault on a defective by reason of that incapacity to consent, if that person knew or had reason to suspect her to be a defective.

Section 15 of the Sexual Offences Act 1956: indecent assault on a man

(2) A boy under the age of 16 cannot in law give any consent which would prevent an act being an assault for the purposes of this section.

(3) A man who is a defective cannot in law give any consent which would prevent an act being an assault for the purposes of this section, but a person is only to be treated as guilty of an indecent assault on a defective by reason of that incapacity to consent, if that person knew or had reason to suspect him to be a defective.

From these provisions it can be seen that consent can only prevent an assault from being indecent if the 'victim' has attained the age of 16 and is not mentally defective.

Faulkner v Talbot [1981] 3 All ER 468 (DC)

Lord Lane CJ: ... The way in which the case arises is this. The appellant was convicted by the justices on 5 February 1980 of indecent assault on a boy, who was then aged 14 years, contrary to s 15(1) of the Sexual Offences Act 1956. The events happened at the appellant's home, and there is no dispute as to the material facts. The 14-year-old boy was living in the appellant's home, having left his parents. The appellant and the boy watched a horror film on the television; the boy was scared, or said he was scared, by the film. As a result of that the appellant told the boy that he could sleep with her if he wished. That he chose to do.

Once they were in bed together, the appellant invited the boy to have sexual intercourse with her. The boy's account, in so far as it was material, was this: the appellant tried to put her hand on his penis, but he would not let her. She then pulled the boy on top of her; she took hold of his penis and put it inside her vagina. On those facts the charge was laid.

[His Lordship quoted s 15(1), (2) of the Sexual Offences Act 1956 and, having considered a number of authorities, went on:]

... First of all what is an assault? An assault is any intentional touching of another person without the consent of that person and without lawful excuse. It need not necessarily be hostile or rude or aggressive, as some of the cases seem to indicate. If touching is an indecent touching, as in this case it plainly was because the appellant took hold of the boy's penis, then the provisions of s 15(2) of the Sexual Offences Act 1956 come into play: 'A boy under the age of 16 cannot in law give any consent which would prevent an act being an assault for the purposes of this section'. Consequently, the touching undoubtedly being indecent, the boy in this case, being aged 14, could not consent to it. It was intentional touching; it was touching without lawful excuse, and in view of s 15(2) it was a touching to which the boy could not in law consent and therefore did not consent. Accordingly, as I see it, one has all the necessary ingredients of the offence of indecent assault ...

... The question which is asked by the case is as follows:

> ... whether the acts of the appellant to which the complainant consented in pulling him on top of her and touching his penis immediately before sexual intercourse by him with her were an indecent assault by the appellant on the complainant contrary to s 15 of the Sexual Offences Act, 1956?

The answer I would give to that is 'Yes', it was an indecent assault ...

Boreham J: Without going into detail, there is, in my judgment, now ample authority for this general proposition: where, in a charge of indecent assault on a person under the age of 16, the act complained of is indecent that act would, if it were done without consent, be an assault, then the offence is made out ...

R v McCormack [1969] 2 QB 442 (CA)

Fenton Atkinson LJ: ... The facts, shortly, were these. The girl was aged 15, and the appellant was 22. It was common ground that they spent the night of 10/11 August 1968 in bed together ... The girl ... said that with her full consent the appellant had intercourse with her ...

... [H]e said himself in the plainest terms that they had indulged in certain acts of sexual intimacy, including this, that he admittedly on his own evidence had inserted a finger into the girl's vagina ...

... [I]n the view of the members of this court, it is plain beyond argument that if a man inserts a finger into the vagina of a girl under 16 that is an indecent assault, in view of her age, and it is an indecent assault however willing and co-operative she may in fact be.

Consent and assault

Where actual injury is caused to the victim, consent does not prevent the act from amounting to an assault: see *R v Brown* [1994] 1 AC 212. However, where no injury is caused, so the only charge is one of indecent assault, consent may operate to prevent the act from being an assault in the first place (irrespective of the provisions of ss 14(2) and 15(2) of the Sexual Offences Act 1956).

R v Sutton [1977] 1 WLR 1086 (CA)

Lord Widgery CJ: ... The appellant was the coach and manager of a football club for small boys. Three of the boys who played for the club, all 11 or 12, were taken by the applicant to his home in order that he might photograph them. Each of them was photographed partially unclothed and two of them were photographed in the nude. The photographs, whether partially clothed or in the nude, were taken so as to draw attention to the boys' genitals. The appellant's purpose was to sell the photographs to Scandinavian magazines. The appellant remained fully clothed throughout and did not invite any of the boys to touch him in any way at all, nor did he stroke or fondle any of the boys. He did, however, touch each one of them on the hands, arms, legs or torso for the purpose of indicating how he wished them to pose. These actions were not threatening or hostile in any ordinary sense of the word and none of the three boys showed any unwillingness, indeed they consented.

... The 1956 Act bars consent from preventing an act being an indecent assault [see below]. Hence, if the act alleged to constitute the assault is itself an indecent act, consent will not avail. But in the present case the touching, which was merely to indicated a pose, was not in itself indecent, and was consented to. It was not hostile or threatening. Consent, therefore, does avail to prevent it being an assault and the question of indecency does not arise ...

SOME OTHER SEXUAL OFFENCES

Sexual intercourse with a girl under 13

Section 5 of the Sexual Offences Act 1956

It is an offence for a man to have unlawful sexual intercourse with a girl under the age of 13.

Maximum penalty: life imprisonment (s 37 and Schedule 2 of the Sexual Offences Act 1956). The word 'unlawful' adds nothing, since all acts of sexual intercourse with a girl under the age of 13 are unlawful.

Sexual intercourse with a girl under 16

Section 6 of the Sexual Offences Act 1956

(1) It is an offence, subject to the exceptions mentioned in this section, for a man to have unlawful sexual intercourse with a girl under the age of 16.

(3) A man is not guilty of an offence under this section because he has unlawful sexual intercourse with a girl under the age of 16, if he is under the age of 24 and has not previously been charged with a like offence, and he believes her to be of the age of 16 or over and has reasonable cause for that belief.

In this subsection, 'a like offence' means an offence under this section or an attempt to commit one ...

Maximum penalty: imprisonment for up to 2 years following conviction on indictment; imprisonment for up to 6 months following summary conviction: see s 37 and Schedule 2 of the Sexual Offences Act 1956; s 32 of the Magistrates' Courts Act 1980). The word 'unlawful' in s 6(1) adds nothing, since all acts of sexual intercourse with a girl under the age of 16 are illegal.

For the defence in s 6(3) to apply:

(1) the defendant must be under 24 at the time he is alleged to have committed the offence; and

(2) the defendant must not have been charged with such an offence at any time in the past (note that the defence does not apply if the defendant has been *charged* with such an offence: he does not have to have been *convicted* in the past); and

(3) the defendant must have believed that the girl was at least 16; and

(4) the defendant's belief must be based on reasonable grounds.

CHAPTER 24

OFFENCES INVOLVING WEAPONS

Section 1 of the Prevention of Crime Act 1953: possessing an offensive weapon

(1) Any person who without lawful authority or reasonable excuse, the proof whereof shall lie on him, has with him in any public place any offensive weapon shall be guilty of an offence.

(4) In this section, 'offensive weapon' means any article made or adapted for use for causing injury to the person, or intended by the person having it with him for such use by him or by some other person.

In this section 'public place' includes any highway and any other premises or place to which at the material time the public have or are permitted to have access, whether on payment or otherwise ...

Under s 1 of the Prevention of Crime Act 1953, it is for the Crown to prove that:

(1) that the accused was in a public place; and

(2) that the accused had in his possession an article which was either:

   (a) offensive *per se* (that is, either made for use as an offensive weapon or adapted for use as an offensive weapon); or

   (b) an ordinarily innocuous article but one which the accused intended to be used to cause injury to someone.

If the prosecution can establish these things, the defendant will be convicted unless he can show (on the balance of probabilities) that he had either lawful authority (eg a police officer carrying a truncheon) or a reasonable excuse.

Has with him

The phrase 'has with him' includes, by implication, a requirement that the defendant knows that he has the article with him. This is, however, subject to the proviso that if a person knew at one time that he had something with him and then forgot about it, he still has it with him for the purpose of s 1 of the 1953 Act.

R v Cugullere [1961] 1 WLR 858 (CA)

Salmon J: ... This court is clearly of the opinion that the words 'has with him in any public place', must mean 'knowingly has with him in any public place'. If some innocent person has a cosh slipped into his pocket by an escaping rogue, he would not be guilty of having it with him within the meaning of the section because he would be quite innocent of any knowledge that it had been put into his pocket. In the judgment of this court, the section cannot apply in circumstances such as those. It is, therefore, extremely important in any case under this section for the judge to give a careful direction to the jury on the issue of possession. The first thing the jury have to be satisfied about – and it is always a question for the jury – is whether the accused person knowingly had with him the alleged offensive weapon.

R v McCalla (1988) 87 Cr App R 372 (CA)

May LJ: [The defendant's car had been stopped by the police.] It was not disputed that when the vehicle was searched there was found in the glove compartment a cosh, the subject of the count with which this appeal is concerned. The appellant accepted that it was in the car. According to the prosecution, when he was asked why it was there he replied: 'Well, some of my mates have been attacked before and I don't want that to happen to me'. He was asked; 'If someone attacked you, would you use the cosh?', and he said: 'Yes, but only to defend myself'.

During his evidence the appellant denied that that conversation had taken place. He said that he had told the police the truth, which was that he had picked up the cosh on a building site where he worked, that he had put it in the car about a month before the incident with the Fiesta, and that he had forgotten about it ...

[His Lordship referred to *R v Martindale* (1986) 84 Cr App R 31, a case involving alleged possession of illegal drugs:]

It is unnecessary to read the whole of the judgment of the Lord Chief Justice in that case, but it is appropriate to read a substantial part of it, particularly at 33:

> In the judgment of this court that argument [that the lack of memory or knowledge negatives possession] is fallacious. It is true that a man does not necessarily possess every article which he may have in his pocket. If for example some evil-minded person secretly slips a portion of cannabis resin into the pocket of another without the other's knowledge, the other is not in law in possession of the cannabis. That scarcely needs stating. But the present situation is different. Here the applicant himself put the cannabis into his wallet knowing what it was and put the wallet into his pocket. In our judgment, subject to the authorities, to which reference will have to be made in a moment, he remained in possession, even though his memory of the presence of the drug had faded or disappeared altogether. Possession does not depend upon the alleged possessor's powers of memory. Nor does possession come and go as memory revives or fails. If it were to do so, a man with a poor memory would be acquitted, he with the good memory would be convicted.

[His Lordship, having referred to three other cases on the meaning of possession, went on:]

As to the law as stated in those four cases one comment must first be made. In those concerning drugs the consideration is that of possession. In those concerning offensive weapons it is having them in a public place. To have something with one necessarily requires, we think, closer contact, as it were, than mere possession. Every case of 'having' is one of 'possessing', but it does not necessarily follow that every case of 'possessing' is one of 'having' within the meaning of the relevant statutory provisions. However, for the purposes of the instant case, and having regard to the earlier decisions to which we have referred, in our view the relevant considerations as to recollection and forgetfulness are the same ...

We think that the basic principle underlying those cases is that once one has or possesses something, be it an offensive weapon or a drug, one continues to have or possess it until one does something to rid oneself of having or possessing it; that merely to have forgotten that one has possession of it is not sufficient to exclude continuing to have or to possess it ...

... There was no need to leave to the jury the question whether he had forgotten that he had it with him. He knew that he had it, because he had picked it up at the building site and continued to have it with him in his car; and by the statutory provisions he had it with him in a public place.

... [Furthermore], we are quite satisfied that to have forgotten that one has an offensive weapon in the car that one is driving is not in itself a reasonable excuse under the Act. But when such forgetfulness is coupled with particular circumstances relating to the original acquisition of the article, the combination of the original acquisition and the subsequent forgetfulness of possessing it may, given sufficient facts, be a reasonable excuse for having the offensive weapon with one.

For instance ... if someone driving along a road where earlier there had been a demonstration were to see and pick up a police truncheon which had obviously been dropped there and were to put it in the boot of his car, intending to take it to the nearest police station, and then were to be stopped within a few minutes, he would have a reasonable excuse for having the truncheon with him in the boot of the car. If he were to forget that it was there and two years later were to be stopped and the truncheon were then found in the boot of the car, the circumstances of the original acquisition of the truncheon and the time for which that person had completely forgotten that it was in the car could constitute a reasonable excuse for possessing the truncheon two years after its acquisition ...

Public place

Knox v Anderton (1982) 76 Cr App R 156 (DC)

Webster J: ... It was not disputed before the justices that on [27 July 1981] the defendant, when standing on an upper landing of a block of flats on the Langworthy Estate in Salford, had a claw hammer in his hand, and that this was an offensive weapon. The only issue raised before the justices, which was raised at the close of the prosecution evidence, was whether that landing was a public place within the meaning of that expression in the Prevention of Crime Act 1953 ... The question for the opinion of this court is whether the justices' finding that the landings to the Langworthy Estate flats in Salford are a public place was wrong in law ...

The facts found by the justices, so far as material, are as follows ... There is nothing to prevent a member of the public from entering the estate, there is nothing to stop members of the public from entering the stairways of the blocks of flats, there is no barrier to prevent members of the public walking along the landings which give access to the individual flats, and there are no doors to the stairways or landings, which are open to the atmosphere. There are no notices to suggest that there is any restriction of access to the landings and stairways or to the whole estate except that there are notices on some of the buildings at the entrance to the estate which read: 'Parking of vehicles above 10 cwt on the estate is prohibited; access is restricted to tenants and their visitors only' ...

... At what point, short of the front door of the individual flats, can it be said as a matter of inevitable inference from the facts found to have ceased to have been a public place? And in particular can it be said, as a matter of inevitable inference from those facts, to have ceased to have become a public place before the landings are reached? In our view there is no inevitable inference that it ceased to become a public place at any point before the landings are reached, in view of the justices' findings that there was nothing to stop members of the public from entering the stairways of the blocks, that there was no barrier to prevent members of the public walking along the landings which give access to the individual flats, that there were no doors to the stairways or landings which were open to the atmosphere and that there were no notices to suggest that there was any restriction of access to the landings and stairways or indeed to the whole estate except the notices posted on some of the buildings at the entrance to the estate to which we have already referred.

For all these reasons we would, slightly rewording the question for the opinion of this court, answer it by saying that the justices have not been shown to have made any error of law in finding that the landings were a public place and we, therefore, dismiss this appeal.

Williams v DPP (1992) 95 Cr App R 415 (DC)

Jowitt J: This is an appeal by way of case stated from a decision of the Liverpool justices convicting the appellant of disorderly behaviour while drunk in Rutland House, a block of flats in Liverpool, contrary to s 91(1) of the Criminal Justice Act 1967. The section requires that the offending conduct is committed in a public place and defines a public place to include premises to which, at the material time, the public have or are permitted to have access whether on payment or otherwise ...

The facts are these. First, Rutland House is a block of flats and the appellant lives in Flat 39 on the 10th floor. There are other flats on that floor, as there are on other floors. Access is gained from a landing which is common to the flats on the floor. Second, there is a staircase and, I would assume, a lift by which access can be gained between the different storeys of the block of flats and between any storey and the ground floor. Third, access to the block of flats from the street is through a locked door and there are three ways in which entry can be gained through that door. First, by operating the security lock by someone who has the key or the security code, whichever may be the case. Though not stated in the case, there is an obvious inference that possession of the key or knowledge of the security code is not something available to members of the public. The second method of entry is by use of an intercom between the entrance door and each of the flats, which enables anyone wishing to enter the building to communicate with one of the flats. The occupier of the flat can then release the security lock to allow entry into the building. Again this is not stated in the case, but the obvious inference is that the intercom and the lock-release mechanism controlled from the flats has the purpose of allowing the flat-dwellers to screen would-be visitors so as to exclude those who have no legitimate business from entering the building. The third method of entry is through the caretaker, who is able to and does admit visitors who satisfy him that they have a legitimate reason to be admitted, for example, the postman and the milkman. The fourth fact which emerges is that on the date charged in the summons, 6 February 1990, and when he was out of his flat on the 10th floor landing, the appellant, while drunk, was guilty of disorderly behaviour. The justices concluded that this landing was a public place; that is to say, a place to which the public have or are permitted to have access. The question for this court is whether, on the facts and inferences which I have related, it was open to them to reach this conclusion.

Ignoring authority and looking only at the statutory definition of 'public place' and making use of my own common sense, I would say assuredly that it is not a public place. Am I then constrained by authority to abandon common sense and reach the opposite conclusion? I do not think so ...

The appropriate starting point to the resolution of the issue in this case is to ask who had or who was permitted to have access to this block of flats and why, and to ask whether the methods by which access was to be gained shed light on the answer to that question. Approached in this way, the question, was the landing in this case a public place, admits of only one answer. It was not. People are not permitted to enter this building and be on the landings as they please. The manifest purpose of the control exercised over entry from the outer door (or it may be doors) from the street is to prevent entry, save by those who visit the building for social, business or professional dealings with those who live in the flats (for example, the friend, the milkman or the doctor) or for purposes connected with the building itself, such as maintenance. This connection with the occupiers or the building takes visitors out of the general public and gives a private (as opposed to public) nature to their access ...

On the facts of this case, as they so plainly appear, in my judgment, the questions which the justices pose for us, whether the landing outside flat 39 Rutland House, Croxteth Drive, Liverpool 17, is a public place or, alternatively, whether the evidence justified a finding by us that this is a public place, both have to be answered, no. The evidence, as it seems to me, is quite overwhelmingly in the opposite direction, that this was not a public place. I would therefore allow this appeal.

Nolan LJ: I agree. The position, as it seems to me, is that residents of the block of flats are entitled and their visitors are allowed to enter the block for reasons personal to them, and not as members of the public. The clear purpose of the barriers on entry was to restrict entry to those persons and to exclude the public. I, too, would allow the appeal.

Weapons which are offensive *per se*: meaning

A weapon is offensive *per se* if it does not have any innocent use, eg a truncheon: see *Houghton v Chief Constable of Greater Manchester* (1986) 84 Cr App R 319 or, in a country where rice is not grown, a rice flail: see *Copus v DPP* [1989] Crim LR 577. A razor which can be used for shaving has an innocent purpose and so is not offensive *per se* : see *R v Petrie* [1961] 1 WLR 358; the same applies to an ordinary penknife: see *R v Humphreys* [1977] Crim LR 225.

Houghton v Chief Constable of Greater Manchester (1986) 84 Cr App R 319 (CA)

Facts: The plaintiff, a former airport police officer, went to a fancy dress party dressed in a police constable's uniform and wore, as part of that uniform, a police truncheon. On his way home from the party he was stopped by two police officers. At trial, the prosecution offered no evidence against him and the plaintiff was acquitted and he was awarded costs. He brought a civil action claiming damages, *inter alia*, for unlawful arrest.

May LJ: ... The definition of 'offensive weapon', as is well-known to those who practise in the criminal courts, draws a distinction between those articles which are offensive weapons *per se*, as is said, and those articles which are brought within the definition because the person having them with him intends to use those articles as offensive weapons, although *per se* they may not be such. An example taken in some cases is that of a sandbag. That can be an effective weapon if it is intended to be used as such; on the other hand it has a purpose and a use wholly devoid of any offensive nature. It is therefore not an offensive weapon *per se*. In order to obtain a conviction of a person for possessing a sandbag, it must be proved that that person intended to use that sandbag as an offensive weapon on the relevant occasion.

The first [question] is whether a policeman's truncheon is an offensive weapon *per se* within the comments that I have just made in relation to s 1(3) of the Act. I for my part have no doubt that it is. One trusts, and fortunately it is the fact, that police officers rarely use their truncheons for the purpose of defence. But that is what they are for. It is not an article which, as I think, can be equated to a sandbag, or even to a razor. A razor is not intended to be used as an offensive weapon, although unfortunately it is so often put to that purpose. A razor is intended to enable a person to shave. A truncheon, in my judgment, cannot be said to possess *per se* any such innocent quality. It is intended, if it is going to be used at all, to be used for the purposes of offence, albeit that offence may be part of defence on the part of the police officer concerned. Consequently I reach the conclusion without hesitation that a police officer's truncheon is an offensive weapon *per se*.

R v Petrie [1961] 1 WLR 358 (CA)

Facts: The defendant had been charged with being in possession of an offensive weapon, namely a 'cut-throat' razor, in a public place.

Salmon J: ... It is clear that the definition section of the Act contemplates offensive weapons of at any rate two classes, namely (a) an article which *per se* is an offensive weapon, that is to say, an article made or adapted for use for causing injury to the person; and (b) an article which, though it is not made or adapted for such use, is carried with the intent so to use it. A cosh, a knuckle-duster and a revolver are examples of articles in the first class. A sandbag and a razor are examples of articles in the second class. No jury could find that a sandbag was in the first class because there would be no evidence to support such a finding. It seems to this court that the same is true about an ordinary razor. There are some articles which are equivocal, for example, knives. It would always be for a jury to say whether a knife was made or adapted for use for causing injury to the person. It would depend upon the view the jury took of the knife.

It is absolutely essential in summing up to the jury in a case of this sort not to muddle up the definition of 'offensive weapon'. If the article in question is an offensive weapon *per se*, once possession in a public place is proved, the onus shifts to the defence to prove on a balance of probability that there was lawful authority or reasonable excuse for carrying the weapon. If the accused fails to discharge this onus the jury must convict him. On the other hand, if the article is something like a sandbag or a razor, the onus is on the prosecution to show that it was carried with the intention of using it to injure. The onus remains on the prosecution throughout, and if at the end of the day the jury are left in doubt about the intent of the accused, he is entitled to be acquitted ...

It is clear, as already indicated, there was abundant evidence that the appellant was carrying this razor with the intent necessary to make it an offensive weapon within the meaning of the Act. Indeed, if a man is found carrying a razor in a public place, there is, at any rate, some evidence on which a jury could say that he had the necessary intent. It would be entirely a matter for the jury. But it was quite wrong for the chairman to direct the jury as a matter of law that the appellant was in possession of an offensive weapon, and that the onus was on him to prove lawful authority or reasonable excuse ...

Weapons which are offensive *per se*: a question of fact

Whether a weapon is offensive *per se* (ie it was made or has been adapted for use in causing injury to the person) is a question of fact for the jury to decide. However, some weapons (such as a flick-knife) are so clearly 'offensive' within this definition of the term that judges are entitled to direct juries accordingly.

R v Williamson (1977) 67 Cr App R 35 (CA)

Facts: The trial judge had held that a sheath knife is offensive *per se* (whereupon the defendant changed his plea to guilty).

Lane LJ: ... It is for the jury to decide whether a weapon held by the defendant was an offensive weapon, bearing in mind the definition in the section which I have just read. Consequently whether the object in the possession of the defendant in any case can properly be described as an offensive weapon is a matter not for the judge but for the jury to decide. The jury must determine whether they feel sure that the object was made or adapted for use in causing injury to the person or was intended by the person having it with him for such use by him. There may perhaps be circumstances in which it is possible to say that there is no evidence to the contrary in a particular case. But that is not the case here. If there is such a case, then in those circumstances the judge might, unobjectionably, direct the jury in those terms, but such cases must be rare. In the normal case of this sort, it remains a question for the jury, although the judge, after proper warnings to the jury, may add his own view on the subject ...

One only has to pause for a moment to consider what is meant by a sheath knife ... It means a knife in a sheath. That is not what the jury ... should be worried about. They should be concerned with the nature of the knife which is in the sheath. To suggest that this court can determine in advance the nature of every knife which may be in a sheath demonstrates the absurdity of the situation in which this court finds itself ... [I]t is not for us to usurp the functions of the jury and to decide into which category [this knife] falls under the Prevention of Crime Act 1953 ...

Gibson v Wales [1983] 1 WLR 393 (DC)

Griffiths LJ: ... [T]here is no reasonable alternative to the view that a flick-knife is an offensive weapon *per se*. It is made for the purpose of causing injury to the person. It may sometimes be used for wholly innocent purposes, even possessed for innocent purposes, but there will be a very heavy burden on any person in possession of a flick-knife to satisfy any court that he had it for such an innocent purpose ...

McCullough J: Whether a flick-knife is an article made for use for causing injury to the person is a question of fact, but in my judgment it is a question which admits of only one answer; it is.

R v Simpson [1983] 1 WLR 1494 (CA)

Lord Lane CJ: ... It was admitted at the trial that the appellant was in possession of the flick-knife and in possession of it in a public place. In the event ... he raised as his defence reasonable excuse for the possession of that weapon, the flick-knife, on the basis that he had it in his possession for nothing more sinister than the carrying out of electrical repairs to his motor car. This defence was, as is apparent, rejected by the jury ...

... It has first to be observed that the mere fact that a particular weapon can be, and perhaps often is, used for an innocent purpose does not necessarily take it out of the offensive *per se* category. That is the reason why we emphasise 'made' in the definition in the Prevention of Crime Act 1953 which I have read. For instance a bayonet may be used to poke the fire, a stiletto may be used as a letter knife, and indeed a handgun to shoot vermin. They remain nevertheless in the first category; they are 'made for use for causing injury to the person' ...

... [I]t is the purpose for which they are made, not that for which they may be used, which is the question ...

We think that the flick-knife falls ... into the category of weapons which are offensive *per se*, namely the first category which is raised by the definition in s 1(4) of the Prevention of Crime Act 1953. These weapons are plainly designed by the manufacturers to be carried conveniently in the hand or in the pocket and there concealed, to be brought into use with the minimum of delay to the assailant and the minimum of warning to the victim. There is no pause while the blade is pulled out from the handle against the spring or is removed from its sheath by hand. By their very design in this way they betray the purpose for which they were made ...

Once one reaches the conclusion, as we have done, that a knife proved to be a flick-knife necessarily is one made for use for causing injury to the person, we take the view that that is a matter of which judicial notice can be taken and the jury can be directed accordingly.

Weapons which become offensive because of the intention with which they are carried

A weapon which is not offensive *per se* can be an offensive weapon if it is carried for the purpose of causing injury to the person. Thus, an apparently innocuous article (eg a comb) can become an offensive weapon if carried with the requisite intent. For such an article to become an offensive weapon, the defendant must have intended to use the article as a weapon at the time specified in the charge: the defendant cannot be convicted if, by the time specified in the charge, he no longer intended to use the article as a weapon: see *R v Allamby* [1974] 1 WLR 1494. Furthermore, where an innocuous article is used as a weapon, the defendant can only be convicted of possessing an offensive weapon if the intention to use the article as a weapon was formed some time before its use: see *R v Dayle* [1974] 1 WLR 181; *Ohlson v Hylton* [1975] 1 WLR 724.

R v Allamby; R v Medford [1974] 1 WLR 1494 (CA)

Facts: The two defendants travelled by car on 20 July 1973 from Reading to Cornwall in order to persuade Medford's former girlfriend to return to him. On the following day, on their way back from Cornwall, their car was stopped and searched on the A303 in Wiltshire by police officers who found three domestic knives.

[Note: Since the knives were domestic knives they were not offensive *per se* and could only be offensive weapons if carried with the intention that they be used to cause injury to someone. The defendants apparently conceded that they had intended to use the knives to cause injury to the new boyfriend of Medford's former girlfriend. However, that intention was no longer in existence by the time the defendants were stopped by the police and the knives were found.]

James LJ: ... The effect of the recorder's direction was to tell the jury that they could convict in relation to the domestic knives if they were satisfied that the intent necessary to give those knives the character of 'offensive weapons' was present at any time during the period commencing when the defendants left Reading for Cornwall and ending at the time of their arrest, although that intention to use the knives for causing injury to the person was not proved to exist at a time and place of the offence charged ...

The question whether a defendant had at the relevant time and place the intention necessary to bring the article in his possession within the definition of an offensive weapon is a question of fact for the jury ... But proof of that intention must be related to the time and place of the offence charged. The intention in relation to such an article may change from time to time. The place in which a defendant has the article with him may be a 'public place' at one time but not at another. 'Reasonable excuse' for having the article may exist at one time but be absent at another. 'Time' and 'place' are material elements in the particulars of this offence, and the issue of guilt has to be decided by the jury in respect of the offence as charged. In the present case it was open to the prosecution to frame the charge in such a way as to cover a period of time when the defendants were in Cornwall. They did not do so. They proceeded on the narrow basis of the particulars on the indictment [namely that on 21 July 1973 they 'had with them in a public place, namely the A303 at Winterbourne Stoke in the county of Wilts offensive weapons ...']. This being so it was open to counsel for the defendants to invite the jury to find that the domestic knives were not offensive weapons at the time charged because any intent to use them for causing personal injury which may have existed at an earlier point of time had been abandoned. This was an issue which ought to have been left to the jury ... It was a misdirection to tell the jury as the recorder did 'the question really boils down to this – why were they taking the knives to Cornwall?' By stating the issue in that way the recorder withdrew from the jury the issue of fact of the intention of the defendants at the time and place relevant to the charge, and the defendants were thereby deprived of the opportunity, to which they were entitled, of obtaining the decision of the jury on the question whether the domestic knives were at the relevant time and place offensive weapons within the meaning of the statute.

R v Dayle [1974] 1 WLR 181 (CA)

Kilner Brown J: ... It was alleged that an injury to the complainant was caused by the appellant throwing the car jack or wheel brace which he took from the boot of his car in the course of a fight ...

The terms of s 1(1) of the Prevention of Crime Act 1953 are apt to cover the case of a person who goes out with an offensive weapon without lawful authority or reasonable excuse and also the person who deliberately selects an article ... with the intention of using it as a weapon without such authority or excuse. But, if an article, already possessed lawfully and for good reason, is used offensively to cause injury, such use does not necessarily prove the intent which the Crown must establish in respect of articles which are not offensive weapons *per se*. Each case must depend on its own facts.

Ohlson v Hylton [1975] 1 WLR 724 (DC)

Lord Widgery CJ: ... The relevant facts are as follows. At about 4.40 pm on 9 January 1974, the defendant was on the platform of Blackfriars underground station intending to board a train going east on his way home from work. It was an occasion when the trains were very crowded, and the defendant had difficulty in boarding a train. Already on the train was a Mr Malcolm, who was standing close to the doors waiting for them to be closed. The defendant attempted to board the train, notwithstanding the protests of Mr Malcolm, and the upshot of the difference between them was that Mr Malcolm either fell from, or stepped from, the train and both he and the defendant finished up on the platform.

The defendant was a carpenter and in his briefcase he had some of the tools of his trade, including a hammer. When he and Mr Malcolm fell out of the train on to the platform, the defendant immediately took the hammer from his briefcase and deliberately struck Mr Malcolm on the head so that he fell to the ground. It is evident that on those facts the defendant was properly convicted of the first charge of assault, but his contention before the Crown Court was that he was not guilty of the second charge, namely a charge of having with him in a public place an offensive weapon ...

[Section 1 of the Prevention of Crime Act 1953] thus divides offensive weapons into two categories. First, the type of weapon which is often described as offensive *per se*, namely an article made or adapted for causing injury to the person. The second category relates to articles not so made or adapted and which have a perfectly innocent and legitimate use but which nevertheless may come into the category of offensive weapons if the person having the weapon with him has it with an intention to use it for causing injury to the person ...

In the absence of authority I would hold that an offence under s 1 is not committed where a person arms himself with a weapon for *instant* attack on his victim. It seems to me that the section is concerned only with a man who, possessed of a weapon, forms the necessary intent before an occasion to use actual violence has arisen. In other words, it is not the actual use of the weapon with which the section is concerned, but the carrying of a weapon with intent to use it if occasion arises ...

I accept that it is unnecessary for the prosecution to prove that the relevant intent was formed from the moment when the defendant set out on his expedition. An innocent carrying of, say, a hammer can be converted into an unlawful carrying when the defendant forms the guilty intent, provided, in my view, that the intent is formed before the actual occasion to use violence has arisen ...

... Accordingly, no offence is committed under the Act of 1953 where an assailant seizes a weapon for instant use on his victim. Here the seizure and use of the weapon are all part and parcel of the assault or attempted assault. To support a conviction under the Act the prosecution must show that the defendant was carrying or otherwise equipped with the weapon, and had the intent to use it offensively before any occasion for its actual use had arisen.

R v Humphreys [1977] Crim LR 225 (CA)

Facts: Following a dance at a youth club a fight broke out during the course of which Humphreys, who had been attacked by another person, stabbed that other person in the back with a penknife which he had managed to extract from an inside jacket pocket while being assaulted by several youths.

Held, allowing the appeal: if a person merely happened to have with him an inoffensive weapon like a penknife and in desperation or in the heat of the moment drew that weapon *ad hoc*, and used it for injuring a person intending then and there to cause injury to another person, he was not guilty of the offence of having an offensive weapon in a public place, because he had not been carrying in a public place that weapon with the necessary intent to cause injury. His intention was formed, as it might be said, *ad hoc*. The jury should have been directed that if the appellant only formed the intent to use the knife defensively after the occasion had arisen he was entitled to be acquitted because his seizure and use of the weapon, taking it out of his pocket and using it, were part and parcel of the wounding of the victim.

Intention to intimidate

In very rare cases, it can be said that an intention to intimidate amounts to an intention to injure, and so converts an article into an offensive weapon. This will only be the case if the intention is to use the article to cause nervous shock (in the tortious sense).

R v Rapier (1979) 70 Cr App R 17 (CA)

Facts: The trial judge had directed the jury that 'an intention to intimidate with the use of the knife' was sufficient to make the knife an offensive weapon.

Park J: ... [His Lordship quoted from *R v Edmonds* [1963] 2 QB 142 where Winn J says, at 150–51:]

> ... it seems to the court that it is, to put it at its lowest, unsafe and undesirable that directions to juries based upon s 1(4) of the Act should include any reference to intent to frighten unless it be made clear in the passage in which such reference is made that the frightening must be of a kind for which the term 'intimidation' is far more appropriate and of a sort which is capable of producing injury through the operation of shock ...

... In our view, in directing a jury in respect of an offence under this section the use of the word 'intimidate' should be avoided unless the evidence discloses that the intention of the person having with him the article alleged to be an offensive weapon was to cause injury by shock and hence injury to the person; it would seem that circumstances giving rise to that situation must be exceedingly rare ...

Lawful authority or reasonable excuse: burden of proof

It must be remembered that s 1(1) of the Prevention of Crimes Act 1953 places the burden of proof on the defence to show either lawful authority or reasonable excuse. The standard of proof is on the balance of probabilities (not beyond reasonable doubt): see *R v Brown* (1971) 55 Cr App R 478.

R v Brown (1971) 55 Cr App R 478 (CA)

Cairns LJ: ... [I]t is clear law that the accused has to satisfy the jury only on a balance of probabilities and not beyond a reasonable doubt as to his having a reasonable excuse for having with him offensive weapons.

Lawful authority

A police officer has lawful authority to carry a truncheon (note that a private security guard does not): see *Bryan v Mott* (1975) 62 Cr App R 71.

Reasonable excuse

The law is prepared to sanction the carrying of a weapon for personal protection where there is an imminent danger of attack and the mode of defence chosen is reasonable in all the circumstances. However, the law will not permit the carrying of a weapon 'just in case'. The scope of the 'reasonable excuse' defence has been considered in a number of cases.

Evans v Hughes [1972] 1 WLR 1452 (DC)

Lord Widgery CJ: ... The facts found were that in the afternoon of 24 February the defendant was in a public place, a public highway in Uxbridge Road, Ealing, and he had in his possession a metal bar about six inches long; it was made, as the justices describe it, of quite light metal. Two police officers saw him with this bar and asked him what he had with him; he replied it was an iron bar; asked where he had got it from and why, he said, 'I have just collected it from a friend of mine who took it from my house'. That proved to be an incorrect statement, because he went back on it later on and said that the truth of why he had the bar was that about a week before:

> I was on my way home and got done by three blokes, so I've been carrying the iron bar about with me for self-protection. I wouldn't carry a knife because that would be silly. If the blokes had attacked me again I would have used the iron bar on them.

He elaborated the earlier incident when he had been attacked by three men and his case was that he carried the bar as a weapon, but his sole purpose was to use it in self-defence if he were subjected to the kind of experience to which he had been subjected the previous week, namely being attacked by three men.

The justices obviously took a favourable view of the defendant; they found that he had reasonable cause for fear, and did fear that he would be violently attacked, and they further found that he carried the bar for the purpose and with the intention of using it for the purpose of self-defence only and not for any aggressive purpose.

The first task of the justices was to decide whether this bar was an offensive weapon at all, because the question whether it was carried with lawful authority or reasonable excuse does not arise unless and until it is shown to be an offensive weapon.

It was obviously, and I turn to the definition, not an 'article made or adapted for use for causing injury to the person'. It was a metal bar and not made or adapted for use as a weapon at all, but on this young man's own admission it was intended by him to be used for self-defence if he was attacked, and therefore in my view it was intended by him for use for causing injury to the person, and the justices when they concluded, as they did, that this was not an offensive weapon, were in my judgment wrong. The fact that the carrier of the weapon only intended to use it defensively does not prevent it from being an offensive weapon within the meaning of the definition, and I have no hesitation for myself in saying that the justices made a mistake in their first conclusion that this was not an offensive weapon at all.

However, they did not leave the matter there because they also said in the case that even if the bar was an 'offensive weapon' within the Act, the defendant had 'a reasonable excuse for having it with him', and the argument in this court has turned on whether it was open to the justices to say in these circumstances that the defendant had a reasonable excuse for having this offensive weapon with him.

[Having considered *Evans v Wright* [1964] Crim LR 466 and *Grieve v Macleod* [1967] Crim LR 424, his Lordship continued:]

The outcome of those authorities, and my own reading of the Act ... is that it may be a reasonable excuse for the carrying of an offensive weapon that the carrier is in anticipation of imminent attack and is carrying it for his own personal defence, but what is abundantly clear to my mind is that this Act never intended to sanction the permanent or constant carriage of an offensive weapon merely because of some constant or enduring supposed or actual threat or danger to the carrier. People who are under that kind of continuing threat must protect themselves by other means, notably by enlisting the protection of the police, and in order that it may be a reasonable excuse to say, 'I carried this for my own defence', the threat for which this defence is required must be an imminent particular threat affecting the particular circumstances in which the weapon was carried.

That being so, a nice point arises as to whether this young man could possibly have pleaded reasonable excuse for carrying this weapon seven days after the attack which he says had previously been made upon him. The story of course was that he remained in fear. To have carried the weapon for a day or two perhaps would have been a case in which he could claim reasonable excuse on the justices' finding without very much difficulty; when you get to eight days you get in my judgment very close to the borderline, but at the borderline it is the good sense of the justices which must ultimately determine whether or not there was reasonable excuse. I am not sure that I should have reached the same conclusion had I been sitting among the justices, but I think we must leave the decision to them. I would accordingly dismiss the appeal.

Malnik v DPP [1989] Crim LR 451 (DC)

Facts: The appellant went to repossess a car unlawfully taken by a man known to have a violent and irresponsible disposition. The appellant took with him a rice flail, which consisted of two pieces of wood joined by a chain. Such weapons were sometimes used in connection with martial arts in which the appellant had a long-standing interest, and some expertise.

Held, dismissing the appeal, the magistrate had correctly concluded that as a matter of law the defence of reasonable excuse was not available to the appellant. Ordinarily, individuals could not legitimately arm themselves with an offensive weapon in order to repel unlawful violence which such individual had knowingly and deliberately brought about by creating a situation in which violence was liable to be inflicted. It was quite different where those concerned with security and law-enforcement were concerned. If private citizens set out on expeditions such as this, armed with offensive weapons, the risk of unlawful violence and serious injury was great, and obvious. The policy of the law therefore must be against such conduct, which conclusion was consistent with the very narrow limits which previous decisions had imposed on the freedom of the citizen to arm himself against attack. It had been rightly concluded that the risk of violence could have been avoided and thus the need to carry weapons, by inviting the appropriate agency to repossess the cars by the usual means.

Southwell v Chadwick (1986) 85 Cr App R 235 (CA)

Stephen Brown LJ: [The appellant was charged with] being in possession in a public place of offensive weapons without lawful authority or reasonable excuse; that is to say, a machete knife and a catapult, contrary to s 1 of the Prevention of Crime Act 1953 ...

... [T]he justices found that the said knife was a heavy machete, having a five-inch wooden handle, with an almost razor-sharp Birmingham steel blade of a little over 12 inches. The said blade was straight except for the cutting edge which was slightly curved. [The justices also found that] 'the said catapult was of the manufactured type known as a "Black Widow". It consisted, *inter alia*, of two strong pieces of rubber tubing, a leather sling, and a forearm rest. It was of great power.'

... Then the justices found:

> that [the defendant's] ambition ... on the said afternoon was limited to killing grey squirrels (of which there were plenty) with missiles from his catapult

and to chopping down tree branches upon which to carry any squirrels so killed with his unsheathed knife.

... [The justices also] found 'that the said knife and catapult were both dangerous articles capable of causing grave personal injury' ...

... It is not suggested by the Crown that either of these two articles was adapted for use in the language of the subsection for causing injury to the person. Plainly, they were not. The machete was in a scabbard or sheath and the catapult was manufactured as described. The question was not, therefore, whether there was evidence that they could be used but whether they were *made* for the use of causing injury to the person. In my judgment there was no such evidence. They were articles which had a legitimate use and, although it was a remarkable sight no doubt for police constables to come across a young man with these particular articles in this wood, nevertheless, the justices have to apply the strict words of the section. It does not in fact appear that this young man had any malicious intent directed to persons at all on their findings, so far as the use of these articles was concerned; that is to say, any use directed towards causing injury to any person ... In my judgment, the magistrates erred in coming to the conclusion that these two articles, or either of them, were dangerous *per se*.

Houghton v Chief Constable of Greater Manchester (1986) 84 Cr App R 319 (CA)

For facts see above.

May LJ: ... The second question which arises ... is whether it can be said on the facts of this particular case that this plaintiff had reasonable excuse for having the truncheon in his possession at the material time.

... [I]t is quite clear why he had [the truncheon] it on him, namely as a theatrical prop to support the verisimilitude of his fancy dress ... I stress that the only facts which are proved are that it is being carried as a prop for his fancy dress. The situation would be different if there was any other evidence, for instance as to the amount of drink taken, or as to the presence of opposing factions at the particular party to which the accused had been, or that the weapon had been used in a threatening way. But where the weapon, offensive *per se*, is carried merely as a theatrical property, as part and parcel of a fancy dress worn by a person going to a fancy dress party, I think that that does constitute a reasonable excuse for carrying that particular prop. I ask myself rhetorically, what other reason has he got for carrying that particular article at that time? The only answer that one can give is that he has it to add, as I say, verisimilitude to his fancy dress. That, as I think, is a reasonable excuse in itself ...

Cases where injury actually inflicted

Where an offensive weapon is used (rather than merely carried) and injury is caused, it is preferable to charge an offence under the Offences Against the Person Act 1861 rather than an offence under the Prevention of Crime Act 1953.

Bates v Bulman [1979] 1 WLR 1190 (DC)

Stocker J: ... The facts as found by the justices were these. The defendant slapped and punched a man called Anthony Kevin Rivett in Westlode Street, Spalding on the day in question. The defendant then at his request was handed an unopened clasp knife by another man, the defendant having formed the intention to use that knife to cause injury to Rivett, his opponent. The defendant then opened the clasp knife and held it against Rivett's head. Finally, the justices found that the clasp knife was not made or adapted for use for causing injury to the person. Upon those facts the justices were of the opinion that the offence was proved ...

...[I]t seems to me that the purport of the Act ... is to cover the situation where an accused person – a defendant – has with him and is carrying an offensive weapon intending that it shall be used, if necessary, for offensive purposes. Where an assault in fact takes place, whether it amounts to an assault causing actual bodily harm or a lesser or greater criminal substantive offence, and the only circumstances in which the weapon used are converted or could be converted into an offensive weapon for the purposes of the definition are its use itself in the assault concerned, then an alternative or second charge under the Prevention of Crime Act 1953 would be more likely to confuse than to resolve the situation.

Therefore, in my judgment, the real purpose of this Act is to prevent the carrying of offensive weapons. Their use would almost inevitably be better dealt with by a substantive offence ...

POSSESSION OF BLADES, ETC

Section 139 of the Criminal Justice Act 1988

(1) Subject to subsections (4) and (5) below, any person who has an article to which this section applies with him in a public place shall be guilty of an offence.

(2) Subject to subsection (3) below, this section applies to any article which has a blade or is sharply pointed except a folding pocket-knife.

(3) This section applies to a folding pocket-knife if the cutting edge of its blade exceeds three inches.

(4) It shall be a defence for a person charged with an offence under this section to prove that he had good reason or lawful authority for having the article with him in a public place.

(5) Without prejudice to the generality of subsection (4) above, it shall be a defence for a person charged with an offence under this section to prove that he had the article with him:

(a) for use at work;

(b) for religious reasons; or

(c) as part of any national costume.

Has with him in a public place

The same form of words is used in s 1 of the Prevention of Crime Act 1953 and so the cases cited above on the meaning of 'has with him' and 'public place' apply equally to s 139 of the Criminal Justice Act 1988.

Folding pocket-knife

Where the length of the blade of the knife is less than 3 inches, no offence is committed if the knife is a folding pocket-knife; it follows that an offence is only committed in respect of a knife with a blade less than three inches if it is a fixed-blade knife.

Harris v DPP; Fehmi v DPP (1993) 96 Cr App R 235 (DC)

These two appeals concerned 'lock knives'.

McCowan LJ: [The question to be decided in both cases was whether] a folding knife ... having a pointed blade of less than three inches in length and capable of being secured in an open position by a locking device [is] a folding pocket-knife within the meaning of s 139 of the Criminal Justice Act 1988.

[The justices in the second case made the following findings of fact:]

(a) that the article was a knife with a blade the cutting edge of which was less than three inches.

(b) that the blade was capable of being folded.

(c) that when the blade was fully opened it automatically locked in that position.

(d) that to fold the blade back into the handle it was necessary to activate a button-triggered mechanism.

... We were shown one of the knives in question, there being no difference between the two. What we observed was that when you first open it manually you cannot then fold it back. You have first to press a button on it in order to fold it back, so that when fully opened, the result is that it requires to be unlocked.

... [Counsel for the Crown submitted that] [w]hen the knife is locked it becomes in effect a fixed-blade knife and the intention of the statute is to prevent the carrying of such a knife. I accept that point.

In my judgment, the right approach to the matter is this. To be a folding pocket-knife the knife has to be readily and indeed immediately foldable at all times, simply by the folding process. A knife of the type with which these appeals are concerned is not in this category because, in the first place, there is a stage, namely when it has been opened, when it is not immediately foldable simply by the folding process and, second, it requires that further process, namely the pressing of the button.

For these reasons ... I would dismiss the appeals.

Lawful authority or good reason

The defences (apart from the specific ones of work, religion and national costume) are lawful authority or good reason. 'Lawful authority' is a defence under s 1 of the Prevention of Crime Act 1953, and so the same principles apply here. However, the other defence ('good reason') is worded differently from the 'reasonable excuse' defence under the Prevention of Crime Act 1953. It follows that cases which define 'reasonable excuse' cannot be used to define 'good reason'. The cases decided under s 139 make it clear that it is for the defendant to prove (on the balance of probabilities) that he had a good reason; the fact that he had forgotten that he had the knife does not amount to a good reason.

Godwin v DPP (1993) 96 Cr App R 244 (DC)

McCowan LJ: ... According to the case, [the justices] found the following facts:

(1) On 24 October 1990, at approximately 9.00 am the defendant was attacked ... The assailant was known to the defendant who knew that the assailant was aggrieved by the defendant's association with a relative of the assailant.

(2) The defendant had with him a red-handled kitchen knife, which had a pointed blade, and a cutting edge which exceeded three inches.

(3) When interviewed by the police the defendant stated that he required the knife for use at his home. He invited a search of his flat to establish lack of kitchen utensils including knives.

... The justices say:

> We were of the opinion that 'the reason put forward by the defendant for having the knife, namely for food preparation later that evening, was most improbable having regard to the circumstances of the case'. Accordingly, we convicted the defendant ...

The questions for the opinion of the High Court are stated as follows:

(1) Whether there was any evidence before the court entitling us to disbelieve the defendant on the balance of probabilities.

(2) Whether it is right in principle where a defendant has given an explanation which is not contradicted by any evidence and is not inherently unlikely and which could have been checked by the prosecution at a time when such a check would have been conclusive either way, and the prosecution decline to make such checks, that the prosecution should then invite the court to disbelieve the defendant's explanation, and whether it is right in such circumstances for the court to disbelieve such explanation.

[Having criticised the form of these questions, his Lordship continued:]

Mr Blake's argument for the defendant in a nutshell was this. The justices, having received no evidence rebutting the explanation given by the defendant which, according to Mr Blake, was not an inherently incredible explanation, the presumption of innocence is resurrected.

For my part, I entirely reject this suggestion. Once the Crown has discharged the burden upon him under s 139, the defendant is guilty of the offence unless he can discharge the burden put upon him by subsection (4). In this case, it is obvious that he failed, in the view of the justices, to discharge that burden. They were fully entitled to reach that conclusion, and having reached it, they would be bound to convict him.

... In my judgment, this is an unarguable appeal and I would dismiss it.

DPP v Gregson (1993) 96 Cr App R 240 (DC)

McCowan LJ: ... The facts found by the justices were these:

(a) At about 6.25 pm on the date specified ... police were called to the defendant's address and outside that address saw the respondent arguing with another person. After some discussion, the police left the scene but returned later and again saw the defendant outside the address.

(b) On this latter occasion police officers intended to search the respondent but before doing so a knife which had a fixed blade of some four inches in length fell from the respondent's clothing, that is his jeans.

(c) On this latter occasion the defendant offered no specific reason or excuse for having the knife with him.

(d) The defendant habitually used the knife for purposes of his work in cutting cork floor tiles and habitually carried the knife in the pocket of the jacket he was wearing at the time of the incident and which he wore for work.

(c) The defendant had last worked six days prior to the incident ... and he had forgotten to remove the knife before entering the street on this occasion.

It appears that it was contended by the defendant that he had a good reason for having the knife with him in a public place, in that he used it for his work and had forgotten it was with him on this occasion. The justices say:

> We were of opinion that the respondent had satisfied us on a balance of probabilities that he had a good reason for having the knife with him.
>
> The questions for the opinion of this court are stated as follows:
>
> (1) Whether, in order to establish a defence of good reason within s 139(4) of the Criminal Justice Act 1988 a defendant has to prove a specific reason for his having the article with him in a public place on the occasion alleged.
>
> (2) Whether a defendant who has forgotten that he has with him an article to which s 139 of the Criminal Justice Act 1988 applies can rely upon that forgetfulness as constituting a defence of good reason within s 139(4) of the said Act.
>
> (3) Whether on the facts we found we made a correct determination and decision in law.
>
> ... In my judgment, [counsel for the Crown] is right to say that it is important to concentrate on the time in respect of which the defendant is charged. Six days earlier, no doubt this man had the knife on him for a good reason, because the justices found that it was a knife that he used in his work and would have had with him at his work and might well have put into his pocket at work six days earlier. But did he have it with him for a good reason at the time of his arrest? Having it for work reasons six days earlier cannot, in my judgment, be a good reason for having it on him six days later when not at work. The question, therefore, it seems to me, boils down to whether forgetfulness at the relevant time was a good reason. It does appear that the justices found that he had forgotten that he had it on him ...
>
> In my judgment, forgetfulness may be an explanation. It cannot be a good reason. I would therefore answer the second question, by saying that the fact that a defendant has forgotten that he has an article to which s 139 applies cannot constitute a defence of good reason within s 139(4) of the Act. I would therefore go on to answer question 3, that they did not make a correct determination and decision in law. As to question 1, which poses the question, whether in order to establish a defence of good reason a defendant has to prove a specific reason for having the article with him in a public place on the occasion alleged, I prefer to give no answer to that question. I would prefer to hear the point much more fully argued. It is unnecessary to answer it for the purposes of this appeal, which I would allow.

Offensive Weapons Act 1996

Section 2 increases the maximum penalty for carrying an offensive weapon (s 1 of the Prevention of Crime Act 1953) to 4 years' imprisonment.

Section 3 increases the maximum penalty for having an article with a blade or point in a public place (s 139 of the Criminal Justice Act 1988) to 2 years' imprisonment.

Section 4 creates a new offence (s 139A of the Criminal Justice Act 1988) of having an article with a blade or point, or an offensive weapon, on school premises:

Criminal Justice Act 1988, s 139A

(1) Any person who has an article to which section 139 of this Act applies with him on school premises shall be guilty of an offence.

(2) Any person who has an offensive weapon within the meaning of section 1 of the Prevention of Crime Act 1953 with him on school premises shall be guilty of an offence.

(3) It shall be a defence for a person charged with an offence under subsection (1) or (2) above to prove that he had good reason or lawful authority for having the article or weapon with him on the premises in question.

(4) Without prejudice to the generality of subsection (3) above, it shall be a defence for a person charged with an offence under subsection (1) or (2) above to prove that he had the article or weapon in question with him -

(a) for use at work,

(b) for educational purposes,

(c) for religious reasons, or

(d) as part of any national costume.

Section 6 of the Offensive Weapons Act 1996 also creates a new offence (s 141A of the Criminal Justice Act 1988) of selling a knife or article with a blade or point to a person under 16:

Criminal Justice Act 1988, s 141A

(1) Any person who sells to a person under the age of sixteen years an article to which this section applies shall be guilty of an offence ...

(2) Subject to subsection (3) below, this section applies to -

(a) any knife, knife blade or razor blade,

(b) any axe, and

(c) any other article which has a blade or which is sharply pointed and which is made or adapted for use for causing injury to the person.

(3) [Allows the Secretary of State to make an order exempting certain articles from the scope of this Act]

(4) It shall be a defence for a person charged with an offence under subsection (1) above to prove that he took all reasonable precautions and exercised all due diligence to avoid the commission of the offence.

INDEX